W9-BRD-172

REVISITING THE WHITE CITY

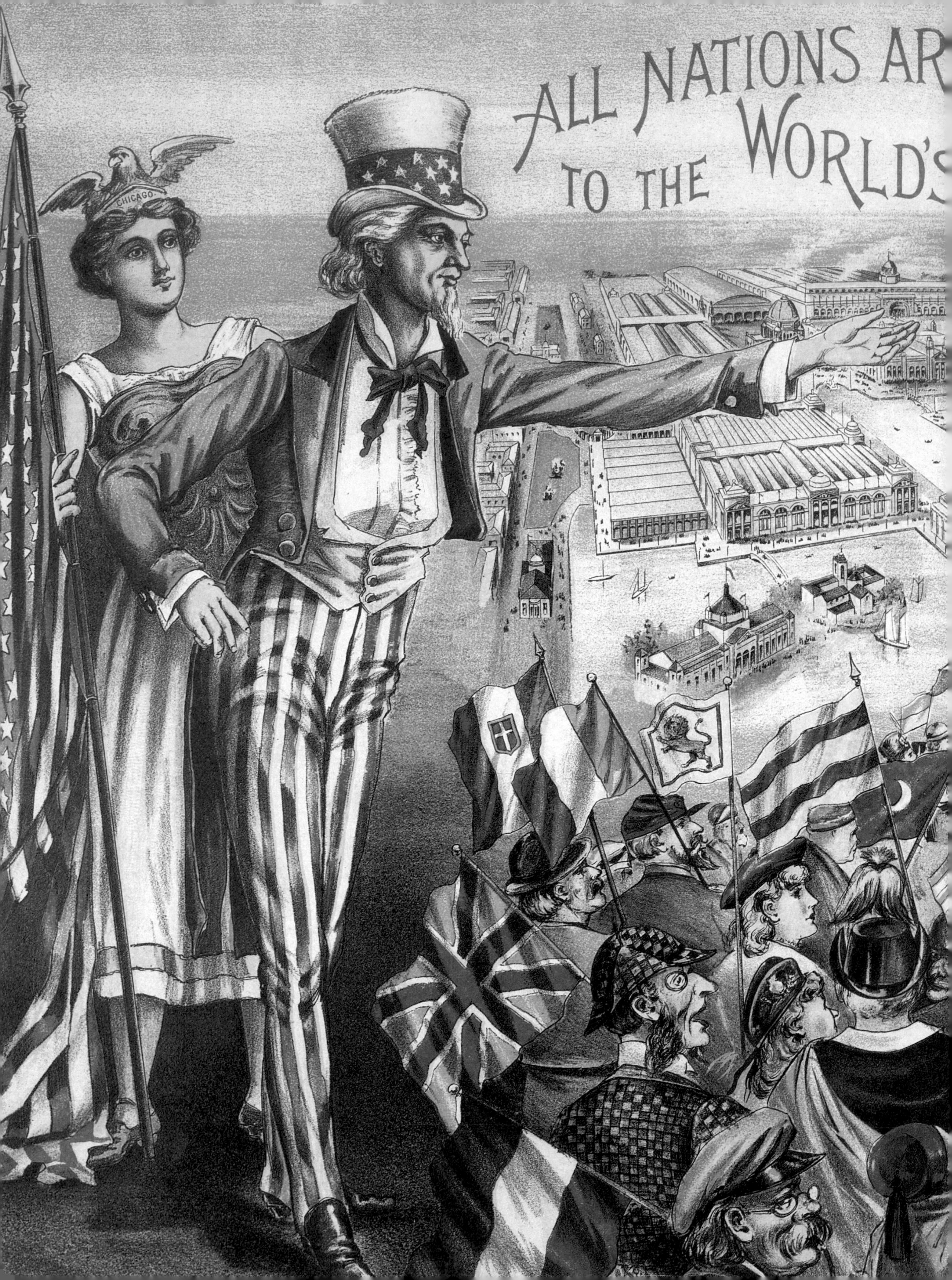
ALL NATIONS AR
TO THE WORLD'S
CHICAGO

WELCOME COLUMBIAN EXPOSITION CHICAGO 1893

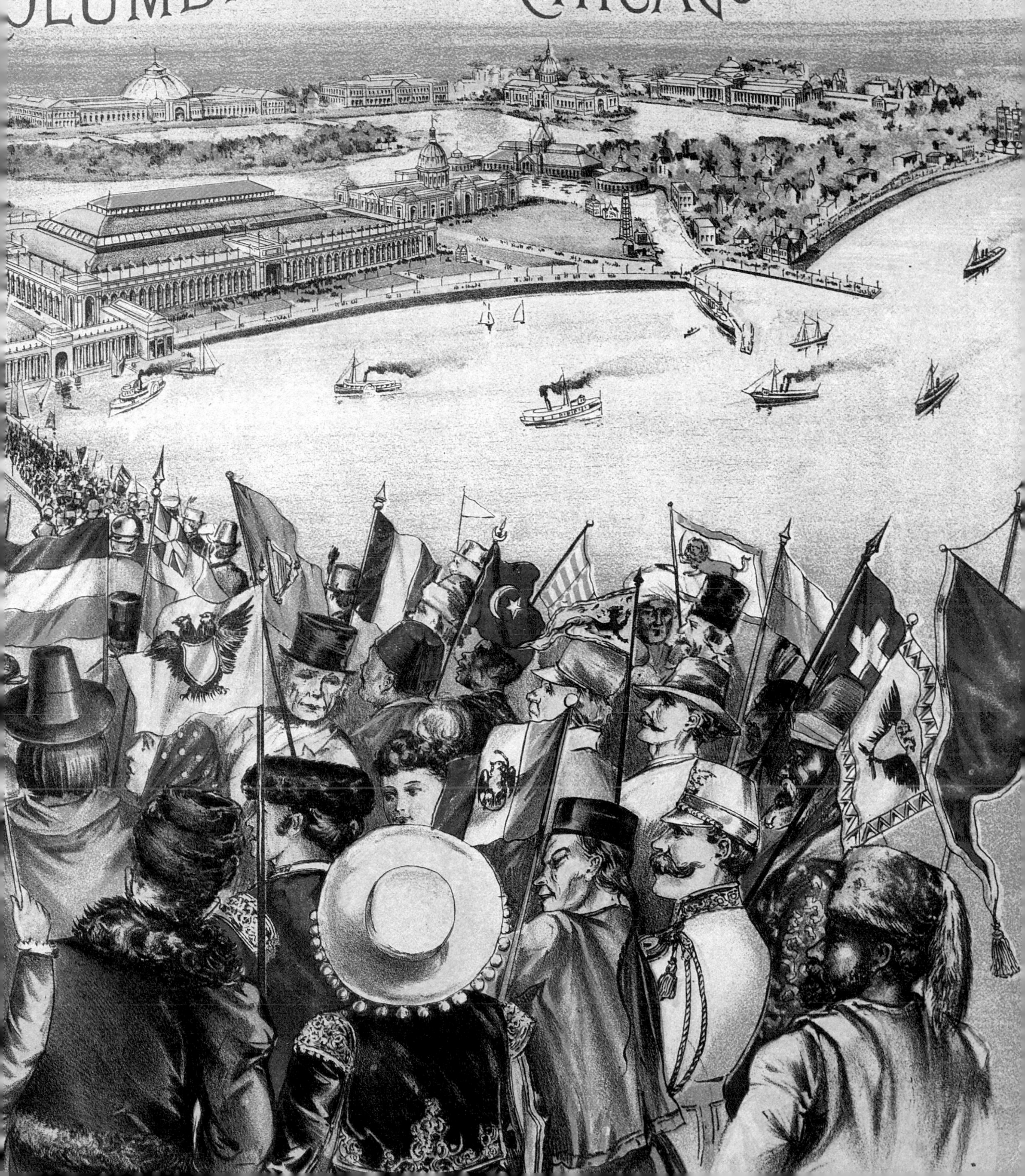

Organized by CAROLYN KINDER CARR AND GEORGE GURNEY

Essays by ROBERT W. RYDELL AND CAROLYN KINDER CARR

Catalogue of Works by BRANDON BRAME FORTUNE AND MICHELLE MEAD

NATIONAL MUSEUM OF AMERICAN ART

AND

NATIONAL PORTRAIT GALLERY

SMITHSONIAN INSTITUTION,

WASHINGTON, D.C.

1993

DISTRIBUTED BY THE UNIVERSITY PRESS OF NEW ENGLAND

HANOVER AND LONDON

REVISITING THE WHITE CITY

AMERICAN ART AT THE 1893 WORLD'S FAIR

THIS PUBLICATION IS MADE POSSIBLE THROUGH
THE GENEROUS SUPPORT OF
THE ELIZABETH F. CHENEY FOUNDATION.

Published on the occasion of the exhibition *American Art at the 1893 World's Fair*, organized by the National Museum of American Art and the National Portrait Gallery of the Smithsonian Institution, and shown in their galleries from 16 April to 15 August 1993. The exhibition is made possible with the support of the Smithsonian Institution Special Exhibition Fund.

Library of Congress Cataloging-in-Publication Data
Revisiting the white city : American art at the 1893 World's Fair / contributors, Carolyn Kinder Carr . . . [et al.].
p. cm.
Includes bibliographical references and index.
ISBN 0-937311-01-4. – ISBN 0-937311-02-2 (pbk.)
1. Art, American–Exhibitions. 2. Art, Modern–19th century–United States–Exhibitions. 3. World's Columbian Exposition (1893 : Chicago, Ill.) I. Carr, Carolyn Kinder. II. National Museum of American Art (U.S.) III. National Portrait Gallery (Smithsonian Institution)
N6510.R48 1993
709'.73'07477311–dc20 92-37218
CIP

All paintings are oil on canvas unless otherwise indicated. Complete credit lines and alternate titles for objects in the color plate section are found in the catalogue section.

Cover: *The Court of Honor, Looking East from the Administration Building with the Columbian Fountain by Frederick MacMonnies in the Foreground.* Photograph by the United States Exposition Board, Committee on Photography: Thomas W. Smillie, Frances Benjamin Johnston, and Lt. Henry Harris. Courtesy of the Smithsonian Institution Archives, RV95, Box 64, folder 3, neg. no. 10237.

Pages 2–3: *All Nations Are Welcome to the World's Columbian Exposition, Chicago, 1893. World's Columbian Exposition Illustrated* 3, no. 3 (May 1893): following 80.

CONTENTS

LENDERS

The Addison Gallery of American Art, Phillips Academy,
Andover, Massachusetts
Albright-Knox Art Gallery, Buffalo, New York
Amon Carter Museum, Fort Worth, Texas
The Art Institute of Chicago, Illinois
The Berkshire Museum, Pittsfield, Massachusetts
The Brooklyn Museum, New York
The Carnegie Museum of Art, Pittsburgh, Pennsylvania
The Century Association, New York, New York
Chesterwood, a Museum Property of the National Trust for Historic Preservation,
Stockbridge, Massachusetts
Sterling and Francine Clark Art Institute, Williamstown, Massachusetts
Cleveland Public Library, Ohio
The Columbia Club Foundation, Indianapolis, Indiana
Columbus Museum of Art, Ohio
Rogers L. and Sally Lorensen Conant
The Corcoran Gallery of Art, Washington, District of Columbia
The Couse Family
Danforth Museum of Art, Framingham, Massachusetts
Davis Museum and Cultural Center, Wellesley College, Massachusetts
Deutsches Historisches Museum, Berlin, Germany
The Duquesne Club, Pittsburgh, Pennsylvania
The Fine Arts Museums of San Francisco, California
Mr. and Mrs. Joel Finn
Collection of Rita and Daniel Fraad
Harvard University Law School Art Collection, Cambridge, Massachusetts
Jane Addams' Hull-House Museum, University of Illinois at Chicago, Illinois
Jefferson Medical College of Thomas Jefferson University,
Philadelphia, Pennsylvania
Herbert F. Johnson Museum of Art, Cornell University, Ithaca, New York
Los Angeles County Museum of Art, California
Louisville Free Public Library, Kentucky
Gloria Manney
John J. McMullen

The Metropolitan Museum of Art, New York, New York
The Montclair Art Museum, New Jersey
Museo de Arte de Ponce, Luis A. Ferré Foundation, Inc., Puerto Rico
Museum of Art, Rhode Island School of Design, Providence
Museum of Fine Arts, Boston, Massachusetts
Museum of Fine Arts, Springfield, Massachusetts
National Museum of American Art, Smithsonian Institution,
Washington, District of Columbia
National Portrait Gallery, Smithsonian Institution,
Washington, District of Columbia
New Britain Museum of American Art, Connecticut
New Jersey State Museum, Trenton
The New-York Historical Society, New York
Northwestern University Library, Evanston, Illinois
Pennsylvania Academy of the Fine Arts, Philadelphia
Estate of George W. and Evelina B. Perkins
Philadelphia Museum of Art, Pennsylvania
The Phillips Collection, Washington, District of Columbia
Private Collection, courtesy of Berry-Hill Galleries, Inc., New York, New York
Private Collection, courtesy of the Spanierman Gallery, New York, New York
Mrs. John Dowling Relfe
Mr. and Mrs. Thomas Rosse
Salem County Historical Society, Salem, New Jersey
Scripps College, Claremont, California
Sheldon Swope Art Museum, Terre Haute, Indiana
Staten Island Institute of Arts and Sciences, New York
Tate Gallery, London, England
Tennessee Wesleyan College, Athens
Timken Museum of Art, San Diego, California
Union League Club of Chicago, Illinois
United States Naval Academy Museum, Annapolis, Maryland
University Art Museum, University of California at Berkeley
The University Club of New York, New York
Utah Museum of Fine Arts, University of Utah, Salt Lake City
Valparaiso University Museum of Art, Indiana
Wadsworth Atheneum, Hartford, Connecticut
The Walters Art Gallery, Baltimore, Maryland
The Warner Collection of Gulf States Paper Corporation,
Tuscaloosa, Alabama
Washington and Lee University, Lexington, Virginia
Jay H. Weibel
Chris Whittle
Graham Williford
Richard York Gallery, New York, New York
Twelve anonymous lenders

INTRODUCTION

WHEN WE FIRST BEGAN TO THINK ABOUT HOW THE NATIONAL Portrait Gallery and the National Museum of American Art could take note of the 500th anniversary of the voyage of Christopher Columbus, it became clear that many of the usual observances would be of little lasting interest. As far as portraits are concerned, no lifetime images of Columbus have been authenticated, and most of the posthumous ones reveal more about the imaginative powers of the artists who made them than about the appearance or character of the subject. The drawings and prints of the New World made by explorers came, for the most part, from later voyages and, in any case, were shown in depth in Washington at the time of the nation's Bicentennial. "Historical" paintings of Columbus and his encounters in the Indies seemed a tired subject, and one with little substance.

A conjunction of interests emerged from a consideration of this problem. Elizabeth Broun, some time ago, had studied the art of the 1893 World's Columbian Exposition in Chicago, and when Carolyn Carr started looking into the portraiture done in the 1890s as a possible source of inspiration for an exhibition, it occurred to both of them that our adjoining museums might collaborate on a project to reassemble a portion of the 1893 exhibition, and through this selection to reveal something of American intellectual and cultural attitudes of the time. The Chicago fair was the nation's major celebration of the 400th anniversary of the voyage of Columbus, and it was a watershed in American visual arts. What could we learn from it today?

In our quincentennial observation of the Columbus voyage, attitudes in America seem very different from those of a century earlier. Most of us no longer view history as the inevitable march of progress toward an ideal condition. In today's world we no longer can celebrate a single culture, religion, or moral code as models to which all others must aspire. The notions that men are superior to women, that towns are better than farms, that technology is an unalloyed benefit, or that there even are such things as "primitive" societies have evaporated, and most Americans have come to accept the premise that no single nation has an inevitable claim to occupy the center of the world's stage. Perhaps in the 1890s there were as many people who questioned these "certainties" as there are now, but their views were clearly absent from the organizing committees of the World's Columbian Exposition, and they were minority views among the recorded responses of contemporary spectators. One such response came from the poet and editor Harriet Monroe, who felt "an overmastering sense of the power derivable from arts in sisterhood and men in brotherhood . . . the feeling that . . . this triumph marked not the climax but the beginning of a day full of light and love and beauty. Surely the most impressive thing about the fair was not what it gave but what it promised."[1]

The purpose of this book, and the exhibition that has inspired it, is to look back at the American art displayed at the fair. We cannot avoid doing this with the eyes of twentieth-century observers, yet we also need to recapture something of the spirit of the time in which the art was originally created, recalling the principles that motivated the selection of these objects for this special showing. To do this, we may be advised, in Harriet Monroe's words, to seek both "what it gave" as well as "what it promised."

At the World's Columbian Exposition, visitors were invited to see the largest and most elaborately selected exhibition of American art ever assembled in this country, and to reflect on what this revealed of the progress of culture in our land. To explore and document the myriad implications of this showing of art, our colleagues attempted to locate as many objects from the exposition as they could find, selecting from these a group of paintings and sculptures that could epitomize the original selection. The results are here, and they are intriguing. In presenting new visual art to mark the 400th anniversary of the Columbus voyage, the organizers of the fair were clearly asserting the arrival of American painting and sculpture on the world scene and signaling the emergence of the young nation from its long dependence on Europe. When we reviewed this same art a hundred years later, other themes emerged as well. Looking back, it is clear that in 1893 women were asserting their professional standing in the arts, demanding inclusion in both the administrative and artistic areas with unprecedented energy and determination. American artists were finding new sources of inspiration in Europe and at home and were substantially changing accepted aesthetic norms, veering away from those that had prevailed in the 1876 Centennial Fair, when the last large American art exhibition had been organized. And art patronage among the emerging American mercantile leaders was presenting new opportunities for artists and their dealers.

Chicago had risen from the ashes of its disastrous fire just twenty-two years before the World's Columbian Exposition. The rebuilding and expansion of the city involved the construction of a network of parks, roads, and railways, the building of skyscrapers of exceptional size and power, the establishment of universities and other cultural institutions, and the consolidation of the metropolis as a national transportation hub. The new planning and architecture were hailed by some theorists of the time as a model for "the city beautiful," an alternative to the haphazard and unlovely admixture of commercial, industrial, and residential functions that was turning older towns into crowded, unpleasant, and unhealthy environments. The organizers of the fine art component of the fair wanted it to be as ambitiously scaled as the White City and the emergent city surrounding it.

As we look at what was chosen for the American portion of the fine arts exhibition, it is difficult at first to discern a clear pattern of selection. What do Thomas Eakins's *The Gross Clinic* and Abbott H. Thayer's *Virgin Enthroned* have in common? How does one reconcile the theatrical historical works with the idyllic landscapes? These are issues with which the essayists in this book have grappled as they explore the significance of the fair, the themes foremost in the organizers' minds, and the politics of art that affected the composition of the exhibition. In thinking about these works of art and reading these essays, one should keep in mind that the day is long past when such an undertaking is possible. Our current exhibition, generous by today's standards, is nonetheless only one-twelfth the size of the original display of American painting and sculpture.

World's fairs on a grand scale have undergone a dramatic evolution in the turbulence of today's national realignments and international economies. The time may come again when nations are certain enough of their identity to wish to proclaim it in the context of an international fair, but perhaps the stresses involved today in the accommodation of various ethnic groups within national boundaries, the threats of armed conflict that seem to underlie every international confrontation, and the earnestness of international economic competition have combined to make governments lukewarm to the considerable investment of funds and planning required to make an impressive showing. One has only to compare the enormous difficulty with which the United States managed to cobble together a pitiful pavilion and an inconsequential exhibition at the 1992 world's fair in Seville with the amazing spectacles of the American presence at the fairs in Montreal, Osaka, Brussels, or (as far back as 1939) New York to see how profound the change has been.

In those days, world's fairs were natural expressions of national pride, evidence that a country had crossed the barrier separating the developed from the nondeveloped, primarily through the excellence of its arts and manufactures. Moreover, arts and manufactures were viewed as interrelated; excellence in one would point toward achievement in the other. Creativity, innovation, and craftsmanship were all part of a national identity and the primary means—apart from military conquest—for increasing a country's prestige.

It is important to realize, if one is truly to recapture the spirit of the 1893 World's Columbian Exposition, that while organizationally it followed a brilliant series of international fairs, reaching back to the Crystal Palace in London in 1851, it was fundamentally different from them in focus. In London the idea had been to bring together under one spectacular roof the finest in manufacturing and the arts from all nations, so craftsmen, industrialists, artists, and ordinary citizens could compare what they saw and work toward a higher standard. Fairs in France, Germany, Italy, and America followed in rapid succession, each offering its own signature innovation. The Eiffel Tower was just one of the structural innovations in Paris in 1889, just as the 1851 Crystal Palace in London had amazed the public with its enormous glass and iron structure created by a renowned designer of greenhouses.

The Chicago fair had its architectural signature as well, but it was more backward looking than futuristic. Ironically, in a city that had already earned a reputation for structural innovation in the balloon-frame skyscrapers of pioneers like William Le Baron Jenney or the powerful yet delicately decorated buildings of Louis Sullivan, the guiding spirits of the World's Columbian Exposition selected the Beaux-Arts style of Daniel Burnham and McKim, Mead & White as the predominant expression of their purpose, grouping their magnificent white confections around a lagoon reminiscent of Venice. Almost as a conscious corrective, the Chicago fair had another signature structure: the first Ferris Wheel, towering above the new University of Chicago buildings on the Midway perpendicular to the main lagoon. The

Ferris Wheel was both an entertainment and a demonstration of the application of advanced mechanical engineering to modern living.

But for most visitors, the White City remained the enduring memory of the fair. As closing day approached, the editor of a New York journal asked a number of well-known men and women of letters to share their impressions of the fair. In these responses we can begin to sense how informed Americans of the time reacted to the presentations in Chicago.[2] Virtually everyone remarked on the magical quality of the buildings, which for many, rivaled anything to be seen in Europe. Others commented on the decorum of the crowds, the nighttime illumination of the area, and the diversity of the exhibits. E. C. Stedman, alluding to the architecture of the fair and the objections of foreign critics to its "antique perfection," observed that "they should comprehend that to rouse the sense of beauty itself among our faraway plain people was the highest mission of the Fair. It sent thousands back to unlovely homes with the beginning of a noble discontent."[3]

The rapt attention of the masses of public visitors to this overwhelming celebration of human endeavor, and the new experiences visitors carried away from the fair, must certainly have had a transforming effect on many aspects of American life thereafter. For this was predominantly an American fair, and although it did celebrate the 400th anniversary of the arrival of Columbus in the Western Hemisphere, this observance conveyed a substantially different attitude toward the image and legend of Columbus than had characterized the 1792 celebration. The legacy of that commemoration, as many writers today have pointed out, is found in the name of the seat of our federal government (District of Columbia) and cities named Columbus or Columbia in several states, not to mention Columbia University and a host of other derivations. The legacy of the World's Columbian Exposition, in contrast, was the assertion of the maturity of American art, which now could stand beside manufacturing, transportation, and commerce as a national achievement. Nevertheless, in those days the understanding was emphatically that "Columbus had discovered America," and we will not fully comprehend the intention of the organizers or the responses of the public unless we try to recapture the spirit of a time very different from the present day. The older civilizations of Europe were to be admired for their arts and traditions; the New World was uniquely vital and technologically positioned to create a life-style hitherto unimagined. The World's Columbian Exposition would demonstrate that with a power and clarity never before seen, and on an unforgettable scale.

The large ambitions of the fair were carried through with great fervor in the Fine Arts Building. Painter Will Low explained how the arts embodied the central tenet of the exposition, announcing the completion of the civilizing process begun in America by Columbus 400 years earlier:

> When the White City was built in 1893 art assumed a definite place in our national life. Then for the first time we awoke to a realisation that art of the people, by the people, for the people had come to us. It came to this New World in the old historic way. From the seed sown in the Orient, through Greece, through Italy from Byzantium, wafted ever westward, its timid flowering from our Atlantic seaboard had been carried a thousand miles inland to find its first full eclosion; not as a single growth, but as the triple flower of architecture, painting, and sculpture.[4]

The aesthetic "triple flower" displayed in Chicago was proof that America was no longer just a provincial nation of manufacturers and small businessmen. Although the fair buildings were crowded with new technical marvels, it was the arts that were to make America the exemplar of modern democracy, ready for leadership in international affairs. No less a sage than Henry Adams, seeking the deepest meaning of the fair, wrote, "If the people of [Chicago] actually knew what was good when they saw it, they would some day talk about Hunt and Richardson, La Farge and St. Gaudens, Burnham and McKim, and Stanford White when their politicians and millionaires were otherwise forgotten."[5]

Perhaps no other public event in America was presented more self-consciously with an eye on the future, confident of making a mark in history. Everything about the fair resonated with history and culture, trumpeting its distinguished ancestry in the civilizations of Europe. Even the Venetian-inspired waterways and imported gondolas, for instance, were not just romantic attractions; they evoked the centuries-old role of Venice as a crossroads of commerce between East and West. For the fair planners, demonstrating mastery of the past was a way to lay claim to the future.

In this century we have sometimes considered the past an oppressive burden, but the late nineteenth century deeply revered history—an attitude rooted in the Enlightenment idea of rational progress. The evolution of nations particularly fascinated civic-minded Americans, who found their history intimately linked to modern developments in Europe: Greece rediscovering democracy, France in the century after its revolution, Germany and Italy in the process of unification. A generation that grew up reading Sir Walter Scott's Anglo-Saxon romances found the study of ancient tribal peoples particularly significant, inaugurating an intensive study of early migration patterns and linguistics that traced the ethnic origins of modern nations. For those with a scientific bent, the theories of Charles Darwin and Alexander Humboldt extended the study of history back to prerecorded time.

Against this backdrop, America had proceeded with its own ambitious westward expansion and nation-building, widely recognized as important "history in the making." Antecedents were significant for their symbolic associations—the older, the better. Greece and Rome provided prototypes for democracy on the frontier, and ancient Teutonic forest gatherings were considered the germ of that peculiarly American form of self-governance, the New England town meeting. America's emerging democratic institutions, no less than its monuments and buildings, were rooted in a deep reverence for historical associations.

Nineteenth-century histories often focused on heroic or tragic events inspired by personal courage and ambition, very different from the contemporary emphasis on social histories. The last century honored leaders whose decisive action changed the world, even though it sometimes caused their downfall, as was the case for Napoleon and Bismarck. The 1876 Centennial celebrations in Philadelphia had already canonized America's Founding Fathers, great men whose vision had brought a nation into being. By 1893 the truly modern industrialist, art patron, or politician drew inspiration from larger-than-life figures sweeping majestically across history's pages. Like modern Medicis, Chicago's civic leaders had the confidence to lay ambitious plans, raise millions, and build a remarkable "Dream City" in Jackson Park without waiting for the government to act.

"Great men" had traditionally been commemorated in grand portraiture, conceived first for aristocracies and easily adapted to the new focus on personal vitality and character. Anders Zorn of Sweden, Giovanni Boldini of Italy, Carolus-Duran of France, and the American John Singer Sargent all specialized in portraying not only the men who had "created" history but also the "geniuses" and "masters" who excelled in the arts. The demise of the grand portrait tradition in our century, often attributed to the invention of photography, was no less the result of our self-consciousness at the very idea of genius transforming an age. Social and economic forces now dominate history, but the fair planners saw themselves in the older tradition as great men (and a few great women) shaping a world in their image. They built Renaissance-style palazzos and Beaux-Arts hotels, founded museums to collect history in a concrete way, and posed for portraits with an aspect of assurance. They unabashedly recast their world in historical and biblical terms, as when Augustus Saint-Gaudens sculpted Admiral David Farragut in the form of Donatello's St. George.

Today these ideas seem at odds with the democratic promise of equality as we understand it. We are inclined to point out that many "great men" were not self-made; they enjoyed a life of privilege and inherited wealth. Those who were genuinely self-made often achieved prominence through ruthless or callous means. We wonder whether their remarkable philanthropies reflect self-validation or true generosity. The names Frick, Peabody, Freer, Huntington, Cornell, and others that identify many of our nation's museums, libraries, and universities elicit mixed emotions. How, for instance, should we view Andrew Carnegie, whose passion for written history made possible our free library system, but who also believed that God granted him immense wealth to hold in trust for ordinary men who would not know how to use it for their own betterment?

It wasn't just American art that staked a claim for international supremacy at the fair; no aspect of human endeavor was ignored in the proud assertion of America's global ascendancy. When Anheuser-Busch won the championship cup for the best beer, for instance, it was pointedly noted that the competition included not only domestic beers but also the finest brews of Germany and Austria. Such an insistence on primacy, we now see, could lead to unforeseen and devastating results, as when the rush to world dominance fostered imperialist expeditions around the globe. The insistence on the Founding Fathers' racial stock (a latent theme in several artworks at the fair) was exclusionary, so that Filipinos and Cubans soon to be conquered by our navy in the Spanish-American War of 1898 were judged incapable of sustaining democratic traditions and were denied the vote. Fear of weakening the Founders' bloodlines as the result of immigration from Eastern Europe (especially pervasive in the years after the 1890 census, with its statistics on ethnic origins) led to the Immigration Act of 1924, which closed our gates and fostered lingering prejudices that we still struggle to eradicate. Even the triumph of American art at the fair, based expressly on its devotion to European traditions, soon posed a dilemma for American culture when Fauvist and Cubist modernists debuted at the 1913 Armory Show in New York. And today, confronted with the long-ignored subjugation of native peoples that flowed from Columbus's "discovery," we find it impossible to present a celebratory 500th anniversary of his voyage, preferring instead to commemorate the "encounter of cultures." How surprised the planners of 1893 would be to know that a century later Columbus, the "great man" they so honored, is all but absent from his own anniversary.

Because the legacy of the World's Columbian Exposition is ambivalent, a contemporary examination of it is necessarily a revisionist enterprise, revealing both the triumphant and troubling aspects of our history. Yet as we map some of the fault lines beneath the fair's dazzling surface, we should remember that no generation sees around the corner of the future, not even ours. In recapturing the dreams and ambitions that animated Americans a century ago, we can find connections across our past and present and clarify our vision for the future.

Elizabeth Broun, Director, National Museum of American Art
Alan Fern, Director, National Portrait Gallery

NOTES

1. *The Critic* 23, no. 614 (25 Nov. 1893), 333.
2. Ibid., 331–34.
3. Ibid., 334.
4. Will Low, *A Painter's Progress* (New York: Charles Scribner's Sons, 1910), 251.
5. *The Education of Henry Adams: An Autobiography* (Boston: Houghton Mifflin, 1918), 341.

REVISITING THE WHITE CITY

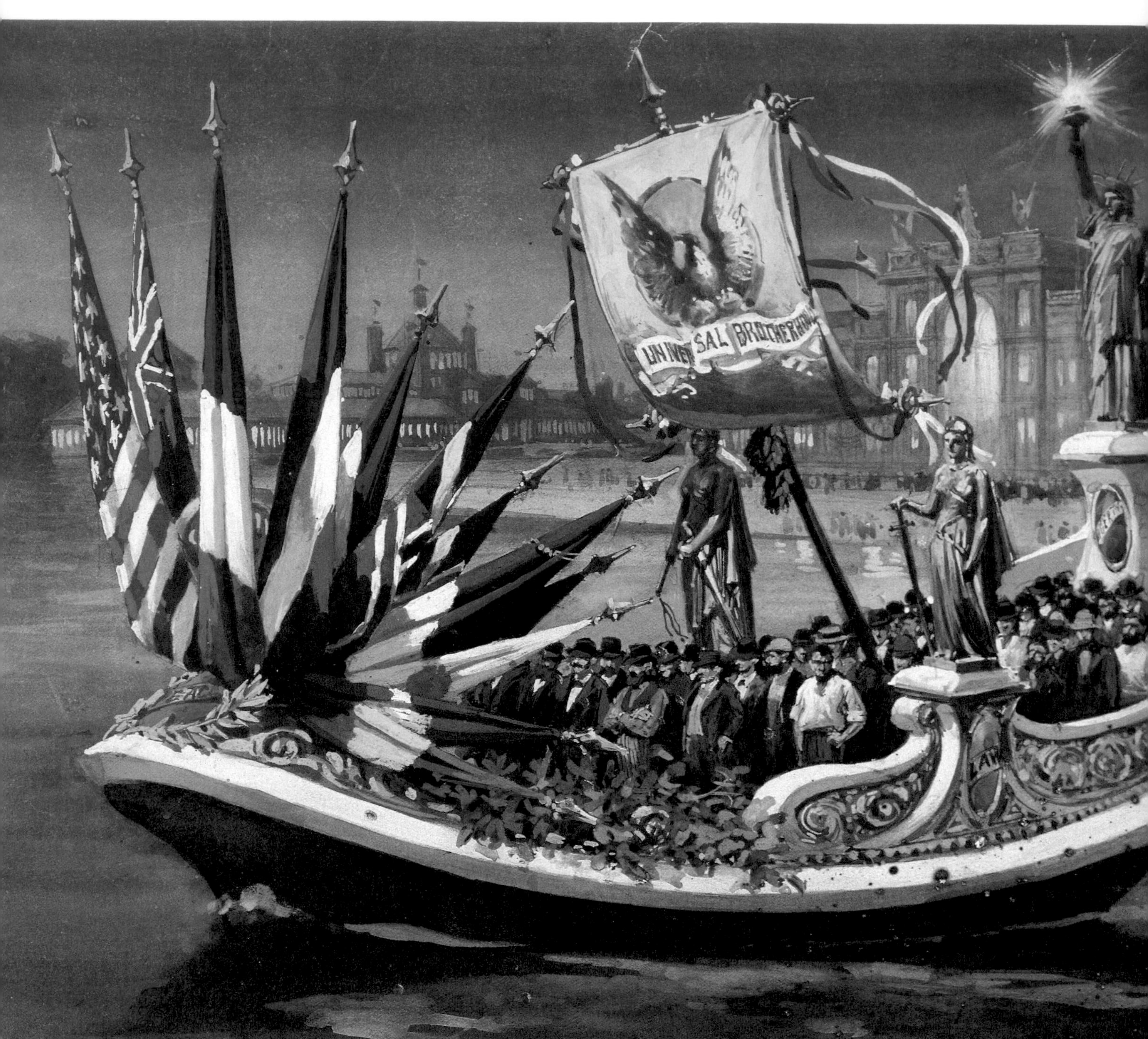
UNIVERSAL BROTHERHOOD

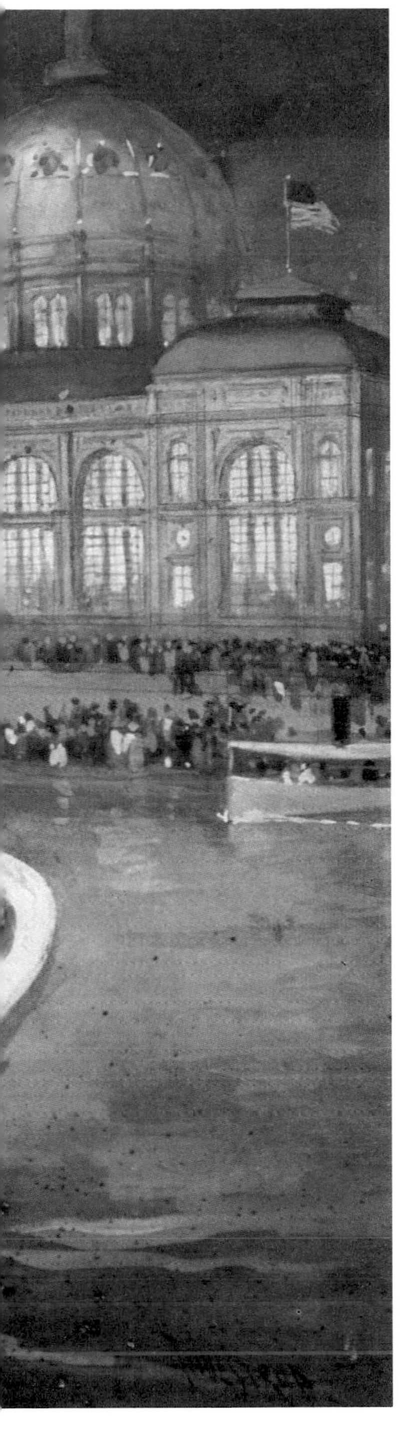

REDISCOVERING THE 1893 CHICAGO WORLD'S COLUMBIAN EXPOSITION

ROBERT W. RYDELL

One of the few institutions which has survived the changes brought about by centuries of time is the Fair. The fairs of yesterday, large and small, have all played a part in present day civilization. Aside from enlarging commerce, entertainment, and education, one particular Fair in our history brought to light a band of men who dedicated themselves to truth, loyalty and love of country and flag. This Fair was the Columbian Exposition of 1893, held in Chicago; and the band of men was The Youth's Companion. *From these two emerged "the Pledge of Allegiance."*

— Margarette Miller, 1946 [1]

..1..
Thur de Thulstrup,
Universal Brotherhood Barge World's Columbian Exposition,
1893, tempera on board. Courtesy of the Chicago Historical Society.

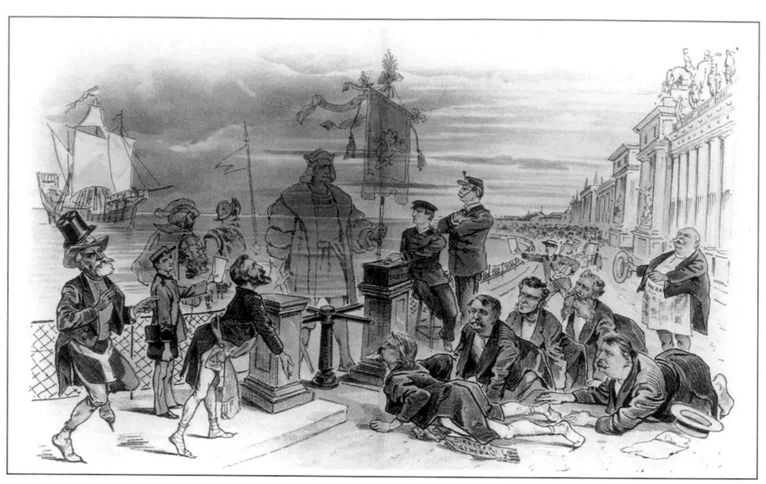

DURING THE WORSENING DEPRESSION OF 1893, CHICAGO HELD a world's fair that commemorated the four hundredth anniversary of Columbus's landfall in the New World (fig. 2). Coming only thirty years after the Civil War, the fair was a stunning achievement. Monumental Beaux-Arts exhibition palaces constructed out of plaster of Paris dotted the 686-acre site in Jackson Park, seven miles south of downtown Chicago, and projected a vision of national unity and universal brotherhood (fig. 1). As if to raise fairgoers' horizons above the realities of economic collapse and growing class tensions, an enormous wheel designed by engineer George Ferris lifted visitors 260 feet above the exposition grounds for spectacular views of the city, Lake Michigan, the University of Chicago campus (taking form immediately adjacent to the exposition grounds), and, of course, the world's fair proper (fig. 3). The fair lasted only six months, but before its gates closed in October, the Chicago World's Columbian Exposition attracted an audience of some twenty million, reaching a secondary audience of millions more through publicity releases and souvenir sales. By all accounts, the fair was an instrumental force in defining American culture.[2]

As such, it is tempting to regard the Chicago fair as a singular event, and in certain respects it was. But the fair was also part of a broader tradition of world's fairs that dated back to London's 1851 Crystal Palace Exhibition (fig. 4). Following the triumph of the London exhibition, world's fairs proliferated throughout the industrialized world, including areas colonized by Europe's imperial powers. By the end of the nineteenth century, nearly one hundred international fairs had taken place, attracting hundreds of millions of visitors (the 1900 Paris Universal Exposition alone recorded some fifty million admissions) (fig. 5). So powerful were these events that the American historian Henry Adams could proclaim the existence of a "religion of world's fairs"—an observation that Umberto Eco has recently echoed in calling the nineteenth-century world's fair the "Missa Solemnis of capitalist culture."[3]

.. 2 ..
"The New Landing of Columbus. When great Columbus' doughty ghost 's new welcomed to Chicago's shore,/ He'll find his present World's Fair hosts are copying those of days of yore—/ Though somewhat hampered in their movements/ By what they think are modern improvements," The World's Fair Puck, *no. 11 (17 July 1893): 126–27.*

Within this universe of fairs, the Chicago World's Columbian

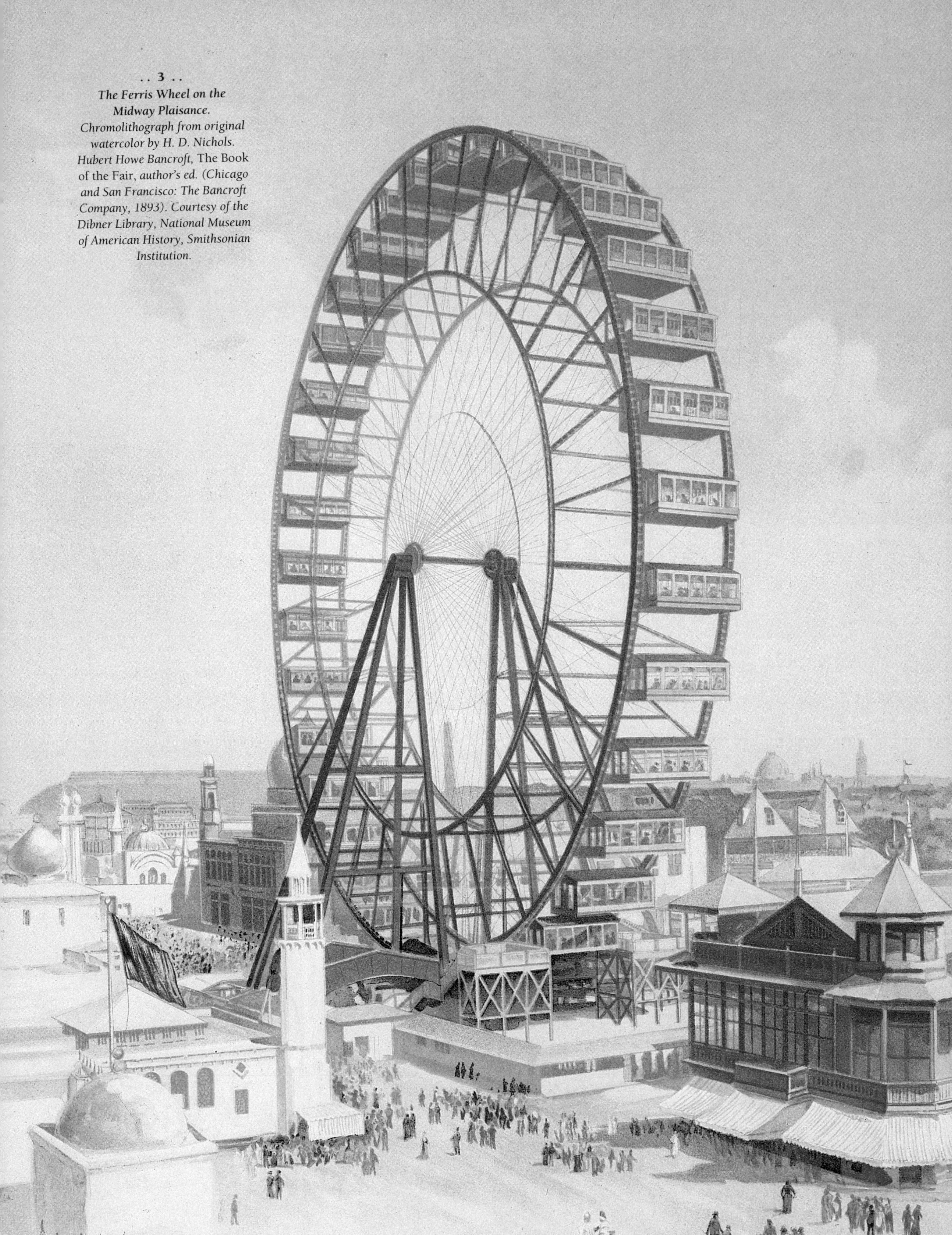

.. 3 ..

The Ferris Wheel on the Midway Plaisance.
Chromolithograph from original watercolor by H. D. Nichols. Hubert Howe Bancroft, The Book of the Fair, *author's ed. (Chicago and San Francisco: The Bancroft Company, 1893). Courtesy of the Dibner Library, National Museum of American History, Smithsonian Institution.*

Exposition of 1893 formed a galaxy of its own and has generated many compelling explanations of its significance.[4] The late historian Warren Susman considered the Chicago World's Columbian Exposition a liminal event, a national "rite of passage," ushering in a new value system that helped put America on the road to becoming a society that valued consumption above production. Historian Neil Harris, in examining Victorian-era fairs as "educational pleasure grounds," has noted the centrality of Chicago's fair for crafting the modern "urban idea," while historian James Gilbert has argued that the fair manifested an essential tension between high culture and commercial values and served as the seedbed for the creation of modern American mass culture. An equally compelling case can be made that

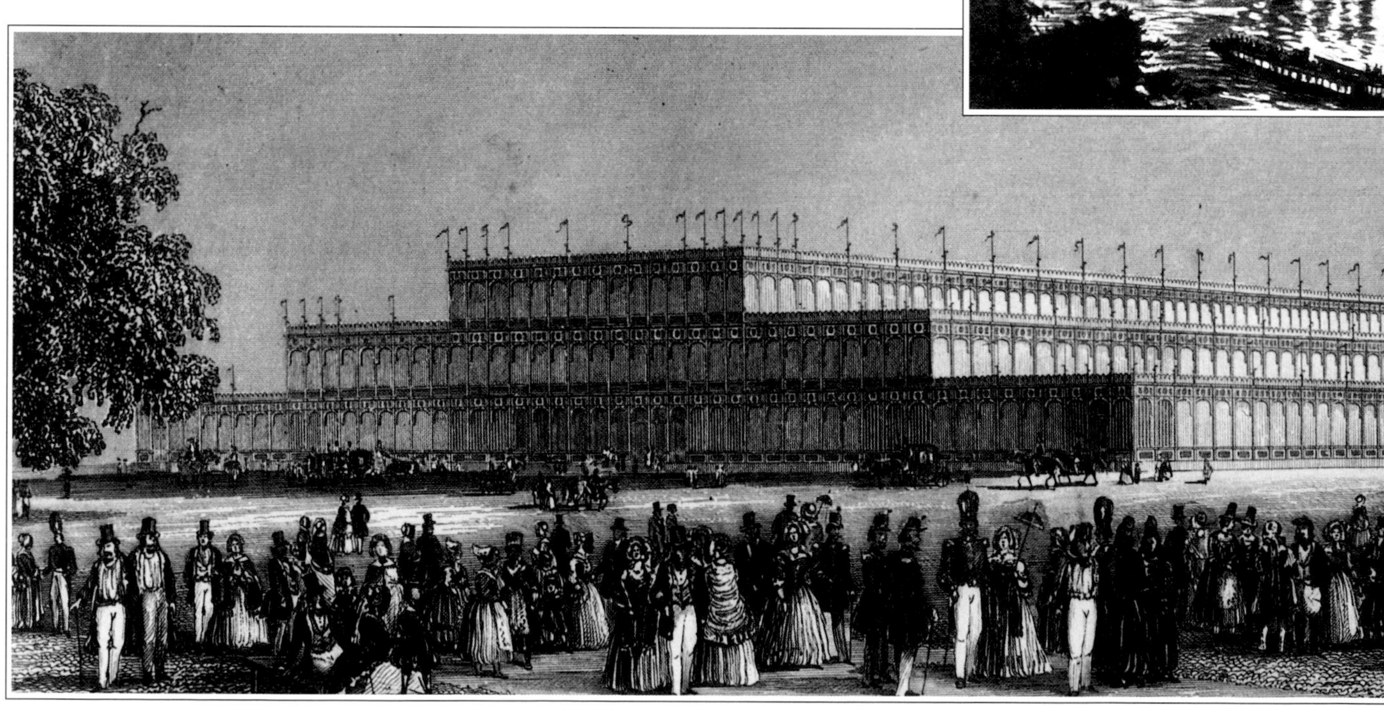

.. 4 ..
"The Great Exhibition of the Industry of All Nations," Tallis's History and Description of the Crystal Palace and the Exhibition of the World's Industry in 1851 *(London and New York: John Tallis and Co., n.d.), frontispiece.*

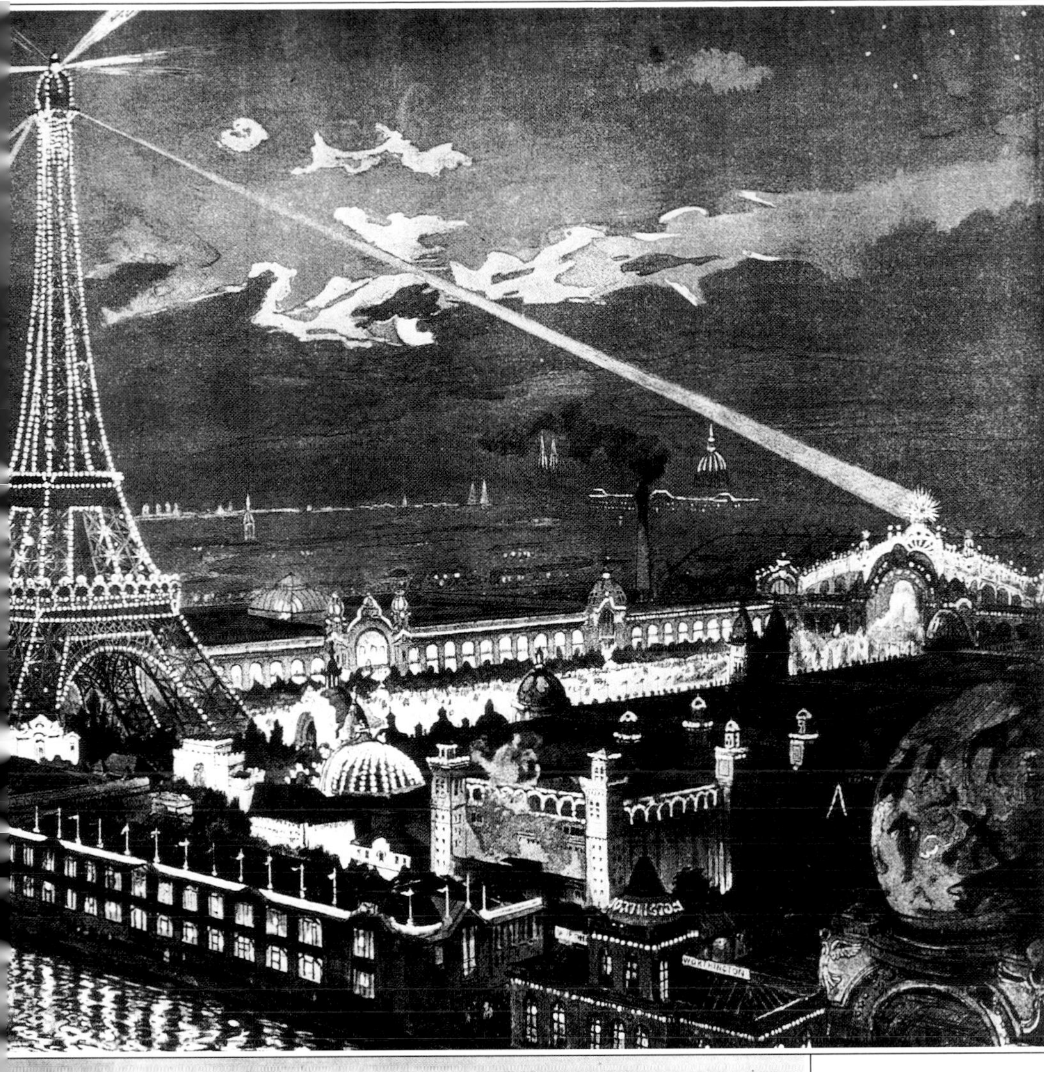

..5..
"Night view of the Eiffel Tower, Paris, 1900,"
L'exposition de Paris (1900), *vol. 1 (Paris: Montgredien et cie, n.d.).*

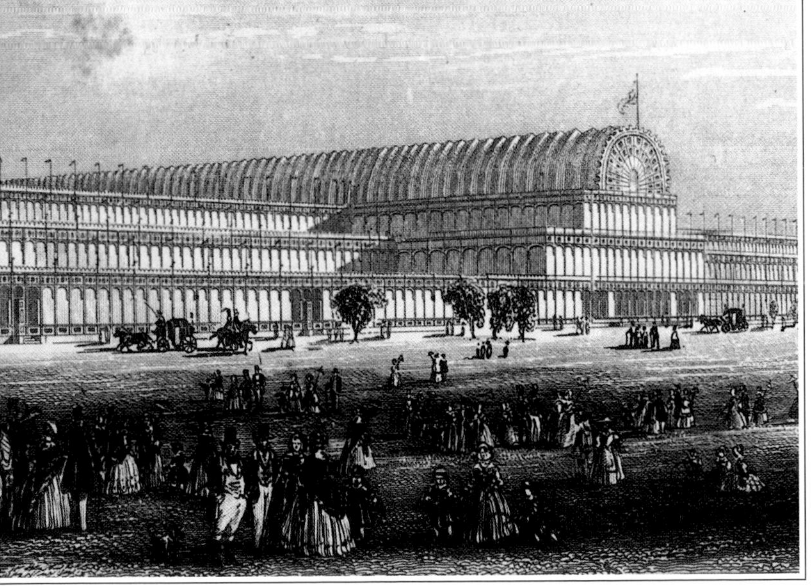

. . 6 . .

"The Centennial—Balloon View of the Fair Grounds." Photographs by R. Newell & Sons and sketches by Theo R. Davis. Harper's Weekly, *30 Sept. 1876, supplement.*

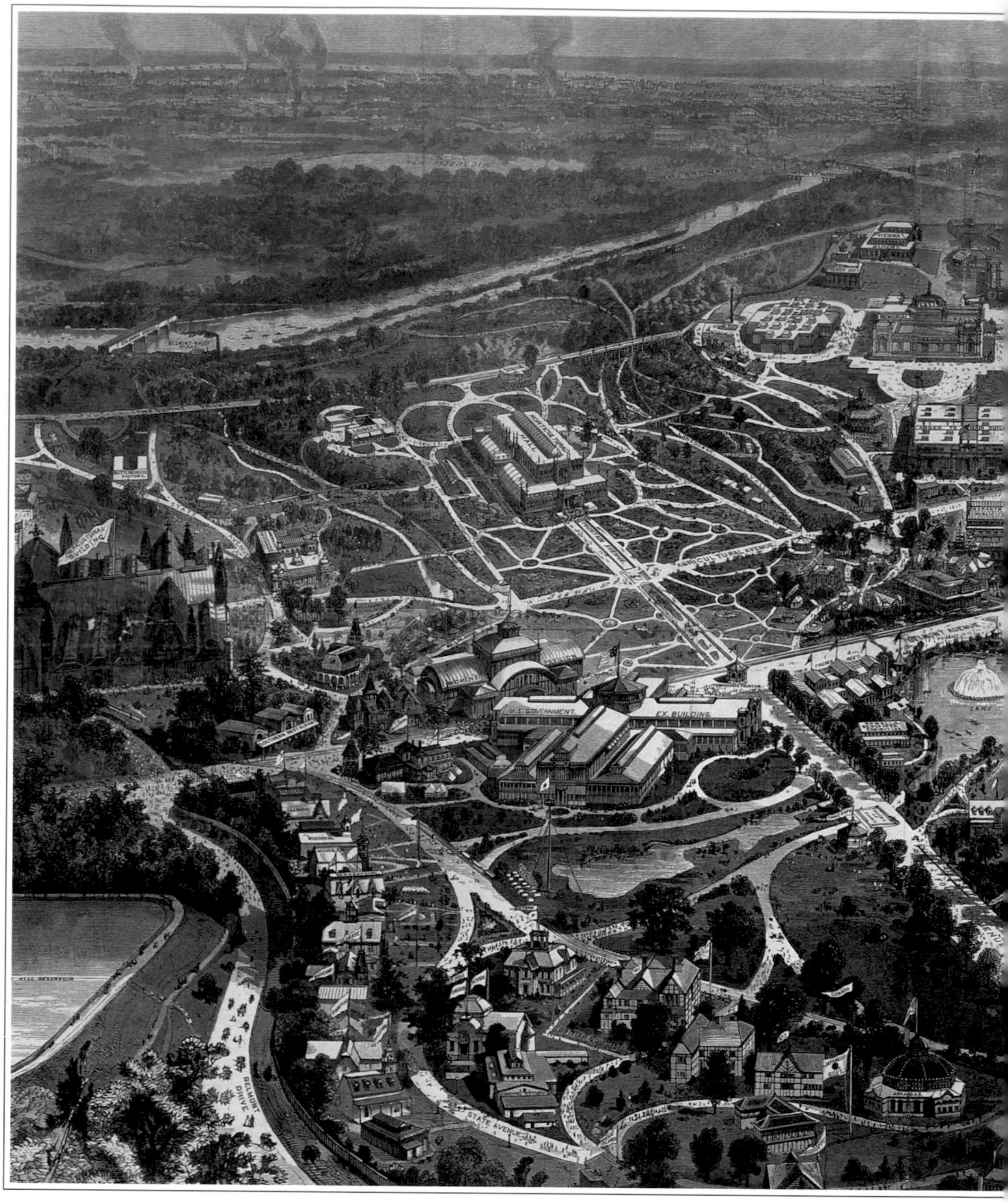

. . 7 . .

"Judge's Suggestion for 1892. Let each State be properly represented in the proposed Exposition,"

Judge *(n.d.): 328. Courtesy of George Gurney.*

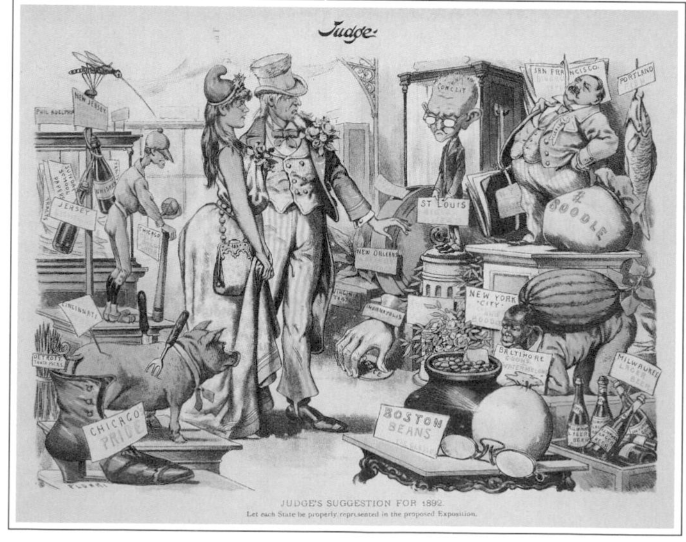

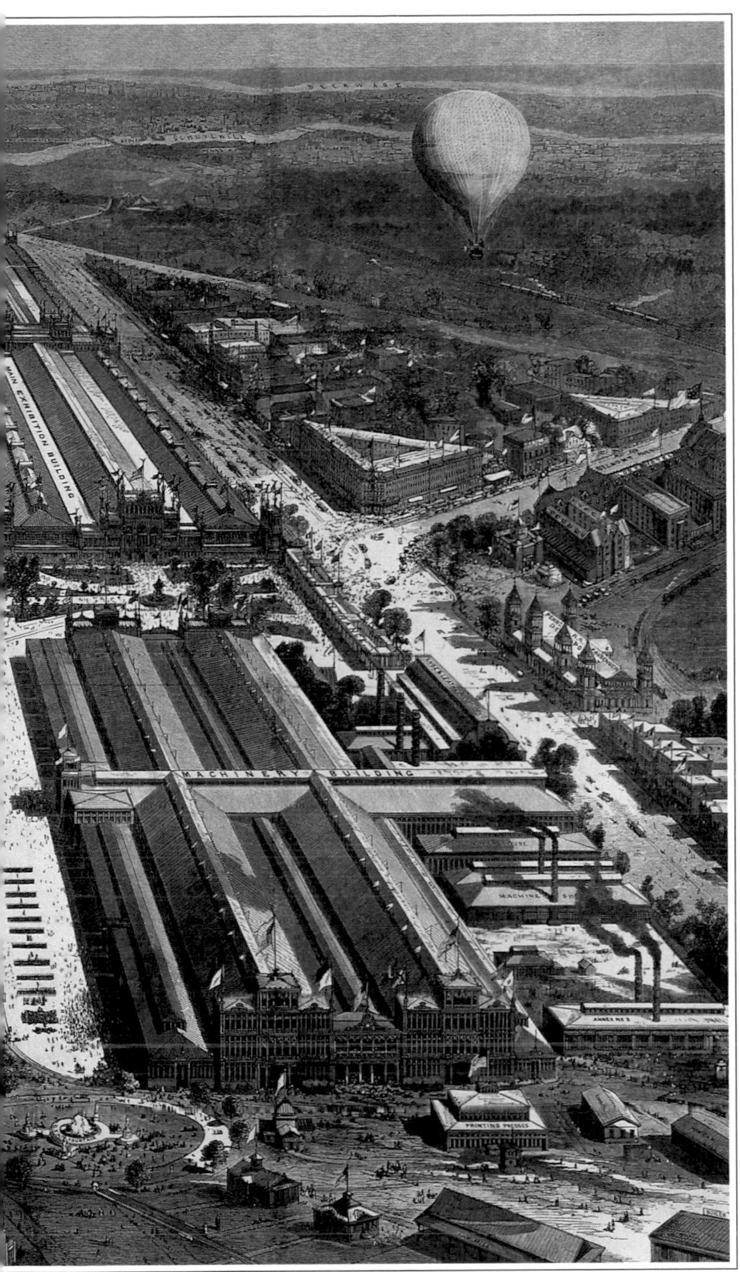

the fair accelerated what sociologist Tony Bennett has called an "exhibitionary complex"—a process initiated by national elites in the context of the massive dislocations associated with industrialization to win the hearts and minds of Americans by convincing them that they could, as Bennett writes, "identify with power, to see it as, if not directly theirs, then indirectly so, a force regulated and channeled by society's ruling groups but for the good of all." With its magisterial White City, consisting of monumental Beaux-Arts buildings overflowing with signs of material and artistic "progress," and its mile-long Midway Plaisance, an outdoor ethnological museum conjugated into an entertainment strip, the Chicago fair offered a blueprint for utopia that linked the promise of future material abundance and prosperity to popular acceptance of prevailing power relationships in American society. The Chicago fair, a work of art in its own right, was an ideological construct, an exercise in cultural representation, that hastened what Alan Trachtenberg has aptly called "the incorporation of America."[5]

The idea to hold a world's fair in conjunction with a national celebration of Columbus's landing in the New World originated in the early 1880s while memories of the Philadelphia Centennial Exhibition were still dancing in people's minds (fig. 6). The centennial had not only stimulated a tremendous outpouring of nationalism, it had pumped millions of dollars into Philadelphia's depression-laden economy. Throughout the 1880s, a parade of civic leaders from Minneapolis/St. Paul, St. Louis, and Washington, D.C., announced plans to compete for authorization by the U.S. Congress to host the Columbian fair. But the uncertain state of the national economy in the 1880s undercut most of these efforts, leaving prominent citizens in Chicago and New York as the main contenders for the prize that one exposition enthusiast described as "the greatest event since the birth of our Saviour" (fig. 7).[6]

.. 8 ..

Architects, Artists and Officials of the World's Columbian Exposition, 1892.

Photograph by C. D. Arnold. From the left: Daniel H. Burnham, director of works; George B. Post of New York, architect; Montgomery B. Pickett, secretary of works; Henry Van Brunt of Kansas City, architect; Frank D. Millet, director of decoration; Maitland Armstrong, artist; Col. Edmund Rice, commandant; Augustus Saint-Gaudens, sculptor; Henry Sargent Codman, landscape architect; George Willoughby Maynard, artist; Charles F. McKim of New York, architect; Ernest R. Graham, assistant director of works; Dion Geraldine, general superintendent. World's Columbian Exposition Photographs by C. D. Arnold, bk. 1, p. 98. Courtesy of the Ryerson and Burnham Libraries, The Art Institute of Chicago, neg. no. E21585.

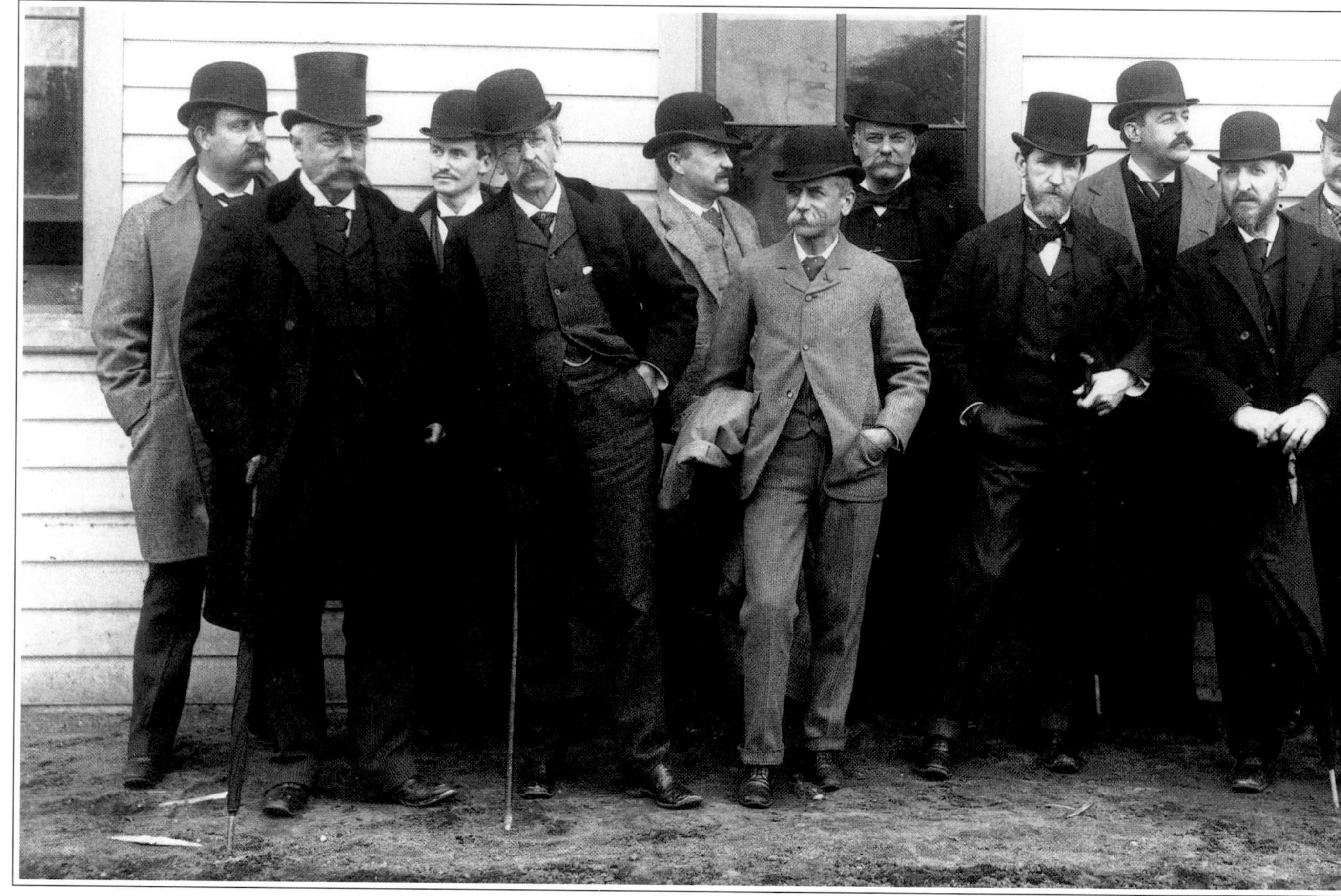

Much has been written about the brutal war of words that developed between the two cities. The New York press ridiculed Chicago's pretentiousness, while the Chicago papers attacked New York's political corruption. As the 1890 congressional deadline for bids approached, New York probably had the inside track because of its financial resources. But political infighting among New York politicians, coupled with the ability of Chicago boosters to raise a $10-million pledge in twenty-four hours from "thirty or more citizens whose aggregate wealth was known to be more than a hundred millions of dollars" led Congress to grant its approval to Chicago as the site for the fair.[7]

The control and direction of the fair was set from the start. In advance of presenting their case to Congress, Chicago elites—led by department store magnate Marshall Field, banker Lyman Gage, industrialist Cyrus McCormick, railroad baron George Pullman, and meat packers Gustavus Swift and Philip Armour—had organized a corporation to produce the fair and had raised $5 million from the first stock subscription. As cost estimates spiraled higher, exposition directors were compelled to turn to the state legislature, which authorized Chicago to sell $5 million in bonds, and to the U.S. Congress, which authorized the coinage of 2.5 million souvenir Columbian half dollars. Exposition authorities then sold the half dollars for one dollar apiece. As costs soared, a subsequent bond issue, purchased in large quantities by railroad corporations, together with interest-free loans from Chicago banks, gave exposition managers the necessary financial margin to proceed with their plans, underscoring the concentration of corporate and financial power that directed the fair.[8]

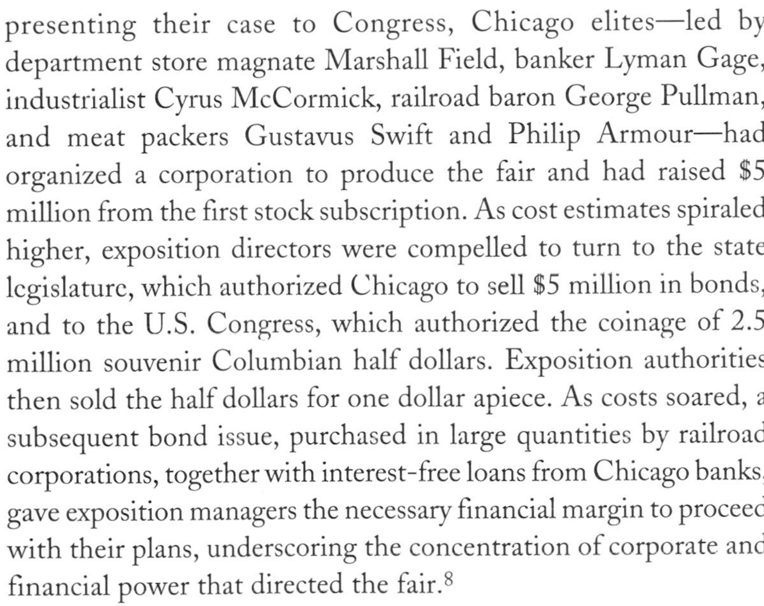

As their financial resources fell into place, exposition directors turned to the task at hand: building the fair and nurturing popular support for their endeavor. To design the exposition, they selected Chicago architect Daniel H. Burnham (fig. 8). Under his guidance, a group of nationally prominent architects and artists (Augustus Saint-Gaudens called one of their early assemblages "the greatest meeting of artists since the fifteenth century") produced the designs for the neoclassical wonderland that constituted the White City. Exposition palaces, however, were not the sum of the design story. The buildings, in addition to being constructed, had to be stocked with exhibits. For advice on arranging tons of exhibition material into a meaningful whole, exposition directors turned to the Smithsonian Institution, which had been the mainstay of the federal government's participation in fairs for nearly two decades. With the aid of an elaborate classification scheme developed by the Smithsonian's assistant secretary, G. Brown Goode, exposition directors developed a taxonomy by which exhibit materials were organized into a narrative structure that equated progress with material growth.[9]

The next steps in the design process were no less significant. To build public interest in the fair, exposition authorities selected Philadelphia journalist Moses P. Handy to organize a publicity department to promote the fair. Thanks to

Handy's department, more than five million words appeared in print about the fair before it even opened. Of equal importance to the fair's success was the decision by exposition organizers to give countless numbers of ordinary Americans a stake in the fair by involving them in the preparation of exhibits. In many states, governors and legislatures appointed world's fair committees; these groups in turn created county committees for gathering exhibition material from local citizens and for raising funds, often among school children, to help offset the costs of the state's display at the fair. Well in advance of its opening, the fair had become part of ordinary life in communities across the nation. Through its dedication day ceremonies it would leave a lasting impression on the ritualistic practices of the nation as well.[10]

The exercises held to dedicate the World's Columbian Exposition could have been an enormous embarrassment to all concerned. The truth was that, because of financial problems, debates over architectural styles, threatened strikes, and weather delays, the fair was behind schedule. As if to rub that fact in, New York City was threatening to steal Chicago's thunder by organizing massive festivities on October 12th—the day set aside for national observance of Columbus Day. Deeply concerned about these turns of fortune, Chicago civic leaders quickened their preparations for a week-long celebration that would serve as a dress rehearsal for the actual opening of the fair the following May.

Initial plans included a grandiose parade of floats devoted to the "procession of centuries." The order of the floats in the procession was revealing, proceeding from representations of the Stone and Bronze Ages, through the rise of Western civilization, to final floats representing the arts and sciences and "liberty enlightening the world." As costs for the spectacle mounted and as the logistical difficulties of getting the floats across and around bridges to Jackson Park became clearer, the directors abandoned this portion of the pageantry; left intact, however, were the hierarchical ideas about progress that governed the floats' thematic groupings in the first place.[11]

The week in late October 1892 set aside for dedication festivities was thick with intersecting webs of cultural and political significance. It began with Chicago's major churches holding what were billed as "Columbian services" as part of the regular worship schedules. Then, the public schools held special Columbus Day exercises which, as the week continued, were followed by civic and military parades, public receptions, and the formal dedication of the buildings.[12]

The civic parade was an astonishing sight to behold, even for a society in which parades were a routine part of the political culture (fig. 9). This parade stretched for almost ten miles with people marching sixteen to twenty abreast, including representatives of "[a]lmost every European nationality resident in Chicago, a division of colored citizens, and even the Indian boys from the Government school at Carlisle, Pa." The immensity of the spectacle was such that it required three hours for the vice president of the United States to witness the parade from his reviewing stand, which stood immediately adjacent to

thousands of Chicago school girls who had been organized into a "living American flag." The orderliness of the day's events received widespread notice, as did the presence of ten thousand federal and state troops. Ostensibly on hand for the military parade scheduled for the following day, the troops—following the precedent established at the 1851 exhibition when the British government stationed ten thousand regulars within a mile of the Crystal Palace in case the crowds, in the highly charged political atmosphere of the day, became mobs—could be mustered into service at a moment's notice.[13]

There was no need, however, for the military to use force. Instead, the troops escorted politicians and world's fair dignitaries through streets lined with more than a half million spectators to the exposition grounds, where between 100,000 and 150,000 people jammed into the Manufactures and Liberal Arts Building. What they saw inside that structure was staggering. On the speakers' platform, no fewer than 2,500 dignitaries took their seats. Immediately below them, nearly seven hundred reporters sat at tables documenting the proceedings. One thousand feet away, a 5,500-voice choir stood on a platform immediately behind the Chicago Orchestra, which had swollen to nearly two hundred performers (fig. 10). The crowd quickly filled the sixty thousand chairs and benches that lined the main floor of the building as well as the fifteen thousand chairs and benches placed in the gallery. Multitudes filled the available standing room. By the time the orchestra struck up the "Columbian March," composed by John K. Paine especially for the occasion, this indoor audience of unprecedented size was primed for the speeches attributing world historical importance to the Chicago fair.[14]

The common theme of the speeches, punctuated with Handel's "Hallelujah Chorus" and Mendelsohn's "To the Sons of Art," suggested that the exposition was a product of, and force behind, civilization. "The ceaseless, resistless march of civilization westward—ever westward—has reached and passed the Great Lakes of North America," Director General George Davis told the audience. In an artful rewriting of recent history, which only two years before had witnessed the massacre of Indians at Wounded Knee, Davis emphasized that "what we are and what we possess as a nation is not ours by purchase, not by conquest, but by virtue of the rich heritage that was spread out beneath the sun and stars . . . by the gift of the Infinite." The fair, he added, was "the national outgrowth of this nation's place in history. . . . And that this city was selected as the scene of this great commemorative festival was the natural outgrowth of predestined events." Other presentations—especially the musical rendition of Harriet Monroe's epic "Columbian Ode"—made clear that America's manifest destiny to fashion a New Jerusalem had been realized on the shores of Lake Michigan.[15]

These parades and ceremonies focused national attention on Chicago, but what gave the festivities added resonance was a dramatic act conceived by James B. Upham and Francis J. Bellamy, editors of *The Youth's Companion.* When plans for the Chicago fair were first taking form, Upham consulted with world's fair directors about making the exposition the centerpiece for a national demonstration of patriotism and offered his journal as the official organ for promoting the celebration. Exposition directors concurred and Upham put

.. 9 ..

Dedication Day Parade, 22 Oct. 1892—The Minnesota Militia Passing in front of the Transportation Building. Photograph by C. D. Arnold. *Official Photographs of the World's Columbian Exposition by C. D. Arnold*, vol. 4, pl. 7. Courtesy of The Chicago Public Library, Special Collections Department.

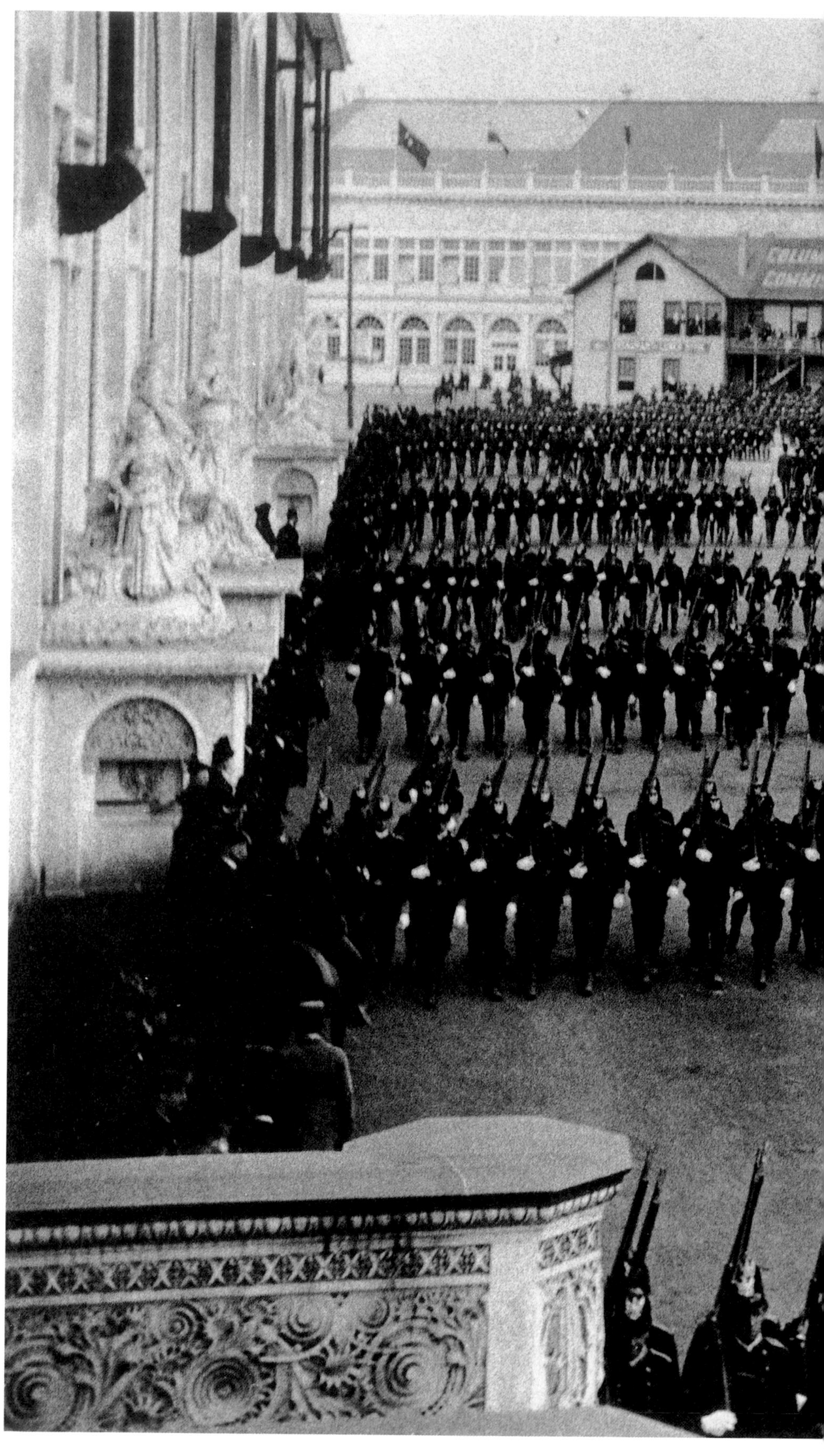

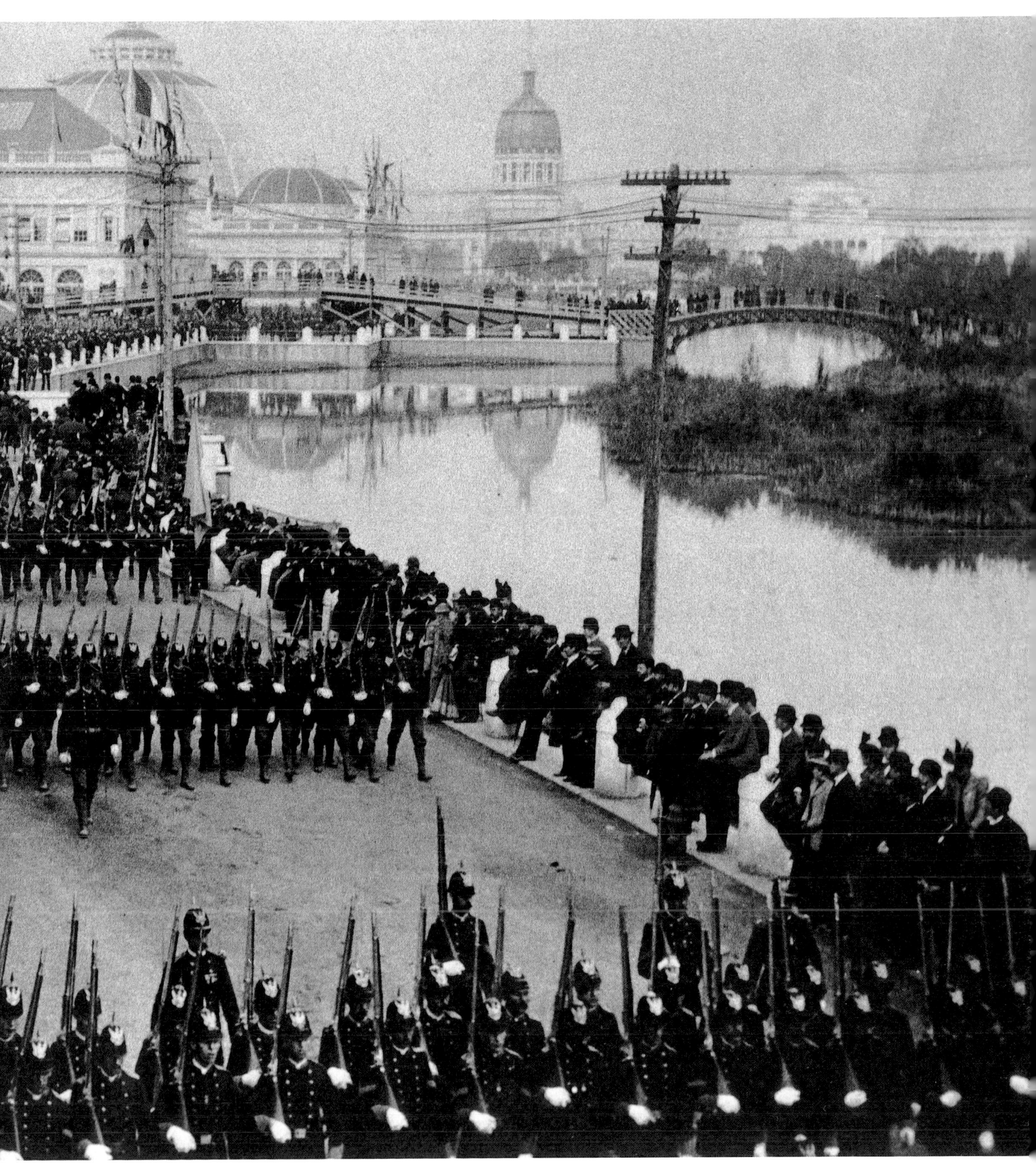

.. 10 ..

Dedication Day—Looking North from the Orchestra inside the Manufactures and Liberal Arts Building.
Photograph by C. D. Arnold. Official Photographs of the World's Columbian Exposition by C. D. Arnold, vol. 4, pl. 1. Courtesy of The Chicago Public Library, Special Collections Department.

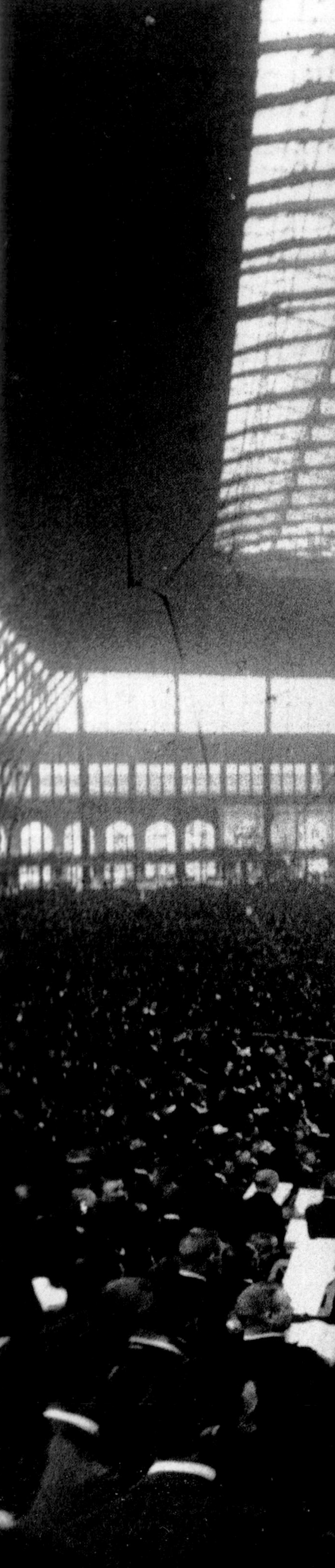

.. 11 ..

Text for "Salute to the Flag, by the Pupils" from "The Official Programme for the National School Celebration of Columbus Day," The Youth's Companion *65 (8 Sept. 1892): 446. Courtesy of the Trustees of Boston Public Library.*

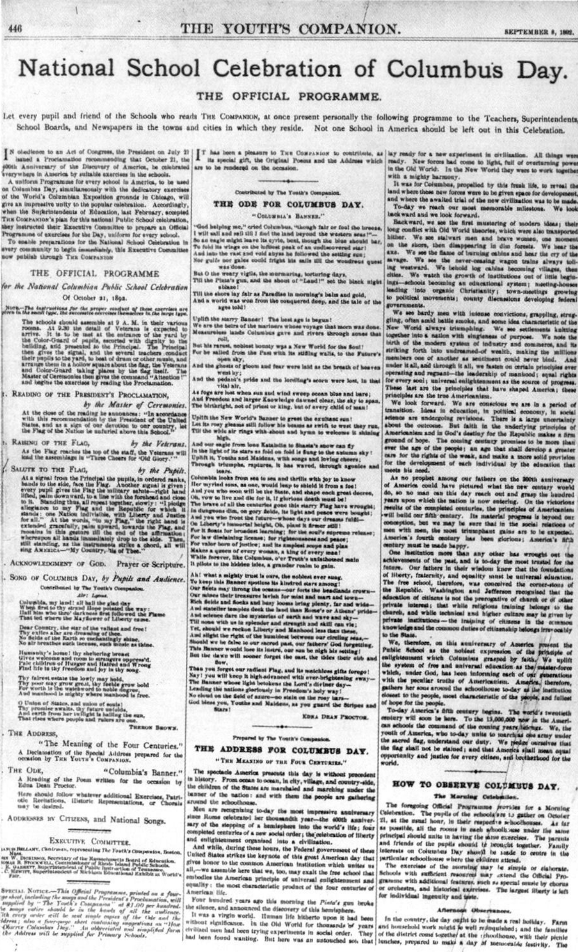

446 THE YOUTH'S COMPANION. SEPTEMBER 8, 1892.

National School Celebration of Columbus Day.

THE OFFICIAL PROGRAMME.

Let every pupil and friend of the Schools who reads THE COMPANION, at once present personally the following programme to the Teachers, Superintendents, School Boards, and Newspapers in the towns and cities in which they reside. Not one School in America should be left out in this Celebration.

IN obedience to an Act of Congress, the President on July 21 issued a Proclamation recommending that October 21, the 400th Anniversary of the Discovery of America, be celebrated everywhere in America by suitable exercises in the schools.

A uniform Programme for every school in America, to be used on Columbus Day, simultaneously with the dedicatory exercises of the World's Columbian Exposition grounds in Chicago, will give an impressive unity to the popular celebration. Accordingly, when the Superintendents of Education, last February, accepted THE COMPANION's plan for this national Public School celebration, they instructed their Executive Committee to prepare an Official Programme of exercises for the Day, *uniform for every school.*

To enable preparations for the National School Celebration in every community to begin *immediately*, this Executive Committee now publish through THE COMPANION.

THE OFFICIAL PROGRAMME

for the National Columbian Public School Celebration

Of October 21, 1892.

NOTE.—*The instructions for the proper conduct of these exercises are given in the small type; the successive exercises themselves in the large type.*

The schools should assemble at 9 A.M. in their various rooms. At 9.30 the detail of Veterans is expected to arrive. It is to be met at the entrance of the yard by the Color-Guard of pupils, escorted with dignity to the building, and presented to the Principal. The Principal then gives the signal, and the several teachers conduct their pupils to the yard, to beat of drum or other music, and arrange them in a hollow square about the flag, the Veterans and Color-Guard taking places by the flag itself. The Master of Ceremonies then gives the command "Attention!" and begins the exercises by reading the Proclamation.

1. READING OF THE PRESIDENT'S PROCLAMATION, *by the Master of Ceremonies.*

At the close of the reading he announces: "In accordance with this recommendation by the President of the United States, and as a sign of our devotion to our country, let the Flag of the Nation be unfurled above this School."

2. RAISING OF THE FLAG, *by the Veterans.*

As the Flag reaches the top of the staff, the Veterans will lead the assemblage in "Three Cheers for 'Old Glory.'"

3. SALUTE TO THE FLAG, *by the Pupils.*

At a signal from the Principal the pupils, in ordered ranks, hands to the side, face the Flag. Another signal is given; every pupil gives the Flag the military salute—right hand lifted, palm downward, to a line with the forehead and close to it. Standing thus, all repeat together, slowly: "I pledge allegiance to my Flag and the Republic for which it stands: one Nation indivisible, with Liberty and Justice for all." At the words, "to my Flag," the right hand is extended gracefully, palm upward, towards the Flag, and remains in this gesture till the end of the affirmation; whereupon all hands immediately drop to the side. Then, still standing, as the instruments strike a chord, all will sing AMERICA—"My Country, 'tis of Thee."

4. ACKNOWLEDGMENT OF GOD. Prayer or Scripture.

5. SONG OF COLUMBUS DAY, *by Pupils and Audience.*

Contributed by The Youth's Companion.
Air: Lyons.

Columbia, my land! all hail the glad day
When first to thy strand Hope pointed the way.
Hail him who thro' darkness first followed the Flame
That led where the Mayflower of Liberty came.

Dear Country, the star of the valiant and free!
Thy exiles afar are dreaming of thee.
No fields of the Earth so enchantingly shine,
No air breathes such incense, such music as thine.

Humanity's home! thy sheltering breast
Gives welcome and room to strangers oppress'd.
Pale children of Hunger and Hatred and Wrong
Find life in thy freedom and joy in thy song.

Thy fairest estate the lowly may hold,
Thy poor may grow great, thy feeble grow bold:
For worth is the watchword to noble degree,
And manhood is mighty where manhood is free.

O Union of States, and union of souls!
Thy promise awaits, thy future unfolds,
And earth from her twilight is hailing the sun,
That rises where people and rulers are one.

THERON BROWN.

6. THE ADDRESS, "The Meaning of the Four Centuries."

A Declamation of the Special Address prepared for the occasion by THE YOUTH'S COMPANION.

7. THE ODE, "Columbia's Banner."

A Reading of the Poem written for the occasion by Edna Dean Proctor.

Here should follow whatever additional Exercises, Patriotic Recitations, Historic Representations, or Chorals may be desired.

8. ADDRESSES BY CITIZENS, and National Songs.

EXECUTIVE COMMITTEE.

FRANCIS BELLAMY, Chairman, representing The Youth's Companion, Boston.
JOHN W. DICKINSON, Secretary of the Massachusetts Board of Education.
THOMAS B. STOCKWELL, Commissioner of Rhode Island Public Schools.
W. R. GARRETT, Superintendent of Public Instruction of Tennessee.
W. C. HEWITT, Superintendent of Michigan Educational Exhibit at World's Fair.

SPECIAL NOTICE.—*This Official Programme, printed on a four-page sheet, including the songs and the President's Proclamation, will be supplied by "The Youth's Companion" at $1.00 per hundred. The songs entire should be in the hands of all the audience. With every order will be sent single copies of the Ode and the Address; also a four-page sheet containing suggestions on "How to Observe Columbus Day." An abbreviated and simplified form of the Address will be supplied for Primary Schools.*

IT has been a pleasure to THE COMPANION to contribute, as its special gift, the Original Poems and the Address which are to be rendered on the occasion.

Contributed by The Youth's Companion.

THE ODE FOR COLUMBUS DAY.

"COLUMBIA'S BANNER."

"God helping me," cried Columbus, "though fair or foul the breeze,
I will sail and sail till I find the land beyond the western seas!"—
So an eagle might leave its eyrie, bent, though the blue should bar,
To fold its wings on the loftiest peak of an undiscovered star!
And into the vast and void abyss he followed the setting sun;
Nor gulfs nor gales could fright his sails till the wondrous quest was done.
But O the weary vigils, the murmuring, torturing days,
Till the Pinta's gun, and the shout of "Land!" set the black night ablaze!
Till the shore lay fair as Paradise in morning's balm and gold,
And a world was won from the conquered deep, and the tale of the ages told!

Uplift the starry Banner! The best age is begun!
We are the heirs of the mariners whose voyage that morn was done.
Measureless lands Columbus gave and rivers through zones that roll,
But his rarest, noblest bounty was a New World for the Soul!
For he sailed from the Past with its stifling walls, to the Future's open sky,
And the ghosts of gloom and fear were laid as the breath of heaven went by;
And the pedant's pride and the lordling's scorn were lost, in that vital air,
As fogs are lost when sun and wind sweep ocean blue and bare;
And Freedom and larger Knowledge dawned clear, the sky to span,
The birthright, not of priest or king, but of every child of man!

Uplift the New World's Banner to greet the exultant sun!
Let its rosy gleams still follow his beams as swift to west they run,
Till the wide air rings with shout and hymn to welcome it shining high,
And our eagle from lone Katahdin to Shasta's snow can fly
In the light of its stars as fold on fold is flung to the autumn sky!
Uplift it, Youths and Maidens, with songs and loving cheers;
Through triumphs, raptures, it has waved, through agonies and tears.
Columbia looks from sea to sea and thrills with joy to know
Her myriad sons, as one, would leap to shield it from a foe!
And you who soon will be the State, and shape each great decree,
Oh, vow to live and die for it, if glorious death must be!
The brave of all the centuries gone this starry Flag have wrought;
In dungeons dim, on gory fields, its light and peace were bought;
And you who front the future—whose days our dreams fulfil—
On Liberty's immortal height, Oh, plant it firmer still!
For it floats for broadest learning; for the soul's supreme release;
For law disdaining license; for righteousness and peace;
For valor born of justice; and its amplest scope and plan
Makes a queen of every woman, a king of every man!
While forever, like Columbus, o'er Truth's unfathomed main
It pilots to the hidden isles, a grander realm to gain.

Ah! what a mighty trust is ours, the noblest ever sung,
To keep this Banner spotless its kindred stars among!
Our fleets may throng the oceans—our forts the headlands crown—
Our mines their treasures lavish for mint and mart and town—
Rich fields and flocks and busy looms bring plenty, far and wide—
And statelier temples deck the land than Rome's or Athens' pride—
And science dare the mysteries of earth and wave and sky—
Till none with us in splendor and strength and skill can vie;
Yet, should we reckon Liberty and Manhood less than these,
And slight the right of the humblest between our circling seas,—
Should we be false to our sacred past, our fathers' God forgetting,
This Banner would lose its lustre, our sun be nigh its setting!
But the dawn will sooner forget the east, the tides their ebb and flow,
Than you forget our radiant Flag, and its matchless gifts forego!
Nay! you will keep it high-advanced with ever-brightening sway—
The Banner whose light betokens the Lord's diviner day—
Leading the nations gloriously in Freedom's holy way!
No cloud on the field of azure—no stain on the rosy bars—
God bless you, Youths and Maidens, as you guard the Stripes and Stars!

EDNA DEAN PROCTOR.

Prepared by The Youth's Companion.

THE ADDRESS FOR COLUMBUS DAY.

"THE MEANING OF THE FOUR CENTURIES."

The spectacle America presents this day is without precedent in history. From ocean to ocean, in city, village, and country-side, the children of the States are marshaled and marching under the banner of the nation: and with them the people are gathering around the schoolhouse.

Men are recognizing to-day the most impressive anniversary since Rome celebrated her thousandth year—the 400th anniversary of the stepping of a hemisphere into the world's life; four completed centuries of a new social order; the celebration of liberty and enlightenment organized into a civilization.

And while, during these hours, the Federal government of these United States strikes the keynote of this great American day that gives honor to the common American institution which unites us all,—we assemble here that we, too, may exalt the free school that embodies the American principle of universal enlightenment and equality: the most characteristic product of the four centuries of American life.

Four hundred years ago this morning the *Pinta's* gun broke the silence, and announced the discovery of this hemisphere.

It was a virgin world. Human life hitherto upon it had been without significance. In the Old World for thousands of years civilized men had been trying experiments in social order. They had been found wanting. But here was an untouched soil that lay ready for a new experiment in civilization. All things were ready. New forces had come to light, full of overturning power in the Old World. In the New World they were to work together with a mighty harmony.

It was for Columbus, propelled by this fresh life, to reveal the land where these new forces were to be given space for development, and where the awaited trial of the new civilization was to be made.

To-day we reach our most memorable milestone. We look backward and we look forward.

Backward, we see the first mustering of modern ideas; their long conflict with Old World theories, which were also transported hither. We see stalwart men and brave women, one moment on the shore, then disappearing in dim forests. We hear the axe. We see the flame of burning cabins and hear the cry of the savage. We see the never-ceasing wagon trains always toiling westward. We behold log cabins becoming villages, then cities. We watch the growth of institutions out of little beginnings—schools becoming an educational system; meeting-houses leading into organic Christianity; town-meetings growing to political movements; county discussions developing federal governments.

We see hardy men with intense convictions, grappling, struggling, often amid battle smoke, and some idea characteristic of the New World always triumphing. We see settlements knitting together into a nation with singleness of purpose. We note the birth of the modern system of industry and commerce, and its striking forth into undreamed-of wealth, making the millions members one of another as sentiment could never bind. And under it all, and through it all, we fasten on certain principles ever operating and regnant—the leadership of manhood; equal rights for every soul; universal enlightenment as the source of progress. These last are the principles that have shaped America; these principles are the true Americanism.

We look forward. We are conscious we are in a period of transition. Ideas in education, in political economy, in social science are undergoing revisions. There is a large uncertainty about the outcome. But faith in the underlying principles of Americanism and in God's destiny for the Republic makes a firm ground of hope. The coming century promises to be more than ever the age of the people; an age that shall develop a greater care for the rights of the weak, and make a more solid provision for the development of each individual by the education that meets his need.

As no prophet among our fathers on the 300th anniversary of America could have pictured what the new century would do, so no man can this day reach out and grasp the hundred years upon which the nation is now entering. On the victorious results of the completed centuries, the principles of Americanism will build our fifth century. Its material progress is beyond our conception, but we may be sure that in the social relations of men with men, the most triumphant gains are to be expected. America's fourth century has been glorious; America's fifth century must be made happy.

One institution more than any other has wrought out the achievements of the past, and is to-day the most trusted for the future. Our fathers in their wisdom knew that the foundations of liberty, fraternity, and equality must be universal education. The free school, therefore, was conceived the corner-stone of the Republic. Washington and Jefferson recognized that the education of citizens is not the prerogative of church or of other private interest; that while religious training belongs to the church, and while technical and higher culture may be given by private institutions—the training of citizens in the common knowledge and the common duties of citizenship belongs irrevocably to the State.

We, therefore, on this anniversary of America present the Public School as the noblest expression of the principle of enlightenment which Columbus grasped by faith. We uplift the system of free and universal education as the master-force which, under God, has been informing each of our generations with the peculiar truths of Americanism. America, therefore, gathers her sons around the schoolhouse to-day as the institution closest to the people, most characteristic of the people, and fullest of hope for the people.

To-day America's fifth century begins. The world's twentieth century will soon be here. To the 13,000,000 now in the American schools the command of the coming years belongs. We, the youth of America, who to-day unite to march as one army under the sacred flag, understand our duty. We pledge ourselves that the flag shall not be stained; and that America shall mean equal opportunity and justice for every citizen, and brotherhood for the world.

HOW TO OBSERVE COLUMBUS DAY.

The Morning Celebration.

The foregoing Official Programme provides for a Morning Celebration. The pupils of the schools are to gather on October 21, at the usual hour, in their respective schoolhouses. As far as possible, all the rooms in each schoolhouse under the same principal should unite in having the same exercises. The parents and friends of the pupils should be brought together. Family interests on Columbus Day should be made to centre in the particular schoolhouse where the children attend.

The exercises of the morning may be simple or elaborate. Schools with sufficient resources may extend the Official Programme with additional features, such as special music by chorus or orchestra, and historical exercises. The largest liberty is left for individual ingenuity and taste.

Afternoon Observances.

In the country, the day ought to be made a real holiday. Farm and household work might be well relinquished; and the families of the district come together at the schoolhouse, with their picnic lunches, prepared to make a day of memorable festivity. The

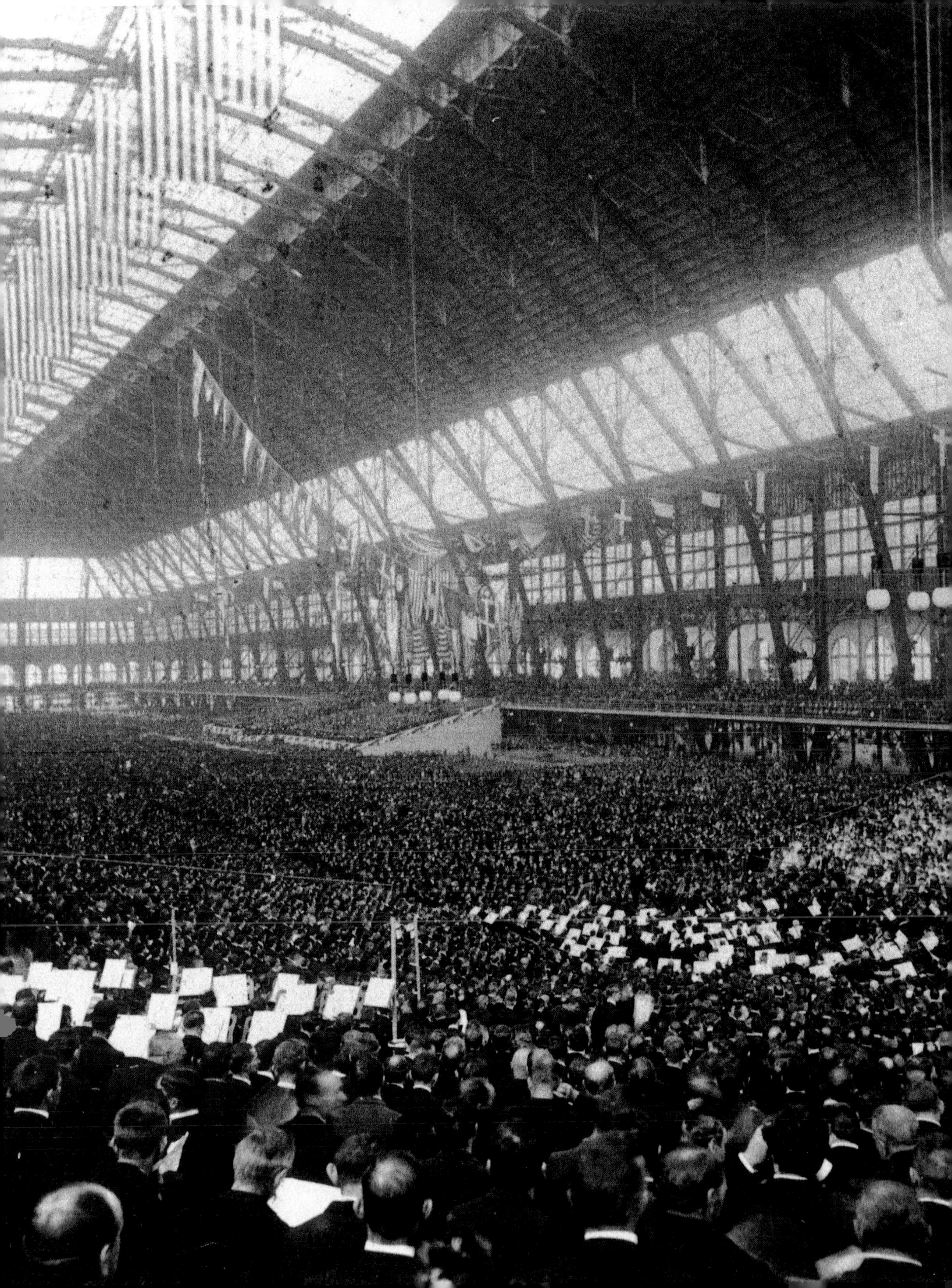

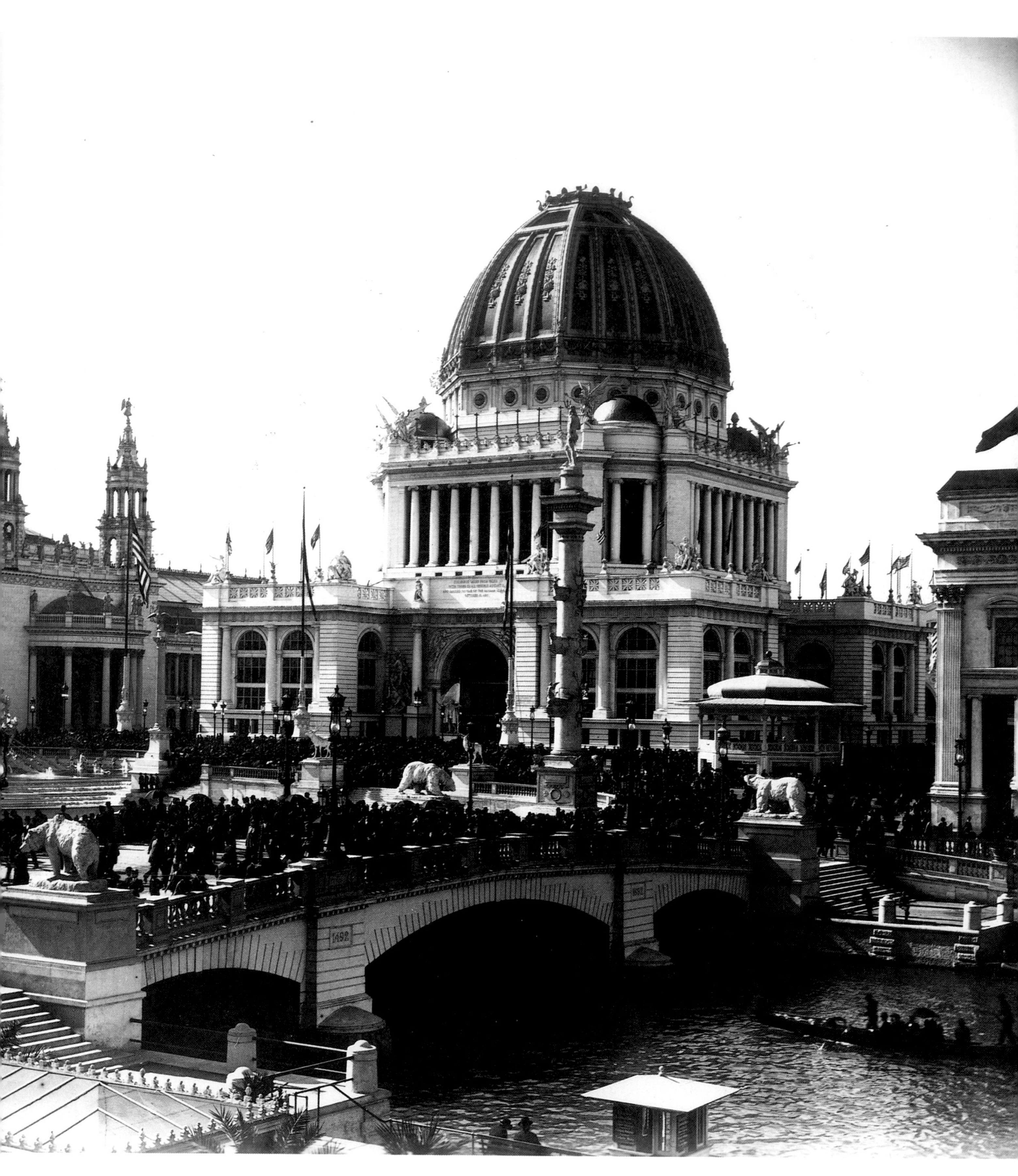

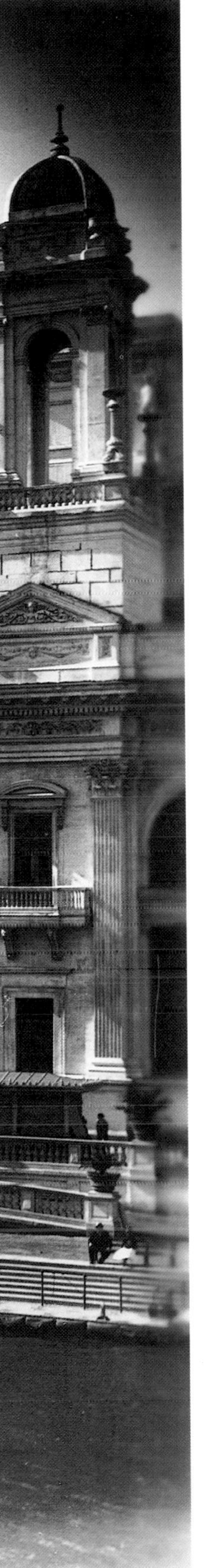

Bellamy, a cousin of utopian novelist Edward Bellamy, in charge of the planning committee. As Bellamy thought about the quadrocentennial celebrations of Columbus's landfall planned for the upcoming year, he was deeply worried by widening fissures of ethnic tension and industrial violence in American society. What Americans, especially their children, needed, Bellamy concluded, was some kind of grand dramatic ritual that would involve children across the land reaffirming their loyalty to their nation—an "affirmation" of allegiance, for example, that schoolchildren could recite as part of the national celebration of the dedication of the World's Columbian Exposition. In the course of one evening, Bellamy jotted down the words that would resonate so deeply in a society torn by conflict: "I pledge allegiance to my Flag and the Republic for which it stands: one Nation, indivisible, with Liberty and Justice for all." When Bellamy brought his idea to the attention of politicians and world's fair directors, they seized it as their own. The Federal Bureau of Education launched a nationwide campaign to get schools to include the salute to the flag as part of their Columbian celebrations. *The Youth's Companion* (fig. 11) was explicit about what children should say and do:

.. 12 ..
The Administration Building from the Manufactures and Liberal Arts Building. *Photograph by the United States Government Exposition Board, Committee on Photography: Thomas W. Smillie, Frances Benjamin Johnston, and Lt. Henry Harris, Photographers. Courtesy of the National Museum of American History, Smithsonian Institution, neg. no. 12135.*

At a signal from the Principal, the pupils, in ordered ranks, hands to the side, face the Flag. Another signal is given; every pupil gives the Flag the military salute—right hand lifted, palm downward, to a line with the forehead and close to it. Standing thus, all repeat together, slowly: "I pledge allegiance to my Flag and the Republic for which it stands: one Nation indivisible, with Liberty and Justice for all." At the words, "to my Flag," the right hand is extended gracefully, palm upward, towards the Flag, and remains in this gesture till the end of the affirmation; whereupon all hands immediately drop to the side. Then, still standing, as the instruments strike a chord, all will sing AMERICA—"My Country, 'tis of Thee."

The result of the pledge was that while a mass audience assembled in Chicago and demonstrated its enthusiasm for the fair, a far larger—and more impressionable—audience performed a ritualistic act of fealty in school ceremonies that wedded images of flag and fair into mutually reinforcing national icons.[16]

As important as they were, these preliminary ceremonies only hinted at the true power of the fair—the power of its organizers to constitute, or construct, national identity. By opening day, the full force of that power to manufacture national identity—through highly charged visual representations of American civilization and the "otherness" of different cultures—was everywhere on view at the fair, especially in the contrast between the White City and the Midway Plaisance.

The White City—a cluster of palatial Beaux-Arts, neoclassical architectural representations of civilization as conceived by the exposition's master builders—comprised the inner core of the exposition (fig. 13). Richard Morris Hunt's Administration Building (fig. 12); Charles F. McKim, William R. Mead, and

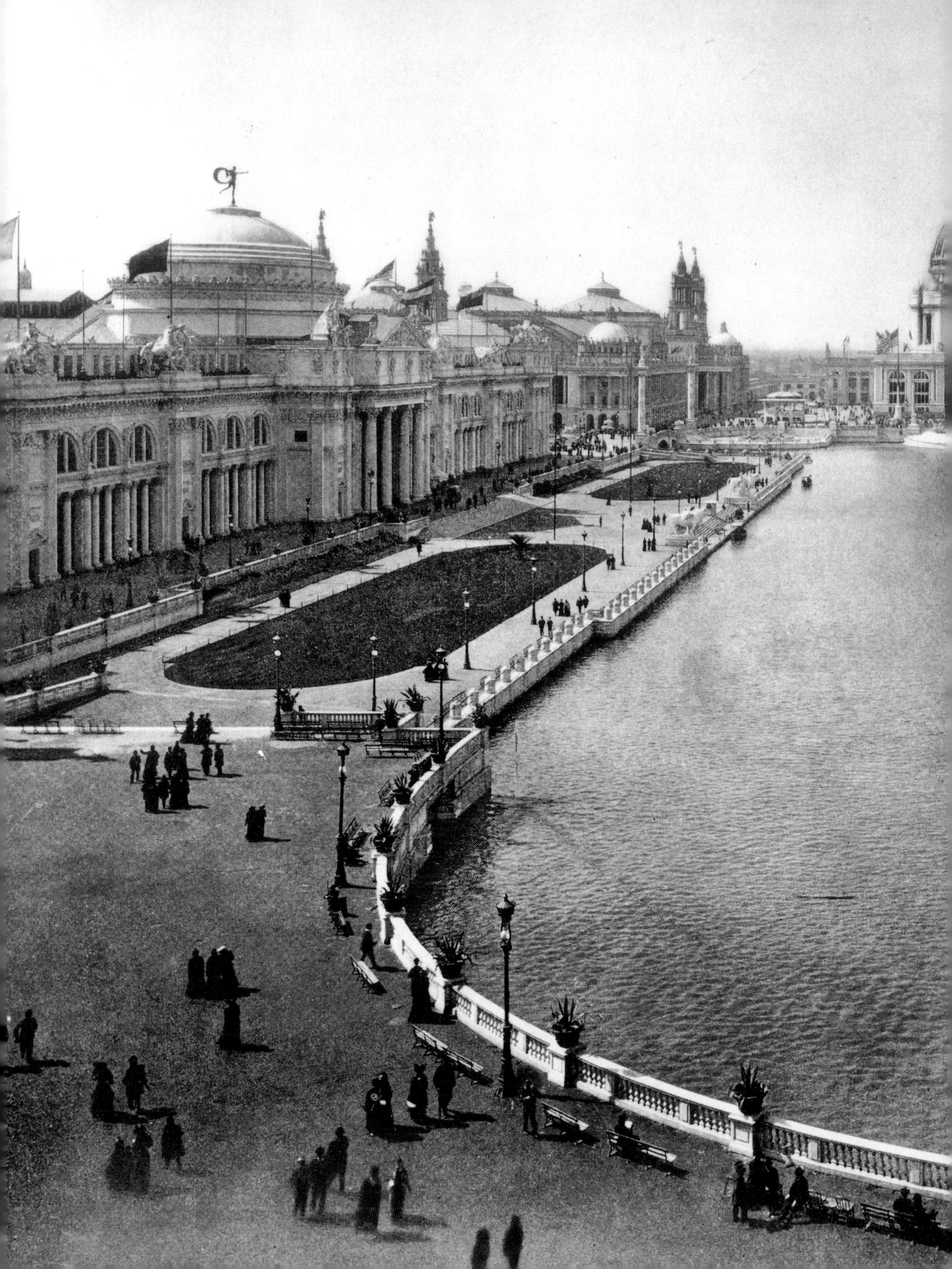

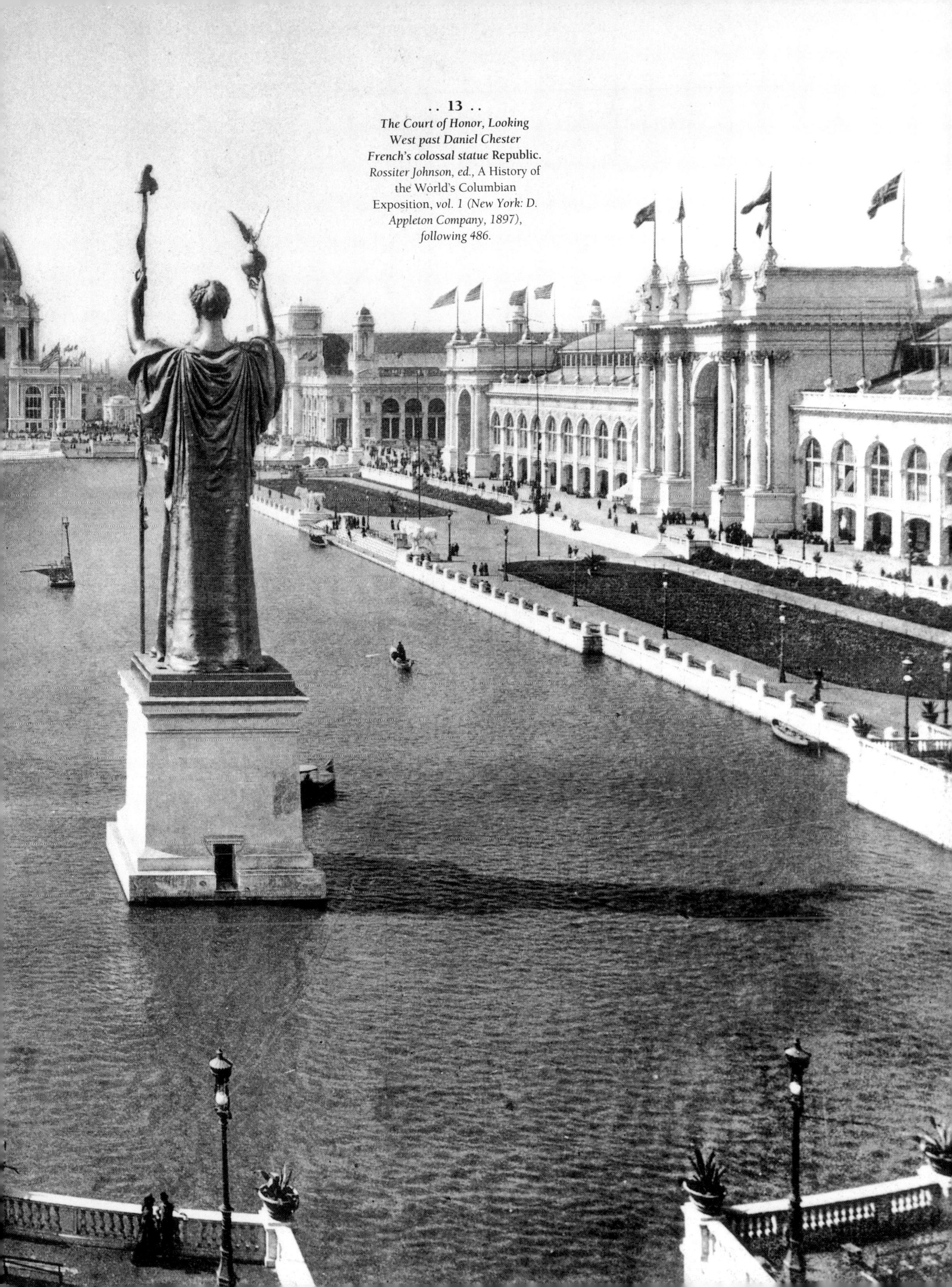

.. **13** ..

***The Court of Honor, Looking West past Daniel Chester French's colossal statue* Republic.**

Rossiter Johnson, ed., A History of the World's Columbian Exposition, *vol. 1 (New York: D. Appleton Company, 1897), following 486.*

Stanford White's Agricultural Building; Henry Van Brunt and Frank M. Howe's Electricity Building; Henry Ives Cobb's Fisheries Building; William Le Baron Jenney's Horticultural Building; Robert Swain Peabody and John Stearns's Machinery Building; George B. Post's Manufactures and Liberal Arts Building; Solon S. Beman's Mines and Mining Building; Dankmar Adler and Louis H. Sullivan's Transportation Building; Charles Atwood's Fine Arts Building; and Sophia G. Hayden's Woman's Building—these exhibition palaces reflected a view that at its core equated civilization with commercial abundance and racial hierarchy.

Signs of America's commercial prosperity were everywhere on view at the fair. In a sense, the fair's great exhibition buildings, full of displays emblematic of America's material prosperity, were nothing more than grandiose versions of Chicago's department stores. Among the sights at the fair were giant exhibits of California fruits, maps made of pickles, immense spreads of machinery and glassware, model kitchens, 160-lb. elephant tusks, multitudes of pyramids built out of soaps and copper wires, and obelisks constructed out of sardine cans. This was a veritable "dream world of mass consumption" (fig. 14).[17]

The fair also projected a dream world of another dimension. At precisely the moment that industrialists and farmers were being criticized for overproducing goods beyond the capacity of the marketplace to absorb them (and thus for causing the cycle of industrial depressions that began in 1873 and were still gripping the country in 1893), the fair held out a solution: foreign markets. Much of the rest of the world, at least as represented in displays at the fair, seemed ripe for American economic penetration. This side of the fair was so clearly in evidence that when the exposition closed, Philadelphia scientist William P. Wilson persuaded that city's civic leaders to erect a commercial museum stocked with displays from the Chicago fair. The museum would help American manufacturers and farmers to assess overseas market possibilities for their goods. On this score, the exposition was clear: there was nothing wrong with the American economy that more markets could not cure. This conviction, in turn, rested upon another—namely, that obtaining those markets was part of an inexorable civilizing process that America had a duty to perform.[18]

The moral imperative that accompanied this imperialistic way of thinking came to light in the contrast presented by the White City and the Midway Plaisance. There is disagreement among scholars who have studied this mile-long entertainment strip and its relationship to the rest of the fair and to the broader culture. Some have argued that the Midway, with its villages of nonwhites located between food and amusement concessions, appeared to be organized into a social Darwinian ladder, stretching from the "savagery" of Native Americans and Africans, to the "civilization" represented by the Woman's Building, located just inside the grounds of the White City. Historian James Gilbert, on the other hand, argues that the ethnological motivations that underlay the original plan for the Midway were subverted by its commercial possibilities. "[A]s the Midway evolved and changed," Gilbert writes, "it became more chaotic and confused in purpose, with the initial order of exhibits disrupted, and the gradual triumph of commercial over pseudoscientific considerations." The Midway Plaisance, Gilbert concludes, is best regarded as "a coherently

.. 14 ..

Interior of the California Building.

Photograph by C.D. Arnold. The statue of California (right) and the knight on horseback made of prunes (left) are surrounded by the bounteous displays of various California counties. Official Photographs of the World's Columbian Exposition by C.D. Arnold, vol. 3, pl. 77. Courtesy of The Chicago Public Library, Special Collections Department.

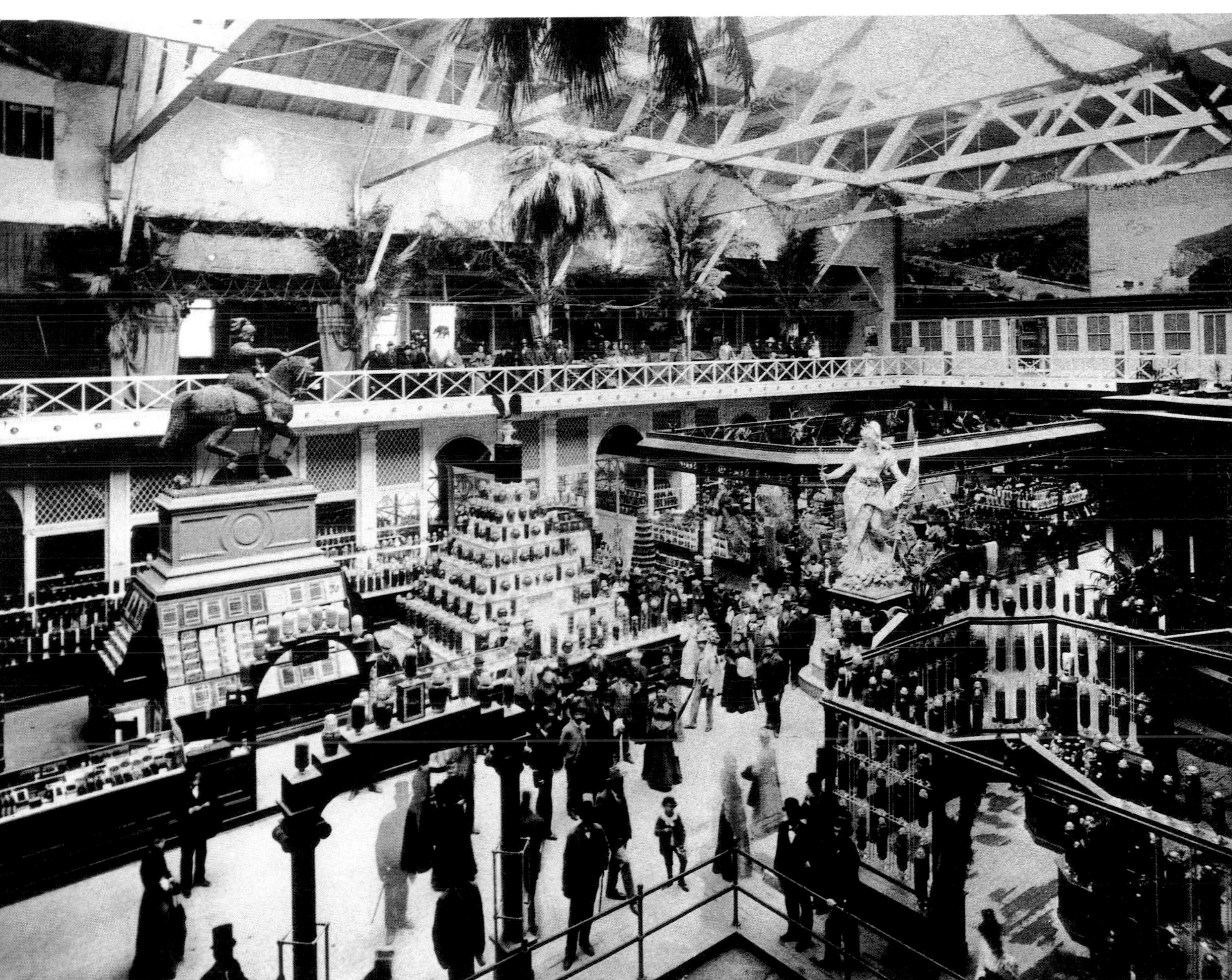

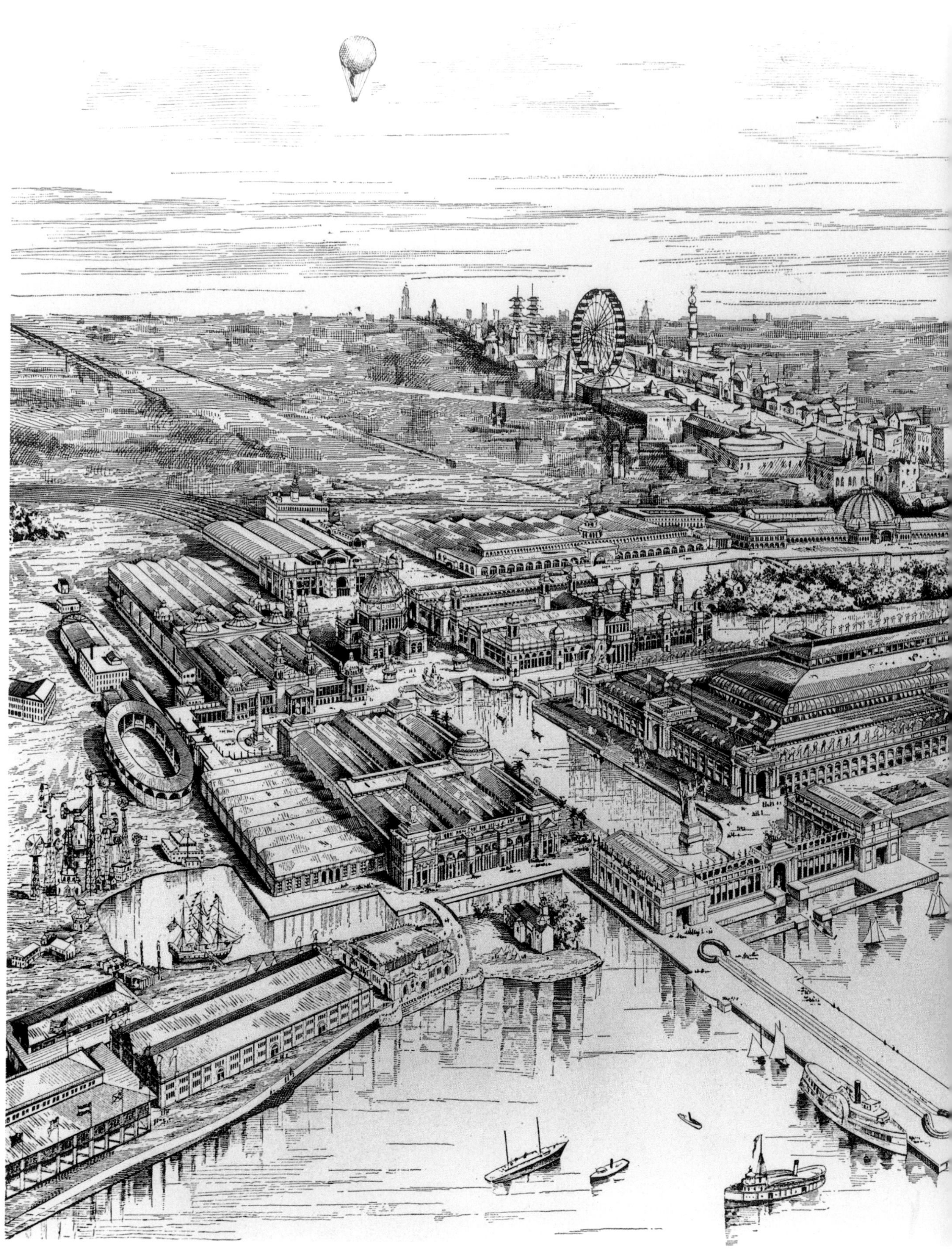

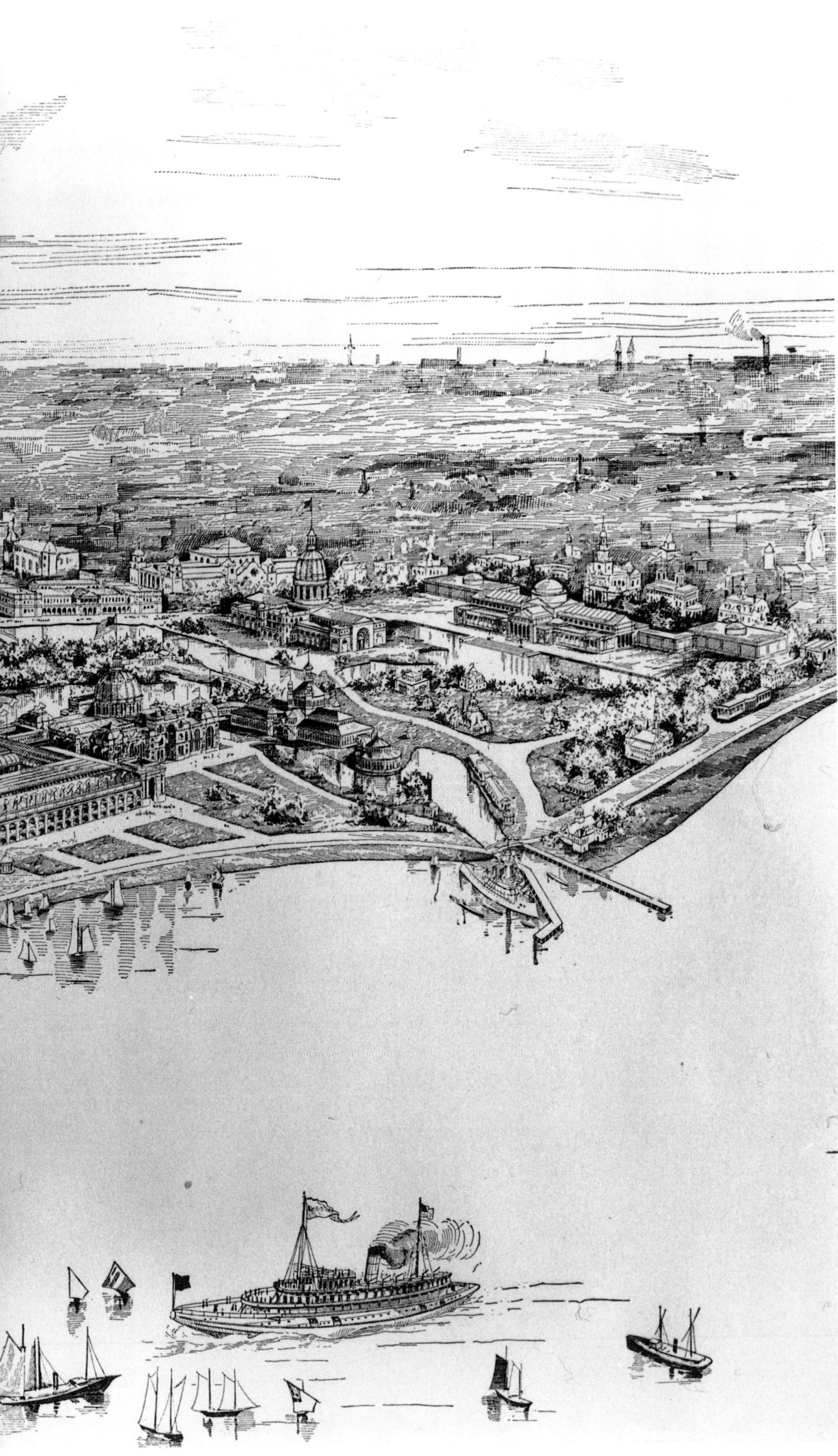

.. 15 ..

Bird's Eye View of World's Columbian Exposition.

Engraving after watercolor by Charles Graham. Court of Honor surrounded by Official Exposition Buildings (lower left to right), Midway Plaisance with Ferris Wheel (upper left), and Fine Arts Building surrounded by state and foreign buildings (far right). Hubert Howe Bancroft, The Book of the Fair, *vol. 1 (Chicago and San Francisco: The Bancroft Company, 1893), 71.*

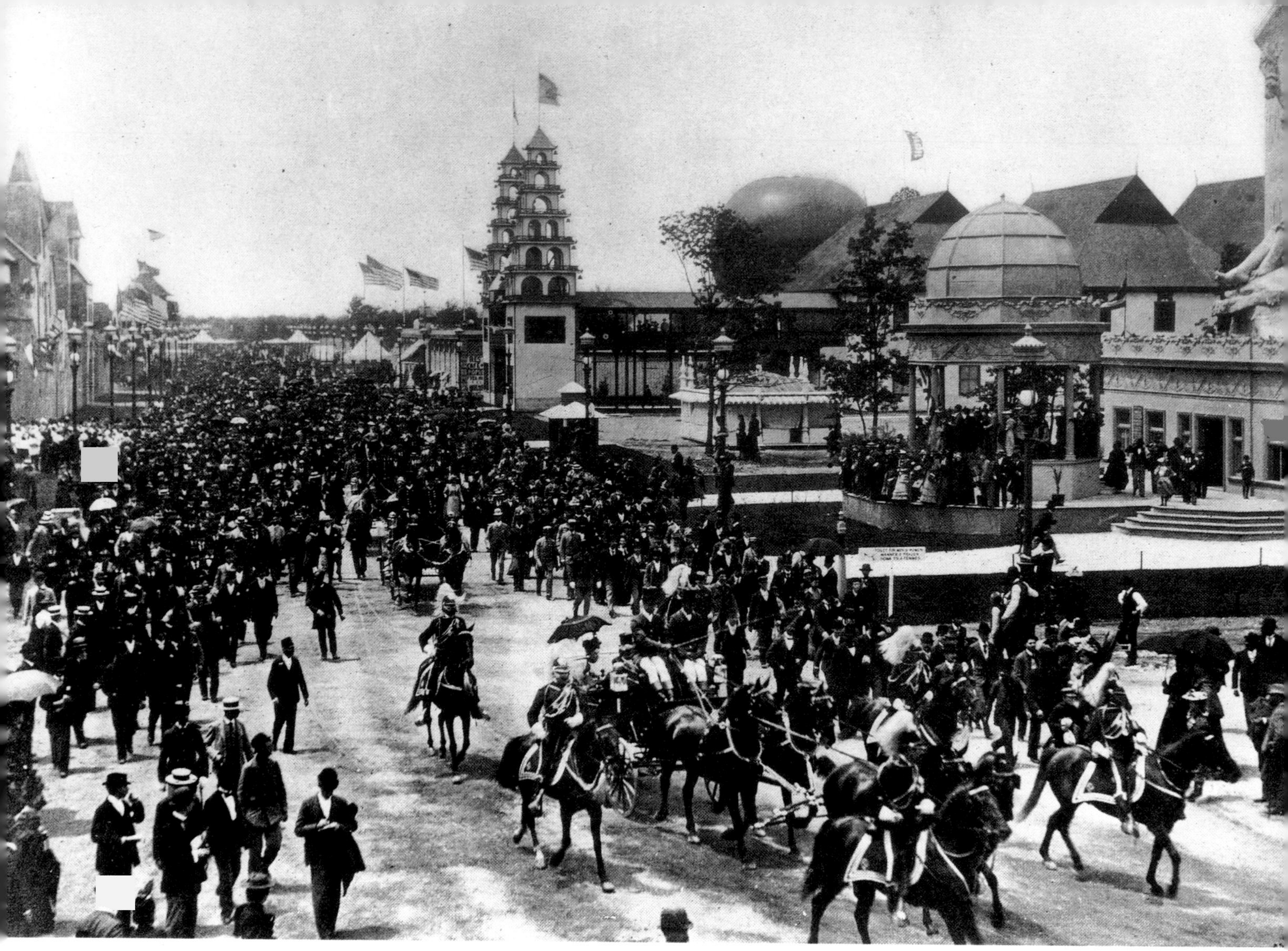

.. **16** ..

On Princess Eulalia Day, 8 June 1893, the Princess of Spain and Escort on the Midway Plaisance, moving past (left to right) the Venetian Village, the Chinese Theater, the Captive Balloon, and the Volcano of Kilauea.
Rossiter Johnson, ed., A History of the World's Columbian Exposition, *vol. 1 (New York: D. Appleton Company, 1897), following 408.*

.. **17** ..

The Dahomey Village on the Midway Plaisance.
Photograph by C. D. Arnold. Official Photographs of the World's Columbian Exposition by C. D. Arnold, vol. 3, pl. 54. Courtesy of The Chicago Public Library, Special Collections Department.

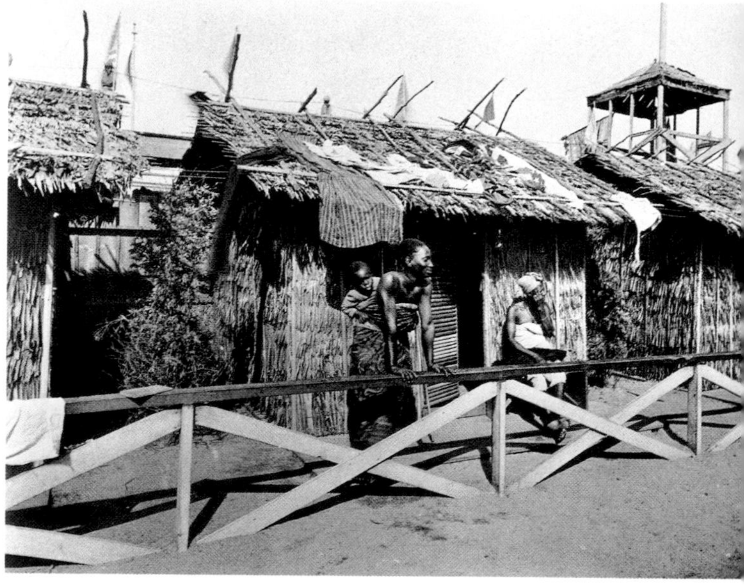

designed city of pleasures" that, while standing in contrast to Burnham's White City, had the effect of reinforcing the consumerism and commercialism that lay at the core of the fair (fig. 15). The Midway's central ideological axis, in other words, did not run between savagery and civilization, but between high and low culture.[19]

Both arguments have merit. The very idea of a Midwaylike avenue (fig. 16) put exposition directors in a bind. They certainly did not want cheap amusements detracting from the splendor of their overcivilized rendition of American abundance on display in the White City. By the same token, exposition authorities were certainly aware of the tremendous popularity and revenue potential of such shows after their success at the 1889 Paris Universal Exposition. Torn between disdain and rational economic calculations, the directors hit upon a compromise. Inspired by the example of the Paris fair, where displays of French colonials had been treated by anthropologists as ethnological field camps, Chicago's exposition directors decided to combine their Midway shows with the displays of the exposition's anthropology department, which was under the direction of one of America's foremost ethnologists, Frederic W. Putnam of Harvard. By the time the fair opened, the Midway, organized by showman Sol Bloom, included a full complement of "native" villages—so-called living ethnological villages—devoted to highly overdetermined representations of Africans, Native Americans, Javanese, and Samoans, as well as "oriental" shows with "exotic" dances like the *danse du ventre* (figs. 17, 18). Such dances, as Zeynep Çelik and Leila Kinney have suggested, had been integral to the imperialistic logic of French exposition planners, providing fairgoers with "models of possession" that "collaborate[d] in the constitution of a colonized female body." In a sense, mechanical amusements, like the Ferris Wheel, detracted from Putnam's original idea to use the fair to promote a public anthropology. But in another sense, these commercial concessions fit hand in glove with the overarching ideological function of the Midway, namely, what Curtis M. Hinsley calls the "commodification of the exotic" (fig. 19).[20]

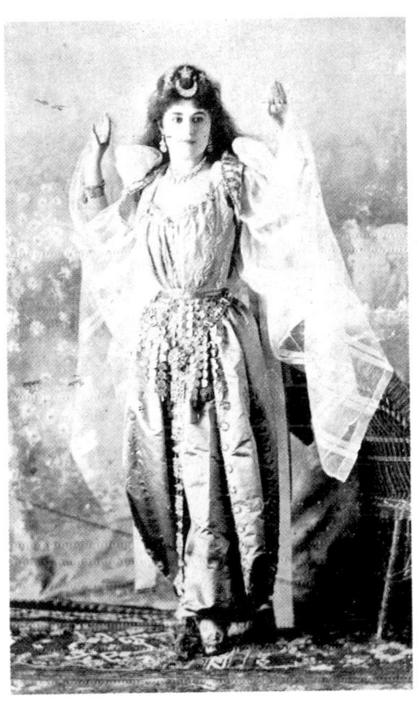

.. **18** ..
"Fatima—An Oriental Type of Beauty."
Photograph by J.J. Gibson.
Pictorial Album and History of the World's Fair and Midway.
Courtesy of the Chicago Historical Society.

The Midway's representation of "otherness" in the context of its sprawling commercialism drew varied responses. As one commentator explained:

> It is a great mistake to regard the Plaisance as a sideshow. A show it certainly is, and the most extensive and varied ever brought together for the entertainment of men; but it is much more. It is an integral part of the Fair: for it is the historical background of the great exposition of the arts and achievements of civilization. The architectural gate of the White City is on the lake front, but its historical gate is at the entrance to the Plaisance. Beginning with the Dahomey village, immediately on the right as one enters the Plaisance, all the barbarous, semi-barbarous, and partially civilized stages of race development are strikingly

illustrated on the broad avenue, a mile in length, lined on either side with communities and villages from the South Sea Islands, Central Africa, and many parts of the Orient. It is, as an acute observer pointed out, a walk through the past history of the race, preparing and conducting one to the highest development which it has attained.[21]

Another commentator stressed the carnival of pleasures afforded by the Midway, which acted as a kind of minstrel show onto which could be projected the licentiousness denied to the "civilized":

> The Plaisance was a medley, a Vanity Fair; it was an "Ethnology Exhibit," according to the catalogue, run riot; it was geography's nightmare; but over and above everything else one found it a playground, a frolic of nationalities, an enormous whirligig of pleasure. . . . For the street was a cauldron into which a giant hand had tossed ingredients of every conceivable kind, sprinkling it all with "the salt of the earth" and a lot of peppery savages. And so it was a bubbling, seething, foaming mass, stirring around faster and faster, boiling, spilling over, sizzling on, ever noisier, swifter, hotter, until it exploded on the last night with a terrible bang of steam and floated away a vapor that we try in vain to seize. You recall only a confused mass of sensations; a passage of amusing and interesting events swifter than you could grasp; a series of scenes that made you laugh because of the comical hopelessness of the effort to comprehend them; a confusion of noise—nay, of hubbub and roar—and a kaleidoscope of color and motion that would have driven one distracted had it not sent his blood leaping in harmony to the uncanny time of its own weird pulse."[22]

Fun contrasted with seriousness of purpose, noise contrasted with serenity, carnival contrasted with culture, male pleasures contrasted with feminized civility—all of these bipolarities characterized the Midway's relationship to the White City. So did the opposition between savagery and civilization—a contrast that bolstered claims by exposition promoters that the fair set the standard for measuring civilized accomplishment and strengthening popular perceptions of underdevelopment in much of the Third World (fig. 20, 21).[23]

As the Midway Plaisance became an ever more vital component of the exposition, it became linked to a larger debate about the nature and organization of American cultural life that turned on the question of whether the fair should be open on Sundays. For exposition directors, there had never been much doubt about the issue. From their perspective, Sunday openings would provide much-needed revenue. Equally to the point, given their conviction that the fair was an educational undertaking, opening the fair on Sundays would afford workers and their families the opportunity to benefit from the lessons taught at the exposition. But not everyone shared the directors' faith. In fact, opponents of the idea marshaled so much support in Congress that the bill authorizing the minting of Columbian half dollars mandated that the fair be closed on Sunday. There matters rested until Congress cut the appropriation for the Columbian half dollars, rendering invalid, at least in the directors' minds, the Sunday closing provision.

Once word leaked out that the fair would be open on Sundays, public debate became ferocious (fig. 22). Opponents of Sunday openings lectured exposition directors that "[t]o corrupt the Sabbath is to debauch the morality of the masses." Supporters of Sunday openings, including many clergy, countered

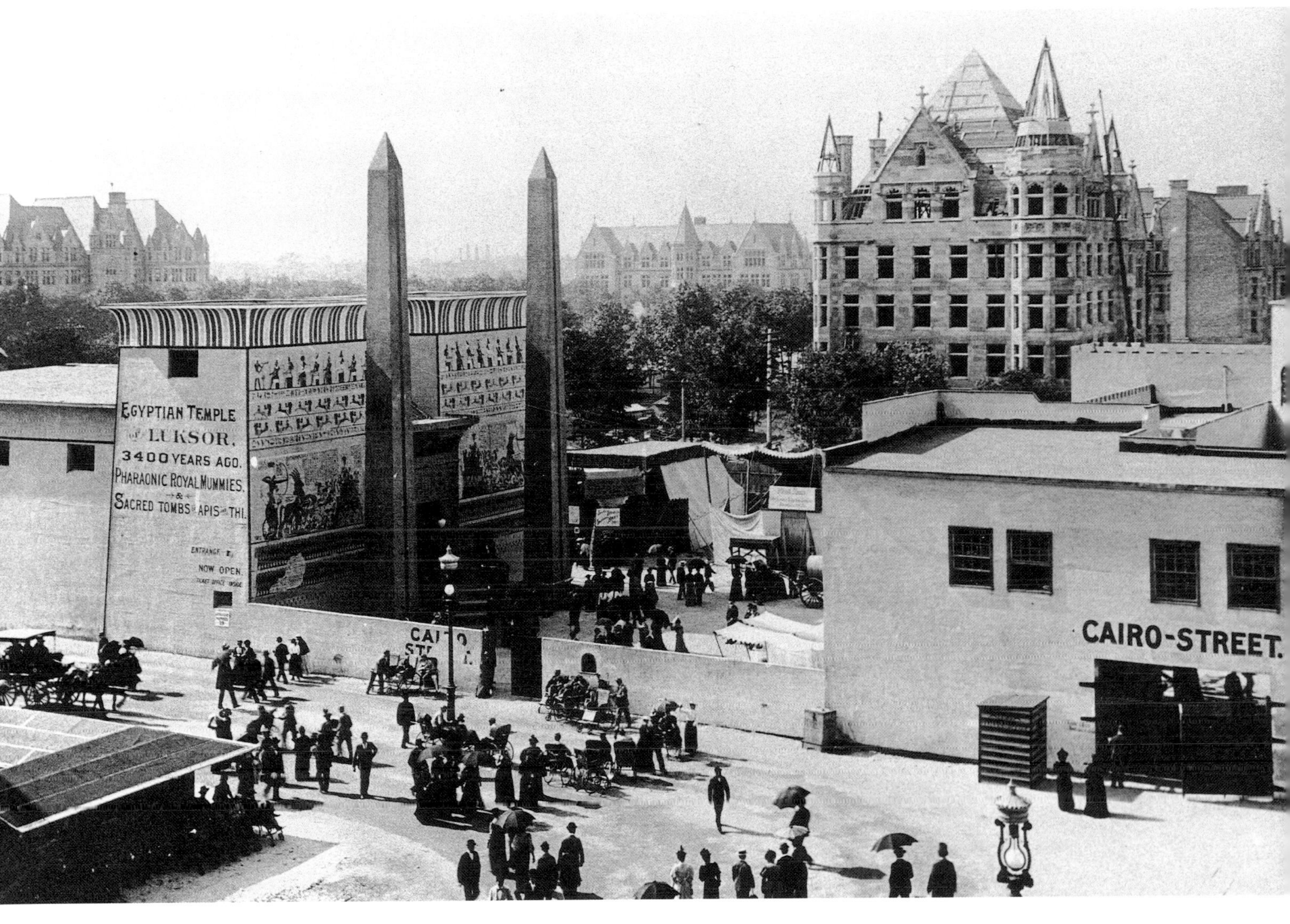

.. 19 ..

"Cairo-Street on the Midway Plaisance."
Photograph by C. D. Arnold. Official Photographs of the World's Columbian Exposition by C. D. Arnold, vol. 10, pl. 54. Courtesy of The Chicago Public Library, Special Collections Department.

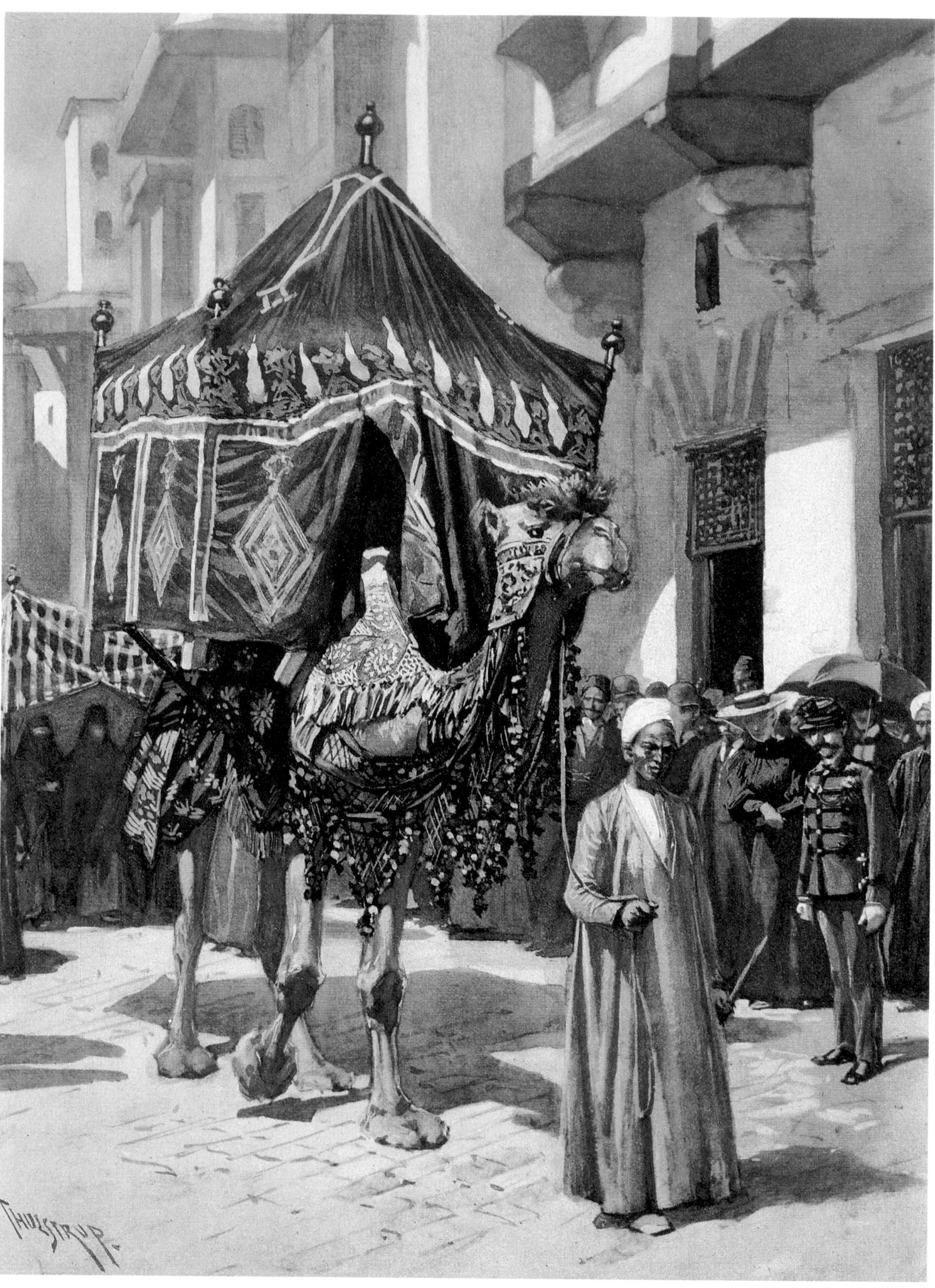
THULSTRUP.

.. 20 ..
"Ship of the Desert."
Chromolithograph from original watercolor by Thur de Thulstrup. Hubert Howe Bancroft, The Book of the Fair, *author's ed. (Chicago and San Francisco: The Bancroft Company, 1893). Courtesy of the Dibner Library, National Museum of American History, Smithsonian Institution.*

.. 21 ..
World's Columbian Exposition Programme.
Published by Shober & Carqueville Litho. Co., Chicago. This poster (48 x 28 in.) shows the serious side of the Midway. Many of its "educational" displays popularized turn of the century ideas about race. Courtesy of the Archive Center, National Museum of American History, Smithsonian Institution.

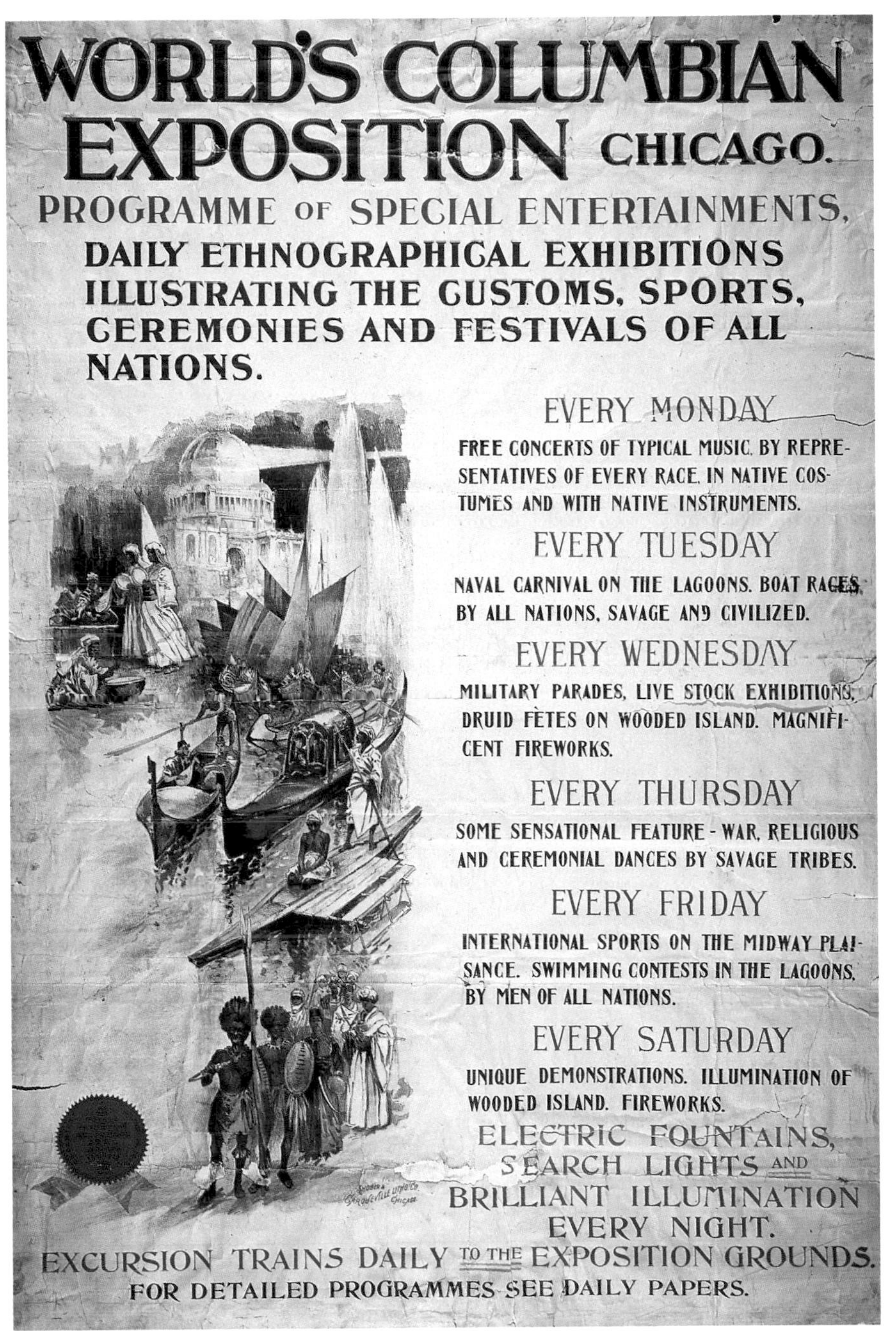

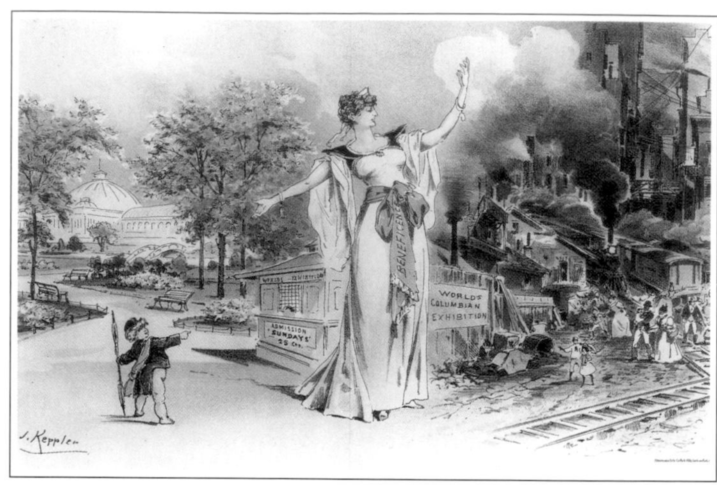

.. **22** ..

"We Don't Give Up the Fight—That's What We Want to See—The Fair Not Only Open For the People on Sunday But at a Popular Price," The World's Fair Puck, *no. 7 (19 June 1893): 78–79.*

with a variety of arguments that stressed the providential design of the fair. "Is it a desecration of the Sabbath to give to the masses a grand object lesson in all the arts and sciences?" one defender of Sunday openings asked. Supporters of Sunday openings regarded the fair as a God-given opportunity to provide uplifting recreational opportunities for the working classes—in their view the fair, far from threatening the authority of religion, actually buttressed Christian values by providing the working classes with "wholesome recreation." One exposition official took a different tack. Chicago, he warned, would have many strangers visiting the city because of the fair, "some of whom, if shut out of the Exposition grounds and thrown upon their own resources, would be likely to spend their time in an unprofitable manner, and perhaps swell the lawless element."[24]

By opening day, exposition authorities thought they had the upper hand and determined to open the fair on Sundays. To underscore the providential qualities of the fair, the exposition's concert band began its first Sunday recital with "Nearer My God to Thee." Despite the fact that "those in the vicinity caught up the air and sang the hymn," the controversy did not end. Opponents of Sunday openings won a preliminary court injunction that prohibited the operation of the fair on Sundays, but ultimately lost their case after several rounds of appeals by exposition authorities. When the dust finally settled, the fair did open on Sunday, but with Midway concessions closed and much of the machinery operating exhibits in the White City shut down.[25]

In certain respects, the directors' victory was hollow. Attendance on Sundays never reached the numbers anticipated until very late in the exposition season. And the closure of so many concessions kept revenues from reaching expected levels. But in a broader sense, the directors' victory was an important triumph in the ongoing struggle over the steady commercialization of American culture.

Dating back at least a decade before the fair, Americans had struggled over the intrusions of commercial culture into their lives. A major battle had been fought over the imposition of railroad, or standard, time zones on the nation. As James W. Carey explains, the victory of the railroads had important consequences. Once standard time was in place, "the new definitions of time could be used by industry and government to control and coordinate activity across the country, infiltrate into the practical consciousness of ordinary men and women, and uproot older notions of rhythm and temporality." Americans also debated the consequences of William Randolph Hearst's decision to market a Sunday newspaper. Carey sees Hearst's creation of a Sunday newspaper in similar light. The Sabbath, Carey writes, had long been a "region free from control of the state and commerce where another dimension of life could be experienced and where altered forms of social relationship could occur." "As such," he notes, "the sabbath [had] always been a major resistance to state and market power." If breaking down that resistance had, by the 1880s, become a major goal of at least some of America's corporate elites, the campaign to keep the fair open on Sunday can be understood as a continuation of this strategy. Midway concessions were closed, but visitors were free to walk through White City palaces and gaze upon the department-store-like displays of America's agricultural and industrial surpluses. These displays of plenitude were visible signs of what it meant to be cultured and civilized—an understanding deepened by the works of art on exhibit in the Art Palace (fig. 23).[26]

The Art Palace occupied a privileged place in the thinking of exposition directors, who were driven by several considerations. After the poor showing of American art at the 1889 Paris fair, in which it was dismissed by many critics as imitative of European styles, these custodians of American culture were determined to use the fair to elevate the international stature of American art. They believed this could be done by showing more than a thousand American oil paintings and hundreds of sculptural works in the context of a massive exhibition that also featured the works of acknowledged European masters. Such a display would not only place American art on an equal footing with European masterworks, but, more important, anchor the impression that exposition promoters were trying to convey about the White City, namely, that the cultural representations that unfolded within its gates were synonymous with civilization and the march of progress.[27]

By the time the Art Palace opened, its walls were "smothered by the works of painters whose talents varied from great to mediocre to worthless." So great was the sheer quantity of art, that most fairgoers probably shared novelist Hildegarde Hawthorne's reaction:

> I have seen more persons looking and hopelessly worn out there than in all the other parts of the Fair put together. I suppose the reason is that so much energy is used up in looking at the pictures and statues that none is left for any other purpose; and to make matters worse, there are not nearly enough seats to rest on.

Hawthorne, however, was not defeated by this "beautiful enchantress, who lures people to her bower, and then deprives them of all appearance of life." She planned her days at the fair in such a way that she could visit the Art Palace

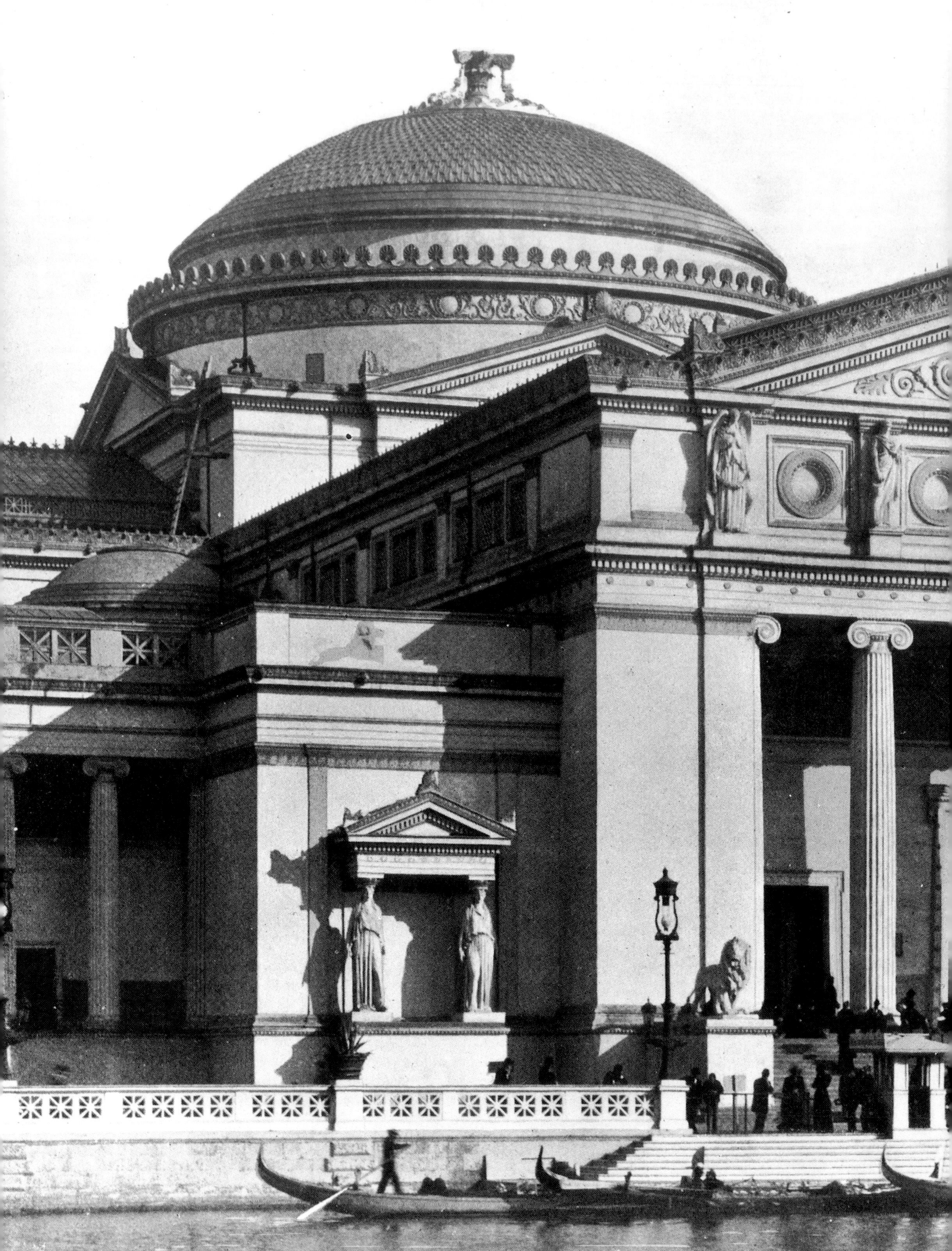

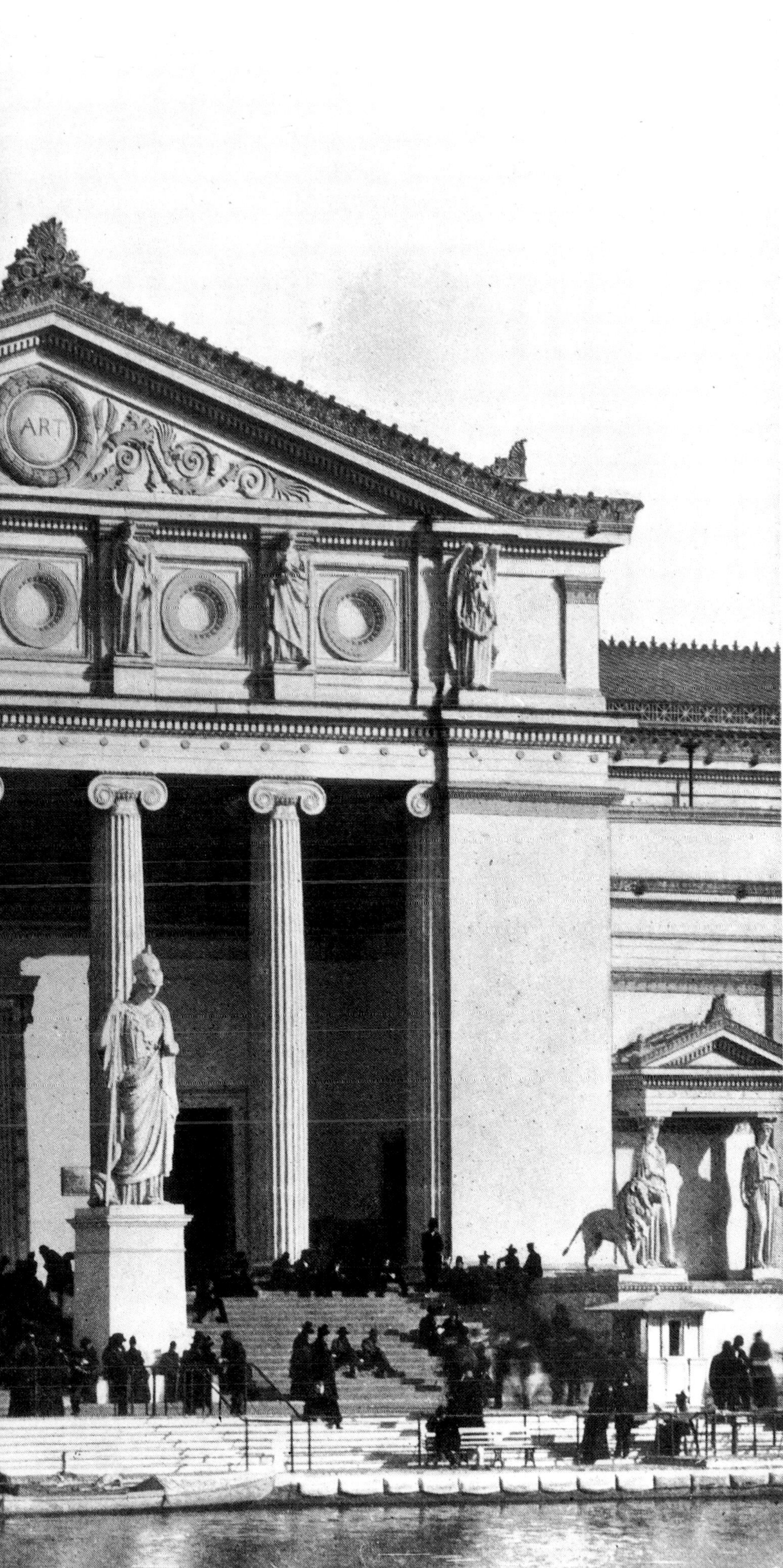

.. **23** ..
Detail of the south façade of the Fine Arts Building,
The Dream City.
Photographic Views of the World's Columbian Exposition
(St. Louis: N. D. Thompson Publishing Co., 1893).

"early in the morning for an hour or two, and thus keep fresh and ready for impressions." Exactly how many fairgoers emulated Hawthorne's strategy is unclear. What is clear is that for many visitors, the Art Palace stood out as an oasis, a refuge from the noise of the Midway, and served as the "civilized" counterpoint to the "exotic otherness" and raw commercialism of the Midway.[28]

Put in slightly different terms, the Art Palace, with the preponderance of gallery space reserved for "civilized" nations (Norway, for instance, was awarded 8,282 square feet of wall space, while Mexico, with 1,500 square feet, received the least amount of any nation), reinforced the ideological messages of the fair. It did so on many different levels: through the jury process that determined which works of art would be displayed; through paintings like Julius L. Stewart's *The Baptism* and Edward Moran's *The First Ship Entering New York Harbor* that encoded images of Anglo-Saxon supremacy; through representations of women that, like the Congress of Beauties on the Midway, featuring "exotic" female dancers, treated them as objects of male pleasure or, like many of the displays within the Woman's Building, as antidotes to America's rampant commercialism; and, through silences—for instance, the relative absence of American paintings that addressed issues of immigration or labor conflict reflected the fact that these disruptive subjects were deemed unpaintable. The Art Palace, in short, occupied a privileged position at the World's Columbian Exposition, joining with the Woman's Building in connecting the narratives of civilization in the White City to narratives of "otherness" along the Midway.[29]

Of all the exposition buildings at the Chicago fair, few excited more controversy than the Woman's Building (fig. 24), which was inspired by the Women's Building constructed for the 1876 Centennial Exhibition in Philadelphia. Prominent women in Chicago—led by Bertha Palmer, wife of Chicago hotel magnate Potter Palmer—determined that the World's Columbian Exposition would also include a pavilion dedicated to advancing women's interests. Exactly how to accomplish this goal proved difficult, and the Board of Lady Managers, consisting of more than one hundred middle- and upper-class women from around the United States, divided into two camps. As Frances K. Pohl relates, one group, composed of the wives of prominent industrialists, wanted the building to emphasize women's work in social reform and philanthropy, and to feature exhibits of women's domestic industries. The other group, consisting of professional women and suffragists, insisted that women's accomplishments be exhibited along with those of their male counterparts and wanted the building to provide meeting rooms for women professionals. Ultimately, the Italian Renaissance-style building, designed by Sophia Hayden, reflected a compromise, with the building housing the administrative offices of Lady Managers and providing exhibit space for "works of 'outstanding' quality created wholly by women." The word "outstanding" was key. For in the realm of art, as Pohl makes clear, the building existed "to provide proof that women could produce 'great' works of art" and that this "'greatness' was to be measured against the famous male European masters."[30]

Greatness, moreover, as Pohl suggests, was a racial category. Mirroring the all-white male boards that ran the fair, no African-American women were

.. **24** ..

East façade of the Woman's Building,
Hubert Howe Bancroft, The Book of the Fair, *vol. 2 (Chicago and San Francisco: The Bancroft Company, 1893), 258.*

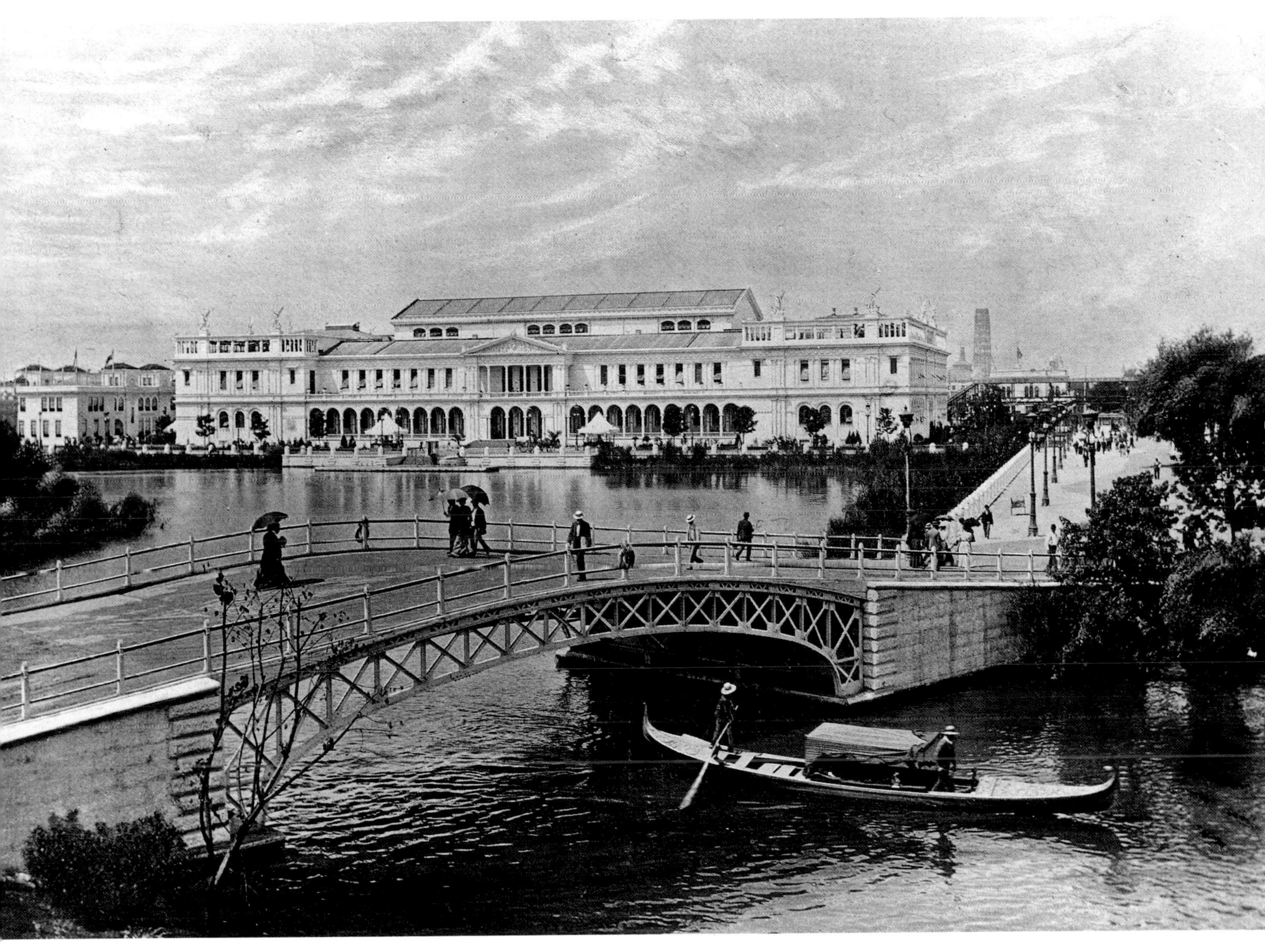

DARKIES' DAY AT THE FAIR.
(A Tale of Poetic Retribution.)

PART I.
THE EVENTS of the Great World's Fair
Impressive went their way.
Time rolled around; at last it was
The Colored People's Day!
The Sons of Ham from far Soudan
And Congo's Sable Kings
Came to the Fair with all the hosts,
Their wives, their plumes, their rings.
From distant Nubia's torrid sands,
From far-famed Zanguebar,
Together with their Yankee Friends,
The Darkies all were dar!

PART II.
But a Georgia coon, named Major Moon,
Resolved to mar the day,
Because to lead the whole affair
He had not had his way.
Five hundred water-melon ripe,
(The Darky's theme and dream,)
He laid on ice so cold and nice
To aid him in his scheme.

PART III.
The plans are laid for a big parade
Of great impressiveness;
With bands, so grand, on every hand,
And gorgeousness in dress.
No eye to right must show the white,
Each head must poise erect.
With proud reserve each must preserve
His dignity circumspect.

PART IV.
'T is a glorious sight, and all goes right;
The ranks are firm and bold—
Until at a turn all eyes discern
Those melons DRIPPING COLD!
Teeth gleamed white. With carver bright
Forth stands the tempter there.
He cuts a melon and starts a-sellin'—
'T is more than flesh can bear.

PART V.
With one load whoop, with one fell swoop,
They swarm down on the stand;
The sons of Ham in the foremost jam,
With a big slice in each hand.
And this is the end. For foe and friend
Give no thought to parade.
As they gaily loot the luscious fruit
And hie them to the shade.

L'Envoi
But Major Moon is a saddened Coon;
For his melons he got no pay.
His successful spite was a boomerang quite—
But it busted up Darkies' Day.

.. 25 ..
"Darkies' Day at the Fair. (A Tale of Poetic Retribution),"
The World's Fair Puck, *no. 16 (21 Aug. 1893): 186–87.*

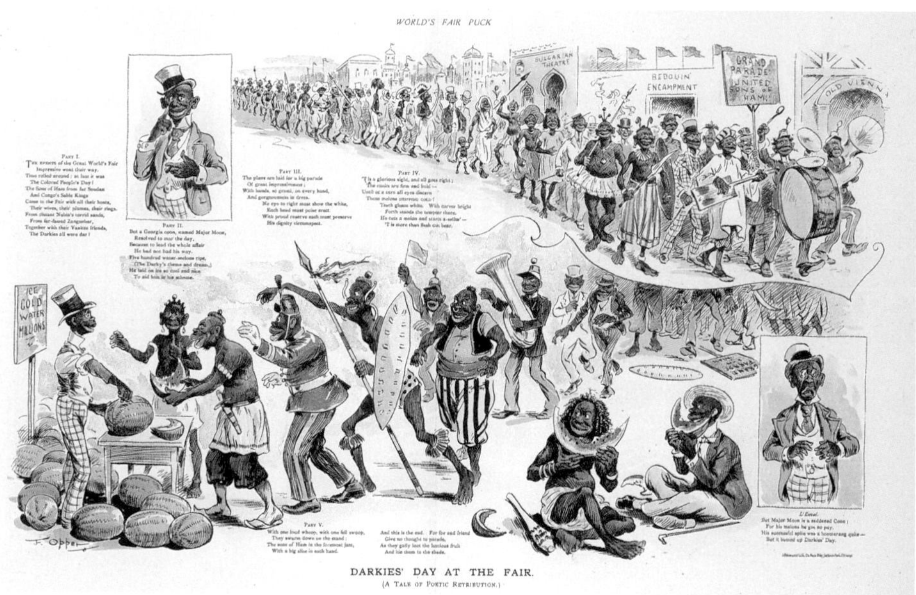

included on the Board of Lady Managers. The interests of African-American women, in theory, were represented by a white woman from Kentucky. And Native American women were represented by ethnologists from the Smithsonian Institution who organized a display on the ground floor of the Woman's Building entitled "The Arts of Women in Savagery."[31]

Like the Art Palace, the Woman's Building presented and represented ideological categories that undergirded the World's Columbian Exposition as a whole. A contemporary novelist, Clara Louisa Burnham, gave voice to the view of the world that shaped the fair when she had one of the characters in *Sweet Clover* exclaim:

> That Midway is just a representation of matter, and this great White City is an emblem of mind. In the Midway it's some dirty and all barbaric. It deafens you with noise; the worst folks in there are avaricious and bad; and the best are just children in their ignorance, and when you're feelin' bewildered with the smells and sounds and sights, always changin' like one o' these kaleidoscopes, and when you come out o' that mile-long babel where you've been elbowed and cheated, you pass under a bridge—and all of a sudden you are in a great, beautiful silence. The angels on the Woman's Buildin' smile down and bless you, and you know that in what seemed like one step, you've passed out o' darkness and into light.[32]

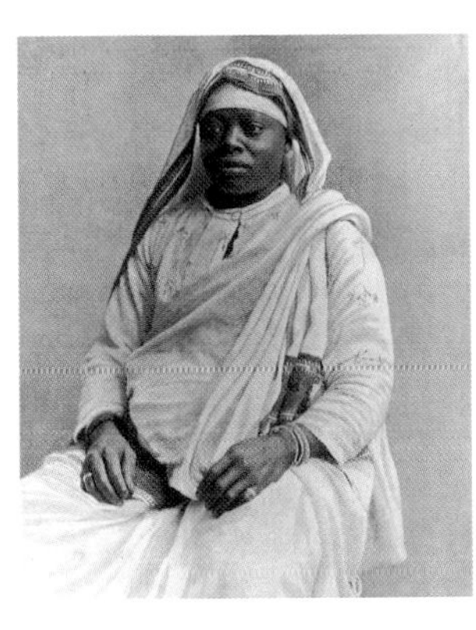

.. 26 ..
"Zaroteffa. (Soudanese Woman). . . . Perhaps one of the most striking lessons that the Columbian Exposition taught was the fact that African slavery in America had not, after all, been an unmixed evil, for of a truth, the advanced social condition of the American Africans over their barbarous countrymen is most encouraging and wonderful." Frederick Ward Putnam, Oriental and Occidental Northern and Southern Portrait Types of the Midway Plaisance *(St. Louis: N. D. Thompson Publishing Co., 1894). Courtesy of Dibner Library, National Museum of American History, Smithsonian Institution.*

The White City, it seemed, was an emblem of civilization.

From the vantage point of African-Americans, the White City was aptly named. Only after strenuous objections from African-Americans was a black person selected to serve on the exposition's National Commission. But Hale G. Parker, a school principal from St. Louis, was relegated to the role of alternate commissioner. The *New York Age* angrily denounced the decision by the Board of Lady Managers not to appoint even one African-American woman to its body. "We object," the newspaper declared. "We carry our objection so far that if the matter was left to our determination we would advise the race to have nothing whatever to do with the Columbian Exposition or the management of it. . . . The glory and the profit of the whole thing is in the hands of the white 'gentlemen' and 'ladies.'" Renowned anti-lynching activist Ida B. Wells agreed and urged African-Americans to boycott Negro Day at the fair—the special day set aside by exposition managers for African-Americans to demonstrate their contributions to the development of the United States (fig. 25).[33]

America's most prominent African-American, Frederick Douglass, disagreed with Wells and urged African-Americans to take advantage of Negro Day to show what they had accomplished since their emancipation from slavery and to call national attention to the hypocrisy of exposition authorities. Douglass followed his own advice in the introduction he wrote for a volume of essays entitled *The Reason Why The Colored American Is Not in the World's Columbian Exposition.* "We would like for instance to tell our visitors that the moral progress of the American people has kept even pace with their enterprise and their material civilization . . .," Douglass declared, "and that to the colored people of America, morally speaking, the world's Fair now in progress, is not a whited sepulcher." But, he concluded, reality would not permit such an interpretation. Douglass recited the horrors of post-Reconstruction America, decrying the lynching and disenfranchisement of African Americans. Then he turned his attention to the exposition proper, condemning the display of Dahomeyans that represented "the Negro as a repulsive savage." He concluded by declaring that the "Americans are a great and magnanimous people and this great exposition adds greatly to their honor and renown, but in the pride of their success they have cause for repentance as well as complaisance, and for shame as well as for glory, and hence we send forth this volume to be read of all men." Despite Douglass's hopes, most Americans, with the aid of captioned souvenir photograph albums featuring White City palaces and Midway villages, would remember a different text—the narrative of American material and racial progress that took visible form in exhibits organized along the Midway and in the White City (fig. 26).[34]

There are any number of ways of documenting the impact of the fair on American culture. The architecture of the White City inspired the City Beautiful movement that swept the country during the Progressive Era around the turn of the century, while that of the Midway probably inspired the "strip" architecture that would increasingly characterize commercial streets in small-town America. Two museums owed their origins directly to the fair, Chicago's Field Museum and the Philadelphia Commercial Museum, while others, like the Smithsonian Institution, augmented existing collections with world's fair exhibits.[35]

On the level of popular beliefs, the legacy of the fair is more difficult to assess. Leo Tolstoy, who never visited the fair, was singularly disgusted by what he read of the spectacle: "The Chicago exhibition, like all exhibitions, is a striking example of imprudence and hypocrisy: everything is done for profit and amusement—from boredom—but noble aims of the people are ascribed to it. Orgies are better." The blind and deaf Helen Keller, on the other hand, delighted in the exposition: ". . . I took in the glories of the Fair with my fingers. It was a sort of tangible kaleidoscope, this white city of the West. . . . All these experiences added a great many new terms to my vocabulary, and in the three weeks I spent at the Fair I took a long leap from the little child's interest in fairy tales and toys to the appreciation of the real and the earnest in the workaday world." Just after the exposition closed, the Hegelian philosopher Denton J. Snider tried to capture the fair's significance in *World's Fair Studies:* "It is true that the outer semblance of the mighty spectacle has quite vanished, and that unseemly heaps of rubbish and ashes lie where the splendid edifices once stood; still they are not lost, but have become internal—the soul's possession, which is immortal." Had the Chicago fair become "the soul's possession?" Millions of Americans returned home with, or otherwise received, world's fair souvenirs—items that ranged from picture postcards, spoons, and buttons to scarves, pop-up cutouts of the White City, and complete table services (fig. 27). In the immediate aftermath of the fair, it is not at all inconceivable that youngsters around the country began their school day with the Pledge of Allegiance, followed a lesson plan drawn from one of several pamphlets generated by the Chicago Kindergarten College, a training institute for prospective kindergarten teachers, and ended it by reading any one of a variety of children's stories written about the fair. Clearly, not everyone saw the fair in the same way, as the responses of Ida Wells and Frederick Douglass demonstrate. And given the industrial violence that continued to characterize American life, not everyone took the exposition's message to heart. But the influence of the fair should not be underestimated. As Donald Horne cautions: "some social groups have greater resources to define 'reality' than others." At the very least, the fair launched an exhibitionary complex of vast proportions that crisscrossed the nation by the onset of America's entry into the World War I.[36]

Soon after the Chicago fair opened, one of the California commissioners to the fair, newspaper publisher Michel de Young, understood its modular significance—that is to say, as cultural critic Jay Blair explains, that its component parts could be "added to, substituted for, or perhaps even rearranged"—and determined to reproduce the essential elements of the fair in San Francisco. In late January 1894, the Midwinter Exposition opened to the public. In addition to its main exhibition buildings, which were offshoots of the White City, the fair included a Midway with living ethnological villages sent, in some cases, directly from Chicago. The San Francisco fair was not an exact copy of its more famous predecessor, but it did mirror the structures of thought and feeling that underpinned the Chicago event. "The concessional attractions were not colonized in any particular geographical section of the Exposition grounds," Midwinter exposition officials insisted in a revealing choice of words, "nor were they incongruously mixed up with the main buildings of the exposition." Rather, the "arrangement assumed something of the character of an inner circle of purely expositional buildings with an outer concentric circle of concessional features." With this arrangement in fact colonizing nonwhites and commercial concessions on the periphery of the fair grounds, San Francisco's exposition promoters did not so much distance themselves from the ideological mapping that shaped the cultural geography of the World's Columbian Exposition as reproduce, in miniature, the imperial vision that gave form to the Chicago fair (fig. 28).[37]

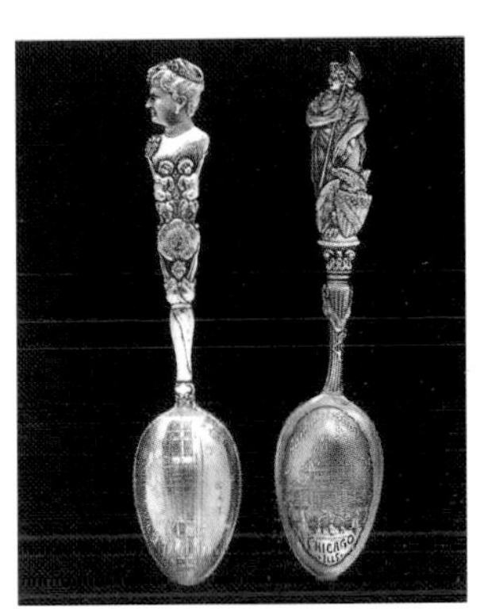

.. 27 ..

Two sterling silver souvenir spoons.

Left: On handle, bust of Bertha Honoré Palmer held by two cherubs above globe with "World's Fair, 1893, Chicago" raised aloft by a figural woman wearing a stars and stripes gown, and in bowl, an image of the Woman's Building. Right: On handle, a figural Miss Liberty with eagle and shield resting on a columnar pedestal form stem with banner reading "Chicago, 1892–3," and in bowl a view of the Administration Building. Larry Zim World's Fair Collection, Division of Community Life, National Museum of American History, Smithsonian Institution.

Subsequent fairs in Atlanta (1895), Nashville (1897), Omaha (1898), Buffalo (1901), St. Louis (1904), Portland, Oregon (1905), Jamestown (1907), Seattle (1909), San Francisco (1915), and San Diego (1915—16) followed suit, reconfiguring the White City/Midway axis into blueprints for imperial dream cities. The full flowering of this tradition occurred at the 1904 St. Louis Louisiana Purchase Exposition where, in a White City even larger than the one at Chicago, the U.S. government installed more than one thousand Filipinos in fake village habitats (fig. 29). The display was part of the government's drive to build popular support for U.S. imperial policies that were evolving in the wake of the war with Spain.[38]

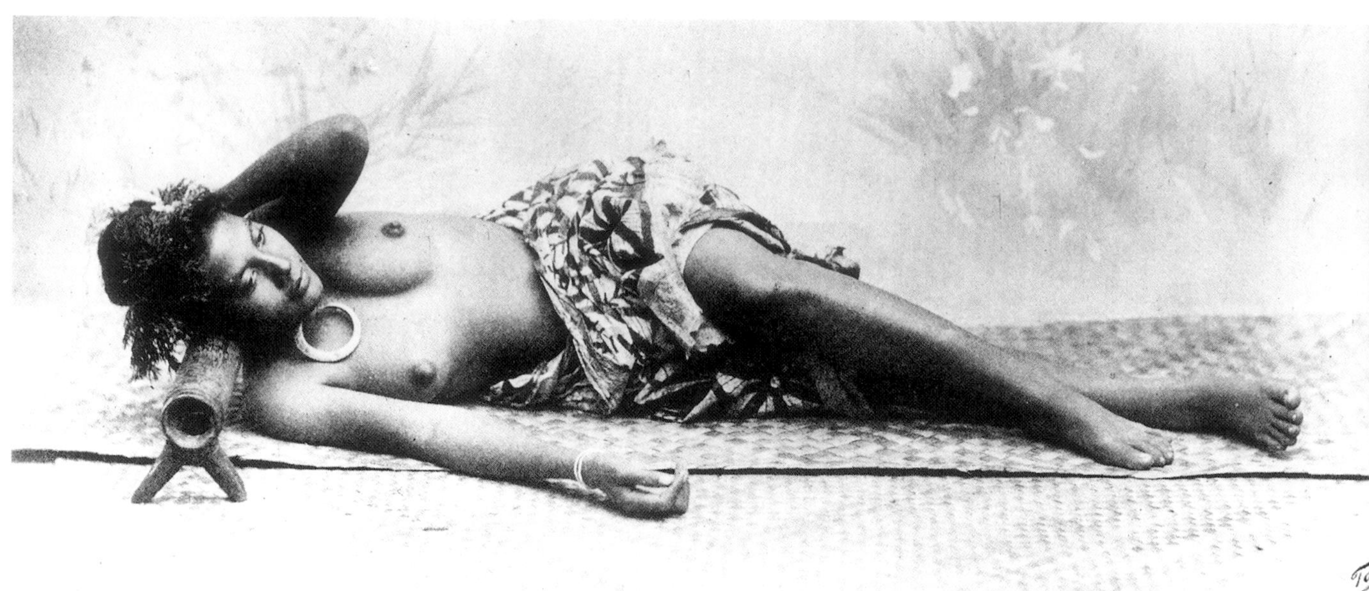

.. 28 ..
"A South Sea Siesta in a Midwinter Concession," The Official History of the California Midwinter International Exposition *(San Francisco: H. S. Crocker Company, 1894), 164.*

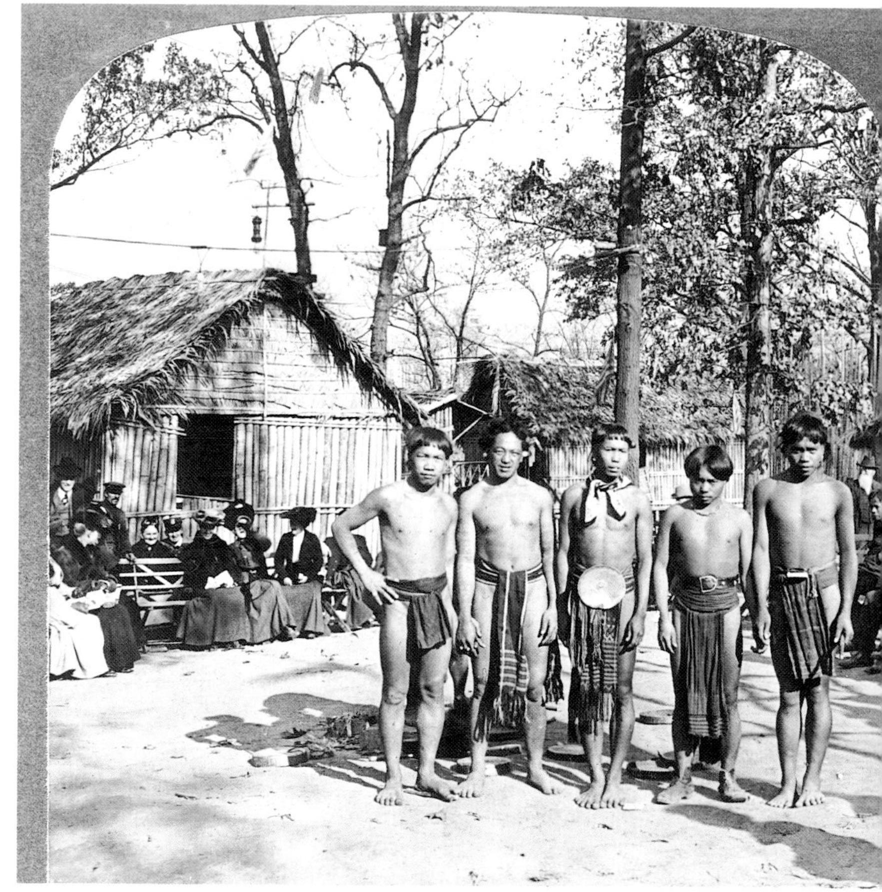

.. 29 ..
"Members of Uncle Sam's Infant Class—Igorrote Filipinos, Igorrote Village. World's Fair, St. Louis. U. S. A." *Stereograph copyrighted 1905 by C. L. Wasson. Courtesy of the Library of Congress.*

Forty years later, in the midst of another depression, builders of another Chicago fair, the 1933 Century of Progress Exposition, provided additional evidence that the World's Columbian Exposition had been an authoritative presence in American culture. With the help of some of the nation's leading scientists, exposition authorities arranged for observatories around the country to beam light from the star Arcturus to photoelectric cells, which in turn produced electrical impulses that started the machinery for exhibits at the 1933 fair. The light received by the observatories was high in symbolic value—it had left Arcturus forty years earlier, exposition authorities claimed, at precisely the moment President Grover Cleveland had opened the 1893 World's Columbian Exposition. With its villages of Africans and Native Americans juxtaposed with modernistic architectural representations of American progress, the 1933 fair bore unmistakable witness to the impress of the White City and Midway Plaisance on the development of American culture.[39]

Because the Chicago World's Columbian Exposition was a defining event in the life of the nation, it is appropriate that it be remembered, especially on the occasion of the Columbian quincentenary. Because of its defining force, it is equally appropriate that the significance of the fair be rediscovered in terms of current interest in how different groups of Americans have struggled to give meaning to American culture.[40] Seen in this light, the centenary of the fair should present less an occasion for nostalgia than a challenge for constructing a better, more inclusive vision of America's future.

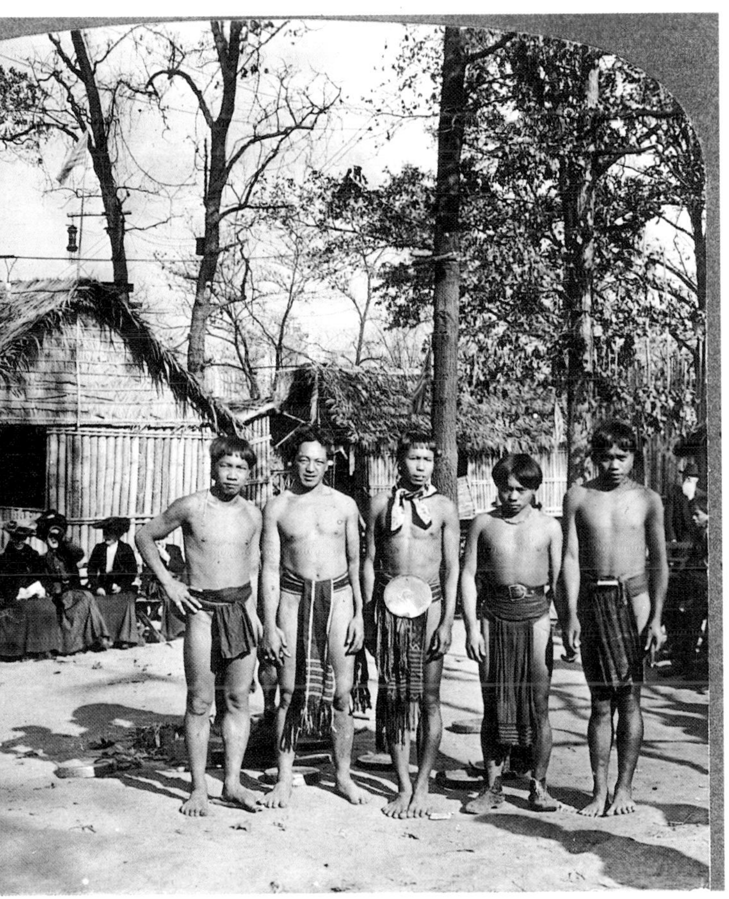

NOTES

I want to express my gratitude to colleagues at the Netherlands Institute for Advanced Study for their comments on this essay. I am also grateful to George Gurney and Carolyn Carr for their support, to James Gilbert for his suggestions for improvement, and to Wim de Witt and Connie Casey at the Chicago Historical Society for sharing their knowledge of the fair.

1. Margarette S. Miller, *I Pledge Allegiance* (Boston: Christopher Publishing House, 1946), 66.

2. There is an impressive literature about the Chicago World's Columbian Exposition. Contemporary histories include Hubert Howe Bancroft, *The Book of the Fair*, 4 vols. (Chicago: Bancroft Company, 1893), and Rossiter Johnson, ed., *A History of the World's Columbian Exposition*, 4 vols. (New York: D. Appleton, 1897). Recent historical interpretations include Reid Badger, *The Great American Fair: The World's Columbian Exposition & American Culture* (Chicago: Nelson Hall, 1979); Malcolm Bradbury, "Struggling Westward: America and the Coming of Modernism (I)," *Encounter* 60 (Jan. 1983): 55–60, and "Struggling Westward: America and the Coming of Modernism (II)," *Encounter* 60 (Feb. 1983): 57–65; David F. Burg, *Chicago's White City of 1893* (Lexington: University of Kentucky Press, 1976); William B. Cronon, *Nature's Metropolis: Chicago and the Great West* (New York: W. W. Norton, 1991), 341–69; Justus D. Doenecke, "Myths, Machines, and Markets: The Columbian Exposition of 1893," *Journal of Popular Culture* 6 (1973): 535–49; Dennis B. Downey, "Rite of Passage: The World's Columbian Exposition and American Life" (Ph.D. diss., Marquette University, 1981); James Gilbert, *Perfect Cities* (Chicago: University of Chicago Press, 1991); Robert Knutson, "The White City--The World's Columbian Exposition of 1893" (Ph.D. diss., Columbia University, 1956); Daniel T. Miller, "The Columbian Exposition of 1893 and the American National Character," *Journal of American Culture* 10 (1987): 17–22; Robert W. Rydell, *All the World's a Fair* (Chicago: University of Chicago Press, 1984); Gertrude M. Scott, "Village Performance: Villages at the Chicago World's Columbian Exposition, 1893" (Ph.D. diss., New York University, 1991).

3. *The Education of Henry Adams* (1907; reprint, Boston: Houghton Mifflin, 1961), 465; Umberto Eco, *Travels in Hyper-Reality: Essays*, trans. William Weaver (1968; reprint, San Diego: Harcourt Brace Jovanovich, 1986), 294.

4. There is a growing body of literature on world's fairs. A good reference source is John E. Findling and Kimberly D. Pelle, eds., *Historical Dictionary of World's Fairs and Expositions, 1851–1988* (Westport, CT: Greenwood Press, 1990). Equally important is Burton Benedict et al., *The Anthropology of World's Fairs: San Francisco Panama-Pacific International Exposition, 1915* (Berkeley and London: Scolar Press, 1983). For an overview of scholarly writings on world's fairs, see Robert W. Rydell, *Books of the Fairs* (Chicago: American Library Association, 1992).

5. See Warren I. Susman, "Ritual Fairs," *Chicago History* 12 (Fall 1983): 4–9; Gilbert, 130; Neil Harris, *Cultural Excursions: Marketing Appetites and Cultural Tastes in Modern America* (Chicago: University of Chicago Press, 1990), 128, 61; Tony Bennett, "The Exhibitionary Complex," *New Formations* 4 (Spring 1988): 76, 80; Alan Trachtenberg, *The Incorporation of America* (New York: Hill and Wang, 1982), 208–34.

6. New York Representative John Quinn, *Congressional Record*, 51st Congress, 1st sess., vol. 21 (20 Feb. 1890), 1558, 1560, quoted in Knutson, "The White City," 13.

7. Robert D. Parmet and Francis L. Lederer II, "Competition for the World's Columbian Exposition: The New York Campaign and the Chicago Campaign," *Journal of the Illinois State Historical Society* 65 (Winter 1972): 364–94; Lyman Gage, *Memoirs of Lyman J. Gage* (New York: House of Field, 1937), 80.

8. Rydell, *All the World's a Fair*, 41–43; Helen Lefkowitz Horowitz, *Culture and the City* (Lexington: University of Kentucky Press, 1976), 43–44; Johnson, *A History*, vol. 1, chs. 3, 6.

9. Thomas S. Hines, *Burnham of Chicago* (New York: Oxford University Press, 1974); Rydell, *All the World's a Fair*, 45–46. Peter Bacon Hales, "Photography and the World's Columbian Exposition: A Case Study," *Journal of Urban History* 15 (May 1989): 247–73, rightly suggests that the fair can be understood as an effort by the elites that controlled it to shape an urban vision for America.

10. For a fuller discussion of efforts to publicize the fair around the country, see Robert W. Rydell, "The Culture of Imperial Abundance: World's Fairs in the Making of American Culture," in *Consuming Visions: Accumulation and Display of Goods in America, 1880–1920*, ed. Simon J. Bronner (New York: W. W. Norton, 1989), 191–216.

11. John J. Flinn, ed., *Handbook of the World's Columbian Exposition* (Chicago: Standard Guide, n.d), 314–15; H. N. Higinbotham, *Report of the President to the Board of Directors of the World's Columbian Exposition* (Chicago: Rand, McNally & Co., 1898), 157–58.

12. Susan G. Davis, *Parades and Power* (Berkeley and Los Angeles: University of California Press, 1986); Burg, *Chicago's White City*, 100.

13. Johnson, *A History*, vol. 1, 260–64; Richard Altick, *The Shows of London* (Cambridge, MA: Harvard University Press, 1978), 457.

14. Johnson, *A History*, vol. 1, 264–65.

15. Johnson, *A History*, vol. 1, 295.

16. Knutson, "The White City," 55–56 first called my attention to the connection of the Pledge of Allegiance with the fair. See also, Miller, "The Columbian Exposition," 107–161; and *Youth's Companion* 65 (8 September 1892): 446–47. Over the course of the twentieth century, the pledge has become more specific in its demands. In the context of the nativism and racially based immigration legislation of the 1920s, the words "the Flag of the United States" were substituted for "my Flag." "This change," Miller writes, "was made on the grounds that some foreign-born children and others born in this Country of foreign parentage, when rendering the Pledge, had in mind the flag of their foreign native land, or that of their parents, when they said my Flag." The next year, the words "of America" were inserted after "United States" for even greater clarity. Then, in the 1950s, amid growing anxiety about the manifest destiny of the country during the Cold War, the phrase "under God" was inserted after "one nation."

17. See Russell Lewis, "Everything Under One Roof: World's Fairs and Department Stores in Paris and Chicago," *Chicago History* 12 (Fall 1983): 28–47; Flinn, *Handbook*, 50; dreamworld quote: Rosalind Williams, *Dream Worlds: Mass Consumption in*

Late Nineteenth Century France (Berkeley and Los Angeles: University of California Press, 1982), 58–106.

18. Doenecke, "Myths, Machines, and Markets," 535–49; Rydell, "The Culture of Imperial Abundance," 210–16.

19. Rydell, *All the World's a Fair*, ch. 2; Gilbert, *Perfect Cities*, 109, 111.

20. Ralph W. Dexter, "Putnam's Problems Popularizing Anthropology," *American Scientists* 54 (1966): 315–32; Zeynep Çelik and Leila Kinney, "Ethnography and Exhibitionism at the Expositions Universelles," *Assemblage* (October 1990): 35–59; Curtis M. Hinsley, "The World as Marketplace: Commodification of the Exotic at the World's Columbian Exposition, Chicago, 1893," in *Exhibiting Cultures*, ed. Ivan Karp and Steven D. Lavine (Washington, D.C., Smithsonian Institution Press, 1991), 344–65. On the representation of "orientalism" at fairs, see also Timothy Mitchell, "The World as Exhibition," *Comparative Studies in Society and History* 31 (1989): 217–36.

21. "Impressions of the White City," *The Outlook* (1 July 1893): 19–20.

22. Charles Mulford Robinson, "The Fair as Spectacle," in Johnson, *A History*, vol. 1, 493–512.

23. Çelik and Kinney, "Ethnography and Exhibitionism," 39.

24. "Hear the Other Side," *Illustrated World's Fair Weekly* 2, 8 (February 1892): 149; "Sunday at the Fair," *Illustrated World's Fair Weekly* 2, 7 (January 1892): 137; Higinbotham, *Report of the President*, 239.

25. Higinbotham, *Report of the President*, 240.

26. James W. Carey, *Communication as Culture* (Boston: Unwin Hyman, 1988), 201–30.

27. Annette Blaugrund, ed., *Paris 1889: American Artists at the Universal Exposition* (Philadelphia: Pennsylvania Academy of the Fine Arts in association with Harry N. Abrams, New York, 1989); Carolyn Kinder Carr, "Prejudice and Pride: Presenting American Art at the 1893 World's Columbian Exposition" in *Revisiting the White City: American Art at the 1893 World's Fair* (Washington, D.C.: National Museum of American Art, National Portrait Gallery), 62–133.

28. Burg, *Chicago's White City*, 185; Hildegarde Hawthorne, *The Fairest of the Fair* (Philadelphia: Henry Altemus, 1897), 98–101.

29. Burg, *Chicago's White City*, 184; Badger, *The Great American Fair*, 121; and Stuart C. Wade and Walter S. Wrenn, comps., *"The Nutshell." The Ideal Pocket Guide...* (Chicago: World's Fair Bureau of Information, 1893), 160.

30. Frances K. Pohl, "Historical Reality or Utopian Ideal? The Woman's Building at the World's Columbian Exposition, Chicago, 1893," *International Journal of Women's Studies* 5 (1982): 289–311. See also Jeanne Madeline Weimann, *The Fair Women* (Chicago: Academy Chicago, 1981); Mary Frances Cordato, "Representing the Expansion of Woman's Sphere: Women's Work and Culture at the World's Fair's of 1876, 1893, and 1904" (Ph.D. diss., New York University, 1989); and Paul Greenhalgh, *Ephemeral Vistas* (Manchester: Manchester University Press, 1988), 174–97.

31. Pohl, "Historical Reality," 295–96; Ann Massa, "Black Women in the White City," *Journal of American Studies* 8 (1974): 319–37.

32. Clara Louisa Burnham, *Sweet Clover* (Chicago: Laird and Lee, 1893), 201.

33. See Rydell, *All the World's a Fair*, 52–55; Elliot Rudwick and August Meier, "Black Man in the 'White City,' Negroes and the Columbian Exposition, 1893," *Phylon* 26 (Winter 1965): 354–61; "The Women and the World's Fair," editorial, *New York Age*, 24 October 1891.

34. Frederick Douglass and Ida Wells, *The Reason Why. The Colored American Is Not in the World's Columbian Exposition* (Chicago, 1893), 2–12.

35. On the influence of the fair on vernacular architecture, see Barbara Rubin, "Aesthetic Ideology and Urban Design," *Annals of the Association of American Geographers* 69 (1979): 339–61.

36. R. F. Christian, ed., *Tolstoy's Diaries* (New York: Charles Scribner's Sons, 1985), 323 (I am indebted to Elise Goldwasser for this reference); Helen Keller, *The Story of My Life* (1902; New York: Doubleday, 1954), 71–72; Denton J. Snider, *World's Fair Studies* (Chicago: Sigman Publishing, 1895), 7; Donald Horne, *The Great Museum: The Re-presentation of History* (London: Pluto Press, 1984), 256.

37. John G. Blair, *Modular America: Cross-Cultural Perspectives on the Emergence of an American Way* (New York: Greenwood Press, 1988); *The Official History of the California Midwinter International Exposition* (San Francisco: H. S. Crocker Company, 1894), 146.

38. Richard Drinnon, *Facing West: The Metaphysics of Indian-Hating and Empire Building* (New York: New American Library, 1980), 333–51; Rydell, *All the World's a Fair*, esp. ch. 6, passim.

39. "Starring a Star," *Literary Digest* 113 (7 May 1933): 24–26.

40. On the importance of matters of cultural representations to broader questions of politics, see Karp and Lavine, *Exhibiting Cultures*.

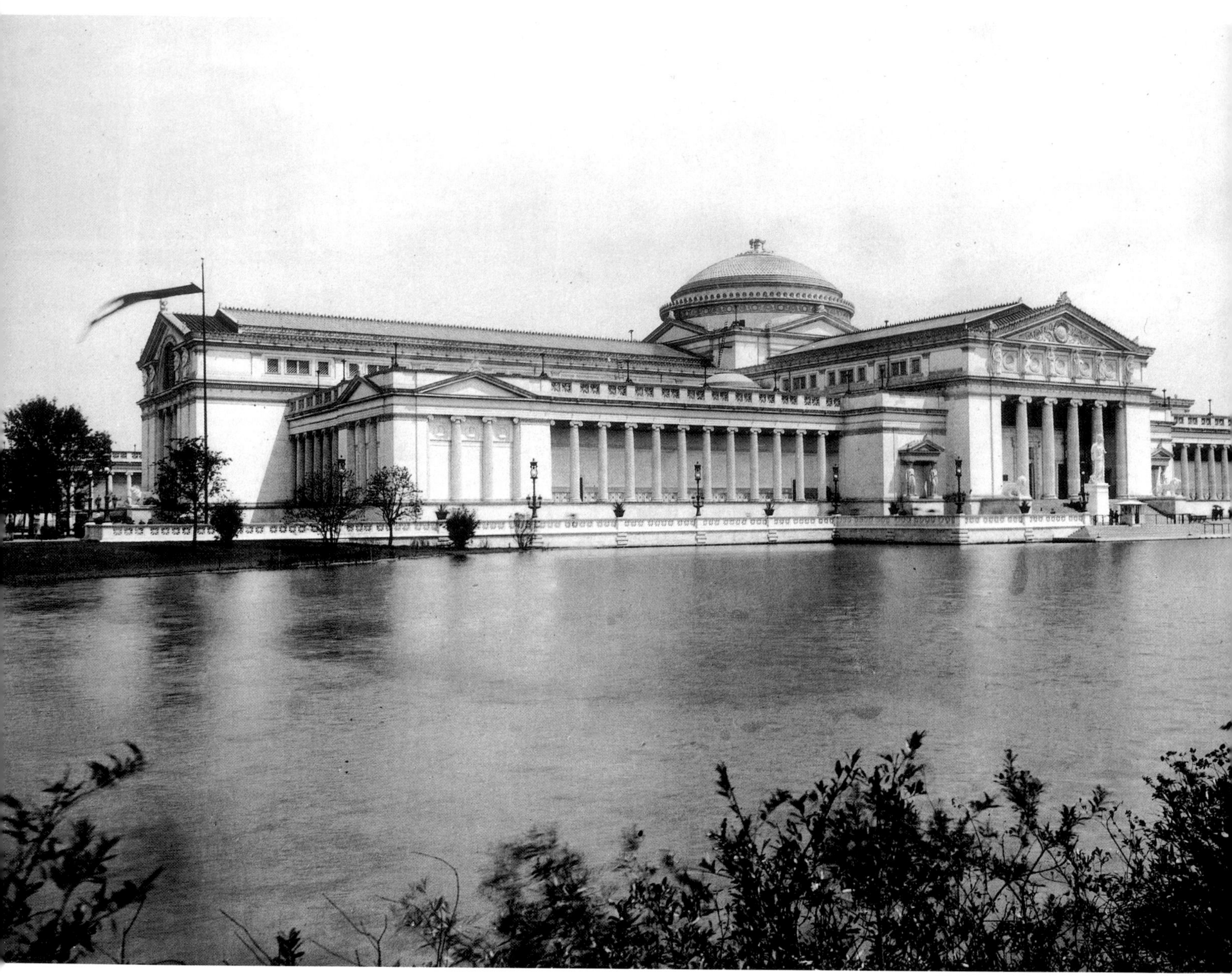

. . 30 . .
Fine Arts Building from the southwest.
Photograph by C. D. Arnold. Official Photographs of the World's Columbian Exposition by C. D. Arnold, vol. 2, pl. 18. Courtesy of The Chicago Public Library, Special Collections Department.

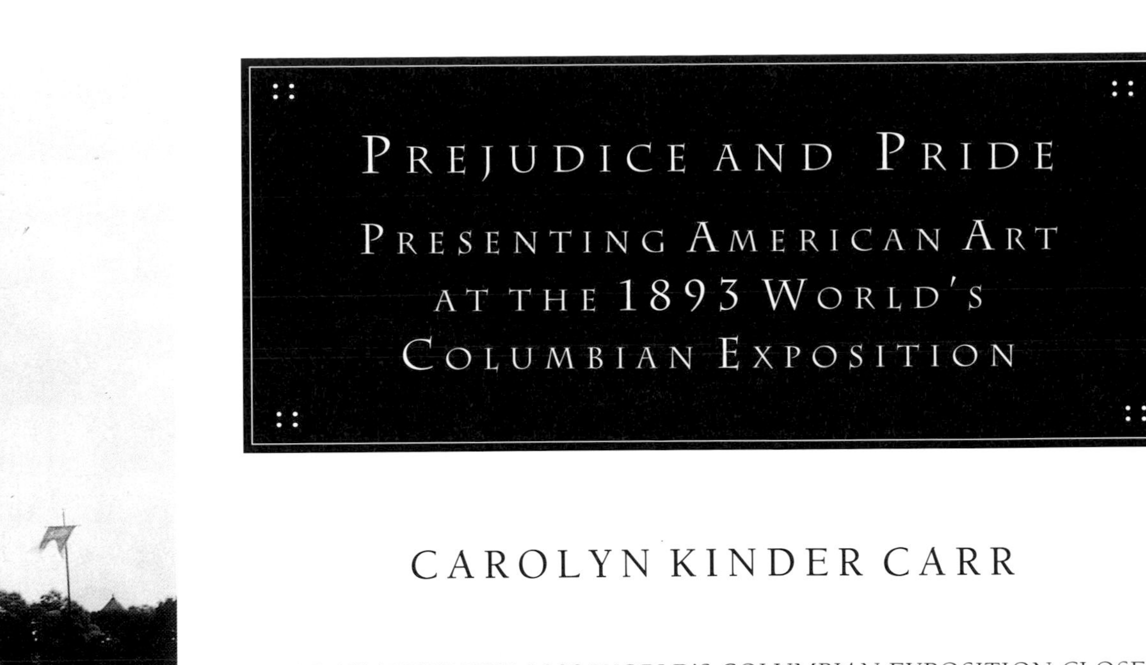

Prejudice and Pride

Presenting American Art at the 1893 World's Columbian Exposition

CAROLYN KINDER CARR

THE DAY AFTER THE 1893 WORLD'S COLUMBIAN EXPOSITION CLOSED, a journalist for the *Chicago Tribune* wrote, "The time for the study of the art work at the Fair virtually has passed. The canvases soon must come down. The buildings . . . must go. Most of the perishable decorations will be lost. But the influence of art at the Columbian Fair will reach far into the future."[1] Not merely the sentiments of a civic chauvinist, these words were prophetic. Many of the works exhibited in 1893 have become icons in the history of American art, emblematic of national achievement in the aesthetic arena; others, while less familiar, command interest and attention as objects that capture the philosophical and intellectual texture of the era. Numerous artists showcased by the sheer number of works they exhibited—William Merritt Chase, Thomas Eakins, Winslow Homer, George Inness, John Singer Sargent, and James McNeill Whistler, to mention only a few—continue to be held in high esteem. Even less well-represented artists—Alice D. Kellogg, Harriet Campbell Foss, Lucy D. Holme, T. C. Steele, Edward E. Simmons, Guy Rose, and S. Seymour Thomas—demand regard as accomplished professionals.

The individuals responsible for selecting the work shown at the fair had a keen sense of important contemporary American art. The story that follows provides a glimpse of the process by which those directing the selection of American art were themselves chosen, and the process by which they created a showcase for American artistic talent.

PROCURING THE PRIZE

On 25 April 1890, after vigorous lobbying and fund-raising by a group of socially and politically well-connected men, mostly from Chicago, President Benjamin Harrison signed into law the act of Congress that provided for "celebrating the four hundredth anniversary of the discovery of America by Christopher Columbus, by holding an international exhibition of arts, industries, manufactures . . . in the city of Chicago."[2] The origin of the 1893 exposition had a long and complex history. Several dates mark the beginning of this movement; various people claimed the honor of first conceiving the idea; and numerous cities, among them New York, St.

Louis, and Washington, vied with Chicago for the privilege of presenting the fair.[3] In August 1889 Thomas B. Bryan, subsequently the first vice-president of the World's Columbian Commission, argued before Congress that Chicago should be selected because of its location and marvelous growth, which "can best typify the giant young nation whose discovery the projected fair is to commemorate." But this midwestern city ultimately won the competition—intellectual justification and political pressure notwithstanding—because the stockholders supporting this location raised the most money in the most timely fashion to assist in underwriting the formidable costs of the exposition.[4]

Two groups were responsible for the governance of the fair: the Board of Directors of the World's Columbian Exposition and the World's Columbian Commission. The former was composed primarily of Chicagoans elected by the shareholders of the group promoting Chicago as the site of the fair; the latter was a national body, appointed by the president upon the recommendation of state governors and composed of two representatives from each state, territory, and the District of Columbia, as well as eight commissioners-at-large.[5] The board had primary fiscal responsibility for the fair and, in many instances, de facto daily management oversight. The commission was "empowered to determine the plan and scope of the Exposition, to prepare a classification of exhibits, to allot space to exhibitors, to appoint all judges and examiners . . . and generally to have charge of all intercourse with the exhibitors and representatives of foreign nations." By mid-September 1890, both the board and the commissioners had selected their officers, formed their oversight committees, begun work on the organizational structure of the fair, and elected George Royal Davis (fig. 31) to be director-general of the exposition.[6] Shortly thereafter, the search for a chief of the Department of Fine Arts was begun by the commission's fine arts committee. This group acted with the advice and consent—and on occasion with the overt interference and manipulation—of various members of the board's committee on fine arts.[7]

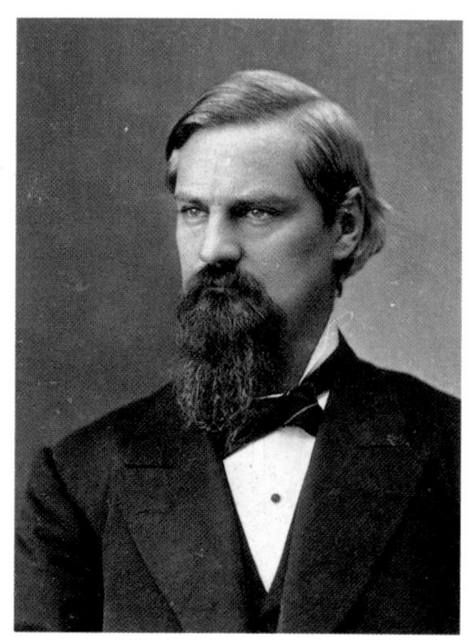

.. **31** ..

***George Royal Davis**, director-general of the World's Columbian Exposition. Photograph by the Brady-Handy Studio. Courtesy of the Prints and Photographs Division, Library of Congress.*

While no position description exists detailing the responsibilities of the chief of the Department of Fine Arts, the duties ultimately assigned to this individual included supervising the organization of three exhibitions that would serve to define America's cultural and aesthetic sophistication. The most important of these exhibitions was the show of contemporary American art, defined as art created since the 1876 Centennial Exhibition in Philadelphia. In addition to the presentation of nearly 1,200 paintings and sculptures, this display also included watercolors, drawings, graphics, engravings on gems and medals, and architecture as fine art. Supplementing this core image-shaping exhibition were the displays of nineteenth-century European art from private collections in America and a retrospective exhibition of important late eighteenth-century and early nineteenth-century American painting. Ultimately, more than 3000 objects were presented in these American shows. Also central to the mission of the chief of the Department of Fine Arts was the ability to convince foreign governments and leading artists to send their best works to

America. For without a foreign context, the American art exhibition would be perceived as having a parochial rather than global resonance.

CHOOSING A CHIEF OF FINE ARTS

The first person known to have applied for the position of chief of the Department of Fine Arts was forty-three-year-old Sara Tyson Hallowell (fig. 32). Born to a prosperous and well-established Philadelphia family, she had distinguished herself in the 1880s as director of the art exhibits at the Chicago Inter-State Industrial Expositions.[8] While organizing these large shows, which often included more than 400 objects, Hallowell came to know major American and European artists, collectors, and dealers. She initiated her campaign to become art director of the fair shortly after opening the last of the Inter-State exhibitions on 3 September 1890. On 30 September Augustus G. Bullock (fig. 33), chairman of the commission's fine arts committee, wrote from Worcester, Massachusetts, to Chicagoan James Ellsworth (fig. 34), a member of the board's fine arts committee:

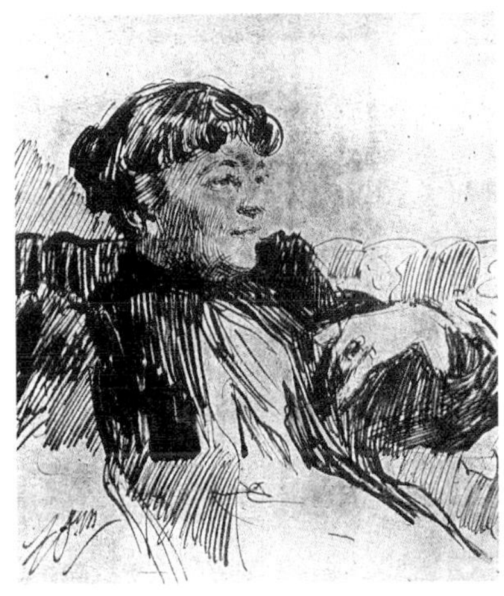

.. 32 ..
Anders Zorn, **Sara Tyson Hallowell**, *1893, ink drawing. Formerly collection Sara Tyson Hallowell, unlocated.* Art Amateur *29, no. 1 (June 1893): 3*

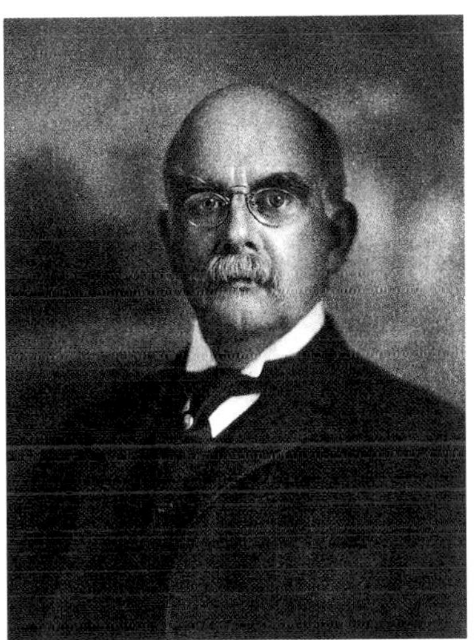

.. 33 ..
Augustus G. Bullock, *chairman of the World's Columbian Commission's Fine Arts Committee. Courtesy of the State Mutual Life Assurance Company of America, Worcester, MA.*

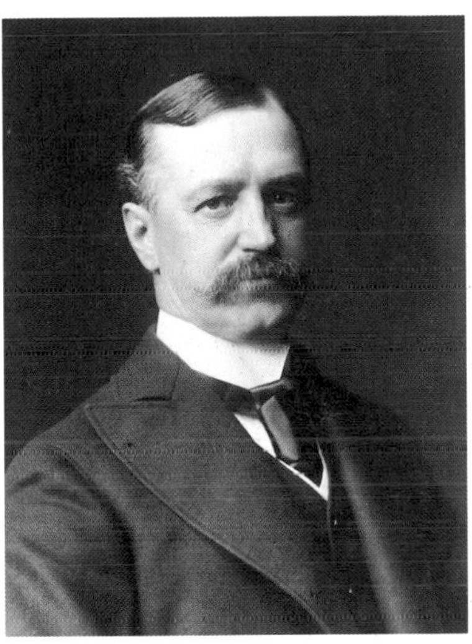

.. 34 ..
James W. Ellsworth, *member of the World's Columbian Exposition's Board of Directors' Fine Arts Committee. Courtesy of the Archives, The Art Institute of Chicago.*

> I have had an interview today with Miss Hallowell who came from Chicago to see me. . . . She has the strong endorsement of almost every one East and West whose name might be expected to lend weight to her petition; not only of leading artists American and foreign but of presidents of Art Museums, like Mr. [Henry G.] Marquand of New York and Mr. [Martin] Brimmer of Boston. She also has the endorsement of the Chicago committee. I gave her a full hearing and told her that all the papers she left with me would be laid before our committee at its October meeting.[9]

When Hallowell's name came up for review in New York at the first meeting of the art committee on 23 October, a petition was read, signed by Marquand and "other well-known lovers of art," advocating her as director. Hallowell's qualifications were praised by a number of the committee members, but, according to newspaper accounts, "the general trend of opinion seemed to be that, owing to the fact that Miss Hallowell was a woman, such a position could not well be filled by her."[10] Hallowell, however, was not one to accept meekly a decision based on gender rather than skill and experience. Over the next four months she waged an intense crusade with a fervor that belies the traditional view of proper, well-bred nineteenth-century women as passive recipients of their fate. Hallowell secured the recommendation of lawyer, collector, patron, and dealer Thomas B. Clarke, who wrote Ellsworth that "if a manageress of the Exposition is to be chosen Miss Hallowell among women applicants is first choice. She has a good knowledge of pictures and knows how to collect and sell some."[11] Support was garnered, too, by the Board of Lady Managers, who offered a petition on her behalf.[12]

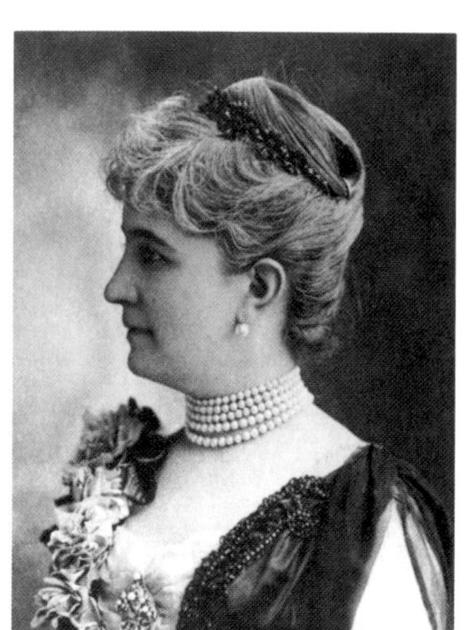

.. **35** ..
Bertha Honoré Palmer (Mrs. Potter Palmer), president of the Board of Lady Managers. Sun and Shade *6, no. 2 (October 1893): pl. 9. Courtesy of the Trustees of the Boston Public Library.*

An early master of the media, Hallowell gathered endorsements in various newspapers, including the *New York Times.*[13] The *Chicago Independent News* was effusive in its praise, saying that Hallowell "has labored so sincerely in the interests of art that artists and art patrons alike agree that she has not her peer in the country as critic, collector, and exhibition manager."[14] Hallowell also obtained the support and active involvement of Bertha Honoré Palmer (fig. 35), Chicago collector, society leader, wife of real estate magnate Potter Palmer, and president of the fair's Board of Lady Managers. As early as 9 October, Mrs. Palmer wrote to artist Gari Melchers: "We are all working for Miss Hallowell for the place at the head of the Art department of the Fair."[15] As the deadline for selection neared, Mrs. Palmer corresponded with powerful New York state commissioner and art committee member Chauncey Depew on Hallowell's behalf. Applying all her social clout and political cunning, Palmer set forth her case for Hallowell. She was the candidate who "has the warm endorsements of both artists and art patrons" and "is strongly endorsed from the practical stand-point by the gentlemen who have worked with her at the . . . [Inter-State] Exposition." Palmer also noted that Hallowell was "absolutely safe, from the business standpoint" and that "there is no man in this country who has had her experience in securing exhibitions and returning pictures from all parts of this country and Europe." Palmer sought "to prevent a gross injustice to a charming woman . . . who should not be shut out from any emoluments and distinctions which lie before her . . . simply because she is a woman," but her words were to no avail.[16] In early February Hallowell, finally convinced that she would not gain the appointment, ended her quest.[17] She may have won the respect of artists and patrons for her managerial talents and aesthetic taste, and females at the end of the nineteenth century may have made great strides professionally, but when it came to representing America in its attempt to challenge the cultural hegemony of Europe, gender was an issue: for the selection committee, a woman, however skilled and knowledgeable, could not be the appropriate symbol of leadership.

From the beginning, the candidate favored by the commission's art committee was the wealthy New York native Henry G. Marquand (fig. 36), collector, arts patron, and president of the Metropolitan Museum of Art. Marquand, who personified America's new, home-grown nobility, was perceived as one who would give class as well as credibility to the art department.[18] A man of means, culture, and erudition, he could convey to the Old World the "progress" of America in developing an aristocracy of its own. In addition, giving an easterner this position would soothe the wounded feelings of New Yorkers still smarting from the loss of the fair to Chicago. In late October 1890 the committee approached Marquand through Metropolitan Museum director General Luigi Palma di Cesnola. Marquand, while flattered, declined the offer, citing age and prior commitments to the museum.[19] Uncertain how to proceed, the committee then sought Marquand's advice regarding the selection of a chief. He had a strong opinion on this subject and responded through Cesnola that

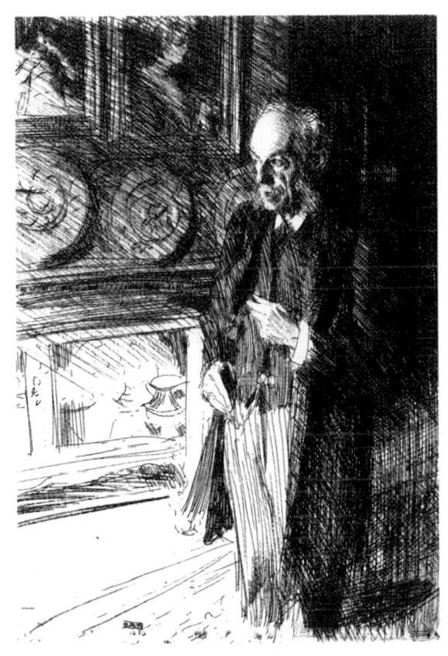

.. 36 ..
Anders Zorn,
Henry Marquand, *1893, etching. Spencer Museum of Art, The University of Kansas, Gift of the Max Kade Foundation.*

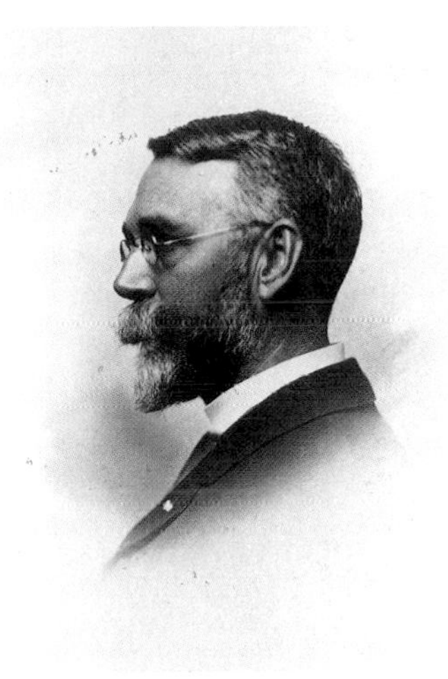

.. 37 ..
Charles M. Kurtz.
Photograph by Howard D. Beach. Courtesy of the Charles M. Kurtz Papers, Archives of American Art, Smithsonian Institution.

> in order to make the art exhibit of your Fair a great success you must have as Art Director an energetic man of great executive ability and endowed with first class powers of organization; this person must be able to devote the whole of his *time* and *thought* to the subject. He should have some experience in art exhibits of the kind the World's Fair requires and a general knowledge of art. A painter, a Sculptor, an architect, a Decorator, an actor, & a musical professor in short any person whose knowledge of art is limited to one branch of it only, no matter how eminent he may be in it, he or she, is not the person qualified . . . to be selected for the position of Art Director of the Chicago Fair, as he would naturally concentrate most of his thoughts mind & time knowledge and activity to that branch of art with which he is professionally connected and the other branches of art would be neglected and deprived of that equal share of time & attention which they have a right to receive from him. Generally speaking "artists" (and under this title I include all the above named professions) are not fit to Direct a general Art Exposition; though they may prove capable enough in directing an exhibition of their own special branch of art. As *assistants* to the Art Director, the services of the above named professionals will not only be invaluable but almost indispensable each in his special branch of art but as Art Directors their services would be worthless—Art collectors & art critics are also unfit for such a position the former are usually narrow-minded & their knowledge of Art [limited] to the class of objects they are collecting for pleasure or speculation; the latter are the pests of the world being ignorant presumptuous and dictatorial.[20]

With Marquand's admonitions in mind, the committee continued its search. Although Marquand and Hallowell were the most publicly discussed candidates for the position of director of fine arts, numerous other names surfaced for consideration.[21] Charles Kurtz (fig. 37), a New York-based art entrepreneur born in western Pennsylvania, applied for the job at the urging of James Ellsworth.[22] Kurtz, who was subsequently to play a major role in the fair's art department, had a background similar to Hallowell's as an organizer of exhibitions. Ellsworth himself, seemingly sensing no conflict of interest with his role as a member of the board's art committee, also submitted a petition for the position.[23] Newspapers mentioned as possible candidates Seth Low, recently appointed ninth president of Columbia College; Rush Hawkins, who assembled the American exhibition of art at the 1889 Paris Universal Exposition; Luigi Palma di Cesnola, the able director of the Metropolitan Museum; William R. French, director of the Art Institute of Chicago; distinguished sculptor Augustus Saint-Gaudens; and "Mr. Walters of Baltimore" (presumably the collector Henry, not his father, William).[24] How seriously the committee entertained these names, or the assemblage of Chicago and New York art personalities—Charles Hutchinson, Martin Ryerson, Samuel P. Avery, Sr., Russell Sturgis, Cyrus J. Lawrence, and Gaston L. Feuardent—mentioned by Thomas B. Clarke in his letters to Ellsworth, can only be a matter of speculation.[25] The committee did, however, follow up on Clarke's suggestion of Sylvester Koehler, then print curator at the Museum of Fine Arts, Boston, but Bullock subsequently reported that "his critics, while acknowledging his 'literary capacity,' suggest that he is 'slow, lacking in execution forces, and could probably not organize the art department.' "[26] Whether the committee approached painter Frank D. Millet, a suggestion made by Marquand (apparently he had overcome his hesitation about artists), is not known.[27]

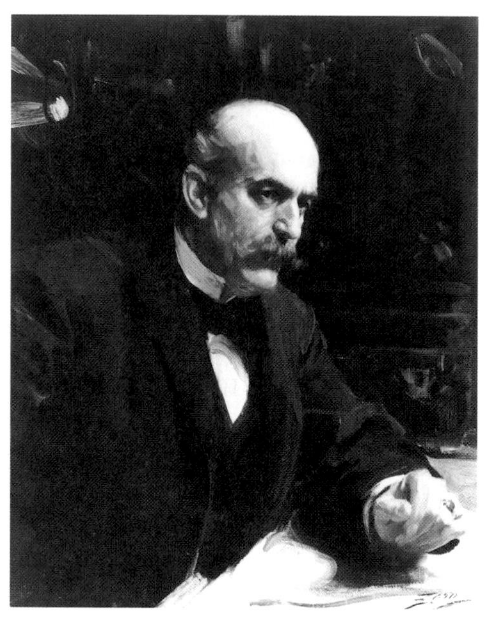

.. **38** ..
Anders Zorn,
Halsey Cooley Ives, *1894–95.*
The Saint Louis Art Museum, Gift of Mrs. Peggy Ives Cole.

As late as February 1891, the committee clung to the hope that Marquand would accept the position. By mid-March, however, the name of forty-two-year-old Halsey C. Ives (fig. 38) had emerged as the committee's first choice for director.[28] Ives, born in 1847 in Havana (Montour Falls), New York, came from a prosperous but not wealthy family that traced its roots in America to 1635. His early years are not well documented, but various biographies indicate that he joined the Union Army as a draftsman in 1864 and subsequently studied art, first in Nashville, Tennessee, with the Polish artist Alexander Piatowski and later in London. Ives went to St. Louis as an instructor at the Polytechnic Institute of Washington University in 1874. When the St. Louis Museum and School of Fine Arts was founded in 1879, he became its first director.[29] William French, who may have nominated Ives as the compromise candidate, praised him eloquently in the *Chicago Herald:*

> Mr. Ives . . . is the very man for the place . . . he has an imposing presence and . . . a peculiarly impressive manner. He has fine judgment and a taste that has been formed on the best models. . . . He is a frequent visitor to Chicago. He sometimes lectures in my place and I lecture . . . in his. He is a very agreeable man personally and his wife,

who is the daughter of a wealthy banker in St. Louis, is a charming woman. They have two children.[30]

The *Chicago Tribune* deemed him "one of the handsomest men in America, tall, of fine figure, with clear-cut feature."[31] Ives, who was known in St. Louis as an energetic and capable administrator, thus possessed not only the professional requirements for the job but also an ample complement of socially and politically proper attributes. Although a midwesterner, he had strong eastern roots; his military record was credible, if not distinguished; he had studied and traveled abroad; and he was a family man who had married well.

Ives's appointment was common knowledge in March, but it was not confirmed until early May 1891 because of the exposition's byzantine bureaucratic structure.[32] The length of the search did not go unnoticed. At issue, according to one journalist, were the old demons that pitted East against West and professional against amateur. Acknowledging, not quite accurately, that the committee initially had sought an artist of the highest rank, the columnist reported that "men of the highest artistic appreciation were not willing to accept the post" because they feared "the embarrassment of being associated in the administration of so responsible a place with laymen having no knowledge whatever of the canons of art and little sympathy with the exigencies that might arise in the proper equipment of the department." In addition, "their reluctance to accept the post arose in some degree from the skepticism of the east toward the west in matters of taste."[33] Ives was aware that his own appointment might not be popular with easterners, but after his first trip east in late May to seek the support of New York artists, both as individuals and members of the art advisory committee, he reported, "I have found . . . not only all absence of opposition, but the most kindly feelings and deep interest in my department."[34] Throughout the course of the fair, Ives's talents as a skilled diplomat and a capable administrator served him well and were, to a large extent, responsible for the high level of success enjoyed by the art department.

SELECTING A STAFF

Ives had many tasks confronting him upon his appointment, among which was the selection of his two primary assistants, one to supervise the exhibition of work by contemporary Americans artists, the other to organize the loan show of foreign masterpieces in American collections.[35] For the first and more important position, his choice was Charles Kurtz, with whom he had maintained a cordial professional and personal relationship since about 1886 (fig. 39). Kurtz, the son of a prominent New Castle, Pennsylvania, lawyer, Davis B. Kurtz, was born in 1855. He received a Bachelor of Arts degree from Washington and Jefferson College in 1876 and a Master of Arts degree from this institution in 1879. In the late 1870s Kurtz also studied at the National Academy of Design and in the studios of Lemuel E. Wilmarth and William Morgan. During the 1880s Kurtz pieced together a living by using his skills as a journalist and his interest in art. For about three years, beginning in late 1879, he was on the staff of the *New York Tribune.* From 1881 to 1889 he published *National Academy Notes,* the illustrated handbook that accompanied the Academy's annual spring exhibitions. In late 1883 he managed the exhibitions of the

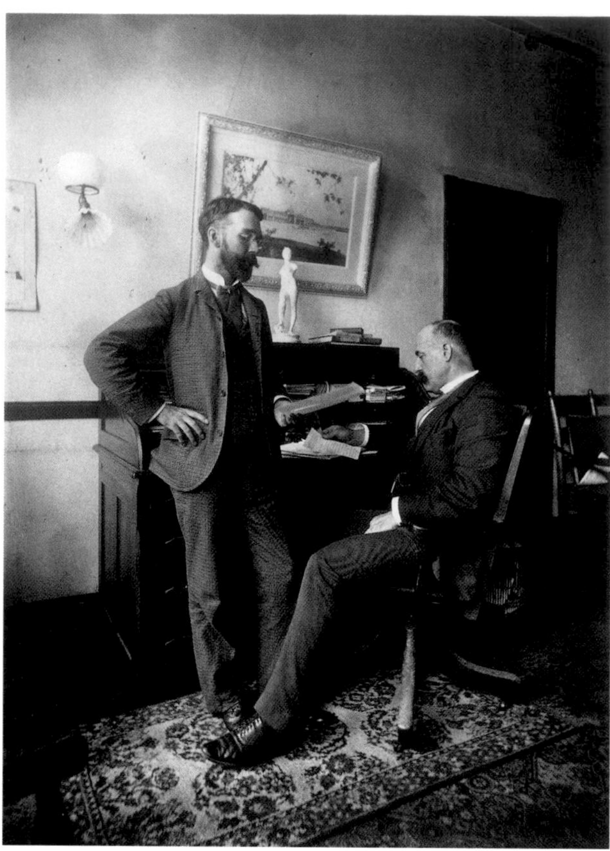

.. 39 ..
Charles M. Kurtz, assistant to the chief of the Fine Arts Department (standing), and Halsey C. Ives, chief of the Fine Arts Department (seated).
Courtesy of the Charles M. Kurtz Papers, Archives of American Art, Smithsonian Institution.

American Art Union and edited its monthly magazine. Between 1884 and 1886, Kurtz was director of art at the Southern Exposition in Louisville, Kentucky. By 1890, after managing a touring exhibition of two paintings by Hungarian-born Milhaly Munkacsy, Kurtz was again living in New York, serving as literary editor of the Sunday *Star.*[36] Ives presumably chose Kurtz as his chief assistant because he knew that they shared an aesthetic viewpoint and that Kurtz's long-standing familiarity with contemporary art would be fundamental to the realization of an exhibition of ambitious American work.

In mid-May Ives wrote to Kurtz, "I want very much to meet you and talk over the possibilities of your joining me, in some capacity, in the World's Fair work." Aware that even the simplest request required political persuasion to work its way through the fair's governing structure, Ives cautioned Kurtz, "Please consider what I have said to you in regard to the World's Fair work as strictly between ourselves. If I can shape things to bring about the desired result, rest assured I will do it."[37] Kurtz and Ives probably met in New York in late May to discuss the position, but Kurtz's appointment was not approved until late June. Even then his starting date and the amount of salary remained problematic. On 30 June, Ives, who was paid $5000 a year as chief, notified Kurtz that he had an official notice of his appointment, but warned him, "Please be in ignorance in regard to the details until you receive my next letter. The reason is that I expect to have to do a little fighting before all is cleared up. I had your salary fixed at $3000.00, the amt. named by the finance com. was $2500."[38] In the end, the latter sum was agreed upon, and Kurtz officially joined the exhibition team in mid-August.[39]

At its 27 June meeting the board also considered Sara Hallowell for a position as an assistant chief. Ives may not have wanted or needed a second assistant, particularly Hallowell, but he survived the fair's administrative wrangling because he was an adroit politician. Ives probably forwarded her appointment to the director-general because he found it expedient to do so as a way of placating the powerful Bertha Palmer and perhaps Charles Hutchinson.[40] As with Kurtz, the Board of Control did not wish to pay Hallowell more than $2500. Ives may not have supported Hallowell's pay request with the same vigor employed to champion Kurtz's petition, for he informed the latter that "Miss Hallowell's appointment is not at all assured. She is inclined to stand on her dignity and the boys are not in the proper humor for that sort of thing."[41] Hallowell initially declined to accept the salary offered her. She wrote from France that "my circumstances do not warrant my considering patriotic motives, and as my personal expenses can hardly be less than $3000 a year, and as I am in a position to earn more than this amount in another channel than that of the great Exposition, I must abandon the idea of connection with a work in which, naturally I would have taken much pride."[42]

Ultimately Ives persuaded Hallowell to accept the job. Hallowell, who had returned to Europe in the spring of 1891 and remained there until mid-September 1892, officially joined the art department in April 1892.[43] Ives assigned her the task of organizing the loan exhibition of foreign masterpieces in American collections. Though she received rave reviews for this display of 131 paintings from such notable collections as those of Alexander Cassatt, Alfred Corning Clark, Jay Gould, Henry Havemeyer, Henry Marquand, Potter Palmer, and Charles Yerkes, this position effectively placed her on the sidelines of the mainstream of American art activity at the fair, which was focused primarily on the nation's contemporary artists.[44]

PROMOTING PARTICIPATION AT HOME

In the summer of 1891, in addition to selecting his assistants and traveling to the East Coast to befriend state commissions and solicit the participation of important artists in the fair (both as individuals and as members of the art advisory committees in New York, Philadelphia, and Boston), Ives turned his attention to advancing the cause of the art department by preparing and publishing *Circular No. 2.*[45] This brochure enumerated the plans for exhibits and summarized the rules and regulations of the art department. It specified that American artists must deposit with the chief of the Department of Fine Arts before 1 November 1892 a list of works that they desired to exhibit. It indicated that all works would be juried, although no details regarding this process were given. It also stated that works produced since 1876 "which have passed the examination of juries of exhibitions of acknowledged standing would be admitted on list, should the jury so determine." The "on list" process, as the phrase implies, consisted of a list of works that the yet-to-be-named jurors wished to see in the show. These objects would have been well-known to art professionals and would not have to be re-judged because they had previously been accorded a favorable response in former exhibitions of note. Extant correspondence suggests that when artists communicated directly with the department, Ives and Kurtz encouraged favored artists to submit work, both before and after the official meetings of the various juries.[46] Likewise, extant documents imply that these two, particularly Kurtz, played a major role in shaping the works admitted "on list."

Circular No. 2, together with a letter of 1 August 1891 from Ives, was mailed to more than 3800 American artists and architects.[47] In this letter Ives articulated his goals for the exhibit of American art, expressing the hope that it would show "many important recent works," which "by bold departure from conventional lines of the old school have become representative of American art." Echoing the theme of the fair as a whole, he envisioned an art exhibition that would be "fully representative of the progress of the country during the last sixteen years." And well aware of the critical drubbing that American art had received in Philadelphia more than a decade earlier,

he wanted the art at the fair "to show what has been accomplished by American artists . . . since the Centennial Exhibition of 1876."

ADVANCING THE ART DEPARTMENT ABROAD

After a whirlwind trip to Washington to secure consular introductions and permission to use a navy ship to transport artworks from Europe, followed by meetings in New York, Boston, and Philadelphia with artists, collectors, and state committees, Ives left on 6 August 1891 for what would ultimately be a seven-month stay in Europe. The purpose of his trip was to meet with fine arts ministers in Europe to encourage their official participation in the fair, including funding for national exhibits. He also sought to secure the participation of major artists, both Americans living abroad and foreigners, and to organize the American advisory committees for France, Germany, and Italy.[48] Kurtz, who with financial support from his father and wife had gone to Europe in mid-July, joined Ives in Paris in mid-August.[49]

Part of the attraction of the job for Ives and Kurtz—idealism, patriotism, and professional advancement aside—was the opportunity to hobnob with important artists, political figures, and socially prominent individuals. Board and commission members also enjoyed these emoluments, particularly those who had plum assignments on committees that dealt with foreign governments. The frenetic but nevertheless glamorous life-style that Ives and Kurtz enjoyed while abroad is glimpsed in the latter's letter to his wife:

> Yesterday forenoon (Sunday) I wrote 16 letters for Professor Ives and then took a walk and visited the "Mauritshuis". . . . After lunch, Minister [Samuel] Thayer invited us to drive with him and took us first to his Club's "summer house" in the beautiful woods near the city, where we heard some splendid music by the Royal Military Band, in the grove near-by, and afterwards took us to call upon the Baroness Ode-Müller, who has a most superb chateau on an enormous and magnificent estate near the Hague . . . after another drive . . . we returned to the city and took tea at the mansion of the Baroness Van Grovestein. . . . We met a lot of . . . prominent Dutch and English people . . . we all went out to Scheveningen and heard a splendid concert at the Kurhaus. . . . This morning . . . we called upon Mr. Mesdag [Hendrik Wilhelm], and went over the details of the Exposition project, and then Mr. Mesdag took us to the Exhibition of the Dutch Water Color Society. . . . From the Exhibition we visited Mr. Tånhoven—Minister of Foreign Affairs. . . . From the Minister's, we went to call upon ISRAELS—Josef Israels, in some respects the greatest painter living. His house like that of Mesdag, is a palace, filled with beautiful things. It is an enormous house, with a long gallery—like the passage across the Ponte Vecchio in Florence, connecting the Uffzzi and Pitti Palace galleries—connecting the front house and the studio building. . . . After lunch, Mr. Thayer's carriage came after us, and we drove out to Delft with him. . . . When we got home I found a note from Ranger [Henry Ward Ranger, an American artist] telling me . . . to see him. W.[illiam] H. Howe, the [American] artist, also called to see us, and invited us to go with him to call upon Mrs. Mauve—the widow of [Anton] Mauve, the artist. . . . We all go to Amsterdam in the morning, with the expectation of visiting the museums, some of the leading artists, and then returning here, via Leyden and Haarlem. The "booring" commissioners of the show expect to be here from St. Petersburg on Thursday.[50]

Five days later the bon vivant Kurtz followed this letter with a description of a three-hour breakfast given by the Belgian minster at Les Trois Frères ("The Delmonico's of Brussels") for his cabinet and the American commission members, who had just arrived from Russia. Kurtz pridefully noted that only he, Bullock, and Minister [Edwin H.] Terrell could speak any French. "We drank toasts to everybody from the King down, and champagne flowed in a continuous sparkling stream. The Belgian cabinet expressed itself as delighted with us, and promised to visit Chicago in a body. You would have thought that they all had an idea of taking out naturalization papers."[51]

SOCIALIZING IN CHICAGO

In early September, while Ives remained in Europe for six more months, Kurtz returned to Chicago to oversee the affairs of the art department.[52] To the press that greeted him, Kurtz spoke glowingly of all that had been accomplished in Europe.[53] That fall Kurtz's activities included attending weekly Tuesday afternoon meetings with the director-general to discuss with other department heads the work of the past week; answering the correspondence of artists who had begun to send in lists of works they wished to be shown; issuing, over Ives's signature, a circular regarding a loan show of oriental objects (which never materialized); and, at Ives's request, reprinting the original *Circular No. 2* in French and German.[54] Although Kurtz also oversaw the progress on the art building, for which plans were finalized in mid-September, he seemed to occupy himself primarily with theater interests, shopping for appropriate attire, writing to earn extra money, and attending ceremonial occasions.[55] While in Chicago, Kurtz shared with Ives apartment 908 in the Pullman Building, which he described as "after the 'Pullman car' fashion, but not *quite* so contracted."[56]

To prove themselves the equals of the European elite, the Chicagoans responsible for the fair entertained their international visitors royally. As in Europe, Kurtz reveled in the opulent atmosphere surrounding these ceremonial occasions. He described as "18K through out" the luncheon for twenty-six, which Director-General Davis gave at the Chicago Club in honor of the English and German imperial commissioners, where the table was embellished with pink silk, an abundance of ferns, yellow chrysanthemums, crimson and pink roses, and a dozen varieties of the white, blue, and crimson lotuses. The dinner the following week at the Palmer House for the English, Danish and German commissioners was likewise deemed "a grand affair."[57]

But if Kurtz was exhilarated by elegant events, he was dismayed by the Chicago that confronted the national and international visitors when they stepped outside the banquet halls, society parlors, and confines of the White City. "Chicago is the dirtiest town in existence. . . . There is more smoke and soot here to the square inch than in either Cincinnati or Pittsburg. It is simply *impossible* to keep clean half an hour at a time. Cuffs that I wear during the forenoon I am ashamed to wear in for lunch." He considered the weather "simply awful . . . hotter than hell . . . *debilitating*."[58] His impression of Chicago had changed little when nearly a year later he wrote of an evening at the opera:

> I bought a seat in "the good part" of the house, but was unable to retain it through the entire evening, because the Chicago citizens at each side never had baths since their birth . . . and the theatre was warm. When I got home I found a bed-bug on my coat! . . . I hate this sink-hole of the sewage of humanity more and more every day. . . . The

> people here live in an atmosphere of sewage which fills river, lake, water-mains and streets; the climate is utterly unreliable and beastly, the city has its foundation in mud and swamp—and how could the people be expected to be decent. Thank God we do not live here![59]

Ever the aesthete, Kurtz did, however, admire the new architecture in Chicago, which he found better than that in New York.[60]

AUGMENTING THE ADVISORY COMMITTEES

The activities of the Department of Fine Arts and its public visibility escalated after the New Year when Kurtz, at Ives's request, went to New York, Boston, and Philadelphia to make final arrangements for the advisory committees in each of these cities and to secure the active participation of other notable artists. While Ives had contacted some artists on his trip east in the summer of 1891, he had not completed all of his arrangements for the advisory committees because many artists were out of town.[61] Strong advisory committees were fundamental to Ives and Kurtz's plan for an exceptional art exhibition. As the committee members were the men from whom the East Coast juries were chosen, it was crucial that they share the aesthetic vision of Kurtz and Ives if the final exhibition was to realize the goal "of showing what has been accomplished by American artists since the Centennial." Although, in retrospect, it is apparent that the artists on the advisory committees reflect Ives's personal choice to a considerable extent, particularly in New York, these selections were made with the consent of the state commissions.[62] That Ives was able to persuade the state commissioners to accept his vision of appropriate individuals for these committees is yet another testimony to his consummate political skills.

After writing a lengthy justification of his forthcoming trip to Director-General Davis, Kurtz arrived in Philadelphia on 25 January 1892.[63] During the next two days on behalf of the department, he visited various artists, collectors, dealers, and Pennsylvania commission members, as well as John Sartain, the director of American art at the 1876 Centennial, and his daughter Emily. He also managed to see the annual exhibition at the Pennsylvania Academy of the Fine Arts and the monthly loan exhibition at the Philadelphia Art Club.[64]

Kurtz maintained this hectic pace in New York. Within the first three days he met with advisory committee members R. Swain Gifford, F. D. Millet, William Merritt Chase, Augustus Saint-Gaudens, and Hugh Bolton Jones, and visited artists Thomas W. Wood, J. G. Brown, William H. Beard, Alban J. Conant, Enoch Wood Perry, John H. Dolph, as well as collectors Samuel P. Avery, Thomas B. Clarke, and James Ellsworth, the latter in town from Chicago. Additionally, he kept up with the auction results of the J. G. Brown and John H. Dolph sales, went to the annual dinner at the Watercolor Society, appeared at a reception at James Wells Champney's home, and attended the regular Saturday night dinner at the Century Club, where he saw William H. Beard again and met Albert Bierstadt. He also called on personal friends not connected with the art world.[65]

While in New York, one of Kurtz's formidable assignments was "to strengthen the art committee by the addition of Eastman Johnson and J. Q. A. [John Quincy Adams] Ward (figs. 40, 41)—to more satisfactorily represent the older element of the Academy." Kurtz invested much time and energy in this project. "Ward promptly

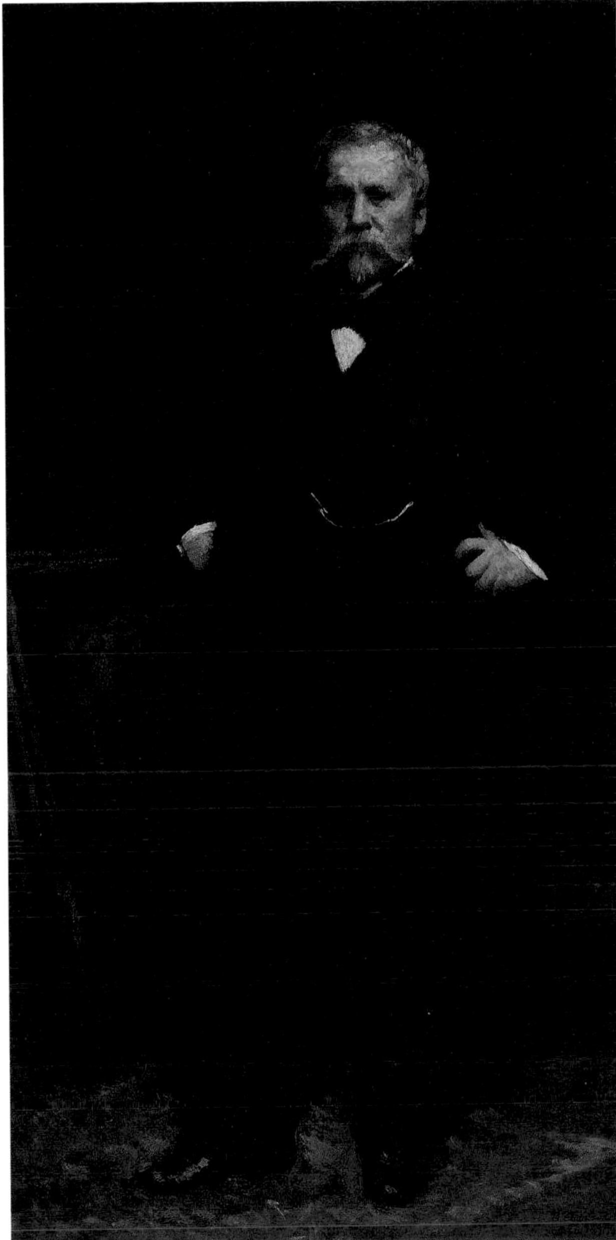

.. 40 ..
Eastman Johnson,
Portrait of the Artist, *1891.*
Hirshhorn Museum and Sculpture Garden,
Smithsonian Institution,
Gift of the Joseph H. Hirshhorn Foundation, 1966.
Photograph by Lee Stalsworth.

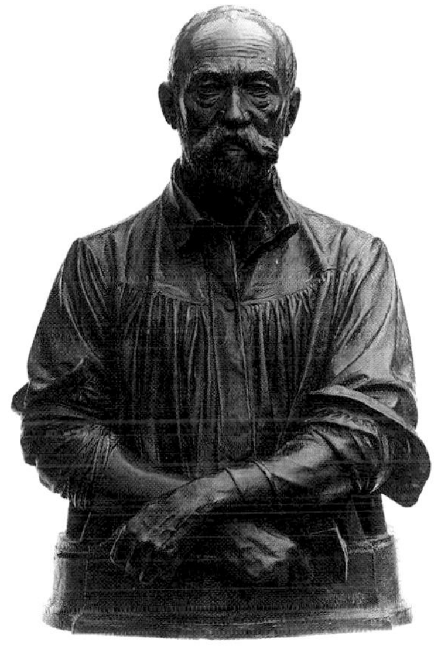

.. 41 ..
Charles H. Niehaus,
John Quincy Adams Ward,
modeled ca. 1900, cast 1911,
bronze.
National Portrait Gallery,
Smithsonian Institution.

accepted, but Eastman Johnson said he *could not* be a member of the committee for a lack of *time*," he wrote to his wife. Ultimately, to accomplish his goal, Kurtz got Gifford and Ward to persuade Johnson to join the committee. Justifying his efforts and the political and intellectual rationale behind them, Kurtz believed that "with Johnson a member, our committee would be an ideal one:—able, broad, liberal.

Nobody, I think, could object to it, and yet it would accept only *good* pictures."[66] Clearly for both Ives and Kurtz, obtaining work of recognized critical stature from prominent New York artists was a key ingredient in their plans. This is apparent in both their words and actions. While they traveled to Boston and Philadelphia to give advice and gain consent, in no other city did the advisory committee and the jury receive as much attention and manipulation.

On 5 February at the National Academy of Design, Kurtz publicly presented the names of the members of the New York advisory committee. The event, in his opinion, had gone "*exactly right*."[67] This was an overly optimistic assessment. Numerous artists, led by Thomas W. Wood, president of the National Academy of Design, held that artists, not Ives, should have selected the advisory committee. Moreover, this group complained that the committee was too small and dominated by individuals representing the Society of American Artists. Hence, they felt it was too heavily weighted toward younger men who had received a substantial amount of their training abroad.[68] The discontent of Wood and his sympathizers reflected an ongoing complaint that the art at the fair was not sufficiently "American," a term that could refer either to style or subject matter or both.

The following week Kurtz went to Boston to finalize the composition of the Massachusetts advisory committee and to seek the assistance of local artists in obtaining a state appropriation to defray the expense of the fine arts exhibit from this area.[69] While there, Kurtz gave a speech that fanned the flames of the long-standing rivalry between artists in New York and Boston. He touched the nerve of the latter's barely hidden sense of inferiority by stating that the work of the Massachusetts advisory committee would be subject to review by its New York counterpart.[70]

QUELLING THE STORM

Thus, when Ives returned to Chicago from Europe in late February, one of his first tasks was to exercise damage control.[71] Addressing the concerns of the more conservative ranks of New York artists, he told the press that the art exhibition "would be thoroughly representative of American art," adding that "if I could talk to Mr. Wood, in a few minutes I could convince him that our action and judgment are proper." To calm the Boston artists he stated that "the New York Jury has nothing to do with Philadelphia or Boston art, and vice versa."[72] Kurtz, by contrast, was no politician and only complicated matters when he tried to explain his position on the jury issue. He wanted a jury composed of the best men, and "it was not his personal responsibility if those same 'best men' all chanced to live in New York."[73]

Aware that words were not enough and that the success of the art department depended upon the good will of the artists and the advisory committees in the East, Ives left Chicago on 8 March to garner fiscal support for the art department in Washington and to visit Philadelphia, New York, and Boston to placate these artistic communities.[74] Kurtz, who left a week later to join him in Philadelphia after first visiting his wife in Kentucky, maintained that Ives "upholds all I have done. Tells me it was just right." In his heart of hearts, however, Ives must have thought that his assistant was a bit of a loose cannon, for he underscored his written plea to him to "*say nothing and do nothing* in Philadelphia until I join you."[75] With the

Pennsylvania advisory committee seemingly on track, the two journeyed to New York on 21 March, where they wined and dined those whose good will they sought. The visit, according to Kurtz, went "*exactly right,*" a phrase he had used before when things were, in truth, not quite right.[76] This time, however, the two seemed to have smoothed ruffled feathers, at least momentarily, and on 27 March Ives left for Boston to calm the tempest in that teapot while Kurtz returned to Chicago.

On 30 March Ives spoke to Boston-area artists at the St. Botolph Club and, on the following evening, at the Art Club. Enough groundwork must have been laid before these speeches, as Ives reported to Kurtz that "all was serene."[77] Likewise, E. C. Hovey of the Massachusetts Commission told the press:

> With regard to the disagreement in the department of fine arts, . . . there seems to have been a misunderstanding on the part of the Boston artists as to what Mr. Kurtz intended to convey. . . . My repeated talks with Professor Ives convinced me that the arrangements which he intends to make with the representatives of the artists in our Eastern cities will be highly satisfactory, just and fair.[78]

It may have been in response to this political crisis that Ives conceived the notion printed in *Circular No. 3*, the June 1892 update on the activities and regulations of the art department, that two men from each city would serve on the juries of the other cities, and "there will be in Chicago no revision as to quality in the works of art passed by these juries."[79]

EXPANDING THE ART PALACE

In the spring of 1892, in addition to pacifying eastern artists, scuttling a proposed competing exhibition in New York, and soliciting money from the New York State committee for expenses related to the judging and transporting of this state's art, Ives's major task was to finalize the allocation of space and the revised plans for the

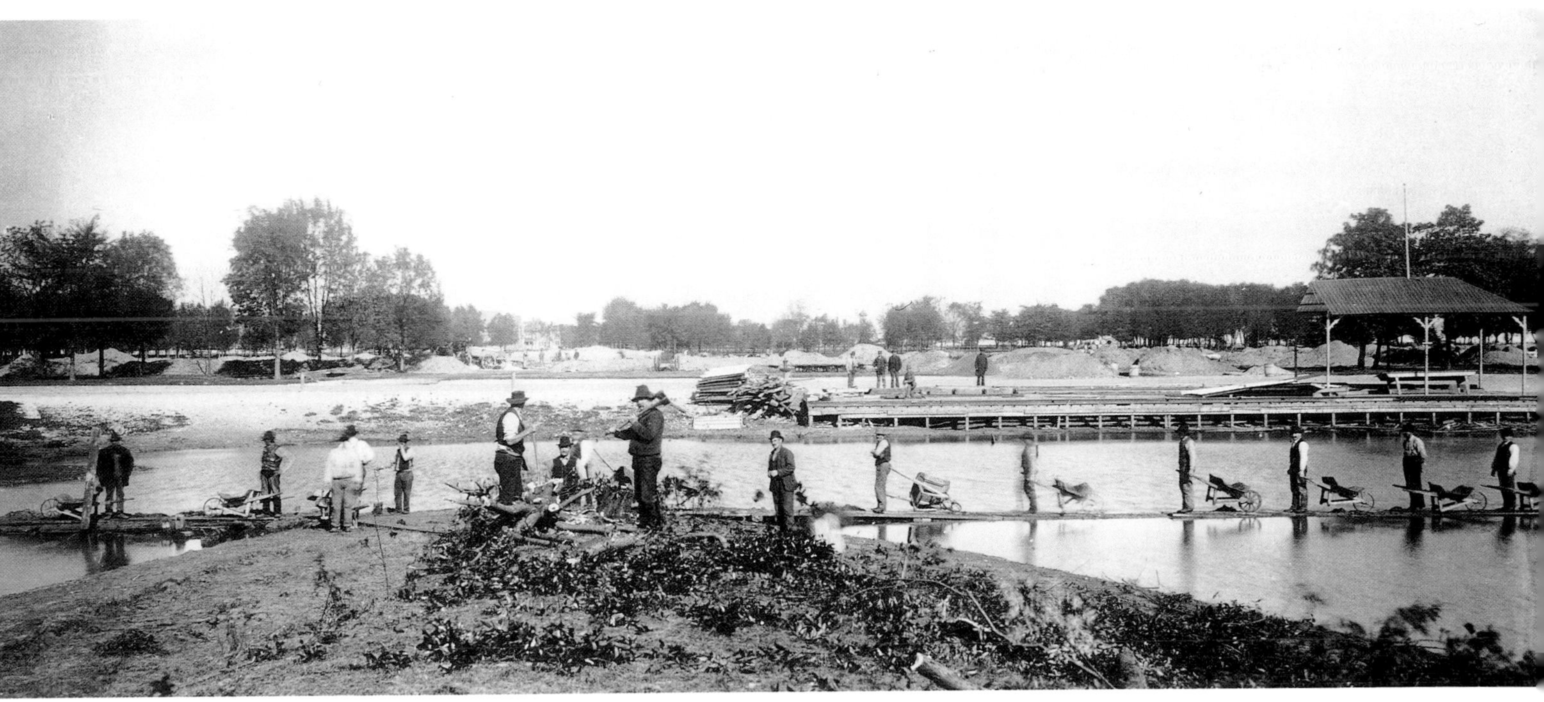

. . 42 . .
Site of the Fine Arts Building looking north, October 1891. *Photograph by C. D. Arnold. Official Photographs of the World's Columbian Exposition by C. D. Arnold, vol. 1, pl. 14. Courtesy of The Chicago Public Library, Special Collections Department.*

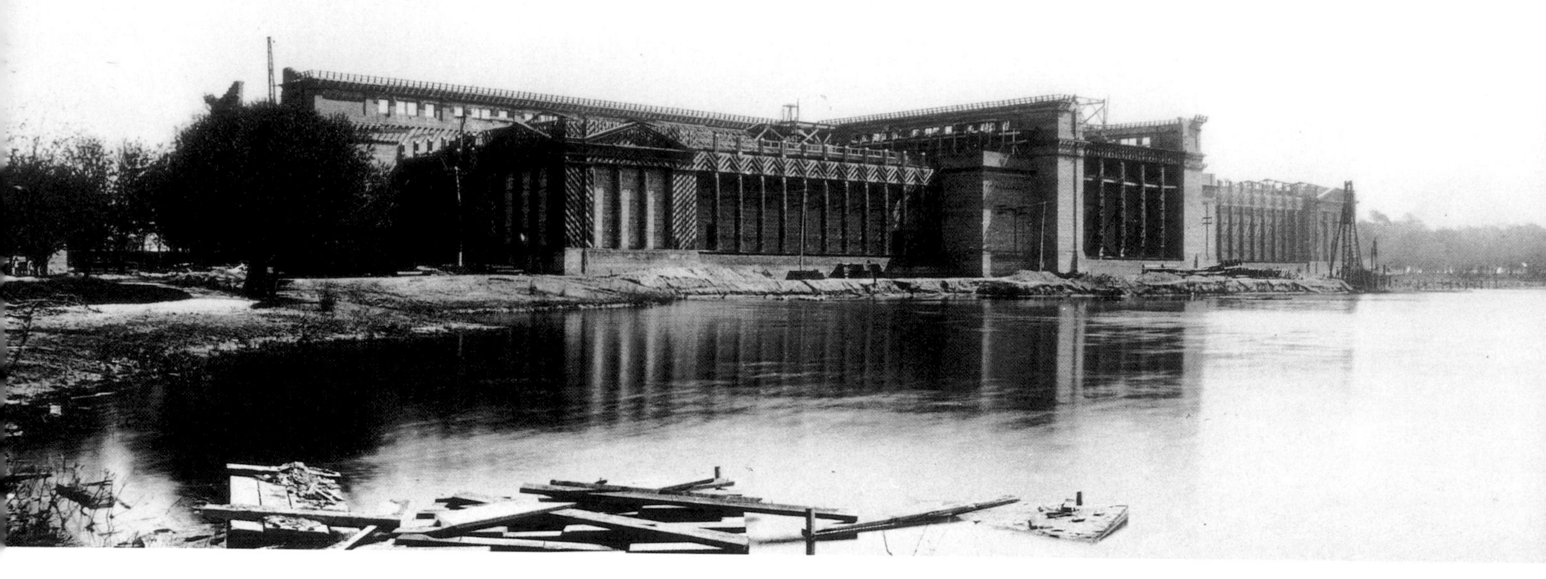

.. 43 ..
The Fine Arts Building under construction, looking northeast, May 1892. Photograph by C. D. Arnold. Official Photographs of the World's Columbian Exposition by C. D. Arnold, vol. 1, pl. 46, I. Courtesy of The Chicago Public Library, Special Collections Department.

art building.[80] At the time of Ives's appointment the previous spring, the art building was the subject of much debate. At issue was whether it should be in Jackson Park or on Michigan Avenue (on the site of the former Inter-State Exposition's building); whether it should be a permanent structure; and, if so, whether it should subsequently be the home of the Art Institute of Chicago. Ultimately it was resolved that the Art Institute of Chicago and the Palace of Fine Arts would be separate buildings, with the Institute located on its present Michigan Avenue site and the Fine Arts Building placed at the north end of Jackson Park.[81]

Construction of the art building, designed by Charles B. Atwood, began in the fall of 1891 (fig. 42), but by the time Ives returned from Europe in February, it was apparent that the building was too small to accommodate the amount of space assigned by Director-General Davis to various foreign governments. To meet the demand, east and west wings were added beginning in May 1892 (fig. 43).[82] When it was completed, the art pavilion, built of steel and brick and covered with staff (a white plaster-like material used on most of the major buildings at the fair), occupied more than five acres and included 145,000 square feet of exhibition space. During the fair it housed more than 10,000 works of art by American and foreign artists (fig. 44). It cost approximately $670,000. The building was thought to be fireproof, a major concern to lenders.[83] The American art exhibition was allocated the most wall space, followed by that given to France.[84] It was no coincidence that the American pavilions were next to the French, separated only by the exhibition of foreign masterpieces from American collections; an important purpose of the exhibit was to demonstrate that American artists were at long last capable of competing head on with this aesthetic rival—and winning the contest.

SUMMER OF 1892 AND *CIRCULAR NO. 3*

With decisions regarding the art building well in hand, Ives returned to Europe in late May to negotiate for copies of medieval French sculptures from the Trocadero

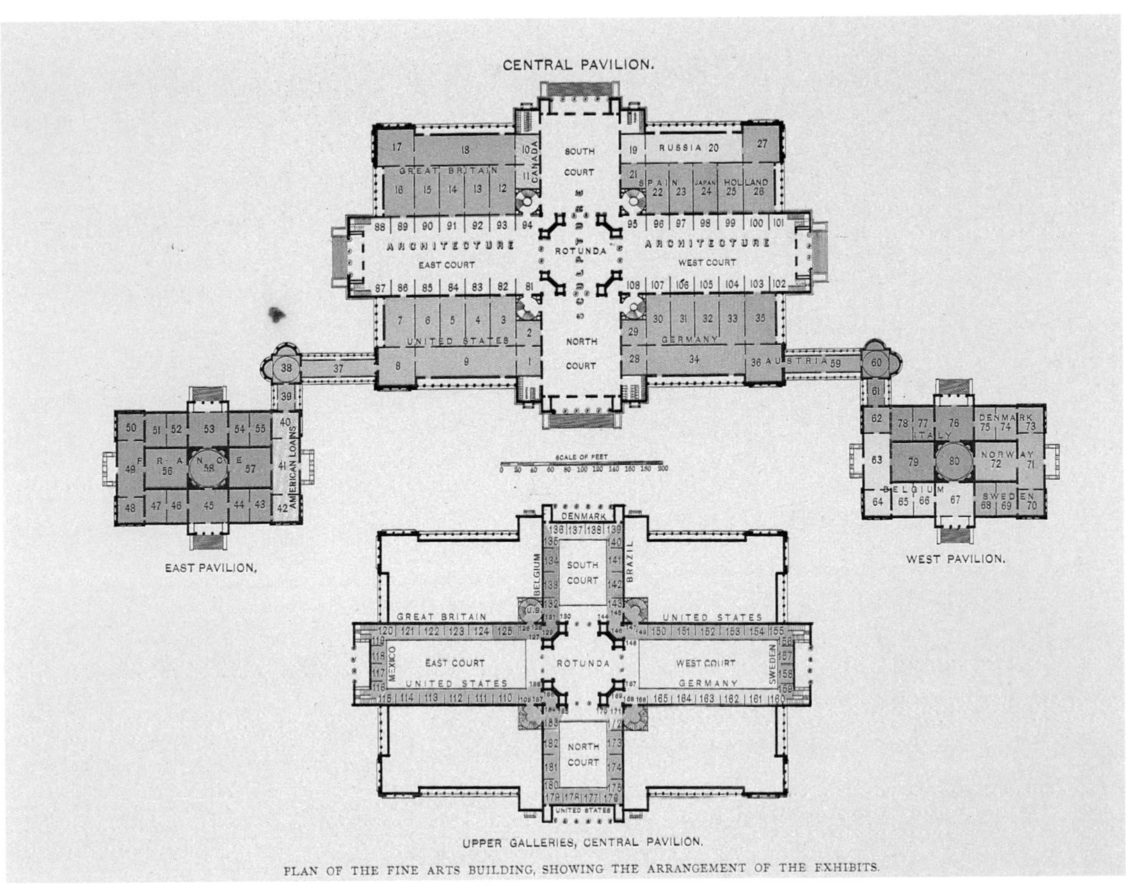

.. 44 ..

Ground plan of the Fine Arts Building.

American oil paintings were exhibited in galleries 1, 3–9, 37–39, and upper alcoves 109–115, 173–76, 179–84, 186–87. American sculpture was shown in the rotunda, the north and west courts, the passage to the east court, and galleries 7 and 38. Ripley Hitchcock, The Art of the World, *vol. 1 (New York: D. Appleton, 1895), following 32.*

Museum in Paris and to meet again with the French, English, Spanish, and Italian ministers and with various American advisory committees.[85] Before he left, he and Kurtz were together briefly in New York, where the latter spent time finalizing the roster of advisory committee members. Among those asked to assist the department at this time were Louis Comfort Tiffany, J. C. Nicoll, Charles A. Platt, Samuel Colman, and John Ferguson Weir.[86] When he returned to Chicago, Kurtz began to draw up lists of works (although none had been selected by any juries!) that he wished to see illustrated in his book, *Official Illustrations from the Art Gallery of the World's Columbian Exposition,* which would be published the following May.[87]

While Ives was abroad, Kurtz published and distributed on 15 June *Circular No. 3,* the most important document to emerge from the art department during the summer of 1892. *Circular No. 3* detailed the names of the individuals serving on the various advisory committees, the rules for the formation of the juries in each city, shipping instructions for artists living abroad (fig. 45), provisions for making selections in the event of space limitations, the presentation of both a retrospective

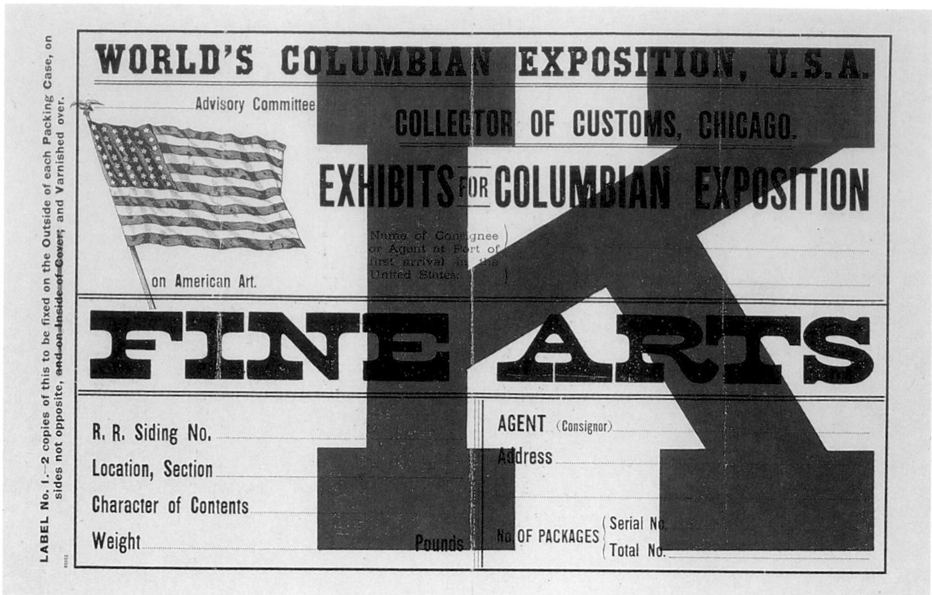

LABEL No. 1.–2 copies of this to be fixed on the Outside of each Packing Case, on sides not opposite, ~~and on Inside of Cover,~~ and Varnished over.

WORLD'S COLUMBIAN EXPOSITION, U.S.A.

Advisory Committee

on American Art.

COLLECTOR OF CUSTOMS, CHICAGO.

EXHIBITS FOR COLUMBIAN EXPOSITION

Name of Consignee or Agent at Port of first arrival in the United States.

K

FINE ARTS

R. R. Siding No.

Location, Section

Character of Contents

Weight ... Pounds

AGENT (Consignor)

Address

No. OF PACKAGES (Serial No. / Total No.

.. 45 ..
Department K shipping label.
Courtesy of Dr. Stephen M. Sheppard.

exhibition of American art and a loan exhibition of European works in American collections, and the size and shape of the art building. It noted that space had been allocated to all countries and underscored the fact that the United States section would occupy over one-quarter of the space in the central pavilion in galleries not far from those reserved for French art. It justified the space allocations to foreign nations, which had requested substantially more space than was given, by saying that the more limited space would make foreign countries "more closely draw the line as to high artistic quality in the works sent to Chicago." It also recounted Ives's earlier trip abroad. By noting the juxtaposition of the American and French pavilions, *Circular No. 3* signaled the forthcoming competition between American and French art; by giving the reasoning behind limiting space to foreign exhibitors, it touched upon the American fear that foreign countries would flood the art building with lesser-quality works because they did not take this exposition seriously. By implication it designated New York, Massachusetts, and Pennsylvania as the most important art centers in America, for these states had their own art juries. With only the national jury in Chicago to judge art from the rest of the American states and territories, it is no wonder that artists in the Midwest, West, and South felt they were given short shrift at the fair.[88]

Additionally, *Circular No. 3* addressed the fear of the three East Coast advisory committees that they would be overruled by the national jury or a hanging committee, for it stated that the national jury would pass only on work not judged by any other committee and that there would be no hanging committee. While Ives was willing to accept the decisions of the various juries as final, he nevertheless provided himself with an escape hatch. Citing space limitations, he requested that all art be ranked, so that "all works marked 'No. 1' will be provided for first, and works marked 'No. 2' and 'No. 3' will be taken care of, in order, so far as the space available may permit." Essentially regulations to soothe artists, particularly those in Boston, these two rules gave Ives and Kurtz final authority to decide what was hung when the installation of artworks took place in the spring of 1893. Out of political expediency,

Ives had created another win-win situation for himself, calming the artistic waters and creating an arrangement that would give him more control, albeit indirectly, over the art shown at the fair.

"THE SEX LINE IN ART"

Circular No. 3 also made apparent the fact that no women served on any of the advisory committees in the United States. Because the final selecting juries were drawn from the membership of the advisory committees, this meant that no women would serve on the juries that passed on the works to be exhibited at the fair. This crisis faced Ives when he returned to Chicago from Europe in mid-July. John Boyd Thacher—a former mayor of Albany, a commissioner, and chairman of the New York State Board of Managers, which had legal and fiscal control over the New York advisory committee—was sympathetic to the position of the fair's Board of Lady Managers, who had objected to the absence of women on the advisory committees. Ives, who had strong feelings on the subject, responded to sculptor J. Q. A. Ward, a member of the New York advisory committee:

> I have an impression that there is a law somewhere in existence . . . that women receive a place on all *juries* considering work by women. That being the case, we shall be obliged to appoint a female or two on each of the juries, but not on the advisory committees. I have spent 22 long years in doing business with interests connected with the female element, and I draw the line here—No Women on the Advisory Committees.[89]

Ives also enlisted the sympathy of F. D. Millet, who, he reported to Kurtz, "had a good deal to say about the 'gall' of the Albany man [Thacher], and his personal feeling against the appointment of women on the jury."[90]

The issue did not die, and in November an open letter was written to the New York State board declaring that while the committee "did not in any way oppose the introduction of women to the committees or juries, it opposed their introduction at the present on a number of grounds." These included the fact that the committees had been appointed and approved the previous February and that the petition did not come from New York women artists but from the Board of Lady Managers, and thus "was not an expression of those most intimately interested." This letter also maintained that just because "a large proportion of art work in the country was executed by women, [and] that women formed the bulk of the pupils in the studios," this was no reason to put women on juries. To do so was "merely the reintroduction of the sex line in art." It then asserted that "the very best encouragement that could be given to any artist, man or woman, . . . was the acceptance of his or her work on the grounds of . . . art value alone, and the awarding of them of a place more or less notable among the works of the best masters of the land."[91]

Pragmatism rather than personal feeling ultimately triumphed, and the appointment of two women to the New York jury was accepted in exchange for a guarantee from the state committee to fund the expenses of the New York art advisory committee.[92] Ives capitulated to *realpolitik* and in mid-December sent Ward two letters requesting the appointment of Mary Hallock Foote to the jury on chalk, charcoal, pastel and other drawings, and Mary Cassatt to the jury on painting.[93] By

selecting these two artists, Ives must have known that there was a good chance that neither woman would serve. Not only was Cassatt living in Paris and unlikely to return, but it was well known that she did not approve of juried exhibitions.[94] Since Foote lived in Idaho, the distance, as well as her own restricted fiscal circumstances, made it unlikely that she would be able to travel to New York without financial support.[95] Although Ives subsequently conceded to the appointment of three women—Foote, Emily Sartain, and Mary Solari—to the International Committee of Judges, which convened in July 1892, he had nevertheless again created a win-win situation for himself by appointing two women who would not or could not serve on the selecting juries.

As for the success—or lack of it—of women painters and sculptors before the all-male juries, 104 women exhibited in the Palace of Fine Arts, or approximately nineteen percent of the 521 American painters and sculptors represented. This number, while seemingly low considering the number of women enrolled in art schools, was not uncharacteristic; an examination of the exhibition records of the annual shows of the National Academy of Design and the Pennsylvania Academy of the Fine Arts in the years preceding the fair reveals that usually between fourteen and eighteen percent of the exhibitors were women. Like the majority of men who participated in the exposition, most of these women began their professional careers by studying in the major art schools in America, and the vast preponderance of these women solidified their careers and their claim to professional standing by continuing their studies abroad. By the time of the fair, many had established a credible exhibition record, showing at the National Academy of Design, the Pennsylvania Academy of the Fine Arts, or in the Paris Salons. Several women also had close affiliations with mainstream establishment artists, such as painter William Merritt Chase and sculptors Lorado Taft and Augustus Saint-Gaudens. Although their careers paralleled those of the men who exhibited at the fair, unlike their male counterparts, only four women—painters Lilla Cabot Perry and Amanda Brewster Sewell and sculptors Caroline S. Brooks and Theo Alice Ruggles—exhibited more than three works.[96]

FINALIZING DETAILS IN THE FALL OF 1892

The fall of 1892 continued to be hectic for Kurtz and Ives, with the latter frequently traveling between the East Coast, Chicago, and St. Louis.[97] Both men attended the festive events surrounding the ceremonies to dedicate the exposition buildings in mid-October. In November Ives spoke at the National Academy of Design about his foreign trips and progress on the art building, among other topics.[98] When Ives returned to Chicago, he sought to maintain control over the New York jury process by sending Kurtz to assist the jury with its work. Realizing that it was not politically wise to make this decision unilaterally, Ives wrote to Ward, somewhat ingenuously:

> I am still considering the propriety of having Mr. Kurtz join you and devote his time to a careful canvass of the city—giving his time to the men of acknowledged standing. We have made out a list of four or five hundred names from which to select such as the members of the committee think best. . . . If you think wise I will ask Mr. Kurtz to join the eastern contingent next week.[99]

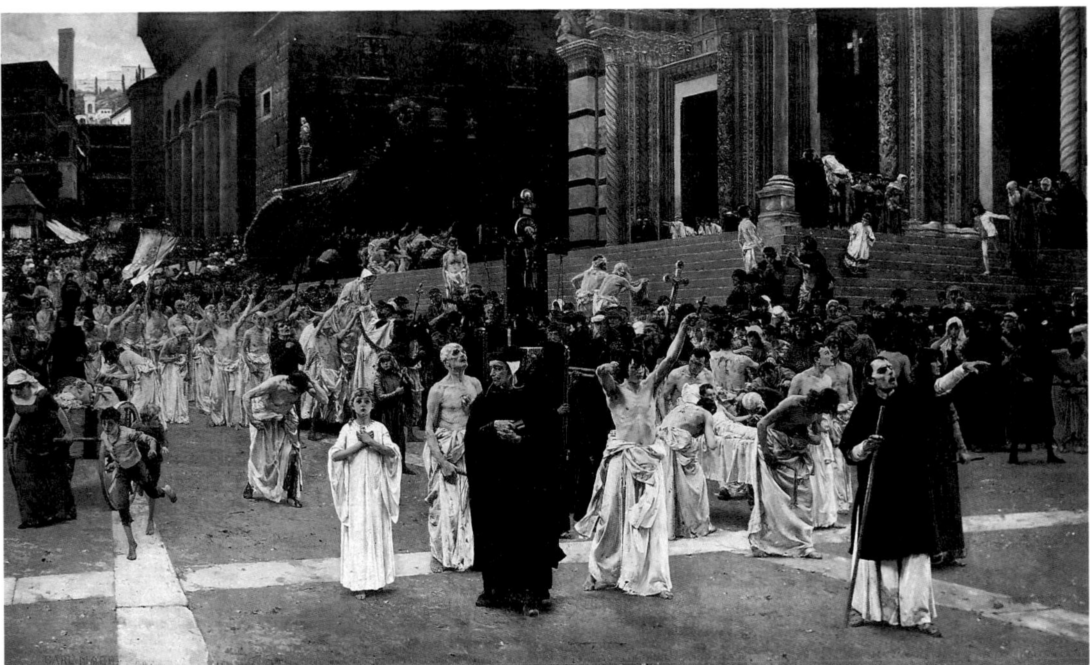

. . 46 . .
Carl Marr,
The Flagellants, *1889.*
City of Milwaukee, permanent loan to West Bend Gallery of Fine Arts.

Clearly Ives believed that Kurtz's presence would enhance the likelihood that men "of acknowledged standing" and "important recent works," which "by bold departure from conventional lines have become representative of American art," would make their way through the jury process.

Kurtz had been working on his vision of the American show at least since the summer of 1892, for he wrote his wife that he had been making a list of "only the *best* men, and . . . their most noteworthy works produced during the past *16* years—as I remember them *via* refreshment of memory given by old catalogues, Academy notes, Art Ass'n catalogues, etc."[100] He also wrote J. Q. A. Ward that he was developing a list of artists and that, among others, he envisioned the show containing the works of "Weeks, Gay, Pearce, Dannat and others of the Paris colony," as well as Carl Marr's *The Flagellants* (fig. 46), "which has brought him so many favorable notices from European critics."[101] As the 1893 show contained an overwhelming number of works that had appeared in previous exhibitions that Kurtz knew well, in addition to works from his collection and from lenders who had bought from him, the cumulative evidence reinforces the notion that Ives and Kurtz either directly or by successfully manipulating the jury system assured themselves that their choices would be included in this mammoth show of American art.[102] Adding credibility to this supposition is the fact that the Kurtz papers contain his handwritten list indicating which artists had been included and which names should be added to the list of artists to be considered by the New York jury.

Before Kurtz left for New York on 10 December, he was invited to a party at the Palmers' home.

> Last night I went to the big Bazaar held at Mrs. Potter Palmer's establishment. There was an enormous crowd and everything was very gorgeous. The Palmer residence, in

> its general scheme of decoration, is the quintessence of ostentation and vulgarity. I do not believe its equal in these respects exists on the face of the earth. Still, it was interesting to see what ignorance could accomplish with a fortune at its disposal, and to observe the "social Chicagoan" on his native heath.[103]

Kurtz may genuinely have disliked Mrs. Palmer's art, but fuel to the fire of his intellectual loathing may have been added because she never purchased any work from him. Also fanning the flames of his biting remarks was the fact that Bertha Palmer was the staunch supporter of his archrival, Sara Hallowell.[104]

So eager was Kurtz to participate in the jurying process that he was willing to forgo the Christmas holidays with his family in Kentucky. He arrived in New York about 15 December and stayed east until late February 1893. Ives had many tasks for him to accomplish while he was in New York. On 19 December Ives asked him to make arrangements with Thomas W. Dewing and Dwight W. Tryon for their exhibits. These two men "of acknowledged standing" and part of the younger generation of "bold innovators" were initially reluctant to participate in the exhibition.[105] But Ives, exercising his considerable charm, persuaded them that it would be worthy of their participation: "I had a very pleasant interview with them, and I think they left the city feeling better disposed toward the work than when they came. They really were very belligerent when they reached here, [but] I related to them what we were trying to do. This seemed to mellow them considerable [*sic*]."[106] Ives also asked Kurtz "to take steps leading to a representation of [Alexander H.] Wyant's work."[107] A minor departmental chore included picking up at Ortgies & Co.'s Fifth Avenue Art Galleries a painting by Frederick A. Bridgman that had been selected by the Paris jury.[108]

THE NEW YORK JURY

According to William Tuthill, an architect and secretary of the New York art bureau (the legally designated collection agency of the state, composed of advisory committee members), New York artists submitted 1,480 paintings and 73 sculptures, of which 758 paintings and 50 sculptures were sent forth to be judged by the New York State jury at the Seventh Regiment Armory after a preliminary competition.[109] Kurtz must have been intimately involved in the winnowing process, for prior to the beginning of the official judging on 16 January, he wrote of the chaos caused by the committees and of the long nights he and Hugh Bolton Jones, secretary of the New York painting jury, spent going over lists of works submitted by artists. At three o'clock in the morning of 10 January, Kurtz wrote, "I am almost overwhelmed with work. The various 'committees' here have things in a most confused condition, and there is an enormous amount of labor necessary to straighten them out. The amount of work I am doing each day sometimes surprises myself." The art committee met again on the next three nights, and Kurtz reported: "Last night it was 4 o'clock before I got to bed. Tonight, I fear it will be almost as late. There is simply an *enormous* amount of detail to be gone through, and, really," he concluded with his characteristic lack of modesty, "there is no one here to attend to it—who knows *how* to attend to it properly—but me."[110]

During the official jury proceedings, Kurtz's role was to keep the jury record and the accepted lists and to correspond with owners about works accepted or rejected or requested for submission "on list."[111] The letters from artists and collectors among Kurtz's papers—not usually addressed to him because official correspondence went out over the signature of Jones, Tuthill, or Ward—reflect the kinds of details with which he was involved.[112] Typical is a letter from Elliott Shepard in which he indicates his willingness to lend John Singer Sargent's portrait of his daughter Alice Vanderbilt Shepard.[113] Shepard was probably contacted in response to Sargent's previous letter to the art department in which he had enclosed a list of pictures in New York that he wished to show, "or such as those which the owners will lend for the purpose."[114] Kurtz, at Ives's request, persuaded the committee to accept the works of Dewing before the artist contacted the collector Charles Freer because Dewing did not "desire to ask the owner for the use of a work for six or eight months and then submit it to the jury and be obliged to humiliate himself by returning it."[115] Kurtz probably used this potentially awkward situation to ask Tuthill, as secretary of the art bureau, to compose the letter to collectors stating that if the committee wrote requesting a work, this meant that it had been accepted "on list."[116] Acceptance "on list" was undoubtedly the intention of the 11 January letter the committee sent prior to the convening of the jury (yet another sign of the control Kurtz exercised over "on list" choices), which requested from the National Academy of Design the loan of George Willoughby Maynard's *Civilization.*[117] But this procedure was not always followed. Daniel Huntington wrote to Seth Low requesting his portrait, and John Ferguson Weir wrote to the owners of *Admiral Farragut, Forging the Shaft,* and *The Flowers (Roses)* asking for these loans.[118] As these letters are dated after the New York committee met, presumably the paintings had been officially accepted "on list" and the resulting confusion minimal.

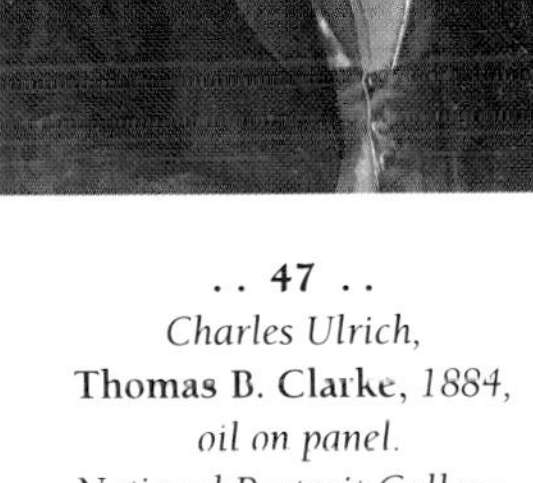

.. 47 ..
Charles Ulrich,
Thomas B. Clarke, *1884, oil on panel. National Portrait Gallery, Smithsonian Institution.*

From the beginning of the New York jury process, Kurtz was optimistic about the art that would be shown. At first he was impressed with the selectivity of the jury, noting that "a large number of paintings was considered, but very few works were accepted—and these not at a high rating. The jury is *very* conservative—sometimes too much so—though, in the main, this is to the advantage of the prospective art exhibit." By the third day Kurtz became a bit anxious about the rigorous nature of the jury: "The selection of works has been made very carefully. Some things have been retained that should have gone out, and others have been 'fired' that should have been retained. The percentage of 'accepted' works, among all which were examined has been *small.* As a result, we may yet have to 'hustle' to fill the American section in a creditable manner."[119]

Kurtz need not have worried, as the problem was just the opposite in May when he began to hang the exhibition. Nevertheless, a supplemental meeting of the painting jury was held on 23 January to make certain no important work or artist had been overlooked.[120] In addition, Kurtz spent most of the next month, before his return to Chicago on 22 February, contacting New York collectors about loans. He was particularly pleased with the generosity of William T. Evans, who ultimately lent sixteen canvases.[121] He visited and wrote to Thomas B. Clarke (fig. 47) several times.[122] Clarke, who lent forty-nine paintings, including fifteen by George Inness, received a list of artists that the organizers wished to exhibit, but within this context he was more or less free to choose what he wanted to send from his collection.[123] The

New York jury ultimately sent more than 600 works to Chicago, of which 324 paintings and thirty-seven sculptures had been judged at the armory and 281 works, mostly paintings, had been admitted "on list."[124] The jury members, for the most part ignoring the "rule of three" noted in *Circular No. 3,* saw that they themselves were well represented.[125]

Kurtz foresaw that "there will be a great deal of weeping and wailing and gnashing of false teeth when the 'Jury returns' are published. Some of the men will feel *very* savage. But it can't be helped!" He anticipated that "a protest will be sent to the Exposition authorities and to Albany, by the 'soreheads' " and that "the particularly resentful brethren" would be Thomas W. Wood, Enoch Wood Perry, William H. Beard, Albert Bierstadt, and James M. and William M. Hart and "the rest of that pre-historic crowd"—that is, the same group who had previously complained about the composition of the New York painting jury. At the Century Club on Saturday, 21 January, Kurtz "had rather a lively time with the disgruntled artists," reporting that "several who did not send work through fear of rejection, are so disgusted with themselves for *not* having sent, and complain the jury was so 'narrow' in its construction that they did not dare *risk* possible 'affront' by sending."[126]

Ives, too, anticipated discontent, but he was particularly annoyed that the list of works chosen by the New York jury had been published in New York and Chicago papers before he had received official word from William Tuthill.[127] Kurtz, who did not like Tuthill and frequently fought with him over issues of power and authority in the administration of the jury process, was horrified that Tuthill had given out the New York jury report with grades on it, raging that

> he has annoyed, no hindered and damaged our work beyond measure, by stupidly giving out "lists" of accepted works before the lists were *completed.* He gave them out also with the *grades* given them by the juries—a matter that *never* is made public. Some of the artists, therefore, seem to be rated as *third-class* men. You can imagine what a commotion all this has created! Some of the men are ordering their accepted pictures returned to them. Like the ass that he is, Tuthill allowed some *accepted* pictures to go. . . . I *never* have known any affairs to get into worse condition—and all on account of one little fool, incompetent officious ass. *I* am *worn out!* [128]

"FRENCH NOTIONS" AND "REAL" AMERICAN ART

When the New York jury list was published, the most vigorous protestor was J. G. Brown.[129] The jury had initially admitted only one of his well-known works, *The Stump Speech* (fig. 48). Thomas Moran took up Brown's cause, citing his treatment as an example of the jury's narrow-mindedness and aesthetic prejudices. Reiterating a theme that was to reappear in the media's criticism of the exhibition, Moran complained that "the committee would accept nothing that isn't according to modern French notions," and that the exhibition as presently constituted "does not in any way represent American art." He continued his harangue: "See how they treated J. G. Brown. Of the four he submitted they took one picture, and that the one he thought the poorest. He withdrew that, and then they came around and patched it up with him by accepting some more." Moran saw William Merritt Chase as the villain who led the group that refused to consider Frederic Remington at all, observing that "whatever Mr. Chase thinks of Mr. Remington's art he cannot say that he is not original, popular and a representative American. But no. Remington

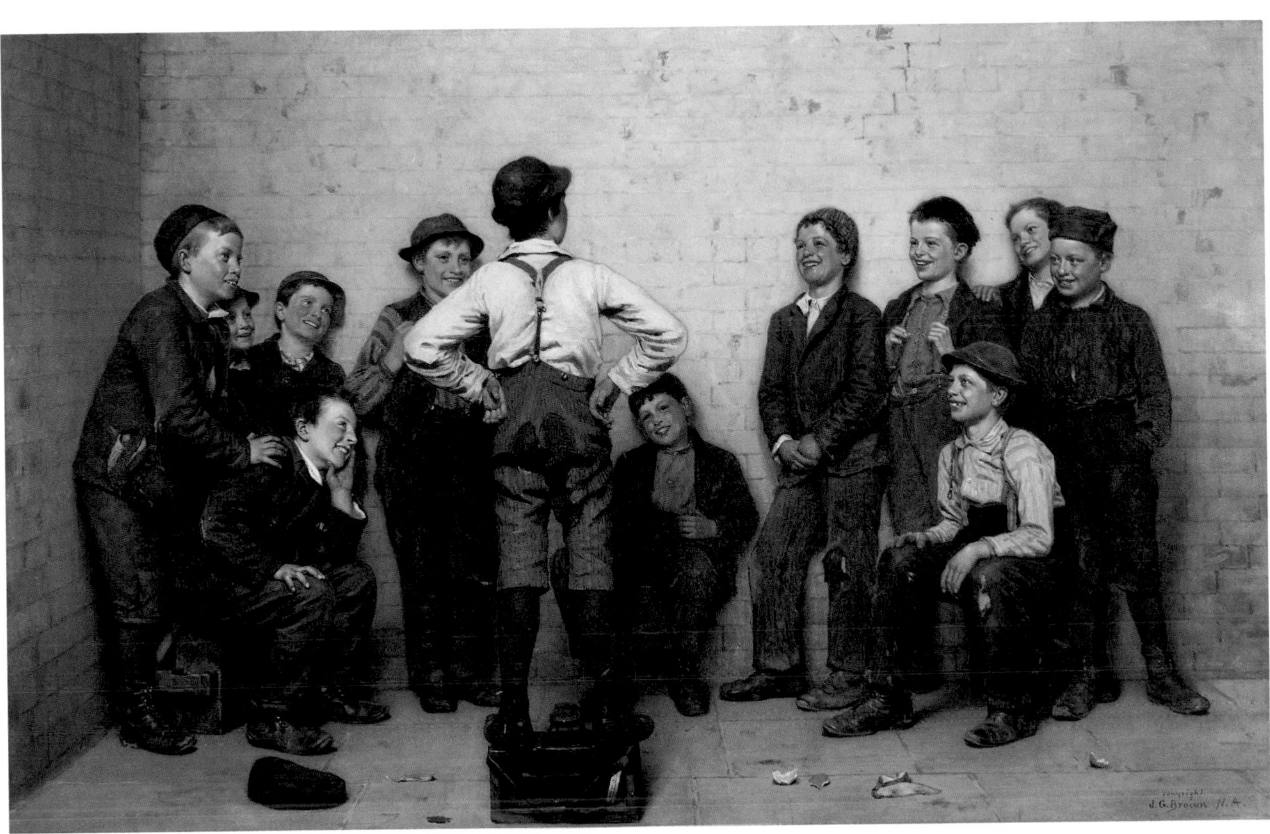

.. **48** ..
J. G. Brown, The Stump Speech, *early 1880s.*
Private Collection. Courtesy of Spanierman Gallery, New York, NY.

isn't French enough, so he can not exhibit at Chicago." Summing up his anger, he concluded:

> My idea of an exhibition of the work of American painters at the great American exposition is that it would fairly represent American art; it should show what this country has accomplished and what it is accomplishing. To do this it is necessary to show the work of all or many of the most prominent artists of the country, not to judge paintings submitted by the standard of a school. [130]

With regard to Brown, it is uncertain *who* ultimately capitulated to public pressure, but a compromise was finally reached permitting him to exhibit seven paintings at the fair. Ives also calmed the storm by placing Brown on the national jury in Chicago.[131] As for Chase, he was of the opinion that "the war [is] not strife between foreign and American ways of painting, but between the good and the bad—and only incidentally between the old and the new."[132]

THE BOSTON JURY

On 24 January, although the work of the New York committee was not completely finished and the issue of who would send out the rejection notices unresolved, Kurtz undertook a one-day trip to Boston. He justified this visit and one to Philadelphia by rationalizing that a familiarity with the works selected by the eastern juries would be useful when hanging the show in Chicago.[133] Judgment Day for Boston artists was 9 January, at which time the Boston painting jury selected approximately half of the 250 works submitted.[134] After a private preview of the jury-approved works at the Massachusetts Charitable Mechanic Association Building on Friday, 13 January, pride of place was in full evidence as a local critic boasted, "If New York and Philadelphia do as well, there is no question about the great and glorious triumph of American art over all competitors at the Chicago show. Our painters have put their best foot forward." Winslow Homer, who was at the opening, was quoted as saying to painter and jury member John J. Enneking that the exhibition "was the best-hung collection of paintings he had ever seen in this country, and it impresses everyone in the same way."[135] Indeed, it may have been the quality of this showing that induced Homer, who appears to have submitted no works to the jury in Boston, to write to Ives and suggest other of his paintings to add to the seven being sent by Thomas B. Clarke.[136]

Kurtz knew what had been selected and how the works had been ranked by the Boston jury because prior to his visit he had received a marked catalogue from Frederic P. Vinton, chairman of the Boston jury.[137] Vinton, aware of the jury issue that had arisen the previous year and sensitive to the criticism that Boston was a city with artists of the second rank, wrote to Kurtz, "You will observe that Boston found very few up to *No. 1* or even '*2*.' Now if N.Y. has been smart she will have marked hers all *No 1 + 2*—then Phila. and Boston will be where N.Y. thinks we belong—*on the shelf*."[138] When he saw the exhibition with Enneking, he was pleasantly surprised, candidly writing to his wife that "the exhibition was *very* interesting and excellent—averaging better, I think—than would an exhibition of the New York pictures." Unwilling to give up his long-held prejudices, however, he concluded with the caveat that "I can hardly be certain about that without having seen the New York works hung advantageously together."[139]

THE PHILADELPHIA PARTICIPANTS

In Philadelphia approximately 650 paintings were submitted to the jury, of which 160 were chosen and immediately afterwards exhibited, along with ten sculptures, at the Pennsylvania Academy of the Fine Arts beginning 16 January.[140] Kurtz does not mention his reactions to the Philadelphia selection, but the critic for the *Philadelphia Press* loved the show and deemed the exhibit one that presented "the strongest work of the best artists of the city. . . . No inferior work has been admitted and the best work of good men has been freely taken without reference to the number of examples of one man's work which might crowd the catalogue."[141] Clearly the Philadelphia jury, unlike the Boston jury, paid no attention to the instructions in *Circular No. 3* to limit to three the number of works sent to Chicago by each artist. Thomas Eakins showed ten paintings and Robert W. Vonnoh thirteen. Between them, according to the *Press* critic, they commanded "a fifth of the works in the exhibition" and "a full third by extent of canvas." Acknowledging Eakins's "primacy," he concluded that "it would be difficult to gather from the work of any man painting in this country pictures and portraits of equal originality and power." Given the demise of Eakins's public reputation after he was asked to resign in 1886 from his position at the

Pennsylvania Academy of the Fine Arts, the selection of this large number of works to be sent to Chicago is an extraordinary testimony to the continued support given to him by his peers. That the jury chose to send *Portrait of Dr. Gross (The Gross Clinic)*—whose graphic realism had led to its being exhibited in the medical rather than the art display at the 1876 Centennial—as well as his recently completed commission, *Portrait of Dr. Agnew (The Agnew Clinic)*, underscores their commitment to presenting his best work, regardless of its "difficult" subject matter.

SELECTING THE NATIONAL JURY

While regional and foreign juries were finalizing their selections, Ives turned his attention to the composition of the national jury, which would convene in Chicago in March to select the work of American artists who were ineligible to compete in Boston, New York, or Philadelphia. On 5 January he wrote Kurtz:

> I have about concluded to announce the full jury, which please understand is given to you in strict confidence—it is subject to amendments: [J. Alden] Weir, [John H.] Twachtman and [Dwight W.] Tryon, one man each from the Philadelphia, New York and Boston committees ([Thomas] Allen, [F. D.] Millet and [Thomas] Hovenden) to which list will be added [Frederick W.] Freer, of Chicago, Douglas Volk, of Minneapolis, and John Fry, of St. Louis, [Arthur H.] Matthews [sic], of San Francisco, and [Gari] Melchers and [Walter] MacEwen, of Europe. As an eleventh man, I shall undoubtedly ask one of the "old fogies" of the New York "bunch" to come—though not T. W. [Thomas Wood]—very likely J. G. B [J. G. Brown].[142]

More than a month later Ives wrote letters to the potential jurors and requested Kurtz to deliver them, suggesting that he first determine if an individual selected wished to serve. Alluding to the recent J. G. Brown contretemps, he opined:

> It goes a little against the grain to send a letter to J. G. Brown. No one is more willing to make a concession than myself when it will save trouble, but it seems to me he has given us no end of annoyance; in fact, he has gone the full length, and to appoint him now would seem to be a full surrender. However, I am disposed to be broad-minded and liberal in the matter, so I will send them on to you and you may do as you *"damn"* please.[143]

Kurtz had some misgivings about having both Brown and Twachtman on the jury, presumably because of their disparate aesthetic approaches—the former known for his crisply delineated narratives, the latter for his evocative, softly contoured landscapes—but this was of no concern to Ives. In the end, Twachtman consulted with Weir, and they both declined to serve. Dwight W. Tryon also refused the invitation to participate, and George Willoughby Maynard substituted for Millet. As for Brown's participation, Ives, the great political tactician, commented: "Putting myself in Brown's place, in the light of recent events, I would take especial pleasure in declining to serve. Indeed, from my standpoint, it seems that the public and the disgruntled element among the artists would hail his appointment as a complete surrender to that which they see fit to term 'the enemy.'" On 15 February Kurtz, who together with Ives represented "the enemy," reported to his wife that he had called on J. G. Brown (fig. 49), whom he found *"Very Pleasant* and very funny," and who agreed to serve as a member of the national jury.[144]

.. 49 ..
Gilbert Gaul,
John George Brown, *1907.*
National Portrait Gallery, Smithsonian Institution.

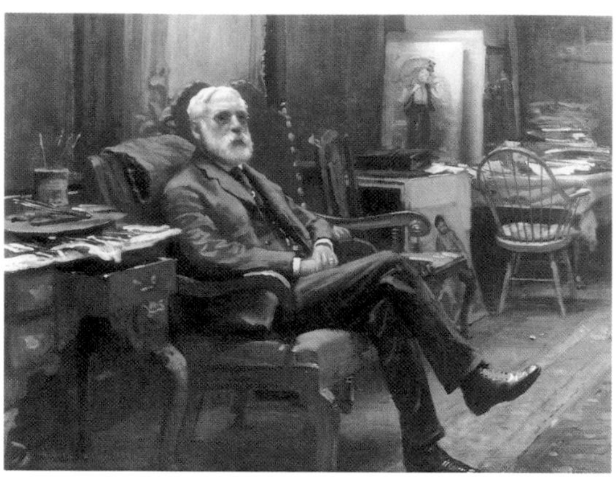

THE NATIONAL JURY CONVENES

By 5 March the majority of works from the states without juries had arrived at the Art Institute of Chicago, where they were to be judged. As in New York, Kurtz was frantically busy.

> Every morning Prof. Ives and I have been out at 7 o'clock, and we have worked over "lists," etc., late almost every night. . . . When I entered upon this work . . . I found things in a perfectly *chaotic* state. I never saw such a mess. Pictures, packing cases, sculptures filled rooms, doors and passage ways. Everything was simply *clogged. Tonight* everything is in order for the jury meeting tomorrow, but I worked all day today (with five "helpers") to bring about this condition.[145]

The jury began by judging sculpture on 8 March and no sooner had it completed its work on 11 March than the newspapers were reporting dissatisfaction, probably not without justification. Of the nearly 500 oil paintings submitted, only seventy-three were selected for exhibit, of which fifteen were by members of the jury. Of the forty-seven sculptures submitted, twenty-seven were accepted. None of the eastern painting juries turned down such a large percentage of works. One newspaper reported that "bribery is hinted at and it was rumored today that one of the rejected had sworn out a warrant for the arrest of one of the jury, charging criminal libel and defamation of character." Leo Mariotti, an angry artist who was carefully identified as having a brother who was a member of the household of King Humbert of Italy, was quoted as saying, "It is just like America. They know nothing about art."[146] Chicago-based critic Lucy Monroe reported that the Chicago jury created as much rancor as did the New York jury and, because less than half the paintings and sculptures submitted by Chicago artists were accepted, "the result was disastrous to the ambition of the city to be . . . an art center."[147]

Juror John H. Vanderpoel defended the committee, saying that "the jury showed no discrimination against any one." He vigorously vindicated himself and the other jury members whose work had been selected and declared that so many works were rejected because they were "not fit to be considered." He indicated that Archibald A. Anderson, who was upset that his large painting *A Woman Taken in Adultery* had been rejected, had no cause for complaint. According to Vanderpoel, the jury had made special provisions to view this work in the large galleries at Jackson Park rather than in the cramped spaces of the Art Institute of Chicago, but still it did not find the painting up to its standards. Blaming the large number of rejections on the art submitted by women, he concluded, "Every girl in the West that had taken a few lessons wanted to be represented in the exposition, and some of the pictures we received were copies of old chromos."[148] Without an extant list of works submitted, it is, of course, impossible to tell whether the committee acted responsibly in its selectivity or whether it was intrinsically prejudiced against lesser-known artists not from the East Coast.

Painter Henry Farny, who had come from Cincinnati to be on the jury, was clearly enthralled by his experiences. Responding to the desire of those in his hometown to hear the latest news from the fair, Farny spoke at the Art Club on the night of his return from Chicago. "I met a lot of bright, artistic people, was entertained at dinners that were poetry in Gorham silver and china, and wouldn't have missed it for a cold, clammy $500 bill." Farny praised Kurtz and Ives, who "unite a wonderful critical acumen with most remarkable executive ability," and he thought the jury "honest, fearless and unprejudiced," although it did have an inclination toward Impressionism. According to him, "the only picture . . . that received the number one vote, was a landscape [*On the Muscatatuck*] by a man from Indianapolis, T. C. Steele . . . whom no one had ever heard of." As to the work seen:

> Of course, there were "russet apples" and "concord grapes" and "pansies" and "sponge cake on silver cake dishes, with a pink claret glass and butter-knife" by the million. The South sent us cotton branches with half-opened pods, and magnolia blossoms. There were yards of roses and bunches of lilac blossoms 'til you couldn't rest, and as the procession of white cotton-gloved porters marched by with these triumphs of feminine horticultural art, the Chairman's eye would glance along the line for a raised hand and then after a pause the brief sentence, "Out" rang out like a pistol shot, and the next porter marched up with some other pomological horror.[149]

Capturing the rhetoric of the organizers, Farny had no doubt that "this Chicago fair will start a new era in American art."

Complaints about the composition of the juries was not limited to artists living in America. Ives heatedly denounced "asinine, idiotic George Hitchcock," who had two pictures accepted "on list." He explained to Kurtz that Hitchcock had written some very venomous letters in abuse of [Edwin A.] Abbey, stating that Sargent and all the other men were disgruntled at the action of the department in appointing a "black and white" man to be in charge of affairs in England. But Ives had letters from Sargent, Mark Fisher, and John McLure Hamilton, stating "that Hitchcock is an unmitigated liar and rascal; that he has no standing among American artists in England, and that there is no man for whom they have greater respect than for Abbey." Ives attributed Hitchcock's "venom" to the fact that he wanted to be appointed chairman of the English advisory committee.[150]

With the work of the national jury completed, the art department began the arduous task of moving its offices from the Rand McNally Building in downtown Chicago to Jackson Park.[151] Kurtz spent the next six weeks completing the lists of works to be shown, finishing the illustrated catalogue, answering correspondence to and from collectors and artists, and dealing with works not sent by the state committees but shipped by private collectors and artists, presumably as part of the "on list" process.[152] In mid-March the shipment of sculptures and paintings from

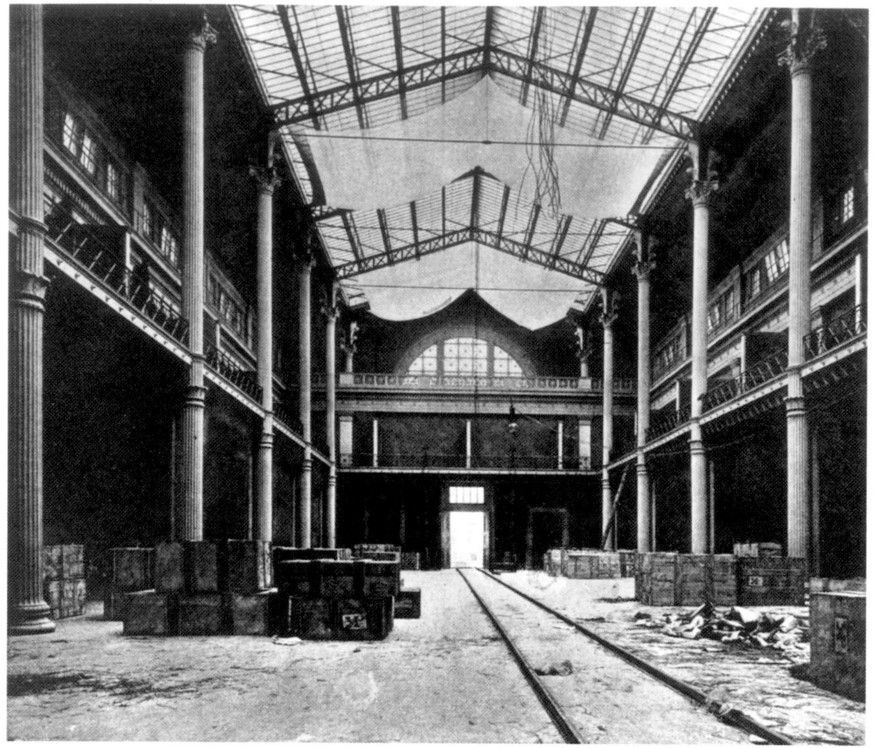

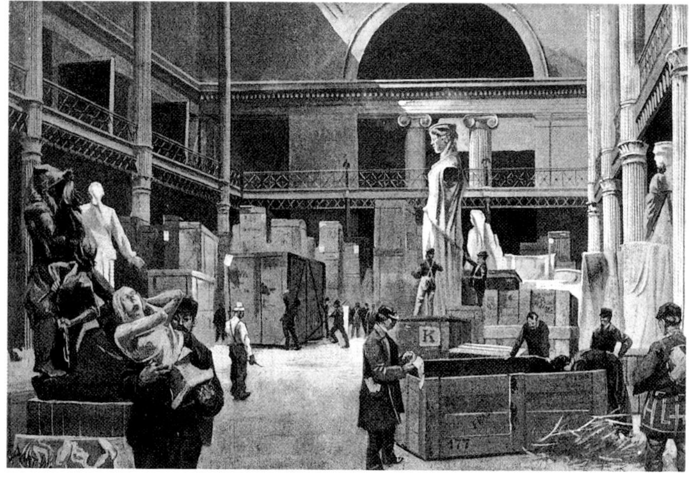

.. 50 ..
"Showing How Exhibits Are Received," east court of the Fine Arts Building. The Art Interchange *30, no. 5 (May 1893): 127. Courtesy of the Library of Congress.*

.. 51 ..
"Unpacking Exhibits in the Art Gallery," north court of the Fine Arts Building. Harper's Weekly, *15 April 1893, 357. Courtesy of the Library of Congress.*

Europe arrived in Chicago (fig. 50).[153] Kurtz began installing the galleries in late March (fig. 51). The first of the more than a thousand accepted paintings to be hung was Edwin H. Blashfield's *Christmas Bells* (fig. 52).[154] Kurtz was particularly annoyed that as of 18 March the New York pictures had not arrived; when two full boxcars arrived more than a month later, on 23 April, he was distressed because the paintings "ran larger" than he had anticipated, and he was not quite certain how he would hang all of them.[155]

As there was no committee to supervise the hanging of the paintings, Ives and Kurtz were the final arbiters of what was displayed in the American art exhibit. Although Ives had stated in *Circular No. 3* that works would be hung based on space considerations and on their rankings, rarely was a painting eliminated if it had been

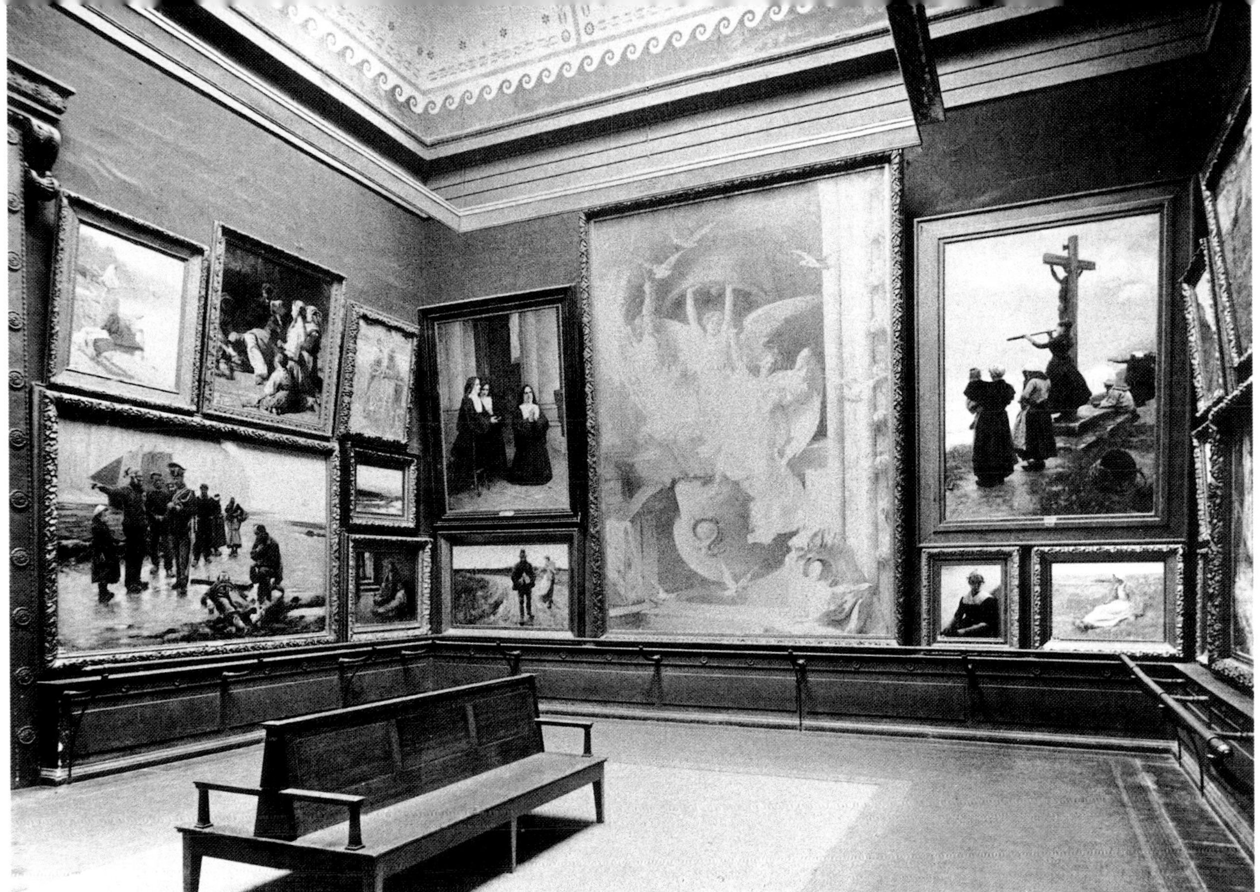

approved by a jury. More usually, numerous artists—among them Chase, Sargent, Whistler, Homer, and Inness—were permitted to exhibit far more than three paintings. While the large showing by Thomas Eakins and Robert W. Vonnoh can be explained by the actions of the Philadelphia jury, many of the works by the seventy-nine artists represented by more than three objects each cannot be accounted for by extant records. One can assume that many of these were accepted "on list" and that the documents supporting this action are simply missing. Possibly the East Coast juries remained active long after the "official" selection process, although more probably Ives and Kurtz accepted numerous pieces on their own long after the juries had met. A case in point would seem to be Thomas Hovenden's *Bringing Home the Bride,* which he was still painting in late March 1893.[156] But regardless of how the work of those who exhibited more than the technical limit of three came to be displayed at the exposition, there is a correlation between the large number of works exhibited by artists and their standing, not only with Ives and Kurtz but also with their peers serving on the selection juries.

.. 52 ..
Gallery 1, west and north walls.
Photograph by C. D. Arnold. Edwin H. Blashfield's Christmas Bells *hangs in the center of the north wall. Official Photographs of the World's Columbian Exposition by C. D. Arnold, vol. 8, pl. 89. Courtesy of The Chicago Public Library, Special Collections Department.*

While Ives and Kurtz made the final decision regarding what was hung, Kurtz decided how to hang the paintings.[157] He gave prime, first-floor gallery space in highly visible locations to works that he found particularly pleasing, including Edmund C. Tarbell's *In the Orchard,* Sargent's *Portrait of Ellen Terry as Lady Macbeth,* and Julius L. Stewart's *The Baptism* (figs. 53, 54, 55). He bragged that the effect of his hanging was "very fine, but very misleading—the best pictures are all arranged so as to catch the eye at once, while the less meritorious are not noticed

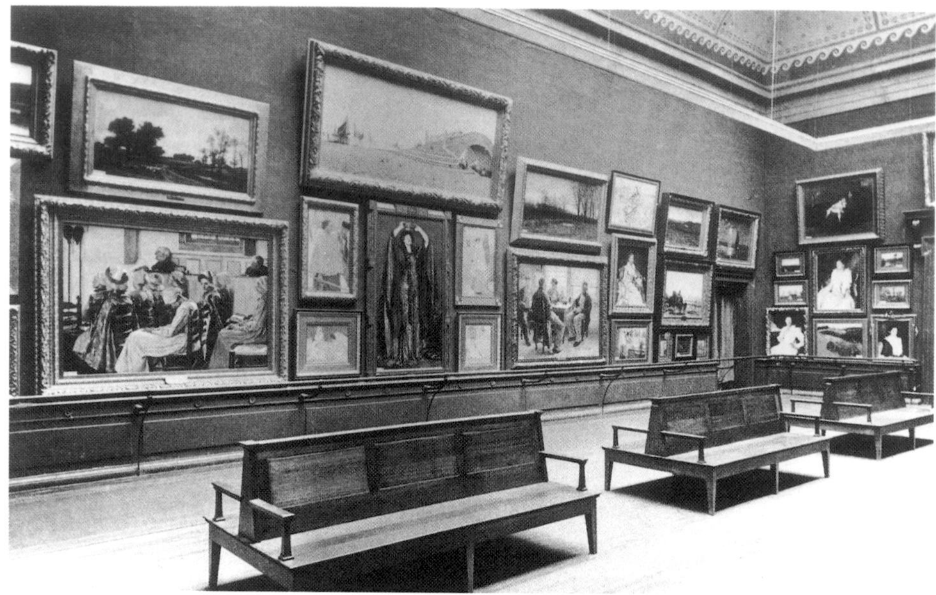

.. 53 ..
Below
Gallery 3, north and east walls.
Photograph by C. D. Arnold. Edmund C. Tarbell's In the Orchard *hangs in the center of the east wall. Official Photographs of the World's Columbian Exposition by C. D. Arnold, vol. 8, pl. 83. Courtesy of The Chicago Public Library, Special Collections Department.*

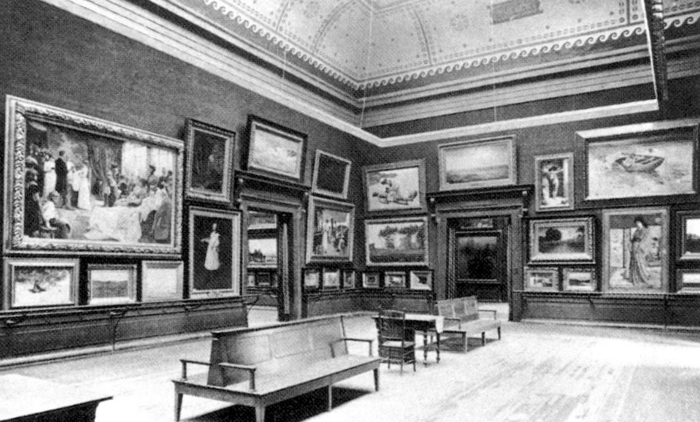

.. 54 ..
Above
Gallery 3, west and north walls.
Photograph by C. D. Arnold. John Singer Sargent's Portrait of Ellen Terry as Lady Macbeth *hangs in the center of the west wall. Official Photographs of the World's Columbian Exposition by C. D. Arnold, vol. 8, pl. 87. Courtesy of The Chicago Public Library, Special Collections Department.*

.. 55 ..
Left
Gallery 9, south and west walls.
Photograph by C. D. Arnold. Julius Stewart's The Baptism *hangs prominently on the south wall. Official Photographs of the World's Columbian Exposition by C. D. Arnold, vol. 8, pl. 88. Courtesy of The Chicago Public Library, Special Collections Department.*

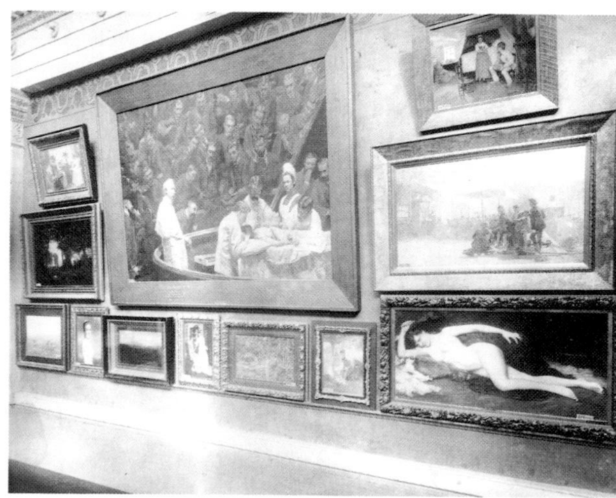

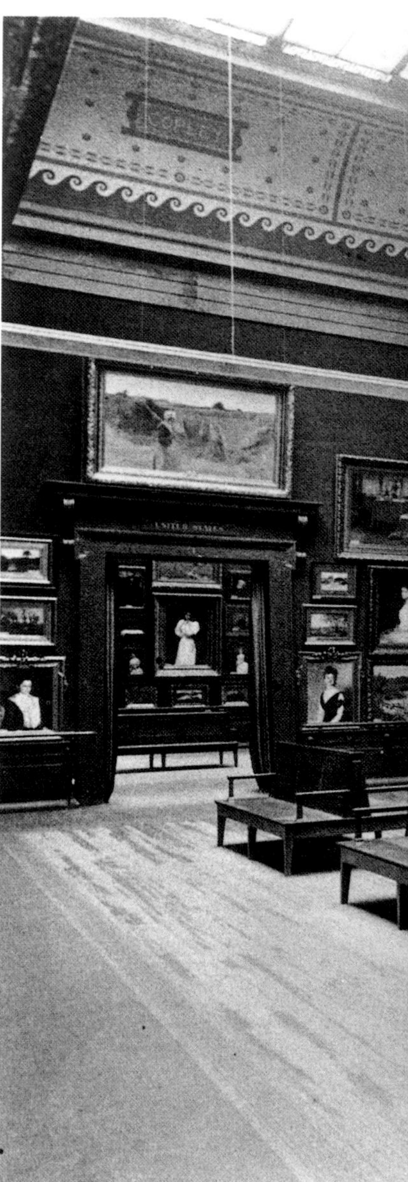

.. 56 ..
Alcove 113.
Photograph by Frances Benjamin Johnston. Thomas Eakins's Portrait of Dr. Agnew *is displayed in the center of this second-floor alcove. Courtesy of the Prints and Photographs Division, Library of Congress, lot 2959.*

until one begins to analyze the pictures."[158] Pressed for space, he chose to hang large paintings on a primary wall, then fill in as space permitted. Disparate imagery did not seem to concern him, as landscapes, portraits, and figure paintings were freely intermingled. Although Kurtz personally admired Eakins's *Portrait of Dr. Gross* and *Portrait of Dr. Agnew* (fig. 56), he probably hung these two works on the balcony to mitigate the controversy surrounding their subject matter.[159] Whether deliberately or inadvertently, he also placed nearly half of the paintings by women on the second floor balcony. (fig. 57).[160]

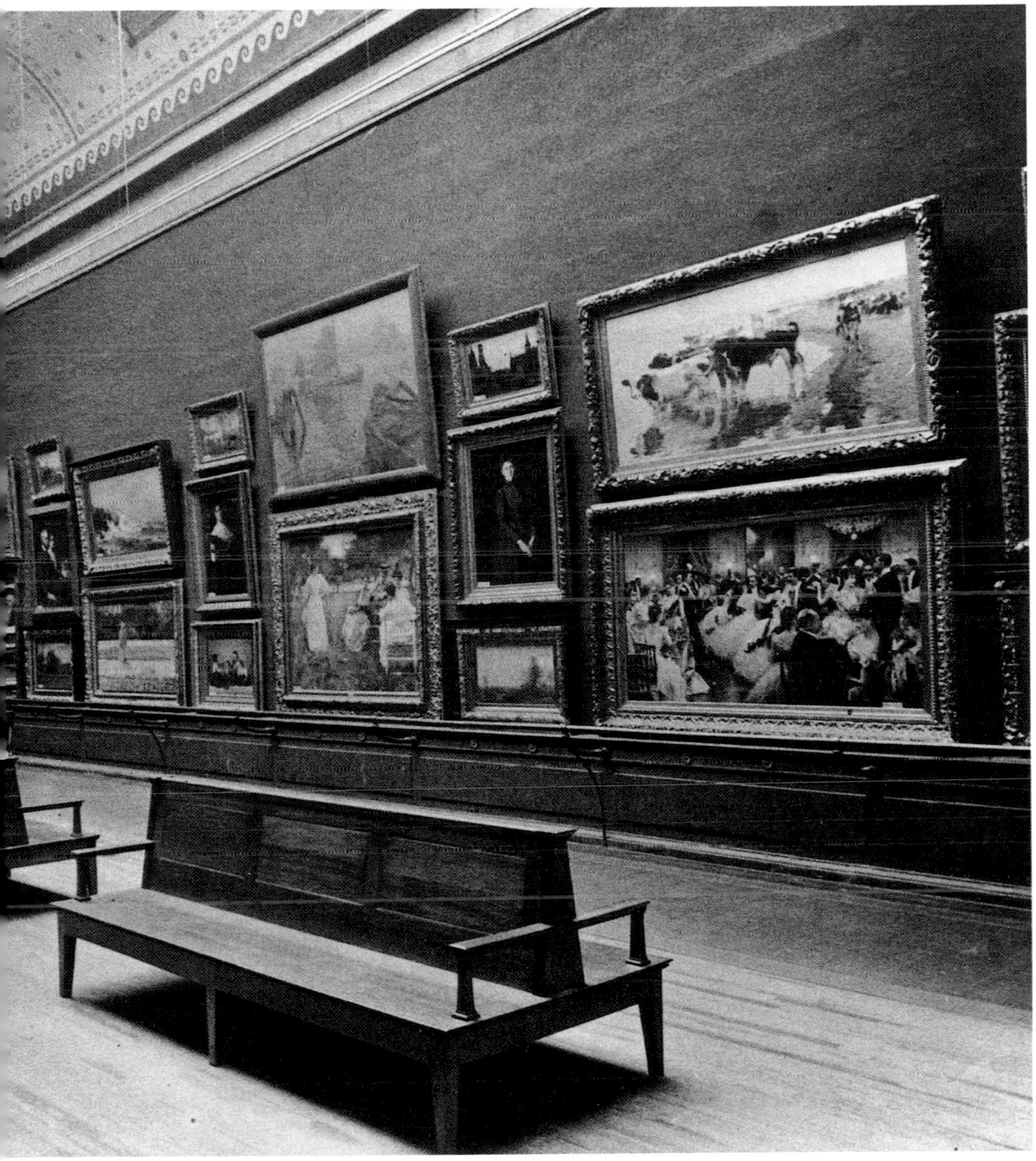

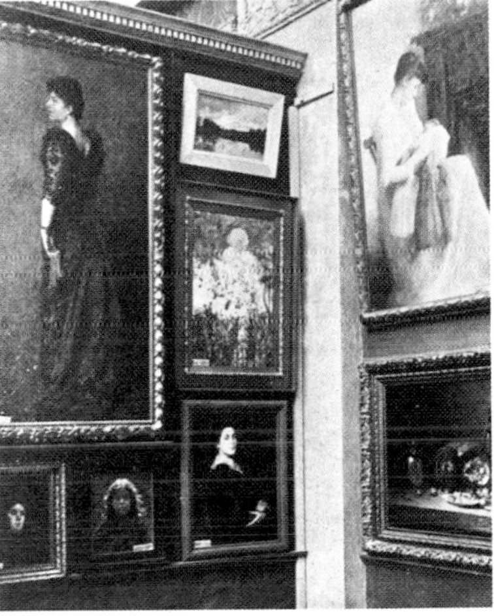

.. 57 ..
Above
Alcove 174.
Over forty-five percent of the 139 paintings by women accepted for the exhibition were hung in the upper alcoves. This photograph shows works by Annie Whepley Renouf (upper left), Ida Joy Didier (lower left), Sophie Bendalari de Peralta (center), Rose Clark (upper right), and Mattie Dubé (lower right). Hubert H. Bancroft, The Book of the Fair, *vol. 3 (Chicago: Blakely Printing Co., 1893), 678.*

As the deadline for the 1 May opening of the exposition neared, Kurtz became increasingly frantic and fearful that the installation would not be completed on time:

> It will be absolutely *impossible* for us to have our galleries ready by May 1. I have about 700 pictures [paintings] to hang, besides about 600 black-and-white drawings and all the watercolors. It almost makes me crazy to think of it. Moreover, we have far more pictures than space. We have secured some space from other nations to add to the U.S. section, but still lack having near enough to accommodate the work we have to hang. I do not believe the Exposition will be anything *near* ready before the latter part of May. I imagine *we* will be busy with our "installation" until the middle of May, and I am told that we are further advanced than are some of the other departments.[161]

Among the many vicissitudes endured by the art department were the damage to some paintings caused by a leak in the roof after a heavy rainstorm in late April and walls that sometimes "sweated vigorously" in warm, damp weather.[162]

Despite of the stress of hanging and the lack of space, Kurtz was particularly proud of his installation:

> This week I have been getting up every morning at 5 o'clock and Rhodes [a department secretary] and I work getting things ready for the picture hangers. Since the N.Y. pictures (from private collections) have come my work has gone on much better. I have done some superb hanging in the past three days. Prof. Ives says it is the best he has ever seen. Zorn [Anders Zorn, the Swedish commissioner], Vos [Hubert Vos, the Dutch commissioner] and others also have complimented it enthusiastically. Actually, I believe the United States will surpass in interest and *merit* the art section of any other country! Never before has such a collection of American work been seen! . . . I suppose the bad artists will want to mob me, however, when they learn that I have acted as a "committee." Ives now leaves all the hanging to me. Such as it is, it is *all* mine, and I am hanging "strictly according to merit," and so as to produce a harmonious composition in form and color—without regard to a man's reputation or my previous acquaintance with him. I do not believe that this has *ever* been done before![163]

Kurtz may have overstated the uniqueness of his efforts, but photographs of several foreign installations indicate that he did give more thought to the whole look of the American exhibition space than other exhibitors gave to their national displays. Unfortunately not everyone appreciated his efforts. Kurtz must have been devastated when Chicago critic Lucy Monroe savaged his installation. Mincing no words, she wrote:

> The motives which governed the hanging of American pictures at the Fair are unfathomable; the harmony of the whole arrangement was certainly not considered, and the fame of the artist had quite as little influence, apparently, in placing his pictures, as the merit of the works themselves. . . . If the good pictures of the collection had been massed together they would have made an imposing array; but, as it is, one finds the most extraordinary combinations and the most infelicitous groupings. Great pictures are often tucked away into obscure corners or surrounded by inferior and discordant works; and even in the main gallery much is included that is unworthy of so conspicuous a position. One finds a cut-and-dried boat-load of J. G. Brown's puppets actually forced into juxtaposition with a fine sea thing by Winslow Homer; and I might mention any number of instances almost as flagrant. A superb study of a nude Egyptian girl, by Sargent, is hung on the second floor, where comparatively few visitors discover it, and almost all of Winslow Homer's paintings—an admirable collection, including the best work he has done—meet the same fate.[164]

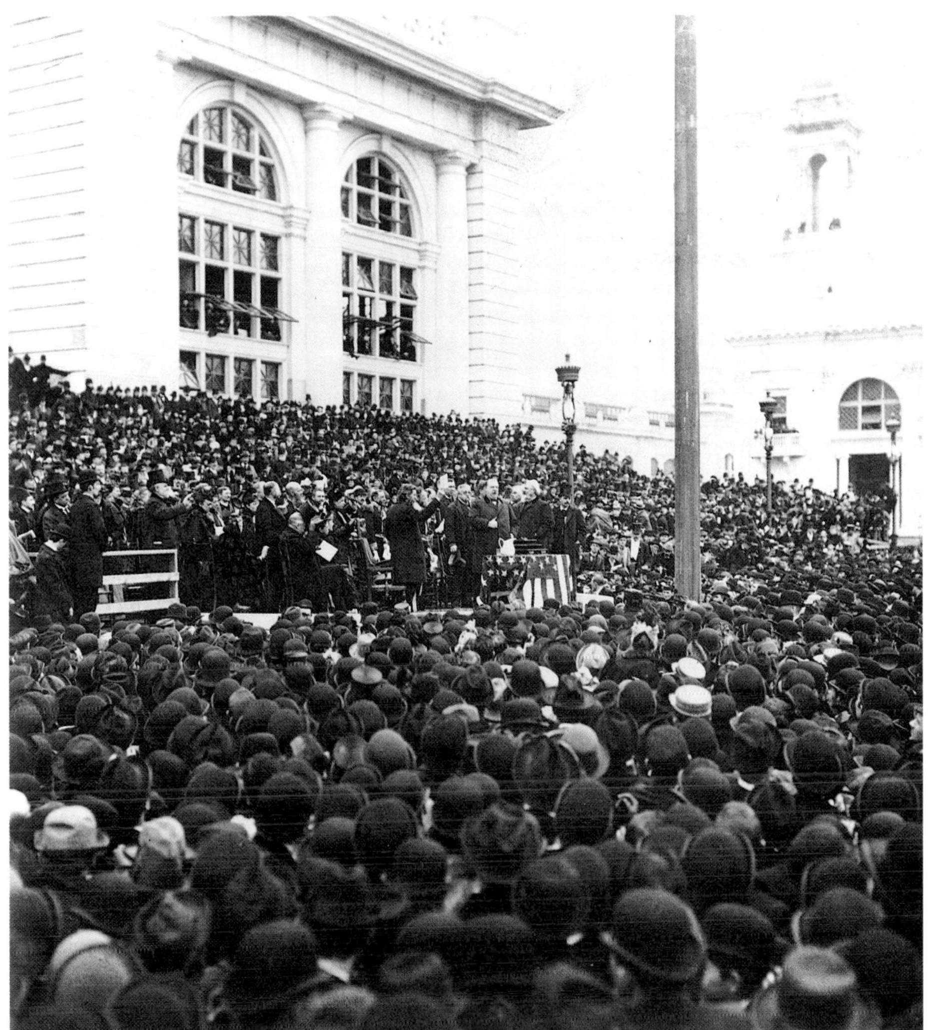

.. 58 ..
Opening Day Ceremonies, 1 May 1893. *Photograph by C. D. Arnold. President Grover Cleveland prepares to press the button to open the exposition. Courtesy of the Prints and Photographs Division, Library of Congress, lot 10559.*

Kurtz's prophecy that he would not be finished by opening day came true. As the 1 May deadline approached, he took an increasingly pragmatic approach: "Today we will hustle up enough pictures to finish five galleries in readiness for the 'opening' tomorrow. In the other four galleries of this portion of the American section we crowded the pictures yet 'unhung.'" His strategy was to "formally open" five galleries on Monday, 1 May, and "informally close" them on Tuesday, and keep them closed "until the whole section is completed, which will be at least ten days or two weeks hence." While in New York, Kurtz had feared the lack of enough good work; his initial fears were groundless. He despaired of finding a place for everything, writing to his wife that "we have about twice as many paintings as we ought to try to hang. It is simply *dreadful!* and more pictures are pouring in upon us every day!"[165]

In the midst of the hanging, Kurtz and Ives received an unexpected visit on 29 April from President Grover Cleveland, who was in town for the formal opening of the exposition. Kurtz concluded at the end of the tour that "Grover is not much of a connoisseur."[166] Given Kurtz's love of ceremony and his penchant for elaborate narratives, his description of the opening ceremonies is uncharacteristically laconic:

"Grover Cleveland pressed a button, and the engines started, the steam whistles blew, flags were unfurled, the cotton shirt dropped from French's gilded statue of 'The Republic,' the people cheered and the Exposition was afloat" (fig. 58).[167] But then Kurtz was unable to participate fully in the festivities, for he had to continue hanging the art when the galleries closed at 6:00 p.m. The original plan was to close the galleries to complete the hanging, but after one day, despite the cold weather and the small crowd, "the closing has caused such a howl that Prof. Ives will open part of it tomorrow." As of mid-May, Kurtz had not yet hung the upper galleries.[168]

THE SHAPE OF THE SHOW

The exhibition that Kurtz proudly installed can best be described as diverse, both stylistically and iconographically. Landscape, portraiture, genre, history painting, and allegory all found their way into the show. While nearly four times as large as the display of paintings and sculpture at the 1889 Paris Universal Exhibition, the American installation at Chicago contained a similar "variety of temperaments" and "diversity of the pictures."[169] Thus one could sample the dispassionate realism of Winslow Homer, Thomas Eakins, Charles F. Ulrich, and Frederic P. Vinton or the cloying sentimentality of William T. Smedley and S. Seymour Thomas. The rural world could be experienced in the American scenes of Eastman Johnson, as well as in the Barbizon-inspired portrayals of peasants by Edward E. Simmons and Charles Sprague Pearce. The crisply contoured renderings of F. D. Millet and Frederick James were given equal billing with the bravura brushwork in portraits by John Singer Sargent and William Merritt Chase. The highly narrative work of Thomas Hovenden found a home here, as did the allusive imagery of H. Siddons Mowbray and Thomas W. Dewing. Palettes ranged from the sober and restrained of men like Stacy Tolman and Charles T. Webber to the fresh, brighter hues of J. Alden Weir and John H. Twachtman. Although the show excluded the work of those whom Kurtz had called "that pre-historic crowd"—the group of still-practicing artists of the American scene who had gained prominence just prior to the 1876 Centennial—most of the artists who had achieved public acceptance in the last decade and a half were included.

The acceptance of a wide range of styles, schools, and subject matter was by no means unique to the 1893 fair. As Linda Docherty has amply illustrated, the art criticism of the prior decade was all-encompassing in its acceptance of a variety of styles and subjects, so long as artists exhibited technical ability and used it to manifest satisfactorily their "ideals."[170] Thus when New York artist and jury member William Merritt Chase, presumably articulating the intentions of that committee, said, "In this country, if anywhere, we should be superior to narrowing notions about schools and styles. The individual merit of a picture is the only final standard," he was merely expressing the commonly understood approach to judging the art of the times.[171] Kurtz presumably shared this point of view. In his 1890 review of an exhibition at New York's Union League Club, he demonstrates that he was equally at home giving kudos to such divergent artists as Eastman Johnson, Thomas W. Dewing, H. Siddons Mowbray, Childe Hassam, Carl Marr, Daniel Ridgway Knight, and Frederick A. Bridgman.[172] As for the use of the world "merit" by both Kurtz and Chase, one can presume that, like numerous critics of the day, they were referring to an artist's ability to render form in a convincing manner regardless of the specific narrative content.

If there is a unifying element among the American artists who exhibited in Chicago, it is their professionalism. They were indeed "men of acknowledged standing," to use Ives's phrase. These artists (both men and women) had, for the most part, been trained in the best schools in New York, Boston, Philadelphia, and Chicago, solidifying their training by then working with noted artists abroad, usually either in Paris or Munich. Their careers and reputations were enhanced by showing regularly in prestigious exhibitions in America and abroad. Moreover, a majority of the paintings selected for the Chicago exposition were "of acknowledged standing." This show was not conceived as an annual in which artists were encouraged to send their most recent creation (although some such as Hovenden did). A majority of works had exhibition histories, and several were regarded as choice because of their place in notable collections. Many had previously won prizes or medals, and many had a critical track record in the popular press. In their attempt to best France, the American jurors, undoubtedly coached but also adhering to the same credo as Ives and Kurtz, did not want to go into the aesthetic battle with France with a large number of unproven foot soldiers. The weapon of choice was seemingly a belief in professionalism rather than method or image. While Kurtz may have claimed that he hung his show without regard to an individual's reputation, caring only for form and color, reputation—that of the artist, the work, or both—was integral to the dominant collective consciousness that formed the show. That he did consider form and color in his installation suggests that Kurtz, despite his rather catholic tastes in art, did have a particularly strong sympathy for those who worked in a tonal mode. Certainly artists who employed this approach, stressing a personal and evocative interpretation of subject matter and a highly painterly rendering of images, among them William Merritt Chase, Dwight W. Tryon, George Inness, Willard L. Metcalf, J. Francis Murphy, Theodore Robinson, James McNeill Whistler, and Alexander H. Wyant, were not only well represented but also well placed at the exposition.[173]

THE CRITICAL RESPONSE

Although the galleries did not fully open to the public until late May, the reviews began almost immediately.[174] Kurtz and Ives must have been ecstatic when Lucy Monroe declared that "careful study of the French and American sections of the Exposition art department only serves to confirm the first impression that the latter is the stronger of the two."[175]

Writing in *The Critic*, Monroe captured the themes that were to be the leitmotifs of the reviews of American art at the fair—the progress of American art since the 1876 Centennial, the lessons learned from study abroad, and the triumph of American over French art. What Monroe admired in American art, in addition to technical skill learned abroad, was "poetic sincerity," an individuality that was a product of American "race and clime," and painting that, regardless of subject, was national and showed "the influence of birth and heredity—this insistent unconscious patriotism." She was particularly taken by the landscapes, by their "freshness in atmosphere," their color, and their originality and vitality.

Not everyone agreed with Monroe that foreign training was an unmitigated blessing. "Mere imitators . . . as clever as their masters, but . . . imitators, nevertheless," decried one critic. Another, disturbed by a large number of works with European-based subject matter, harangued: "Where is our American national art? If we find it at all, we must find it in the clap, clap, clap of wooden shoes. If we see it at all, we must hunt for it in the dikes of Holland, the downs of Brittany, the taverns of the south of France, the boulevards and attics of the French capital."[176]

In truth, with 1,024 paintings on display, there was enough diversity to substantiate both claims—and neither. There were as many paintings with subjects rooted in the American landscape and experience as there were of European vistas and peasants. Moreover, while a vast number of exhibiting artists had studied abroad, to rail against all who had such training as "mere imitators" was to overlook the diversity of styles that emerged within this large contingent. To paint Daniel Ridgway Knight and Thomas Eakins with the same critical brush, both of whom had their work sent by the Philadelphia jury, was to misunderstand the nature of the European experience and its translation and transformation within the work of various American artists. But whatever their point of view, whether they praised or denigrated the "artistic qualities" of French art, critics used it as the primary standard against which to judge American art at the fair.[177]

Reaping reward among the critics who championed a homegrown American art was Winslow Homer, who was repeatedly complimented for merging technique with American subject matter. Homer was praised as an artist "who affiliates with no particular group in the home school, but is a law unto himself in technical methods and individuality of expression." His scenes of New England coastal life (fig. 59) generated adulation for their "unyielding individuality" and "homely poetry." Homer was embraced as "a painter of strength whose works command attention" because "they are American without preface or apology. They breathe of the soil and the sea, tell of their place of origin, give the American point of view."[178] George Inness, too, was characterized as authentically American. Inness knew "the secrets of our storms and sunsets." Repeatedly deemed a "genius," he was extolled as one of the older men whose work had transcended the past. While his "beginnings were sown amid the now antiquated tenets of the Hudson River school," his art was seen as "released from [these] analytic shackles" and rivaling "the great landscape work of France on its own ground."[179]

If Inness and Homer were viewed as the most "American" of the native painters at the exhibition, the most talked about were John Singer Sargent and James McNeill Whistler. Sargent was singled out for his sure, luminous brushwork, as well as his ability to capture a sitter's character: "This is the first requisite with Sargent—to show the influence of his sitter's history upon his mind, to select the dramatic moment which tells his story. His method and coloring are simple where his subject is simple, and complicated when he wishes to express varied emotions." One critic called him "a modern Velasquez." Another said of his *Portrait* (Homer Saint-Gaudens and his mother) that "few portraits have ever been painted which equal this in the living quality which enables the artist to . . . retain in his painting the fleeting, momentary expression on his sitter's face, which . . . contains some indication of the mind and personality." Yet another enthusiastic writer proclaimed his full-length

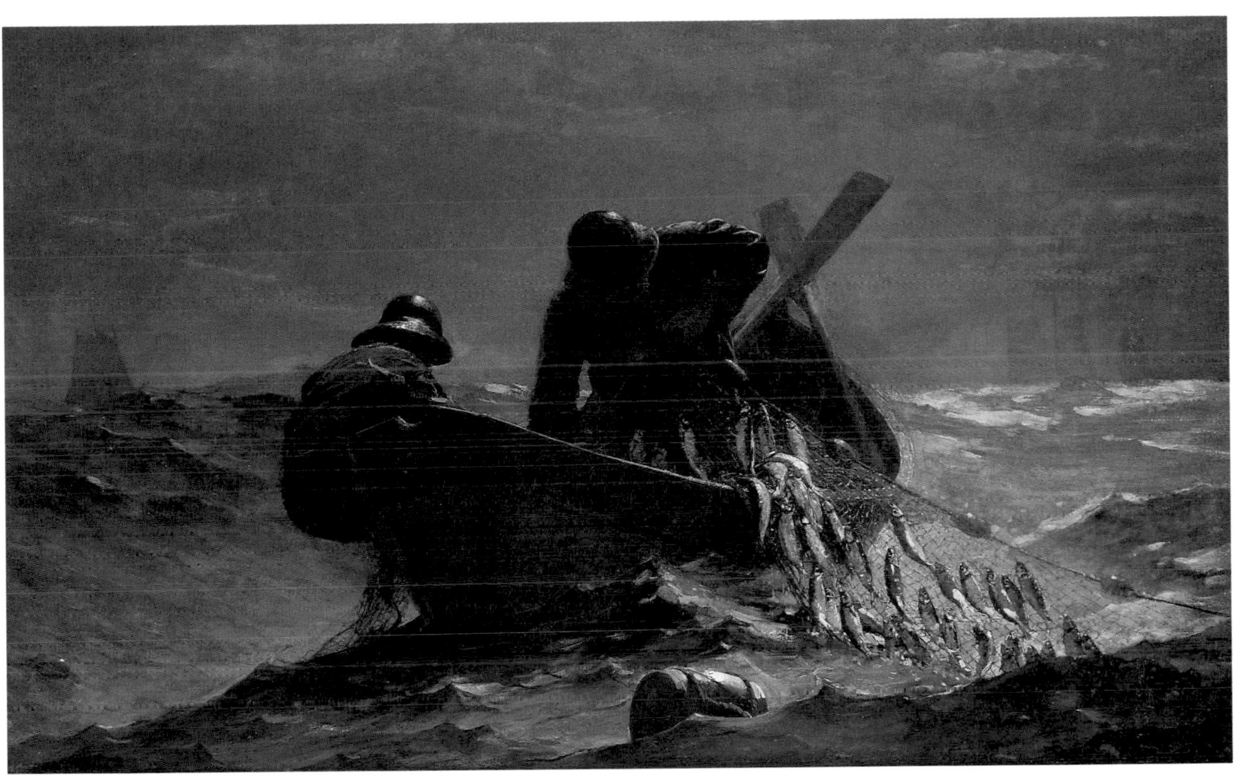

.. 59 ..

Winslow Homer, **Herring Fishing,** *1885.*
The Art Institute of Chicago,
Mr. and Mrs. Martin A. Ryerson Collection.

double portrait of Mrs. Edward L. Davis and her son "remarkable for its beautiful and dignified composition, for the beauty of expression in the faces" and for "the splendid swing of the brush which envelops every part of the picture in a harmonious ensemble."[180] *Portrait of Ellen Terry as Lady Macbeth* was mentioned as many times as its creator, usually favorably but sometimes not. One writer admired the brushwork and the "wonderful robe, wrought with blue and green in a showy barbaric pattern," and announced that every stroke was an inspiration.[181] Another reviewer saw the painting as a thing which captivated artists by its commanding talent, "but which is unbeautiful, and disagreeable to the ordinary observer." For him, "the picture gives us neither the real Miss Terry, nor the real Lady Macbeth, but the dyed and painted and bewigged stage semblance of Shakespeare's mighty heroine, with powder and rouge visible in the complexion, and long braids of mock red hair such as never grew on any human head."

With Whistler, there was some concern that his unfinished, sketchy style might not be comprehensible to the casual observer lacking an intimate knowledge of his aims and intentions. But to more tutored eyes, there was no hesitation. One commentator wrote that Whistler's "genius is universal" and singled out *The Lady with the Yellow Buskin* (fig. 60) for its "certain elusive charm." He also admired the background, which was "not dark paint but mysterious space," and pointed out that while "there are few colors on the canvas, it is rich with color harmony." Not one to restrain his words, he let his readers know that "each time that I approach this painting I feel a repetition of that first thrill of pleasure in its spontaneity and in the indescribably beautiful color-harmony. . . . It will be forever a joy." Tracing the source of Whistler's inspiration, he proclaimed: "It is a man's personality which makes his art." According to him, Whistler's original vision was "nature's gift to the artist."[182]

Writers constantly compared Whistler and Sargent. One wrote, "If Sargent stands for the triumph of bravura in painting, Whistler stands for the triumph of its antithesis." Another characterized Whistler as "subtle, fanciful, elusive above all things, essentially delicate and reserved in his thoroughly comprehended art" and described Sargent as "bold, masterful, at times to the edge of violence; not always secure in his effects, but with a splendid reckless dash and confidence about him, which make one forgive him a great deal." Despite their differences—and their expatriate status—both Sargent and Whistler were invariably claimed as American painters in spirit and style.[183]

Among other expatriate artists capturing favorable comment was marine and landscape painter Alexander Harrison, who garnered respect for his "poetic and refined" work, such as *In Arcadia*.[184] Julian Story received kudos for his portrait of opera star Emma Eames (his new bride), and *Mlle. de Sombreuil (Episode of the French Revolution—)* (fig. 61) was noticed for its melodramatic subject matter.[185] Julius L. Stewart's portraits and large figural groups of Parisian society usually attracted attention, as did the paintings of Gari Melchers, Walter McEwen, and George Hitchcock, known for peasant subjects based on their study in Holland and Brittany. Of this trio, Melchers commanded the most discussion, not all of it favorable. One critic was disturbed by the "newness" of *The Pilots, The Sermon, Skaters*, and *Married*. He was "vexed by Melchers's hard outlines, his harsh color, and his inclination to omit all those delicate nuances which in nature blend tone with tone."[186] Similarly,

. . 60 . .

James McNeill Whistler,

The Lady with the Yellow Buskin, *ca. 1883.*

Philadelphia Museum of Art: W. P. Wilstach Collection.

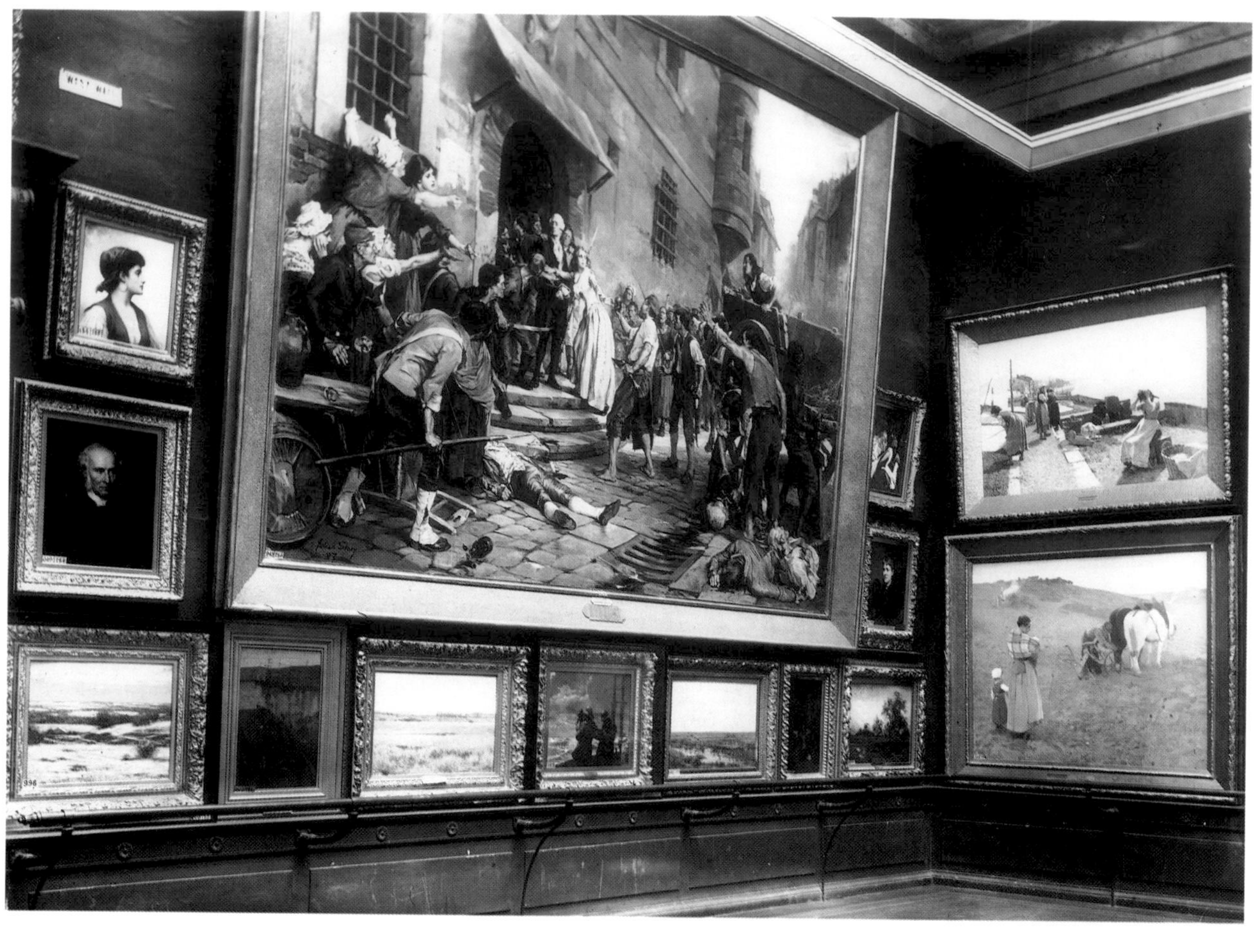

.. 61 ..
Gallery 8, west and north walls. Julian Story's Mlle. De Sombreuil (Episode of the French Revolution—) *hangs in the center of the west wall. Courtesy of the National Museum of American History, Smithsonian Institution, neg. no. 12141.*

William T. Dannat's *Spanish Women* received mixed reviews for its neon palette. One writer called it a fascinating but unwholesome picture; another, "a rich harmony—a vibration of color in a full light—iridescent in its brilliancy."[187]

Of the works by artists who spent more time at home than abroad, Chase's portrait of *Alice* was said to belong "to the whole kingdom of childhood" and to possess "the rare tenderness of a poem by Longfellow."[188] Abbott H. Thayer's *Virgin Enthroned* and George de Forest Brush's *Mother and Child* were often mentioned together as types of gentle beauty and sentiment and as examples of the ideal focus of some of the best American painting.[189] Thomas W. Dewing's work, such as *Lady in Blue,* appealed to many because his subjects also captured the late nineteenth-century notion of the ideal female.[190]

If the paintings of Chase, Dewing, and Thayer reinforced accepted cultural values, Thomas Eakins's *Portrait of Dr. Gross* and *Portrait of Dr. Agnew* challenged them. Thus while one critic could admire Eakins for his skill and versatility, another called these two paintings "unfit for a public exhibition of art" and lamented that "there can be little that is esthetic in representations of probing and dissecting."[191] Propriety did not seem to be the issue with art by women, yet only the two large Impressionist canvases—*Tea al Fresco* and *June Morning*—by Mary Fairchild MacMonnies, the artist who contributed one of the two major mural decorations for

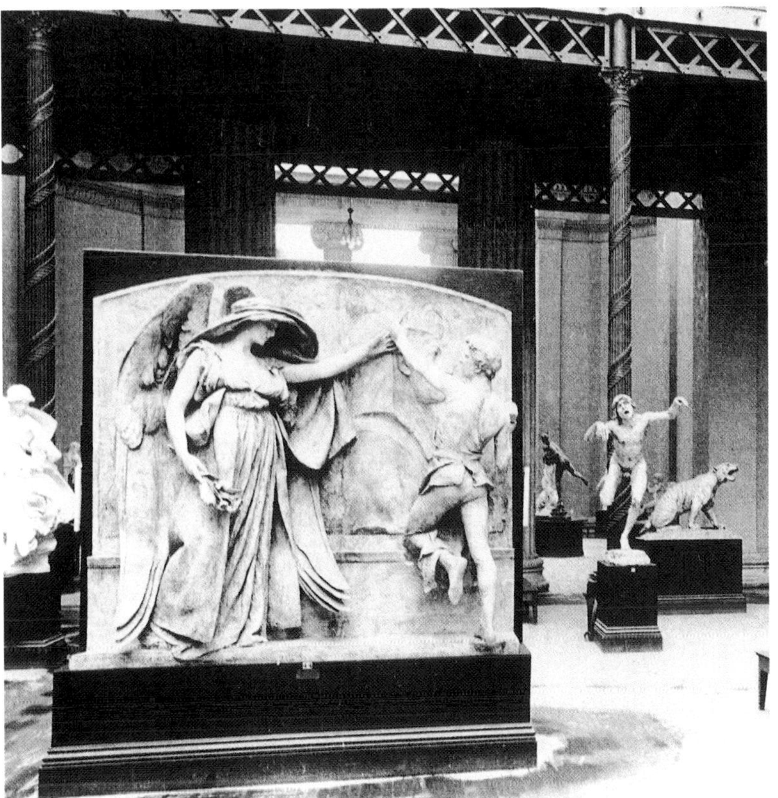

.. **62** ..
West court looking east.
Photograph by C. D. Arnold. Daniel Chester French's The Angel of Death and the Sculptor *is exhibited in the foreground. Official Photographs of the World's Columbian Exposition by C. D. Arnold, vol. 8, no. 62. Courtesy of The Chicago Public Library, Special Collections Department.*

the Women's Building, were mentioned with any regularity. If it had not been for a hometown critic, Lilla Cabot Perry would have received virtually no notice of her seven portraits.[192]

Ironically, the most *popular* works in the American galleries were not always examples of perfect "French style" or American subject matter but rather were the overwhelming narrative and theatrical pieces. Disdained by some and praised by others, the crowd-pleasers were distinguished by their emphasis on anecdote and sentiment. Thomas Hovenden's *Breaking the Home Ties,* a must-see for the average citizen, was described by one enthusiastic admirer as a work "which affects the crowd in much the same way as does the song of 'Home, Sweet Home,' when sung by Adelina Patti." Competing with *Breaking the Home Ties* for crowds was Carl Marr's enormous canvas, *The Flagellants.*[193]

The American sculpture submitted for display in the art building received comparatively little attention from the press. Its conservative nature struck one critic, who commented that "sculpture, which must be produced by slower processes and from more enduring materials, has not been so readily influenced by the spirit of the times, which has left its mark on the painting."[194] Painter and critic William A. Coffin considered French sculpture "the best at the Fair," but conceded that the American sculpture was "next in importance and general excellence to the French." While disdaining "such miserable stuff" as *Lady Godiva, Lady Godiva Returning,* and *"La Rosa" (Vanderbilt Group)* by Caroline S. Brooks, and a few other "cheap and vulgar" works, he was otherwise complimentary, particularly about Daniel Chester French's *The Angel of Death and the Sculptor* (fig. 62) and the work of Paul W. Bartlett,

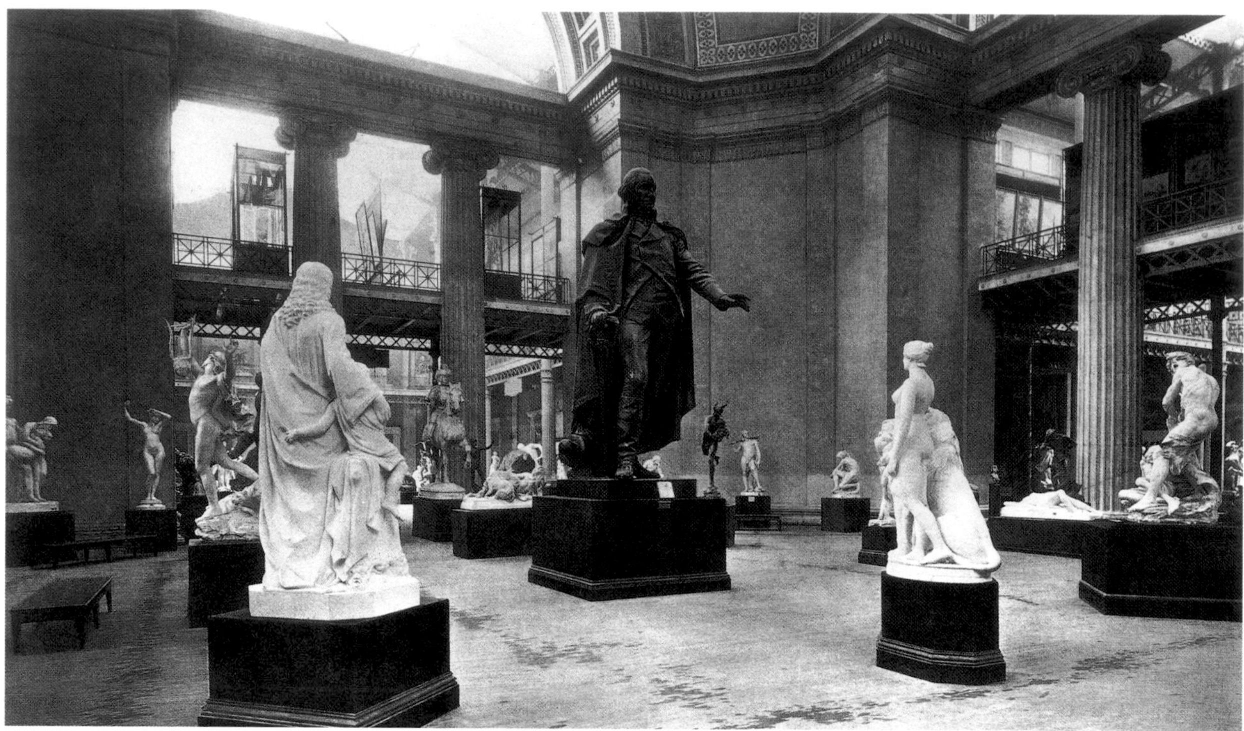

.. 63 ..
International Rotunda in the Fine Arts Building.
Thomas Ball's Colossal Statue of Washington _is exhibited in the center, while his_ Christ and the Little Child _and F. Edwin Elwell's_ Intellect Dominating Brute Force; or Diana and the Lion _are exhibited in the left and right foreground, respectively. Ripley Hitchcock,_ The Art of the World, _vol. 2 (New York: D. Appleton, 1895), following 63._

.. 64 ..
Opposite
North court looking south.
Photograph by C. D. Arnold. The majority of the sculptures by Americans were exhibited in the north court. The large works are (clockwise from center) H. K. Bush-Brown's The Buffalo Hunt, _Douglas Tilden's_ Indian Bear Hunt, _F. Edwin Elwell's_ Charles Dickens and Little Nell, _John Rogers's statue of Abraham Lincoln, Thomas Shields Clarke's_ The Cider Press, _and Johannes Gelert's_ The Struggle for Work. _Courtesy of Jane F. Allen._

Douglas Tilden, Herbert Adams, John Donoghue (especially *The Young Sophocles Leading the Chorus of Victory After the Battle of Salamis*), Philip Martiny, and Olin Levi Warner. He noted, as did other journalists, that important sculptors such as Augustus Saint-Gaudens, J. Q. A. Ward, and the much younger Frederick MacMonnies had no works in the exhibition, although, with the exception of Ward, they were represented elsewhere on the exposition grounds. For another reviewer, who must have wearied of the cacophony of more than a thousand paintings, the sculptural works in the great courts and rotundas of the Fine Arts Building (figs. 63, 64) provided "a cool and restful retreat, where the eye, tired with color, can be relieved."[195]

ART SALES

Favorable criticism did not have a significant impact on the sale of work at the fair. The day after the fair closed, the *Chicago Tribune* reported that only thirty-five works by Americans had been purchased, admitting, however, that "quite a number are now under consideration."[196] Among the artists whose paintings were cited as newly belonging to collectors were J. G. Brown, *A Stump Speech* ($2500), *A Card Trick* ($1200), and *Training the Dog* (not priced); Henry S. Bisbing, *Lapsing Waves on a Quiet Shore* ($200); John J. Enneking, *November* ($350); Mrs. Kenyon [Louise King] Cox, *A Rondel* ($300); Frederick A. Bridgman, *In a Village at El Biar, Algiers* ($2200); R. Swain Gifford, *The Sea-weed Gatherers* ($1500); William J. Whittemore, *Autumn Sunshine* ($400); and Charles Yardley Turner,

Washing Day ($300). The two sculptures designated as sold were by Herbert Adams, *St. Agnes Eve* ($1000), and William G. Turner, *A Dream* ($300).[197] On the whole, the prices were modest. Size rather than price may have been the determining factor for purchases by private collectors. Clearly, those who believed that American art influenced by the "French method" would rule the day had nothing to fear when it came to sales. Of greater concern to them should have been the fact that European artists sold approximately ten times as many works as did the Americans.[198] The American art exhibit may have been a critical and intellectual triumph, but it was clearly not a commercial one. The fair itself may have been about the selling of

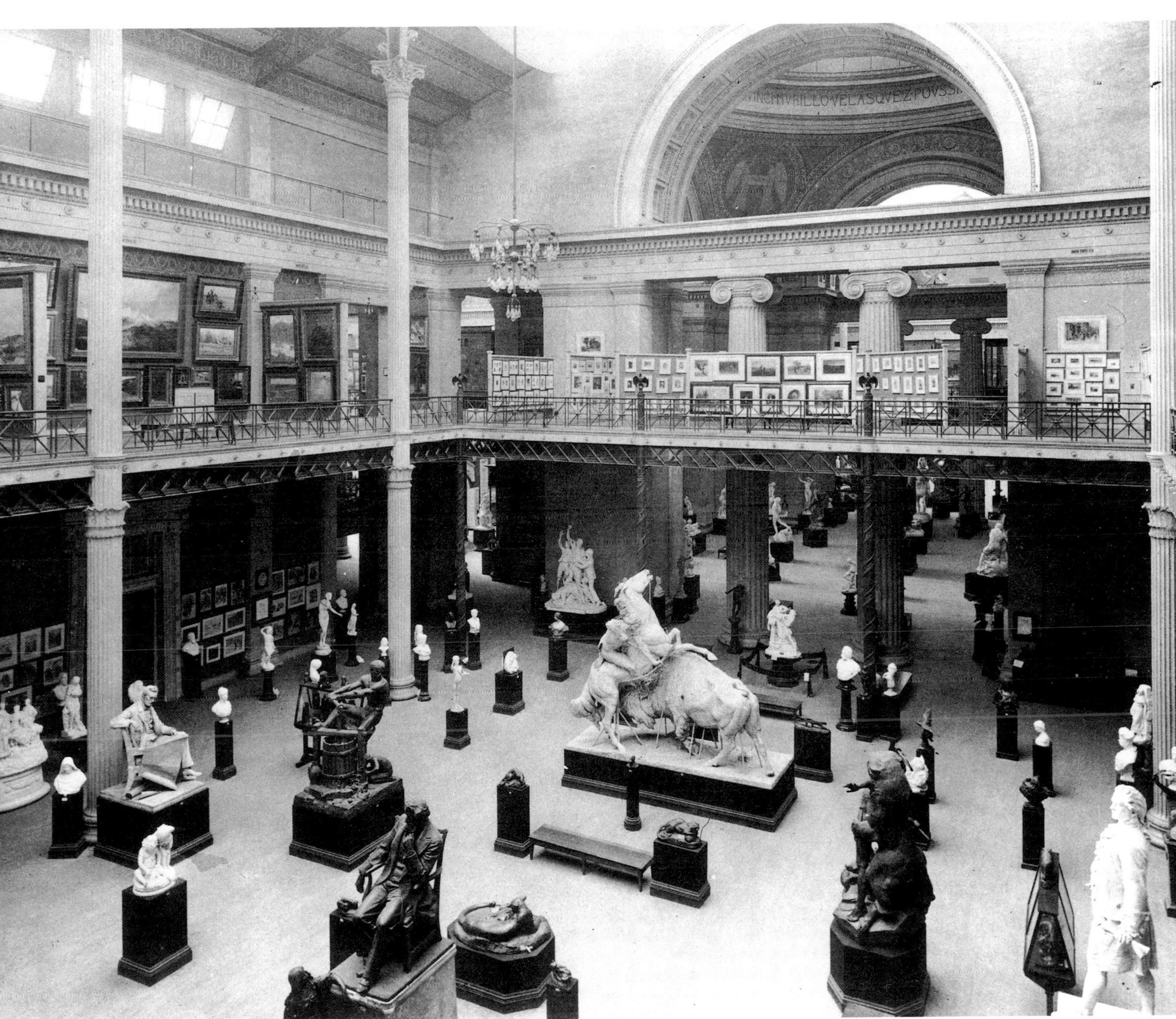

American culture, but the marketing of American art was greater at the ideological than the literal level of selling objects.

In part, American art may not have sold as well as foreign art because the Americans were apparently less organized for sales than the foreigners, whose commissioners were acting as agents.[199] It may also have been the case that the great eastern collectors did not wish to purchase at this "western" exhibit, and, conversely, that wealthy western collectors preferred to buy in the eastern galleries or directly from artists' studios, just as collectors outside New York tend to do today. Sales may also have been affected by the economic turmoil that erupted shortly after the opening of the fair. When Hallowell wrote to Auguste Rodin to explain why there had been no buyers for his three sculptures, which she had brought to America for the loan exhibition of foreign masterpieces in American collections, she lamented that "the Exposition has been a grand success, but the financial crisis which exists yet in our country has been very bad for artists."[200]

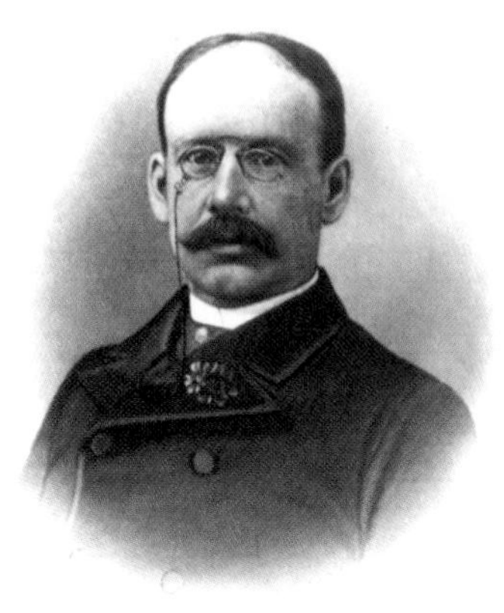

.. 65 ..
John Boyd Thacher, chairman of the Executive Committee on Awards. Engraving by H. B. Hall's Sons. Courtesy of the McKinney Library Book Collection, Albany Institute of History & Art.

THE MEDALS MELEE

The brouhaha surrounding the judging system and the awarding of medals could not have helped sales either. In August 1892, when Ives's nemesis, New York commissioner John Boyd Thacher (fig. 65), assumed chairmanship of the Executive Committee on Awards, he plunged the awards proceedings into controversy by defining and defending what he termed an "American system." Under his plan, an entire category of works (e.g. oil paintings) would be judged by a single juror, and winners would be given the same medal. There would be no distinction between honors of the first and second rank.[201] According to Thacher, his "American" plan was "the same as was recommended at the Philadelphia Exposition."[202] He believed that it was superior to the "old Continental or European system," an allusion to the use of consensus judging by jurors and multiple levels of awards, most recently employed at the 1889 Paris Universal Exposition.[203] Thacher was convinced that an "American system" would cost less because fewer people would have to be employed.[204] He also maintained that because reports would be signed by individual judges, and thus would not represent the collective opinion of "an irresponsible and indefinite judgment of a jury," they would make "fears and dissatisfaction . . . disappear, and trust and confidence . . . take their place." He also thought the information in the reports would be an excellent way to educate people. Thacher advocated one medal rather than a hierarchy of awards because he believed that the sole criterion for an award should be "excellence in a certain direction or improvement over the past." Championing the twin notions of nationalism and progress, he aspired to set a standard of judging that would endure beyond the World's Columbian Exposition and be recognized internationally both as American and superior.[205]

Department K was seriously affected by Thacher's determination to adopt this "American system," and Ives was outspoken in his opposition. In mid-December 1892 Ives complained bitterly to Kurtz, who was in New York, about "the asinine

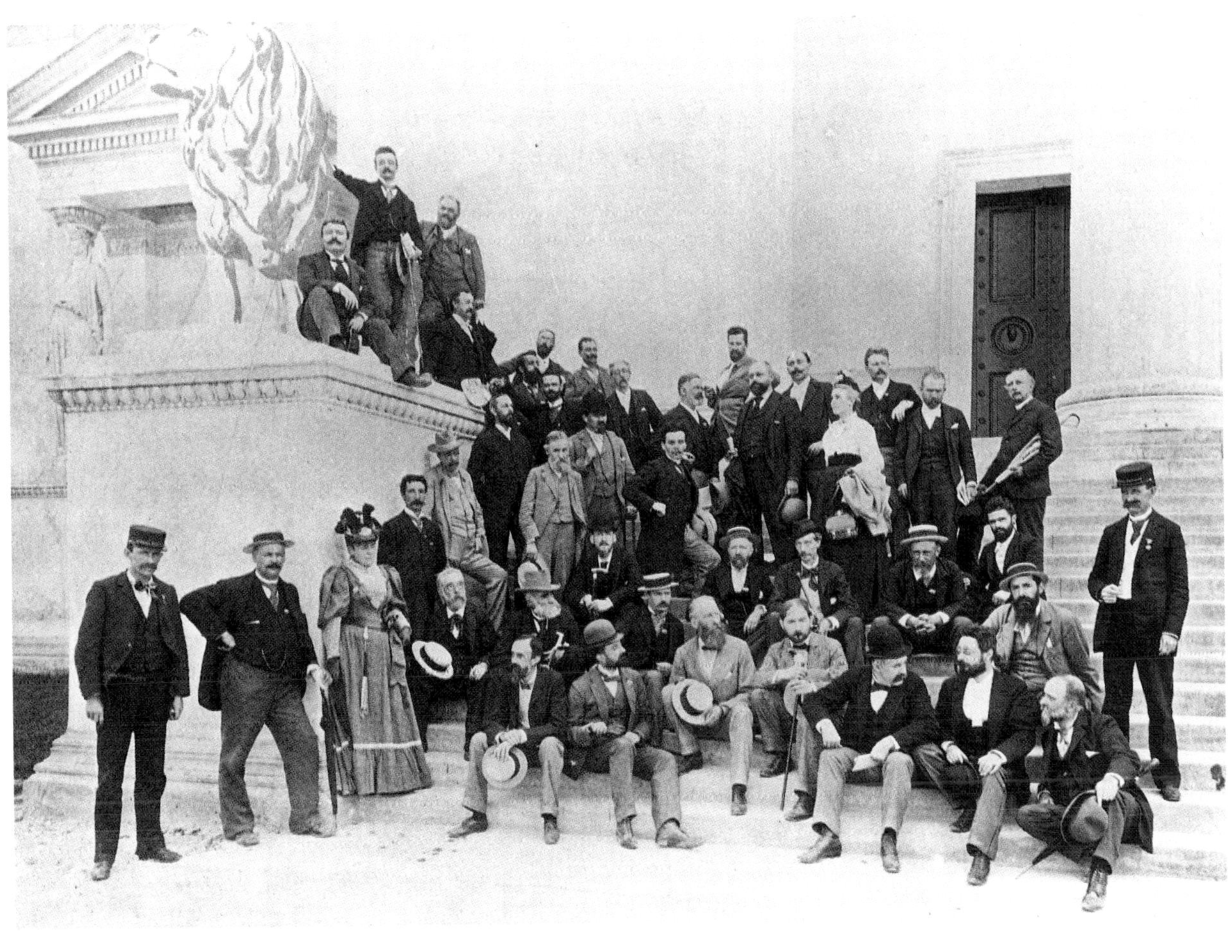

.. 66 ..
Members of the International Committee of Judges for Fine Arts on the steps of the Fine Arts Building. Hubert H. Bancroft, The Book of the Fair, *vol. 4 (Chicago: Blakely Printing Co., 1893), 960.*

errors contained in the scheme [of awards] as presented by the Albany man [Thacher]." Working behind the scenes to obtain his way, Ives asked Kurtz to "stir the fellows up a bit about the one judge plan of J. B. T.," telling him also that "I have *wired*—yes, *wired*—the officers of the various advisory committees, asking them to send me, before the 4th of January, strong resolutions opposing the plan."[206] In early January 1893 Ives made public his antagonism to the Thacher plan when he spoke before the fair's Board of Control, stating that "the adoption of the 'American system' would deprive him of all the first-class exhibits now in site." He explained, "Artists of a class are jealous and are full of prejudices. They know their own weaknesses, however, and will not submit their creations to any one member of their own craft for final judgment. They demand a decision from a jury composed of experts."[207]

Ives correctly anticipated the reaction of artists. As the *New York Times* subsequently reported, artists feared that "painters and sculptors whose work barely reached the mark . . . [will win] exactly the same distinction as artists who show masterpieces."[208] Among the expatriate artists displeased with the one-judge, single-medal system who withdrew their works from competition in the spring of 1893 were Charles Sprague Pearce, George Hitchcock, Frederick A. Bridgman, Elizabeth Gardner, and Julius L. Stewart. Among the American artists living in the United

States who chose not to be judged were Walter Shirlaw, J. G. Brown, Edwin H. Blashfield, Will H. Low, Kenyon Cox, Gilbert Gaul, and Theodore Robinson.[209] In addition, the artists who served on the International Committee of Judges (fig. 66) were not permitted to be judged. Ironically, however, many of the artists who voluntarily withdrew from competition received awards; they were, according to the *New York Times,* "medaled against their will."[210] Kurtz, who worked on the final edition of the catalogue for the art department, included a list of artists who had withdrawn from competition, as if to signify how the debate over the jury system had inestimably damaged the reputation of the American exhibit.[211] It was as if he wished to answer in his catalogue the criticism that "a large number of eminent artists" did not receive awards, while "a large number of mediocre artists have been able to decorate themselves with meaningless bronze."[212]

The withdrawal from competition of many notable artists and foreign countries led to a rethinking by many on the board and commission. In late May it appeared as if those opposing Thacher had won the war, but the battle continued to the end of the awards process.[213] Thus on 18 July the artist-members of the International Committee of Judges in the Department of Fine Arts, together with Ives, again had to denounce Thacher's system as "impractical" and announce their intention to go forward with a plan "founded on past experiences."[214] As Thacher stood his ground, his contentious personality—one newspaper called him the "pugnacious New Yorker"—became an issue: "Mr. Thacher has by this time wrought those who have dealings with him into such a state that they are ready to oppose whatever he

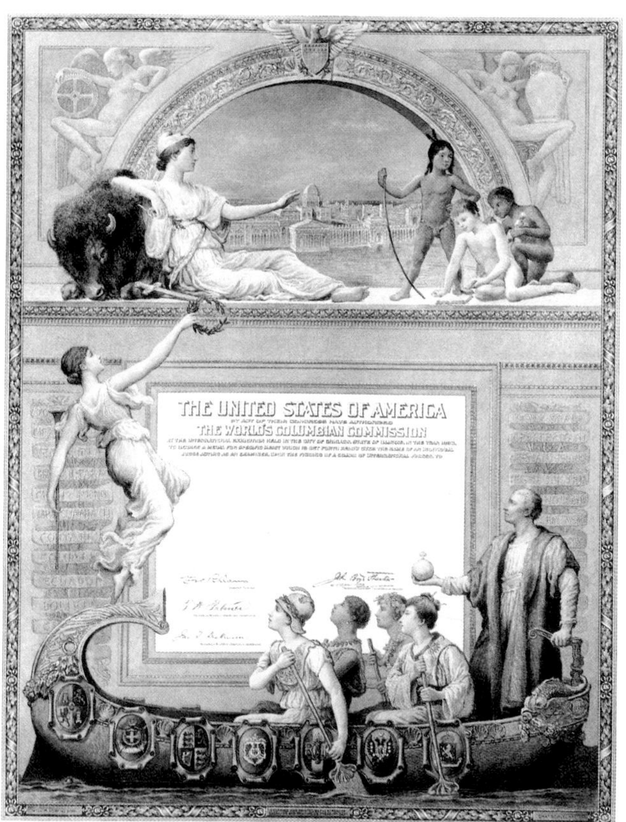

.. **67** ..
World's Columbian Exposition Awards Diploma, *1893–96. Designed by Will H. Low, engraved by Charles Schlect. Courtesy of the Bureau of Engraving and Printing, Department of the Treasury, Washington, D.C.*

proposes on the ground that he proposes it."[215] As the unrelenting, albeit weary Thacher had previously lamented to a fellow member of the committee, "Jordan is a macadamized passageway compared to the uneven way our committee on awards had [*sic*] had to travel from its first step."[216]

To add to the cacophony of controversy, Thacher's appointment of a large percentage of eastern—mostly New York—judges for the Department of Fine Arts irritated a large number of artists. Thacher countered the criticism, with its roots in the persistent competition between eastern and western art circles, by arguing that "the gentlemen were very highly recommended by the leading art institutes and artists of the country. Western men were not recommended very strongly and we did

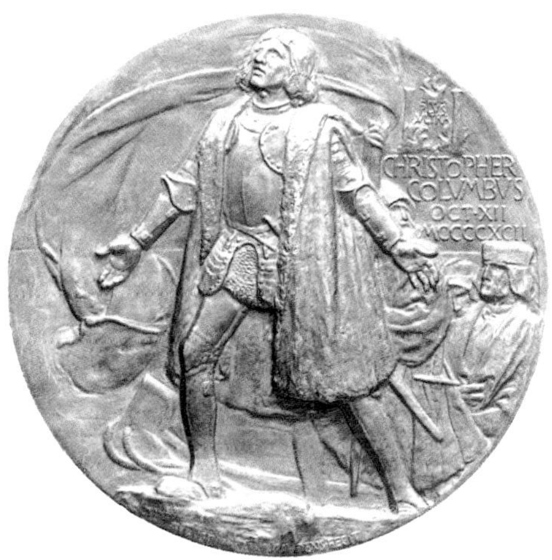

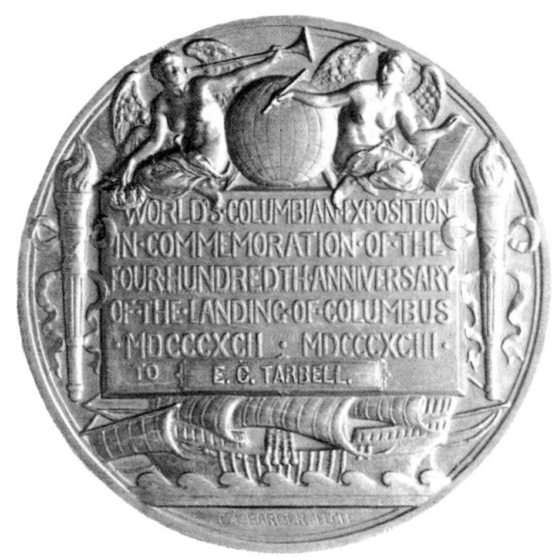

.. **68** ..
World's Columbian Exposition Awards Medal, 1893, awarded to Edmund C. Tarbell. Obverse designed by Augustus Saint-Gaudens, reverse designed by Charles E. Barber. Courtesy of the National Numismatic Collection, Smithsonian Institution.

not take any of them."[217] Indeed, the composition of the committee of judges must have been the one thing that Ives and Thacher agreed upon, for most of the individuals had served on previous selection juries, the composition of which had been quite carefully crafted by Ives.

By August, although all the issues surrounding the judging had not been resolved, the awards process was well under way. In the end a compromise was effected. An award was given by consensus, but only a single medal (accompanied by a diploma) was awarded. To win a medal, an artist needed to have his or her work nominated by a member of the International Committee of Judges for Fine Arts, be seconded by a second member, and then given a vote of approval by a majority of the committee. The diploma accompanying the medal was signed by the nominating juror. By 11 August all decisions by the jury had been ratified and submitted to the Executive Committee on Awards.[218] But if the wrangling over the jury process introduced a degree of skepticism regarding the validity of the awards as symbols of meritorious achievement, then the enthusiasm of the artists who were entitled to a fair reward must have been diminished by the fact that they did not immediately receive a token of their talent. Two mementos had been created to honor the award-winning artists: a diploma (fig. 67), designed by Will H. Low and engraved by the U. S. Government's Bureau of Engraving and Printing, and a medal (fig. 68), designed by Augustus Saint-Gaudens with modifications by a mint engraver, Charles E. Barber.[219] Unfortunately neither the medal nor the diploma were handed out to the appropriate recipients until late April 1896, nearly three years to the day after the 1893 exposition had opened in Chicago.[220]

CLOSING THE FAIR

Attendance at the fair began slowly but picked up momentum as the 31 October deadline approached.[221] Ives spent the summer of 1893 mostly haggling over the judging process. Kurtz was engaged in rewriting the art catalogues, both to correct inaccuracies and to create a version that listed the paintings and sculptures in the sequence in which they appeared in the galleries rather than purely alphabetically.[222] He answered numerous queries about the return of works, but he also began to focus his attention on his next job as art agent for the annual exhibitions at the St. Louis Exposition and Music Hall Association.[223] Both men were busy entertaining foreign visitors and American artists who came to see the exposition. Kurtz particularly enjoyed the lavish banquet Ives gave on 3 August at a Swedish restaurant on the fair grounds for the members of the International Committee of Judges for the Fine Arts Department. He captured the seductive charm of the fair grounds when he wrote, "Before the dinner, we all went aboard a couple of electric launches and rode through all the lagoons and out over the lake. After the dinner we came over to the art building, which tonight was illuminated throughout for the first time. Is simply *superb* when illuminated."[224]

Kurtz's letters, the main source of behind-the-scenes information about the fair, tell little of the effort that went into dispersing the artworks between November 1893 and January 1894. Kurtz was clearly a man who liked to plan the party and enjoy it, but he evidenced no interest in "doing the dishes" afterwards. Only Sara Hallowell's letter to Bertha Palmer gives a sense of the monumental and fatiguing nature of the task. "The rush that we have been in—in fact are still in—has prevented my doing anything whatever outside of this building. There will probably be plenty to keep me busy here until the middle of January. . . . This closing up matter is a terrible experience."[225]

The 1893 World's Columbian Exposition ended not in a panoply of ceremonial triumphs but in a shroud of despair with the assassination on 28 October of Carter H. Harrison, the mayor of Chicago.[226] But the pall cast over the fair was only temporary, and as the events of the previous six months entered history, it soon became apparent that the exposition's impact was far reaching. As artist F. D. Millet told a Yale University audience a decade later, "Never has there been in the history of art any such object lesson as was there shown to the millions of people, eager for information, hungry for the beautiful."[227]

Indeed, in retrospect, it is apparent that the American art at the fair achieved the organizers' goal of showing "what has been accomplished by American artists . . . since the Centennial Exposition of 1876." It also succeeded—for the first time on such a large scale—as an agent of ideology and a tool for cultural assertion. Never before had American art and artists competed so successfully in the international arena. Moreover, the artists acclaimed at the fair, by sheer number of works shown, if not by medals, continued to be represented in major national and international exhibitions during the following decade, among them the 1900 Paris Universal

Exposition, the 1901 Pan-American Exposition, and the 1904 Louisiana Purchase Exposition. Some even found their work in the 1915 Panama-Pacific Exposition, although by the time of that fair, the 1913 Armory show had initiated the death knell for the stylistic hegemony of late nineteenth-century American art among younger artists.

For Halsey Ives and Charles Kurtz, the two who orchestrated this panoply of American artistic talent, the fair solidified their reputations in the art world as important, capable, and knowledgeable men who could be relied upon to organize exhibitions that would reinforce America's image of itself as a place of artistic sophistication. After the fair, Ives and Kurtz both returned to St. Louis, where Ives became director of the St. Louis Museum and School of Fine Arts, and Kurtz became director of exhibitions for the St. Louis Music Hall Association. Both were subsequently called upon to participate in various international expositions.[228] As a team, they were most visible at the 1904 Louisiana Purchase Exposition in St. Louis, where, as director and assistant director respectively of the art department, they relied on the organizational lessons they had employed more than a decade earlier at the World's Columbian Exposition. By contrast, the Chicago fair signaled the end of Hallowell's meteoric rise in the art world, although she continued to work with collectors and served as an agent for the Art Institute of Chicago from her home in Paris until the outbreak of World War I.

As for the impact of the art of the fair today, it is apparent, despite the many stylistic and iconographic transformations that American art has undergone since the 1893 exposition, that the paintings and sculptures shown in Chicago continue to command attention. They serve not only as a richly textured symbol of past cultural concerns and national aesthetic aspirations but also, as they become increasingly prized by museums and private collectors, as objects with enduring visual and intellectual resonance.

NOTES

This essay owes much to the gracious assistance of Brandon Brame Fortune, who has collaborated with me on numerous aspects of the research for this exhibition and catalogue.

1. *Chicago Tribune,* 1 Nov. 1893, 4.

2. U.S. Congress, Fifty-first Congress, Session I, Chs. 153, 156, 1890, *United States Statutes at Large,* 26 Stat 62, 25 Apr. 1890.

3. Harlow N. Higinbotham, *Report of the President to the Board of Directors of the World's Columbian Exposition 1892–1893* (Chicago: Rand McNally, 1898), 7. The two major nineteenth-century histories of the exposition are Hubert Howe Bancroft, *The Book of the Fair,* 2 vols. (New York: Bancroft Books, 1894), and Rossiter Johnson, ed., *A History of the World's Columbian Exposition,* 4 vols. (New York: Appleton, 1898). Additional information can be found in *The Official Directory of the World's Columbian Exposition, May First to October Thirtieth, 1893,* ed. Moses P. Handy (Chicago: W. B. Conkey, 1893); Thomas W. Palmer, "Final Report of the World's Columbian Commission, Thomas W. Palmer, President," Record Group 43, Box 2343, National Archives, Washington D.C. (hereafter NA); and John T. Dickinson, "World's Columbian Exposition. Final Report of the World's Columbian Commission, John T. Dickinson, Secretary," 2 vols., Record Group 43, Box 2348, NA.

4. Higinbotham, *Report of the President,* 9; see also *Official Directory,* 41–72; and Robert D. Parmet and Francis L. Lederer II, "Competition for the World's Columbian Exposition: The Chicago Campaign," *Journal of the Illinois State Historical Society* 65, no. 4 (Winter 1972): 364–94.

5. Higinbotham, *Report of the President,* 18, 113ff. The history of the fair is characterized by a series of differences between the commission and the board, which, as Higinbotham tersely noted in his final report, "delayed the work and at times imperiled the success of the enterprise." See also Frank A. Cassell and Marguerite E. Cassell, "The White City in Peril: Leadership and the World's Columbian Exposition," *Chicago History* 12, no. 3 (Fall 1983): 10–27; and Johnson, *A History,* vol. 2, 408, as this conflict related to the art department. To deal with the demands of women, the act of Congress also authorized a Board of Lady Managers, who reported to the commission. For a history of this group, see Jeanne Madeline Weimann, *The Fair Women* (Chicago: Academy Press, 1981).

6. The fair, with minor variations, followed the organizational models established for earlier world's fairs, such as the 1876 Centennial Exhibition in Philadelphia and the 1889 Universal Exposition in Paris. New to the 1893 fair was the Department of Publicity and Promotion, headed by Moses P. Handy. The Department of Fine Arts was known as Department K. George Royal Davis, a former Illinois congressman, was also a leader in the group that brought the fair to Chicago. His official exposition papers have not been located. For their location in the late nineteenth century, see *New York Times,* 24 May 1897; Dickinson, "World's Columbian Exposition," 121; and Palmer, "Final Report," 129.

7. The *Official Manual of the World's Columbian Commission Containing the Minutes and Other Official Data of the Commission from the Date of Its Organization, June 16, 1890 to Its Third Session, November 26, 1890* (Chicago: Rand McNally, 1890), 107, lists the commission committee on fine arts as follows: at-large-delegate Augustus G. Bullock (insurance executive and son of a former Massachusetts governor), Worcester, Mass., chairman; Thomas J. Woodward, New Orleans, Louisiana; James M. Hodges, Baltimore, Maryland; William I. Buchanan (subsequently appointed chief of the fair's Agricultural Department), Sioux City, Iowa; Orson V. Tousley, Minneapolis, Minnesota; Albert A. Wilson, Washington, D.C.; Michel H. de Young (newspaper publisher and second vice-president of the commission), San Francisco, California; and Chauncey M. Depew (railroad magnate and head of the committee advocating New York as the site of the fair), New York. In April 1890 the board's committee on fine arts consisted of Charles L. Hutchinson (who was simultaneously president of the board of trustees of the Art Institute of Chicago), chairman; Robert A. Waller and Potter Palmer (both art museum trustees); and Chicago collectors James W. Ellsworth and Charles T. Yerkes. In March 1891 Hutchinson's friend, Martin A. Ryerson, also a museum trustee and collector, took Waller's place. At the April 1892 annual board meeting, Palmer and Ryerson were replaced by Elbridge G. Keith, a banker and insurance executive, and Eugene S. Pike, a real estate speculator and museum trustee, who was instrumental in raising support for the exposition (Higinbotham, *Report of the President,* 16, 122, 143).

8. Hallowell (1846–1924) was the fourth of six children and the first daughter born to Caleb W. Hallowell and his wife, Mary Morris Tyson. Hallowell's father died in 1857, thus depriving the family of its customary level of financial support. This and other family circumstances presumably led to Hallowell's decision to supplement her income with a paid position. The Chicago Inter-State Industrial Expositions were industrial fairs with an art component. They began in 1873 and ended in the fall of 1890, when the site of the expositions became that of the present Art Institute of Chicago, which opened in 1893. Hallowell appears to have initially aided the art department in 1878 by assisting with art sales (see *Catalogue of Paintings, Engravings, Designs and Casts in the Art Hall of the Inter-State Industrial Exposition* [Chicago: Rand McNally, 1878]). From 1880, when she was promoted to clerk of the art committee, until 1890 (with the exception of the year 1886), she was responsible for curating the Inter-State art exhibitions. Many paintings shown at the 1893 World's Columbian Exposition were first shown in Chicago at an Inter-State art exhibition. A biography of Hallowell, the first major female curator in America, is being written by this author.

9. Bullock to Ellsworth, 30 Sept. 1890, Ellsworth Papers, Special Collections, Chicago Public Library (hereafter CPL). The papers that Hallowell left with Bullock may have included a letter of support signed by sixty-nine American artists, including Augustus Saint-Gaudens, William Merritt Chase, Dwight W. Tryon, Albert Bierstadt, Abbott H. Thayer, Edwin A. Abbey, Louis Comfort Tiffany, Edward Moran, John Singer Sargent, J. Francis Murphy, F. S. Church, and Daniel Chester French. One copy of the letter is now in the possession of Ursus Rare Books, Ltd., New York;

another, in the papers of the Board of Lady Managers, Box 5, at the Chicago Historical Society (hereafter BLM/CHS).

10. *Commercial Advertiser*, New York, 23 Oct. 1890, William I. Buchanan Papers, Buffalo and Erie County Historical Society, Buffalo, NY. See also *New York Times*, 24 Oct. 1890, 8.

11. Clarke to Ellsworth, 6 Oct. 1890, Ellsworth Papers, CPL.

12. "Board of Lady Managers Official Record," vol. 1, 38, 21 Nov. 1890, CHS; Weimann, *Fair Women*, 183.

13. *New York Times*, 18 Oct. 1890, 1. Long after another director had been chosen, the critic for the *Daily Evening Transcript*, Boston, 16 February 1893, 4, lamented the discrimination against Hallowell.

14. Susan Hayes Ward, *Chicago Independent News*, 11 Dec. 1890, Art Institute of Chicago Scrapbook, Ryerson and Burnham Libraries, Art Institute of Chicago (hereafter AIC). This article concludes by alluding to the fact that the commission will consider a foreign art director imported from Paris. It is not clear from extant documents who "the director from Paris" might have been.

15. Palmer to Melchers, 9 Oct. 1890, Archives, Belmont, The Gari Melchers Memorial Gallery, Mary Washington College, Fredericksburg, VA.

16. Palmer to Depew, Jan. 1891, quoted in Weimann, *Fair Women*, 184–85.

17. Hallowell to Charles Hutchinson, 10 Feb. [1891], Palmer Papers, AIC.

18. Calvin Tomkins, *Merchants and Masterpieces: The Story of the Metropolitan Museum of Art* (New York: E. P. Dutton, 1970), 73, calls Marquand "the most discriminating collector and art patron of his time." Marquand acquired his enormous resources by myriad means, including a jewelry business, real estate, banking, brokerage, and railroad financing. After 1882, when he lost control of the St. Louis and Iron Mountain Railroad to Jay Gould, he devoted a great deal of his time and attention to art and philanthropy.

19. Marquand to Cesnola, 29 Oct. [1890]. Metropolitan Museum of Art Archives, New York (hereafter MMAA).

20. Cesnola to W[illiam] I. Buchanan, 31 Oct. 1890, MMAA. Determined to use Marquand and Cesnola's connections in the art world, Buchanan wrote to the latter and requested a list of the directors and officers of art museums and associations, as well as a list of artists living in America and abroad, in order to send a circular about the art department to each of them (Buchanan to Cesnola, 31 Oct. 1890). Subsequently he requested a list of the names of the possible salaried assistants Marquand and Cesnola would have used if the fair had been held in New York. He then proceeded to chastise them for their support of Hallowell's petition (Buchanan to Cesnola, 7 Nov. 1890).

21. *The Magazine of Art* 14 (1891): xxiv, snidely commented on the debate over the director for the fair by posing the question, "Who is to be the scapegoat for bad art at the World's Fair? . . . It was hoped that good Mr. Marquand, who is a little hard of hearing, would accept the position, but in spite of his deafness, that gentleman hears quite enough blame regarding the Metropolitan Museum to be content with such fault-finding as comes his way. . . . Miss Holliwell [*sic*] is still in the race it appears, but the authorities are not anxious to have a woman in command."

22. Kurtz to Bullock, 24 Oct. 1890, Charles Kurtz Papers, Archives of American Art, Smithsonian Institution (hereafter AAA). Unless otherwise specified, all letters to or from Charles Kurtz are from the Charles Kurtz Papers. These papers provide the most intimate glimpse of the activities of the art department known to date.

23. Clarke to Ellsworth, 10 Oct. 1890. Clarke also wrote that he was not in the running for the position, which suggests that his name may have been mentioned. Bertha Palmer was aware of Ellsworth's interest in the position, implying that it may have been rather common knowledge (Palmer to Melchers, 9 Oct. 1890, AIC). Hallowell was aware that Hutchinson did not care for Ellsworth as a candidate and also that Hutchinson had no interest in the position himself (Hallowell to Palmer, quoted in Weimann, *Fair Women*, 187).

24. *New York Times*, 24 Oct. 1890, 8; *Chicago Herald*, 9 Oct. 1892, 10; *Kansas City Star*, 28 Jan. 1891, Scrapbook, AIC. A description of Walters in the *Chicago Tribune*, 7 Jan. 1891, 6, as "somewhat younger than Marquand" (1819–1902), suggests that the reference is to Henry (1848–1919), not his father, William T. (1820–1894). Bertha Palmer also mentioned Walters as a candidate, and "four men other men not nearly so well qualified" (Palmer to Depew, in Weimann, *Fair Women*, 184–85). The four men are not otherwise identified.

25. Clarke to Ellsworth, 6, 10 Oct. 1890, CPL. Samuel P. Avery, Sr., and Russell Sturgis were both trustees of the Metropolitan Museum, Cyrus J. Lawrence was a collector, and Gaston L. Feuardent was a collector and the son of a well-known antiquities dealer. Clarke reconsidered the name of Feuardent, however, because of the suit against him by Cesnola (Calvin Tomkins, *Merchants and Masterpieces*, 62ff.). The *Chicago Tribune*, 31 Mar. 1891, 7, indicates that Hutchinson was offered the job but refused to take it.

26. Clarke to Ellsworth, 10 Oct. 1890; Bullock to Ellsworth, 21 Jan. 1891, CPL.

27. Ibid.

28. *Chicago Tribune*, 27 Jan. 1891, 8. This article stated that the choice of a director rested between Ives and Hallowell, but concluded that "Miss Hallowell will hardly secure that place." Johnson, *A History*, vol. 2, 65, dates the work of the Department of Fine Arts from 18 March 1891, "at which time Halsey C. Ives . . . was called to Chicago to consult with a joint committee composed of representative members of the Committees on Fine Arts." Public speculation on his appointment appeared shortly thereafter (*New York Times*, 28 Mar. 1891, 1, and 29 Mar. 1891, 2; *Chicago Tribune*, 31 Mar. 1891, 7).

29. Ives, who organized the 1904 art exhibition at the Louisiana Purchase Exposition, remained as director of the St. Louis Museum until his death in 1911. Unfortunately Ives's official correspondence from the time of the fair, which he refers to in a letter to Charles Kurtz, 26 Oct. 1892, has not been located. Johnson, *A History*, vol. 2, 408, mentions Ives's final report written to Director-General Davis at the close of the fair, but this also remains unlocated. It may have been part of the now unlocated papers Davis submitted to the congressional committee on printing.

30. Undated article, *Chicago Herald*, John Barrett Kerfoot Scrapbook, Manuscript Division, CHS.

31. *Chicago Tribune*, 30 Mar. 1891, 6. The *Chicago Tribune*, 9 May 1891, 1, described Ives as having "strong but delicately chiseled features, a perfect nose, deep brown eyes, and a fine artistic head." If physique and family status were require-

ments for the position, it should be noted that Hallowell was short, stout, husbandless, and childless.

32. *Chicago Tribune,* 3 May 1891, 2; 9 May 1891, 1; 20 June 1891, 9; 20 June 1891, 9. Johnson, *A History,* vol. 2, 65, dates Ives's appointment to 10 May. Although Ives had been granted a three-year leave of absence by Washington University to take the position in Chicago, he had ongoing commitments in St. Louis (*Chicago Tribune,* 13 May 1891, 7). He discovered, as he juggled his new responsibilities with his old, "that seventeen years as a member of the faculty of Washington University, fifteen years Director of the art school and eleven years as Director of the museum leaves me in a condition which I cannot shed my duties as we do an old coat when our tailor brings us a new one" (Ives to Kurtz, 22 May 1891).

33. *Chicago Herald,* 9 Oct. 1892, 10.

34. *New York Recorder,* 31 May 1891, Kurtz Papers. In this statement Ives also outlined his ambitious plans for the art department and his desire to have a showing in art "as never before has been seen in this country." For the issue of East v. West, see also Ives to Kurtz, 26 Mar., 7 May 1891.

35. The concept of a retrospective exhibition was not formulated until late spring of 1892. Ultimately, Ives appointed a committee consisting of Charles Henry Hart, a director of the Pennsylvania Academy of the Fine Arts, Charles G. Loring, director of the Museum of Fine Arts, Boston, and Thomas B. Clarke, a New York lawyer and collector, to organize this display. For the activities of the retrospective committee, see the Charles Henry Hart Letters, New York Public Library, microfilm copy, AAA, roll N10, frames 646–1346, and roll N11, frames 1–788.

36. The earliest letter between these two colleagues in the Kurtz Papers is Ives to Kurtz, 23 October 1886. After the fair, Kurtz became director of art exhibitions for the St. Louis Exposition and Music Hall Association. At the time of his death in 1909, Kurtz was director of the Albright Art Gallery in Buffalo, NY. In 1885 Kurtz married Julia Stephenson of Harrodsburg, Kentucky. They had three children: Elizabeth Stephenson (1886–1897), Julia Wilder (1889–after 1963), and Isabella Starkweather (1901–1991) (Kurtz Papers).

37. Ives to Kurtz, 15 May 1891. Ensuing correspondence between Ives and Kurtz indicates that Ives's biggest problem was keeping the garrulous Kurtz from publicly announcing his role in the art department before it was a fait accompli.

38. Ives to Kurtz, 30 June 1891.

39. Johnson, *A History,* vol. 2, 387.

40. The genesis of Hallowell's appointment is unclear. Bertha Palmer first proposed the idea of Hallowell's working as an assistant to the as yet unappointed director in January 1891 (Palmer to Hallowell, 24 Jan. 1891, BLM/CHS). Speculation about Hallowell's appointment as an assistant to Ives appeared in the *Chicago Tribune,* 31 Mar. 1891, 7, and she herself had acknowledged this possibility to Mrs. Palmer (Weimann, *Fair Women,* 187). Earlier Mrs. Palmer had tried to get Hallowell to take the position as director of art at the Woman's Building, but Hallowell declined, saying that she had a clear vision of what she wanted to do with the fine art exhibit, "But in thinking of any other department of work, a sense of vagueness comes over me which fairly stupefies me and utterly obscures my vision" (Hallowell to Palmer, 5 Jan. 1891, Palmer Papers, CHS).

41. Kurtz to Ives, 30 June 1891.

42. Hallowell to Ives, 6 Aug. 1891, Palmer Papers, CHS.

43. *Chicago Tribune,* undated clipping, "The Fair Today," Kurtz Papers. Ives saw Hallowell in Paris in mid-October, although he had avoided her when she tried to see him the previous August (Hallowell to Potter Palmer, 15 Aug. 1891, Palmer Papers, AIC; Palmer to Hallowell, 17, 29 Oct. 1891; and Hallowell to Palmer, 10 Nov. 1891, Palmer Papers, CHS). Ives and Hallowell concluded negotiations in Paris in February 1892, at which time she was assigned the task of organizing the loan exhibition (Johnson, *A History,* vol. 2, 393). The first salary payment to Hallowell is recorded in an "Itemized Account of Expenses of Department K" for the month ending 30 June 1892, Kurtz Papers. There is no evidence that Hallowell was included in the work of Kurtz and Ives when they were in Paris, nor is there any evidence that she assisted the American advisory committee in Paris. For Hallowell's activities at the fair on behalf of Mrs. Palmer, the Board of Lady Managers, and the Woman's Building, see Palmer Papers, AIC; BLM/CHS.

44. See *Chicago Tribune,* 20 Sept. 1893, 11; and the *Daily Evening Transcript,* Boston, 26 May 1893, 5.

45. *Information for Exhibitors and Others Interested in the Department of Fine Arts of the World's Columbian Exposition. Circular No. 2* (Chicago: Globe Lithographing and Printing Co., n.d. [1891]). Library of Congress, Paul Wayland Bartlett Papers, Box 31. These regulations were approved 12 July 1891. Bartlett was a member of the Paris committee on sculpture, and his papers contain numerous official documents sent from the art department. If *Circular No. 1* was published, no copy has been located.

46. For example, Ives to Kurtz, 19, 23 Dec. 1892 (re: Thomas W. Dewing, Dwight W. Tryon, and Ross Turner); George Inness to Kurtz, 12 Jan. 1893; Edward Moran to Kurtz, 4 Mar. 1893; Hovenden to Kurtz, 15 Mar. 1892.

47. Letter from Department of Fine Arts, Chicago, 1 Aug. 1891, Ellsworth Papers, CPL; Johnson, *A History,* vol. 2, 386.

48. Ives's forthcoming European trip and his itinerary were discussed in the *Chicago Tribune,* 6 June 1891, 9; 12 July 1891, 8; 18 July 1891, 18; and 22 July 1891, 5. Between Kurtz's letters, newspaper accounts, and Johnson, *A History,* vol. 2, 387ff., one can reconstruct most of Ives's itinerary. Between mid-August and early December Ives traveled to London, Paris, The Hague, Amsterdam, Copenhagen, Stockholm, Berlin, St. Petersburg, Moscow, Warsaw, Cracow, Vienna, and Munich. In late August Ives and his assistant Kurtz were joined by A. G. Bullock and other commissioners, who were abroad on behalf of the exposition. In December, prior to his planned return to America, Ives, who was in Italy, received a cable telling him to meet Harlow N. Higinbotham and Thomas B. Bryan in Rome. This group then traveled to Spain. From there, Ives returned to America in mid-February 1892, after stopping first in Paris, where he met with Sara Hallowell, and then in London, where he met with Sir Frederic Leighton regarding the English exhibition.

49. Ives and Kurtz discussed the possibility of a trip abroad even before the latter's confirmation (Ives to Kurtz, 13 May 1891). Because Kurtz's appointment had not been secured, Ives suggested that he assume the fiscal responsibility for his trip to Europe (Ives to Kurtz, 8 June 1891). Kurtz, whose

income before the fair was somewhat erratic, had previously written to his father requesting money for the trip. His father indulged his eldest, but not without commenting that he wished his thirty-five-year-old son would be economically self-sufficient (D. B. Kurtz to Charles Kurtz, 24 May 1891). Kurtz also borrowed money from his wife for the trip (Charles Kurtz to Julia (Judy) Kurtz, 30 Sept. 1891; hereafter Kurtz to Kurtz).

50. Kurtz to Kurtz, 24 Aug. 1891. In a previous letter Kurtz had described the artist Mesdag as "perhaps the first marine painter in the world and also the owner of the finest collection of pictures by the Barbizon painters that exists" (Kurtz to Kurtz, 22 Aug. 1891). Kurtz bought two works from him. Throughout this trip, Kurtz's greatest regret was his inability to buy more work from the artists he saw. His letters reveal that he continued to buy and sell art throughout the period he was employed by the art department at the fair.

51. Kurtz to Kurtz, 29 Aug. 1891.

52. Kurtz to Kurtz, 16 Sept. 1891; *Chicago Tribune,* 15 Sept. 1891, 8. During the summer Professor E. A. Engle, a member of the Washington University art faculty, had been in charge of the Fine Arts Department (*Chicago Tribune,* 12 July 1891, 8; 18 July 1891, 12).

53. *Chicago Tribune,* 17 Sept. 1891, 8; 19 Sept. 1891, 12. A less optimistic note was sounded by Levy Mayer, a Chicago attorney, who complained that the fair had not been sufficiently advertised in Europe (*Chicago Tribune,* 26 Sept. 1891, 4).

54. Kurtz to Kurtz, 19, 21 Sept., 12 Oct. 1891. The 28 September 1891 letter announcing a loan show focusing on Oriental art in American collections reflects neither Ives's earlier description of a loan show from private collections nor the loan show subsequently organized by Hallowell (Kurtz Papers).

55. Kurtz to Kurtz, 20 Sept.–16 Dec. 1891. The *Chicago Tribune,* 4 Sept. 1891, 1, reported that the plans for the art building would be perfected in a day or two and that construction would begin "in a fortnight."

56. Kurtz to Kurtz, 16 Sept. 1891. After her stay in Europe, Mrs. Kurtz returned to Harrodsburg, Kentucky, to live with her family for the duration of the fair, rarely visiting Chicago.

57. Kurtz to Kurtz, 24, 30 Sept. 1891.

58. Kurtz to Kurtz, 19, 20 Sept. 1891.

59. Kurtz to Kurtz, 16 July 1892.

60. Kurtz to Kurtz, 20 Sept. 1891.

61. Kurtz to Kurtz, 5 Jan. 1892; C. M. K. [Charles M. Kurtz], "News and Notes," *The Art Amateur* 26, no. 4 (Mar. 1892): 111. No located documents indicate with whom Ives met on his two trips to the East Coast in the summer of 1891, but it would appear from Kurtz's letters that Ives met or contacted New York artists R. Swain Gifford, William Merritt Chase, Hugh Bolton Jones, and Augustus Saint-Gaudens, for they were in place as members of the state art advisory committee by the time Kurtz went to New York in January 1891 (Kurtz to Kurtz, 29, 30 Jan. 1892).

62. William Tuthill, "Report of the Fine Arts Exhibit," *Report of the Board of General Managers of the Exhibit of the State of New York, at the World's Columbian Exposition; Transmitted to the Legislature April 18, 1894* (Albany: J. B. Lyon, 1894), 381. See also Johnson, *A History,* vol. 2, 394.

63. Kurtz to Davis, 19 Jan. 1892.

64. Kurtz to Kurtz, 25, 26 Jan. 1892.

65. Kurtz to Kurtz, 29, 31 Jan. 1892. While in New York, Kurtz was also trying to promote his written but as yet unproduced opera.

66. Kurtz to Kurtz, 31 Jan. 1892.

67. Kurtz to Kurtz, 6 Feb. 1892; Johnson, *A History,* vol. 2, 394. Some of those present, in addition to committee members, were artists J. G. Brown, T. Addison Richards, H. W. Robbins, Frederick Dielman, Charles Yardley Turner, J. B. Bristol, Louis Comfort Tiffany, George Willoughby Maynard, J. C. Nicoll, C. Harry Eaton, R. M. Shurtleff, H. W. Ranger, W. A. Collins, and Irving R. Wiles (*New York Times,* 6 Feb. 1892, 2). Olin Levi Warner was not added to the committee on sculpture until mid-March (*Chicago Herald,* 29 Mar. 1892).

68. *New York Herald,* 19 Feb. 1892, 6; 20 Feb. 1892, 10. In truth, Jones, Chase, Gifford, Johnson, Millet, and Saint-Gaudens were members of *both* the Society of American Artists and the National Academy of Design, while sculptor J. Q. A. Ward was a member only of the NAD.

69. Kurtz to Kurtz, 13 Feb. 1982. Johnson, *A History,* vol. 2, 394, states that Kurtz played a major role in organizing the Massachusetts advisory committee, implying that it was not as securely established as the New York committee by the time Ives had left for Europe the previous summer. Kurtz requested an appropriation of $20,000 from the state committee to underwrite the cost of sending art to the fair from Massachusetts and returning it to the artists after the fair's close; in late summer 1892 Ives finally got a commitment for $10,000 for this expense.

70. "Boston Artists Protest," undated clipping, Kurtz Papers. According to this article, fifty or sixty artists attended this meeting at the Boston Art Club.

71. Unidentified article, Kurtz Papers, featuring an interview with Ives in St. Louis, suggests that it was only upon his return that Ives received the first hint of "the trouble growing out of the desire of a New York jury to judge the work of artists in other cities." Kurtz had returned to Chicago about 21 February via New York and Philadelphia (Kurtz to Kurtz, 13, 22 Feb. 1892; *Philadelphia North American,* 18 Feb. 1892, 1). Kurtz and Ives may have timed their return to Chicago to coincide with the arrival of a group of national commissioners. While on the East Coast, Kurtz had been kept abreast of fair politics by the art department secretary, John K. Murphy, who took a decidedly cynical view of various fair leaders, as well as the artists who came to petition for their cause. Murphy's letter to Kurtz is typical: "Am sorry you shall not be here on the 22nd.—when the law-makers from the capital will hold high revelry in the Windy City. They will arrive on Saturday next and remain three days. Mrs. Potter Palmer will hold a reception, and the members from Podunk, Squatters Hollow and other seaport towns will catch a comprehensive glimpse of life in a big town 'where they burn gas.' If they should drop in on the art department and express a desire to satisfy their cravings for 'the nude in art' I will open to their morbid gaze a few works which brother Spiel [a photographer] has here, some of the pictures which would make Mother Eve and her fig leaf blush" (Murphy to Kurtz, 16 Feb. 1892).

72. *Inter-Ocean,* Chicago, 24 Feb. 1892, 5; *Chicago Herald,* 26 Feb. 1892.

73. *Inter-Ocean,* Chicago, 27 Feb. 1892, 13. See also Charles M. Kurtz, "The American Art Exhibit at the Columbian Exposition," *The Studio* 7 (5 Mar. 1892): 130–31, where his remarks are of a much more conciliatory nature.

74. Ives to Kurtz, 18 Mar. 1892

75. Kurtz to Kurtz, 22 Feb. 1892; Ives to Kurtz, 18 Mar. 1892.

76. Kurtz to Kurtz, 22, 25 Mar. 1892.

77. Ives to Kurtz, 30 Mar. 1892. Not all artists were antagonistic to the two from Chicago. Ross Turner wrote to Ives: "I do not know of any personal feelings antagonistic to you or against your plans—and I feel certain that the Boston men will take hold . . . and everything will be done to assist you in your arrangements" (Turner to Ives, 6 Mar. 1892, Kurtz Papers).

78. Unidentified newspaper clipping, Kurtz Papers.

79. *Circular No. 3.* Department of Fine Arts, World's Columbian Exposition, Chicago, 25 June 1892, Kurtz Papers.

80. Ives to Kurtz, 16 Apr. 1892. While in New York, Ives went with Ward to call on [Richard Morris] Hunt to convince him to "take a hand" with the architectural committee. He dined on Friday [15 April] with Augustus Saint-Gaudens, Thomas W. Dewing, Stanford White and Edward E. Simmons. On 16 April Ives spoke in Philadelphia to about 150 people regarding his plans for the art exhibitions at the fair (Ives to Ward, 16 May 1892, Ward Papers, AAA, roll 509, frame 279, microfilm copy of originals in the New York Public Library).

81. Charles Hutchinson favored locating the museum at its present lakeside site. As president of the board's fine arts committee and the board of trustees of the Art Institute of Chicago, Hutchinson clearly played a role in determining the final decision, which was made by mid-June 1891. For an excellent overview of the early history of the museum, see Linda S. Phipps, "The 1893 Art Institute Building and the 'Paris of America': Aspirations of Patrons and Architects in Late Nineteenth-Century Chicago," *The Art Institute of Chicago Museum Studies* 14, no. 1 (1988): 28–45, 99–102. After the fair, the Fine Arts Building became the Columbian Field Museum; today it is the location of the Museum of Science and Industry.

82. Johnson, *A History,* vol. 2, 382–83, 397; *Inter-Ocean,* Chicago, 4 Mar. 1892, 5; 22 Apr. 1892, 5. In early April Kurtz wrote to his wife that he was sending off instructions to the advisory committees and working on plans for the annexes to the building (Kurtz to Kurtz, 11 Apr. 1892). In May he informed her that "we have completed our space assignments and the Director-General has approved them" (Kurtz to Kurtz, 5 May 1892).

83. Lenders' concerns about the safety of their works, particularly the possibility of a fire, led the board of directors to guarantee insurance (Higinbotham, *Report of the President,* 199–200; Johnson, *A History,* vol. 2, 401).

84. Johnson, *A History,* vol. 2, 397. The United States had 12,747 square feet of floor space and 57,357 square feet of wall space; France had more square feet of floor space (16,325) but less square feet of wall space (33,393). Presumably the larger amount of floor space given to France was to accommodate the sculpture casts from the Trocadero Museum.

85. Johnson, *A History,* vol. 2, 398–99; *Inter-Ocean,* Chicago, 29 May 1892, 9; 15 June 1892, 5; 19 June 1892, 9; and 28 June 1892, 5. Ives returned to Chicago 11 July (Kurtz to Kurtz, 6 July 1892).

86. Johnson, *A History,* vol. 2, 297; Tiffany to Kurtz, 25 May 1892; Nicoll to Kurtz, 23 May 1892; Weir to Kurtz, 27 May 1892. Although *Circular No. 3* was printed 15 June 1892 with these names and those of Charles Platt and Samuel Colman, it was not until late June that Platt wrote to Kurtz accepting the etching committee appointment (Platt to Kurtz, 25 June 1892); Colman, who had been in Mexico, did not respond to Kurtz until the end of July (Colman to Kurtz, 30 July 1892).

87. *Official Illustrations from the Art Gallery of the World's Columbian Exposition,* ed. Charles M. Kurtz (Philadelphia: George Barrie, 1893). Kurtz appears to have discussed this project with his publisher, George Barrie, at least as early as January 1892 (Kurtz to Kurtz, 25 Jan. 1892). In May and August of that year Kurtz again met with Barrie (Kurtz to Kurtz, 12 May, 15 Aug. 1892). As part of this project, he wrote a letter of introduction for a Mr. Spiel, a photographer, to enable him to take pictures of work "likely to be exhibited" by foreign artists and Americans living abroad (Kurtz to Walter McEwen [secretary of the Paris advisory committee], 29 June 1892). Kurtz was frantically writing biographies for the book in March 1893, and photographs were still being taken at this time (Kurtz to Kurtz, 23 Mar. 1893; George Barrie to David B. Walkley, 11 Mar. 1893, Walkley Family Archives). The first edition of the catalogue appeared shortly after the exhibition opened (see *The Studio* 8 [20 May 1893]: 224). Kurtz was paid $1000 for his efforts as editor (Kurtz to Kurtz, 9 June 1893). Eastman Johnson was annoyed that the New York committee had played no part in the selection of the final illustrations (Johnson to Kurtz, 14 June 1893).

88. Of the 1,024 paintings and 160 sculptures in the American exhibition, only seventy-three paintings and twenty-seven sculptures from the Midwest, the South, and the West were chosen for the show by the national jury when it met in Chicago in March 1893.

89. Kurtz to Ward (postscript, Ives to Ward), 18 July 1892, Ward Papers, roll 509, frame 294. The topic was to preoccupy Ives throughout the fall, and it was one of his several arguments with Thacher (Ives to Kurtz, 26 Oct. 1892). Ives must have forgotten that sculptor Harriet Hosmer served on the advisory committee in Rome. As jurors for the painting and sculpture committees were, for the most part, drawn from the advisory committees, to have no women on an advisory committee was, de facto, to eliminate them from the jury of selection.

90. Ives to Kurtz, 22 Dec. 1892. Millet's paintings at the fair also show that he clearly preferred his women cloistered at home, e.g., *Old Harmonies, Sweet Melodies, Rook and Pigeon, A Difficult Duet, At the Inn,* and *The Window Seat.*

91. Open letter to the Executive Committee of the [New York] State Board of Managers, 22 Nov. 1892, Ward Papers, roll 509, frames 215–16.

92. New York was the last advisory committee to get an appropriation from the state committee (unsigned letter to the Executive Committee of the State Board of Managers, World's Columbian Exposition, 22 Nov. 1893, Ward Papers, roll 509, frames 225–27, 242ff.). The Ward Papers also indicate that the state committee had not paid for many of the expenses associated with the art exhibit as late as January 1894.

93. Ives to Ward, 20 Dec. 1892, Ward Papers, roll 509, frame 295. See also Tuthill, "Report of the Fine Arts Exhibit," 381.

94. Bertha Palmer, who had probably signed the request to put women on the advisory committee, knew Cassatt's distaste for juries but wrote to her twice, arguing that even if she was unwilling to travel

to America and actively participate, it was important that she lend her name (Palmer to Cassatt, 15 Dec. 1892, 31 Jan. 1893). Cassatt, who was in the midst of finishing her mural for the Woman's Building, mistakenly thought the telegram she received asked her to be on the jury for American paintings in Paris. "Naturally I will refuse in spite of the desire that I have to be agreeable. It seems to me that I have enough of Chicago for the moment" (Cassatt to Paul Durand-Ruel, 19 Dec. 1892). In her 1904 letter to Harrison Morris, director of the Pennsylvania Academy of the Fine Arts, Cassatt gives the most explicit description of her long-held and well-known position on prizes for art (Cassatt to Morris, 15 Mar. 1904). These letters have been published in Nancy M. Matthews, ed., *Cassatt and Her Circle: Selected Letters* (New York: Abbeville Press, 1984).

95. New York-born Mary Hallock Foote, a good friend of Helena deKay Gilder, wife of the publisher of the *Century Magazine*, Richard Watson Gilder, was known for her illustrations in *Scribner's Monthly, Century Magazine,* and *Harper's Weekly*. In 1876 she married Arthur DeWint Foote, a mining engineer, and moved west with him. She mentions declining the New York jury appointment in a letter to Mrs. R. Swain Gifford (Foote to Gifford, 19 Dec. 1892, R. Swain Gifford Papers, AAA, roll 594, frame 506). Foote ultimately accepted a post on the International Committee of Judges, which convened to award medals in August 1892. She describes this experience in *A Victorian Gentlewoman in the Far West: The Reminiscences of Mary Hallock Foote*, ed. Rodman W. Paul (San Marino, CA: Huntington Library, 1972), 354ff.

96. NPG intern Mary Fearon undertook a statistical analysis of the American women artists who exhibited paintings and sculptures in the Fine Arts Building. A copy of her research paper is in the NMAA/NPG library's World's Columbian Exposition files.

97. Johnson, *A History*, vol. 2, 401; Ives to Kurtz and Kurtz to Kurtz, various letters, Sept.–Nov. 1892. In September Ives was in St. Louis helping the museum's school of fine arts to initiate its new semester. Exasperated at Ives's frequent absences and schedule changes, Kurtz wrote to his wife that Ives was "utterly unreliable" (Kurtz to Kurtz, 23 Sept. 1892).

98. *New York Times*, 11 Nov. 1892, 8.

99. Ives to Ward, 1 Dec. 1893 [1892], Ward Papers, roll 509, frame 284.

100. Kurtz to Kurtz, 18 Aug. 1892.

101. Kurtz to Ward, 15 July 1892, Ward Papers, roll 509, frame 289.

102. See Kurtz to Kurtz, 25 Aug. 1892. For example, Carleton Wiggins's *Evening, Village at Grez* was loaned by Mrs. Charles M. Kurtz. Both William Semple, who loaned Frederick Dielman's *A New York Arab*, and R. J. Menefee, who loaned Hugh Bolton Jones's *The Flax Breaker*, were personal friends and frequently bought art through Kurtz.

103. Kurtz to Kurtz, 9 Dec. 1892.

104. Hallowell, who had returned from Europe in mid-September, was in Chicago at the time of the opening ceremonies. Kurtz was unhappy at her reappearance: "Miss Hallowell has arrived and has been given a desk in the office where I am. . . . I have an instinctive feeling that I would rather she did not belong in this department" (Kurtz to Kurtz, 6 Oct. 1892). The rivalry between the two assistants was at a peak when Ives wrote to remind Kurtz that while in New York, "Please understand that you are not engaged in any way in the making or collecting a loan exhibit. . . . You are there to act under the direction of . . . the advisory committee, in making the strongest possible exhibit from New York. . . . Above all, be careful not to tread upon Miss Hallowell's bailiwick" (Ives to Kurtz, 14 Dec. 1892). Conversely, Ives had to reassure Kurtz that Hallowell would not interfere with his activities (Ives to Kurtz, 19 Dec. 1892).

105. For a thorough examination of the "new" approach to art represented by Dewing and Tryon, see Wanda M. Corn, *The Color of Mood: American Tonalism 1880–1910* (San Francisco: de Young Memorial Museum and California Palace of the Legion of Honor, 1972).

106. Ives to Kurtz, 14, 19 Dec. 1892. After Kurtz called on Tryon, the artist wrote to collector Thomas B. Clarke requesting works from his collection (Tryon to Clarke, 23 Dec. 1892, Charles Henry Hart Autograph Collection, AAA, roll D5, frame 316). Ultimately Dewing was to exhibit seven paintings and Tryon fourteen.

107. Murphy to Kurtz, 20 Dec. 1892. Mrs. Wyant had written previously suggesting a group of her recently deceased husband's pictures (A. L. Wyant to Ives, 16 Dec. 1892, Kurtz Papers).

108. Charles Rhodes (an art department secretary) to Kurtz, 4 Jan. 1893. The instructions for artists living in Paris stated that all works were to be submitted for judging on 13 December, and if not selected, were to be picked up by 23 December (Bartlett Papers, LC, Box 31). The Paris jury accepted about 150 works (Ives to Kurtz, 3 Jan. 1892). Because of shipping requirements, foreign juries had to make their decisions earlier than the American juries. The *Roman Herald*, 19 November 1892, 1, reported dissatisfaction among American artists in Rome and Florence because they had not expected such an early departure date; many had not finished works when the *Constellation* left Naples on 18 November and Genoa on 23 November. The *Constellation* departed from Le Havre on 11 January and docked in New York 10 March. As the Bridgman example demonstrates, it is difficult to determine what was sent from abroad by foreign juries because some works accepted by foreign juries were already in New York. There are no extant customs records.

109. Tuthill, "Report of the Fine Arts Exhibit," 379–81. Symptomatic of the chaos surrounding the New York committee was the fact that as late as 6 January, J. Q. A. Ward had not been appointed chairman of the art bureau. Without this appointment, the art bureau could not enter into contracts with artists, and the jury would have no work to evaluate (Ives to Kurtz, 9 Jan. 1893). Works began arriving at the armory on 11 January (*Mail and Express*, New York, 12 Jan. 1892, Thomas B. Clarke Papers, AAA, roll N597, frame 486). For a description of the jury process, see *New York Recorder*, 17 Jan. 1893, Clarke Papers, AAA, roll N597, frame 491.

110. Kurtz to Kurtz, 10, 12 Jan. 1893.

111. Kurtz to Kurtz, 16 Jan. 1893.

112. Kurtz to Tuthill, 4 Feb. 1893.

113. Elliott Shepard to Hugh Bolton Jones, 18 Jan. 1893.

114. John Singer Sargent, 27 Sept. 1892. Sargent's list of suggestions is not attached to this letter. As there is no record that *Ellen Terry as Lady Macbeth* was in America prior to the time of the fair, Sargent must have submitted the painting through the English advisory committee.

115. Ives to Kurtz, 4 Jan. 1893.

116. Tuthill to "To the Private Owners

of Works of Art," [Jan. 1893], Kurtz Papers.

117. Hugh Bolton Jones to the Council [National Academy of Design], 11 Jan. 1893, Archives of the National Academy of Design, New York.

118. Huntington to Low, 28 Jan. 1893, 31 Jan. [1893], Seth Low Papers, Rare Book and Manuscript Collection, Butler Library, Columbia University, New York; Weir to Tuthill, 25 Jan. 1893, Kurtz Papers.

119. Kurtz to Kurtz, 10, 16, 18 Jan. 1893.

120. Some artists had not previously sent their work to be judged because they had assumed that it would be collected by the art bureau, as was customary with local exhibits (Tuthill to Ward, 21 Jan. 1893, Ward Papers, roll 509, frame 244).

121. Kurtz to Kurtz, 30 Jan. 1893.

122. Ives to Kurtz, 23 Jan. 1893, 2 Feb. 1892; Kurtz to Kurtz, 7 Feb. 1893.

123. Hugh Bolton Jones [Kurtz] to Clarke, 10 Feb. 1893. Clarke also sent numerous works to the fair's retrospective exhibition of American art made prior to 1876.

124. Tuthill, "Report of the Fine Arts Exhibit," 381; Kurtz's figures are a bit different (Kurtz to Kurtz, 19 Jan. 1893). NPG intern Claire Tieder undertook a comparison of the works in the exposition catalogues listed as having been sent by New York artists with the lists published in *The Art Amateur* 28, no. 4 (Mar. 1893): 116; *The Studio* 8, no. 11 (11 Feb. 1893): 93–95; *New York Times,* 29 Jan. 1893, 16; and "Report on the Fine Arts Exhibit." It is impossible to reconcile these lists and to tell *precisely* what was sent from New York by the state committee and what ended up coming from New York, either directly from the artist or from a collector. This fact adds to the supposition that, in numerous cases, artists dealt directly with Ives and Kurtz when they wished to place a work. *The Art Amateur* 28, no. 4 (Mar. 1893): 116–17, contains a list of works sent from Boston and Philadelphia, and similar contradictions are apparent, although to a lesser degree.

125. R. Swain Gifford, perhaps as recompense for the time and effort he spent on behalf of the committee, sent eleven paintings; Eastman Johnson, seven; F. D. Millet, eight; and William Merritt Chase, five; only Hugh Bolton Jones, with a modest two works forwarded to Chicago, adhered to the published rule of no more than three. The artists on the Boston and Philadelphia juries were more discreet; only John J. Enneking, of Boston, sent five paintings.

126. Kurtz to Kurtz, 19, 23 Jan. 1893.

127. Ives to Kurtz, 23 Jan., 2 Feb. 1893.

128. Kurtz to Kurtz, 3 Feb. 1893. Kurtz was also angry that Tuthill had permitted John H. Dolph to remove a work (Kurtz to Tuthill, 2 Feb. 1893; Tuthill to Kurtz, 3 Feb. 1893).

129. *New York Herald,* 3 Feb. 1893, 9.

130. *Brooklyn Daily Eagle,* 26 Feb. 1893, 5.

131. Kurtz to Kurtz, 7 Feb. 1892.

132. *Inter-Ocean,* Chicago, 5 Mar. 1893, 15.

133. Kurtz to Kurtz, 23 Jan. 1893; Kurtz's expense report shows that he purchased a train ticket to Philadelphia, 11 Mar. 1893.

134. *Daily Evening Transcript,* Boston, 10 Jan. 1893, 10. The *Catalogue of the Massachusetts Fine Art Exhibit at the Massachusetts Charitable Mechanics' Association Building from January 16 to 28 Inclusive,* Kurtz Papers, lists 159 works exhibited, of which approximately 125 were paintings.

135. *Daily Evening Transcript,* Boston, 14 Jan. 1893, 12.

136. Ives wrote to Kurtz, 23 Jan. 1893, "I want to allude to the enclosed from Winslow Homer (letter and list) and I would be glad if you would see that both works named are passed on list and made part of his group." No "letter and list" exist in the Kurtz Papers and no extant records indicate how *Sailors Take Warning (Sunset), Hound and Hunter, Lost on the Grand Banks, The Fog Warning, Herring Fishing,* and *Return from the Hunt* became part of the exhibition. The additional works that Homer wished to display are not indicated in the list of those accepted by the New York jury published in *The Studio* 8, no. 11 (11 Feb. 1893): 93–95, or *The Art Amateur* 28, no. 4 (Mar. 1893): 116. Moreover, Tuthill's "Report on the Fine Arts Exhibit," 388, lists only five of the seven pictures loaned by Clarke. While Kurtz had ample time to consult with the New York committee about the acceptance of Homer's work "on list" during February, it is also possible that he and Ives accepted the additions unilaterally, without the formal approval of the New York committee.

137. *Catalogue of the Massachusetts Fine Art Exhibit,* Kurtz Papers. This catalogue is marked with the designations "1," "2," and "3" beside most works.

138. Vinton to Kurtz, 19 Jan. 1893.

139. Kurtz to Kurtz, 26 Jan. 1893. During his visit Kurtz found Vinton and his wife "very agreeable, not at all like traditional Yankees."

140. *Philadelphia Press,* 15 Jan. 1893, 8; Pennsylvania Academy of the Fine Arts, *Catalogue of Works of Art To Be Exhibited at the World's Columbian Exposition, Chicago, 1893* (Philadelphia, 16 Jan. to 4 Feb. 1893). The catalogue indicates that Edwin Lord Weeks showed only *Three Beggars of Cordova,* implying that the other five pictures he exhibited in Chicago came directly from Europe; similarly, Julius L. Stewart showed only *The Hunt Ball* and *The Yacht Namouna, Venice, 1890,* suggesting that *The Baptism* was likewise shipped from Europe.

141. *Philadelphia Press,* 15 Jan. 1893, 8.

142. Ives to Kurtz, 5 Jan. 1893.

143. Ives to Kurtz, 10 Feb. 1893.

144. Ives to Kurtz, 7, 13 Feb. 1893; Twachtman to Kurtz, 17 Feb. 1893; Tryon to Kurtz, 23 Feb. 1893; Kurtz to Kurtz, 15 Feb. 1983.

145. Kurtz to Kurtz, 5 Mar. 1893. According to Kurtz, the "mess" had been created by George Corliss, who had previously worked at the Pennsylvania Academy of the Fine Arts.

146. *Chicago Evening Post,* 14 Mar. 1893, unpaged clipping, Kurtz Papers. See also *Inter-Ocean,* Chicago, 11 Mar. 1893, 5, and *Chicago Tribune,* 11 Mar. 1893, 9.

147. Lucy Monroe, "Chicago Letter," *The Critic* 22, no. 579 (25 Mar. 1893): 185–86.

148. *Chicago Evening Post,* 14 Mar. 1893. The *New York World,* 29 May 1893, 1, stated that *A Woman Taken in Adultery,* which won a medal at the 1889 Paris Salon, was subsequently hung in the French galleries. A crimson piece of cloth covered the painting because "it was too immoral for exhibition." Ives was "roundly criticized" for this act of censorship.

149. *Cincinnati Commercial Gazette,* 12 Mar. 1893. Unpaged copy, Henry E. Farny Papers, AAA, roll 1233, frame 467. Steele's painting is identified in the *Chicago Tribune,* 8 Mar. 1893, 3.

150. Ives to Kurtz, 15 Feb. 1893. Little is known about the English advisory com-

mittee, and there was no official English jury as in Paris, Munich, and Rome.

151. Kurtz to Kurtz, 15 Mar. 1983.

152. For example, Hugh Bolton Jones inquired about the insurance for three paintings by Elihu Vedder (Hugh Bolton Jones to Kurtz, 29 Mar. 1893); Douglas Volk inquired whether Thomas B. Clarke had lent his *Witchcraft* (Volk to Kurtz, 18 Apr. 1893); and Kurtz wrote to his wife that William Semple, his close friend from Louisville, had sent his Dielman and that three Tryons and three Dewings had arrived from Freer (Kurtz to Kurtz, 18 Apr. 1893).

153. *Chicago Evening Post,* 14 Mar. 1893, unpaged clipping, Kurtz Papers.

154. *Chicago Evening Journal,* 29 Mar. 1893, 12. The *Chicago Tribune,* 4 Mar. 1893, 9, reported that of the approximately 1000 paintings to be hung at the exposition, 500 came from New York, 139 from Boston, 112 from Philadelphia, 140 from Paris, 20 from Florence and Rome, 40 from Munich, 50 from London, and the remaining 73 from Chicago.

155. Kurtz to Kurtz, 18 Mar., 24 Apr. 1893. The exhibition of forty-seven accepted paintings at the New York Union League Club, mostly from the Thomas B. Clarke collection, might explain some of the delay (*A Group of Paintings by American Artists Accepted for the Columbian Exposition* [New York: Union League Club, 9–11 Mar. 1893]). See also "American Pictures at the Union League Club" *The Critic* 22, no. 578 (18 Mar. 1893), 168.

156. Hovenden to Kurtz, 16, 22 Mar., 7 Apr. 1893.

157. Earlier the *Daily Evening Transcript,* Boston, 14 Nov. 1892, 6, detailed a hanging plan (ultimately not followed) and reported that a hanging committee would be chosen. Ives reiterated his stand against a hanging committee in a telegram to J. Q. A. Ward: "The installation of collections, that is hanging pictures and placing other works of art, is in the hands of the chief of Dept. This is fixed by law" (Ives to Ward, 15 Dec. 1892, Ward Papers, roll 509, frame 306).

158. Kurtz to Kurtz, 11 May 1893.

159. In an unpublished essay on *The Gross Clinic* and *The Agnew Clinic* in the Kurtz Papers, the author admires "their admirable technical skill" and says that these two paintings take the observers "into a province seldom penetrated by lovers of art."

160. See Department of Fine Arts, ed., *Revised Catalogue,* 39–78.

161. Kurtz to Kurtz, 24 Apr. 1893.

162. Julia Kurtz to Charles Kurtz, 22 Apr. 1893; Kurtz to Kurtz, 23 Mar. 1893.

163. Kurtz to Kurtz, 26 Apr. 1893.

164. Monroe, "Chicago Letter," *The Critic* 23, no. 598 (5 August 1893): 90–91.

165. Kurtz to Kurtz, 30 Apr. 1890.

166. Ibid.

167. Kurtz to Kurtz, 1 May 1893. After the opening ceremonies, Kurtz and Ives accompanied Cleveland on "another short visit" to the art department. Kurtz reported, "There is one thing about Grover, he hasn't any 'swagger.'"

168. Kurtz to Kurtz, 2, 11 May 1893.

169. Theodore Child, quoted in D. Dodge Thompson, " 'Loitering Through the Paris Exposition': Highlights of the American Paintings at the Universal Exposition of 1889," in Annette Blaugrund, *Paris 1889: American Artists at the Universal Exposition* (New York: Harry N. Abrams, 1989).

170. Linda Jones Docherty, "A Search for Identity: American Art Criticism and the Concept of the 'Native School,' 1876–1893," (Ph.D. diss., University of North Carolina at Chapel Hill, 1985).

171. *New York Herald,* 18 Sept. 1892, 30.

172. C. M. K., *New York Star,* 16 Feb. 1890, Clarke Papers, AAA, roll N597, frame 317.

173. See Corn, *The Color of Mood,* for a discussion of "tonalism" in late nineteenth century American painting.

174. Reviews of the American art exhibition can be found in various newspapers, including the *Chicago Tribune, Chicago Evening Journal, Chicago Herald, Inter-Ocean,* Chicago, *New York Times, Philadelphia Press, Brooklyn Daily Eagle,* and *Daily Evening Transcript,* Boston. Other, often lengthier, more sophisticated critical reviews appeared in national magazines, such as *The Nation* and *Century Magazine,* as well as in leading art journals, including *The Art Amateur* and *The Critic.* As Docherty, in "A Search for Identity," demonstrates, the issues addressed in these reviews were not dissimilar to the topics discussed in other criticism of the era. The European art exhibits were also reviewed, but far less frequently. See, for example Lucy Monroe, "Chicago Letter," *The Critic* 22, no. 585 (6 May 1893): 297, and *The Critic* 23, no. 608 (14 Oct. 1893): 243; John C. Van Dyke, "Painting at the Fair," *The Century Magazine* 48 (July 1894), 439–446; *Daily Evening Transcript,* Boston, 15 July 1893, 7; and *Chicago Herald,* 23 July 1893, 11.

175. Monroe, "Chicago Letter," *The Critic* 22, no. 588 (27 May 1893): 351. Among the other critics who supported her point of view were William A. Coffin, "The Columbian Exposition II. Fine Arts: The United States Section," *The Nation* 57, no. 1467 (10 Aug. 1893): 96; Van Dyke, "Painting at the Fair," 445; and William Forsyth, "Some Impressions of the Art Exhibit at the Fair," *Modern Art* 1, no. 4 (Autumn 1893): n.p.

176. *Chicago Herald,* 15 June 1893, 2. Similar sentiments are also expressed in the *Chicago Herald,* 18 June 1893, 2. An attempt to reconcile the thorny issue of national origins was proposed in the *Daily Evening Transcript,* Boston, 21 July 1893, 5.

177. See, for instance, Monroe, "Chicago Letter," *The Critic* 22, no. 587 (20 May 1893): 329; and *New-York Daily Tribune,* 21 June 1893, 7.

178. *Daily Evening Transcript,* Boston, 24 May 1893, 6; Coffin, "The Columbian Exposition," 97; Van Dyke, "Painting at the Fair," 446.

179. Monroe, "Chicago Letter," *The Critic* 22, no. 598 (5 Aug. 1893): 92; *New-York Daily Tribune,* 19 June 1893, 5.

180. See Monroe, *The Critic* 22 (27 May 1893): 351, *Chicago Tribune,* 8 Oct. 1893, 27; *Daily Evening Transcript,* Boston, 21 July 1893, 5; Coffin, "The Columbian Exposition," 96–97.

181. *Daily Evening Transcript,* Boston, 21 July 1893, 5; "American Painting. IV. Whistler, Dannat, Sargent," *The Art Amateur* 29 (Nov. 1893): 134.

182. *Chicago Evening Journal,* 4 Apr. 1893, 4. This critic also noted that this was a rare opportunity to see Whistler oils in America, as in this country he was better known for his etchings and watercolors. For other comments on Whistler, see *Inter-Ocean,* Chicago, 6 Aug. 1893, 23; "American Painting. IV.," 134; *Chicago Tribune,* 8 Oct. 1893, 27; *Chicago Evening Journal,* 26 Aug. 1893, 4.

183. *New-York Daily Tribune,* 19 June 1893, 5; *Daily Evening Transcript,* Boston, 21 July 1983, 5; *Chicago Tribune,* 25 June 1893, 27.

184. Coffin, "The Columbian Exposition," 97–98; *New-York Daily Tribune,* 19 June 1893, 5; *Daily Evening Transcript,* Boston, 26 May 1893, 5. Walter C. Larned, *Art Clippings from the Pen of Walter Cranston Larned and other critics at the Fair,* arranged by J. S. Merrill (Chicago, 1893), 8, took a less sympathetic point of view.

185. *Chicago Tribune,* 8 Oct. 1893, 27.

186. "American Painting. III. Melchers, McEwen, Shirlaw, Chase, Marr, Duveneck," *The Art Amateur* 29 (Aug. 1893): 56. See also Coffin, "The Columbian Exposition III," *The Nation* 57, no. 1468 (17 Aug. 1893): 114–16.

187. "American Painting. IV," 134; *Chicago Tribune,* 20 Aug. 1893, 24.

188. *Chicago Tribune,* 20 Aug. 1893, 24. See also Monroe, "Chicago Letter," *The Critic* 22 (5 Aug. 1893): 92; and *Chicago Tribune,* 30 Apr. 1893, 42.

189. *Chicago Tribune,* 30 Apr. 1893, 42; "Painting and Sculpture at the World's Fair," *The Inland Architect and News Record* 22, no. 4 (Nov. 1893): 35–36.

190. *Chicago Tribune,* 14 May 1893, 37. For a discussion of images of women in the late nineteenth century, see Martha Banta, *Imaging American Women: Idea and Ideals in Cultural History* (New York: Columbia University Press, 1987).

191. *Chicago Tribune,* 17 Sept. 1893, 13; *Chicago Tribune,* 8 Oct. 1893, 27; *Chicago Tribune,* 27 Sept. 1893, 35.

192. *Daily Evening Transcript,* Boston, 26 May 1893, 5; *Brooklyn Daily Eagle,* 29 June 1893, 2; Coffin, *The Nation* 57, no. 1486, 116; William H. Downes, "New England Art at the World's Fair," *New England Magazine,* n.s., 8 (July 1893): 363–64.

193. *Chicago Tribune,* 16 July 1893, 14; see also *Chicago Tribune,* 28 Oct. 1893, 35; *Inter-Ocean,* Chicago, 14 May 1893, 23.

194. *Chicago Tribune,* 6 Aug. 1893, 14.

195. Coffin, "The Columbian Exposition I. Fine Arts: French and American Sculpture," *The Nation* 57 (3 Aug. 1893): 80; *Daily Evening Transcript,* Boston, 15 July 1893, 7; *Chicago Tribune,* 17 Sept. 1893, 34.

196. *Chicago Tribune,* 1 Nov. 1893, 10–11. This list may not be wholly accurate. For instance, William Merritt Chase's *Alice* was purchased from the fair in September 1893 and given to the Art Institute of Chicago.

197. Department of Publicity and Promotion, M. P. Handy, Chief, *World's Columbian Exposition, 1893, Department K, Fine Arts, Halsey C. Ives, Chief* (Chicago: W. B. Conkey Company, 1893). The Kurtz Papers contain a copy of this catalogue marked with prices by Kurtz.

198. *Chicago Tribune,* 1 Nov. 1893, 10.

199. *Chicago Tribune,* 11 June 1893, 27.

200. Hallowell to Auguste Rodin, 8 Dec. 1893, Rodin Archives, Musée Rodin, Paris. Hallowell was not entirely candid with Rodin. His three sculptures, *Cupid and Psyche, The Sphinx,* and *Andromeda,* belonged to no American collector (the premise for works selected for this show), and because they were sufficiently controversial, they were removed from view and could be seen only by special request (*Chicago Tribune,* 17 May 1893, 3).

201. The history of the Executive Committee on Awards is somewhat obscure prior to Thacher's appointment (*Chicago Herald,* 12 Aug. 1893, 1). In the summer of 1890 the commission asked journalist Robert Porter to present a plan for an awards system (*Plan for the Organization of a Bureau of Awards for the World's Columbian Exposition, September 12, 1890,* microfilm, National Museum of American History, Smithsonian Institution). In November 1891 a subcommittee of the Executive Committee was asked to review the awards system used in former international expositions "with reference to their demonstrated excellencies and short comings" (Thomas W. Palmer, "Final Report," Part I, 86). Thacher's actions as chairman can be followed in "Letters Sent by Executive Committee on Awards," Record Group 56, Entry 509, vol. 1 (Oct. 1892–Apr. 1893), NA, and in the "Minutes of the Executive Committee on Awards: November–December 1892," Record Group 56, Entry 508, NA. See also John T. Dickinson, "World's Columbian Exposition. Final Report." Ives's conflict with Thacher over the jury system was reported as early as October 1892 (*Chicago Herald,* 11 Oct. 1892). Unreported in the press was Thacher's plan to "make up a jury among connoisseurs and collectors . . . among whom Messrs Marquand and Walters had been mentioned" (Ives to Kurtz, 26 Oct. 1892). The unpublished paper by NPG intern Judy Shindel, "Fair Reward: Art and Argument," in the NMAA/NPG library's World's Columbian Exposition files, provides an in-depth look at the awards system at the fair and served as the basis for many of the references that follow in this essay.

202. Thacher to Smalley, 4 Nov. 1892, "Letters Sent," 42–43. See also "Investigations of the Management of the World's Columbian Exposition Hearings," Record Group 133, HR 52 A F3.5 (ca. Feb./Mar. 1892), 1599, NA. For a discussion of the awards system at the 1876 Centennial, see Susan Hobbs, *1876: American Art of the Centennial* (Washington, D.C.: Smithsonian Institution Press, 1976), 12.

203. Thacher to the Indicator Company, Chicago, "Letters Sent," 23 Nov. 1892, 108–9, and 18 Jan. 1893, 248. For a discussion of the jury system at the 1889 exhibition, see Annette Blaugrund, "Behind the Scenes: The Organization of the American Paintings," 27–29, in Blaugrund, ed., *Paris 1889.*

204. The *Chicago Tribune,* 4 Apr. 1893, 6, reported that the proposed budget for the awards process at the fair was $570,000. This amount was only about $100,000 less than the cost of the art building.

205. Thacher to the Hon. Levi K. Fuller, "Letters Sent," 17 Nov. 1892, 90; Thacher to George R. Davis, "Letters Sent," 7 Nov. 1892, 51–53.

206. Ives to Kurtz, 19, 30 Dec. 1892.

207. *Inter-Ocean,* Chicago, 14 Jan. 1893, 5.

208. *New York Times,* 27 Aug. 1893, 16.

209. Foreign exhibitors were just as outspoken as their American counterparts (*New York Times,* 27 Aug. 1893, 16). France, Belgium, Norway, and Russia were among the countries that refused to be bound by Thacher's rule and withdrew their art from competition (*Chicago Herald,* 4 Aug. 1893, 9; 12 Aug. 1893, 1).

210. *New York Times,* 27 Aug. 1893, 16.

211. Department of Fine Arts, ed., *Revised Catalogue,* 10–12, 23–24. The *Chicago Tribune,* 27 Aug. 1893, 12, stated that Thacher's system had "a pitiable" outcome where it applied to the Fine Arts Department.

212. *Chicago Tribune,* 27 Aug. 1893, 12.

213. *Chicago Tribune,* 22 May 1893, 1; 24 May 1891, 1; 28 May 1893, 3; 31 May 1893, 1.

214. "Minutes of Meeting of The International Committee of Judges in the

Department of Fine Arts (K)," Manuscript. Record Group 56, Entry 512, National Archive, 3–4.

215. *Chicago Herald,* 18 July 1893, 1; *New York Times,* 19 July 1893, 4. The fine arts judges also clashed with Thacher over the issue of awards for art in the Women's Building. The committee, with Ives—no champion of women's rights—as one of the most outspoken protagonists, stated (not quite accurately) that because the art in that building had not been passed by any of the pre-fair juries (a requirement for entry into the American art exhibits) or, in some instances, had "been rejected by them," these works were "not proper subject for examination for award by this committee." In the end, however, the committee capitulated and judged not only art in the Woman's Building but also art that was exhibited in such unlikely places as the Midway ("Minutes," 16–17, 20–23, 31, 34–36).

216. Thacher to Britton, "Letters Sent," 9 Mar. 1893, 470. Not all American artists were displeased with Thacher's efforts. Edgar S. Cameron, a Chicago artist who showed in the Fine Arts Palace but did not win an award, supported Thacher's system, believing that "a single juryman naturally would be extremely careful that he should not be reproached for any injustice or favoritism," but admitted that "artists did not wish to give up the old shifty, wire-pulling politics" (Edgar Spier Cameron Papers, AAA, roll 4292, frame 127).

217. *Chicago Herald,* 12 July 1893, 3. Eventually "westerners" Henry F. Farny, the Cincinnati artist who had been on the national jury, and Mary Hallock Foote were named to serve.

218. *New York Times,* 20 July 1893, 5; *Chicago Herald,* 4 Aug. 1893, 9; "Minutes," 11 Aug. 1893, 37–41. The few records that identify award recipients do not necessarily agree. Fourteen more names are listed in the awards section of the Department of Fine Arts, ed., *Revised Catalogue,* 14–15 than appear in the individual proofs at the National Archives ("Awards of the World's Columbian Exposition, 1893," Record Group 43, vol. 38, entry 578). For additional information, see the *Final Report of Executive Committee of Awards, World's Columbian Commission* (Washington, D.C.: John F. Sheiry, 1895), the *Report of the Committee on Awards of the World's Columbian Commission,* vols. 1, 2 (Washington, D.C.: Government Printing Office, 1901), as well as the bibliographic listing in this publication under the manuscript entry for the National Archives.

219. A history of the diploma can be partially reconstructed in the letters of Thacher (Thacher to Charles Foster, 23 Dec. 1892, "Letters Sent," 191–92; Thacher to Smalley, 14 Apr. 1893, 699–700; Thacher to Low, 19 Apr. 1893, 758; A. M. Britton to Claude M. Johnson, Superintendent, Bureau of Engraving and Printing, 4 Jan. 1895). Pertinent newspaper articles include the *Chicago Tribune,* 27 Apr. 1893, 1; *New-York Daily Tribune,* 30 June 1893, 2; and *Chicago Herald,* 15 Aug. 1893, 9, which contains an extensive description of the diploma. Will H. Low's original artwork for the diploma is in the archive of the Bureau of Engraving and Printing. For an early history of the medal, see Thacher to E. O. Leech (director of the Mint), 10 Oct. 1892, "Letters Sent," 10–11; Thacher to J. M. Forbes (chairman of the Shaw Monument Committee), 29 Oct. 1892, 14–16, 19; Thacher to Saint-Gaudens, 4 Dec. 1892, 146–47; and Thacher to Charles Foster (Treasury Department), 23 Dec. 1892, 191–92. For the controversy surrounding the design, see *New York Times,* 20 Jan. 1894, 4; 21 Jan. 1894, 1; 28 Jan. 1894, 9; and 28 Mar. 1894, 1, as well as John H. Dryfhout, *The Work of Augustus Saint-Gaudens* (Boston and London: University Press of New England, 1982), 151, 201–2. The National Numismatic Collection at the National Museum of American History, Smithsonian Institution, has a galvano of the rejected design. A copy of the final medal, given to Edmund Tarbell, is also in this collection.

220. Palmer, "Final Report," 94; the *New York Times,* 28 Apr. 1896, 1, reported that distribution of the medals had begun the previous day. Thacher's role with the awards committee diminished greatly after the close of the fair. Most of the final work of the committee was left to A. T. Britton, the commissioner from Washington, D.C.

221. The *Chicago Tribune,* 1 Nov. 1893, 4, estimated the attendance during the 179 days the fair was open at over 21 million; Johnson, *A History,* vol. 1, 364–65.

222. Kurtz to Kurtz, 30 June, 28 July, 3 Aug. 1893. For a lengthy complaint against the alphabetical catalogues published by the art department, see Elizabeth Arnold, "The Art Catalogue of the World's Fair," *Woman's Progress in Literature, Science Art, Education and Politics* 2, no. 1 (Oct. 1893): 16–19. The *Chicago Tribune,* 16 July 1893, 14, mentions that a revised catalogue listing works as installed in the exhibition is about to be issued, but this does not appear to have taken place until after the awards were made by the jury.

223. Kurtz to Kurtz, 9 June 1893; Kurtz to William H. Howe, 9 June 1893; J. Francis Murphy to Kurtz, 21 Aug. 1893; Douglas Volk to Kurtz, 23 Oct. 1893; Benoni Irwin to Kurtz, 26 Dec. 1893; Harrison S. Morris to Mrs. Kurtz, 13 July 1893.

224. Kurtz to Kurtz, 3 Aug. 1893.

225. Hallowell to Palmer, 20 Dec. 1893, AIC.

226. Higinbotham, *Report of the President,* 274.

227. F. D. Millet, "Conventions and Possibilities of Art in the United States," delivered before the faculty of Yale University, 1 June 1904 (Millet Papers, AAA, roll 1099, frame 548).

228. Kurtz, for instance, became the assistant to the American Commissioner of Fine Arts, John R. Cauldwell, at the 1900 Paris Universal Exposition, but took ill before he could assume his responsibilities (*Report of The Commissioner-General for the United States to the International Universal Exposition, Paris, 1900,* vol. 2 [Washington, D.C.: Government Printing Office, 1901], 516).

Color Plates
The 1993 Exhibition

Portraying America's History

The World's Columbian Exposition celebrated 400 years of progress since Columbus's voyage. Art, considered the highest expression of civilization, played a key role in presenting the nation's history from the perspective of the fair planners. Indeed, they believed that the demonstration of America's new accomplishments in the aesthetic realm would in part persuade viewers that the nation had completed the civilizing process begun by Columbus.

Many American artworks shown at the fair depicted historic events and figures from colonial to contemporary times. Rarely history paintings in the grand manner, they were instead more concerned with individual lives than with momentous events. At first glance many works fit more comfortably into genre, landscape, or portrait traditions. Even though their relationship to history is often oblique, it is no less potent. By not appearing to be intentionally didactic, these works could more subtly reinforce certain cultural and social themes, presenting the historic past as an appropriate prelude to America's future.

The underlying message was the idea of the nation's progress from simple, quaint beginnings to a level of supreme accomplishment in industry and the arts. Artists told the story by drawing on such literary figures as John Alden and Antony Van Corlear, recalling the Puritan and Knickerbocker settlers. These paintings abound in details of costume and domestic furnishings, evidence of the colonial revival that swept the nation in the 1880s and 1890s, which in turn signaled a new fascination with the country's early days.

Such charmingly anecdotal works were balanced by images showing America as an advanced nation ready for a leadership role in world affairs. Artworks referring to naval heroism and triumphs, for example, took many forms but always served to ennoble the subject. An invented "historic" view of Henry Hudson entering New York Harbor paralleled Columbus's voyage to the New World, and the imposing ships of the White Squadron, which encircled the globe proclaiming America's naval prowess in the 1890s, signaled expansionist military adventures to come.

In general, problematic subjects in history were glossed over or ignored by artists at the fair, but occasionally they are presented as inevitable if regrettable aspects of America's predestined march toward civilization. Thus Olin Levi Warner's medallions of Columbia River Indians are devoid of any reference to the bloody Indian wars so recently concluded; rather, they present these Indians as noble warriors in defeat, reminiscent of ancient Greeks or Romans. This reluctance to acknowledge ambivalent aspects of recent American history was typical of the fair, which was overwhelmingly celebratory in spirit.

Having studied in European academies to master traditional techniques, American artists sought to apply their skills to depicting events in the nation's past that would foretell future greatness. The nineteenth century, often called the "Age of History," witnessed the flourishing of this discipline, from the work of G. W. F. Hegel and Karl Marx in Europe to Francis Parkman, Charles A. Beard, and Frederick Jackson Turner in America. This keen sense of connection to the past lay behind the idea of staging an exposition honoring Columbus's voyage. Taken together, the paintings and sculptures with American historical themes can be considered an early attempt to sketch a national identity for Americans that would serve their future ambitions.

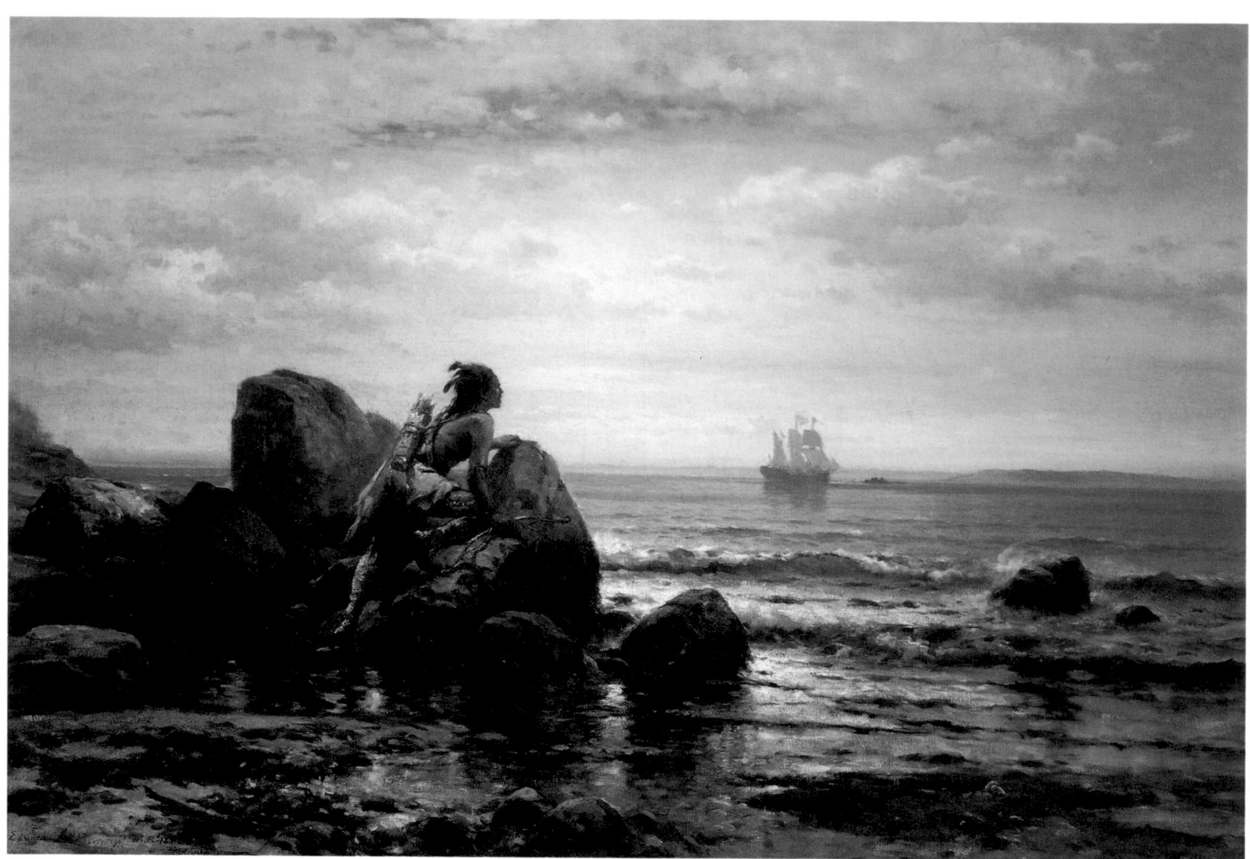

Plate 1.
Edward Moran,
The First Ship Entering New York Harbor, 1892.
The Berkshire Museum, Pittsfield, MA.

At the south end of Staten Island, an American Indian is depicted looking across Raritan Bay toward Sandy Hook on 11 September 1609, witnessing the historic and ultimately fateful approach of Henry Hudson's ship, the *Half Moon*. At the time of the 1893 exposition, Hudson's discovery of New York was directly linked to the celebration of Columbus's landing and the ensuing development of the New World. Unlike Columbus's landings, however, Hudson's soon led to trading expeditions, permanent colonization, and the founding of New York.

This painting and *The White Squadron's Farewell Salute to Commodore John Ericsson*, also shown at the fair, were part of a series of thirteen historical paintings by Edward Moran representing important epochs in the maritime history of the United States. The series also included the *Debarkation of Columbus*, not exhibited at the fair. These paintings reflect the importance then given to naval power on the world scene.

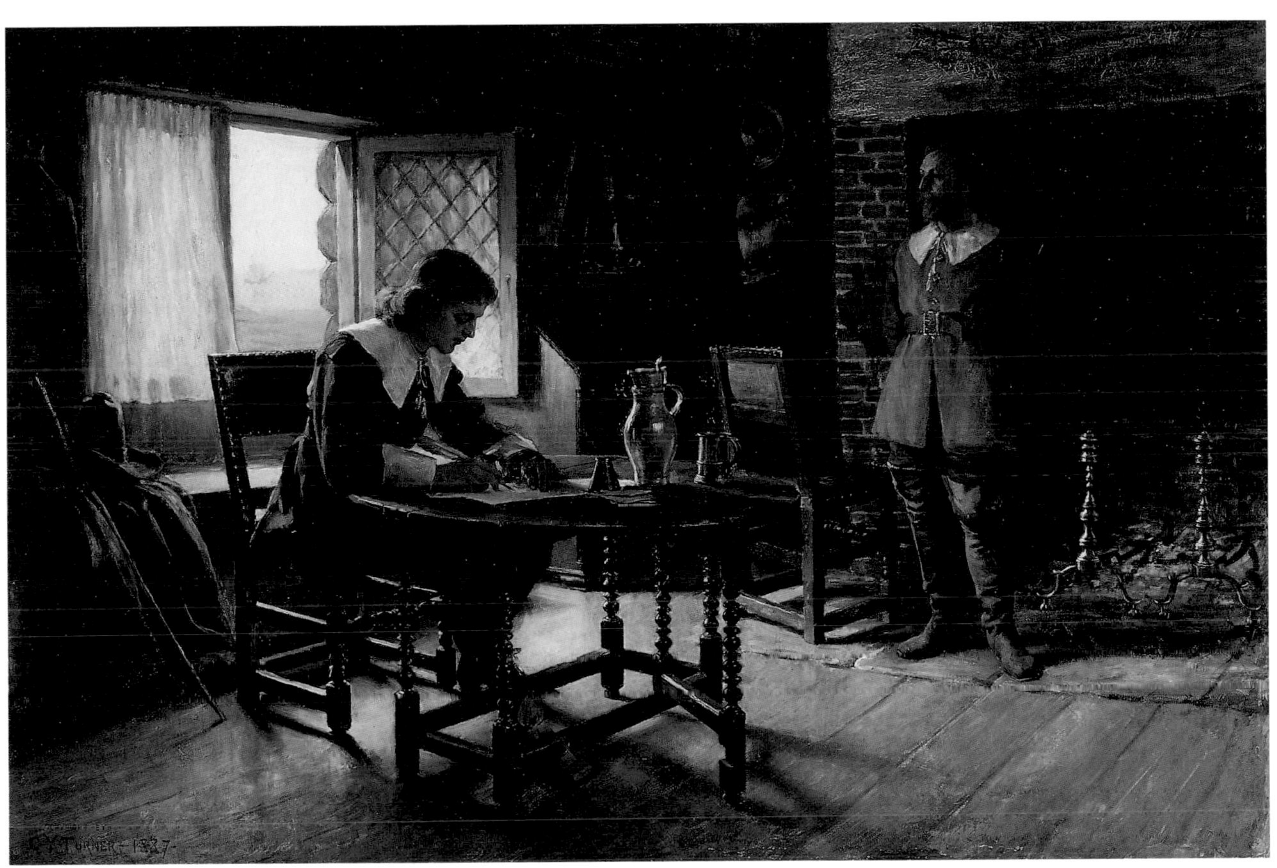

Plate 2.
C. Y. Turner,
John Alden's Letter, ca. 1888.
Union League Club of Chicago.

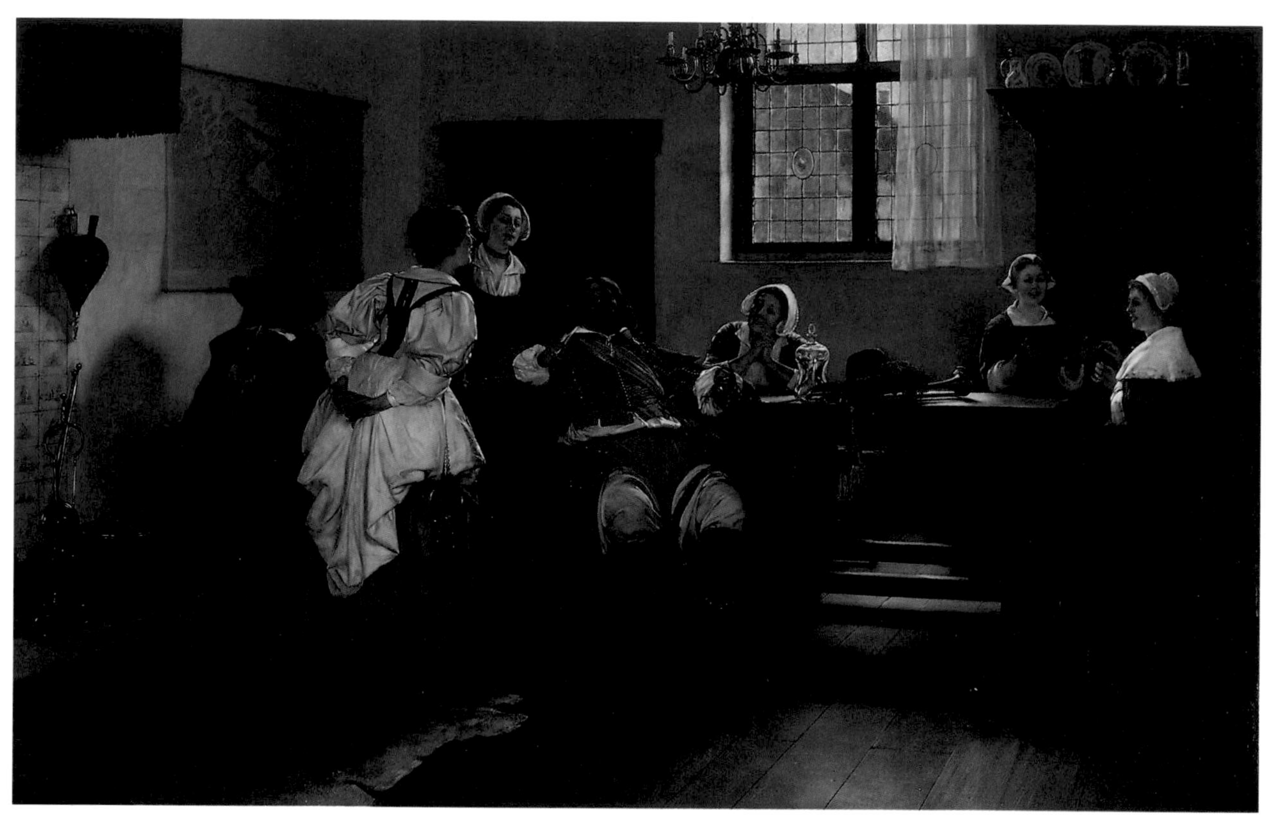

Plate 3.
F. D. Millet,
Antony Van Corlear, the Trumpeter, ca. 1889.
The Duquesne Club, Pittsburgh, PA.

Millet, like many other artists during this period, chose to portray a scene derived from a literary source. *Antony Van Corlear, the Trumpeter* is based on an episode in Washington Irving's *A History of New-York*, first published in 1809. Though a fictional account of the founding of New York City by Dutch settlers, the book and Millet's painting were based on fact. The picture, containing known historical figures and costumes, would have been viewed as largely accurate by fair-goers. According to a *Harper's Weekly* critic, the painting "relates so closely to the history of New York under the quaintest conditions of its earlier life, that it should become a public possession." As the critic relates, the past has become quainter, and more idealized, through fiction.

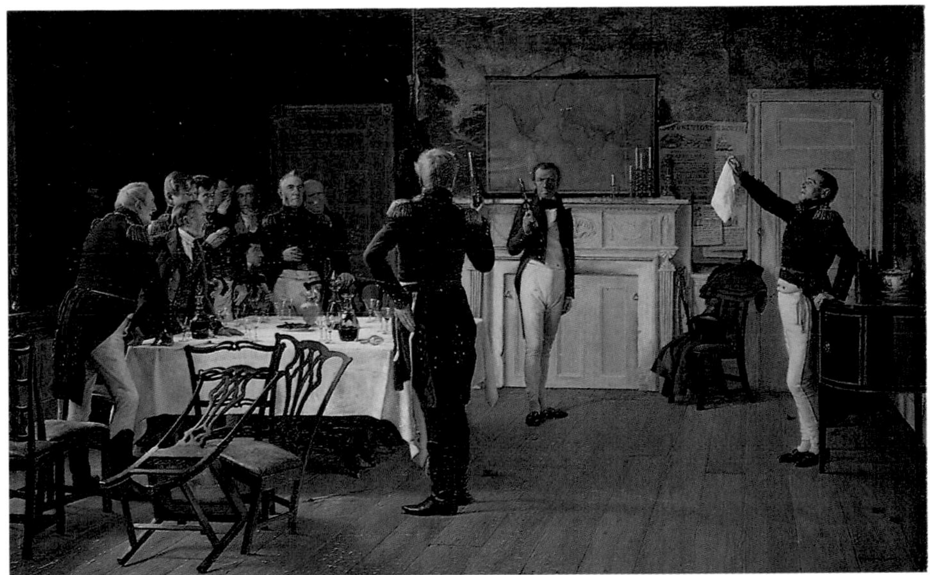

Plate 4.
Frederick James,
An Impromptu Affair in the Days of "The Code," ca. 1890.
The Museum of Fine Arts,
Springfield, MA.

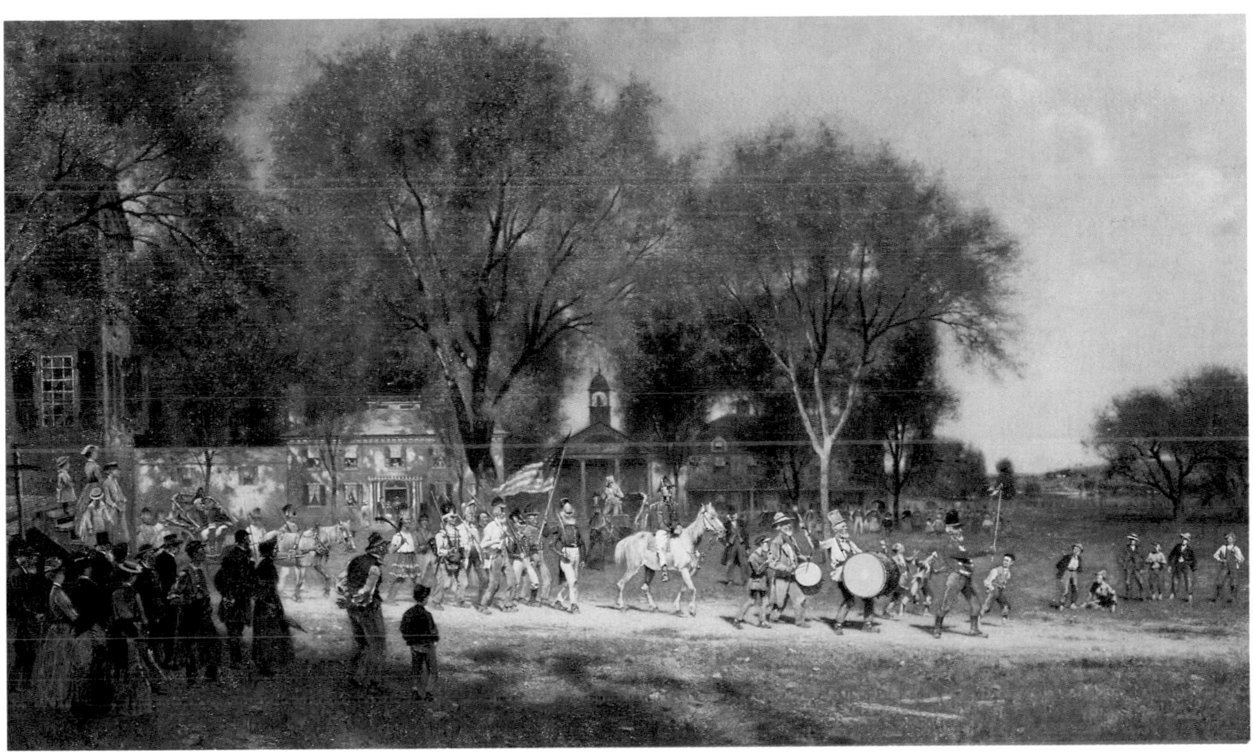

Plate 5.
A. C. Howland,
Fourth of July Parade, ca. 1886.
Private Collection.

Plate 6.
Gilbert Gaul,
Charging the Battery, ca. 1882.
The New-York Historical
Society, New York City.

Plate 7.
William T. Trego,
The Pursuit, 1885.
Private Collection.

This picture was painted from a sketch made near the battlefield of Cedar Creek in the Shenandoah Valley in Virginia. Major General Philip H. Sheridan is shown commanding the Union cavalry in hot pursuit of the retreating Confederates on the valley turnpike road to Winchester on 19 October 1864. The force of Sheridan's charge leaves little doubt about the outcome of the battle and, symbolically, the war. The painting therefore also becomes a reminder of the nation's unity and strength as it prepared to bid for a position of world leadership toward the end of the nineteenth century.

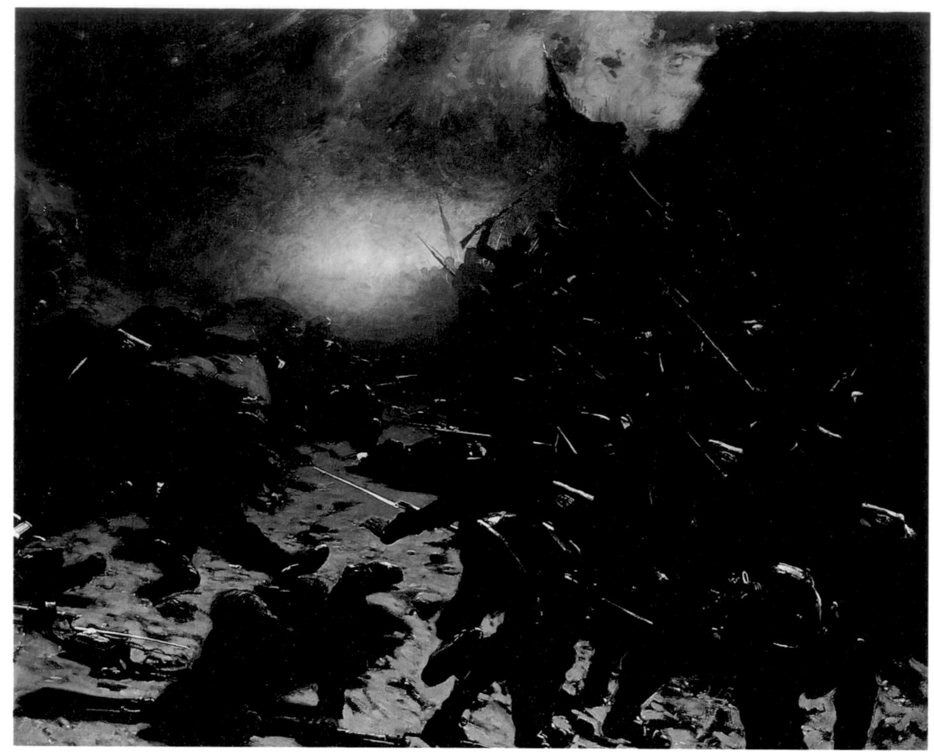

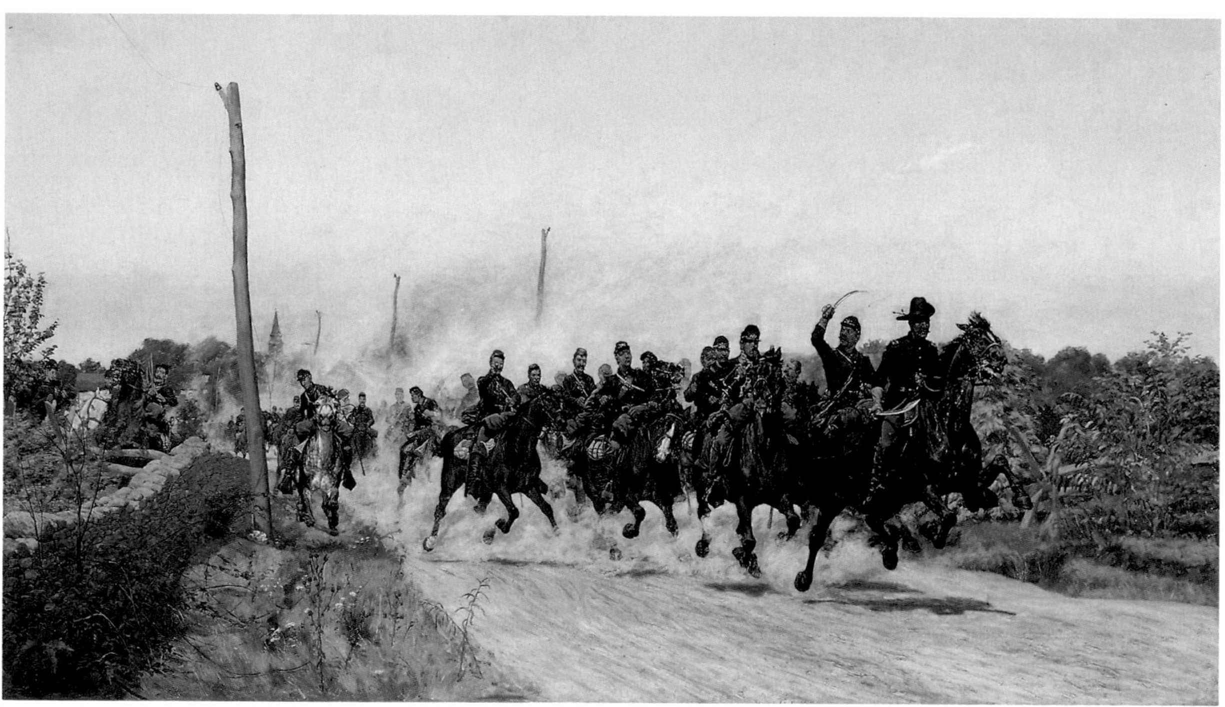

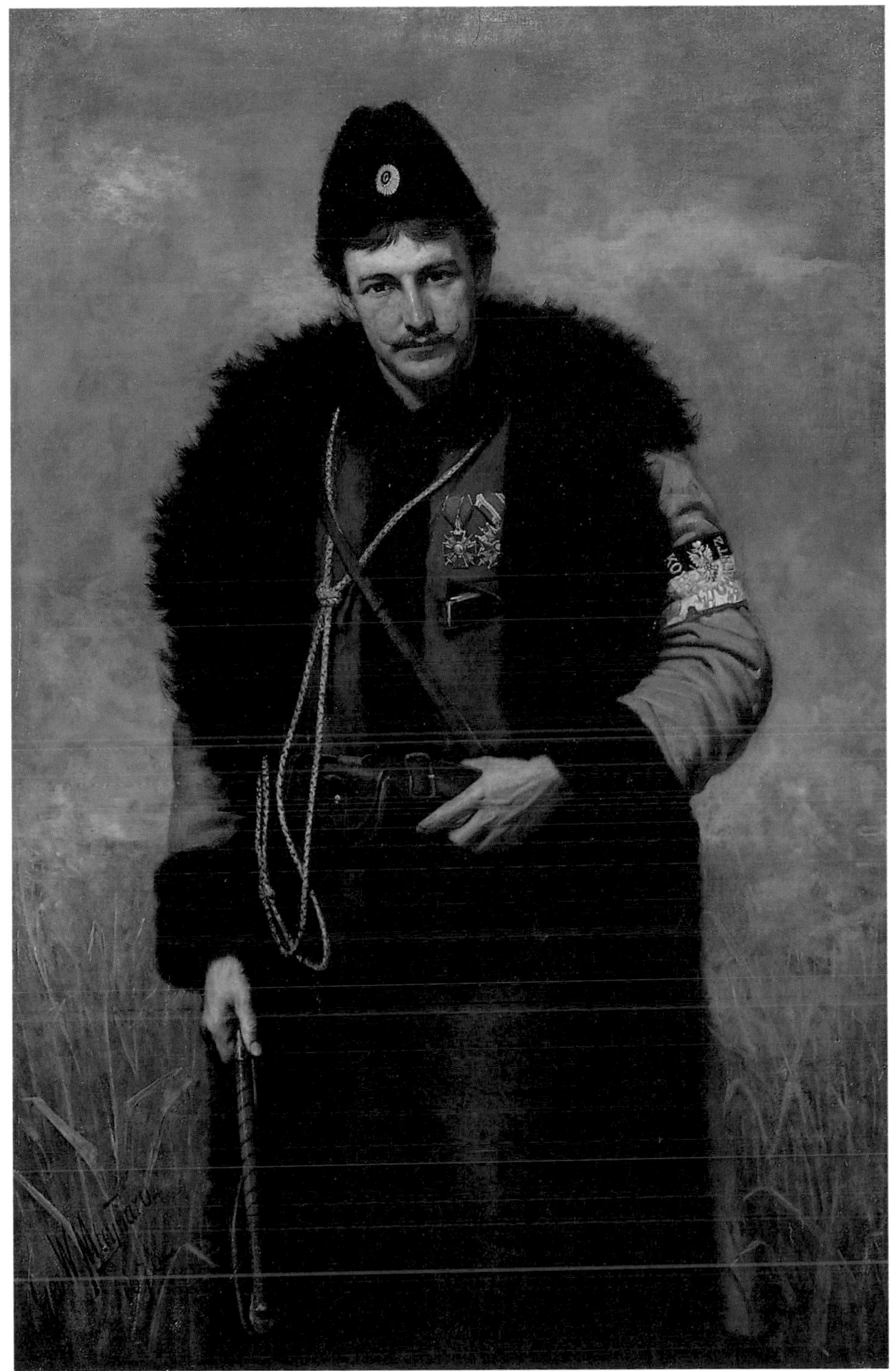

Plate 8.
George Willoughby Maynard,
Portrait of F. D. Millet, 1878.
National Portrait Gallery,
Smithsonian Institution.

In this portrait Maynard has depicted his good friend and fellow painter, not with the tools of his usual trade but in his role as a foreign correspondent during the 1877 Russo-Turkish War. Millet is shown wearing the military uniform of the Russian troops whom he reported on while serving as a correspondent at the front for the *New York Herald* and *London Daily News* and as an artist for the *London Graphic*. Both the artist and his subject were active participants at the fair, exhibiting works in the Fine Arts Palace and also contributing to the larger decorative program of the exposition. As director of decorations and functions, Millet oversaw the production of the numerous mural paintings that enlivened the walls and ceilings of several official buildings. Maynard created a mural for the Agriculture Building, while Millet executed another for the New York State Building. During the course of the fair, Millet also assumed charge of the outdoor amusements, such as parades, swimming contests, and fireworks displays.

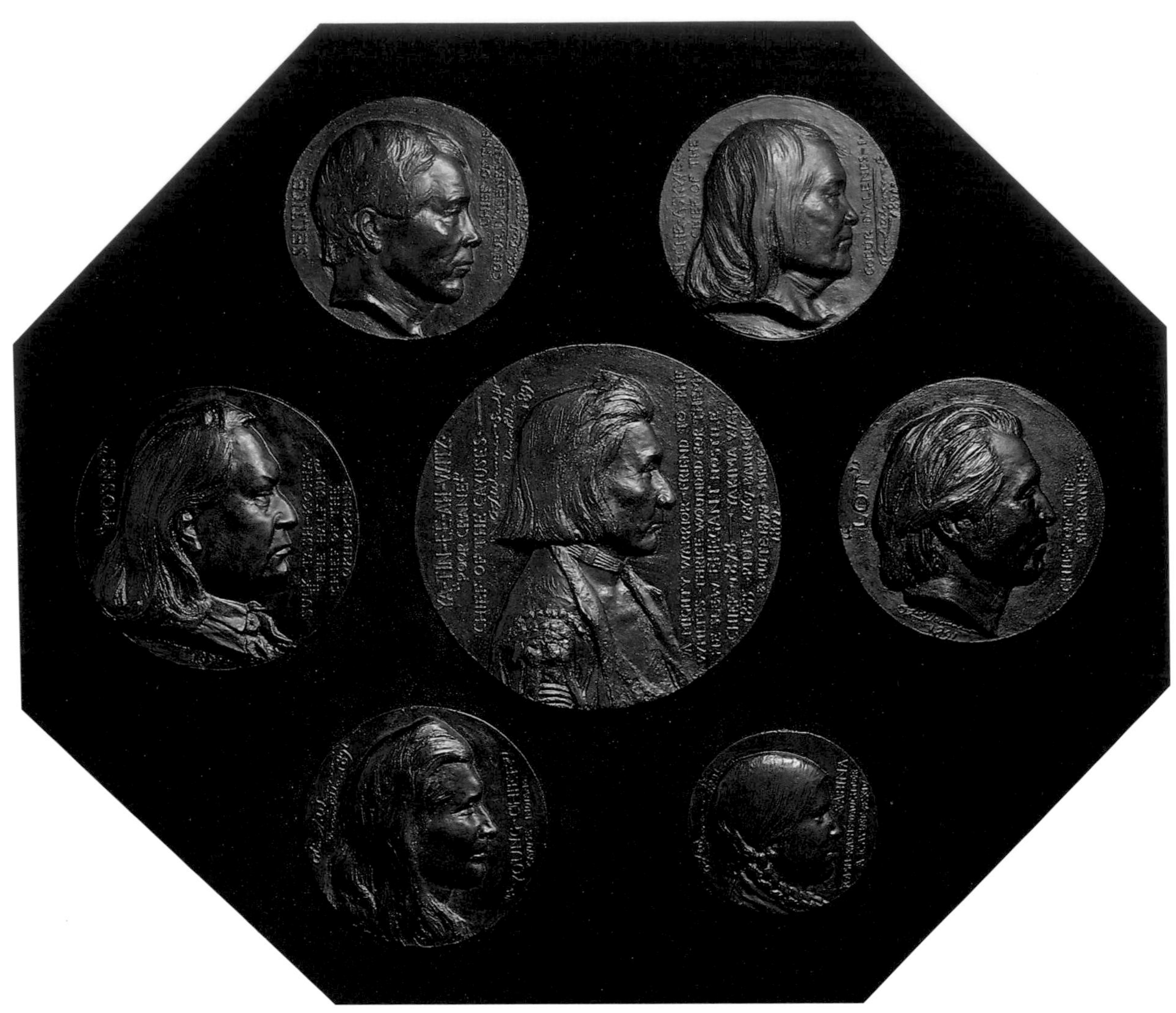

Plate 9.
Olin Levi Warner,
Medallions of Columbia River Indians, 1891.
National Museum of American Art, Smithsonian Institution.

On a trip to the Northwest, Warner modeled each of these portraits from life in the incredibly brief period of one or two hours. These images of Native Americans must have seemed all the more poignant after nearly a century of the devastating subjugation and defeat of these people, as well as the recent closing of the frontier that had been their home. The reliefs, in the tradition of Italian Renaissance medallions but larger, may be viewed as both ethnological records and artistic portrayals commemorating the nobility of Native Americans.

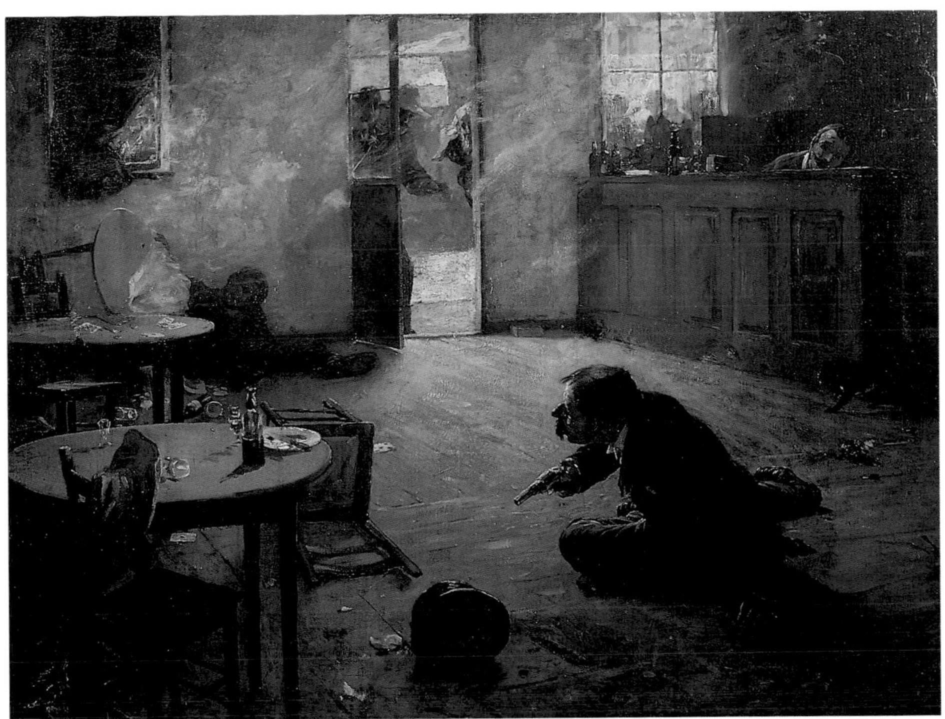

Plate 10.
William R. Leigh,
The End of the Play, 1892.
Collection John J. McMullen.
Photograph by Wayne Geist.

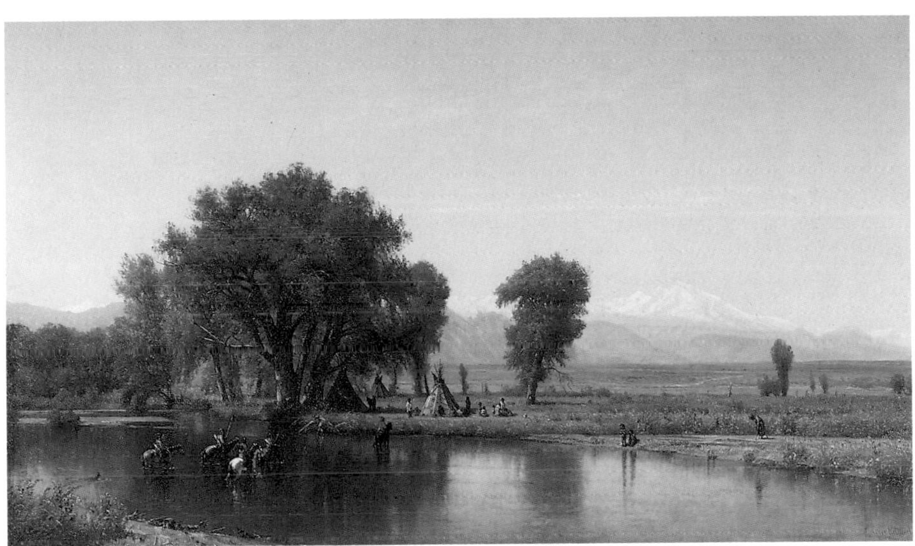

Plate 11.
Worthington Whittredge,
The Plains, 1868–70.
The Century Association, New York.

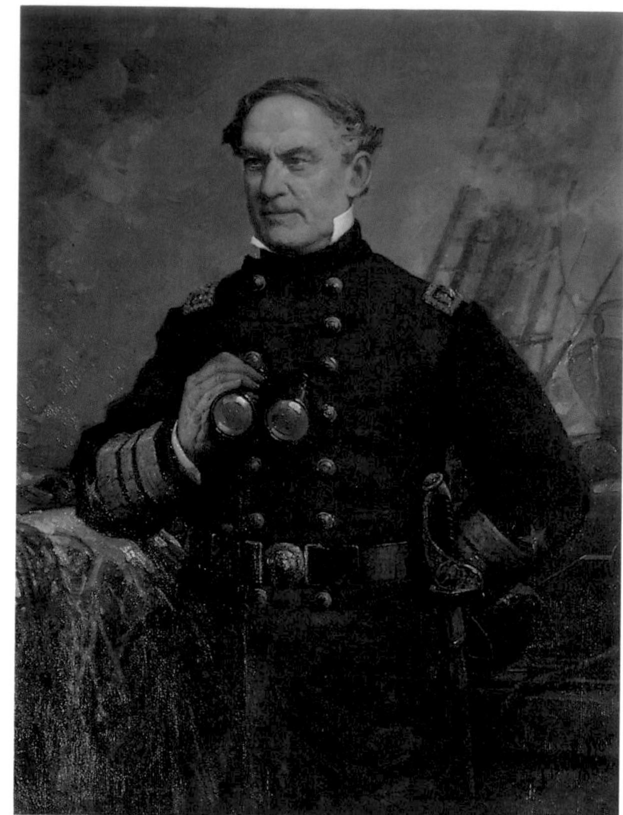

Plate 12.
John F. Weir,
Portrait of Admiral Farragut,
1889.
The University Club,
New York, NY.

Renowned for his ingenuity and courage during the Civil War, Admiral David Farragut was one of the most famous heroes in American naval history. By the end of the nineteenth century, the legendary Farragut had become a popular symbol of American patriotism. Although he died in 1870, artistic tributes to his heroism continued to be fashioned throughout the remainder of the century, including prominent public statues in New York, Washington, and Boston. Admiral Farragut's exploits also made their way into the popular verses of Oliver Wendell Holmes and Henry Howard Brownell and prompted a biography by naval historian Alfred Thayer Mahan in 1892. Portraying Farragut in full regalia, standing with consummate poise and confidence on the deck of his battleship, Weir's likeness clearly captures the officer's aura of power and authority.

Plate 13.
Edward Moran,
The White Squadron's Farewell Salute to Commodore John Ericsson, ca. 1891.
United States Naval Academy Museum.

Moran's picture strikes an elegiac note as it memorializes the funeral cortege conveying the remains of renowned naval engineer and inventor John Ericsson back to his native Sweden in 1890. Leading the procession is the gleaming white hull of the *Baltimore*, one of the navy's late-model protected cruisers, lent to the cortege by the U.S. government as a tribute to Ericsson's contributions to American naval technology. The armed cruisers of the White Squadron loomed as tangible evidence of the beginning of a new era in American naval history and expansionist foreign policy, as American diplomacy in the 1890s underwent the transition from a continental focus to a global framework. Ericsson's fame rested on his development of the ironclad battleship for the Union navy during the Civil War. His first experimental ironclad, the *Monitor*, had emerged as the victor in a much lauded gun duel with the Confederate frigate *Merrimac* at Hampton Roads, Virginia, in 1862. Ericsson's contributions to technology also included the invention of the screw propeller in 1837.

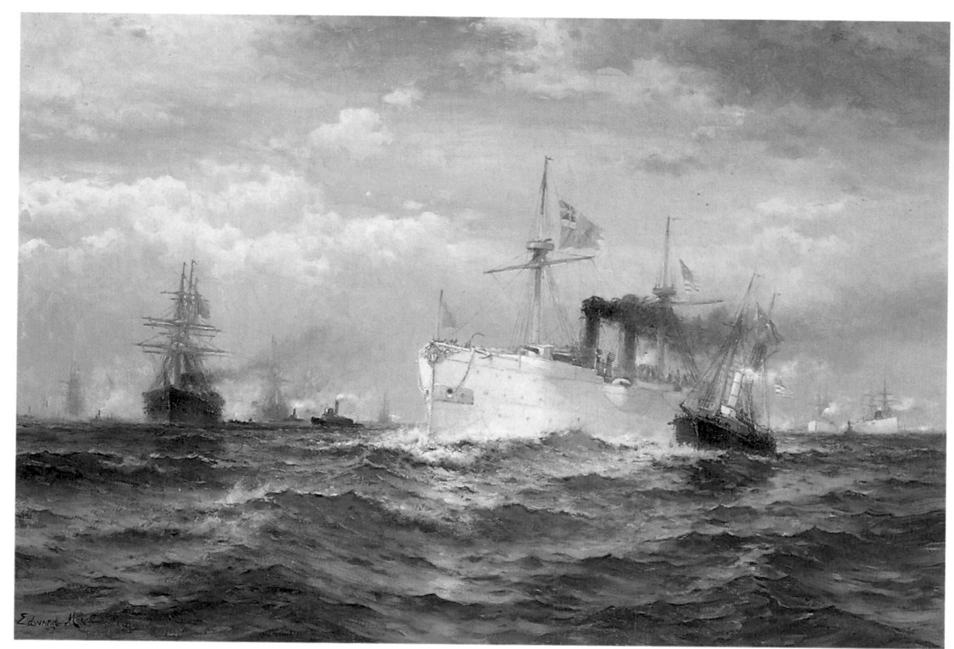

Cycles of Nature, Cycles of Life

Images focusing on the dependable cadences of the seasons, the times of day, and the predictable rhythms of the human life cycle emphasize continuity rather than progress. They convey the nostalgia people felt for an earlier, more dependable or familiar way of life and their apprehensions about rapid social change in post-Civil War America.

Whereas the history paintings highlight the male-dominated public arenas, these depictions focus on the domestic sphere where women predominate. In all epochs, cyclical patterns in life and nature are related to themes of reproduction and periodicity commonly associated with women, but the decades immediately preceding the fair are particularly significant for women, as they witnessed the birth of modern feminism. It was a time when many women began to assert themselves in the public aspects of life. Nonetheless, perhaps in response to changing gender roles, many artists (both male and female) reinforced the traditional view of women as daughters, wives, and mothers, whose special realm was the home—the temple of traditional values. Alice D. Kellogg's *The Mother*, Gari Melchers's *Married*, and Thomas Hovenden's *Bringing Home the Bride*, are among the works that restated traditional feminine subjects for a modern audience.

Portraits and genre scenes in the Fine Arts Palace embodied every phase of life from pregnancy to old age. Paralleling these images, landscapes emphasized ideas of stability and continuity—reassuring rhythms for a culture trying to adjust to mass immigration, transition from a rural to an urban economy, territorial expansionism, and extreme fiscal instability. This desire for continuity helps to explain why seasonal landscapes accounted for fully a quarter of the total number of American paintings on view. They were a reassuring contrast to the dynamic insistence on progress elsewhere at the fair, where the rush to use the latest technologies often involved a willed subversion of nature's rhythms.

The landscapes were rarely views of identifiable locations, as had been common before the Civil War. They were "mood" pieces dependent on evocative color, and the mood was often somber, tinged with melancholy. Artists were fascinated by transitional times of day or seasons—twilight, dawn, fall, and spring—and also by the more physically or emotionally chilling aspects of nature, as depicted in Walter Launt Palmer's *An Early Snow*, Winslow Homer's *March Wind*, and Dwight W. Tryon's *Night*. In such veiled but powerful references we find the anxieties of late nineteenth-century American society that were so often left unaddressed in figure or history painting.

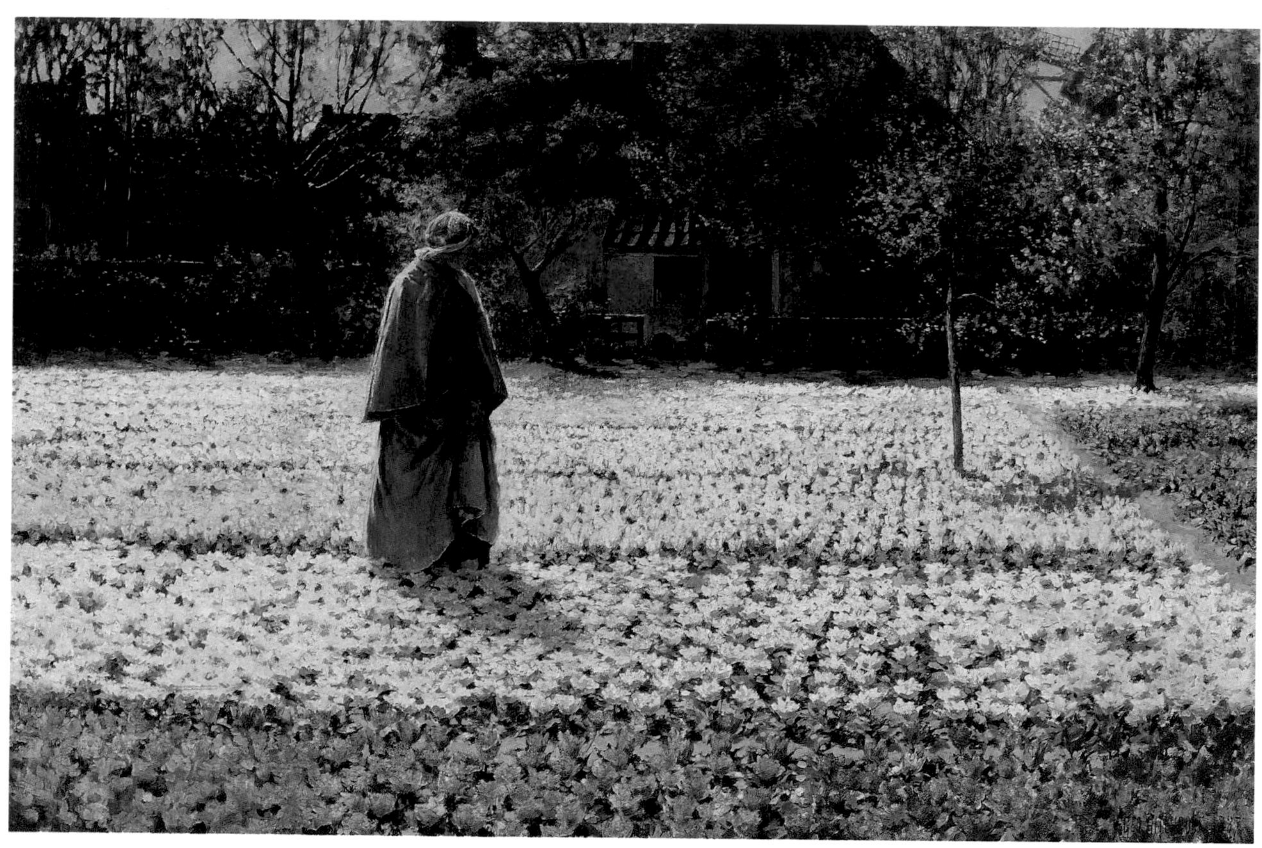

Plate 14.
George Hitchcock,
Tulip Culture, Holland, 1887.
Private Collection.

Last exhibited publicly a century ago, *Tulip Culture, Holland* is one of the many important paintings that have remained hidden in private collections since the fair. When first shown in the 1887 Paris Salon, Hitchcock's work received stunning reviews from the press; an American collector who had not even seen it firsthand immediately cabled to purchase it. The well-known French artist Jean Léon Gérôme praised it as the "best American picture of the year."

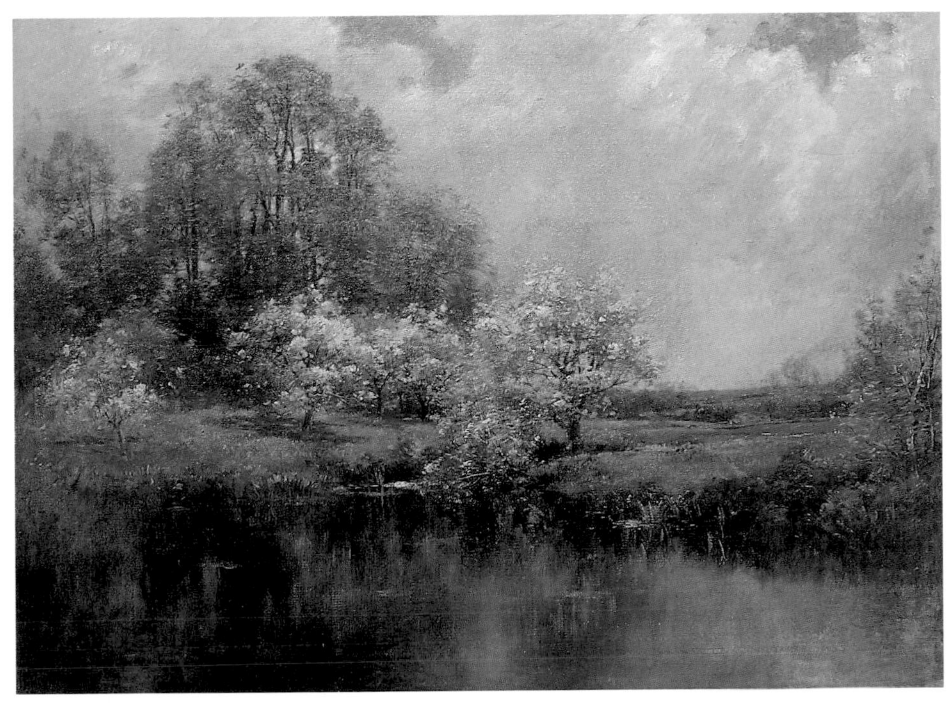

Plate 15.
J. Appleton Brown,
Springtime, n.d.
Collection Mr. and
Mrs. Thomas Rosse.

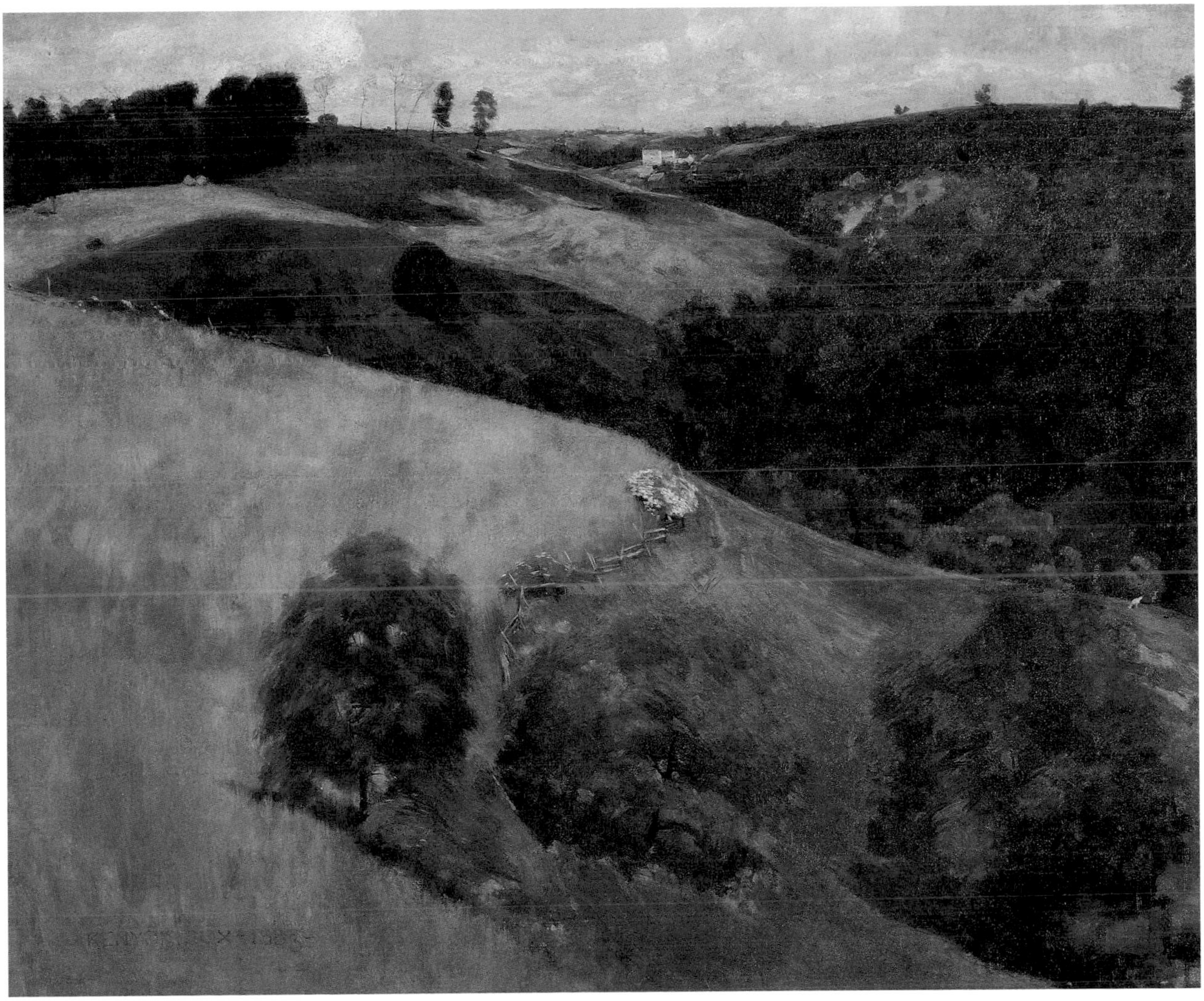

Plate 16.
Kenyon Cox,
Flying Shadows, 1883.
The Corcoran Gallery of Art.

Plate 17.
George Inness,
A Gray Lowery Day, ca. 1877.
Davis Museum and Cultural
Center, Wellesley College.

At the time of the fair, George Inness was lauded by many reviewers as "the dean of the landscape painters" and consistently praised for the indigenous character of his work. He was thus accorded due respect by the exposition's selection committee, who chose fifteen of his canvases for exhibiton—a number matched only by Winslow Homer. Critics were quick to note Inness's thematic loyalty to "the changing moods of nature," a predilection exemplified in this painting.

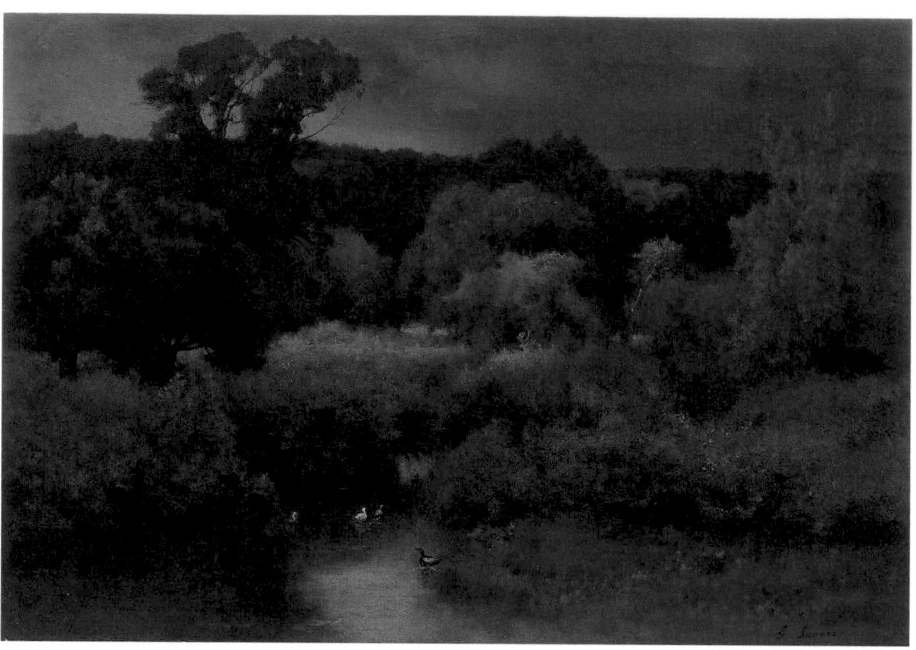

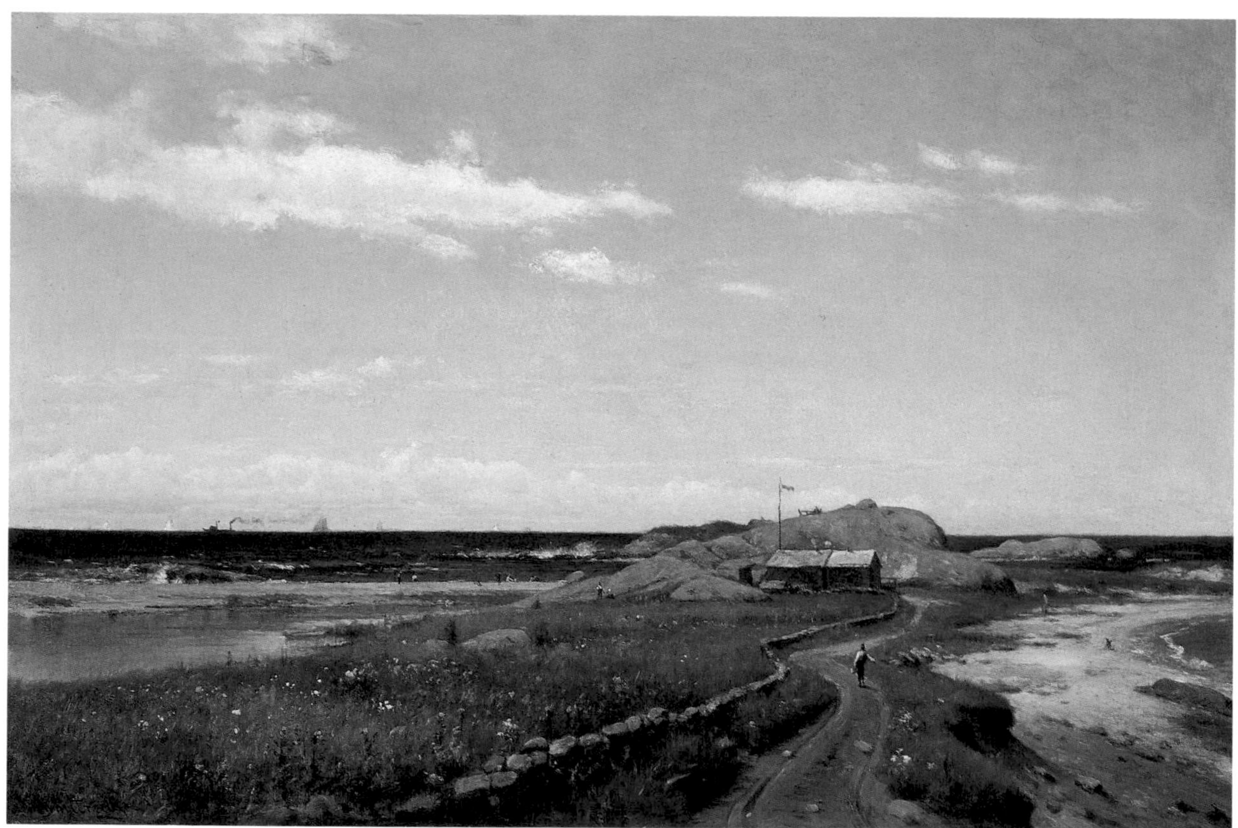

Plate 18.
Worthington Whittredge,
Rhode Island Coast, ca. 1880.
Amon Carter Museum,
Fort Worth.

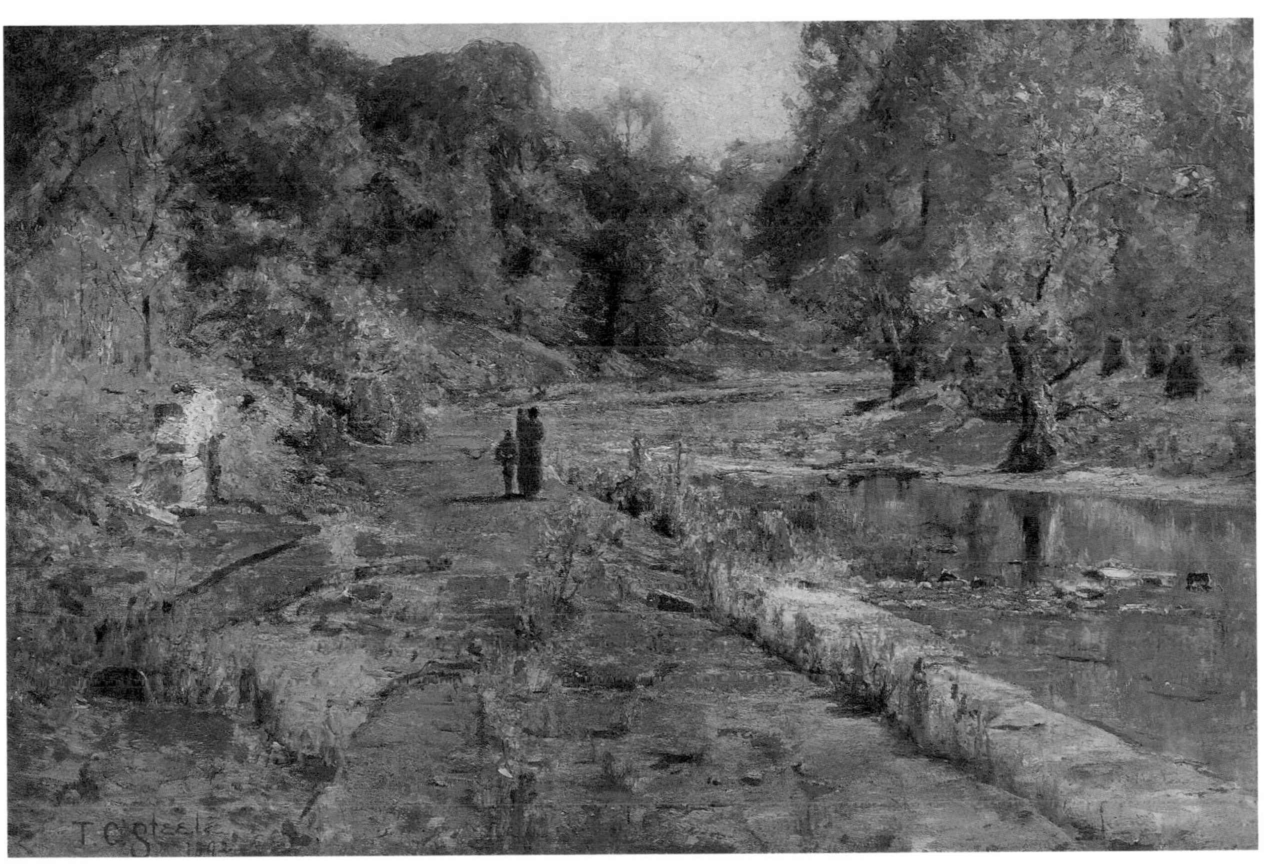

Plate 19.
T. C. Steele,
***On the Muscatatuck*, 1892.**
The Columbia Club Foundation, Indianapolis, IN.
Photograph by John Geiser.

When artworks from the Midwest, South, and West were assembled in Chicago to be judged for inclusion in the Fine Arts Palace, only seventy-three of 638 oil paintings submitted were accepted by the jury. Among these, a single painting, *On the Muscatatuck*, was given the highest "number one" rating. Jury member Henry Farny noted that "the majority of the jury seemed inclined to impressionism," and "the only picture that received the number one vote, was a landscape by a man from Indianapolis, T. C. Steele . . . whom no one had ever heard of."

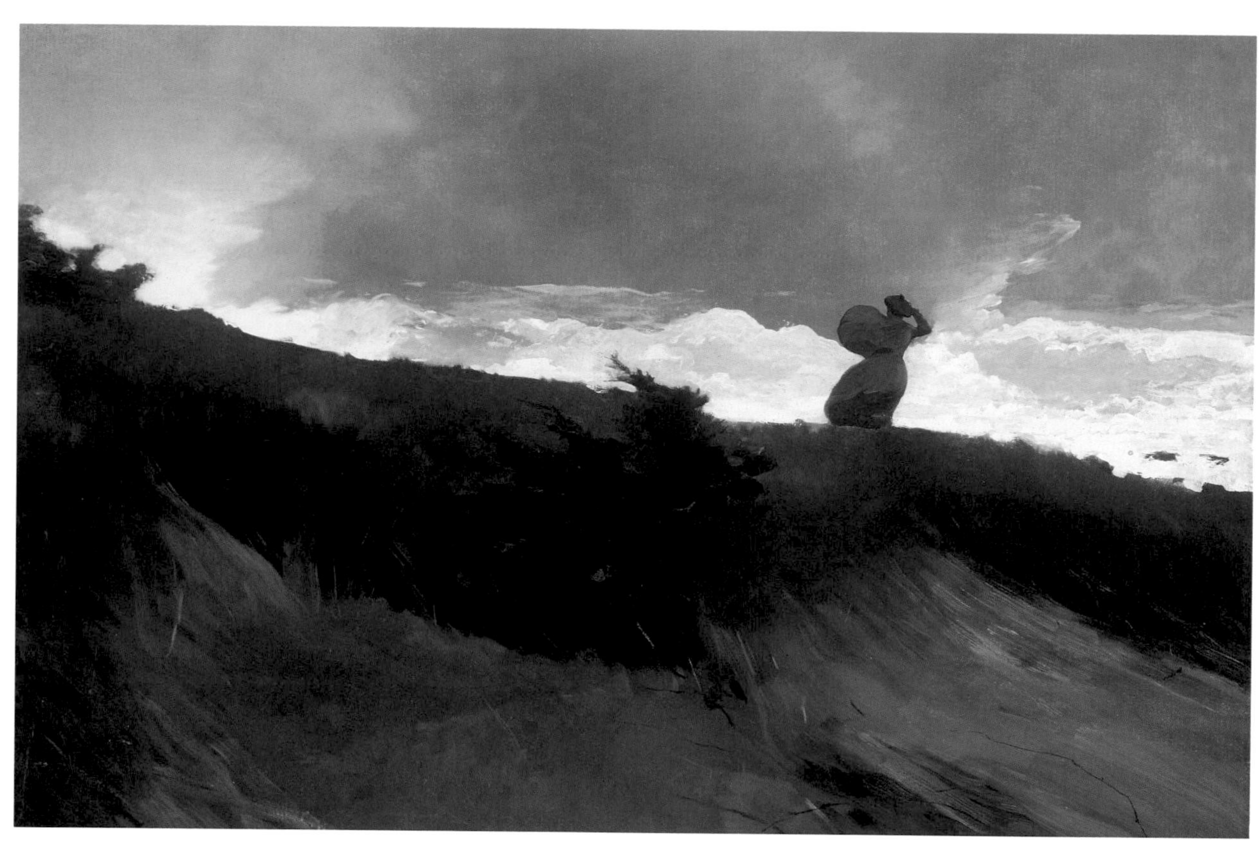

Plate 20.
Winslow Homer,
March Wind, 1891.
©Addison Gallery of American Art, Phillips Academy, Andover, MA. All Rights Reserved.

Plate 21.
George Inness,
September Afternoon, 1877.
National Museum of American Art, Smithsonian Institution.

Plate 22.
George Inness,
Winter Morning, 1882.
The Montclair Art Museum.

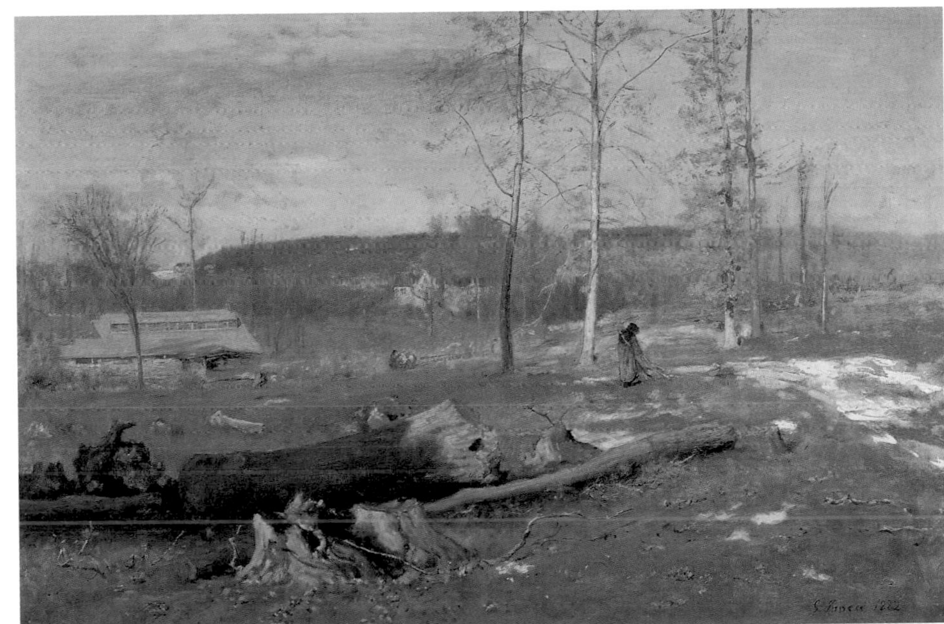

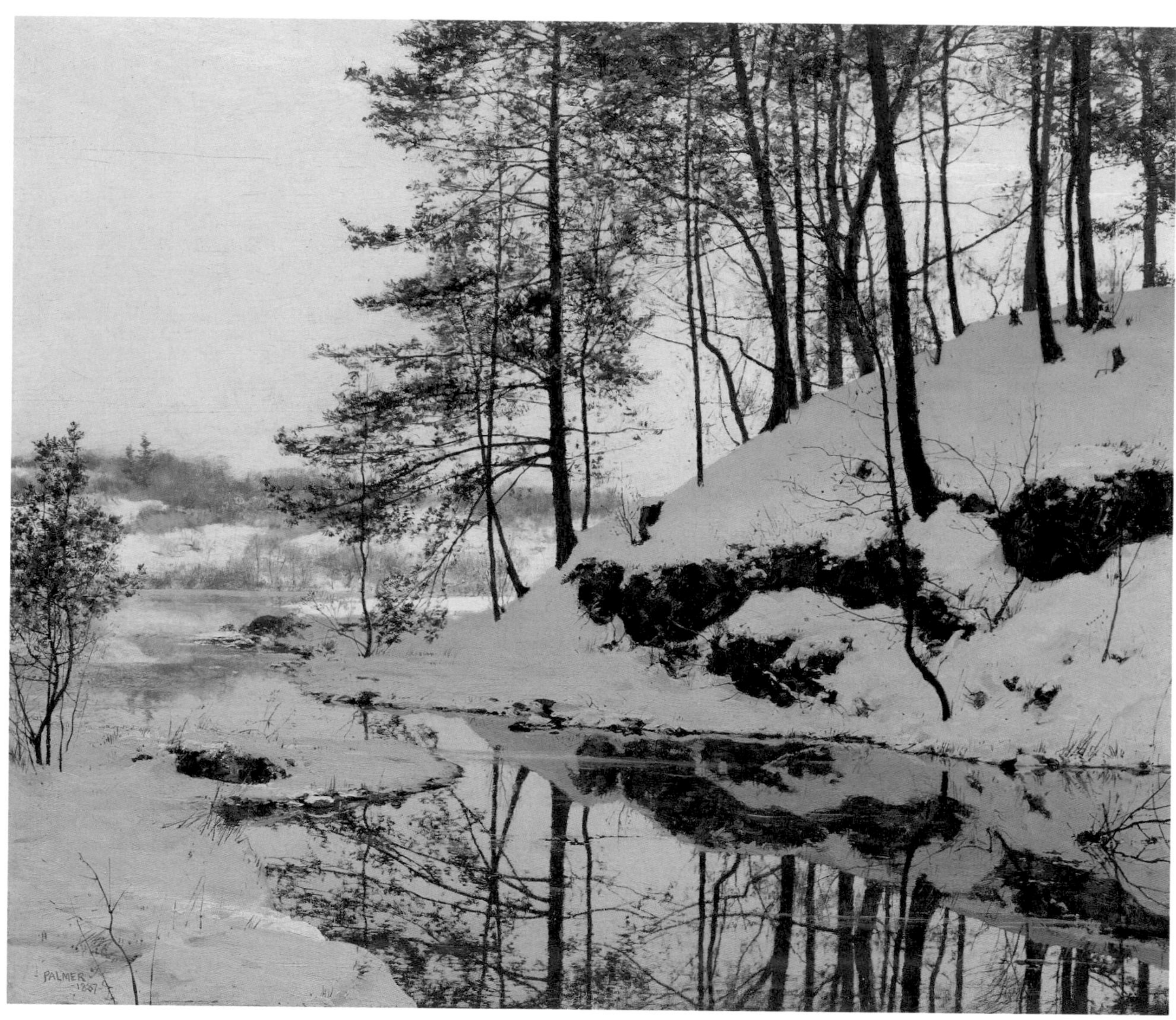

Plate 23.
Walter Launt Palmer,
An Early Snow, 1887.
Collection Mr. and
Mrs. Joel Finn.

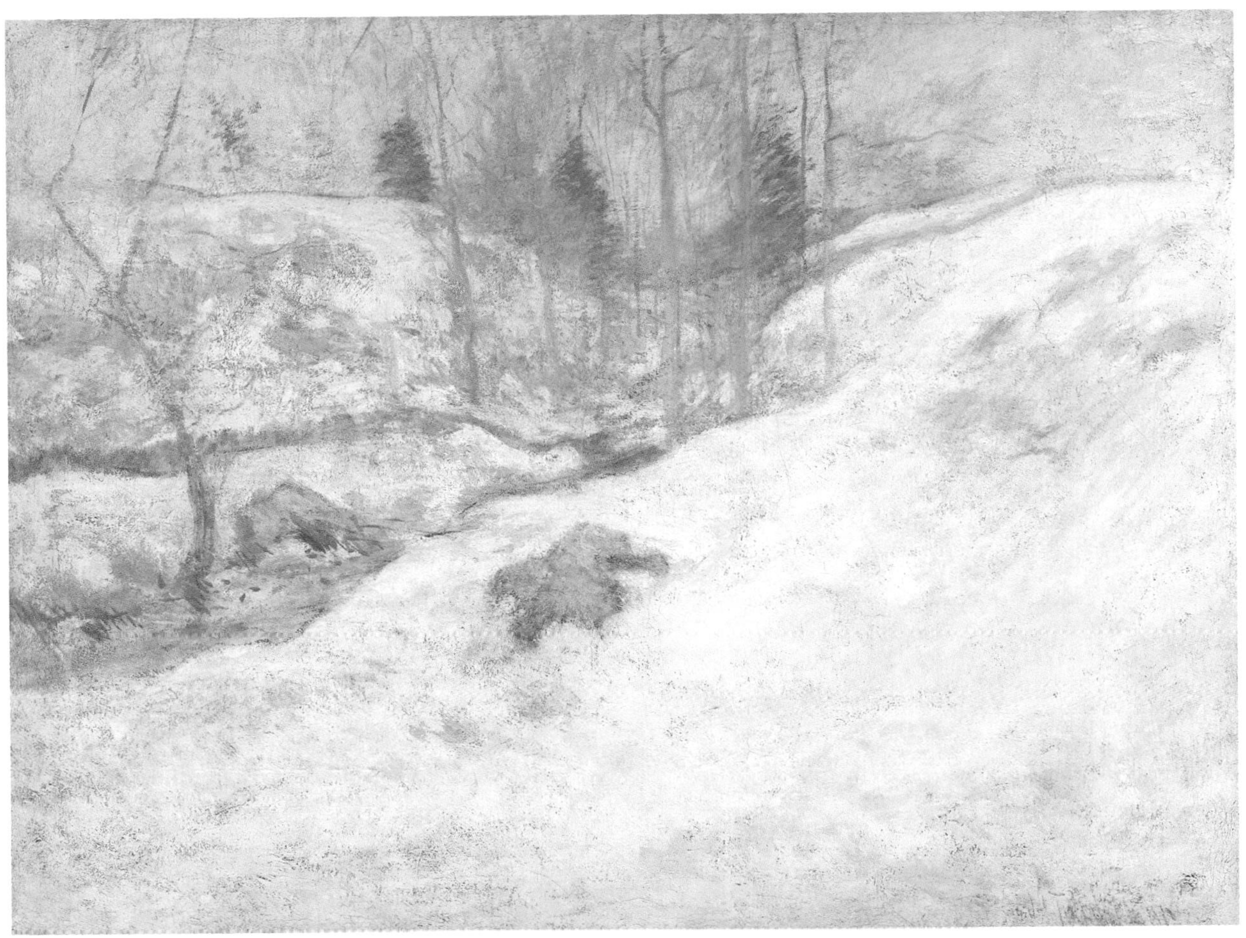

Plate 24.
John H. Twachtman,
Brook in Winter, ca. 1892.
Museum of Fine Arts, Boston.

In this painting (now entitled *February*) Twachtman presents an el egant synthesis of French Impressionist techniques, Oriental motifs, and native subject matter. Twachtman's debt to Impressionism can be discerned in the painting's light palette, broken forms, and gestural brushwork. Its Oriental legacy appears in its high horizon, abstracted natural elements, limited tonal range, and flattened, highly decorative design.

Twachtman's devotion to painting various forms of water, represented by the frozen snow, the brook, and the moisture-laden haze, is consonant with the Zen Buddhist belief that fugitive and amorphous effects of nature symbolize the spiritual essence of the world. The Oriental character of *Brook in Winter* would have been appreciated by many viewers at the fair, as Eastern mysticism was increasingly influential in late nineteenth-century America. Nonetheless, Twachtman affirmed his American identity by making his farm in Greenwich, Connecticut, the subject of *Brook in Winter* and other paintings in the 1890s.

Plate 25.
Dwight W. Tryon,
Daybreak, New Bedford Harbor,
1885.
Museum of Art, Rhode Island
School of Design.

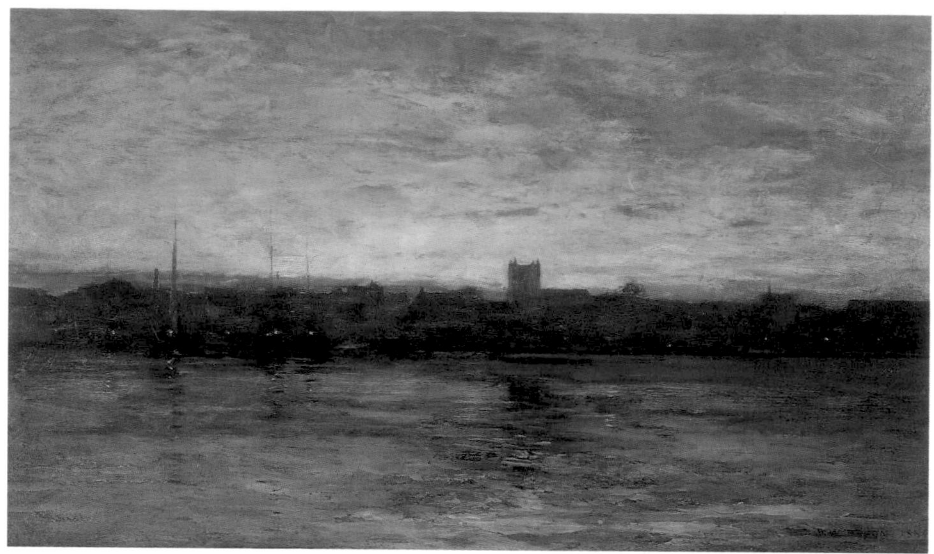

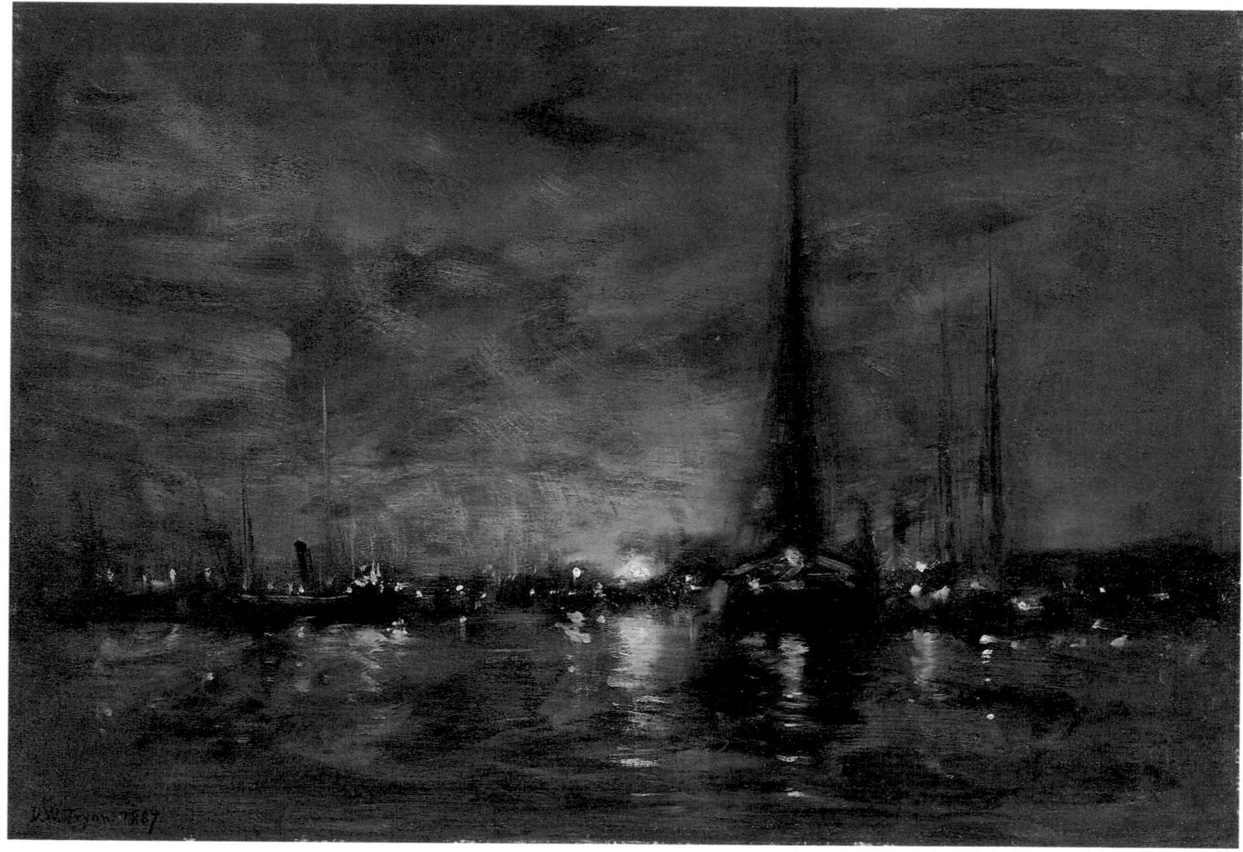

Plate 26.
Dwight W. Tryon,
Night, 1887.
Collection Rogers L. and Sally
Lorensen Conant.
Photograph by Michael Agee.

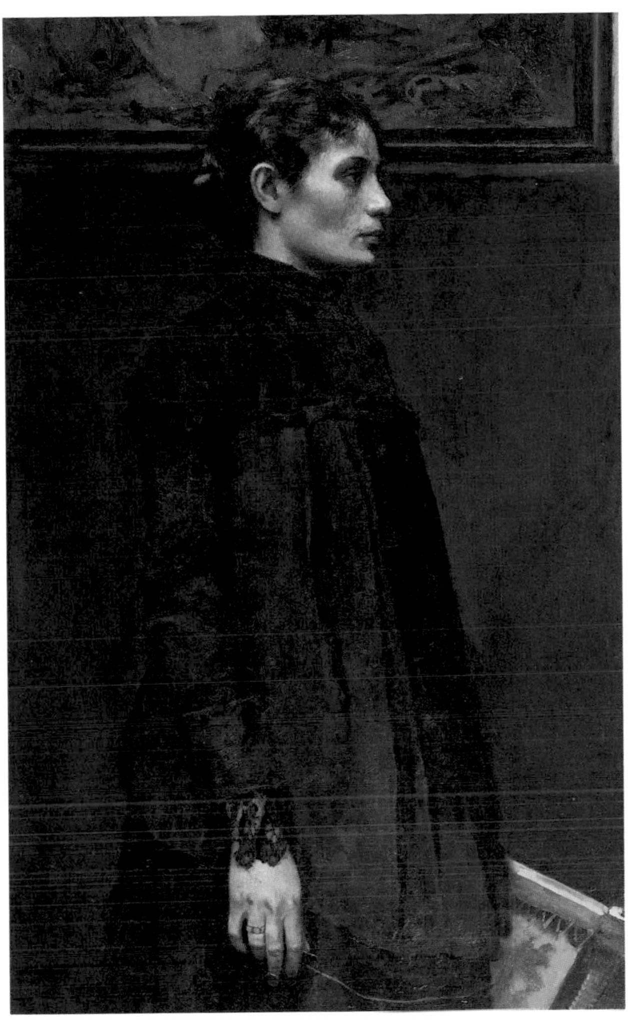

Plate 27.
Gari Melchers,
Portrait of Mrs. H. **(Mrs. George Hitchcock)**, ca. 1890
Collection Rita and Daniel Fraad.

Melchers depicts his favorite model, Henriette Hitchcock, who was the wife of the painter with whom Melchers shared a studio in Egmond-aan-zee, Holland. The portrait shows *Mrs. H.* as an expectant mother, wearing a dark maternity smock and engaged in her decorative needlework.

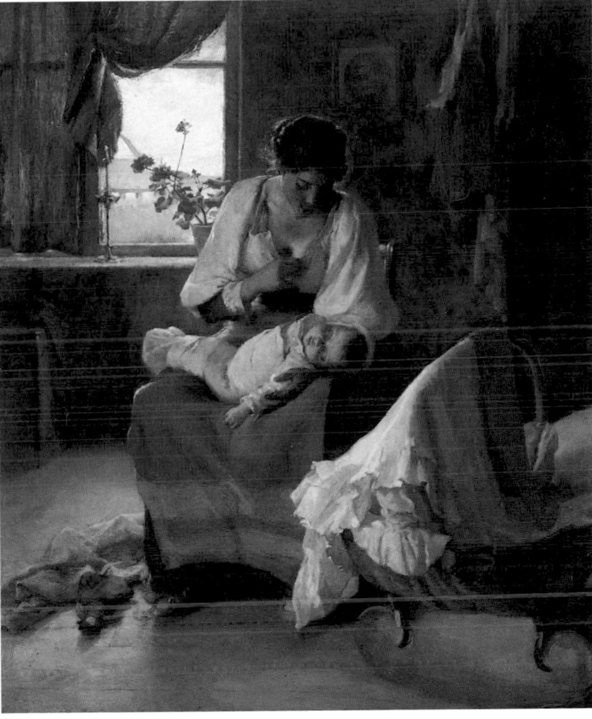

Plate 28.
Alice D. Kellogg,
The Mother, 1889.
Jane Addams' Hull-House Museum, University of Illinois at Chicago.
Photograph by Michael Tropea.

As an art student in Paris, Chicago native Alice Kellogg executed this variation on the popular modern madonna theme just as her two-year sojourn there was ending. When she returned to the United States, the work was well received and helped launch her career as a painter and art instructor. In 1891 *The Mother* was selected for the annual exhibition of the Society of American Artists, whose duly impressed members soon elected Kellogg to the group, a distinction rarely conferred upon midwesterners or women. *The Mother* gained added recognition just before the fair opened when it was reproduced as the frontispiece to the *Century Illustrated Magazine* in January 1893.

Plate 29.
Douglas Tilden,
Young Acrobat, ca. 1890–92.
National Museum of American Art, Smithsonian Institution.

This statuette by Tilden, a deaf San Francisco sculptor, was modeled in Paris and sent as a gift to his California benefactor. Like his *Base-ball Player* and *Tired Boxer*, also exhibited at the fair, this conceit suggests an athletic association. With one foot up and the other steadied against the brawny arm and with hands half outstretched, the timid baby weighs the insecurity of his seat and his immediate future. Yet held aloft on the hand of a working man with his sleeve rolled up, the young acrobat symbolizes the hopes and fears of the next generation.

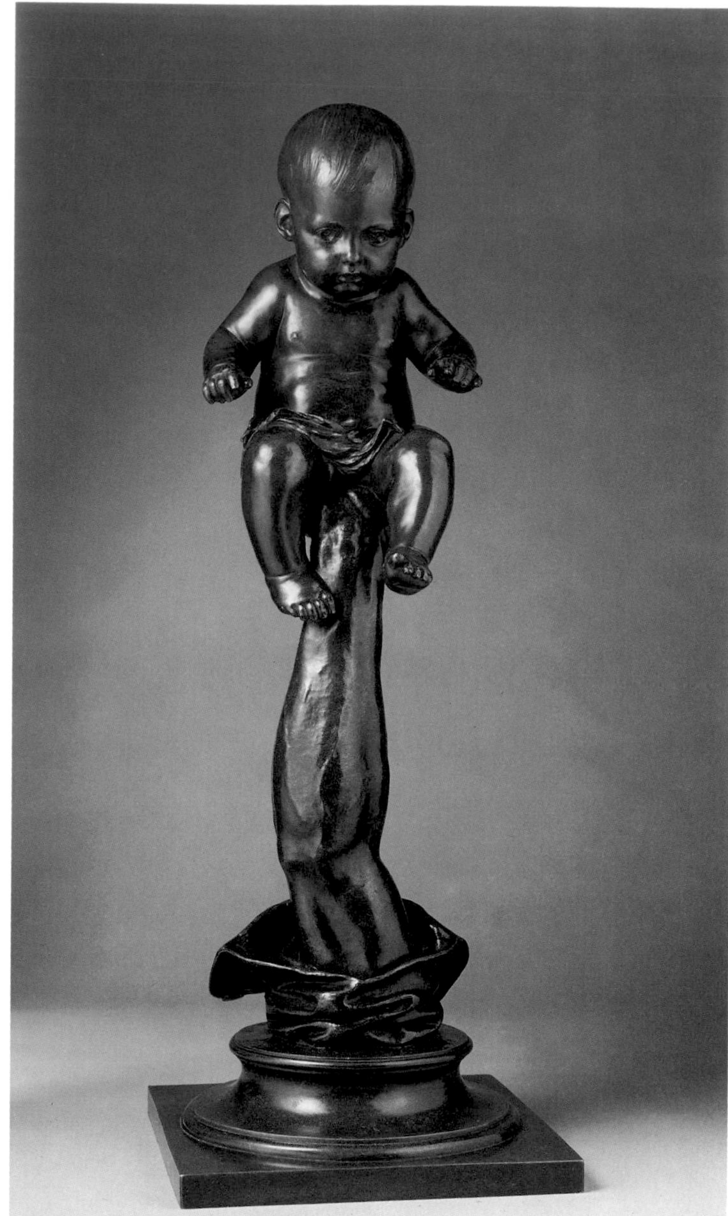

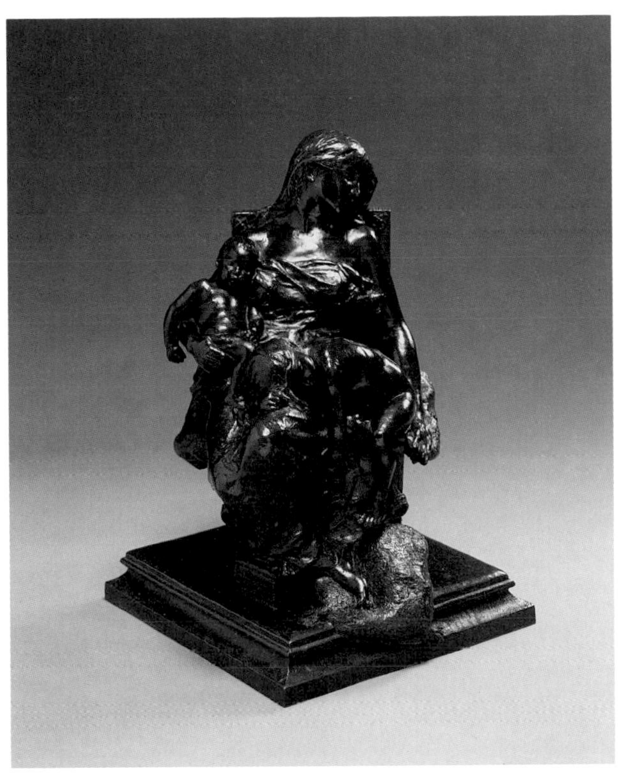

Plate 30.
John J. Boyle,
Tired Out, 1887.
Pennsylvania Academy of the
Fine Arts, Philadelphia.

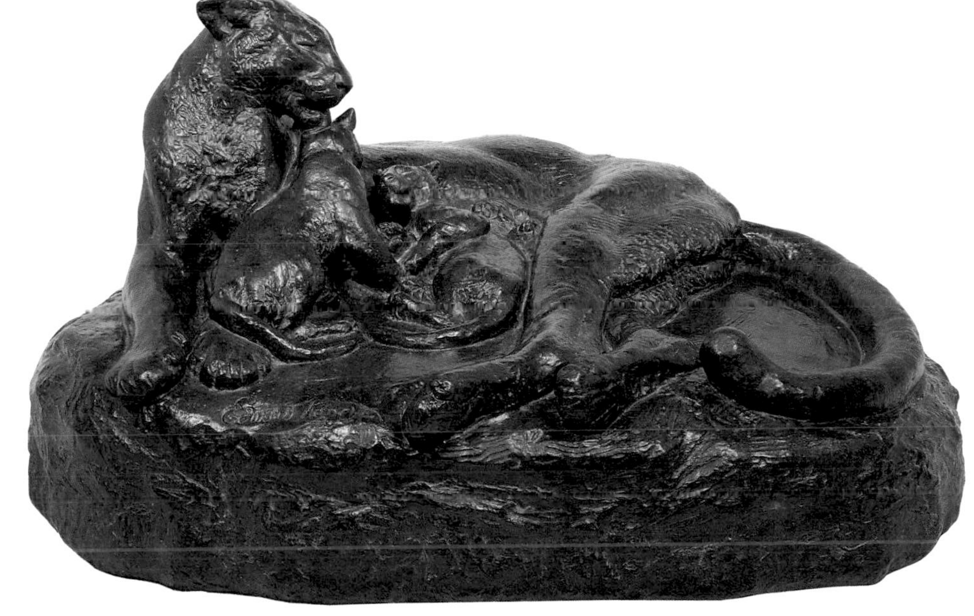

Plate 31.
Edward Kemeys,
American Panther and Her Cubs,
1878.
National Museum of American
Art, Smithsonian Institution.

A self-taught sculptor, Kemeys holds the distinction of being the first American to specialize in animal sculpture. Knowledge of his subjects came from firsthand study in the wild before the encroachment of civilization. Although often compared to the refined, idealized style of the great French *animalier* Antoine-Louis Barye, Kemeys's impressionistic realism conveyed his psychological understanding of the creatures he modeled. His works also reflect the growing nineteenth-century interest in the scientific study of the behavior of animals in their environment. Here the feline mother lavishes attention on her infant cubs with an intimacy not unlike that found in the paintings of human subjects.

At the exposition, Kemeys sculpted numerous heroic statues of native American animals as decorations for the bridges over the waterways.

Plate 32.
Carl Marr,
Summer Afternoon, 1892.
University Art Museum,
University of California at
Berkeley.

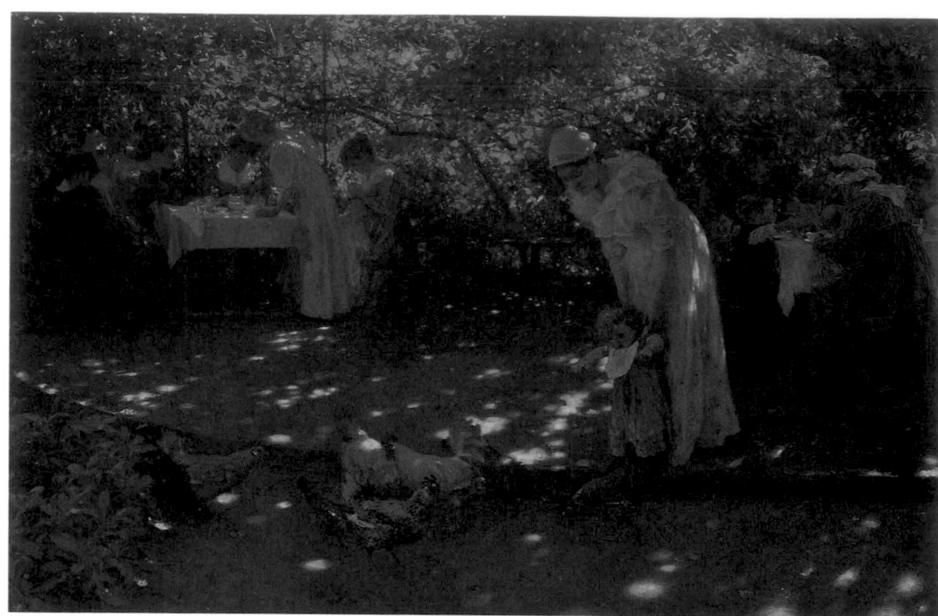

Plate 33.
Cecilia Beaux,
Last Days of Infancy, 1885.
Pennsylvania Academy of the
Fine Arts, Philadelphia.

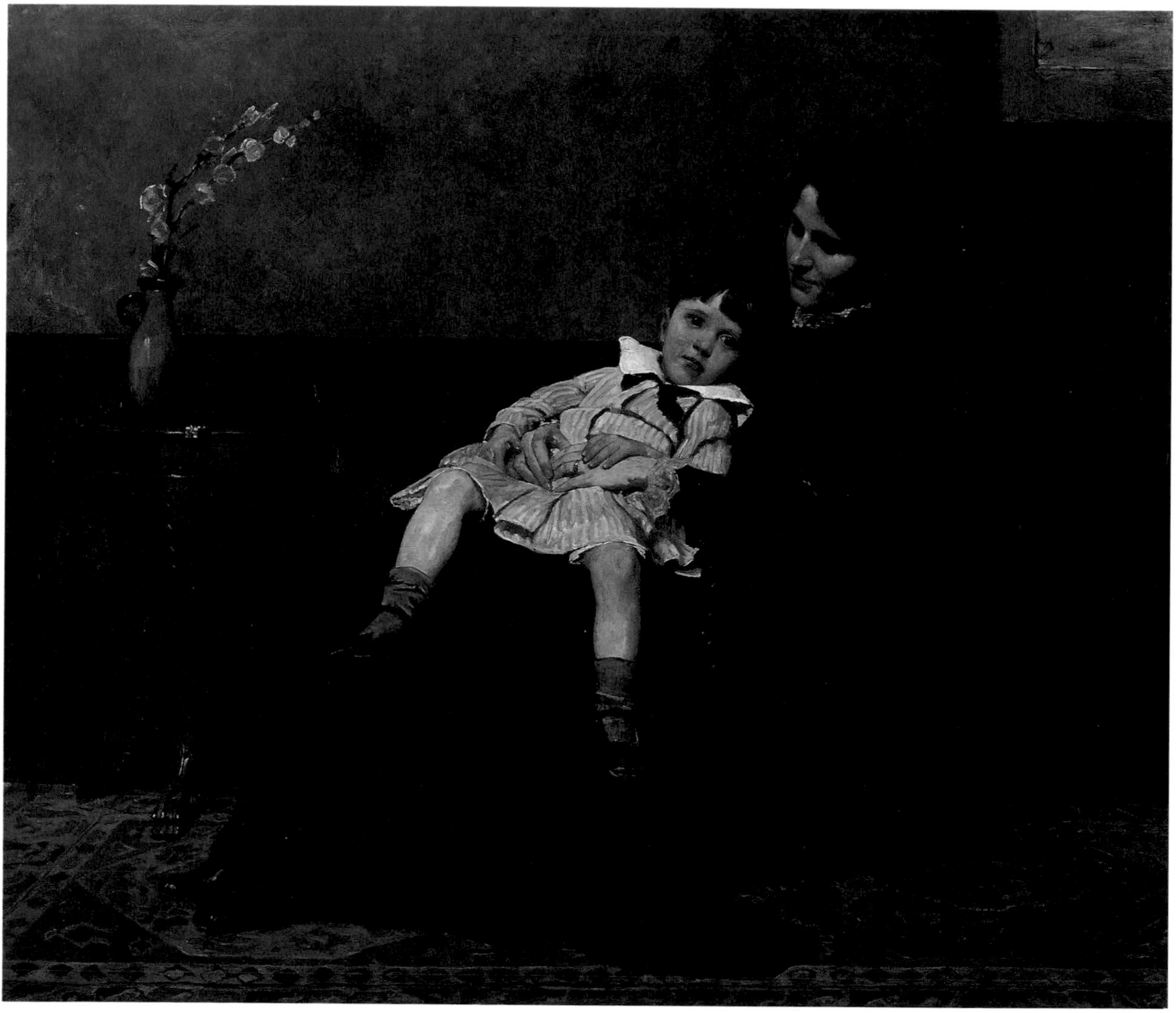

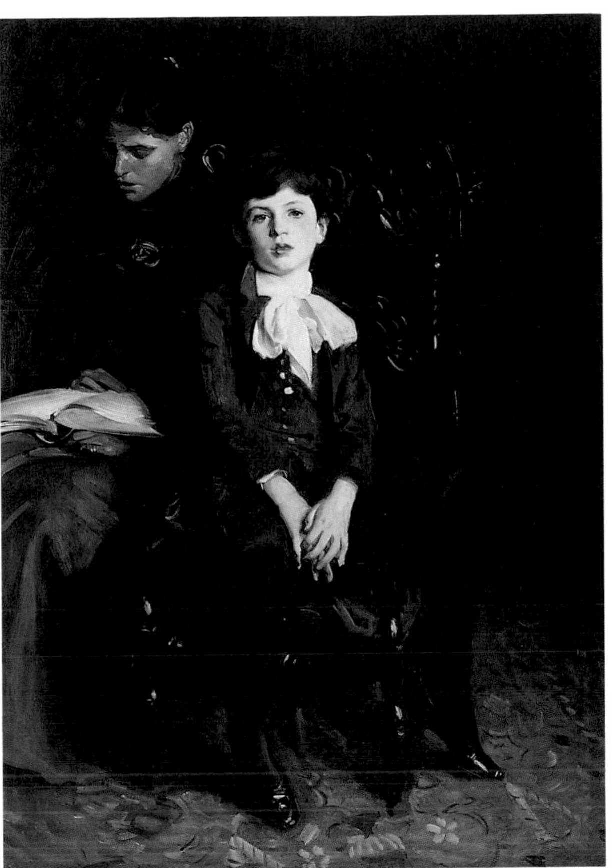

Plate 35.
John Singer Sargent,
***Portrait* (Homer Saint-Gaudens)**, 1890.
The Carnegie Museum of Art, Pittsburgh.

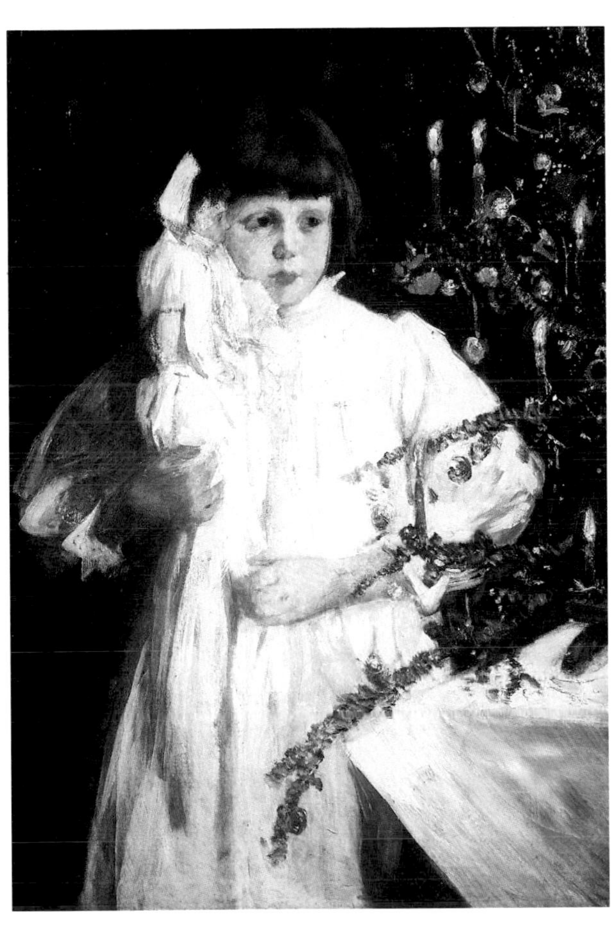

Plate 34.
J. Alden Weir,
The Christmas Tree, 1890.
Private Collection.

Sargent and the sculptor Augustus Saint-Gaudens were lifelong friends. In the summer of 1890, when both artists were negotiating for commissions to decorate the new Boston Public Library, Saint-Gaudens did a bas-relief portrait of Sargent's sister, Violet. In return, Sargent painted Saint-Gaudens's son, a portrait that was much praised and exhibited. Critics mentioned the vitality and naturalness of the pose, in which the boy's mother is shown reading to him. At least one writer linked the picture to depictions of the Madonna and Child, noting that it "avows the divinity of the maternal tie as seen in the thoughtful boy leaning with simple trust at his mother's side. The costume sinks away, the accidents of time and place count nothing. . . . it breathes the human significance which makes one soul stand for all."

Plate 36.
Lucy Holme,
A Holiday Occupation,
ca. 1892–93.
Salem County Historical Society,
Salem, NJ.

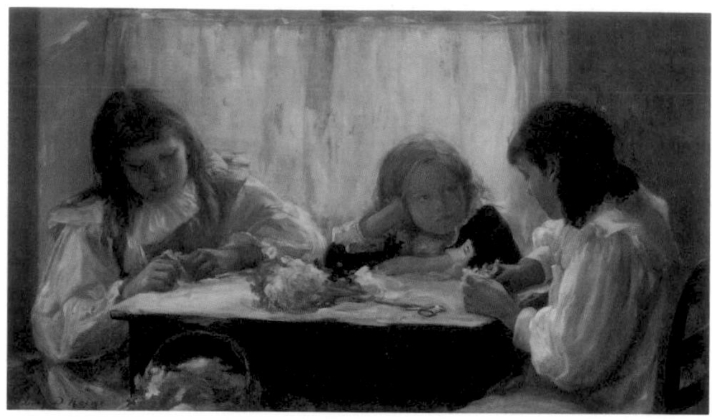

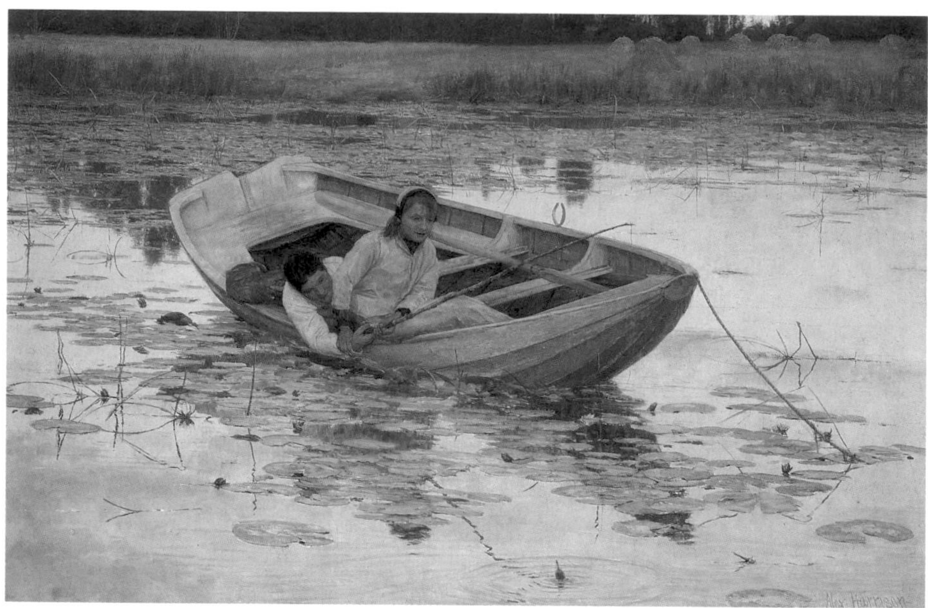

Plate 37.
Alexander Harrison,
The Amateurs, 1882–83.
Valparaiso University Museum
of Art.

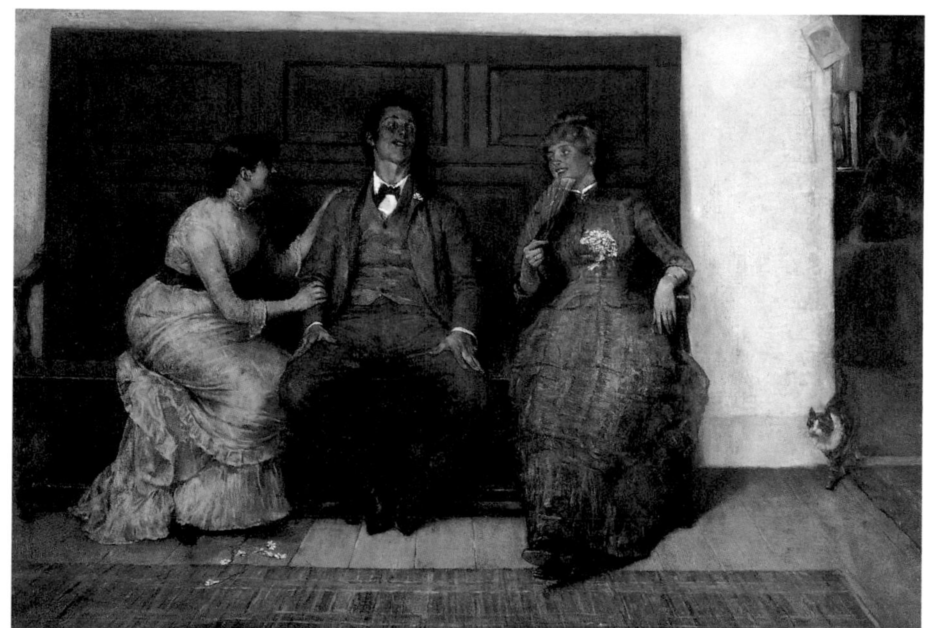

Plate 38.
William T. Smedley,
Embarrassment, 1883.
The New Jersey State Museum,
Trenton.

Smedley's painting fits squarely into the tradition of comic courtship scenes, which were popular in American literature and art throughout most of the nineteenth century. Contemporary reviewers were quick to laud Smedley's talent as an astute chronicler of American social rituals. In *Embarrassment*, as one critic described it: "Two sportive girls, American to the heart, have caught an inexperienced beau between them, and are giving him all the mingled emotions of ecstasy and fear. These beauties are well up in their parts; they understand each other completely, and are amused from head to foot. She with the daisies on her breast is the one on whom the swain has fixed his affections. To her he would fain say and do the sweetest things. She has made a little game with her friend, however, to torment the bashful beau out of his senses."

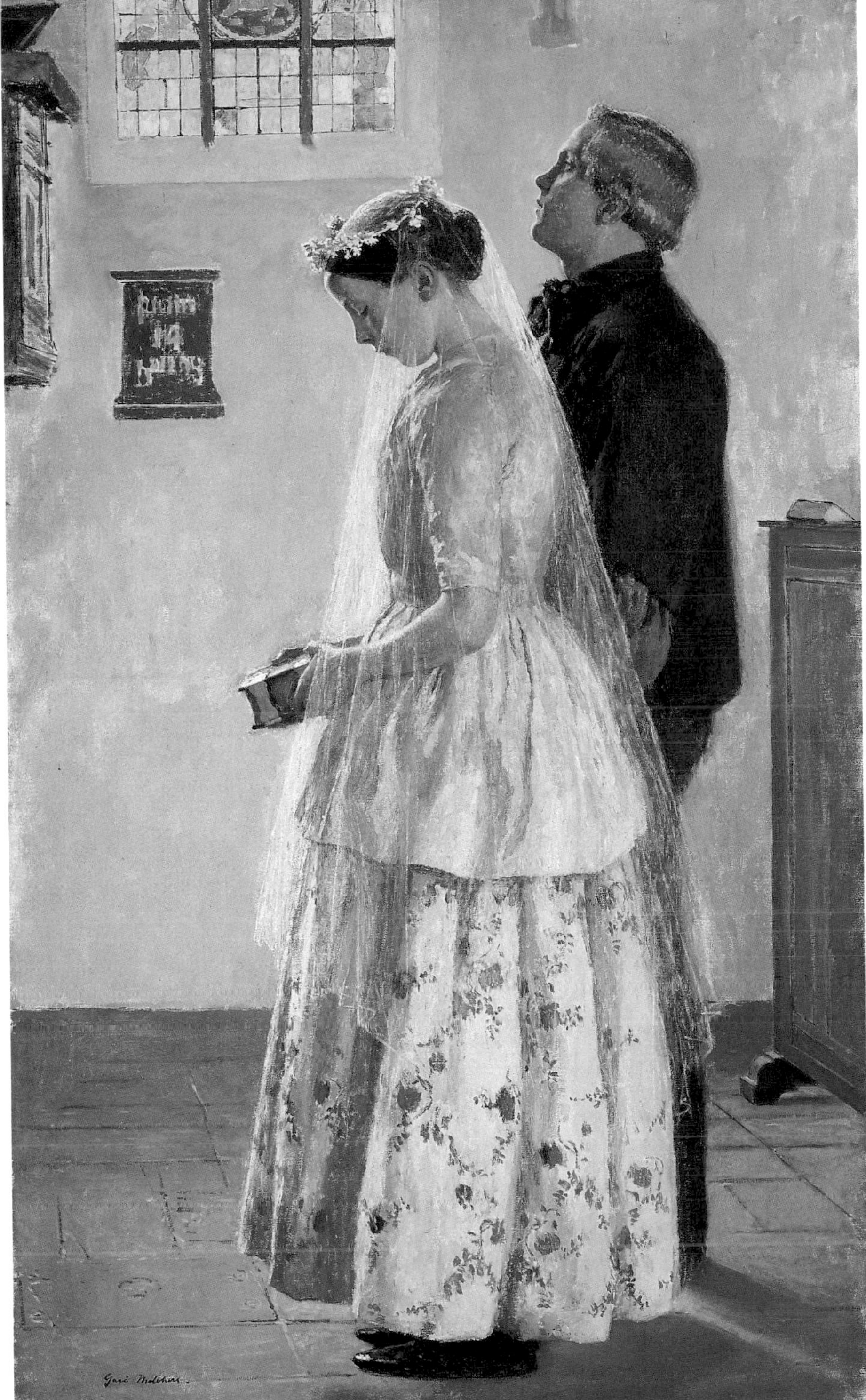

Plate 39.
Gari Melchers,
Married, ca. 1892.
Albright-Knox Art Gallery,
Buffalo, NY.

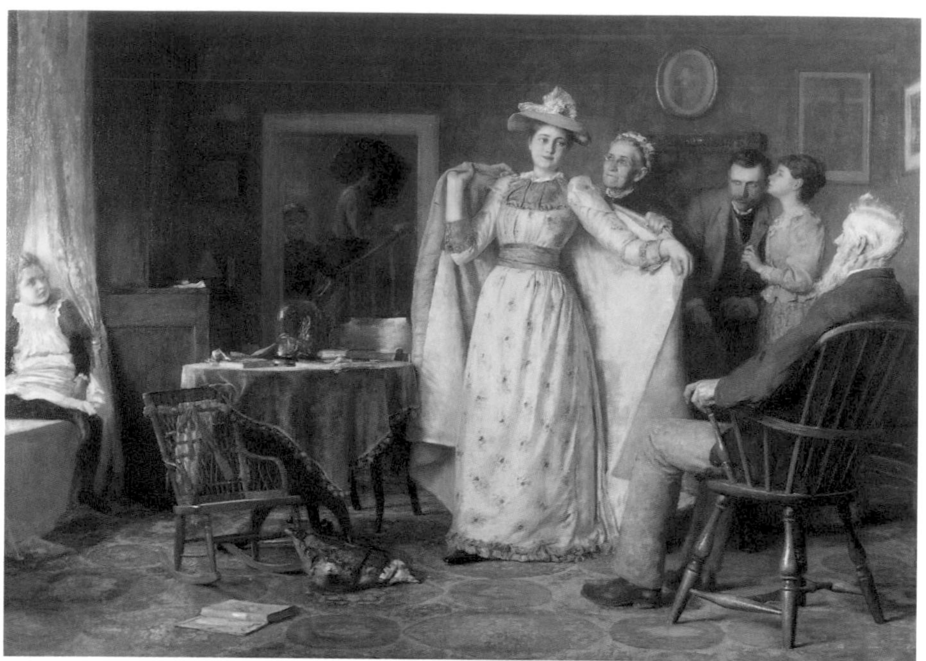

Plate 40.
Thomas Hovenden,
Bringing Home the Bride, 1893.
Collection Jay Weibel,
Newport, RI.

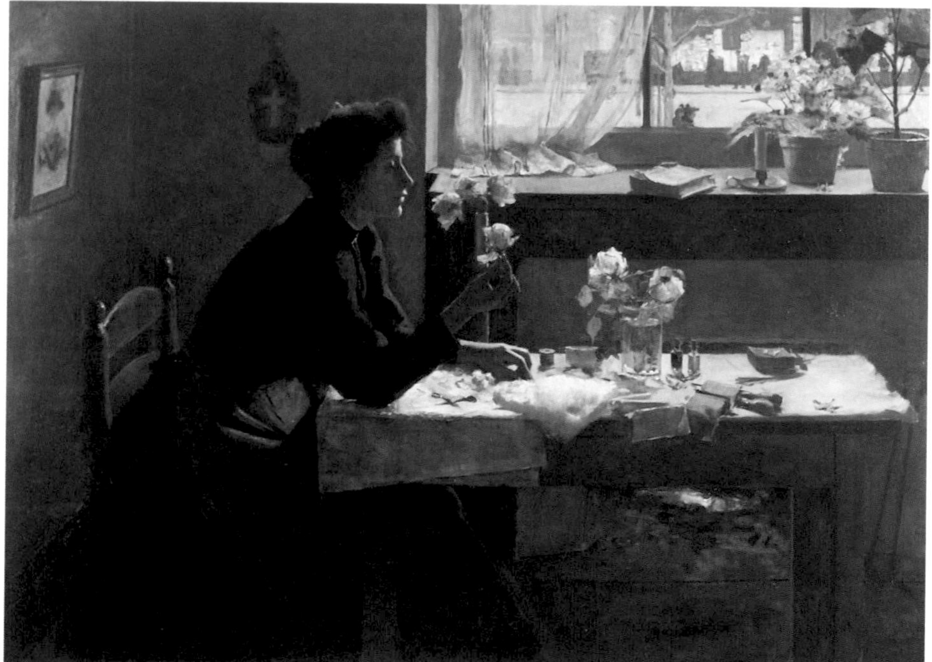

Plate 41.
Harriet Campbell Foss,
A Flower Maker, 1892.
Private Collection.

Foss painted *A Flower Maker* in Paris, where the production of artificial flowers was a booming industry that employed tens of thousands of women in the late nineteenth century. Flower-making was a common variety of low-paying piecework, which also included jobs like finishing trousers and trimming hats. Such work was often the only employment option for urban working women in the United States as well as Europe, particularly those with children. Like traditional female labor, it was often done in the home, where women could look after infants or aging parents and enlist the assistance of older children.

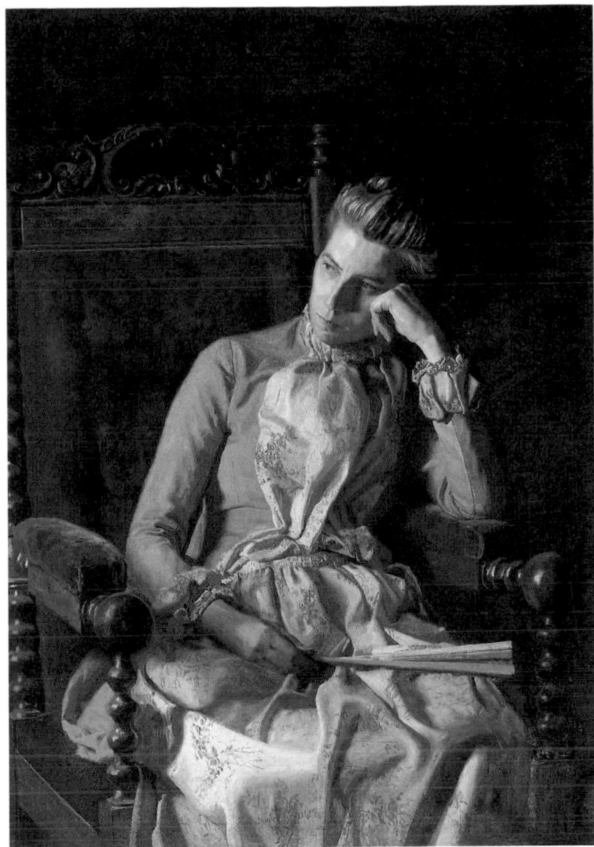

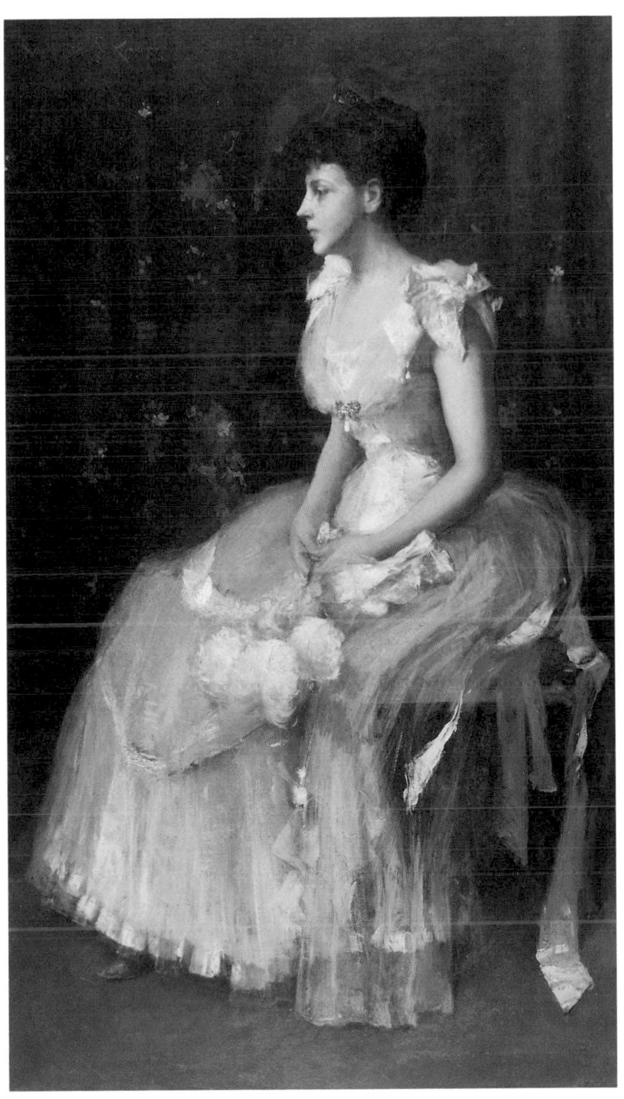

Plate 42.
William Merritt Chase,
Lady in Pink **(Mrs. Leslie Cotton)**, ca. 1888–89.
Museum of Art, Rhode Island School of Design.

Plate 43.
Thomas Eakins,
Portrait of a Lady **(Amelia Van Buren)**, ca. 1889–91.
©The Phillips Collection, Washington, D.C.

This painting clearly expresses Chase's interest in the work of James McNeill Whistler and his debt to the Aesthetic Movement, with its emphasis on decorative surfaces. As in Whistler's work, the color of the sitter's dress, not her identity, is the basis for the painting's title. Attention is given to painterly effect and the delineation of texture, with Chase's seemingly artless facility highlighted in the treatment of the gauzy layers of the sitter's dress. Mariette Benedict Cotton was one of Chase's students and a portraitist, but he gives the viewer no sense of her role as an artist. Instead she is merely the demure vehicle for the demonstration of his technical skill.

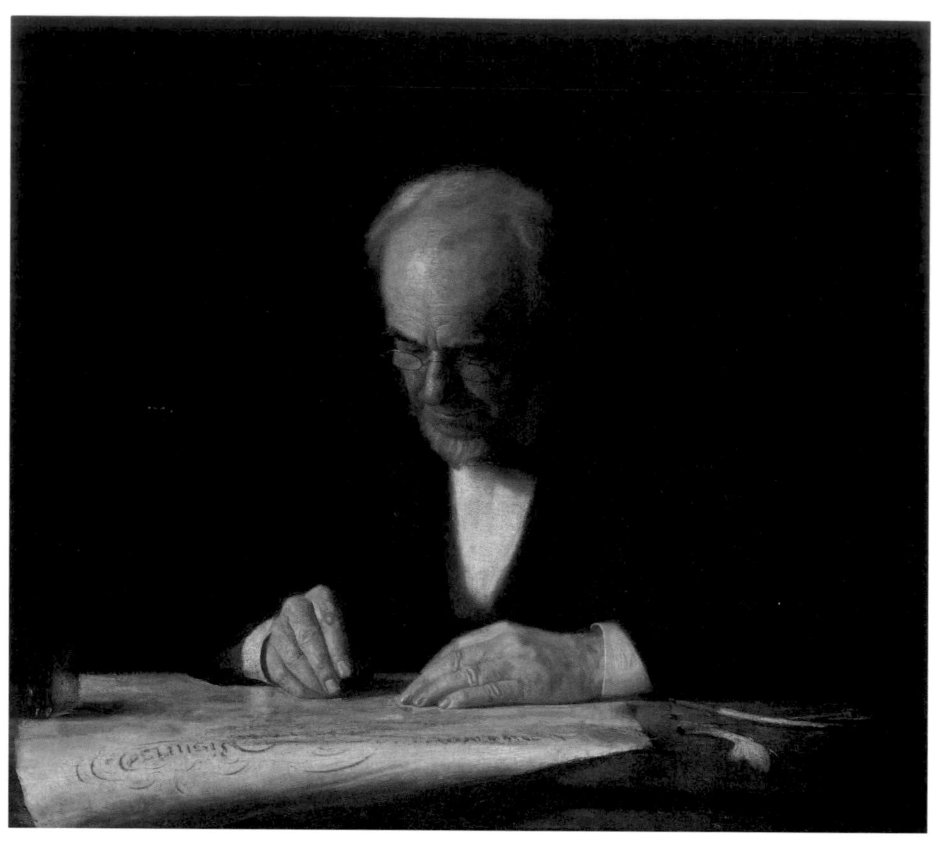

Plate 44.
Thomas Eakins,
The Writing Master, 1882.
The Metropolitan Museum of Art.

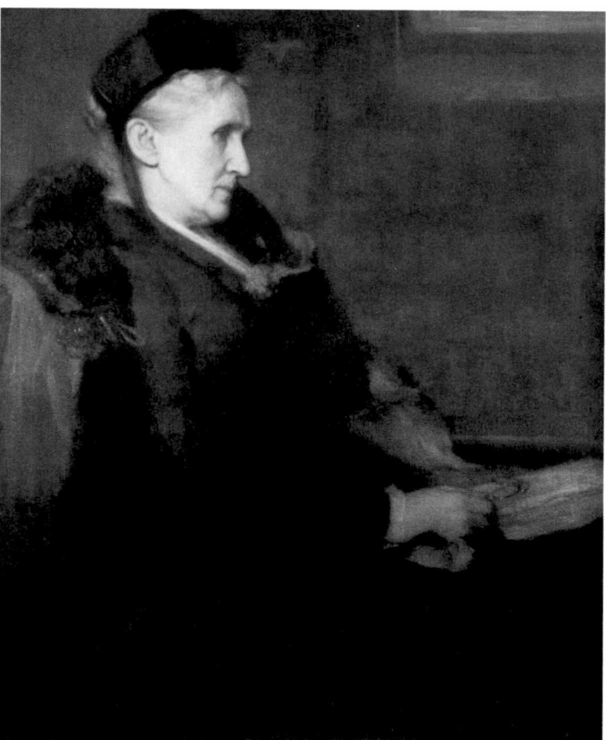

Plate 45.
Adeline Albright Wigand,
Portrait of Mrs. J. Albright,
ca.1890–92.
Staten Island Institute of Arts & Sciences.

A large number of paintings and sculptures were exhibited in Chicago by young women, but only a few of these artists went on to develop professional careers. Some stopped exhibiting after marriage; others continued to work but, like Adeline Albright Wigand, never attained a great reputation. Wigand never surpassed this portrait of her mother. It is a subtle evocation of James McNeill Whistler's famous portrait of his own mother, which had been purchased by the French government in 1891. According to one critic, "Mrs. Wigand succeeded in portraying herself as well as her mother in the same picture; for only a loving and revering daughter could do such a masterpiece."

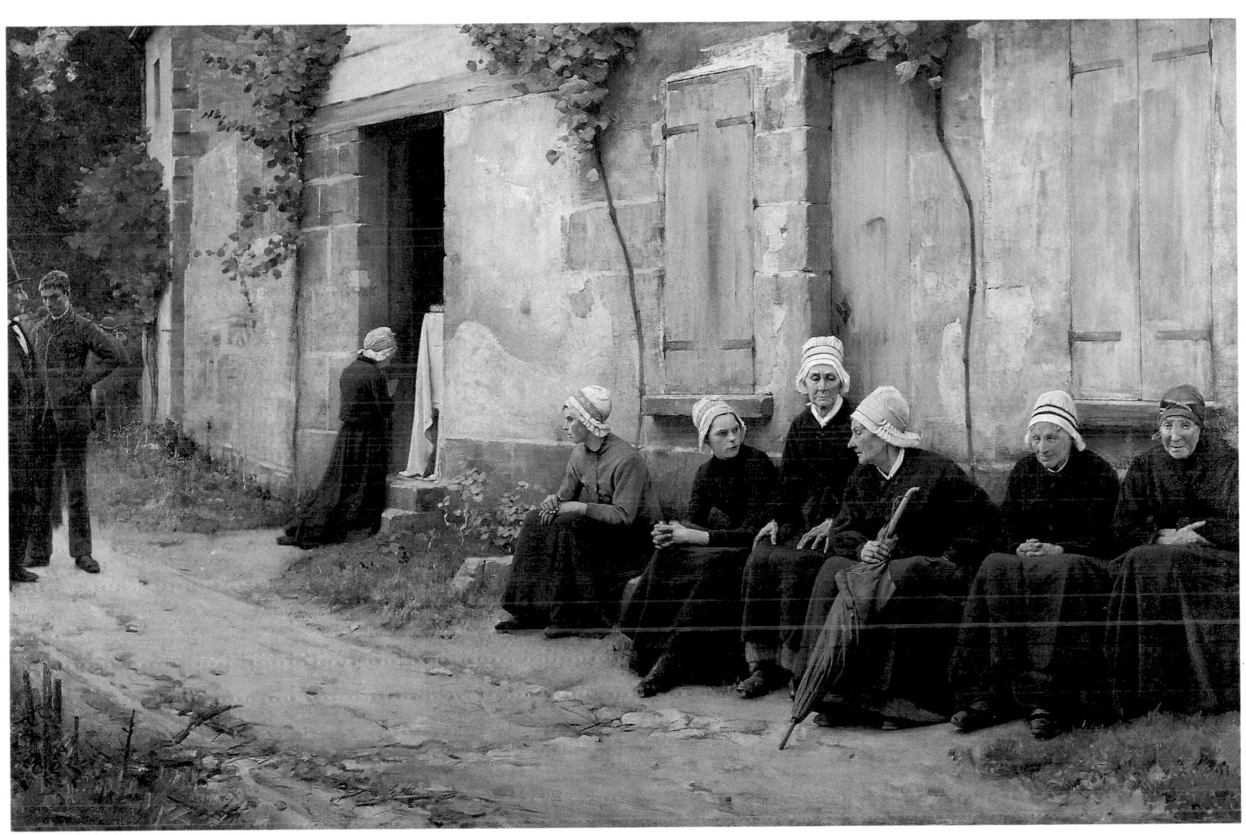

Plate 46.
Charles Sprague Pearce,
A Village Funeral, Brittany, 1891.
Danforth Museum of Art Collection, Framingham, MA.

French villagers gather to mourn the passage of one of their members in this depiction of a traditional burial rite. Pearce alludes to the procession of time by recording the aging process in the faces of the women seated outside the home. The somber, brooding atmosphere reflects late nineteenth-century America's fear of a loss of tradition, as life in the United States grew increasingly complex and modern.

Body and Soul

For American artists trained in European academies, the human figure was the worthiest subject of art, symbolically evoking eternal truths and ideals. The figure might serve as an object of spiritual reverence, visual pleasure, colonial appropriation, or scientific investigation, but whatever the ultimate purpose, it almost always provided the focus for a larger complex of associations.

The human figure most frequently encountered in the Fine Arts Palace—and in the monumental sculptural decorations and murals of the fair buildings—was the idealized classical nude. Olin Levi Warner's *Diana* and John Donoghue's *The Young Sophocles Leading the Chorus of Victory After the Battle of Salamis* demonstrated familiarity with the ideal proportions and unifying classical style of antique art. Such nudes established a standard of beauty that followed Western visual traditions; this standard also implied social and cultural harmony for a developing America, associating contemporary life with ancient Greece and Rome.

After Darwin's revolutionary theories seemed to displace God from his position at the center of the universe, the roles of religion and art were revised and somewhat merged. The elevated sentiments inspired by art occasionally substituted for the higher feelings usually associated with religion. Contemporary life was often recast in terms of spiritual feeling, as when Abbott H. Thayer painted his daughter and titled the picture *Virgin Enthroned*—one of innumerable modern madonnas painted during this period.

Moral inspiration was provided by representations of biblical stories and episodes in the lives of monks and nuns. However, artists also gave expression to the disruptions of faith that marked the age, as in Elihu Vedder's allegories of the soul. Indeed, the entire fair was examined from a spiritual point of view in a book entitled *If Christ Came to Chicago*, suggesting the moral judgment that was never far from the surface in late nineteenth-century life.

At the other extreme were figure paintings that frankly portrayed the human figure as an object of desire, appropriation, or study. John Singer Sargent's life-size *Study of an Egyptian Girl* is just one example of a large category of works that depict exoticized foreigners. In many cases the images supply the subordinate positions of colonial people in an age of imperialist expansion.

In the tension between idealized and objectified portrayals of the figure, we find further suggestions of the ambivalence with which people greeted scientific progress, materialism, expansionism, and the future. While works at the fair rarely confronted such issues directly, the widely varying approach to such a time-honored subject as the human form is testimony enough to the divided feelings of many artists.

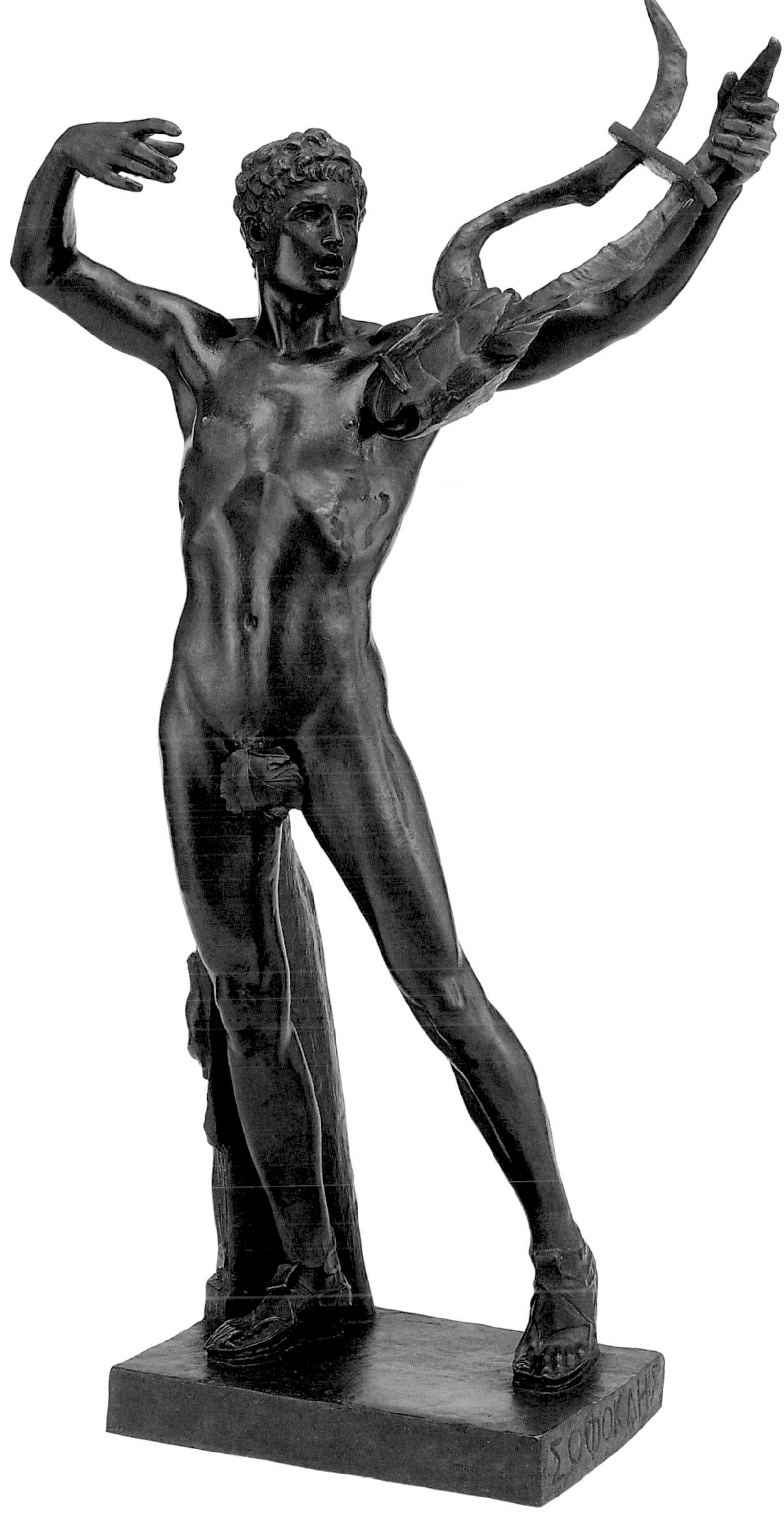

Plate 47.
John Donoghue,
The Young Sophocles Leading the Chorus of Victory After the Battle of Salamis, 1885.
The Art Institute of Chicago.

Plate 48.
Frederick Wellington Ruckstuhl,
Evening, 1891.
The Metropolitan Museum
of Art.

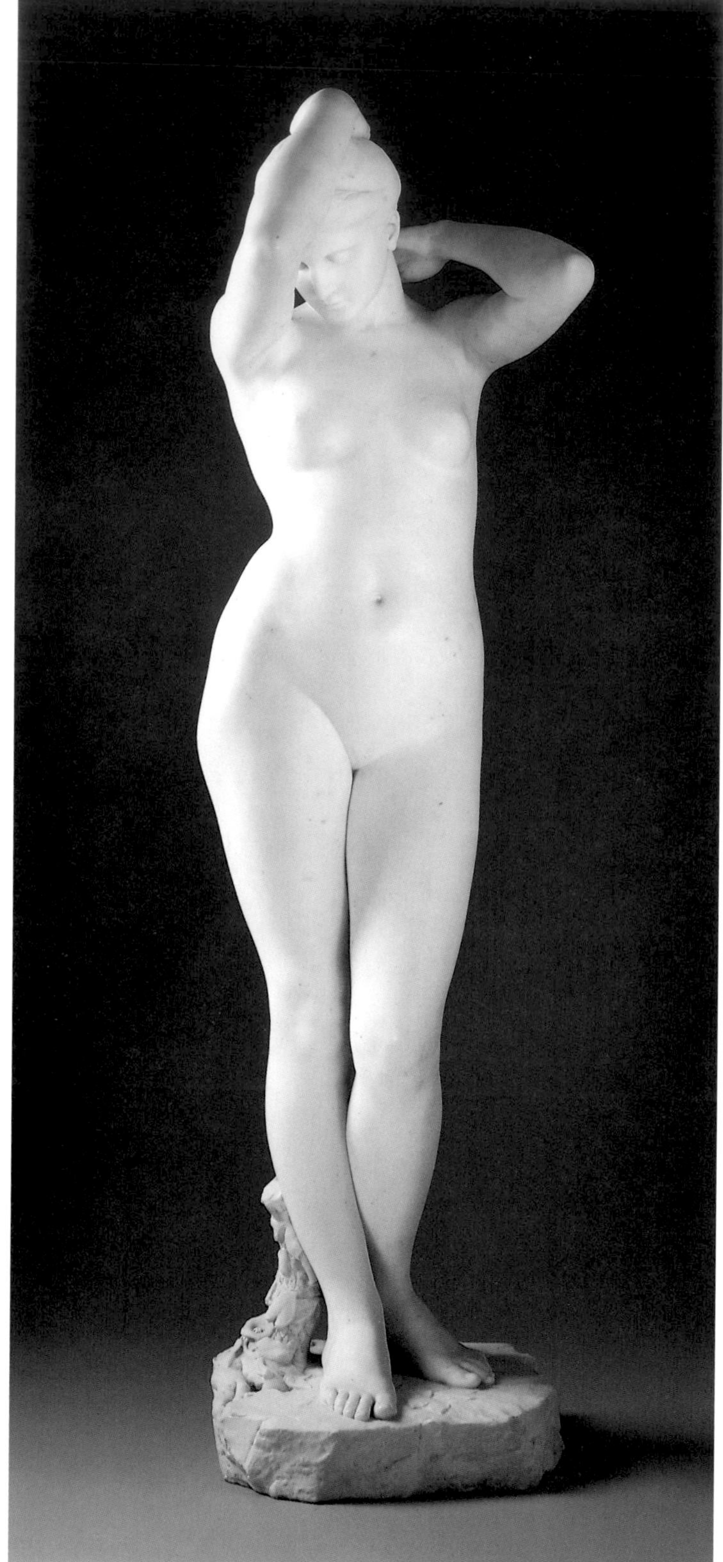

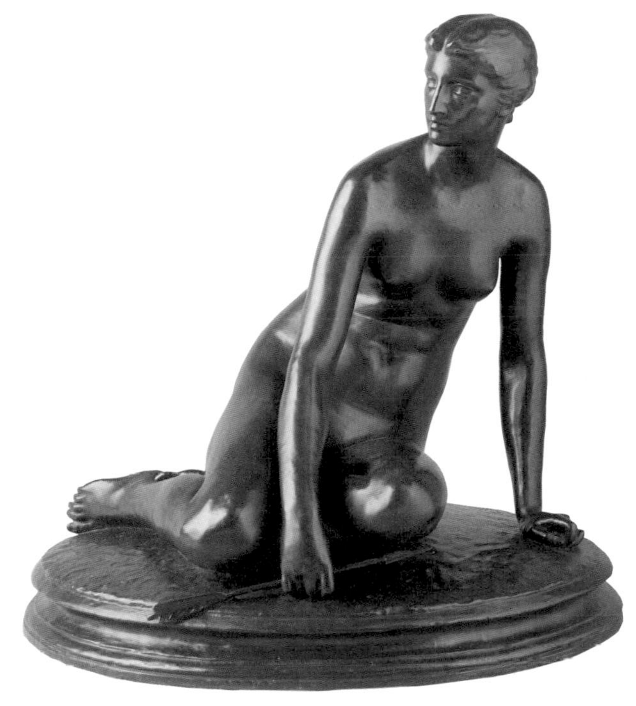

Plate 49.
Olin Levi Warner,
Diana, 1887.
The Metropolitan Museum
of Art.

Plate 50.
Douglas Tilden,
Tired Boxer, 1890.
The Fine Arts Museums of
San Francisco.

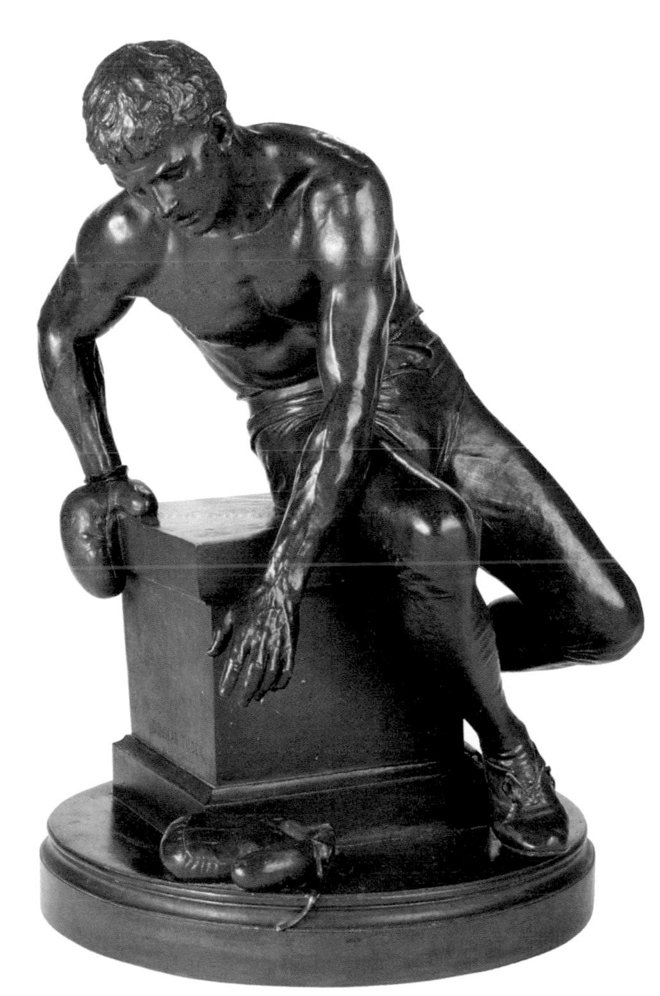

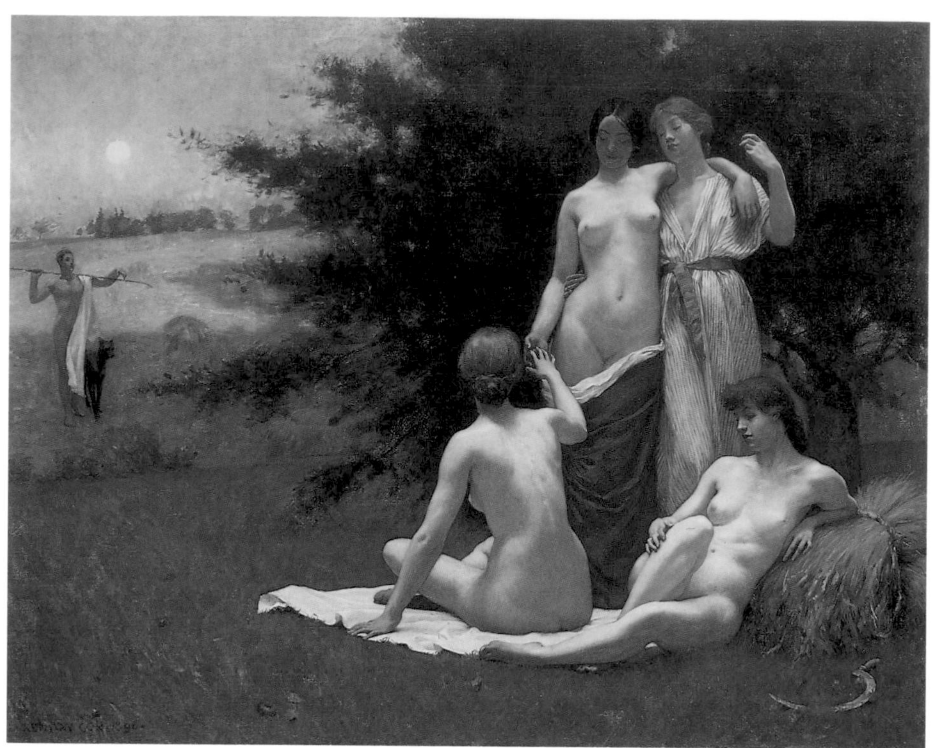

Plate 51.
Kenyon Cox,
An Eclogue, 1890.
National Museum of American Art, Smithsonian Institution.

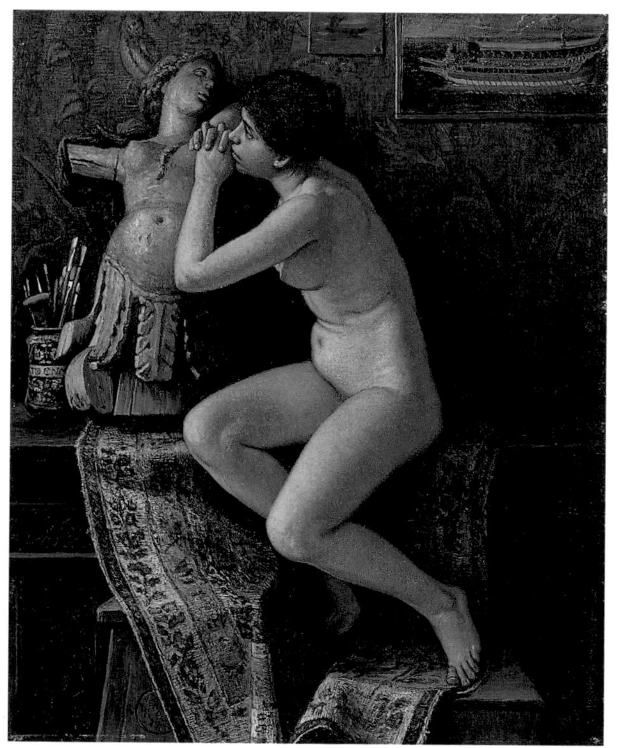

Plate 52.
Elihu Vedder,
A Venetian Model, 1878.
Columbus Museum of Art, Ohio.

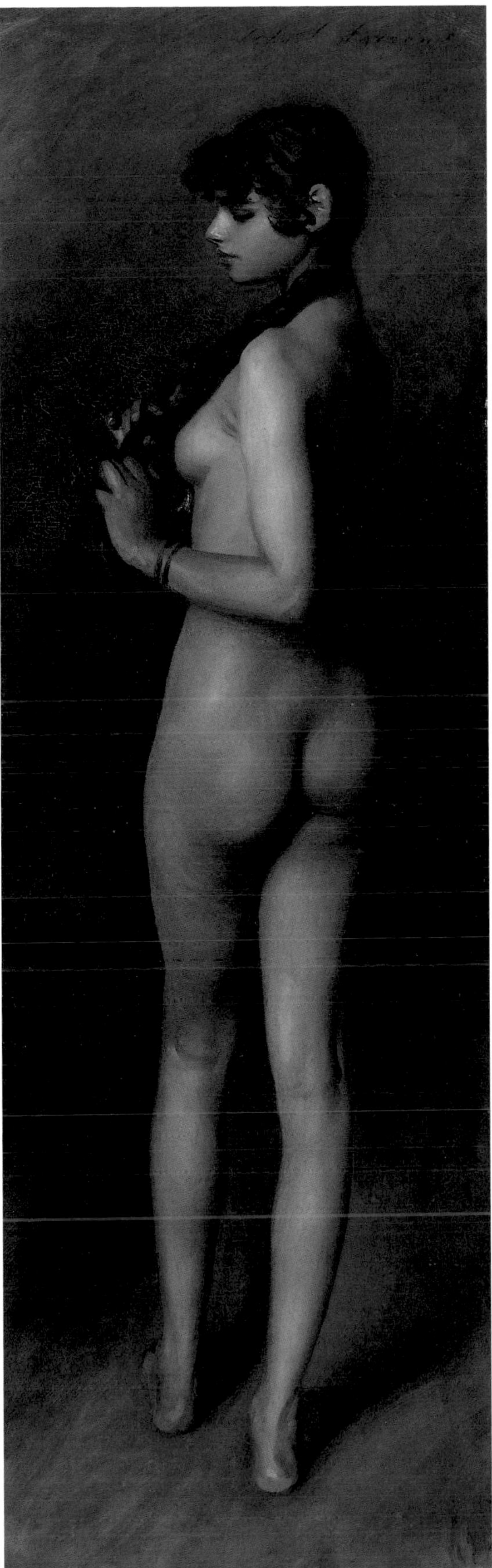

Plate 53.
John Singer Sargent,
***Study of an Egyptian Girl*, 1891.**
The Art Institute of Chicago.
Lent by an anonymous donor.

In search of subjects for murals commissioned by the Boston Public Library, Sargent traveled to Egypt in 1891, where he painted this work. Its exotic tenor is akin to his earlier paintings of Spanish and Javanese dancers, which reflect the artist's fascination with the alluring costumes and movements of the women. The pose of the *Egyptian Girl* also relates to the classical tradition of the idealized female figure.

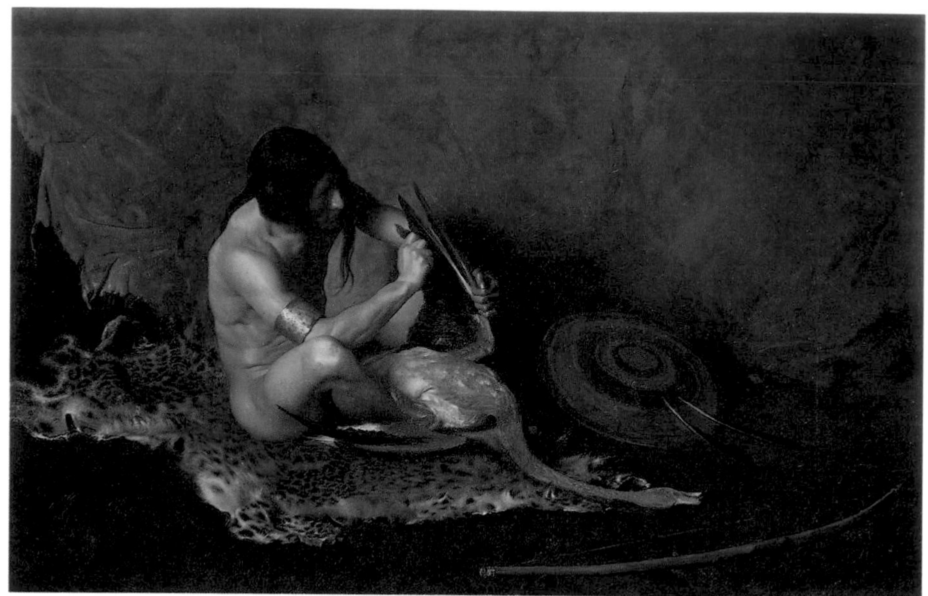

Plate 54.
George de Forest Brush,
The Head Dress, 1890.
The Warner Collection of Gulf States Paper Corporation, Tuscaloosa, AL.

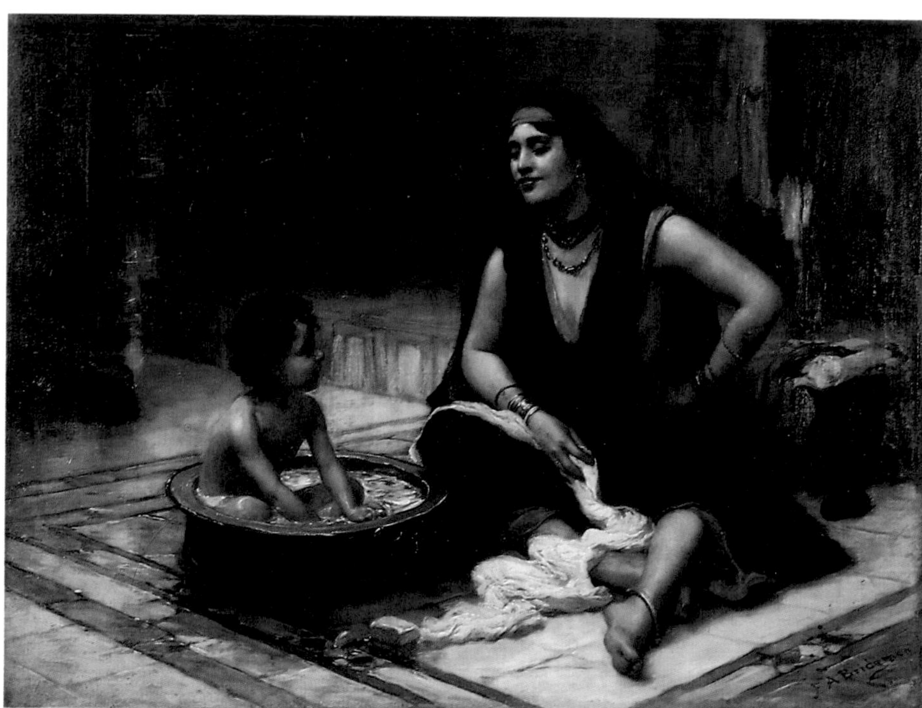

Plate 55.
Frederick A. Bridgman,
Fellahine and Child—the Bath, Cairo, ca. 1892.
Private Collection, Princeton, NJ.

Bridgman is best known for his Orientalist figures and scenes, of which this painting is a typical example. The artist made the first of his regular sojourns to Algeria in 1872 and toured Egypt in 1873. Bridgman compiled his recollections of these visits in a book entitled *Winters in Algeria*, published in 1890. During these trips he made numerous sketches of Algerian scenes, but most of his finished paintings were executed in his Paris studio. Bridgman combined details from a random variety of figures, costumes, and settings, striving for visual effect rather than ethnographic authenticity. Along with the fair's enormously popular Street in Cairo and Algerian Theater built on the Midway, Bridgman's paintings and writings helped create a vivid mythology about the Near East. Despite its fictive origins, this popular Orientalist imagery played an important role in shaping American attitudes toward the region well into the twentieth century.

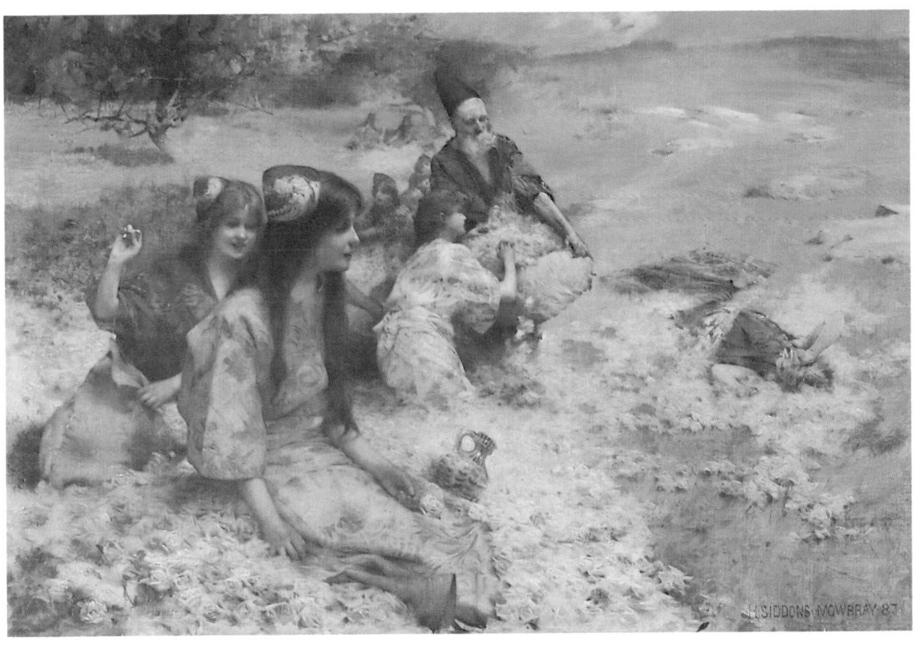

Plate 56.
H. Siddons Mowbray,
Rose Harvest, 1887.
Richard York Gallery,
New York, NY.

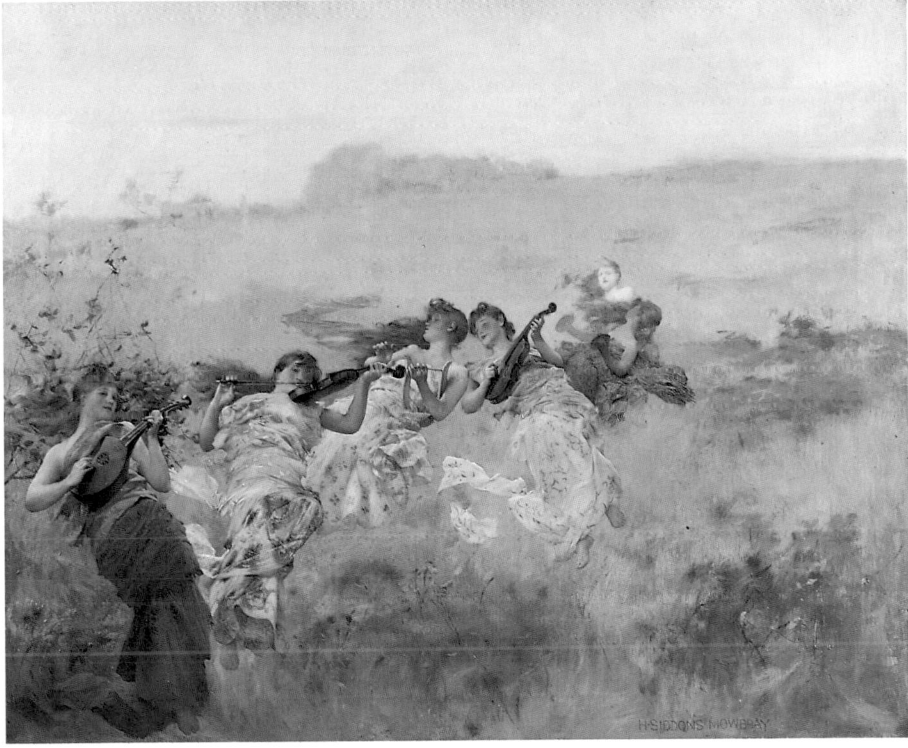

Plate 57.
H. Siddons Mowbray,
The Evening Breeze, 1887.
Private Collection.

Mowbray's interest in the decorative qualities of classicism is conveyed in this allegorical painting. The six maidens who personify the evening breeze are clothed in the delicate hues of twilight as they float softly through the dreamlike landscape.

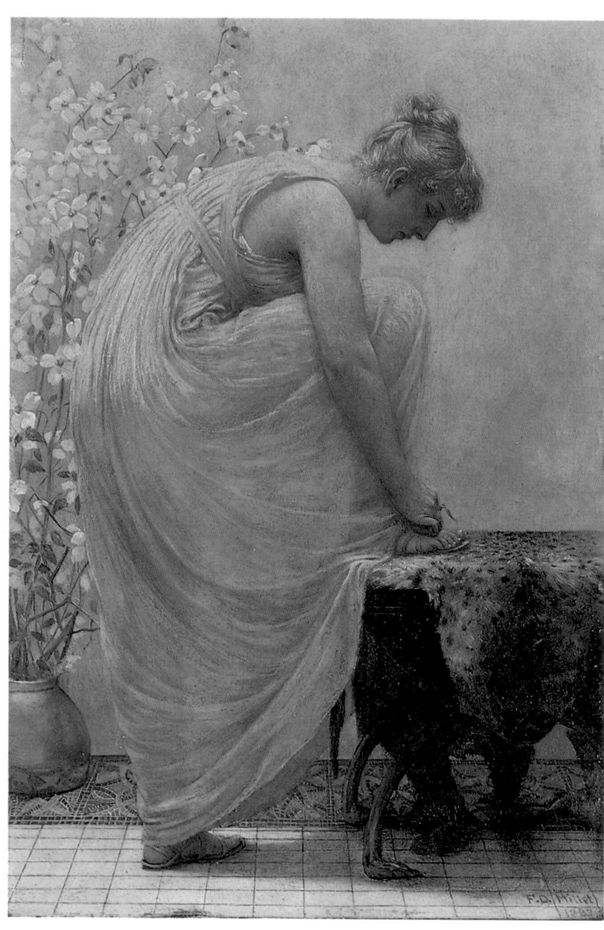

Plate 58.
F. D. Millet,
Lacing the Sandal, 1883.
Private Collection.

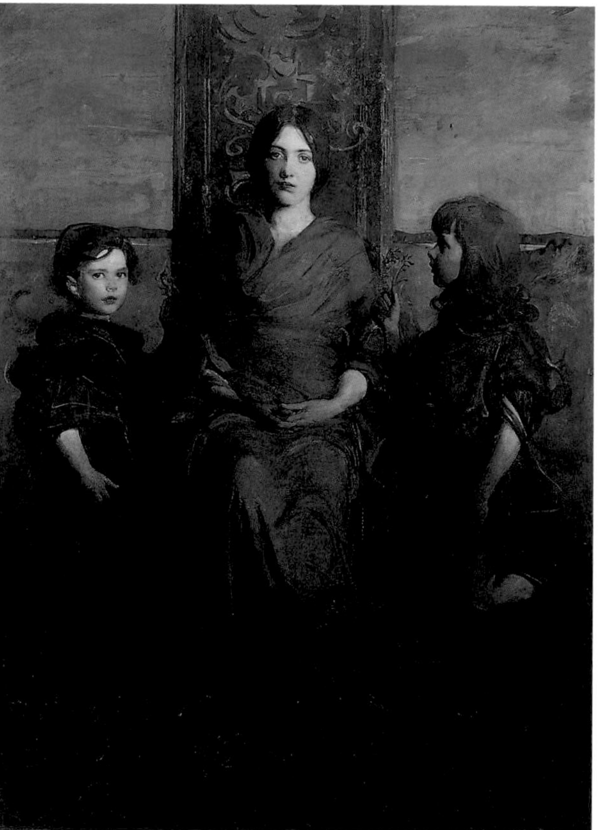

Plate 59.
Abbott H. Thayer,
Virgin Enthroned, 1891.
National Museum of
American Art,
Smithsonian Institution.

In *Virgin Enthroned* Thayer entwined personal and biblical references by painting his own three children as the Madonna flanked by young Jesus and John the Baptist. Another updated religious theme may be found in Alice D. Kellogg's *The Mother*, where the swaddling worn by the newborn infant recalls the wrapping of the Christ child and the mother's position echoes the traditional pose of the Pietà. Both paintings, like those of many other late nineteenth-century artists, were inspired by Renaissance altarpieces.

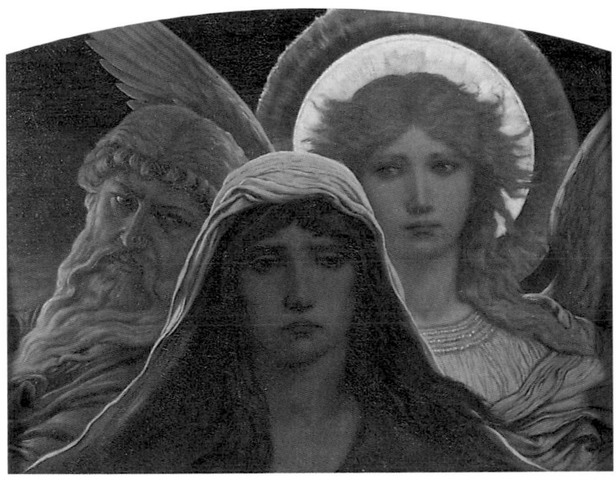

Plate 60.
Elihu Vedder,
Sorrowing Soul Between Doubt and Faith, ca. 1887.
Herbert F. Johnson Museum of Art, Cornell University.

Elihu Vedder gave visual form to the spiritual dilemmas confronting many late nineteenth-century Americans. In this allegorical image a dark and troubled figure hovers on the edge between Doubt, incarnated in the face of a learned, worldly old man, and Faith, symbolized by a beautiful young woman whose calm facial expression and angelic halo radiate confidence. Offering no clue as to the final resolution of the soul's agonizing struggle, Vedder implies that her spiritual turmoil will be endless.

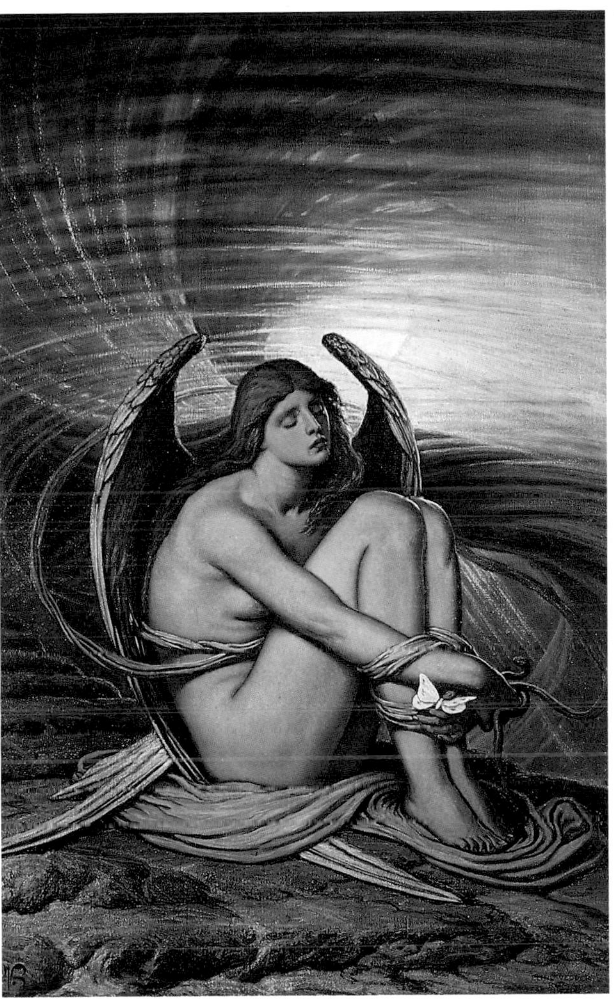

Plate 61.
Elihu Vedder,
A Soul in Bondage, 1891.
The Brooklyn Museum.

Plate 62.
John La Farge,
Halt of the Wise Men from the East, after 1868.
Museum of Fine Arts, Boston.

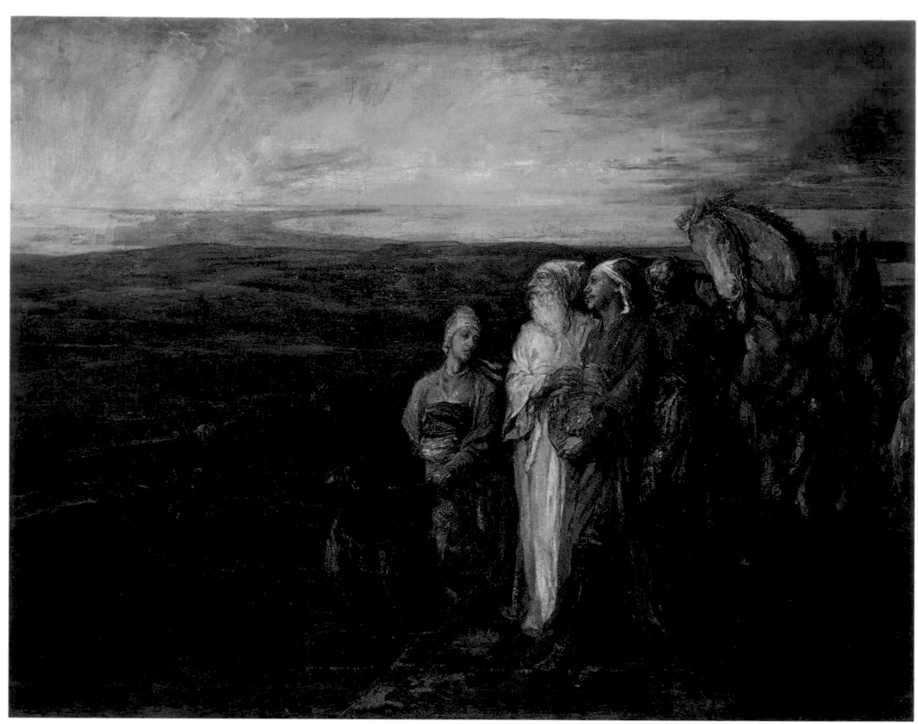

Plate 63.
Gari Melchers,
The Sermon, 1886.
National Museum of American Art, Smithsonian Institution.

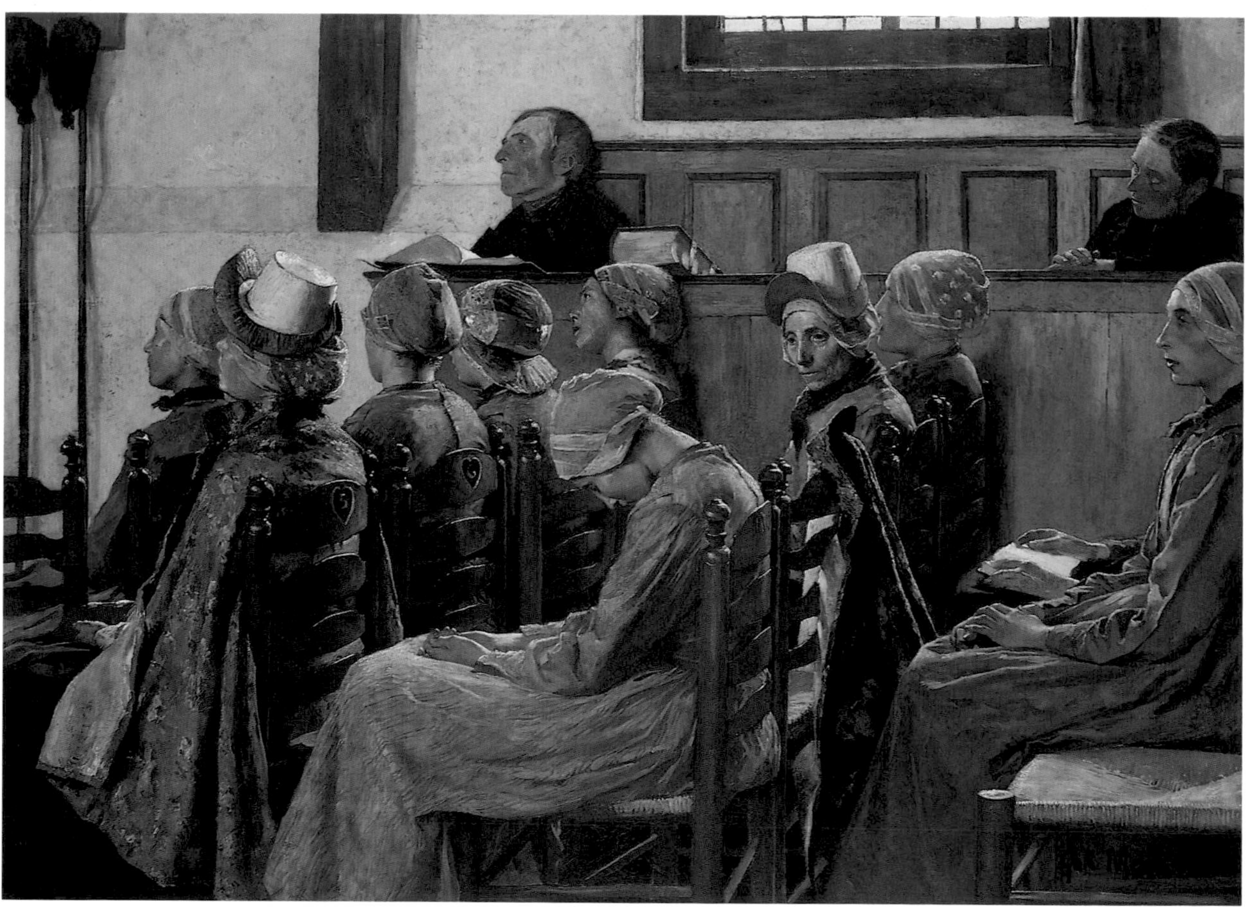

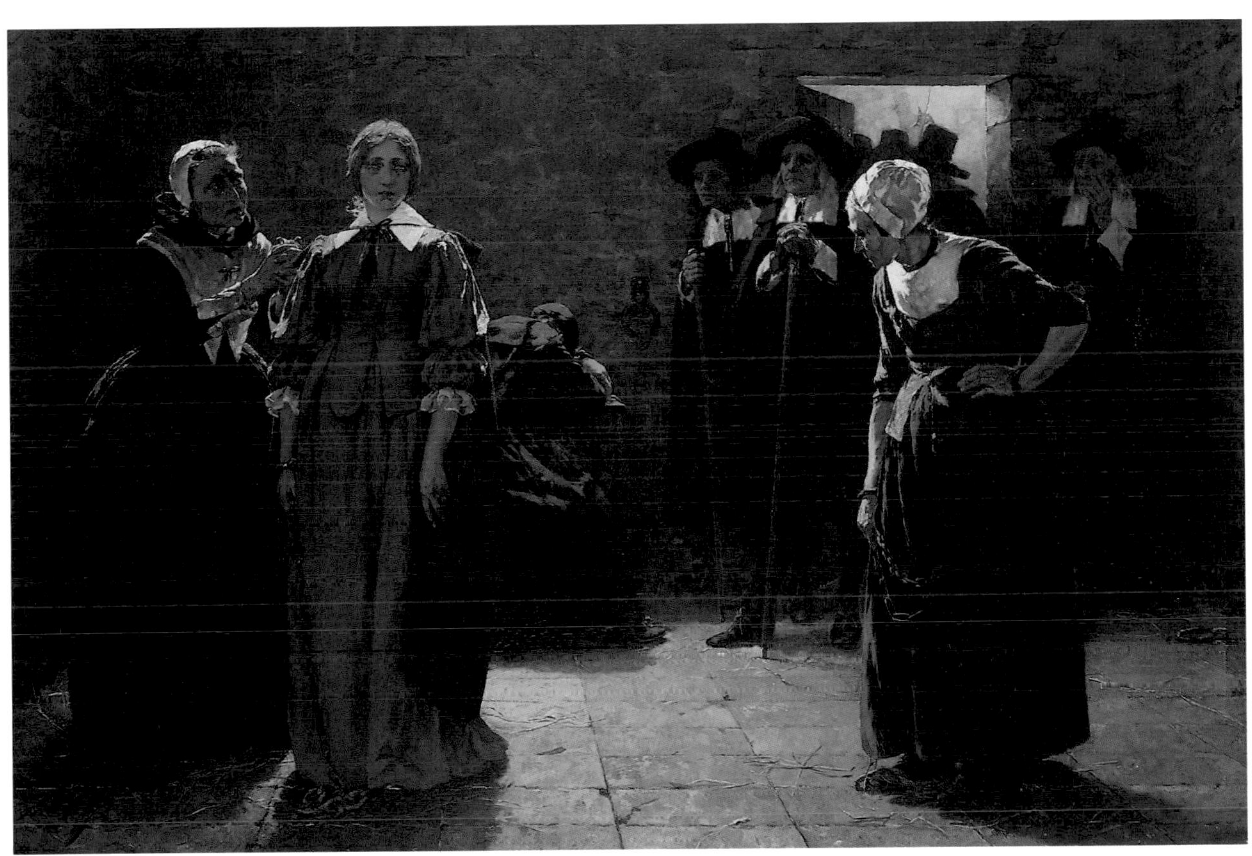

Plate 64.
Walter McEwen,
The Witches, ca. 1892.
Collection Mr. Graham Williford.

One of the most discussed works in the Fine Arts Palace, this painting re-creates an episode from the notorious witch trials that were held in Salem, Massachusetts, in the 1690s. While the monumental scale of the picture certainly made it hard to miss, its popularity was also fueled by a resurgence of interest in the witch trials, which accompanied the colonial revival. At the exposition this interest was heightened by a period-room installation in the Massachusetts Building, mounted by the Essex Institute of Salem, which featured a table from the historic trials.

Rural Traditions and Urban Transformations

In the galleries of the Fine Arts Palace, images of America's urban and industrial centers were all but absent. The laborers, machines, and factories that made the products displayed in the Manufacturing Building at the fair were still not considered appropriate subjects for art, which preferred moral themes and classical subjects. The few exceptions, such as Robert Koehler's *The Strike* or John F. Weir's *Forging the Shaft*, represent unusual attempts to integrate art and industrial life.

Few paintings were as obvious as Charles F. Ulrich's *In the Land of Promise* in treating the subject of immigration, which fueled the labor disputes and economic pressures of the age. Many paintings, however, conceal references to the immigrant experience and its impact on this period. J. G. Brown, for instance, often portrayed poor street urchins learning the most basic lessons of enterprise and social interchange—a charming child's-eye view of life's harsh realities for America's new laboring classes.

Although labor disputes were a major part of national life (the bloody 1886 Haymarket Square riot was still a vivid memory in Chicago), most images of labor at the 1893 fair centered on European peasantry, which automatically meant removing the subject from an urban environment to a rustic setting. Rural labor suggested physical stamina, refined skills, moral discipline, dignity, and honesty; as such, it was an example for American workers. Not surprisingly, such pictures, whether imported from European artists or produced by their American disciples, were popular with the industrialist-collectors who also sought to make a mark in the field of culture.

Charles F. Ulrich's *Glass Blowers* and Edward E. Simmons's *The Carpenter's Son* (another secularized religious subject) provided examples of toil and tradition popular at the time, with an emphasis on manual skills taught by one generation to another, and on continuity within families and communities. In canvases by John J. Enneking, Eastman Johnson, and Guy Rose, outdoor workers moved in timeless harmony with nature's rhythms, whether digging clams, harvesting cranberries, or gathering potatoes. The effect of such portrayals was to gloss over issues of class struggle, wage disputes, and competition for jobs, which characterized American industry at this period—one of the most violent in the nation's history.

Many paintings at the fair showed the elegant pursuits of the leisure class. Julius L. Stewart was the artist most associated with depicting the pleasures and pastimes of society, but other artists also delighted in showing the parade on the way to the Grand Prix (Childe Hassam) or the relaxed ambience of teatime (Mary MacMonnies). The society portrait flourished as the last manifestation of the grand portrait tradition that began in the Renaissance, which was rapidly giving ground to the new medium of photography.

In addition, a large number of portraits highlighting the accomplishments of the rapidly expanding class of professionals were exhibited. These portraits, such as those of the eminent surgeon Dr. Samuel Gross or the distinguished lawyer Christopher C. Langdell, were primarily of men. A rare exception was John Singer Sargent's portrait of Ellen Terry as Lady Macbeth.

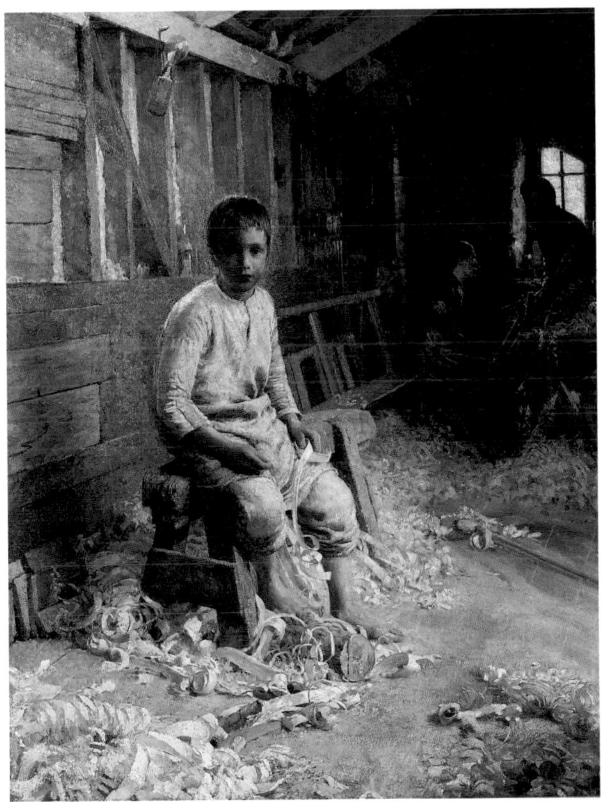

Plate 65.
Edward E. Simmons,
The Carpenter's Son, 1888.
Private Collection.

Influenced by German painter Friedrich von Uhde, who often modernized the Scripture in his religious subjects, Simmons painted his son as the youthful Christ in present-day peasant garb. The light entering through the crude walls of the carpenter's shop creates a halo effect; the turtledoves above his head represent those that were sacrificed when the young Christ was taken to the temple for purification.

When first exhibited in 1888 at the Royal Academy in London, and later in Glasgow, many were outraged at the "low-typed boy, who, with the old hag . . . are supposed to represent Christ and his mother." The artist defended his position in an 1892 letter to the painting's purchaser: "I know very little of how the details of Christ's surroundings should be told. Therefore we younger men fall back upon our own time—believing that man has always been fundamentally the same."

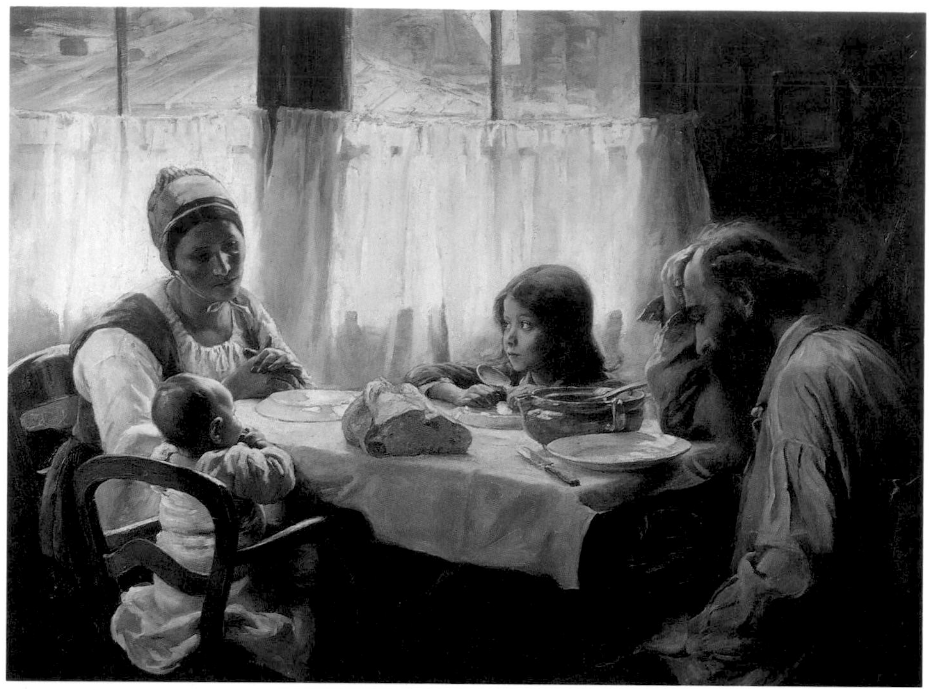

Plate 66.
Elizabeth Nourse,
A Family Meal, 1891.
Estate of George W. and Evelina B. Perkins. Photograph by Wayne Geist.

Nourse took several sketching trips to remote European villages in order to render faithfully the peasants, whose costumes and customs greatly interested her. She and her American patrons believed that the struggles and labors of these people embodied a piety toward which they should all strive. This reverence for peasant life was particularly strong in late nineteenth-century America when the population was rapidly forsaking rural areas for higher-paying jobs in the cities, creating considerable social upheaval in urban areas.

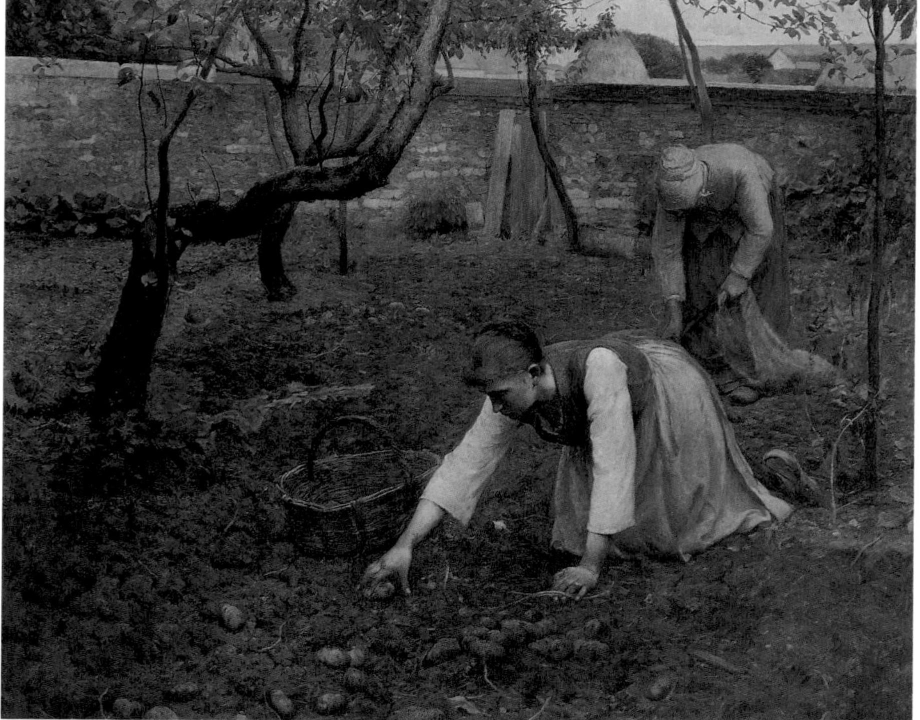

Plate 67.
Guy Rose,
Potato Gatherers, 1891.
Collection Mrs. John Dowling Relfe. Photograph by Schopplein Studio.

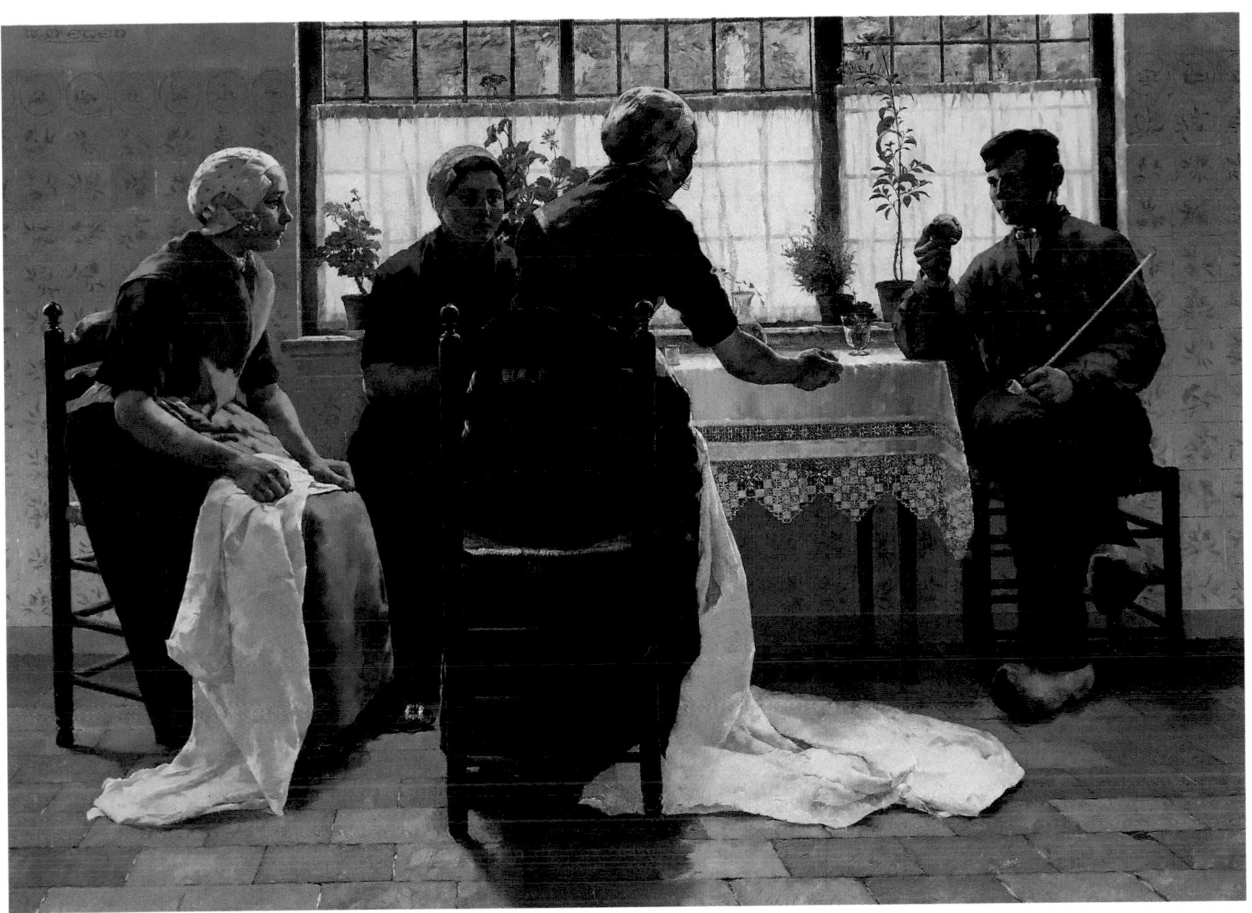

Plate 68.
Walter McEwen,
The Judgment of Paris, ca. 1886.
Tennessee Wesleyan College, Athens, TN.

Walter McEwen updated a venerable tale from Greek mythology by rendering it as a genre scene in a rural Dutch domestic interior. The myth focuses upon a beauty contest in which the Trojan prince Paris was called upon to choose one of three goddesses—Hera, Athena, or Aphrodite—to receive the coveted golden apple; the ensuing jealousies resulted in the Trojan War. By substituting contemporary figures, McEwen simultaneously ennobled the Dutch peasants and called attention to the modern relevance of the myth's moral lessons. The painting was well received by critics and won an honorable mention at the Paris Salon of 1886.

Plate 69.
Henry S. Bisbing,
On the River Bank, ca. 1891.
Collection Mrs. Betty Williams.

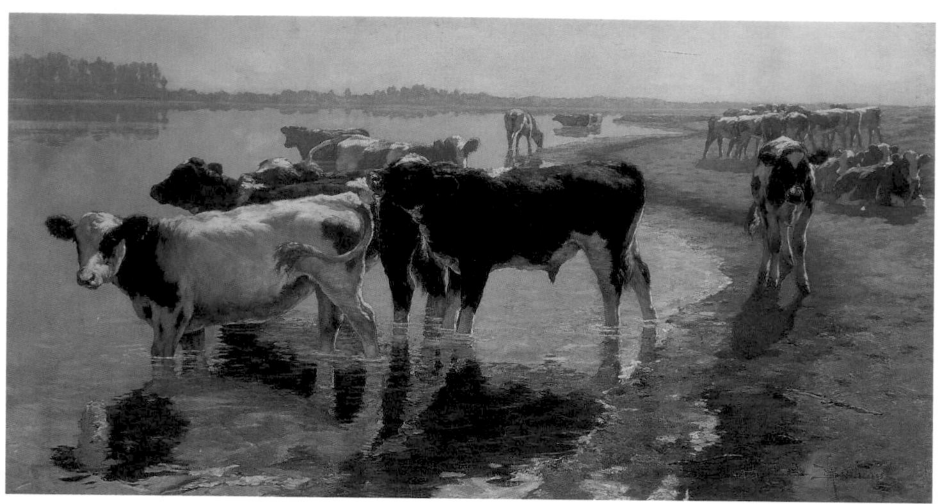

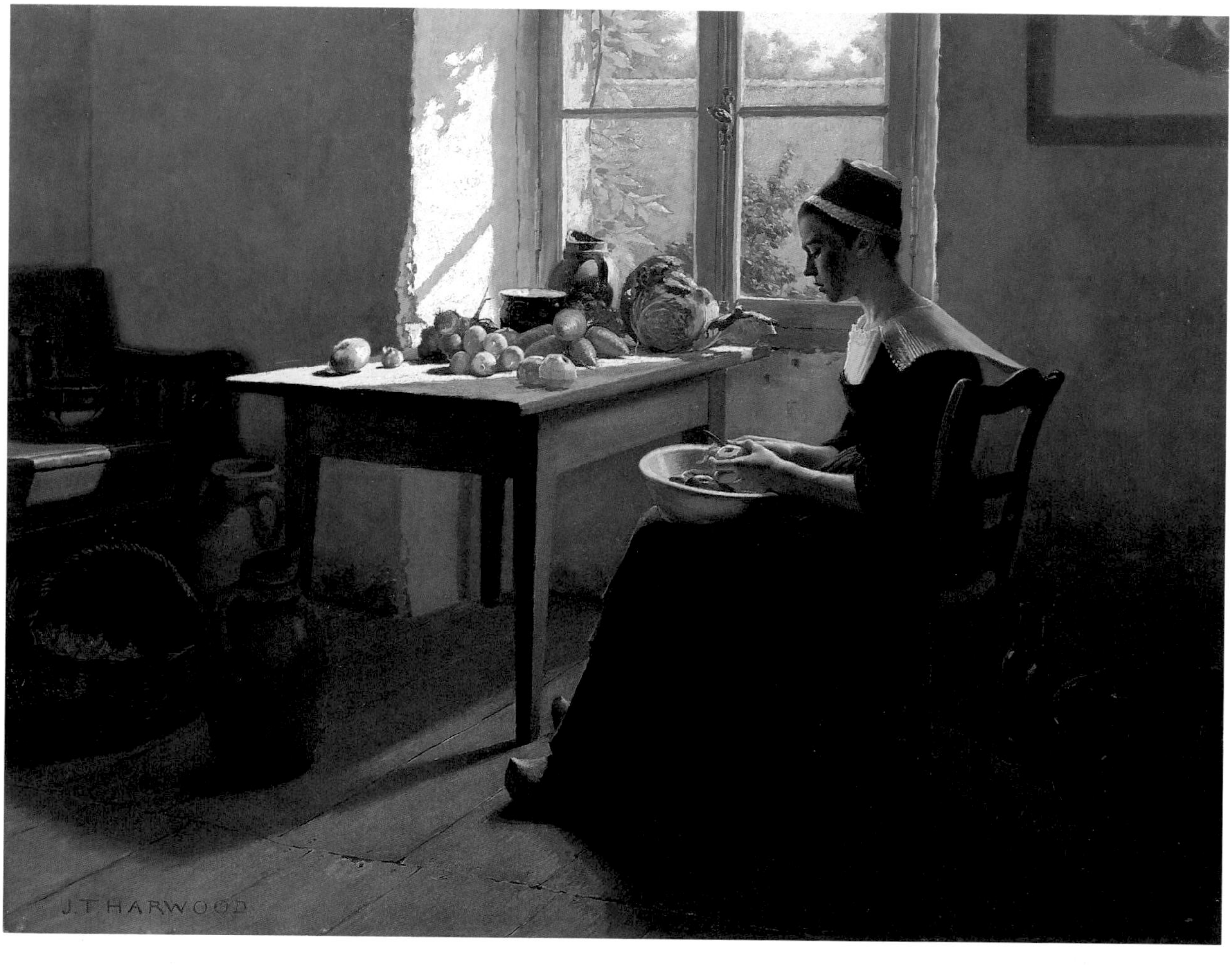

Plate 70.
J. T. Harwood,
Preparing Dinner, 1891.
University of Utah Union Collection/Utah Museum of Fine Arts, University of Utah.

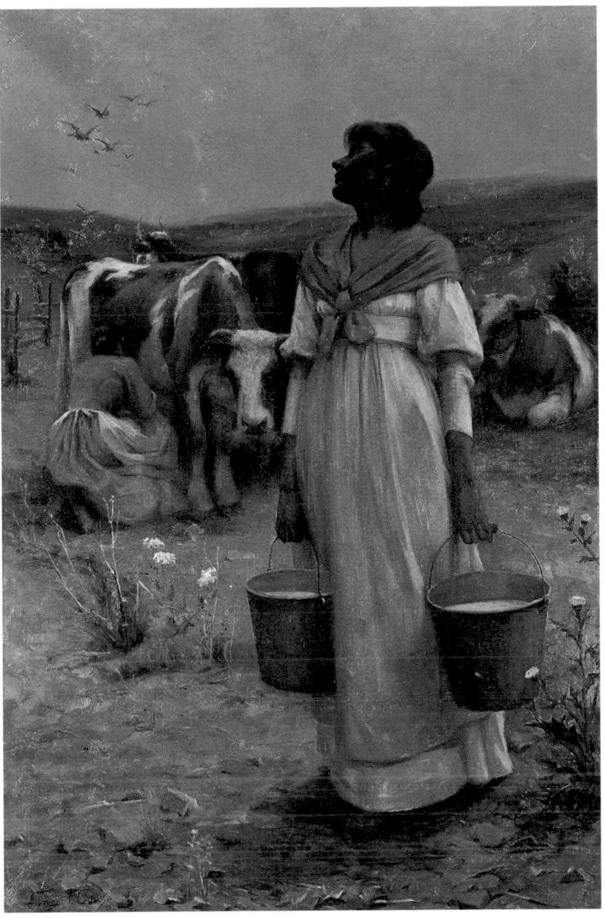

Plate 71.
Eanger Irving Couse,
Milking Time, 1892.
Couse Family Collection.

Plate 72.
Winslow Homer,
The Two Guides, ca. 1875.
Sterling and Francine Clark Art Institute, Williamstown, MA.

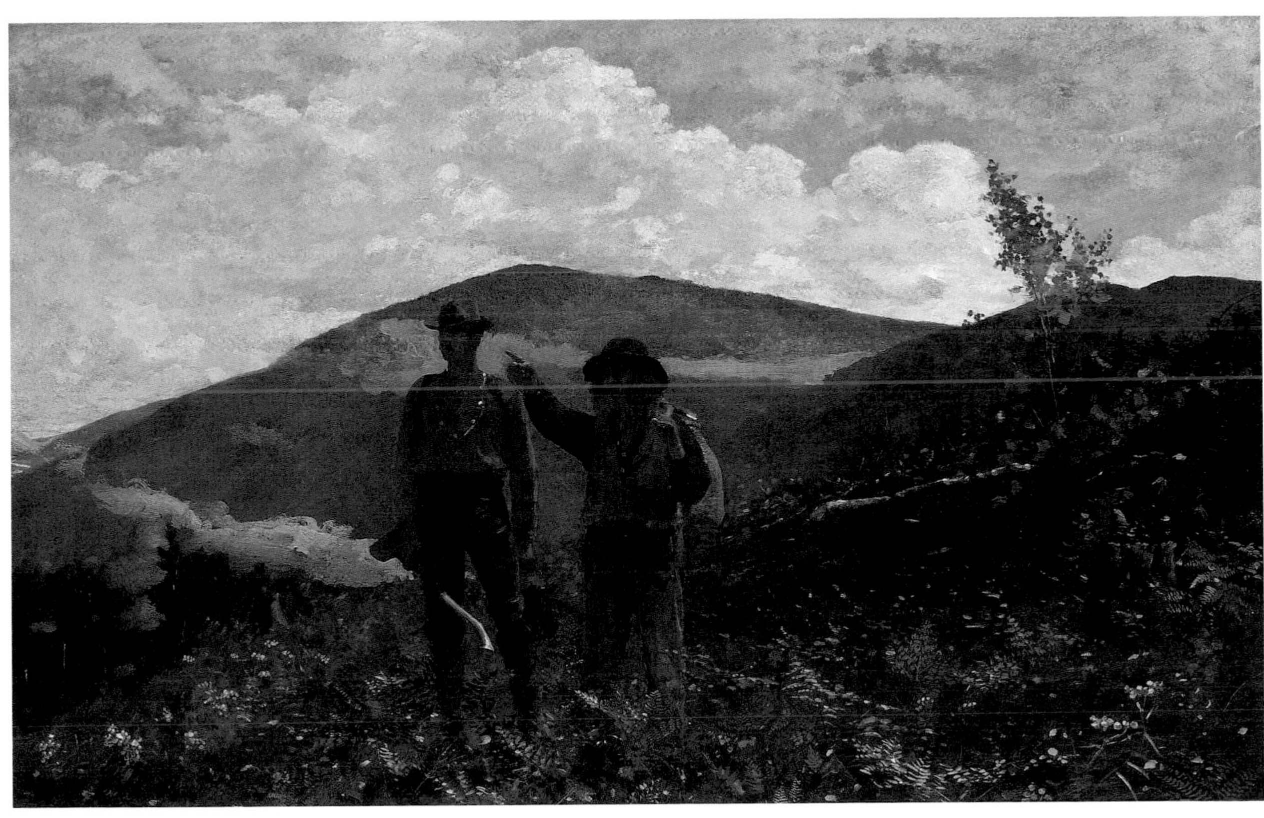

Plate 73.
John J. Enneking,
A South Duxbury Clam Digger,
1892.
Scripps College, Claremont, CA.

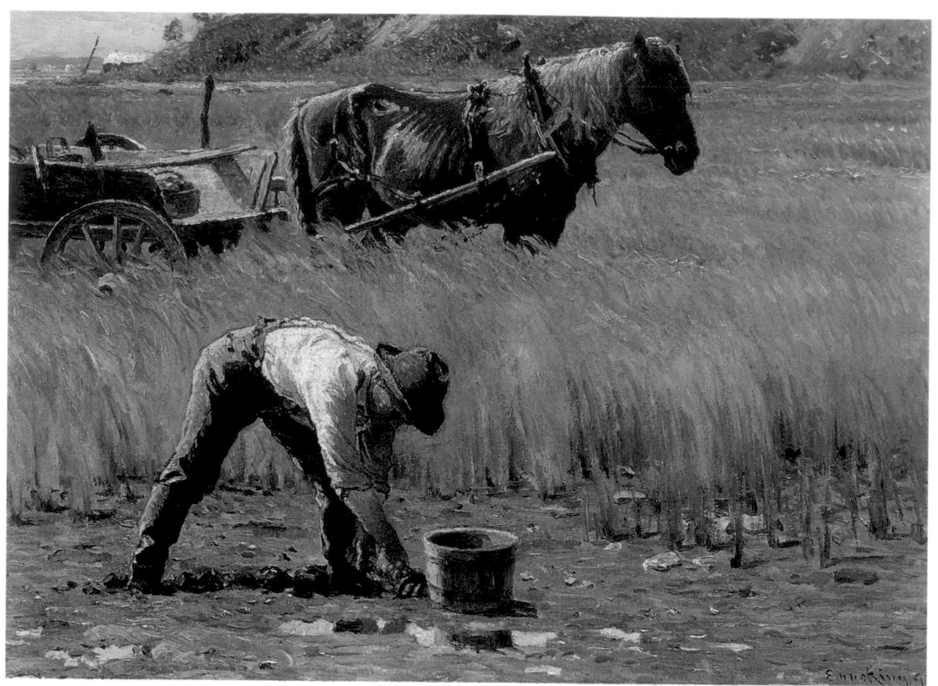

Plate 74.
Eastman Johnson,
The Cranberry Harvest, Nantucket Island, Mass., 1880.
Putnam Collection, Timken Museum of Art, San Diego.

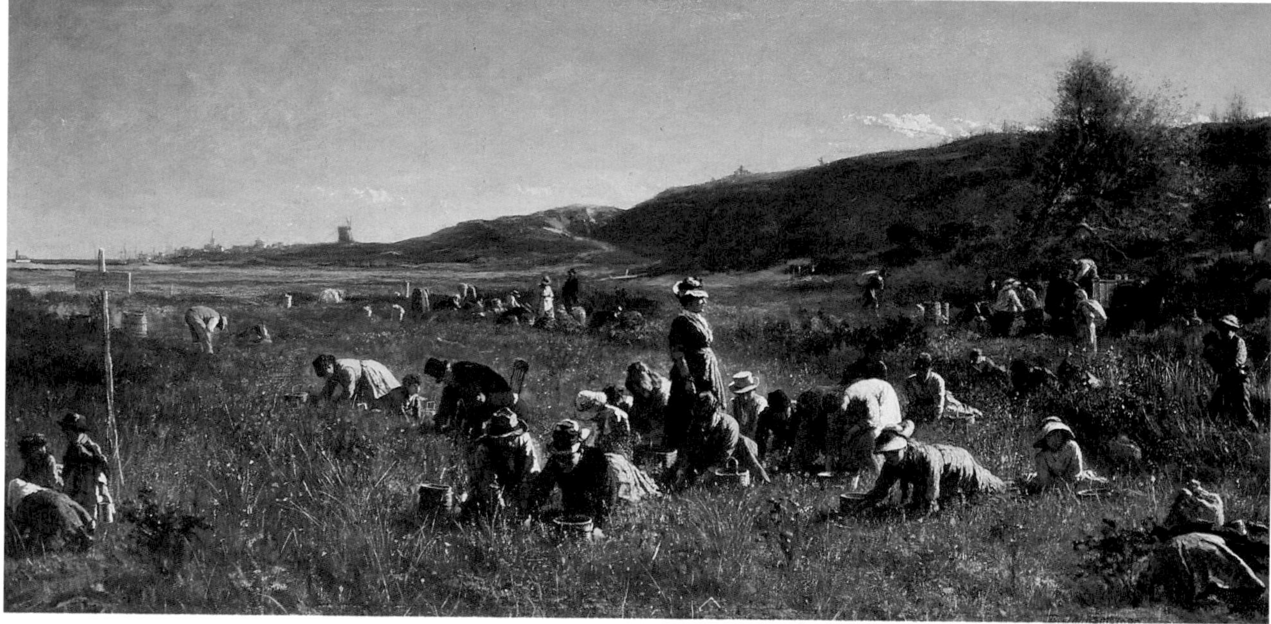

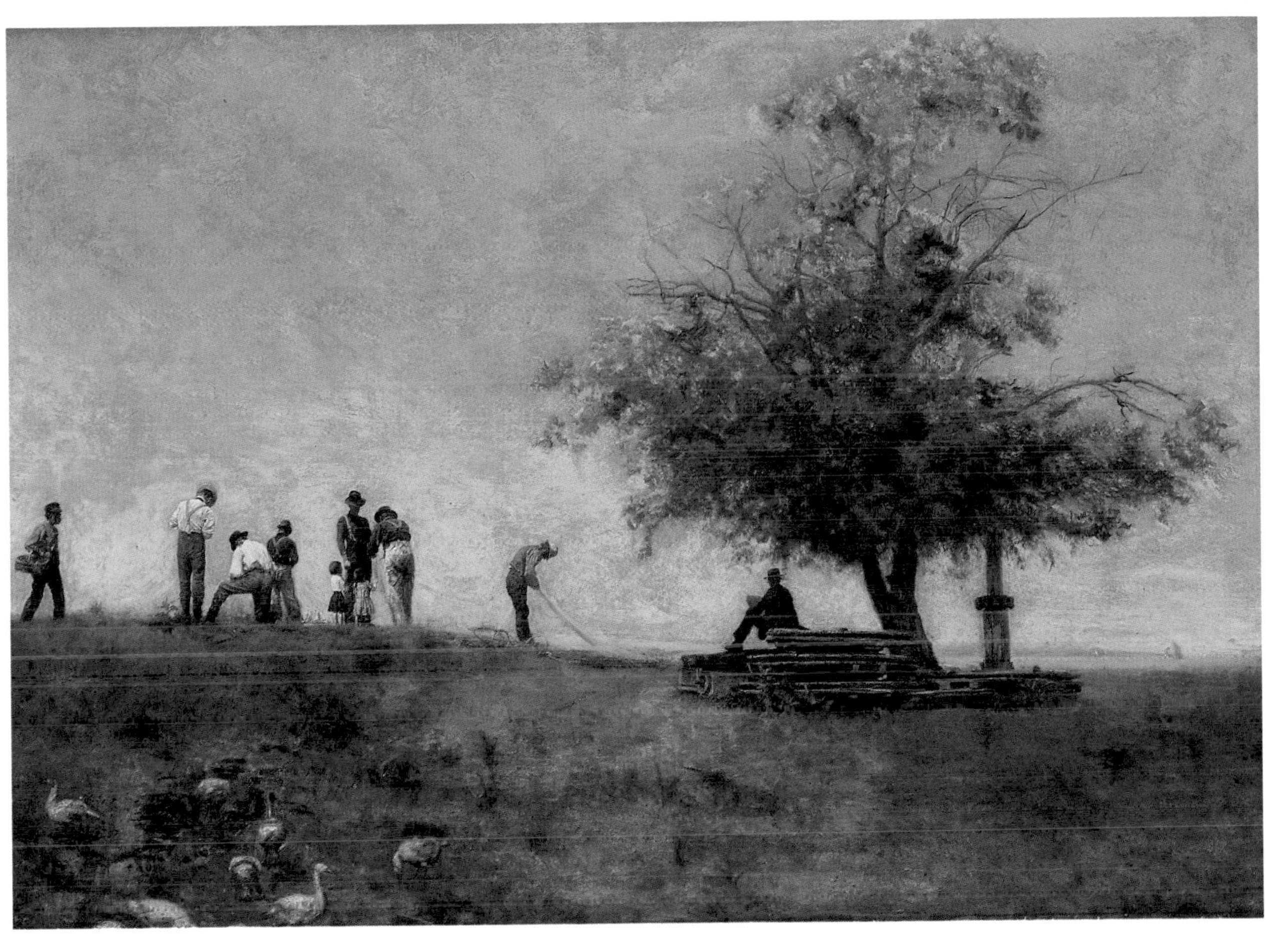

Plate 75.
Thomas Eakins,
Mending the Nets, 1881.
Philadelphia Museum of Art.

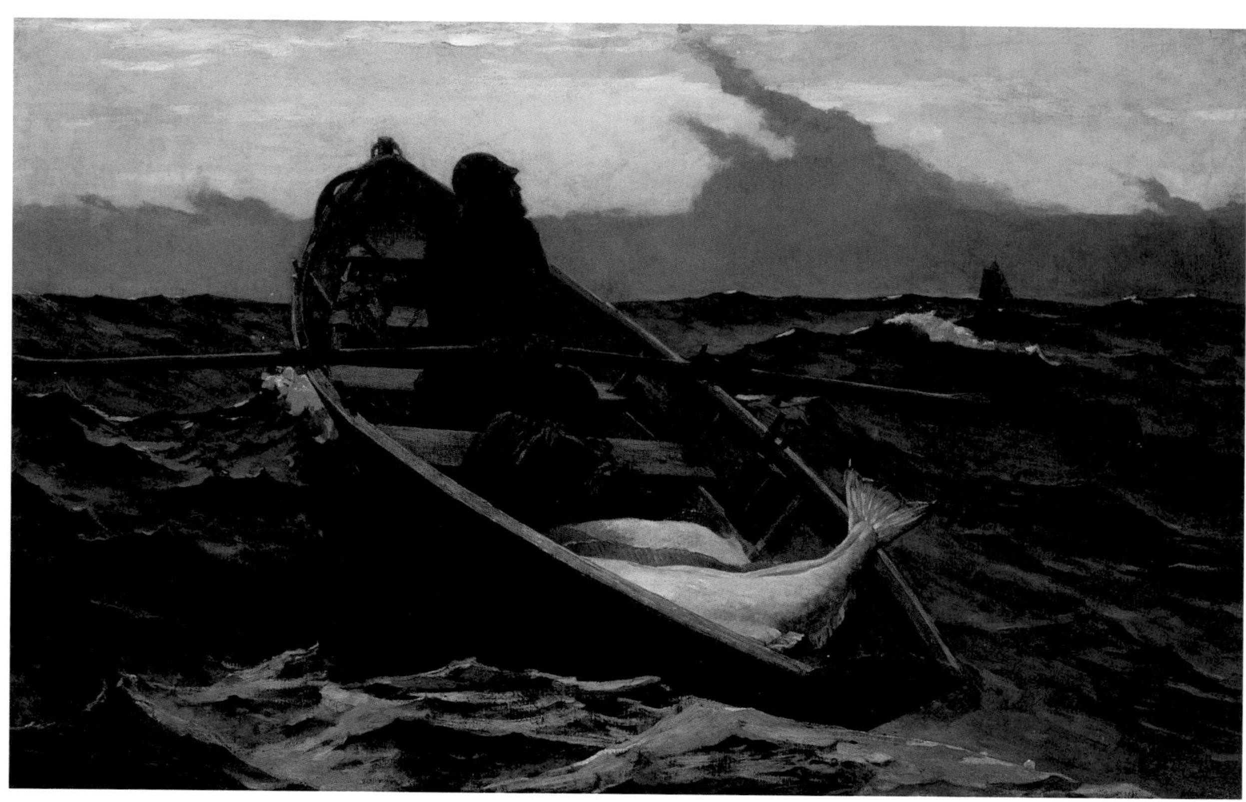

Plate 76.
Winslow Homer,
The Fog Warning, 1885.
Museum of Fine Arts, Boston.

Of the fifteen paintings Winslow Homer exhibited at the fair, ten have as their theme the people and environment of the New England coast. Four works, including *The Fog Warning*, focus upon the activities of fishermen at sea. This painting depicts a lone fisherman rowing a dory back toward its mother schooner. While the two large halibut lying in the bottom of the boat assure us that his quest for fish has been successful, the threatening fog on the horizon indicates that his safe return to the ship is less certain.

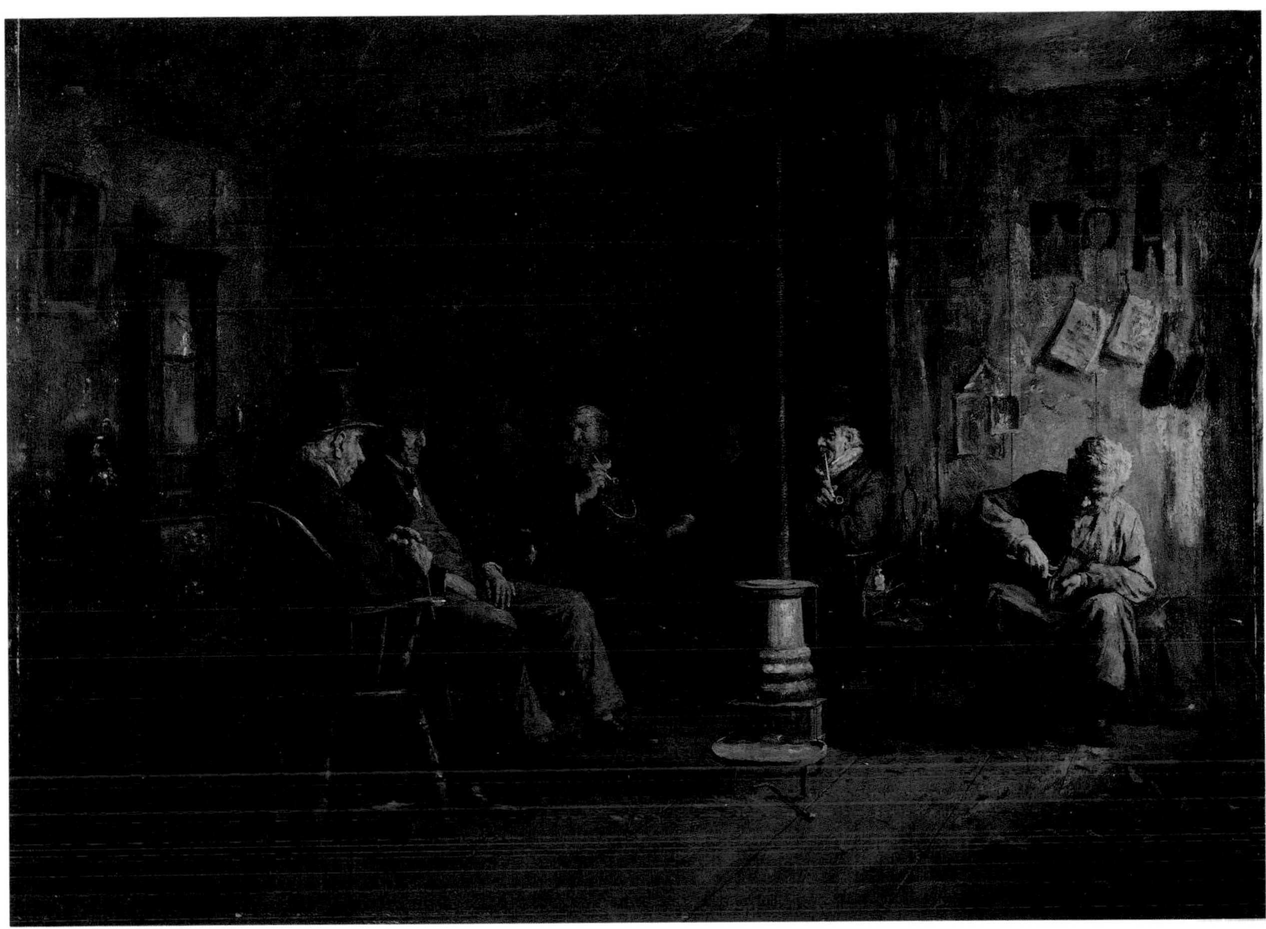

Plate 77.
Eastman Johnson,
The Nantucket School of Philosophy, ca. 1886.
The Walters Art Gallery,
Baltimore.

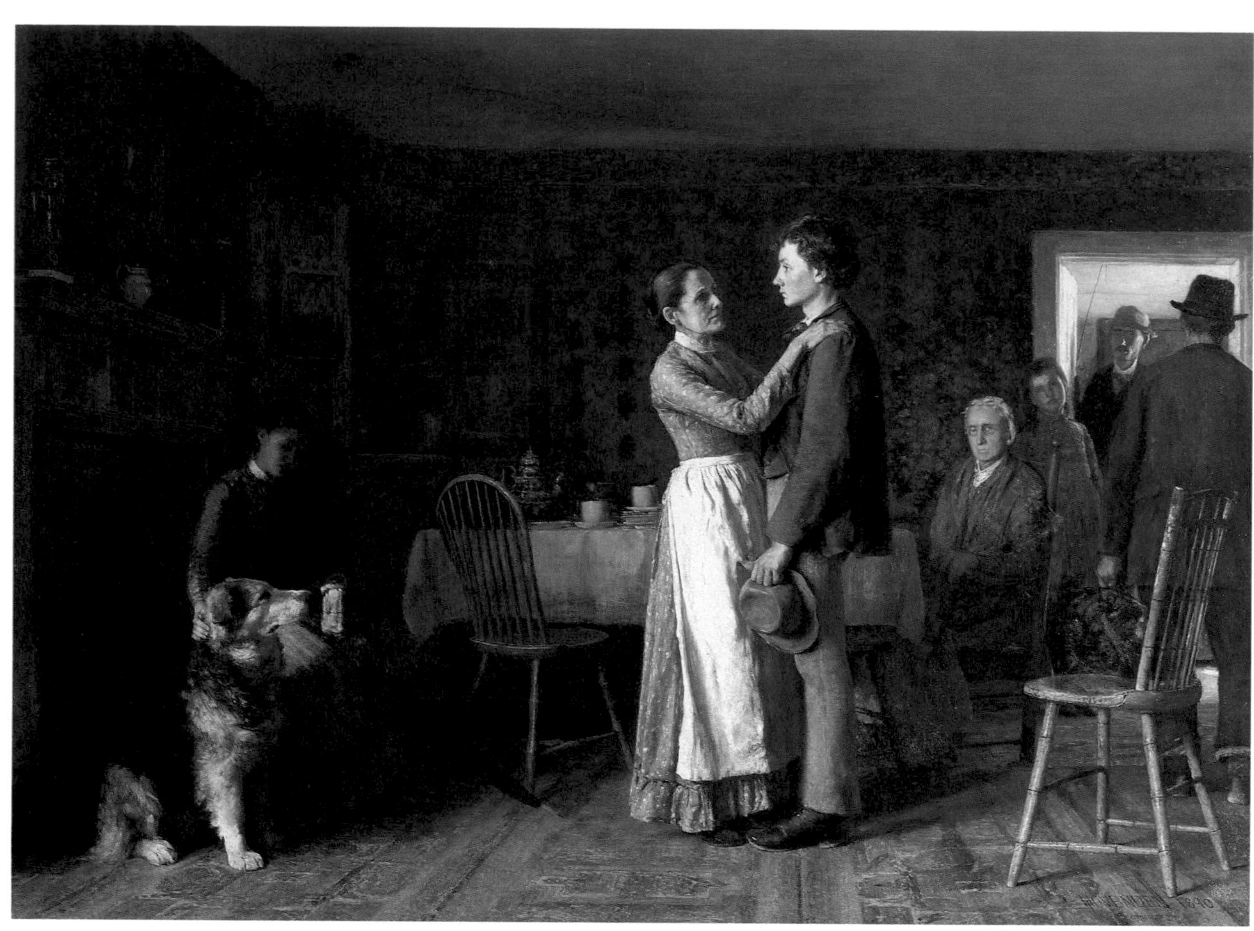

Plate 78.
Thomas Hovenden,
Breaking the Home Ties, 1890.
Philadelphia Museum of Art.

Although dismissed as too anecdotal by some critics, this was the single most popular picture at the fair, pronounced their favorite by an overwhelming majority of visitors. A reporter for the *Pittsburgh Press* noted: "It did not surprise me to see tears running down many a motherly-looking face, and to hear one self-made man exclaim: 'By George, I'd rather have that than all the rest of the collection!'" Another critic agreed: "A community cannot be entirely gone to the dogs when it is enthralled by a simple, homely scene like this."

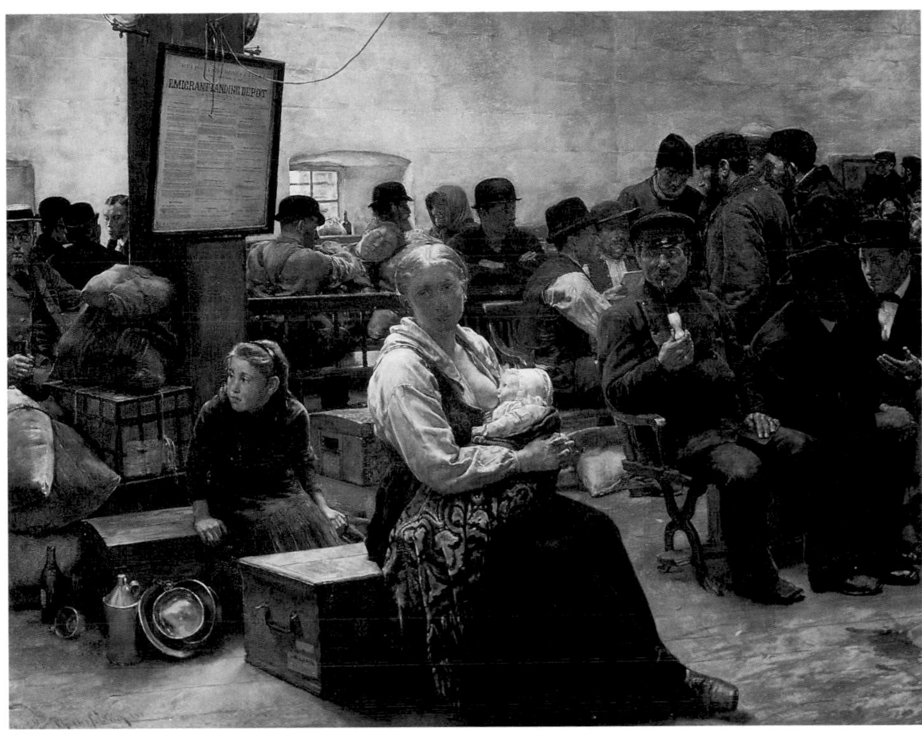

Plate 79.
Charles F. Ulrich,
In the Land of Promise, 1884.
Corcoran Gallery of Art.

When it was exhibited at the National Academy of Design in 1884, this work garnered for Ulrich the first Thomas B. Clarke Prize, awarded for the best figure painting shown that year. The painting features a variety of national and ethnic types anxiously waiting at the Castle Garden immigration station on the lower tip of Manhattan. Castle Garden served as the primary landing depot for immigrants from 1855 to 1892; seven and a half million people passed through the station before it was replaced by the new facility at Ellis Island.

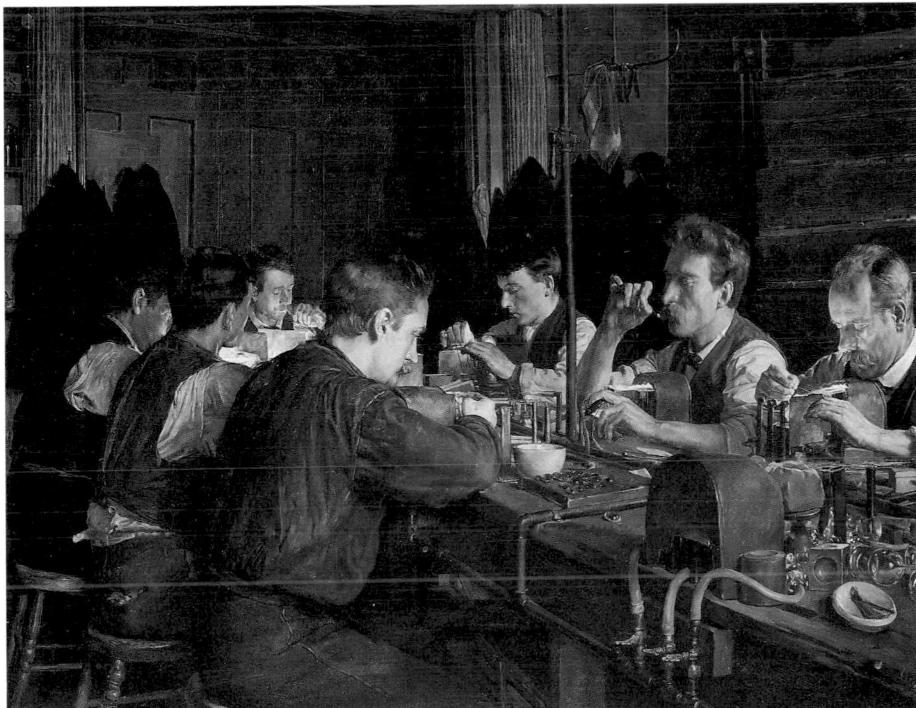

Plate 80.
Charles F. Ulrich,
Glass Blowers, 1883.
Museo de Arte de Ponce, Luis A. Ferré Foundation, Ponce, PR.
Photograph by Antonio de Jesús.

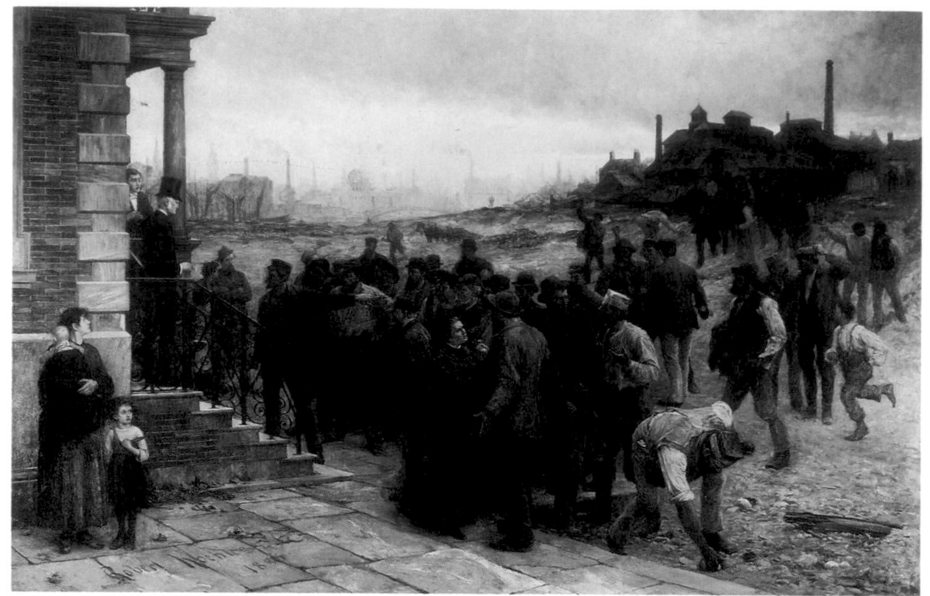

Plate 81.
Robert Koehler,
The Strike, 1886.
Deutsches Historisches
Museum, Berlin.

This was one of the few pictures at the fair, and in American art of that period in general, to address the issues of industrial labor and workers' unrest. Originally inspired by the 1877 strike of railroad workers in Pittsburgh, the painting caused a sensation in 1886 when its exhibition at the National Academy of Design coincided with the outbreak of a general strike in Chicago. Culminating in a violence-filled rally at Haymarket Square, the Chicago strike was part of a national campaign of organized laborers to establish the eight-hour workday as a legal standard. Koehler's painting would have served to mirror yet another contemporary situation when it was shown at the exposition, where the construction of the buildings and grounds had been delayed by several strikes.

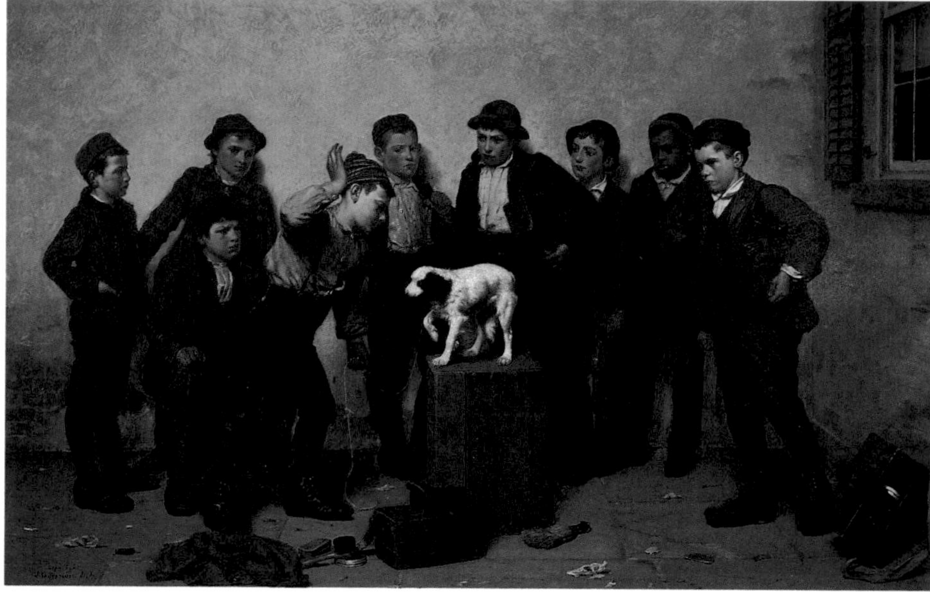

Plate 82.
J. G. Brown,
Training the Dog, n.d.
Washington and Lee University,
Lexington, VA.

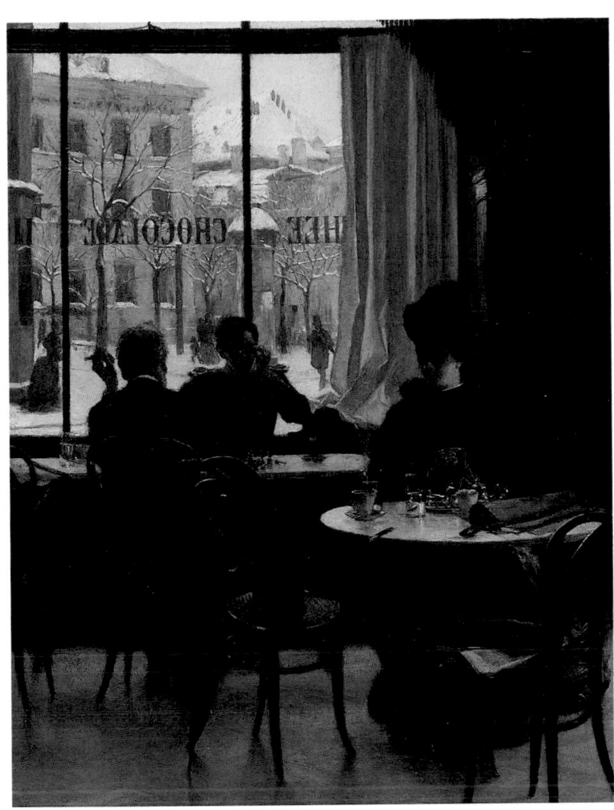

Plate 83.
Robert Koehler,
At the Cafe, ca. 1887.
Private Collection.

Plate 84.
Eugene L. Vail,
On the Thames, 1886.
Collection Chris Whittle,
Knoxville, TN.

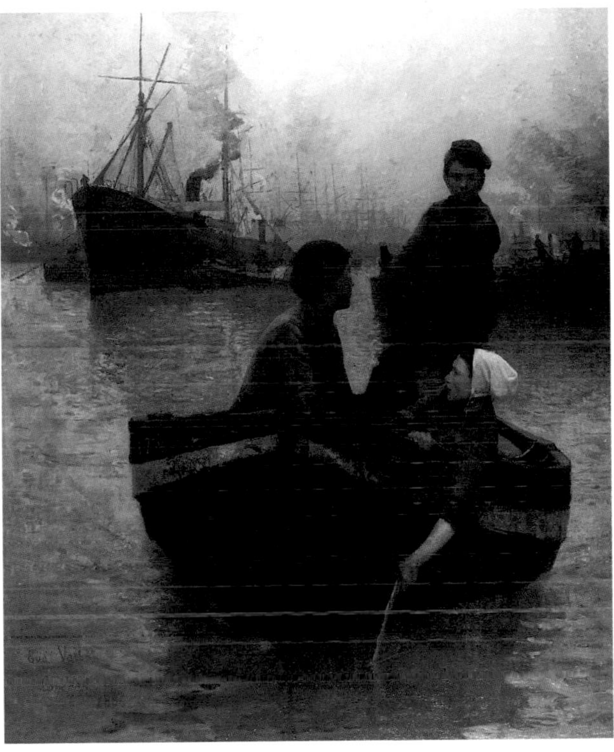

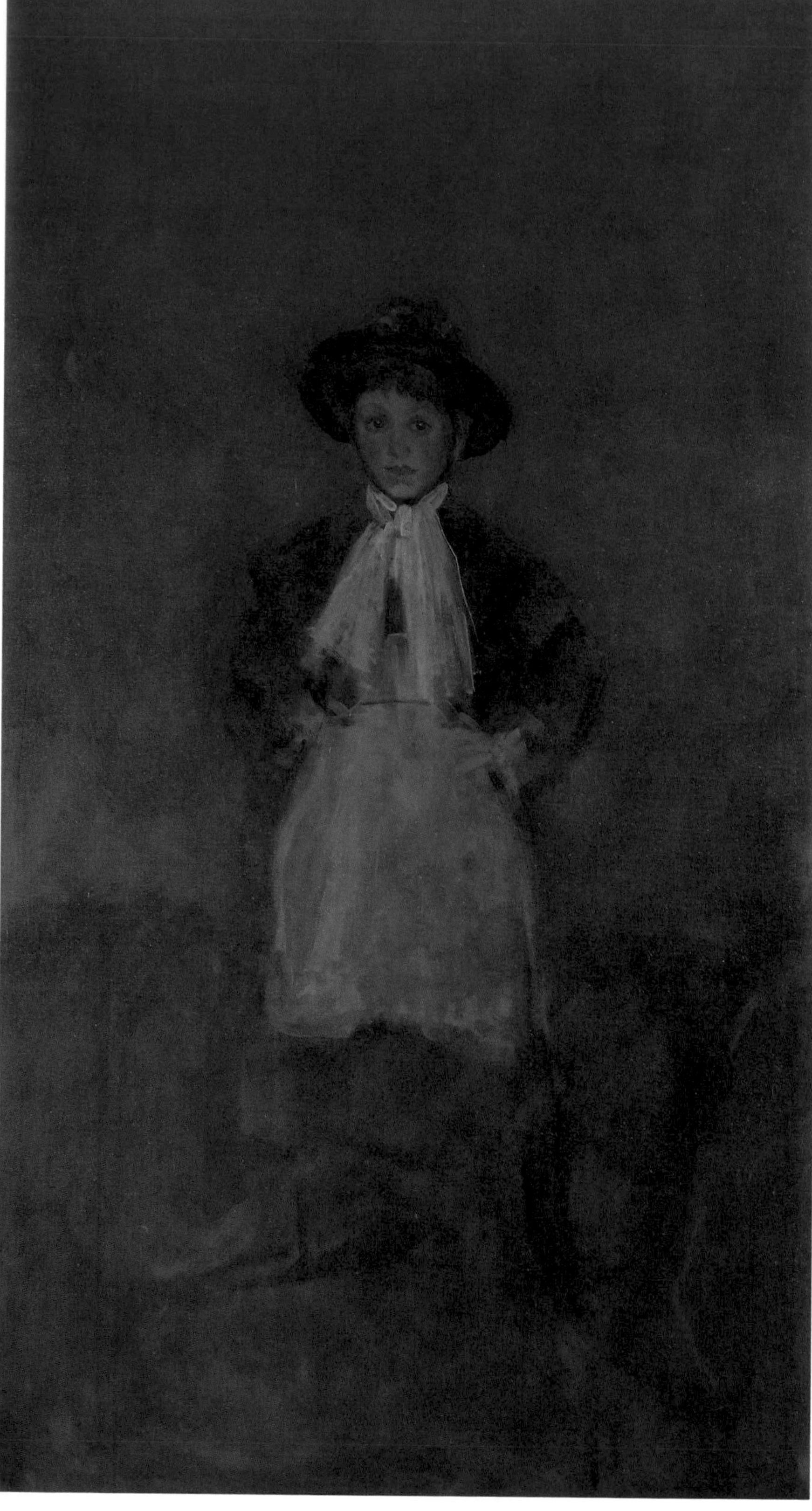

Plate 85.
James McNeill Whistler,
The Chelsea Girl,
ca. 1884–86.
Private Collection. Photograph by Christopher Burke.

The Chelsea Girl was described as a "veritable daughter of the people, with all the defiance of an offspring of the *prolétaire* in her attitude" and as a little "coster child," or fruitmonger's daughter. As an image taken from the streets of London, the subject was one unencumbered by middle-class conventions of decorum. The painting was praised for its beautiful brushwork. Whistler, as well as critics writing about it during the summer of 1893, saw it as a sketch, a "work for artists." Whistler, in fact, was a bit miffed that it had been sent to the fair, as it was "the sketch of *one afternoon*—or rather the first statement or beginning of a painting—I am not *excusing* it mind—for of course it is a damn fine thing . . . [but not] a *representative* finished picture!"

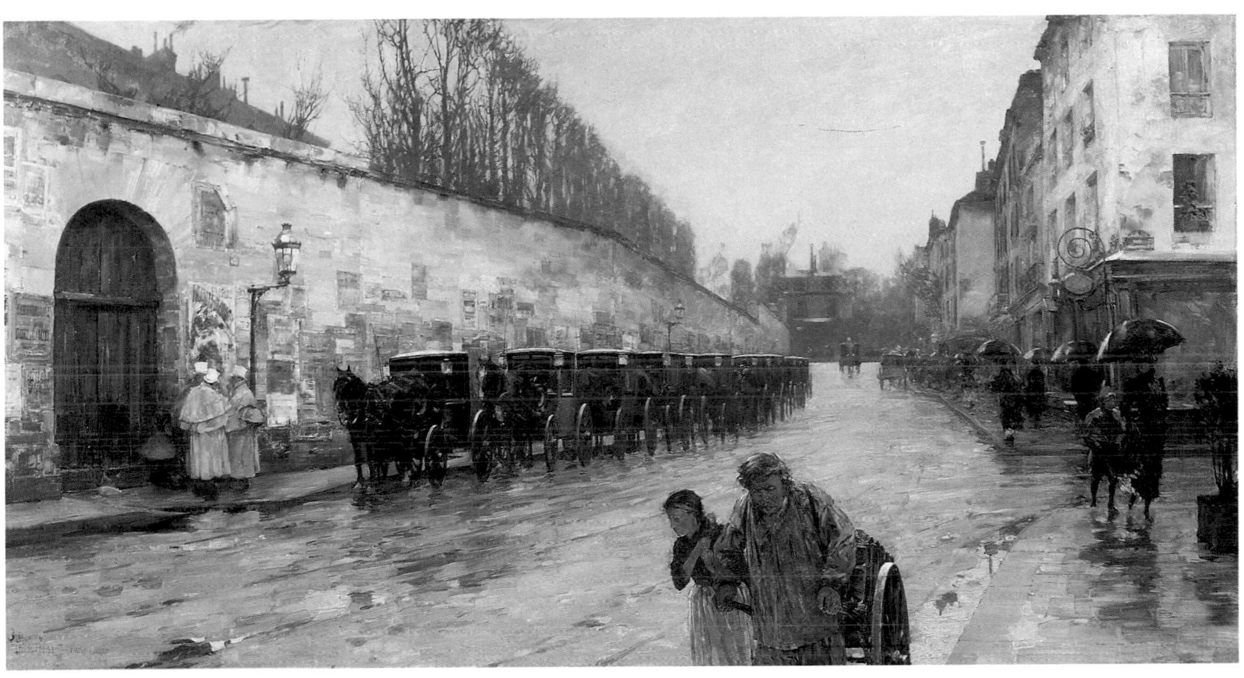

Plate 86.
Childe Hassam,
Cab Station, Rue Bonaparte, Paris, 1887.
Collection Gloria Manney.

Plate 87.
Thomas Eakins,
Portrait of Dr. Gross, 1875.
Jefferson Medical College of
Thomas Jefferson University,
Philadelphia, PA.

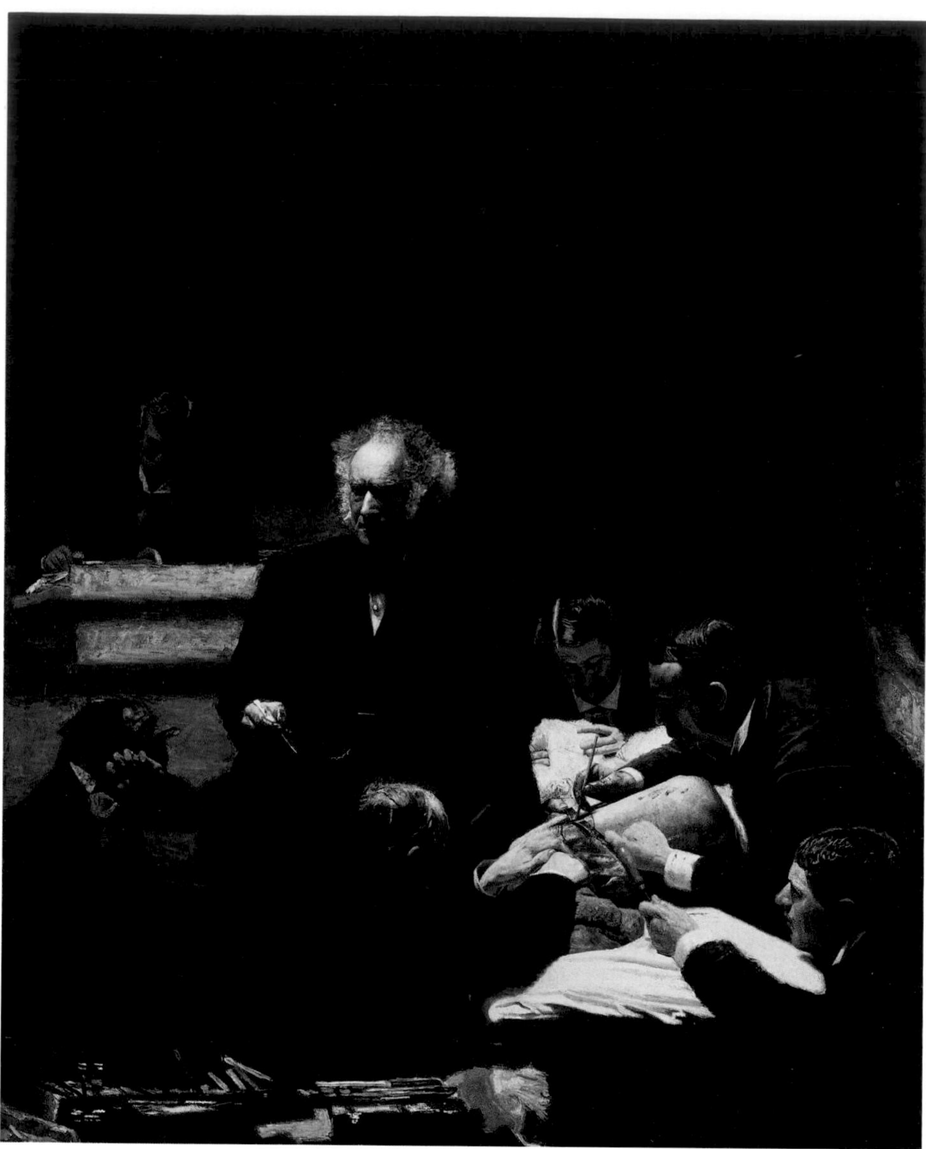

When the Philadelphia jury met in January 1893 to select the artworks to represent the region at the World's Columbian Exposition, they chose ten paintings by Thomas Eakins. Less than a dozen other American painters were accorded this honor at the fair. The decision to present Eakins's work in such depth was an extraordinary testimony to the continued support given him by his peers after 1886 when he was asked to resign from his teaching position at the Pennsylvania Academy of the Fine Arts.

The Philadelphia committee was equally courageous in selecting *Portrait of Dr. Gross* (now entitled *The Gross Clinic*) as one of Eakins's entries. The artist originally created this work for the 1876 Centennial Exposition in Philadelphia as an example of American surgical excellence. The Centennial art jury, offended by the picture's directness, refused to allow it to hang in the regular art exhibition. Dr. Gross, an admirer of Eakins's work, arranged for it to be exhibited in the medical section, where it was described as an illustration of "an operation for the removal of dead bone from the femur of a child." By 1893, although critics commended Eakins's portraits for their "originality and power" and praised his skill and versatility, many still felt that *The Gross Clinic*, despite being "admirably painted," was "unfit for a public exhibition of art" because "there can be little that is esthetic in representations of probing and dissecting."

Plate 88.
John Singer Sargent,
Portrait of Ellen Terry as Lady Macbeth, 1889.
Tate Gallery, London.

Sargent was present on 29 December 1888, at the first performance of Sir Henry Irving's new production of *Macbeth*, in which Ellen Terry played Lady Macbeth. Her silk and tinsel costume oversewn with beetle wings and Celtic designs was so stunning that the painter resolved to do her portrait. The finished work was a sensation when it was exhibited in London; four years later in Chicago it was one of the most talked about paintings in the Fine Arts Palace, both praised and reviled by the critics. The crux of all arguments was the picture's artificiality. As one writer pointed out: "It is a *tour de force* of realism applied to the artificial, the actress caught and fixed, not as the individuality assumed, but as herself seen through and outside of the assumption."

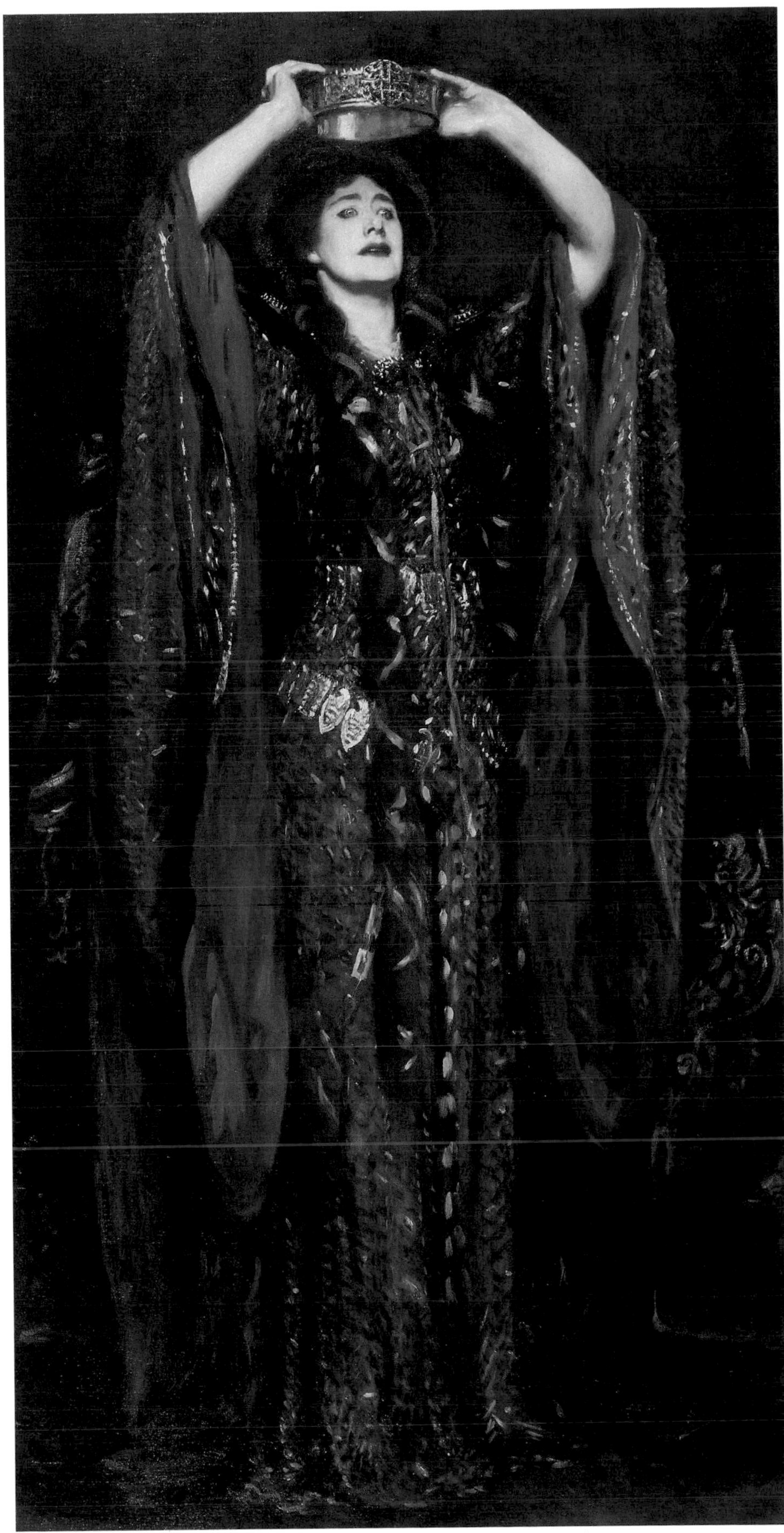

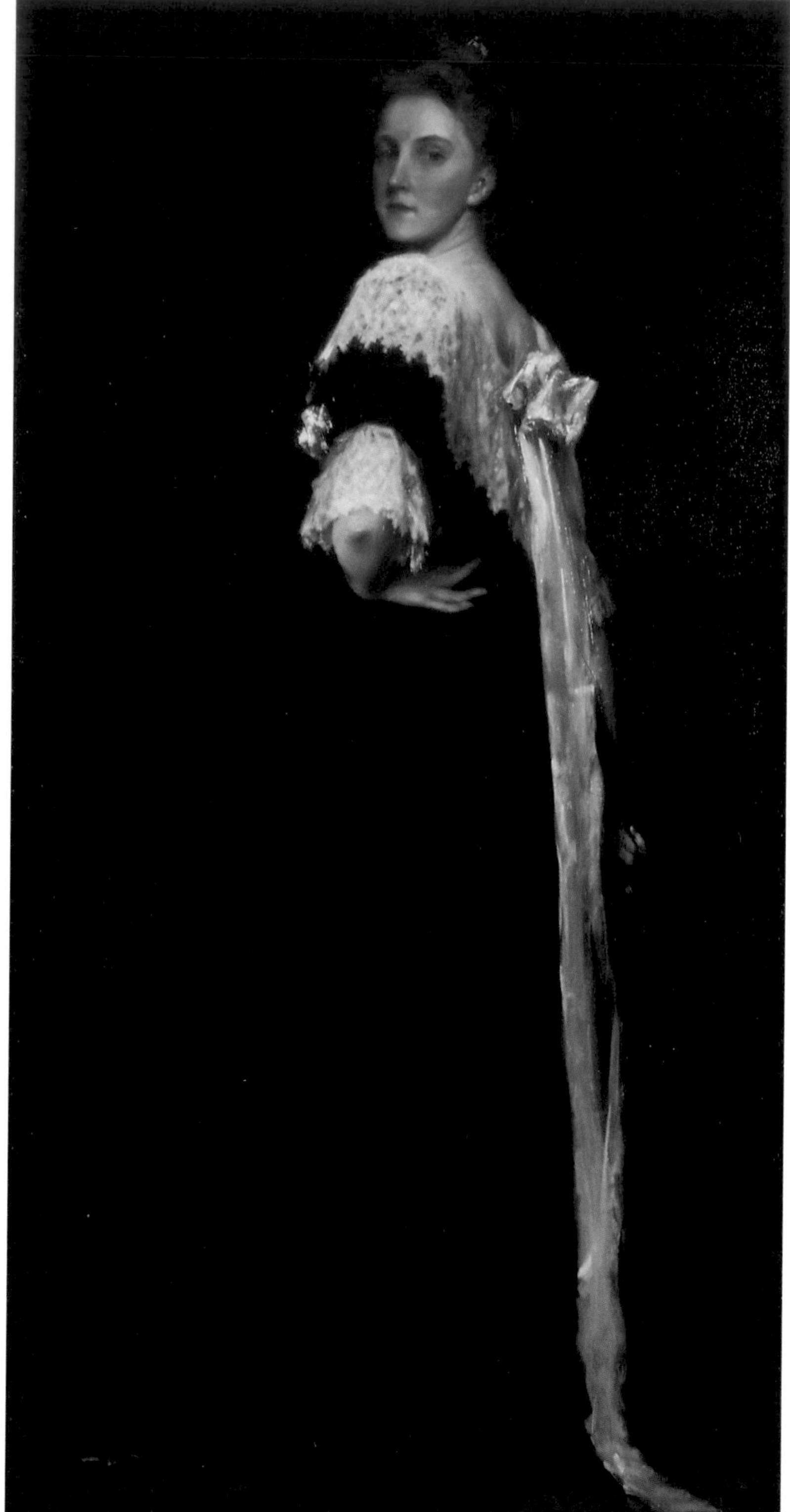

Plate 89.
William Merritt Chase,
***Portrait of Mrs. E.* (Lydia Field Emmet)**, ca. 1893.
The Brooklyn Museum.

William Merritt Chase, the unofficial leader of the more progressive New York artists in 1893, was also a member of the fair's International Committee of Judges, which awarded medals to exhibiting artists. With regard to his own paintings, Chase's technical virtuosity led to assertions that he "carried his picture making into his portraiture," creating decorative compositions that expressed the artist's admiration for the work of Whistler. Yet, unlike the aestheticized portraits by such contemporaries as Thomas W. Dewing and Frank W. Benson, Chase's representations of women are often forthright depictions of individuals of purpose and intellect. This is the case in his portrait of Lydia Field Emmet, who was not only Chase's student at the Art Students League in New York from 1889 to 1895, but also contributed a mural for the decoration of the Woman's Building at the fair. With its dramatically dark background and fluent handling of paint, the subject's assertive posture, and the precisely modeled face, *Portrait of Mrs. E.* is one of Chase's most arresting works.

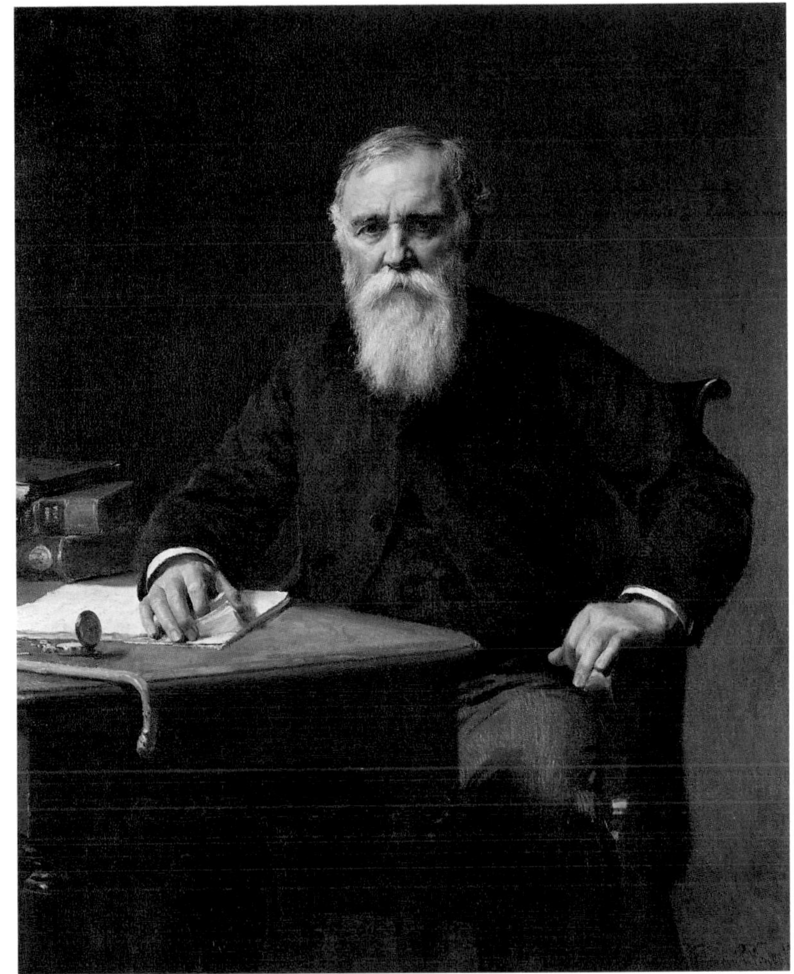

Plate 90.
Frederic Porter Vinton,
Portrait of C. C. Langdell **(Christopher Columbus Langdell)**, 1892.
Harvard University Law School Art Collection.

Vinton's portrait of the venerable dean of the Harvard Law School is one of several likenesses of well-established, middle-aged professional men exhibited at the fair. Depicted as men of intellectual or political accomplishment rather than wealth, they represented late nineteenth-century cultural ideals. Vinton has presented Langdell as though he has been momentarily interrupted in his work—with law books at his side, an open pocketwatch, and one finger marking his progress through a sheaf of papers. These attributes, combined with the dramatic lighting on his formidable brow, contribute to the impression of vitality and activity that pervades Vinton's masterful portrait.

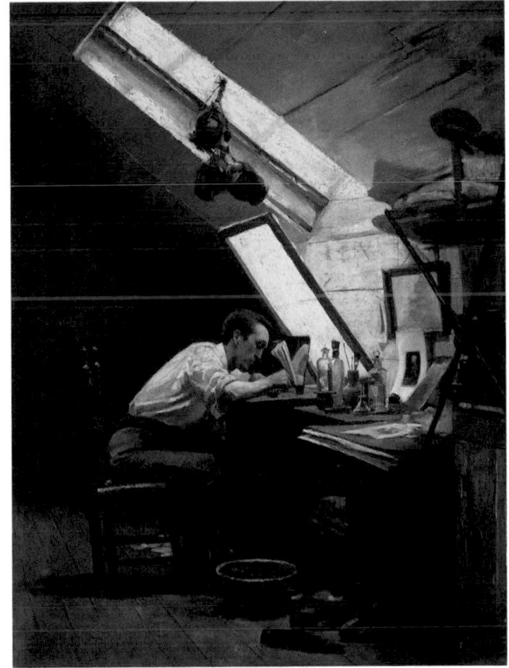

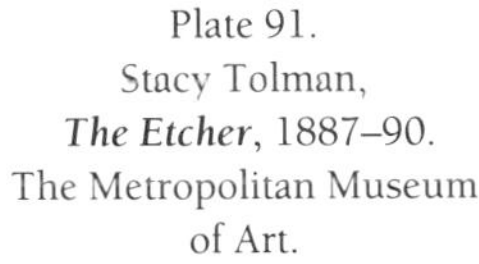

Plate 91.
Stacy Tolman,
The Etcher, 1887–90.
The Metropolitan Museum of Art.

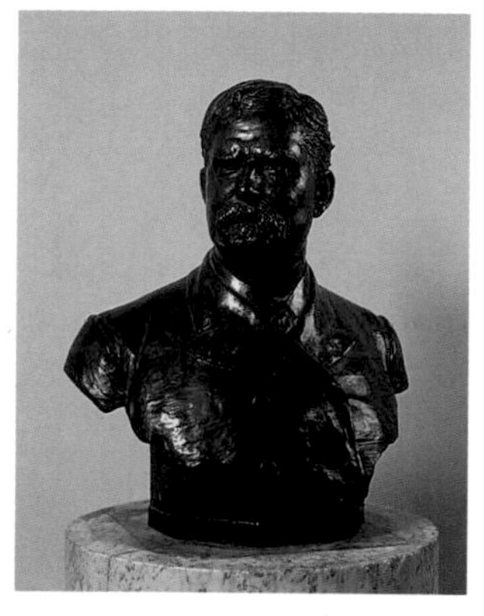

Plate 92.
Carl Rohl-Smith,
Bust of Henry Watterson, 1890.
Louisville Free Public Library, Louisville, KY. Photograph by Richard Bram.

Henry Watterson (1840–1921), statesman and editor of the influential *Louisville Courier-Journal*, was renowned for his exceptional powers as a public speaker and political debater. He delivered the inaugural oration at the dedication ceremonies for the exposition in October 1892. In this bust the Danish-born sculptor caught the energy and striking appearance of the journalist, who was described as having "fierce blue eyes under penthouses of bushy eyebrows" and a flaring mustache and slight goatee. Watterson reflected the noble self-image of the confident and ambitious shapers of the nation's social and economic future.

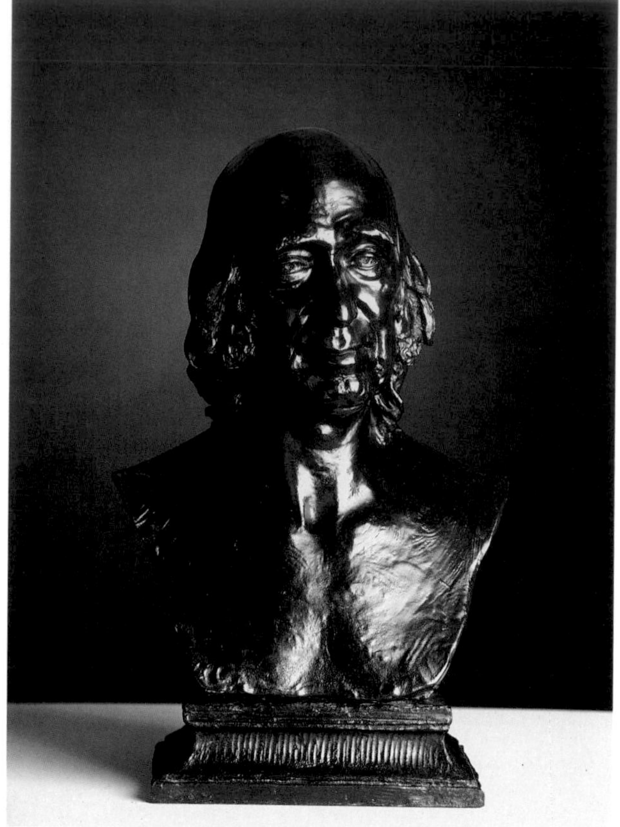

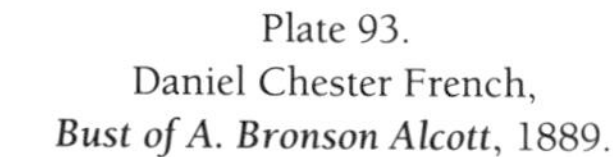

Plate 93.
Daniel Chester French,
Bust of A. Bronson Alcott, 1889.
Chesterwood, a Museum Property of the National Trust for Historic Preservation, Stockbridge, MA. Photograph by Nicholas Whitman.

Amos Bronson Alcott (1799–1888), the noted New England transcendentalist and co-founder of the Concord School of Philosophy, was a family friend of the artist. In 1880 when French first modeled a bust of Alcott, the sitter objected to being portrayed in "modern coat and cravat." In this posthumous bust, based on the earlier version and photographs, French gave his subject a more classical form by omitting clothing. Yet his naturalistic treatment of Alcott's age and appearance and the broadly modeled, irregular surfaces with their flickering play of light imbue the bust with a timeless, artistic life that celebrates the memory of the venerable philosopher.

French received more attention for his sculptural decorations on the fair grounds, particularly his monumental statue of the *Republic*, which was installed in the lagoon in the Court of Honor. A smaller version of this sculpture now stands on the fair site in Chicago's Jackson Park.

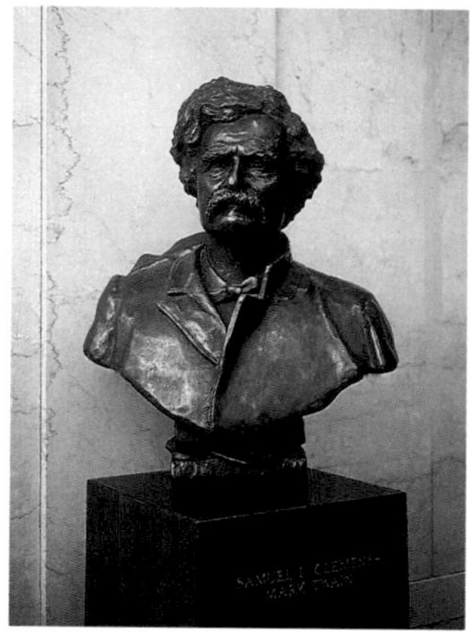

Plate 94.
Luella M. Varney,
Mark Twain, 1892.
Cleveland Public Library.
Photograph by Lynn Chambers Freska.

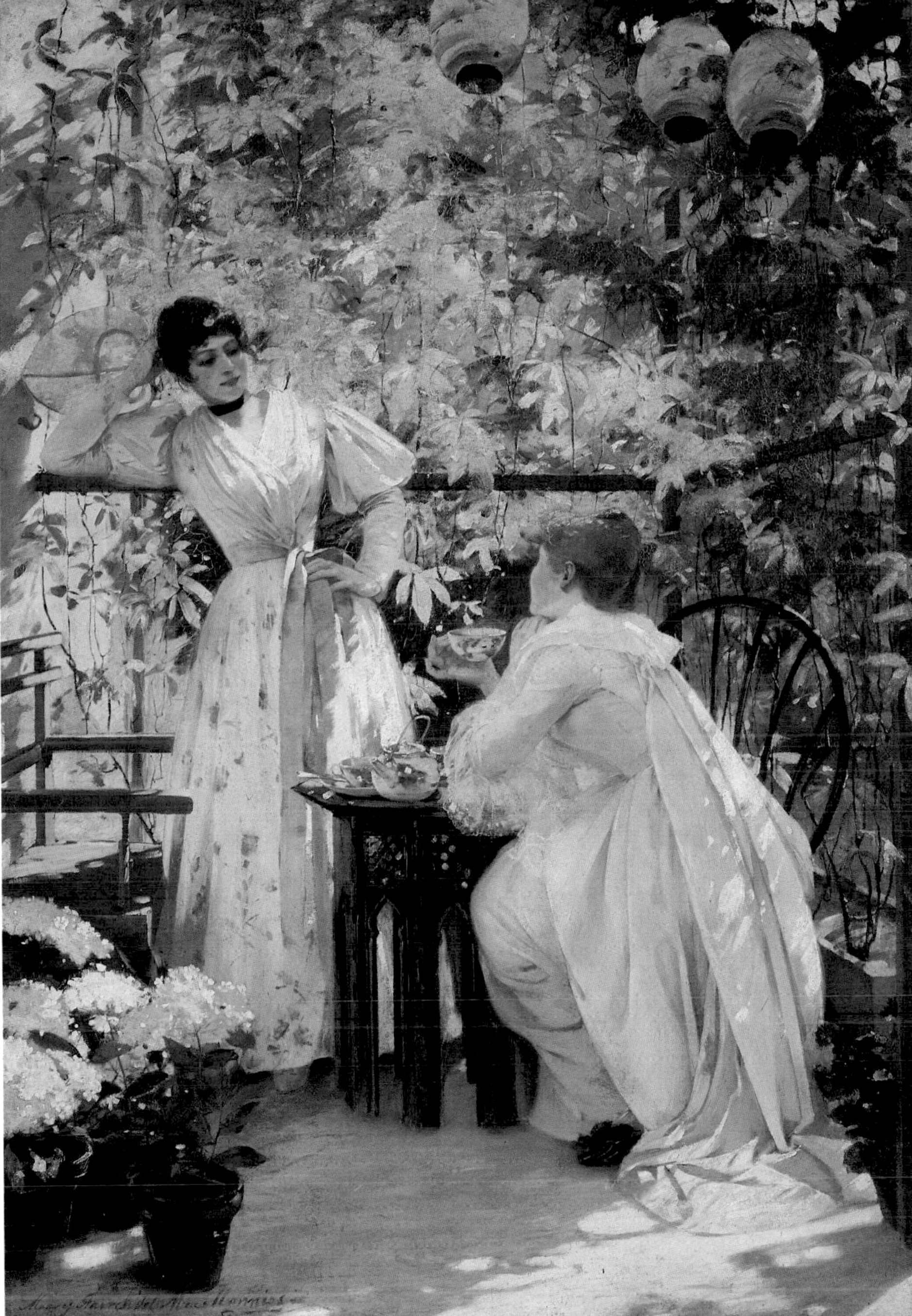

Plate 95.
Mary Fairchild MacMonnies,
Tea al Fresco, 1891.
Sheldon Swope Art Museum,
Terre Haute, IN.

This painting occupied a central position in the gallery that Department of Fine Arts assistant director Charles Kurtz had designated to display the works most closely associated with American Impressionism and other *plein-air* painting. Both the picture and the artist, who also executed a large mural for the Woman's Building at the fair, received favorable critical attention during the summer of 1893.

The ambiguous role of a professional woman artist at this time is expressed in the way MacMonnies represented herself in this painting—not as a working painter but as a fashionable woman participating in the social ritual of afternoon tea.

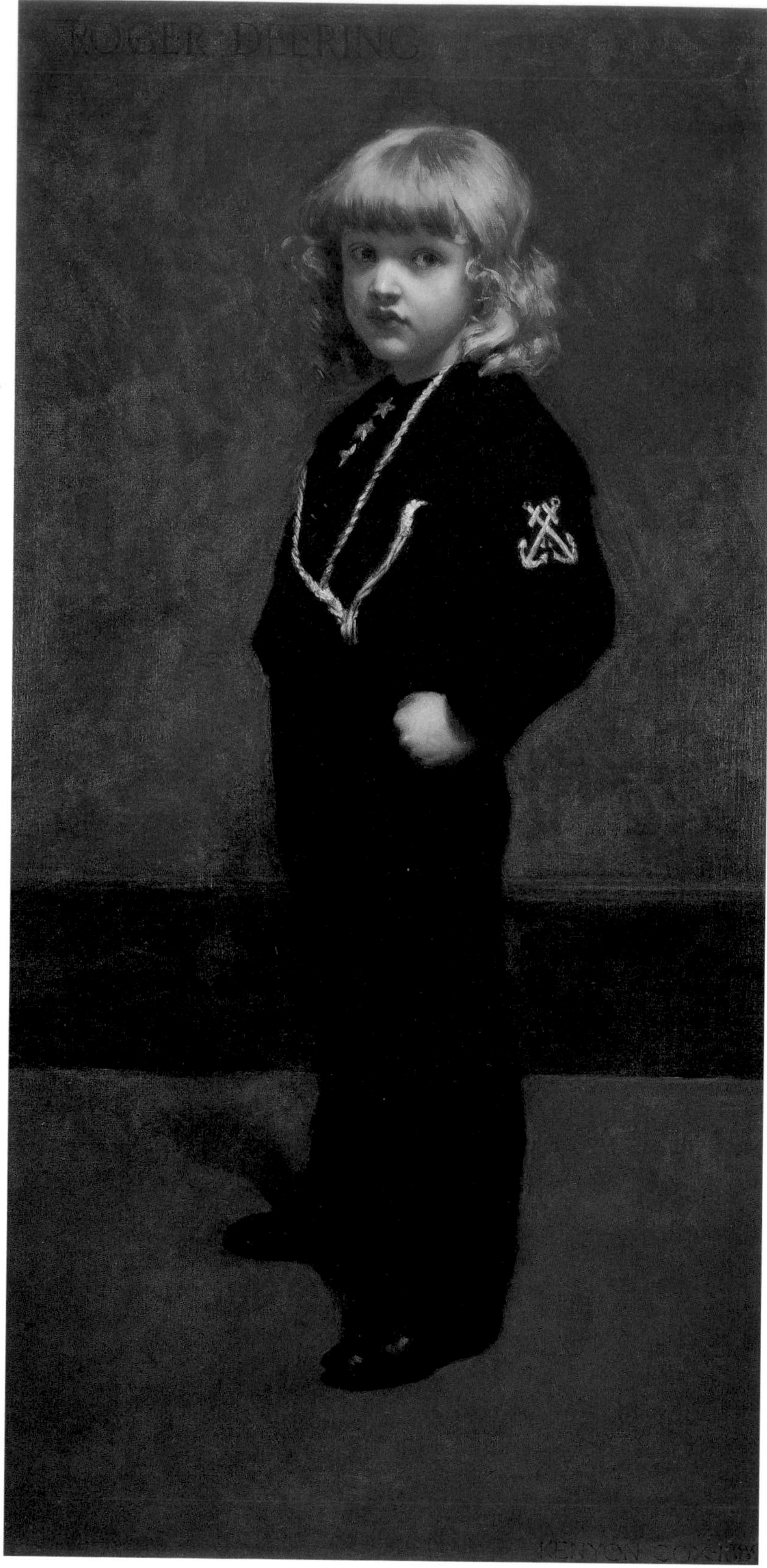

Plate 96.
Kenyon Cox,
***Portrait of Roger D.* (Roger Deering)**, 1889.
Special Collections Department, Northwestern University Library, Evanston, IL.
Photograph by Michael Tropea.

Roger Deering's father, Charles, a wealthy Chicago manufacturer, was also a talented amateur painter who enjoyed the friendship of many contemporary artists, including John Singer Sargent and Kenyon Cox. *Portrait of Roger D.*, praised at the 1893 fair, was representative of a large number of children's portraits exhibited there. The preponderance of these images may bear witness to Harrison Morris's comments, published in 1901, on the appeal of such portraits in an age of great upheaval: "The purity of sentiment which lives in beauty are nowhere expressed so simply as in a little child. He stands as he was fashioned, unaltered from Nature's mould. He twines the problem of existence with charm of form and character, and to catch his changing moods is half to solve the mystery of beauty."

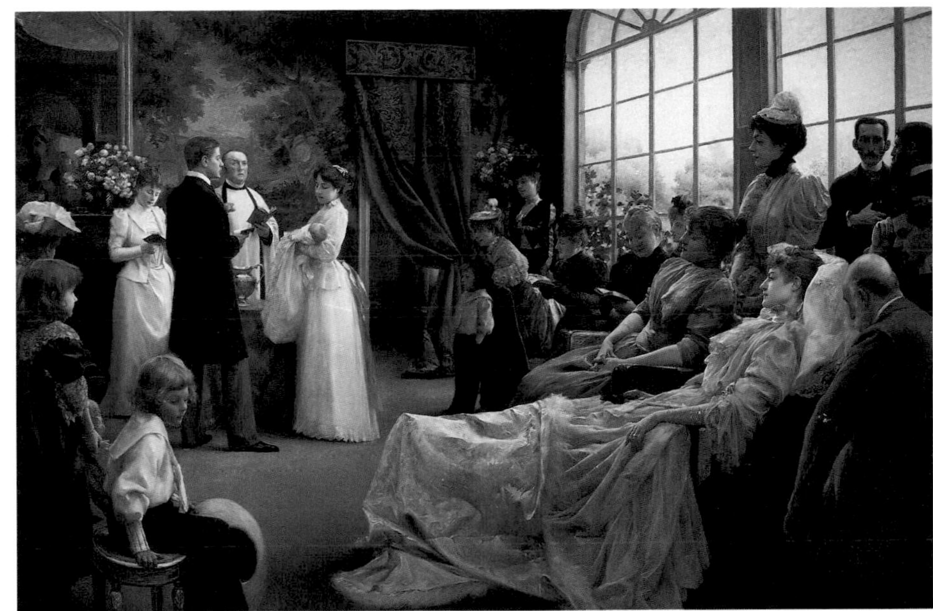

Plate 97.
Julius L. Stewart,
The Baptism, 1892.
Los Angeles County Museum of Art.

An American expatriate living in Paris, Stewart often turned to the elegant rituals of high society for the subjects of his art. His personal wealth gave him the freedom to paint as he chose, without the need to secure commissions or respond to the demands of the art market. The inscription of the day and time of the event on the back of the canvas indicates that the painting may have recorded the baptism of a friend's child. While the religious ceremony provided the ostensible occasion for the painting, the relegation of the christening to the back of the room intimates that the more important rite is to be found in the social gathering of glamorously attired people in the foreground.

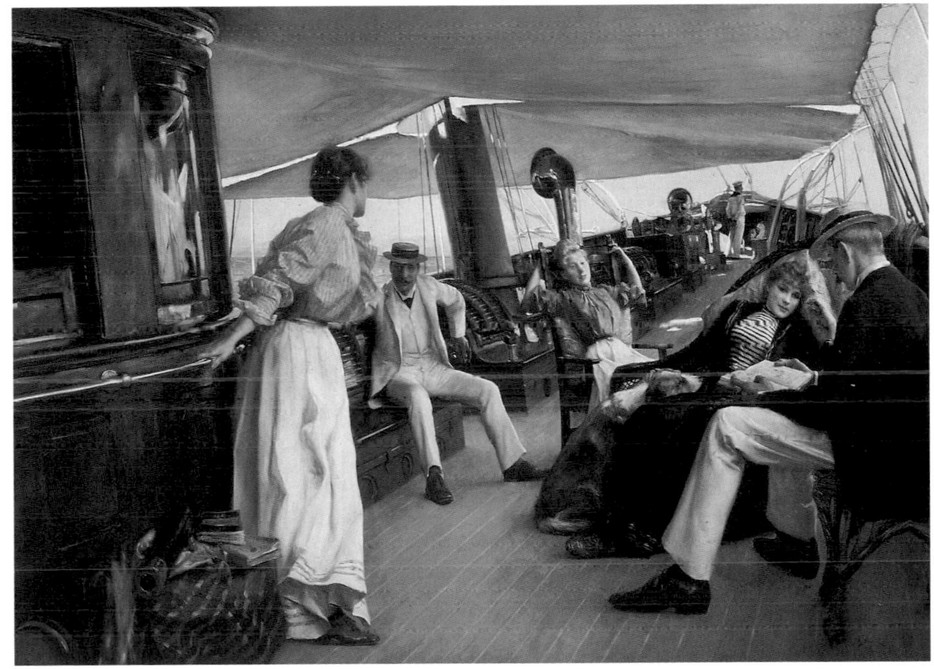

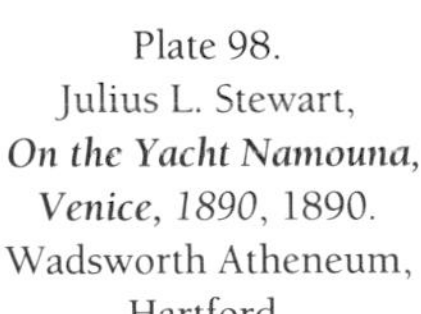

Plate 98.
Julius L. Stewart,
***On the Yacht Namouna, Venice,** 1890*, 1890.
Wadsworth Atheneum, Hartford.

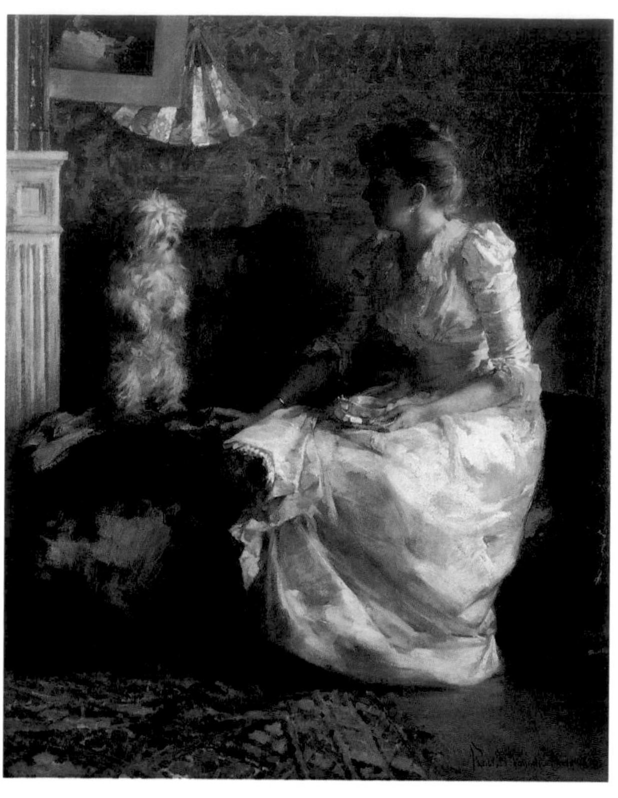

Plate 99.
Robert W. Vonnoh,
"Show What You Can Do!",
1890.
Private Collection. Photograph courtesy of Berry-Hill Galleries, Inc., New York, NY.

Plate 100.
Childe Hassam,
On the Way to the Grand Prix,
1888.
New Britain Museum of American Art, Connecticut.

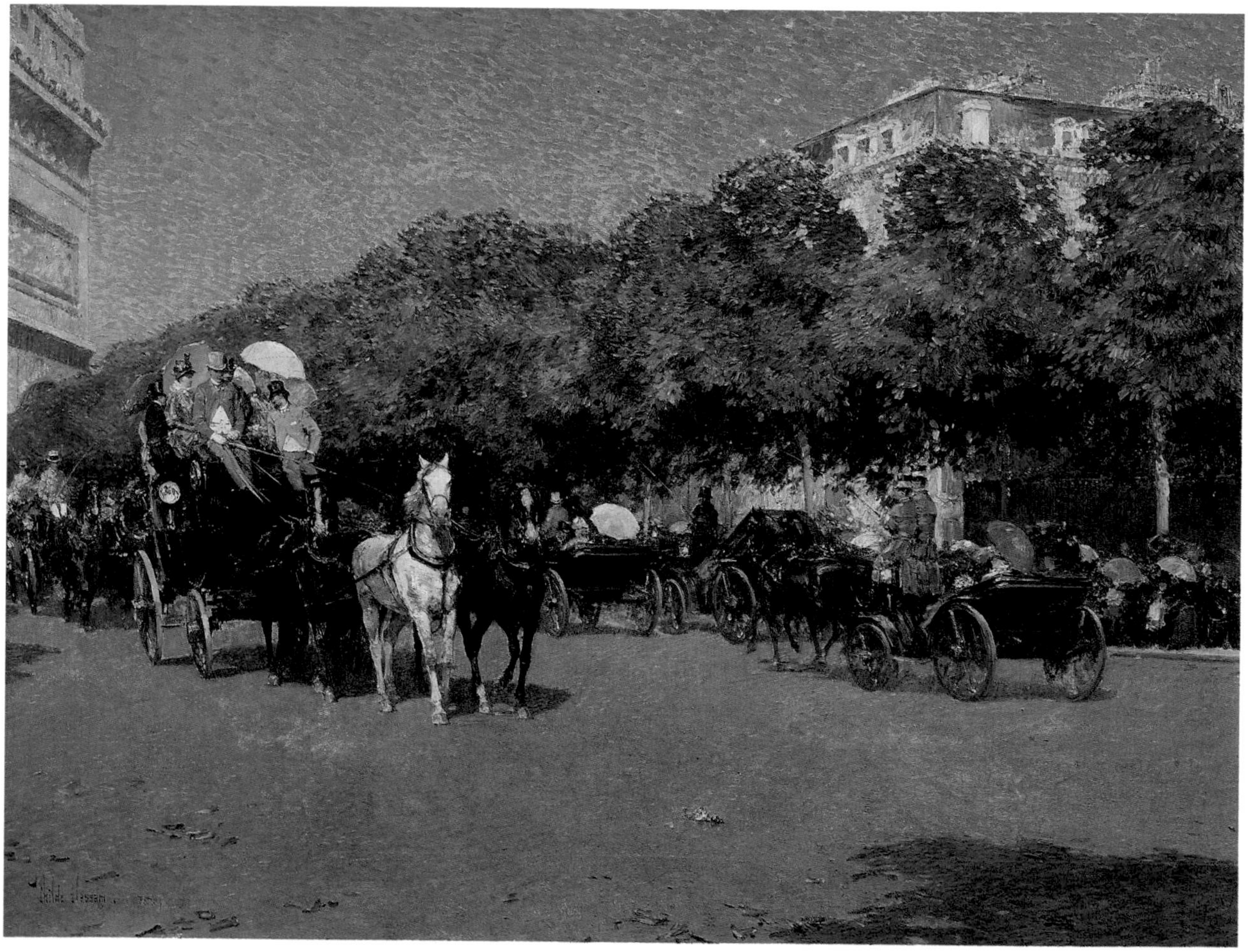

CATALOGUE OF AMERICAN PAINTINGS AND SCULPTURES EXHIBITED AT THE WORLD'S COLUMBIAN EXPOSITION

Revised and Updated

THE FINE ART OF DETECTION

AN INTRODUCTION TO THE CATALOGUE OF AMERICAN PAINTINGS AND SCULPTURES EXHIBITED AT THE WORLD'S COLUMBIAN EXPOSITION

> Detection is, or ought to be, an exact science, and should be treated in the same cold and unemotional manner. You have attempted to tinge it with romanticism, which produces much the same effect as if you worked a love-story or an elopement into the fifth proposition of Euclid.
> —Sherlock Holmes, in Sir Arthur Conan Doyle, *The Sign of Four*, 1890

Despite Holmes's injunction, the thrill of discovery and the misery of failure did intrude upon our generally quiet and meticulous research into the present location of American works of art exhibited at the 1893 World's Columbian Exposition. How could it be otherwise? A hundred years ago the works shown at this remarkable exhibition were highly valued, but now many of them are extremely difficult to find. After exhaustive attempts, we were indeed saddened by the failure to find not only a particular work but, in some cases, the biographical record of an artist, which remains lost to the written history of art. And who could deny the happiness that followed the reclamation of another work or artist for that same larger history?

Clearly, for the last six years this search for 1,184 paintings and sculptures has been the obsession of a dedicated team of curators, research assistants, interns, and volunteers, goading otherwise calm persons into research so imaginative that an account of how the picture or sculpture was found became, at times, more interesting than fiction! This work has carried the deputy director of the National Portrait Gallery, for instance, into the recesses of the Surrogate's Court record rooms in Manhattan, and a former intern into a little-known shop for artists' supplies in Paris. Certainly our research has been a team effort, and one that we are happy to have coordinated for most of the project's life. The resulting catalogue is not just a compendium of information on artists and their work but one that presents much new material and serves as merely the tip of the iceberg in terms of information that we have gleaned on little-known artists and formerly lost works of art.

Unfortunately the official records of the exposition's Department of Fine Arts have not been located, forcing us to rely on varied sources in order to determine the exact objects of our quest. First we consulted the published catalogues of the department, only to find that these exist in several versions. The earliest catalogue, arranged alphabetically by artist within each country, was hurriedly compiled from lists of accepted works bound for Chicago and was probably ready for fair-goers by the time the exposition opened on 1 May 1893. Since at that point much of the art had not yet been installed in the galleries, the catalogue contains numerous errors. Several editions of the alphabetical catalogue followed, each attempting to correct previous mistakes.

These catalogues sold swiftly (by the end of the fair, the catalogues of the art department had outsold those of all other departments at the fair combined), although visitors complained that the alphabetical arrangement of the catalogue paired with the seemingly unsystematic installation of the artwork made it difficult to locate information about the objects while visiting the galleries. The *Revised Catalogue* (fig. 69) was therefore published in late August or early September. In this catalogue, works of art are arranged numerically according to their location in the galleries. As far as we can tell, the United States section is nearly perfect, with only a few mistakes in spelling and one omission from the sculpture galleries.

After sorting out the official catalogues, we supplemented the information contained in them by examining lists of the works accepted for the exposition. These were published in the winter and early spring of 1893 in various newspapers and art journals such as *The Art Amateur* and *The Studio*. Further material was found in exhibition catalogues published when works gathered for Chicago in Boston, Philadelphia, and New York were exhibited in those cities. From all of these sources, we obtained basic information concerning artist, title, and, when pertinent, lender.

Extensive use was made of the installation photographs of the United States galleries taken by C. D. Arnold and

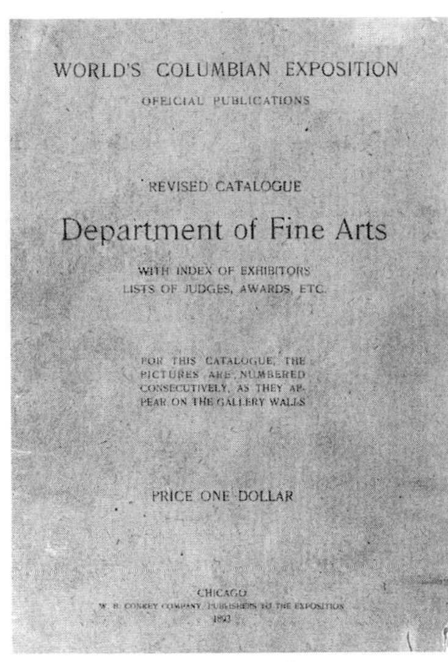
WORLD'S COLUMBIAN EXPOSITION

OFFICIAL PUBLICATIONS

REVISED CATALOGUE

Department of Fine Arts

WITH INDEX OF EXHIBITORS
LISTS OF JUDGES, AWARDS, ETC.

FOR THIS CATALOGUE, THE PICTURES ARE NUMBERED CONSECUTIVELY, AS THEY APPEAR ON THE GALLERY WALLS

PRICE ONE DOLLAR

CHICAGO
W. B. CONKEY COMPANY, PUBLISHERS TO THE EXPOSITION
1893

. . **69** . .
Cover page of Department of Fine Arts, ed., World's Columbian Exposition, Official Publications, Revised Catalogue, Department of Fine Arts *(Chicago: W. B. Conkey Company, 1893).*

. . **70** . .
World's Columbian Exposition label used by the advisory committees in Massachusetts, Pennsylvania, and all of Europe.

. . **71** . .
World's Columbian Exposition label used by the New York advisory committee.
Photograph by Cathy Carver, courtesy Museum of Art, Rhode Island School of Design.

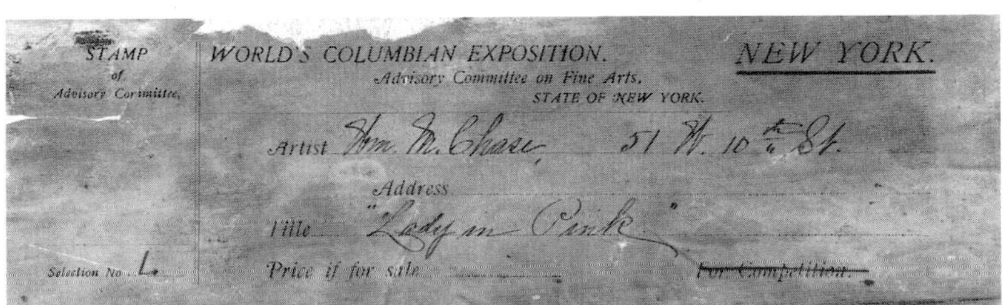
STAMP of Advisory Committee
WORLD'S COLUMBIAN EXPOSITION. NEW YORK.
Advisory Committee on Fine Arts.
STATE OF NEW YORK.
Artist Wm. M. Chase 51 W. 10th St.
Address
Title "Lady in Pink"
Selection No. 4
Price if for sale
For Competition.

Frances Benjamin Johnston. Approximately forty percent of the paintings and eighty percent of the sculptures appear in these photographs. We used the *Revised Catalogue,* much like an 1893 visitor to the art palace, to identify the works in the photographs. Since the catalogue did not give the dimensions of objects, we used the dimensions of known works in the photographs to estimate the dimensions of the unknown works adjacent to them. This painstaking process has allowed us to offer estimated dimensions of more than 200 of the objects in this catalogue that remain unlocated.

In several cases, the installation photographs provided confirmation of the success of our quests or led us to the correct work by an artist when there were many possible candidates among his or her oeuvre for the one shown in Chicago. For instance, John H. Twachtman's *Brook in Winter* could have been any number of winter scenes that he painted in the early 1890s near his home in Greenwich, Connecticut. When we viewed the original installation photograph at the Chicago Public Library, however, the details in the painting emerged and led us to Twachtman's *February* at the Museum of Fine Arts in Boston.

The existence of a World's Columbian Exposition label on a painting's stretcher or frame also enabled us to verify many of our searches. There were at least two versions of this label. One was a more generic label (fig. 70) used for works sent to Chicago from various cities in Europe and possibly used most generally for works gathered in the United States. The other (fig. 71), designed specifically for the use of the New York Advisory Committee, has the place name "New York" and the words "World's Columbian Exposition" printed on it. Once we had seen a few of these labels, we began to recognize them, even though the owners of the paintings often did not know that the label was from the Chicago fair.

In addition, we gathered photographs of individual works shown in Chicago from illustrated books and journals published around the time of the exposition and gleaned descriptions of objects from exhibition reviews published from about 1885 to 1895. The works often had considerable exhibition histories before being chosen for display at the Columbian Exposition. In the United States many of the paintings and sculptures had earlier been shown in annual exhibitions held, for instance, by the National Academy of Design, the Society of American Artists, the American Art Association (entitled Prize Fund Exhibitions and presented annually from 1885 to 1889), the Art Institute of Chicago, the Chicago Inter-State Industrial Expositions, the Pennsylvania Academy of the Fine Arts, the Philadelphia Art Club, the Boston Art Club, and the Massachusetts Charitable Mechanic Association. They were often shown abroad in the Paris Salons and in annual exhibitions in Munich and Berlin, and many had been exhibited in the 1889 Universal Exposition in Paris.

Once we knew to some extent *what* we were looking for, the question became *how* to find it. First we consulted published sources on better-known artists, as well as scholars specializing in their work. We relied frequently upon the Inventory of American Paintings, the Inventory of American Sculpture, and the Catalog of American Portraits, computerized databases available at the National Museum of American Art and the National Portrait Gallery.

Artists' papers held by the Archives of American Art were searched, as were materials found in the National Museum of American Art/National Portrait Gallery library's vertical files, the Witt Computer Index, located at the Courtauld Institute of Art, London, and the New York Public Library's Artists File, which was recently placed on microfiche. Major American art dealers were contacted, and recent auction records were checked through the use of the computer database "ArtQuest," available from Art Sales Index Ltd. in Surrey, England. Through these disparate means, as well as by sending copies of the 1893 exposition catalogue to countless museums, galleries, and other institutions throughout this country, we managed to locate about fifteen percent of the 1,184 works exhibited (forty percent of the total works located). After this initial sifting of information, our progress slowed. Although some works turned up through sheer serendipity, most of our "finds" were hard-earned.

At least 150 works shown in 1893 were sold at auction between 1893 and 1930, and several resources facilitated the process of tracing them. The American Art Association Papers, held by the Archives of American Art, contain the actual sales ledgers of the American Art Association, giving price and purchaser information on the many important auctions held by this New York City organization. Two sales that were especially relevant to our work were those of Thomas B. Clarke, held in February 1899, and of William T. Evans, held in January and February 1900. Clarke and Evans lent a total of sixty-five paintings to the exposition, of which all but one were sold in these auctions. The American Art Association sales ledgers supplied us with the names of the purchasers of these paintings and the prices at which they sold.

Similar to this source are the lists of "Paintings Sold at Auction" that appear in Florence N. Levy's *American Art Annual*, which began publication in 1899. These lists contain results of sales held at the American Art Association as well as at other major auction houses and galleries throughout the United States from 1899 until 1930. A card index to these lists in the European paintings department at the Metropolitan Museum of Art provides an easy way to trace the sale and purchase of works by a particular artist.

Finally, extensive use was made of Harold Lancour's *American Art Auction Catalogues, 1785–1942, A Union List*, which was compiled from approximately 6000 catalogues. The list of catalogues is arranged chronologically, each entry concluding with a list of the libraries in which the catalogue is held. The index of owners allows one to search for sales of specific artists and collectors.

Aside from tracing sales records of works, most of our research involved tracking down families of artists, lenders, purchasers, and portrait subjects by making use of biographical dictionaries, obituaries, social registers, city directories, newspaper indexes, census materials, birth, death, and marriage records, and probate records. Very often local historical societies and public libraries provided extremely useful information that was unobtainable elsewhere. In fact, we often found more material on an artist's life and career than on the specific works we were seeking. This was especially true in the case of some of the younger women artists (who often had married by 1900 and dropped from sight) and those artists who spent much of their lives abroad. For example, we found birth and death dates as well as a husband for expatriate artist Lucy Lee Robbins, and similar biographical information for Annie Vincent Davenport Whelpley Renouf, whose protofeminist lifestyle and numerous ways of signing her name led us astray for years. Research assistant Claire Tieder located the French will made and revised by William T. Dannat, who died in Monte Carlo; and another will, that of Frank Holman, revealed that Charles Holman-Black, who was identified as Holman's brother in early twentieth-century biographical accounts, and who shared his Paris house until Holman's death in 1930, was actually his lifelong companion. Such information was not only useful in helping us to write the biographical portions of our catalogue but also often proved invaluable in tracking down works of art.

One of the noteworthy women whom we have rediscovered is Amy Aldis Bradley, who exhibited two plaster busts at the World's Columbian Exposition. Her name, as far as we can tell, has never appeared in an artists' biographical dictionary. She was raised in Brattleboro, Vermont, and went to Paris in her early twenties to study sculpture. According to family legend, Miss Aldis desired to study with the famous French sculptor Auguste Rodin, but her parents, upon inspection of his studio, deemed it inappropriate for her to study with an unmarried man.

Amy Aldis married Richards Merry Bradley and moved to Boston in 1892. She seems to have produced little or no sculpture after this time, and only one piece of her work has been located today. The mother of seven children, she became well known in Boston for her interest in a number of women's issues and as a speaker calling for more hygienic methods of food preparation. Her career was cut short when she died of pneumonia in 1918, but her life is illustrative of the many women in this catalogue who may have given up their artistic careers after marriage but who nonetheless continued to be recognized for their contributions to society.

In addition to valuable biographical information on artists who showed work in Chicago, our efforts often turned up the specific works of art for which we were searching. Our quest for Clinton Peters's likeness of Dr. George J. Bull was one of the most detailed and rewarding. We discovered material on the artist at the Mattatuck Historical Society in Waterbury, Connecticut; included was a reproduction in *Dixie* (April 1899) of the painting, shown at the Salon of 1888 and the Universal Exposition of 1889. Since Peters was in Paris from around 1886 until 1896, it seemed possible that Dr. Bull had also resided there. He was indeed listed in one of the French social registers, *Bottin-Mondain*, in 1906 as an ophthalmologist living with his wife "née Montague-Caldwell," but he dropped out of the registers about 1912. A brief obituary for Dr. Bull was located in the *New York Times*, 2 January 1911. As luck would have it, we found a biography of Dr. Bull (born 1848 in Hamilton, Ontario) in *Who's Who in Paris. Anglo-American Colony* for 1905. His 15 December 1898 marriage (in Washington, D.C.) to Susan Montague Caldwell of Greenville, South Carolina, was recorded there. We obtained the marriage license from the District of Columbia Marriage Bureau, which gave Susan's age as thirty-four and listed her parents as Howard Hayne Caldwell and Agnes Montague Caldwell. Through Penny Forrester of the Greenville County Library, we learned that Susan Caldwell's roots were solidly in South Carolina. She was born in 1859, the year before her father's tragic death. Forrester was also able to trace Susan Caldwell Bull to Richmond, Virginia, in 1917. In the Richmond social register she was listed with a daughter, Miss Agnes Montague Bull. We traced them through the social register and, after 1927, through city directories until 1930, at which time we found that Mrs. Bull was living with her daughter and her daughter's new husband, William Frazier. At her death in 1949, she left no will, but her daughter's will was filed for probate in 1985. In this document was a provision that the portrait of Dr. Bull be left to Harcourt Wesson Bull or to his son Anthony Seaton Bull. Agnes Bull Frazier's executor provided us with Tony Bull's address—and indeed the portrait was hanging in his house in Santa Fe. In fact, we learned that Dr. Bull had been married once before, in 1870, to Sarah Wesson, daughter of Daniel, inventor of the Smith & Wesson revolver, and it was his grandson from this marriage to whom the portrait was initially given.

Many of our biggest finds resulted from combining a little bit of Sherlock Holmes's "exact science" with a little bit of luck. The search for S. Seymour Thomas's once celebrated painting, *An Innocent Victim*, was one such discovery. In 1915 Thomas settled in La Crescenta, California, where he lived until his death in 1956. An exhibition of his work was held at the Los Angeles Museum in 1935, and *An Innocent Victim* was listed in the accompanying exhibition pamphlet having been lent by the artist. Because Thomas still owned the work more than forty years after it had been painted, it seemed likely that he would have kept the painting until his death in 1956 rather than selling it. *The National Cyclopedia of American Biography* notes that Thomas designed and built the Church of St. Luke of the Mountain in La Crescenta. Fortunately, the church still exists. We called, spoke with the rector, and described *An Innocent Victim*. He told us that he would talk with some of the elderly members of the congregation to see if they recalled the painting. When the rector telephoned a week later, he had spoken with a woman in her eighties who remembered seeing the painting forty years ago when it hung in St. Vincent's Hospital in Los Angeles. She went back several years later to see the work and was told that it was in storage. Another telephone inquiry located a St. Vincent's Medical Center in Los Angeles, where we spoke with Sister Mary Joseph in the public affairs office and described the painting to her. She said that she was familiar with *copies* of it. How striking that in 1990 she was familiar with copies of a painting that had been so extensively reproduced in 1893. Was a wall in every room at St. Vincent's adorned with prints of *An Innocent Victim*? It seemed too good to be true. Sister Mary Joseph called again later that day to report that she had located *An Innocent Victim* in the provincial house of the Daughters of Charity (the same order as that portrayed in the painting) in Los Altos Hills, California. We had succeeded in locating one of the most popular and widely illustrated paintings that hung in the 1893 fair!

In other cases, unfortunately, we were not so lucky. After mounting intensive searches for nearly half of the works still listed as unlocated, we have been unable to find them or to be absolutely sure that we had located the correct painting or sculpture. For example, we have searched for more than four years for Thomas Eakins's portrait of his friend William Rudolf O'Donovan, which depicts him sculpting a bust of Eakins. We assumed that the portrait, along with another Eakins painting given to O'Donovan, must have remained with the sculptor. Although we attempted to trace O'Donovan's first and second wives, his son, and their respective families, we have not succeeded in finding his descendants or the painting. In the case of Orrin Peck's *Portrait of Mrs. H.*, it is most likely the portrait of his patron Phoebe Apperson Hearst in the collection of the University of California at Berkeley. However, with no installation photograph available and no label on the painting's stretcher to verify this, we cannot be certain and must list it in the catalogue as unlocated.

Other works remain lost because we cannot trace them beyond a specific sale, often the result of their having been deaccessioned from museum collections. Many of the most notable paintings and sculptures shown in Chicago were purchased by or given to museums in the decade following the fair. Although many of them remain in museum collections, a number were deaccessioned, due to changes in taste, around 1940. These works, as well as others from private collections, were often sold through the Parke-Bernet Galleries (now Sotheby's) in New York City, which does not release sales records, or through small galleries no longer in existence, making it impossible to trace these important works further.

Still other unlocated objects have been destroyed. It was particularly difficult to locate the many sculptures that had been exhibited in plaster. Sixty-three of the 160 American sculptures shown were plasters, and of these, only *two* have been located. We can verify that some of the missing sculptures were destroyed and must assume that the majority of them met the same fate. In some cases, we discovered that paintings, too, had been destroyed, long ago or as recently as the tragic Oakland, California, fire of 1991.

Once we had gathered all of this information on the art and artists, we began to put it together in legible form. Our most important task before the catalogue could be assembled was to verify the information. For example, in the area of artists' training, we consulted several specific sources in order to produce as accurate a record as possible. These include the archives of the Akademie der Bildenden Künste, Munich; the enrollment records of the National Academy of Design, New York City; the enrollment records of the Pennsylvania Academy of the Fine Arts, Philadelphia; Lois Marie Fink's *American Art at the Nineteenth-Century Paris Salons* (Cambridge and New York: Cambridge University Press, 1990); *The Julian Academy, Paris, 1868–1939* (New York: Shepherd Gallery, 1989); and H. Barbara Weinberg's "Nineteenth-Century American Painters at the École des Beaux-Arts," *American Art Journal* 13 (Autumn 1981): 66–84.

In formulating approximate dates for some works, lacking additional external information, we consulted other exhibition records to ascertain when a work was first shown publicly. Many of these records are now published. Most helpful were Janice H. Chadbourne, Karl Gabosh, and Charles O. Vogel, eds., *The Boston Art Club Exhibition Record 1873–1909* (Madison, CT: Sound View Press, 1991); Peter Hastings Falk, ed., *The Annual Exhibition Record of the Pennsylvania Academy of the Fine Arts*. Vol. II, 1876–1913 (Madison, CT: Sound View Press, 1989); Peter Hastings Falk and Andrea Ansell Bien, eds., *The Annual Exhibition Record of the Art Institute of Chicago 1888–1950* (Madison, CT: Sound View Press, 1990); Lois Marie Fink's *American Art at the Nineteenth-Century Paris Salons* (Cambridge and New York: Cambridge University Press, 1990); and Maria Naylor, ed., *The National Academy of Design Exhibition Record 1861–1900* (New York: Kennedy Galleries, 1973).

The complicated and controversial awards system instituted for the Columbian Exposition was very different from the form of awards generally used for exhibitions of art. By the late nineteenth century the French system of graduated awards, adapted for American use, was standard, with gold, silver, and bronze medals, as well as honorable mentions, being given to specific works. Thus when John Boyd Thacher, chairman of the Executive Committee on Awards for the Chicago fair, decided to use what he called an "American system," complaints were voiced throughout the country, particularly by artists. Thacher's system called for only one class of medal, cast in bronze, which would be bestowed on work of excellence by a single judge rather than a jury. In the Department of Fine Arts, Thacher's system decreed that an artist would receive an award, but not for a single work. The symbol we have used to designate the recipient of an award is therefore located beside the name of the artist rather than beside the title of a specific work.

With the completion of this catalogue, our research must come to a halt, if only temporarily. We have attempted to locate an enormous number of disparate works of art and to verify or discover biographical information about a substantial number of American artists of the late nineteenth century. In doing so, we have incurred many debts and owe much more than token thanks to those who have helped us along the way. We hope that other scholar-detectives will correct any errors we have inadvertently made, and that the paintings and sculptures we were unable to locate will emerge at some future date, providing unseemly thrills to those, like us, who attempt to follow Holmes's exact science but find themselves caught up in the romance of the quest.

Brandon Brame Fortune
Michelle Mead

KEY TO THE CATALOGUE

All text in bold type is a reproduction of information from Department of Fine Arts, ed., *World's Columbian Exposition, Official Publications, Revised Catalogue, Department of Fine Arts* (Chicago: W.B. Conkey Company, 1893). If clear typographical errors appeared in this catalogue, they were corrected. Throughout the key, this source is referred to as the *Revised Catalogue.*

Sample entry:

BRIDGMAN, Frederic A. (Frederick Arthur).
Paris, France.
1847 Tuskegee, AL–1928 Rouen, France
Training— New York: NAD; Brooklyn: Brooklyn Art School; Paris: Jean-Léon Gérôme, Atelier Suisse.

******Fellahine & Child—The Bath, Cairo.* #430.** n.d. (ca. 1892). 23¾ x 31⅞. Private Collection, Princeton, NJ.

***A Hot Day at Mustapha, Algiers.* #432.** [$1400]. *L'Aprés Midi, Algier,* n.d. 21½ x 29. Private Collection. Photograph courtesy Mathaf Gallery, London, England.

***Women at the Mosque, Algiers.* #937.** [$1600]. 1887. 29 x 25. Sold, American Art Association, New York, NY, 10 March 1899, lot 44, to M. Knoedler & Co. Unlocated.[7] Illus (as *Algerian Women*): George W. Sheldon, *Recent Ideals of American Art* (New York: Appleton, 1890).

1. A dagger preceding the name of an artist (†) indicates that the artist received an award from the Department of Fine Arts for his or her work shown at the World's Columbian Exposition. The award consisted of a single bronze medal and an engraved certificate called a "diploma." Carolyn Kinder Carr's essay, in this publication, explains the awards system and the controversy surrounding it.

2. **Name.** The artist's name as it appears in the *Revised Catalogue* is listed first. When known, the artist's full first and middle names have been added in parentheses. Married or maiden names of women are given following their full names. If a misspelling occurs in the name in the *Revised Catalogue*, it is corrected in the additional information.

3. **Address.** This place name, taken from the *Revised Catalogue*, indicates the address each artist gave to the Department of Fine Arts. It was used in the catalogue and on labels attached to the back of the artworks.

Since artists sometimes kept several studios, both in the United States and abroad, the address may not reflect their actual place of residence at the time of the exposition. For example, Robert Koehler sent his paintings to Chicago from Munich, where he lived at the time, but he gave his address as 128 East 93rd Street, New York City. Thus, his address in the *Revised Catalogue* is listed as **New York,** where he most likely kept a studio, rather than Munich, where he actually resided at the time of the exposition.

4. **Birth and Death Dates and Places.** Date and place of birth are followed by date and place of death. If no date or place is given, none is known.

When no information on the artist's death is available, but the artist has been traced beyond the address he or she gave in 1893, the last known date and place of residence are listed.

1860 New York, NY–Residing 1926 Paris, France

If the artist's death date is known, but the place of death cannot be verified, the artist's place of residence closest to the date of death is given, followed by a question mark.

1860 Newark, NJ–1895 New York, NY?

5. **Training.** The cities (or sometimes only the countries) where an artist trained are listed, followed by specific schools in that city. If the persons with whom the artist studied at a specific school are known, those names are listed in parentheses following the name of the school. Please see the introduction to this section for a list of sources consulted for this information. The following abbreviations are used for frequently cited institutions:

AIC	Chicago Academy of Design, Chicago, IL (1867–1882)/Art Institute of Chicago, Chicago, IL (1882 onward)

ASL	Art Students League, New York, NY
EcBA	École des Beaux-Arts, Paris, France
EcAD	École des Arts Decoratif, Paris, France
MIT	Massachusetts Institute of Technology, Cambridge, MA
MFA	School of Drawing and Painting, Museum of Fine Arts, Boston, MA
NAD	National Academy of Design, New York, NY
PAFA	School of the Pennsylvania Academy of the Fine Arts, Philadelphia, PA

6. **Endnote.** A notes section for both paintings and sculptures follows the catalogue listings.

7. An asterisk [*] preceding the title of an object indicates that it is included in the exhibition *Revisiting the White City: American Art at the 1893 World's Fair*, held 16 April–15 August 1993 at the National Portrait Gallery and the National Museum of American Art, Washington, D.C. These works are illustrated in the color plate section of this publication.

8. **Title and Lender.** This information is taken directly from the *Revised Catalogue*. If the painting or sculpture is currently known by another title, that title follows the original information. If the name of the subject of a portrait is not given in the title of the work, the name, when known, is given in parentheses following the title taken from the *Revised Catalogue.*

9. **Catalogue Number.** The catalogue number, taken from the *Revised Catalogue*, refers to the position of the work within the Fine Arts Building. See the introduction to this section for a more complete description of the installation of the galleries.

10. **Price.** The price given in brackets after the catalogue number in some entries is taken from a marked catalogue, published in the spring or early summer of 1893, found in the Charles M. Kurtz Papers, Archives of American Art, Smithsonian Institution. Kurtz had labeled it "PRICED CATALOGUE." It is assumed that the price given in the "PRICED CATALOGUE" was usually taken from the label that was affixed to each work, on which there was a space for a price. There are indications, however, that in some cases the figure given may have been an insurance value.

11a. **Medium/Paintings.** All paintings are oil on canvas unless otherwise indicated.

11b. **Medium/Sculpture.** The medium for sculptures is taken directly from the *Revised Catalogue* and is listed immediately following the title. If a sculpture, as it was shown at the World's Columbian Exposition, is unlocated or destroyed, a located version in another medium may follow the main entry. Reductions or later versions are cited only when all original versions are unlocated or destroyed.

12. **Date.** If the date of a work is unknown, it is simply not given, or an approximate date is suggested. If an unqualified date is given for a located work, that date is inscribed on the work. If an unqualified date is given for an unlocated work, documentary evidence exists confirming that the date was/or is inscribed on the work.

In the case of located works that have no date on them, "n.d." is used, sometimes followed by an approximate date or an established date in parentheses. Unless miscellaneous information from research files was used to formulate an approximate date for a work, exhibition records have been relied upon as a basis for these dates. For a list of published exhibition records which were helpful, please see the introduction to this section.

13. **Dimensions.** Dimensions are listed in inches, with height preceding width for paintings and height followed by width and depth for sculptures. If exact dimensions could not be obtained, "(approx.)" follows the given dimensions. "Est." listed before the dimensions indicates that the work is unlocated but that the dimensions have been estimated from installation photographs of the galleries by comparing works of known size to works of unknown size.

14. **Location.** If a work is located, the credit line is given. If a work remains unlocated, the last known owner or location is included.

For sculpture, the location given refers to a located version of the sculpture but not necessarily to the exact object that was shown at the World's Columbian Exposition in 1893. For example, the bronze cast of Olin L. Warner's *Portrait of J. Alden Weir* at the American Academy and Institute of Arts and Letters may not be the same bronze which was exhibited in 1893.

15. **Illustration, Photograph or Description Source.** If an illustration of an unlocated work has been found, it is reproduced above the printed information on the work, and the source is given after the notation "Illus." In the case of located works, the photograph has been provided by the owner unless another source is cited. If a painting or sculpture is unlocated but a description has been discovered, the description and its source are cited.

OIL PAINTINGS

† **ABBEY,** **Edwin A.** (Edwin Austin). **Fairford, Gloucestershire, England.**
1852 Philadelphia, PA–1911 London, England
Training — Philadelphia: Isaac L. Williams, PAFA (Christian Schussele).

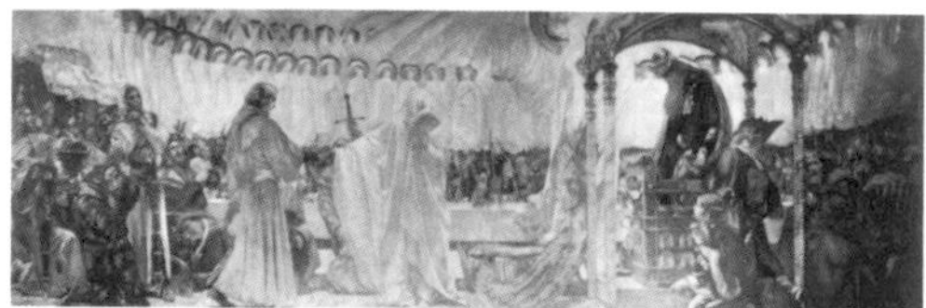

Galahad Brought to Arthur's Court. (Section of frieze for the Delivery Room of the Public Library, Boston). **#503. Lent by the Public Library, Boston.** n.d. (ca. 1890–93). 96 x 288. Boston Public Library. Photograph courtesy of the Trustees of the Public Library of the City of Boston.

ALBRIGHT, A. E. (Adam Emory). **Chicago.**
1862 Monroe, WI–1957 Warrenville, IL
Training — Chicago: AIC (Henry F. Spread, John Vanderpoel); Philadelphia: Thomas Eakins; Munich: Royal Academy (Carl von Marr); Paris: Acad. Julian (Jean-Joseph Benjamin-Constant).

Morning Glories. **#437.** [$100]. Est. 28 h. Unlocated.

ALEXANDER, **Henry. New York.**
1860 San Francisco, CA–1894 New York, NY
Training — San Francisco: California School of Design (Toby Rosenthal); Munich: Royal Academy.

Chinese Interior. **#1231.** [$2000]. Unlocated. Possibly destroyed in San Francisco, CA, earthquake and fire, 1906. "A deal of low-toned lacquer panels and much rich carving and gilding, all very well painted" —*Art Amateur* 28 (Jan. 1893): 44.

ALLEN, **Thomas. Boston.**
1849 St. Louis, MO–1924 Worcester, MA
Training — Paris; Dusseldorf: Royal Academy (Decker, Léon Germain Pelouse).

Moonrise. **#489.** [$1000]. Est. 40 h. Unlocated. "A well conceived and executed composition, full of repose and tranquility, one in which the stillness and intangible hues of twilight have been rendered by a master's hand" —Hubert H. Bancroft, *The Book of the Fair,* vol. 3 (Chicago: Blakely Printing Co., 1893).

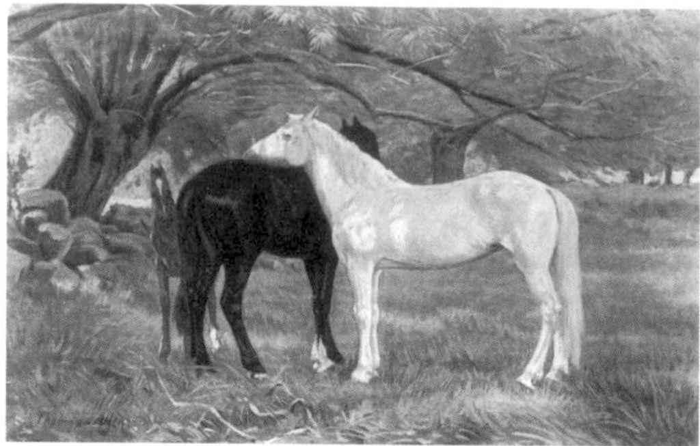

Under the Willows. **#738.** [$350]. n.d. 17½ x 28¼. Collection Lisa Nowell, Boulder, CO. Illus: Ripley Hitchcock, *The Art of the World* (New York: Appleton, 1895), 85.

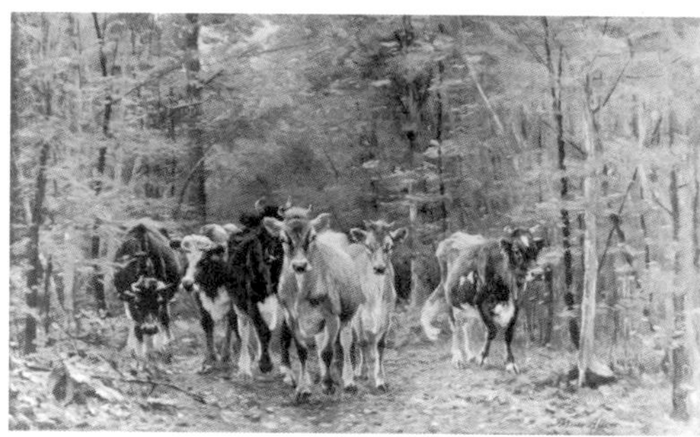

Coming Through the Woods. **#889.** [$350]. Unlocated. Illus: Daniel H. Burnham, *The Art of the World,* vol. 3 (New York: Appleton, 1893–95).

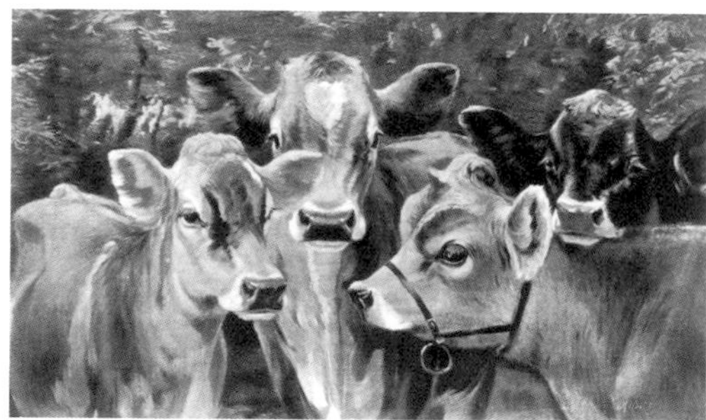

Thoroughbreds. **#1038. Lent by Mrs. Thomas Allen, Pittsfield, Mass.** n.d. (ca. 1888). 17 x 27½. Collection John Conley, San Francisco, CA. Illus: George W. Sheldon, *Recent Ideals of American Art* (New York: Appleton, 1890).

ALLEN, W. S. (William Sullivant Vanderbilt). **New York.**
1860 New York, NY–1931 New York, NY?
Training — Paris: Jean-Léon Gérôme, William Bouguereau, Jules Joseph Lefebvre, Claude Monet.

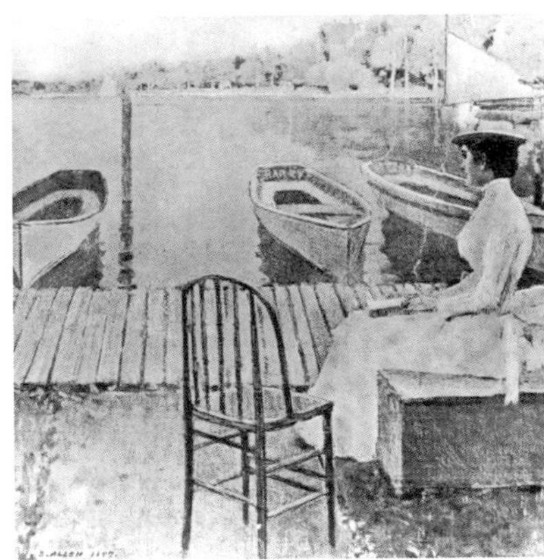

Evening at the Lake. **#993.** 1887. Unlocated. Illus: William Walton, *Chefs-d'oeuvre de l'Exposition Universelle de Paris, 1889,* vol. 10 (Philadelphia: G. Barrie, 1889), 109.

AMSDEN, William T. (William King). **New York.**
Unknown–Residing 1901 Rockland Lake, NY
Training — Paris: Fernand Cormon.

Spanish Meadows. **#445.** [$200]. Unlocated.

ANDERSON, David J. Woodridge, N.J.[1]

Landscape. **#761.** Unlocated.

ARMSTRONG, Maitland (David Maitland). **New York.**
1836 Newburg, NY–1918 New York, NY
Training — Rome; Paris: Luc Olivier Merson.

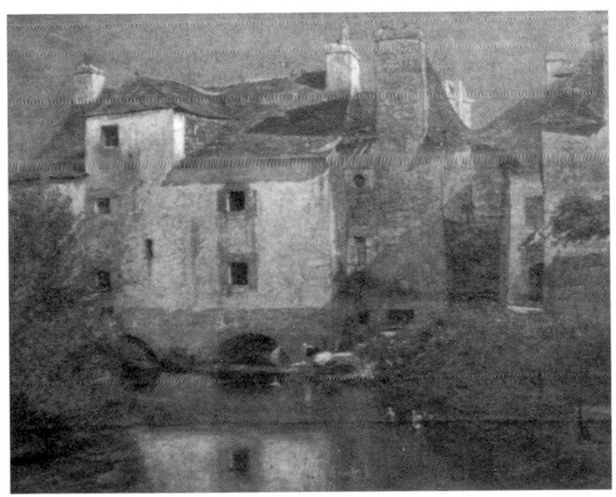

White House at Pont Aven, Brittany. **#467.** 1878. 21 x 24¾. Collection Gregor A. Gamble, New Brunswick, ME.

BAER, William J. (William Jacob). **New York.**
1860 Cincinnati, OH–1941 East Orange, NJ
Training — Cincinnati: McMicken School of Design; Munich: Royal Academy.

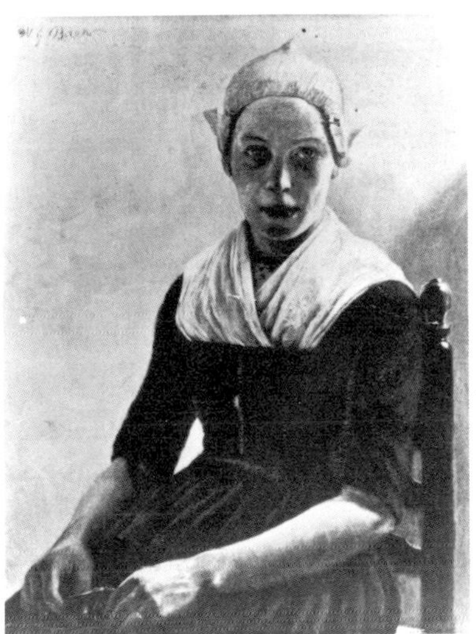

Day Dreams. **#600.** [$350]. Est. 30 x 20. Unlocated. Illus: *Art Interchange* (Jan. 1895): cover.

BAIRD, W. B. (William Baptiste). **Paris, France.**
1848 Scotland–Residing 1899 Paris, France
Training — Paris: Adolphe Yvon.

Waiting Their Turn. **#1073.** [$100]. Unlocated.

BAKER, Ellen Kendall (Mrs. Harry Thompson). **Puteaux, France.**
1839 Fairfield, NY–1913 Chalfont St. Giles, England
Training — Paris: Paul Soyer, Charles Müller, Harry Thompson.

Sans Souci. **#313.** [$800]. Est. 80 x 60. Unlocated.

BAKER, Mary K. (Mary Katherine). **Boston.**
ca. 1841 New Bedford, MA–1934 Melrose, MA
Training — self-taught

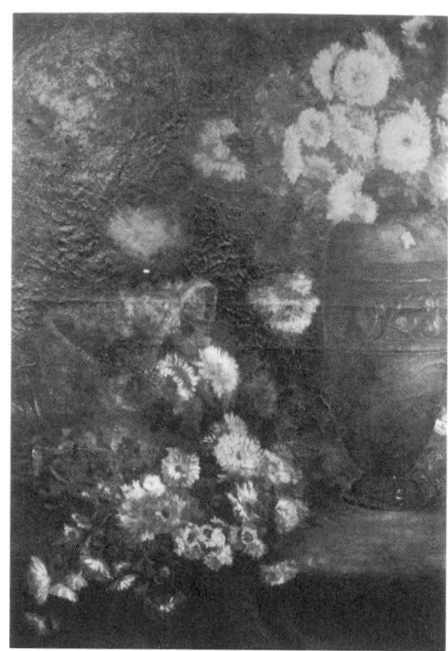

Chrysanthemums. **#884.** [$1000]. *Autumn Flowers (Chrysanthemums),* n.d. 55 x 44. Melrose Public Library, Melrose, MA.

BAKER, William Bliss. deceased.
1859 New York, NY–1889 Ballston, NY
Training — Albert Bierstadt, M. F. H. De Haas.

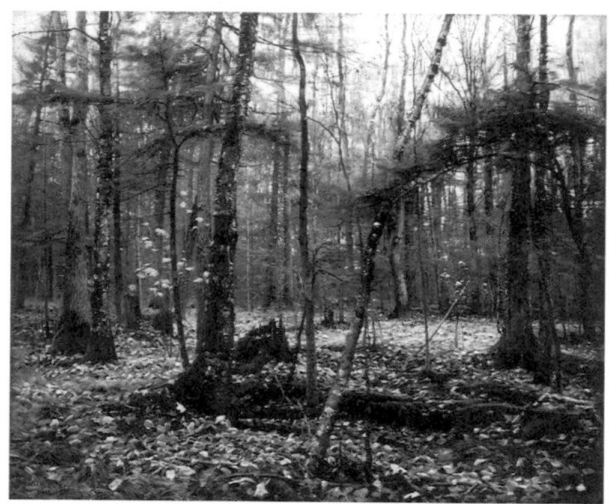

Silence. **#904. Lent by Mr. Thomas B. Clarke, New York.** 1883. 25 x 30. Private Collection.

BARNARD, E. H. (Edward Herbert). **Boston.**
1855 Belmont, MA–1909 Westerly, MA
Training — Boston: John B. Johnston, Otto Grundmann, MFA; Paris: Acad. Julian (Gustave Boulanger, Jules Joseph Lefebvre), Raphaël Collin.

Mid-day. **#281.** [$1000]. Est. 40 x 30. Unlocated.

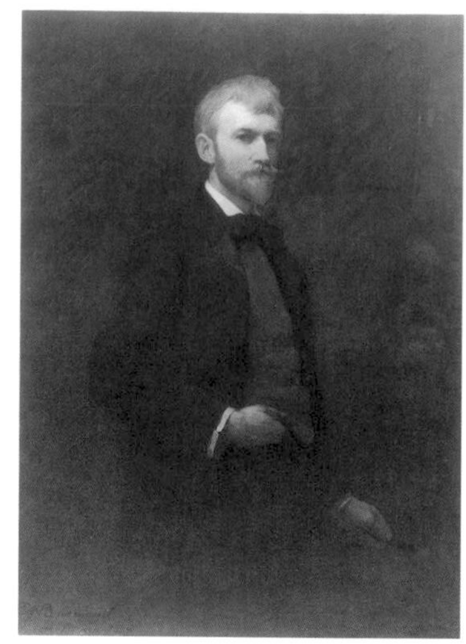

Portrait of E. H. B. **#1104.** 1889. 51 x 35. Collection Charles C. Butt, San Antonio, TX.

BATES, Dewey. Cookham Dene, Berkshire, England.
1851 Philadelphia, PA–1899 Rye, England
Training — Antwerp: Royal Academy; Paris: Jean-Léon Gérôme.

Spring. **#750.** [$500]. **Lent by Mrs. A. C. C. Bere, London.** Unlocated.

BEAUX, Cecilia. Philadelphia.
1855 Philadelphia, PA–1942 Gloucester, MA
Training — Philadelphia: School of Adolf van der Whelen (Mrs. Thomas Janvier), William Sartain; Paris: Acad. Julian (William Bouguereau, Tony Robert-Fleury, Jean-Joseph Benjamin-Constant), Acad. Colarossi.

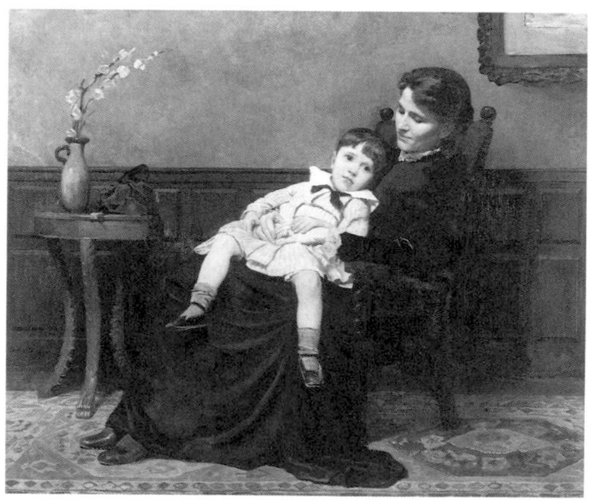

******Last Days of Infancy.* **#512. Lent by Mr. W. F. Biddle, Philadelphia.** *Les Derniers Jours d'Enfance,* 1885. 45¾ x 54. Pennsylvania Academy of the Fine Arts, Philadelphia, Gift of Cecilia Drinker Saltonstall.

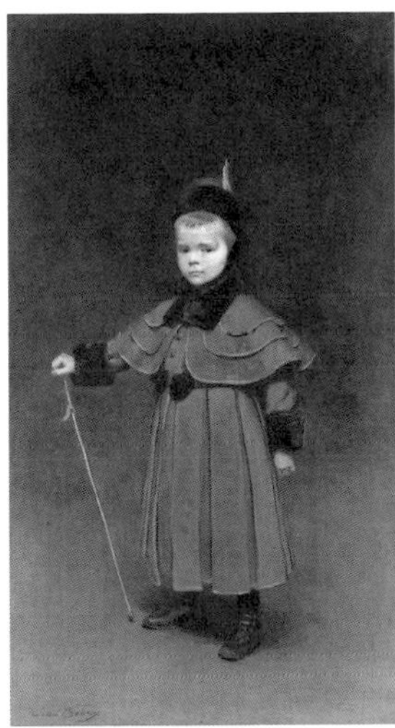

Portrait of a Boy. **#1232.** *Portrait of Cecil Drinker*, 1891. 64 x 34½. Philadelphia Museum of Art, Purchased: Joseph E. Temple Fund.

BECK, **Carol H. Philadelphia.**

1859 Philadelphia, PA–1908 Philadelphia, PA
Training — Philadelphia: PAFA; Dresden; Paris.

Portrait. **#566.** Unlocated.

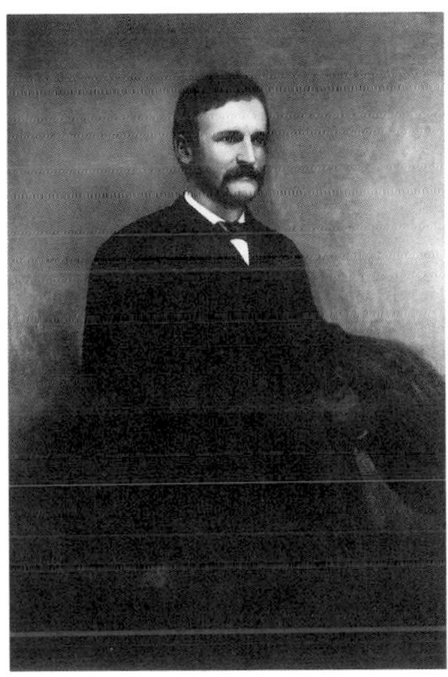

Portrait of Governor Pattison, of Pennsylvania. **#841. Lent by the Hon. R. E. Pattison, Harrisburg, Pa.** *Governor Robert Emory Pattison*, n.d. (ca. 1891). 55 x 38. The State Museum of Pennsylvania, Pennsylvania Historical and Museum Commission.

BECKWITH, **Carroll** (James Carroll). **New York.**

1852 Hannibal, MO–1917 New York, NY
Training — New York: NAD (Walter Shirlaw); Paris: Carolus-Duran, EcBA.

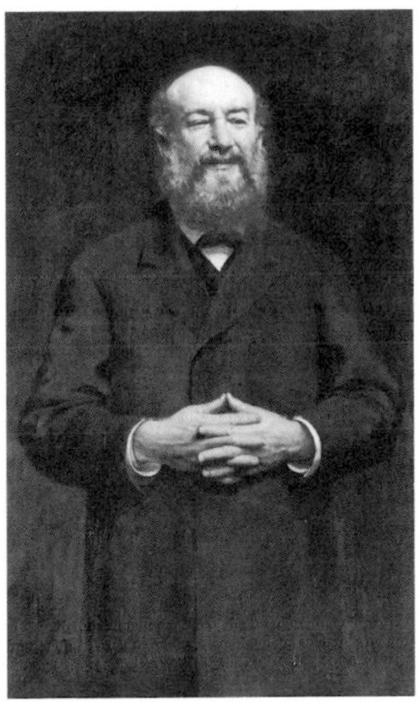

Mr. Isaacson. **#491.** [$1000]. *Portrait of Professor Isaacson*, 1889. 48 x 28. Wadsworth Atheneum, Hartford, Gift of Herbert L. Satterlee.[2]

Portrait of Miss E. A. H. (Elisa Adams Hall). **#968. Lent by Miss Hall, New York.** 1889.[3] ca. 79 x 43. Unlocated. "A 'Portrait of Miss Hall,' gorgeous in fur-edged gown beside a sumptuous curtain" — "Monthly Record of American Art," *The Magazine of Art* 16 (Dec. 1892–Nov. 1893): vi.

BELL, E. A. (Edward August). **New York.**

1861/62 New York, NY–1953 Peconic, NY
Training — New York: NAD, ASL; Munich: Royal Academy.

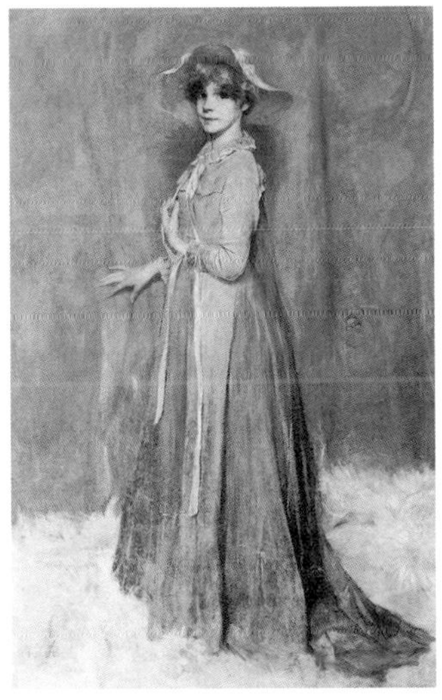

Portrait. Study of a Lady in Gray. **#508.** [$500]. *Lady in Gray*, 1889. 76⅛ x 49½. Memphis Brooks Museum of Art, Memphis, TN, Gift of the Artist.

BENEDICT, Enella. Lake Forest, Ill.
1858 Chicago, IL–1942 Richmond, VA
Training—Chicago: AIC; New York: ASL; Paris: Acad. Julian (Jules Joseph Lefebvre, J. P. Laurens, Jean-Joseph Benjamin-Constant).

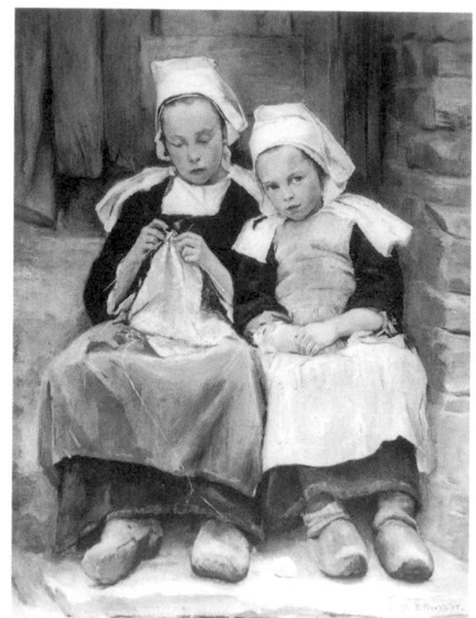

Brittany Children. **#436.** [$150]. n.d. 31 ½ x 24 ¼. The National Museum of Women in the Arts, Gift of Elizabeth Sita. Photograph by Carl J. Thome Photography.

† **BENSON, Frank W.** (Frank Weston). **Salem, Mass.**
1862 Salem, MA–1951 Salem, MA
Training—Boston: MFA; Paris: Acad. Julian (Gustave Boulanger, Jules Joseph Lefebvre).

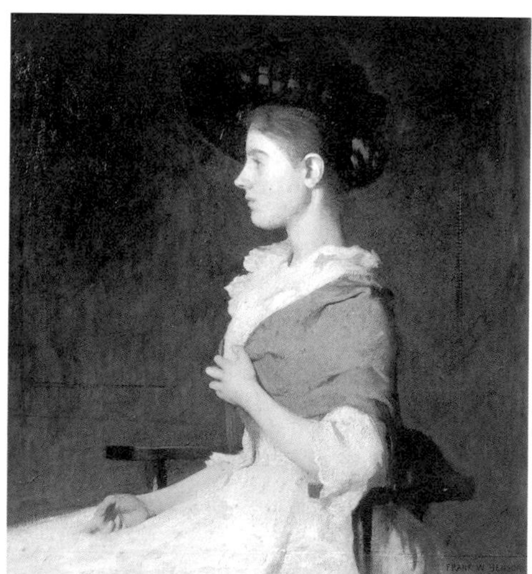

Girl with a Red Shawl. **#552. Lent by Mrs. David Kimball, Boston.** *Girl in a Red Shawl,* 1890. 32¼ x 32¼. Museum of Fine Arts, Boston, Bequest of David P. Kimball in memory of his wife Clara Bertram Kimball.

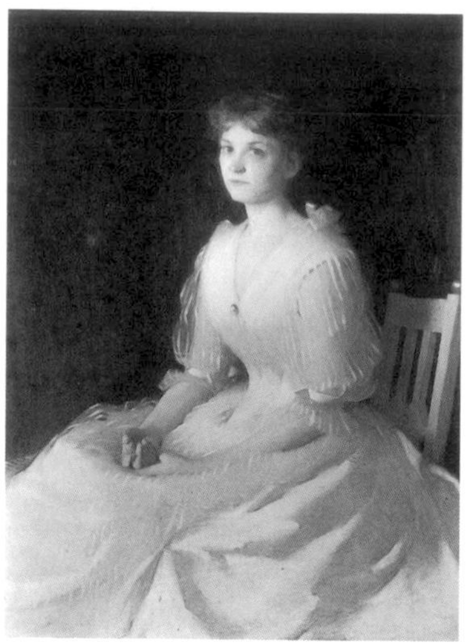

Portrait of a Lady in White (Ellen Perry Peirson Benson). **#561.** *Portrait in White,* 1889. 48½ x 38¼. National Gallery of Art, Washington, Gift of Sylvia Benson Lawson.

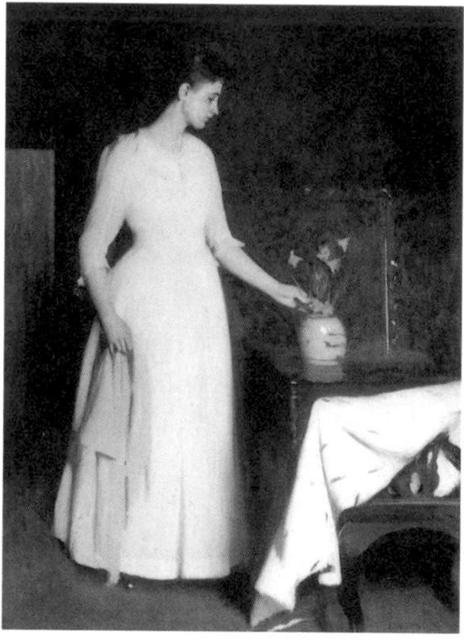

Figure in White. **#1283.** [$500]. 1890. 40 x 30. Trustees of the Salem Public Library, Salem, MA. Photograph by Mark Sexton.

BICKNELL, Frank A. (Frank Alfred). **Paris, France.**
1866 Augusta, ME–1943 Essex, CT
Training— Malden, MA: Albion H. Bicknell; Paris: Acad. Julian (William Bouguereau, Tony Robert-Fleury).

Along the River Oise. **#610.** [$325]. Unlocated.

An Old Apple Orchard. **#1245.** [$325]. Est. 32 x 34. Unlocated.

BIGELOW, D. F. (Daniel Folger). **Chicago.**
1823 Peru, NY–1910 Chicago, IL
Training — largely self-taught.

***Lake Champlain and the Adirondacks.* #618.** [$350]. Unlocated. "Far in the distance over the placid waters of the lake can be seen the green-clad hills that form a base for the wooded Adirondacks. . . . The foreground represents a hillside pasture on which a flock of sheep is feeding, and the tints of Autumn are seen in grass and shrub. . . . The sky is filled with fleecy summer clouds that shade the fields and hills from the direct sunlight, and yet allow sufficient of the rays to bring out in relief the tender greens of the meadows and the darker shades of the highlands" —*The Chicago Evening Journal,* 24 Feb. 1893.

† **BISBING, Henry S.** (Henry Singlewood). **Paris, France.**
1849 Philadelphia, PA–1933 Ledyard, CT
Training — Philadelphia: PAFA; Brussels: M. F. H. De Haas; Paris: Felix de Vuillefroy; Munich: Royal Academy (Franz Xaver Barth, Ludwig von Löfftz).

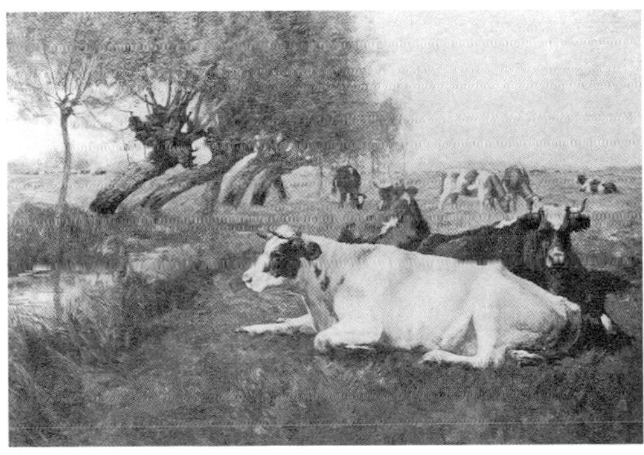

***Afternoon in the Meadow.* #284.** [$400]. Est. 30 x 45. Unlocated. Illus: Charles M. Kurtz, ed., *Illustrations from the Art Gallery of the World's Columbian Exposition* (Philadelphia: G. Barrie, 1893), 13.

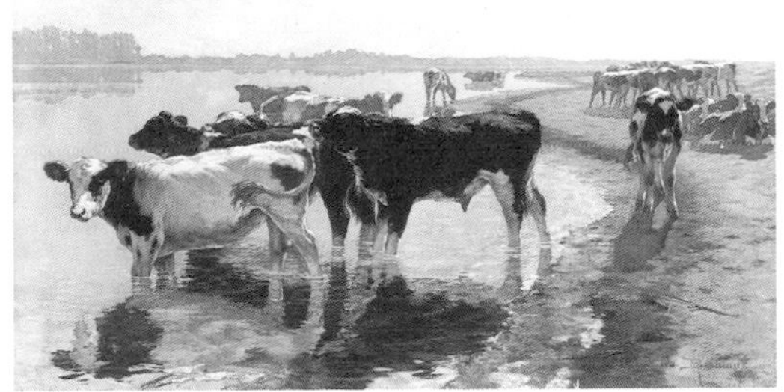

* ***On the River Bank.* #543.** [$1000]. n.d. (ca. 1891). 44 x 81. Collection Betty Williams, Concord, NC. Illus: Charles M. Kurtz, ed., *Illustrations from the Art Gallery of the World's Columbian Exposition* (Philadelphia: G. Barrie, 1893), 144.

***Lapsing Waves on a Quiet Shore.* #990.** [$200]. Sold, World's Columbian Exposition, Chicago, IL, 1893. Unlocated.

BLACKMAN, Walter. London, England.
1847 New York–1928 Chicago, IL
Training — Paris: Jean-Léon Gérôme.

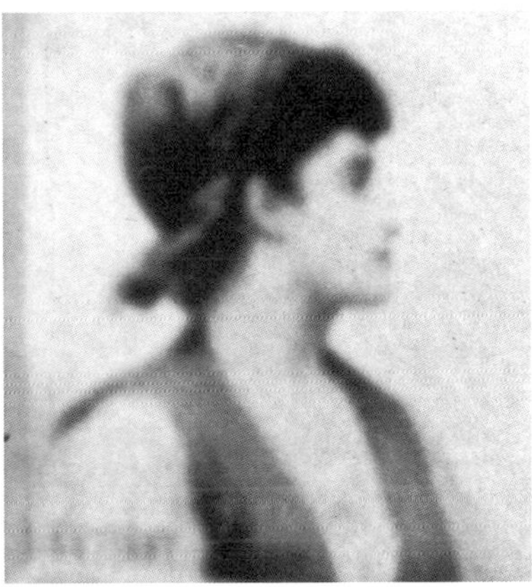

***A Capri Belle.* #785.** [$500]. Est. 22 x 20. Unlocated. Illus: Office of Printing and Photographic Services, National Museum of American History, Smithsonian Institution, neg. 12141.

BLAKELOCK, R. A. (Ralph Albert). **Cloverdale, N.Y.**
1847 New York, NY–1919 near Elizabethtown, NY
Training — self-taught.

***Landscape.* #935. Lent by Mr. Thomas B. Clarke, New York.** *Near Cloverdale,* n.d. 12 x 17½. Collection Ernest Closuit, Fort Worth, TX, ca. 1973. Unlocated.[4] "Twilight descends, curtaining a sky still pulsating with the glimmer of sunset. Trees are massed in the left foreground, and a line of dusky verdure marks the line of a water course, a range of hills showing on the horizon beyond" —American Art Association, *Catalogue of the Private Art Collection of Thomas B. Clarke, New York* (New York: American Art Association, 1899), lot 288.

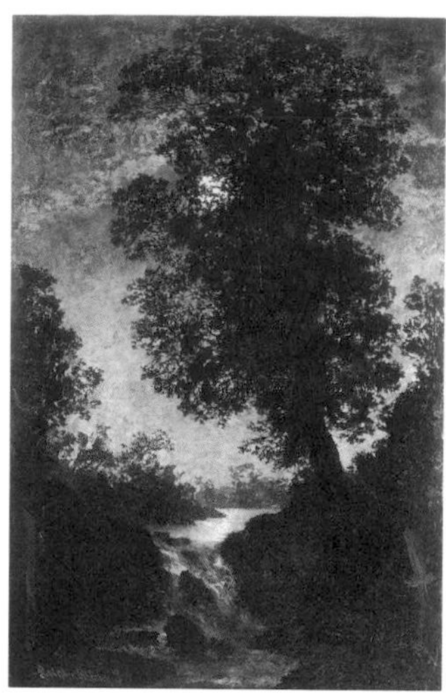

Moonlight. **#948. Lent by Mr. W. M. Laffan, New York.** *A Waterfall, Moonlight,* n.d. (by 1886). 56¼ x 35¾. The Metropolitan Museum of Art, Bequest of Eda K. Loeb, 1952.

† **BLASHFIELD, Edwin H.** (Edwin Howland). **New York.**
1848 New York, NY–1936 South Dennis, MA
Training — Philadelphia: PAFA; Paris: Léon Bonnat, Jean-Léon Gérôme, H. M. A. Chapu.

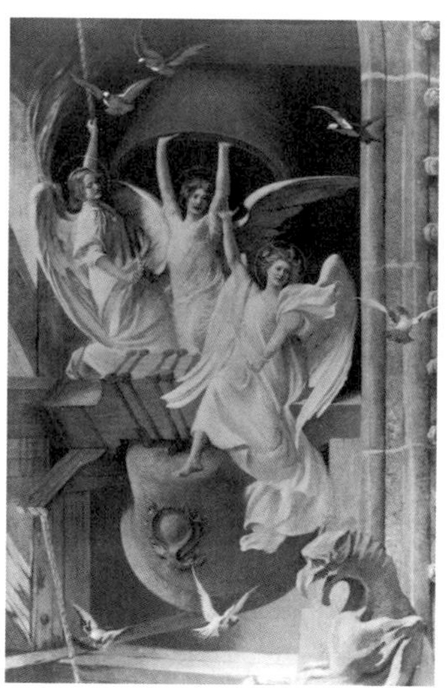

Christmas Bells. **#599.** 1892. 180⅞ x 123½. The Brooklyn Museum, Gift of the Artist. Illus: Daniel H. Burnham, *The Art of the World,* vol. 9 (New York: Appleton, 1893–95).

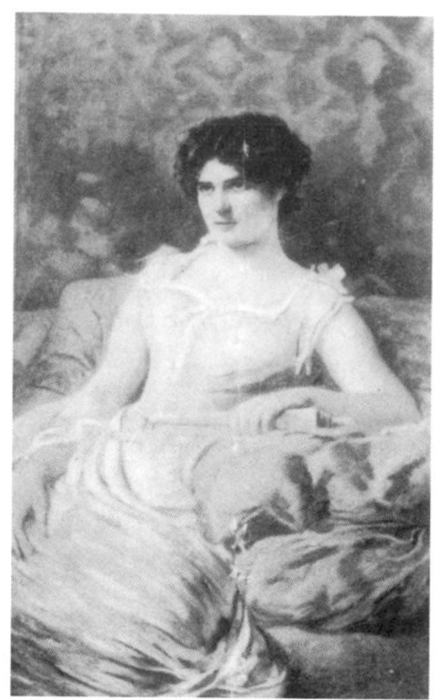

Portrait (Evangeline Wilbour Blashfield). **#625.** Collection of the artist, 1936. Unlocated.[5]

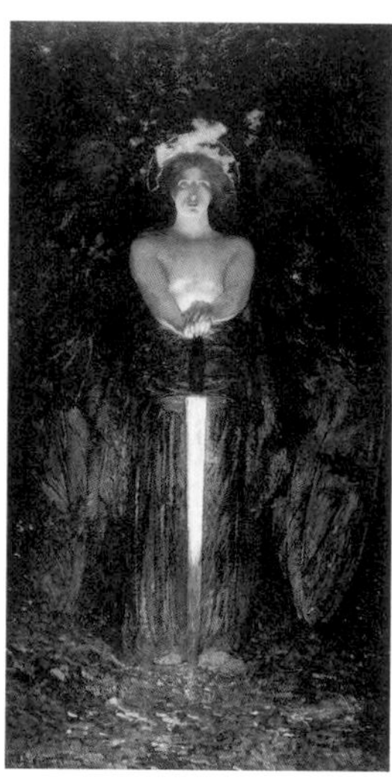

The Angel with the Flaming Sword. **#1130.** 1891. 110 x 57½. The Church of the Ascension, New York, NY. Photograph courtesy The Sterling and Francine Clark Art Institute, Williamstown, MA.

BLENNER, Carle J. (Carle Johann). **New York.**
1864 Richmond, VA–1952 New Haven, CT
Training — New Haven, CT: Yale School of the Fine Arts; Paris: Edmond-François Aman-Jean, A. F. A. Schenck, Acad. Julian (William Bouguereau, Tony Robert-Fleury).

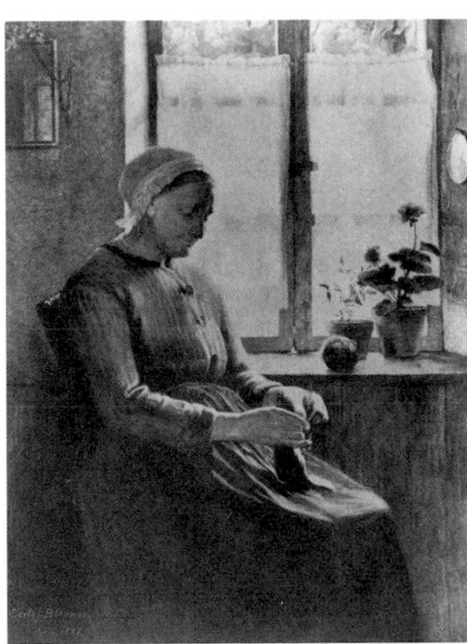

Contentment. **#381.** [$800]. 1888. 52½ x 38. Sold, American Art Association, New York, NY, 3 Feb. 1921, lot 64, to George d'Utassy. Unlocated. Illus: American Art Association, *Illustrated Catalogue of Notable Paintings . . . To Be Sold . . . February 3rd, 1921* (New York, 1921), lot 64.

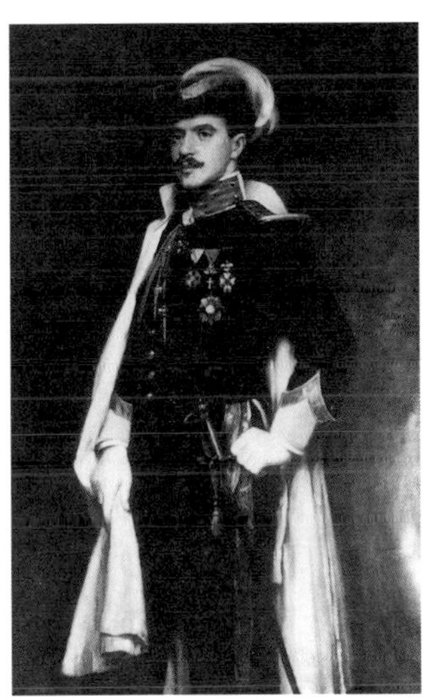

Portrait of El Señor Don Roderigo de Saavedra, Jr. **#1244. Lent by Señor Roderigo de Saavedra, Jr., Royal Spanish Legation, Washington.** *Don Rodrigo de Saavedra, Marqués de Villalobar.* Est. 70 x 35. Collection Marqués de Villalobar, Madrid, Spain.

BOGERT, **George H.** (George Hirst). **New York.**
1864 New York, NY–1944 New York, NY
Training — New York: NAD; Paris: Gustave Colin, Aimé Morot, Puvis de Chavannes, Eugène-Louis Boudin.

Moonlight, Etaples, France. **#741.** 18 x 26. Sold, Fifth Avenue Art Galleries, New York, NY, 24 Feb. 1910, lot 64, to J. G. Monroe. Unlocated. "A canvas of colored grays; a play of greenish blue and rose with some darker brownish notes. At the right are the houses of a fishing village with a windmill in the distance. Above them the yellow moon, the sky about it rosy and greenish blue. Against its misty light the sails of the fishing fleet show dark. One of the boats has a light near the base of a mast. Astern of it, and a little nearer the observer, is a man in a rowboat. To the right, and nearer the foreground, another rowboat is moored, its bow where the reflections of the moon light the water" —Fifth Avenue Art Galleries, *Catalogue of Oil Paintings . . . of the Late Charles M. Kurtz, Ph.D . . . To Be Sold . . . February 24 and 25, 1910* (New York, 1910), lot 64.

Morning. **#1206.** [$500]. Unlocated. "An expanse of river flowing through a flat country, edged with trees, and fresh and dewy, still, although the sun is up . . ." —*Brooklyn Daily Eagle*, 27 June 1893.

BOGGS, **Frank M.** (Frank Myers). **Paris, France.**
1855 Springfield, OH–1926 Paris, France
Training — Paris: Jean-Léon Gérôme, Jean Baptiste Antoine Guillemet, William Bouguereau.

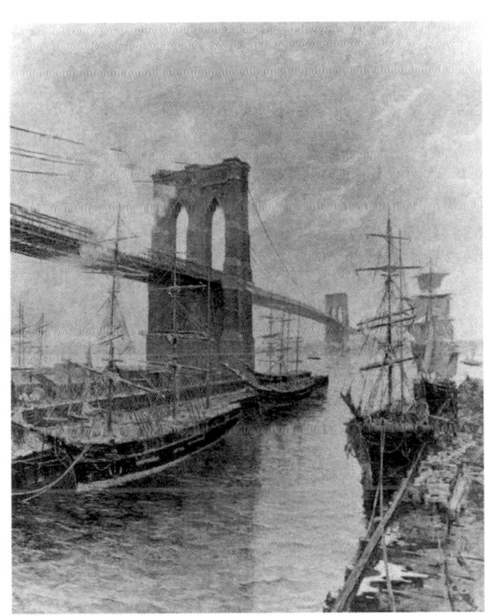

The Brooklyn Bridge, New York. **#468.** [$1000]. ca. 1889. 73 x 60. Sold, Fifth Avenue Art Galleries, New York, NY, 12 March 1906, lot 111, to Dr. Francis J. Quinlan. Unlocated. Illus: Daniel H. Burnham, *The Art of the World*, vol. 1 (New York: Appleton, 1893–95).

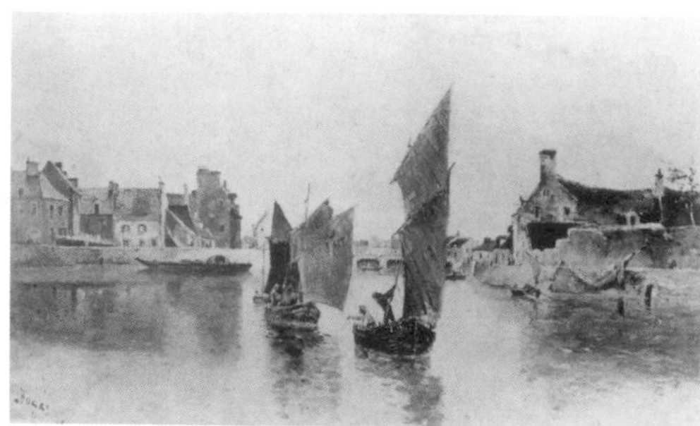

Fishing Boats Going Out, Isigny, France. **#863. Lent by Mr. James H. Dole, Chicago.** Unlocated. Illus: *Buildings and Art at the World's Fair* (Chicago: Rand, McNally, 1894), 171.

BOSTON, Joseph H. Brooklyn, N.Y.
1860 Bridgeport, CT–1954 New York, NY
Training — New York: NAD.

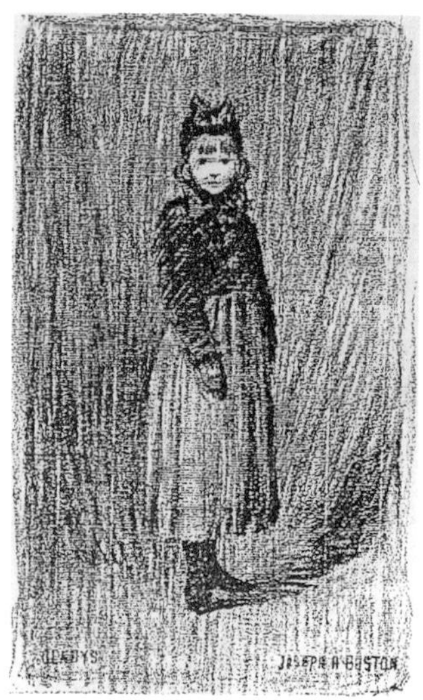

Gladys. A Portrait. **#1086.** Unlocated. Illus: *Discussions on American Art and Artists* (New York: American Art League, 1893), 110. "The most important work of Joseph H. Boston is his portrait of a child — 'Gladys.' The painting is now in the World's Fair art exhibition. The little girl, rosy-cheeked and large-eyed, dressed in some dark brown stuff, stands before a dark green background. The picture is of the size of life, and is an admirable piece of brush-work" —*Discussions on American Art and Artists* (New York: American Art League, 1893), 110.

BOUGHTON, George H. (George Henry). **London, England.**
1833 Norwich, England–1905 London, England
Training — Paris: Edouard May, Pierre Edouard Frère.

An English Spring Day. **#486.** Unlocated.

BOUTWOOD, Charles E. (Charles Edward). **Chicago.**
England–Residing 1913 Chicago, IL
Training — London: Royal Academy; Paris: William Bouguereau, Tony Robert-Fleury.

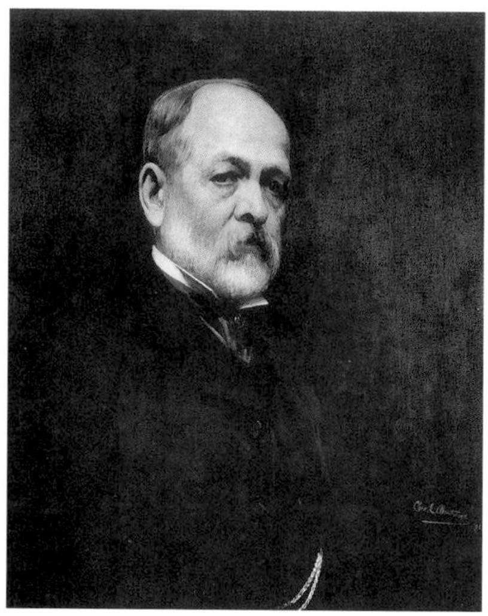

Portrait of the Hon. Charles B. Farwell. **#603. Lent by Mrs. Dudley Winston, Chicago.** 1893. 26¼ x 21⅛. Collection Mrs. James O. Heyworth, Lake Forest, IL. Photograph by Michael Tropea.

BOYDEN, Dwight Frederic (also Dwight Frederick). **Paris, France.**
1860 Boston, MA–1933 Baltimore, MD
Training — Paris: Acad. Julian (Gustave Boulanger, Jules Joseph Lefebvre).

The Pines of Mauve. **#701.** [$1000]. ca. 1892. Unlocated.

BREGLER, Charles. Philadelphia.
1864 Philadelphia, PA–1958 Philadelphia, PA
Training — Philadelphia: PAFA (Thomas Eakins).

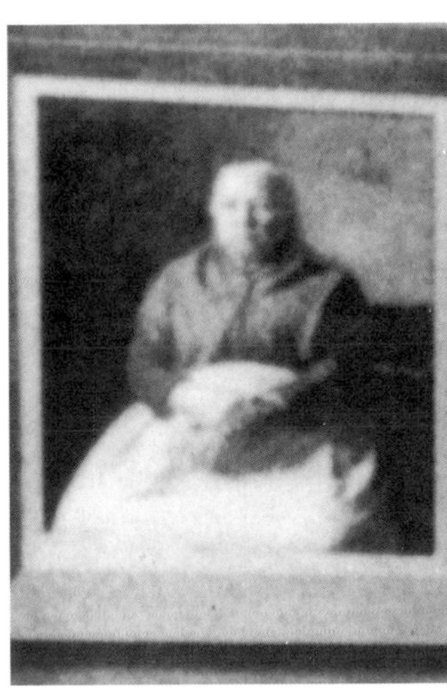

Portrait of a Woman.[6] **#1279. Lent by Mrs. Wm. Bregler, Philadelphia.** *Grandmother.* Est. 40 x 36. Estate of Mrs. Charles Bregler. Illus: Office of Printing and Photographic Services, National Museum of American History, Smithsonian Institution, neg. 12338.

BRIDGMAN, Frederic A. (Frederick Arthur). **Paris, France.**
1847 Tuskegee, AL–1928 Rouen, France
Training — New York: NAD; Brooklyn: Brooklyn Art School; Paris: Jean-Léon Gérôme, Atelier Suisse.

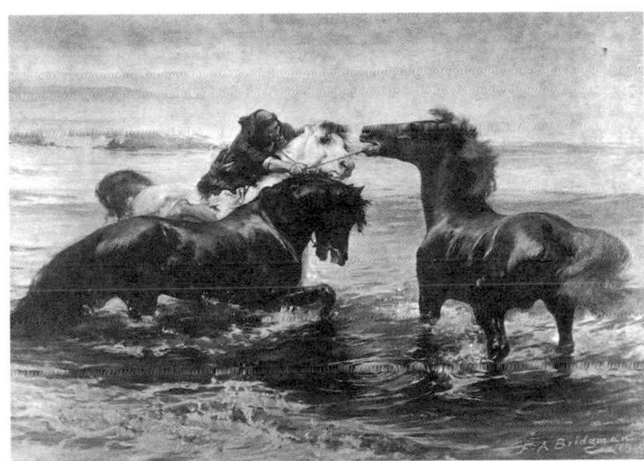

***Coast of Algiers — The Morning Bath.* #428.** 1891. 23 x 34. Sold, American Art Association, New York, NY, 10 March 1899, lot 12, to E. S. Ullman. Unlocated. Photograph courtesy Dr. and Mrs. Frederic Bridgman.

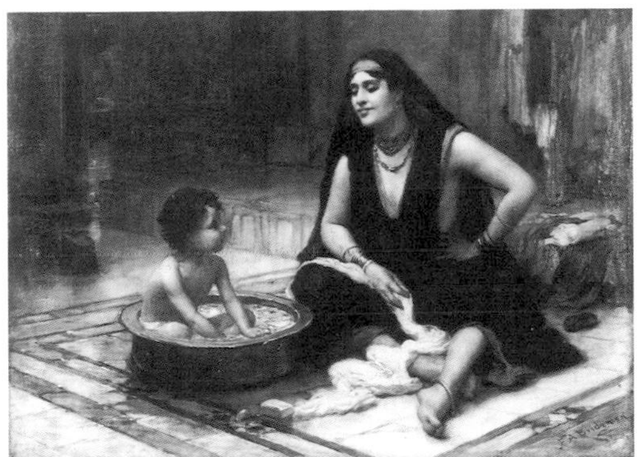

***Fellahine & Child — The Bath, Cairo.* #430.** n.d. (ca. 1892). 23¾ x 31⅞. Private Collection, Princeton, NJ.

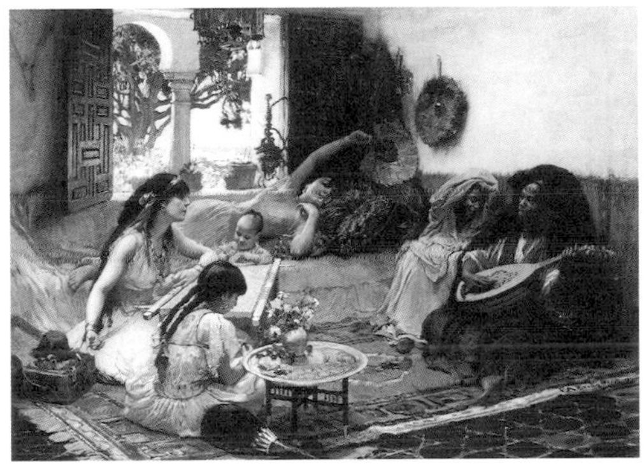

***A Hot Day at Mustapha, Algiers.* #432.** [$1400]. *L'Aprés Midi, Algier,* n.d. 21½ x 29. Private Collection. Photograph courtesy Mathaf Gallery, London, England.

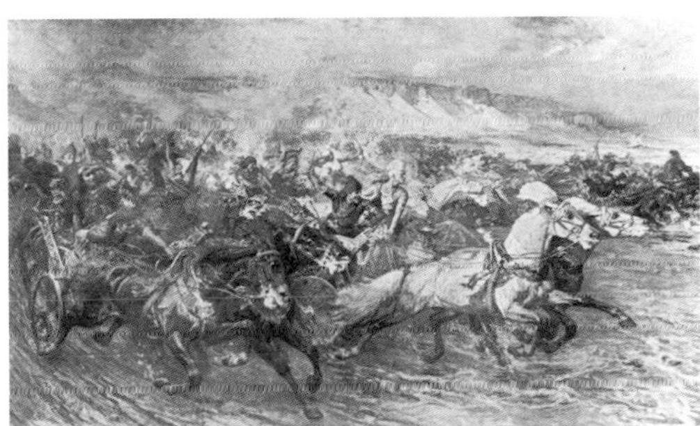

***Passage of the Red Sea.* #433.** [$8000]. 1891–92. 108 x 168. Columbia University in the City of New York, Gift of J. Ackerman Coles, 1914. Partially destroyed. Illus: John C. Ridpath, ed., *Art and Artists of All Nations* (New York: Arkell Weekly Company, 1894), 384.

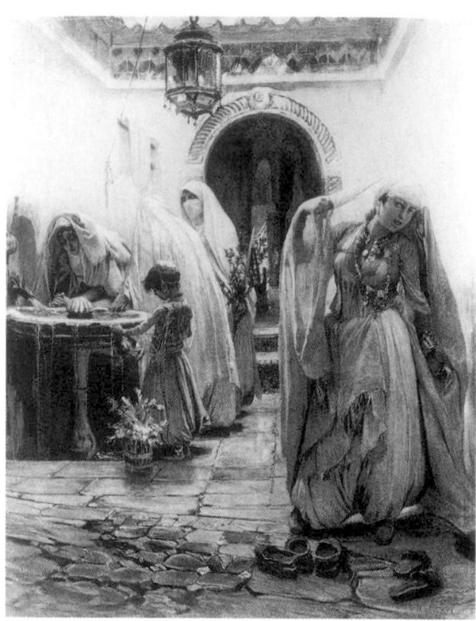

Women at the Mosque, Algiers. **#937.** [$1600]. 1887. 29 x 25. Sold, American Art Association, New York, NY, 10 March 1899, lot 44, to M. Knoedler & Co. Unlocated.[7] Illus (as *Algerian Women*): George W. Sheldon, *Recent Ideals of American Art* (New York: Appleton, 1890).

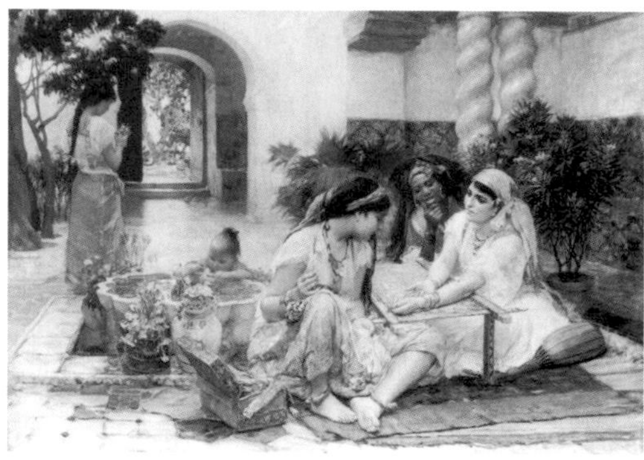

In a Village at El Biar, Algiers. **#955.** [$2200]. 1889. 36 x 52. Private Collection. Photograph courtesy Richard Green Gallery, London, England.

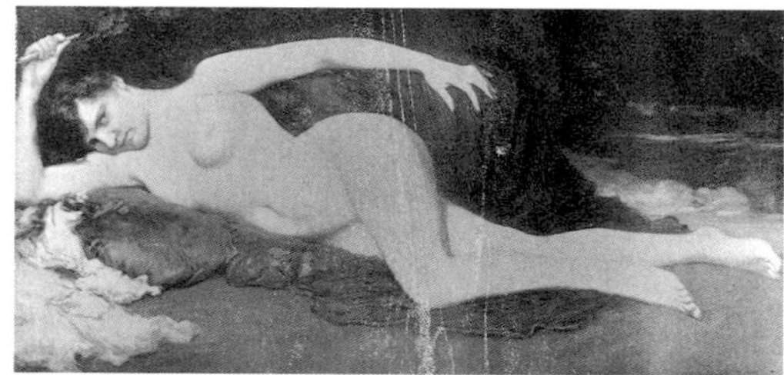

Day Dreams. **#1049.** [$1800]. Est. 36 x 80. Collection Harmonie Club, New York, NY, 1899. Unlocated. Illus: William Walton, *Art and Architecture,* vol. 1 (Philadelphia: G. Barrie, 1893–95), 21.

BRISTOL, J. B. (John Bunyan). **New York.**
1826 Hillsdale, NY–1909 New York, NY
Training — Henry Ary; largely self-taught.

Mount Chocorua, N.H. **#442.** [$800]. Unlocated.

BROOKS, A. F. (Alden Finney). **Chicago.**
1840 West Williamsfield, OH–1932 Kenilworth, IL?
Training — Edwin White; Paris: Carolus-Duran.

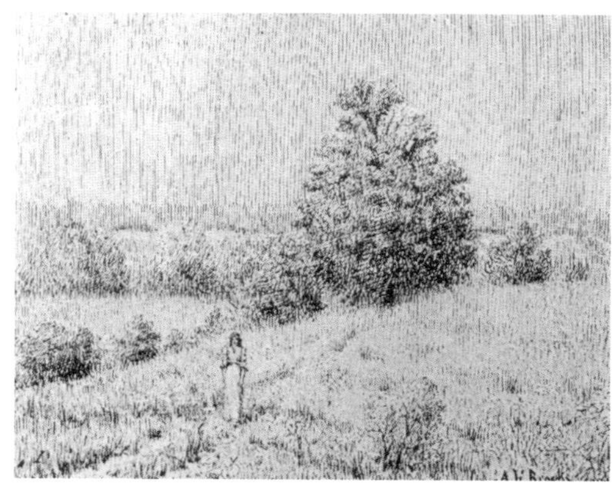

The Primrose Way. **#1126.** [$150]. Unlocated. Illus: Trumbull White and William Igleheart, *The World's Columbian Exposition, Chicago, 1893* (Philadelphia and St. Louis: P. W. Ziegler, [1893]), 359. "Coming along a half-worn track through a field yellow with buttercups, and backed by a sky that is still filled with the dewy haze of morning, is a young girl clad in white. The figure is not prominent enough to attract much attention, though cleverly executed. The charm of the picture lies in the langorous ease that seems to pervade the entire scene" — *The Chicago Evening Journal,* 24 Feb. 1893.

BROUWER, T. A., Jr. (Theophilus Anthony). **East Hampton, L.I.**
1864 New York, NY–1932 Westhampton, NY
Training — New York: Cooper Union, NAD

Musk Melons. **#425.** [$600]. Est. 25 x 35. Unlocated.

BROWN, J. Appleton (John Appleton). **New York.**
1844 Newburyport, MA–1902 New York, NY
Training — Benjamin Curtis Porter; Paris: Emile Lambinet.

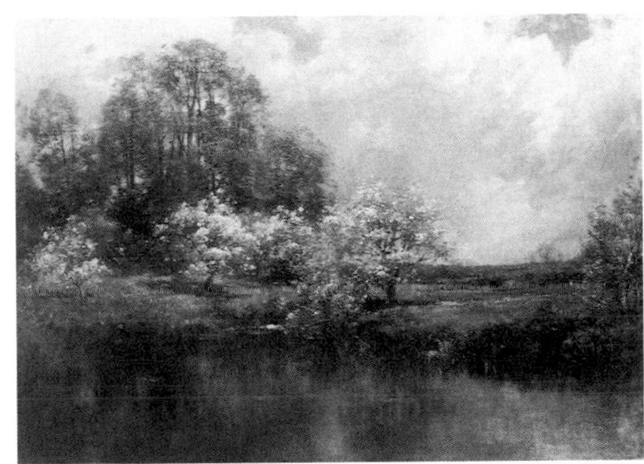

Springtime.* **#334. [$800]. n.d. 30⅞ x 41⅞. Collection Mr. and Mrs. Thomas Rosse.

BROWN, J. G. (John George). **New York.**
1831 Durham, England–1913 New York, NY
Training — New York: NAD; Newcastle-upon-Tyne: Scott Lauder; Edinburgh: Royal Academy (William B. Scott).

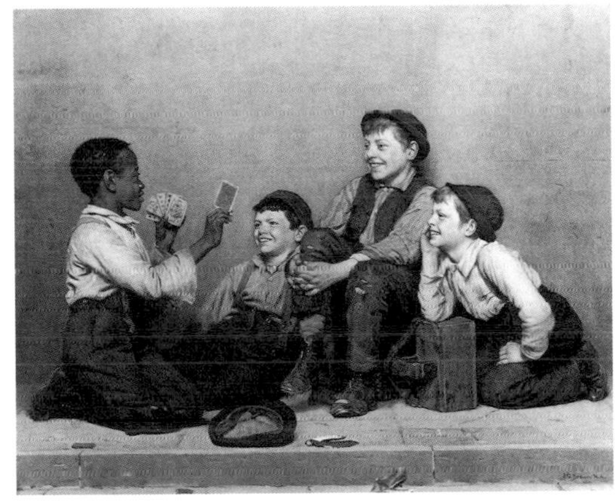

A Card Trick. **#536.** [$1200]. n.d. (ca. 1880s). 26 x 31. Joslyn Art Museum, Omaha, NE.[8]

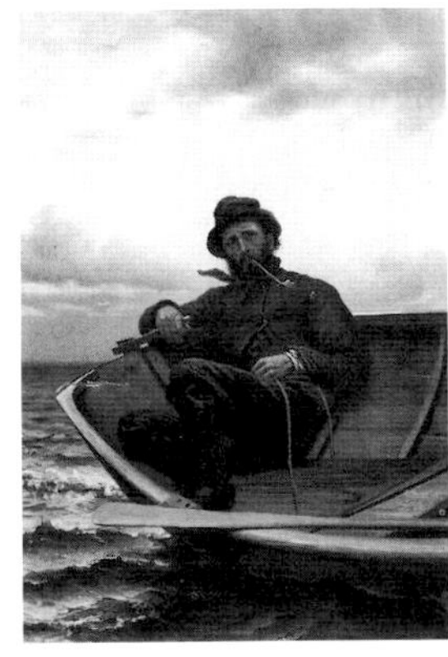

Homeward Bound. **#557. Lent by Mr. W. T. Evans, New York.** 1878. 30 x 19⅞. Society for the Preservation of New England Antiquities.

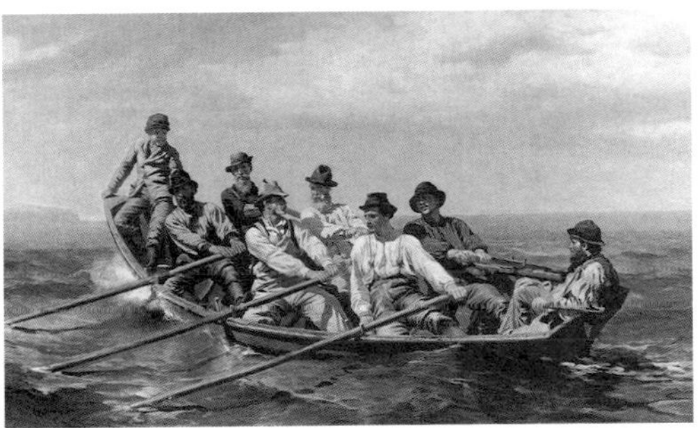

Pull for the Shore. **#691. Lent by Mr. Isidore Strauss, New York.** n.d. (ca. 1878). 23⅞ x 39¾. Collection of the Santa Barbara Museum of Art, Museum Exchange for the Preston Morton Collection.

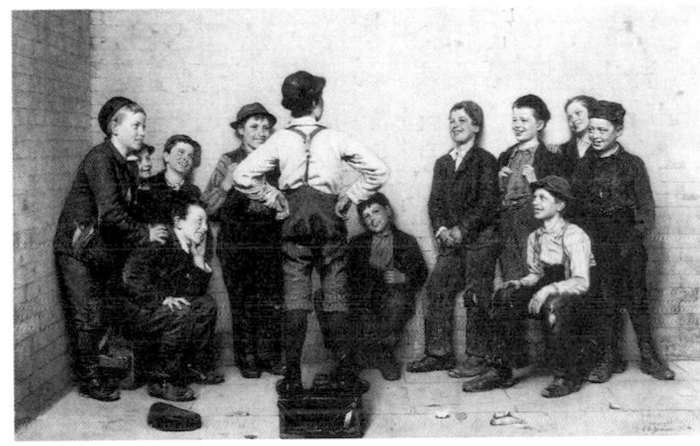

The Stump Speech. **#871.** [$2500]. n.d. (early 1880s). 28 x 44. Private Collection. Photograph courtesy Spanierman Gallery, New York, NY.

When We Were Girls. **#873. Lent by Mr. E. Asiel, New York.** ca. 1890. 25 x 30. Unlocated. "Two very old women in a homely farm house interior, one with a pipe, the other with her knitting, talking over the seemingly hard-to-realize time when they were buxom, blooming belles of the village. There is a whole lifetime story told in each of these faces, with regret for the days that are past, and pleasure in the remembrance of the enjoyment that was in them" — *New York Star*, 16 Feb. 1890.

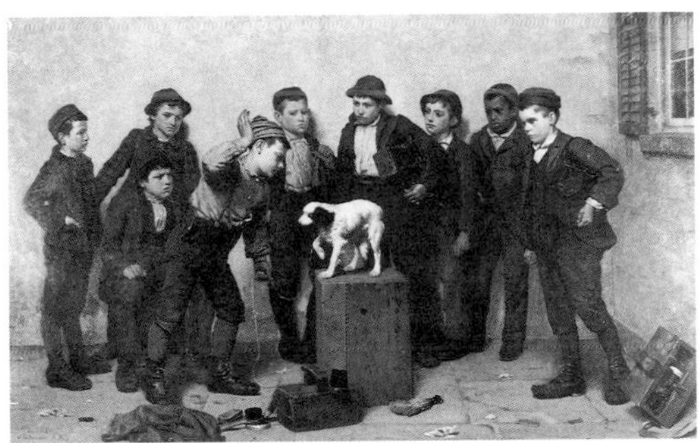

Training the Dog.* **#876. *Teaching Tricks,* n.d. 29 x 45. Washington and Lee University, Lexington, VA.

At the Old Cottage Door. **#944. Lent by Mr. Gilbert Gaul, New York.** Unlocated.

BROWN, Matilda (Matilda C. Browne/Mrs. Frederick Van Wyck). **New York.**
1869 Newark, NJ–1947 Greenwich, CT
Training — Charles M. Dewey, Frederick Freer, Eleanor and Kate Greatorex, Carleton Wiggins; Paris: Acad. Julian (William Bouguereau), Julien Dupré; the Netherlands: Henry Bisbing.

An Unwilling Model. **#356.** [$175]. ca. 1892. Unlocated. "[The artist and her mother] bought calves at a near-by fair and the young artist painted these and then exchanged them for others. One little animal objected to being put to this use and never ceased to tug at the rope which held it in the shade of a small fruit tree. She painted a picture of it in spite of its display of will power and called the canvas 'Unwilling Model.' When she came back to this country the picture represented her at the Columbian Exposition in 1893 and was sold there" —*International Studio* (Nov. 1923): 130.

BROWN, Walter Francis. Venice.
1853 Providence, RI–1929 Venice, Italy
Training — Providence, RI: Brown University; Paris: Jean-Léon Gérôme, Léon Bonnat.

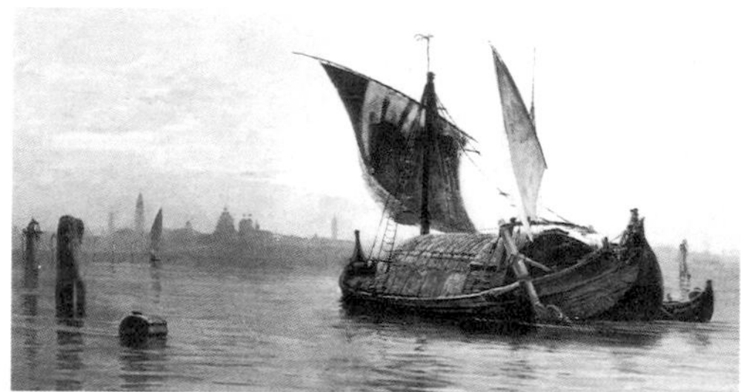

***Roscona, Sunrise.* #332.** [$500]. *Roscona Sunrise, Venice,* n.d. 30 x 50. Vanderpoel Memorial Gallery, John H. Vanderpoel Art Association, Chicago, IL.

BROWNE, Charles Francis. Chicago.
1859 Natick, MA–1920 Waltham, MA
Training — Boston: MFA; Philadelphia: PAFA (Thomas Eakins, Thomas P. Anshutz); Paris: Gustave Boulanger, Jules Joseph Lefebvre, Jean-Léon Gérôme, A. F. A. Schenck, EcBA; Auvers-sur-Oise; Ecouen: August Friedrich Albrecht.

***Old Poplar Trees.* #621.** [$350]. Unlocated.

***On the Oise, France.* #883.** [$250]. Unlocated.

***Sand Dunes of Drummadoon, Arran.* #928.** [$400]. Est. 20 x 30. Unlocated.

***Back from the Beach, Cape Ann.* #967.** [$200]. Unlocated.

† **BRUSH, George de Forest. New York.**
1855 Shelbyville, TN–1941 Hanover, NH
Training —New York: NAD; Paris: Jean-Léon Gérôme, EcBA.

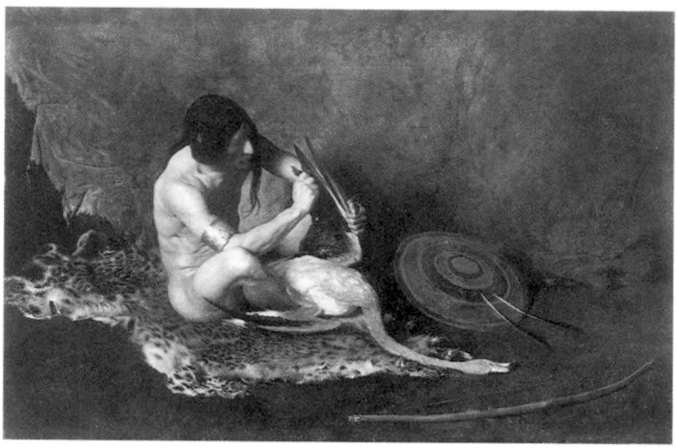

* ***The Head Dress.* #586. Lent by Mr. H. H. Fay, Boston.** *The Shield Maker,* 1890. 10⅞ x 16⅛. The Warner Collection of Gulf States Paper Corporation, Tuscaloosa, AL.

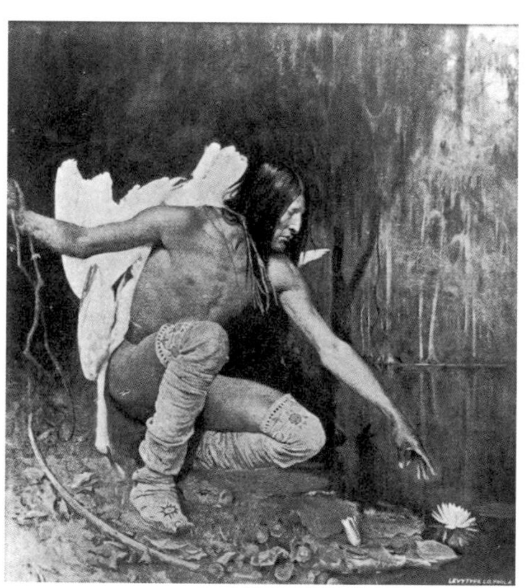

***The Indian and the Lily.* #664. Lent by Mr. C. D. Miller, Jersey City.** 1887. 21¼ x 19⅞. Collection Pierre Bergé. Illus: Pennsylvania Academy of the Fine Arts, *Forty Works of Art from the Sixty-third Annual Exhibition of the Academy of the Fine Arts* (Philadelphia: The Levytype Company, 1894).

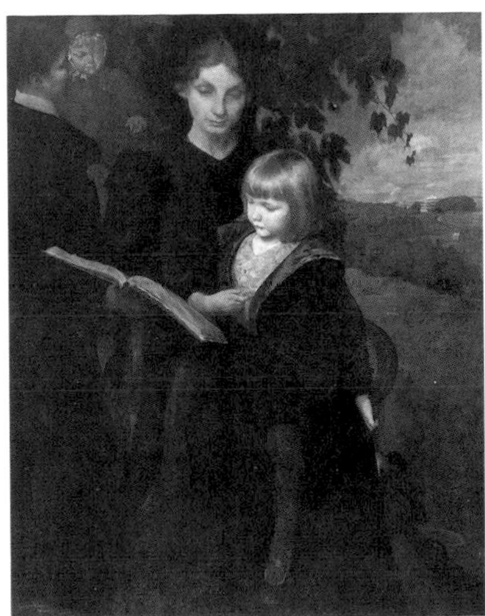

Mother and Child. **#705. Lent by Mr. J. M. Sears, Boston.** 1892. 42¼ x 35⅜. ©Addison Gallery of American Art, Phillips Academy, Andover, MA. Gift of anonymous donor. All rights reserved.

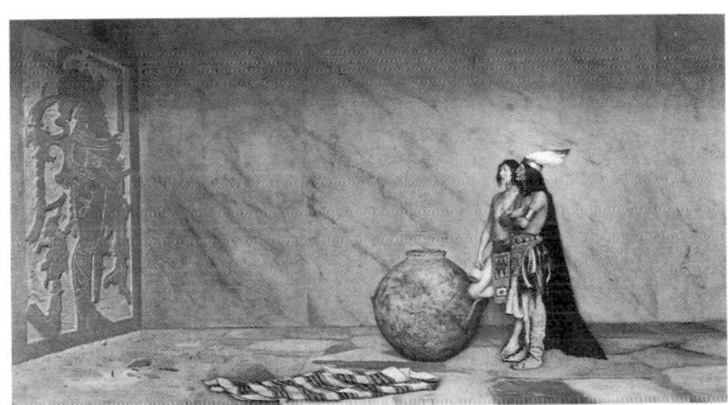

The Sculptor and the King. **#745. Lent by Mr. Henry Failing, Portland, Ore.** 1888. 20 x 36. Portland Art Museum, bequest of Mary Forbush Failing.

BRYANT, **Wallace. Boston.**
1864 Melrose, MA–1953 Gloucester, MA
Training — Paris: Acad. Julian (William Bouguereau, Jean-Joseph Benjamin-Constant, J. P. Laurens, Tony Robert-Fleury).

Noon. **#1111.** [$600]. Unlocated.

BUNKER, **Caroline. Boston.**
Maine–1930 New York, NY

Goosefield. **#1012.** [$75]. Est. 14 x 20. Unlocated.

Wheat Stacks, Afternoon Sunshine. **#1068.** [$75]. Unlocated.

Study of Snowballs. **#1235. Lent by Mrs. F. D. Cross, Providence.** ca. 1890. Unlocated.

BUTLER, **George B.** (George Bernard). **New York.**
1838 New York, NY–1907 Croton Falls, NY
Training — New York: Thomas Hicks, NAD; Paris: Thomas Couture.

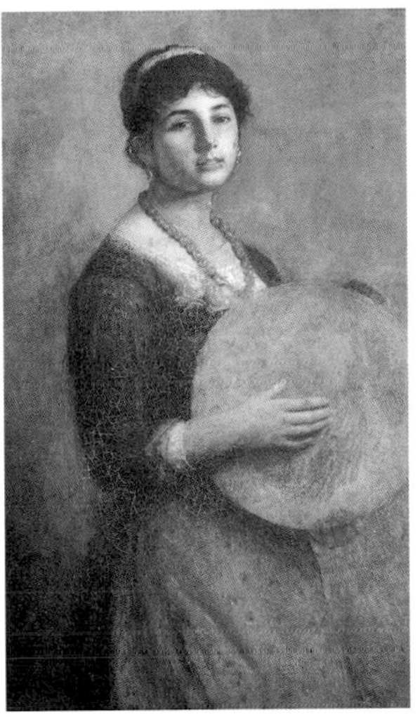

Girl with Tambourine. **#640.** n.d. 43¾ x 26. Barnard College, New York, NY. Photograph by Gregory W. Schmitz.

BUTLER, **Herbert** (Herbert E.). **Chicago.**
1860 London, England–Residing 1915 Polperro, England
Training —London: Heatherley's, Royal Academy.

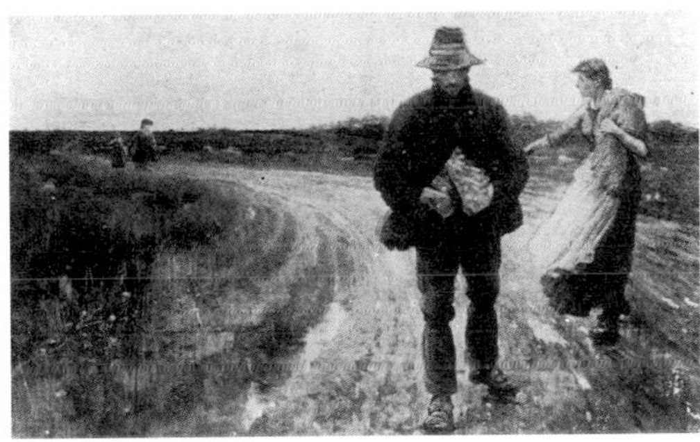

Hard Times. **#597.** Est. 40 x 55. Unlocated. Illus: Trumbull White and William Igleheart, *The World's Columbian Exposition, Chicago, 1893* (Philadelphia and St. Louis: P. W. Ziegler, [1893]), 346.

BUTLER, **Howard Russell. New York.**
1856 New York, NY–1934 Princeton, NJ
Training —Alexander Harrison, Charles Lasar; New York: ASL (J. Carroll Beckwith, George de Forest Brush); Mexico: Frederic Church; Paris:

P. A. J. Dagnan-Bouveret, Henri Gervex, Alfred Philippe Roll; Concarneau, France; St. Ives, England.

Church of Guadalupe, Aguas Calientes. **#409.** [$300]. ca. 1890. Sold, World's Columbian Exposition, Chicago, IL, 1893. Unlocated.

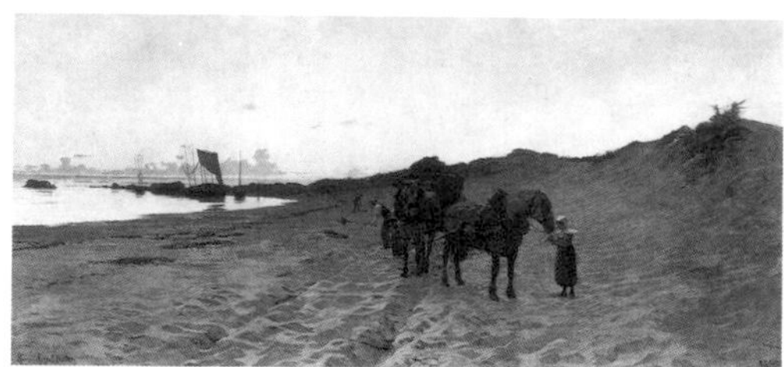

Sea Weed Gatherers, Finistere, France. **#411.** *The Seaweed Gatherers,* 1886. 46¾ x 96¼. National Museum of American Art, Smithsonian Institution, Gift of Howard Russell Butler, Jr.

Marine. **#1098.** [$300]. Unlocated.

BUTTLES, Mary. New York.
Columbus, OH–Residing 1895 New York, NY
Training — Paris: Jean-Joseph Benjamin-Constant, Jules Joseph Lefebvre.

Peasant Woman of Alsace. **#859.** [$500]. ca. 1892. Unlocated. "A three-quarter length of a woman in the apron and big black bows of Alsatian peasants" —*New York Times,* 1 May 1892.

Julie. **#1039.** Unlocated.

CADY, Henry N. (Henry Newell). **Philadelphia.**
1849 Warren, RI–1935 Warren, RI
Training — self-taught.

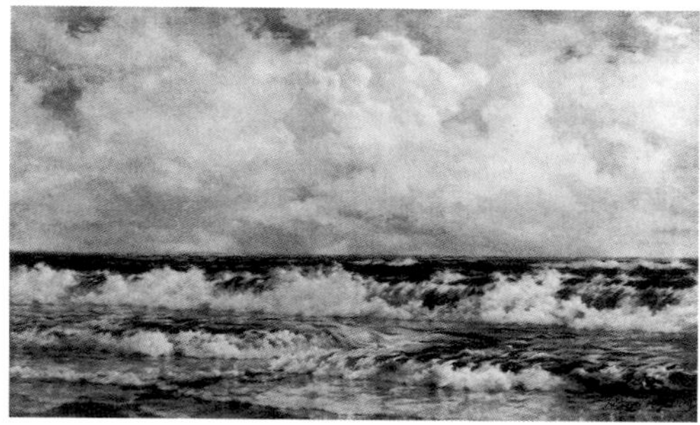

Sunset at Narragansett Pier, Rhode Island. **#418.** [$250]. 1892. 18 x 30. Collection Robert and Marjorie Catanzaro, Narragansett, RI.

CAIN, Neville. Louisville.
Louisville, KY–1935 Louisville, KY
Training — Paris: Carolus-Duran.

The Satyr and the Traveler. **#1095.** ca. 1890. Est. 100 x 125. Unlocated.

CALIGA, I. H. (Isaac Henry).[9] **Boston.**
1857 Auburn, IN–1944 Provincetown, MA
Training — Munich: Royal Academy (Wilhelm Lindenschmidt).

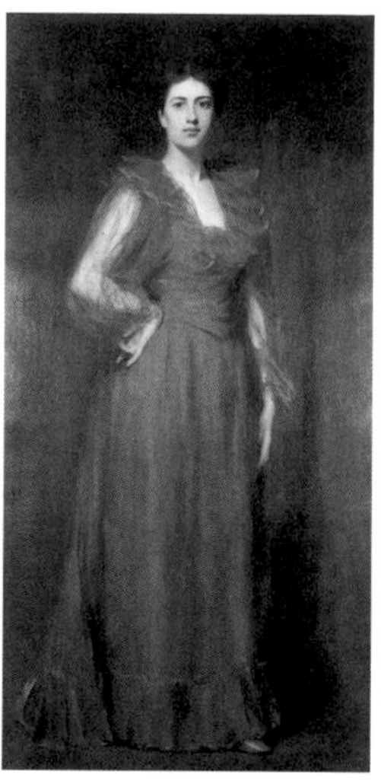

Portrait (Alice Taft Herrick). **#651. Lent by Mrs. Robert F. Herrick, Brookline, Mass.** n.d. (ca. 1892). 83 x 47. Private Collection. Photograph by Joe O'Connell.

CAMERON, Edgar S. (Edgar Spier). **Chicago.**
1862 Ottawa, IL–1944 Chicago, IL
Training — Chicago: Academy of Design (Newton M. Carpenter, Lawrence Carmichael Earle, Henry F. Spread); New York: ASL (William Merritt Chase, Thomas Dewing); Paris: Acad. Julian (Gustave Boulanger), EcBA (Alexandre Cabanel), Jean-Joseph Benjamin-Constant, Acad. Colarossi.

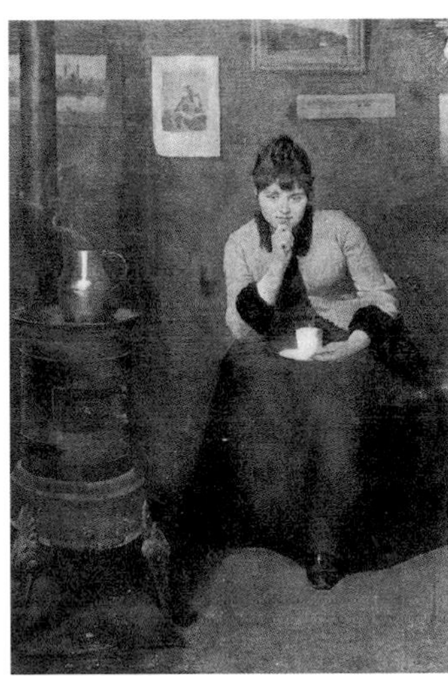

In the Studio. **#1161.** [$500]. ca. 1888. Est. 30 x 20. Unlocated. Illus: John C. Ridpath, ed., *Art and Artists of All Nations* (New York: Arkell Weekly Company, 1894), 340.

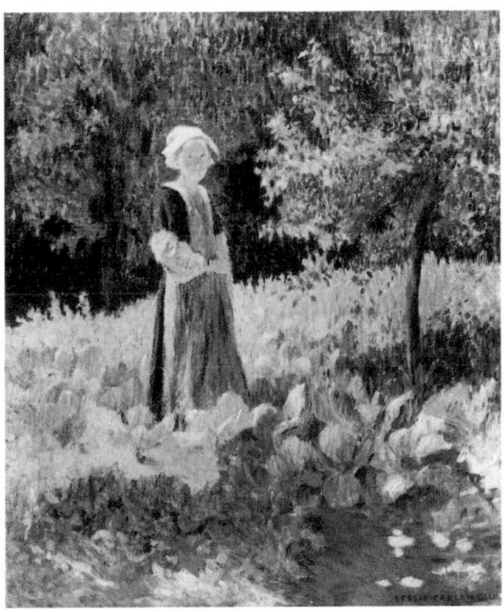

A Breton Garden. **#1185.** [$300]. 1892. 22 x 18. Private Collection. Photograph courtesy D. Wigmore Fine Art, New York, NY.

CANDIDUS, **Harry W. T. Munich, Bavaria.**
1867 New York–1902 Munich, Germany
Training — Cronberg, Germany: Schuler A. Burgers.

Landscape. **#559.** [$100]. Unlocated.

CARL, **Kate A.** (Katharine Augusta). **Paris, France.**
ca. 1862 New Orleans, LA–1938 New York, NY
Training — Paris: Acad. Julian (J. P. Laurens, William Bouguereau), Hector LeRoux, Gustave Courtois, Tony Robert-Fleury.

Head of a Man. **#611.** Unlocated.

CAULDWELL, **Leslie** (Leslie Giffen). **Paris, France.**
1861 New York, NY–1941 Paris, France
Training — Paris: Acad. Julian (Gustave Boulanger, Jules Joseph Lefebvre), Carolus-Duran.

A Sun Bath. **#694.** [$350]. Unlocated.

A Daughter of Eve. **#695.** [$300]. Unlocated.

CHAPMAN, **Carlton T.** (Carlton Theodore). **New York.**
1860 New London, OH–1925 New York, NY
Training — New York: NAD, ASL; Paris: Acad. Julian (Gustave Boulanger, Jules Joseph Lefebvre), Jean-Léon Gérôme; London: National Gallery, South Kensington Museum School; the Netherlands.

On Cape Ann. **#520. Lent by Mrs. John Hutton, New York.** Est. 10 x 14. Unlocated.

Five O'clock at St. Ives, England. **#1066.** [$400]. ca. 1892. Unlocated. "A rich-colored townscape with shadowed foreground, the light falling strong on a row of pinkish houses on higher ground" —*New York Times,* 1 May 1892.

CHASE, **Harry** (Harry S.). **deceased.**
1853 Woodstock, VT–1889 Sewanee, TN
Training — St. Louis: J. M. Stuart; New York: NAD; Munich: Royal Academy (Konstantinos Bolonachi, Wilhelm von Kaulbach); The Hague: Royal Academy (Hendrik Willem Mesdag); Paris: Paul Constant Soyer.

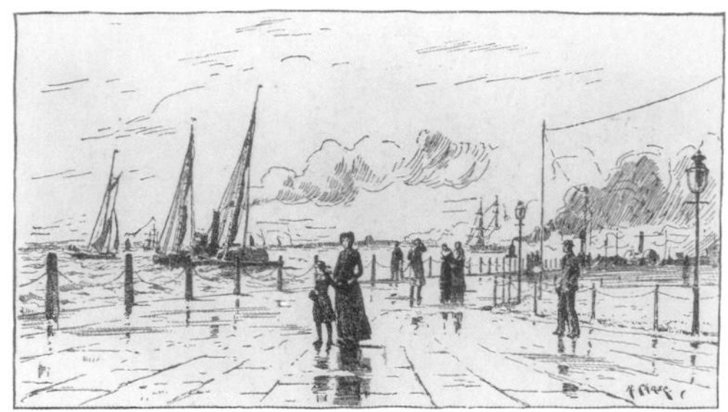

The Battery Park, New York. **#852. Lent by Mrs. Harry Chase, St. Louis.** 1884. 30 x 50. Unlocated. Illus: Charles M. Kurtz, ed., *National Academy Notes, Including the Complete Catalogue of the Fifty-Ninth Spring Exhibition, National Academy of Design New York* (New York: Cassell & Co., 1884), 37.

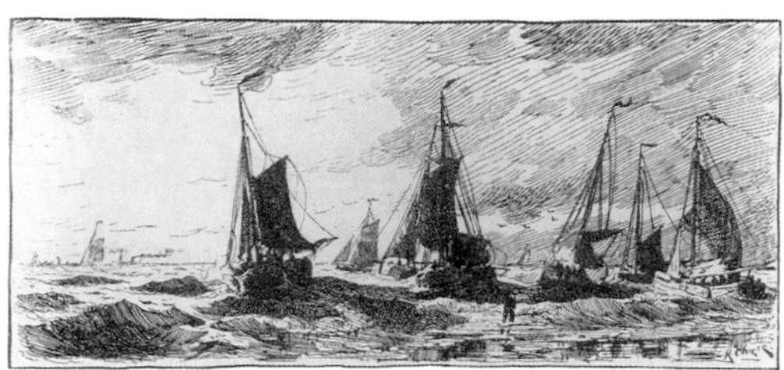

At Anchor off Scheveningen. **#854. Lent by Mrs. Harry Chase, St. Louis.** ca. 1885. 26 x 60. Unlocated. Illus: American Art Association, *Illustrated Catalogue of the Prize Fund Exhibition* (New York: J. J. Little, 1885), no. 67.

CHASE, William M. (William Merritt). **New York.** 1849 Nineveh, IN–1916 New York, NY *Training* — Indianapolis: B. F. Hayes; New York: NAD (J. O. Eaton); Munich: Royal Academy (Karl von Piloty, Alexander Wagner); Venice.

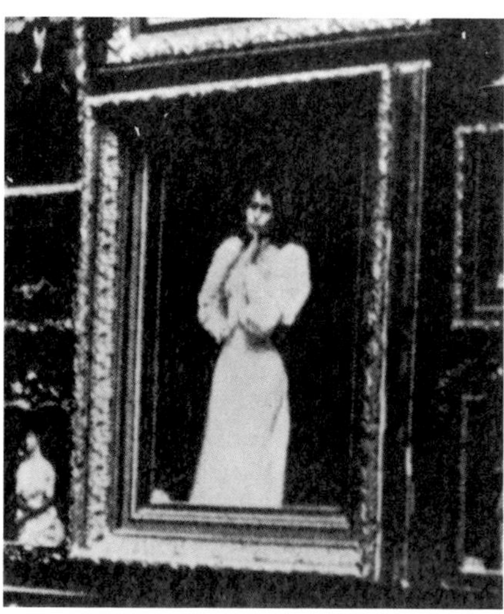

Portrait of Mrs. L.[10] **#657.** ca. 1891–92. Est. 50 x 35. Unlocated. Illus: J. W. Buel, *The Magic City* (St. Louis: Historical Publishing Company, 1894). "A portrait of Miss Lawrence, painted by William Merritt Chase, which is in some respects the best in the exhibition. The lady stands in white, with some gold embroidery about the body of her dress, and regards the world with a sweet but alert pensiveness very flattering to the artist's skill. A dark blue background throws out face and figure nicely" — *New York Times,* 1 April 1892; "Miss Lawrence, a slender, nervous American girl in white with gold bodice, her hand to her face in an irresolute gesture, her eyes shadowy and thoughtful" — "Monthly Record of American Art," *The Magazine of Art* 15 (Dec. 1891–Nov. 1892): xxii.

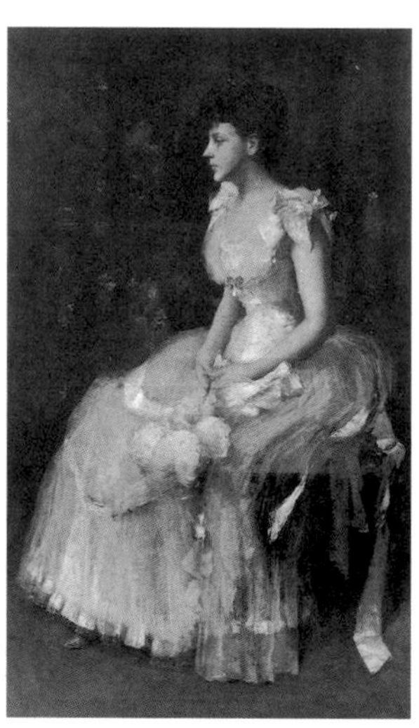

Lady in Pink.* **#684. *Portrait of a Lady in Pink* (Mrs. Leslie Cotton), n.d. (ca. 1888–89). 70 x 40. Museum of Art, Rhode Island School of Design, Gift of Isaac C. Bates.

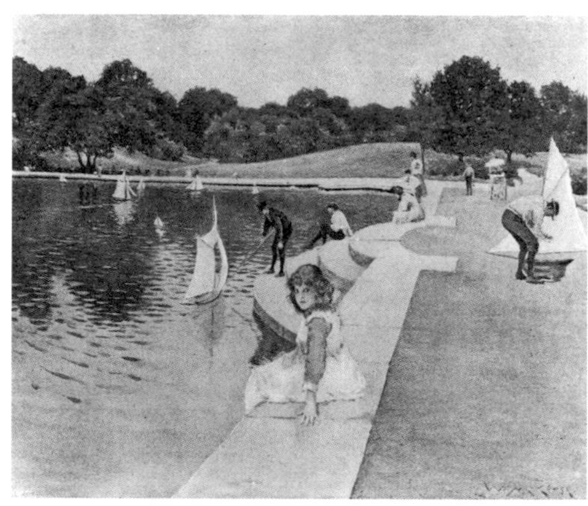

Lilliputian Boats in the Park. **#725. Lent by Mr. R. L. Knoedler, New York.** 19 x 22¾. Collection Miss Anna C. Meyer, New York, NY, 1917. Unlocated. Illus: Clarence C. Cook, *Art and Artists of Our Time,* vol. 3 (New York: S. Hess, [1888]), 281.

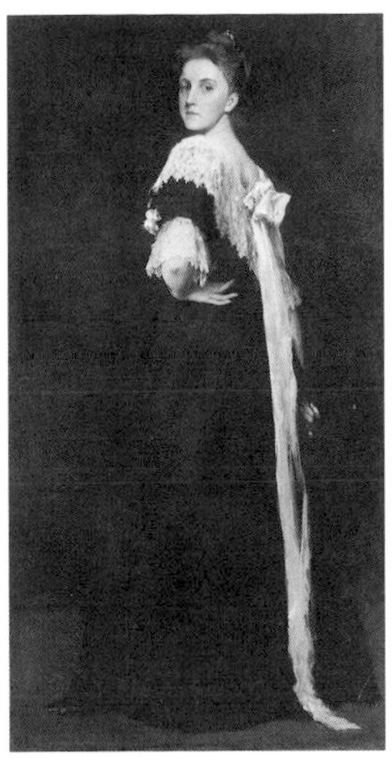

Portrait of Mrs. E. **#764. Lent by Mrs. E.** *Lydia Field Emmet,* n.d. (ca. 1893). 71⅞ x 36¼. The Brooklyn Museum, Gift of the Artist.

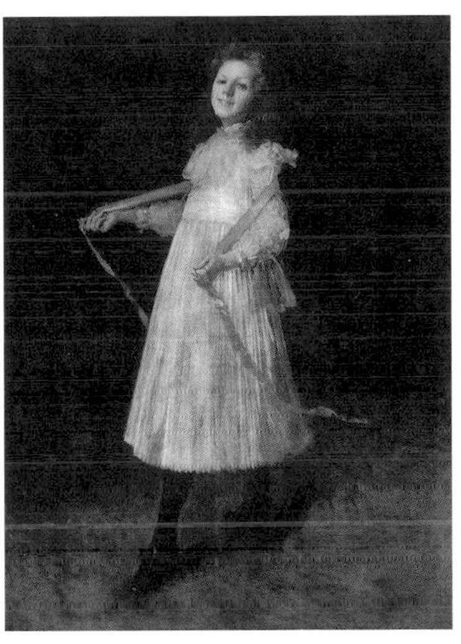

Alice (a portrait). **#769.** *Alice,* n.d. (ca. 1892). 67⅝ x 49⅜. The Art Institute of Chicago, Gift of Ernest A. Hamill.

† **CHURCH, F. S.** (Frederick Stuart). **New York.**
1842 Grand Rapids, MI–1924 New York, NY
Training — Chicago: Academy of Design; New York: NAD (Lemuel E. Wilmarth, Walter Shirlaw).

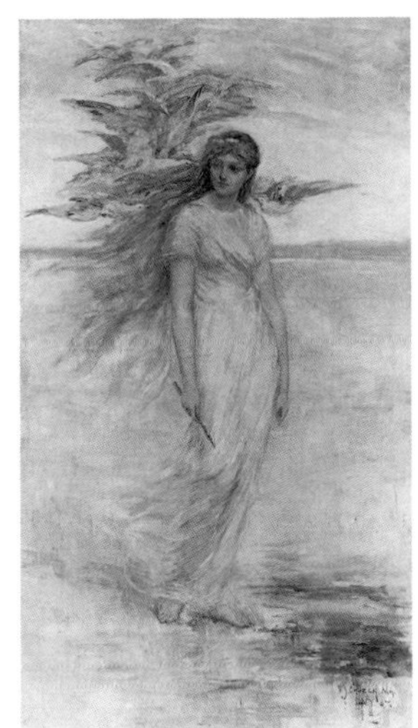

The Viking's Daughter. **#471. Lent by Mr. John Gellatly, New York.** 1887. 35½ x 19¼. National Museum of American Art, Smithsonian Institution, Gift of John Gellatly.

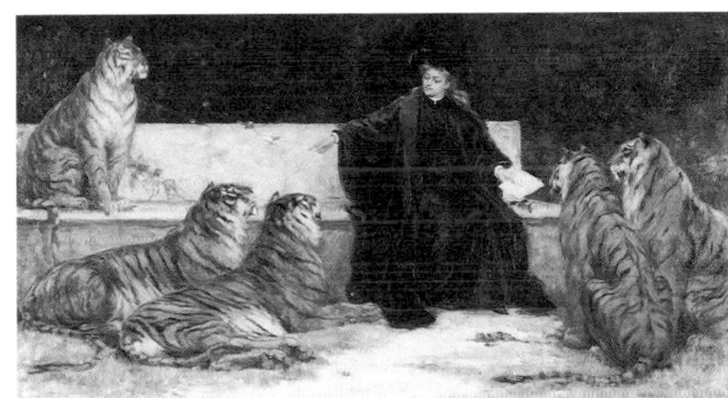

Knowledge is Power. **#740. Lent by Mr. C. L. Freer, Detroit.** 1889. 20⅛ x 36. Grand Rapids Public Library, Grand Rapids, MI.

CHURCHILL, W. W., Jr. (William Worcester). **Boston.**
1858 Jamaica Plain, MA–1926 Washington, DC
Training — Cambridge, MA: MIT; Paris: Léon Bonnat.

Portrait. **#1135.** Unlocated.[11]

CLARK, Rose (Harriette Candace). **Buffalo.**
1852 La Porte, IN–1942 Buffalo, NY
Training — New York: NAD.

Mother and Child. **#1252.** [$1500]. Est. 66 x 45. Collection of the artist, 1914. Unlocated.[12]

CLARK, **Walter** (Walter A.). **New York.**
1848 Brooklyn, NY–1917 Bronxville, NY
Training— J. S. Hartley, George Inness; New York: NAD, ASL.

Spring. **#359.** Sold, World's Columbian Exposition, Chicago, IL, 1893. Unlocated.

† CLARKE, **Thomas Shields. Pittsburg.**
1860 Pittsburgh, PA–1920 New York, NY
Training— Princeton; New York: ASL; Paris: P. A. J. Dagnan-Bouveret, Tony Robert-Fleury, William Bouguereau, Henri-Lucien Doucet, Denys Puech, Jean-Joseph Benjamin-Constant, H. M. A. Chapu, Acad. Julian (Jules Joseph Lefebvre), Jean-Léon Gérôme.

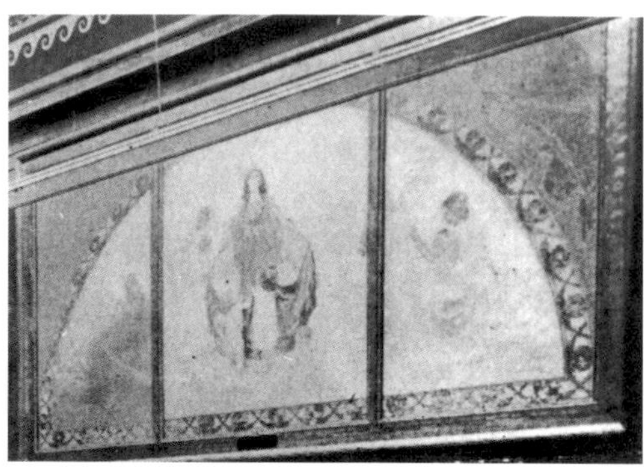

Morning, Noon and Night. **#475.** [$3500]. Est. 120 x 300. Unlocated. Illus: Rossiter Johnson, *A History of the World's Columbian Exposition,* vol. 2 (New York: Appleton, 1897), 400.

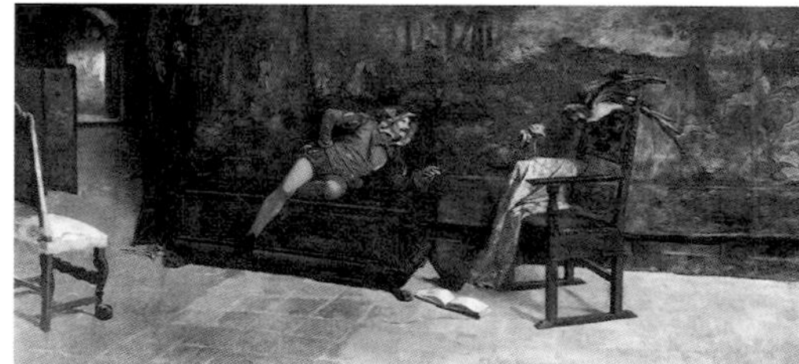

A Fool's Fool. **#732. Lent by the Pennsylvania Academy of the Fine Arts, Philadelphia.** 1887. 39½ x 83. Pennsylvania Academy of the Fine Arts, Philadelphia, Gift of Charles J. Clarke.

Portrait of Madame d'E. **#1079.** ca. 1890. Unlocated. "An interesting portrait of the back of an apparently handsome lady . . ." — *Yankee Doodle at the Fair* (Philadelphia: George Barrie & Son, 1896), 195.

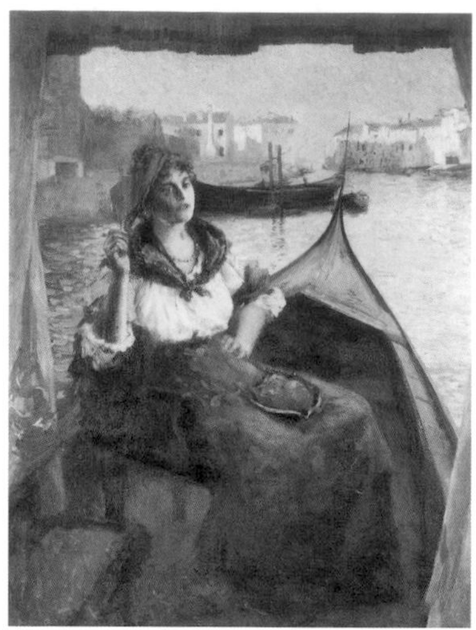

A Gondola Girl. **#1212.** [$750]. 1892. 34¾ x 26. Collection Mrs. George C. T. Remington, Wynnewood, PA and Palm Beach, FL. Photograph by Peter Hughes.

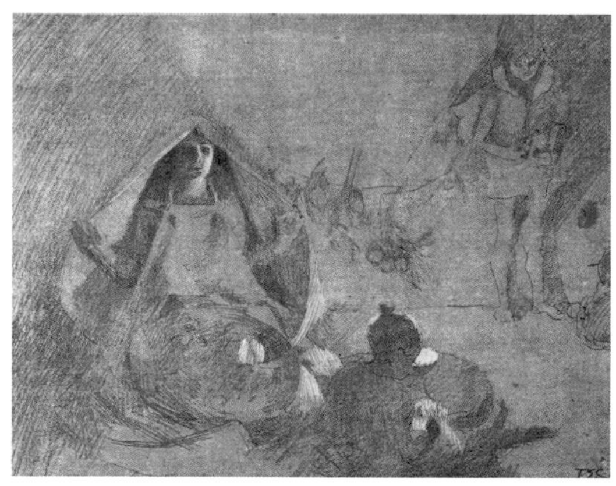

Night Market, Morocco. **#1248.** [$3000]. ca. 1892. Est. 60 x 70. Formerly Collection Philadelphia Art Club. Unlocated. Illus: Ludovic Baschet, ed., *Catalogue Illustré de Peinture et Sculpture, Salon de 1892* (Paris: Chamerot & Renouard, 1892), 198. "The scene, except for its Moorish figures, might have been in any city where peddlers hawk their goods amid the flare of smoking torches" — Hubert H. Bancroft, *The Book of the Fair,* vol. 3 (Chicago: Blakely Printing Co., 1893), 683.

CLAWSON, **John W.** (John Willard). **Paris, France.**
1858 Salt Lake City, UT–1936 Salt Lake City, UT
Training— Utah: George Ottinger; New York: NAD; Paris: Jean-Léon Gérôme, Acad. Julian (Jules Joseph Lefebvre).

Santa Maria della Salute, Venice. **#342.** [$300]. Est. 30 x 35. Unlocated. Probably destroyed in studio in San Francisco, CA, earthquake and fire, 1906.

CLEMENTS, Gabrielle D. (Gabrielle de Veaux). **Philadelphia.**
1858 Philadelphia, PA–1948 Rockport, MA
Training — Philadelphia: The Philadelphia School of Design for Women, PAFA (Thomas Eakins, Stephen Parrish); Paris: Acad. Julian (William Bouguereau, Tony Robert-Fleury); Italy.

Andarina. **#1140.** [$200]. Unlocated.

CLINEDINST, B. W. (Benjamin West). **New York.**
1859 Woodstock, VA–1931 Pawling, NY
Training — Paris: Alexandre Cabanel, Léon Bonnat.

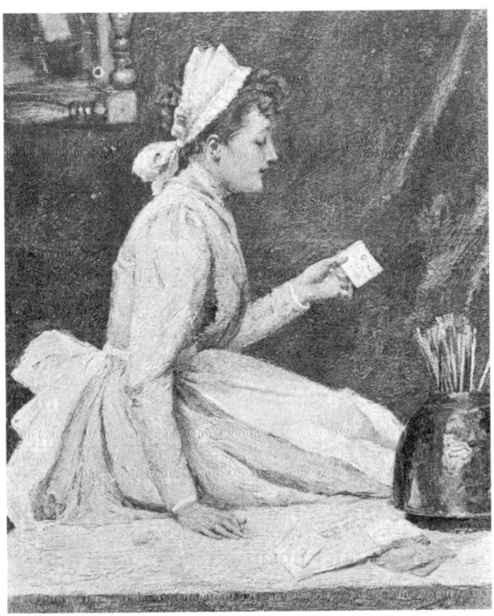

Monsieur's Mail. **#548.** [$275]. Unlocated. Illus: Ripley Hitchcock, *The Art of the World,* vol. 2 (New York: Appleton, 1895), 53.

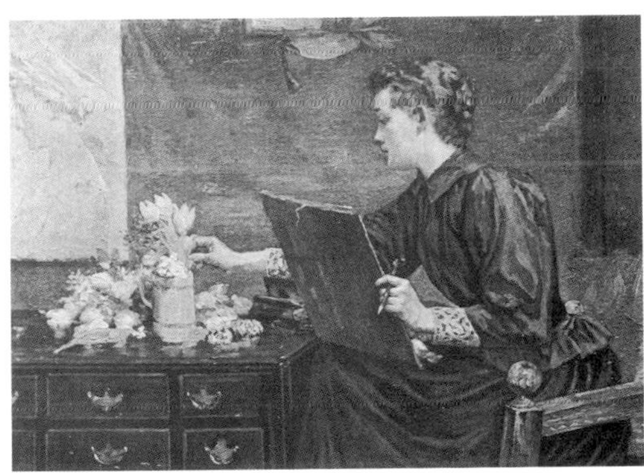

The Water Colorist. **#885.** [$300]. ca. 1891. Unlocated. Illus: Ripley Hitchcock, *The Art of the World,* vol. 2 (New York: Appleton, 1895), 179.

COBB, Arthur Murray. Giverny, France.
1861 Cleveland, OH–1951 Orange, NJ

First Snow. **#310.** [$50]. Est. 22 x 20. Unlocated.

COCHRANE, J. G. (Josephine Granger). **Boston.**
1864 Philadelphia, PA–1953 Preston, CT
Training — George Hitchcock; Paris: Acad. Julian.

Old Stone Stairway, Pont Aven, France. **#1046.** [$150]. Est. 16 x 10. Unlocated.

COFFIN, Elizabeth R. (Elizabeth Rebecca). **Brooklyn, N.Y.**
1850/51 Brooklyn, NY–1930 Nantucket, MA
Training — New York: ASL (William Merritt Chase); Brooklyn: Brooklyn Art Guild; Philadelphia: PAFA; The Hague: Royal Academy.

Hanging the Net. **#1088.** [$300]. ca. 1892. Unlocated. "Winner of the Norman W. Dodge Prize for the best picture by a woman . . . her picture being that of a fisherman's hut with fishermen 'Hanging the Nets.' Barrels full of nets are about, and while one sits and the other stands, the two men are at work on a length of seine. The figures are nicely painted and so is the shadowy interior"— *New York Times,* 1 May 1892; "A dark interior of a loft or country store, full of barrels, cordage and other picturesque truck, and with two figures engaged in getting fishing nets ready for use. One is seated, with a pipe in his mouth, and is hanging a net on a cord which is held taut by another, younger, man standing in the rear of the store. The light comes from behind the first-mentioned figure, and falls sideways on the second"— *Art Amateur* 27 (June 1892): 5.

COFFIN, Esther L. (Esther Lawton/Mrs. Caleb Coffin). **New York.**
1838–1921 New York, NY

Grapes. **#1149.** [$100]. ca. 1889. Unlocated.

COFFIN, William A. (William Anderson). **New York.**
1855 Allegheny, PA–1925 New York, NY

Training — New Haven, CT: Yale School of the Fine Arts; Paris: Léon Bonnat.

Evening. **#632.** [$1000]. **Lent by Mr. J. M. Lichtenauer, New York.** By 1888. 14 x 20. Sold, American Art Association, New York, NY, 27 Feb. 1913, lot 126, to Miss E. R. Wellington. Unlocated. "High at the left the crescent moon . . . is seen in a pale-blue sky above the rosy blush of sunset along the horizon. A landscape of trees and a stream in the foreground is almost in darkness, so deep is the shadow, but the shallow stream reflects the light and the rosy pink of the western sky" — American Art Association, *Collection of the Late J. M. Lichtenaur, Esq. of New York* (New York, 1913), lot 126.

Twilight. **#637. Lent by Mr. John B. Ladd, Brooklyn, N.Y.** Est. 14 x 20. Unlocated.

Early Morning. **#687. Lent by Mr. W. Seward Webb, New York.**[13] *Early Moonrise.* 30 x 40. Unlocated.

September Breeze. **#743. Lent by Mr. W. Seward Webb, New York.** ca. 1890. 41 x 30. Unlocated. "Beautiful in subject and in color, the bluish greens of the trees being well harmonized with the brighter color of the long grass and touch of yellow in the growing flowers" —*Chicago Times,* 9 June 1890.

Moonlight in Harvest. **#970.** [$750]. ca. 1886. 30 x 40. Sold, Fifth Avenue Art Galleries, New York, NY, 9 Dec. 1904, lot 119, to G. B. Daniel. Unlocated. "A clear, star-studded sky of blue. Here and there over the fields of rolling ground are great bundles of wheat that gleam faintly gold in the moonlight. The inequalities of ground under an uncertain light are well rendered and the impression of space and distance beyond the hills, admirable" — *Chicago Times,* 26 May 1888.

A Pennsylvania Farm After a Thunder Shower. **#1139.** [$1500]. ca. 1890. 40 x 55. Sold, Fifth Avenue Art Galleries, New York, NY, 9 Dec. 1904, lot 120, to Isaac Newton Seligman. Unlocated. "An immense subject, a veritable tour de force. If one considers that splendor of light on the fields and of darkness in the sky. The rushing clouds through gray depths of air is powerfully rendered, and the shining wetness of the green and yellow fields . . ." — *Chicago Tribune,* 15 June 1890.

COHEN, George W. New York.

1861 New York, NY–Residing 1927 New York, NY
Training — Paris: Acad. Julian (Jules Joseph Lefebvre), Gustave Boulanger, Jean-Joseph Benjamin-Constant, Henri-Lucien Doucet; Munich.

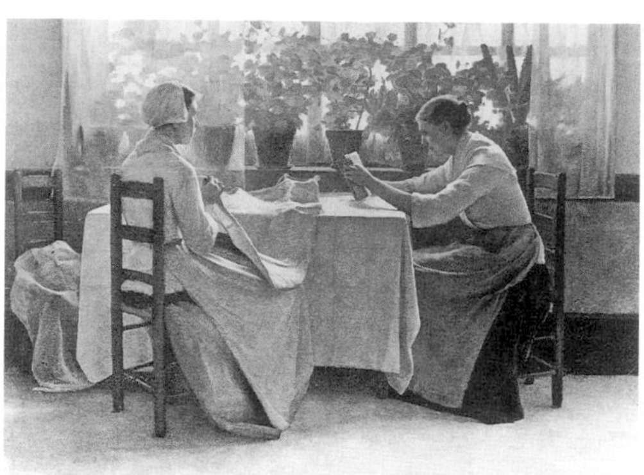

A Tale of the Sea. **#362.** [$500]. Unlocated. Illus (as *The Reading*): George W. Sheldon, *Recent Ideals of American Art* (New York: Appleton, 1890).

COLLINS, Alfred Q. (Alfred Quinton). New York.

1855 Portland, ME[14] –1903 Cambridge, MA
Training — Paris: Acad. Julian (Jules Joseph Lefebvre), Henri-Lucien Doucet, Tony Robert-Fleury, Jean-Joseph Benjamin-Constant, William Bouguereau, Léon Bonnat.

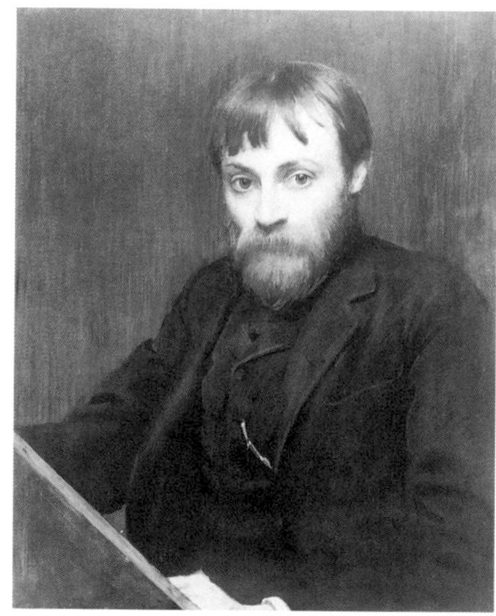

Portrait of Joe Evans. **#377. Lent by Mr. Joseph Evans, New York.** n.d. (ca. 1891–92). 26¼ x 21. Art Students League of New York, Gift of Mr. Burling. Photograph courtesy Peter A. Juley & Son Collection, National Museum of American Art, Smithsonian Institution.

COLMAN, Samuel. Newport.
1832 Portland, ME–1920 New York, NY
Training — New York: Asher B. Durand; Paris; Spain.

The Inner Gorge of the Grand Cañon of the Colorado. **#380.** [$1000]. Unlocated.[15]

Mt. Tacoma from Puget Sound. **#551.** [$1200]. Unlocated. "The scale of color rising from the deep blue of the water to the rosy tints of the sky is managed with skill of a virtuoso" — Samuel P. Avery Papers, Archives of American Art, roll NMM26, frame 342.

Mexican Hacienda. **#560.** [$1200]. Unlocated.

COMAN, Mrs. Charlotte B. (Charlotte Buell/ Mrs. J. B.Coman). **Waterville, N.Y.**
1833 Waterville, NY–1924 Yonkers, NY
Training — James Renwick Brevoort; Paris: Harry Thompson, Emile Vernier; the Netherlands.

A Stony Brook. **#722.** [$300]. Unlocated.

The Road to Town, Florida. **#919.** [$250]. ca. 1892. Unlocated.

CONANT, Lucy S. (Lucy Scarborough). **Boston.**
1867 Brooklyn, CT–1920 Boston, MA
Training — Boston; Paris: Hector Le Roux, Julien Dupré.

The Orchid Meadow. **#1177.** [$75]. Unlocated.

CONNAH, Douglas John. New York.
1871 New York, NY–1941 New York, NY
Training — Weimar, Germany: Weimar Academy; Dusseldorf: Royal Academy; Paris: Acad. Julian (Jean-Joseph Benjamin-Constant, J. P. Laurens), Léon Bonnat, Jules Joseph Lefebvre, Henri-Lucien Doucet.

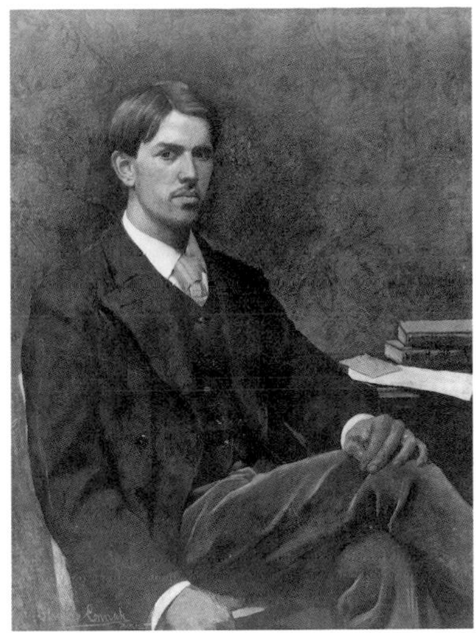

Douglas John Connah. **#682. Lent by Mrs. John Connah.**
Self-portrait, Douglas John Connah, 1890. 40½ x 31. Private Collection. Photograph by David H. Ramsey.

COOPER, Colin C. (Colin Campbell). **Philadelphia.**
1856 Philadelphia, PA–1937 Santa Barbara, CA
Training — Philadelphia: PAFA (Thomas Eakins); Paris: Acad. Julian (William Bouguereau), Auguste-Joseph Delecluse, Henri-Lucien Doucet.

Portrait (St. Clair A. Mulholland). **#1239. Lent by Gen. St. Clair A. Mulholland, Philadelphia.** Est. 55 x 30. Unlocated.

Portrait of a Lady. **#1290.** Unlocated.

CORNER, Thomas C. (Thomas Cromwell). **Baltimore.**
1865 Baltimore, MD–1938 Baltimore, MD
Training — Baltimore: Maryland Institute of Art; New York: ASL (Kenyon Cox, J. Alden Weir); Paris: Acad. Julian (Jean-Joseph Benjamin-Constant, Jules Joseph Lefebvre), François Flameng, G. J. M. A. Ferrier.

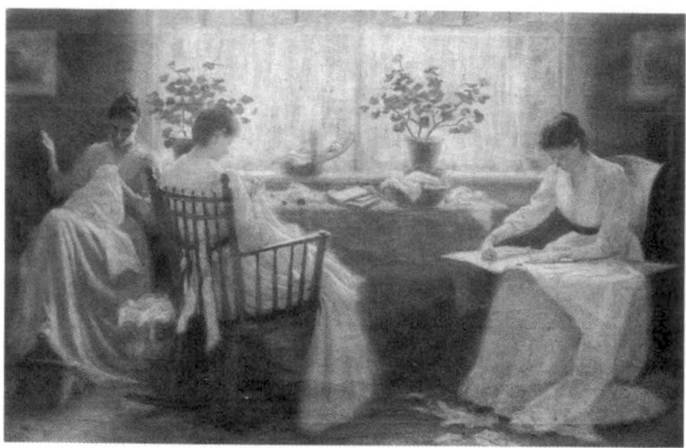

Industry. **#1060.** [$500]. n.d. 24 x 36. Collection Tom Corner, Columbia, MD. Photograph by George Gurney.

Mother and Child. **#1278.** [$500]. Est. 40 x 35. Unlocated.

CORWIN, Charles A. (Charles Abel). **Chicago.**
1857 Newburgh, NY–1938 Chicago, IL
Training — Munich: Royal Academy, Frank Duveneck.

Edge of the Clearing. **#672.** [$200]. Unlocated.

COUSE, Eanger I. (Eanger Irving). **Paris, France.**
1866 Saginaw, MI–1936 Albuquerque, NM
Training — Chicago: AIC; New York: NAD (Lemuel E. Wilmarth, Edgar M. Ward); Paris: Acad. Julian (William Bouguereau, Tony Robert-Fleury), EcBA (Pierre Victor Galland).

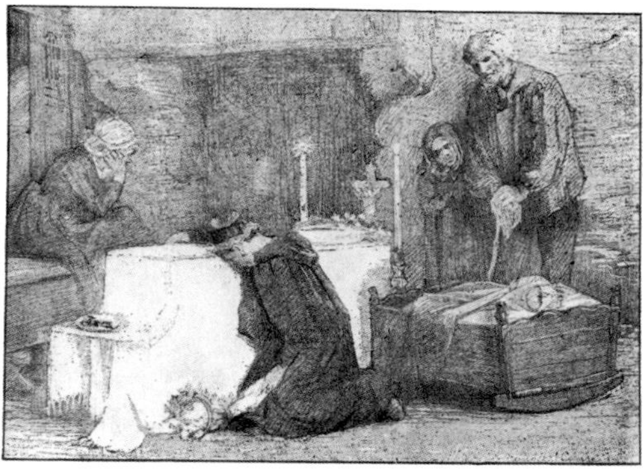

My First Born. **[$1000]. #614.** ca. 1890. Unlocated. Illus: Ludovic Baschet, ed., *Salon de 1890, Catalogue Illustré, Peinture & Sculpture* (Paris: Georges Chamerot, 1890), 255.

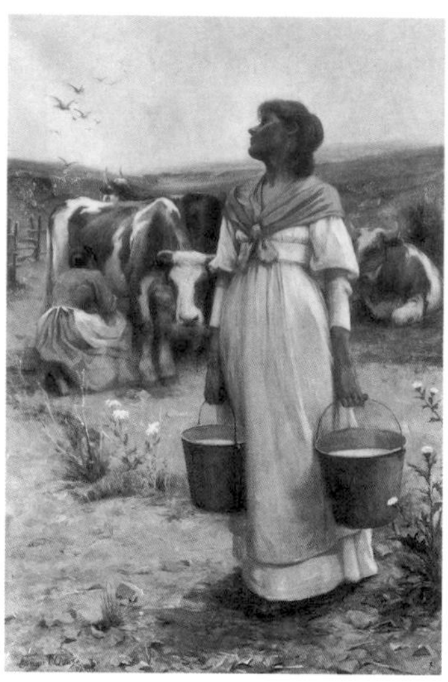

Milking Time*. **#1018. [$500]. n.d. (1892). 47 x 32. Couse Family Collection.

---

† **COX, Kenyon. New York.**
1856 Warren, OH–1919 New York, NY
Training — Cincinnati: Ohio Mechanics' Institute School of Design (Frank Duveneck); Philadephia: PAFA; Paris: Carolus-Duran, Jean-Léon Gérôme. Alexandre Cabanel, Acad. Julian (Jules Joseph Lefebvre, Henri-Lucien Doucet), EcBA.

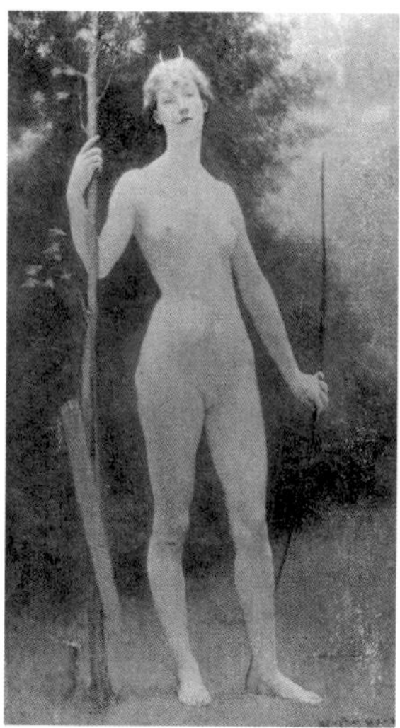

Diana. **#393.** [$750]. 1892. 30 x 18. Sold, Anderson Auction Company, New York, NY, 29 Feb.–1 March 1912, lot 116, to W. D. Fraul. Unlocated. Illus: William Walton, *Art and Architecture*, vol. 1 (Philadelphia: G. Barrie, 1893–95), 21.

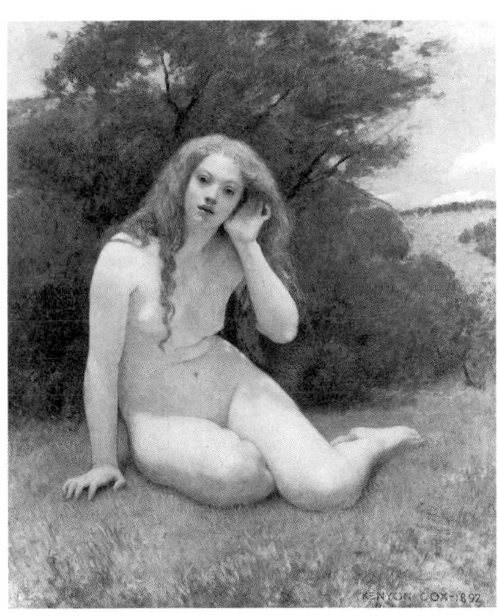

Echo. **#466.** [$750]. 1892. 35½ x 29¾. National Museum of American Art, Smithsonian Institution, Gift of Mrs. Ambrose Lansing.

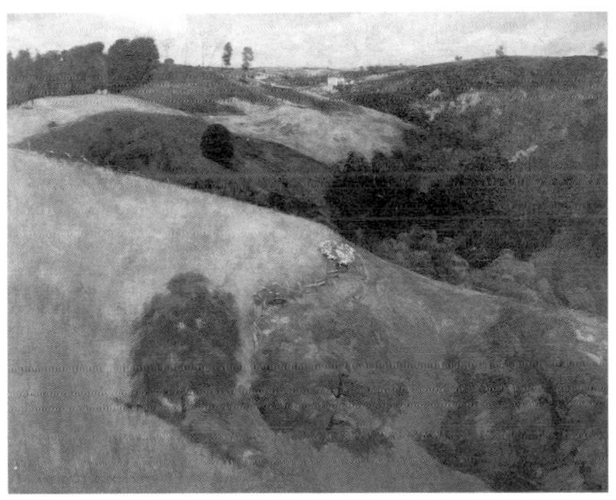

******Flying Shadows.* **#514. Lent by Mr. Stanford White, New York.** 1883. 30 x 36¼. The Corcoran Gallery of Art, Museum Purchase, Gallery Fund, 1922.

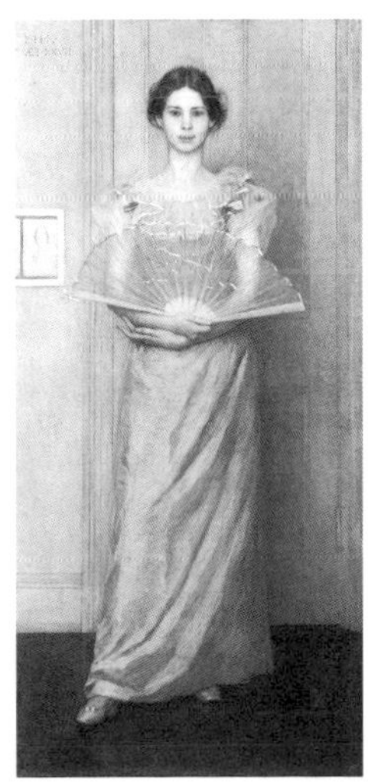

Portrait of L. H. K. **#564. Lent by Mrs. Kenyon Cox.** *Louise Howland King (Mrs. Kenyon Cox),* 1892. 38⅝ x 18. National Museum of American Art, Smithsonian Institution, Bequest of Allyn Cox.

Music. **#706. Lent by Mr. F. N. Finney, Milwaukee.** Est. 18 x 18. Unlocated.

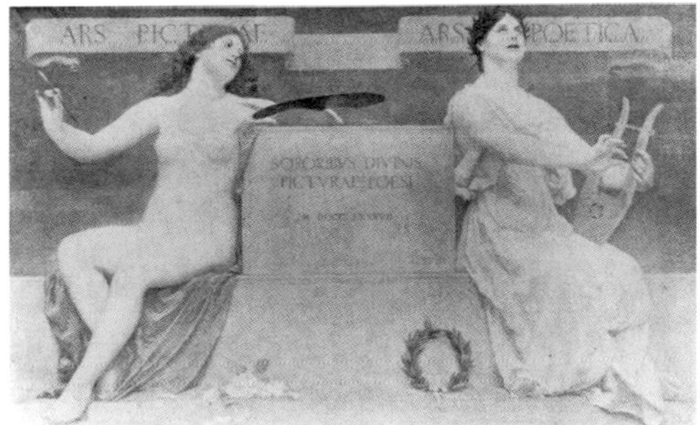

Painting and Poetry. **#810.** [$2000]. Est. 55 x 80. Unlocated. Illus: Charles M. Kurtz, ed., *Illustrations from the Art Gallery of the World's Columbian Exposition* (Philadelphia: G. Barrie, 1893), 289.

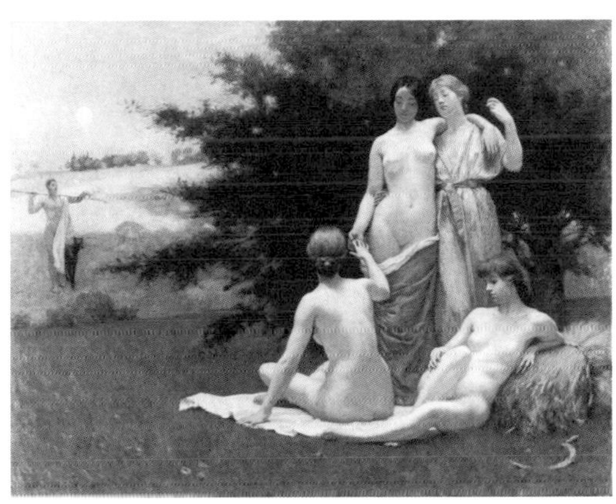

An Eclogue.* **#811. [$1500]. 1890. 48 x 60½. National Museum of American Art, Smithsonian Institution, Gift of Allyn Cox.

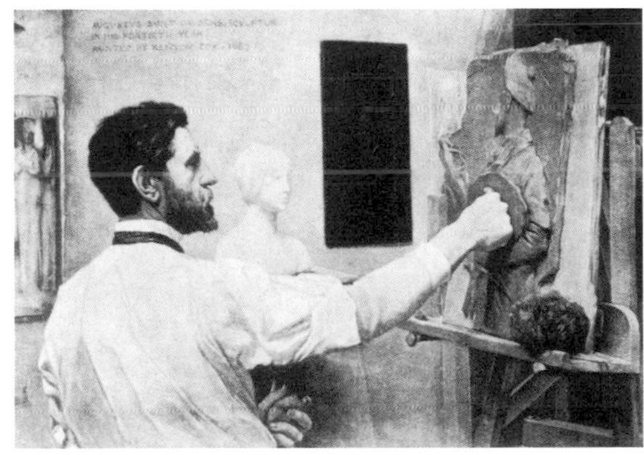

Portrait of St. Gaudens. **#829. Lent by Mr. Augustus St. Gaudens, New York.** 1887. Destroyed in fire, 1904.[16] Illus: Homer Saint-Gaudens, ed., *The Reminiscences of Augustus Saint-Gaudens* (New York: The Century Co., 1908), frontispiece.

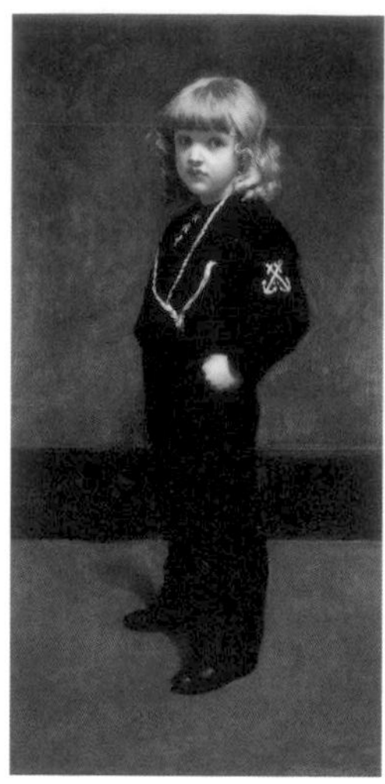

******Portrait of Roger D.* **#848. Lent by Mr. Charles Deering, Evanston, Ill.** *Portrait of Roger Deering,* 1889. 54⅛ x 27⅜. Special Collections Department, Northwestern University Library, Evanston, IL. Photograph by Michael Tropea.

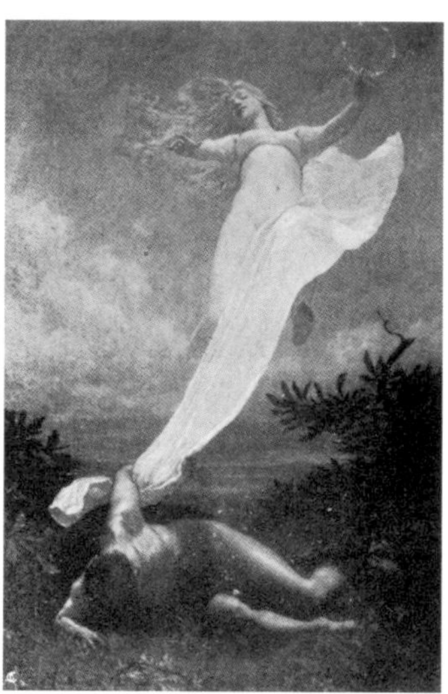

The Pursuit of the Ideal. **#856.** [$1500]. ca. 1891. Destroyed. Illus: H. Hobart Nichols, ed., *Official Illustrated Catalogue. Fine Arts Exhibit, United States of America, Paris Exposition of 1900* (Boston: Noyes, Platt, & Company, 1900).

A Vision of Moonrise. **#866. Lent by Mr. Charles Deering, Chicago.** ca. 1891. Unlocated. "Fearful and wonderful . . . in which the nude, winged figure in the air may be supposed the personification of the moon. It is a female person; its wings are magenta and look like porcelain. On the ground lies a man of large muscularity more or less draped in a red mantle, who peers at his nude visitor from under his arm. The floating figure's hair is yellowish-red and 'swears' horribly with the color of its wings. There is no harmony in heaven if such discord between the hair and wings of angelic beings are allowed" — "Monthly Record of American Art," *The Magazine of Art* 14 (Dec. 1890–Nov. 1891): xxi.

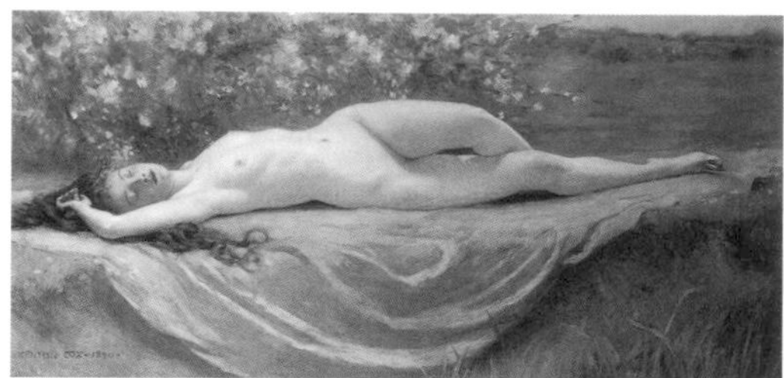

May. **#1041.** [$500]. 1890. 15 x 30. Private Collection. Photograph by Wayne Geist.

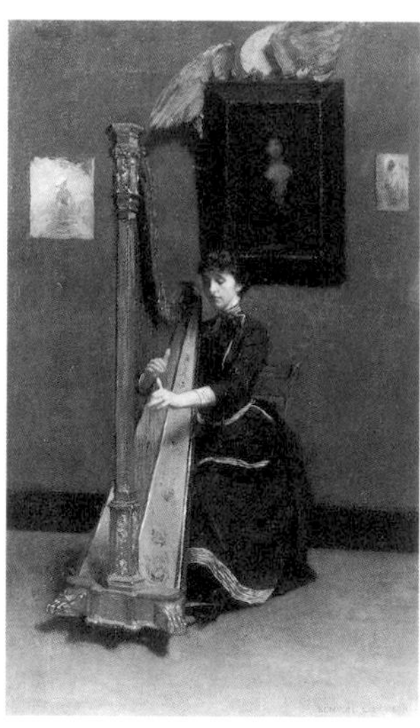

A Solo. **#1159.** [$500]. *The Harp Player (A Solo),* 1888. 30 x 17⅞. The Metropolitan Museum of Art, Rogers Fund, 1912.

COX, Mrs. Kenyon (Louise H. King) (Louise Howland King). **New York.**
1865 San Francisco, CA–1945 Windham, CT
Training — Kenyon Cox; New York: ASL, NAD.

The Lotos Eaters. **#901.** [$750]. ca. 1887. Est. 30 x 55. Unlocated.

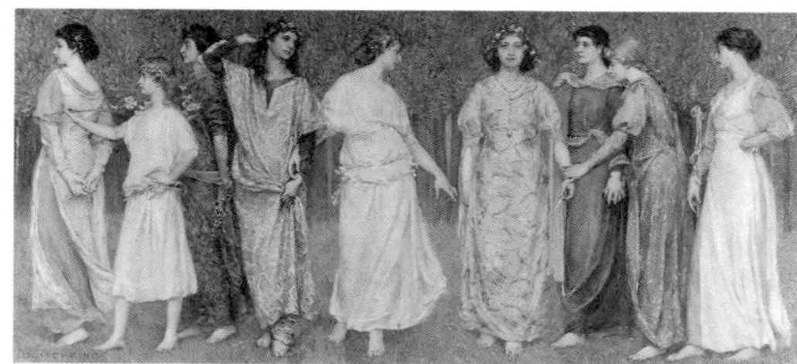

A Rondel. **#1025.** [$300]. *Primavera,* 1892. 18 x 38⅝. Collection High Museum of Art, Atlanta, Purchase with funds from The Phoenix Society.

CRAIG, Thomas B. (Thomas Bigelow). **New York.**
1849 Philadelphia, PA–1924 Woodland, NY
Training — self-taught.

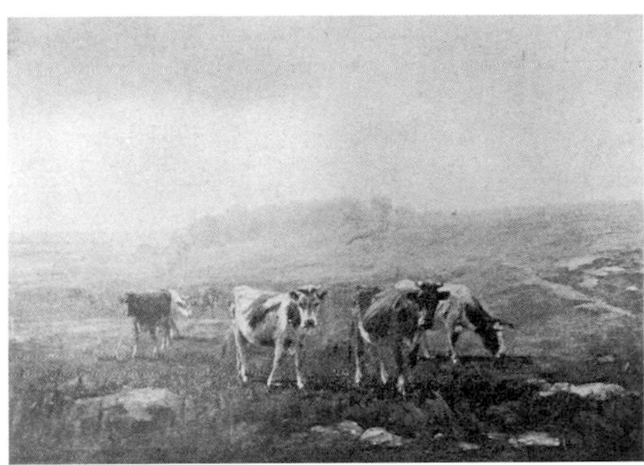

An Upland Pasture (Morning). **#1058.** [$600]. ca. 1892. Unlocated. Illus: The Art Club of Philadelphia, *5th Annual Exhibition Oil Paintings and Sculpture* (Philadelphia, 1893), 85.

CRANCH, Mrs. Caroline A. (Miss Caroline Amelia). **Boston.**
1853 Fishkill Landing, NY–1931 Auburndale, MA
Training — Boston: Christopher Pearse Cranch, Helen Knowlton, William Morris Hunt; New York: Cooper Union, ASL (William Merritt Chase); Paris: Carolus-Duran, Jean-Jacques Henner.

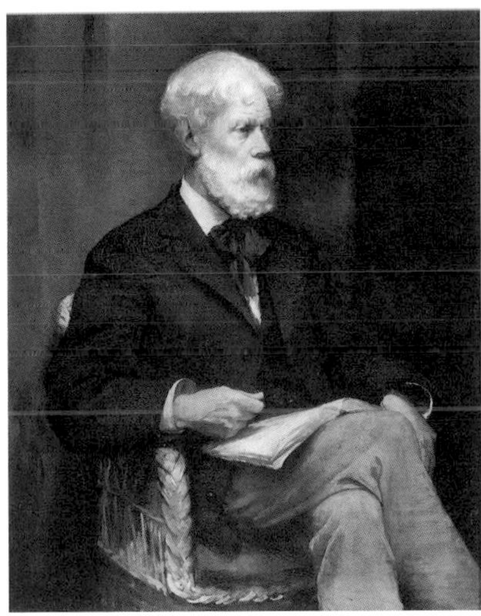

Portrait of Mr. Christopher Cranch. **#485.** ca. 1883. 39 x 31. Collection Mrs. Samuel L. Biddle, Bellevue, WA. Photograph by Richard Nichol.

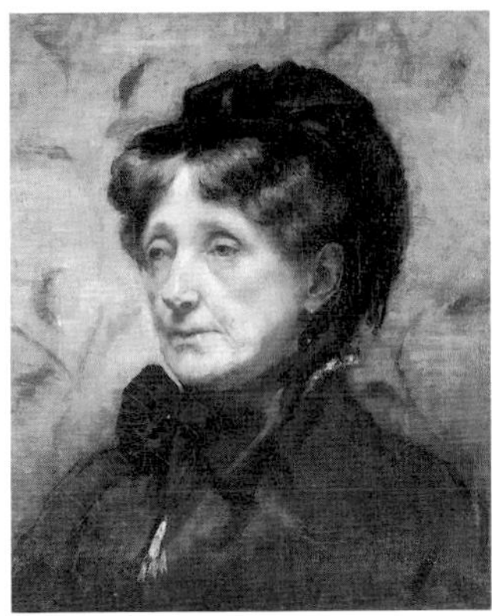

Portrait of Mrs. E. D. Cranch. **#550. Lent by Mrs. Caroline A. Cranch.** *Portrait of Her Mother, Elizabeth De Windt Cranch (Mrs. Christopher Pearse Cranch),* n.d. 17½ x 14½. Private Collection. Photograph by Fay Foto.

CRANE, Bruce (Robert Bruce). **New York.**
1857 New York, NY–1937 Bronxville, NY
Training — Alexander Wyant; New York: ASL; Grez, France: J. C. Cazin.

The Harvest Field. **#571. Lent by Mr. Andrew Carnegie.** Unlocated.

CUNNINGHAM, J. Wilton (John Wilton).[17] **Paris, France.**
St. Louis, MO–1903 Camp Reliance, TX
Training — St. Louis: School of Fine Arts; Paris: Acad. Julian (Jules Joseph Lefebvre), Jean-Jacques Benjamin-Constant, Henri-Lucien Doucet, Tony Robert-Fleury.

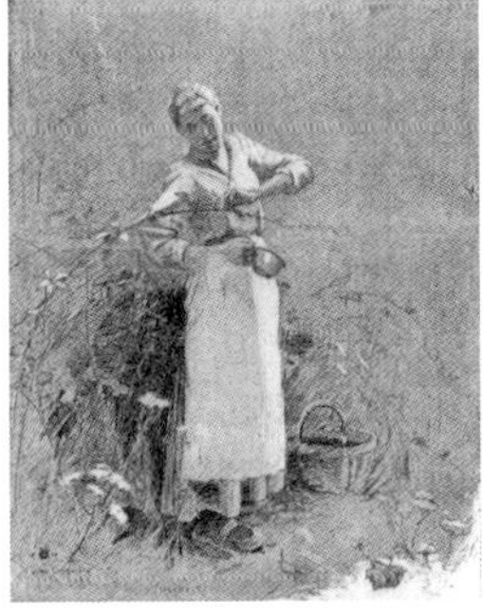

Caught in the Briers. **#697.** [$1000]. ca. 1892. Unlocated. Illus: Ludovic Baschet, ed., *Catalogue Illustré de Peinture et Sculpture, Salon de 1892* (Paris: Chamerot & Renouard, 1892), 143.

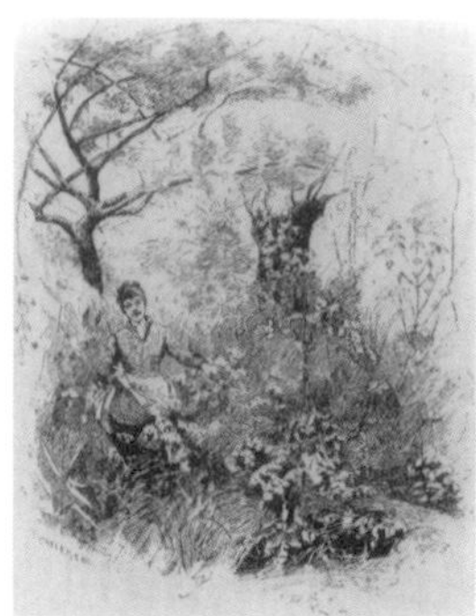

For My Rabbits. **#831.** [$600]. ca. 1890. Unlocated. Illus: Ludovic Baschet, ed., *Salon de 1890, Catalogue Illustré, Peinture & Sculpture* (Paris: Georges Chamerot, 1890), 173.

---

† **CURRAN, Charles C.** (Charles Courtney). **New York.**
1861 Frankfort, KY–1942 New York, NY
Training — Cincinnati: McMicken School of Design; New York: NAD, ASL; Paris: Acad. Julian (Jules Joseph Lefebvre, Henri-Lucien Doucet, Jean-Jacques Benjamin-Constant).

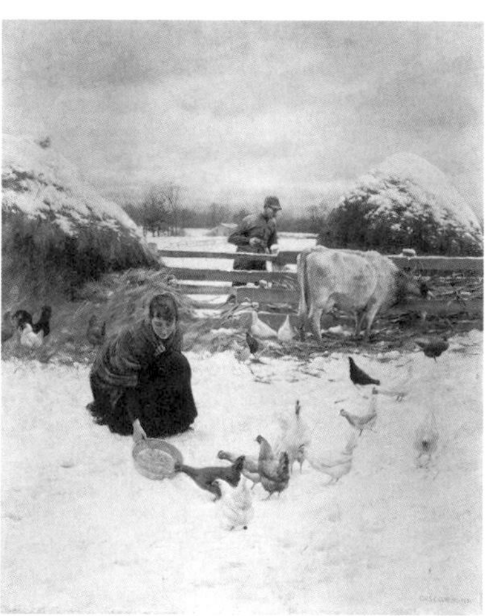

Winter Morning in a Barnyard. **#357. Lent by Mr. George I. Tyson, New York.** 1891. 22 x 18. Collection Spanierman Gallery, 1983. Unlocated. Illus: Daniel H. Burnham, *The Art of the World,* vol. 4 (New York: Appleton, 1893–95).

A Corner in a Barnyard. **#649. Lent by Mr. Thomas B. Clarke, New York.** 9 x 12. Sold, American Art Association, New York, NY, 14–18 Feb. 1899, lot 255, to John G. Beirning. Unlocated. "Leaning over the rails of a barnyard, a man is looking at a horse, which is under a straw-thatched shelter roof. In the yard are some chickens and a calf. A typical American country scene" —American Art Association, *Catalogue of the Private Art Collection of Thomas B. Clarke, New York* (New York: American Art Association, 1899), lot 255.

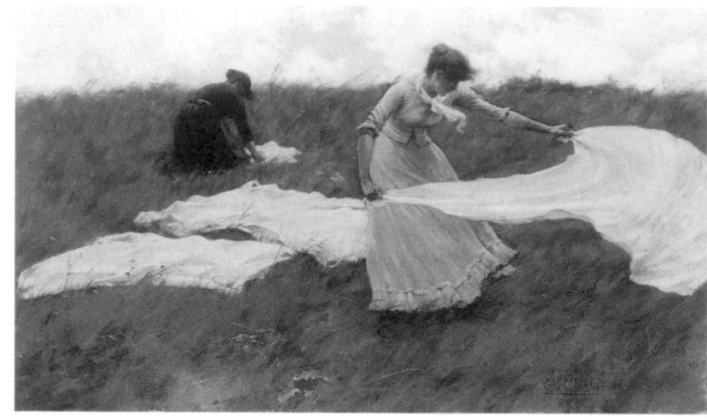

A Breezy Day. **#656. Lent by Mr. Thomas B. Clarke, New York.** 1887. $11^{15}/_{16}$ x 20. Pennsylvania Academy of the Fine Arts, Philadelphia, Henry D. Gilpin Fund.

A Cabbage Garden. **#930. Lent by Mrs. J. A. Hewlett, Brooklyn, N.Y.** ca. 1887. Unlocated.

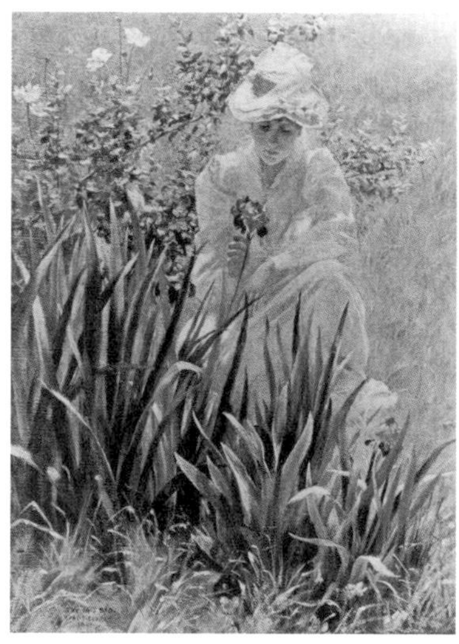

The Iris Bed. **#951. Lent by Mr. William S. Hollingsworth, New York.** 1891. Unlocated. Illus: Daniel H. Burnham, *The Art of the World,* vol. 1 (New York: Appleton, 1893–95).

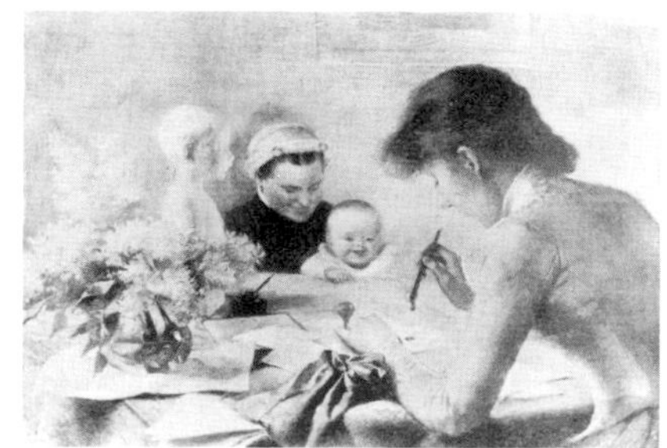

Sealing the Letter. **#961. Lent by Mr. Henderson, Minneapolis.** ca. 1890. Unlocated. Illus: Charles M. Kurtz, ed., *Illustrations from the Art Gallery of the World's Columbian Expostition* (Philadelphia: G. Barrie, 1893), 129.

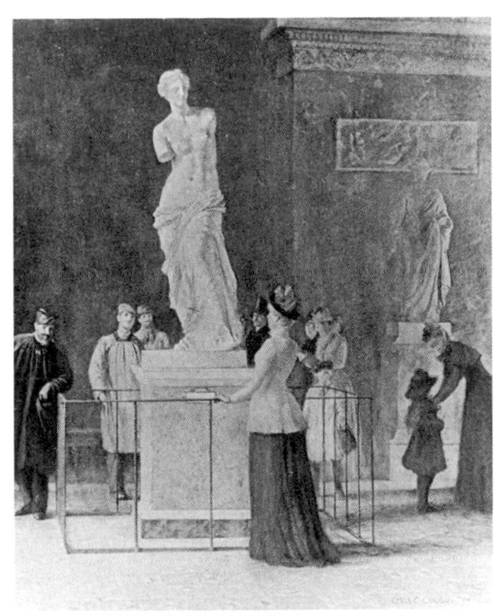

Hall of the Venus de Milo, in the Louvre, Paris. **#974.** [$450]. **Lent by Mr. H. T. Shriver, New York.** 1889. Unlocated. Illus: Daniel H. Burnham, *The Art of the World,* vol. 6 (New York: Appleton, 1893–95).

A Winter Fog. **#1022.** [$500]. ca. 1892. Unlocated.

Early Morning in June. **#1128. Lent by Mr. Samuel T. Shaw, New York.** 1891. 18 x 22. Collection T. R. Baird Gallery, 1977. Unlocated. " The cold air is swept in the distance by gray mist which is slowly clearing away from the meadowland. In the foreground scattered brown and black cows are browsing in the long grass; a ditch with young willows, and a fence rail bounds the field at the right" —American Art Association, *The Samuel T. Shaw Collection of American Paintings* (New York, 1928), lot 148.

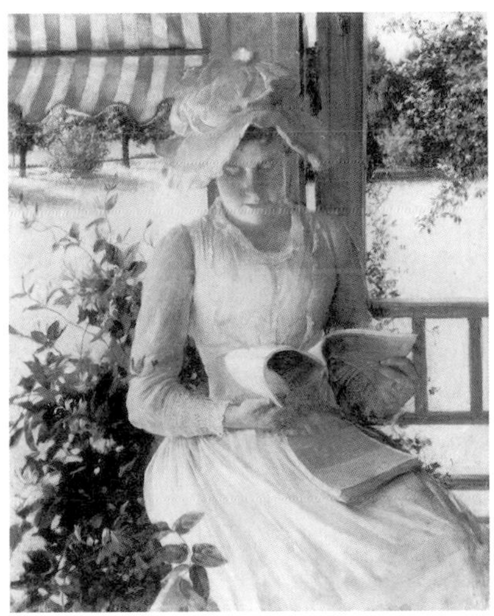

Under the Awning. **#1146. Lent by Mrs. K. R. Papin, Chicago.** 1891. 22 x 18. Collection Mr. and Mrs. John Hoerner. Photograph courtesy Edward and Deborah Pollack.

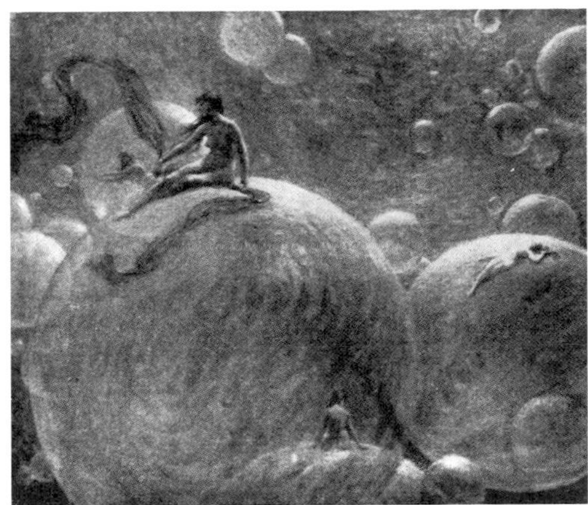

A Dream. **#1191.** [$800]. 1892. 18 x 22. Sold, American Art Association, New York, NY, 31 Jan.– 2 Feb. 1900, lot 76, to Baroness d'Alexandre d'Oreangiani. Unlocated. Illus: *Harper's Weekly,* 17 Dec. 1892, 1212.

DANNAT, **Wm. T.** (William Turner). **Paris, France.**
1853 New York, NY–1929 Monte Carlo, Monaco
Training — Munich: Royal Academy; Florence; Paris: Carolus-Duran, Mihaly Munkacsy.

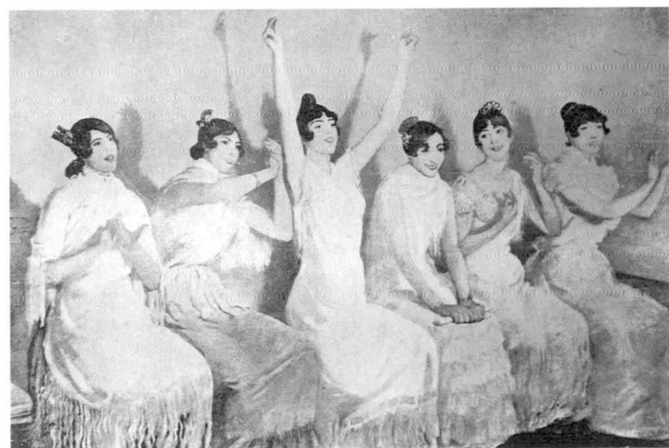

Spanish Women. **#300.** [$8000]. ca. 1892. Est. 70 x 90. The Philadelphia Museum, 1915.[18] Unlocated. Illus: William Walton, *Art and Architecture,* vol. 1 (Philadelphia: G. Barrie, 1893–95), 23.

---

† DAVIS, **Charles H.** (Charles Harold). **Mystic, Conn.**
1856 Amesbury, MA–1933 Mystic, CT
Training — Boston: MFA (Otto Grundmann); Paris: Acad. Julian (Gustave Boulanger, Jules Joseph Lefebvre).

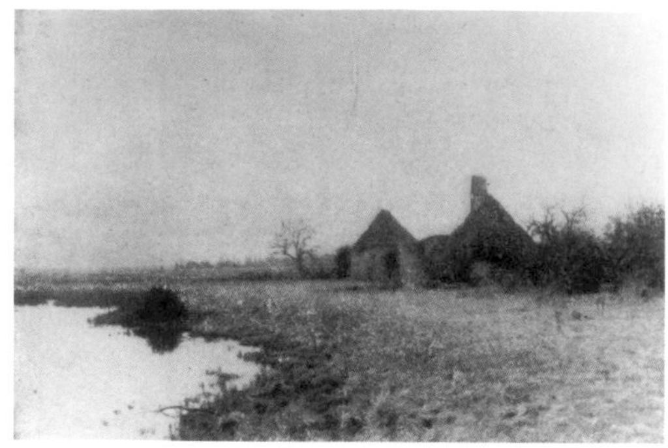

Abandoned. **#367.** [$2500]. n.d. 62½ x 94. Omaha Public Library, Omaha, NE. Illus: William H. Downes, "New England Art at the World's Fair," *New England Magazine* 8 (July 1893): 360.

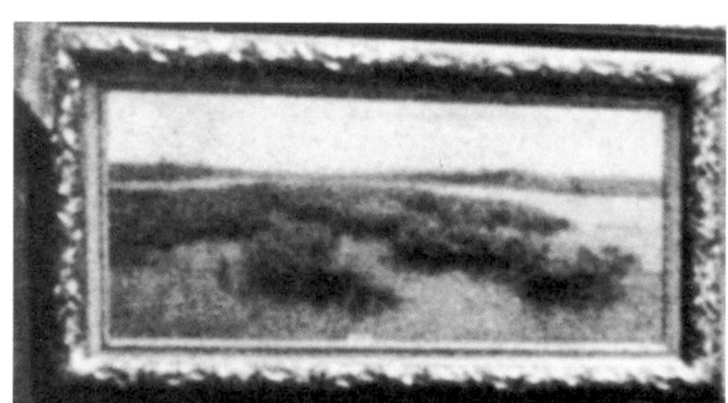

A Winter Evening. **#403. Lent by Mr. Thomas E. Waggaman, Washington, D.C.** 1888. 38 x 76. Sold, American Art Association, New York, NY, 27 Jan. 1905, lot 70, to H. Allaway. Unlocated. Illus: Official Photographs of the World's Columbian Exposition by C. D. Arnold, vol. 8, pl. 91. Courtesy of The Chicago Public Library, Special Collections Department.

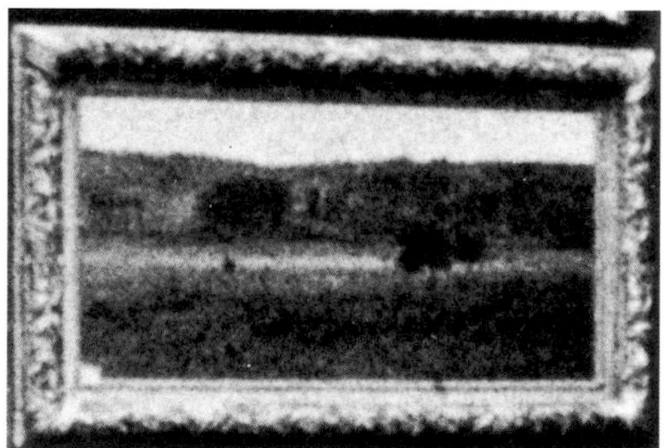

The Valley. **#413.** [$2000]. Est. 38 x 76. Unlocated. Illus: Official Photographs of the World's Columbian Exposition by C. D. Arnold, vol. 8, pl. 91. Courtesy of The Chicago Public Library, Special Collections Department.

April. **#721.** [$2000]. ca. 1888. Unlocated.

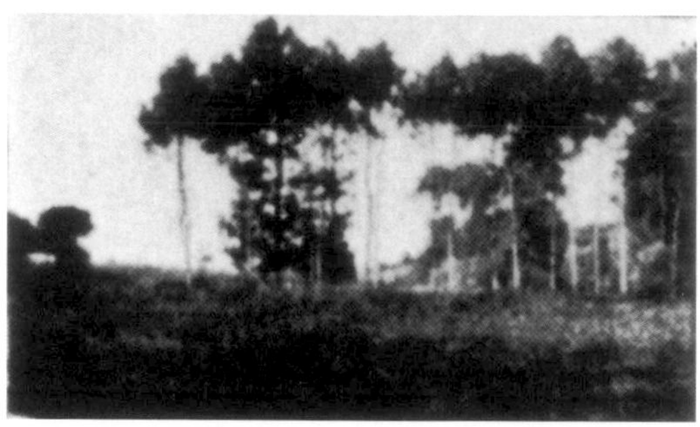

Summer Morning. **#780.** [$2000]. ca. 1890. Est. 55 x 80. Unlocated. "A delightful rendering of morning sunshine on green meadows and tall trees . . ." —*The Nation,* 17 Aug. 1893, 115. Illus: J. W. Buel, *The Magic City* (St. Louis: Historical Publishing Company, 1894).

On the New England Coast. **#941.** [$1500]. Unlocated.

DAY, Francis (James Francis). **New York.**
1863 LeRoy, NY–1942 Lanesboro, MA
Training — New York: ASL; Paris: A. A. E. Hébert, Luc Olivier Merson.

A Table d'Hote. **#372.**[19] Unlocated.

DEAN, Walter L. (Walter Lofthouse). **Boston.**
1854 Lowell, MA–1912 East Gloucester, MA
Training — Boston: Walter Smith; Paris: Acad. Julian (Gustave Boulanger, Jules Joseph Lefebvre), Achille François Oudinot.

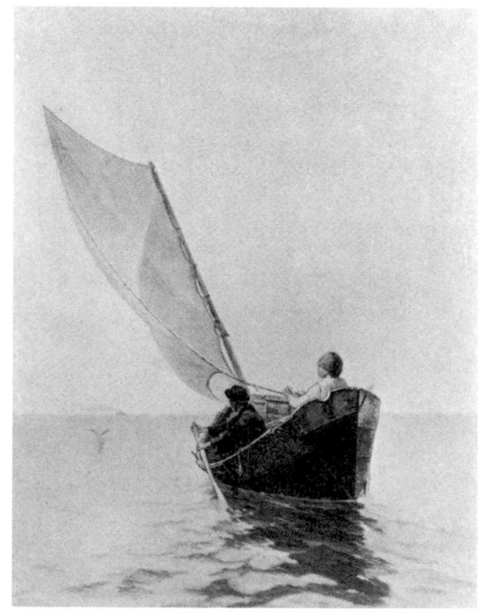

The Open Sea. **#322.** [$1000]. ca. 1890. Unlocated. Illus: Charles M. Kurtz, ed., *Illustrations from the Art Gallery of the World's Columbian Exposition* (Philadelphia: G. Barrie, 1893), 207.

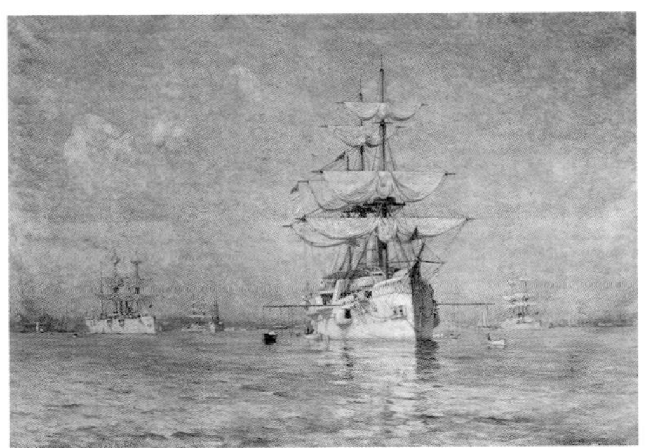

Peace (Represented by the White Squadron of United States Navy at anchor in Boston harbor). **#339.** [$7000]. 1893. 75 x 108. Architect of the Capitol, U.S. House of Representatives Collection.

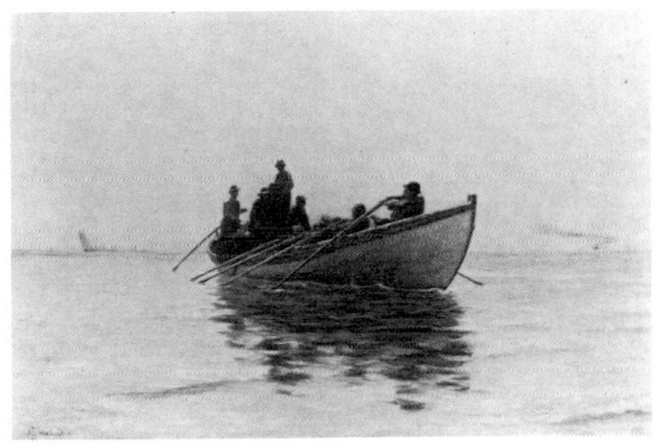

The Seiners' Return. **#347.** [$1200]. ca. 1892. Est. 50 x 70. Unlocated. Illus: Charles M. Kurtz, ed., *Illustrations from the Art Gallery of the World's Columbian Exposition* (Philadelphia: G. Barrie, 1893), 184.

DEARTH, Henry J. (Henry Golden). **East Hampton, L.I.**
1864 Bristol, RI–1918 New York, NY
Training — Waterbury, CT: Horace Johnson; Paris: A. A. E. Hébert, Aimé Morot.

Autumn. **#766. Lent by Mr. George G. Tillotson.** Est. 25 x 35. Unlocated.

A Long Island Garden. **#1153.** Est. 25 x 36. Unlocated.

DE CAMP, Joseph (Joseph Rodifer). **Boston.**
1858 Cincinnati, OH–1923 Boca Grande, FL
Training — Cincinnati: McMicken School of Design, Ohio Mechanics' Institute School of Design (Frank Duveneck); Munich: Royal Academy; Florence; Venice.

Carnation and Black. **#1236.** [$500]. Est. 39 x 28. Unlocated. "A profile head of a lady arrayed in black and scarlet of the most positive description" — *Boston Evening Transcript,* 8 Oct. 1892.

DE CRANO, F. F. (Felix F.). **Philadelphia.**
ca. 1845 France–1908 Wallingsford, PA
Training — Philadelphia: PAFA (Christian Schussele); Paris; London; Rome.

Mentone, France. **#920.** [$150]. ca. 1889. Unlocated.

DE FOREST, Lockwood. New York.
1850 New York, NY–1932 Santa Barbara, CA
Training — New York: Frederic Church, James Hart; Rome: Hermann Corrodi.

Moonrise Among the Ruins of Palmyra. **#646.** [$800]. ca. 1891. Est. 45 x 50. Unlocated. "With the stark columns of a temple stretching into the east and a wolf prowling in the foreground, and his ruins at Philese half buried in the sand . . . "—*Brooklyn Daily Eagle,* 13 March 1892.

DE HAAS, M. F. H. (Mauritz Frederick Hendrick). **New York.**
1832 Rotterdam, the Netherlands–1895 New York, NY
Training — Louis Meyer; Rotterdam: Academy of Fine Arts; The Hague: Royal Academy.

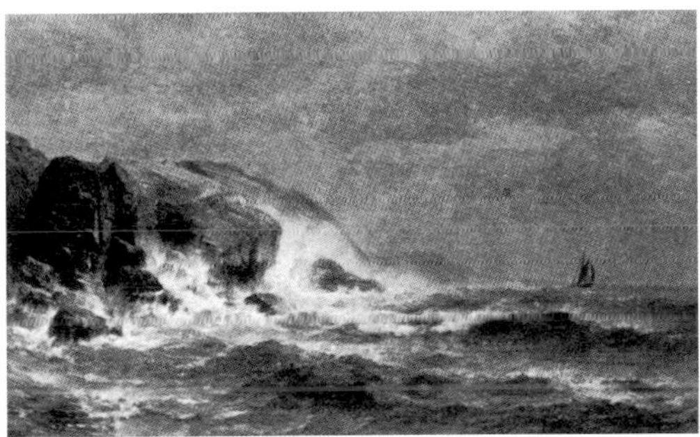

New England Coast. **#533.** [$2000]. n.d. 38⅛ x 60¼. Sold (as *Ship Off a Stormy Coast),* Christie's, New York, NY, 3 Dec. 1982, lot 47. Unlocated. Illus: National Academy of Design, *Illustrated Catalogue with Short Letters on Art Topics, Sixty-ninth Annual Exhibition 1894* (New York, 1894), 51.

DELACHAUX, Leon (also Léon). **Paris, France.**
1850 United States–1919
Training — Paris: Ernest Duez, P. A. J. Dagnan-Bouveret.

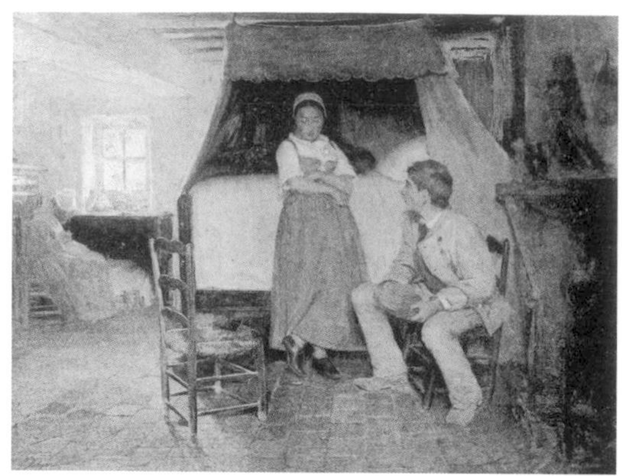

The Miller's Son. **#1051.** [$400]. ca. 1891. Est. 32 x 40. Unlocated. Illus: *Catalogue Illustré des Ouvrages de Peinture, Sculpture et Gravure* (Paris: A. Lemercier et Cie, 1891), 34.

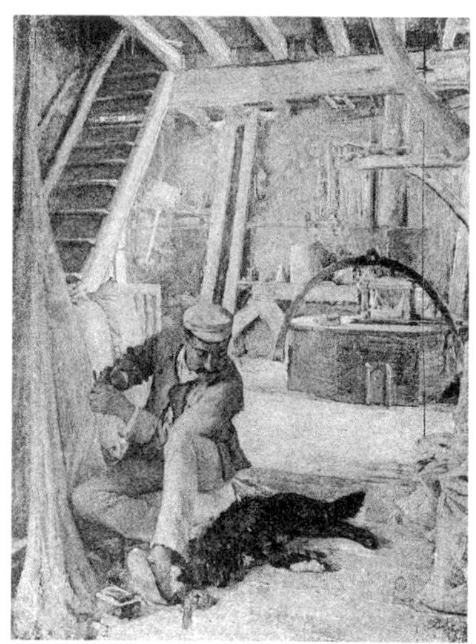

The Mill in the Meadows. **#1287.** [$300]. ca. 1891. Unlocated. Illus: *Catalogue Illustré des Ouvrages de Peinture, Sculpture et Gravure* (Paris: A. Lemercier et Cie, 1891), 195.

DELLENBAUGH, Frederick S. (Frederick Samuel). **New York.**
1853 McConnelsville, OH–1935 New York, NY
Training — Buffalo, NY; New York; Munich: Royal Academy; Paris: Carolus-Duran, Acad. Julian (Jules Joseph Lefebvre).

On the Moquis Cliffs, Arizona. **#1096.** [$350]. Unlocated.

DEMING, E. W. (Edwin Willard). **New York.**
1860 Ashland, OH–1942 New York, NY
Training — New York: ASL; Paris: Acad. Julian (Gustave Boulanger, Jules Joseph Lefebvre).

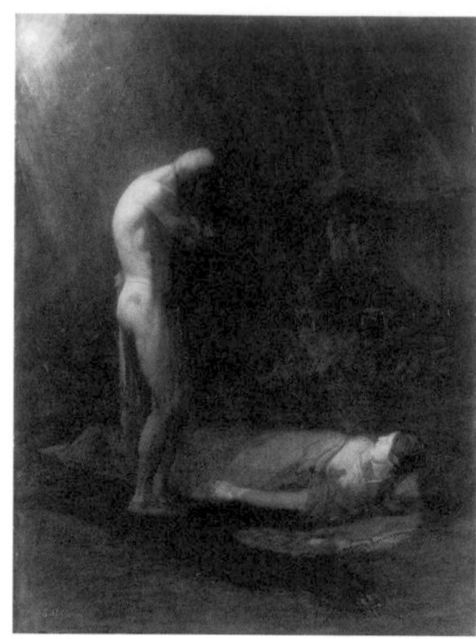

A Mourning Brave. **#609.** [$400]. *The Mourning Brave,* n.d. (ca. 1892). 39½ x 30½. National Museum of American Art, Smithsonian Institution, Gift of William T. Evans.

DENMAN, Herbert. New York.
1855 Brooklyn, NY–1903 Idylwild, CA
Training — New York: ASL; Paris: Carolus-Duran.

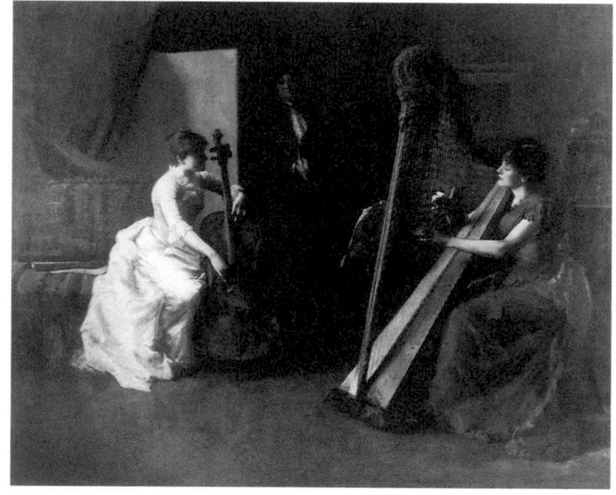

The Trio. **#803.** [$5000]. 1886. 83 x 96½. The Brooklyn Museum, Gift of C. H. Genung, E. Carlson, H. Howard, and W. L. Carrigan.

---

† **DESSAR, Louis P.** (Louis Paul). **Paris, France.**
1867 Indianapolis, IN–1952 Preston, CT
Training — New York: NAD (J. Q. A. Ward, Lemuel E. Wilmarth); Paris: Acad. Julian (William Bouguereau, Tony Robert-Fleury), EcBA.

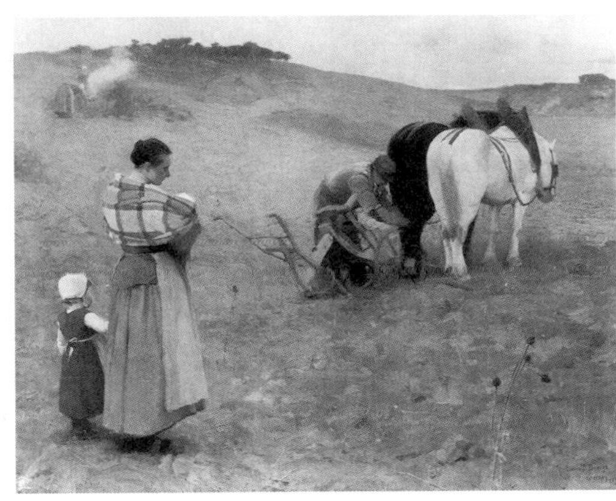

Evening. **#796.** [$3000]. 1892. Est. 55 x 65. Collection Udall & Ballou, Jewellers, New York, NY, 1925. Unlocated. Illus: Charles M. Kurtz, ed., *Illustrations from the Art Gallery of the World's Columbian Exposition* (Philadelphia: G. Barrie, 1893), 39.

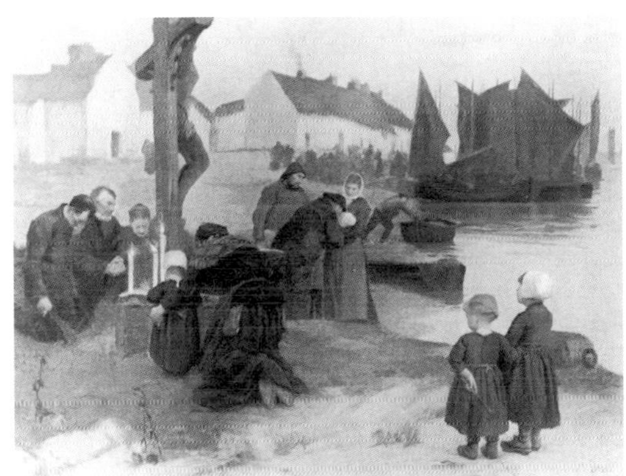

The Fishermen's Departure (Étaples, France). **#799.** [$4000]. 1891. 68 x 86. Omaha Public Library, Omaha, NE. Partially destroyed. Illus: Daniel H. Burnham, *The Art of the World,* vol. 10 (New York: Appleton, 1893–95).

Study —French Peasant Girl's Head. **#1020.** [$300]. **Lent by Mr. Meyer Jonasson, New York.** Unlocated.

DEWEY, Charles Melville. New York.

1849 Lowville, NY–1936 New York, NY
Training— New York: NAD; Paris: Carolus-Duran.

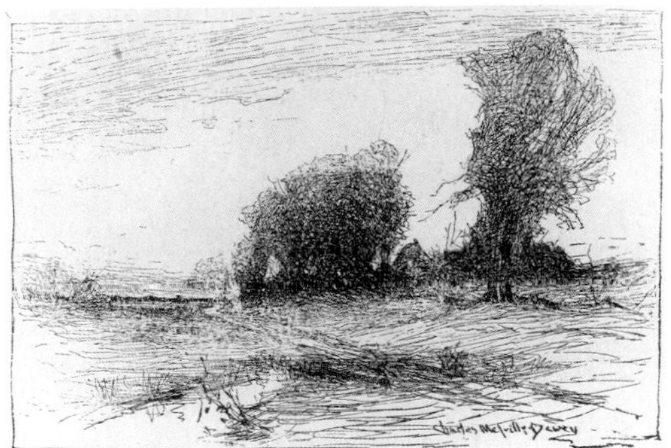

The Hush of Day. **#541. Lent by Mr. L. A. Ault, Cincinnati.** Est. 25 x 35. Unlocated. Illus: American Art Galleries, *The Second Prize Fund Exhibition for the Promotion and Encouragement of American Art* (New York: J. J. Little, 1886), no. 77.

Shadows of the Evening Hour. **#562. Lent by Mr. W. T. Evans, New York.** 18 x 24. Sold, American Art Association, New York, NY, 31 Jan.– 2 Feb. 1900, lot 138, to J. M. Simonson. Unlocated. "Rarely delicate in treatment and poetic in feeling. The foreground of waste pasture land rises to a slight eminence in the middle distance, where slender trees denuded of leaves, and a house, with wood smoke rising from the chimney, are in vague silhouette against the evening sky of greenish blue with rose tints at the horizon and gray clouds above. The landscape is wrapped in a misty haze, the sign of fast-falling night, and the picture shows in all its parts the impress of the artist's poetic temperament" —American Art Association, *Catalogue of American Paintings Belonging to William T. Evans* (New York: Press of J. J. Little, 1900), lot 138.

The Return of the Hay Boats. **#1100. Lent by Mr. W. T. Evans, New York.** ca. 1891. 20 x 30. Sold, American Art Association, New York, NY, 31 Jan.– 2 Feb. 1900, lot 247, to J. M. Simonson. Unlocated. "A celebrated picture. Two men seated in the bow of a barge loaded high with dried marsh grass are pulling down the river with long sweeps. The flat country and some low-lying hills occupy the middle distance, while above is the sky of clouds and broken masses of light. The misty atmosphere is admirably rendered, and the general effect is exquisitely poetic. Exhibited at the Munich International Exhibition, 1895"— American Art Association, *Catalogue of American Paintings Belonging to William T. Evans* (New York: Press of J. J. Little, 1900), lot 247.

The Prelude of Night. **#1167.** [$1000]. ca. 1890. Unlocated.

† **DEWING, T. W.** (Thomas Wilmer). **New York.**
1851 Boston, MA–1938 New York, NY
Training — Paris: Acad. Julian (Jules Joseph Lefebvre, Gustave Boulanger).

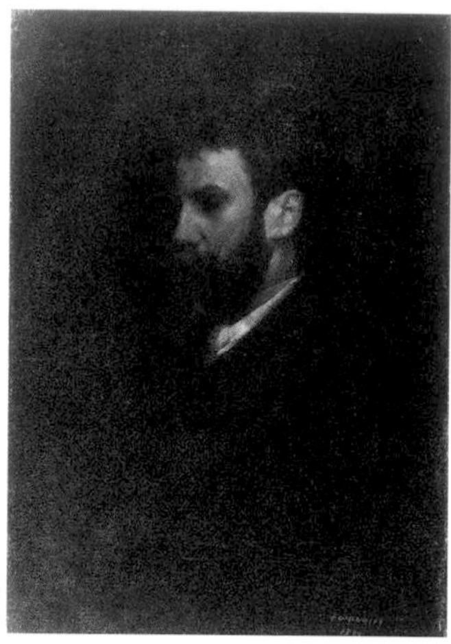

Portrait of W. M. Chase. **#554. Lent by Mr. W. M. Chase, New York.** 1890. 13¼ x 9½. Cincinnati Art Museum, Bequest of Mr. and Mrs. Walter J. Wichgar.

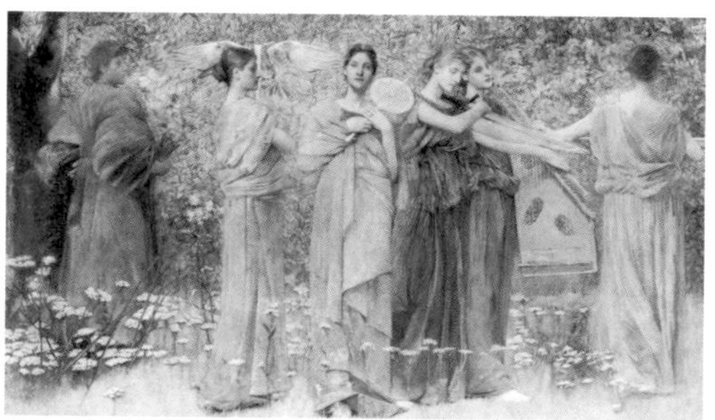

The Days. **#698. Lent by Miss A. W. Cheney and Miss Louise Cheney, South Manchester, Conn.** 1887. 43 3/16 x 72. Wadsworth Atheneum, Hartford, Gift from the Estates of Louise Cheney and Anne W. Cheney.

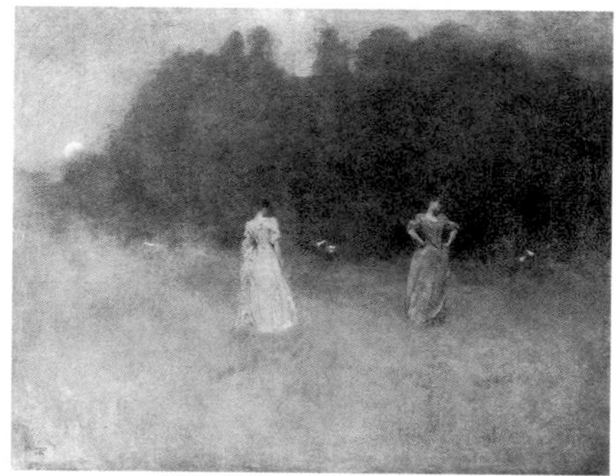

Summer Twilight. **#712. Lent by Mr. C. L. Freer, Detroit.** *After Sunset,* 1892. 20 x 15⅝. Freer Gallery of Art, Smithsonian Institution.

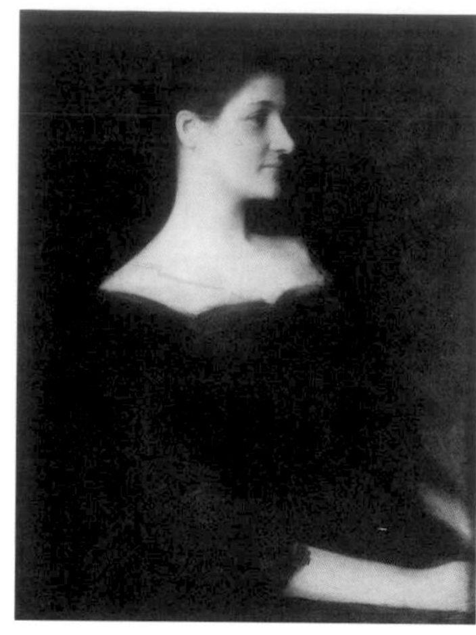

A Portrait. **#713. Lent by Mr. Stanford White, New York.** *Portrait of Mrs. Stanford White,* 1886 (oil on wood panel). 13½ x 10¼. Collection of Erving and Joyce Wolf.

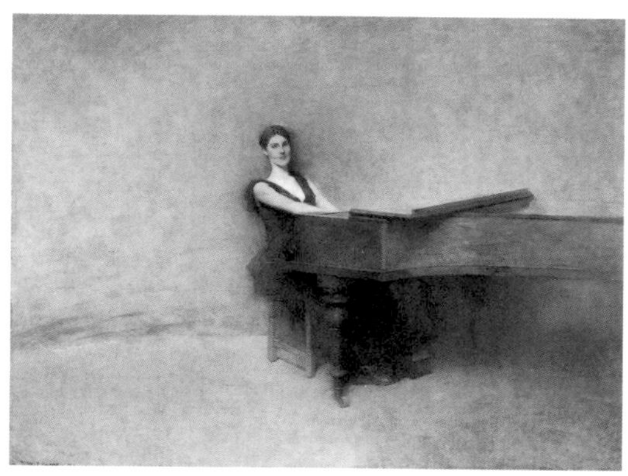

A Musician. **#714. Lent by Mr. C. L. Freer, Detroit.** *The Piano,* 1891 (oil on wood panel). 20 x 26 9/16. Freer Gallery of Art, Smithsonian Institution.

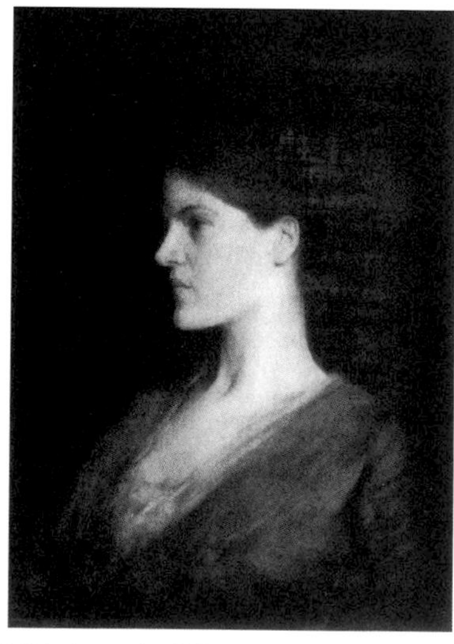

A Portrait. **#720. Lent by Mr. Stanford White, New York.** *Portrait of Ella Emmet,* ca. 1888–89. 13 x 10¼. Private Collection.

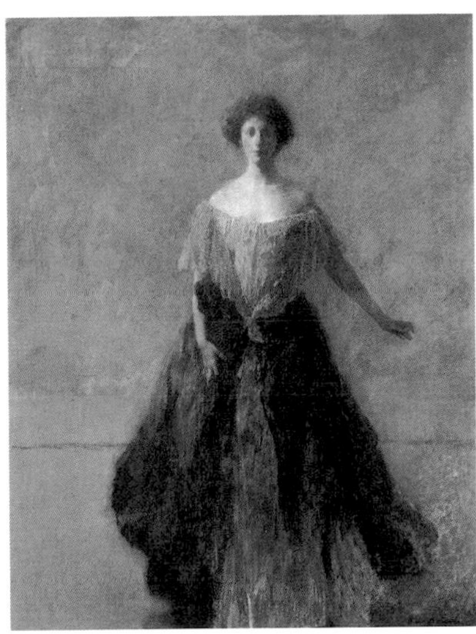

A Lady in Blue. **#997. Lent by Mr. C. L. Freer, Detroit, Mich.** *The Blue Dress,* 1892 (oil on wood panel). 20 x 15⅞. Freer Gallery of Art, Smithsonian Institution.

DIDIER, **Ida Joy.** (Mrs. N. A. Didier). **Allegheny, Pa.**
Unknown–Residing 1897 Allegheny, PA[20]
Training — Paris.

Portrait. **#1259.** Est. 18 x 14. Unlocated.

DIELMAN, **Frederick. New York.**
1847 Hanover, Germany–1935 Ridgefield, CT
Training — Munich: Royal Academy (Wilhelm Diez).

A New York Arab. **#726. Lent by Mr. William Semple, Louisville, Ky.** Unlocated.

DILLON, **Julia** (Julia McEntee/Mrs. John Dillon). **New York.**
1834 Rondout, NY–1919 Kingston, NY
Training — Paris: Harry Thompson, Georges Jeannin.

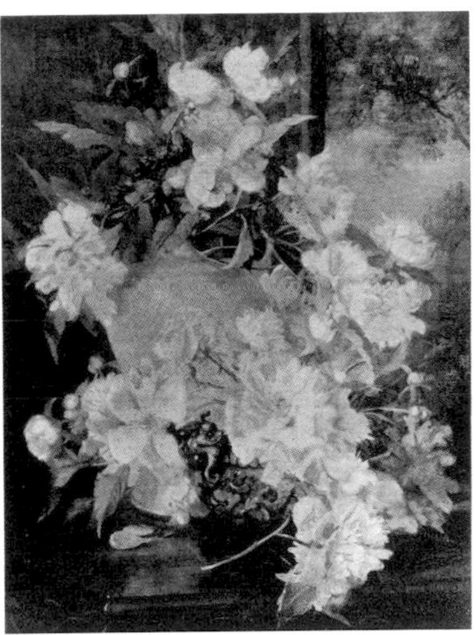

Peonies. **#1210.** ca. 1890. Unlocated. Illus: Charles M. Kurtz, ed., *Illustrations from the Art Gallery of the World's Columbian Exposition* (Philadelphia: G. Barrie, 1893), 326.

DODSON, **Sarah P. Ball** (Sarah Paxton Ball). **Brighton, England.**
1847 Philadelphia, PA–1906 Brighton, England
Training — Philadelphia: PAFA (Christian Schussele); Paris: Acad. Julian (Jules Joseph Lefebvre), Évariste Vital Luminais, Maurice Boutet de Monvel.

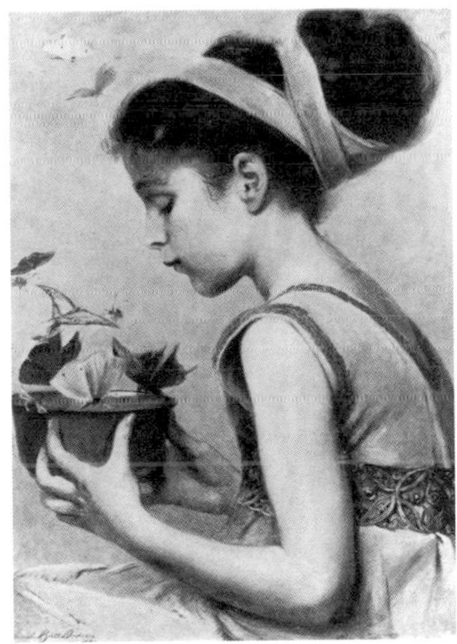

Honey of Hymettus. **#416.** 1891. Unlocated. Illus: American Art Galleries, *Catalogue of the Exhibition of Paintings by Sarah Ball Dodson* (New York: The Lent & Graff Company, 1911), no. 82.

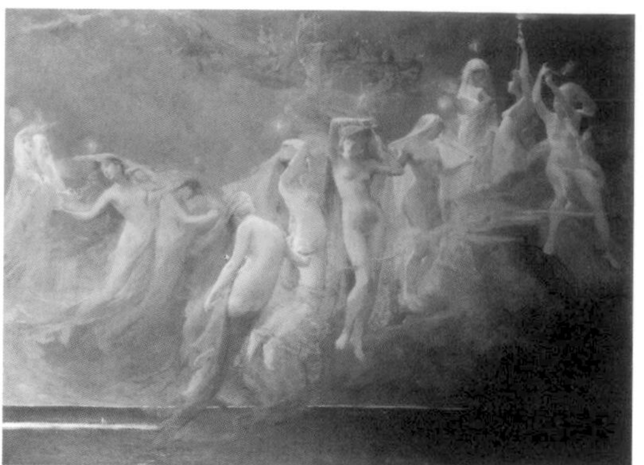

The Morning Stars. **#1094.** [$750]. 1887. 23 x 30. Private Collection. Photograph by Wayne Geist.

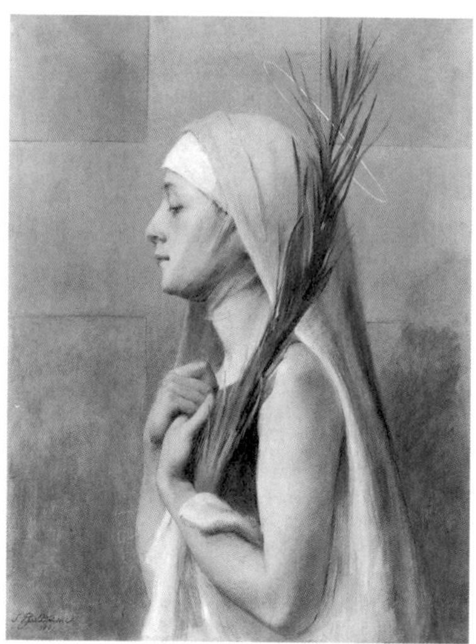

Saint Thekla. **#1230.** *Une Martyre (Saint Thechla),* 1891. 29½ x 21½. National Museum of American Art, Smithsonian Institution, Gift of Richard Ball Dodson.

DOHN, **Pauline A.** (Mrs. Franklin Rudolph). **Chicago.**
1865 Chicago, IL–1934 Los Angeles, CA
Training — Philadelphia: PAFA (Thomas Anshutz, Thomas Eakins); Chicago: Henry F. Spread, J. Roy Robertson; Paris: Gustave Boulanger, Thomas Couture, Charles Lasar, Jules Joseph Lefebvre.

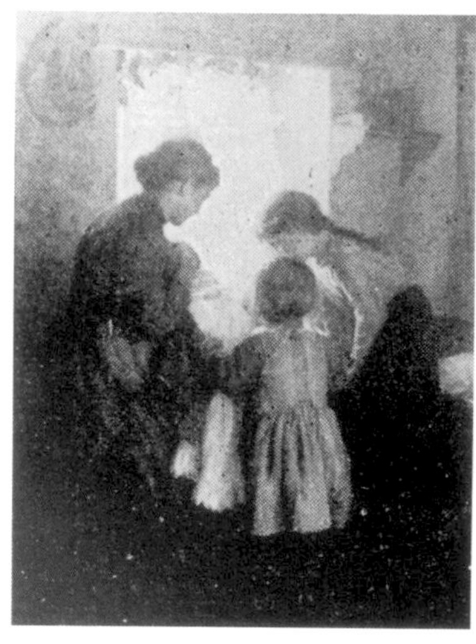

What the Stork Brought. **#886.** [$500]. ca. 1892. Unlocated. Illus: Trumbull White and William Igleheart, *The World's Columbian Exposition, Chicago, 1893* (Philadelphia and St. Louis: P. W. Ziegler, [1893]), 359.

---

† **DONOHO, G. Ruger** (Gaines Ruger). **New York.**
1857 Church Hill, MS –1916 New York, NY
Training — New York: R. Swain Gifford, ASL; Paris: Acad. Julian (William Bouguereau, Gustave Boulanger, Jules Joseph Lefebvre, Tony Robert-Fleury).

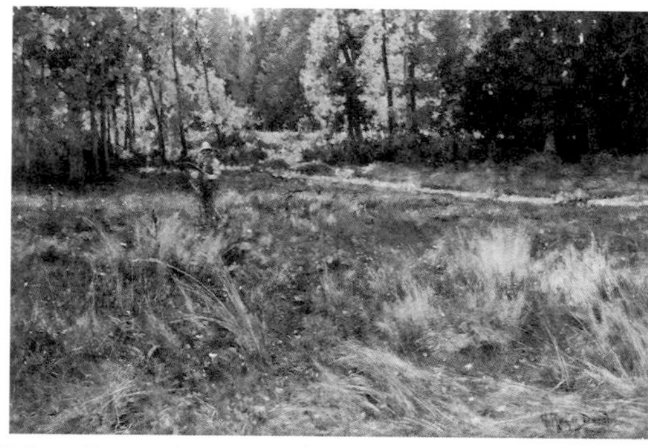

La Marcellerie. **#724.** n.d. (ca. 1882). 51⅜ x 77⅛. The Brooklyn Museum, Gift of George A. Hearn.

The Explorers. **#849. Lent by Mr. J. Hull Browning, New York.** ca. 1892. Unlocated. "A bit of thin woods is shown with the big leaves in a brown carpet among gray rocks and a pasture in the background. Sheep have strayed from the pasture to explore the piece of timber where one stunted and queerly branching tree forms a picturesque center for the rest of the bare woodland" — "Monthly Record of American Art," *Magazine of Art* 15 (Dec. 1891–Nov. 1892): xxvi.

DOW, Arthur W. (Arthur Wesley). **Ipswich, Mass.**
1857 Ipswich, MA–1922 New York, NY
Training — Paris: Acad. Julian (Gustave Boulanger, Jules Joseph Lefebvre), Paul-Louis Delance, Henri-Lucien Doucet.

Marsh Islands. **#1031.** [$1000]. Unlocated.

DUBÉ, Mrs. Mattie (Mrs. Louis Théodore Dubé). **New York.**
1861 Florence, AL–Residing 1919 Paris, France
Training —Paris: Acad. Julian (William Bouguereau, Tony Robert-Fleury).

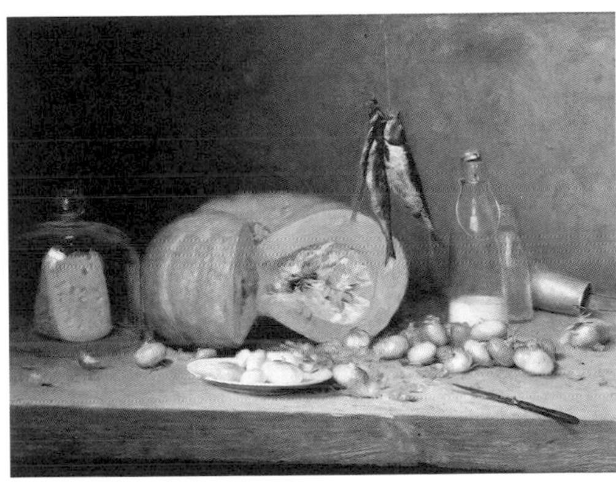

Pumpkins and Onions. **#1253.** [$800]. *Still Life With Pumpkin and Fish,* 1891. 34¼ x 45¼. Greenville County Museum of Art.

DUMOND, Frank Vincent. New York.
1865 Rochester, NY–1951 New York, NY
Training — New York: ASL (J. Carroll Beckwith, William Sartain); Paris: Acad. Julian (Gustave Boulanger, Jean-Jacques Benjamin-Constant, Jules Joseph Lefebvre), Henri-Lucien Doucet.

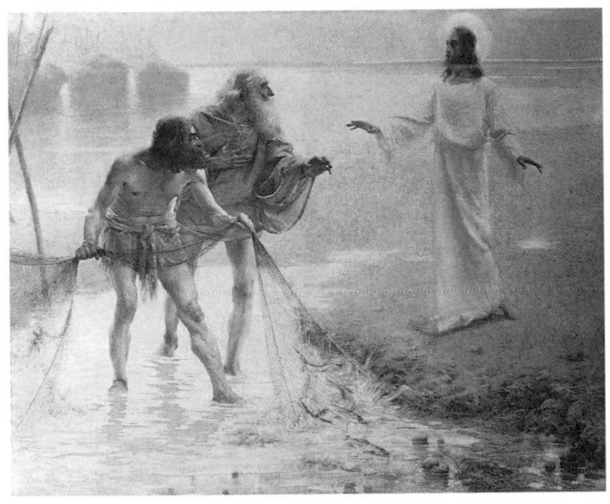

Christ and the Fishermen. **#291.** [$2000]. 1891. 51 x 64. Collection Stephen V. DeLange and N. Robert Cestone, Rowayton, CT. Photograph courtesy Peter A. Juley & Son Collection, National Museum of American Art, Smithsonian Institution.

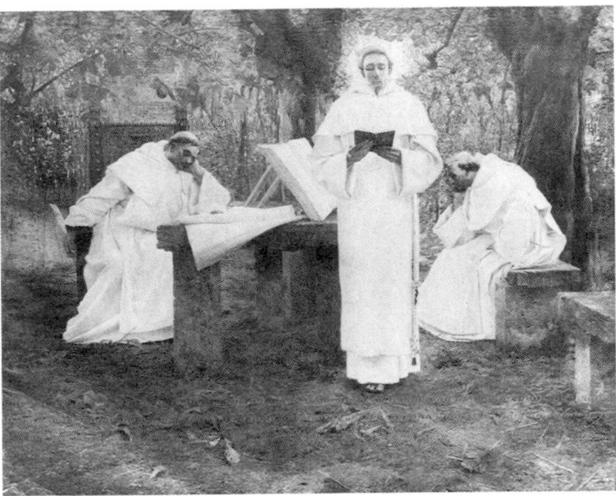

Monastic Life. **#1036.** n.d. (ca. 1891). 64¼ x 80. Collection Alexander R. Raydon, Raydon Gallery, New York.

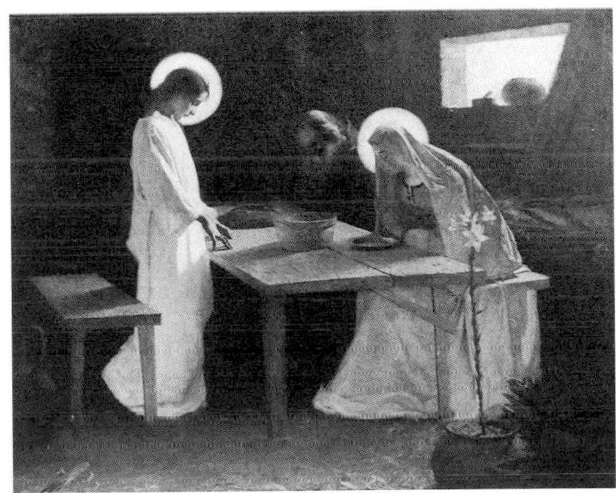

Holy Family. **#1093.** [$2500]. 1890. 51 x 64. St. Paul's On the Green, Norwalk, CT. Photograph by George Gurney.

DUMOND, Fred Melville (Frederic Melville). **Paris, France.**
1867 Rochester, NY–1927 Monrovia, CA
Training — Paris: Acad. Julian (Jean-Joseph Benjamin-Constant, Henri-Lucien Doucet, J. P. Laurens, Jules Joseph Lefebvre), F. A. P. Cormon, EcBA.

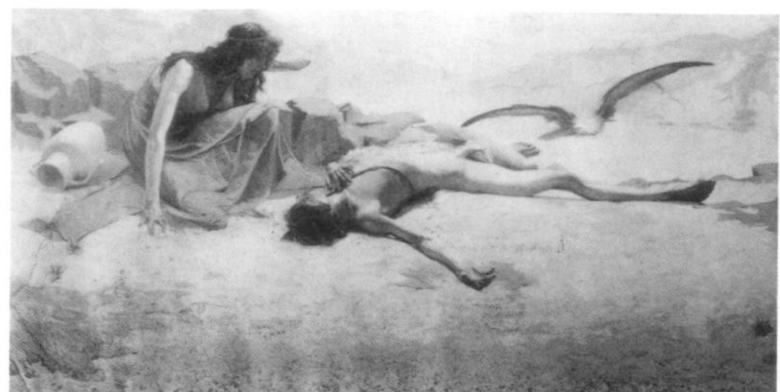

A Legend of the Desert. **#1184.** 1892. 59⅜ x 113½. Los Angeles County Museum of Art, Gift of Joseph Szymanski in memory of Dr. Joseph McLain and Roger Smoot.

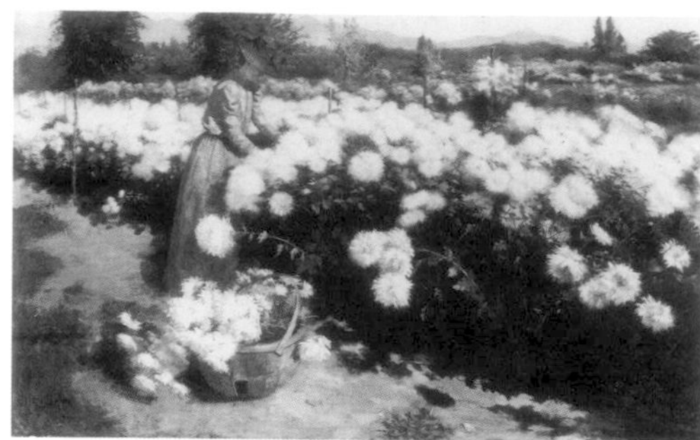

Chrysanthemum Garden in California. **#1082.** [$500]. 1891. 42½ x 68¼. Formerly Collection of James L. Coran and Walter A. Nelson-Rees. Destroyed in Oakland, CA, fire, 1991.

DUNSMORE, John Ward. Detroit.
1856 Reilly, OH–1945 Dover, NJ
Training — Cincinnati: McMicken School of Design; Paris: Thomas Couture, Aimé Millet.

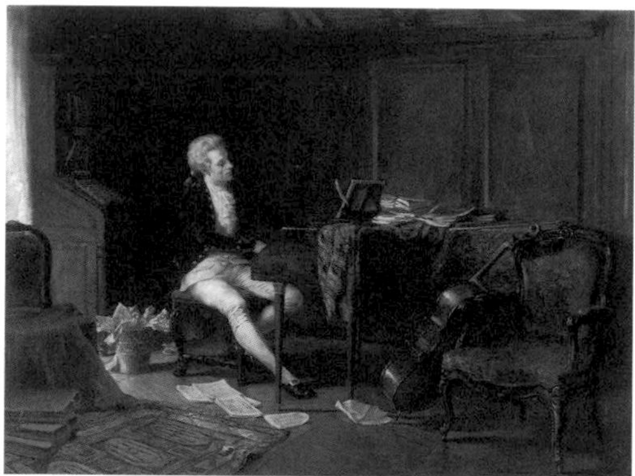

Mozart. **#1021.** [$500]. *Mozart at the Piano,* n.d. 38¾ x 51½. The Wagnalls Memorial, Lithopolis, OH.

DUVALL, Fannie E. (Fannie Eliza). **Los Angeles, Cal.**
1861 Port Byron, NY–1934 Los Angeles, CA
Training — New York: ASL (William Sartain), Cooper Union; Paris: Whistler School, Grand Chaumière (J. Francis Auburtin, Antonio de la Gandara, Olga de Bozananska).

Study of Onions. **#763.** [$100]. Unlocated.

---

† **DUVENECK, Frank. Cincinnati.**
1848 Covington, KY–1919 Cincinnati, OH
Training — Munich: Royal Academy (Wilhelm Diez).

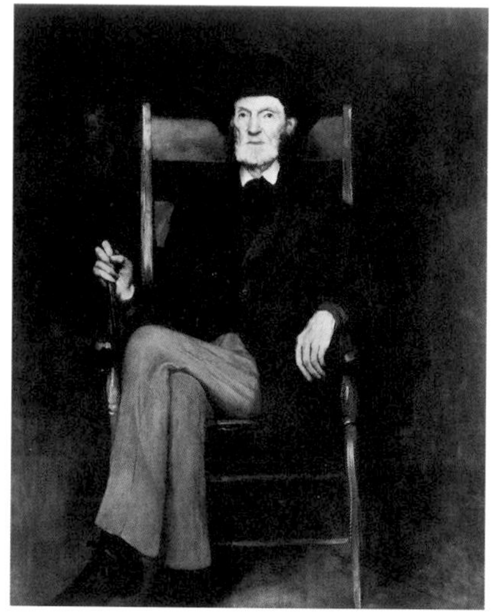

Portrait of William Adams. **#391.** 1874. 60⅛ x 48¼. Milwaukee Art Museum, Gift of Mr. and Mrs. Myron Laskin, Mr. and Mrs. George G. Schneider and Dr. and Mrs. Arthur J. Patek, Jr. in memory of Dr. and Mrs. Arthur J. Patek.

DVORAK, Frant. Chicago.
1862 Prelouc, Bohemia–Residing 1911 London, England
Training — Munich: Royal Academy (Otto Seitz, Wilhelm Lindenschmit); Vienna: Vienna Academy.

Mother's Pleasure. **#917.** [$1200]. Unlocated. "It represents the mother and child lying in the shade under trees. It is a bright day and the mother is playing with the child. The coloring is very brilliant, but harmonious as a whole" —*Chicago Tribune,* 11 March 1893; "Shows a mother, lying in the grass holding her baby above her and laughing at its antics" —*The Graphic* [Chicago], 29 Oct. 1892, 312.

EAKINS, Mrs. Thomas (Susan Hannah Macdowell). **Philadelphia.**
1851 Philadelphia, PA–1938 Philadelphia, PA
Training— Philadelphia: The Philadelphia School of Design for Women, PAFA (Christian Schussele, Thomas Eakins).

Reflection. **#748. Lent by Mr. W. H. MacDowell, Philadelphia.** Unlocated.[21]

---

† **EAKINS, Thomas** (Thomas Cowperthwaite). **Philadelphia.**
1844 Philadelphia, PA–1916 Philadelphia, PA
Training— Philadelphia: PAFA; Paris: Jean-Léon Gérôme, Léon Bonnat, Augustin Dumont.

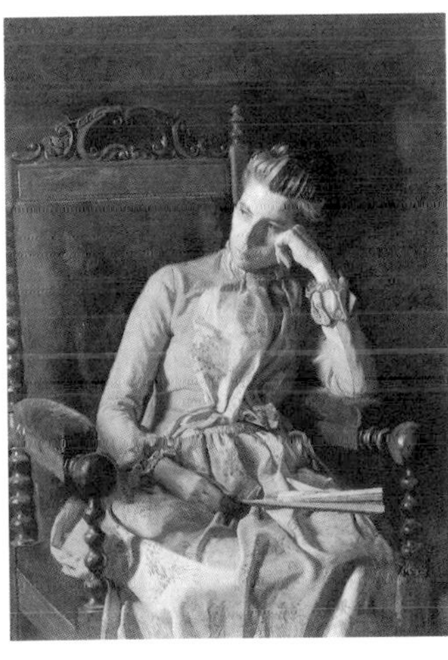

Portrait of a Lady.* **#667. Lent by Miss A. B. Van Buren, Detroit, Mich. *Miss Amelia Van Buren,* n.d. (ca. 1889–1891). 44½ x 32. ©The Phillips Collection, Washington, DC.

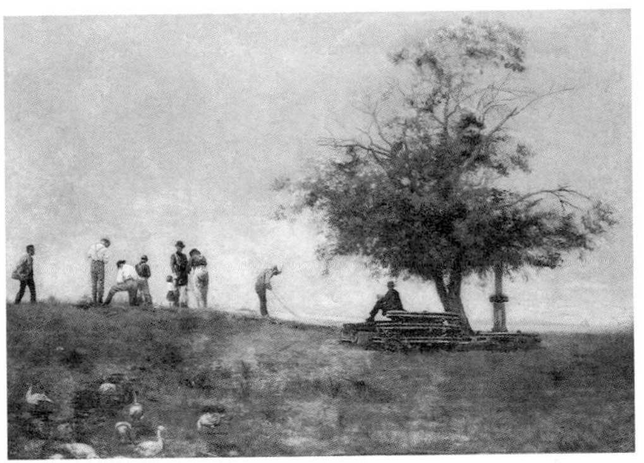

Mending the Nets.* **#747. [$800]. *Mending the Net,* 1881. 32⅛ x 45⅛. Philadelphia Museum of Art, Gift of Mrs. Thomas Eakins and Miss Mary Adeline Williams.

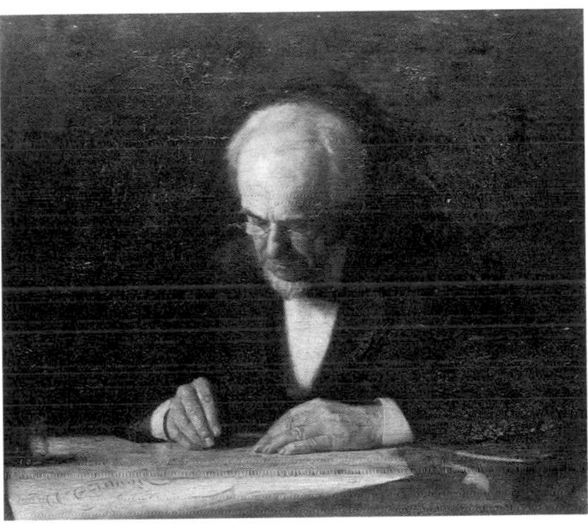

The Writing Master.* **#867. 1882. 30 x 34¼. The Metropolitan Museum of Art, John Stewart Kennedy Fund, 1917.

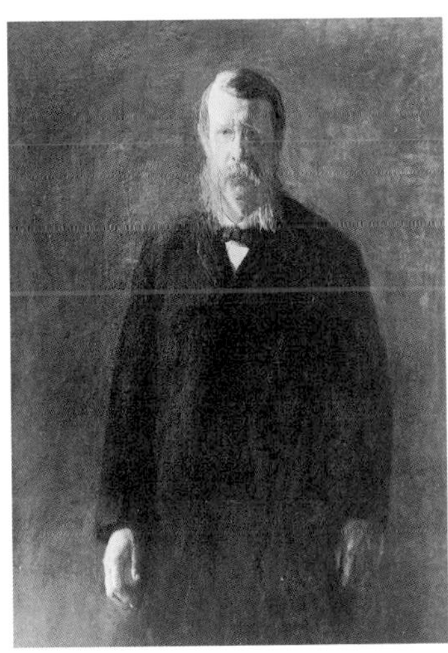

Portrait of Prof. George Barker. **#1033. Lent by Prof. George Barker, Philadelphia.** 1886.[22] Mitchell Museum, John R. and Eleanor R. Mitchell Foundation.

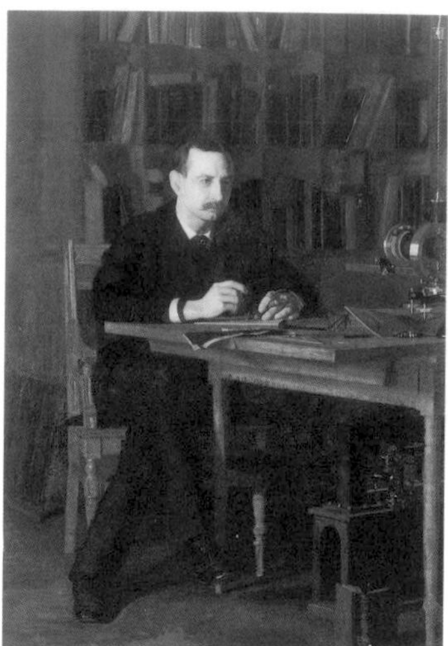

Portrait of Mr. William D. Marks. **#1044. Lent by Mr. William D. Marks, Philadelphia.** *Portrait of Professor William D. Marks,* 1886. 76⅜ x 54⅛. Washington University Gallery of Art, St. Louis.

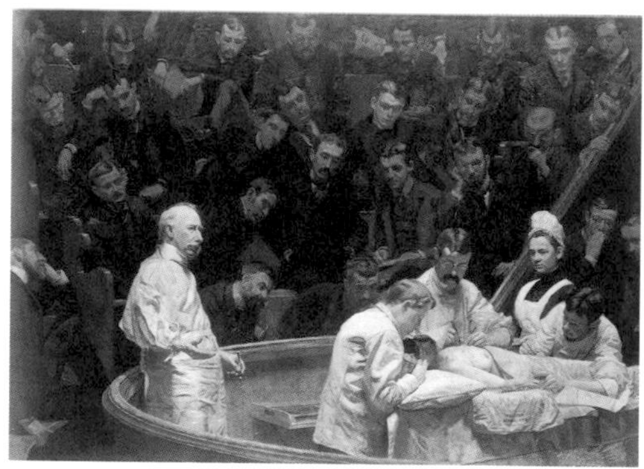

Portrait of Dr. Agnew. **#1052. Lent by the University of Pennsylvania.** *The Agnew Clinic, Portrait of David Hayes Agnew,* 1889. 84⅜ x 118⅛. Collection University of Pennsylvania School of Medicine, Philadelphia, PA.

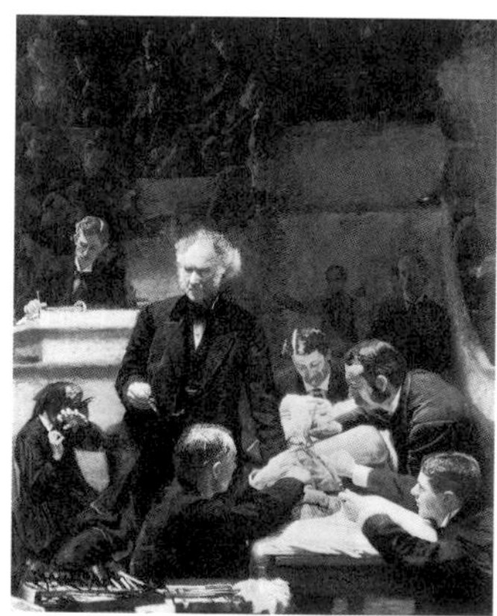

Portrait of Dr. Gross.* **#1061. Lent by the Jefferson Medical College, Philadelphia. *The Gross Clinic,* 1875. 96 x 78. Jefferson Medical College of Thomas Jefferson University, Philadelphia.

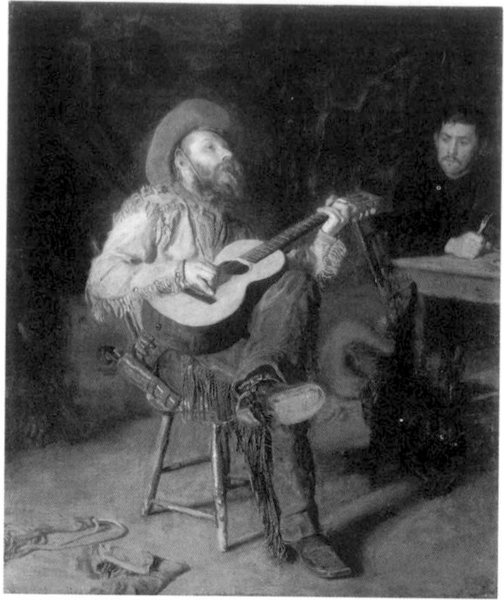

Cowboys at Home on a Ranch. **#1083.** [$800]. *Cowboys at Home Ranch,* 1892. 24 x 20. Philadelphia Museum of Art, Gift of Mrs. Thomas Eakins and Miss Mary Adeline Williams.

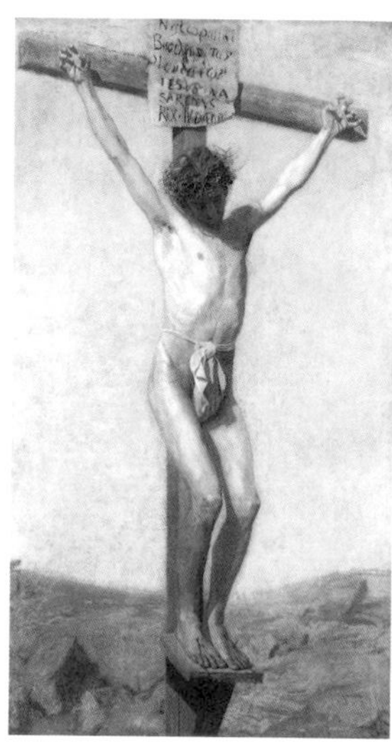

The Crucifixion. **#1132.** [$1200]. 1880. 96 x 54. Philadelphia Museum of Art, Gift of Mrs. Thomas Eakins and Miss Mary Adeline Williams.

The Sculptor. **#1211. Lent by William R. O'Donovan, New York.** ca. 1891. Unlocated. "Mr. William Rudolph O'Donovan has had his portrait painted by Mr. Thomas Eakins as he worked in sculptor's apron at a portrait bust; but that bust was a portrait of the painter himself. Thus, as one hand washes another, the sculptor modeled the painter while the painter put on canvas the sculptor" —*New York Times,* 5 April 1892.

EATON, **C. Harry** (Charles Harry). **New York.**
1850 Akron, OH–1901 Leonia, NJ
Training — self-taught.

Normandy Landscape. **#663. Lent by Mr. W. T. Evans, New York.** 1885. 24 x 36. Sold, American Art Association, New York, NY, 30 Jan.– 2 Feb. 1900, lot 31, to Marcus Stine. Unlocated. "The meadow which occupies the foreground is traversed by a brook, which in the middle distance flows past a farmhouse on the left embowered among the trees. Overhead a noble sky with masses of white cloud. Cool and restrained in color and very attractive in general aspect, this is one of Mr. Eaton's most beautiful and successful landscapes. Exhibited at the Paris Exposition of 1889, and at the World's Fair, Chicago, in 1893" —American Art Association, *Catalogue of American Paintings Belonging to William T. Evans* (New York: J. J. Little, 1900), lot 31.

Landscape. **#851. Lent by Mr. Henry A. Rust, Chicago.** Unlocated.

EATON, **Charles Warren. New York.**
1857 Albany, NY–1937 Glen Ridge, NJ
Training — New York: NAD, ASL.

Woods in Winter. **#299.** [$200]. Est. 18 x 25. Unlocated.

Moonrise. **#389.** [$1000]. Unlocated.

October. **#642.** [$150]. Est. 18 x 12. Unlocated.

On the Maine Coast. **#817.** [$300]. Est. 18 x 22. Unlocated.

ELWELL, **D. Jerome. Boston.**
1847 Gloucester, MA–1912 Naples, Italy
Training — Antwerp: Royal Academy.

Country of Calmpthout, Belgium. **#305.** [$200]. ca. 1888. Est. 8 x 12. Unlocated.

Bruges, Belgium. **#539.** [$1000]. Est. 20 x 30. Unlocated.

The Moorlands, Cape Ann. **#643.** [$500]. Est. 10 x 16. Unlocated.

Moonrise at Domberg, Zeeland, Holland. **#1222. Lent by the St. Botolph Club, Boston.** ca. 1883. Unlocated.

This work "was executed while [he was] a student at the Antwerp academy. Its weird and sombre tones, suggesting rather than portraying an almost invisible landscape, at once established his reputation among Belgian critics when displayed at the Cercle Artistique" —Hubert H. Bancroft, *The Book of the Fair*, vol. 3 (Chicago: Blakely Printing Co., 1893), 369; "The big 'Moonrise in Holland,' which is Elwell's masterpiece" —*Art Interchange* (April 1895): 110.

EMMET, **Lydia Field. New Rochelle, N.Y.**
1866 New Rochelle, NY–1952 New York, NY
Training — New York: ASL (William Merritt Chase), H. Siddons Mowbray, Kenyon Cox, Robert Reid; Paris: Acad. Julian (William Bouguereau, Tony Robert-Fleury), Gustave Colin, Frederick MacMonnies.

Noonday. **#1074. Lent by Miss A. B. Phelps, Wilkes-Barre, Pa.** Unlocated.

The Mere. **#1262.** [$100]. Unlocated.

ENNEKING, **John J.** (John Joseph). **Boston.**
1841 Minster, OH–1916 Hyde Park, MA
Training — Boston: Professor Richardson; Munich: Royal Academy (Eduard Schleich, Adolphe-Heinrich Lehr); Paris: Léon Bonnat, Charles François Daubigny, Eugène Louis Boudin.

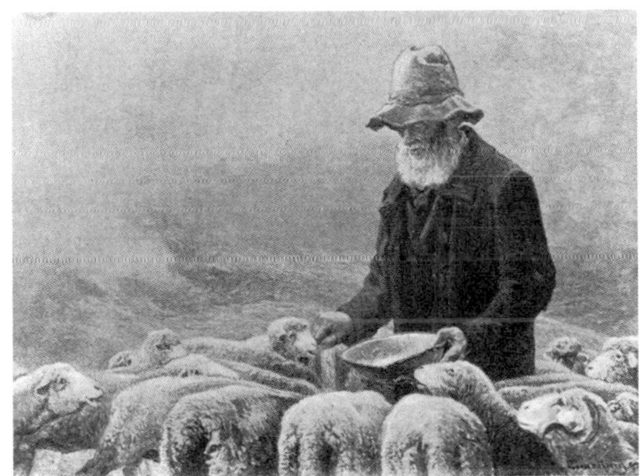

Salting Sheep. **#315.** [$650]. 1892. 34¼ x 45¾. Private Collection. Illus: Charles M. Kurtz, ed., *Illustrations from the Art Gallery of the World's Columbian Exposition* (Philadelphia: G. Barrie, 1893), 190.

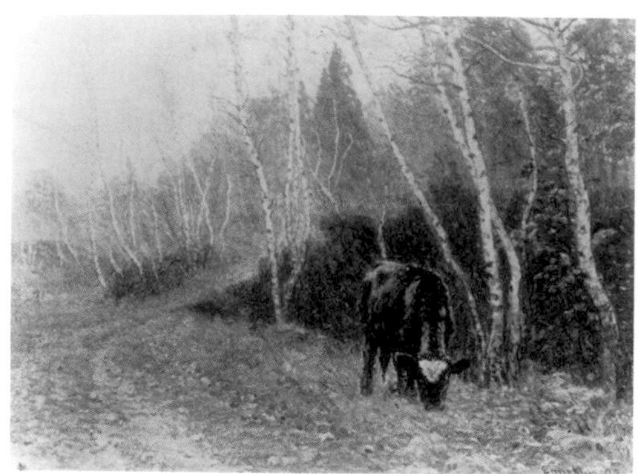

Autumn Afternoon. **#395.** [$650]. Unlocated. Illus: William H. Downes, "New England Art at the World's Fair," *New England Magazine* 8 (July 1893): 359.

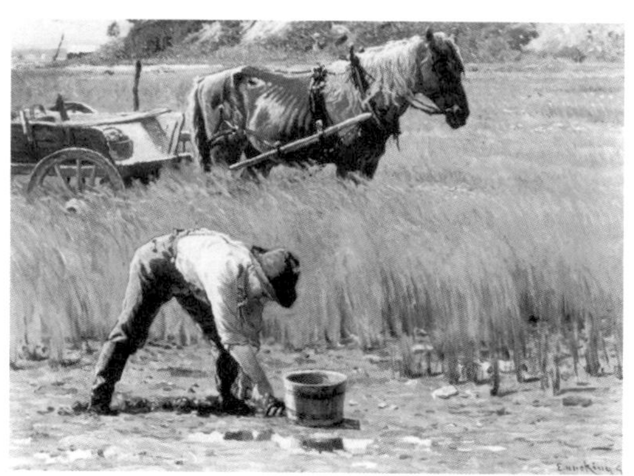

******A South Duxbury Clam Digger.* **#450.** [$350]. *Duxbury Clam Digger,* 1892. 22½ x 30½. Scripps College, Claremont, CA.

November. **#451.** [$350]. Est. 23 x 33. Sold, World's Columbian Exposition, Chicago, IL, 1893. Unlocated.

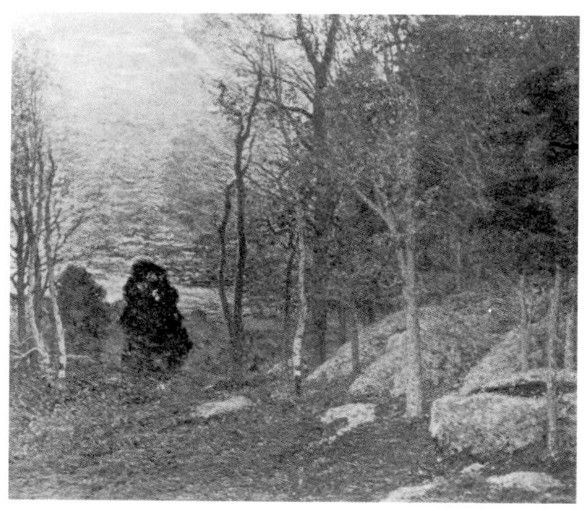

October Twilight. **#452.** [$2000]. ca. 1891. 60 x 65. Unlocated. Illus: Charles M. Kurtz, ed., *Illustrations from the Art Gallery of the World's Columbian Exposition* (Philadelphia: G. Barrie, 1893), 183.

ERTZ, **Edward** (Edward Frederick). **Paris, France.**
1862 Canfield, IL–1954 England
Training — Chicago: Academy of Design; Paris: Georges Callot, Paul-Louis Delance, Acad. Julian (Jean-Joseph Benjamin-Constant, Jules Joseph Lefebvre).

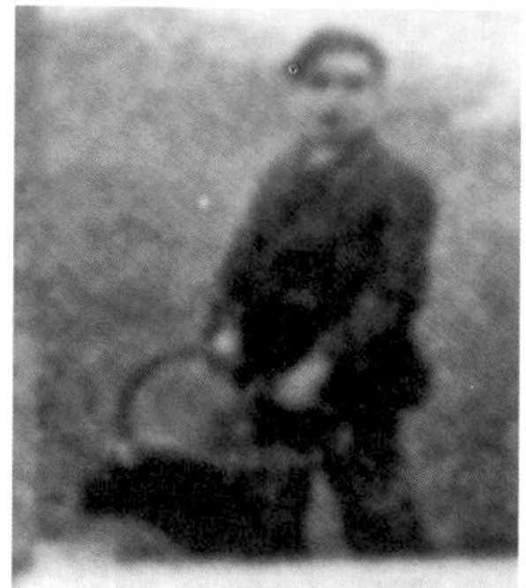

The Potato Gatherer. **#490.** [$1000]. Est. 35 x 30. Unlocated. Illus: William Walton, *Art and Architecture,* vol. 1 (Philadelphia: G. Barrie, 1893–95), opposite 25.

EVANS, **E.** (Edwin). **Lehi, Utah.**
1860 Evansville, UT–1946 Venice, CA
Training — Utah: University of Utah (George Ottinger, Danquart A. Weggeland); Paris: Acad. Julian (Jean-Jacques Benjamin-Constant, J. P. Laurens, Jules Joseph Lefebvre).

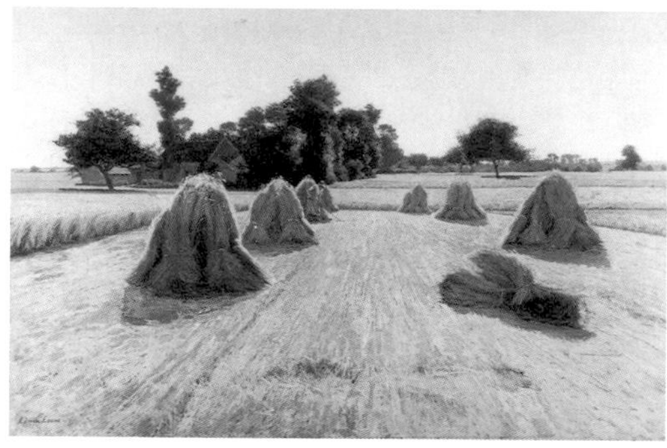

Harvest. **#297.** *Grain Fields,* 1893. 39 x 58. ©Museum of Fine Arts Brigham Young University. All rights reserved.

EVANS, Joe (Joseph T.). **New York.**
1857 New York, NY–1898 New York, NY
Training — New York: NAD, ASL; Paris: Jean-Léon Gérôme.

The Red Gate. **#460.** [$200]. ca. 1891. Est. 25 x 18. Unlocated.

The Plainfield Road. **#984.** [$300]. ca. 1892. Unlocated.

EVANS, Mrs. M. E. (M. Eleanor/Mrs. R. C. P. Evans). **New York.**
Unknown –Residing 1917 New York, NY[23]
Training — New York: NAD, ASL; Paris: Daniel Bouvet, Thomas Couture, Acad. Julian (J. P. Laurens, Jean-Joseph Benjamin-Constant).

September Lane. **#279.** [$300]. Est. 19 x 27. Unlocated. "A picture of Indian summer in Connecticut. It is a dreamy, poetic thing full of tenderness and sentiment, yet vigorous in handling and true to the facts of nature. The trees and rocks, as well as the hedge of goldenrod, are simply and effectively massed. This color scheme, with its recurring note of gray, is delightful and harmonius" —*Los Angeles Times,* 10 June 1906, Sec. 6.

FAIRCHILD, Lucia (Mrs. Henry Brown Fuller). **Boston.**
1870/72 Boston, MA–1924 Madison, WI
Training — Boston: Cowles Art School (Dennis M. Bunker); New York: ASL (H. Siddons Mowbray, William Merritt Chase).

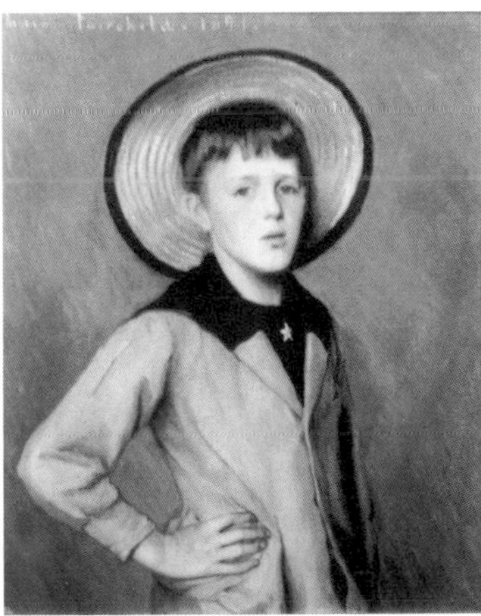

Portrait of a Boy with a Hat. **#1260. Lent by Mrs. C. Fairchild, Boston.** *Portrait of a Boy with a Hat: Neil Fairchild,* 1891. 28½ x 23. Collection Mrs. Lucia T. Miller, Evanston, IL.

FAXON, William Bailey. New York.
1849 Hartford, CT–1941 New York, NY
Training — Paris: Jacquesson de la Chevreuse, EcBA.

Maia. **#638.** [$250]. ca. 1892. Est. 14 x 9. Unlocated.

Lady in Profile. **#1142.** [$300]. ca. 1891. Unlocated.

† **FISHER, Mark** (William Mark). **Stockbridge, England.**
1839 Boston, MA–1923 London, England
Training — George Inness; Boston: Lowell School of Practical Drawing; Paris: Charles Gleyre.

Summer Afternoon. **#295.** [$400]. Est. 22 x 35. Unlocated.

Moonrise. **#368.** [$200]. Unlocated.

Timber Wagon, Normandy. **#371.** [$325]. Unlocated.

A Hampshire Dairy. **#458. Lent by Mr. McCulloch, London.** Est. 25 x 35. Unlocated.

A Small Holding. **#492.** [$400]. Est. 20 x 30. Unlocated.

Teste Valley Meadows. **#510.** [$200]. Est. 14 x 20. Unlocated.

Orchard in Normandy. **#516.** [$150]. Est. 14 x 20. Unlocated.

Sorting the Flock. **#521.** [$150]. Est. 14 x 20. Unlocated.

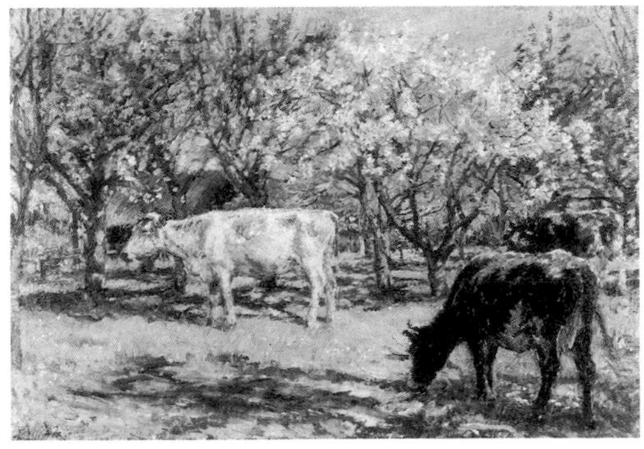

Cows in Orchard (Winter). **#534.** [$250]. *Cows in the Orchard,* n.d. 18 x 25. Tate Gallery, London.

Evening. **#891.** [$350]. Unlocated.

Cattle Crossing a Stream. **#1027.** [$3000]. Est. 50 x 70. Unlocated.

FITZ, **B. R.** (Benjamin Rutherford). **deceased.**
1855 New York, NY–1891 Peconic, NY
Training — New York: NAD; Munich: Royal Academy.

Autumn Showers. **#925. Lent by Dr. George W. Fitz, Cambridge, Mass.** Est. 12 x 22. Unlocated.

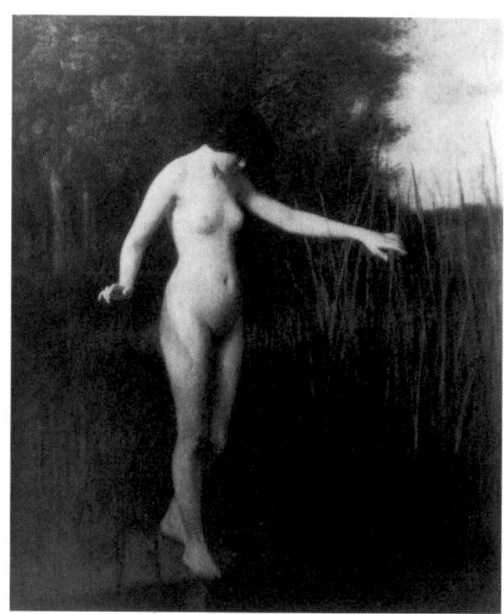

The Reflection. **#985. Lent by Mr. W. T. Evans, New York.** 1890. 30 x 25⅛. Private Collection.

FLAGG, **Charles Noel. Hartford, Conn.**
1848 Brooklyn, NY–1916 Hartford, CT
Training — Paris: Jacquesson de la Chevreuse.

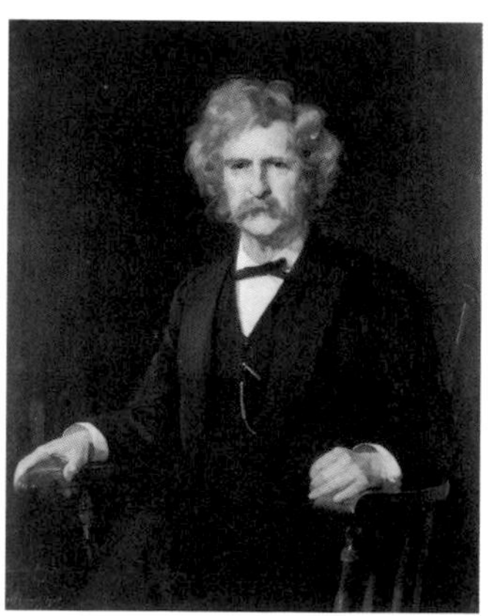

Portrait of Mark Twain. **#570. Lent by Mr. Samuel L. Clemens, Hartford, Conn.** *Mark Twain,* 1890. 40¼ x 32⅜. The Metropolitan Museum of Art, Gift of Miss Ellen Earle Flagg, 1917.

FORSYTH, **W.** (William). **Indianapolis.**
1854 Hamilton, OH–1935 Indianapolis, IN
Training — Indianapolis: Indiana School of Art (John W. Love, James F. Gookins); Munich: Royal Academy (Gyula Benczur, Nikolaus Gysis, Ludwig von Löfftz).

Edge of the Woods. **#329.** [$300]. Unlocated.

In the Garden. **#527. Lent by Mr. Carl H. Lieber, Indianapolis, Ind.** ca. 1892. Est. 14 x 20. Unlocated.

Landscape. **#1186. Lent by Mr. L. Weisenberger, Indianapolis.** Unlocated.

FOSS, **Harriet Campbell. New York.**
1860 Middleton, CT–1938 Darien, CT
Training — New York: J. Alden Weir; Paris: Gustave Courtois, Alfred Stevens, Tony Robert-Fleury.

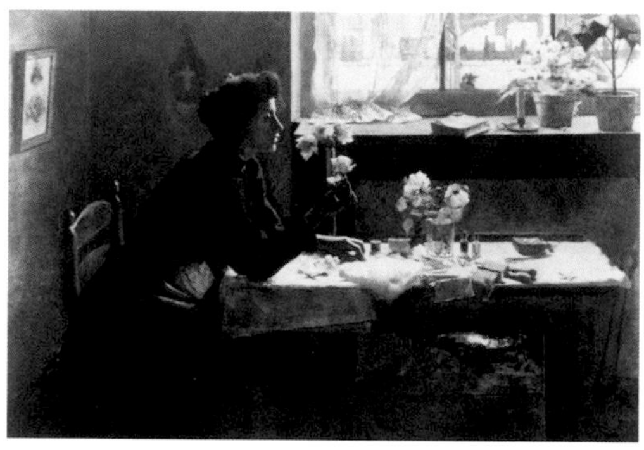

A Flower Maker.* **#897. [$1500]. 1892. 51½ x 72¼. Private Collection. Photograph courtesy Spanierman Gallery, New York, NY.

† FOSTER, **Ben** (Benjamin). **New York.**
1852 North Anson, ME–1926 New York, NY
Training — New York: Abbott H. Thayer; Paris: Aimé Morot, Luc Olivier Merson.

A Maine Hillside. **#378. Lent by Mr. James T. Pettus, New York.** ca. 1889. 29 x 34½. Sold, Ortgies Fifth Avenue Art Galleries, New York, NY, 12 Jan. 1897, lot 102. Unlocated.

The Returning Flock. **#668.** [$400]. Unlocated.

First Days of Spring. **#683. Lent by Mr. James T. Pettus, New York.** 29 x 34½. Sold (as *Early Spring on Staten Island*), Ortgies Fifth Avenue Art Galleries, New York, NY, 12 Jan. 1897, lot 120. Unlocated.

In Fontainebleau Forest. **#1246. Lent by Mr. J. F. Drummond, New York.** ca. 1887. Est. 40 x 30. Unlocated.

FOWLER, **Frank. New York.**
1852 Brooklyn, NY–1910 New Canaan, CT
Training — Florence: Edwin White; Paris: Carolus-Duran, EcBA (Alexandre Cabanel).

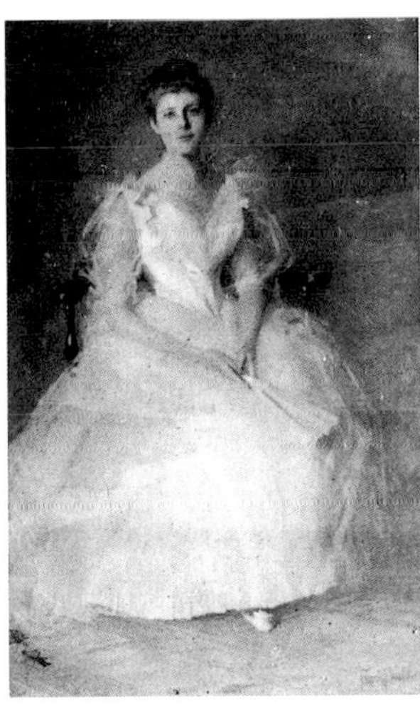

Portrait —A Figure in White. **#420. Lent by Mrs. William A. Fowler, Brooklyn, N.Y.** *Mary Aymar Fowler,* ca. 1889. Est. 60 x 45. Destroyed. Photograph courtesy Mr. & Mrs. Aymar H. Fowler, Warren, CT.

Portrait. **#464. Lent by Dr. Neftel, New York.** Est. 40 x 30. Collection Mrs. Miriam T. Neftel Ellison, Tallahassee, FL.[24]

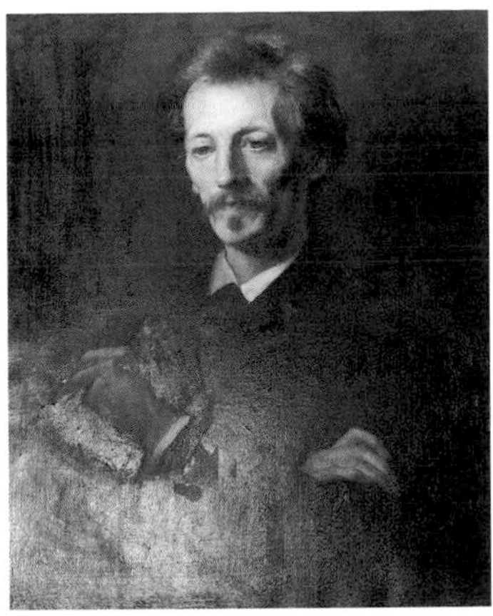

Portrait of Walter Shirlaw. **#525. Lent by Mr. Walter Shirlaw, New York.** 1890. 30¼ x 25. National Academy of Design, New York City.

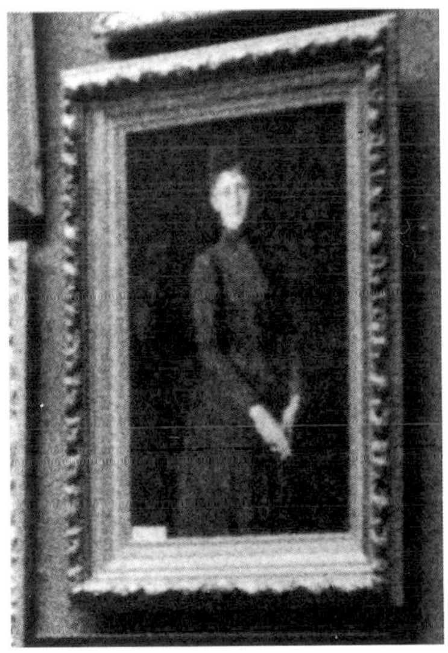

Portrait, Girl in Black. **#540.** Est. 45 x 28. Unlocated. Illus: Official Photographs of the World's Columbian Exposition by C. D. Arnold, vol. 8, pl. 83. Courtesy of The Chicago Public Library, Special Collections Department.

Portrait. **#926. Lent by Mr. H. W. Goodrich, New York.** ca. 1892. Est. 15 x 10. Unlocated.[25]

FOWLER, Mary B. O. (Mary Berrian Odenheimer/ Mrs. Frank Fowler). **New York.**
Philadelphia, PA–1898 Nutley, NJ
Training — Philadelphia: Philadelphia Art School [probably The Philadelphia School of Design for Women]; Paris: Carolus-Duran, Jean-Jacques Henner.

Marie. **#556.** [$200]. Unlocated.

FRASER, John A. (John Arthur). **New York.**
1838 London, England–1898 New York, NY
Training — London: Royal Academy (F. W. Topham, R. Redgrave).

An English Spring Morning. **#847.** [$350]. ca. 1890. Unlocated.

† **FREER, Frederick W.** (Frederick Warren). **Chicago.**
1849 Chicago, IL–1908 Chicago, IL
Training — Munich: Royal Academy; Paris.

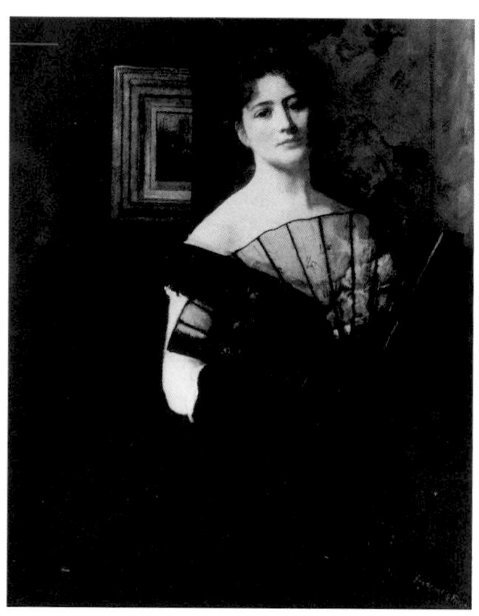

Portrait of a Lady in Black. **#535. Lent by the Boston Art Club.** n.d. (ca. 1886–87). 44 x 26. Collection Mr. and Mrs. Norton W. Mailman, New York, NY.

Portrait. **#793. Lent by Mr. Henry C. Champlin, Chicago.** Est. 27 x 20. Unlocated.

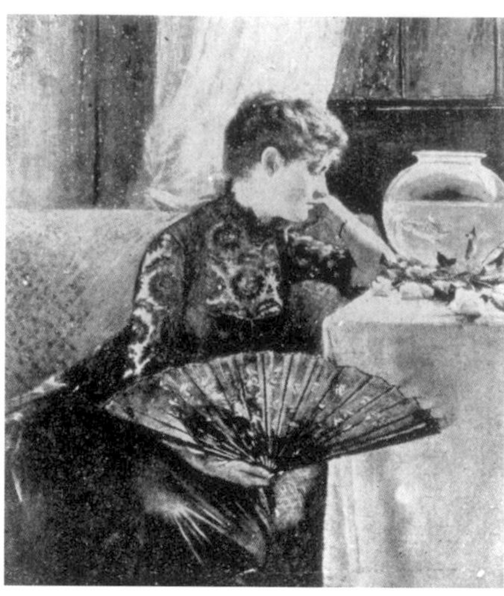

Gold Fish. **#929. Lent by Mr. James C. Brooks, Chicago.** ca. 1885. Unlocated. Illus: Trumbull White and William Igleheart, *The World's Columbian Exposition, Chicago, 1893* (Philadelphia and St. Louis: P. W. Ziegler, [1893]), 335.

FRY, John H. (John Hemming). **St. Louis.**
1861 Green County, IN–1946 Greenwich, CT
Training — St. Louis: School of Fine Arts; Paris: Acad. Julian (Gustave Boulanger, Jules Joseph Lefebvre), Fernand Cormon, Jean-Jacques Benjamin-Constant, Augustin Dumont.

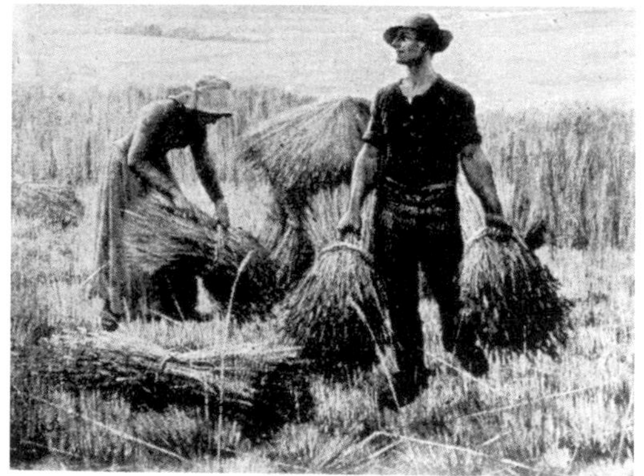

Labor. **#448.** [$400]. Unlocated. Illus: Trumbull White and William Igleheart, *The World's Columbian Exposition, Chicago, 1893* (Philadelphia and St. Louis: P. W. Ziegler, [1893]), 359.

FRYE, Miss Gertrude (Gertrude Harrison/Mrs. Frederick O'Brien). **Philadelphia.**
1863 Belfast, ME–1956 Los Angeles, CA
Training — Boston: John J. Enneking; Vienna; Paris: Paul-Louis Delance, Georges Callot, Jules Joseph Lefebvre, Tony Robert-Fleury, William Bouguereau, Jean-Joseph Benjamin-Constant.

Portrait of Miss E.[26] **#673. Lent by Mr. F. Evans, Philadelphia.** Unlocated.

GARDNER, Elizabeth (Elizabeth Jane/Mrs. William Bouguereau). **Paris, France.**
1837 Exeter, NH–1922 Saint Cloud, France
Training — Auburndale, MA: Lasell Seminary (Imogene R. Morrell) Paris: Acad. Julian (William Bouguereau, Jules Joseph Lefebvre), Hugues Merle, Antoine-Louis Baryé.

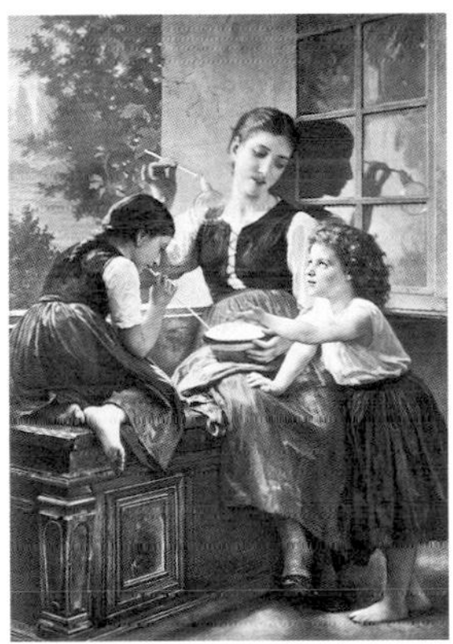

Soap Bubbles. **#617.** [12,500 francs]. **Lent by Mr. Arthur Tooth, London.** n.d. (ca. 1891). 64 x 46. The Jefferson Hotel, Richmond, VA. Illus: William Walton, *Art and Architecture,* vol. 1 (Philadelphia: G. Barrie, 1893–95), 21.

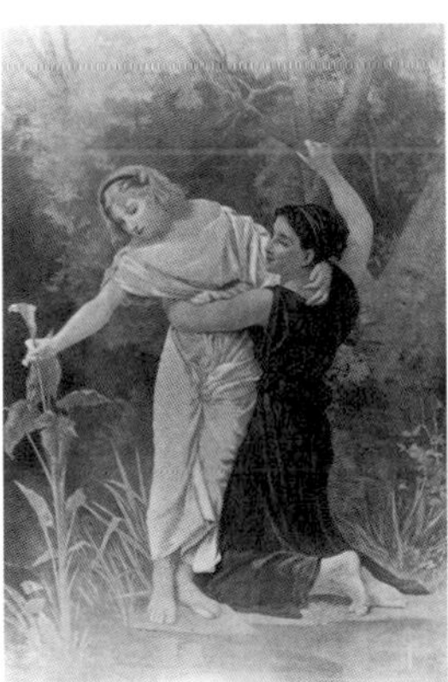

The Water's Edge. **#865. Lent by Mr. W. H. Tailer, Dobb's Ferry, N.Y.** 45 x 30. Sold, James P. Silo Fifth Avenue Art Galleries, New York, NY, 2 Jan. 1907, lot 225, to F. A. Watson. Unlocated. Illus: Daniel H. Burnham, *The Art of the World,* vol. 7 (New York: Appleton, 1893–95).

GAUGENGIGL, I. M. (Ignaz Marcel). **Boston.**
1855 Passau, Germany–1932 Boston, MA
Training — Munich: Royal Academy (Wilhelm Diez, Johann Leonhard Raab).

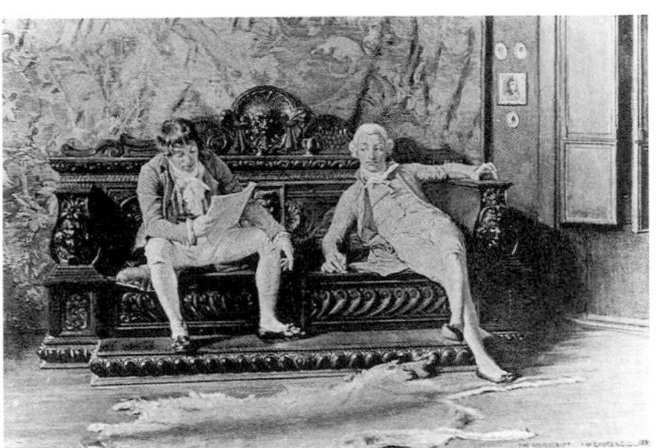

The Manuscript. **#777. Lent by Mr. Wm. A. Slater, Norwich, Conn.** 1889. Est. 6 x 10. Unlocated. Illus: Daniel H. Burnham, *The Art of the World,* vol. 6 (New York: Appleton, 1893–95).

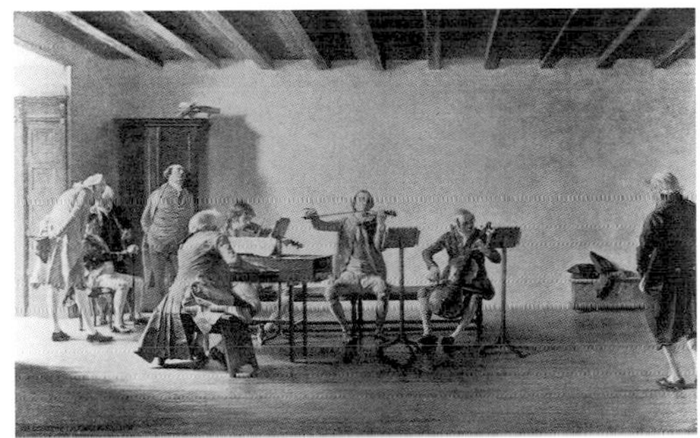

The Rehearsal. **#778.** [$6000]. 1893 (oil on panel). 13½ x 21½. Sold (as *The Quartette*), Vose Galleries, Boston, MA, 1931 to R. J. Flick of California. Unlocated. Illus: Daniel H. Burnham, *The Art of the World,* vol. 9 (New York: Appleton, 1893–95).

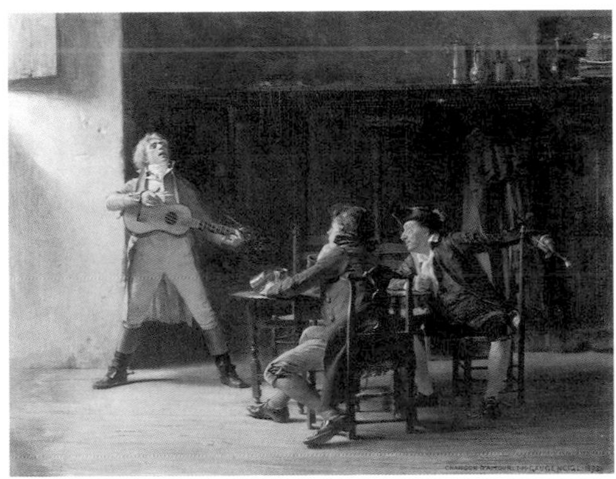

The Love Song. **#779. Lent by the Tavern Club, Boston.** 1892. Est. 12 x 18. The Tavern Club.

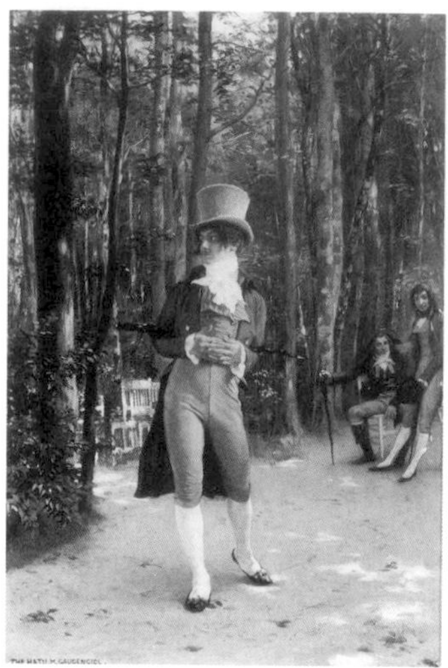

The Hat. **#960. Lent by Mr. W. F. Weld, Boston.** n.d. (oil on panel). 9⅞ x 6⅞. Collection Edward T. Wilson, Fund for Fine Arts, Inc., Chevy Chase, MD.

---

† **GAUL, Gilbert** (William Gilbert). **New York.**
1855 Jersey City, NJ–1919 New York, NY
Training — New York: J. G. Brown, NAD (Lemuel E. Wilmarth).

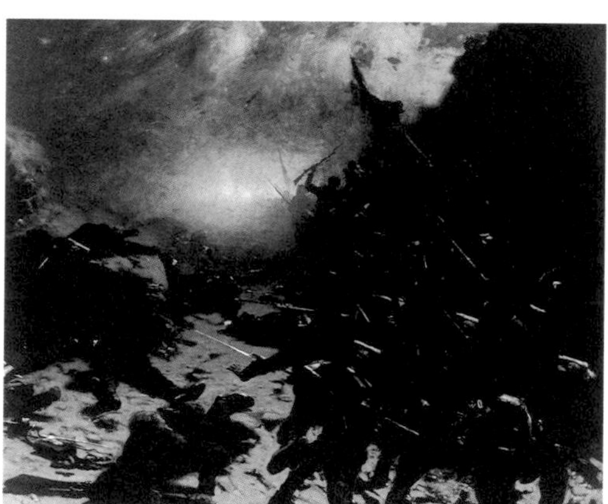

Charging the Battery.* **#899. Lent by Mr. W. T. Evans, New York. n.d. (ca. 1882). 36 x 44. The New-York Historical Society, New York; Gift of Donald Anderson.

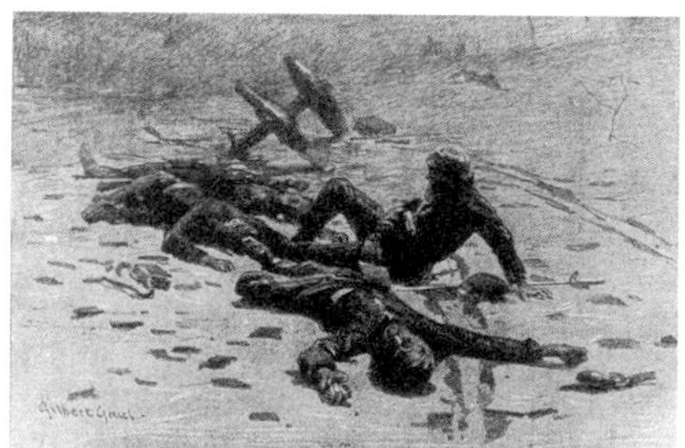

Silenced. **#1205. Lent by Mr. W. M. Chase, New York.** ca. 1883. 28 x 40. Unlocated. Illus: Charles M. Kurtz, ed., *Illustrated Art Notes Upon the Fifty-Eighth Annual Exhibition of the National Academy of Design, New York* (New York: Cassell, Petter, Galpin, 1883), 22.

GAY, Edward. Mt. Vernon, N.Y.
1837 Dublin, Ireland–1928 Mt. Vernon, NY
Training — Albany: J. M. Hart; Karlsruhe, Germany: Johann Wilhelm Schirmer, Carl Friedrich Lessing.

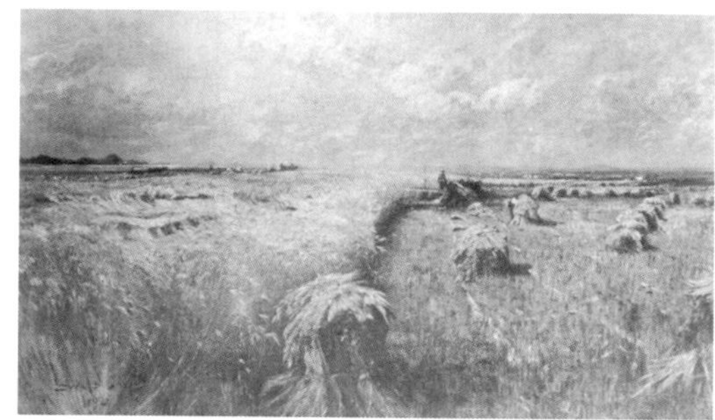

Mother Earth. **#1203.** 1892. 70 x 96. Canajoharie Library and Art Gallery, Canajoharie, NY.

GAY, Walter (Walter L.). **Paris, France.**
1856 Boston, MA–1937 Chateau Breau, France
Training — Boston: William Morris Hunt; Paris: Léon Bonnat.

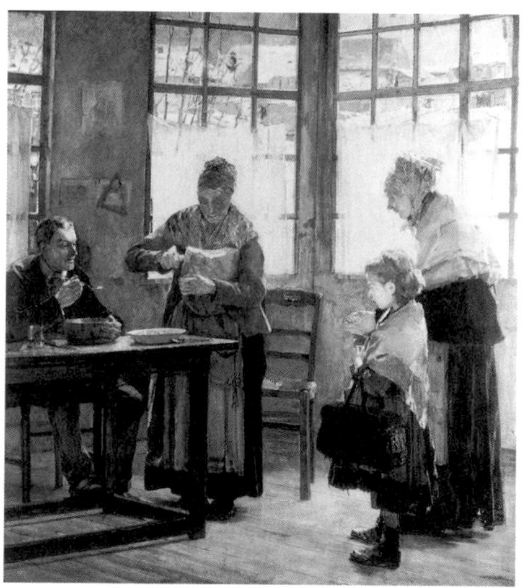

Charity. **#488.** [$2000]. 1889. 102 x 88. Collection Gloria Manney.

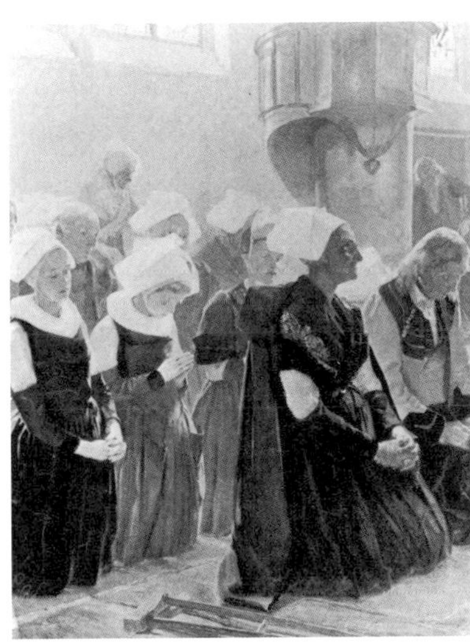

A Mass in Brittany. **#495.** [$2000]. ca. 1892. Est. 70 x 55. Unlocated. Illus: Charles M. Kurtz, ed., *Illustrations from the Art Gallery of the World's Columbian Exposition* (Philadelphia: G. Barrie, 1893), 74.

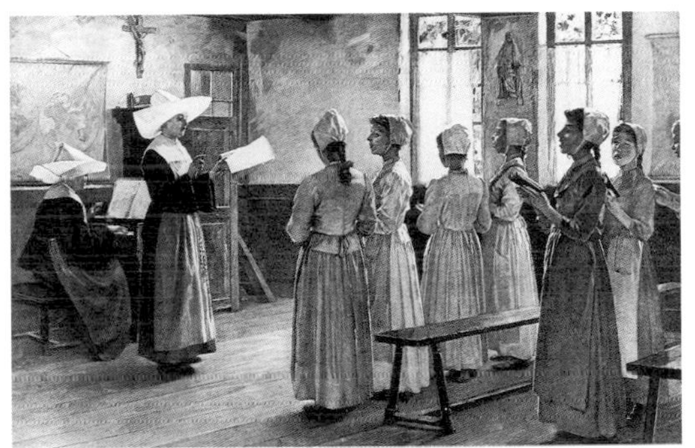

A Gregorian Chant. **#742.** [$3000]. 1891. 98 x 125½. Jordan-Volpe Gallery, Inc., New York, NY.

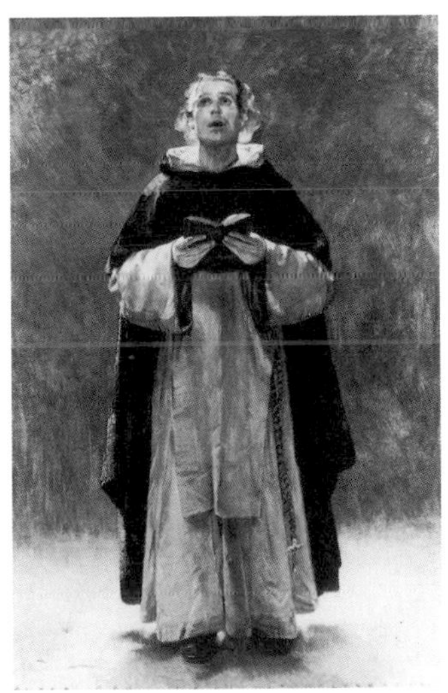

A Dominican Monk. **#1136.** [$1200]. 1888. 57⅛ x 38. Collection Arthur T. Garrity, Jr., Hingham, MA.

GIFFORD, R. Swain (Robert Swain). **New York.** 1840 Island of Naushon, MA–1905 New York, NY *Training* — New Bedford, MA: Albert van Beest, William Bradford, B. Russell.

Over the Summer Sea. **#487.** [$550]. Sold, World's Columbian Exposition, Chicago, IL, 1893. Unlocated.

Telegraph Station at Sandy Hook. **#526.** [$350]. Est. 12 x 23. Sold, World's Columbian Exposition, Chicago, IL, 1893. Unlocated.

Landscape. **#644. Lent by Mr. J. B. Wheeler, New York.** Est. 14 x 16. Unlocated.

Autumn. **#662. Lent by Mr. Thomas B. Clarke, New York.** 1888. 10 x 14. Sold, American Art Association, New York, NY, 14–18 Feb. 1899, lot 28, to James Obermeyer. Unlocated. "A typical American coast forest of scrubby trees is made splendid by the colors of autumn. The foreground is a clearing overgrown with brush. Toward the right is a pile of firewood, stacked up for removal, and a man with an axe on his shoulder advances into the wood to continue the work of destruction" —American Art Association, *Catalogue of the Private Art Collection of Thomas B. Clarke, New York* (New York: American Art Association, 1899), lot 28.

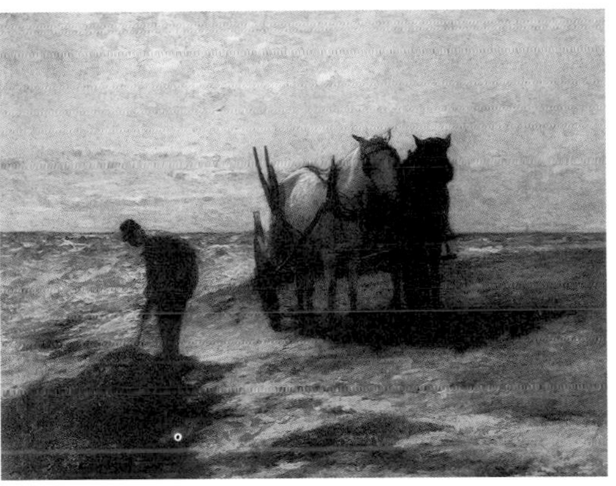

The Sea-weed Gatherers. **#685.** [$1500]. *Seaweed Gatherer,* 1886. 25 x 38. Washington and Lee University, Lexington, VA.

Sand Dunes. **#707. Lent by Mrs. Robert Carter, New York.** Unlocated.[27]

Salt Works of Padanaram. **#727.** Unlocated.[28]

The Cove Road, Naushon Island, Mass. **#757. Lent by the Detroit Club.** 1888. 19½ x 39½. Sold, Sotheby's, New York, NY, 3 Dec. 1992, lot 45. Unlocated.

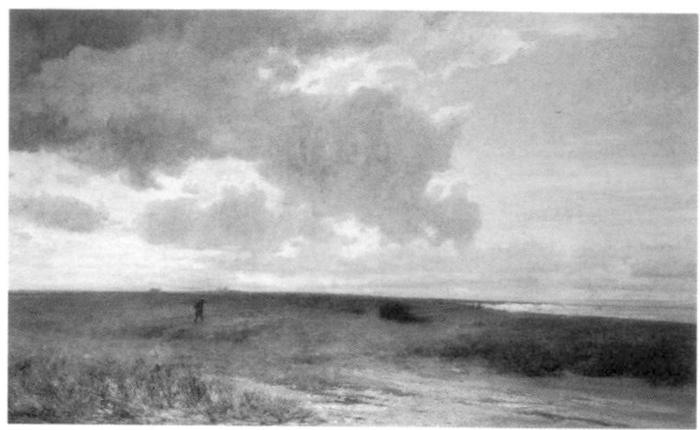

Moorlands. #819. [$1800]. n.d. (ca. 1892–93). 30 x 50. New Bedford Whaling Museum.[29]

The Rock of Gibraltar. **#986. Lent by Mrs. H. E. Lawrence, New York.** ca. 1872. Unlocated.

Nashawena. **#1080. Lent by Mr. Thomas B. Clarke, New York.** ca. 1887. 14 x 26. Sold (as *Nashawena Island*), American Art Association, 14–18 Feb. 1899, lot 335, to O. H. Durrell. Unlocated. "From the superior elevation of the foreground, the eye follows a coast line broken by projecting points of rock, between which the breakers play in flashing foam upon the beach. From the foreground, on the left, the moor extends its undulating surface variegated with heather. A sunny sky brightens the scene" —American Art Association, *Catalogue of the Private Art Collection of Thomas B. Clarke, New York* (New York: American Art Association, 1899), lot 335.

GILL, **Mariquita** (Mariquita S.). **Giverny, France.**
1861 Montevideo, Uruguay–1915 Salem, MA
Training— Ross Turner; New York: ASL; Paris: Acad. Julian, M. Lahaye, M. Dumoulin.

A Midsummer Morning, Giverny. **#709.** [$50]. Unlocated.

A Gray Day, Giverny, France. **#1233.** [$50]. Unlocated.

GILL, **Rosalie Lorraine** (Mme. René Lara, Comptesse de Chaban). **New York.**
1867 Baltimore, MD or Elmira, NY–1898 Paris, France
Training— New York: ASL (William Merritt Chase); Paris: Alfred Stevens, James M. Whistler.

Twilight on St. Ives Bay. **#868.** [$200]. Unlocated.

Portrait of Miss Inglis. **#1202.** Unlocated.

GILMAN, **B. F.** (Benjamin Ferris). **Philadelphia.**
1856 Salem, NJ or New York, NY–1934 New York, NY?
Training— Paris: Alexandre Cabanel, Henri Lehmann, Jean-Léon Gérôme.

Portrait Study. **#659.** [$100]. Est. 20 x 15. Unlocated.

GOLDMAN, **Martha. Pittsburg, Pa.**
1860 Norway–Residing 1899 Allegheny, PA

Study Head. **#613.** [$250]. Unlocated.[30]

GOTTWALD, **F. C.** (Frederick Carl). **Cleveland.**
1860 Vienna, Austria–1941 Pasadena, CA
Training— New York: ASL; Munich: Royal Academy.

Along the Docks. **#529.** [$150]. ca. 1891. Est. 18 x 20. Unlocated.

Sunday on the Docks. **#1050.** [$500]. Est. 40 x 70. Unlocated.

GRAVES, **Abbot** (Abbott Fuller). **Boston.**
1859 Weymouth, MA–1936 Kennebunkport, ME
Training— Cambridge, MA: MIT; Paris: Fernand Cormon, Georges Jeannin, Paul Jean Gervais, Acad. Julian (J. P. Laurens).

Poppies. **#1145.** [$400]. Unlocated.

GRAYSON, **Clifford P.** (Clifford Prevost). **Philadelphia.**
1857 Philadelphia, PA–1951 Old Lyme, CT
Training— Philadelphia: PAFA; Paris: Léon Bonnat, Jean-Léon Gérôme, Alfred Phillipe Roll, EcBA.

November. **#616. Lent by the Art Club, Philadelphia.** Unlocated.

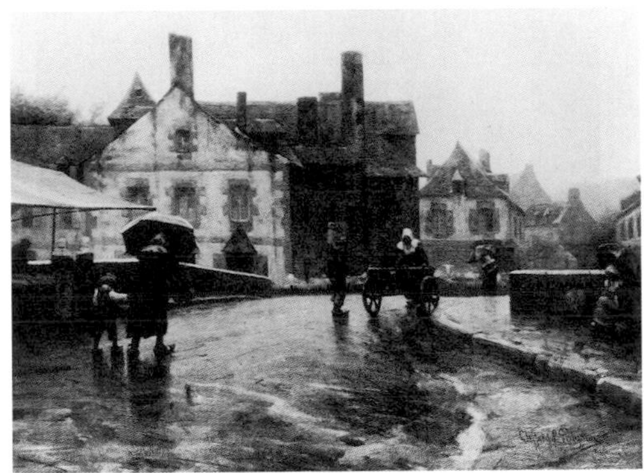

A Rainy Day at Pont Aven. **#814. Lent by Mr. Charles J. Singer, Chicago.** 1882. 41½ x 65. Collection Art Institute of Chicago, 1896. Sold, Grant Art Galleries, Chicago, IL, 1950. Unlocated. Photograph courtesy Sellin Archives.

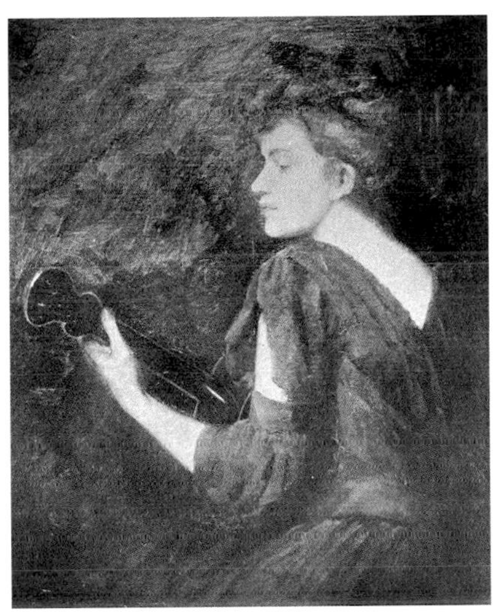

Idle Hours. **#888.** [$300]. ca. 1891. Unlocated. Illus: The Art Club of Philadelphia, *Third Annual Exhibition of Oil Paintings and Sculpture* (Philadelphia: Isaiah Price, 1891), 20.

GREEN, **C. A.** (Caroline A., also Caroline H.). **Brooklyn.**
Unknown–Residing 1902 Brooklyn, NY

Peonies. **#1127.** [$75]. ca. 1891. Unlocated.

GREEN, **Frank Russell. New York.**
1856 Chicago, IL–1940 New York, NY
Training — Paris: Acad. Julian (Gustave Boulanger, Jules Joseph Lefebvre), Acad. Colarossi (Gustave Courtois, Raphaël Collin).

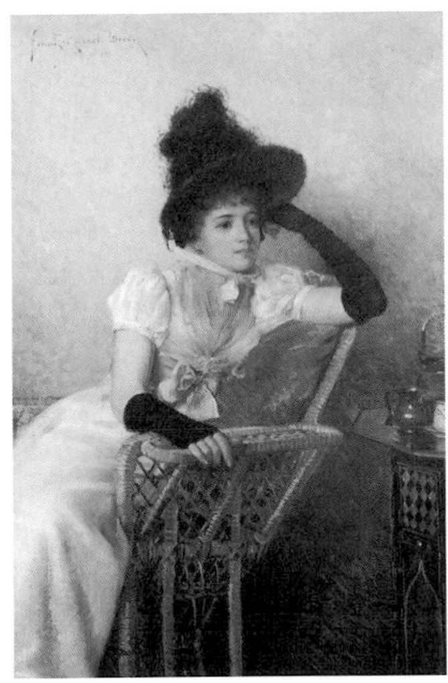

My Sweetheart. **#953. Lent by Mr. Thomas B. Clarke, New York.** n.d. 30 x 20. Private Collection. Photograph by Rolland White.

GREENE, **Lillian. Boston.**[31]
1856 Albany, ME–1940 Waltham, MA
Training — Boston: MFA; Paris: Acad. Julian (Tony Robert-Fleury, Jules Joseph Lefebvre, G. J. M. A. Ferrier).

A Brittany Landscape. **#1240.** [$400]. Est. 38 x 22. Unlocated.

GREENWOOD, **Joseph H. Worcester, Mass.**
1857 Spencer, MA–1927 Worcester, MA
Training — R. Swain Gifford; Boston.

Autumn Oaks. **#273.** [$350]. Est. 20 x 30. Unlocated.

GRENET, **Edward** (Edward Louis). **Levallois-Perret, France.**
1857 San Antonio, TX–1922 Paris, France
Training — New York; Paris: Acad. Julian (William Bouguereau, Tony Robert-Fleury), Alexandre Cabanel.

Forgotten. **#1047.** [$100]. Est. 16 x 18. Unlocated.

Evening Harmony. **#1207.** [$125]. Unlocated.

Portrait Study. **#1277.** [$80]. Est. 6 x 4. Unlocated.

Grandmother's Return. **#1289.** [$100]. Unlocated.

GROSS, P. A. (Peter Alfred). **Paris, France.**

1849 Allentown, PA–1914 Chicago, IL
Training — Paris: E. C. J. Yon, Edmund Marie Petitjean.

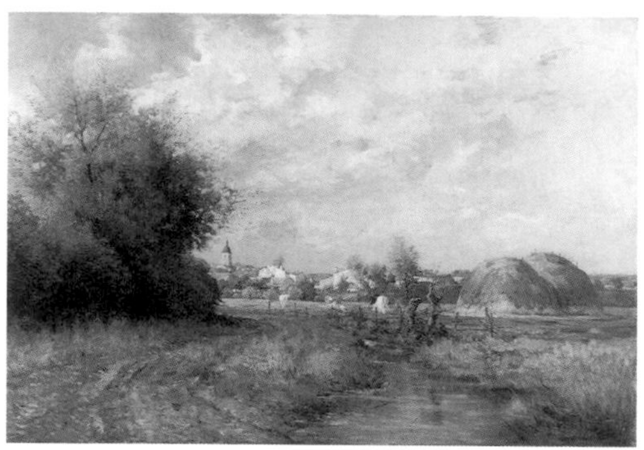

Essegney near Charmes, Vosges. **#361.** [$1000]. *Autumn,* 1892. 55½ x 80. Allentown Art Museum, Gift of the Artist to the City of Allentown, 1909; transferred to Allentown Art Museum in 1959.

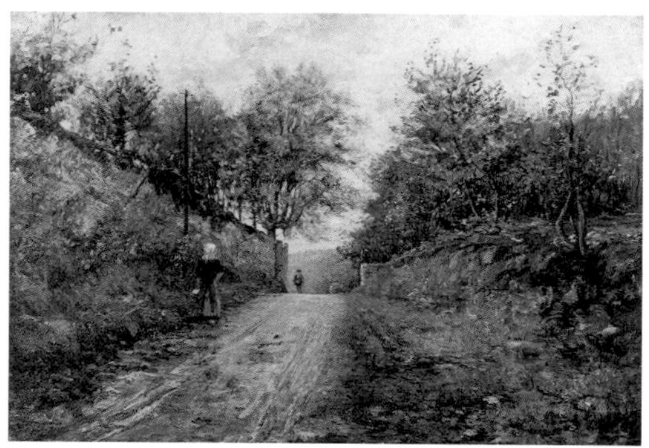

Road to the Spring, Liverdun, France. **#605.** [$500]. n.d. (ca. 1890). 27½ x 39. Collection Mr. and Mrs. Benjamin L. Walbert III, Jim Thorpe, PA.

A Rainy Day. **#620.** [$500]. Unlocated.

GROVER, Oliver Dennett. **Chicago.**

1861 Earlville, IL–1927 Chicago, IL
Training — Chicago: Academy of Design, University of Chicago; Munich: Frank Duveneck, Royal Academy; Paris: Acad. Julian (Gustave Boulanger, Jules Joseph Lefebvre, J. P. Laurens).

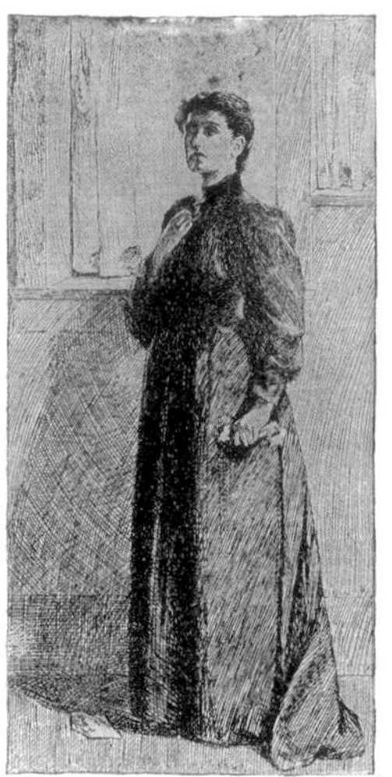

Thy Will Be Done. **#446.** [$1000]. Unlocated. Illus: Trumbull White and William Igleheart, *The World's Columbian Exposition, Chicago, 1893* (Philadelphia and St. Louis: P. W. Ziegler, [1893]), 352. "It represents a young woman in black holding a telegram just received. The expression is of grief tempered by resignation" —*Chicago Tribune,* 11 March 1893.

GUTHERZ, Carl. **St. Paul.**

1844 Schoftland, Switzerland–1907 Washington, DC
Training — Paris: Isodore Pils, Guillaime-Adolphe Cabassan, Acad. Julian (Gustave Boulanger, Jules Joseph Lefebvre); Antwerp; Munich: Royal Academy (Wilhelm von Kaulbach); Rome: Alfonso Simonetti.

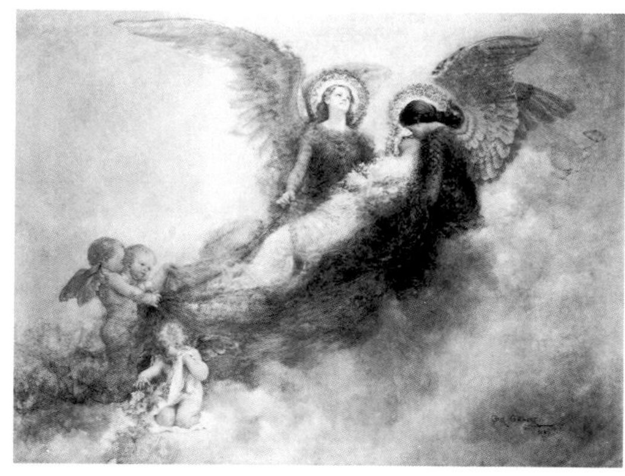

Arcessita ab Angelis. **#319.** [$5000]. 1889. 59¼ x 79¼. Memphis Brooks Museum of Art, Gift of Mr. and Mrs. Marshall F. Goodheart.

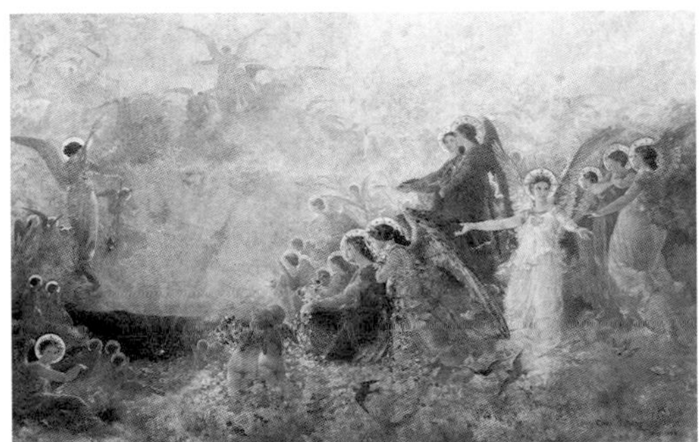

Light of the Incarnation. **#388.** [$10,000]. 1888. 77 x 114. Memphis Brooks Museum of Art, Gift of Mr. and Mrs. Marshall F. Goodheart.

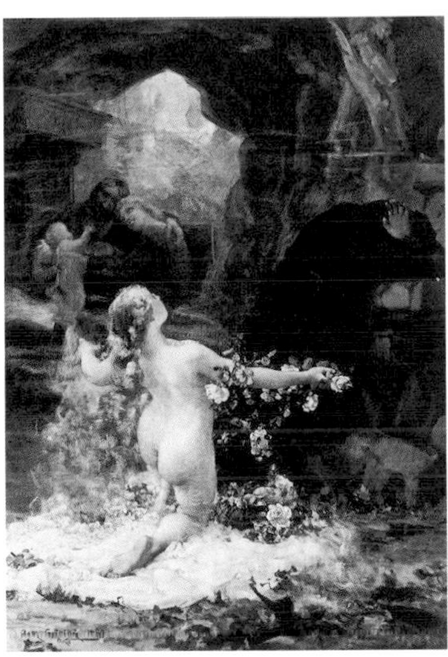

The Temptation of St. Anthony. **#927.** [$3000]. 1890. 54 x 40. Collection Mrs. Marshall Goodheart, Memphis, TN. Photograph courtesy the Memphis Brooks Museum of Art.

HALE, **Ellen Day. Boston.**
1855 Worcester, MA–1940 Brookline, MA
Training — Boston: William Morris Hunt, Helen Knowlton, William Rimmer; Philadelphia: PAFA; Paris: Acad. Colarossi (Raphaël Collin, Gustave Courtois), Acad. Julian (William Bouguereau, Tony Robert-Fleury), Félix-Henri Giacomotti, Jean-Jacques Henner, Carolus-Duran, Pierre-Auguste Cot, Gabrielle de Vaux Clements.

Under the Vine. **#289.** [$200]. Est. 25 x 30. Unlocated.

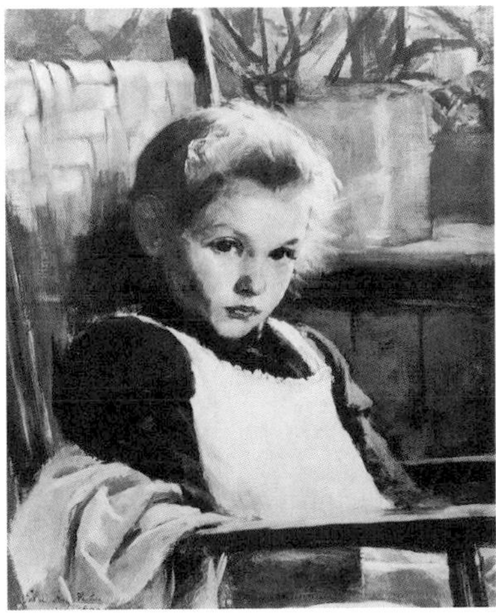

Bessy. **#1190.** [$100]. 1890. 24 x 18. Private Collection. Photograph courtesy Richard York Gallery, New York, NY.

HALE, **Philip** (Philip Leslie). **Paris, France.**
1865 Boston, MA–1931 Boston, MA
Training — Boston: Ellen Day Hale, MFA; New York: ASL (J. Alden Weir); Paris: Acad. Julian, Gustave Boulanger, Jules Joseph Lefebvre, Jean-Joseph Benjamin-Constant.

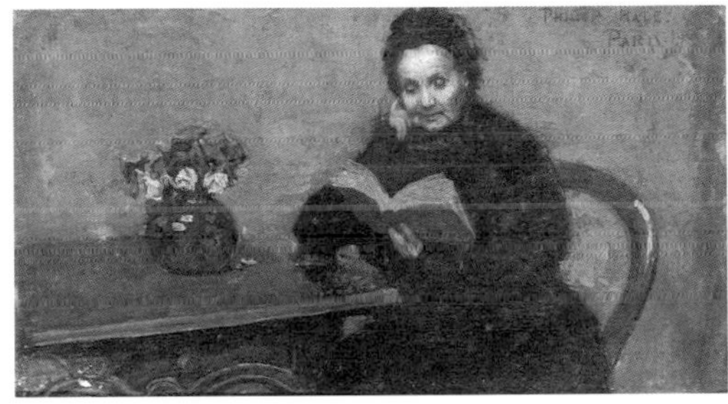

Old Woman Reading. **#1226.** [$100]. **Lent by Rev. E. E. Hale, Roxbury, Mass.** 1890 (oil on panel). 4 15/16 x 8 9/16. Private Collection.

HALLOWELL, **Maria** ("May"/Mrs. Joseph P. Loud). **West Medford, Mass.**
1860 West Medford, MA–1916 West Medford, MA
Training — Boston: MFA, Cowles Art School; Paris: Acad. Julian, Tony Robert-Fleury, Félix-Henri Giacomotti, Louis Deschamps.

Portrait. **#379. Lent by Miss A. N. Hallowell, West Medford, Mass.** Unlocated.

Portrait. **#1208.** [$500]. Unlocated.

HAMILTON, E. W. D. (Edward Wilbur Dean). **Boston.**
1864 Somerfields, PA–1948 Kingston, MA
Training — Paris: Acad. Julian, William Bouguereau, Tony Robert-Fleury, Jean-Jacques Henner, EcBA (Elie Delaunay).

Landscape. **#314.** Unlocated.

Evening. **#1192.** Unlocated.

HAMILTON, **John McLure. London, England.**
1853 Philadelphia, PA–1936 Mandeville, Jamaica
Training — Philadelphia: PAFA; Antwerp: Royal Academy (Jan van Lerius); Paris: Jean-Léon Gérôme.

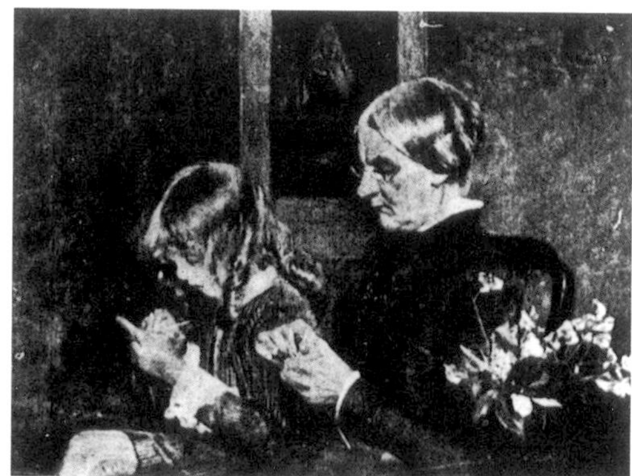

The Knitting Lesson. **#1042.** 1892. Unlocated. Illus: The New York Public Library, *The Artists File* (Alexandria, VA: Chadwyck-Healey, 1989). "Quite a small canvas . . ." — The New York Public Library, *The Artists File* (Alexandria, VA: Chadwyck-Healey, 1989).

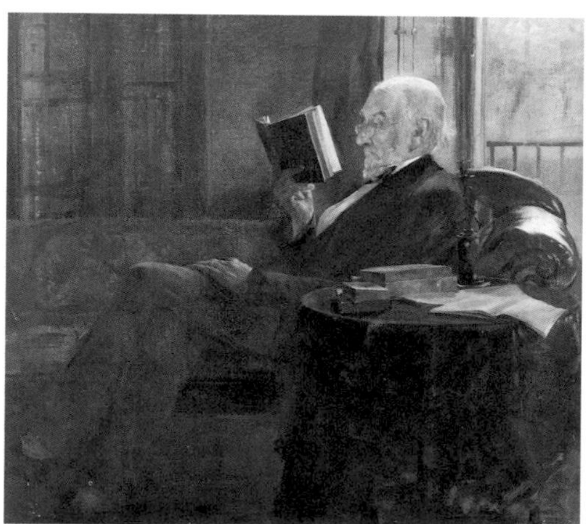

The Rt. Hon. W. E. Gladstone, at Downing Street. **#1154.** *The Right Hon. William Ewart Gladstone at Downing Street,* 1893. 31¼ x 35⅛. Pennsylvania Academy of the Fine Arts, Philadelphia, Henry D. Gilpin Fund.

HAMMER, **John J. New York.**
1838/42 Westhofen, Germany –1906 New York
Training — Munich: Royal Academy (Ludwig von Löfftz, Alexander Wagner).

Spring Flowers. **#1187.** [$500]. ca. 1890. Unlocated.

HARDIE, **Robert Gordon. New York.**
1854 Brattleboro, VT–1904 Brattleboro, VT
Training — New York: NAD; Paris: Jean-Léon Gérôme, Henri Lehmann, Alexandre Cabanel.

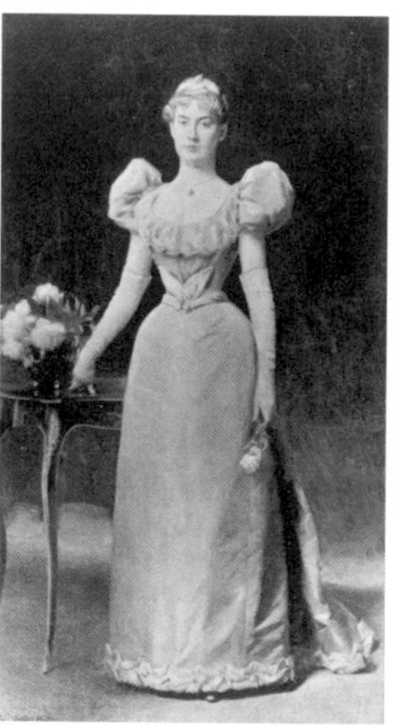

Portrait of the Artist's Wife. **#914.** *Portrait of Catherine Cullom Hardie.*[32] Collection Mr. John Phelps Clark, Guilford, CT. Illus: Charles M. Kurtz, ed., *Illustrations from the Art Gallery of the World's Columbian Exposition* (Philadelphia: G. Barrie, 1893), 335.

HARPER, **W. St. John** (William St. John). **Easthampton, L.I.**
1851 Rhinebeck, NY–1910 New York, NY
Training — Brooklyn: Brooklyn Art School (John Barnard Whittaker); New York: NAD (Lemuel E. Wilmarth), William Merritt Chase, Walter Shirlaw; Paris: Léon Bonnat, Mihaly Munkacsy.

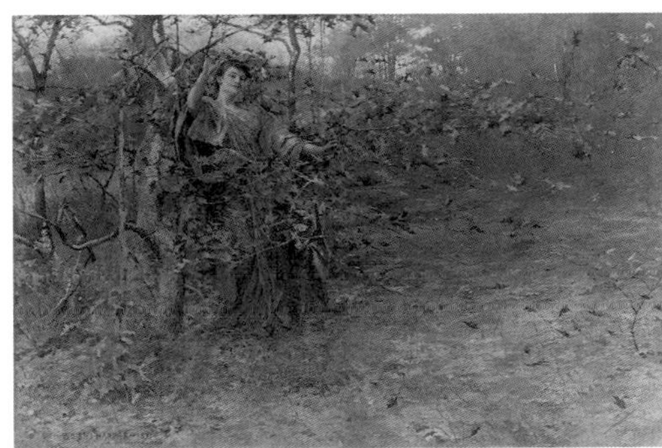

Autumn, Easthampton. **#1217. Lent by Mr. W. T. Evans, New York.** 1891. 30⅜ x 44. Private Collection, Princeton, NJ.

HARRIS, Charles X. (Charles Xavier). **New York.**
1856 Foxcroft, ME–During/After 1934[33]
Training — Paris: Alexander Cabanel.

The Mowers. **#555. Lent by Mr. Frederick James, New York.** Unlocated.

HARRISON, Alexander (Thomas Alexander). **Paris, France.**
1853 Philadelphia, PA–1930 Paris, France
Training —Philadelphia: PAFA; San Francisco: California School of Design (Virgil Williams, Raymond Yelland); Paris: Acad. Julian, Jean-Léon Gérôme, Jules Bastien-Lepage.

Marine. **#317.** [$2000]. Unlocated. "A small 'Marine'. . ." —Henry D. Northrop, *The World's Fair as Seen in One Hundred Days* (Philadelphia: Ariel Book Co., 1893), 293.

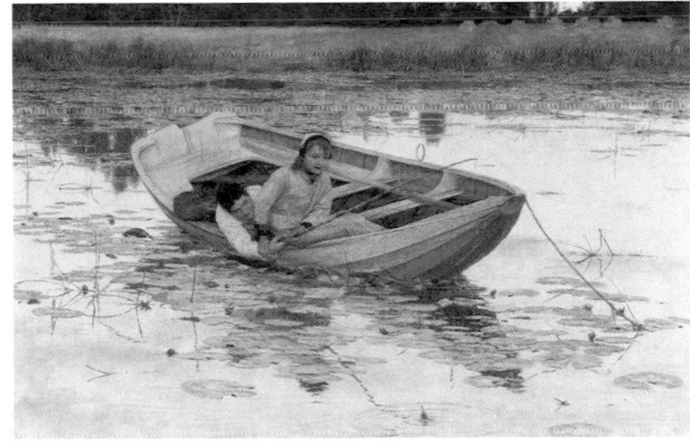

******The Amateurs.* **#635.** 1882–83. 58 5/16 x 90. Sloan Collection of American Paintings, Valparaiso University Museum of Art, Bequest of Percy H. Sloan.

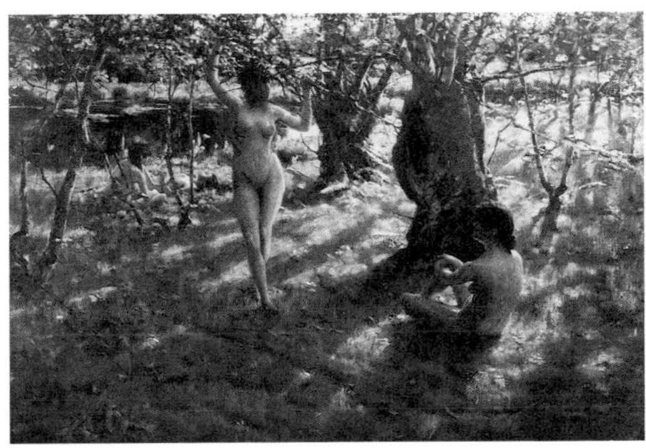

In Arcadia. **#802.** [$10,000]. *En Arcadie,* 1885. 77½ x 114¼. Musée d'Orsay.

The Bathers. **#806.** Unlocated. "'The Bathers,' by Alexander Harrison, represents a number of women, in the water or on the sand, beckoning to each other and enjoying themselves to their hearts' content in nature's garb and in communion with nature. The coloring is excellent, especially that of the water, for in his rendition of moving waters and the play of light upon them Harrison has no superior. Beautiful is the glow of the setting sun reflected from the tranquil waves, whose aspect suggests the majesty of ocean even in its restful mood. These gently curling billows and the foam that crests them seem to be permeated with light . . ." —Hubert H. Bancroft, *The Book of the Fair,* vol. 3 (Chicago: Blakely Printing Co., 1893), 681; "A new 'Bathers,' — the same scene [long lines of summer waves breaking on the beach] and nearly the same evening hour but enlivened by the presence of five or six young women, some of whom splash each other in the knee deep water while two sit on the sand and look on" — William Walton, *Art and Architecture,* vol. 1 (Philadelphia: G. Barrie, 1893–95), 19.

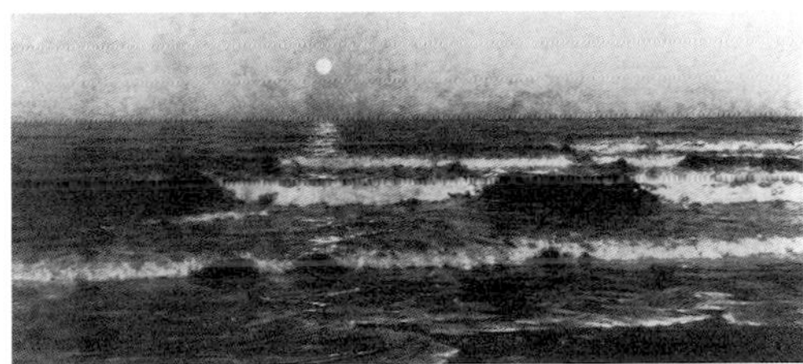

Twilight. **#807. Lent by the St. Louis Museum of Fine Arts.** *Le Crêpuscule,* 1885. 59 x 126. Collection Washington University, St. Louis, MO, by 1924. Sold, Selkirk's, St. Louis, MO, 1946. Unlocated. Illus: *Brush and Pencil* (June 1899): 141.

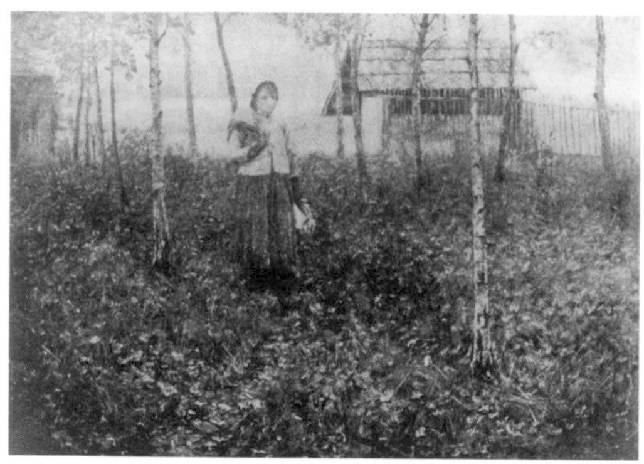

A Misty Morning. **#1105.** [$1600]. ca. 1884. Unlocated. Illus: *International Studio* (June 1912): 280. "A charming wood interior of yellowish tone" —*The Nation,* 10 Aug. 1893, 97.

HARRISON, Birge (Lowell Birge). **Paris, France.**
1854 Philadelphia, PA–1929 Woodstock, NY
Training— Philadelphia: PAFA; Paris: Carolus-Duran, EcBA (Alexandre Cabanel).

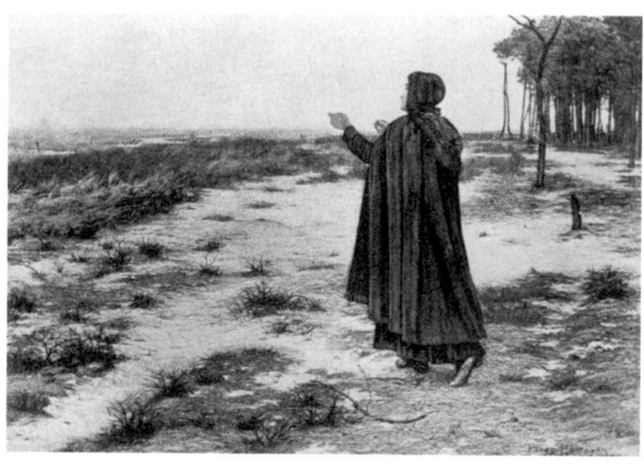

The Return of the Mayflower. **#506.** [$1100]. 1887. 67 x 96½. Swarthmore College, Swarthmore, PA. Illus: Ripley Hitchcock, *The Art of the World* 1 (New York: Appleton, 1895), 60.

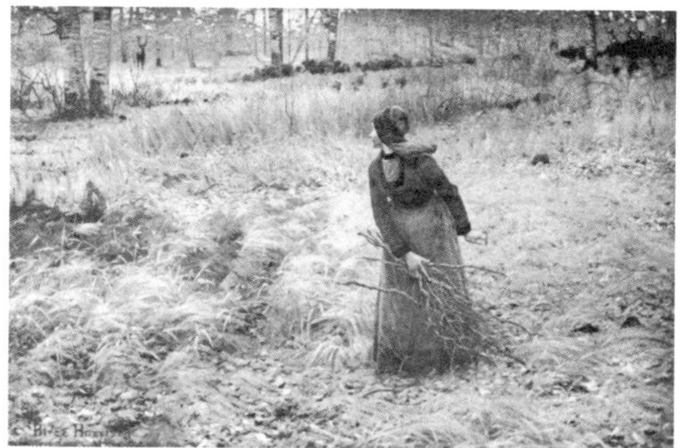

A Surprise in the Forest of Compiègne. **#813.** [$750]. ca. 1888. Est. 55 x 75. Unlocated. Illus: The Art Club of Philadelphia, *Second Special Exhibition* (Philadelphia: Gebbie, 1890), 70. "Has for its scene the forest of Compiegne in autumn tide, the ground covered with russet leaves, of which only a few remain on the branches above. A peasant girl is gathering wood, and glancing upward for a moment sees an antlered stag within a few rods of where she stands. They are looking at each other, and admirable is the expression of astonishment and fear in the face of each, for both girl and stag are thoroughly alarmed, and a moment later will be running from each other as fast as their limbs will carry them" —Hubert H. Bancroft, *The Book of the Fair,* vol. 3 (Chicago: Blakely Printing Co., 1893), 683.

HARTWICH, Herman (also Herman Hartwick). **Munich, Bavaria.**
1853 New York, NY–1926 Munich, Germany
Training— George Hartwich; Munich: Royal Academy (Wilhelm Diez, Ludwig von Löfftz).

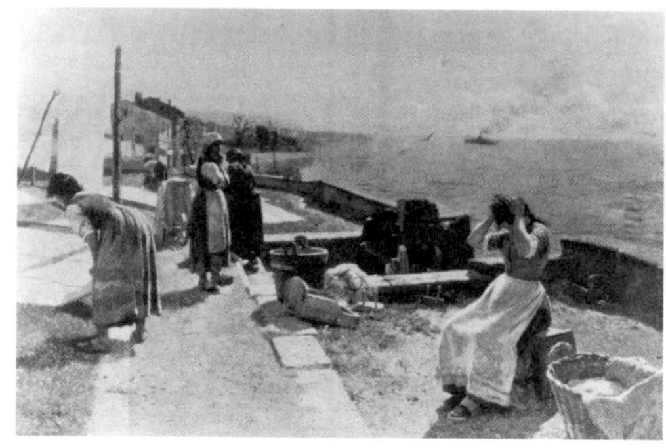

A Bleachery in Lombardy. **#795.** [$5000]. ca. 1892. 51 x 75. Sold, American Art Association, New York, NY, 4 April 1929, lot 95. Unlocated. Illus: American Art Association, *Oil Paintings, Fine Canvases by Distinguished European and American Artists, Collections Formed by the Late Hermon Simon and by Mirabeau L. Towns with Additions* (New York, 1929), 53.

HARWOOD, J. T. (James Taylor). **Salt Lake City.**
1860 Lehi, UT–1940 Salt Lake City, UT
Training— Salt Lake City: Alfred Lambourne, Danquart A. Weggeland; San Franciso: California School of Design (Virgil Williams); Paris: Léon Bonnat, Acad. Julian (Jean-Joseph Benjamin-Constant, Jules Joseph Lefebvre, Henri-Lucien Doucet).

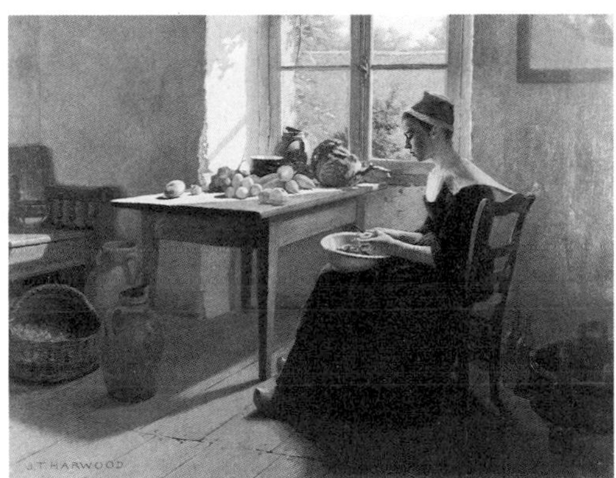

Preparing Dinner.* **#366. [$1000]. *Preparations for Dinner,* 1891. 37½ x 50. University of Utah Union Collection/Utah Museum of Fine Arts, University of Utah.

HASBROUCK, **D. F.** (DuBois Fenelon). **New York.**
1860 Pine Hill, NY–1917 Stamford, NY
Training — self-taught.

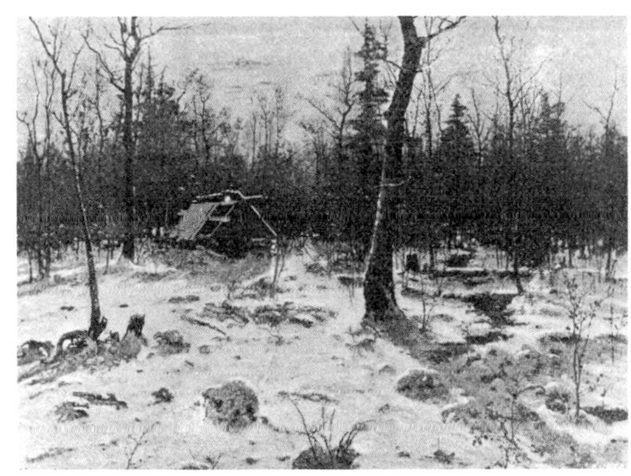

A Winter Morning in the Catskills. **#870.** [$3000]. **Lent by Mr. E. W. Gillett, Chicago.** 1888. 34½ x 45½. Unlocated. Illus: Charles M. Kurtz, ed., *National Academy Notes and Complete Catalogue, Sixty-third Spring Exhibition, National Academy of Design, New York* (New York: Cassell & Co., 1888), 29.

HASKELL, **Ida C. New York.**
1861 Cumberland, CA–1932 Brookhaven, NY
Training — Chicago: Academy of Design; Philadelphia: PAFA; New York: ASL; Paris: Gustave Courtois, Jean-André Rixens, Acad. Julian (William Bouguereau, Gustave Boulanger, P. A. J. Dagnan-Bouveret, Jules Joseph Lefebvre).

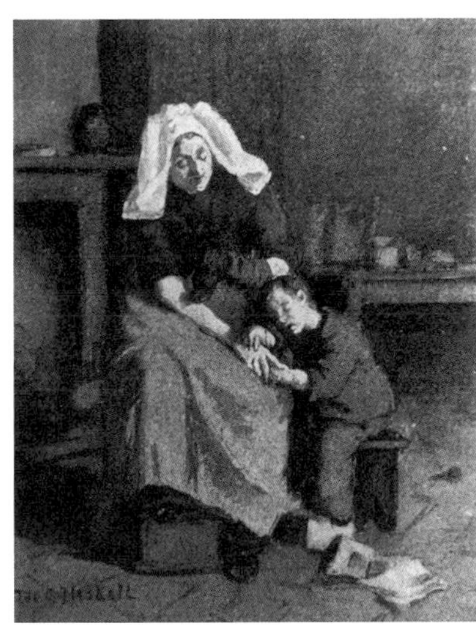

Mother Love. **#404.** [$250]. Est. 28 x 25. Unlocated. Illus (as *Where Trouble Ends*): *The Quarterly Illustrator* 2 (Apr.–June 1894): 119.

---

† HASSAM, **Childe** (Frederick Childe). **New York.**
1859 Boston, MA–1935 East Hampton, NY
Training — Boston: I. M. Gaugengigl, Boston Art Club, Lowell School of Practical Drawing; Paris: Acad. Julian (Gustave Boulanger, Jules Joseph Lefebvre, Henri-Lucien Doucet).

Mid-summer Morning. **#326.** Unlocated.[34]

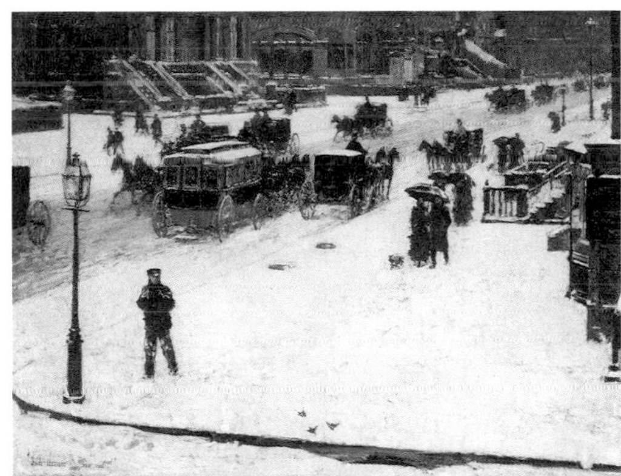

A Snowy Day on Fifth Avenue, New York. **#337.** [$1200]. *Fifth Avenue in Winter,* n.d. (ca. 1892). 21⅝ x 28. The Carnegie Museum of Art, Pittsburgh, Purchase.

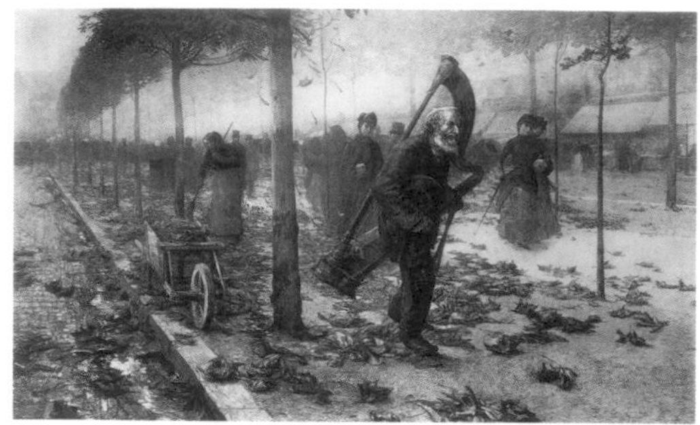

Autumn. **#666.** 1888–89. 118 wd. Sold, American Art Association, New York, NY, 6–7 Feb. 1896, lot 205. Unlocated. Illus: George W. Sheldon, *Recent Ideals of American Art* (New York: Appleton, 1890), opposite 148.

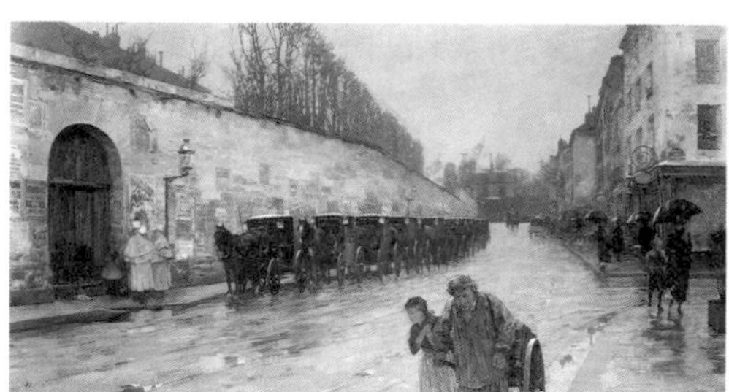

Cab Station, Rue Bonaparte, Paris.* **#833. 1887. 40¼ x 77¼. Collection Gloria Manney.

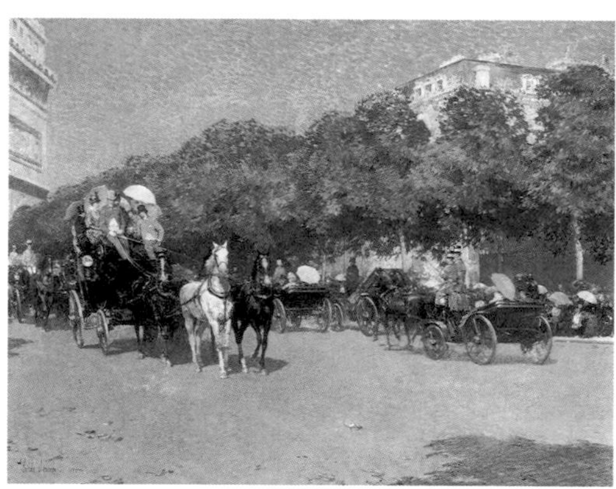

On the Way to the Grand Prix.* **#931. [$1500]. *Le Jour du Grand Prix,* 1888. 36 x 48. From the collection of the New Britain Museum of American Art, Connecticut (Grace Judd Landers Fund).

HATFIELD, J. H. (Joseph Henry). **Canton Junction, Mass.**
1863 Kingston, Ontario–1928 Canton Junction, MA
Training— Paris: Acad. Julian (Jean-Joseph Benjamin-Constant, Henri-Lucien Doucet, Jules Joseph Lefebvre).

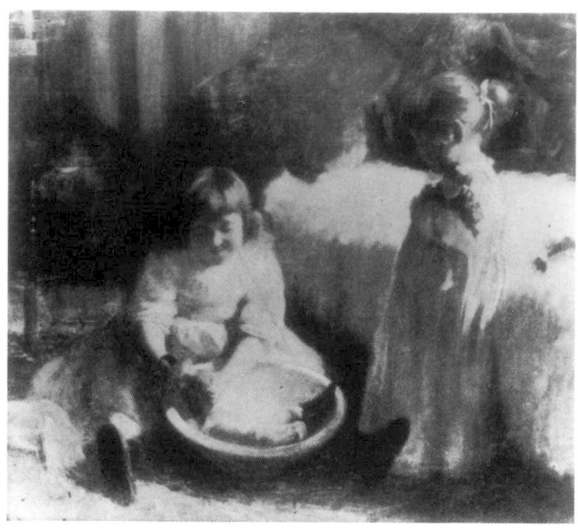

The Doll's Bath. **#1065.** [$1000]. ca. 1891. Unlocated. Illus: William H. Downes, "New England Art at the World's Fair," *New England Magazine* 8 (July 1893): 362.

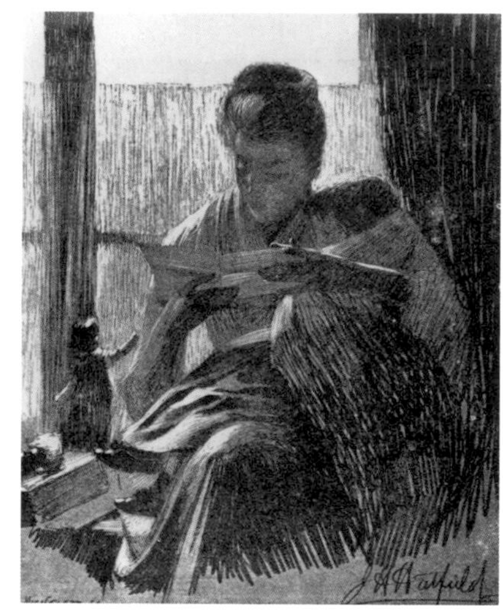

A Letter from Papa. **#1219.** [$1000]. ca. 1891. Unlocated. Illus: Ludovic Baschet, ed., *Catalogue Illustré de Peinture et Sculpture, Salon de 1891* (Paris: Georges Chamerot, 1891), 155. "Misty . . . something of the true ring of sentiment in it . . ." —*Boston Daily Evening Transcript,* 19 Jan. 1893; "A sweet home scene, mother and child, and doll in the window" —*Canton Journal,* n.d.

HAYDEN, Charles H. (Charles Henry). **Boston.**
1856 Plymouth, MA–1901 Belmont, MA
Training— John B. Johnston; Boston: MFA (Otto Grundmann); Paris: Raphaël Collin, Acad. Julian (Gustave Boulanger, Jules Joseph Lefebvre).

Cattle and Landscape. **#275.** [$400]. Est. 25 x 30. Unlocated.

Pasture Land, Connecticut. **#303.** [$1000]. Est. 40 x 60. Unlocated.

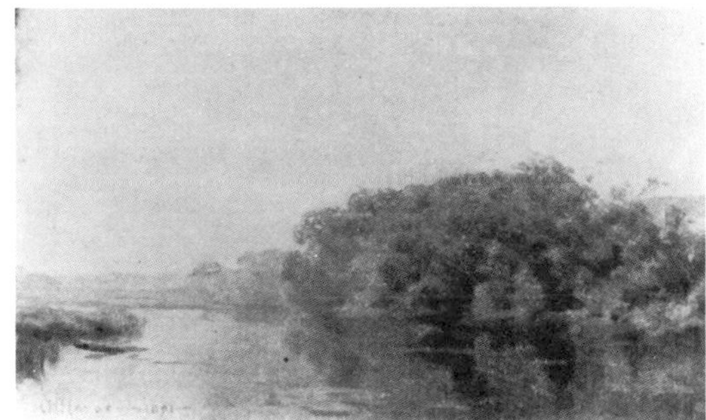

A Quiet Morning, October. **#348.** [$400]. 1891. Est. 25 x 40. Unlocated. Illus: William H. Downes, "New England Art at the World's Fair," *New England Magazine* 8 (July 1893): 360.

HAYDEN, Edward Parker.
1858 Haydenville, OH–1921 Haydensville, MA
Training — William L. Picknell; New York: ASL.

October Sunlight. **#895.** [$600]. Unlocated.

HAYNES, C. Coventry (Caroline Coventry). **New York.**
1857/58 New York, NY–1951 New York, NY
Training — New York: ASL; Paris: Alfred Stevens, Gustave Courtois.

Poplars. **#549.** [$75]. ca. 1891. Unlocated.

Portrait. **#652. Lent by Mrs. F. W. Haynes.** Est. 31 x 19. Unlocated.[35]

At Home. **#1055.** [$130]. 26 x 18. Unlocated.

HEALY, G. P. A. (George Peter Alexander). **Chicago.**
1813 Boston, MA–1894 Chicago, IL
Training — Paris: Baron Gros, Thomas Couture.

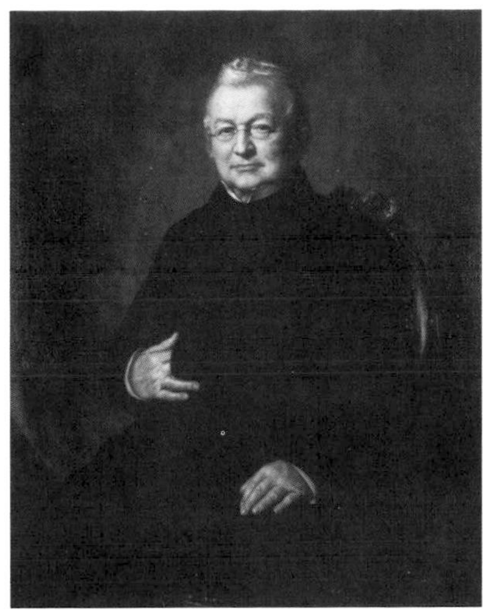

Portrait of Adolphe Thiers. **#1144. Lent by the Newberry Library, Chicago.** 1874. 42 x 36. The Newberry Library.

HEBERER, Charles. St. Louis.
St. Louis, MO–Unknown
Training — St. Louis: School of Fine Arts; Paris: Gustave Boulanger, Henri-Lucien Doucet, Felix de Vuillefroy, Acad. Julian (Jules Joseph Lefebvre, Jean-Joseph Benjamin-Constant).

The End of November. **#308.** [$400]. Est. 40 x 60. Unlocated.

HELMOLD, Adele von (Mrs. Read). **Philadelphia.**
1858 Philadelphia, PA Residing 1931 Landsdowne, PA
Training — William Merritt Chase; Philadelphia: PAFA (Thomas Anshutz).

Marigolds. **#964.** [$125]. Unlocated.

HENRY, Edward L. (Edward Lamson). **New York.**
1841 Charleston, SC–1919 Ellenville, NY
Training — Philadelphia: Paul Weber, PAFA; New York: William Oddi; Paris: Charles Louis Suisse, Charles Gleyre, Gustave Courbet, Acad. Julian (Tony Robert-Fleury, Jean-Joseph Benjamin-Constant).

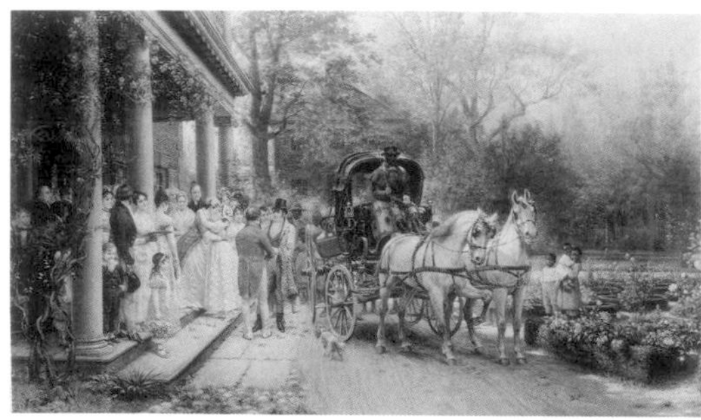

The Wedding Day. **#441. Lent by Mr. Dickinson, Mt. Holyoke, Mass.** *A Virginia Wedding,* 1890. 21½ x 36. Private Collection. Photograph courtesy The R. W. Norton Art Gallery, Shreveport, LA.

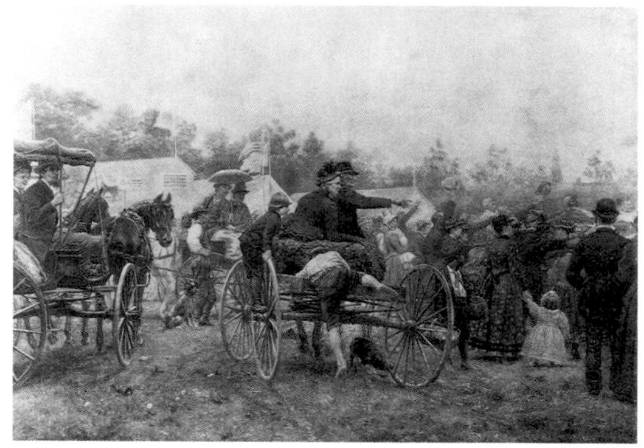

The County Fair. **#493. Lent by Mr. W. F. Havemeyer, New York.** 1891. Est. 18 x 26. Unlocated. Illus: John C. Ridpath, ed., *Art and Artists of All Nations* (New York: Arkell Weekly Company, 1894), 29.

HERTER, **Albert. New York.**
1871 New York, NY–1950 Santa Barbara, CA
Training — New York: ASL (J. Carroll Beckwith); Paris: Acad. Julian (J. P. Laurens), Fernand Cormon, Albert Besnard.

Portrait of Mrs. H. (Adele McGinnis Herter). **#360.** Unlocated.

HESS, **Lydia Purdy** (Mrs. Charles Doak Lowry). **Chicago.**
ca. 1866 Newago, MI–1936 Chicago, IL
Training — Chicago: AIC; Paris: Charles Lasar, Georges Laugée, Paul-Louis Delance.

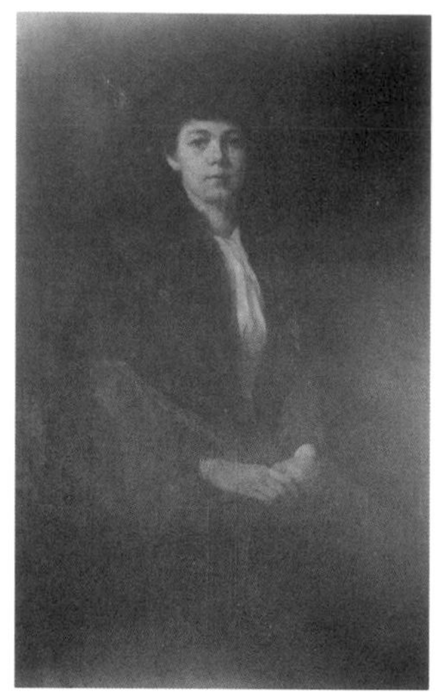

Portrait of Miss E. H. **#1270. Lent by Miss Ena Hutchison, Mineral Point, Wis.** *Miss Ena Hutchison,* n.d. 47¼ x 30. Mineral Point Historical Society, Mineral Point, WI. Photograph by Patrick Ripp.

HETZEL, **George. Pittsburg.**
1826 Alsace, France–1899 Pittsburgh, PA
Training — Dusseldorf: Royal Academy.

Wood Scene. **#478.** [$150]. Est. 18 x 27. Unlocated.

Study from Nature. **#1200.** [$150]. Unlocated.

HILL, **Roswell S.** (Roswell Stone). **New York.**
1861 Lawrence, KS–1907 Bridgeport, CT
Training — New York: ASL; Paris: Jean-Léon Gérôme, Acad. Julian (William Bouguereau, G. J. M. A. Ferrier).

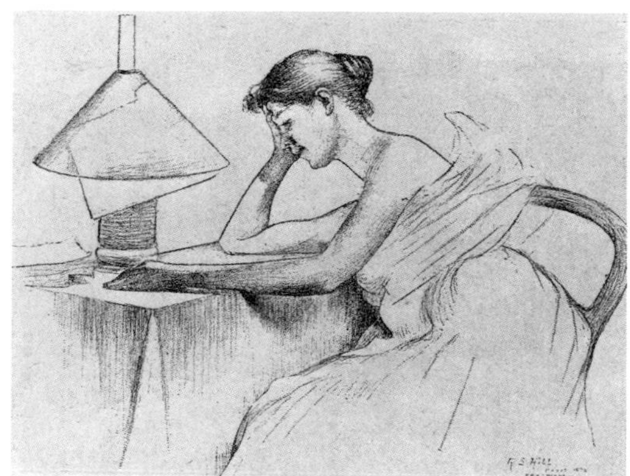

Young Girl Reading. **#1032.** [$800]. ca. 1892. Destroyed in studio fire. Illus: Ludovic Baschet, ed. *Catalogue illustré de peinture et sculpture, Salon de 1892* (Paris, 1892), 196.

HIPPLE, Sarah Levis (Sarah P. Levis/Mrs. Frank K. Hipple). **Philadelphia.**
Philadelphia, PA–Residing 1901 Philadelphia, PA
Training — Philadelphia: PAFA, The Philadelphia School of Design for Women; Paris: Harry Thompson.

Sardine Fishing Boats. **#623. Lent by Mrs. F. K. Hipple, Philadelphia.** ca. 1887. Unlocated.

The Road to Puteaux. **#842. Lent by Mrs. F. K. Hipple, Philadelphia.** Unlocated.

† **HITCHCOCK, George.**
1850 Providence, RI–1913 Island of Marken, the Netherlands
Training — The Hague: Royal Academy (Hendrik Willem Mesdag); Paris: Acad. Julian (Gustave Boulanger, Jules Joseph Lefebvre); London; Dusseldorf.

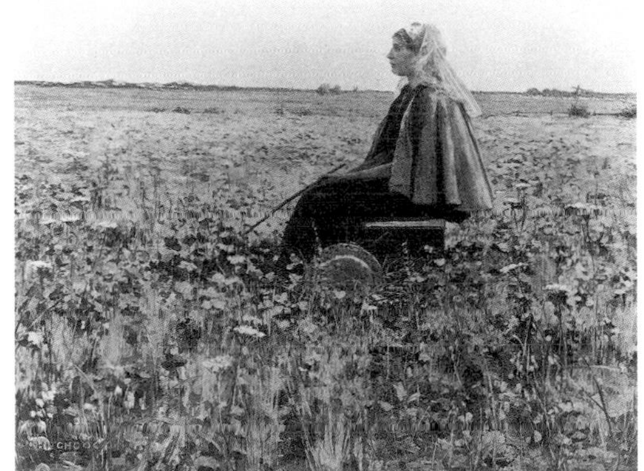

The Scarecrow. **#292.** 51¼ x 65. Repainted by the artist as *The Poppy Field.*[36] Illus: Daniel H. Burnham, *The Art of the World,* vol. 6 (New York: Appleton, 1893–95).

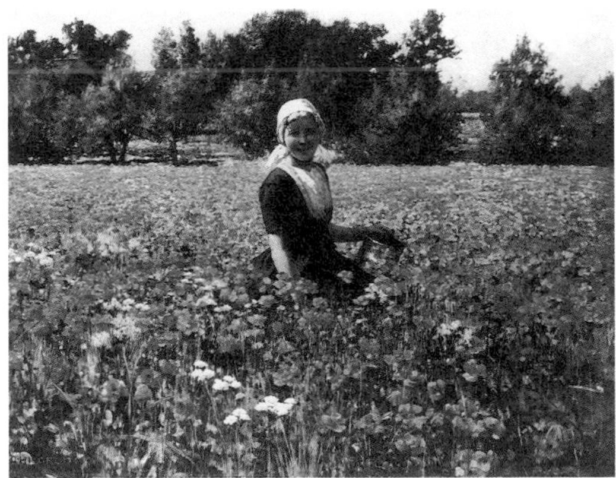

The Poppy Field, n.d. 51¼ x 65. Collection Richard L. Fisher, New York.

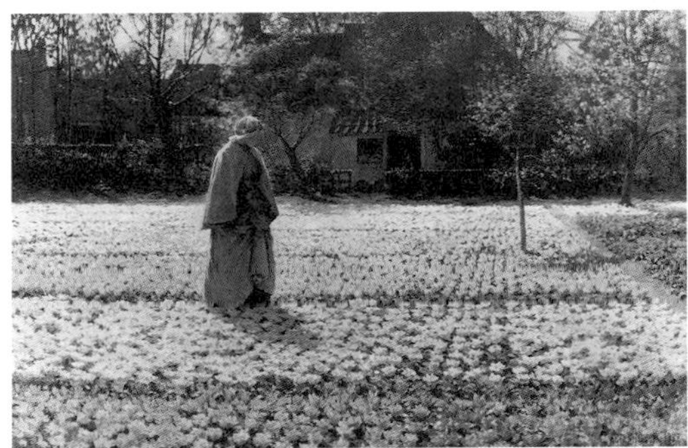

Tulip Culture, Holland.* **#532. 1887. 43 x 66. Private Collection.

HITCHCOCK, Lucius (Lucius Wolcott). **Paris, France.**
1868 West Williamsfield, OH–1942 New Rochelle, NY
Training — New York: ASL; Paris: Acad. Julian (Jean-Joseph Benjamin-Constant, J. P. Laurens, Jules Joseph Lefebvre), Acad. Colarossi.

Summer. **#343.** [$1000]. Est. 85 x 50. Unlocated.

HODGKINS, Belle D. Salem, Mass.
Unknown–Residing 1909 Gloucester, MA

Low Tide at Annisquam. **#1103.** [$30]. Unlocated.

HOLMAN, Frank (Samuel Francis). **Paris, France.**
1865 Attleboro, MA–1930 Paris, France
Training — New York: NAD; Paris: Alexandre Cabanel, Carolus-Duran.

Venice. **#1141.** [$250]. Unlocated.

Young Warrior. **#1155.** [$300]. Est. 9 x 18. Unlocated.

HOLME, Lucy D. Philadelphia.
1848 Salem County, NJ–1928 Salem, NJ
Training — Philadelphia: PAFA (Thomas Eakins); Paris.

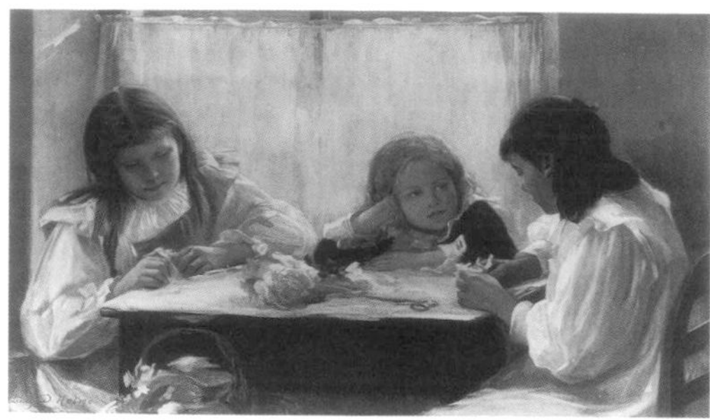

A Holiday Occupation. **#386.** [$600]. n.d. (ca. 1892–93). 28½ x 49. Salem County Historical Society.

---

† **HOMER, Winslow. Scarboro, Me.**
1836 Boston, MA–1910 Prout's Neck, ME
Training — Frederic Rondel, J. H. Buford; New York: NAD; Brooklyn: Brooklyn Art School.

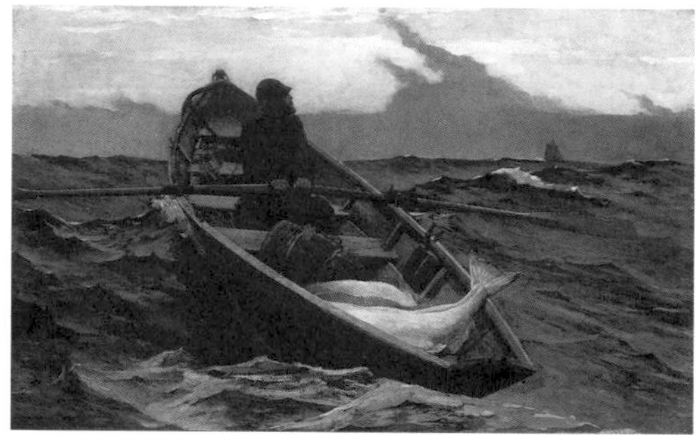

The Fog Warning.* **#423. 1885. 30 x 48. Museum of Fine Arts, Boston, Otis Norcross Fund.

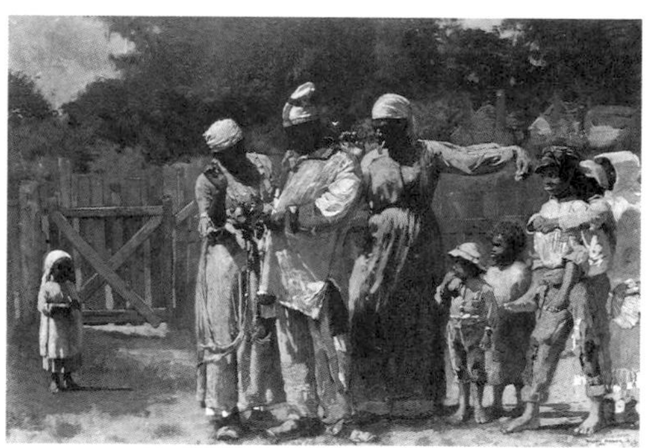

Dressing for the Carnival. **#459. Lent by Mr. Thomas B. Clarke, New York.** 1877. 20 x 30. The Metropolitan Museum of Art, Amelia B. Lazarus Fund, 1922.

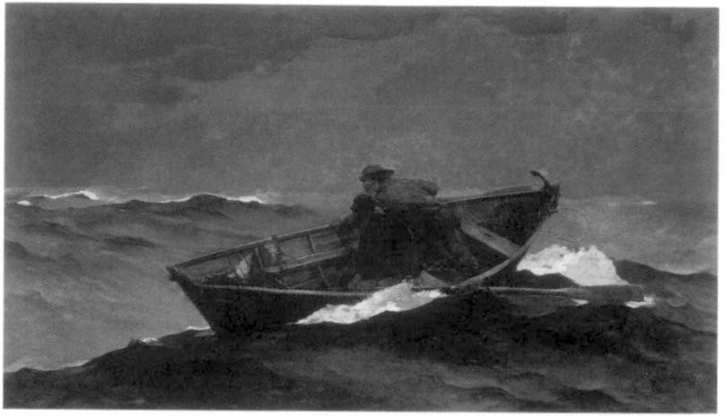

Lost on the Grand Banks. **#693.** 1885. 30½ x 49⅜. Los Angeles County Museum of Art, lent by Mr. and Mrs. John S. Broome.

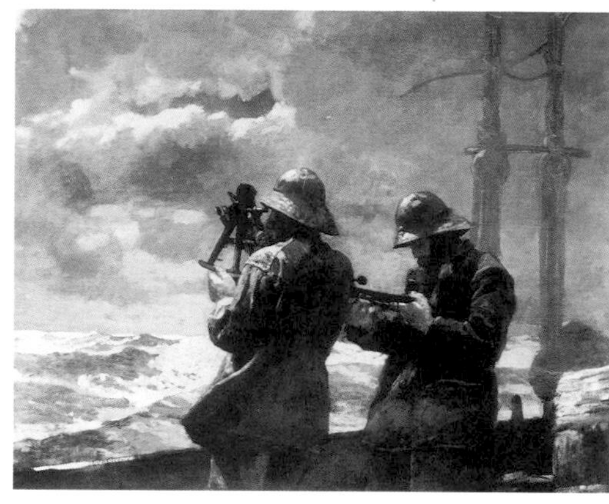

Eight Bells. **#789. Lent by Mr. Thomas B. Clarke, New York.** 1886. 25¼ x 30⅛. ©Addison Gallery of American Art, Phillips Academy, Andover, MA, Gift of anonymous donor. All rights reserved.

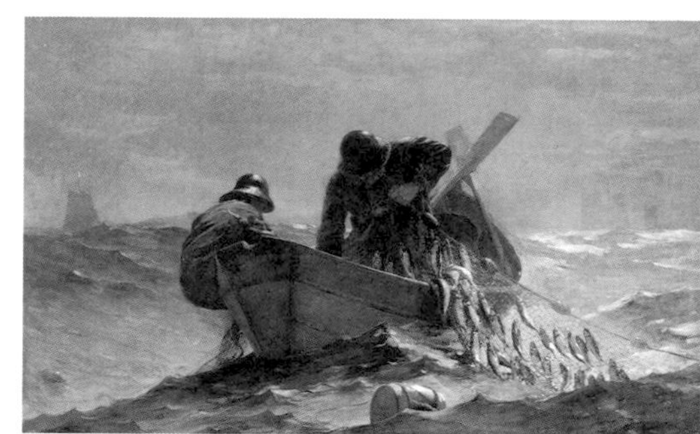

Herring Fishing. **#860.** *The Herring Net,* 1885. 30⅛ x 48⅜. The Art Institute of Chicago, Mr. and Mrs. Martin A. Ryerson Collection.

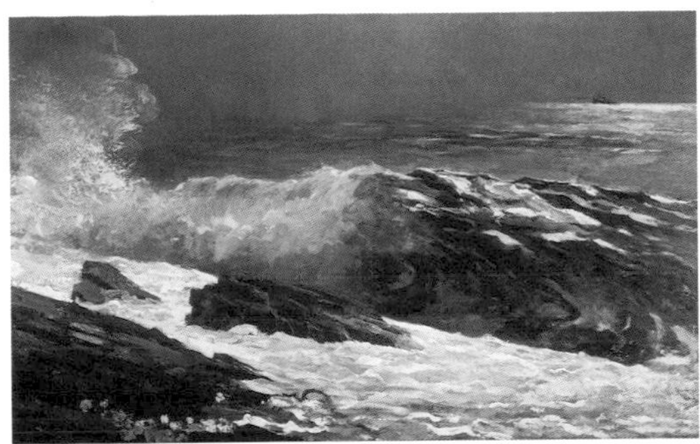

Sunlight on the Coast. **#1070. Lent by Mr. John G. Johnson, Philadelphia.** 1890. 30 x 40. The Toledo Museum of Art, Gift of Edward Drummond Libbey.

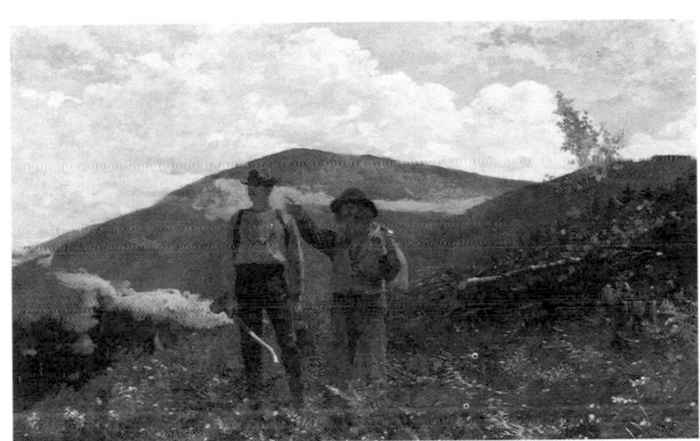

The Two Guides.* **#1081. Lent by Mr. Thomas B. Clarke, New York. 1875?. 24¼ x 38¼. Sterling and Francine Clark Art Institute, Williamstown, MA.

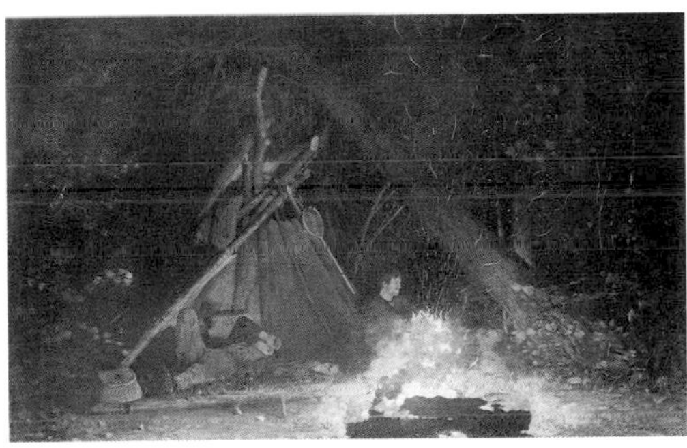

The Camp Fire. **#1106. Lent by Mr. Thomas B. Clarke, New York.** *Camp Fire,* 1880. 23¾ x 38⅛. The Metropolitan Museum of Art, Gift of Henry Keney Pomeroy, 1927.

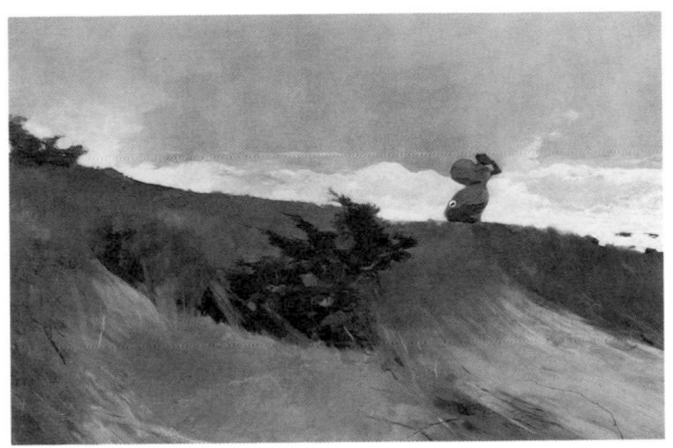

March Wind.* **#1108. Lent by Mr. Thomas B. Clarke, New York. *The West Wind,* 1891. 30 x 44. ©Addison Gallery of American Art, Phillips Academy, Andover, MA, Gift of anonymous donor. All rights reserved.

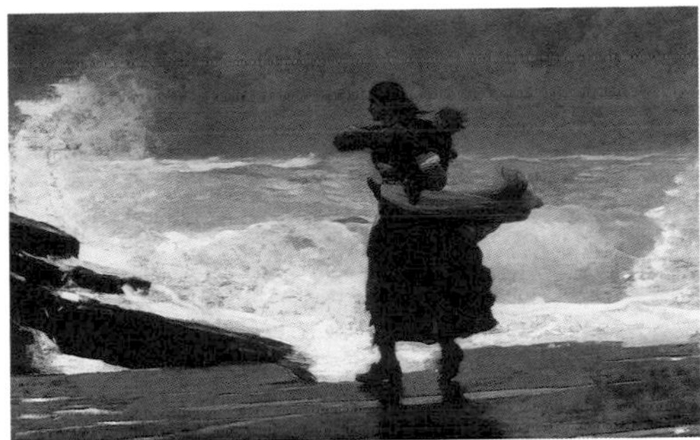

A Great Gale. **#1112. Lent by Mr. Thomas B. Clarke, New York.** *The Gale,* 1893. 30¼ x 48⅜. Worcester Art Museum, Worcester, MA.

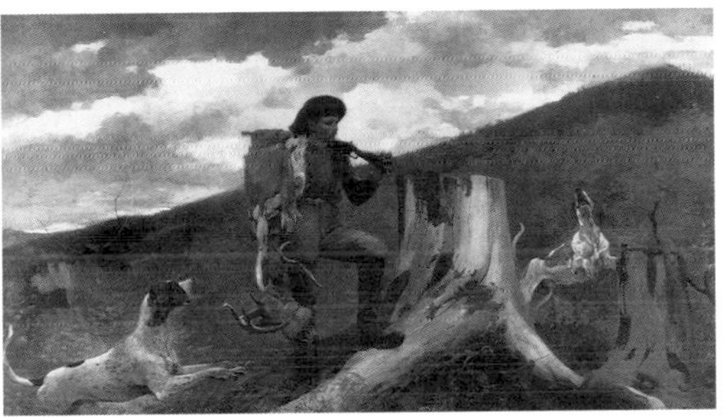

The Return from the Hunt. **#1116. Lent by Messrs. Reichard & Co., New York.** *Huntsman and Dogs,* 1891. 28 x 48. Philadelphia Museum of Art, The William L. Elkins Collection.

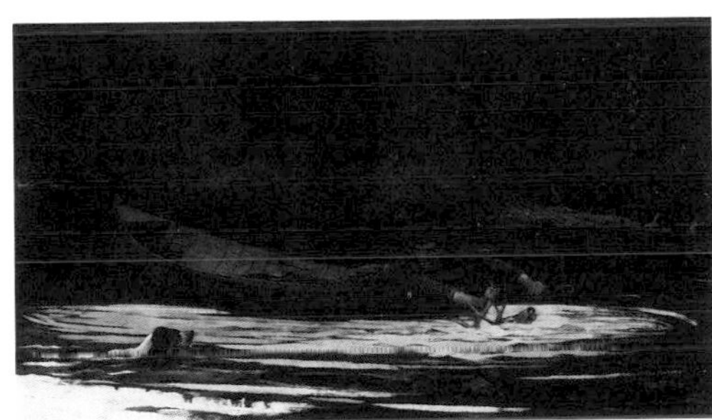

Hound and Hunter. **#1118.** 1892. 28¼ x 48⅛. National Gallery of Art, Washington, Gift of Stephen C. Clark.

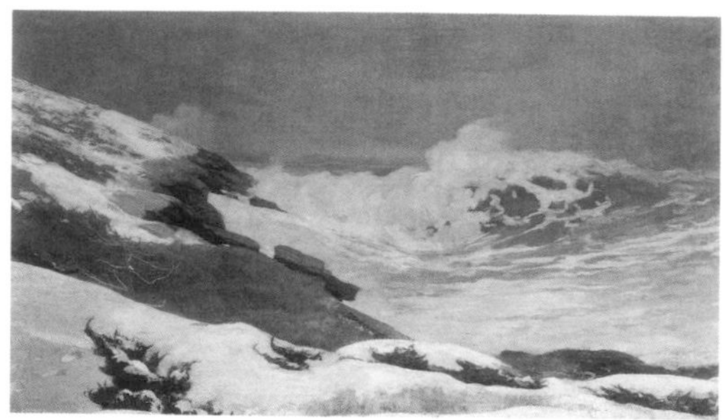

Maine Coast in Winter. **#1119. Lent by Mr. Thomas B. Clarke, New York.** 1892. 28⅜ x 48⅜. Worcester Art Museum, Worcester, MA.

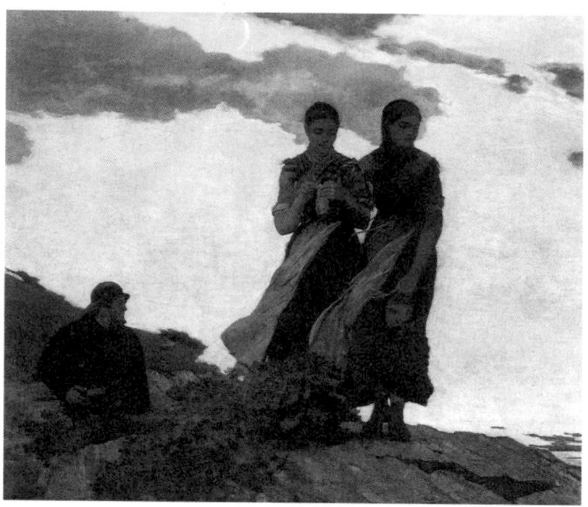

Sailors Take Warning (Sunset). **#1124.** ca. 1881. Repainted by the artist as *Early Evening,* 1907.[37] 33 x 38¾. Freer Gallery of Art, Smithsonian Institution.

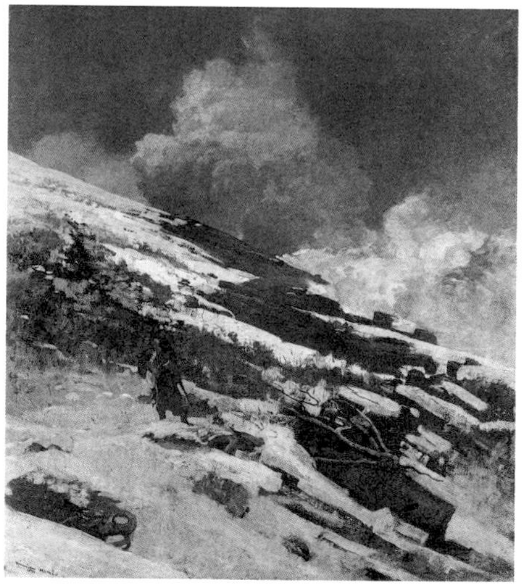

Coast in Winter. **#1137. Lent by John G. Johnson, Philadelphia.** 1890. 36 x 31⅝. Philadelphia Museum of Art, The John G. Johnson Collection.

HORSFALL, **Bruce** (Robert Bruce). **Clinton, Iowa.**

1868 Clinton, IA–1948 Long Branch, NJ
Training — Cincinnati: Art Academy of Cincinnati (L. C. Lutz, Thomas Noble); Munich: Royal Academy (Nikolaus Gysis); Paris: Acad. Colarossi, Acad. Julian (William Bouguereau, G. J. M. A. Ferrier).

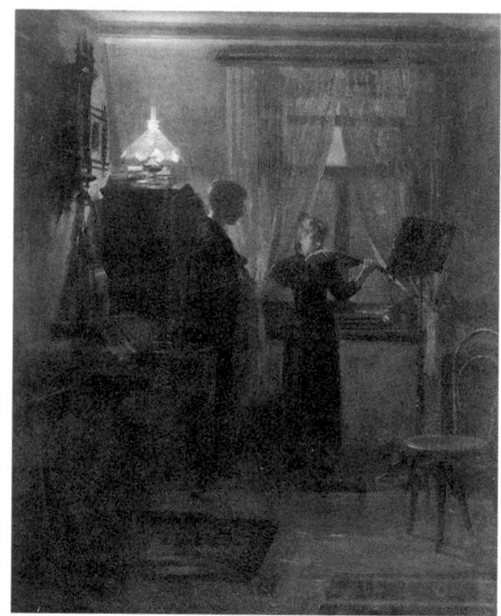

The Musical Hour. **#1201.** [$500]. n.d. (ca. 1893). 48 x 38. The Jane Voorhees Zimmerli Art Museum, Rutgers, The State University of New Jersey, Gift of Dr. Helgi Johnson.

HOVENDEN, **Thomas. Plymouth Meeting, Pa.**

1840 Dunmanway, Ireland–1895 near Norristown, PA
Training — Cork, Ireland: Cork School of Design; New York: NAD; Paris: Alexandre Cabanel; Pont-Aven.

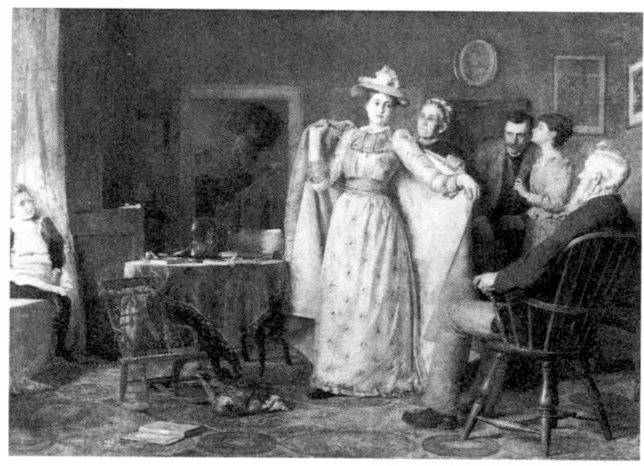

Bringing Home the Bride.* **#277. n.d. (1893). 56 x 78. Collection Jay Weibel, Newport, RI.

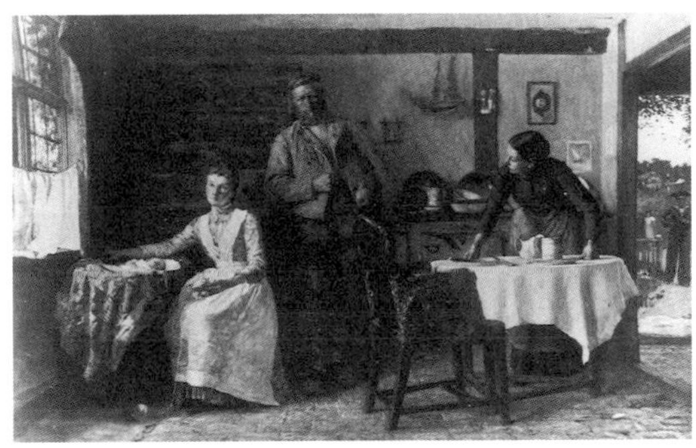

When Hope Was Darkest. **#472.** [$5000]. 1892. 36 x 57. Sold (as *The Sailor's Return*), Christie's, New York, NY, 30 Sept. 1988, lot 122. Unlocated. Illus: *The Graphic* [Chicago], 5 Aug. 1893, 110.

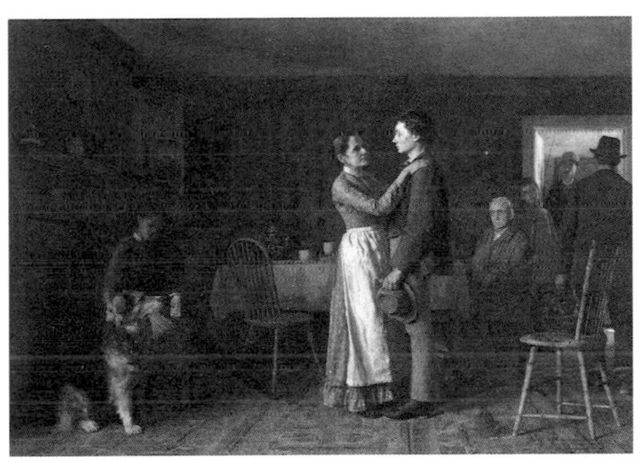

Breaking the Home Ties.* **#846. Lent by Mr. Charles C. Harrison, Philadelphia, Pa. *Breaking Home Ties,* 1890. 52¼ x 72¼. Philadelphia Museum of Art, Gift of Ellen Harrison McMichael in memory of C. Emory McMichael.

---

† **HOWE, William H.** (William Henry). **Paris, France.** 1846 Ravenna, OH–1929 Bronxville, NY
Training — Dusseldorf: Royal Academy; Paris: Felix de Vuillefroy, Otto de Thoren, Léon Germain Pelouse.

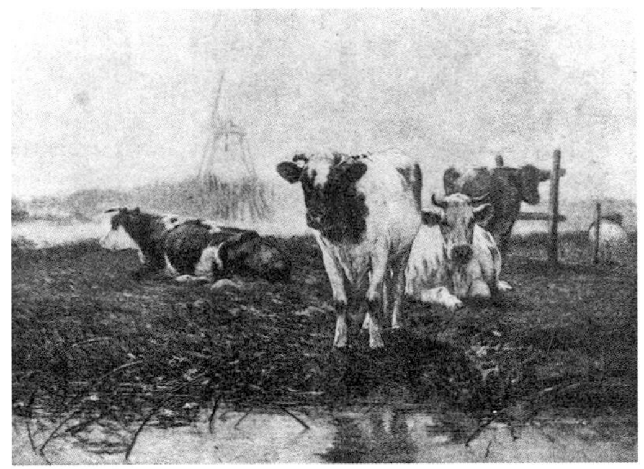

Morning, Karton Hof Meadows, Holland. **#483.** [$1200]. ca. 1892. 72 x 96. Unlocated.[38] Illus: *Art Interchange,* May 1892, 133. "A picture which many good judges consider to be the strongest he has ever done. It is called 'Early Morning,' and is a composition with four cows. The scene is laid in a dune or meadow on the lowlands near Lauren. In the foreground, just at the edge of the water, a handsome red-and-white cow is standing peacefully, whilst behind there are two other cows, a white one and a red-and-white one, lying on the grass, and the fourth is standing up against a rail. In addition he has shown us a very fine misty Dutch effect in the background, where we see a couple of mills almost shrouded in the thick haze of morning" —*New York Herald* [Paris], 26 March 1892.

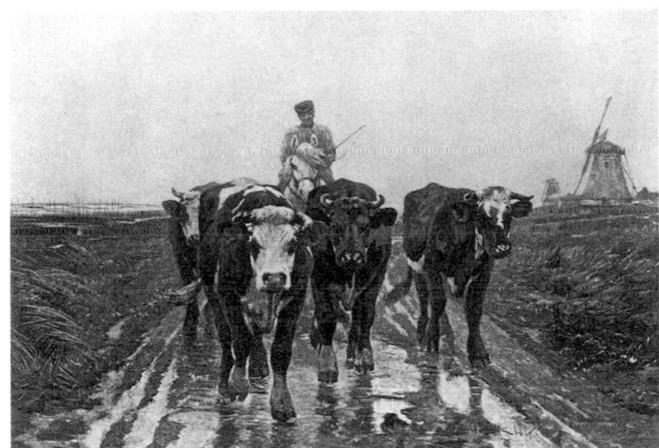

Early Start to Market, Holland. **#499.** ca. 1888. Est. 70 x 144. Formerly Collection Grand Rapids (Michigan) Art Association. Stolen from gallery in 1922. Unlocated. Illus: Henri Sylvestre, Jr., *Marvels in Art of the Fin de Siècle,* vol. 2 (Philadelphia: Gebbie, 1893), part 20.

Return of the Herd. **#689.** ca. 1887. Unlocated. "A large and very well painted canvas of a group of cattle on a grassy slope in noonday. The individual cows are admirably handled, firmly and without affection, and the feeling of the landscape is quiet and agreeable. Yet, there is little of pictorial interest or of poetic suggestion and the effect is rather dull" —*New York Times,* 30 Jan. 1890; "Canvas of three meters and represents a herdess driving her cattle home. The new moon shows on the horizon, and makes a delicate twilight effect" —*New York Herald* [Paris], 14 Dec. 1890.

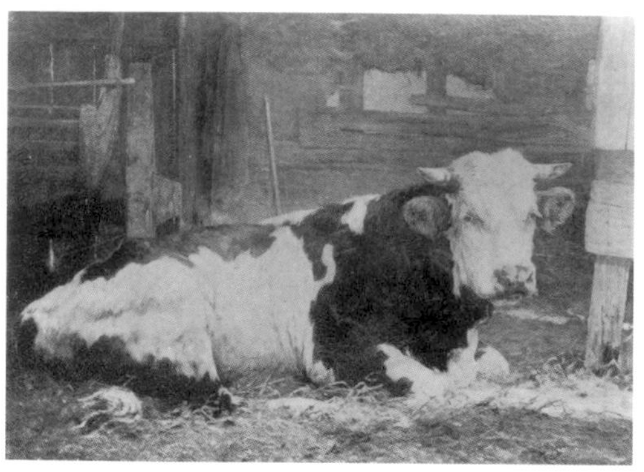

A Norman Bull. **#896.** [$2500]. 1891. 36½ x 49¼. Repainted as *Monarch of the Farm* by artist.[39] Illus: Charles M. Kurtz, ed., *Illustrations from the Art Gallery of the World's Columbian Exposition* (Philadelphia: G. Barrie, 1893), 50.

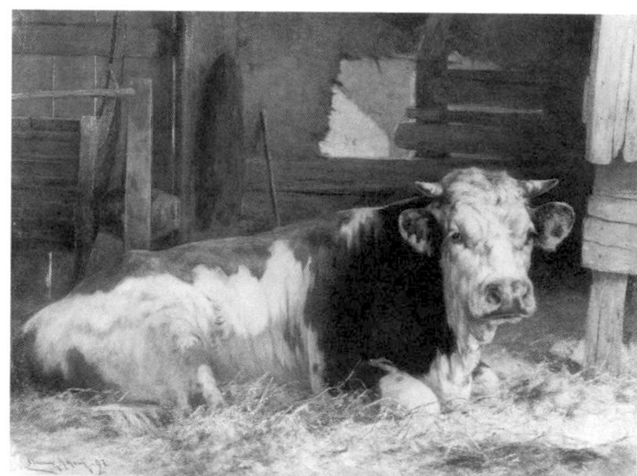

Monarch of the Farm, 1891 (ca. 1901). 36½ x 49¼. National Museum of American Art, Smithsonian Institution, Gift of Mrs. William Henry Howe.

HOWES, Edith M. Boston.

Unknown–Residing 1907 Boston, MA

In the Orchard. **#323.** [$150]. Unlocated.

HOWLAND, A. C. (Alfred Cornelius). New York.

1838 Walpole, NH–1909 Pasadena, CA
Training — New York; Dusseldorf: Royal Academy (Andreas Muller), Albert Flamm; Paris: Emile Lambinet.

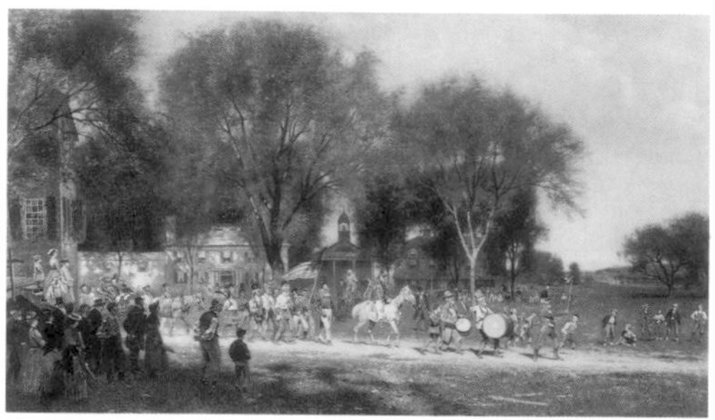

Fourth of July Parade.* **#1062. Lent by Mr. W. H. Fuller, New York. n.d. (ca. 1886). 26 x 44½. Private Collection.

HUNTINGTON, Daniel. New York.

1816 New York, NY–1906 New York, NY
Training — Hamilton College; New York: Samuel F. B. Morse, Henry Inman, NAD.

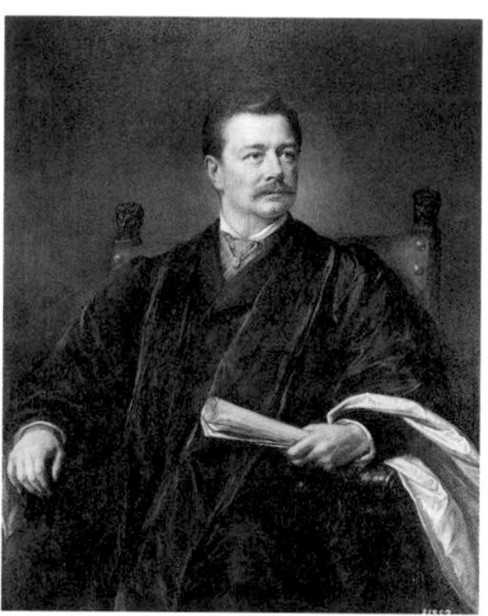

Portrait of the Hon. Seth Low. **#383.** 1891. 49½ x 39½. Columbia University in the City of New York, Gift of Seth Low, 1899, at the invitation of the Trustees. Photograph courtesy the Frick Art Reference Library.

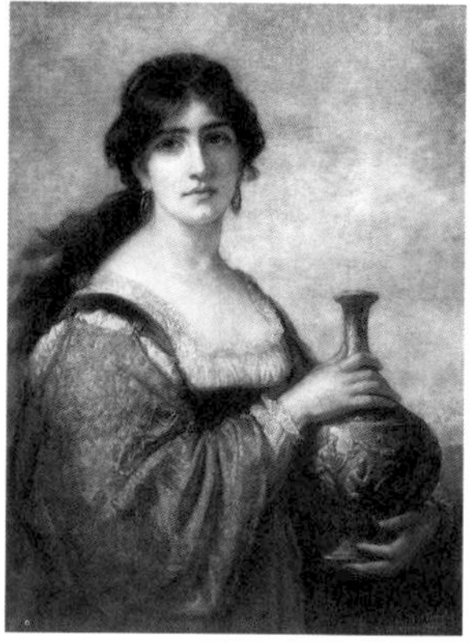

The Goldsmith's Daughter. **#837.** [$1200]. 1883. 36 x 26. Collection Mrs. Edgar Irving Bostwick, Richmond, VA. Photograph by Ronald Jennings.

Portrait of Mr. Elliott F. Shepard, Jr. **#947.** ca. 1891–92. 50 x 36 .[40] Unlocated.

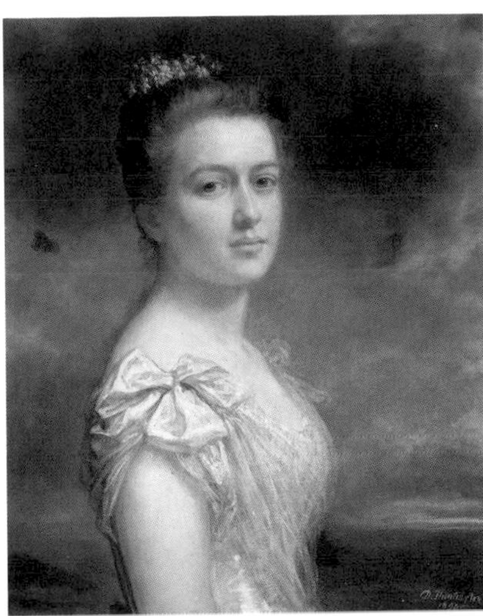

Elise (Elise Huntington Franck Tappin). **#1057.** [$750]. n.d. (ca. 1891). 27 x 22. Private Collection. Photograph by Gregory W. Schmitz.

---

† **INNESS, George. Montclair, N.J.**
1825 Newburgh, NY–1894 Bridge-of-Allan, Scotland
Training — largely self-taught; Brooklyn: R. Gignoux.

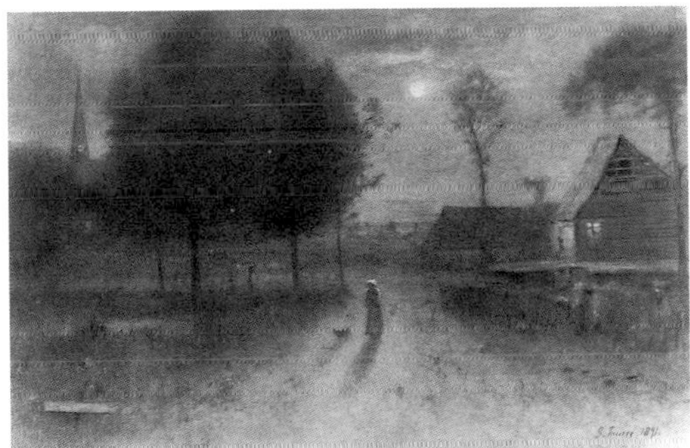

Nine O'Clock. **#633. Lent by Mr. Thomas B. Clarke, New York.** 1891. 30 x 45. Sold, American Art Association, New York, NY, 30 Jan.– 2 Feb. 1900, lot 179, to George E. Morris. Unlocated. Illus: Daniel H. Burnham, *The Art of the World,* vol. 6 (New York: Appleton, 1893–95).

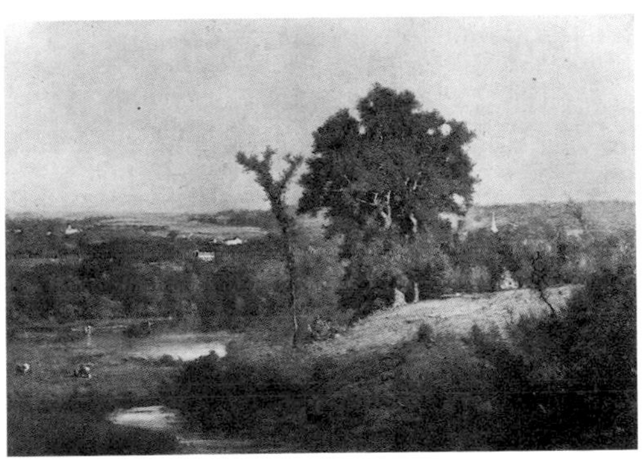

Near Marshfield. **#690. Lent by Mr. Thomas B. Clarke, New York.** *Autumn, Near Marshfield,* 1876. 16 x 24. Sold, American Art Association/Anderson Galleries, New York, NY, 30 April 1936, lot 26. Unlocated. Illus: Elliot Daingerfield, *Fifty Paintings by George Inness* (New York, 1913; privately printed), plate 13.

Sunburst. **#692. Lent by Mr. Thomas B. Clarke, New York.** 1878. Unlocated. " The rain clouds, hanging low along the crests of the distant hills, a portion of which they actually obscure, have been rent asunder to give passage to a brave burst of the sun. The rays of the luminary light the broad meadow in the middle distance, and the line of trees and the hillsides behind it, and leave the foreground in shade. The scene is a spacious valley, dotted with farms and enlivened with grazing cattle and the figures of haymakers. In the immediate foreground, at the right, a boy lands in a boat from a little creek, and at the left, through a gate shaded by two lofty and noble elm trees, a shepherd drives a flock of sheep. To a fertile country, smiling even under the frown of the stormy heavens, the artist, by the mere contrast between nature and the elemental conflict which is waging above the earth, gives a distinct dramatic character and expression. Signed at the left" —The Pennsylvania Academy of the Fine Arts, *Catalogue of the Thomas B. Clarke Collection of American Pictures* (Philadelphia, 1891), 68–69.

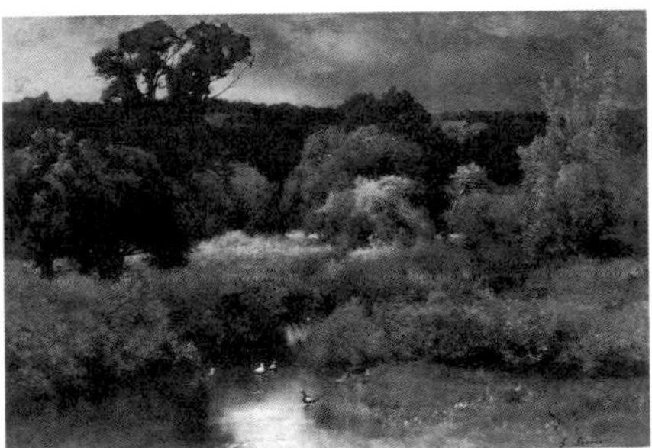

A Gray Lowery Day.* **#731. Lent by Mr. Thomas B. Clarke, New York. 1877. 17½ x 25½. Davis Museum and Cultural Center, Wellesley College,

Gift of Mr. and Mrs. James B. Munn (Ruth C. Hanford, Class of 1909) in the name of the class of 1909.

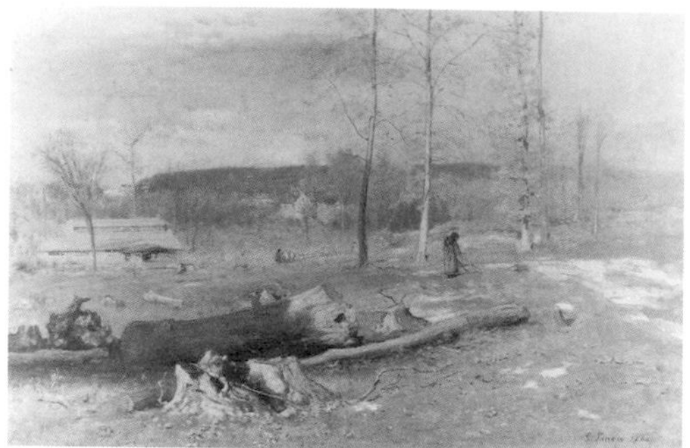

******Winter Morning*. **#943. Lent by Mr. Thomas B. Clarke, New York.** *Winter Morning, Montclair,* 1882. 30¼ x 45¼. Collection of The Montclair Art Museum, Gift of Mrs. Arthur D. Whiteside.

Sundown in the Lane. **#950. Lent by Mr. Thomas B. Clarke, New York.** 1892. 30 x 45. Collection of The Montclair Art Museum, Gift of Mrs. S. Barksdale Penick, Jr.

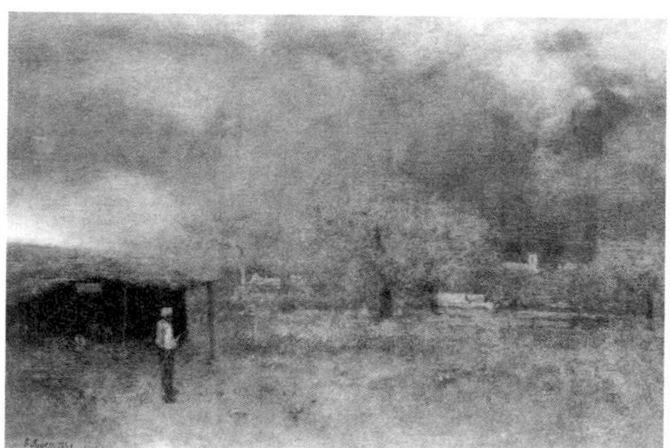

Threatening. **#958. Lent by Mr. Thomas B. Clarke, New York.** 1891. 30¼ x 45¾. The Art Institute of Chicago, Edward B. Butler Collection.

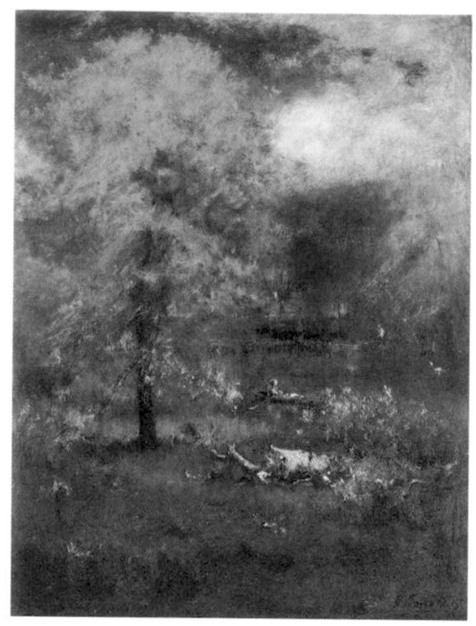

Millpond. **#969. Lent by Mr. Thomas B. Clarke, New York.** *The Mill Pond,* 1889. 37¾ x 29¾. The Art Institute of Chicago, Edward B. Butler Collection.

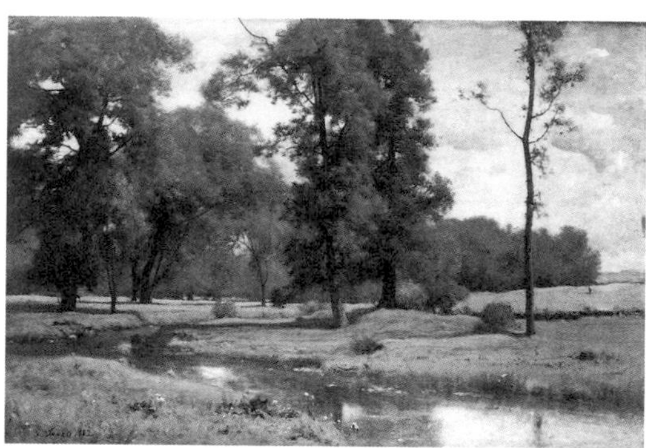

A Day in June. **#973.** 1882. 30¼ x 45. The Brooklyn Museum, Bequest of Mrs. William A. Putnam.

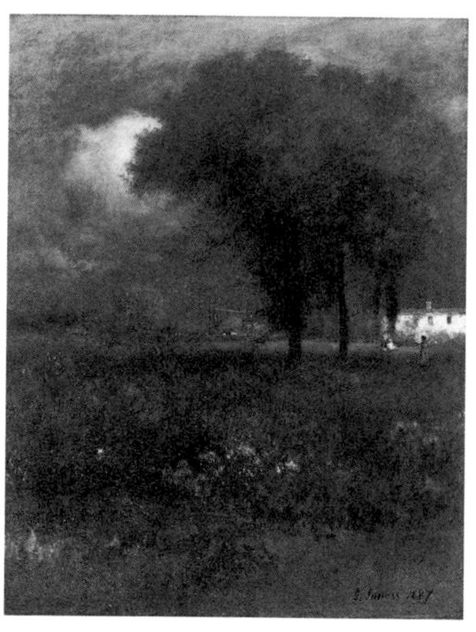

September Afternoon*. **#977. Lent by Mr. Thomas B. Clarke, New York. 1877. 36½ x 28½. National Museum of American Art, Smithsonian Institution, Gift of William T. Evans.

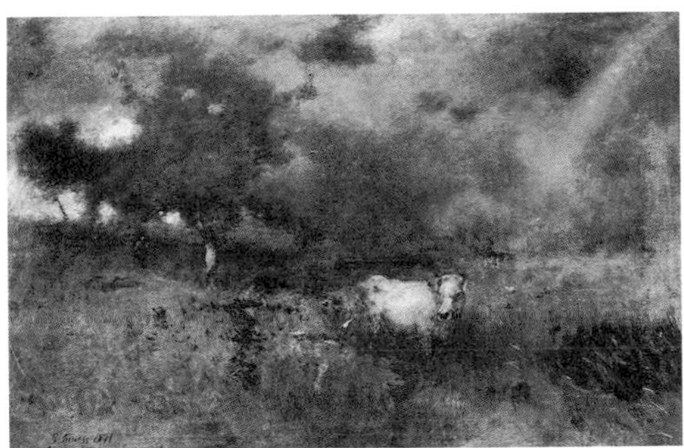

End of the Shower. **#994. Lent by Mr. Thomas B. Clarke, New York.** *End of the Rain,* 1891. 29½ x 44½. Collection of The University of Arizona Museum of Art, Tucson, Gift of T. E. Hanley.

Twilight. **#995. Lent by Mr. Thomas B. Clarke, New York.** *Twilight Medfield,* 1876. 16 x 24. Sold, American Art Association, New York, NY, 14–18 Feb. 1899, lot 231, to George Blumenthal. Unlocated. "The expiring fires of the day are smouldering among cloud banks whose forms have the brooding heaviness of mid-summer heat. The marshlands, which reach away from the foreground to the horizon, are growing dusky with the extending shade. The sluggish waters of the winding creek are yet slightly flushed by the reflection of the sky, and the leafy bulk of a clump of trees in the middle ground makes a massive landmark on the background of crimsoned cloud. In the profound and pervading calm, the wild ducks on the water float fearless of intrusion or peril. Signed at the left, 1876" —The Pennsylvania Academy of the Fine Arts, *Catalogue of the Thomas B. Clarke Collection of American Pictures* (Philadelphia, 1891), 68.

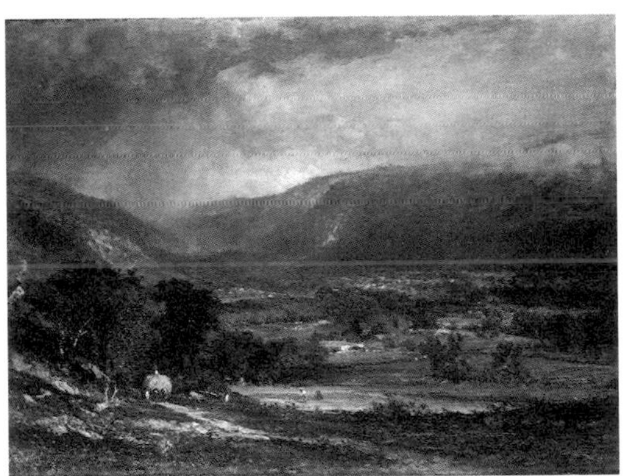

The Delaware Valley. **#996. Lent by Mr. Thomas B. Clarke, New York.** 1863?. 22¼ x 30⅜. The Metropolitan Museum of Art, Gift of Several Gentlemen, 1899.

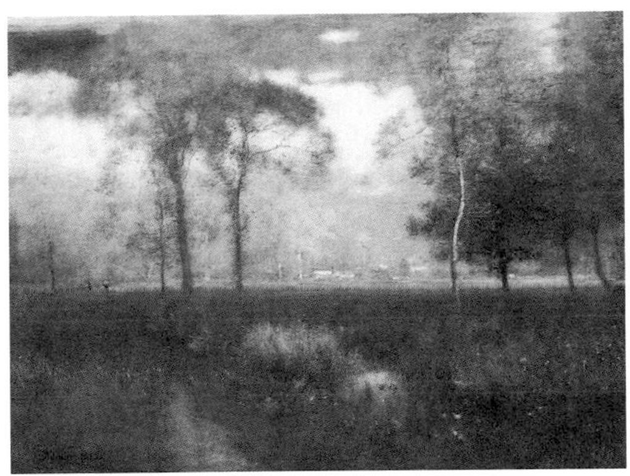

Sunny Autumn Day. **#998. Lent by Mr. Thomas B. Clarke, New York.** 1892. 32 x 42. The Cleveland Museum of Art, Anonymous Gift.

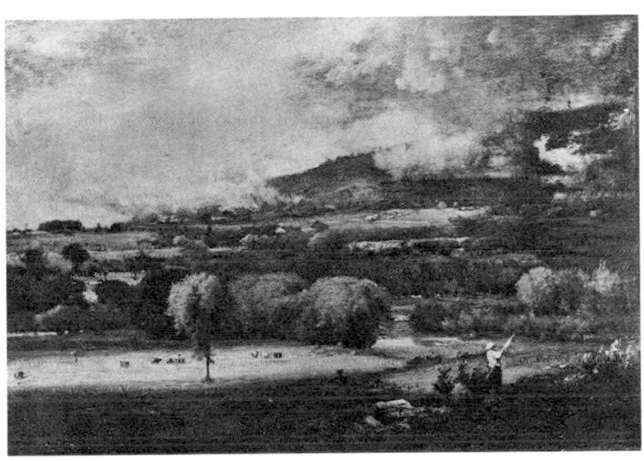

White Mountain Valley. **#999. Lent by Mr. Thomas B. Clarke, New York.** 1875–78. 20 x 30. Sold, American Art Association, New York, NY, 14–18 Feb. 1899, lot 50, to Henry Sampson. Unlocated. Illus: Elliot Daingerfield, *Fifty Paintings by George Inness* (New York, 1913; privately printed), plate 14.

IPSEN, Ernest (Ernest Ludwig). **Boston.**
1869 Malden, MA–1951 Miami, FL
Training — Boston: MFA (Frederic Vinton); Copenhagen: Royal Academy.

Interior of a New England Blacksmith Shop. **#1266.** [$500]. Est. 45 x 60. Unlocated.[41]

IRWIN, Benoni. New York.
1840 Newmarket, Ontario–1896 South Coventry, CT
Training — New York: NAD; Paris: Carolus-Duran.

Portrait of Hubert Herkomer. **#827.** ca. 1883.[42] Est. 30 x 20. Unlocated.

Sweet Sixteen. **#962.** Unlocated.

ISHAM, Samuel. New York.
1855 New York, NY–1914 East Hampton, NY
Training — New Haven: Yale School of the Fine Arts; Paris: Jacquesson de la Chevreuse, Acad. Julian (Gustave Boulanger, Jules Joseph Lefebvre).

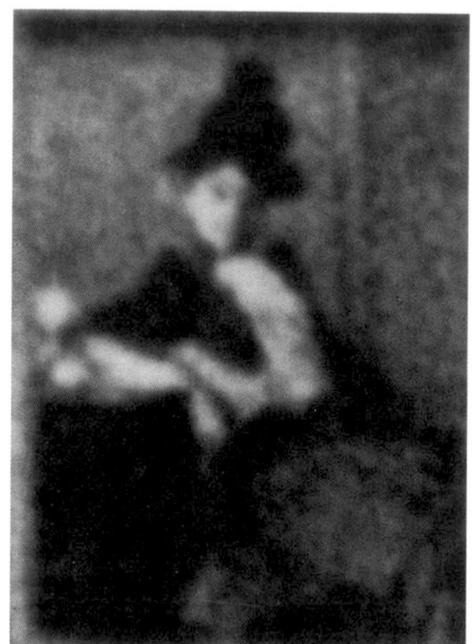

Portrait of a Lady. **#269.** Est. 30 x 25. Unlocated. Illus: Official Photographs of the World's Columbian Exposition by C. D. Arnold, vol. 8, pl. 90. Courtesy of The Chicago Public Library, Special Collections Department.

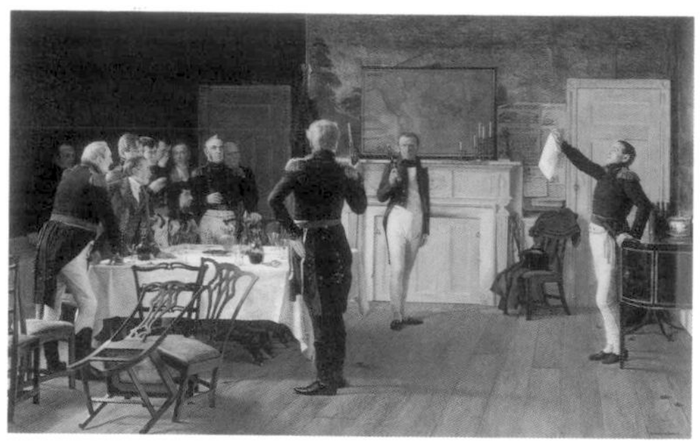

An Impromptu Affair in the Days of "The Code."* **#1077. [$1500]. *An Impromptu Affair in the Days of the Code,* n.d. (ca. 1890). 26¼ x 41⅜. The Museum of Fine Arts, Springfield, MA, Gift of Charles T. and Emilie Shean.

IVES, Percy (Percival). **Paris, France.**
1864 Detroit, MI–1928 Detroit, MI
Training — Detroit: Lewis T. Ives [his father]; Philadelphia: PAFA (Thomas Eakins); Paris: Acad. Julian (Gustave Boulanger, Jean-Joseph Benjamin-Constant, William Bouguereau, Jules Joseph Lefebvre, Tony Robert-Fleury), Fernand Cormon, Jean-Léon Gérôme, EcBA.

Brittany Fishermen. **#1209.** [$500]. Unlocated.

JAMES, Frederick. New York.
1845 Philadelphia, PA–1907 Peru, Quebec
Training — Philadelphia: PAFA; Paris: Jean-Léon Gérôme.

JAMISON, Henrietta L. (Henrietta Lewis). **Columbus, O.**
1862 Columbus, OH–1895 Aurora, IL

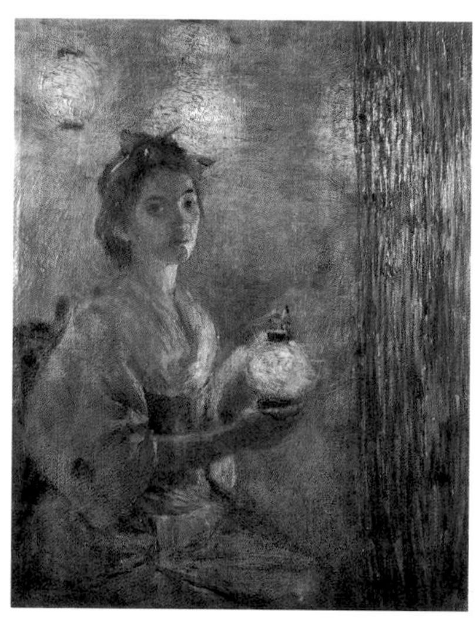

The Lanterns. **#1182.** [$75]. n.d. 16 x 12¾. Columbus Museum of Art, Ohio, Bequest of Effie Duncan.

JENKINS, H. T. (Hannah Tempest/Mrs. Jenkins). **Philadelphia.**
1855 St. Clair, PA–1927 Claremont, CA
Training — Philadelphia: School of Industrial Art, PAFA; Paris: Acad. Julian (Jean-Joseph Benjamin-Constant, Tony Robert-Fleury); Kyoto, Japan: Tackouchi Seiho.

Still Life. **#723.** [$150]. Unlocated.

Landscape. **#756.** [$200]. Unlocated.

JOHNS, Laura A. (Mrs. George C. Danforth). **New York.**
Unknown–Before 1919
Training — Joseph De Camp.

Apple Trees in Sunlight. **#1176. Lent by Mrs. H. C. Johns, Decatur, Ill.** Unlocated.

† **JOHNSON, Eastman** (Jonathan Eastman). **New York.**
1824 Lovell, ME–1906 New York, NY
Training — Dusseldorf: Royal Academy (Emanuel Leutze); Paris: Thomas Couture; The Hague: Royal Academy.

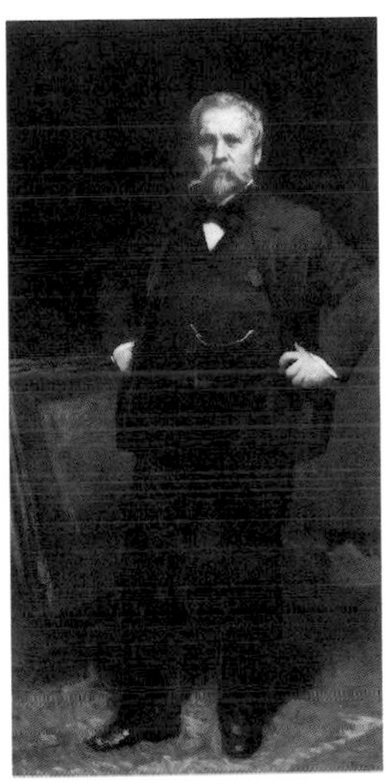

Portrait of the Artist. **#438.** *Self-Portrait,* 1891. 72 x 36. Hirshhorn Museum and Sculpture Garden, Smithsonian Institution, Gift of the Joseph H. Hirshhorn Foundation, 1966. Photograph by Lee Stalsworth.

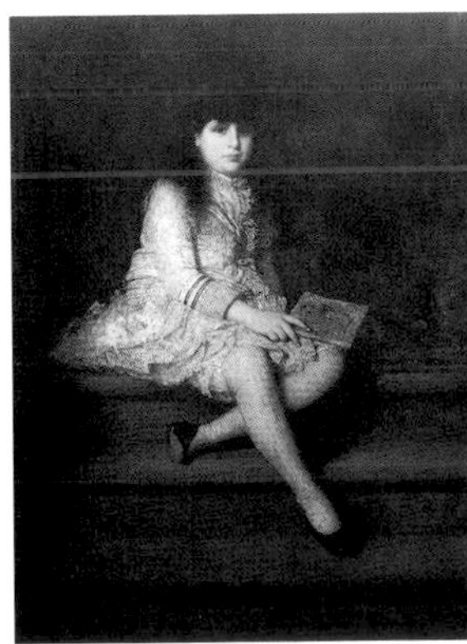

Portrait of a Girl (Florence Einstein). **#669. Lent by Mr. D. L. Einstein, New York.** 1883. 54¼ x 40¼. Private Collection. Photograph courtesy Joan Michelman Ltd.

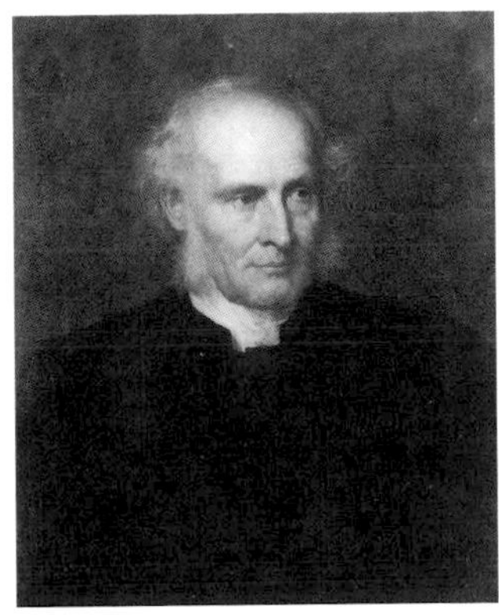

Portrait of Dr. McCosh. **#784. Lent by Mr. Alexander Maitland.** 1883. 27 x 22¼. Princeton University.

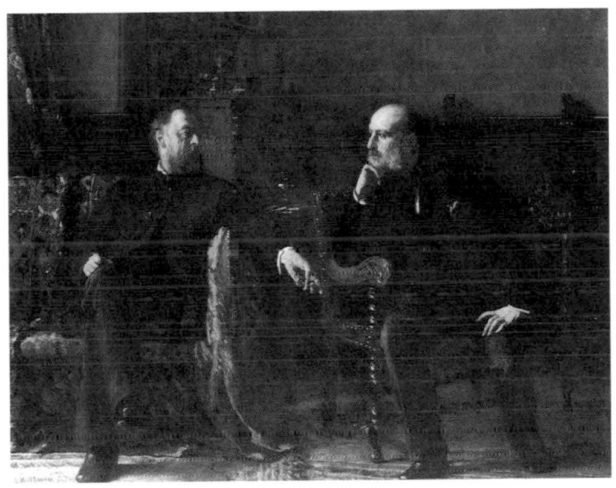

Two Men. **#853.** *The Funding Bill,* 1881. 60½ x 78¼. The Metropolitan Museum of Art, Purchase, Robert Gordon Gift, 1898.

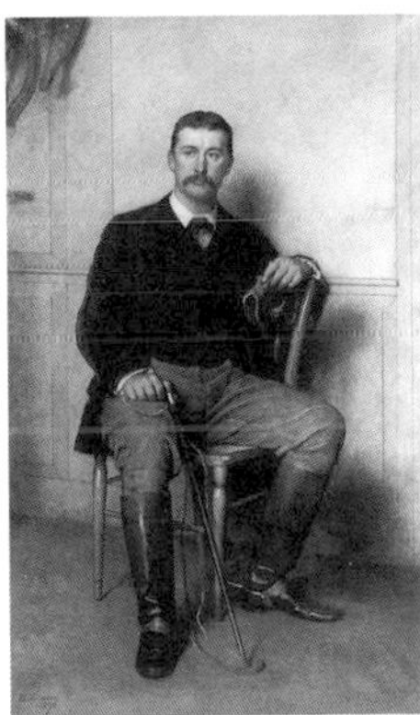

Life size Portrait. **#921. Lent by Mr. Archibald Rogers, Hyde Park, New York.** *Colonel Archibald Rogers at Hyde Park, New York,* 1892. 75 x 49. Collection of the Anne C. Stradling Museum of the Horse in Ruidoso Downs, NM.

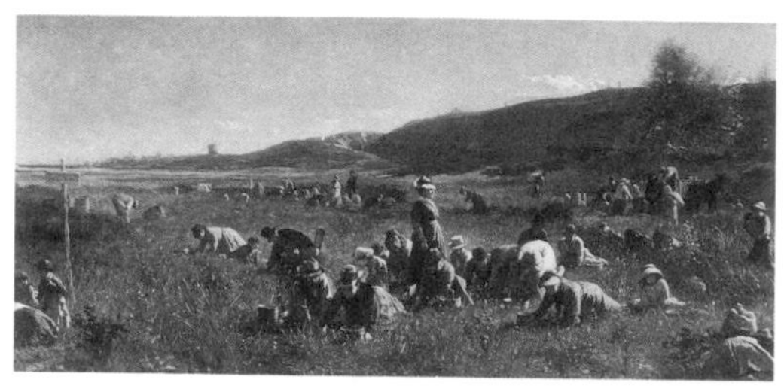

The Cranberry Harvest, Nantucket Island, Mass.* **#954. Lent by Mr. Auguste Richard, New York. *The Cranberry Harvest, Island of Nantucket,* 1880. 27⅜ x 54½. Putnam Collection, Timken Museum of Art, San Diego.

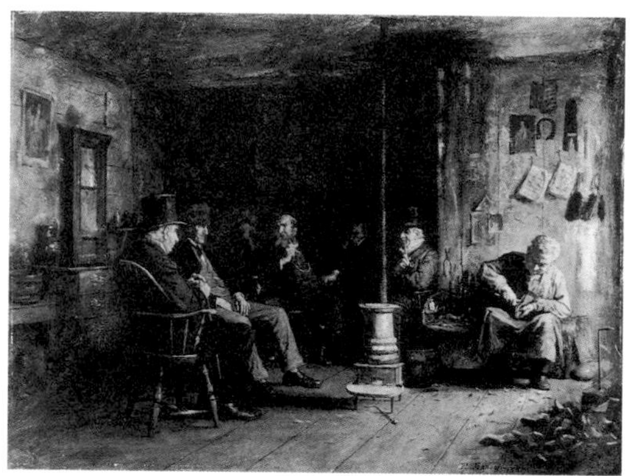

The Nantucket School of Philosophy.* **#983. Lent by Mr. E. D. Adams, New York. ca. 1886 (oil on panel). 23¼ x 31¾. Walters Art Gallery, Baltimore.

JOHNSTON, Humphreys (John Humphreys). Paris, France.

1857 New York, NY–1941 Cannes, France
Training — New York: John LaFarge; Paris: Acad. Julian (Henri-Lucien Doucet, Jules Joseph Lefebvre); Madrid.

Moorish Fountain in the Church of Santa Maria del Alhambra. **#1170.** [$300]. ca. 1892. Unlocated.

Study of Breton Peasants (Late Afternoon). **#1197.** [$250]. Unlocated.

Study in a Grenada Garden. **#1237.** [$500]. Est. 30 x 18. Unlocated.

JONES, Francis C. (Francis Coates). New York.

1857 Baltimore, MD–1932 New York, NY
Training — Paris: Acad. Julian (Gustave Boulanger, Jules Joseph Lefebvre), Henri Lehmann, Adolphe Yvon, EcBA.

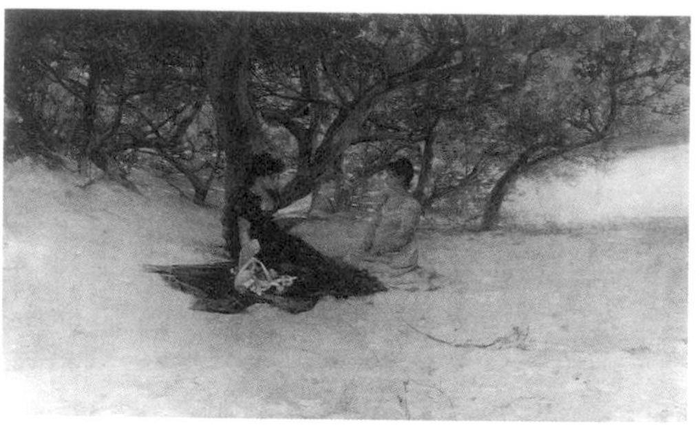

On the White Sand Dunes. **#765. Lent by Mr. John Gellatly.** 1885. 22 x 35. Sold (as *Sand Dunes*), Silo's, New York, NY, 24 Feb. 1928, lot 416, to Mr. Finger and possibly sold (as *Sand Dunes*), National, New York, NY, 4–6 Feb. 1932, lot 51. Unlocated. Illus: Daniel H. Burnham, *The Art of the World,* vol. 10 (New York: Appleton, 1893–95).

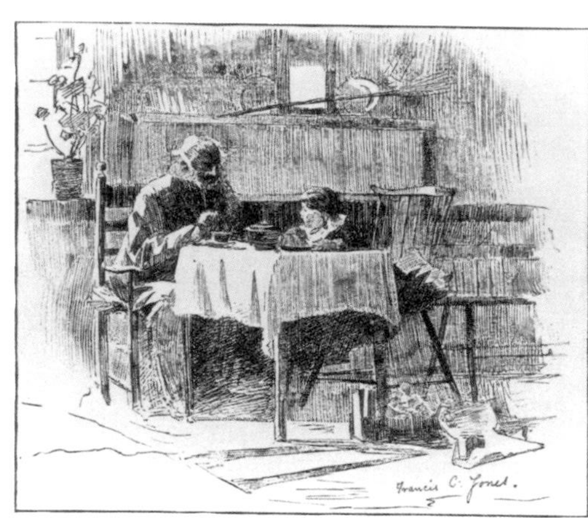

Exchanging Confidences. **#861. Lent by Mr. Thomas B. Clarke, New York.** ca. 1885. 18 x 22. Sold, American Art Association, New York, NY, 14–18 Feb. 1899, lot 45, to W. B. Lockwood. Unlocated. Illus: Charles M. Kurtz, ed., *National Academy Notes and Complete Catalogue, 1885* (New York: Cassell & Co., 1885), 103.

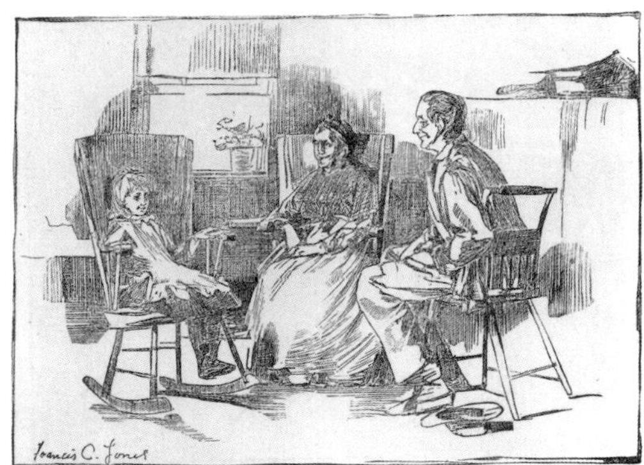

The Favorite Grandchild. **#991.** [$450]. ca. 1888. 20 x 26. Sold, World's Columbian Exposition, Chicago, IL, 1893. Unlocated. Illus: Charles M. Kurtz, ed., *National Academy Notes and Complete Catalogue, Sixty-third Spring Exhibition, National Academy of Design, New York* (New York: Cassell & Co., 1888), 36.

---

† JONES, H. Bolton (Hugh Bolton). New York.

1848 Baltimore, MD –1927 New York, NY
Training — Baltimore: Maryland Institute of Art; New York: Horace W. Robbins; Paris: Acad. Julian.

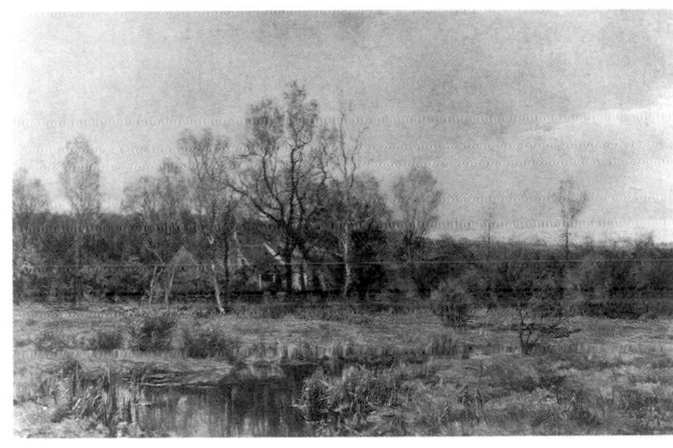

Spring. **#470.** [$1300]. Est. 35 x 60. Unlocated. Illus: Daniel H. Burnham, *The Art of the World,* vol. 5 (New York: Appleton, 1893–95).

The Flax Breaker. **#834.** [$1100]. **Lent by Mr. R. J. Menefee, Louisville, Ky.** Unlocated. "The figure is of no importance, serving merely to give a name to the picture. Against a gray sky of autumn the leafless twigs of a great tree are outlined in most delicate tracery, reminding one of some fine algae. Yet, in spite of the amount of detail here, it is so skillfuly subordinated that it is not at all tiresome. The green thatched huts at the left make an effective background — all boldy done, though so refined" — *The Baltimore Sun,* 14 Oct. 1893.

---

† KAPPES, Alfred. New York.

1850 New York, NY–1894 Yonkers, NY
Training — New York: NAD.

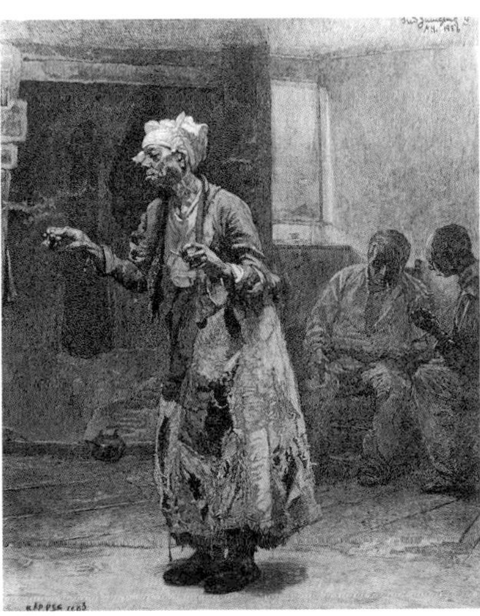

Tattered and Torn. **#881. Lent by the Boston Art Club.** 1886. Unlocated. Illus: *The Magazine of Art* (1887): 93.

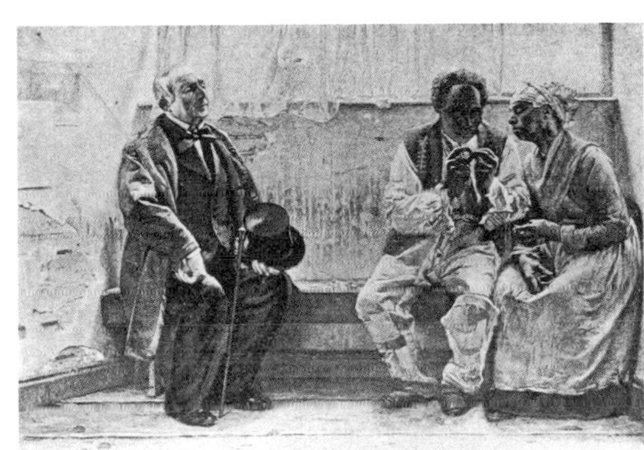

Rent Day. **#922. Lent by Mr. Thomas B. Clarke, New York.** 1885. 32 x 43. Sold, Parke-Bernet Galleries, New York, NY, 14 Jan. 1939, lot 49. Unlocated. Illus: Daniel H. Burnham, *The Art of the World,* vol. 9 (New York: Appleton, 1893–95).

KAVANAGH, John. Cleveland, O.

1854 Prescott, Canada–1898 Cleveland, OH
Training — Cleveland: W. C. Morse; New York: Cooper Union; Munich: Royal Academy (Ludwig von Löfftz); Paris: Acad. Julian (Gustave Boulanger), Fernand Cormon.

Washer-women. **#592.** [$600]. ca. 1891. Est. 50 x 40. Unlocated.

KEITH, **Mrs. Dora Wheeler** (Mrs. Boudinot Keith). **New York.**
1856 Jamaica, NY–1940 New York, NY
Training — New York: ASL (William Merritt Chase), Paris: Acad. Julian.

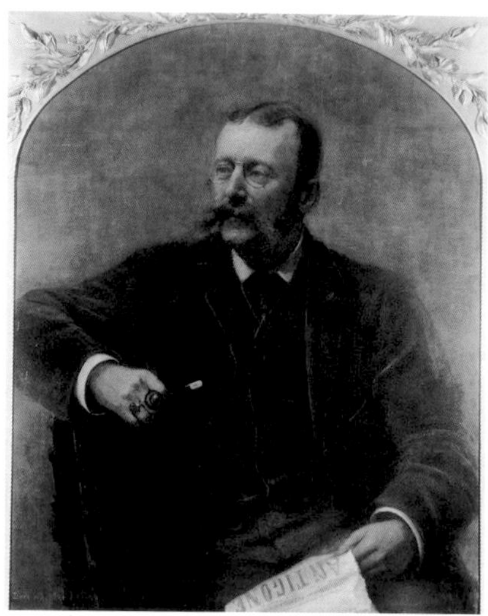

Portrait of Lawrence Hutton. **#688. Lent by Mr. Lawrence Hutton, New York.** 1892. 39 x 31. Princeton University.

KEITH, **William. San Francisco.**
1839 Aberdeenshire, Scotland–1911 Berkeley, CA
Training — Samuel Brookes, Harrison Eastman; Dusseldorf; Munich.

***Autumn Sunset.* #772.** Est. 40 x 60. Unlocated.

KELLER, **Charles F.** (Charles Frederick). **Munich, Bavaria.**
1852 Milwaukee, WI–1928 Franklin Square, NY
Training — Munich: Royal Academy.

***Canal at Schleissheim, near Munich.* #401.** [$150]. Unlocated.

KELLOGG, **Alice D.** (Alice De Wolf/Mrs. Orno James Tyler). **Chicago.**
1862 Chicago, IL–1900 Chicago, IL
Training — Chicago: Academy of Design (Henry F. Spread, Lawrence C. Earle, J. Roy Robertson); Paris: Acad. Julian (Gustave Boulanger, Jules Joseph Lefebvre), Acad. Colarossi (Jean-André Rixens, Gustave Courtois), Charles Lasar, P. A. J. Dagnan-Bouveret.

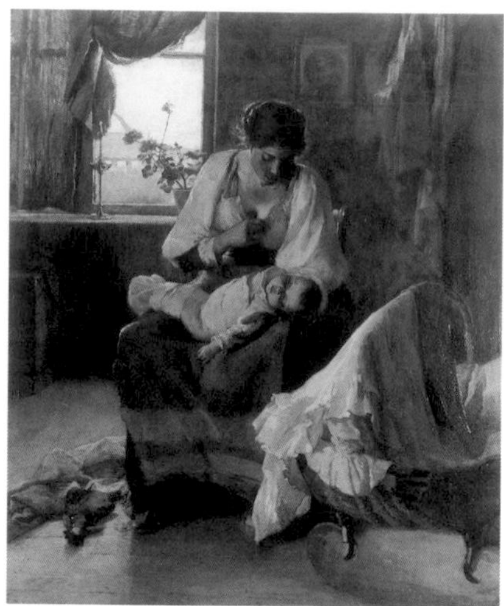

***The Mother.* #838.** [$700]. 1889. 38½ x 32½. Jane Addams' Hull-House Museum, University of Illinois at Chicago.

***Intermezzo.* #1288.** [$200]. ca. 1892. Unlocated. "Alice D. Kellogg has the ability to treat clouds most delightfully, giving the hazy effect so much to be desired. 'Intermezzo' was a charming composition in every way, excellent in drawing and harmonious in coloring" — *The Arts* 1 (Jan. 1893).

† **KENDALL,** **William Sargent** (William Sergeant). **New York.**
1869 Spuyten Duyvil, NY–1938 Hot Springs, VA
Training — Brooklyn: Brooklyn Art Guild; New York: ASL; Philadelphia: PAFA (Thomas Eakins); Paris: Henri-Lucien Doucet, Jules Joseph Lefebvre, Jean-Joseph Benjamin-Constant, Acad. Julian, Luc Olivier Merson, EcBA.

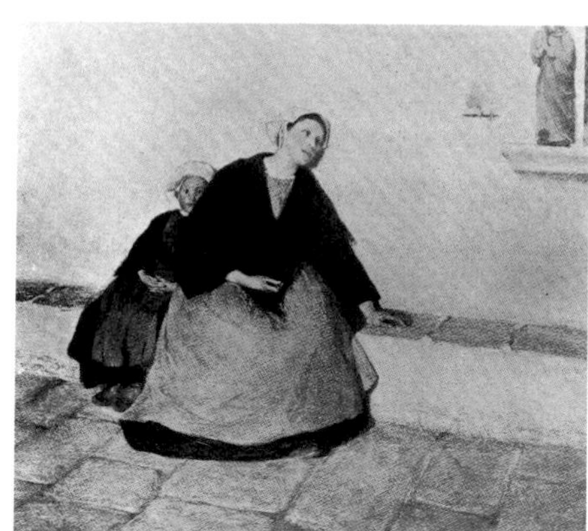

***Saint Yves, Pray for Us.* #1221.** ca. 1890. Est. 37 x 42. Unlocated. Illus: Pennsylvania Academy of the Fine Arts, *Forty Works of Art from the Sixty-third Annual Exhibition of the Academy of the Fine Arts* (Philadelphia: The Levytype Company, 1894).

The Glory of Fair Promise. **#1265.** [$2000]. ca. 1892. Est. 45 x 30. Unlocated.

KETCHAM, Susan M. (Susan Merrill). **New York.**
1841 Indianapolis, IN–1930 Indianapolis, IN
Training — Indianapolis: Indiana School of Art; Chicago: Academy of Design; New York: ASL (William Merritt Chase, Edward A. Bell); Southampton, NY: Shinnecock Summer School of Art (William Merritt Chase); Europe.

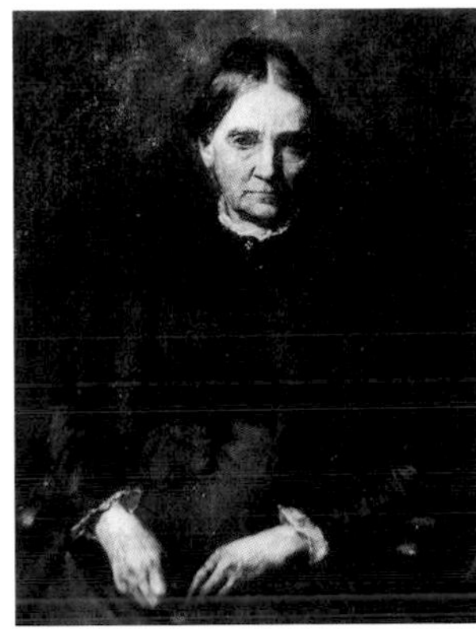

Portrait of a Lady. **#434.** ca. 1890. Est. 30 x 24. Unlocated. Photograph courtesy Indianapolis Museum of Art.

KING, James S. Upper Montclair, N.J.
1852 New York, NY–1925 Upper Montclair, NJ
Training — New York: NAD, ASL; Paris: Léon Bonnat, Jean-Léon Gérôme.

Evening Glow. **#658.** [$500]. Est. 32 x 42. Unlocated.

KNIGHT, Arthur. Milwaukee, Wis.
1867 New York–Residing 1911 Milwaukee, WI
Training — Paris: Jean-Léon Gérôme.

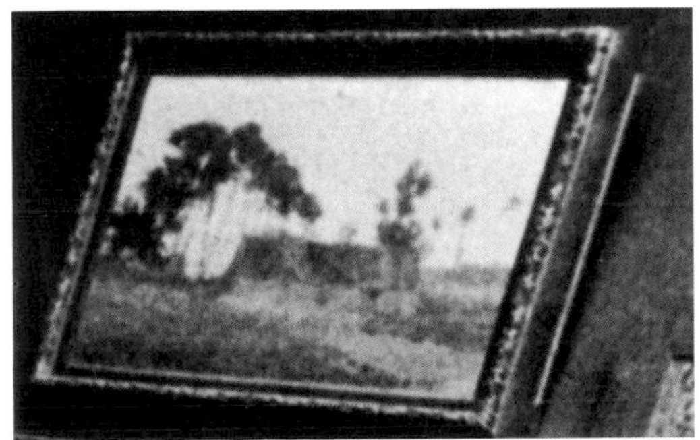

Moonrise in Brittany. **#288.** [$250]. Est. 30 x 48. Unlocated. Illus: Official Photographs of the World's Columbian Exposition by C. D. Arnold, vol. 8, pl. 92. Courtesy of The Chicago Public Library, Special Collections Department.

† **KNIGHT, D. Ridgway** (Daniel Ridgway). **Paris, France.**
1839 Philadelphia, PA–1924 Paris, France
Training — Joseph Woodwell; Pierce Francis Connelly; Philadelphia: PAFA; Paris: Auguste Renoir, Alfred Sisley, Jean-Charles Meissonier, Charles Gleyre, EcBA.

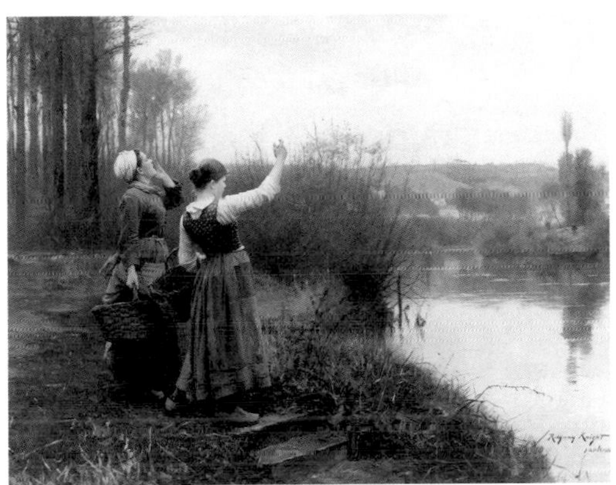

Hailing the Ferry. **#800. Lent by the Pennsylvania Academy of the Fine Arts, Philadelphia.** 1888. 64½ x 83⅛. Pennslyvania Academy of the Fine Arts, Philadelphia, Gift of John H. Converse.

KOEHLER, Robert. New York.
1850 Hamburg, Germany –1917 Minneapolis, MN
Training — Milwaukee: H. Vianden, J. Roese; New York: ASL, NAD (Lemuel E. Wilmarth); Munich: Royal Academy (Alexander Straehuber, Franz Xaver Barth, Ludwig von Löfftz, Franz von Defregger).

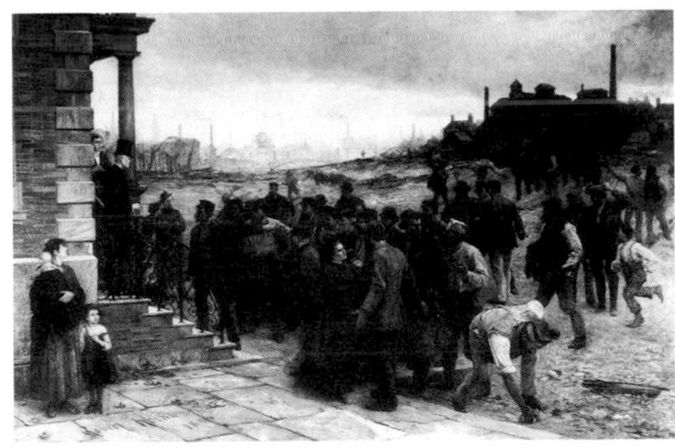

The Strike.* **#482. [$3000]. 1886. 71½ x 108½. Deutsches Historisches Museum, Berlin.

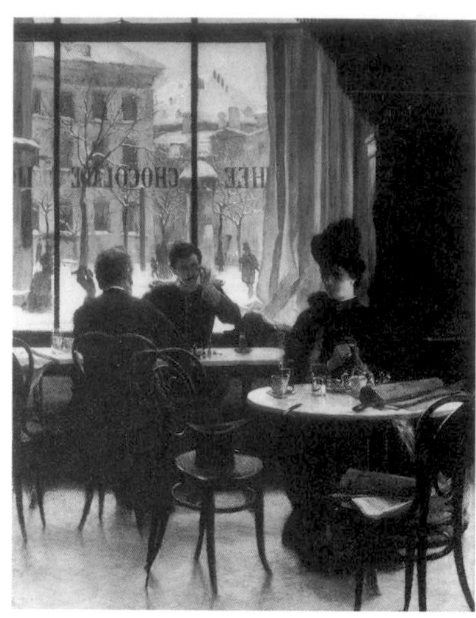

At the Cafe. **#906.** [$250]. n.d. (ca. 1887). 20½ x 16⅛. Private Collection.

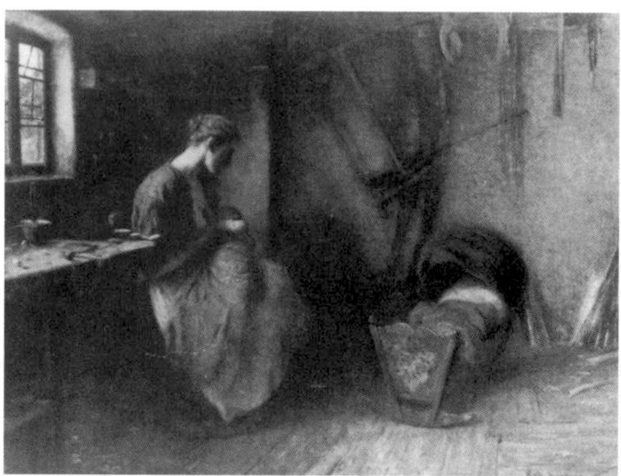

The Carpenter's Family. **#909.** [$500]. 23½ x 32. Collection Mr. and Mrs. Daniel Elliot, Woodland Hills, CA. Illus: *Brush and Pencil* 9 (no. 3): 147.

KOOPMAN, **August B.** (Augustus B.). **New York.**
1869 Charlotte, NC–1914 Étaples, France
Training — Philadelphia: PAFA; Paris: Jean-Joseph Benjamin-Constant, H. Levy, Acad. Julian (William Bouguereau, Tony Robert-Fleury), EcBA.

The Orphan. **#496.** [$500]. Est. 33 x 45. Unlocated. "Effect of sunlight among trees. Brittany" — American Art Galleries, *Pictures and Studies by A. B. Koopman* (New York, 1892), no. 2.

Dreaming of One Afar. **#612.** [$350]. 1891. Sold, World's Columbian Exposition, Chicago, IL, 1893. Unlocated.

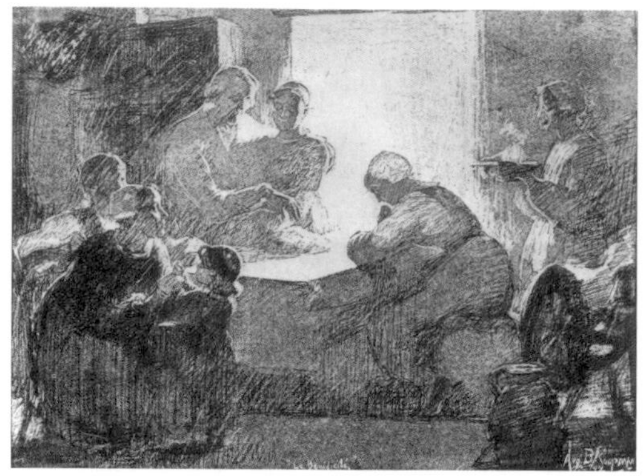

Asking a Blessing. **#1076.** [$10,000]. ca. 1892. Est. 75 x 95. Unlocated. Illus: Ludovic Baschet, ed., *Catalogue Illustré de Peinture et Sculpture, Salon de 1892* (Paris: Chamerot & Renouard, 1892), 162.

KRONBERG, **Louis. Boston.**
1872 Boston, MA–1965 Palm Beach, FL
Training — Boston: MFA; New York: ASL; Paris: Raphaël Collin, Acad. Julian (Jean-Joseph Benjamin-Constant, Jules Joseph Lefebvre).

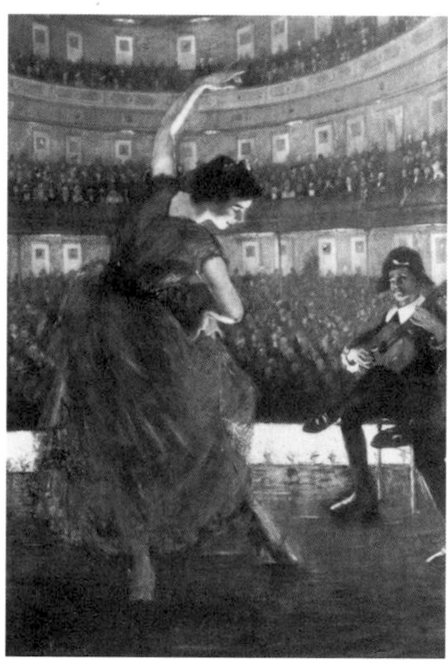

Behind the Footlights. **#1134.** [$2000]. 1892 (oil on canvas, mounted on wood). 84 x 60. Pennsylvania Academy of the Fine Arts, Philadelphia, Gift of Clarence H. Clark.

LA FARGE, **John. New York**
1835 New York, NY–1910 Providence, RI
Training — Newport, RI: William Morris Hunt; Paris: Thomas Couture.

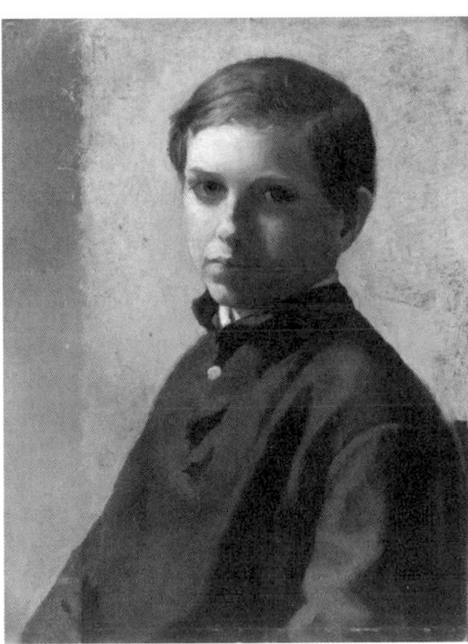

Study of a Boy's Head. **#648. Lent by Mr. Edward W. Hooper, Cambridge, Mass.** *Portrait of a Boy,* n.d.[43] (ca. 1860 62). 21 x 16. Denver Art Museum, Helen Dill Collection.

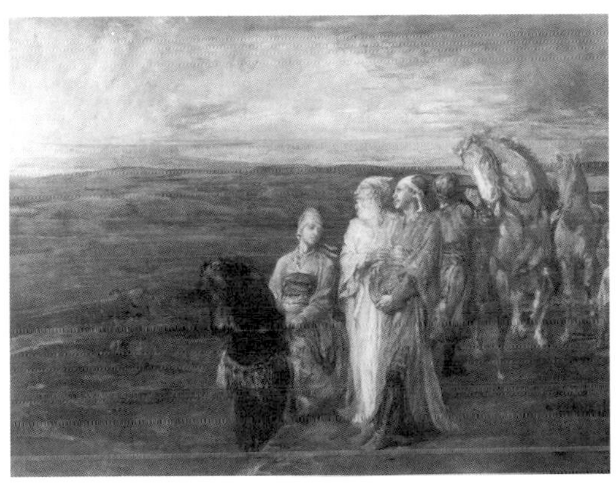

******Halt of the Wise Men from the East.* **#978. Lent by the Museum of Fine Arts, Boston.** n.d. (after 1868). 32¾ x 42. Museum of Fine Arts, Boston, Gift of Edward W. Hooper.

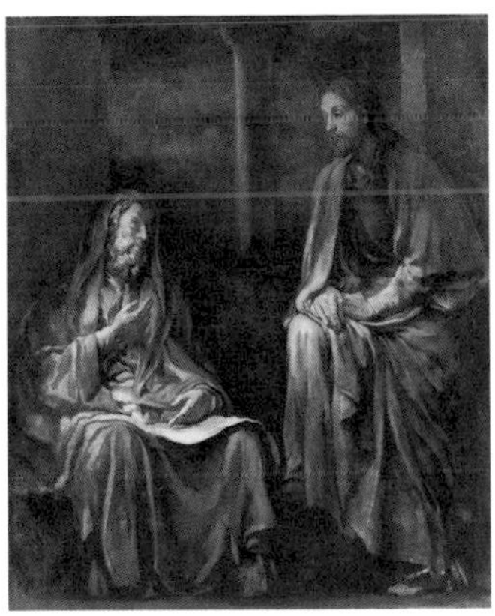

Visit of Nicodemus to Christ. **#980.** [$1500]. n.d. (ca. 1884). 41¾ x 35. National Museum of American Art, Smithsonian Institution, Gift of William T. Evans.

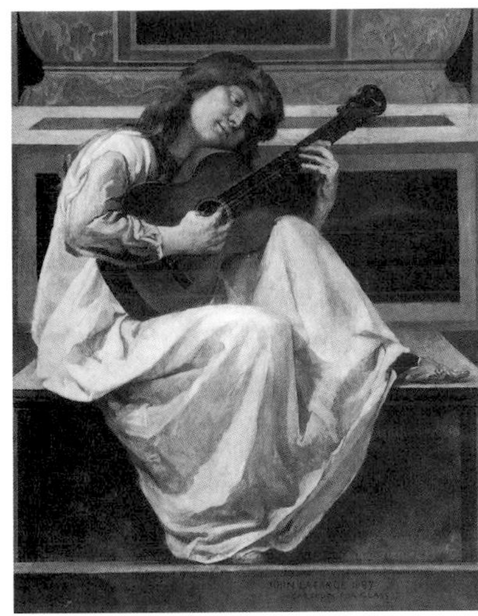

A Venetian Guitar Player (A design for stained glass). **#1005.** [$2000] *The Suonatore,* 1887 (wax colors on prepared board). 46 x 36. Worcester Art Museum, Worcester, MA.

LAMB, Ella Condie (Mrs. Charles Rollinson Lamb). **New York.**
1862 New York, NY–1936 Creskill, NJ
Training—New York: NAD, ASL (William Merritt Chase, Charles Y. Turner); England: Hubert Herkomer; Paris: Raphaël Collin, Gustave Courtois.

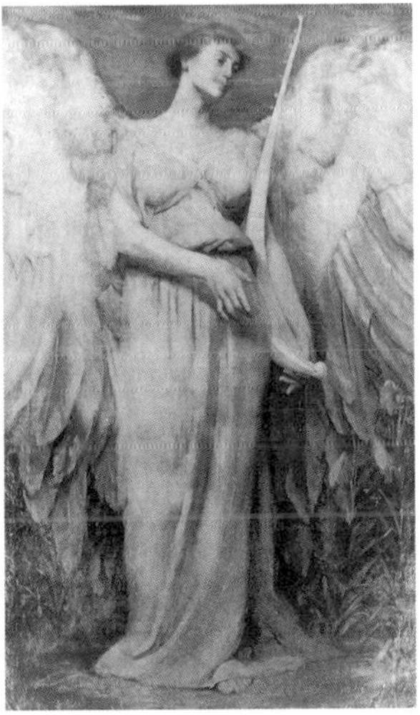

The Advent Angel. **#1251.** 1889. 60 x 35½. Church of the Atonement, Tenafly, NJ.

LAMB, F. M. (F. Mortimer). **Houghton, Mass.**
1861 Middleboro, MA–1936 Stoughton, MA
Training— Boston: Massachusetts Normal Art School, MFA; Paris: Acad. Julian.

End of the Trail. **#1072.** [$500]. ca. 1891. Unlocated. "A life-size painting of hounds picking up a fox . . . [this work] was later shown in San Francisco and numerous exhibitions throughout the country. While being shown in Philadelphia, it was stolen from the gallery and recovered three years later"—*Brockton Enterprise,* 24 June 1936.

LAMBERT, **John, Jr. Philadelphia.**
1861 Philadelphia, PA–1907 Jenkintown, PA
Training— Philadelphia: PAFA; New York: ASL; Paris: EcBA (Luc Olivier Merson), Henri-Lucien Doucet, Jules Joseph Lefebvre, Jean-Joseph Benjamin-Constant, Acad. Julian.

Portrait. **#364. Lent by Mrs. Lambert, Philadelphia.** Unlocated.

Landscape, Midday. **#1179.** [$225]. Unlocated.

A Commissionaire (Public Porter and Messenger). **#1214.** [$300]. Unlocated.

LAMPERT, **Emma E.** (Emma Esther/Mrs. Colin Campbell Cooper). **Rochester, N.Y.**
1860 Nunda, NY–1920 Pittsford, NY
Training— New York: Agnes Abbatt, William Merritt Chase, Cooper Union, ASL; Paris: Harry Thompson, Acad. Delecluse (Luc Olivier Merson); the Netherlands: J. Kever.

Behind the Dunes. **#604.** [$350]. Unlocated. "A charming Dutch scene . . . awarded a medal at the Atlanta Exposition. A soft, misty Dutch landscape, so thoroughly sympathetic that it won instant recognition from artists and laymen alike"—*Arts for America* 7 (April 1898): 470.

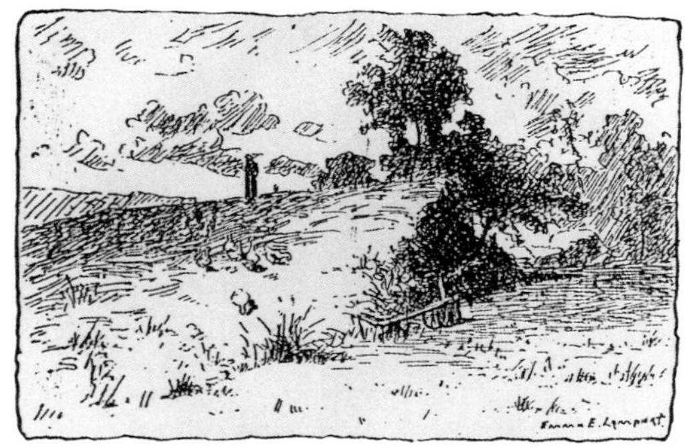

A Hillside in Picardy. **#749.** [$300]. ca. 1887. Unlocated. Illus: Rochester Art Club, *Illustrated Catalogue, Ninth Annual Exhibition of the Rochester Art Club* (Rochester: Scrantom Wetmore, 1888), no. 90.

LATHROP, **Clara W.** (Clara Welles). **Northampton, Mass.**
1853 Northampton, MA–1907 Northampton, MA
Training— New York: ASL; Brooklyn: Pratt Institute; Paris: Tony Robert-Fleury, Julius Rolshoven, William Bouguereau; England; the Netherlands.

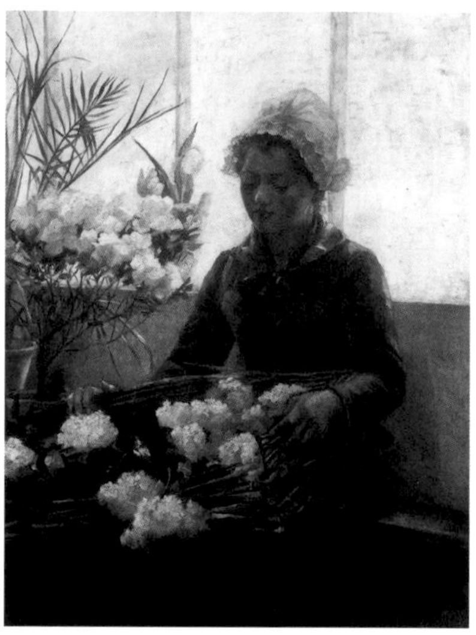

At the Flower Market. **#341.** [$200]. *A French Flower Girl,* 1891. 45¾ x 35⅛. Smith College Museum of Art, Northampton, MA, Purchased from the artist's estate and given by friends of the artist, 1907.

LEE, **Laura. Boston.**
1867 Charlestown, MA–1954 Melrose, MA
Training— Boston: MFA (Frederic Crowninshield, Otto Grundmann, Robert Vonnoh); Paris: Charles Lasar, Acad. Julian (William Bouguereau, Jules Joseph Lefebvre).

Retrospection. **#710.** Unlocated.

LEIGH, **William R.** (William Robinson). **Munich, Bavaria.**
1866 Falling Waters, WV–1955 New York, NY
Training— Baltimore: Maryland Institute of Art (Hugh Newell); Munich: Royal Academy (Karl Raupp, Nikolaus Gysis, Ludwig von Löfftz, Wilhelm Lindenschmidt).

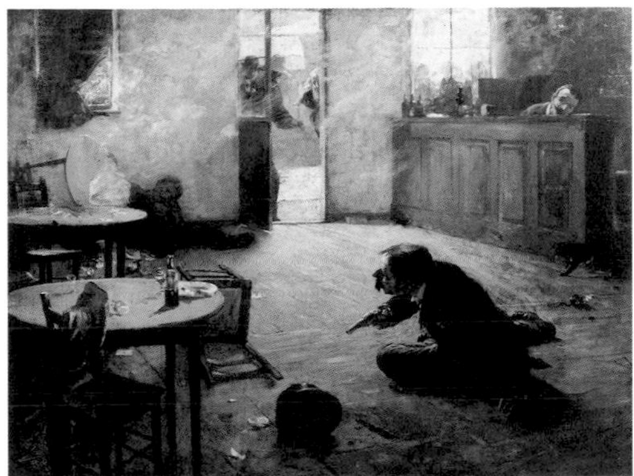

The End of the Play*. **#568. [$1000]. *The End of the Play (The Gambler),* 1892. 38 x 50. Collection John J. McMullen. Photograph by Wayne Geist.

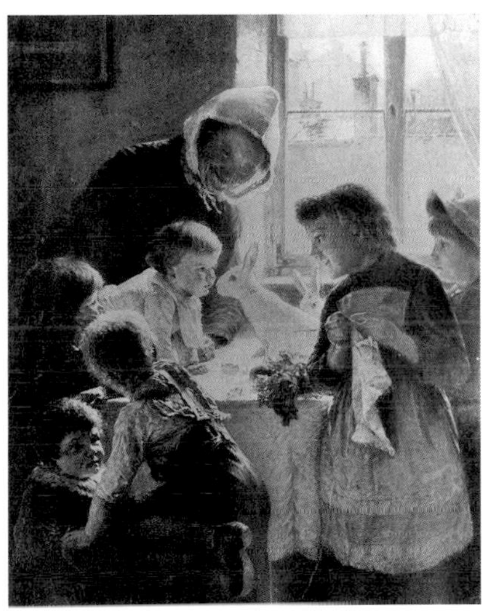

A New Acquaintance. **#1223.** [$1000]. 38 x 31. Unlocated. Illus: William Walton, *Art and Architecture,* vol. 1 (Philadelphia: G. Barrie, 1893–95), 7.

LOOMIS, Chester (Chester Hicks). **Englewood, N.J.**
1852 Syracuse, NY–1924 Englewood, NJ
Training — West Haven, CT; Paris: Harry Thompson, Léon Bonnat, Acad. Julian.

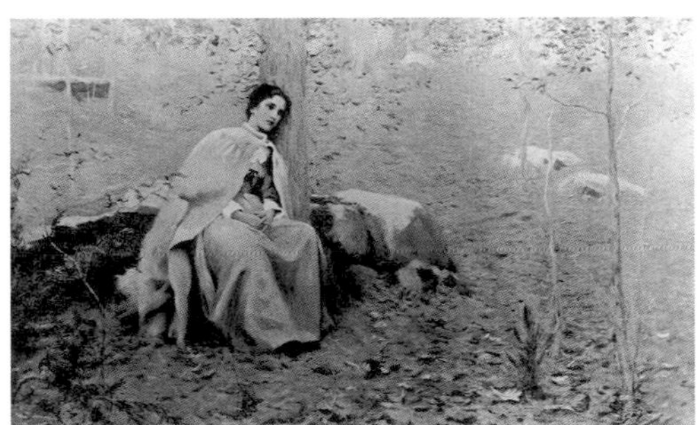

Hester. **#407.** [$500]. ca. 1892. Est. 18 x 32. Unlocated. Illus: *Buildings and Art at the World's Fair* (Chicago: Rand, McNally, 1894), 229. "The figure of a handsome young woman in gray whose dress has the same tone as the rocks among the autumn leaves"— "Monthly Record of American Art," *The Magazine of Art* 15 (Dec. 1891–Nov. 1892): xxvii.

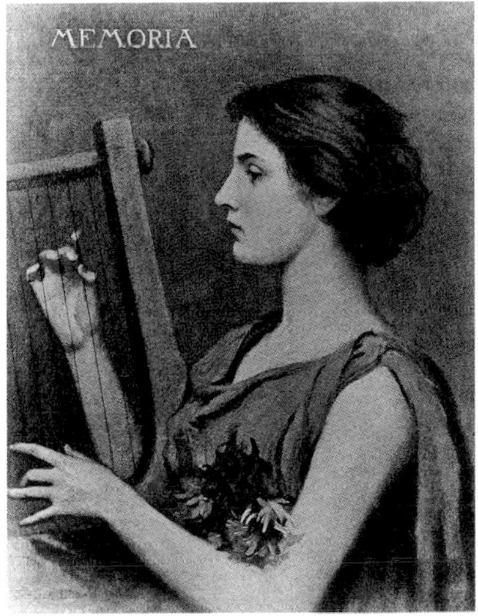

Memoria. **#479.** [$200]. Est. 18 x 15. Unlocated. Illus: Daniel H. Burnham, *The Art of the World,* vol. 5 (New York: Appleton, 1893–95).

LORENZ, Richard. Milwaukee.
1858 Voigstadt, Germany 1915 Milwaukee, WI
Training — Milwaukee: William Wehner; Weimar, Germany: Weimar Academy (Albert-Heinrich Brendel, Marc Thedy, Willem Linnig, Alexander Struys, Theodor-Joseph Hagen).

Alone. **#1163.** [$1500]. Unlocated.

LORING, Francis W. (Francis William). **Florence, Italy.**
1838 Boston, MA–1905 Meran, Austria
Training — Boston; New York; Chicago; Paris: Acad. Colarossi, Léon Bonnat, Gustave Boulanger, Jules Joseph Lefebvre.

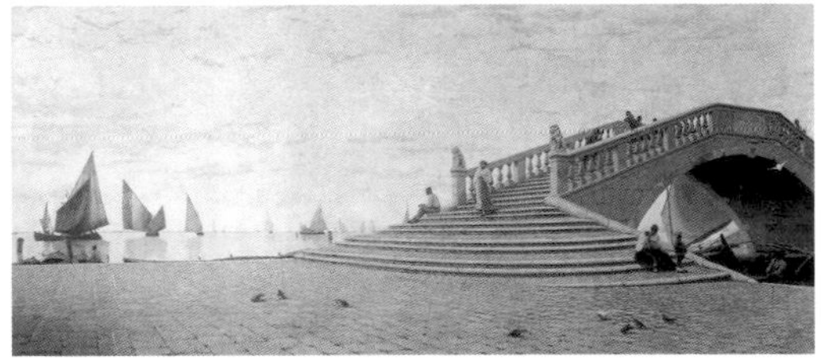

Great Bridge at Chioggia, Italy. **#576.** [$3000]. *Great Bridge at Chioggia,* 1886–87. 57⅞ x 118⅜. Museum of Fine Arts, Boston, Gift of the Artist.

LOW, Will H. (Will Hicok). **New York.**
1853 Albany, NY–1932 Bronxville, NY
Training — Paris: Carolus-Duran, Jean-Léon Gérôme.

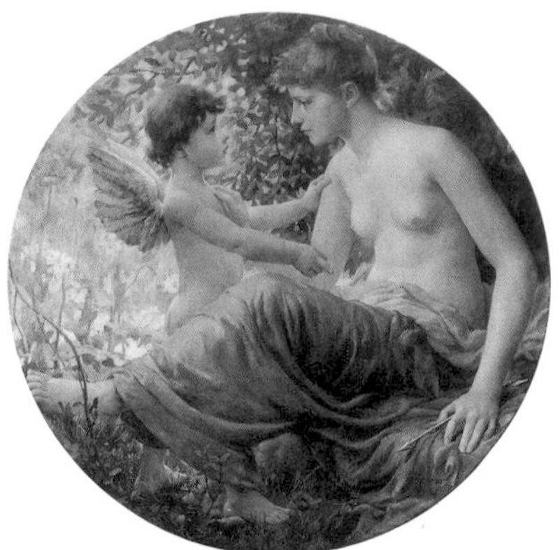

Love Disarmed. **#504. Lent by Mr. Gardiner G. Hubbard, Washington, D.C.** 1889 (oil on panel). 36⅛ x 36⅛. The Brooklyn Museum, Dick S. Ramsay Fund, Augustus Graham School of Design, A. L. Pratt Fund, Charles S. Smith Memorial Fund.

In an Old Garden. **#587. Lent by Dr. C. B. Kelsey, New York.** ca. 1889. Est. 10 x 8. Unlocated. "A pleasant bit of landscape to which the small figures give a certain piquancy"—*Art Amateur* 21 (July 1889): 28.

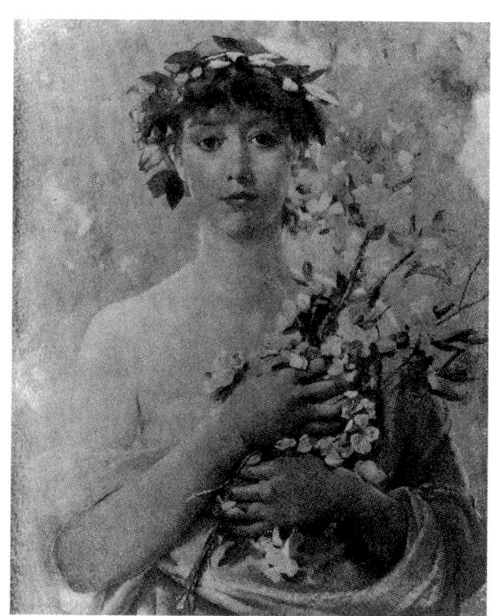

May Blossoms. **#945. Lent by Smith College, Northampton College, Mass.** 25½ x 21. Formerly Collection Smith College Museum of Art. Sold, Kende Galleries at Gimbel Brothers, New York, NY, 1946. Unlocated. Illus: *McClure's Magazine* (Sept. 1895): 296.

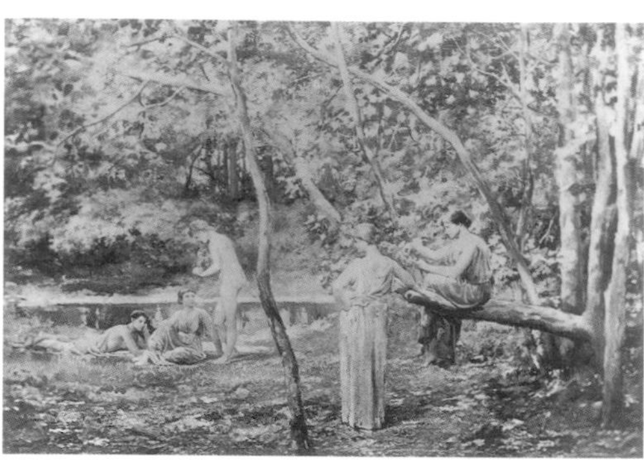

A Woodland Glade. **#1054.** [$1200]. 1891 (oil on panel). 19½ x 30½. Offered for sale (as *An Arcadian Pool*), Christie's, New York, NY, 28 May 1992, lot 92. Unlocated. Illus: William Walton, *Art and Architecture,* vol. 1 (Philadelphia: G. Barrie, 1893–95), opposite 12.

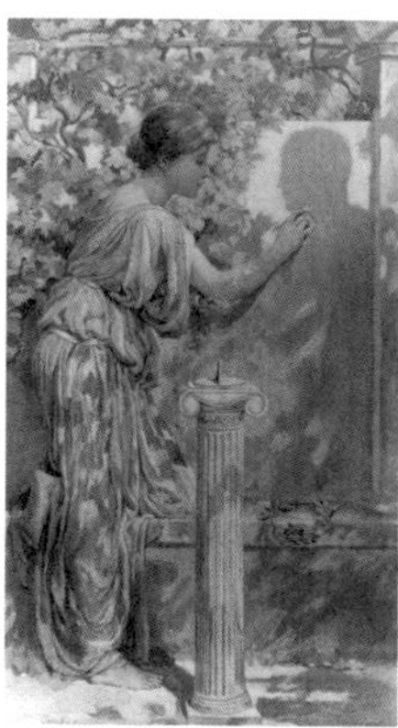

The Portrait. **#1092.** [$1000]. **Lent by Mr. W. T. Evans, New York.** 1890. 25 x 14½. Sold, American Art Association, New York, NY, 12 Jan. 1923, lot 43, to A. Austin. Unlocated. Illus: *Century Magazine* 41 (Nov. 1890): 61.

LOWNES, Anna (also Lowndes). **Philadelphia.**
Unknown–Residing 1910 Media, PA
Training — Philadelphia: The Philadelphia School of Design for Women (Milne Ramsay); Paris: Acad. Delecluse.

The Raven. **#966.** Unlocated.

LUCAS, A. P. (Albert Pike). **Paris, France.**
1862 Jersey City, NJ–1945 New York, NY
Training — Paris: A. A. E. Hébert, Gustave Courtois, P. A. J. Dagnan-Bouveret, Acad. Julian (Gustave Boulanger), EcBA.

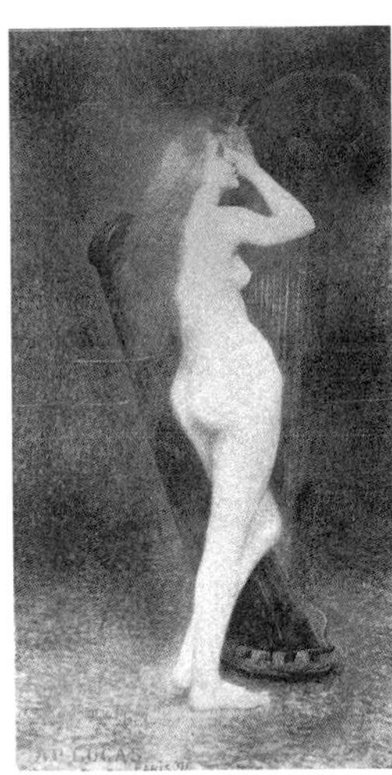

Music. **#333.** [$3000]. 1891. Est. 85 x 50. Unlocated. Illus: The Art Club of Philadelphia, *Third Annual Exhibition of Oil Paintings and Sculpture, 1891, Catalogue of Exhibition* (Philadelphia: Isaiah Price, 1891), 12.

LUTZ, **Lewis C.** (Lewis Cass). **Cincinnati.**
1855 Cambridge City, IN–1893 Cincinnati, OH?
Training — Cincinnati: McMicken School of Design; Munich: Royal Academy; Paris: Acad. Julian (William Bouguereau), Acad. Colarossi, Auguste-Joseph Delecluse.

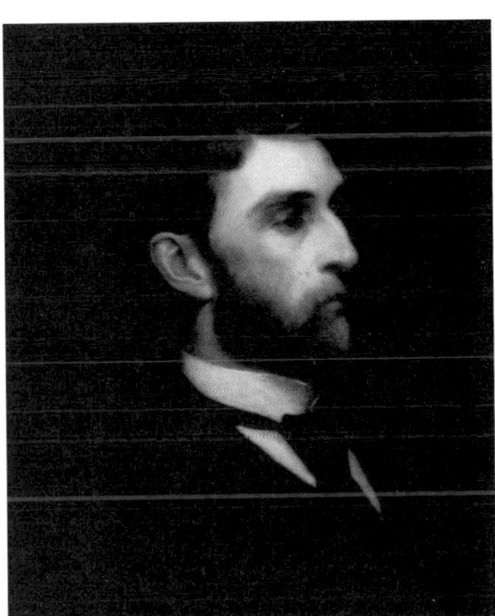

Portrait of J. H. Gest. **#696. Lent by Mrs. J. H. Gest.** 1892. 24 x 20. Private Collection.

LYMAN, **Joseph. New York.**
1843 Ravenna, OH–1913 Wallingford, CT
Training — New York: J. H. Dolph, Samuel Coleman; Europe.

Early Snow in the Adirondacks. **#624.** ca. 1892. Unlocated.

Sand Dunes at Annisquam, Mass. **#808.** [$400]. ca. 1889. Est. 30 x 55. Unlocated.

MACDOWELL, **Elizabeth** (Mrs. Louis Kenton). **Philadelphia.**
1858 Philadelphia, PA–1953 Roanoke, VA
Training — Philadelphia: PAFA (Thomas Eakins).

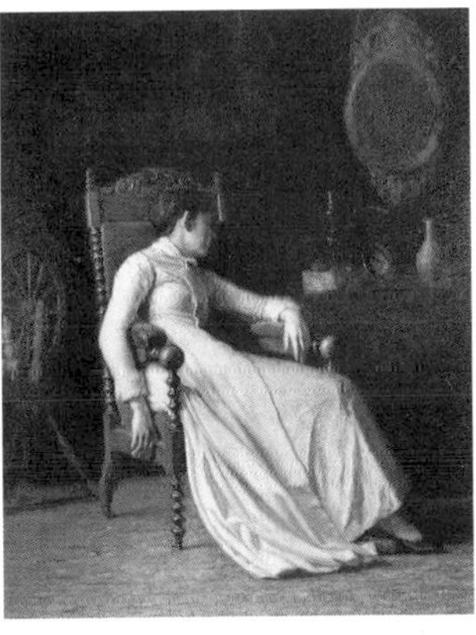

Day Dreams. **#1034. Lent by Mr. Walter Macdowell, Philadelphia.** n.d. 19¼ x 15⅜. Private Collection. Photograph by M. Wayne Newcomb.

---

† MACMONNIES, **Mary Fairchild** (Mary Louise Fairchild/Mrs. Frederick William MacMonnies; after 1909, Mrs. Will Hicok Low). **Paris, France.**
1858 New Haven, CT–1946 Bronxville, NY
Training — St. Louis: School of Fine Arts; Paris: Acad. Julian (Gustave Boulanger, William Bouguereau, Tony Robert-Fleury), Carolus-Duran, Jules Joseph Lefebvre, Harry Thompson.

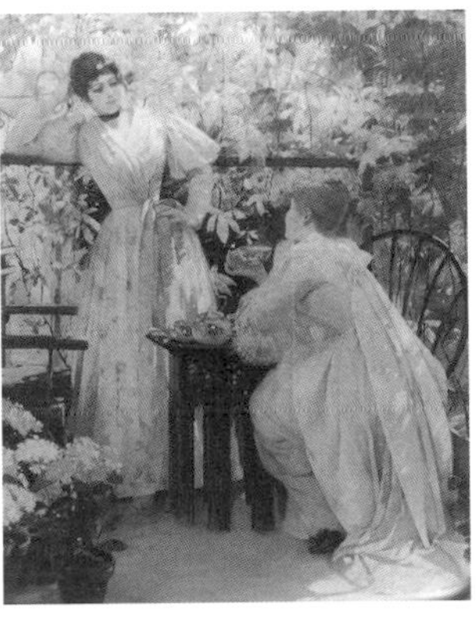

******Tea al Fresco.* **#301.** *Five O'Clock Tea,* 1891. 89 x 61. Sheldon Swope Art Museum, Terre Haute, IN.

June Morning. **#307. Lent by the St. Louis Museum of Fine Arts.** 1888. 56 x 74. Collection The City Art Museum, St. Louis, 1915. Unlocated. "A kitchen-garden in a French village (Cernay-la-Ville). A young women, in the foreground, stoops to pluck a flower, and a nurse-maid with an infant in her arms, stands nearby. The garden is bright with poppies and other blossoms of early summer, growing up amidst various vegetables. The feeling of morning is admirably expressed. A light blue haze is in the air, and the entire color-scheme is light and delicate, ranging through pale pinks, greens, purples and grays, accentuated by touches of red in certain of the flowers"—*Handbook, City Art Museum* (St. Louis, 1915).

MACOMBER, M. L. (Mary Lizzie). **Waverly, Mass.**
1861 Fall River, MA–1916 Boston, MA
Training— Fall River, MA: Robert S. Dunning; Boston: MFA, Frank Duveneck.

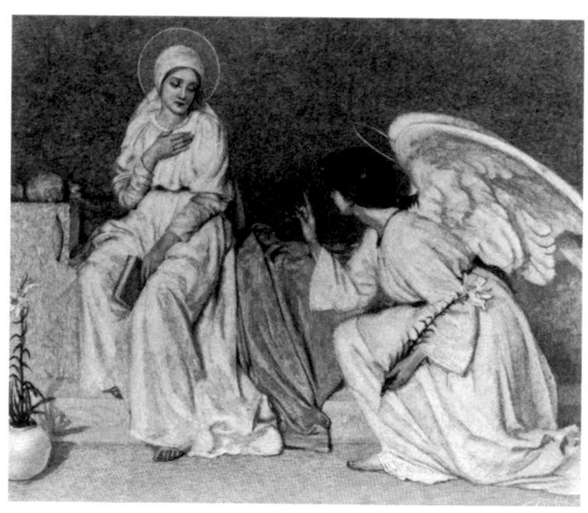

The Annunciation. **#574. Lent by Mrs. D. P. Kimball, Boston.** ca. 1892. Est. 20 x 30. Unlocated.[44] Illus: *Century Magazine* 45 (Dec. 1892): 283. "A modest, shrinking virgin, with her book and her lily, a gentle kneeling angel, a good deal of white on a background of dappled bluish green . . ."— J. S. Merrill, *Art Clippings from the Pen of Walter Cranston Larned and Other Critics at the Fair* (Chicago: J. S. Merrill, 1893).

Love Awakening Memory. **#578. Lent by Miss Elizabeth Howell, Boston.** Est. 30 x 20. Unlocated. "Abounding in white drapery and white wings, with a background of pinkish hue this time and the same naive, pensive charm of treatment, its medievalism helped out by the arches in the background"— J. S. Merrill, *Art Clippings from the Pen of Walter Cranston Larned and Other Critics at the Fair* (Chicago: J. S. Merrill, 1893); "The only attempt at an ideal subject. . . . The two white-robed figures in a white marble cloister are very well composed, but the handling is a little hard and labored"— *Art Amateur* 28 (Jan. 1893): 44.

MAJOR, Ernest L. (Ernest Lee). **Boston.**
1864 Washington, DC–1950 Boston, MA
Training— Washington, D. C.: Corcoran School of Art; New York: ASL (William Merritt Chase); Paris: Acad. Julian (Gustave Boulanger, Jules Joseph Lefebvre), Henri-Lucien Doucet.

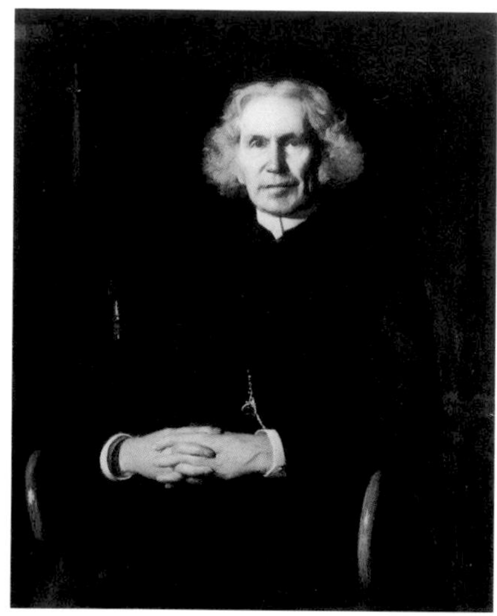

Portrait. **#949. Lent by Mrs. S. Clark, Williamstown, Mass.** *Amos Edward Lawrence,* 1892. 40½ x 32⅛. Yale University Art Gallery, Gift of Mrs. Samuel F. Clarke to the Fence Club.

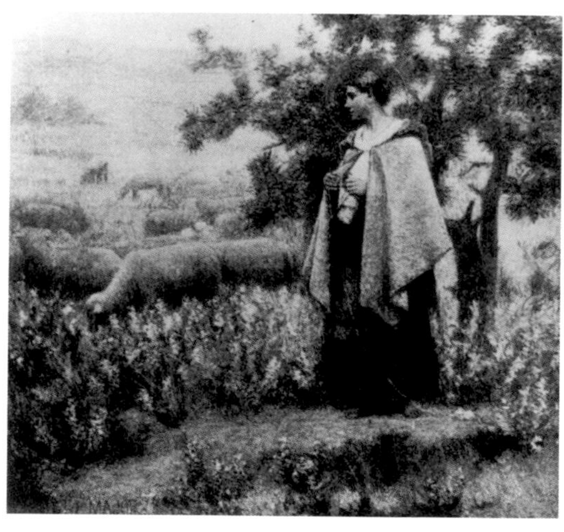

St. Genevieve. **#1090.** [$1000]. ca. 1889. Est. 100 x 120. Unlocated. Illus: William H. Downes, "New England Art at the World's Fair," *New England Magazine* 8 (July 1893): 365.

Youth. **#1148.** [$300]. Unlocated. "Ernest L. Major's 'Youth,' a woman with blond hair combed back in the style of Mrs. Henry M. Stanley — Dorothy Tennant that was — and showing against a spray of apple blossoms, is a work of refinement, wherein one feels that the artist has enobled his subject"— *Brooklyn Daily Eagle,* 12 April 1891.

MARR, Carl (Carl von). **Munich, Bavaria.**
1858 Milwaukee, WI–1936 Munich, Germany
Training — Johann von Marr [his father], Henry Vianden; Weimar, Germany: Weimar Academy (Ferdinand Schauss, Carl Gehrts); Berlin: Berlin Academy (Karl Gussow); Munich: Royal Academy (Otto Seitz, Gabriel Max, Wilhelm Lindenschmidt).

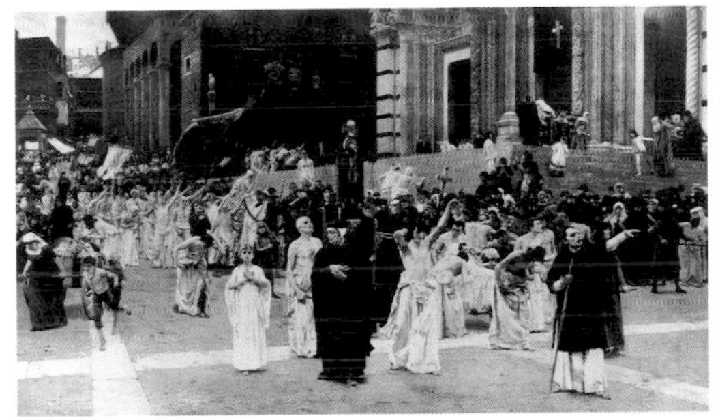

The Flagellants. **#797.** [$20,000]. 1889. 166 x 308. City of Milwaukee, permanent loan to West Bend Gallery of Fine Arts.

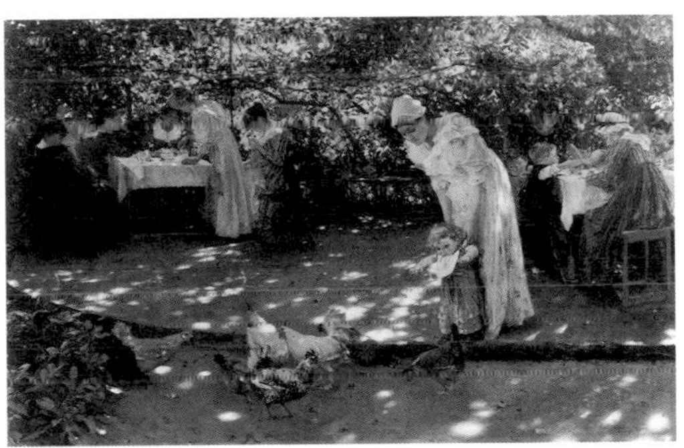

A Summer Afternoon*. **#812. Lent by Mrs. P. A. Hearst, Washington, D.C. 1892. 52¾ x 81½. University Art Museum, University of California at Berkeley, bequest of Phoebe Apperson Hearst, on long-term loan to West Bend Gallery of Fine Arts.

MARTIN, Homer D. (Homer Dodge). **New York.**
1836 Albany, NY–1897 St. Paul, MN
Training — Albany, NY: James MacDougal Hart.

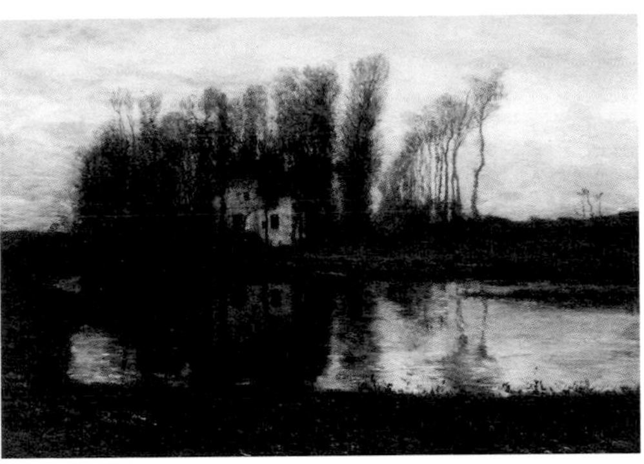

Old Manor at Cricqueboeuf. **#665. Lent by Dr. D. L. Stimson, New York.** *Old Manor of Cricqueboeuf,* n.d. (ca. 1882–86). 25¼ x 37½. The Metropolitan Museum of Art, Bequest of Daniel M. Stimson, 1922.

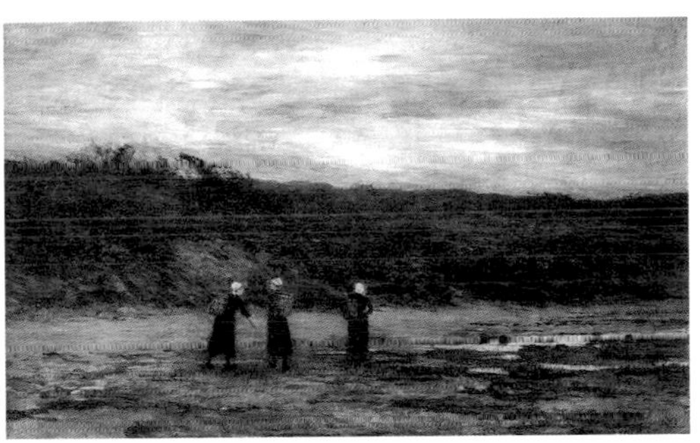

Mussel Gatherers at Villerville, Normandy. **#839. Lent by Mr. F. L. Gunther, New York.** *Mussel Gatherers,* 1886. 29⅛ x 46½. Corcoran Gallery of Art, Bequest of Mabel Stevens Smithers.

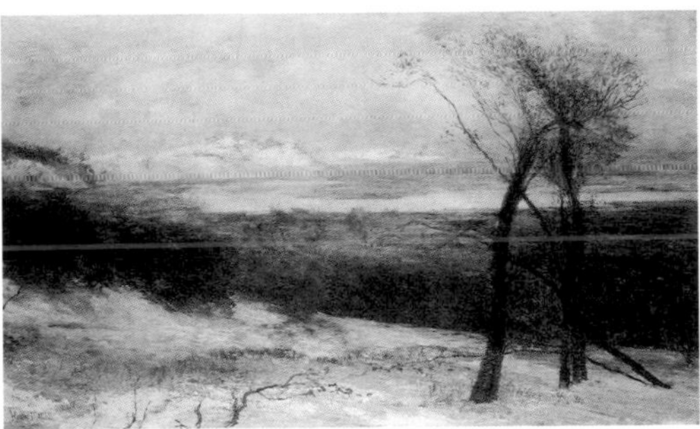

Behind the Dunes, Lake Ontario. **#965.** [$2500]. *Behind Dunes, Lake Ontario,* 1887. 36 x 60½. The Metropolitan Museum of Art, Gift of George A. Hearn, 1906.

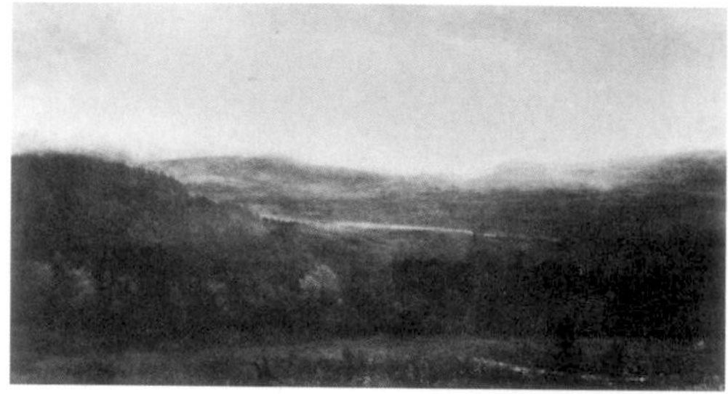

Head-Waters of the Hudson. **#1056. Lent by Mr. Thomas B. Clarke, New York.** 1869. 18 x 32. Formerly Collection St. Louis Art Museum. Sold, Christie's East, New York, NY, 1 October 1986, lot 147. Unlocated. Illus: Dana H. Carroll, *Fifty-eight Paintings by Homer D. Martin* (New York, 1913; privately printed), 48.

MATHEWS, **Arthur F.** (Arthur Frank). **San Francisco.**
1860 Markesan, WI–1945 San Francisco, CA
Training — Paris: Acad. Julian (Gustave Boulanger, Jules Joseph Lefebvre); the Netherlands.

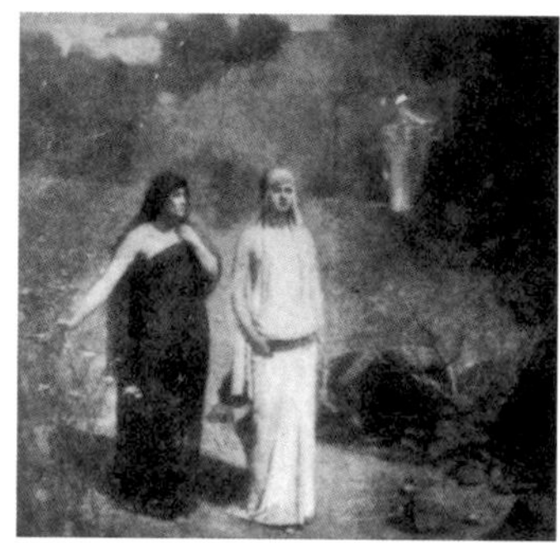

Judith. **#1264.** Est. 40 x 25. Unlocated. Photograph (cropped by one quarter at bottom) courtesy Archives of California Art, The Oakland Museum.

MAYNARD, **George Willoughby. New York.**
1843 Washington, DC–1923 New York, NY
Training — New York: NAD; Florence: Edwin White; Antwerp: Royal Academy (Jan van Lerius).

Flora. **#730. Lent by Mrs. K. R. Papin, Chicago.** ca. 1892. On loan to The Art Institute of Chicago by Mrs. Kate R. Papin, 1896. Unlocated. "The half-length of a nymph crowned with blue and red field flowers"—*Frank Leslie's Illustrated Newspaper,* 12 May 1892, 253.

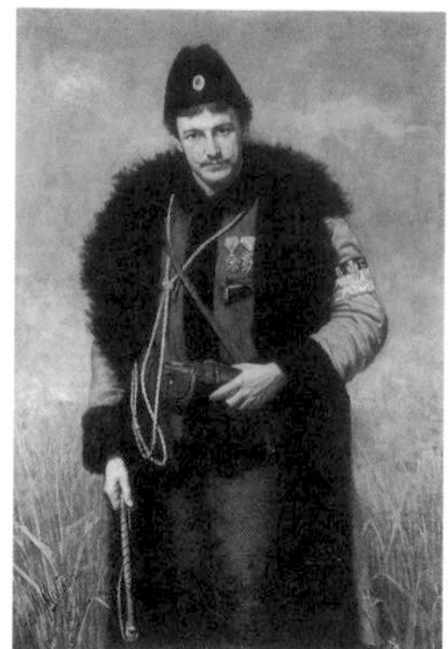

Portrait of F. D. Millet.* **#892. [$1500]. **Lent by Mr. F. D. Millet, New York.** *Francis Davis Millet,* 1878. 59½ x 38¼. National Portrait Gallery, Smithsonian Institution, Bequest of Dr. John A. P. Millet.

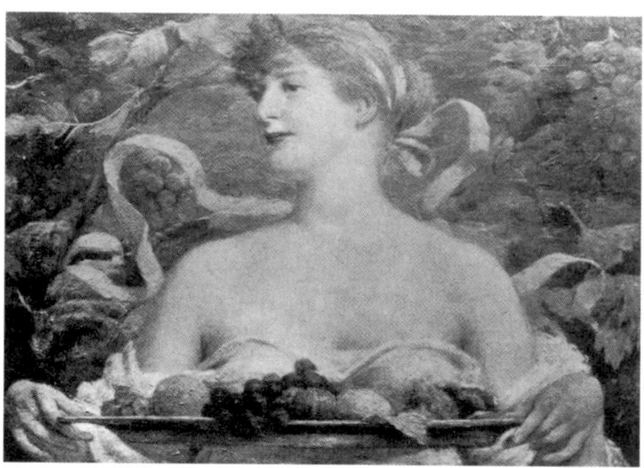

Pomona. **#910.** [$500]. Est. 20 x 30. Unlocated. Illus: Daniel H. Burnham, *The Art of the World,* vol. 9 (New York: Appleton, 1893–95).

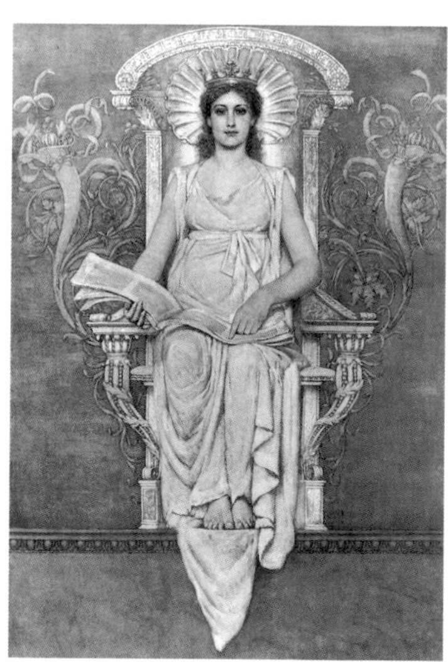

Civilization. **#1274. Lent by the National Academy of Design, New York.** n.d. (ca. 1893). 54¼ x 36. National Academy of Design, New York City.

MAYNARD, Guy F. (Guy Ferris). **Chicago.**
1856 Northampton, MA–1936 Europe?
Training — Chicago: AIC; Paris: Fernand Cormon.

Dutch Interior. **#890. Lent by Mr. P. C. Maynard, Chicago.** Unlocated.

Looking Out. **#981. Lent by Mr. P. C. Maynard, Chicago.** Unlocated.

MCCOMB, R. Lee (Robert Lee MacComb). **Paris, France.**
San Francisco, CA–Unknown
Training — Paris: Albert Gabriel Rigolot.

Summer Time. **#426.** [$250]. Est. 25 x 32. Unlocated.

MCCORMICK, M. Evelyn. San Francisco.
1869 Placerville, CA–1948 Monterey, CA
Training — San Francisco: California School of Design (Emil Carlsen, Virgil Williams, Raymond Yelland); Paris: Acad. Julian.

Afternoon, Old San Luis Rey Mission, California. **#321.** Unlocated.

Morning at Giverny, France. **#933.** Unlocated.

MCEWEN, Walter (also Walter MacEwen). **Paris, France.**
1860 Chicago, IL–1943 New York, NY
Training — Munich: Royal Academy (Frank Duveneck); Paris: Fernand Cormon; Acad. Julian (Tony Robert-Fleury).

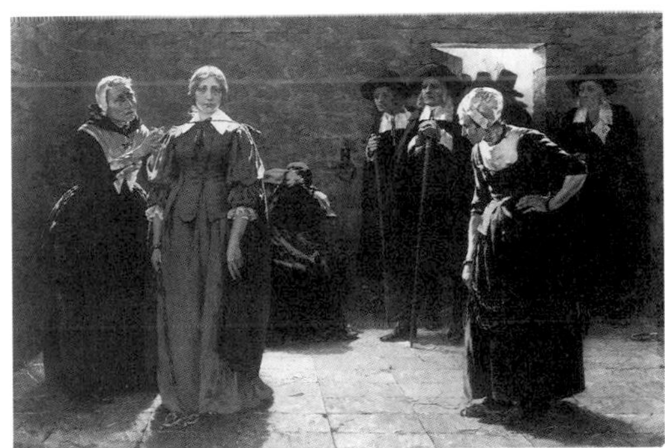

The Witches.* **#502. n.d. 79 x 118¾. Private collection. Illus: Pennslyvania Academy of the Fine Arts, *Forty Works of Art from the Sixty-third Annual Exhibition of the Academy of Fine Arts* (Philadelphia: The Levytype Company, 1894).

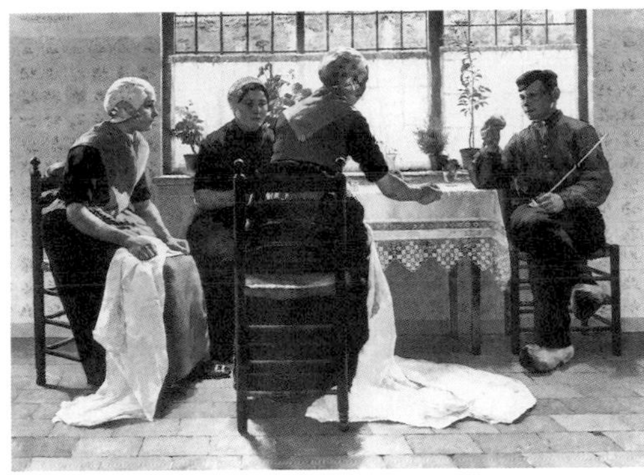

The Judgment of Paris.* **#746. Lent by Mr. Albert A. Munger, Chicago. n.d. (ca. 1886). 36⅜ x 50¼. Tennessee Wesleyan College, Athens, TN.

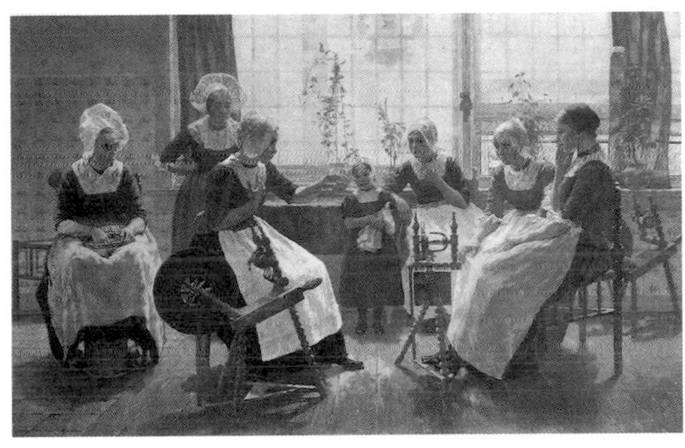

Telling Ghost Stories. **#801.** *The Ghost Story,* 1887. 47¾ x 75¼. The Cleveland Museum of Art, Gift of Mrs. Edward S. Harkness.

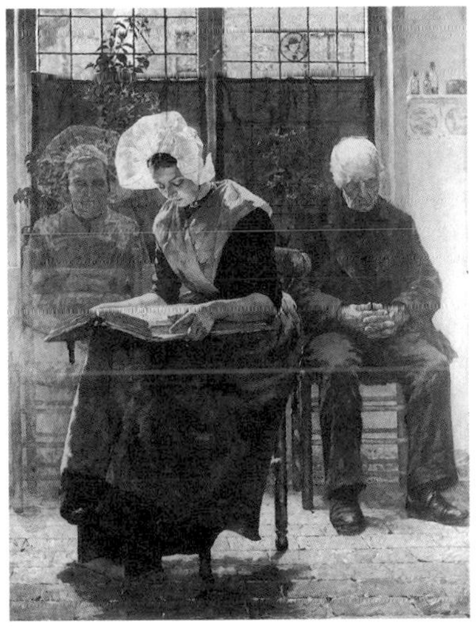

The Absent One (All Soul's Day). **#916.** *"L'absente",* 1889. 63 x 48¼. Museum of Modern Art, Liège.

† McILHENNEY, C. Morgan (Charles Morgan). **Shrub Oak, N.Y.**
1858 Philadelphia, PA–1904 New York, NY
Training — Philadelphia: PAFA.

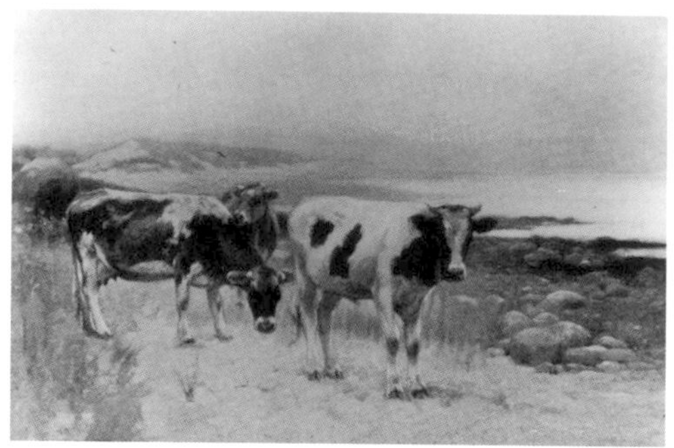

On the Beach. **#670.** [$750]. Sold, World's Columbian Exposition, Chicago, IL, 1893. Unlocated. Illus: Charles M. Kurtz, ed., *Illustrations from the Art Gallery of the World's Columbian Exposition* (Philadelphia: G. Barrie, 1893), 196.

MEEKS, **Eugene. Florence, Italy.**
1843 New York, NY–1916 Florence, Italy
Training — New York; The Hague: Royal Academy; Antwerp: Royal Academy (Nicaise de Keyser, Jan van Lerius).

Macaroni Hot. **#1084.** [$400]. ca. 1888. Unlocated.

Ready for the Chase. **#1267.** [$250]. Est. 30 x 20. Unlocated.

MELCHERS, **Gari** (Julius Gari). **Paris, France.**
1860 Detroit, MI–1932 Fredericksburg, VA
Training — Dusseldorf: Royal Academy (Karl von Gebhardt, Peter Jansen); Paris: Acad. Julian (Jules Joseph Lefebvre, Gustave Boulanger), EcBA.

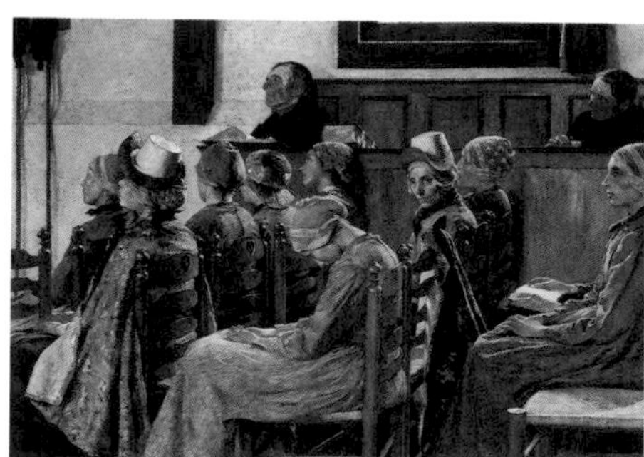

******The Sermon.* **#573. Lent by Mr. Potter Palmer, Chicago.** 1886. 62⅝ x 86½. National Museum of American Art, Smithsonian Institution, Bequest of Henry Ward Ranger through the National Academy of Design.

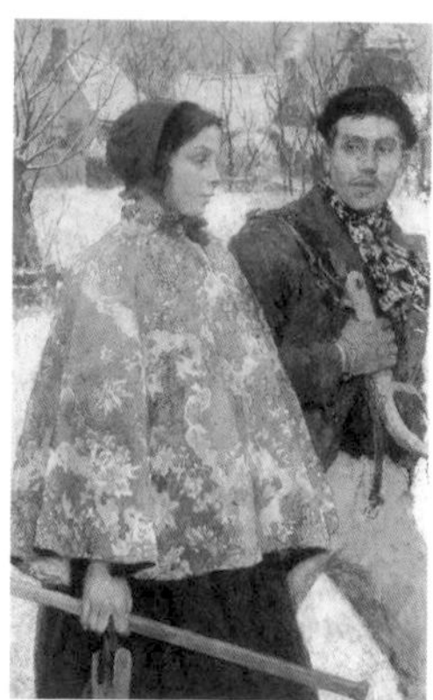

Skaters. **#575.** n.d. (ca. 1893). 43³⁄₁₆ x 27 ⁷⁄₁₆. Pennsylvania Academy of the Fine Arts, Philadelphia, Joseph E. Temple Fund.

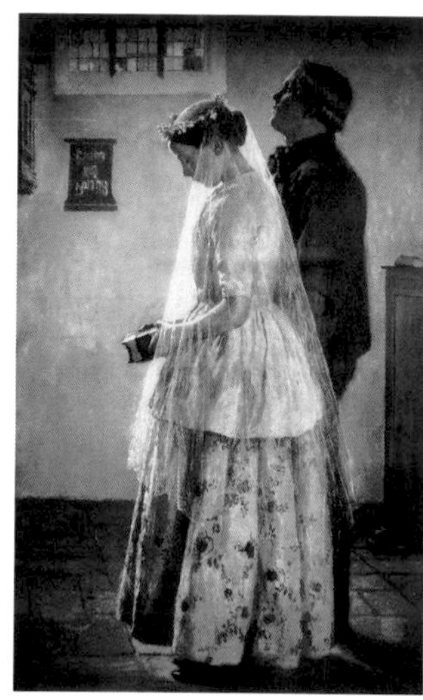

******Married.* **#579. Lent by Mr. Potter Palmer, Chicago.** *The Wedding,* n.d. (ca. 1892). 43 x 26. Albright-Knox Art Gallery, Buffalo, NY, Charles W. Goodyear Fund, 1922.

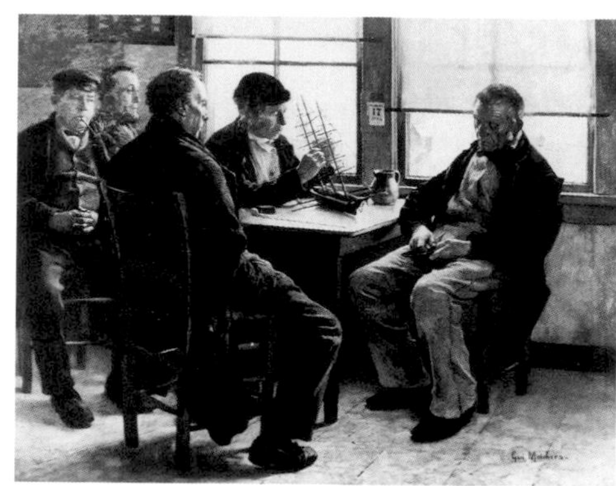

The Pilots. **#580.** 1887. 67 x 83½. Collection of the Charles and Emma Frye Art Museum, Seattle, WA.

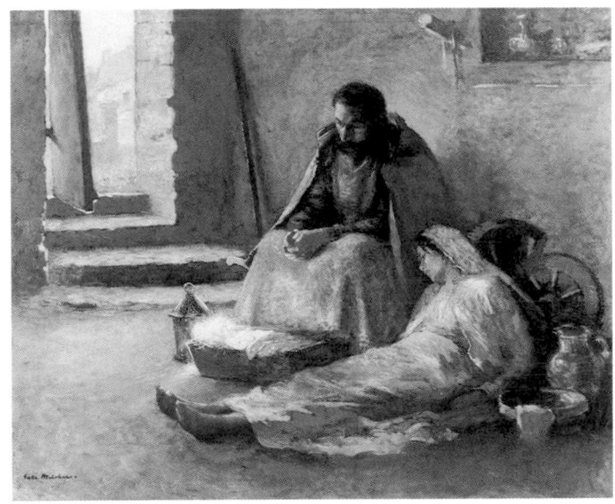

The Nativity. **#596.** [$2000]. n.d. (ca. 1891). 35½ x 43½. Belmont, The Gari Melchers Estate and Memorial Gallery, Mary Washington College, Fredericksburg, VA.

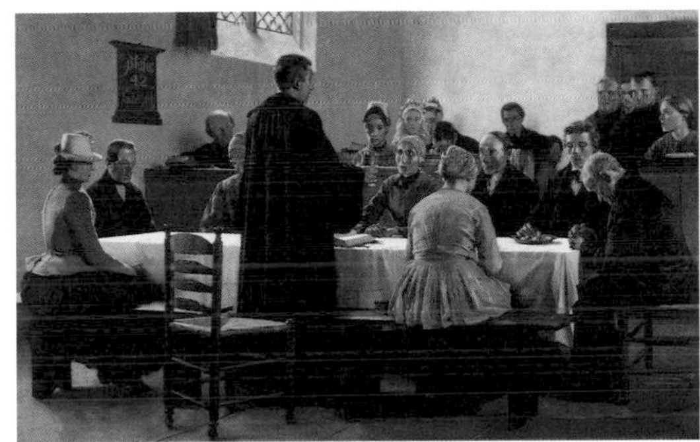

Communion (Holland). **#678.** 1888. 86⅞ x 134¼. College of Arts and Sciences, Cornell University.

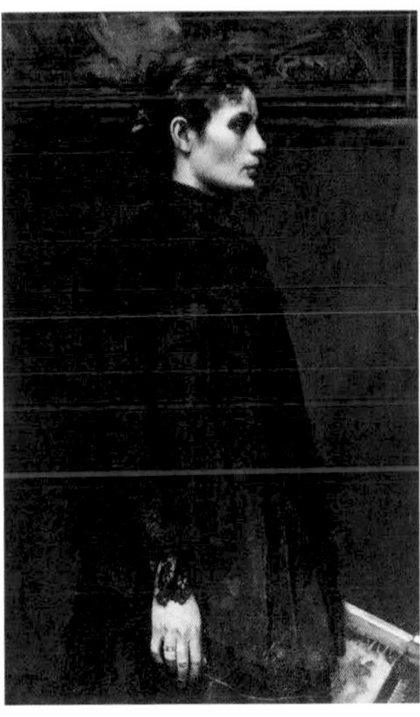

Portrait of Mrs. H*. **#905. *Portrait of Mrs. George Hitchcock,* n.d. (ca. 1890). 35½ x 21¾. Collection of Rita and Daniel Fraad.

MERRITT, **Mrs. Anna Lea** (Anna Massey Lea/Mrs. Henry Merritt). **Andover, Hampshire, England.**
1844 Philadelphia, PA–1930 London, England
Training — Dresden: Heinrich Hoffman; England: Henry Merritt; Paris; Rome.

Portrait of Mrs. Reginald DeKoven. **#370. Lent by Mrs. Joseph Lea, Philadelphia.** ca. 1891. Unlocated.[45]

Love Locked Out. **#634.** [$1250]. 1893. Est. 46 x 26. Unlocated.[46]

METCALF, **W. L.** (Willard Leroy). **New York.**
1858 Lowell, MA–1925 New York, NY
Training — Boston: George Loring Brown, Lowell School of Practical Drawing, Massachusetts Normal Art School, MFA; New Mexico and Arizona: Frank Hamilton Cushing; Paris: Acad. Julian (Gustave Boulanger, Jules Joseph Lefebvre).

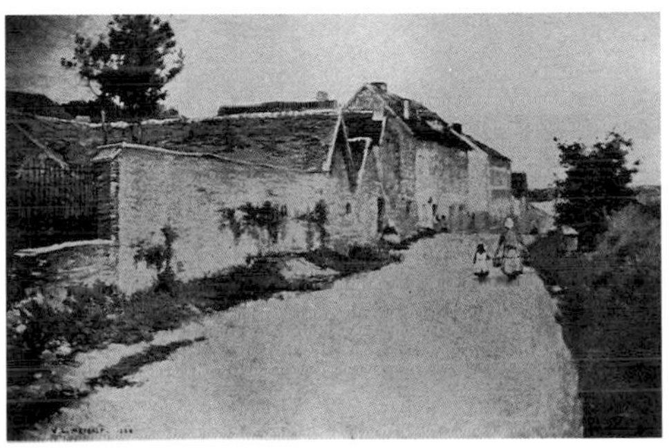

Road to the Village, Normandy. **#344.** [$600]. 32 x 46. Unlocated. Illus (as *Twilight*): The Art Club of Philadelphia, *Third Annual Exhibition of Oil Paintings and Sculpture, 1891, Catalogue of Exhibition* (Philadelphia: Isaiah Price, 1891), 84.

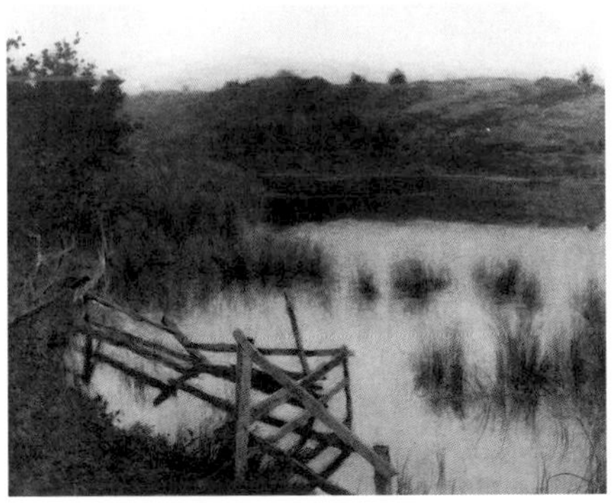

Summer Twilight. **#523.** [$500]. 1890. 34½ x 35. Private Collection, Atlanta, GA.

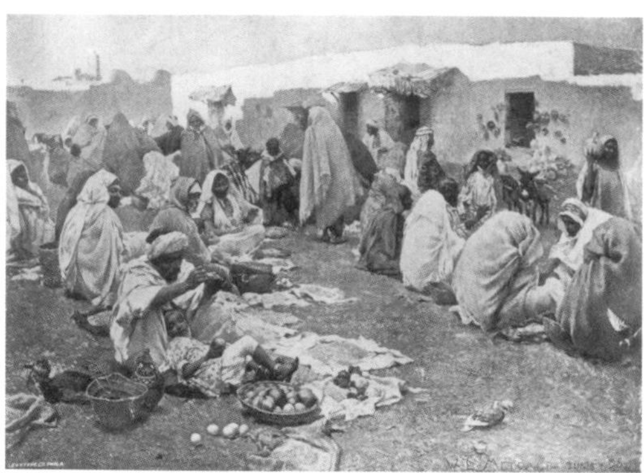

Tunisian Market. **#1030. Lent by Mr. H. R. Astor Carey.** ca. 1888. Est. 60 x 80. Collection St. Boltoph Club, Boston, MA, 1901. Unlocated. Illus: Pennsylvania Academy of the Fine Arts, *Forty Works of Art from the Sixty-third Annual Exhibition of the Academy of Fine Arts* (Philadelphia: The Levytype Company, 1894).

METEYARD, **T. B.** (Thomas Buford). **Paris, France.**
1865 Rock Island, IL–1928 Gilon, Switzerland
Training — Paris: Piérre Bonnard, Claude Monet.

Iris Meadows. **#328.** [$250]. Unlocated.

Road at Giverny. **#1238.** [$150]. Est. 8 x 12. Unlocated.

MIGNOT, **Louis R.** (Louis Remy). **deceased.**
1831 Charleston, SC–1870 Brighton, England
Training — Charleston, SC; The Hague; Paris: Andreas Schelfhout.

Niagara. **#454.** [$3500]. Est. 50 x 120. Unlocated.

MILLER, **Charles H.** (Charles Henry). **New York.**
1842 New York, NY–1922 Queens, NY
Training — Munich: Royal Academy, Adolph Lier.

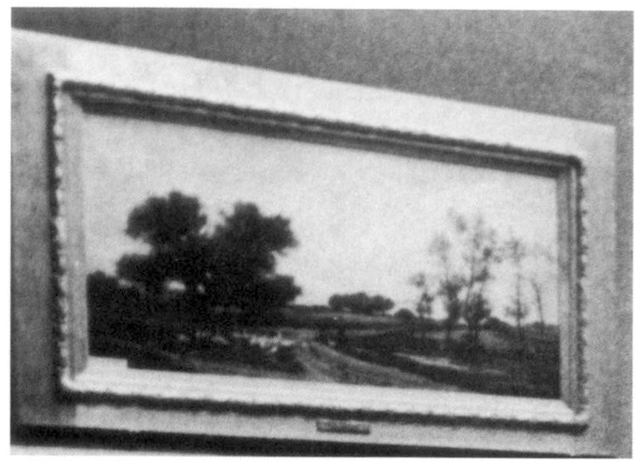

A Gray Day on Long Island. **#572.** [$1000]. ca. 1882. Est. 40 x 70. Unlocated. Illus: Official Photographs of the World's Columbian Exposition by C. D. Arnold, vol. 8, pl. 87. Courtesy of The Chicago Public Library, Special Collections Department. "With its quiet landscape, its rolling ground, its geese in the front of the view, its old farm wagon drawn by two horses and its buildings of a former generation"—*Brooklyn Daily Eagle,* 27 June 1893.

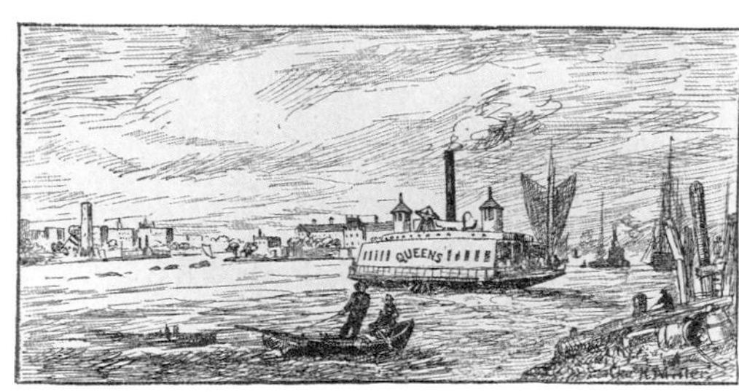

The East River, New York. **#1113.** [$1000]. ca. 1882. 32 x 65. Collection Bloomingdale Brothers, New York, NY, 1909. Unlocated. Illus: Charles M. Kurtz, ed., *Illustrated Art Notes Upon the Fifty-Seventh Annual Exhibition of the National Academy of Design, New York* (New York: Cassell, Petter, Galpin, 1882), 82.

MILLET, **F. D.** (Francis Davis). **New York.**
1846 Mattapoisett, MA–1912 at sea on the *Titanic*
Training — Antwerp: Royal Academy (Jan van Lerius, Nicaise de Keyser).

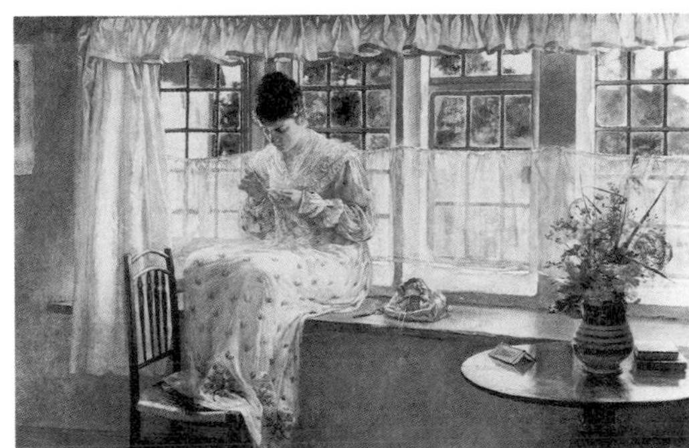

The Window Seat. **#584. Lent by Mr. Charles Fairchild, Boston.** 1883. 20⅛ x 30¼. Manoogian Collection.

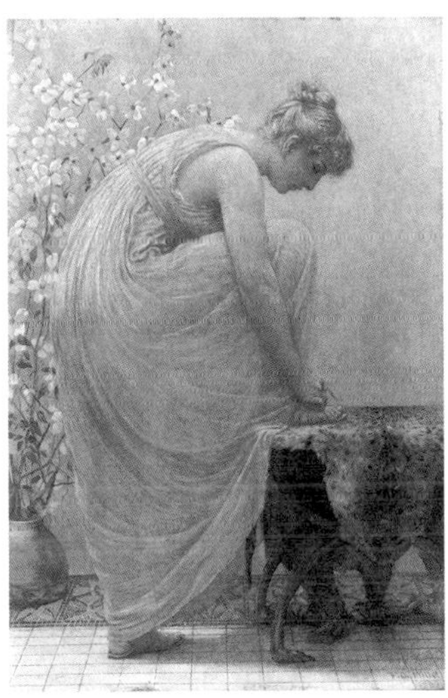

Lacing the Sandal.* **#585. Lent by Mr. Thomas B. Clarke, New York. 1883. 12 x 8. Private Collection.

Sweet Melodies. **#631. Lent by Mr. D. M. Ferry, Detroit, Mich.** Est. 14 x 20. Formerly Collection Vassar College Art Gallery. Sold to Victor Spark, New York, NY, ca. 1964. Unlocated.

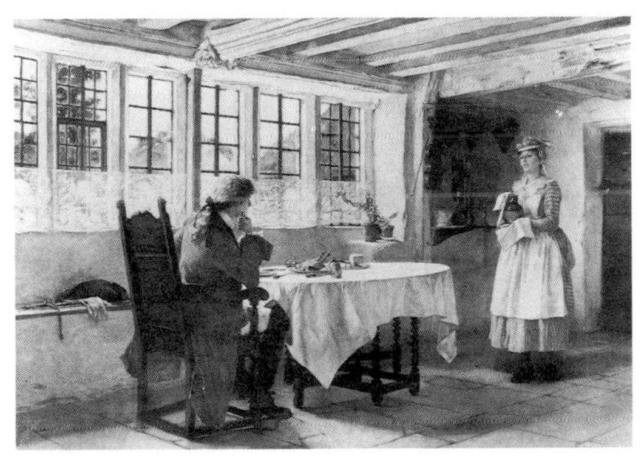

At the Inn. **#677. Lent by the Union League Club, New York.** 1884. 15 x 30. The Union League Club, New York, NY.

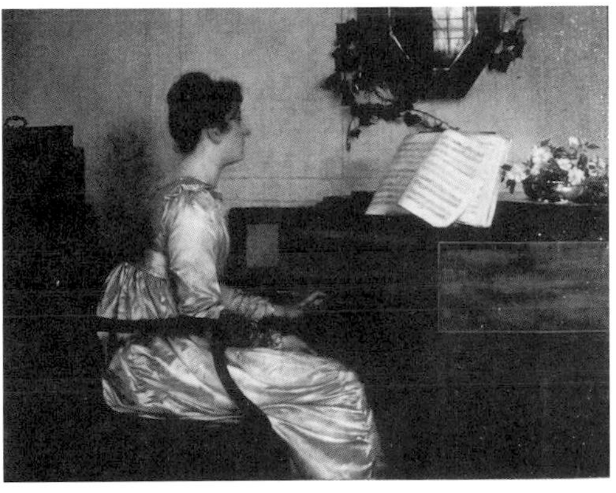

Old Harmonies. **#704. Lent by Mrs. H. K. Porter, Pittsburg.** n.d. (after 1884). 16 x 20½. Collection Karen and Stuart Watson, New Canaan, CT.

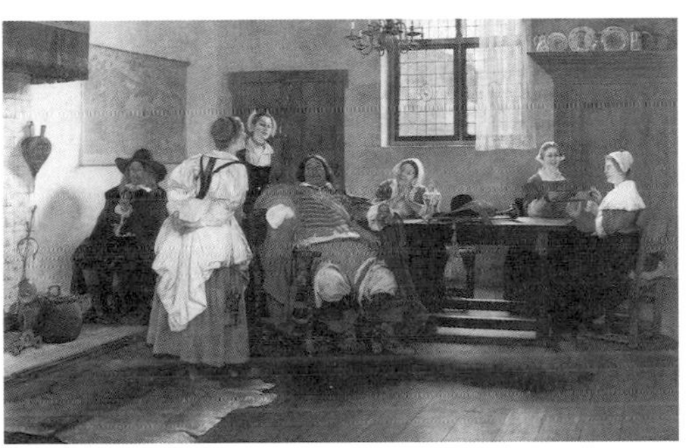

Antony Van Corlear, the Trumpeter.* **#759. [$5000]. n.d. (ca. 1889). 42 x 66. The Duquesne Club, Pittsburgh, PA.

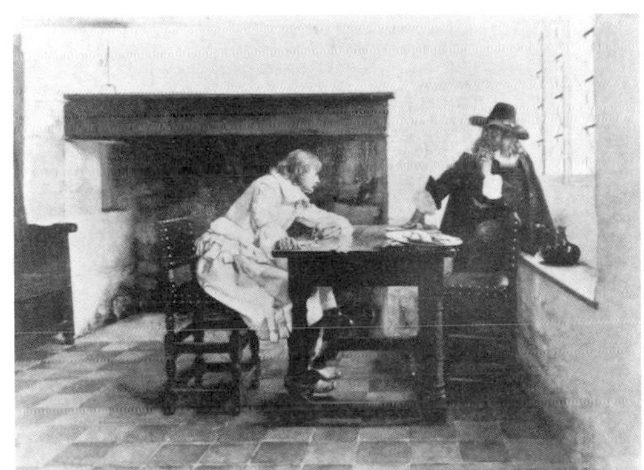

Rook and Pigeon. **#1117. Lent by H. McK. Twombly, New York.** 1889. 27¾ x 37½. Estate of Shirley C. Burden. Illus: *International Studio* (Oct. 1907): cxv.

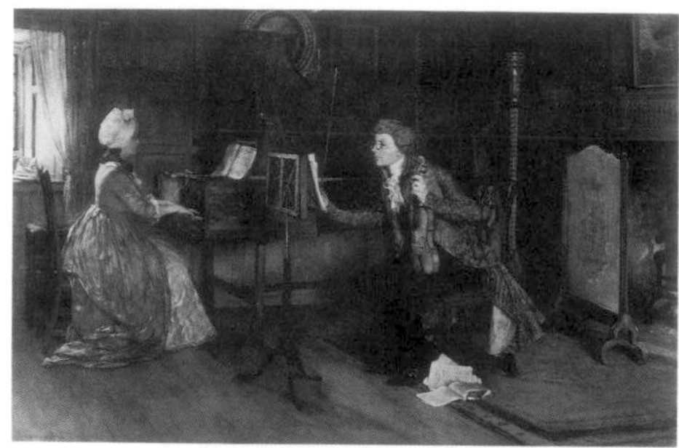

A Difficult Duet. **#1123. Lent by Mrs. C. M. Raymond, New York.** 1886. 24¼ x 36¼. Collection Mr. and Mrs. Richard M. Waitzer.

MINOR, Robert C. (Robert Crannell). **New York.**
1839 New York, NY–1904 Waterford, CT
Training — New York: Alfred Howland; Barbizon, France: Virgilio Narcisso Diaz de la Peña; Paris: Acad. Julian (Gustave Boulanger); Antwerp: G. J. A. Van Luppen.

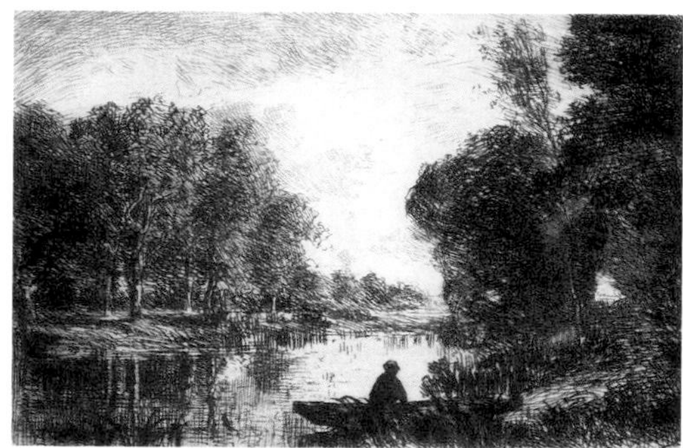

The Close of Day. **#443. Lent by Mr. W. T. Evans, New York.** ca. 1886. 30 x 50. Sold, American Art Association, New York, NY, 31 Jan.–2 Feb. 1900, lot 85, to S. P. Avery. Unlocated. Photograph (from etching after the painting) courtesy of the James Ruddock Collection of American Art and The William Benton Museum of Art, Storrs, CT. "A pastoral of simple beauty of line, mass, and color. A placid stream flows through the meadows, and groups of full-foliaged trees border it on either side and form effective silhouettes, while an evening sky clouded, but very luminous, is reflected on the water. This picture is unified and harmonious, and notable for its golden mellow tone and atmospheric quality. Awarded a medal at the Paris Exposition of 1889"—American Art Association, *Catalogue of American Paintings Belonging to William T. Evans* (New York: Press of J. J. Little, 1900), lot 85.

Evening. **#832.** [$2000]. Unlocated.[47]

Autumn. **#1059.** [$2500]. Est. 36 x 50. Unlocated.

MOELLER, Louis (Louis Charles). **New York.**
1855 New York, NY–1930 Weehawken, NJ
Training — with his father; New York: NAD (Lemuel E. Wilmarth); Munich: Royal Academy (Wilhelm Diez, Frank Duveneck).

Searching. **#650. Lent by Mr. Thomas B. Clarke, New York.** 11 x 14. Sold (as *Inspection*), American Art Association, New York, NY, 14–18 Feb. 1899, lot 352, to P. Doelger. Unlocated. "Having turned it almost inside out, a man is still rummaging in a trunk from which he has extracted all sorts of odds and ends. An elderly man, on a bench near the wall, regards the searcher. Both figures are drawn with insistence on the detail, yet without any evidence of fatigue, for the execution is spirited. The still-life is no less interestingly painted, and the composition is admirably balanced"—American Art Association, *Catalogue of the Private Art Collection of Thomas B. Clarke, New York* (New York: American Art Association, 1899), lot 352.

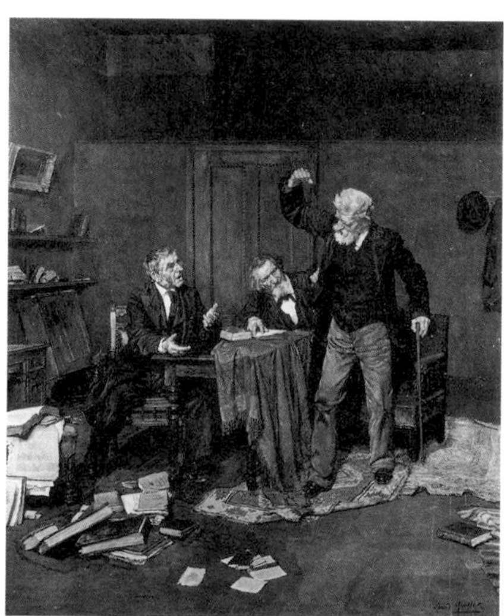

Stubborn. **#938. Lent by Mr. Thomas B. Clarke, New York.** n.d. (ca. 1887). 18 x 15. Collection Mr. and Mrs. Sidney H. Kosann.

MOORE, H. Humphrey (Harry Humphrey). **Paris, France.**
1844 New York, NY–1926 Paris, France
Training — New Haven, CT: Louis Bail; Philadelphia: PAFA (Samuel J. Waugh); San Francisco; Paris: Jean-Léon Gérôme, EcBA (Adolphe Yvon), Acad. Julian (Gustave Boulanger).

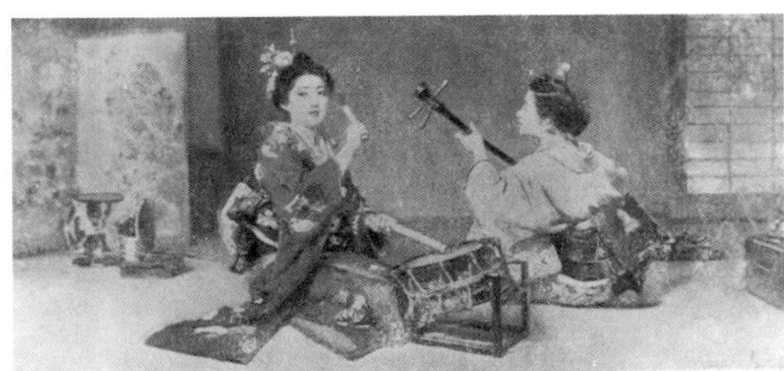

Japanese Musicians. **#815.** [$4500]. Before 1891. Est. 40 x 75. Unlocated.[48] Illus: William Walton, *Art and Architecture,* vol. 1 (Philadelphia: G. Barrie, 1893–95), 9.

MORAN, Edward. New York.

1829 Bolton, England–1901 New York, NY
Training— Philadelphia: James Hamilton, Paul Weber, PAFA; Paris: Acad. Julian.

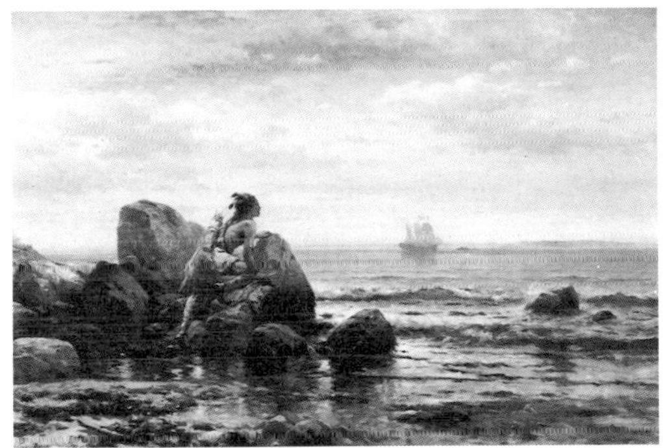

***The First Ship Entering New York Harbor. #588.** [$1500]. *Henrik Hudson Entering New York Harbor, September 11, 1609,* 1892. 35½ x 52½. The Berkshire Museum, Pittsfield, MA, Gift of Zenas Crane.

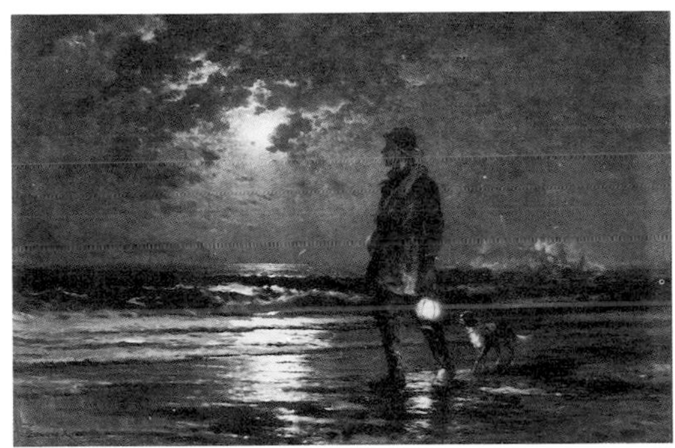

Life Saving Patrol, New Jersey Coast. **#590. Lent by Mr. Amedée Fargis, New York.** n.d. (ca. 1892–93). 36 x 54⅜. National Museum of American Art, Smithsonian Institution, Bequest of Clara L. Tuckerman.

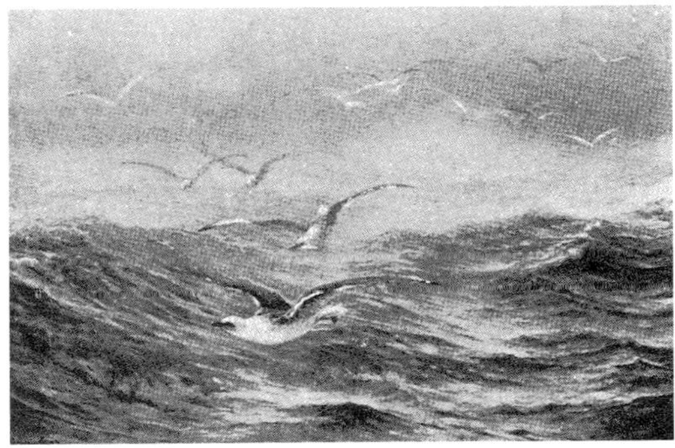

Melodies of the Sea. **#915. Lent by Mrs. Martha E. French, Chicago.**[49] ca. 1890. Unlocated. Illus: *Essays on American Art and Artists* (Temple Court, NY: Eastern Art League, 1896), 28. "Superb dramatic view of a flock of sea-gulls plunging through white foam, dipping their wings in the wild waters, and listening to the 'Melodies of the Sea,' far away from the peopled land" —*Art Amateur* 23 (October 1890): 84.

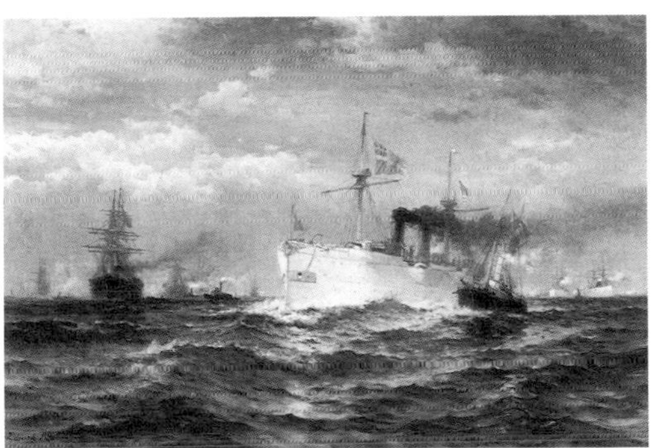

***The White Squadron's Farewell Salute to Commodore John Ericsson.* #1109.** [$1500]. *The White Squadron's Farewell Salute to the Body of John Ericsson in New York Bay, August 25, 1890,* ca. 1891.[50] 36 x 54. United States Naval Academy Museum.

MORAN, Leon (John Leon). New York.

1864 Philadelphia, PA–1941 Plainfield, NJ
Training— Edward Moran [his father]; New York: NAD; France; England.

Back from the Post-office. **#708.** Unlocated.

MORAN, Peter. Philadelphia.

1841 Lancashire, England–1914 Philadelphia, PA
Training— Thomas and Edward Moran [his brothers]; Philadelphia: Herline & Hersel, Lithographers; London.

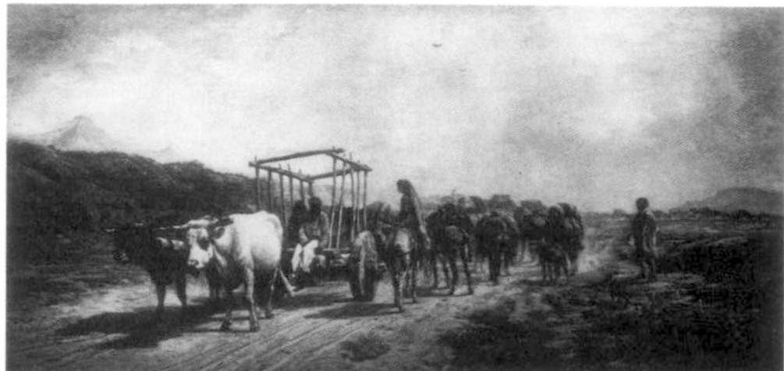

Down the Arroya to Santa Fé. **#1120.** ca. 1885.
Unlocated. Photograph (from photogravure after the painting) courtesy Dr. James Powell, Rosemont, PA.

MORAN, Thomas. New York.
1837 Lancashire, England–1926 Santa Barbara, CA
Training — Edward Moran [his brother]; Philadelphia: James Hamilton; London; Paris; Italy.

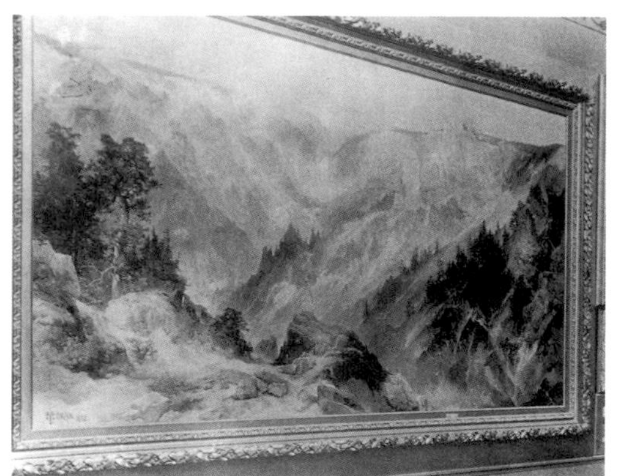

Grand Cañon of the Yellowstone. **#1016.** 1892. 97 x 168⅞.
Repainted as *The Grand Canyon of the Yellowstone.* Illus: Library of Congress, Prints and Photographs Division, lot 2959.

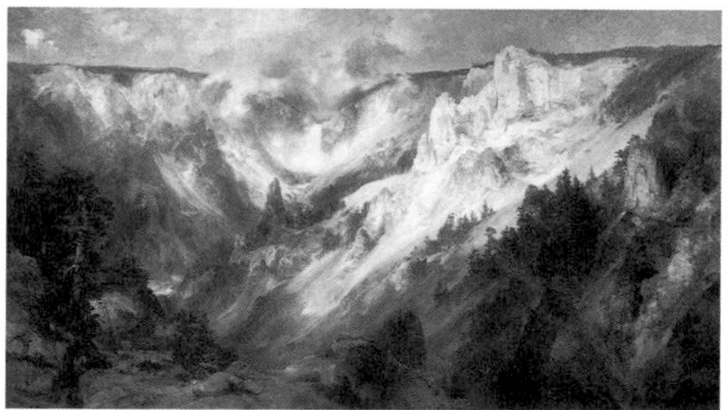

The Grand Canyon of the Yellowstone, 1893. 97 x 168⅞.
National Museum of American Art, Smithsonian Institution, Gift of George D. Pratt.

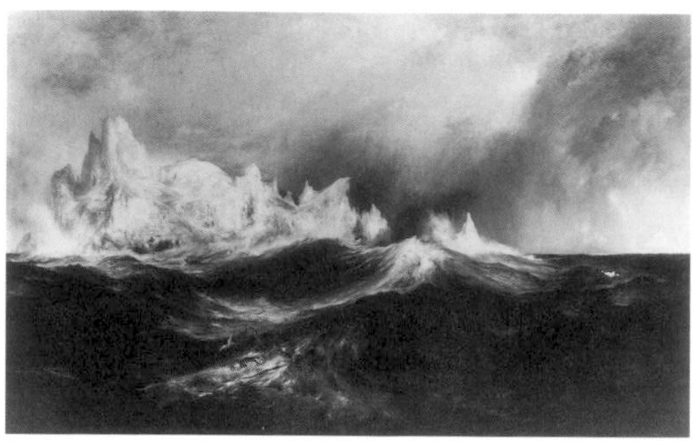

Iceberg in Mid-Atlantic. **#1162.** *Spectres From the North,* 1890. 74 x 118. The Thomas Gilcrease Institute of American History and Art, Tulsa, OK.

MORRIS, Jennie H. Moorestown, N.J.
Unknown–Residing 1905 Moorestown, NJ

Still Life. **#1026.** [$100]. Est. 20 x 18. Unlocated.

A Corner in a Turkish Bazaar. **#1078.** [$150]. Unlocated.

---

† **MOWBRAY, H. Siddons** (Henry Siddons). **New York.**
1858 Alexandria, Egypt–1928 Washington, CT
Training — Paris: Léon Bonnat, Jean-Léon Gérôme.

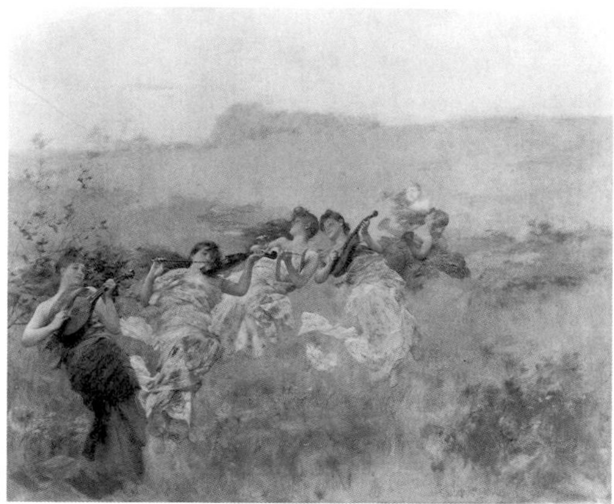

The Evening Breeze.* **#553. Lent by Mr. Thomas B. Clarke, New York. 1887. 23 x 28. Private Collection.

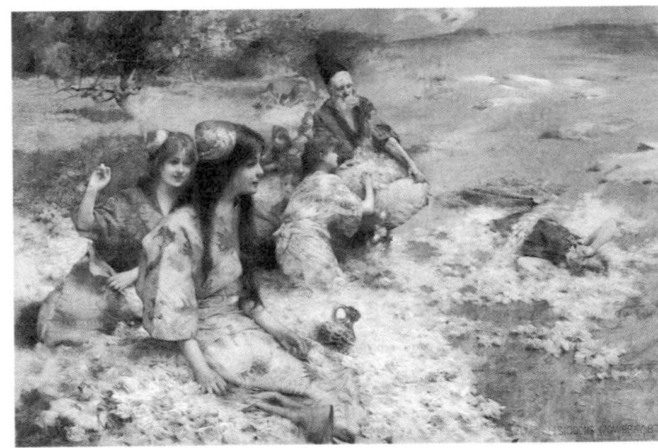

* *The Rose Harvest.* **#774. Lent by Mr. T. Helman, New York.** 1887. 14 x 20. Richard York Gallery, New York, NY.

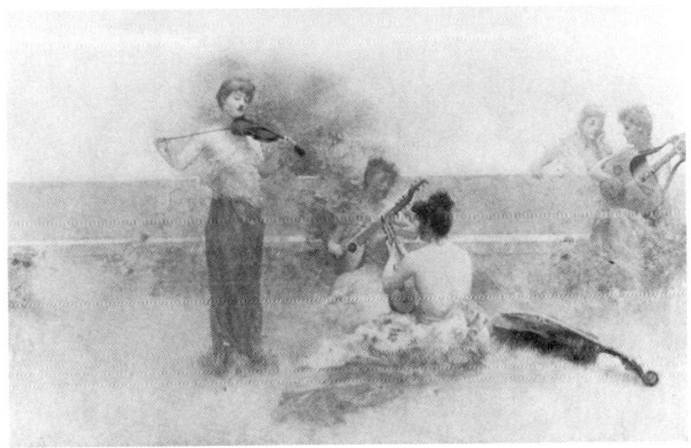

Arcadia. **#775. Lent by Mr. W. T. Evans, New York.** 1888. 17 x 25½. Sold, Sotheby Parke Bernet, New York, NY, 24 May 1990, lot 65. Unlocated. Illus: Charles Caffin, *The Story of American Painting, The Evolution of Painting in America from Colonial Times to the Present* (New York: Frederick A. Stokes, 1907), 176.

Scheherazade ("Arabian Nights"). **#776. Lent by Mr. Thomas B. Clarke, New York.** 1886. 12 x 14. Sold, American Art Association, New York, NY, 19 March 1924, lot 33. Unlocated. "The favorite of the harem is extended on a divan, lapped in cushioned luxury. At the right a refection of oranges and pomegranates on a brazen salver tempts her appetite. Before her, on the floor carpeted with rugs, the romance-weaving heroine of 'The Arabian Nights' recounts one of her fascinating legends. Her attitude is expressive of the climax of a tale, to which her listener attends with languid but absorbed interest. Splendid Oriental colors enrich the composition, and the figures are contrasted types of feminine beauty" —American Art Association, *Catalogue of the Private Art Collection of Thomas B. Clarke, New York* (New York: American Art Association, 1899), lot 16.

MUHRMAN, **Henry. London, England.**

1854 Cincinnati, OH–1916 Meissen, Germany
Training— Munich: Royal Academy.

The Two Trees. **#1250.** [$500]. Unlocated.

MUNGER, **Gilbert** (Gilbert Davis). **Paris, France.**

1836/37 North Madison, CT–1903 Washington, DC
Training— New Haven: Louis Agassiz; largely self-taught.

The Rising Moon. **#1075.** [$500]. Unlocated.

MUNSELL, **Albert H.** (Albert Henry). **Boston.**

1858 Boston, MA–1918 Brookline, MA
Training— Boston: Massachusetts Normal Art School; Rome; Paris: Gustave Boulanger, Jules Joseph Lefebvre, Acad. Julian, EcBA.

The Sea. **#296.** [$600]. Est. 30 x 45. Unlocated.

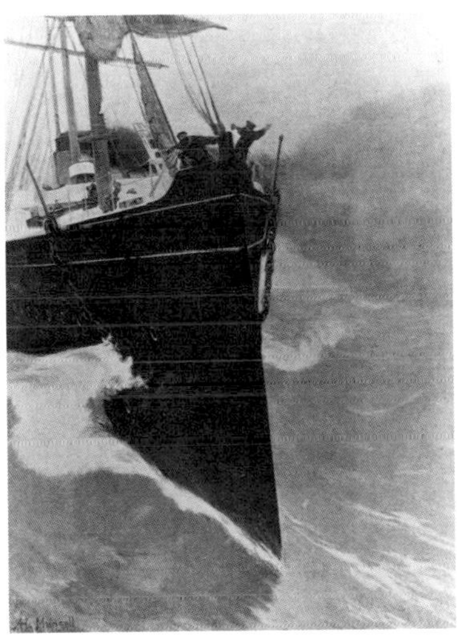

Danger Ahead. **#497.** [$1000]. 1887. Est. 65 x 45. Unlocated. Illus: Daniel H. Burnham, *The Art of the World,* vol. 4 (New York: Appleton, 1893–95).

Beacon Hill in Winter. **#1195.** [$300]. Unlocated.

---

† MURPHY, **J. Francis** (John Francis). **New York.**

1853 Oswego, NY–1921 New York, NY
Training— self-taught.

November Grays. **#531.** [$1000]. Est. 30 x 35. Unlocated.

The Hazy Morn. **#546.** [$800]. Unlocated. "Poetic and Corot-like in quality" — J. S. Merrill, *Art Clippings from the Pen of Walter Cranston Larned and Other Critics at the Fair* (Chicago: J. S. Merrill, 1893).

NEEDHAM, Charles Austin. New York.

1844 Buffalo, NY–1922 Palenville, NY
Training — New York: Free Academy, ASL (August Will).

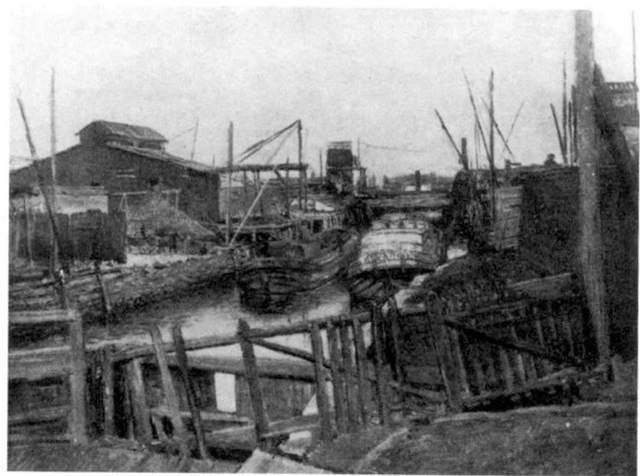

Mott Haven Canal, New York City. **#1107.** ca. 1892. Unlocated. Illus: *International Studio* (Oct. 1906): 363.

A Street in New York City. **#1171.** [$100]. Unlocated.

Near Factory Hollow, Turner's Falls, Mass. **#1225.** [$250]. Unlocated. "A picture that is not helped by the frame he has put around it and that is melancholy without showing why . . . . It looks . . . as it was painted in poverty to represent poverty, and as if poverty was the only thing that the poor devil was in the habit of associating with. The bold execution of the picture, however does not bespeak poverty, or, at least, discouragement for it has every mark of careless confidence"—*Brooklyn Daily Eagle,* 22 November 1892.

NEHLIG, Victor (Michael Victor). New York.

1830 Paris, France–Residing 1909 abroad[51]
Training — Paris: Raimundo de Madrazo y Garreta, Abel de Pujol, Léon Cogniet, EcBA.

Pocahontas Saving the Life of Captain John Smith. **#232.** Est. 100 x 144. Unlocated.

NETTLETON, Walter (Walter Eben). Finistère, France.

1861 New Haven, CT–1936 New Haven, CT
Training — New York: ASL; Paris: Acad. Julian (Gustave Boulanger, Jules Joseph Lefebvre), Carolus-Duran.

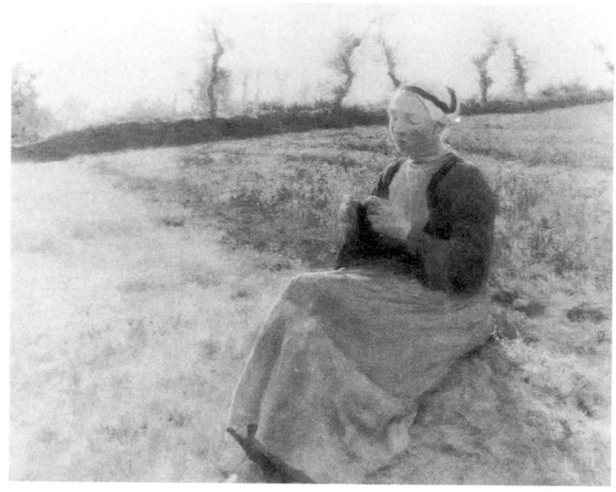

December Sunshine. **#419.** [$500]. 1891. 25¾ x 32. Yale University Art Gallery, Gift of the artist.

Approach of Harvest Time. **#518.** [$900]. 1892. Est. 45 x 75. Unlocated.

Teasel Gatherer. **#563.** [$300]. 1892. Unlocated.

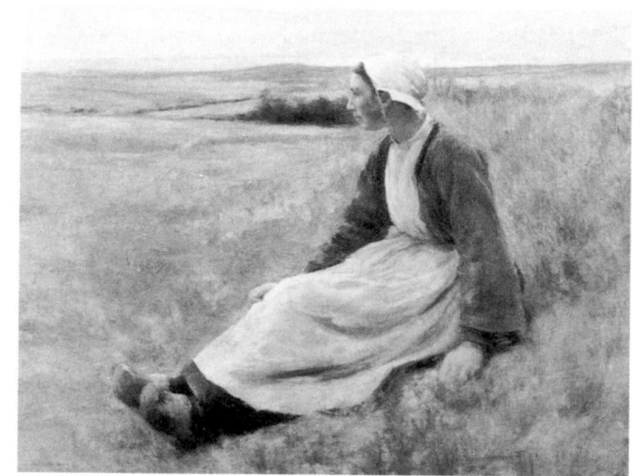

Watching for the Return of the Fishing Fleet. **#602.** [$350]. 1891. 29 x 36⅜. Private Collection, Claremont, CA.

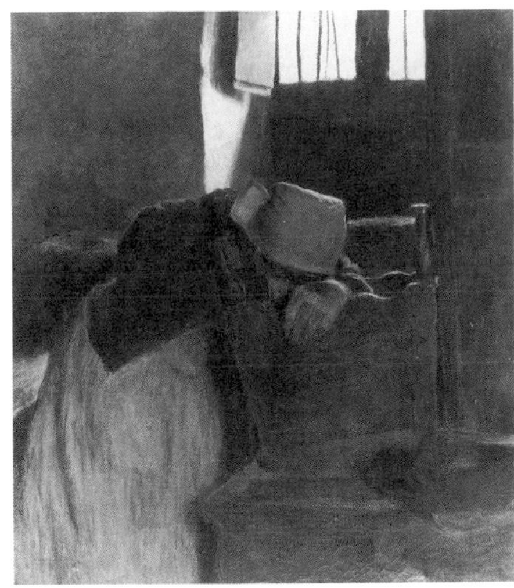

A Dark Interior. **#1099.** [$250]. 1888. 22 x 19¼. Private Collection. Photograph by Joseph Levy.

Left in Charge of the Farmyard. **#1173.** [$250]. 1890. 33 x 36. Unlocated.

NEWCOMB, **Mrs. Marie Guise** (Marie H. Guise/ Mrs. Newcomb). **New York.**
1865 Newark, NJ–1895 New York, NY?
Training— Paris: A. F. A. Schenck, Luigi Chialiva, Edouard Detaille.

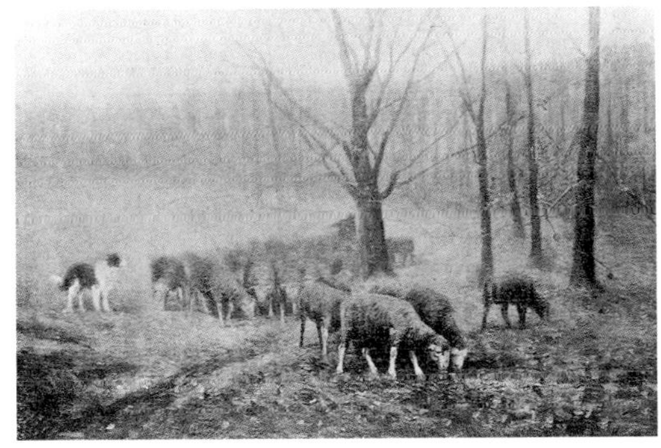

Sheep in the Clearing. **#1013.** [$350]. ca. 1892. Est. 15 x 20. Unlocated. Illus: *Fine Arts at the World's Columbian Exposition, Chicago, 1893* (Chicago: Rand, McNally, 1894).

NEWMAN, **Carl. Philadelphia.**
1858 Philadelphia, PA?–1932 Huntingdon Valley, PA
Training— Philadelphia: PAFA; Paris: Acad. Julian, William Bouguereau, Tony Robert-Fleury.

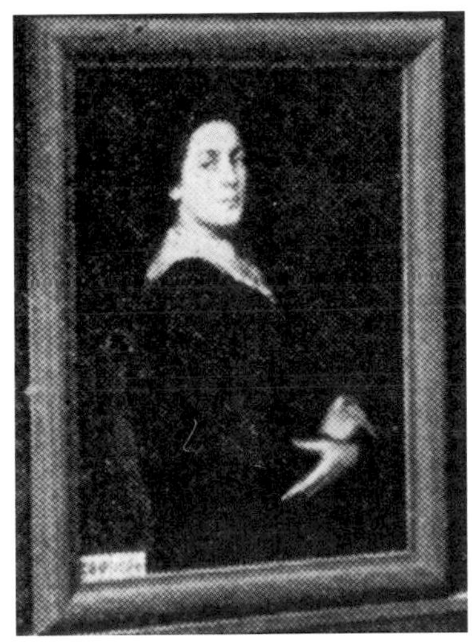

A Study. **#1254. Lent by Mr. Charles M. Chabot.** Est. 30 x 18. Unlocated. Illus: Hubert H. Bancroft, *The Book of the Fair,* vol. 3 (Chicago: Blakely Printing Co., 1893), 678.

NICOLL, **J. C.** (James Craig). **New York.**
1846 New York, NY–1918 Norwalk, CT
Training— M. F. H. De Haas, Kruseman Van Elten.

"Will it Rain To-morrow?" **#840.** [$600]. ca. 1892. Unlocated. "A cloudy sky at evening, and while the clouds seem rather heavy, yet the general effect is good. Particularly noticeable is the green in the water. . . . There is actually a look of rain in the air . . . " —*New York World,* 1 Apr. 1892.

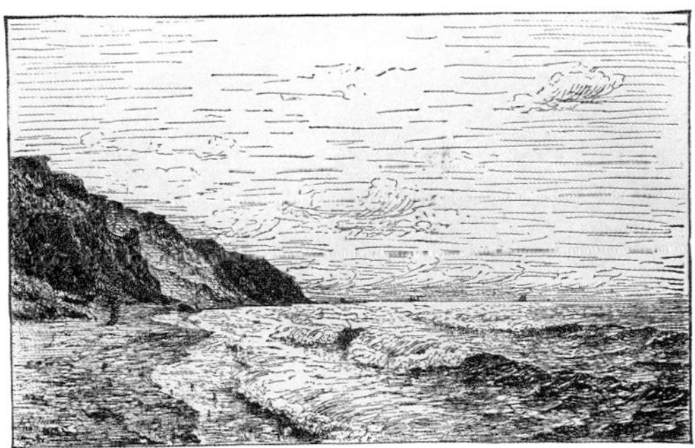

Sunlight on the Sea. **#879.** [$3000]. 1883. 38 x 60. Collection Williams College, Williamstown, MA, ca. 1910. Unlocated. Illus: Charles M. Kurtz, ed., *National Academy Notes, Including the Complete Catalogue of the Fifty-Ninth Spring Exhibition, National Academy of Design New York* (New York: Cassell & Co., Limited, 1884), 45.

NILES, Edward Glover. Boston.
1859 Boston, MA–1908 New Castle, NH
Training — Paris: Gustave Boulanger, Jules Joseph Lefebvre.

Portrait. **#1085.** Unlocated.

NORCROSS, Eleanor. Paris, France.
1854 Fitchburg, MA–1923 Fitchburg, MA
Training — Boston: Massachusetts Normal Art School; New York: ASL (William Merritt Chase); Paris: Alfred Stevens.

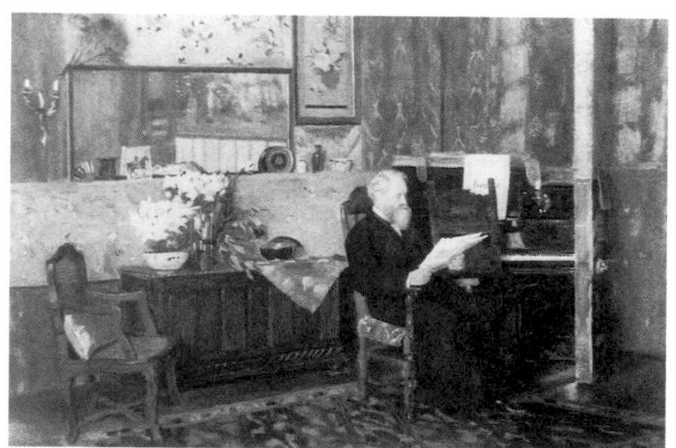

In My Studio. **#1286. Lent by Mr. A. Norcross.** 1891. 45 x 57¾. Fitchburg Art Museum, Fitchburg, MA.

NORTON, S. Mary. Boston.
Fort Edward, NY–1922 Nutley, NJ
Training — New York: ASL; Paris: Acad. Julian, Acad. Colarossi.

A Tea Party. **#627.** [$450]. ca. 1889. Unlocated.

In the Locomotive Cab. **#1168.** [$750]. Unlocated. "Engine driver in his cab, clothed in blue overalls—large free brushwork, light color scheme . . . "—*Brooklyn Daily Eagle,* 27 June 1893.

NORTON, William E. (William Edward). **London, England.**
1843 Boston, MA–1916 New York, NY
Training — George Inness; Boston: Lowell School of Practical Drawing; Paris: Jacquesson de la Chevreuse, Antoine Vollon.

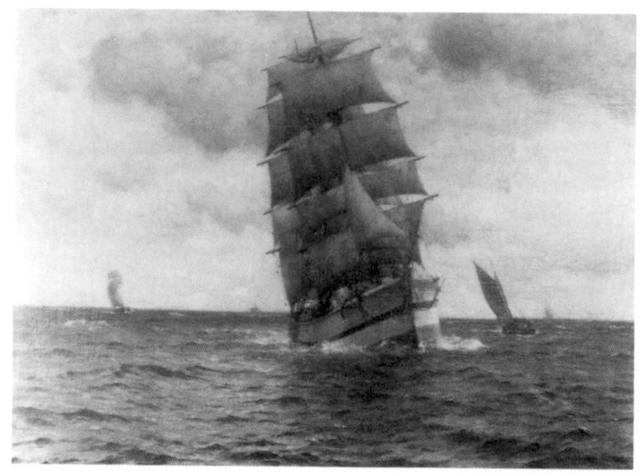

Mid-Channel. **#287.** [$1500]. n.d. 47 x 63. Collection New York Medical College, Valhalla, NY.

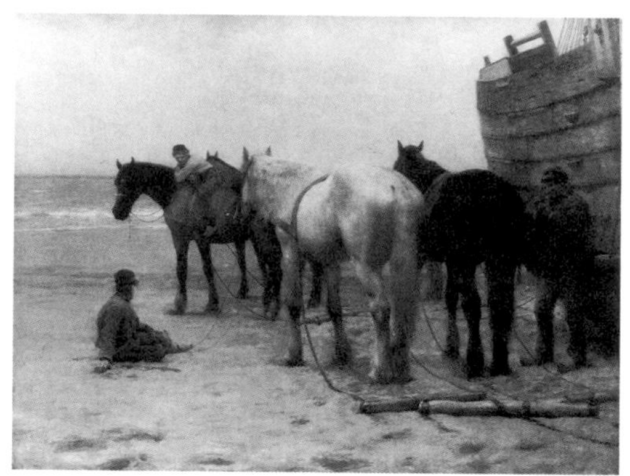

A Moment's Rest. **#400.** n.d. 48½ x 64⅞. National Museum of American Art, Smithsonian Institution, Gift of Dr. Morris F. Wiener.

Off the Dutch Coast. **#565.** [$250]. Unlocated.

Moonlight on the River. **#1122. Lent by Messrs. Williams & Everett, Boston.** Unlocated.

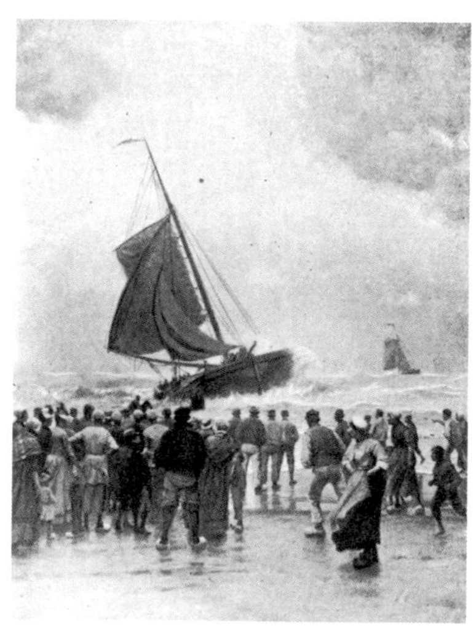

Return of the Herring Fleet, Holland. **#1198.** [$1800]. Unlocated. Illus: Charles M. Kurtz, ed., *Illustrations from the Art Gallery of the World's Columbian Exposition* (Philadelphia: G. Barrie, 1893), 200.

† **NOURSE, Elizabeth. Paris, France.**
1860 Cincinnati, OH–1938 Paris, France
Training — Cincinnati: McMicken School of Design (Thomas Noble, Benn Pitman, Marie Eggers, Will H. Humphreys, Louis Rebisso); New York: ASL (William Sartain); Paris: Acad. Julian (Gustave Boulanger, Jules Joseph Lefebvre), Carolus-Duran, Jean Jacques Henner.

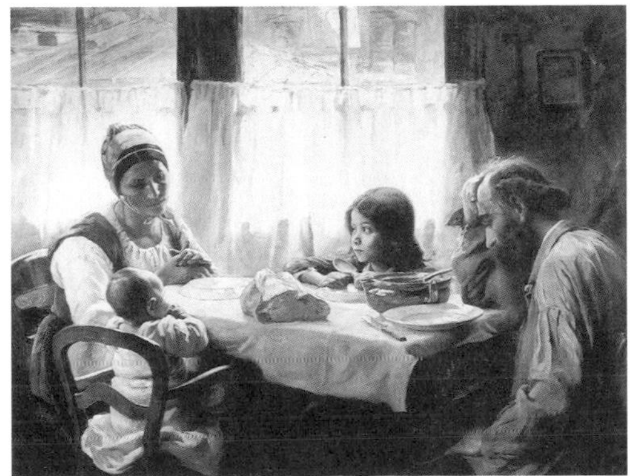

**A Family Meal. #373.* [$500]. *Le Repas en famille,* 1891. 44 x 60. Estate of George W. and Evelina B. Perkins. Photograph by Wayne Geist.

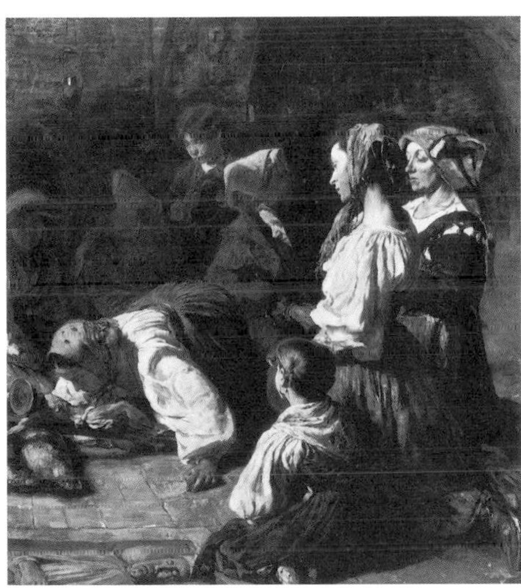

Good Friday, Rome. **#593** [$800]. 1891. 62 x 55. Union League Club of Chicago. Photograph by Michael Tropea.

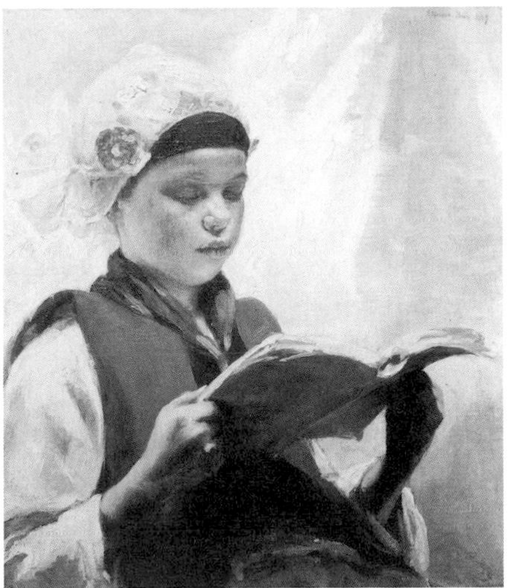

The Reader. **#843.** [$200]. 1889. 22½ x 20. Private Collection, Cincinnati, OH.

NOWOTTNY, Vincent. Cincinnati.
1854 Akron, OH–1908 Alderson, WV
Training — Cincinnati: McMicken School of Design; Munich: Royal Academy (Ludwig von Löfftz, Alexander Straehuber, Johann Leonhard Raab); Paris: William Bouguereau, Acad. Julian (Jules Joseph Lefebvre, G. J. M. A. Ferrier).

Landscape near Munich. **#1147.** Unlocated.[52]

† **OCHTMAN, Leonard. New York.**
1854 Zennemaire, the Netherlands–1934 Greenwich, CT
Training — New York: ASL; largely self-taught.

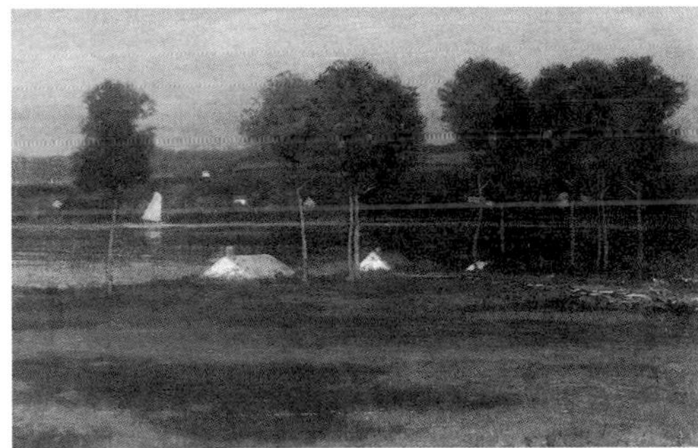

Along the Mianus River. **#500.** [$600]. 1892. 24 x 36. Flint Institute of Arts, Gift of Mr. and Mrs. Jerome O. Eddy.

Harvesting by Moonlight. **#505. Lent by Mr. Frederick Benedict, New York.** ca. 1891. Est. 24 x 36. Unlocated.

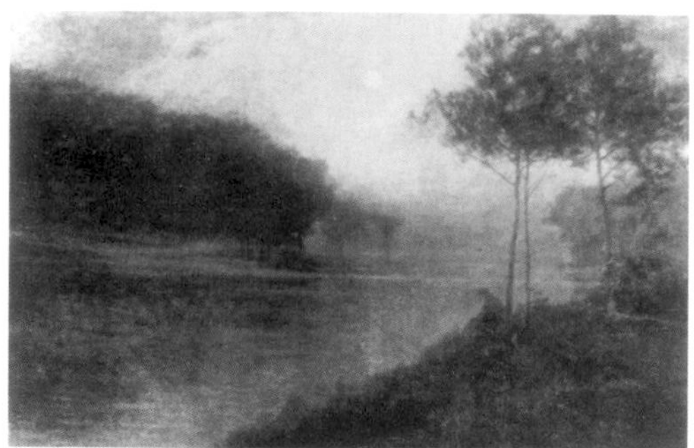

Night. **#987.** [$2500]. 1893. 36 x 52. Sold, Silo's, New York, NY, 18–19 Feb. 1927, lot 435, to George H. Ainslie. Unlocated. Illus: *Brush and Pencil* (Nov. 1901): 69.

---

† **PALMER, Walter L.** (Walter Launt). **Albany, N.Y.**
1854 Albany, NY–1932 Albany, NY
Training — Erastus Dow Palmer [his father], Frederic E. Church; Paris: Carolus-Duran.

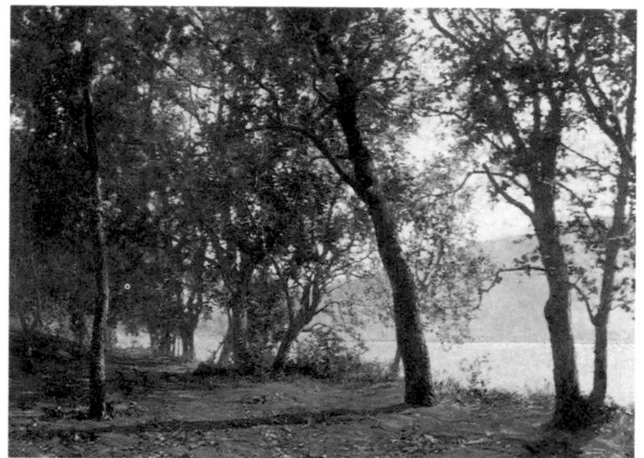

***Autumn Morning; Mist Clearing Away.* #900. Lent by Mr. John G. Myers, Albany.** *Autumn Morning—Mist Clearing Away,* 1892. 38½ x 52½. Collection of the Albany Institute of History & Art, Gift of Jane Samuels.

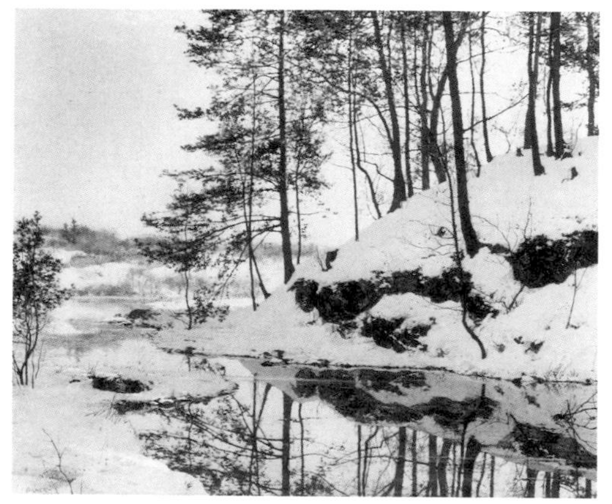

*****An Early Snow.* #975. Lent by Mr. F. D. Hurtt, New York.** 1887. 22 x 27. Collection Mr. and Mrs. Joel Finn.

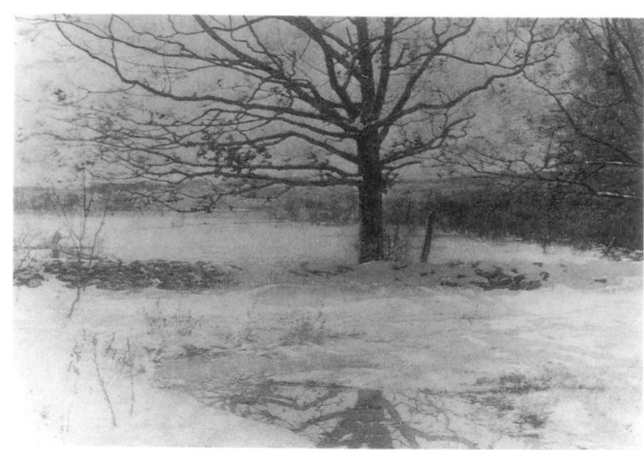

***January.* #1087. Lent by Mr. Thomas B. Clarke, New York.** 1887. 25 x 36. Sold, American Art Association, New York, NY, 14–18 February 1899, lot 67, to H. R. Butler. Unlocated. Illus: Daniel H. Burnham, *The Art of the World,* vol. 7 (New York: Appleton, 1893–95).

PAPE, Frederic L. M. (Frederick "Eric" Ludwig Moritz). **Paris, France.**
1870 San Francisco, CA–1938 New York, NY
Training — San Francisco: California School of Design (Emil Carlsen); Paris: Jules Joseph Lefebvre, Henri-Lucien Doucet, Jean-Joseph Benjamin-Constant, Paul-Louis Delance, Jean-Léon Gérôme, Elie Delaunay, Joseph-Paul Blanc, EcBA.

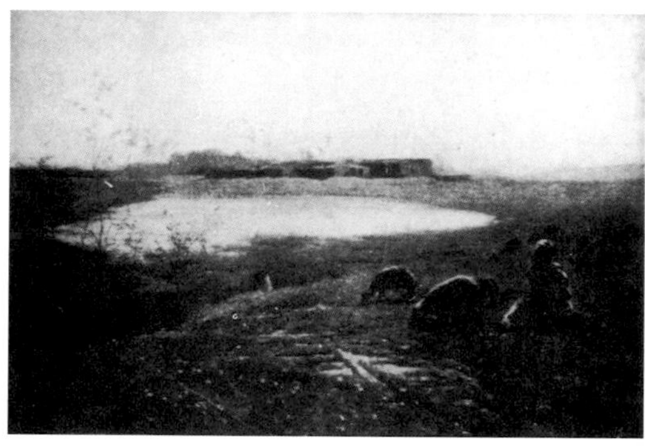

***The Site of Ancient Memphis.* #1249.** [$2500]. Est. 50 x 60. Unlocated. Illus: The New York Public Library, *The Artists File* (Alexandria, VA: Chadwyck-Healey, 1989).

PARRISH, Stephen. Philadelphia.
1846 Philadelphia, PA–1938 Cornish, NH
Training — Philadelphia: Peter Moran; France.

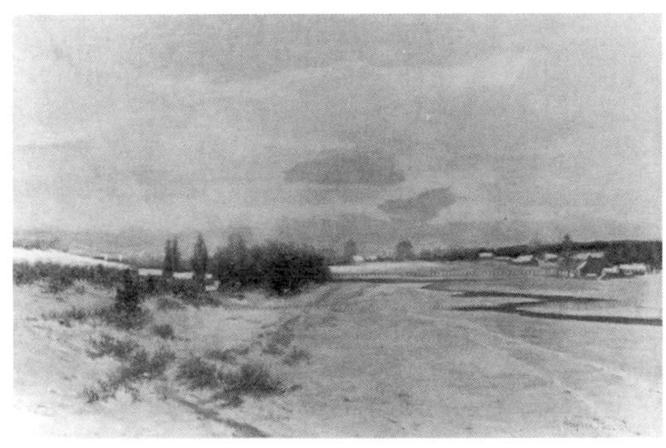

Winter Sunset, Cape Cod. **#290.** [$500]. 1892. 33 x 49½. Private Collection, 1915.[53] Unlocated. Illus: Daniel H. Burnham, *The Art of the World,* vol. 10 (New York: Appleton, 1893–95).

Winter in New Hampshire. **#349.** [$400]. 1891. 30 x 40. Unlocated. "Open fields blue mountain in background"—Stephen Parrish Papers, Dartmouth College Library, Hanover, NH.

Evening. **#431.** [$250]. 1892. 20 x 30. Unlocated. "Clam digger's cabins. Trees & houses (of Riverdale) back. foreground green flat marsh. glow in sky. Cresent moon" — Stephen Parrish Papers, Dartmouth College Library, Hanover, NH.

An Orchard. **#1019.** [$150]. Unlocated.

A Mountain Road. **#1125.** [$500]. Unlocated.

PARSHALL, **De Witt** (DeWitt). **Paris, France.**
1864 Buffalo, NY–1956 Santa Barbara, CA
Training— Alexander Harrison; Paris: Acad. Julian, Fernand Cormon; Dresden: Royal Academy.

The Cliffs of Ayerne. **#1152.** [$400]. Est. 54 x 35. Unlocated.

PARSONS, **Orrin Sheldon. New York.**
1866 Newark, NY–1943 Albuquerque, NM
Training — New York: Will H. Low, Edgar Ward, William Merritt Chase, NAD.

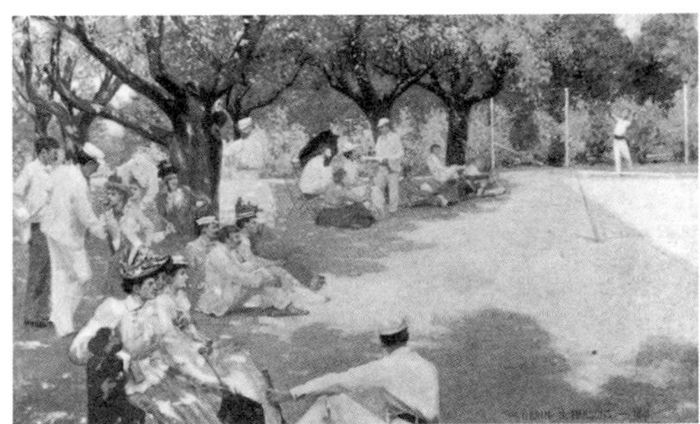

Lawn Tennis. **#324.** [$1000]. 1891. Unlocated. Illus: Charles M. Kurtz, ed., *Illustrations from the Art Gallery of the World's Columbian Exposition* (Philadelphia: G. Barrie, 1893), 185.

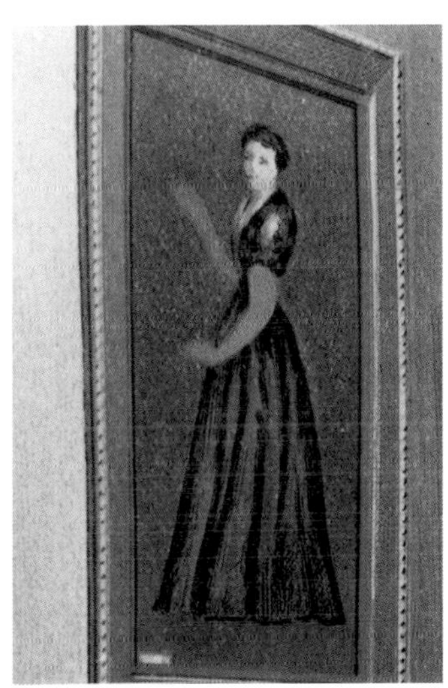

A Lady in Black. **#924. Lent by Mr. J. L. M. Hunt, New York.** Est. 75 x 42. Unlocated. Illus: *Yankee Doodle at the Fair* (Philadelphia: George Barrie & Son, 1896).

PARTON, **Arthur. New York.**
1842 Hudson, NY– 1914 Yonkers, NY
Training — Philadelphia: William T. Richards; Barbizon, France.

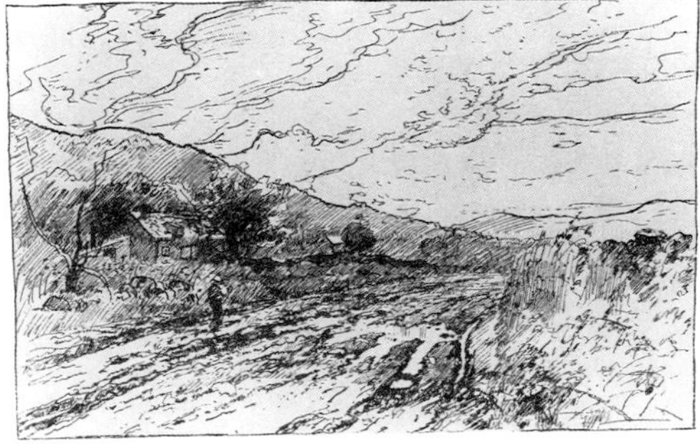

Evening after the Rain. **#507. Lent by Mr. George I. Seney.** ca. 1886. 40 x 60. Offered for sale by a "New

York Collector," Parke-Bernet Galleries, New York, NY, 25–28 Feb. 1942, lot 544. Unlocated. Illus: American Art Galleries, *The Second Prize Fund Exhibition for the Promotion and Encouragement of American Art* (New York: J. J. Little, 1886), no. 203.

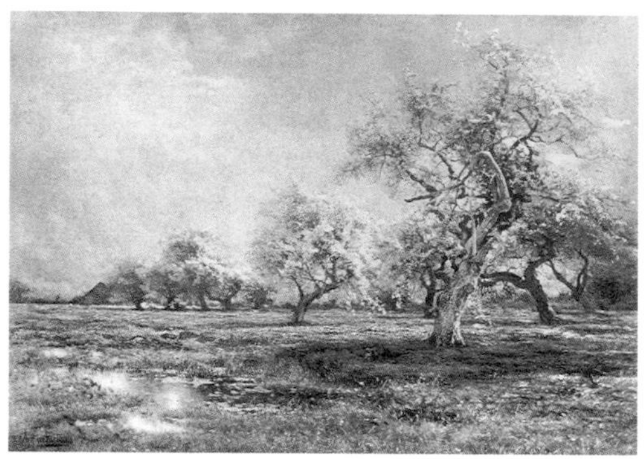

In the Month of May. **#792. Lent by Mr. W. T. Evans, New York.** ca. 1888. 26 x 36. Sold, American Art Association, 31 Jan.–2 Feb. 1900, lot 94, to E. Dwight. Unlocated. Illus: George W. Sheldon, *Recent Ideals of American Art* (New York: Appleton, 1890). "An apple orchard in blossom. A pool in the left foreground reflects the spring sky of blue and white. The tree trunks and branches are crooked and bent, and the delicate pink and white of the blossoms contrast effectively with their gray bark and the sparse, green foilage. Awarded honorable mention at the Paris Exposition of 1889" — American Art Association, *Catalogue of American Paintings Belonging to William T. Evans* (New York: Press of J. J. Little, 1900), lot 94.

PATTISON, **James William. Jacksonville, Ill.**
1844 Boston, MA–1915 Asheville, NC
Training — New York: R. Swain Gifford, George Inness, J. M. Hart; Dusseldorf: Albert Flamm; Paris: Luigi Chialiva.

Sheep. **#439.** [$300]. Est. 22 x 30. Unlocated.

PAULI, **Richard. deceased.**
1855 Chicago, IL–1892 Bergen County, NJ
Training — France: F. L. Francis.

Sunset in New Jersey. **#382.** [$750]. **Lent by Mrs. Pauli, Leonia, N.J.** Unlocated.

PAULUS, **Francis P.** (Francis Petrus). **Munich, Bavaria.**
1862 Detroit, MI–1933 Detroit, MI
Training — Philadelphia: PAFA (Thomas Eakins); Munich: Royal Academy (Ludwig von Löfftz, Nikolaus Gysis); Paris: Léon Bonnat.

A Rainy Day. **#1256.** [$100]. Est. 10 x 14. Unlocated.

PAXTON, **William M.** (William McGregor). **Boston.**
1860 Baltimore, MD–1941 Newton Centre, MA
Training — Boston: Cowles Art School (Dennis M. Bunker); Paris: Acad. Julian, Jean-Léon Gérôme.

An Idyl. **#594.** [$1000]. Est. 50 x 30. Probably destroyed in the Harcourt studio fire, Boston, MA, 1904. "The artist has done something in the study of the figure out of doors, and he shows a number of things in this line. The most noticeable of these is No. 4, 'An Idyl,' a study of two French peasants, a young man and a young woman, leaning against a rustic fence with a sunlit stretch of landscape in the rear. Leaving out the expression of the girl's face, this is a great thing and well worthy of the place that it occupied at the World's fair. While the color is brilliant in the extreme, it is not crude or offensive. The handling of the group of houses in the distance and the bit of road is thoroughly natural" — "A Portrait Show," unidentified newspaper, Worcester, MA, ca. May 1895.

PEARCE, **Charles Sprague. Auvers-sur-Oise, France.**
1851 Boston, MA–1914 Auvers-sur-Oise, France
Training — Paris: Léon Bonnat.

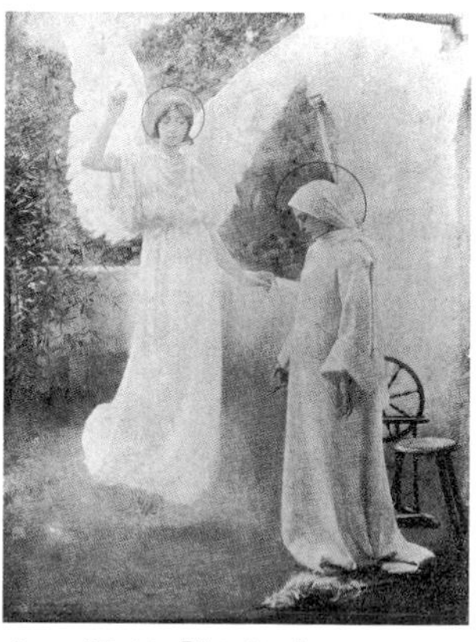

The Annunciation. **#346.** [$2500]. ca. 1892. Est. 60 x 45. Unlocated. Illus: Charles M. Kurtz, ed., *Illustrations*

from the Art Gallery of the World's Columbian Exposition (Philadelphia: G. Barrie, 1893), 204.

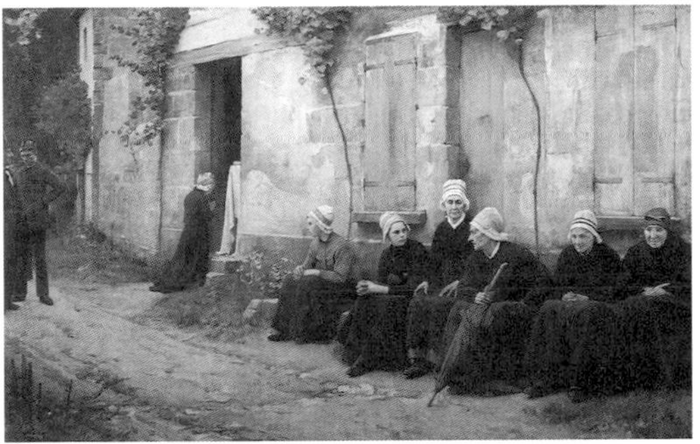

A Village Funeral, Brittany.* **#607. [$3500]. *A Village Funeral in Brittany,* 1891. 65½ x 102. Danforth Museum of Art Collection, Framingham, MA, Gift of Charles F. Scott in memory of Alice Daudelain Scott.

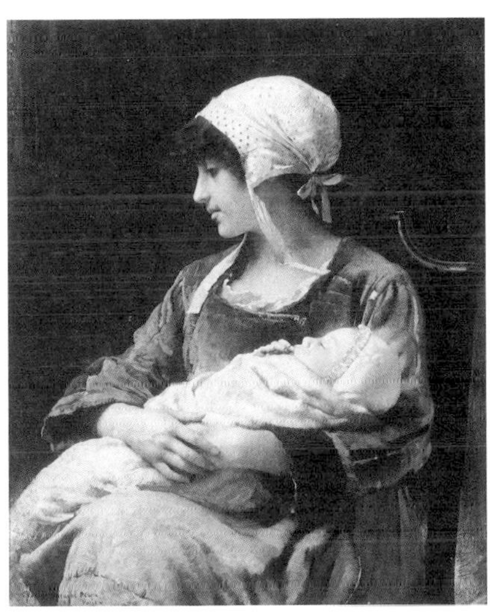

***Mother and Child.* #608. Lent by the Hon. Lewis Emery, Jr., Bradford, Pa.** n.d. 25 x 20½. Collection Mrs. Elaine F. Northrup, Ellicottville, NY. Photograph by Thomas Loonan.

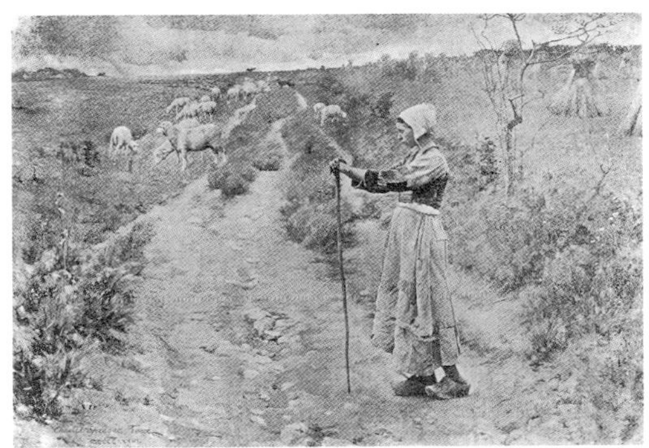

***The Shepherdess.* #755.** [$5000]. Est. 95 x 120. Sold (as *La Bergère*), Propriété Pearce, Auvers-sur-Oise, France, 4 July 1925, lot 86. Unlocated. Illus: Charles M. Kurtz, ed., *Illustrations from the Art Gallery of the World's Columbian Exposition* (Philadelphia: G. Barrie, 1893), 129.

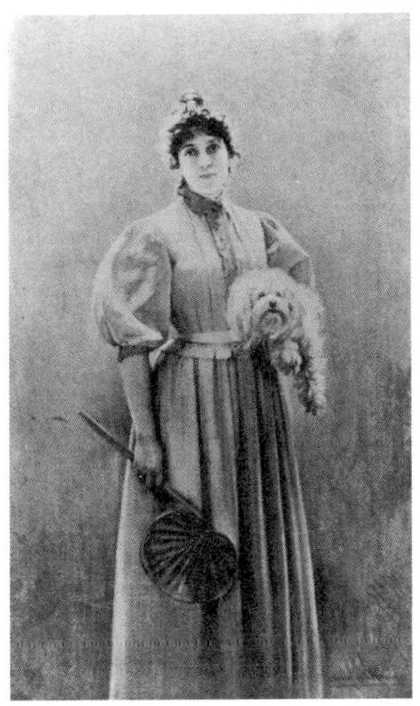

***Portrait of Mrs. P.* #805.** 1889. Est. 75 x 45. Unlocated. Illus: George W. Sheldon, *Recent Ideals of American Art* (New York: Appleton, 1890). "The figure seems to be stepping out of the canvas from a greenish-gray background. . . . No labored details of the steel-blue costume, or palm-leaf fan, or white dog, detract from the effect of the facial expression" — George W. Sheldon, *Recent Ideals of American Art* (New York: Appleton, 1890).

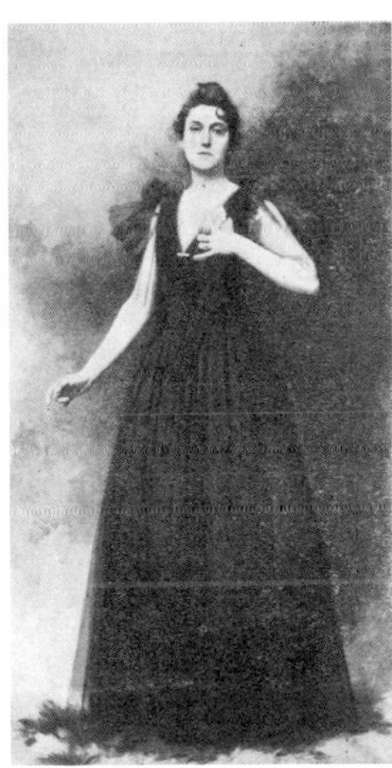

***Portrait of Mrs. P.* #1196.** Unlocated. Illus: Charles M. Kurtz, ed., *Illustrations from the Art Gallery of the World's Columbian Exposition* (Philadelphia: G. Barrie, 1893), 67.

† **PECK, Orrin. Munich, Bavaria.**
1860 Hobart, NY–1921 Los Angeles, CA
Training — California; Munich: Royal Academy (Nikolaus Gysis, Ludwig von Löfftz).

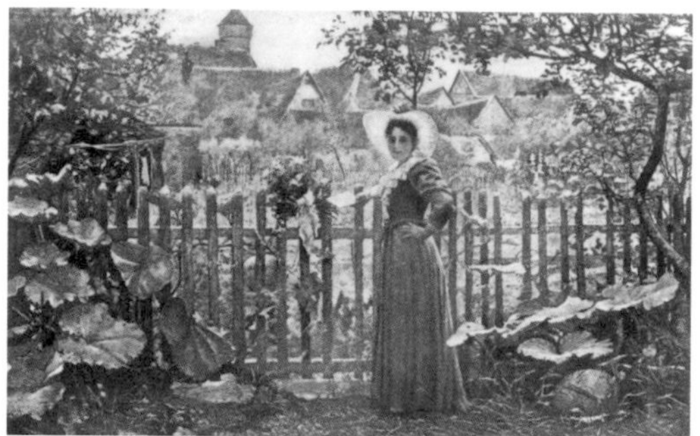

Love's Token. **#476. Lent by Mrs. P. A. Hearst, Washington, D.C.** n.d. (ca. 1892). 84½ x 118. The Phoebe A. Hearst Museum of Anthropology, University of California at Berkeley. Illus: Ferdinand Perret Research Collection, National Museum of American Art/National Portrait Gallery Library, Smithsonian Institution.

Portrait of Mrs. H. **#1291.** Unlocated.[54]

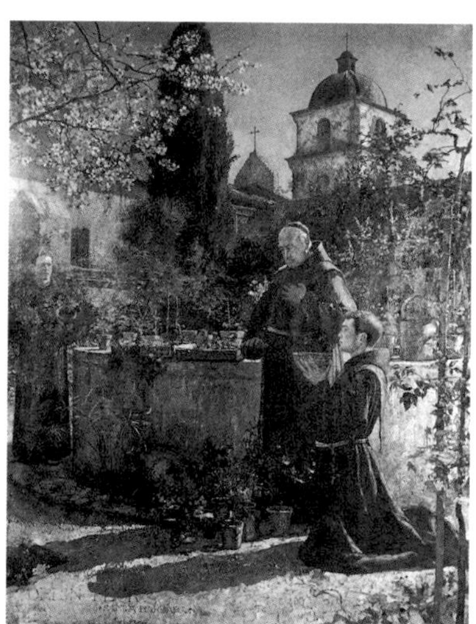

Blessing the Flowers. **#1292.** *Blessing of the Flowers, Santa Barbara Mission,* n.d. 91 x 72⅜. The Oakland Museum, Gift of the Women's Board of the Oakland Museum.

PEIXOTTO, George D. Maduro (George DaMaduro). **Paris, France.**
1858 Cleveland, OH–1937 White Plains, NY
Training — Dresden: Royal Academy; Paris: Jean-Charles Meissonier, Mihaly Munkacsy, Léon Pohle, J. Grosse.

Portrait of a Child. **#1271. Lent by Senator J. P. Jones, California.** *Portrait of Georgina Jones.* Est. 49 x 34. Private Collection, Florida, 1989. Unlocated.

PENFOLD, Frank C. (Francis Chapman). **Buffalo.**
1849 Lockport, NY–1921 Concarneau, France
Training — William Penfold [his father]; Paris: Gustave Boulanger, Jules Joseph Lefebvre.

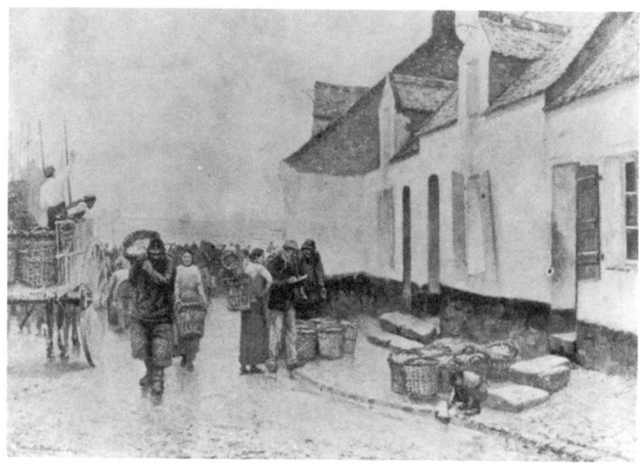

Herring Season, Pas de Calais. **#1178.** [$1000]. Est. 50 h. Unlocated. Illus: Charles M. Kurtz, ed., *Illustrations from the Art Gallery of the World's Columbian Exposition* (Philadelphia: G. Barrie, 1893), 138.

PERALTA, S. B. de (Sophie Bendelari/Mme. de Peralta). **Boston.**[55]
Unknown–Residing 1895 Boston, MA

Among the Lilies. **#1255.** [$500]. Est. 34 x 18. Unlocated.

PERRY, Lilla C. (Lilla Cabot/Mrs. Thomas Sergeant Perry). **Boston.**[56]
1848 Boston, MA–1933 Hancock, NH
Training — Boston: Cowles Art School (Dennis M. Bunker, Robert Vonnoh); Paris: Acad. Julian, William Bouguereau, Tony Robert-Fleury, Acad. Colarossi (Gustave Courtois), Alfred Stevens; Munich: Friedrich von Uhde.

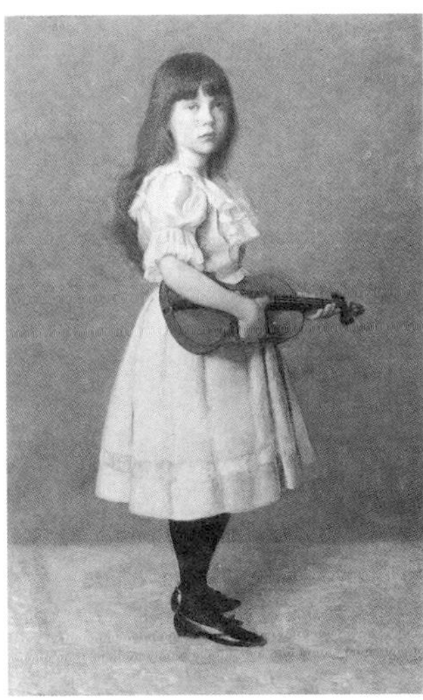

***Portrait of Alice*. #1110.** [$1000]. *Portrait Study of a Child (Alice Perry),* 1891. 60 x 36. Collection Natalie, Brienne, and Chase Rose, Kansas City, MO.

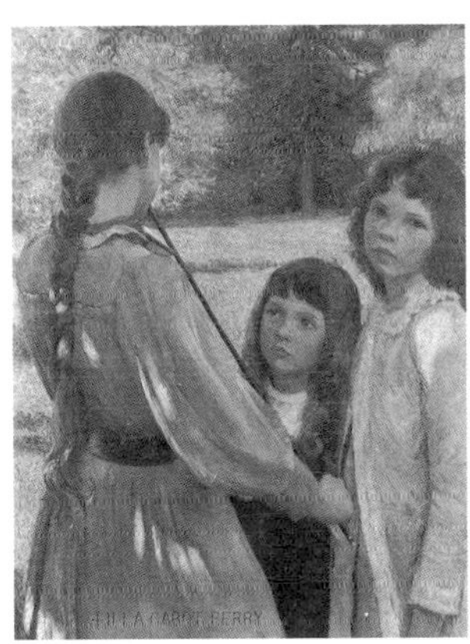

***An Open Air Concert*. #1169.** *Open Air Concert,* 1890. 40 x 30. Museum of Fine Arts, Boston, Gift of Miss Margaret Perry.

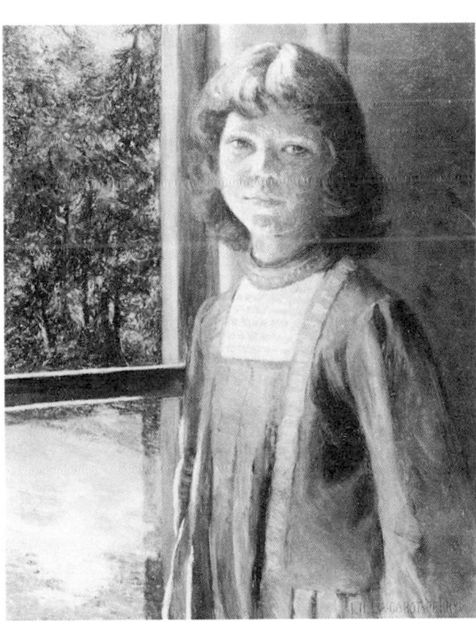

***Reflection*. #1229.** [$550]. n.d. (ca. 1890). 27½ x 22. Private Collection.

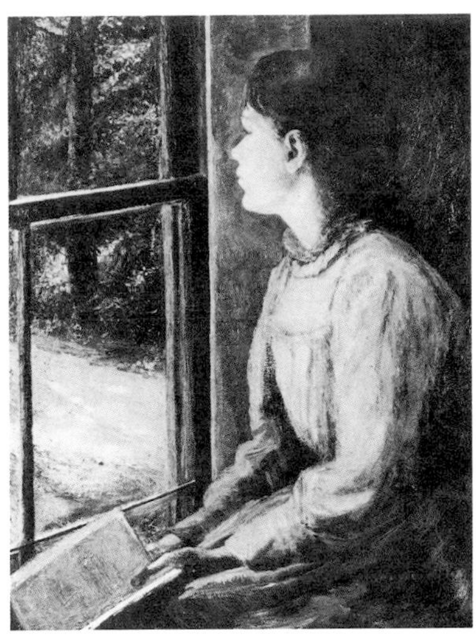

***Child in a Window*. #1234.** [$600]. *At the Library Window,* ca. 1890. 33½ x 26. Sold, Sotheby Parke Bernet, Los Angeles, CA, 12 March 1979, lot 163. Unlocated.

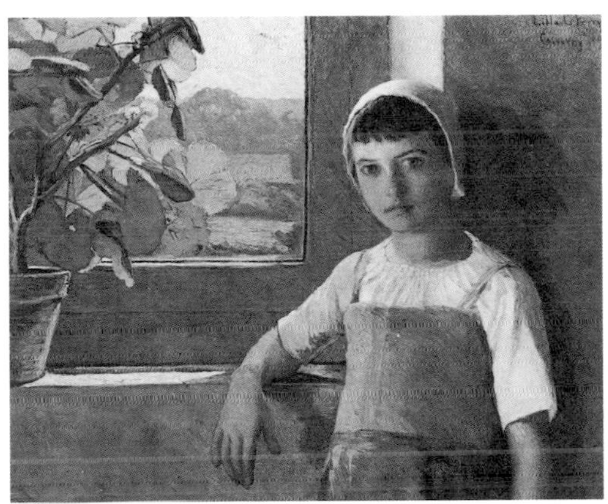

***Little Angèle*. #1261.** [$600]. *La Petite Angèle I,* 1889. 25½ x 32. Unlocated. Photograph courtesy Hirschl & Adler Galleries, Inc., New York, NY.

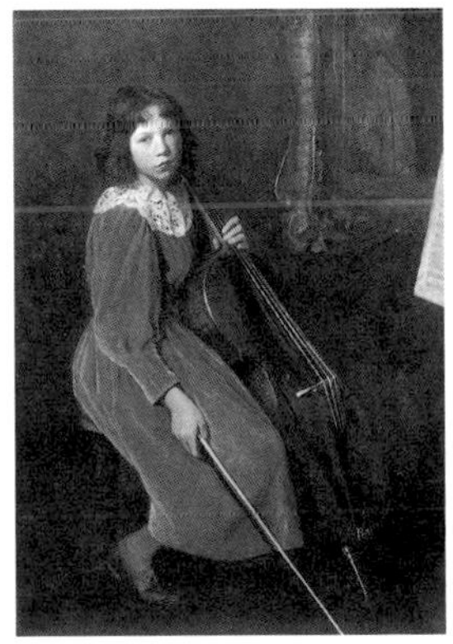

***Child with Violincello*. #1269.** [$1000]. *The Young Violincellist,* 1892. 55 x 39½. Museum of Fine Arts, Boston, Bequest of Dr. Arthur T. Cabot.

Portrait of a Child. **#1280. Lent by Mr. Roger Wolcott, Boston.** Unlocated.[57]

PERRY, **Roland Hinton. Paris, France.**
1870 New York, NY–1941 New York, NY
Training — New York: ASL; Paris: Paul Louis Delance, EcBA (Jean-Léon Gérôme), Acad. Julian (H. M. A. Chapu, Denys Puech), Acad. Delecluse, Georges Callot.

Portrait of Mrs. Perry. **#455.** Est. 42 x 31. Unlocated.[58]

PETERS, **Clinton** (DeWitt Clinton, Jr.). **Paris, France.**
1865 Baltimore, MD–1948 Newtown, CT
Training — New York: ASL, NAD; Paris: Acad. Julian (Gustave Boulanger, Jules Joseph Lefebvre), Raphaël Collin, EcBA (Jean-Léon Gérôme), Jean-Andre Rixens.

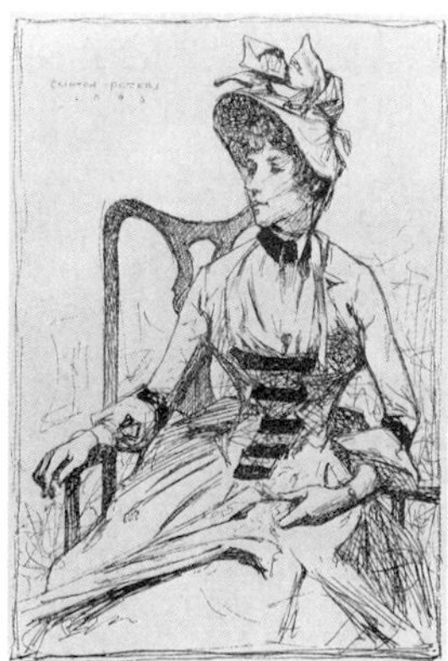

Portrait of Mlle. N. C. **#963.** 1888. Unlocated. Illus: Ludovic Baschet, ed., *Salon de 1889 Catalogue Illustré* (Paris: Georges Chamerot, 1889), 216.

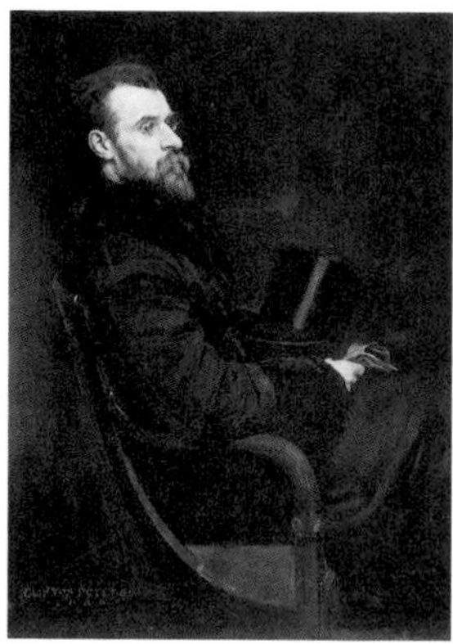

Portrait of Dr. George Bull. **#1071. Lent by Dr. George Bull, Paris.** *Portrait of Dr. George J. Bull,* 1888. 28 x 21¼. Collection Mr. and Mrs. Anthony S. Bull, Santa Fe, NM. Photograph by Dan Morse.

PEYRAUD, **F. C.** (Frank Charles). **Chicago.**
1858 Bulle, Switzerland–1948 Highland Park, IL
Training — Chicago: AIC; Paris: Léon Bonnat.

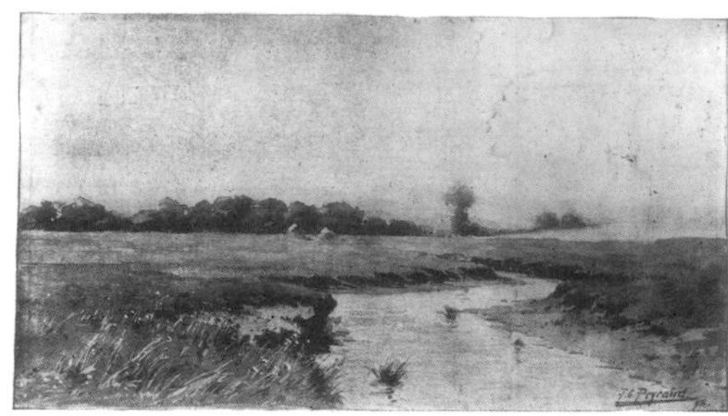

Evening. **#274.** [$180]. Est. 15 x 25. Unlocated. Illus: *The Graphic* [Chicago], 27 May 1893, 349.

Autumn Morning. **#473.** [$120]. Est. 15 x 20. Unlocated.

PHELPS, **Helen Watson. New York.**
1864 Attleboro, MA–1944 New York, NY
Training — Providence, RI; Paris: Raphaël Collin, Tony Robert-Fleury, William Bouguereau, Félix-Henri Giacomotti, Acad. Julian.

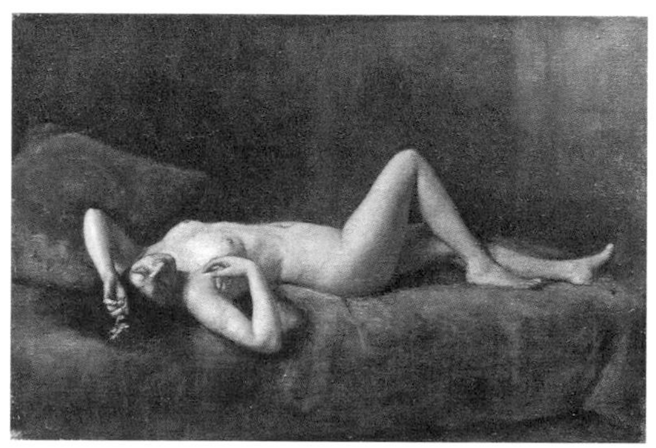

Abandon. **#653.** [$125]. *L'Abandon,* n.d. 8 x 12. Museum of Art, Rhode Island School of Design, Gift of Helen Watson Phelps.

---

† PICKNELL, **William L.** (William Lamb). **New York.**
1853 Hinesburg, VT–1897 Marblehead, MA
Training — Rome: George Inness; Paris: Jean-Léon Gérôme; Pont Aven: Robert Wylie

Early Morning. **#569.** [$650]. Unlocated.

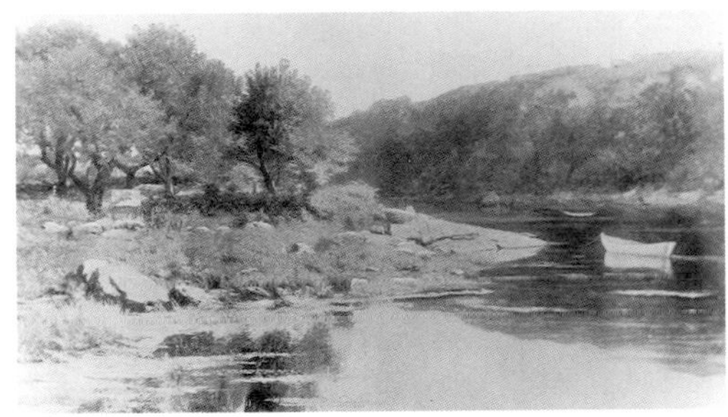

Sunday Morning. **#681.** [$650]. Unlocated. Illus: William Walton, *Art and Architecture,* vol. 1 (Philadelphia: G. Barrie, 1893–95), 8.

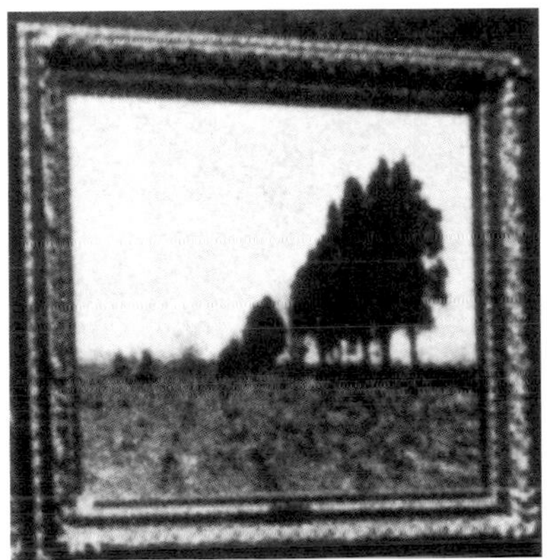

The Edge of Winter. **#798. Lent by Mr. F. A. Hammond, New York.** ca. 1891. Est. 55 x 70. Unlocated. Illus: Official Photographs of the World's Columbian Exposition by C. D. Arnold, vol. 8, pl. 84. Courtesy of The Chicago Public Library, Special Collections Department. "With its stubble of corn, its line of fence and its row of old cedars, [this] is one of the strongest of the recent works of this self contained and admirable realist. He subjects himself in this to nature, but he shows her to be worthy of his worship, and in the touch of distance with its hills he lets the fresh air in upon us" —*New York Times,* 17 May 1891.

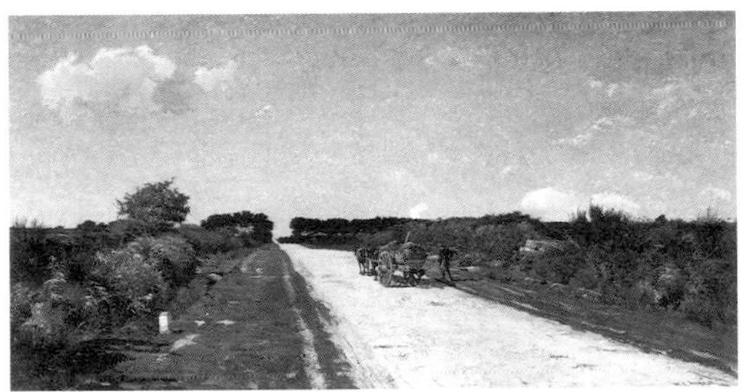

The Road to Concarneau. **#822. Lent by Mr. Thomas B. Clarke, New York.** 1880. 42⅜ x 79¾. Corcoran Gallery of Art, Museum Purchase.

† **PLATT, Charles A.** (Charles Adams). **New York.**
1861 New York, NY–1933 Cornish, NH
Training — New York: NAD, ASL; Paris: Acad. Julian (Jules Joseph Lefebvre, Gustave Boulanger); Italy.

Winter Landscape. **#283. Lent by Mr. Francis M. Jencks, New York.** Est. 20 x 27. Collection Mrs. Francis M. Jencks, 1938. Unlocated.

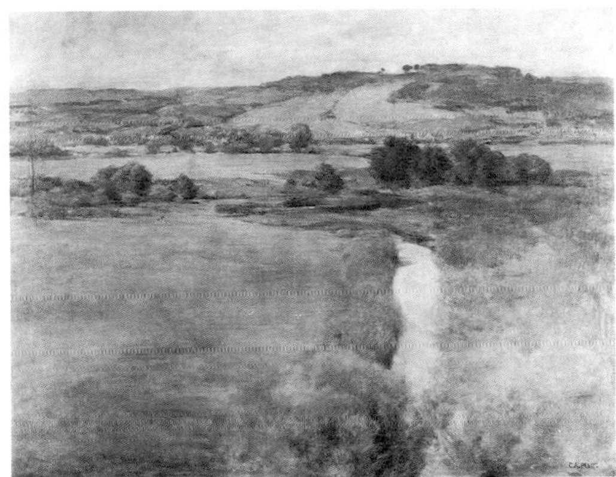

Early Spring. **#293.** n.d. 41¼ x 53¼. Worcester Art Museum, Worcester, MA.

POORE, H. R. (Henry Rankin). **Philadelphia.**
1859 Newark, NJ–1940 Orange, NJ
Training — Philadelphia: Peter Moran, PAFA; New York: NAD; Paris: Évariste Vital Luminais, Acad. Julian (William Bouguereau).

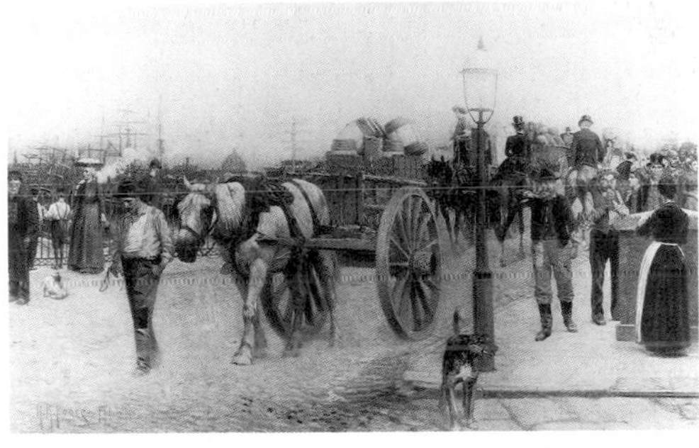

The Bridge (At Close of Day). **#874.** [$1800]. ca. 1886. 48 x 72. Sold (as *The Close of a City Day*), Fifth Avenue Art Galleries, New York, NY, 6–7 April 1899, lot 215. Unlocated. Illus: Daniel H. Burnham, *The Art of the World,* vol. 3 (New York: Appleton, 1893–95).

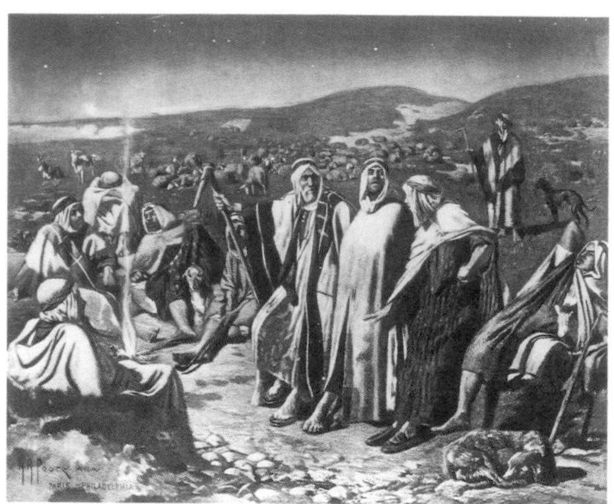

The Night of the Nativity. **#880.** ca. 1889. Unlocated.[59] Illus: George A. Smith, *The Laurelled Chefs-d'Oeuvre d'Art from the Paris Exhibition and Salon, Also from the Royal Academy of London and Other Public Galleries of Europe and America* (Philadelphia: Gebbie, 1889).

PRITCHARD, J. Ambrose. Boston.
1858 Boston, MA–1905 Boston, MA
Training — Boston: Massachusetts Normal Art School; Paris: Acad. Julian (Gustave Boulanger, Jules Joseph Lefebvre), Jean-Léon Gérôme.

Prayer. **#1131.** ca. 1888. Unlocated.

PUTNAM, Sarah G. (Sarah Gooll). **Boston.**
1851 Boston, MA–1912 Chocorua, NH
Training — Boston; New York: J. B. Johnston, Frank Duveneck, William Merritt Chase, Abbott H. Thayer; Munich: Wilhelm Durr; Schevinengen, the Netherlands: Bart-John Blommers.

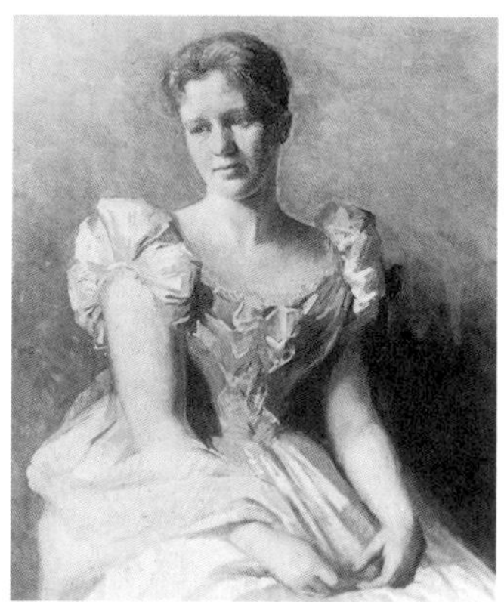

Portrait (Elizabeth Reed Hooper). **#1263. Lent by Elizabeth R. Hooper, Boston.** 1891. Est. 35 x 25. Unlocated. Photograph courtesy Massachusetts Historical Society.

RAMSDELL, F. Winthrop (Frederick Winthrop). **Paris, France.**
1865 Manistee, MI–1915 Manistee, MI
Training — New York: ASL (J. Carroll Beckwith); Paris: Raphaël Collin, EcBA.

Twilight at Grez. **#355.** [$500]. **Lent by Mr. T. J. Ramsdell, Manistee, Mich.** Est. 20 x 30. Unlocated.

Portrait of Mrs. Reynolds. **#1224. Lent by Mr. T. J. Ramsdell.** Unlocated.

RAUGHT, John Willard. New York.
1857 Dunmore, PA–1931 Dunmore, PA
Training — New York: NAD; Paris: Jules Joseph Lefebvre, Gustave Boulanger, Acad. Julian.

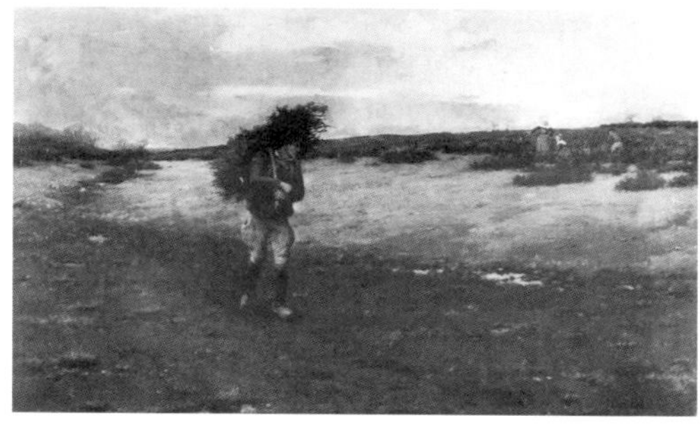

Gorse Cutters, Brittany. **#463.** [$1500]. n.d. (ca. 1892). 45 x 71. Collection Col. (USAF Ret.) and Mrs. John B. Henning.

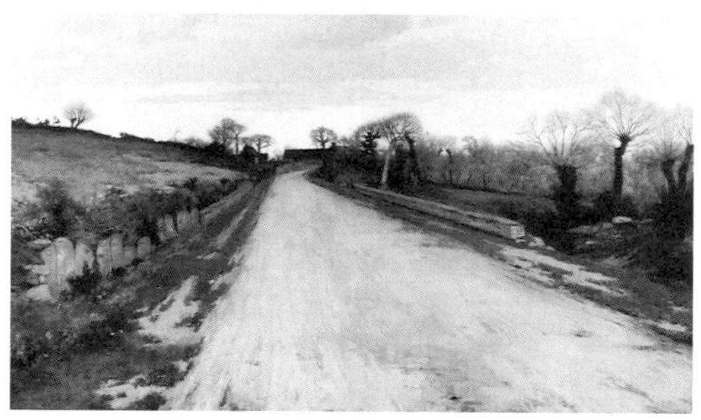

The Highway, Brittany. **#1121.** [$350]. 1889. 23 x 39. Collection Mrs. Isabella R. Scott. Photograph by Paul Jeremias.

REHN, F. K. M. (Frank Knox Morton). **New York.**
1848 Philadelphia, PA–1914 Magnolia, MA
Training — Philadelphia: PAFA.

Where Waves and Sunshine Meet. **#312.** [$800]. Est. 35 x 50. Unlocated.

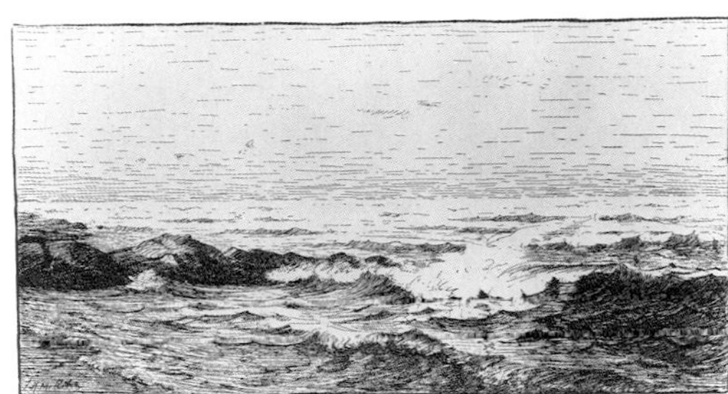

Close of a Summer Day. **#875. Lent by the Buffalo Fine Arts Academy, Buffalo, N.Y.** 1886. 58 x 84. Formerly Collection Albright-Knox Art Gallery. Sold, 1961 to Knoedler's, New York, NY. Unlocated. Illus: American Art Galleries, *The Second Prize Fund Exhibition for the Promotion and Encouragement of American Art* (New York: J. J. Little, 1886), no. 214.

† **REID, Robert** (Robert Lewis). **New York.**
1862 Stockbridge, MA–1929 Clifton Springs, NY
Training — Boston: MFA; New York: ASL; Paris: Acad. Julian (Gustave Boulanger, Jules Joseph Lefebvre).

Portrait of Little Miss S. **#285. Lent by Mrs. L. H. Stevens, New York.** Unlocated.

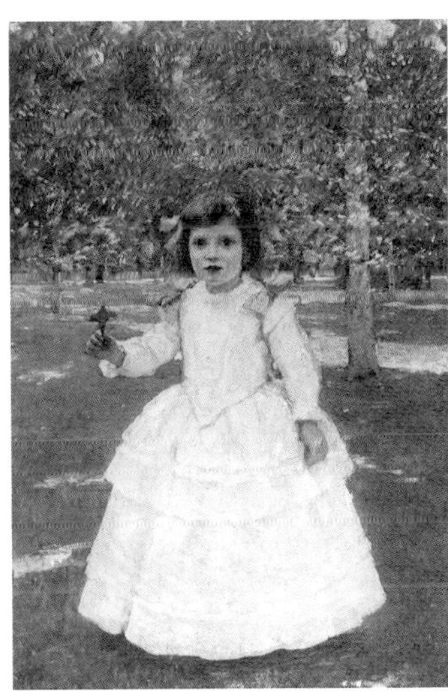

The Red Flower. **#304.** [$1000]. 1890. 50½ x 32¼. Private Collection.[60]

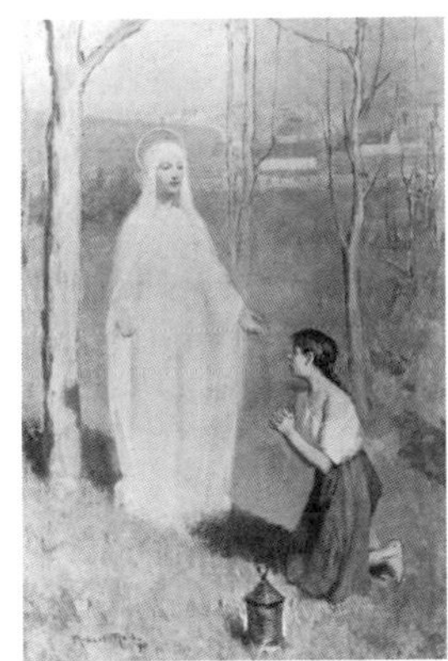

Vision of Saint Angela d'Agnant. **#330.** [$800]. 1890. Est. 75 x 55. Unlocated. Illus: Daniel H. Burnham, *The Art of the World,* vol. 7 (New York: Appleton, 1893–95).

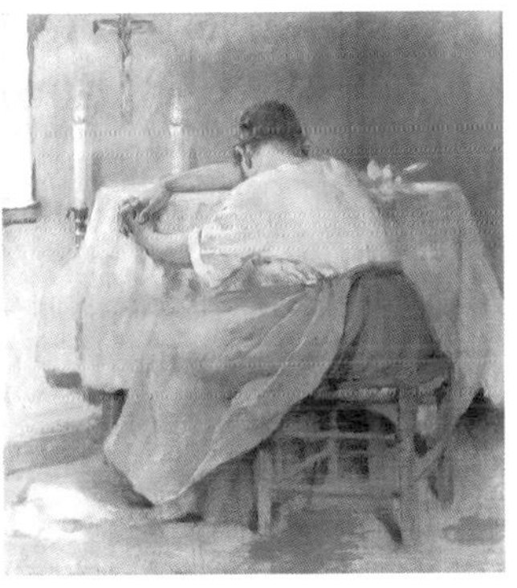

Her First Born. **#959.** [$1000]. 1888. 37⅛ x 33¼. The Brooklyn Museum, Gift of Mr. and Mrs. Sidney W. Davidson.

REINHART, C. S. (Charles Stanley). **New York.**
1844 Pittsburgh, PA–1896 New York, NY
Training — Paris: Charles Louis Suisse; Munich: Royal Academy (Alexander Straehuber, Carl Otto).

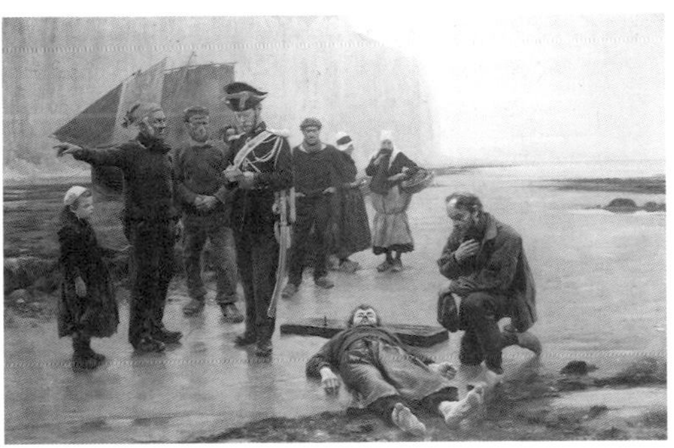

Washed Ashore. **#591.** 1887. 78 x 108½. Corcoran Gallery of Art, 1899. Sold, 1957, to Coleman Auction Galleries, New York, NY. Unlocated. Photograph courtesy Corcoran Gallery of Art.

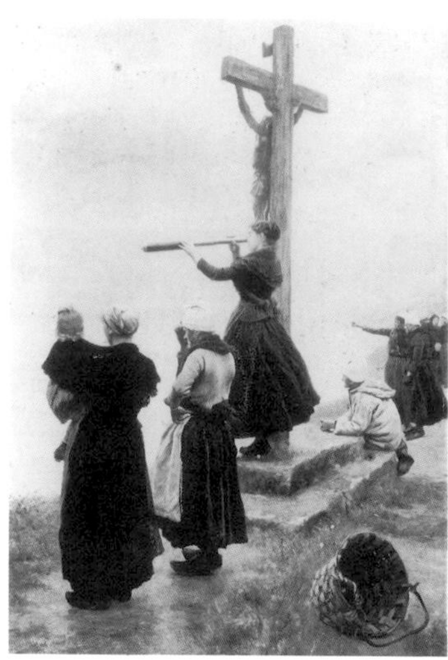

Awaiting the Absent. **#601.** 1888. 107 x 72. Carnegie Museum of Art by 1936. Sold, 1966, to William J. Fischer, New York, NY. Unlocated. Photograph courtesy the Library of Congress, Prints and Photographs Division, Detroit Publishing Co. glass color transparency LC-D415-50397.

RICE, **William M. J.** (William Morton Jackson). **New York.**
1854 Brooklyn, NY–1922 New York, NY
Training—New York: ASL (J. Carroll Beckwith), NAD; Paris: Carolus-Duran.

Landscape; Evening Clouds. **#340.** [$250]. Est. 30 x 30. Unlocated.

Portrait. **#376.** Unlocated. "Portrait — Man" — *New York Tribune,* 29 Jan. 1893.

Portrait. **#1268.** Est. 70 x 35. Unlocated. "Portrait—Woman, Pink and White" — *New York Tribune,* 29 Jan. 1893.

RICHARDS, **Samuel. Denver.**
1853 Spencer, IN–1893 Denver, CO
Training— Indianapolis: Theodore Lietz; Munich: Royal Academy (Alexander Straehuber, Ludwig von Löfftz, Nikolaus Gysis, Gyula Benczur).

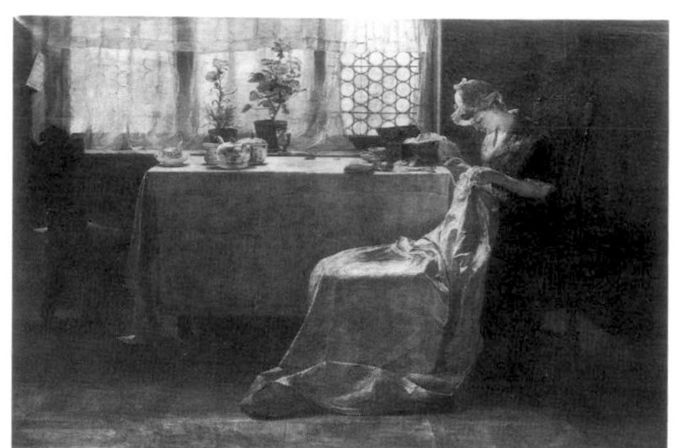

Blissful Hours. **#519. Lent by Mr. David Gebhart, Dayton, Ohio.** 1885. 39½ x 57¼. The Dayton Art Institute, Gift of Mrs. Frank A. Brown.

The Hour of Prayer. **#1220.** [$1500]. **Lent by Mrs. L. Richards, Denver.** 1887. 41 x 34. On loan to The Metropolitan Museum of Art until December, 1934. Unlocated.[61] "Painted in Munich in 1887 and . . . won a gold medal at the Academy. It shows the kneeling figure of a Capauchin monk at his evening devotions in the monastery chapel" —Marguerite Hall Albjerg, "A Nineteenth Century Hoosier Artist Samuel Richards, 1853–1893," *Indiana Magazine of History* 44 (June 1948): 154.

RICHARDS, **William T.** (William Trost). **Newport, R.I.**
1833 Philadelphia, PA–1905 Newport, RI
Training—Philadelphia: Paul Weber; Florence; Rome; Paris.

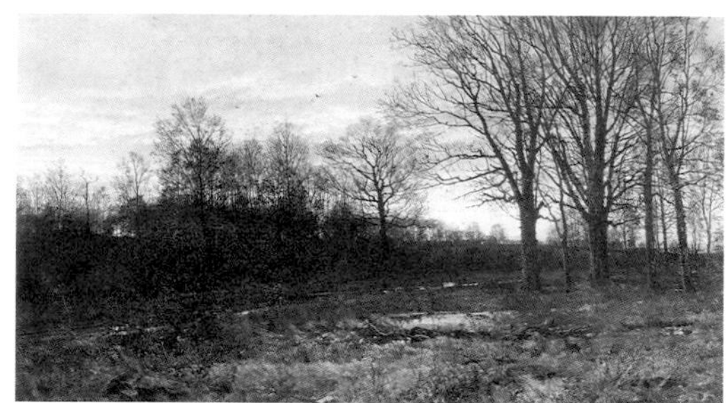

February. **#581. Lent by Mr. Edward H. Coates, Philadelphia.** 1885 (oil on canvas, mounted on wood). 40¼ x 72. Pennsylvania Academy of the Fine Arts, Philadelphia, Gift of Mrs. Edward H. Coates (The Edward H. Coates Memorial Collection).

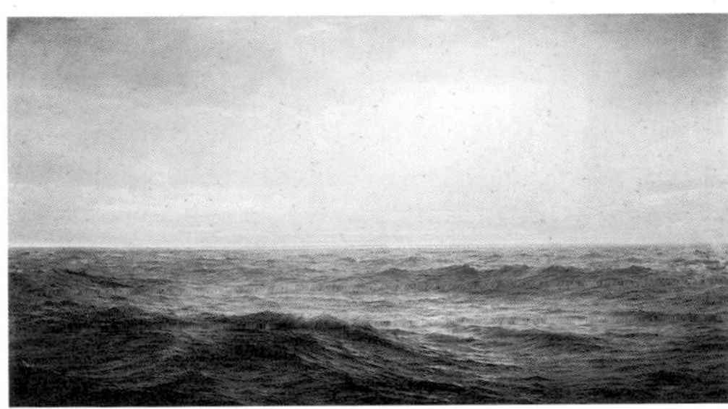

Old Ocean's Gray and Melancholy Waste. **#782. Lent by Mr. Edward H. Coates, Philadelphia.** 1885. 40¾ x 72¼. Pennsylvania Academy of the Fine Arts, Philadelphia, Gift of Mrs. Edward H. Coates (The Edward H. Coates Memorial Collection).

RICHARDSON, F. H. (Francis Henry). **Boston.**
1859 Boston, MA–1934 Ipswich, MA
Training— Boston: William Morris Hunt; Paris: Acad. Julian (Gustave Boulanger, Jules Joseph Lefebvre, J. P. Laurens, Jean-Joseph Benjamin-Constant).

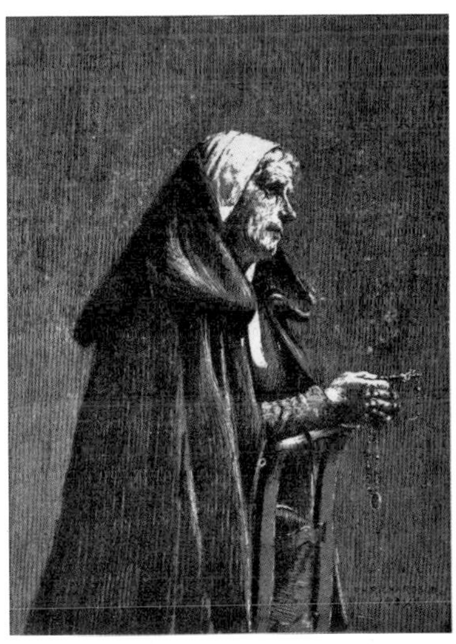

Breton Widow at Prayer. **#619.** [$1000]. ca. 1890. Unlocated. Illus: Ludovic Baschet, ed., *Salon de 1890 Catalogue Illustré* (Paris: Georges Chamerot, 1890), 237.

ROBBINS, Lucy Lee (Mme. Hendrik George van Rinkhuyzen).[62] **Paris, France.**
1865 New York, NY–1943 Paris, France
Training— Paris: Carolus-Duran, Jean-Jacques Henner.

My Portrait. **#700.** Unlocated. " 'My Own Portrait' represents the artist, very decolletée, black bodice, a red cloak, and the background of the same color, with Japanese designs"—*New York Times,* 7 May 1892.

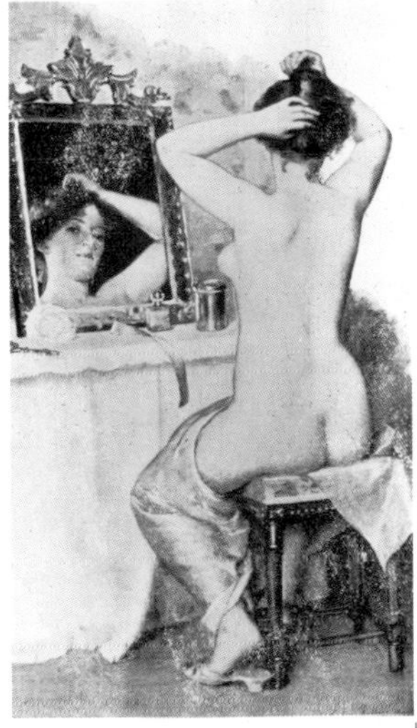

Before the Looking Glass. **#1063.** [$1000]. Est. 50 x 30. Unlocated. Illus: William Walton, *Art and Architecture,* vol. 1 (Philadelphia: G. Barrie, 1893–95), 10. "The background is pale blue, the carpet light green, and the toilet table of white muslin"—*New York Times,* 7 May 1892.

My Mother's Portrait. **#1133.** Unlocated.[63]

ROBBINS, Richard (Richard Smith). **Chicago.**
1863 Solon, OH–Residing 1898 Chicago, IL
Training— Paris: Acad. Julian (Jules Joseph Lefebvre, Jean-Joseph Benjamin-Constant, Henri-Lucien Doucet).

Decorative Panel. **#350.** [$100]. Est. 20 x 30. Unlocated.

---

† **ROBINSON, Theodore. New York.**
1852 Irasburg, VT–1896 New York, NY
Training— Chicago: AIC; New York: NAD; Paris: Carolus-Duran, Acad. Julian (Jean-Jacques Benjamin-Constant), Jean-Léon Gérôme, Henri Lehmann, EcBA.

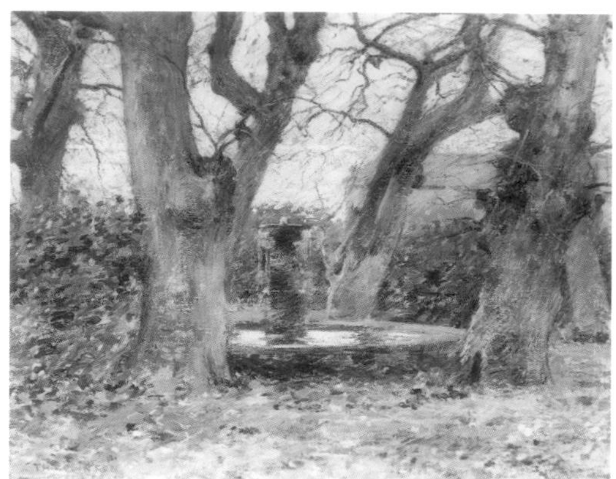

A Roman Fountain. **#336.** n.d. (ca. 1891). 18¼ x 22⅛. The Cornelia and Meredith Long Collection of American Art.

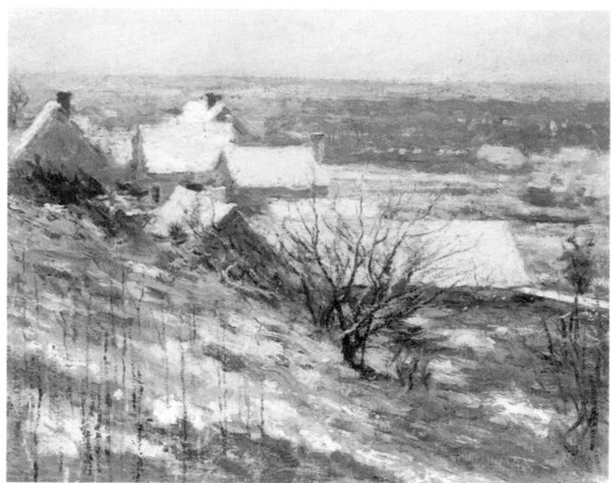

Winter Landscape. **#338. Lent by Mr. J. M. Lichtenauer, New York.** 1889. 18¼ x 22. Daniel J. Terra Collection, Terra Museum of American Art, Chicago.

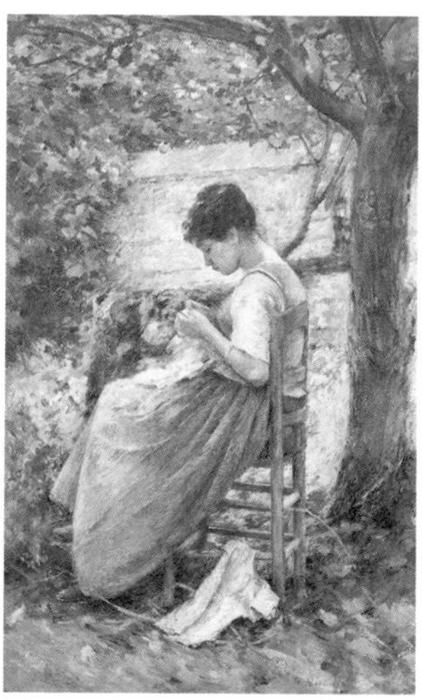

The Layette. **#354.** [$3000]. n.d. (ca. 1892). 58⅛ x 36¼. Corcoran Gallery of Art, Museum Purchase.

---

† **ROLSHOVEN, Julius** (Julius E.). **Paris, France.**
1858 Detroit, MI–1930 New York, NY
Training — New York: Cooper Union; Dusseldorf: Dusseldorf Academy (Hugo Crola); Munich: Royal Academy (Ludwig von Löfftz); Paris: Acad. Julian (Tony Robert-Fleury, William Bouguereau); Florence (Frank Duveneck).

Hall in the Doge's Palace, Venice. **#421.** [$1200]. ca. 1888. Est. 22 x 25. Collection Mrs. Stevens, London, England, 1900. Unlocated.

A Spanish Dancer. **#1101.** [$400]. Unlocated.

ROOK, Edward F. (Edward Francis). **Paris, France.**
1870 New York, NY–1960 Old Lyme, CT
Training — Paris: Acad. Julian (Jean-Jacques Benjamin-Constant, J. P. Laurens), Jean-Léon Gérôme.

Moonrise, Normandy. **#1213.** [$200]. Unlocated.

ROSE, Guy (Guy Orlando). **New York.**
1867 San Gabriel, CA–1925 Pasadena, CA
Training — San Francisco: California School of Design (Virgil Williams, Emil Carlsen); Paris: Acad. Julian (Jules Joseph Lefebvre, Jean-Jacques Benjamin-Constant, J. P. Laurens, Henri-Lucien Doucet).

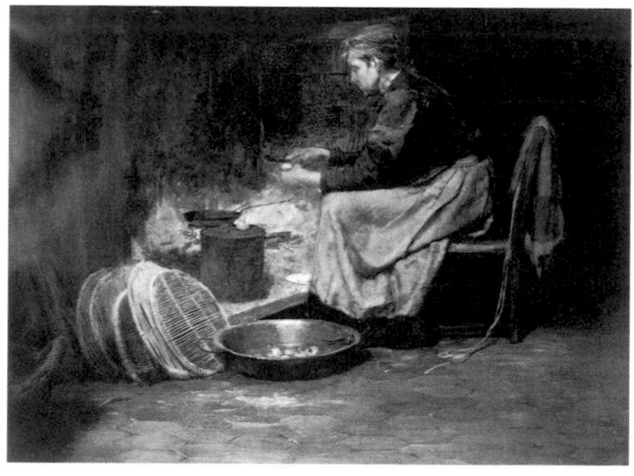

Food for the Laborers. **#453.** [$1000]. n.d. (ca. 1890). 48 x 64. Private Collection.

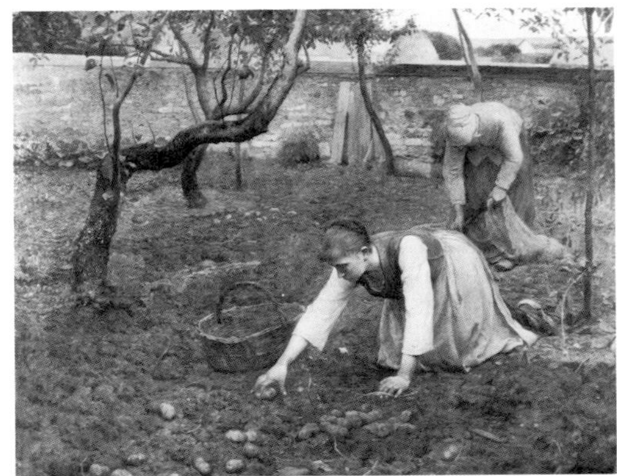

Potato Gatherers. **#606.** [$1500]. 1891. 51 x 64. Collection Mrs. John Dowling Relfe.

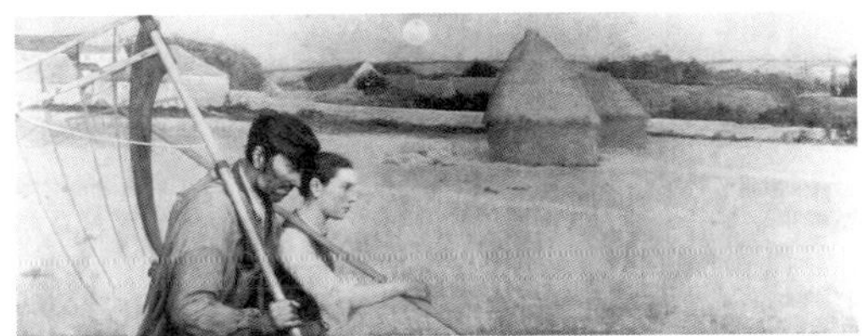

The End of the Day. **#622.** [$2000]. 1890. 39¾ x 98. Formerly Collection James L. Coran and Walter A. Nelson-Rees. Destroyed in the Oakland, CA, fire, Oct. 1991.

ROSENTHAL, Toby (Toby Edward). **Munich, Bavaria.**
1848 New Haven, CT–1917 Munich, Germany
Training — San Francisco: California School of Design (Virgil Williams, Henry Bacon, Fortunato Arriola); Munich: Royal Academy (Karl von Piloty, Alexander Straehuber, Karl Raupp).

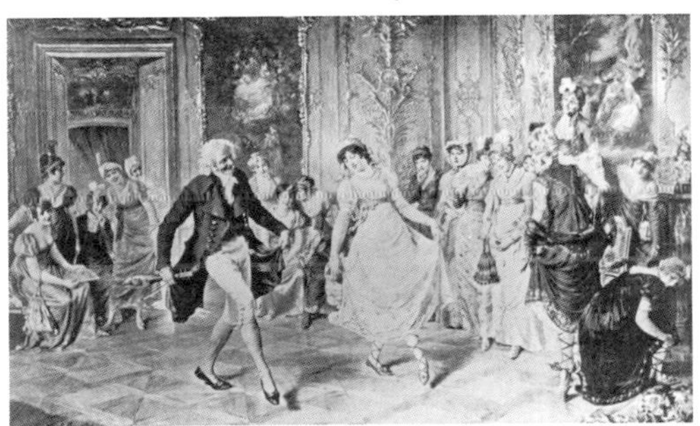

A Dancing Lesson of Our Grandmothers. **#862.** [$10,000]. **Lent by Mr. G. Mannheimer, New York.**[64] 1886. 42 x 69. Collection Mrs. Leonard A. Dessar, New York, NY, 1918. Unlocated. Illus: Hubert H. Bancroft, *The Book of the Fair,* vol. 3 (Chicago: Blakely Printing Co., 1893), 685.

RUDELL, P. E. (Peter Edward). **Greenwich, Conn.**
1854 Preston, Ontario–1899 New York, NY?
Training — A. H. Wyant.

Autumn. **#544.** Unlocated.

A November Day. **#821.** [$800]. Est. 30 x 40. Unlocated.

RYDER, Henry Orme (Henry Orne). **Auburndale, Mass.**
1860 Salem, MA–Residing 1907 Auburndale, MA
Training — Boston: MFA; Paris: Gustave Boulanger, Jules Joseph Lefebvre, P. L. F. Schmitt.

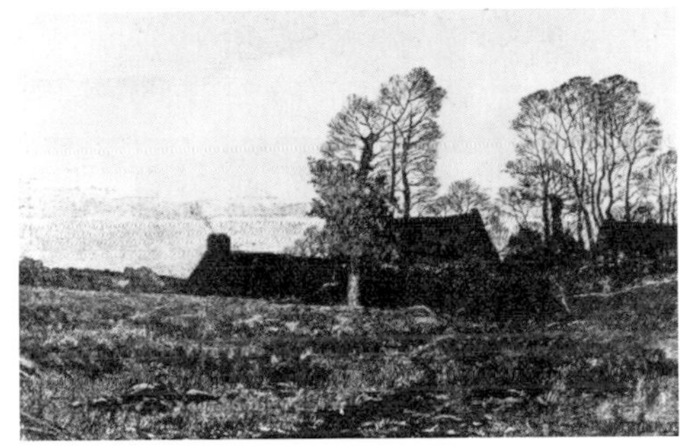

Old Breton Farmhouse, Evening. **#435.** 1889. 40 x 58. Sold, Sotheby Parke Bernet, New York, NY, 4 June 1975, lot 144. Unlocated. Illus: Ludovic Baschet, ed., *Salon de 1889, Catalogue Illustré, Peinture & Sculpture* (Paris: Georges Chamerot, 1889), 169.

SARGENT, John S. (John Singer). **London, England.**
1856 Florence, Italy–1925 London, England
Training — Florence: Accademia delle Belle Arti; Paris: Carolus-Duran, EcBA, Acad. Julian.

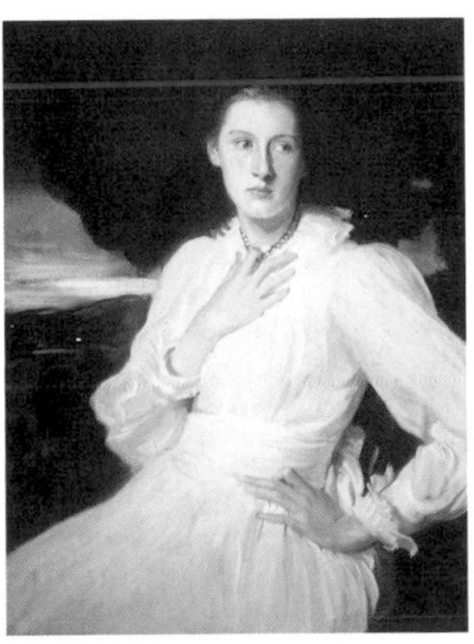

Portrait (Katherine Chase Pratt). **#509. Lent by Mr. F. S. Pratt, Worcester, Mass.** n.d. (1890). 40⅜ x 30⅛. Private Collection.

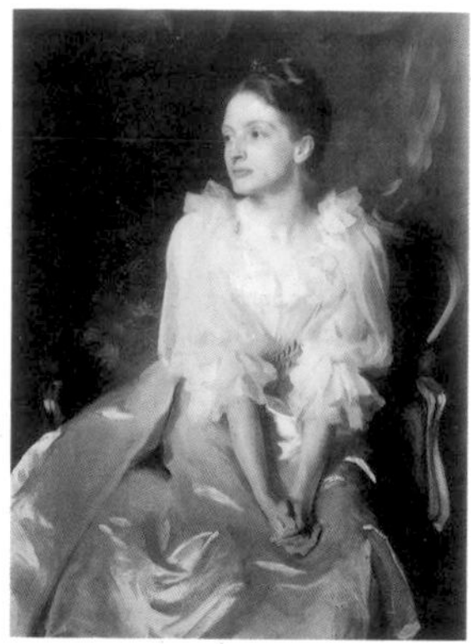

Portrait. **#513. Lent by Mr. Dunham, New York.** *Miss Helen Dunham,* 1892. 50⅜ x 43½. Private Collection.

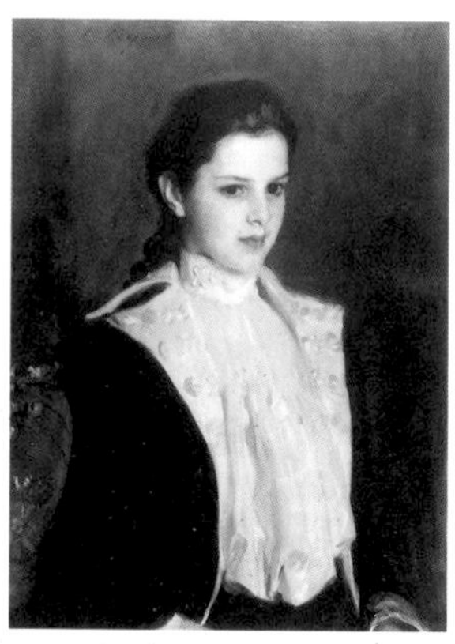

Portrait. **#515. Lent by Mr. Elliott F. Shepard, New York.** *Portrait of Alice Shepard Morris of New York,* 1888. 22 x 20. Private Collection. Photograph courtesy Peter A. Juley & Son Collection, National Museum of American Art, Smithsonian Institution.

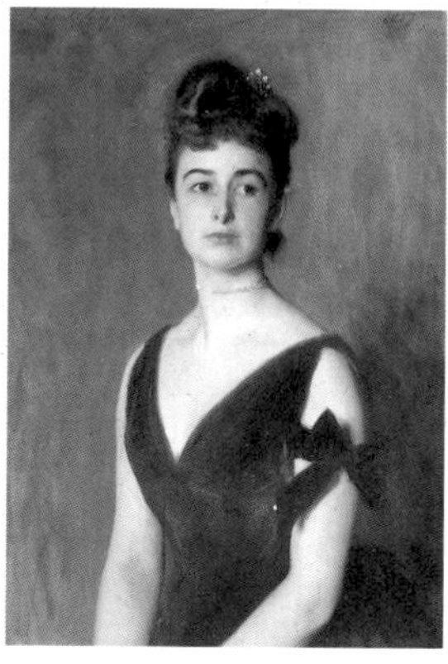

Portrait of Mrs. Inches. **#522. Lent by Dr. C. E. Inches, Boston.** *Mrs. Charles E. Inches (Louise Pomeroy),* 1887. 33⅞ x 24. Museum of Fine Arts, Boston, Anonymous Gift in Memory of Mrs. Charles Inches' daughter, Louise Brimmer Inches Seton.

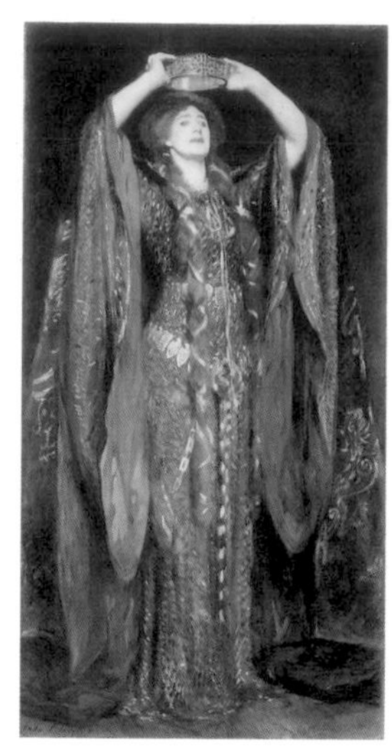

Portrait of Ellen Terry as Lady Macbeth.* **#577. Lent by Mr. Henry Irving, London. *Ellen Terry as Lady Macbeth,* n.d.(1889). 87 x 45. Tate Gallery, London.

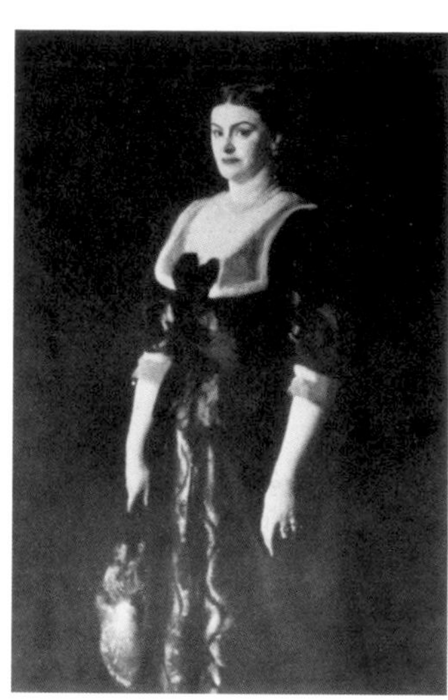

Portrait. **#680.** *Alice Mason (1838–1913),* 1885. 61 x 41. Private Collection.

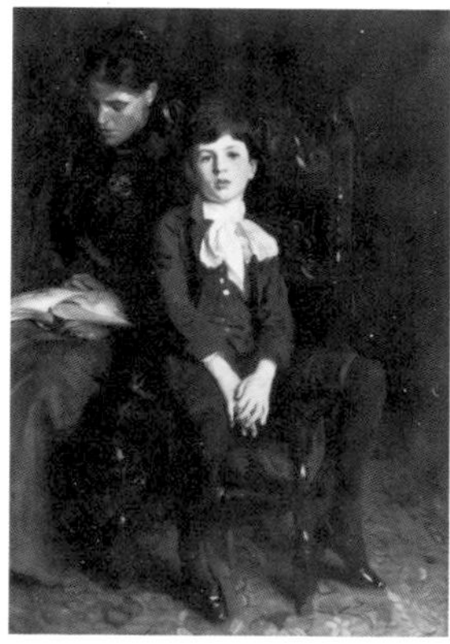

Portrait.* **#686. Lent by Mr. Augustus St. Gaudens, New York. *Portrait of a Boy (Homer St. Gaudens),* n.d. (1890). 56⅛ x 39½. The Carnegie Museum of Art, Pittsburgh, Patrons Art Fund.

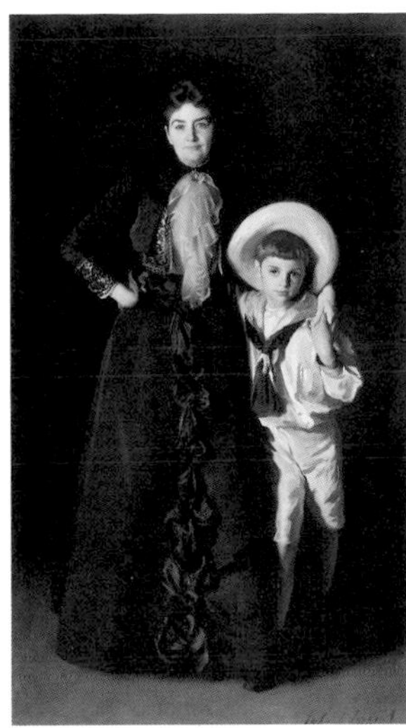

Mother and Child. **#809. Lent by Mr. Edward Davis, Boston.** *Portrait of Mrs. Edward L. Davis and Her Son, Livingston Davis,* n.d. (1890). 86⅛ x 48¼. Los Angeles County Museum of Art, Frances and Armand Hammer Purchase Fund.

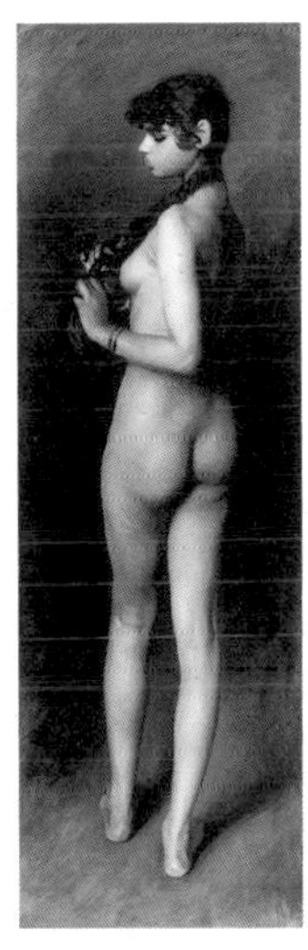

Study of an Egyptian Girl.* **#1043. *Study from Life,* n.d. (1891). 72¾ x 23¼. The Art Insititute of Chicago, Lent by an anonymous donor.

SARTAIN, Emily. Philadelphia.

1841 Philadelphia, PA–1927 Philadelphia, PA
Training — Philadelphia: John Sartain [her father], PAFA (Christian Schussele); Paris: Evariste Vital Luminais.

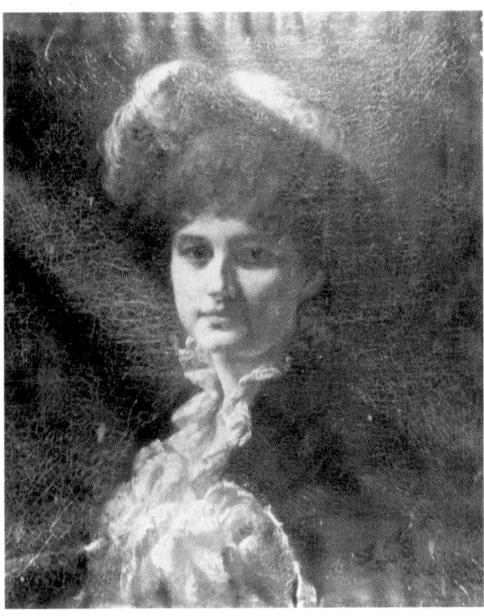

Marie. **#826.** 1881. 25 x 20. Moore College of Art and Design Permanent Collection.

SARTAIN, William (William M.). New York.

1843 Philadelphia, PA–1924 New York, NY
Training — Philadelphia: PAFA (Christian Schussele); Paris: Léon Bonnat, EcBA; Italy; Spain.

Sand Dunes at Manasquan. **#595.** [$1000]. ca. 1890. Est. 25 x 30. Unlocated.

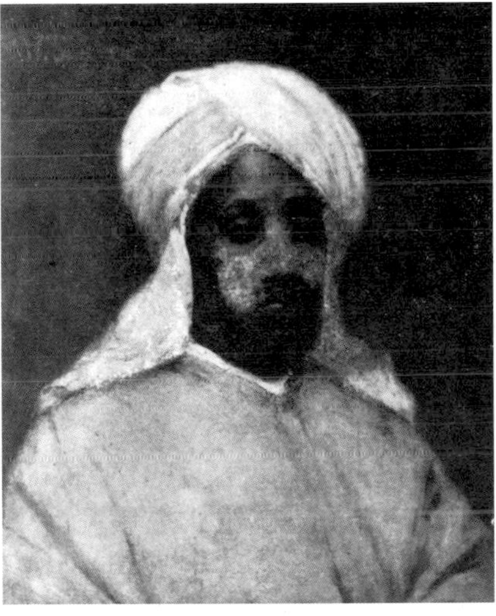

Nubian Sheik. **#1284.** [$1000]. n.d. (ca. 1886). 24 x 19¾. Mairie de Villefranche, France.

SCHILLING, Alexander. New York.

1859 Chicago, IL–1937 New York, NY
Training — Chicago: Henry A. Elkins, AIC; the Netherlands.

A Day in Spring. #728. **Lent by Mr. Alexis Ludwig, Leonia, N.Y.** Sold (as *Spring*), Ortgies Fifth Avenue Art Galleries, New York, NY, 1 Feb. 1898, lot 79. Unlocated.

Landscape. #907. **Lent by Mr. Alexis Ludwig, Leonia, N.Y.** 12 x 16. Sold (as *June*), Ortgies Fifth Avenue Art Galleries, New York, NY, 1 Feb. 1898, lot 7. Unlocated.

SCHWILL, **William V.** (William Valentine Schevill). **Munich, Bavaria.**
1864 Cincinnati, OH–1951 Cincinnati, OH
Training — Cincinnati: McMicken School of Design; Munich: Royal Academy (Ludwig von Löfftz, Wilhelm Lindenschmidt, Nikolaus Gysis); London.

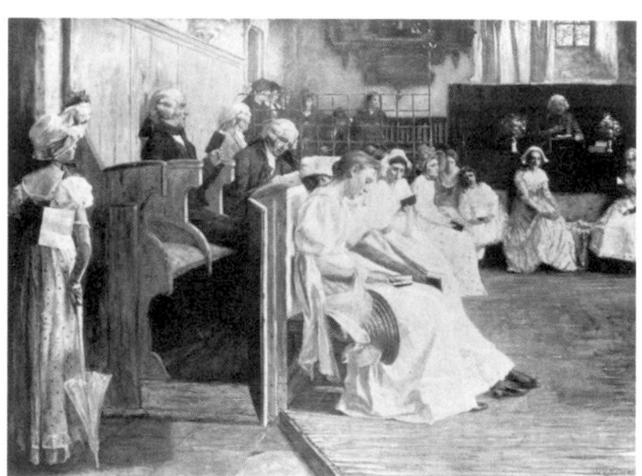

The Closing Hymn. **#402.** [$5000]. Est. 55 x 76. Unlocated. Illus: John C. Ridpath, ed., *Art & Artists of All Nations* (New York: Arkell Weekly Company, 1894), 309.

SCOTT, **Frank Edwin. Paris, France.**
1862 Buffalo, NY–1929 Paris, France
Training — New York: ASL (J. Carroll Beckwith); Paris: Alexandre Cabanel.

Parisian Street Scene. **#282.** [$350]. Est. 37 x 30. Unlocated.

SCOTT, **Jeannette. Paris, France.**
1864 Kincardine, Ontario–1937 Skaneateles, NY
Training —Philadelphia: PAFA, The Philadelphia School of Design for Women, Emily Sartain; Paris: Acad. Colarossi, Rene Prinet, A. M. Mucha; Spain.

Hollyhocks. **#1242.** [$150]. Est. 42 x 18. Unlocated.

SENAT, **Prosper L.** (Prosper Louis). **Philadelphia.**
1852 Germantown, PA–1925 Germantown, PA
Training — Paris: Jean Léon Gérôme; London: E. L. Hampton, South Kensington School.

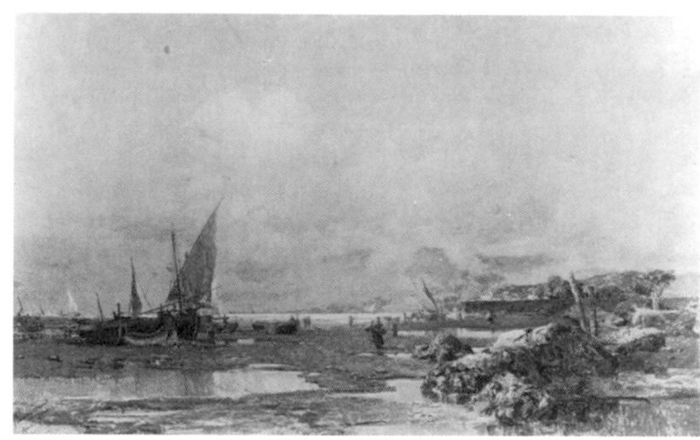

In the Gulf of Ajaccio. **#1174.** Unlocated. Est. 75 x 105. Illus: Charles M. Kurtz, ed., *Illustrations from the Art Gallery of the World's Columbian Exposition* (Philadelphia: G. Barrie, 1893), 153.

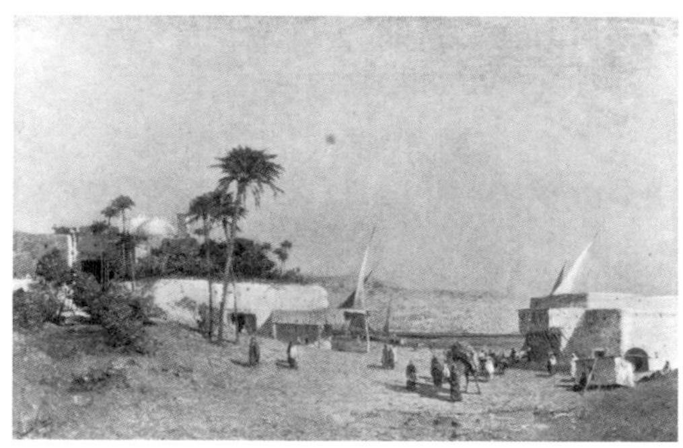

On the Nile near Beni Hassan. **#1194.** [$2500]. 1892. Unlocated. Illus: Charles M. Kurtz, ed., *Illustrations from the Art Gallery of the World's Columbian Exposition* (Philadelphia: G. Barrie, 1893), 57.

SEWELL, **Mrs. Amanda Brewster** (Lydia Amanda Brewster/Mrs. Robert Van Vorst Sewell). **New York.**
1859 North Elba, NY–1926 Florence, Italy
Training — New York: Cooper Union (R. Swain Gifford, Douglas Volk), ASL (William Merritt Chase, William Sartain); Paris: Acad. Julian (William Bouguereau, Tony Robert-Fleury), Carolus-Duran.

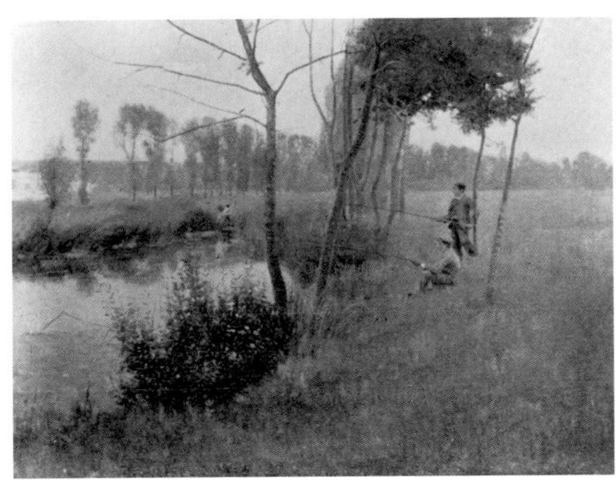

By the River. **#374.** Unlocated. Illus: Charles M. Kurtz, ed., *Illustrations from the Art Gallery of the World's Columbian Exposition* (Philadelphia: G. Barrie, 1893), 208.

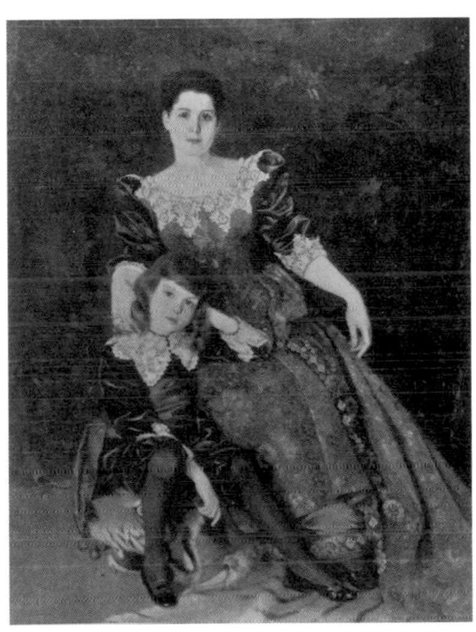

Portrait of Mother and Son. **#398.** [$1000]. ca. 1889. Unlocated. Illus: Charles M. Kurtz, ed., *Illustrations from the Art Gallery of the World's Columbian Exposition* (Philadelphia: G. Barrie, 1893), 168.

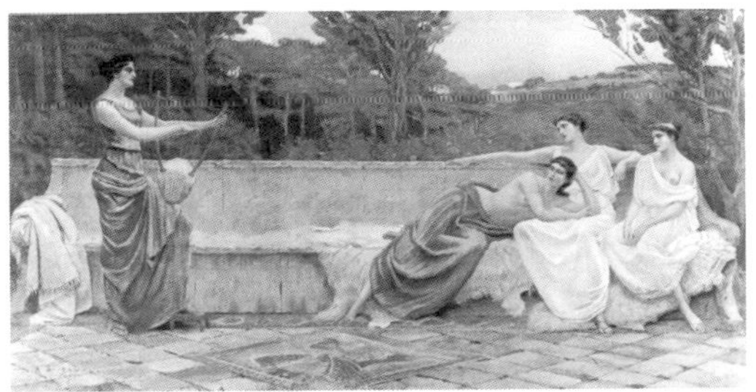

Sappho. **#447.** [$1000]. 1891. Sold, World's Columbian Exposition, Chicago, IL, 1893. Unlocated. Illus: Daniel H. Burnham, *The Art of the World*, vol. 8 (New York: Appleton, 1893–95).

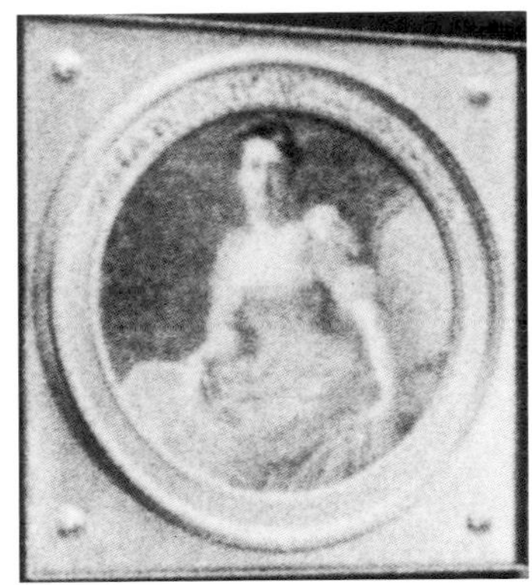

Portrait of Mrs. Boudinot Keith. **#501. Lent by Mrs. J. M. Wheeler [*sic*], New York.**[65] ca. 1888. Circular canvas, est. 36 diam. Unlocated. Illus: Official Photographs of the World's Columbian Exposition by C. D. Arnold, vol. 8, pl. 97. Courtesy of The Chicago Public Library, Special Collections Department.

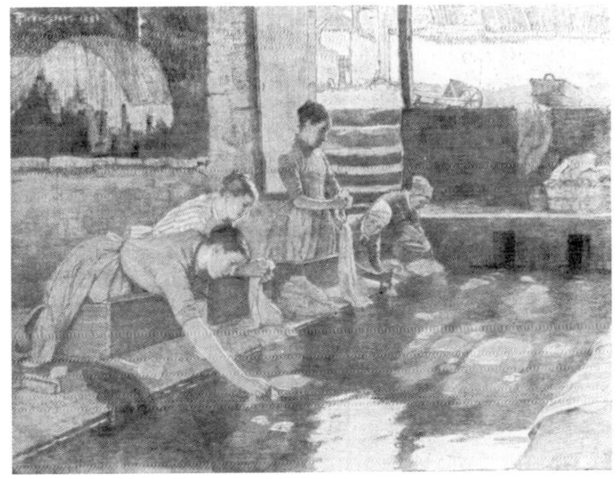

Washing Place in the Gatinais. **#629.** [$1000]. 1886. Unlocated. Illus: American Art Galleries, *Third Prize Fund Exhibition* (New York: J. J. Little, 1887), 40.

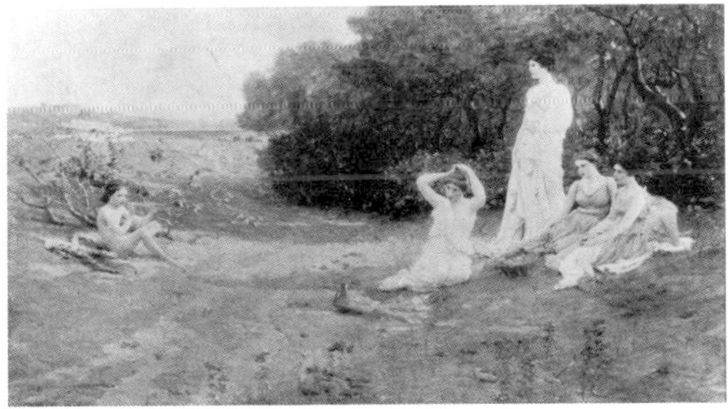

Pleasures of the Past. **#828.** [$1000]. ca. 1890. Est. 30 x 40. Unlocated. Illus: Charles M. Kurtz, ed., *Illustrations from the Art Gallery of the World's Columbian Exposition* (Philadelphia: G. Barrie, 1893), 159.

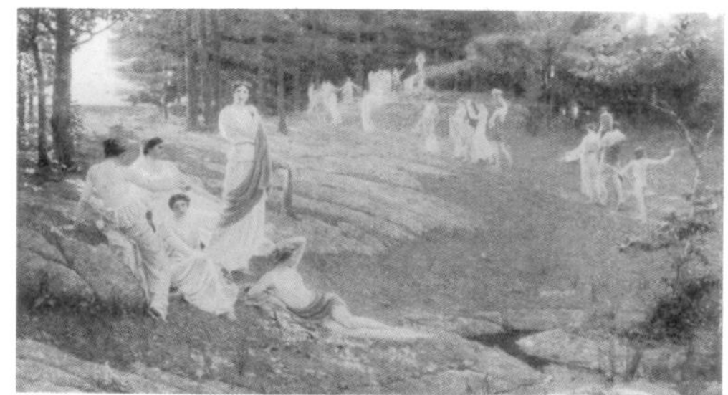

A Sylvan Festival. **#864.** [$1000]. n.d. 30 x 51½. Collection Helen Brady, Gassaway, WV. Illus: Charles M. Kurtz, ed., *Illustrations from the Art Gallery of the World's Columbian Exposition* (Philadelphia: G. Barrie, 1893), 163.

SEWELL, Robert V. V. (Robert Van Vorst). **New York.**
1860 New York, NY–1924 Florence, Italy
Training — Paris: Acad. Julian (Jules Joseph Lefebvre, Gustave Boulanger).

Diana Hunting. **#272.** [$1000]. Est. 25 x 30. Unlocated.

In Shanty-town. **#449.** [$125]. 1888. Unlocated.

Winter. **#626.** [$500]. ca. 1887. Unlocated.

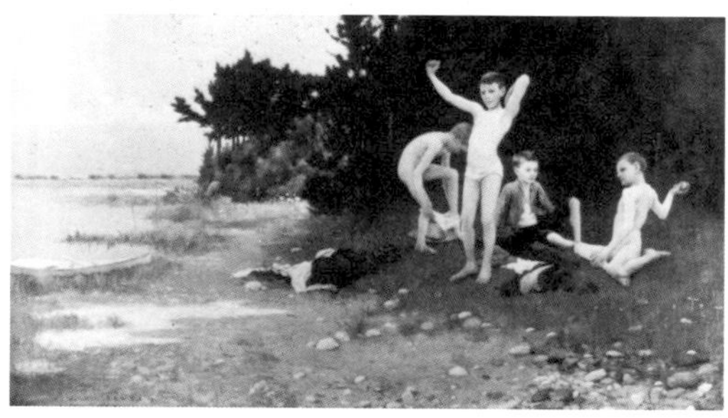

Boys Bathing. **#1188.** 1889. 16¾ x 28¼. Sold (as *At the Swimming Hole*), Sotheby Park Bernet, Los Angeles, CA, 28 Nov. 1973, lot 81. Unlocated.

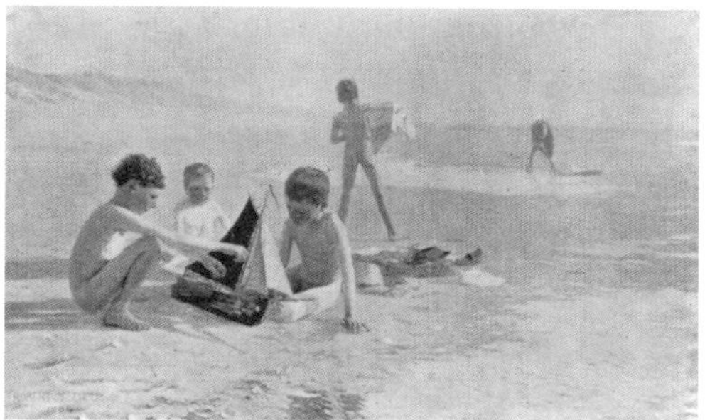

Sea Urchins. **#1189.** 1888. 30 x 51. Sold (as *The Bathers*), American Art Association, New York, NY, 18–19 March 1920, lot 192, to B. Devine. Unlocated. Illus: Charles M. Kurtz, ed., *Illustrations from the Art Gallery of the World's Columbian Exposition* (Philadelphia: G. Barrie, 1893), 293.

SHARP, J. H. (Joseph Henry). **Cincinnati.**
1859 Bridgeport, OH–1953 Pasadena, CA
Training — Cincinnati: McMicken School of Design; Antwerp: Charles Verlat; Munich: Royal Academy (Carl Marr, Nikolaus Gysis); Paris: Acad. Julian (J. P. Laurens, Jean-Joseph Benjamin-Constant), Gustave Courtois; Spain; Italy (Frank Duveneck).

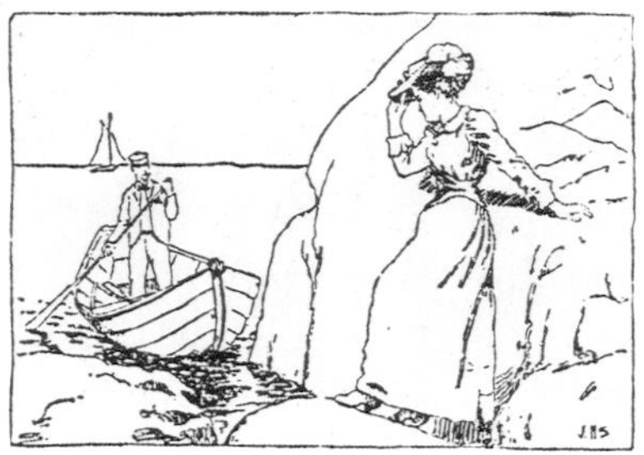

Going to the Race. **#294.** [$450]. Est. 22 x 33. Unlocated. Photograph courtesy Forrest Fenn.

SHEPLEY, Annie B. (Annie Barrows). **New York.**
Unknown–Residing 1905 Worcester, MA
Training — New York: H. Siddons Mowbray; Paris: L. Simon, Acad. Julian (Jules Joseph Lefebvre, Jean-Joseph Benjamin-Constant).

The Wonderful Story. **#1102.** [$1000]. Unlocated.

SHEPPARD, Warren (Warren Wood). **Brooklyn.**
1855 Greenwich, NJ–1920 Brooklyn, NY
Training — M. F. H. De Haas; New York: Cooper Union; Paris.

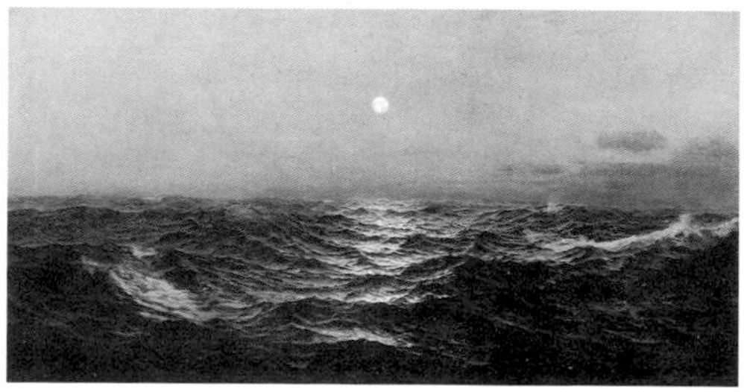

The Restless Sea. **#734.** [$2500]. **Lent by Mr. J. S. Fassett, Tonawanda, N.Y.** n.d. (ca. 1886). 35 x 66. Albright-Knox Art Gallery, Buffalo, NY, Bequest of Theodore S. Fassett, 1908.

SHIELDS, Thomas W. Brooklyn, N.Y.
1849 St. Johns, New Brunswick or Scotland–1920 New York, NY
Training— New York: NAD (Lemuel E. Wilmarth), ASL; Paris: Acad. Julian (Jules Joseph Lefebvre), Jean-Léon Gérôme, Carolus-Duran, Mihaly Munkacsy.

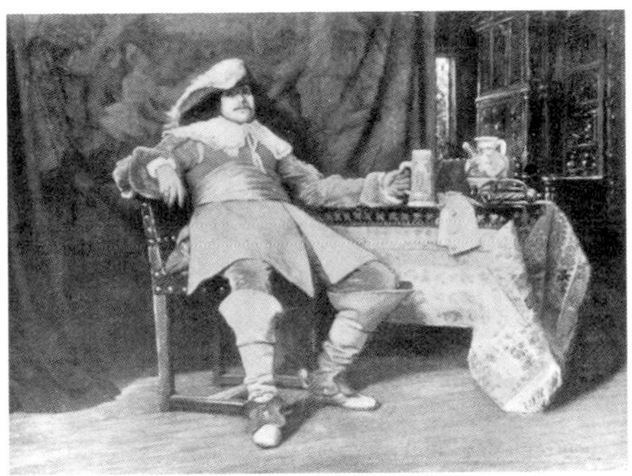

Cavalier, Time of Louis XIII. **#858.** [$750]. ca. 1881. 36 x 48. Unlocated. Illus: Charles M. Kurtz, ed., *Illustrations from the Art Gallery of the World's Columbian Exposition* (Philadelphia: G. Barrie, 1893), 145.

SHIRLAW, Walter. New York.
1837 Paisley, Scotland–1909 Madrid, Spain
Training— New York: NAD; Munich: Royal Academy (Johann Leonhard Raab, Alexander von Wagner, A. G. F. von Romberg, Wilhelm Lindenschmidt, Wilhelm von Kaulbach).

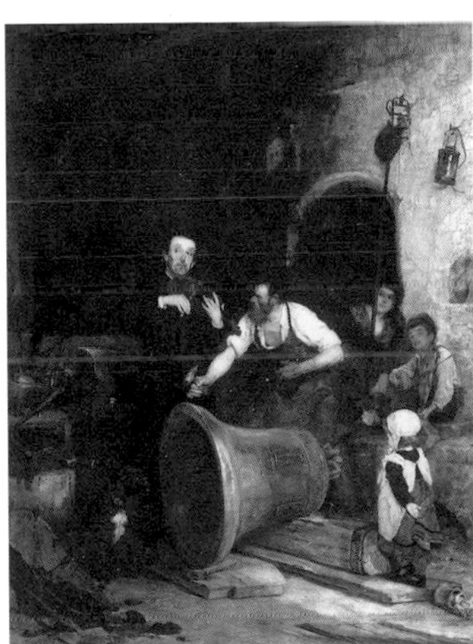

Toning the Bell. **#477. Lent by Mr. J. H. Willing, Chicago.** 1874. 40 x 30. The Art Institute of Chicago, Friends of American Art Collection.

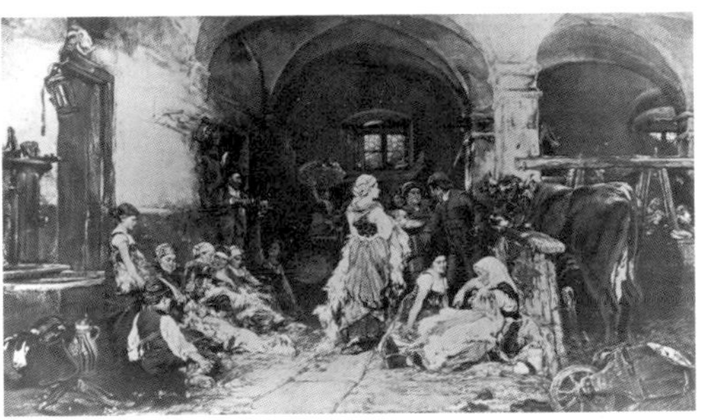

Sheep-shearing in the Bavarian Highlands. **#825.** [$5000]. ca. 1877. 50 x 84. Sold, Kende Galleries at Gimbel Brothers, New York, NY, 4 May 1945, lot 178. Unlocated. Illus: Daniel H. Burnham, *The Art of the World,* vol. 6 (New York: Appleton, 1893–95).

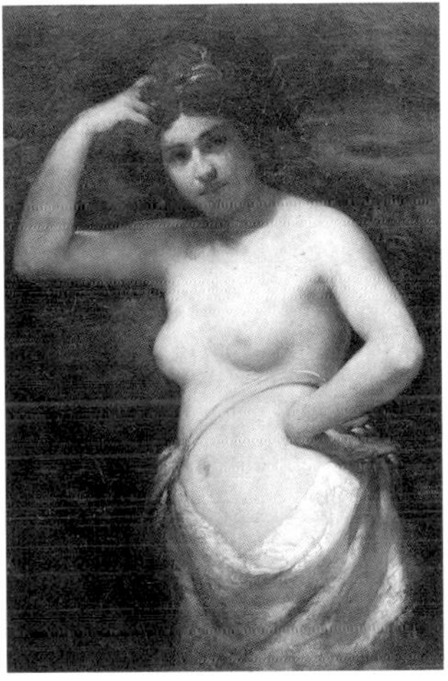

Rufina. **#850.** [$1500]. **Lent by the Century Association, New York.** n.d. (ca. 1887–88). 40⅝ x 27⅜. The Century Association, New York, NY.

SHURTLEFF, R. M. (Roswell Morse). **New York.**
1838 Rindge, NH–1915 New York, NY
Training— Buffalo, NY; Boston: Lowell School of Practical Drawing; New York: NAD; Berlin.

Autumn Forest. **#429. Lent by Mr. W. T. Evans, New York.** ca. 1892. 20 x 25. Sold (as *Woods in Autumn*), American Art Association, New York, NY, 30 Jan.–2 Feb. 1900, lot 53, to Louis Stern. Unlocated. "A forest effect, with the trunks of trees, large boulders, and a pool in the brook in the foreground. Farther into the picture are the green foliage lighted up by the sun and a bit of sky appearing through the leafy recesses of the woods. Charming in color and eminently truthful in effect. This picture represented Mr. Shurtleff at the Chicago World's Fair in 1893, and was his sole exhibit" —American Art Association, *Catalogue of American Paintings Belonging to William T. Evans* (New York: Press of J. J. Little, 1900), lot 53.

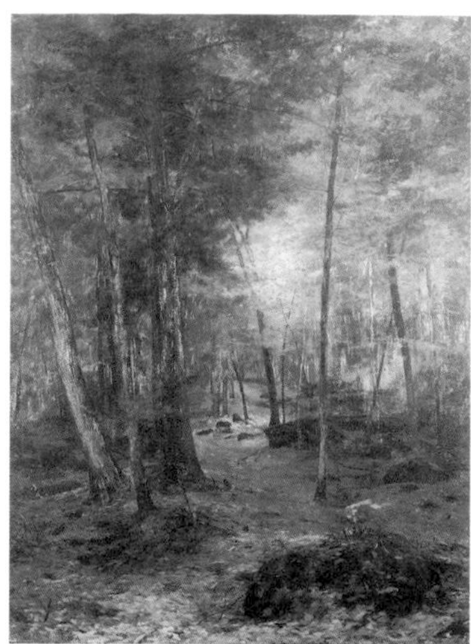

In Autumn Woods. **#770.** [$2000]. *Autumn Woods,* date illegible (ca. 1889). 50 x 38½. The George Walter Vincent Smith Art Museum, Springfield, MA.

Looking East at Sunset. **#893.** [$700]. ca. 1891. 24 x 34. Unlocated. "The 3d picture is 24 x 34 — that I called 'Looking East at Sunset.' Hung on north wall of Academy two years ago. A mountain top lighted by last rays of sun — the valley in shadow" —R. S. Shurtleff to R. S. Gifford, Charles M. Kurtz Papers, Archives of American Art.

---

† **SIMMONS, Edward E.** (Edward Emerson). **New York.**
1852 Concord, MA–1931 Baltimore, MD
Training — Paris: Acad. Julian (Gustave Boulanger, Jules Joseph Lefebvre), EcBA.

Early Moonlight, Bay of St. Ives. **#302.** [$1500]. Est. 35 x 60. Unlocated.

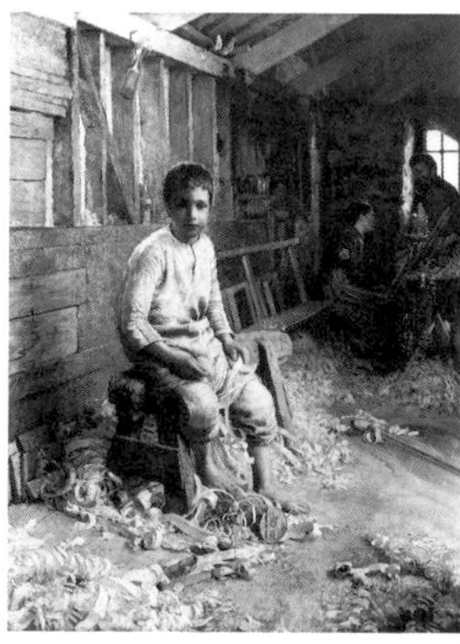

******The Carpenter's Son.* **#645. Lent by Miss Amelia C. Jones, New Bedford, Mass.** 1888. 66 x 50½. Private Collection.

Darby and Joan. **#736.** Unlocated. "A plain interior with a pilot saying goodbye to his old wife who sits at the breakfast table. As he conceals her head and shoulders, and his own face is turned away, we have an interesting scene of elderly affection, but a group without faces" — "Monthly Record of American Art," *The Magazine of Art* 16 (Dec. 1892–Nov. 1893): vi.

SINGER, Winnaretta (Winnaretta Eugenie/Princesse Edmond de Polignac). **Paris, France.**
1865 Yonkers, NY–1943 London, England
Training — Paris: Eugène Le Roux, Félix Joseph Barrias, Paul Mathey.

Spring Study. **#1216.** [800 francs]. Unlocated.

SLADE, Emily. New York.
Philadelphia, PA–Residing 1911 Paris, France
Training — New York: NAD, ASL (J. Carroll Beckwith); Paris: Alfred Stevens.

Portrait of Miss C. C. C. **#1024.** ca. 1887. Unlocated.

SMEDLEY, W. T. (William Thomas). **New York.**
1858 West Bradford, PA–1920 Bronxville, NY
Training — Philadelphia: PAFA; Paris: Acad. Julian (J. P. Laurens).

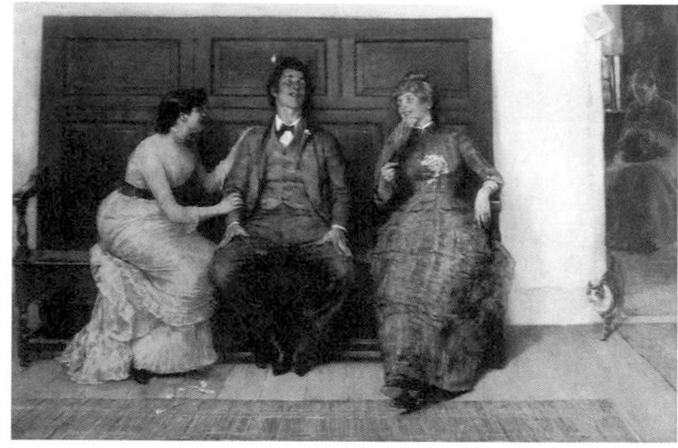

Embarrassment.* **#936. Lent by Mr. Thomas B. Clarke, New York. *The Embarrassment,* 1883. 15¾ x 23½. New Jersey State Museum Collection, Trenton, Gift of Mr. and Mrs. Stuart P. Feld.

SMILLIE, George H. (George Henry). **New York.**
1840 New York, NY–1921 Bronxville, NY
Training —James D. Smillie [his father], James MacDougal Hart.

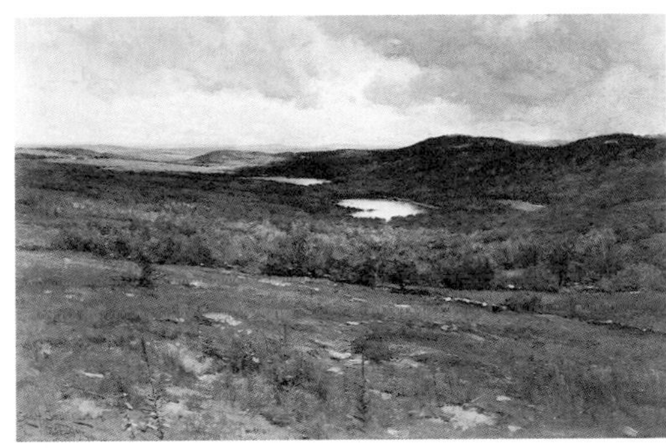

From West Mountain, Conn. **#589.** [$1500]. 1891. 30 x 46. Post Road Gallery, Larchmont, NY.

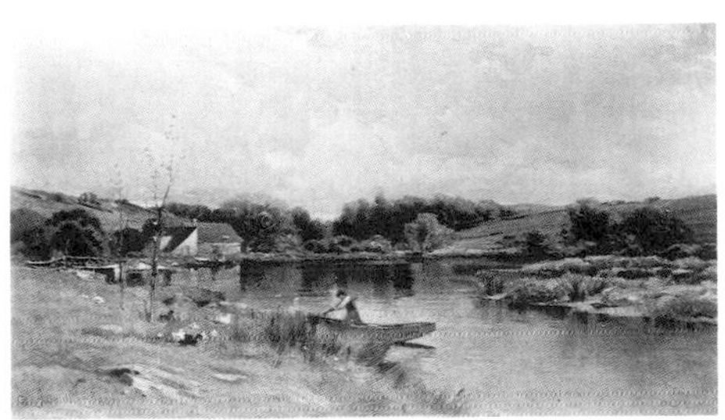

Mill Pond at Ridgefield, Conn. **#674. Lent by Mr. John S. White, New York.** 1887. 19 x 33. Private Collection.

A Lush Place. **#679. Lent by Mr. Washington Wilson, New York.** ca. 1889. Unlocated.

SMITH, **De Cost** (DeCost). **New York.**
1864 Skaneateles, NY–1939 Amenia, NY
Training — New York: ASL, McMullin School; Paris: Acad. Julian (Gustave Boulanger, Jules Joseph Lefebvre), M. H. Lefort.

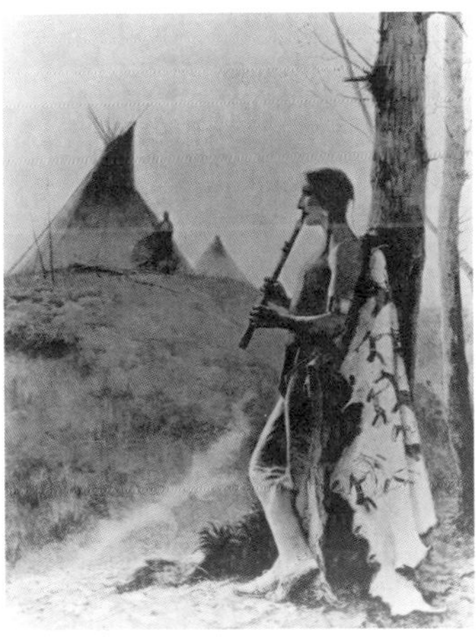

Sioux Lovers. **#1089. Lent by Mr. E. Reuel Smith, New York.** n.d. (ca. 1887). ca. 72 x 48. Private Collection. Illus: Daniel H. Burnham, *The Art of the World,* vol. 3 (New York: Appleton, 1893–95).

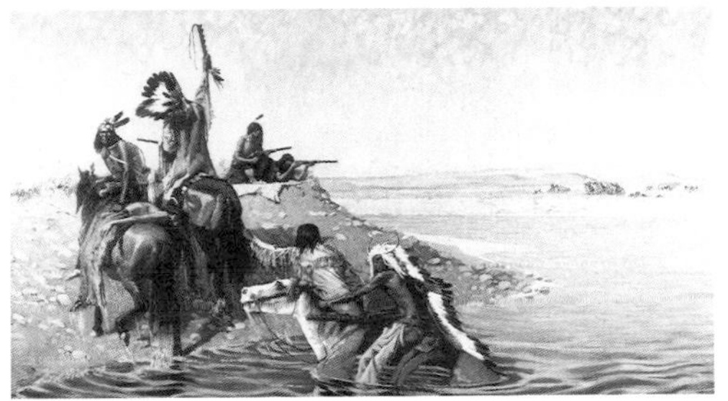

Driven Back. **#1157.** [$400]. *War Party,* 1892. 26 x 46. Collection of the Birmingham Museum of Art, Gift of Dr. and Mrs. Harold E. Simon.

SMITH, **E. Boyd** (Elmer Boyd). **Auvers-sur-Oise, France.**
1860 St. John, New Brunswick, Canada–1943 Wilton, CT
Training — Paris: Acad. Julian (Gustave Boulanger, Jules Joseph Lefebvre), M. H. Lefort.

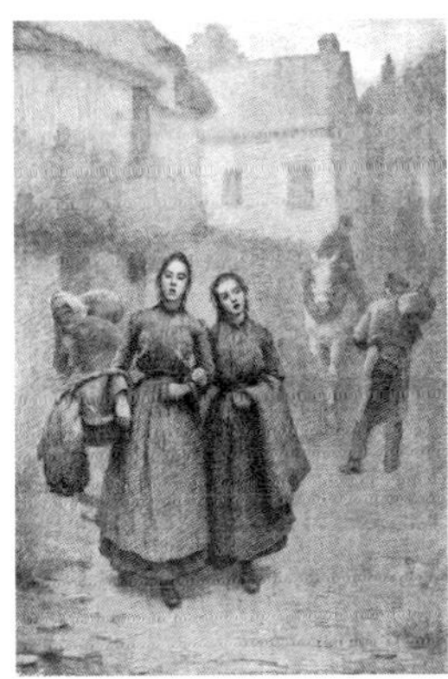

Return from the Fields. **#1215.** [$600]. ca. 1892. Unlocated. Illus: Ludovic Baschet, ed., *Catalogue Illustré de Peinture et Sculpture, Salon de 1892* (Paris: Chamerot & Renouard, 1892), 193.

SMITH, **Frank Eugene.**[66] **Munich, Bavaria.**
1865 New York, NY–1936 Leipzig, Germany
Training — Munich: Academy of Graphic Arts.

Portrait of my Brother (Frederick Lorenz Smith). **#1241.** [$5000]. **Lent by Mr. F. L. Smith, New York.** Est. 35 x 24. Unlocated.

SMITH, **Henry P.** (Henry Pember). **New York.**
1854 Waterford, CT–1907 Asbury Park, NJ
Training — self-taught.

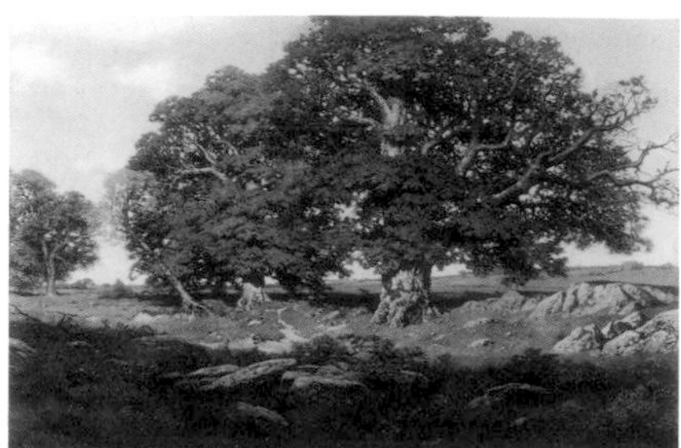

Old Oaks at Waterford. **#857. Lent by Mr. Latham A. Fish, Brooklyn, N.Y.** *Old Oaks,* n.d. (ca. 1889). 36⅛ x 54. Tweed Museum of Art, University of Minnesota, Duluth.

Landscape at Waterford, Conn. **#869.** [$1000]. ca. 1891. Unlocated.

SMITH, J. Francis (John Francis). **St. Louis.**
1868 Chicago, IL or Waukesha, WI–1941 Los Angeles, CA
Training — Paris: Gustave Boulanger, Jules Joseph Lefebvre, Jean-Joseph Benjamin-Constant.

Young Girl of Feuillee. **#387.** ca. 1891. Unlocated.

SONNTAG, William L. (William Louis). **New York.**
1822 near Pittsburgh, PA–1900 New York, NY
Training — Florence; largely self-taught.

Mt. Jefferson and Mt. Adams, White Mountains, New Hampshire. **#417.** [$1200]. Est. 40 x 55. Unlocated.

STEELE, T. C. (Theodore Clement). **Indianapolis.**
1847 Owen County (near Gosport), IN–1926 Brown County, IN
Training — Munich: Royal Academy (Ludwig von Löfftz, Gyula Benczur).

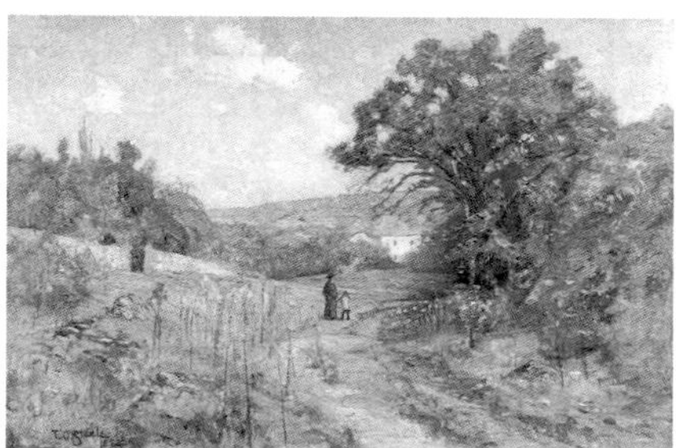

September. **#335.** [$500]. 1892. 30 x 45½. Mr. and Mrs. Theodore L. Steele, Indianapolis, IN.

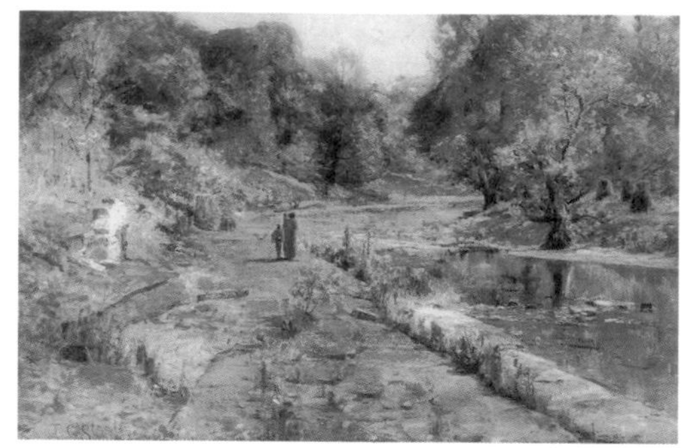

On the Muscatatuck.* **#345. [$500]. 1892. 30 x 45. The Columbia Club Foundation, Indianapolis, IN.

STEPHENS, Alice Barber (Alice Barber/Mrs. Charles H. Stephens). **Philadelphia.**
1858 Salem, NJ–1932 Moylan, PA
Training — Philadelphia: John Sanderson Dalziel, The Philadelphia School of Design for Women; PAFA (Thomas Eakins, Christian Schussele); Paris: Acad. Colarossi, Acad. Julian.

Harvesting in the Meadows. **#405.** [$100]. Est. 15 x 30. Unlocated.

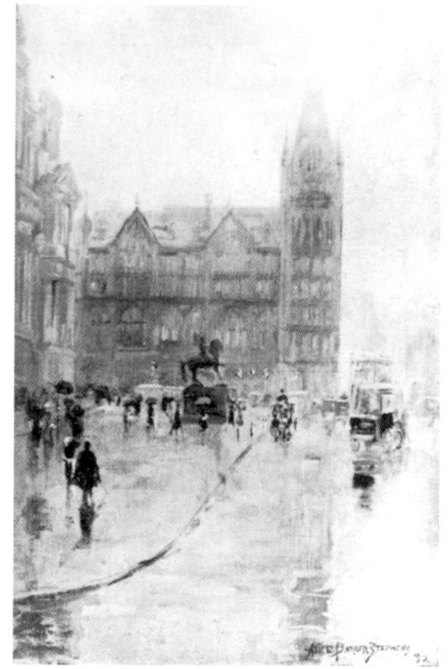

Rainy Day Effect in Philadelphia. **#1175.** [$125]. ca. 1890. Destroyed. Illus: The Art Club of Philadelphia, *Second Special Exhibition* (Philadelphia: Globe Printing House, 1890), no. 79.

STEWART, Jules L. (Julius LeBlanc). **Paris, France.**
1855 Philadelphia, PA–1919 Paris, France
Training — Paris: Eduardo Zamaçois y Zabala, Jean-Léon Gérôme, Raimundo de Madrazo y Garreta.

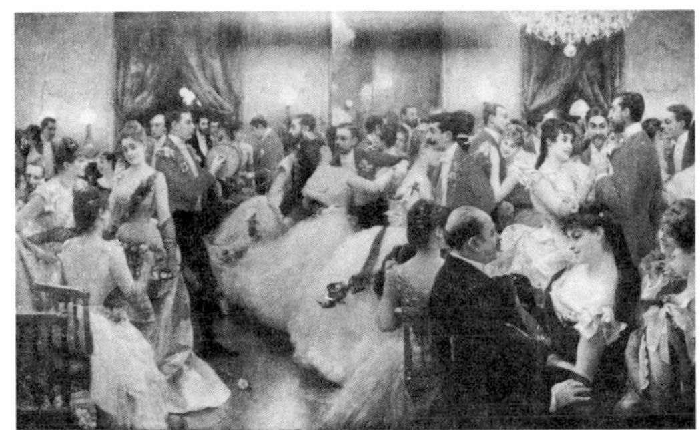

The Hunt Ball. #542. **Lent by the Essex Club, Newark, N.J.** 1885. 49 x 79. Private Collection.

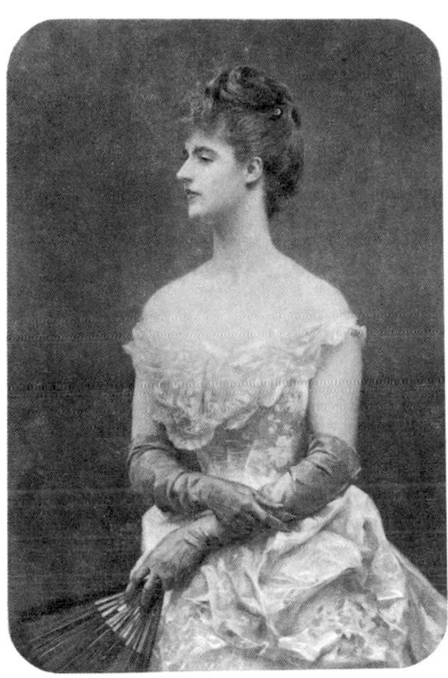

Portrait of the Viscountess de Gouy d'Arcy. **#654. Lent by the Viscountess de Gouy d'Arcy, Paris.** ca. 1888. Est. 18 x 13. Unlocated. Illus: George W. Sheldon, *Recent Ideals of American Art* (New York: Appleton, 1890), opposite 102.

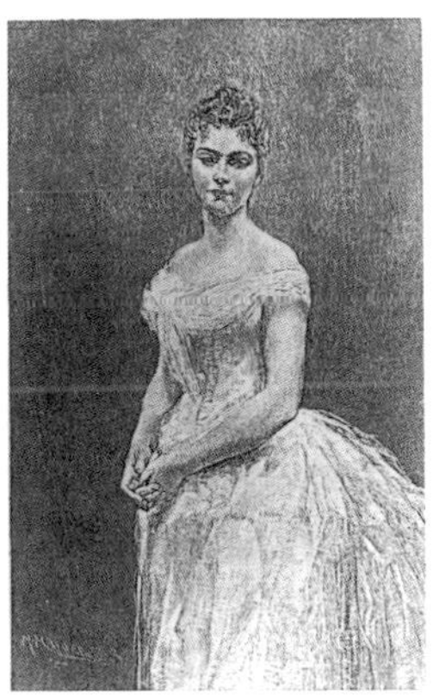

Portrait of the Baroness Benoist Mechin, Paris. **#661. Lent by the Baron Benoist Mechin, Paris.** ca. 1889. Est. 20 x 14. Unlocated. Illus: *Harper's New Monthly Magazine* 79 (Sept. 1889): 507.

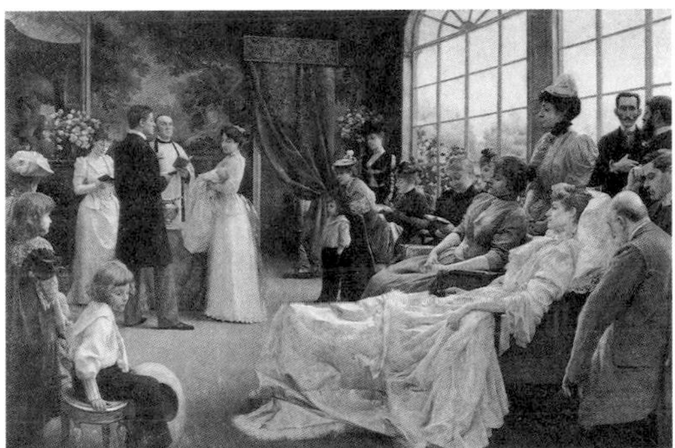

The Baptism.* **#767. [$10,000]. 1892. 79¼ x 118¼. Los Angeles County Museum of Art, purchased with funds provided by the Museum Acquisition Fund.

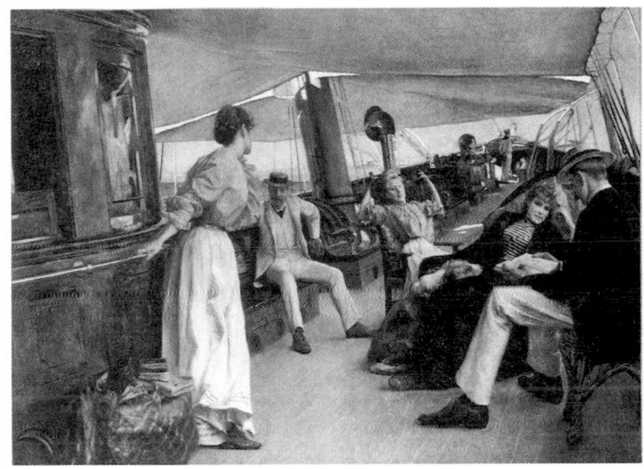

On the Yacht Namouna, Venice, 1890.* **#773. Lent by Mrs. Henry P. Borie, Philadelphia. 1890. 56 x 77. Wadsworth Atheneum, Hartford, The Ella Gallup Sumner and Mary Catlin Sumner Collection.

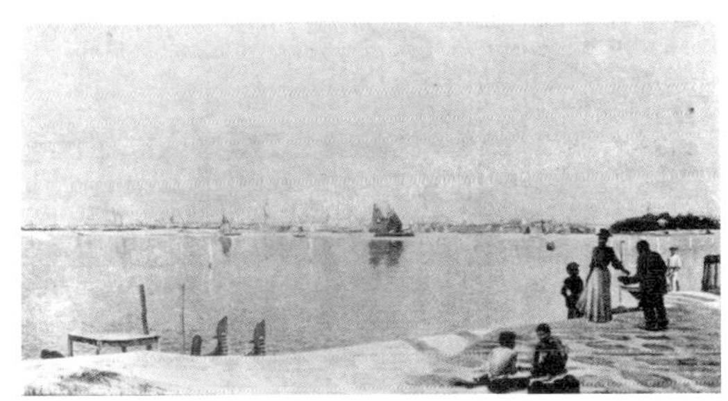

Venice. **#1183.** [$3500]. **Lent by Mr. James Gordon Bennett, Paris.** Unlocated. Illus: Charles M. Kurtz, ed., *Illustrations from the Art Gallery of the World's Columbian Exposition* (Philadelphia: G. Barrie, 1893), 30.

STOKES, **F. W.** (Frank Wilbert). **Philadelphia.**

1858 Nashville, TN–1955 New York, NY
Training — Philadelphia: PAFA (Thomas Eakins); Paris: Acad. Julian (Gustave Boulanger, Jules Joseph Lefebvre), Acad. Colorossi (Raphaël Collin), Jean-Léon Gérôme.

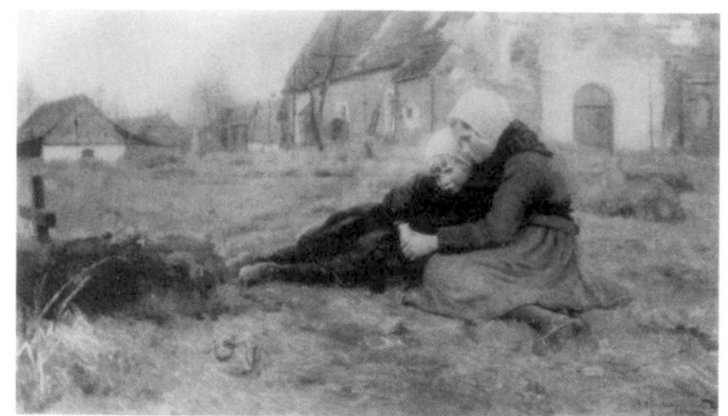

The Orphans. **#444.** [$1000]. Destroyed in the Haseltine studio fire, Philadelphia, PA, 1896. Illus: The American Art Galleries, *Special Exhibition* (New York: 1891), 4. "Is truer and deeper and is painted with a better understanding and sympathy. It represents two girls who have come to a bleak churchyard to place flowers on their mother's grave and who are sitting before it in attitudes of rude and unconscious pathos, clasping each others' hands for comfort . . . unusually moderate in color, temperate in the treatment of his subjects and loose in texture . . ." —*Brooklyn Daily Eagle,* 13 Dec. 1892.

STONE, **J. M.** (James Madison). **Boston.**
1841 Dana, MA–1930 Beverly, MA
Training — New York: NAD, Cooper Union; Munich: Royal Academy (Otto Seitz, Wilhelm Lindenschmidt).

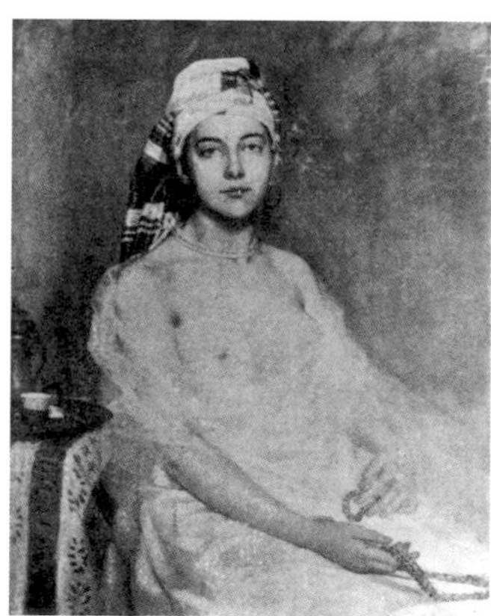

***Leukopis.* #902.** [$1000]. ca. 1889. Est. 32 x 25. Unlocated. Illus: William H. Downes, "New England Art at the World's Fair," *New England Magazine* 8 (July 1893): 357.

***A Summer Dream.* #1218.** [$800]. ca. 1891. Unlocated. "Figure is somewhat scantily draped, with flesh tints sufficiently pronounced, 'A Summer Dream,' representing a brown-haired maiden lost in reverie, and in reclining posture, with eyes half closed and slightly parted lips, one hand resting on her bosom and the other holding in her lap a cluster of roses" —Hubert H. Bancroft, *The Book of the Fair,* vol. 3 (Chicago: Blakely Printing Co., 1893), 678–79.

STORY, **Julian** (Julian Russell). **Paris, France.**
1857 Walton-on-Thames, England–1919 Philadelphia, PA
Training — Paris: Acad. Julian (Gustave Boulanger, Jules Joseph Lefebvre), Henri Gervex, Fernand Humbert; Florence; Venice.

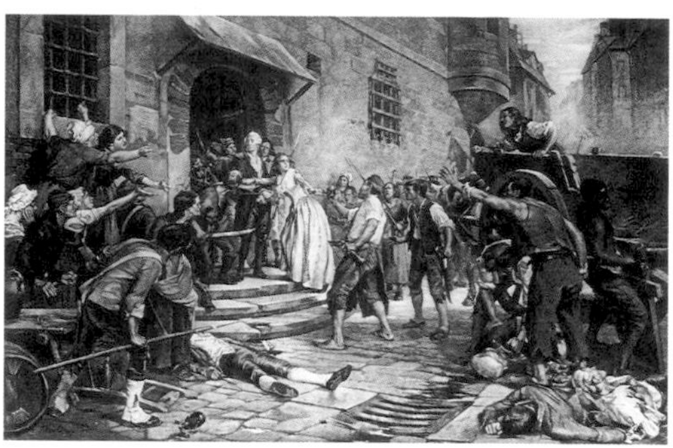

***Mlle. De Sombreuil (Episode of the French Revolution—).* #786.** 1887. 156 x 198. Collection Washington University, St. Louis, MO, by 1920. Sold, Kende Galleries at Gimbel Brothers, New York, NY, 4 May 1945, lot 183. Unlocated. Illus: Henri Sylvestre, Jr., *Marvels in Art of the Fin de Siècle,* vol. 1 (Philadelphia: Gebbie, 1893), part 7.

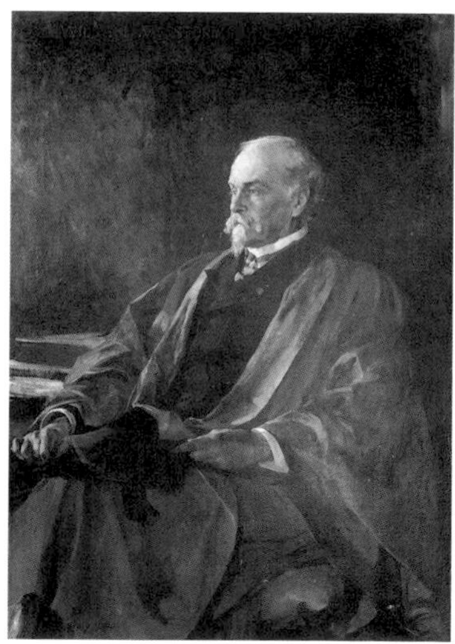

Portrait of the Artist's Father (William Wetmore Story). **#872.** n.d. (ca. 1886–89). 48 x 36. Private Collection. Photograph by Doyle Bush.

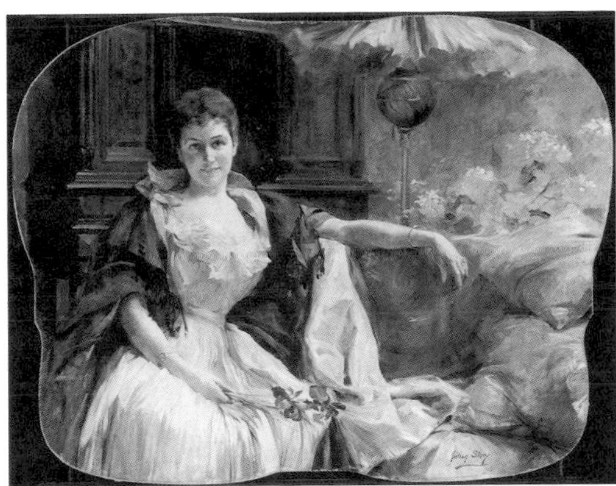

Portrait of Mme. Eames-Story. **#1138.** *Portrait of Mme. Eames Story (Emma Eames),* n.d. (ca. 1891). 51 x 64. Museum of Fine Arts, Boston, Bequest of Matilda E. Frelinghuysen.

STRICKLER, **John R.** (John Ramsey). **Brooklyn.**
1862 Peoria, IL–Unknown
Training — Paris: Jean-Léon Gérôme.

Interrupted. **#1247.** [$500]. Est. 60 x 27. Unlocated. "A portrait of his painter friend Edgar J. Taylor in his studio. Mr. Taylor is seated at his easel and has been chatting with a friend who sits beyond him carelessly rolling a cigarette. Someone has entered, and the painter turns in his chair to see who it is. The suspense of action, without the aspect of a formal pose, the quaint fittings that artists so love, the free brushing and positive, but harmonized color are commendable elements in this picture" —*Brooklyn Daily Eagle,* 27 June 1893.

SWORD, **J. B.** (James Brade). **Philadelphia.**
1839 Philadelphia, PA–1915 Philadelphia, PA
Training — Philadelphia: W. T. Richards, PAFA (Christian Schussele).

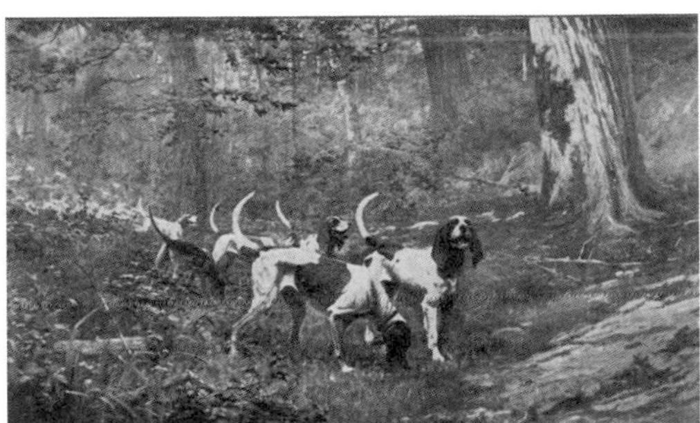

Off the Scent. **#567.** [$750]. ca. 1891. Unlocated. Illus: The Art Club of Philadelphia, *Third Annual Exhibition of Oil Paintings and Sculpture, 1891, Catalogue of Exhibition* (Philadelphia: Isaiah Price, 1891), 88.

TAGGART, **George** (George Henry). **Watertown, N.Y.**
1865 Watertown, NY–1959 Port Washington, NY
Training — Paris: Acad. Julian (William Bouguereau, G. J. M. A. Ferrier, Jules Joseph Lefebvre).

A Portrait. **#932.** Unlocated.

† TARBELL, **Edmund C.** (Edmund Charles). **Boston.**
1862 West Groton, MA–1938 New Castle, MA
Training — Boston: Massachusetts Normal Art School, MFA (Frank Benson, Robert Reid); Paris: William T. Dannat, Acad. Julian (Gustave Boulanger, Jules Joseph Lefebvre).

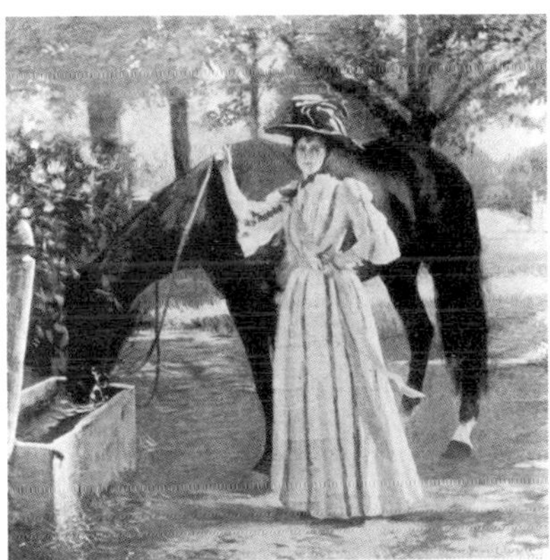

Girl and Horse. **#278.** [$3000]. 93 x 95½. Collection of the artist, 1922. Unlocated. Illus: Charles M. Kurtz, ed., *Illustrations from the Art Gallery of the World's Columbian Exposition* (Philadelphia: G. Barrie, 1893), 323.

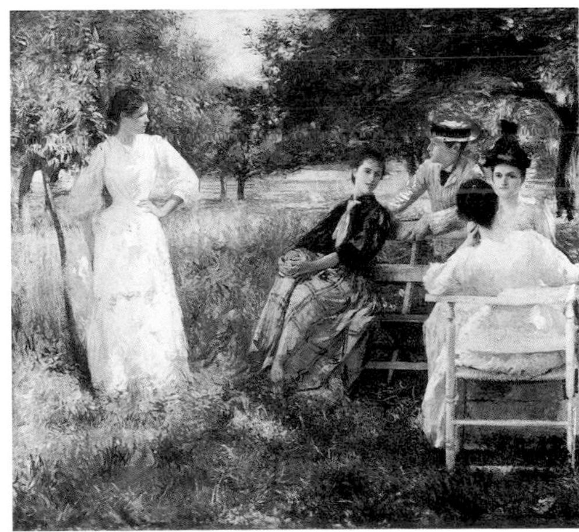

In the Orchard. **#537.** [$2500]. 1891. 60½ x 65¼. Private Collection.

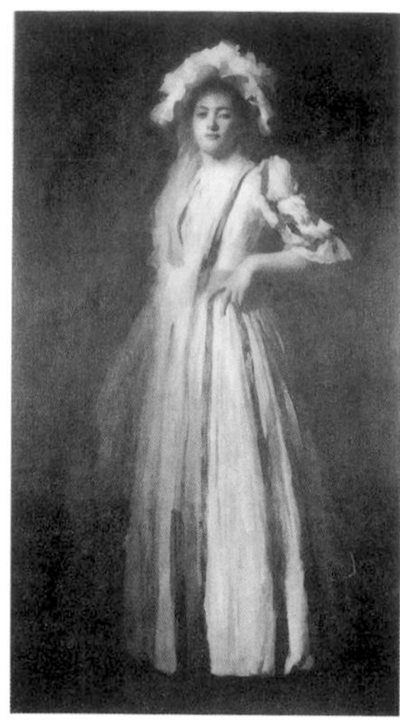

My Sister Lydia. **#671. Lent by Miss Lydia Souther, Dorchester, Mass.** n.d. (ca. 1889). 76 x 43. Private Collection. Photograph by Fay Foto.

† **THAYER, Abbott H.** (Abbott Handerson). **Scarboro, N.Y.**
1849 Boston, MA–1921 Monadnock, NH
Training — Boston: Henry D. Morse; New York: Brooklyn Art School (John Barnard Whittaker), NAD (Lemuel E. Wilmarth); Paris: EcBA (Henri Lehmann, Jean-Léon Gérôme).

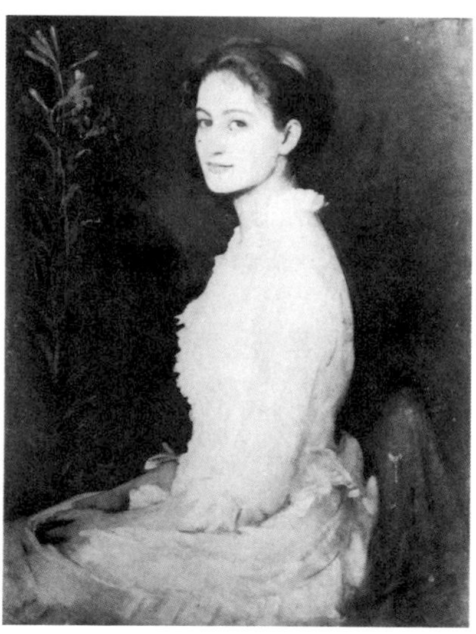

Portrait of a Lady. **#524. Lent by Miss C. F. Stillman, New York.** *Bessie Gray Stillman in 1883,* 1883. 36 x 28. Private Collection.

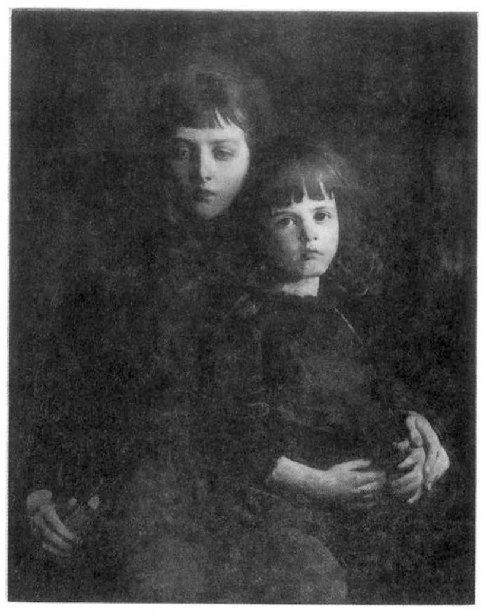

Brother and Sister (Mary and Gerald Thayer). **#699. Lent by Mr. A. A. Carey, Boston.** 1889. 36¼ x 28⅜. National Museum of American Art, Smithsonian Institution, Gift of John Gellatly.

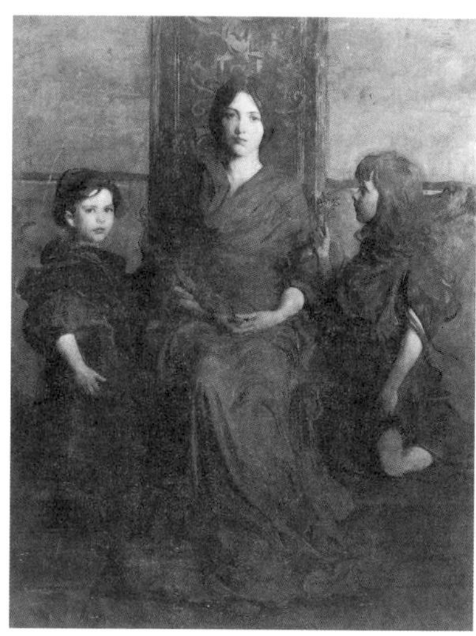

Virgin Enthroned.* **#715. Lent by Mr. J. M. Sears, Boston. 1891. 72⅝ x 52½. National Museum of American Art, Smithsonian Institution, Gift of John Gellatly.

THERIAT, C. J. (Charles James). **Paris, France.**
1860 New York, NY–Residing 1926 Paris, France
Training — Paris: Acad. Julian (Jules Joseph Lefebvre, Gustave Boulanger).

Banks of the Ain Mlili. **#306.** Est. 10 x 8. Unlocated.

Young Girl Spinning (Biskra). **#1158.** [$200]. Est. 15 x 10. Unlocated.

An Arab Goatherd. **#1164.** [$1200]. Unlocated.

Path in the Oasis of Biskra. **#1228.** [$250]. ca. 1892.

Unlocated.

Waiting for Supper. **#1281.** Unlocated.

THOMAS, S. Seymour (Stephen Seymour). **Paris, France.**
1868 San Augustine, TX–1956 La Crescenta, CA
Training— New York: ASL (William Merritt Chase, J. Carroll Beckwith); Paris: Henri-Lucien Doucet, Acad. Julian (Jules Joseph Lefebvre, Jean-Joseph Benjamin-Constant).

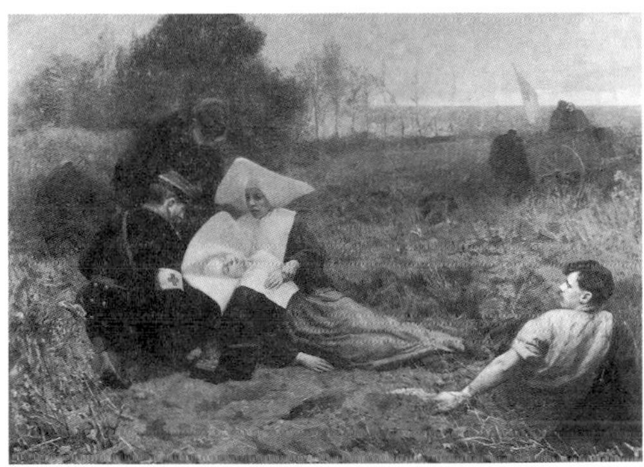

An Innocent Victim. **#615.** 1892. 69¾ x 89¾. Daughters of Charity of St. Vincent de Paul, Seton Provincialate, Los Altos Hills, CA.

THOMPSON, Wordsworth (Alfred Wordsworth). **New York.**
1840 Baltimore, MD–1896 Summit, NJ
Training— Baltimore; Paris: Charles Gleyre, H. F. A. Yvon, Emile Lambinet, Jardin des Plantes (Antoine Bayre), Alberto Pasini.

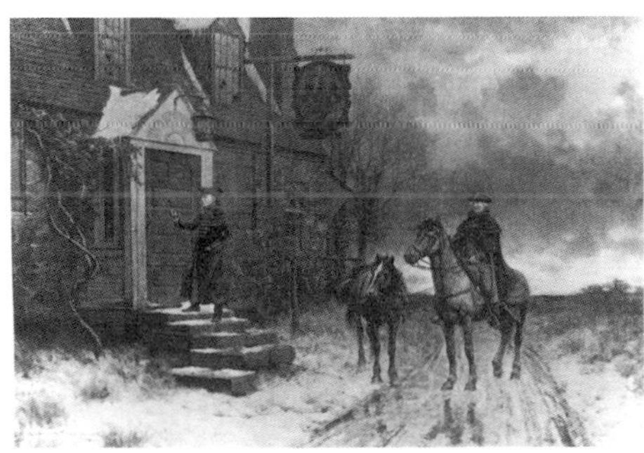

The Deserted Inn. **#394.** [$800]. Unlocated. Illus: Daniel H. Burnham, *The Art of the World,* vol. 7 (New York: Appleton, 1893–95).

In the Sweet Summer Time. **#494. Lent by Mr. George H. Babcock, Plainfield, N.J.** ca. 1892. Est. 16 x 24. Unlocated.

THOURON, Henry (Henry Joseph). **Philadelphia.**
1851 Philadelphia, PA–1915 Rome, Italy
Training— Philadelphia: PAFA; Paris: Léon Bonnat; Rome.

A Precious Bit. **#1064.** [$125]. Unlocated.

Resting. **#1067. Lent by Mrs. E. A. Thouron, New York.** ca. 1881. Unlocated.

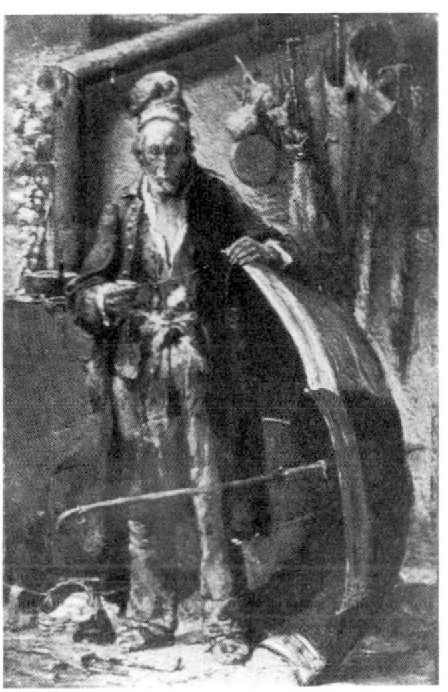

A Rainy Prospect. **#1069. Lent by Mr. Howard Hancock, Philadelphia.** ca. 1881. Unlocated. Illus: *Brush and Pencil* (March 1905): 174.

Up Hill. **#1275. Lent by Miss Moss, Philadelphia.** Est. 7 x 5. Unlocated.

Patches—Soup. **#1276. Lent by Mr. Caleb Cresson, Philadelphia.** ca. 1881. Two panels, est. 3½ x 2 each. Unlocated.

Etruria. Decorative study in Neutral Tints and Complementary Colors. **#1282.** [$1000]. ca. 1890. Sold, World's Columbian Exposition, Chicago, IL, 1893. Unlocated.

THROOP, Frances Hunt (Mrs. Samuel H. Ordway). **New York.**
1860 New York, NY–1933 East Hampton, NY
Training— New York: ASL (J. Carroll Beckwith); Paris: Alfred Stevens.

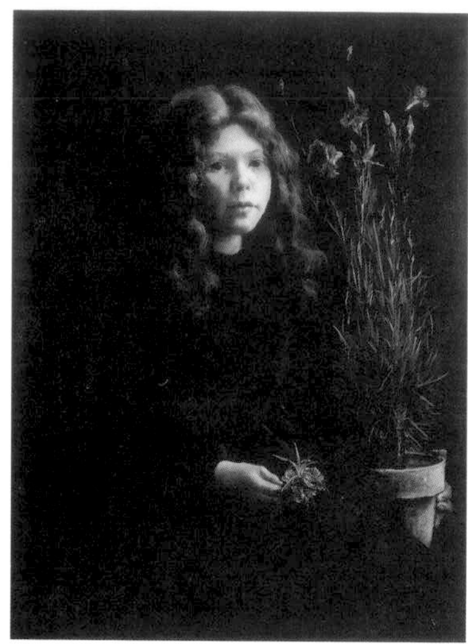

Spring Carnations. **#820.** 1889. 36⅜ x 25¾. Private Collection. Photograph by Wayne Geist.

Portrait of a Lady. **#830.** Unlocated.

† **TIFFANY, Louis C.** (Louis Comfort). **New York.**
1848 New York, NY–1932 New York, NY
Training — New York: George Inness, Samuel Colman; Paris: L. C. A. Bailly.

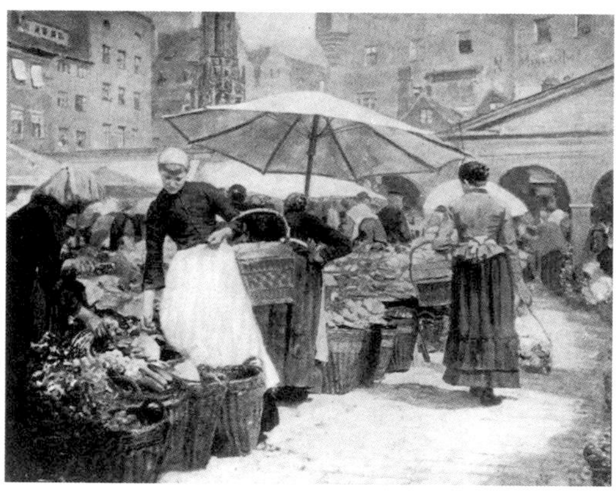

Market at Nuremberg, Bavaria. **#424.** n.d. (ca. 1893; oil on wood). 32 x 40¾. Private Collection. Illus: Charles M. Kurtz, ed., *Illustrations from the Art Gallery of the World's Columbian Exposition* (Philadelphia: G. Barrie, 1893), 348.

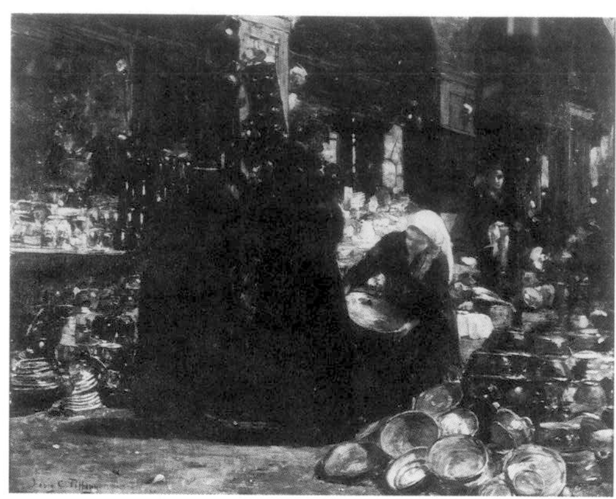

Pottery Market at Wurtzburg. **#461.** [$1000]. *The Pottery Market at Nuremberg,* n.d. (ca. 1892). 23 x 28⅛. Virginia Museum of Fine Arts, Richmond, The Arthur and Margaret Glasgow Fund.

TOASPERN, Otto. New York.
1863 Brooklyn, NY–1940 Brooklyn, NY
Training — New York: Cooper Union; Munich: Royal Academy (Nikolaus Gysis, Heinrich Nauen).

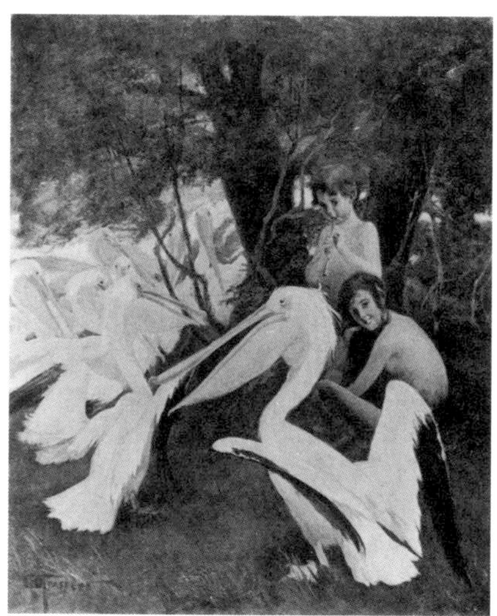

Music. **#794.** [$1000]. ca. 1892. Est. 30 x 20. Unlocated. Illus: Daniel H. Burnham, *The Art of the World,* vol. 1 (New York: Appleton, 1893–95).

TOLMAN, Stacy. Allston, Mass.
1860 Concord, MA–1935 Pawtucket, RI
Training — Boston: MFA (Otto Grundmann); Paris: Acad. Julian (Gustave Boulanger, Jules Joseph Lefebvre), EcBA (Alexandre Cabanel).

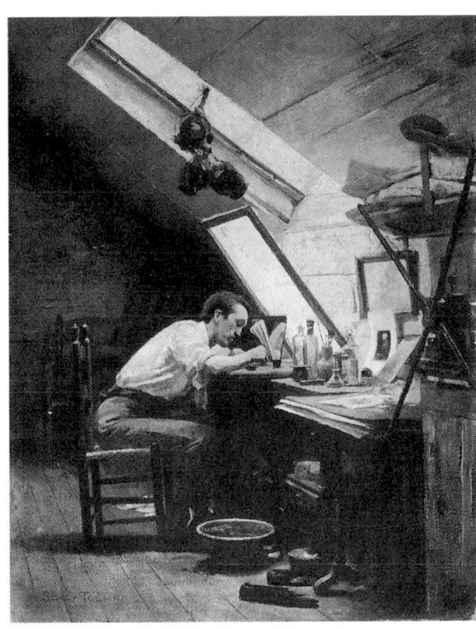

The Etcher.* **#1037. [$300]. n.d. (1887–1890). 40 1/8 x 30 3/16. The Metropolitan Museum of Art, Purchase, Bertram F. and Susie Brummer Foundation, Inc., Gift, 1962.

TOMPKINS, Clementina M. G. New York.
1848 Washington, DC–1931 New York, NY
Training— Baltimore: Peabody Art Institute; Brussels; Paris: Léon Bonnat.

A Beginner in Art. **#1227.** [$900]. ca. 1875. Unlocated.

TOMPKINS, F. H. (Frank Henry). **Boston.**
1847 Hector, NY–1922 Brookline, MA
Training— Cincinnati: McMicken School of Design; New York: ASL (Walter Shirlaw); Munich: Royal Academy (Ludwig von Löfftz).

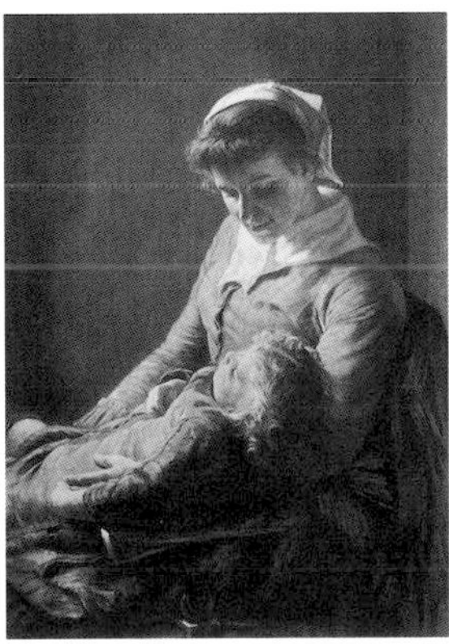

Mother and Child. **#545. Lent by the Boston Art Club.** Collection Boston Art Club, 1922. Unlocated. Illus: Ripley Hitchcock, *The Art of the World,* vol. 2 (New York: Appleton, 1895), opposite 99.

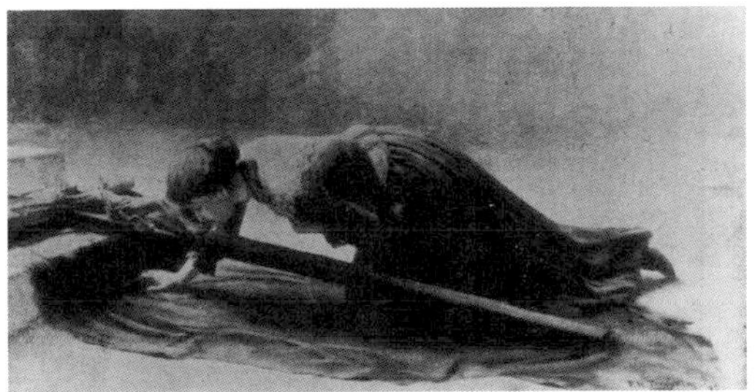

Good Friday. **#855.** ca. 1888. Sold, Leonard & Co., Boston, MA, 26–27 March 1897, lot 36. Illus: William H. Downes, "New England Art at the World's Fair," *New England Magazine* 8 (July 1893): 356.

TOWNER, Flora L. Albany, N.Y.
1855–Residing 1898 Albany, NY

Portrait. **#474.** Est. 15 x 12. Unlocated.

TRACY, John M. (John Martin). **deceased.**
1844 Rochester, OH–1893 Ocean Springs, MS
Training— Chicago: A. L. Rawson; Paris: Adolphe Yvon, Isadore Pils, Carolus-Duran.

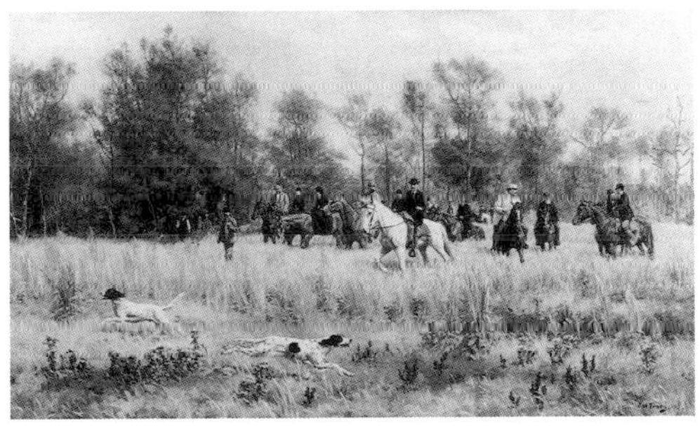

***Southern Field Trials, 1891.* #1156. Lent by Mr. C. Klackner, New York.** 1891. 30 x 50. Private Collection. Photograph courtesy David Ramus Fine Art, Atlanta, GA.

TREGO, William T. (William Brooke Thomas). **North Wales, Pa.**
1859 Yardley, PA–1909 North Wales, PA
Training—Jonathan Trego [his father]; Philadelphia: PAFA; Paris: Acad. Julian (William Bouguereau, Tony Robert-Fleury).

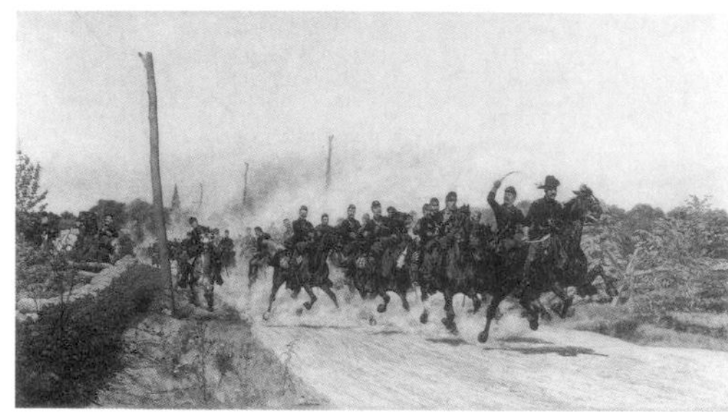

The Pursuit.* **#908. Lent by Mr. J. B. Wheeler, New York. 1885. 30¼ x 43¼. Private Collection.

TROTTER, Mary K. (Mary Kempton). **New York.**
1857 Philadelphia, PA–Residing 1916 Charbres or Chartres, France
Training — Philadelphia: PAFA (Thomas Eakins); Paris: Acad. Julian (Tony Robert-Fleury).

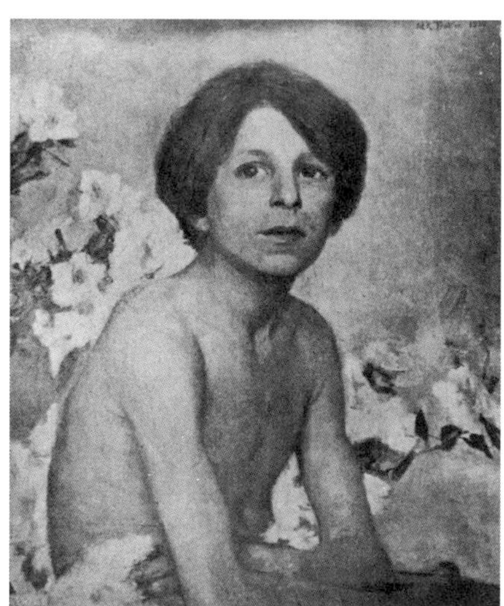

***Daphnis.* #1014.** [$150]. 1890. Est. 20 x 16. Unlocated. Illus: The Art Club of Philadelphia, *Fifth Annual Exhibition, Oil Paintings and Sculpture* (Philadelphia, 1893), 82.

***Lamplight.* #1097.** [$200]. ca. 1890. Unlocated. "A 'Lamplight' study, which is more than a tour de force, being most charming in feeling" —*Art Amateur* 23 (October 1890): 84.

TRUESDELL, Gaylord S. (Gaylord Sangston). **Paris, France.**
1850 Waukegan, IL–1899 New York, NY
Training — Philadelphia: PAFA; Paris: Aimé Morot, Fernand Cormon.

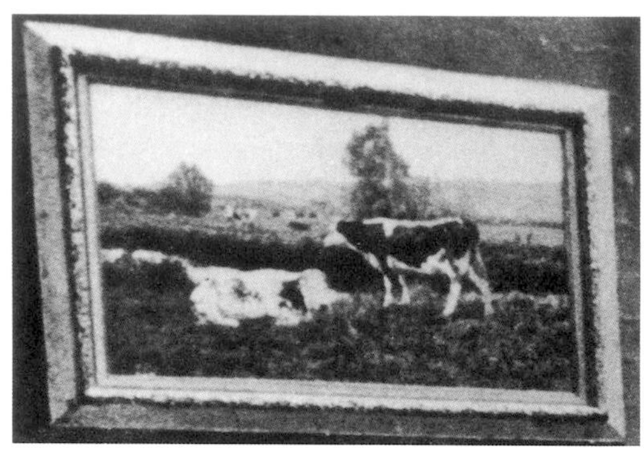

***Cows on the River Bank.* #498.** [$5000]. 1891. 45½ x 69½. Sold, Parke-Bernet Galleries, New York, NY, 17–18 May 1946, lot 122. Unlocated. Illus: Official Photographs of the World's Columbian Exposition by C. D. Arnold, vol. 8, pl. 97. Courtesy of The Chicago Public Library, Special Collections Department.

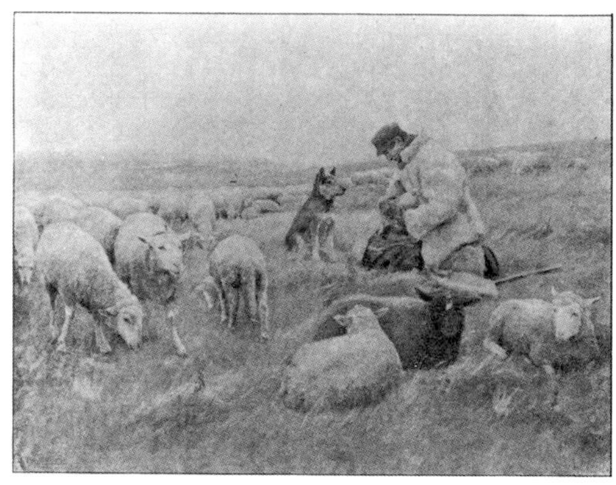

***The Shepherd's Lunch.* #898.** [$2000]. 1892. 72 x 96. Sold, American Art Association, New York, NY, 24 March 1915, lot 273, to John R. Thompson. Unlocated. Illus: Charles M. Kurtz, ed., *Illustrations from the Art Gallery of the World's Columbian Exposition* (Philadelphia: G. Barrie, 1893), 37.

---

† **TRYON, D. W.** (Dwight William). **New York.**
1849 Hartford, CT–1925 South Dartmouth, MA
Training — Paris: Jacquesson de la Chevreuse, Charles François Daubigny, H. Harpignies, Antoine Guillemet.

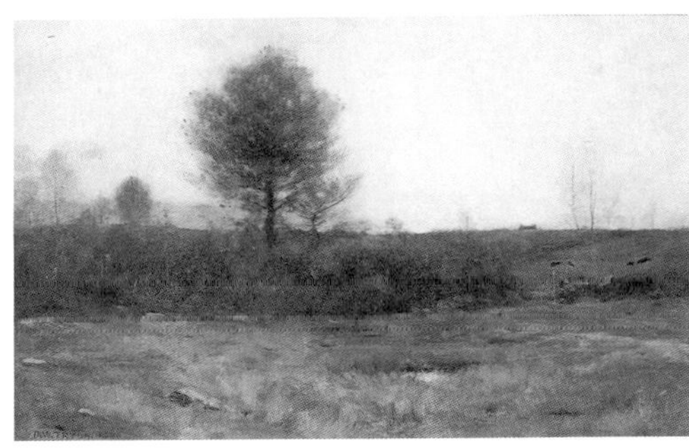

New England Village, Evening. **#422. Lent by Mr. Thomas B. Clarke, New York.** *Evening,* 1886. 16 x 24. Pennsylvania Academy of the Fine Arts, Philadelphia, Henry D. Gilpin Fund.

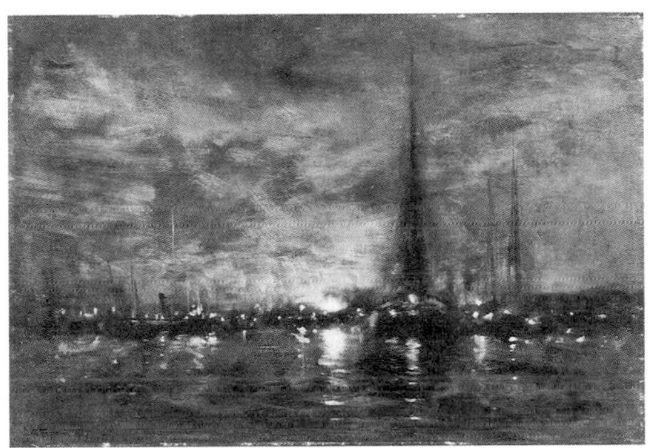

Night.* **#655. Lent by Mr. Thomas B. Clarke, New York. *Newport at Night,* 1887 (oil on wood panel). 10¾ x 15¾. Collection Rogers L. and Sally Lorensen Conant. Photograph by Michael Agee.

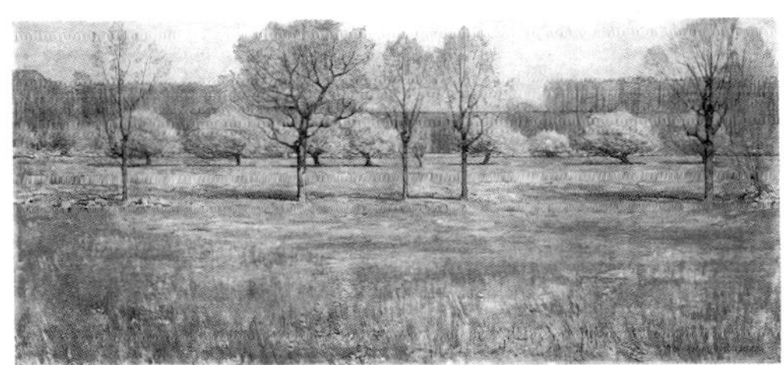

Springtime. **#702. Lent by Mr. C. L. Freer, Detroit.** 1892. 38⅛ x 83⅛. Freer Gallery of Art, Smithsonian Institution.

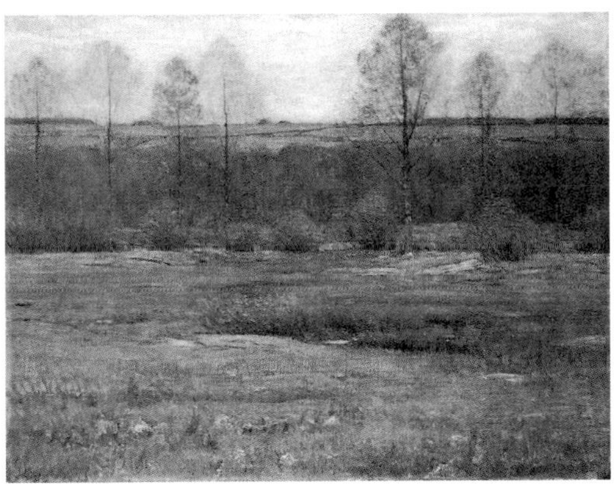

Autumn. **#718. Lent by Mr. C. L. Freer, Detroit.** n.d. 37¾ x 49¼. Freer Gallery of Art, Smithsonian Institution.

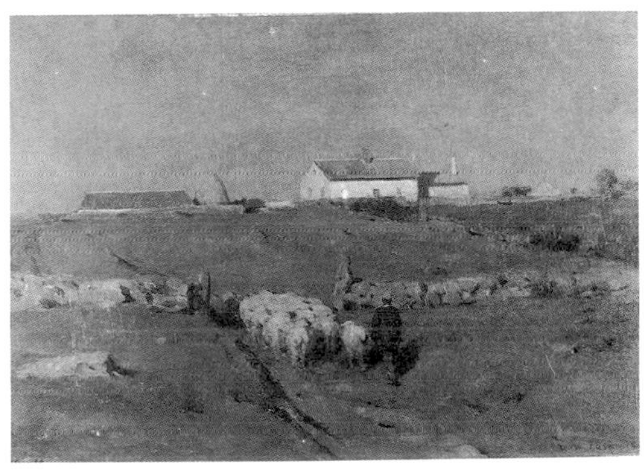

Starlight. **#737. Lent by Mr. Thomas B. Clarke, New York.** 1884. 14 x 20. Sold (as *Moonlight Night*), Sotheby Parke Bernet, New York, NY, 28 Jan. 1982, lot 154. Unlocated. Illus (as *Moonlight—Sheep*): Charles Caffin, *The Art of Dwight W. Tryon, An Appreciation* (New York: Forest Press, 1909).

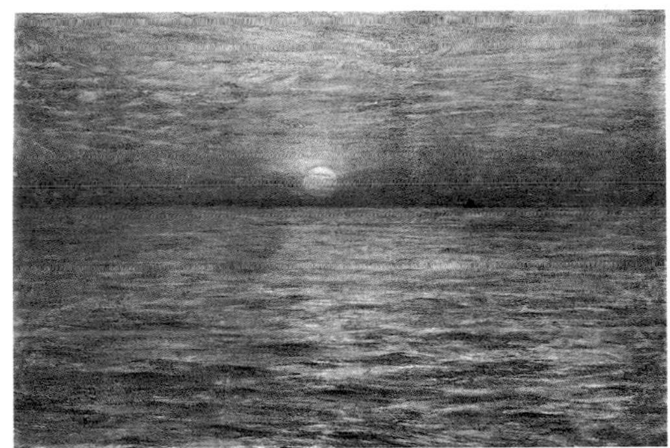

Sunset at Sea. **#739. Lent by Mr. C. L. Freer, Detroit.** *The Sea—Sunset,* 1889 (oil on wood panel). 20 x 30⅛. Freer Gallery of Art, Smithsonian Institution.

Morning. **#752. Lent by Mr. John Newell, Chicago.** Unlocated. "Another 'washed-out' picture, according to the verdict of the average visitor, yet within its borders we find very beautiful, harmonious coloring.

The horizon here is a little above the middle of the picture. The middle ground is occupied by three trees interspersed with low shrubs, among which rise the indistinct silhouettes of two or three farmhouses. There is a Corot-like feeling in this glimpse of early daybreak. The picture is full of the restful quiet that pervades the world just before nature's awakening voices make themselves heard in clamorous morning song. The little pool in the foreground seems to sleep and neglects to nod to the whispering breezes of dawn" —*The Baltimore Sun,* 14 Oct. 1893.

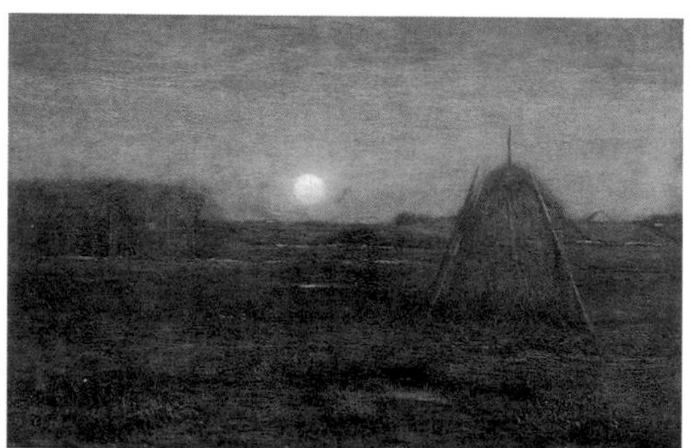

Rising Moon, Autumn. **#753. Lent by Mr. C. L. Freer, Detroit.** 1889 (oil on wood panel). 20 x 31⅝. Freer Gallery of Art, Smithsonian Institution.

Winter Evening. **#754. Lent by Mr. Thomas B. Clarke, New York.** 20 x 32. Sold, American Art Association, New York, NY, 14–18 Feb. 1899, lot 273, to C. L. Freer. Unlocated. "Cold and bleak, a snow-covered field lies under a gray evening sky, enlivened only by the light of the setting sun. A forest on the right, denuded of its leaves, lets some of the light filter through the branches, and on the horizon may be seen a line of dark hills. A fine quality of atmosphere characterizes the landscape, and the sky, with its well-composed masses, is agreeable in color and fine effect" —American Art Association, *Catalogue of the Private Art Collection of Thomas B. Clarke, New York* (New York: American Art Association, 1899), lot 273.

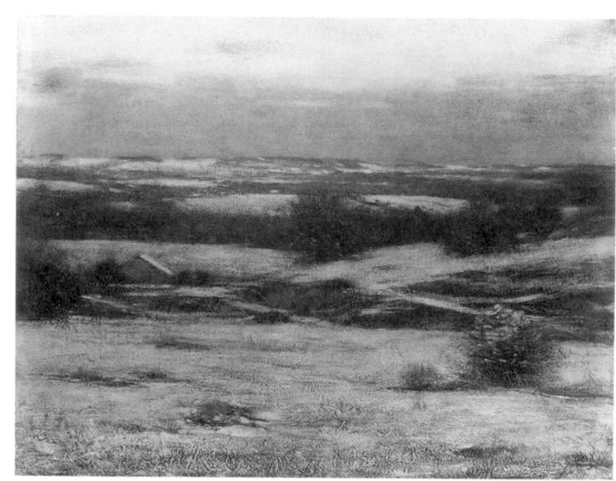

A Winter Afternoon. #783. [$1500]. n.d. (ca. 1892). 24 x 29½. Private Collection.

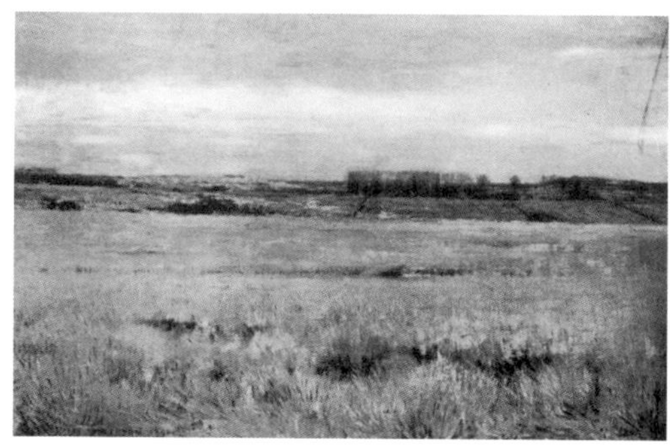

A Salt Marsh. December. #788. 1890 (oil on panel). 24 x 36. Formerly Collection Smith College Museum of Art. Sold (as *Late Autumn Landscape*), Kende Galleries at Gimbel Brothers, New York, NY, 24–25 Jan. 1947, lot 267. Unlocated. Photograph courtesy Smith College Museum of Art.

October. **#818. Lent by Mr. Thomas B. Clarke, New York.** 20 x 30. Sold (as *Autumn*), American Art Association, New York, NY, 14–18 Feb. 1899, lot 252, to H. B. Jennings. Unlocated. "The spectator looks across a fallow field, and over trees to a blue distance. To the right, a group of young oaks and saplings have taken on dark rich reds; to the left, bare branches are softly outlined against the sky, bits of autumn foilage here and there making vibrant notes. The arrangement is graceful, and is heightened by a brilliant burst of light along the horizon, breaking out from a leaden sky. This streak of yellow light runs along the entire length of the composition. Some rocks are seen here and there, with long grasses and weeds. All is sober and toneful, and the color is agreeably subdued" —American Art Association, *Catalogue of the Private Art Collection of Thomas B. Clarke, New York* (New York: American Art Association, 1899), lot 252.

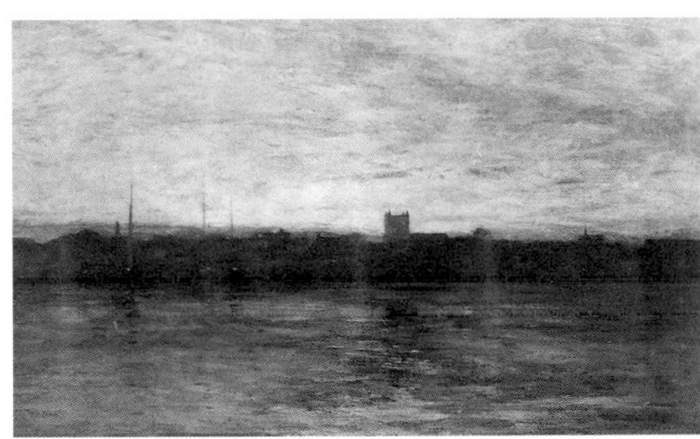

Daybreak, New Bedford Harbor. **#911. Lent by Mr. W. T. Evans, New York.** *Daybreak,* 1885 (oil on wood panel). 17¾ x 30. Museum of Art, Rhode Island School of Design, Jesse Metcalf Fund.

The Rising Moon. **#1091. Lent by Mr. Charles L. Freer, Detroit.**[67] Unlocated.

---

† **TURNER,** C. Y. (Charles Yardley). **New York.** 1850 Baltimore, MD–1919 New York, NY *Training*— Baltimore: Maryland Institute of Art; New York: NAD, ASL; Paris: Mihaly Munkacsy, Léon Bonnat, Acad. Julian (J. P. Laurens).

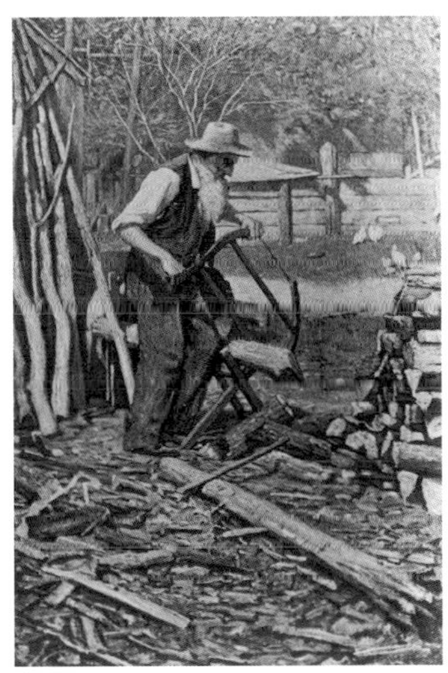

Saw Wood and Say Nothing. **#271.** [$1000]. 1891. 46 x 30. Sold, The Anderson Galleries, New York, NY, 28 April 1920, lot 105. Unlocated. Illus: Daniel H. Burnham, *The Art of the World,* vol. 5 (New York: Appleton, 1893–95).

Washing Day. **#415.** [$300]. Est. 18 x 24. Sold, World's Columbian Exposition, Chicago, IL, 1893. Unlocated.

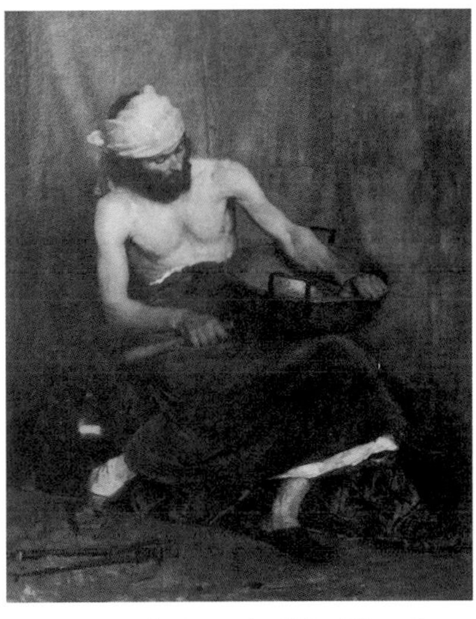

The Coppersmith. **#457. Lent by Mr. Theodore Marburg.** 1880. 39 x 31. Private Collection.

Gossips. **#676. Lent by Mr. Thomas B. Clarke, New York.** 1891. 20 x 26. Sold (as *Gossip in the Lane*), American Art Association, 15–16 Jan. 1914, lot 100, to Clark Brown (or Broun). Unlocated. "In one of the narrow streets of a New England fishing port, three girls are discussing the merits and demerits of a couple of fishermen whose figures appear in the distance, passing up the road. One of the gossips has halted on her way to the store. The others have interrupted their domestic duties to join her. Each is a distinct native type, individual in character, and expressive in attitude and movement. Autumn leaves cover the roadway, which, with the figures themselves, is in shadow" American Art Association, *Catalogue of the Private Art Collection of Thomas B. Clarke, New York* (New York: American Art Association, 1899), lot 73.

On the Beach, Easthampton. **#703. Lent by Mr. W. M. Chase, New York.** 1882. 15 x 24. Sold, American Art Association, New York, NY, 14–17 May 1917, lot 224. Unlocated. "A solitary man stands with his back against a low two-wheeled beach cart in the sparse gray-green beach grass, looking out toward his right over a gray-blue sea whose low combers splash upon a long stretch of yellow sand" —American Art Association, *Catalogue of the Completed Pictures, Studies and Sketches Left by the Late William Merritt Chase, N.A.* (New York, 1917), lot 224.

Afternoon Tea. **#729. Lent by Mr. Chester W. Chapin, New York.** Unlocated.

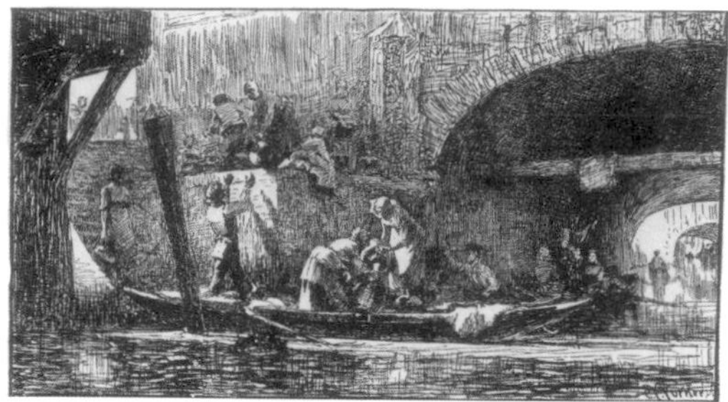

The Grand Canal, Dordrecht, Holland. **#760. Lent by Mr. John Taylor Johnston, New York.** ca. 1882. 38 x 65. Unlocated. Illus: Charles M. Kurtz, ed., *Illustrated Art Notes Upon the Fifty-Seventh Annual Exhibition of the National Academy of Design, New York* (New York: Cassell, Petter, Galpin, 1882), 58.

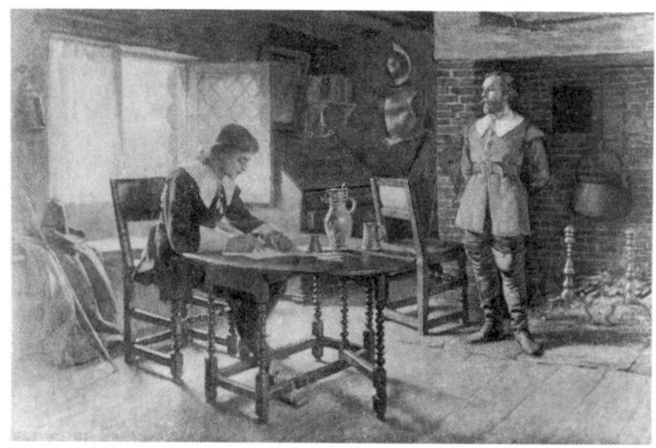

******John Alden's Letter.* **#823.** [$1200]. n.d. (ca. 1888). 30 x 45. Union League Club of Chicago.

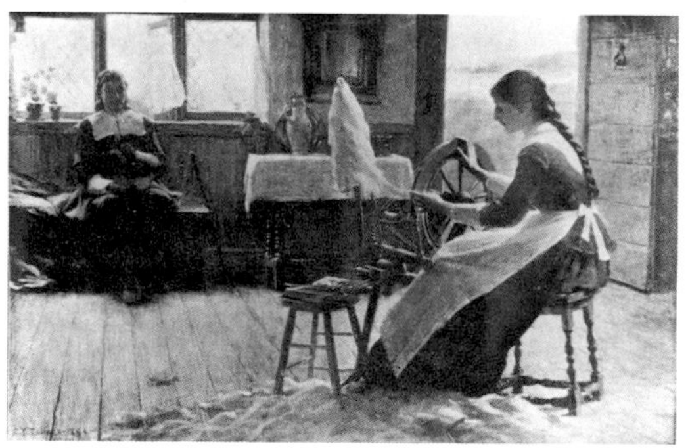

Courtship of Miles Standish. **#835. Lent by Mr. Henry C. Howells, Flushing, L.I.** 1884. 30 x 45. Sold, Parke-Bernet Galleries, New York, NY, 31 Jan. 1946, lot 66. Unlocated. Illus: William Walton, *Art and Architecture,* vol. 1 (Philadelphia: G. Barrie, 1893–95), 25.

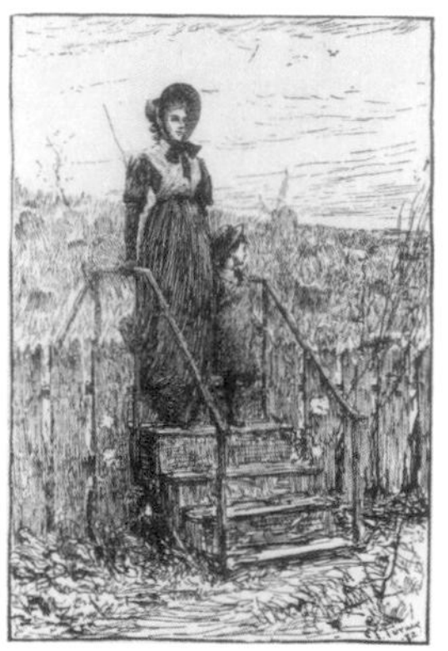

The Days that are no More. **#887.** 1882. 45 x 30. Collection Theodore Marburg, Baltimore, MD, 1914. Unlocated. Illus: Charles M. Kurtz, ed., *Illustrated Art Notes Upon the Fifty-Seventh Annual Exhibition of the National Academy of Design, New York* (New York: Cassell, Petter, Galpin, 1882), 35.

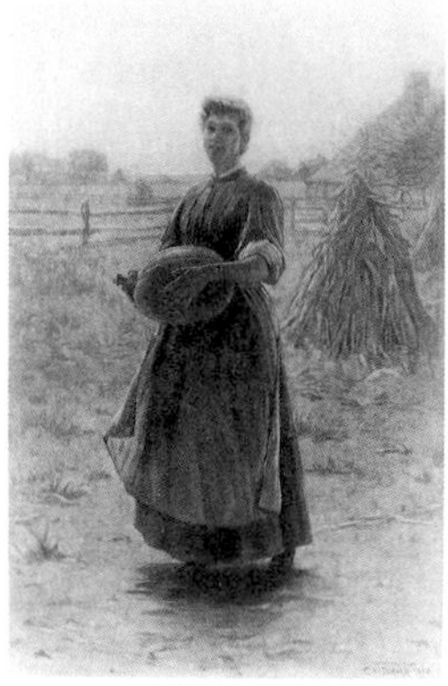

The Pride of the Farm. **#971.** [$750]. ca. 1890. Unlocated. Illus: Daniel H. Burnham, *The Art of the World,* vol. 5 (New York: Appleton, 1893–95).

TURNER, Ross (Ross Sterling). **Salem, Mass.**
1847 Westport, NY–1915 Nassau, Bahamas
Training— Frank Currier; Munich; Italy.

Moonlight. **#320.** [$600]. Unlocated.

TWACHTMAN, J. H. (John Henry). **Greenwich, Conn.**
1853 Cincinnati, OH–1902 Gloucester, MA
Training— Cincinnati: Ohio Mechanics' Institute School of Design (Frank Duveneck), McMicken School of Design (Frank Duveneck); Munich: Royal Academy (Ludwig von Löfftz); Venice (Frank Duveneck, William Merritt Chase); Paris: Acad. Julian (Gustave Boulanger, Jules Joseph Lefebvre).

Winter. **#270.** Est. 17 x 23. Unlocated.

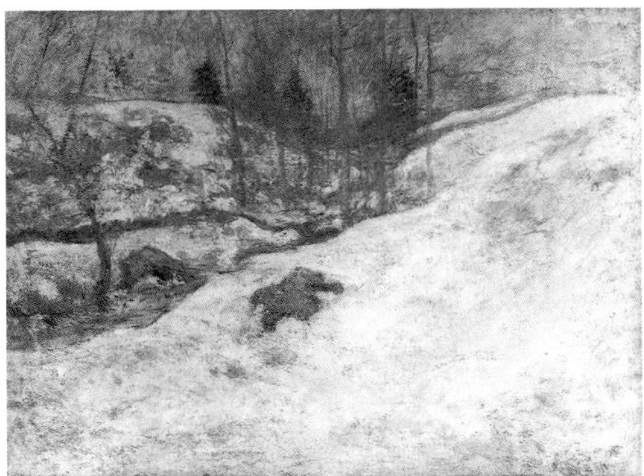

Brook in Winter.* **#276. [$500]. *February,* n.d. (ca. 1892). 36¼ x 48. Museum of Fine Arts, Boston, Charles Henry Hayden Fund.

Decorative Landscape. **#716.** Unlocated. "Here also are J. H. Twachtman's large 'Decorative Landscape,' . . . " —*New York Herald,* 3 Dec. 1892; "Decorated that is with the all-pervading hues of purple and lilac, relieved here and there by a dash of vermilion or a streak of yellow and white" —Hubert H. Bancroft, *The Book of the Fair,* vol. 3 (Chicago: Blakely Printing Co., 1893), 685; "The big 'decorative' landscape was the most curious, being painted in very broad, smooth brush-strokes; low notes of green and gray depict a wet sky, a river and rushy banks" —"Monthly Record of American Art," *The Magazine of Art* 16 (Dec. 1892–Nov. 1893): vi; "A reedy lake with low hills on the farther side, was also, in a way, impressionistic . . . " — *Art Amateur* (Feb 1894): 74.

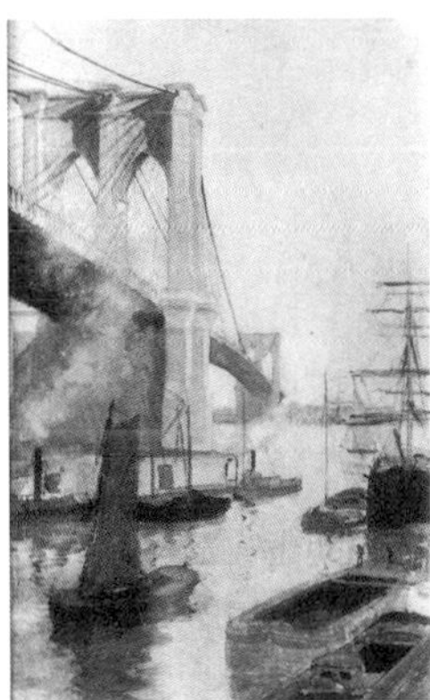

The Brooklyn Bridge. **#1045. Lent by Charles Scribner's Sons, New York.** ca. 1888. 16 x 10. Private Collection. Photograph courtesy Spanierman Gallery, New York, NY.

Autumn Shadows. **#1180.** ca. 1892. Unlocated.

TYLER, **Bayard H.** (Bayard Henry). **New York.**
1855 Oneida, NY–1931 Yonkers, NY
Training — Syracuse, NY: Syracuse University; New York: ASL, NAD.

Waiting. **#988.** [$1000]. Unlocated.

TYLER, **James G.** (James Gale). **New York.**
1855 Oswego, NY–1931 Pelham, NY
Training — New York: A. Cary Smith.

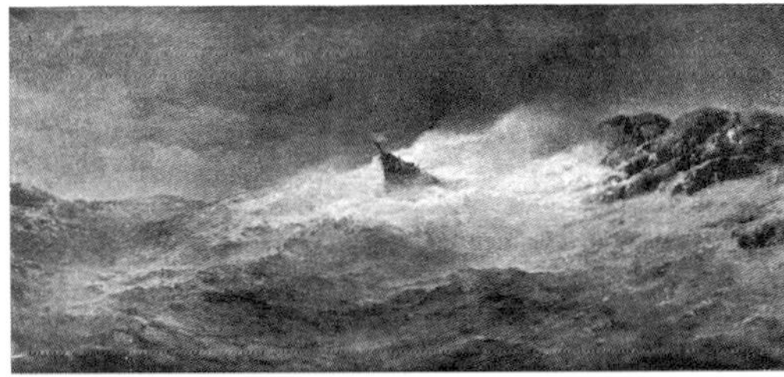

The Norman's Woe. **#771.** [$2000]. **Lent by Mr. J. M. Jones, New York.** Est. 35 x 70. Unlocated. Illus: *The Monthly Illustrator,* n.d.

---

† ULRICH, **Charles F.** (Charles Frederick). **Munich, Bavaria.**
1858 New York, NY–1908 Berlin, Germany
Training — New York: NAD; Munich: Royal Academy (Ludwig von Löfftz, Wilhelm Lindenschmidt).

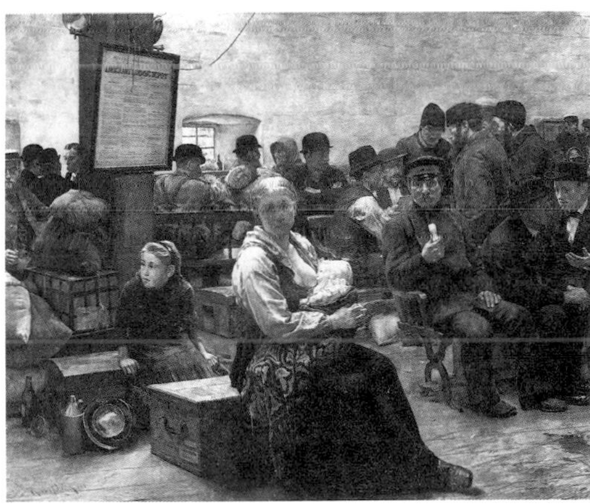

In the Land of Promise (Castle Garden, New York).* **#894. Lent by Mr. W. T. Evans, New York. *In the Land of Promise — Castle Garden,* 1884 (oil on panel). 28⅜ x 35¾. Corcoran Gallery of Art, Museum Purchase, Gallery Fund.

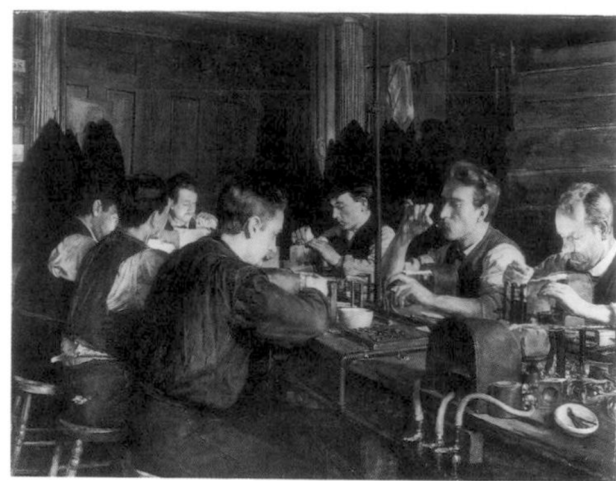

Glass Blowers.* **#913. Lent by Mr. Thomas B. Clarke, New York. 1883 (oil on panel). 17¾ x 22⅝. Museo de Arte de Ponce, Luis A. Ferré Foundation, Inc., Ponce, PR. Photograph by Antonio de Jesús.

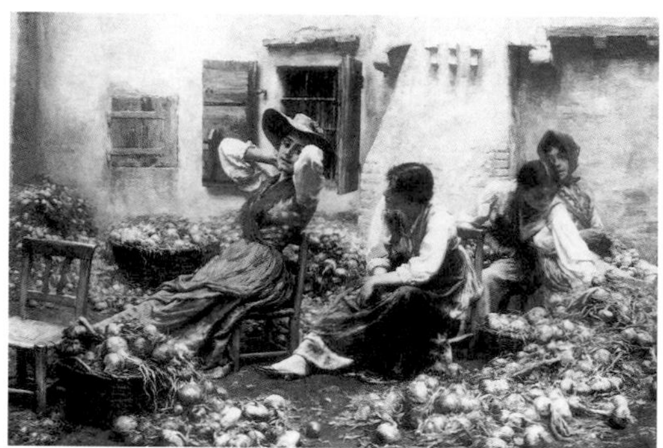

An Italian Idyl. **#923.** [$1500]. n.d. (oil on panel). 29¾ x 43¾. Private Collection.

VAIL, Eugene L. (Eugene Lawrence). **Paris, France.**
1857 Saint-Servan, France–1934 France?
Training — New York: ASL (J. Carroll Beckwith, William Merritt Chase); Paris: Alexandre Cabanel, Raphaël Collin, P. A. J. Dagnan-Bouveret, Acad. Julian.

Dordrecht. **#538.** Est. 65 x 70. Unlocated. "A November night study, showing the river and the town with its lights across the water"—*New York Herald* [Paris], 4 May 1891.

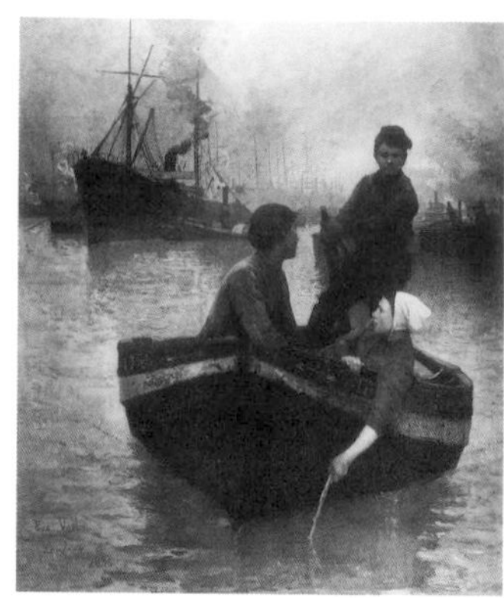

On the Thames.* **#630. [$10,000]. 1886. 82¼ x 69¼. Collection Chris Whittle, Knoxville, TN.

VAN BOSKERCK, Robert W. (Robert Ward). **New York.**
1855 Hoboken, NJ–1932 New York, NY
Training — New York: Alexander H. Wyant, R. Swain Gifford.

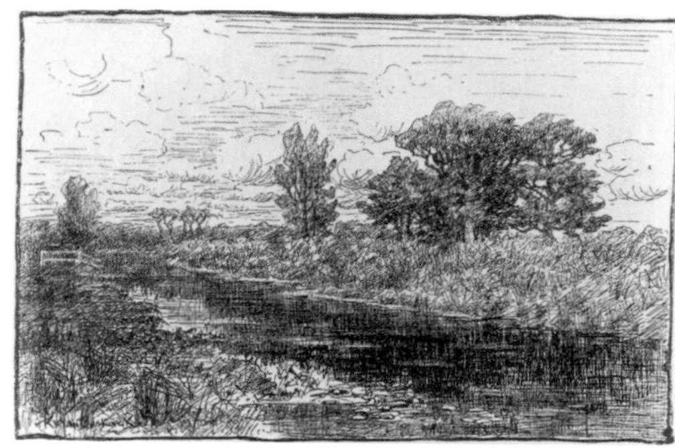

A Rhode Island River. **#733.** [$1500]. n.d. (ca. 1888). 44⅛ x 64½. Graves Art Gallery, Sheffield, England. Illus: Charles M. Kurtz, ed., *National Academy Notes and Complete Catalogue, Sixty-third Spring Exhibition, National Academy of Design, New York* (New York: Cassell & Co., 1888), 82.

The Hackensack Meadows. **#790.** [$600]. Est. 24 x 36. Unlocated.

Sand Road from the Sea. **#845. Lent by Mr. H. R. C. Watson, New York.** Unlocated.

VAN BRIGGLE, A. (Artus). **Cincinnati.**
1869 Felicity, OH–1904 Colorado Springs, CO
Training — Cincinnati: McMicken School of Design, Rookwood Studios; Acad. Julian (J. P. Laurens, Jean-Joseph Benjamin-Constant).

Portrait of Mrs. Charity Van Briggle. **#1272.** Est. 58 x 42. Unlocated.

VANDERPOEL, J. H. (John H.). Chicago.

1857 Haarlemmer-Meer, the Netherlands–1911 University City, MO
Training — Chicago: Herman Hanstein, C. F. Schwerdt, Turner Hall, AIC (J. F. Gookins, Lawrence Earle, Henry F. Spread); Paris: Acad. Julian (Gustave Boulanger, Jules Joseph Lefebvre).

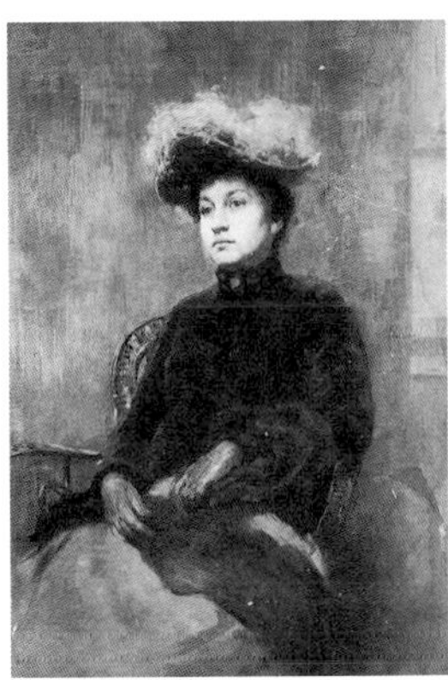

Portrait of a Lady. **#660. Lent by Mr. J. B. Humphreys, Tracy, Cook Co., Ill.** ca. 1892. Est. 24 x 20. Unlocated. Photograph courtesy Vanderpoel Art Association, Chicago, IL.

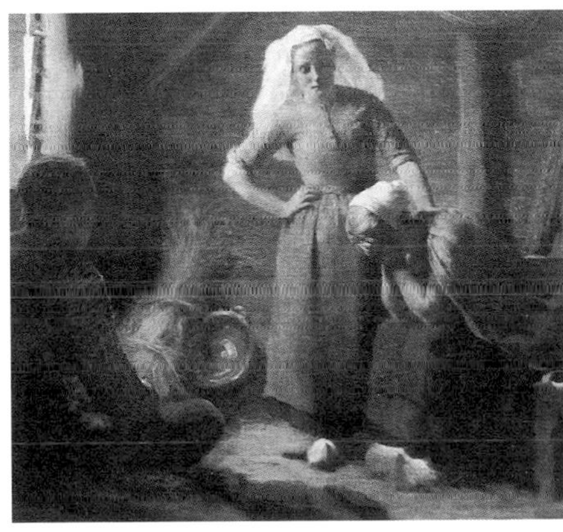

Blessed are They that Mourn. **#762.** [$500]. n.d. 24 x 26⅛. Collection Neilson M. Mathews, Jr., Radnor, PA. Photograph by George Gurney.

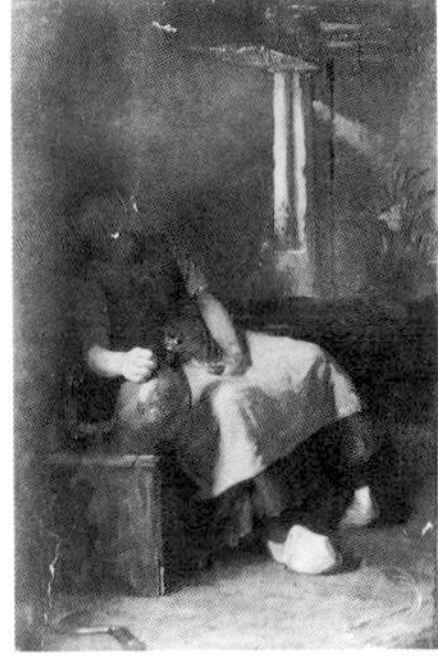

Weary. **#791. Lent by Mr. C. L. Hutchinson, Chicago.** Est. 30 x 20. Unlocated. Photograph courtesy Vanderpoel Art Association, Chicago, IL. "Represents a woman who has returned from the field, seated for her frugal meal within a barn. She leans back against the wall, and from sheer weariness has fallen asleep. The lower portion of her figure is in the full light and the upper part in dark shadow, the artist's idea being evidently to show the harmony of the darkness with sleep" — *The Graphic* [Chicago], 23 Jan. 1892, 70.

Twilight Reverie. **#976.** [$200]. Unlocated. "An agreeable twilight effect in an interior with a young woman seated, subdued light from a curtained window falling over her shoulders. . . . Her work is laid aside as she has given herself up to 'Twilight Reveries' " — *Chicago Tribune,* n.d.

Summer Morning in the Orchard. **#1143.** [$150]. Unlocated.

VAN DER WEYDEN, Harry. Paris, France.

1868 Boston, MA–1952 London, England?
Training — Paris: Acad. Julian (J. P. Laurens, Jules Josesph Lefebvre, Jean-Joseph Benjamin-Constant); London: Fred Brown, Slade School.

Katwijk Herring Boats (Holland). **#956.** [$500]. Unlocated.

VAN ELTEN, Kruseman (Hendrik Dirk Kruseman). New York.

1829 Alkmaar, the Netherlands–1904 Paris, France
Training — Haarlem, the Netherlands: C. Lieste.

Late Autumn. **#628.** [$800]. Unlocated.

VAN GORDER, L. E. (Luther Emerson). New York.

1857 Pittsburgh, PA–1931 Toledo, OH
Training — New York: William Merritt Chase, Charles Y. Turner; Paris: Carolus-Duran; London.

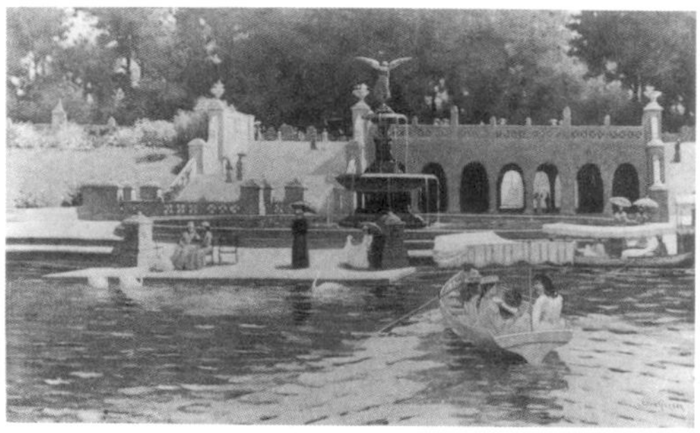

The Terrace, Central Park, New York. **#1172.** [$350]. ca. 1891. Unlocated. Illus: Daniel H. Burnham, *The Art of the World,* vol. 6 (New York: Appleton, 1893–95).

---

† **VEDDER, Elihu. Rome, Italy.**
1836 New York, NY–1923 Rome, Italy
Training — Sherbourne, NY: T. H. Matteson; Paris: Edouard Picot; Florence: Bonaiuti.

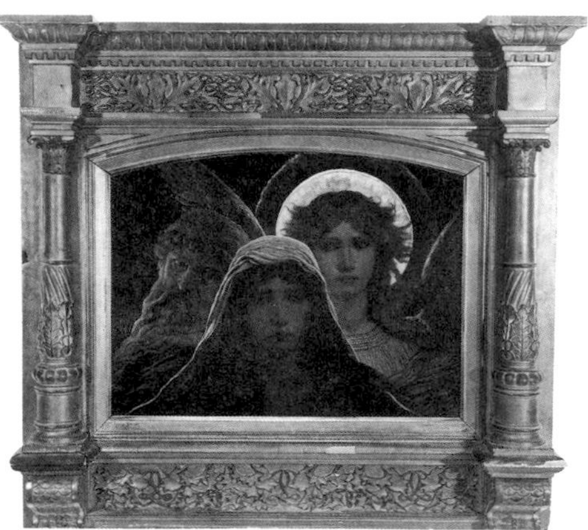

The Sorrowing Soul between Doubt and Faith.* **#1000. Lent by Mr. W. George Webb, Salem, Mass. n.d. (ca. 1886–87). 16 x 21. Herbert F. Johnson Museum of Art, Cornell University, Membership Purchase Fund.

The Cup of Love. **#1001. Lent by Mrs. A. F. Roudebush, New York.** 1887. 12 x 10. Collection Mr. Harold G. Henderson, ca. 1970. Unlocated. "Past lies buried in a sculptured sarcophagus; youth in Greek costume and with crown of vine leaves sits on sarcophagus. To him comes woman holding glass. Cupid with shining globe smiles at them" —Regina Soria, *Elihu Vedder American Visionary Artist in Rome (1836–1923)* (Rutherford, NJ: Fairleigh Dickinson University Press, [1970]), 332–33.

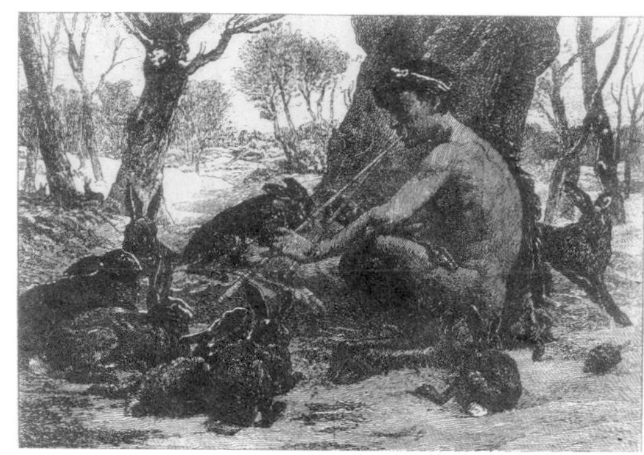

The Young Marsyas. **#1002. Lent by Mrs. A. F. Roudebush, New York.** 1878. 37¼ x 52. Sold, Parke-Bernet Galleries, New York, NY, 21 April 1943, lot 347, to Renaissance Art Gallery, New York, NY. Unlocated. Illus: *Art Amateur* 29 (July 1893): 33.

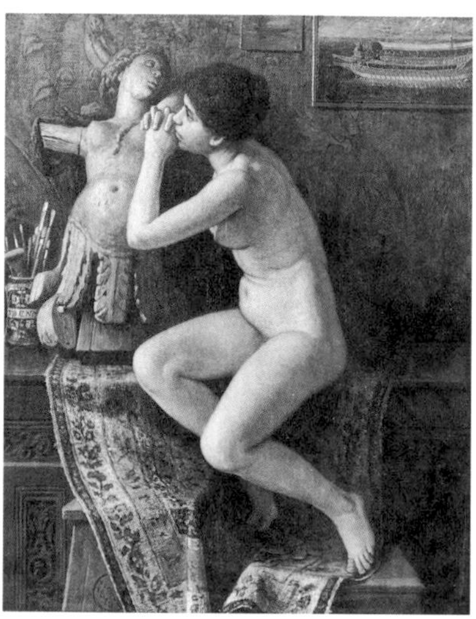

A Venetian Model.* **#1003. Lent by Mr. Davis Johnson, New York. 1878. 18 x 14⅞. Columbus Museum of Art, Ohio, Museum Purchase, Schumacher Fund.

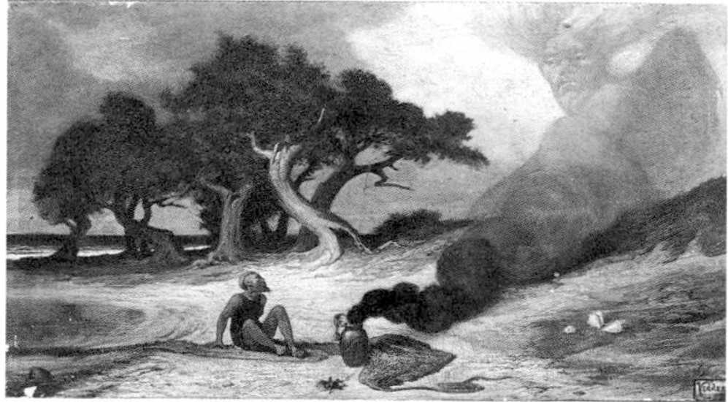

The Fisherman and the Geni. **#1004. Lent by Mr. Martin Brimmer, Boston.** *Fisherman and the Genie,* 1861 (oil on panel). 7½ x 13¾. Museum of Fine Arts, Boston, Bequest of Mrs. Martin Brimmer.

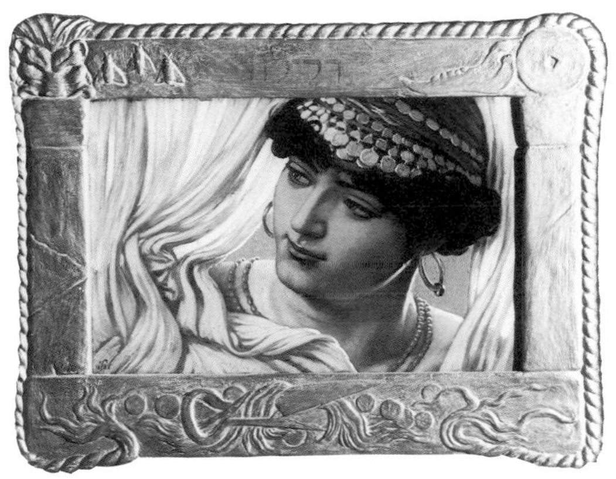

Delilah. **#1006. Lent by Col. J. G. Moore, New York.** 1886 (oil on panel). 18 x 27½. Jordan Volpe Gallery, Inc., New York, NY.

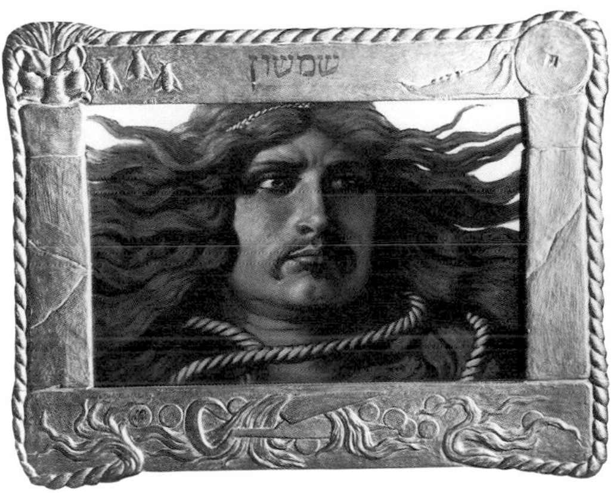

Sampson. **#1007. Lent by Col. J. G. Moore, New York.** 1886 (oil on panel). 18 x 27½. Jordan Volpe Gallery, Inc., New York, NY.

Morning. **#1008. Lent by Mr. J. B. Wheeler, New York.** 1890. 19 x 16. Sold, American Art Association, New York, NY, 18–19 March 1920, lot 143, to F. K. Richards. Unlocated. "Through a high window comes the morning light, with a glimpse of trees and bird, and of morning glories on the window-ledge, and between parted portières of mingled neutral tones the soft light brushes the features of a young woman looking upward, with head thrown back, her face seen a little more than in profile, to the left. She is seated, partly reclining, among cushions, and her classical garment of delicate bluish note partly reveals her bust" —American Art Association, *American and Foreign Oil Paintings* (New York, 1920), lot 143.

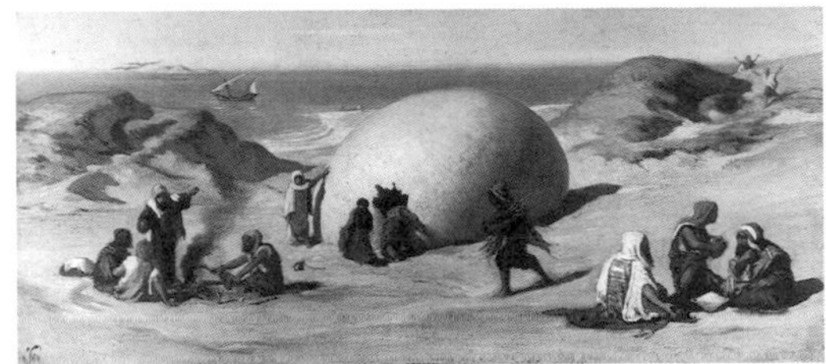

The Roc's Egg. **#1009. Lent by Mr. Martin Brimmer, Boston.** 1868. 7½ x 16. The Chrysler Museum, Norfolk, VA.

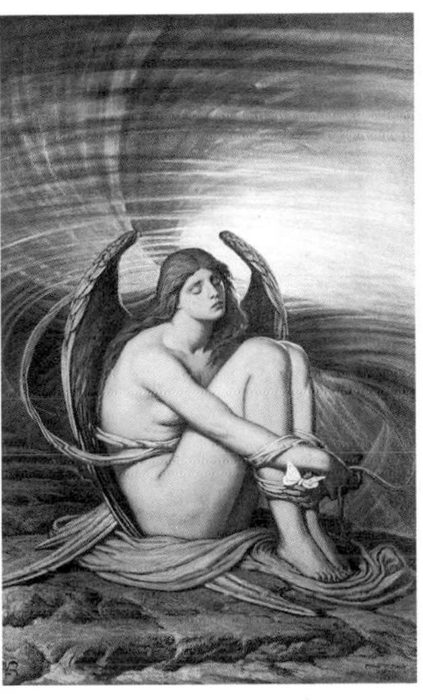

A Soul in Bondage.* **#1010. Lent by Mrs. A. F. Roudebush, New York. *Soul in Bondage,* 1891. 37⅞ x 24. The Brooklyn Museum, Gift of Mrs. Harold G. Henderson.

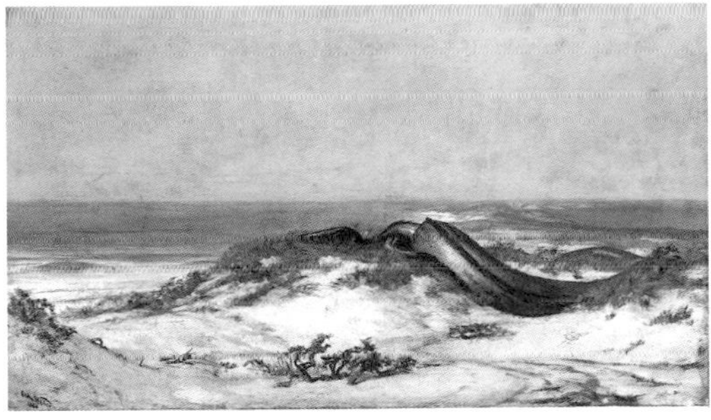

The Lair of the Sea Serpent. **#1011. Lent by the Museum of Fine Arts, Boston.** *Lair of the Sea Serpent,* 1864. 21 x 36. Museum of Fine Arts, Boston, Bequest of Thomas G. Appleton.

VEDDER, Simon Harmon. Paris, France.
1866 Amsterdam, NY–1937 London, England? *Training* — New York: School of the Metropolitan Museum; Paris: Acad. Julian (William Bouguereau, Tony Robert-Fleury), EcBA (Jean-Léon Gérôme).

Indian Head. **#1048.** [$75]. Est. 16 x 10. Unlocated.

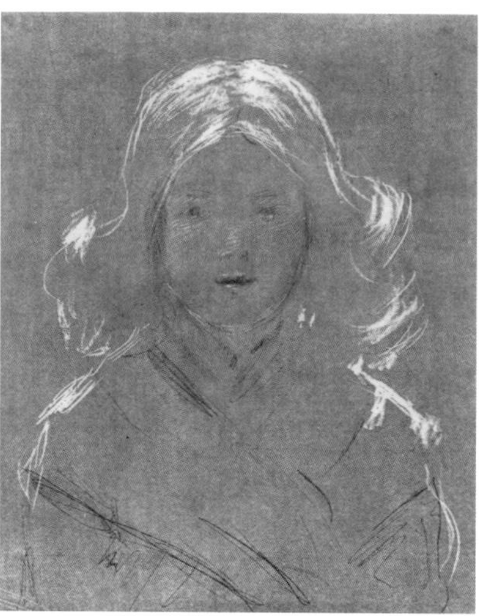

Head of a Young Girl. **#1258.** [$125]. ca. 1892. Est. 16 x 13. Unlocated. Illus: Ludovic Baschet, ed., *Catalogue Illustré de Peinture et Sculpture, Salon de 1892* (Paris: Georges Chamerot, 1892), 101.

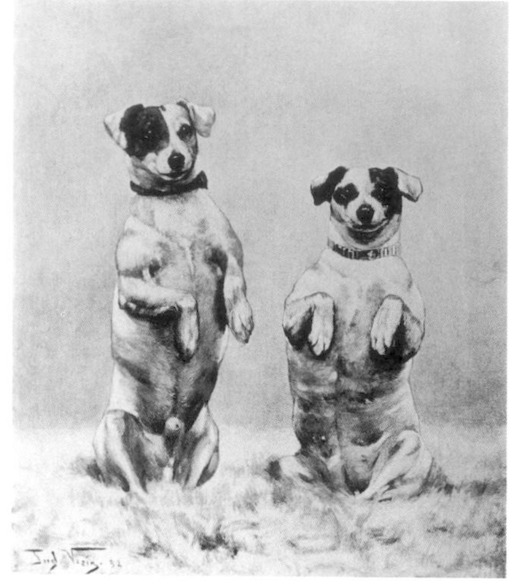

Dogs. **#1181.** [$500]. Sold, World's Columbian Exposition, Chicago, IL, 1893. Unlocated. Illus: *Yankee Doodle at the Fair* (Philadelphia: George Barrie & Son, 1896), 168.

VEZIN, **Fred** (Frederick). **Munich, Bavaria.**
1859 Philadelphia, PA–Unknown
Training — Dusseldorf: Dusseldorf Academy (Karl Gebhardt, Wilhelm Sohn).

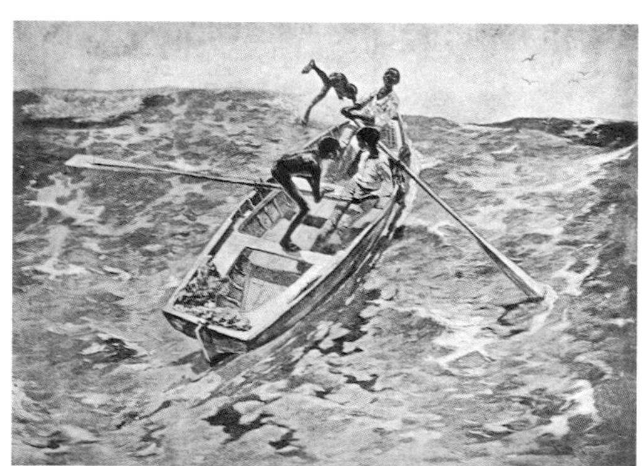

Boys in a Boat. **#582.** [$500]. Est. 43 x 47. Unlocated. Illus: *Yankee Doodle at the Fair* (Philadelphia: George Barrie & Son, 1896), f. 187. "The boat is cleverly tipped up toward you on a mounting billow whose blue and green reflections are better painted than are the merry little negro lads diving into it" — J. S. Merrill, *Art Clippings from the Pen of Walter Cranston Larned and Other Critics at the Fair* (Chicago: J. S. Merrill, 1893).

VINCENT, **H. A.** (Henry/Harry Aiken). **Chicago.**
1864/67 Chicago, IL–1931 Rockport, MA
Training — self-taught.

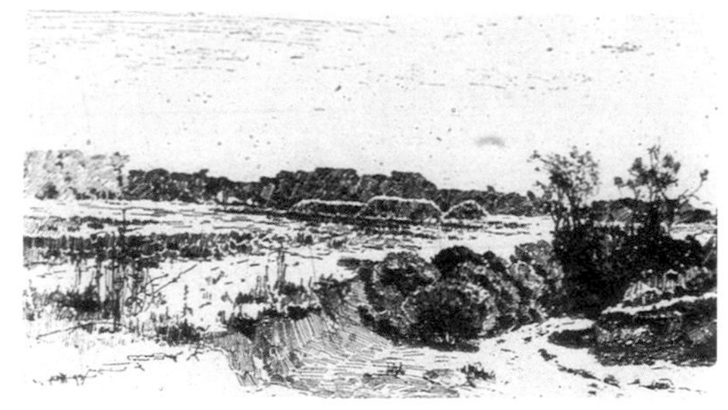

Fields in October. **#331.** [$600]. Est. 40 x 55. Unlocated. Illus: *The Graphic* [Chicago], 27 May 1893, 349.

---

† VINTON, **Frederick P.** (Frederic Porter). **Boston.**
1846 Bangor, ME–1911 Boston, MA
Training — Boston: William Morris Hunt, Lowell School of Practical Drawing (William Rimmer); Paris: Léon Bonnat, Acad. Julian (J. P. Laurens); Munich: Royal Academy (George Mauger, Wilhelm Diez).

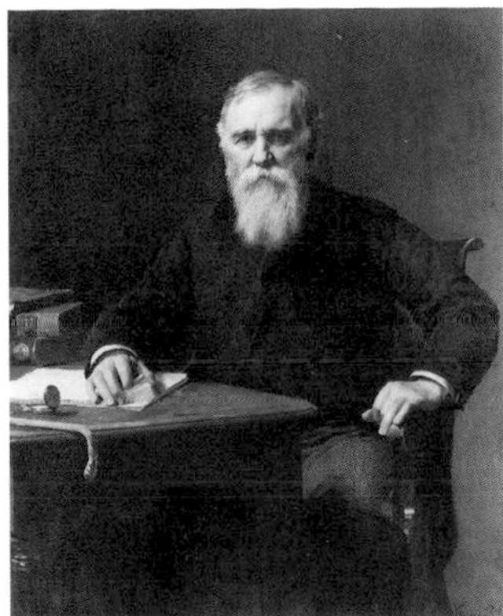

Portrait of C. C. Langdell. **#396.** *Christopher Columbus Langdell,* 1892. 50⅛ x 40¼. Harvard Law Art Collection.

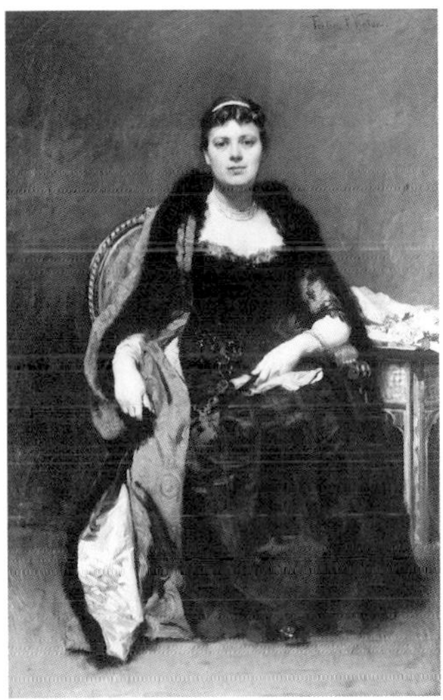

Portrait of a Lady. **#675.** *Portrait of Annie Peirce Vinton, the Artist's Wife,* n.d. (ca. 1890). 68¾ x 43¼. Private Collection, Cape Elizabeth, ME. Photograph by Bernard Meyers.

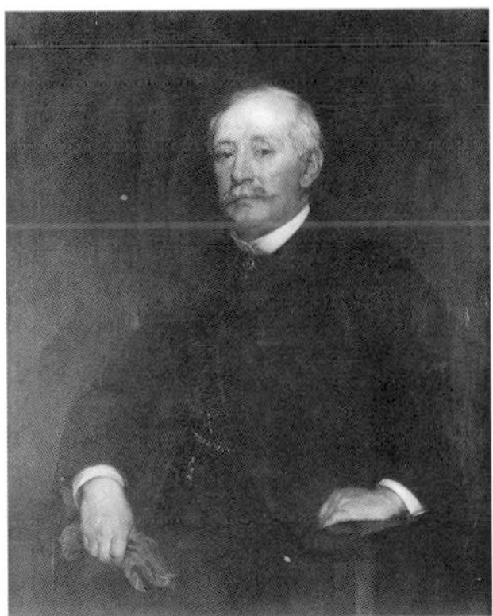

Portrait of Augustus Flagg. **#957. Lent by Mr. Augustus Flagg, Boston.** ca. 72 x 72. Private Family Collection. Photograph by Fay Foto.

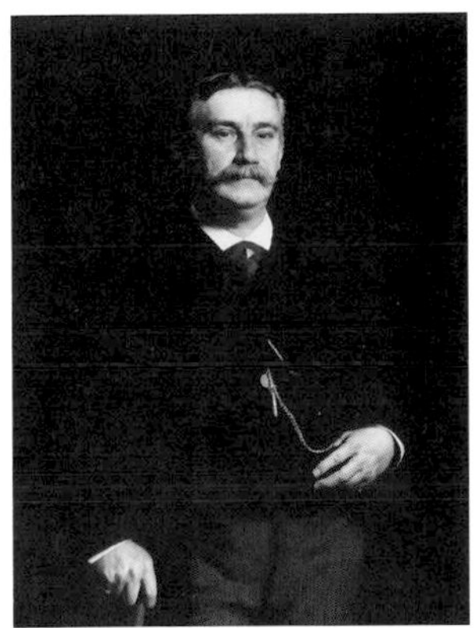

Portrait of Theodore Chase. **#979. Lent by Mr. Theodore Chase, Boston.** 1886. 43 x 32. University of Michigan Museum of Art, Gift of Dr. and Mrs. Irving Levitt.

---

† **VOLK, Douglas** (Stephen Arnold Douglas). **Minneapolis, Minn.**
1856 Pittsfield, MA–1935 Fryeburg, ME
Training — Paris: Jean Léon Gérôme; Rome: St. Luke's Academy.

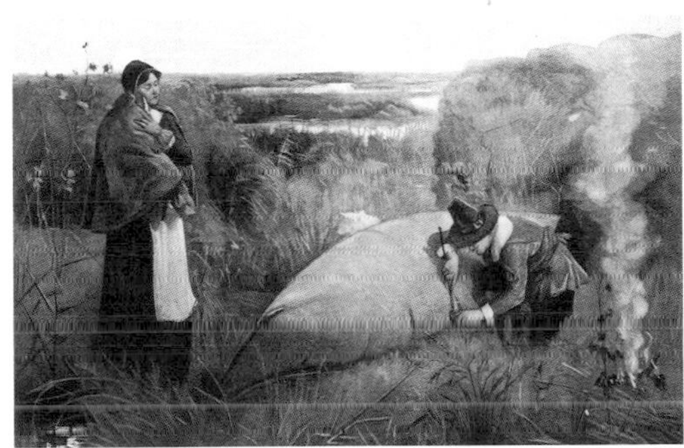

Mending the Canoe. **#469.** [$3000]. Est. 70 x 100. Unlocated. Illus: Henri Sylvestre, Jr., *Marvels in Art of the Fin de Siècle,* vol. 2 (Philadelphia: Gebbie, 1893), part 13.

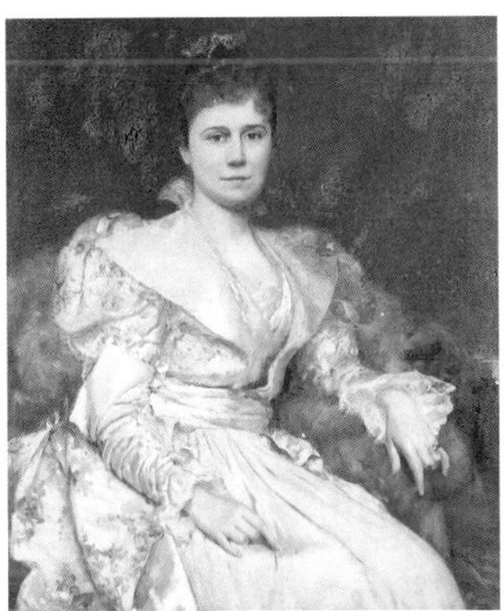

Portrait of Madam X (Beatrice Goodrich Lowry). **#583.** n.d. 36 x 30½. Private Collection. Photograph by Gary Mortensen.

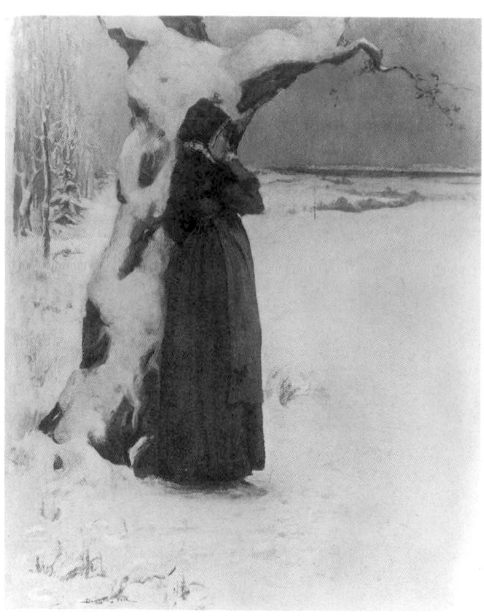

A Puritan Girl. **#824. Lent by Mr. Thomas B. Clarke, New York.** ca. 1883. 30 x 24. Sold, American Art Association, New York, NY, 21–22 Jan. 1926, lot 173, to Muller Galleries. Unlocated. Illus: William Walton, *Art and Architecture,* vol. 1 (Philadelphia: G. Barrie, 1893–95), opposite 26.

---

† **VONNOH, Robert W.** (Robert William). **Philadelphia.**
1858 Hartford, CT–1933 Nice, France
Training — Boston: Massachusetts Normal Art School; Paris: Acad. Julian (Gustave Boulanger, Jules Joseph Lefebvre).

Duxbury Bay. **#309.** [$400]. Est. 22 x 30. Unlocated.

Riva degli Schiavoni, Venice. **#311.** [$500]. ca. 1892. Est. 20 x 30. Unlocated.

Viola. **#327.** [$500]. Unlocated. "Merely the head of a child, in white against a yellow background, but the arrangement is so artistic, the management of the light so skillful, and the characterization of the dreamy child so simple and exquisite, that it is a rare and notable portrait" —Review of an 1894 exhibition at O'Brian's Gallery, Chicago.[68]

A Dull Day. **#351.** [$400]. Est. 30 x 20. Unlocated.

Early Morning. **#352.** [$500]. Est. 20 x 30. Unlocated.

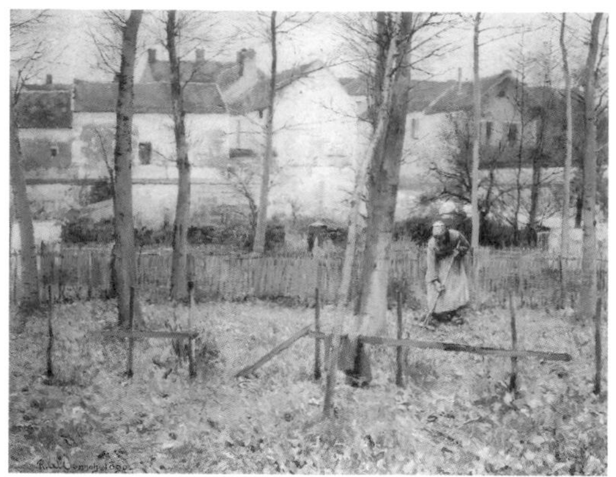

November. **#353.** [$750]. 1890. 31¾ x 39¼. Pennsylvania Academy of the Fine Arts, Philadelphia, Joseph E. Temple Fund.

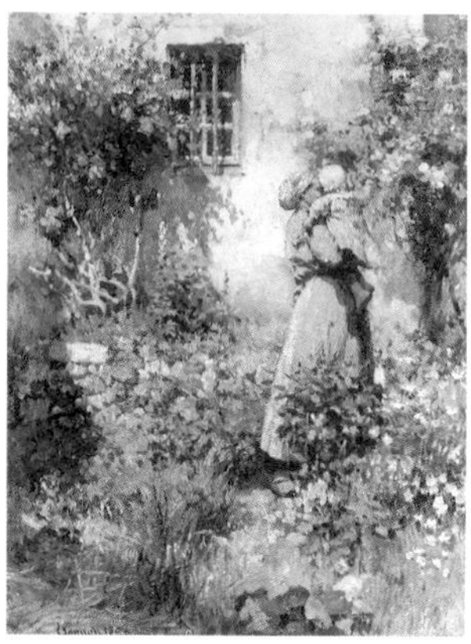

A Peasant Woman's Garden. **#363.** [$400]. *Jardin de Paysanne,* 1890 (oil on canvas board). 25⅝ x 19⅝. Terra Museum of American Art, Chicago.

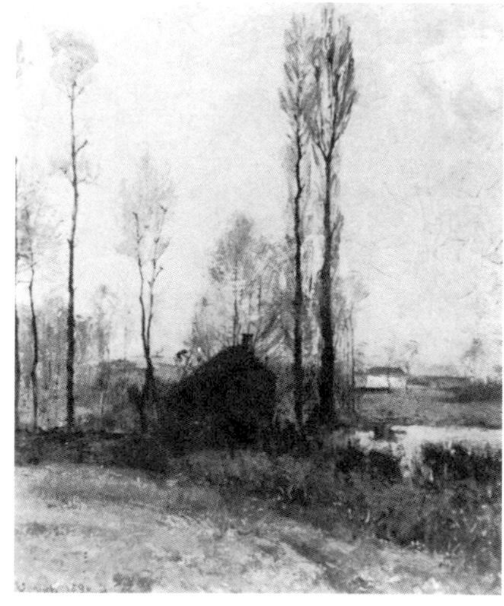

Moist Weather. **#365.** [$400]. 1890. 25½ x 21¼. Sold, Christie's, New York, NY, 4 Dec. 1992, lot 79. Unlocated.

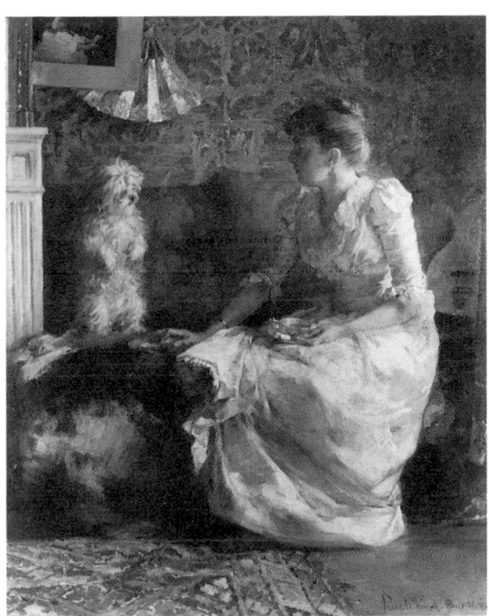

*"Show What You Can Do!". **#484.** [$1500]. *"Fais le Beau!"*, 1890. 64 x 51¼. Private Collection.

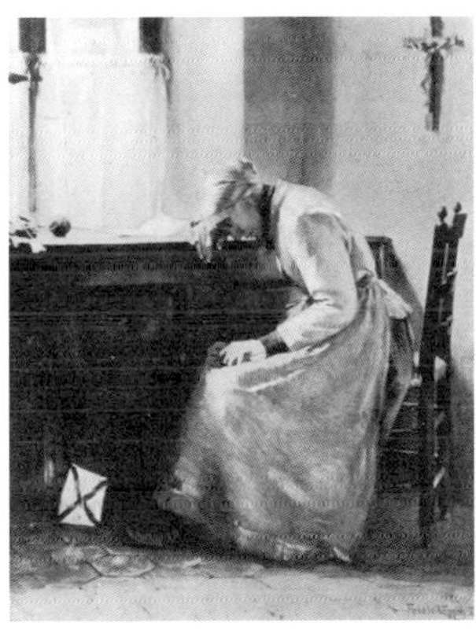

Bad News. **#934.** [$1500]. 1889. Unlocated. Illus (as *Sad News*): Sadakichi Hartmann, *A History of American Art*, vol. 2 (Boston: L. C. Page, 1901), 243.

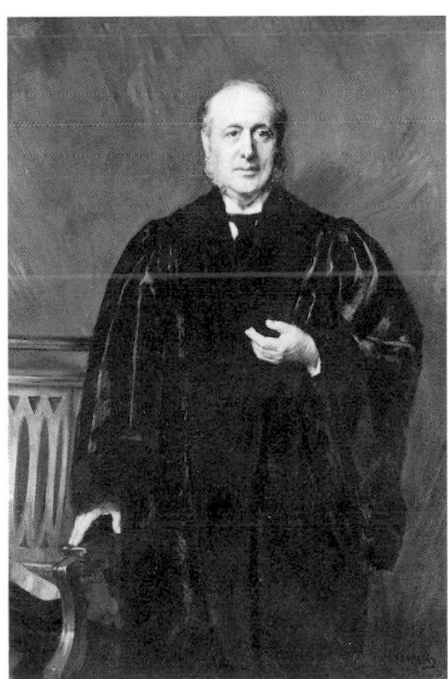

Portrait of Dr. J. M. Da Costa. **#1017. Lent by the Jefferson Medical College, Philadelphia.** 1892. 53¼ x 36¼. Jefferson Medical College of Thomas Jefferson University, Philadelphia, PA.

Blanche. **#1193.** [$300]. Unlocated.

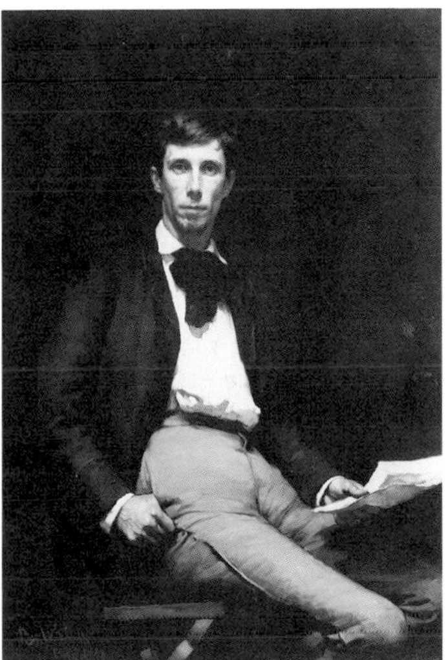

Studio Comrade. **#1273. Lent by the Pennsylvania Academy of the Fine Arts.** *Companion of the Studio*, 1888. 51½ x 36½. Pennsylvania Academy of the Fine Arts, Philadelphia, Joseph E. Temple Fund.

WADE, Caroline D. Chicago.
1857 Chicago, IL–1947 Chicago, IL?
Training — Chicago: AIC (Henry F. Spread, Lawrence Earle), George Robertson; Paris: Acad. Colarossi (Gustave Courtois, Jean André Rixens).

Portrait of a Lady. **#427.** Est. 55 x 35. Unlocated.

WAGNER, Jacob. Boston.
1852 Duthweiler, Germany–1898 New York, NY
Training— Boston: Lowell School of Practical Drawing, MFA.

Over all the Trees is Rest. **#316.** [$800]. Unlocated.

A Bit of a Lark. **#1028.** [$500]. ca. 1891. Unlocated.

WALDEN, Lionel. Paris, France.
1861 Norwich, CT–1933 Chantilly, France
Training — Paris: Carolus-Duran, Acad. Julian.

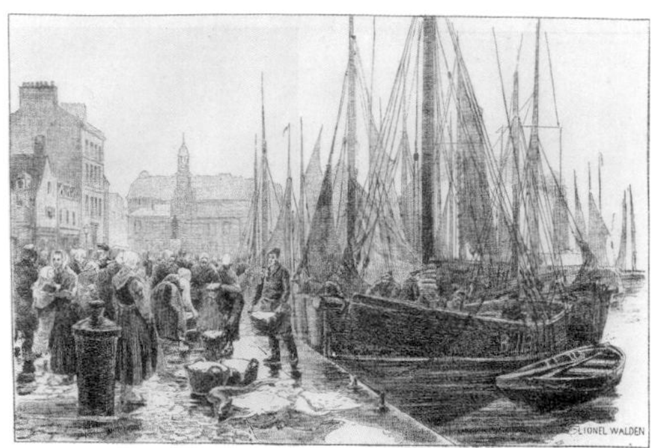

Boulogne Fishing Boats. **#1115.** [$800]. ca. 1890. Unlocated. Illus: Ludovic Baschet, ed., *Salon de 1890, Catalogue Illustré, Peinture & Sculpture* (Paris: Georges Chamerot, 1890), 201.

Fog on the Thames. **#1129.** [$500]. Unlocated.

---

† WALKER, **Henry O.** (Henry Oliver). **New York.**
1843 Boston, MA–1929 Belmont, MA
Training — Paris: Léon Bonnat.

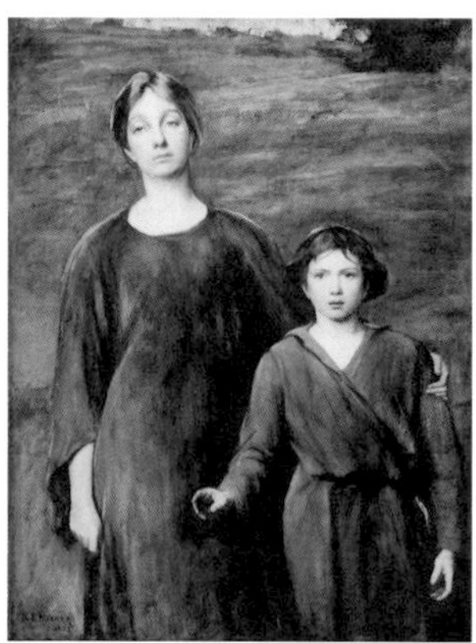

Hagar and Ishmael. **#399.** [$600]. 1892. 24 3/16 x 18¾. Flint Institute of Arts, Gift of Mrs. Arthur Jerome Eddy.

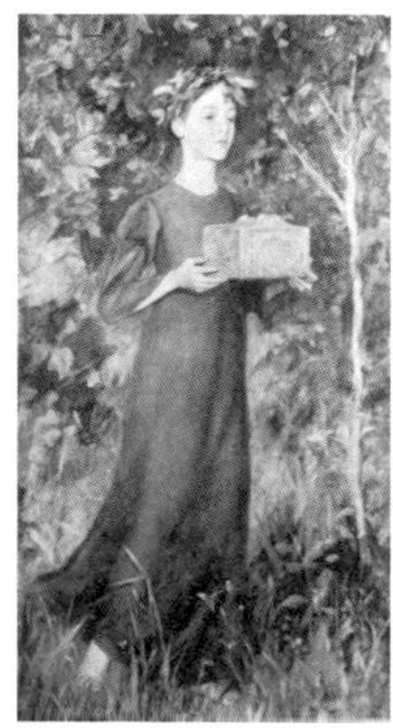

The Gift-Bearer. **#641. Lent by Miss E. H. Bartol, Boston, Mass.** Unlocated. Illus: Charles M. Kurtz, ed., *Illustrations from the Art Gallery of the World's Columbian Exposition* (Philadelphia: G. Barrie, 1893), 227.

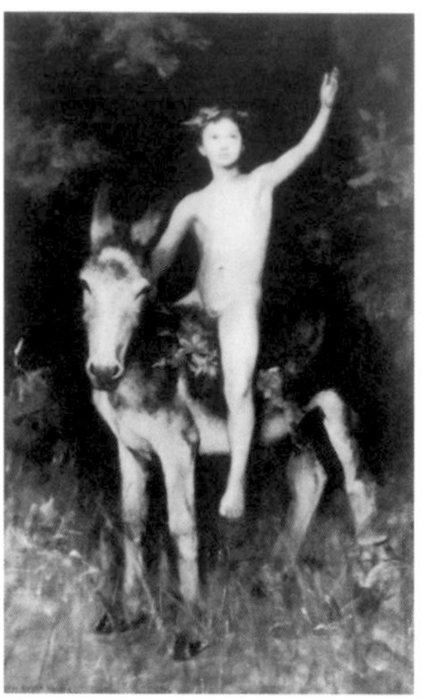

Boy on a Donkey. **#647. Lent by Mrs. S. D. Warren, Boston.** 1889. 30½ x 19. Sold, Richard Oliver Auctioneers, Kennebunk, ME, 6 Nov. 1981, lot 29. Unlocated.

---

† WALKER, **Horatio. New York.**
1858 Listowel, Ontario, Canada–1938 Ile d'Orleans, Quebec, Canada
Training — Toronto: R. F. Gagen, John A. Fraser.

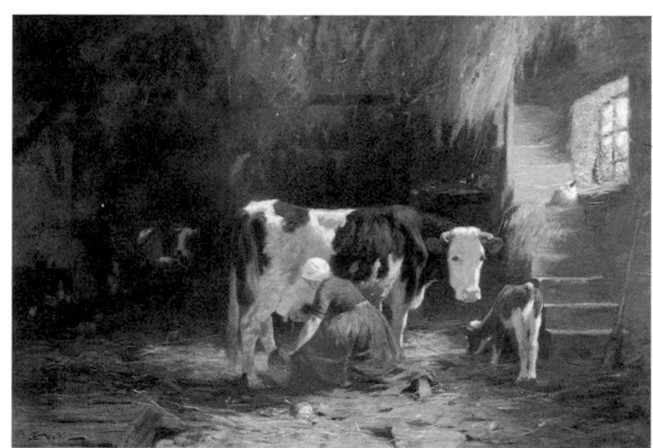

A Stable Interior. **#836.** [$3000]. *Milking*, 1887. 42 1/5 x 66 3/5. Art Gallery of Ontario,Toronto. Gift of Mr. & Mrs. Jules Loeb, 1978.

WALKLEY, **D. B.** (David Birdsey). **Pittsburg.**
1849 Rome, OH–1934 Rock Creek, OH
Training — Philadelphia: PAFA; New York: ASL (William Merritt Chase); Paris: Acad. Julian (Gustave Boulanger, Jules Joseph Lefebvre), Henry Mosler.

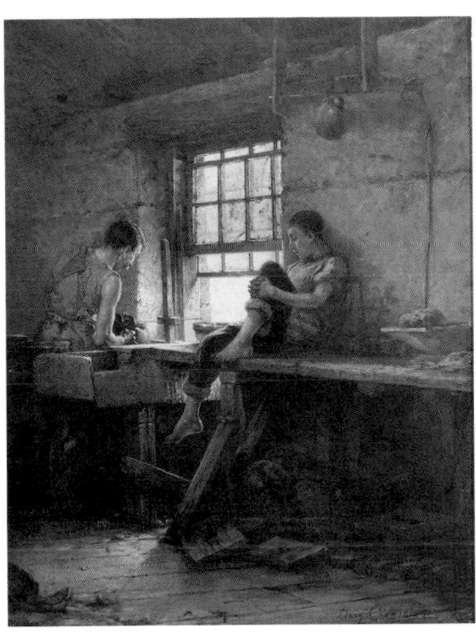

The Potter. **#1029.** [$1000]. **Lent by Mr. W. A. Shaw, Sharpsburg, Pa.** n.d. (ca. 1889). 32 x 25. Private Collection. Photograph by Cathy Carver.

WALL, A. Bryan (Alfred Bryan). **Pittsburg.**
1861 Pittsburgh, PA–1935 Pittsburgh, PA
Training — Alfred S. Wall [his father]; Paris: Acad. Delecluse.

Across the Meadow. **#390.** [$500]. Unlocated.

WALLACE, Laurie (John Laurie). **Omaha.**
1864 Garvagh, Ireland 1953 Omaha, NE
Training — Philadelphia: PAFA (Thomas Eakins).

Portrait of Mr. James W. Scott. **#903. Lent by the Chicago Press Club.** Est. 43 x 35. Unlocated. "After you catch the expression, the power of thought and the strength of will hold you there until it seems almost discourteous to pass on until the head is turned back again to the work lying on the great publisher's desk" —Teresa Dean, *White City Chips* (Chicago: Warren Publishing Co., 1895), 229.

WAUGH, Ida. Philadelphia.
Philadelphia, PA–1919 New York, NY
Training — Philadelphia: Samuel B. Waugh [her father], PAFA; Paris: Acad. Julian (Jules Joseph Lefebvre, Jean-Joseph Benjamin-Constant), Paul-Louis Delance, Georges Callot, Acad. Delecluse.

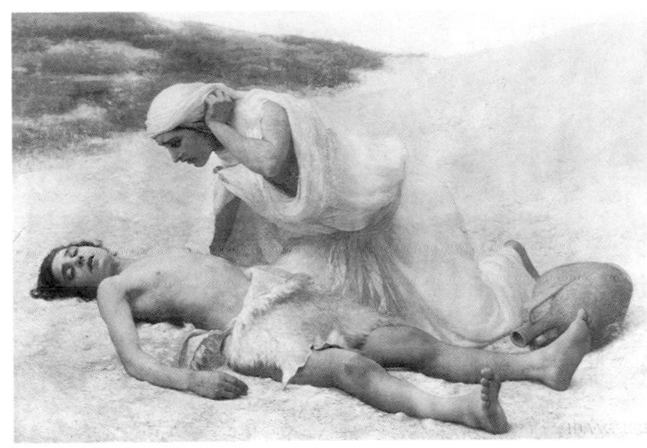

Hagar and Ishmael. **#781. Lent by the Pennsylvania Academy of the Fine Arts.** 1889. 48 x 71. Formerly Collection Pennsylvania Academy of the Fine Arts. Sold, Samuel H. Freeman & Son, Philadelphia, PA, 10 Jan. 1951. Unlocated. Illus: *Arts for America* 7 (Oct. 1897): 71.

WEBBER, C. T. (Charles T.). **Cincinnati.**
1825 Cayuga Lake, NY–1911 Cincinnati, OH
Training — largely self-taught.

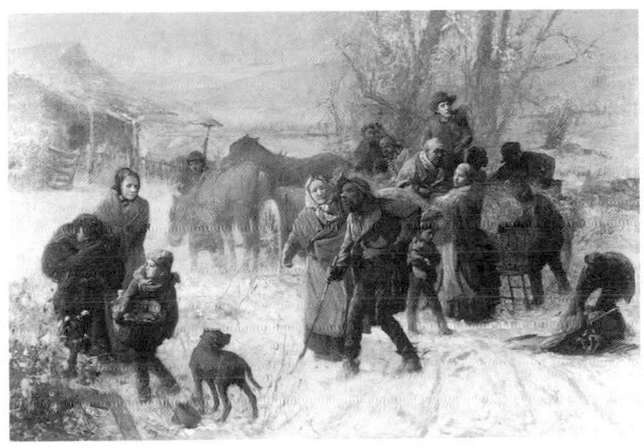

The Underground Railroad (A souvenir of slavery days). **#412.** n.d. (ca. 1891–93). 52 3/16 x 76⅛. Cincinnati Art Museum, Subscription Fund Purchase.

WEBER, Carl. Philadelphia.
1850 Philadelphia, PA–1921 Ambler, PA
Training — Paul Weber [his father]; Frankfurt: Jakob Becker; Vienna: Edward von Steinle; Munich: Karl Raupp; Paris.

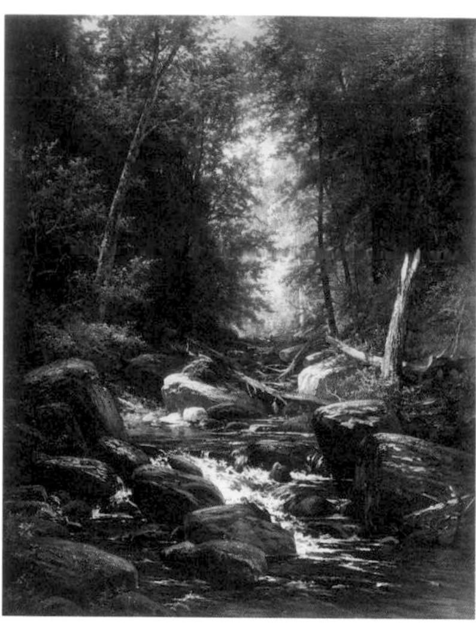

Trout Stream near Dingman's Ferry. **#1015.** [$120]. *The Trout Stream,* n.d. 60 x 48. Reading Public Museum and Art Gallery, Reading, PA.

WEEKS, **Edwin Lord. Paris, France.**
1849 Boston, MA–1903 Paris, France
Training — Paris: Jean-Léon Gérôme, Léon Bonnat.

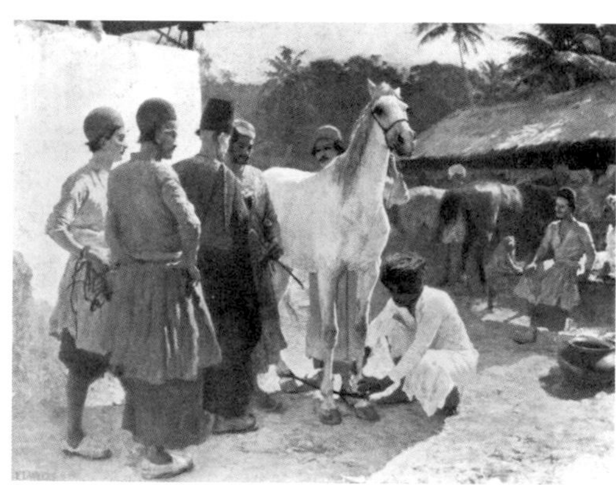

Persian Horse Dealers. **#318.** [$3500]. *Oriental Horse Market,* n.d. 55½ x 74. Sold, American Art Association, New York, NY, 25 Feb. 1918, lot 82, to John Starnbough. Unlocated. Illus: *Catalogue of the Collection of Foreign and American Paintings Owned by Mr. George A. Hearn* (New York, 1908; privately printed), 176.

Interior at Toledo, Spain. **#406.** [$500]. Est. 20 x 20. Unlocated.

Study at Bombay, India. **#408.** [$500]. Est. 25 x 20. Unlocated.

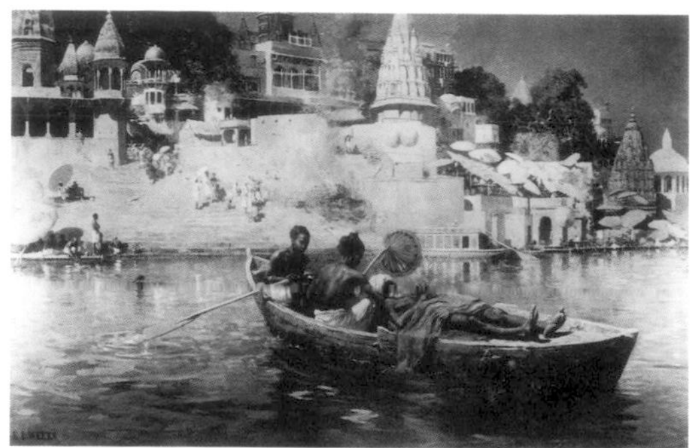

The Last Voyage: A Souvenir of the Ganges. **#410.** [$5000]. *The Last Voyage,* n.d. (ca. 1885). 78½ x 117½. Collection of Stuart Pivar, Courtesy of Bayly Art Museum, University of Virginia, Charlottesville, VA.

Marble Court at Agra, India. **#414.** [$500]. Est. 18 x 16. Unlocated.

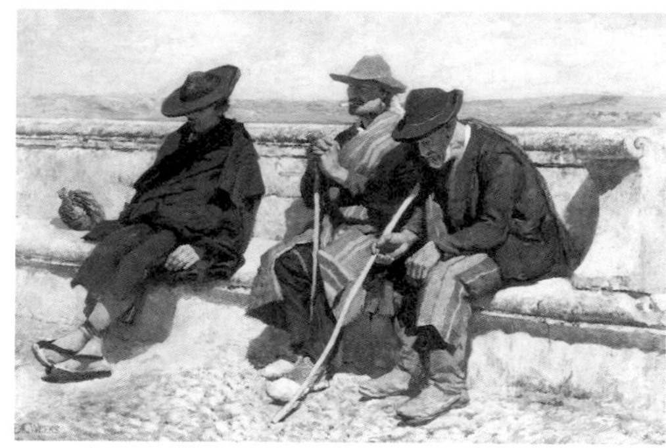

Three Beggars of Cordova. **#462. Lent by the Pennsylvania Academy of the Fine Arts, Philadelphia.** 1892. 65½ x 98½. Pennsylvania Academy of the Fine Arts, Philadelphia, Gift of Charles W. Wharton.

---

† WEIR, **J. Alden** (Julian Alden). **New York.**
1852 West Point, NY–1919 New York, NY
Training — West Point: Robert W. Weir [his father]; New York: NAD; Paris: Jean-Léon Gérôme, Gustave Boulanger, EcBA.

Summerland. **#280.** Est. 23 x 30. Unlocated.

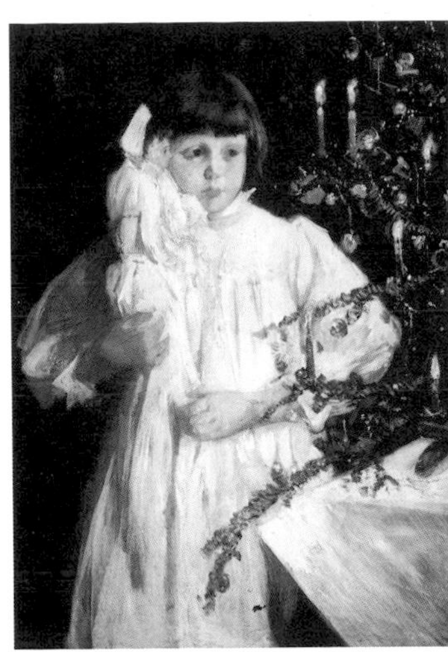

The Christmas Tree.* **#298. 1890. 36¾ x 25½. Private Collection.

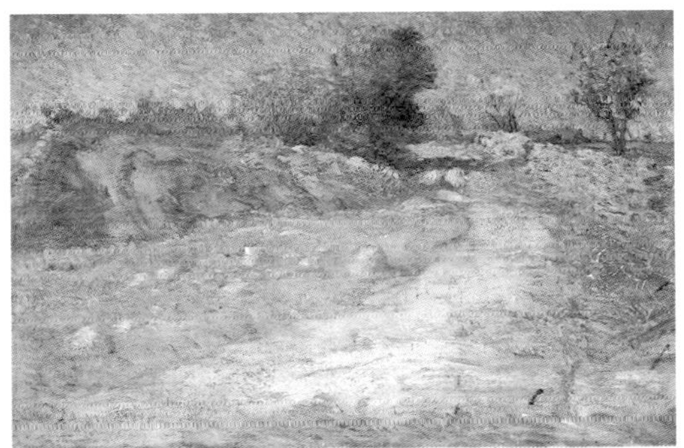

The Lane. **#325.** n.d. (ca. 1890). 10¼ x 15¾. The Phillips Collection, Washington, D.C.

Autumn. **#384.** Unlocated.

The Young Student. **#385.** ca. 1892. Unlocated.

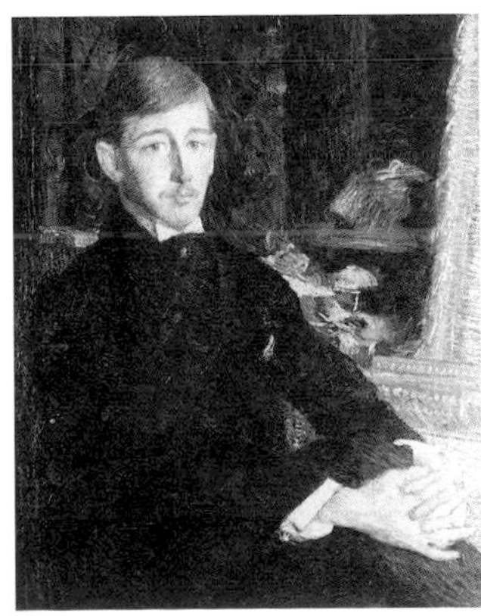

Portrait of Webb Weir. **#717.** *Portrait of Alexander Webb Weir,* 1892. 36 x 29. Spencer Museum of Art, University of Kansas.

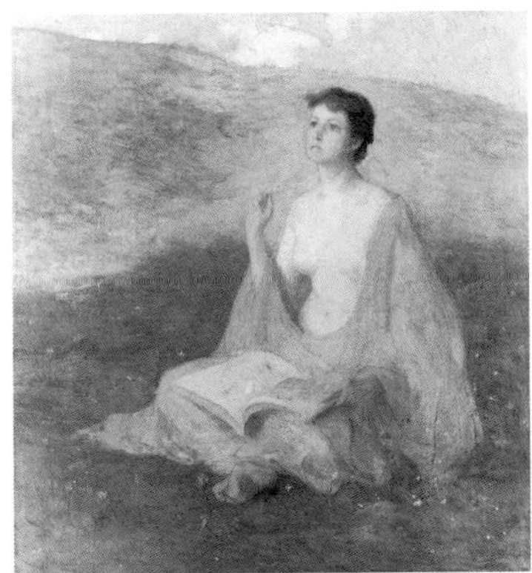

The Open Book. **#1150.** [$2000]. 1891. 31¾ x 29⅛. National Museum of American Art, Smithsonian Institution, Gift of John Gellatly.

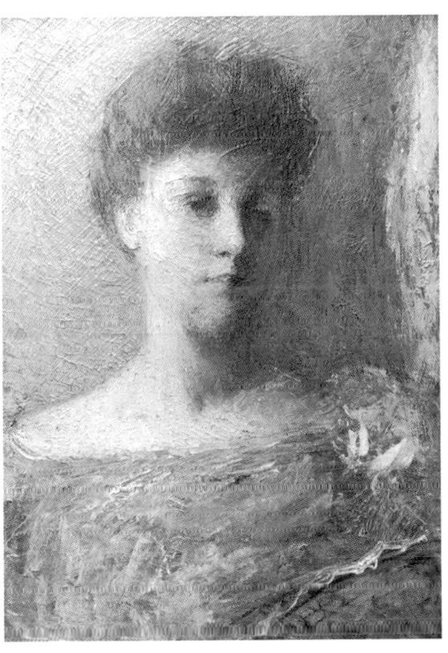

Portrait. **#1199.** *Portrait of a Lady,* n.d. (oil on panel). 16 x 11¼. Vose Galleries, Boston, MA.

WEIR, John F. (John Ferguson). **New Haven, Conn.**
1841 West Point, NY–1926 Providence, RI
Training — West Point: Robert W. Weir [his father]; New York: NAD.

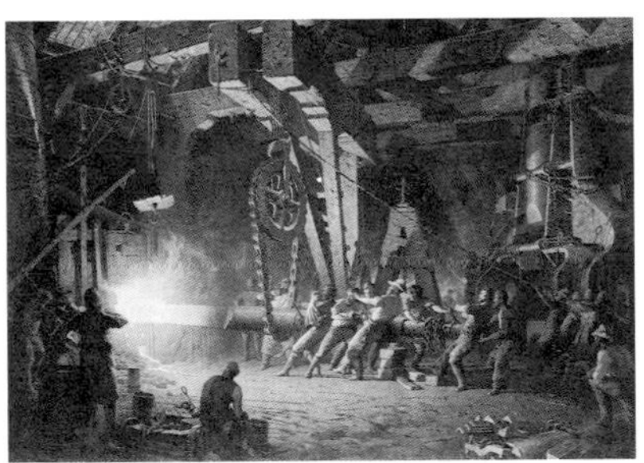

Forging the Shaft. **#816.** [$4000]. n.d. (1874–77). 52 x 73¼. The Metropolitan Museum of Art, Purchase, Lyman G. Bloomingdale Gift, 1901.

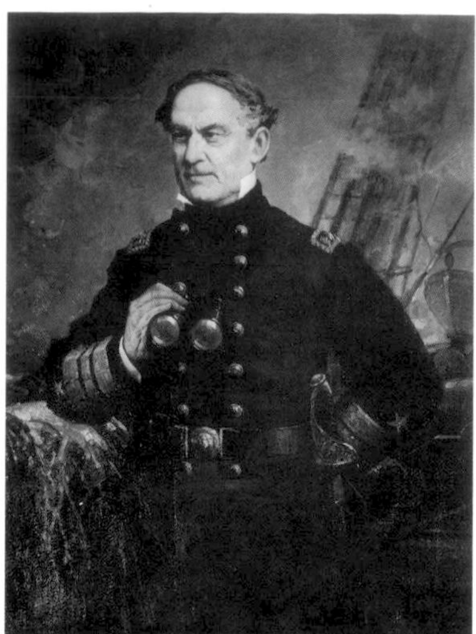

Portrait of Admiral Farragut. **#1151. Lent by the University Club, New York.** 1889. 47½ x 35½. The University Club, New York, NY.

Roses. **#1166.** [$400]. **Lent by Mr. J. R. Ball, New York.** ca. 1882–83. 22 x 33. Unlocated.[69]

WENTWORTH, Cecilia E. (Cecilia E. Smith/ Mrs. Josias Wentworth). **New York.**
1853 New York, NY–1933 Nice, France
Training — Paris: Alexandre Cabanel, Edouard Detaille.

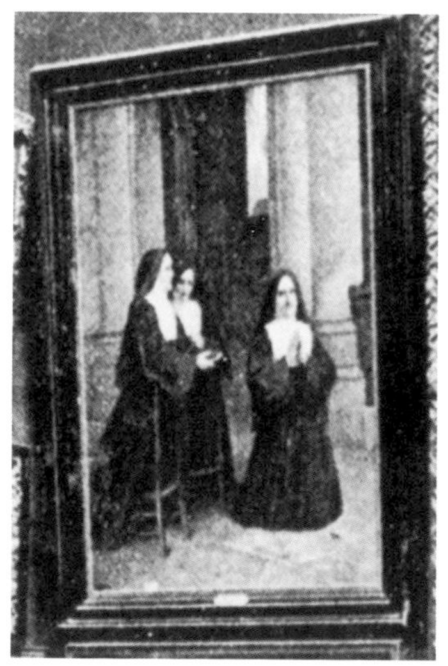

Prayer. **#598.** ca. 1891. Est. 80 x 55. Unlocated. Illus: J. W. Buel, *The Magic City* (St. Louis: Historical Publishing Company, 1894).

WHELPLEY, A. Renouf (Annie Vincent Davenport Whelpley/Mrs. Edward A. Renouf).[70] **Munich, Bavaria.**
1852 Boston, MA–After 1928 Florence, Italy?
Training — Munich: von Hartwick (Herman Hartwich?), Ludwig von Löfftz, Rudolf Maison, Marc Thedy.

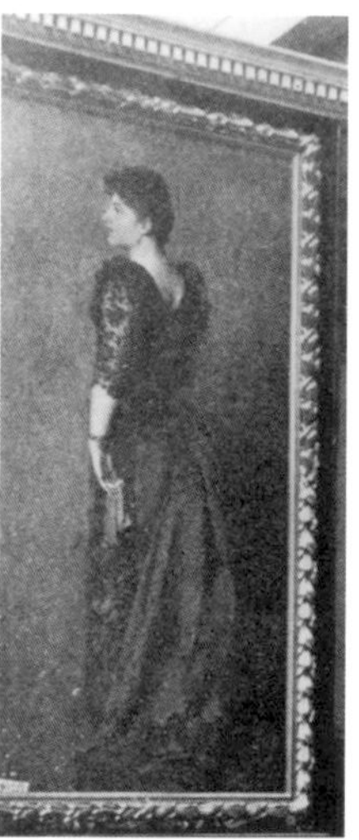

Portrait of Mlle. Hausen. **#1257. Lent by Mlle. Hausen, Brunswick.** ca. 1892. Est. 78 x 35. Unlocated. Illus: Hubert H. Bancroft, *The Book of the Fair,* vol. 3 (Chicago: Blakely Printing Co., 1893), 678.

---

† **WHISTLER, J. McNeill** (James Abbott McNeill). **Paris, France.**
1834 Lowell, MA–1903 London, England
Training — West Point: G. W. Whistler [his father], Robert W. Weir; Paris: École Imperiale de Dessin, Charles Gleyre; St. Petersburg: Imperial Academy of Fine Arts.

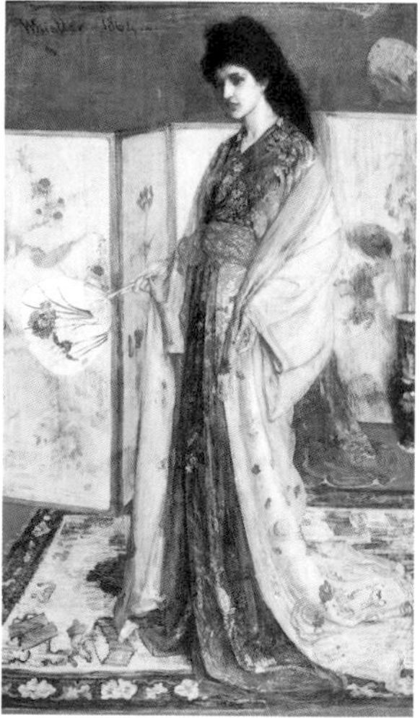

The Princess of the Land of Porcelain. **#636.** [$15,000]. **Lent by Mr. Alexander Reid, Glasgow, Scotland.** *Rose and Silver: The Princess from the Land of Porcelain,* 1864. 78¾ x 45¾. Freer Gallery of Art, Smithsonian Institution.

86 x 43½. Philadelphia Museum of Art, The W. P. Wilstach Collection.

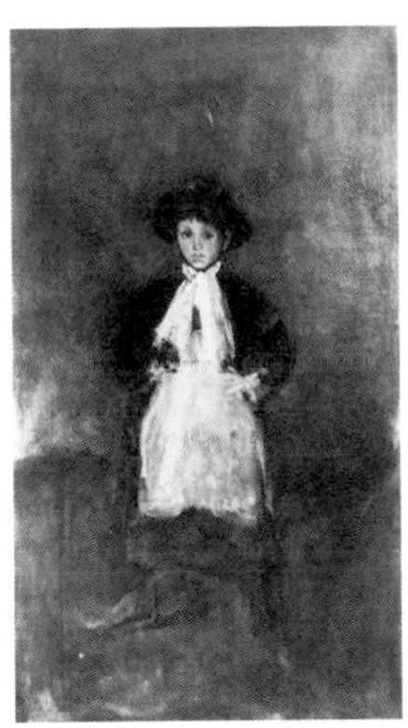

The Chelsea Girl.* **#744. Lent by Mr. A. J. Cassatt, Philadelphia. n.d. (ca. 1884–86). 65 x 35. Private Collection.

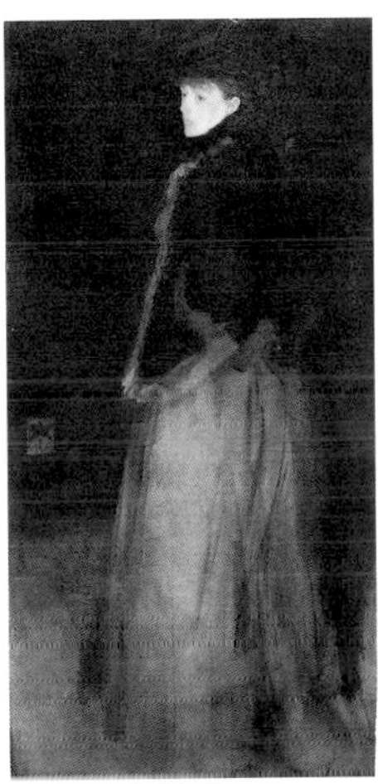

The Fur Jacket. #751. [$15,000]. **Lent by Mr. Alexander Reid, Glasgow, Scotland.** *Arrangement in Black and Brown: The Fur Jacket,* 1876. 76⅜ x 36½. Worcester Art Museum, Worcester, MA.

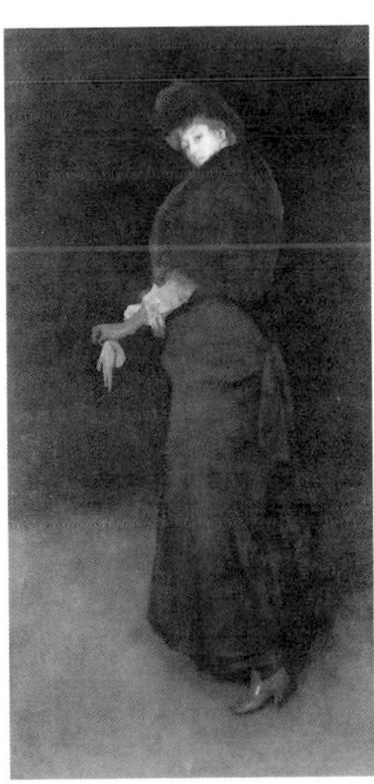

The Lady with the Yellow Buskin. **#758.** [$15,000]. **Lent by Mr. Alexander Reid, Glasgow.** n.d. (ca. 1883).

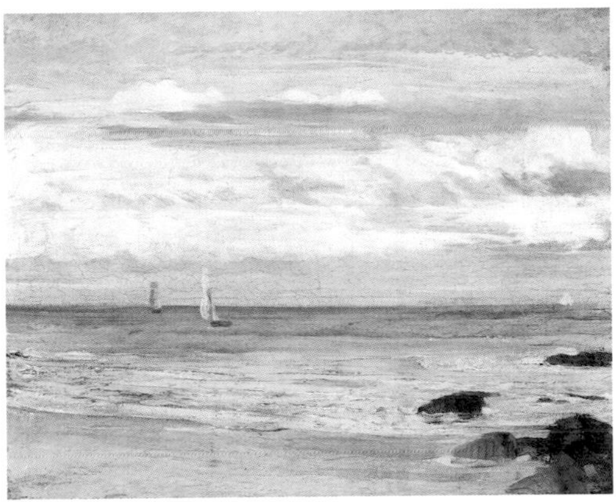

Harmony in Blue and Silver. **#768. Lent by Mr. J. J. Shannon, London.** *Blue and Silver—Trouville,* 1865. 23⅜ x 28⅝. Freer Gallery of Art, Smithsonian Institution.

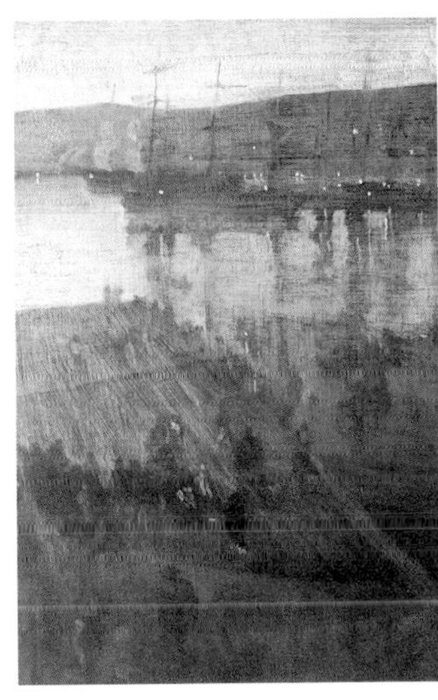

Nocturne, Valparaiso. **#787. Lent by the Hon. Sir John Charles Day, London.** *Nocturne. Blue and Gold—Valparaiso,* 1866. 29¾ x 19¾. Freer Gallery of Art, Smithsonian Institution.

WHITE, Henry C. (Henry Cook). **Hartford, Conn.**
1861 Hartford, CT–1952 Waterford, CT
Training — New York: ASL (Kenyon Cox, George De Forest Brush), Dwight Tryon.

Spring Landscape. **#480.** [$500]. Est. 30 x 35. Unlocated.

WHITE, **Robert H. Camden, N.J.**

Morning in February. **#1243.** [$100]. Est. 15 x 20. Unlocated.

WHITEMAN, **S. Edwin** (Samuel Edwin). **Baltimore.**
1860 Philadelphia, PA–1922 Baltimore, MD
Training — Boston: William Morris Hunt; Paris: Thomas Couture, Acad. Julian (Gustave Boulanger, Jules Joseph Lefebvre, Jean-Joseph Benjamin-Constant).

Over Autumnal Hills. **#528.** [$850]. Est. 50 x 65. Unlocated.

Lowland Pastures. **#547.** [$850]. Unlocated.

WHITMAN, **Sarah W.** (Sarah de St. Prix Wyman/ Mrs. Henry Whitman). **Boston.**
1842 Baltimore, MD–1904 Boston, MA
Training — Boston: William Morris Hunt; Paris: Thomas Couture.

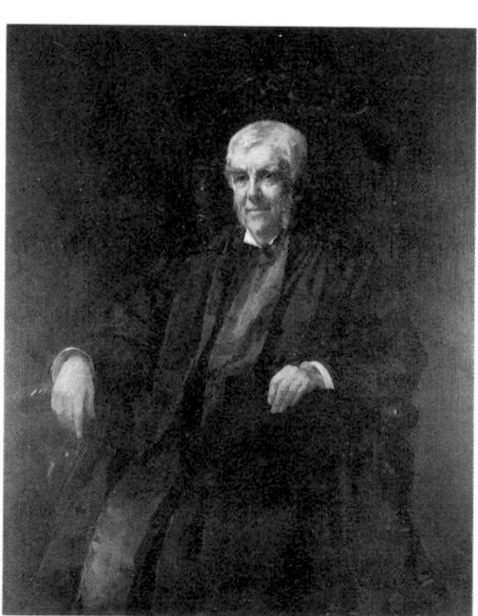

Portrait of Oliver Wendell Holmes. **#877. Lent by the College of Physicians, Philadelphia.** 1892. 50½ x 41½. The College of Physicians of Philadelphia.

Niagara. **#1204.** [$500]. Unlocated. "In the view of Horseshoe fall, Niagara, she belittles her subject especially by magnifying the foliage above it" —*Brooklyn Daily Eagle,* 4 Dec. 1892.

WHITTEMORE, **William J.** (William John). **New York.**
1860 New York, NY–1955 East Hampton, NY
Training — New York: NAD (William Hart, Lemuel E. Wilmarth), ASL (J. Carroll Beckwith); Paris: Acad. Julian (Jules Joseph Lefebvre, Jean-Joseph Benjamin-Constant).

Autumn Sunshine. **#878.** [$400]. ca. 1891. Sold, World's Columbian Exposition, Chicago, IL, 1893. Unlocated.

WHITTREDGE, **W.** (Worthington). **New York.**
1820 near Springfield, OH–1910 Summit, NJ
Training — Cincinnati; Dusseldorf: Andreas Achenbach; London; Paris; Antwerp; Rome.

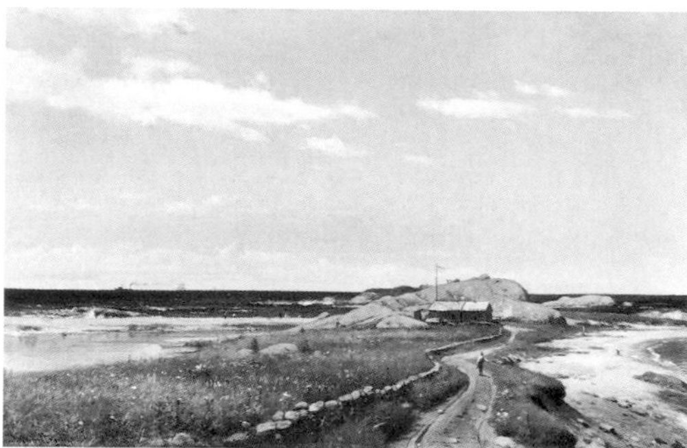

Rhode Island Coast.* **#392. [$300]. *A Breezy Day — Sakonnet Point, Rhode Island,* n.d. (ca. 1880). 25⅜ x 38½. Amon Carter Museum, Fort Worth.

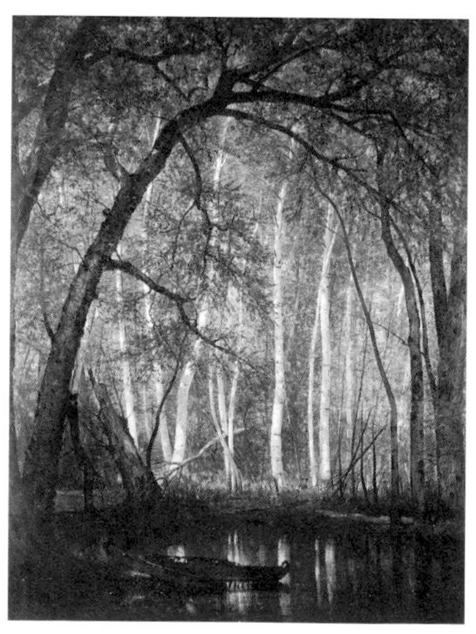

The Old Hunting Ground. **#882. Lent by Mr. J. W. Pinchot, New York.** 1864. 36 x 27. Reynolda House Museum of American Art, Winston-Salem, NC.

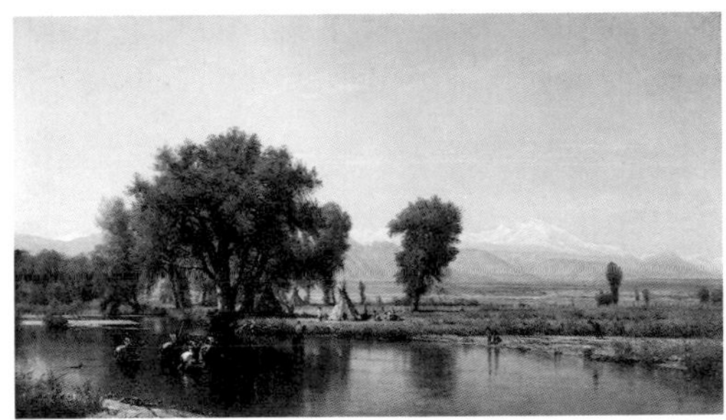

******The Plains.* **#972. Lent by the Century Club, New York.** *Crossing the Ford, Platte River, Colorado,* 1868–1870. 40¼ x 69⅛. The Century Association, New York, NY. Photograph by Geoffrey Clements.

WICKENDEN, **Robert J.** (Robert John). **Paris, France.**
1861 Rochester, England–1931 Brooklyn, NY
Training — Toledo, OH; New York: J. Carroll Beckwith, William Merritt Chase; Paris: A. A. E. Hébert, Luc Olivier Merson, Gustave Courtois, Raphaël Collin.

Whisperings of Spring. **#558.** [$100]. By 1890. Unlocated.

WIGAND, **Albright** (Adeline Albright/Mrs. Otto Charles Wigand). **Mt. Vernon, N.Y.**
1855 Madison, NJ–1944 Staten Island, NY
Training — New York: Cooper Union, NAD, ASL (William Merritt Chase); Paris: Acad. Julian (Gustave Boulanger, Jules Joseph Lefebvre, Tony Robert-Fleury, William Bouguereau).

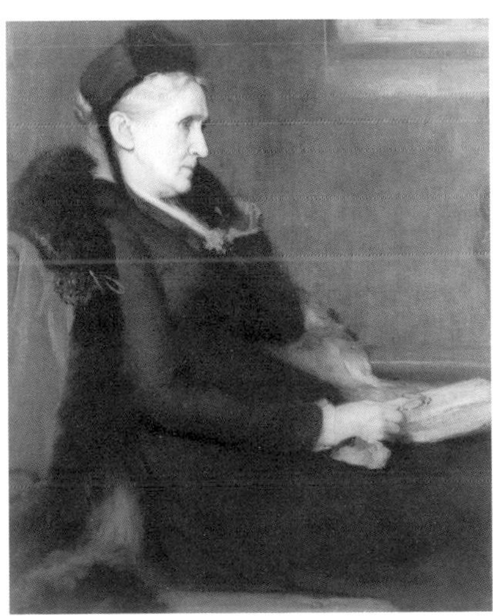

******Portrait of Mrs. J. Albright.* **#711.** *Portrait of My Mother,* n.d. 37½ x 30⅝. Collection of the Staten Island Institute of Arts and Sciences.

WIGAND, **Otto C.** (Otto Charles). **Mt. Vernon, N.Y.**
1856 New York, NY–1944 Staten Island, NY
Training — New York: ASL; Paris: Acad. Julian (Gustave Boulanger, Jules Joseph Lefebvre).

The Old Willow Tree. **#456.** [$250]. Est. 30 x 20. Unlocated.

WIGGINS, **Carlton** (John Carleton). **New York.**
1848 Turners, NY–1932 Old Lyme, CT
Training — Brooklyn: Johann Hermann Carmiencke; New York: NAD; Eagleswood, NJ: George Inness.

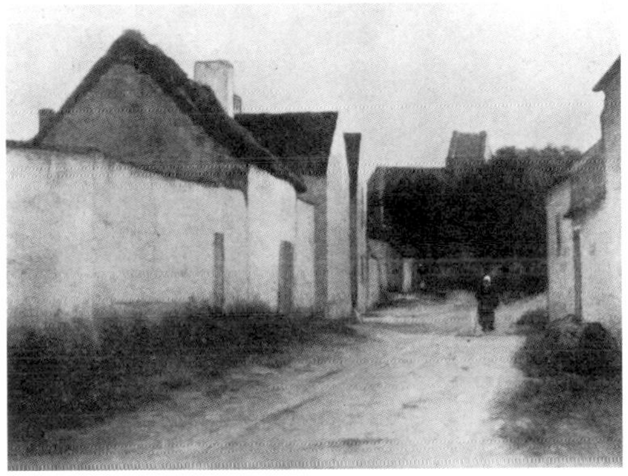

Evening, Village of Grez. **#719. Lent by Mrs. Charles M. Kurtz, New York.** ca. 1881. 20 x 26. Sold, Fifth Avenue Art Galleries, New York, NY, 24 Feb. 1910, lot 146, to F. T. Fleitmann. Unlocated. Illus: Fifth Avenue Art Galleries, *Catalogue of Oil Paintings, Water Colors, and Drawings of the Late Charles M. Kurtz, Ph.D.* (New York, 1910), 109.

Clouds and Sunshine. **#939. Lent by Mr. Charles E. Dingee, Brooklyn.** Unlocated. "Sheep are seen advancing along a sandy road that is lighted by a sunburst falling through a stormy overcast, the rest of the landscape lying dark under the shadow of gathering tempest. Vast, slaty rolls of cloud . . . " —*Brooklyn Daily Eagle,* 27 June 1893.

Midsummer. **#946. Lent by Mr. John F. Dingee, Brooklyn.** Unlocated. "A cow in the shadow of a tree" —*Brooklyn Daily Eagle,* 27 June 1893.

† **WILES, Irving R.** (Irving Ramsay). **New York.**
1861 Utica, NY–1948 Peconic, NY
Training — Lemuel Wiles [his father]; New York: ASL (William Merritt Chase, J. Carroll Beckwith); Paris: Acad. Julian (Jules Joseph Lefebvre), Carolus-Duran.

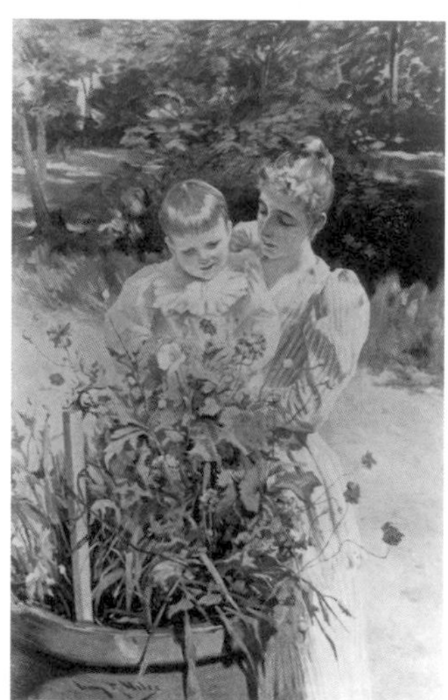

Sunshine and Flowers. **#358.** [$1500]. ca. 1892. Unlocated. Illus: Daniel H. Burnham, *The Art of the World,* vol. 6 (New York: Appleton, 1893–95).

Sunlight in the Studio. **#369. Lent by Mr. Charles D. Miller, Jersey City.** Est. 18 x 22. Unlocated. "A bare-armed model lying on a lounge in a sunny corner of the studio; her loose robe is blue, the bear skin on which she reposes white, the curtain behind her, lit up by the sun, very yellow and the chest of drawers in the corner very red" —*Art Amateur* 20 (Jan. 1889): 29.

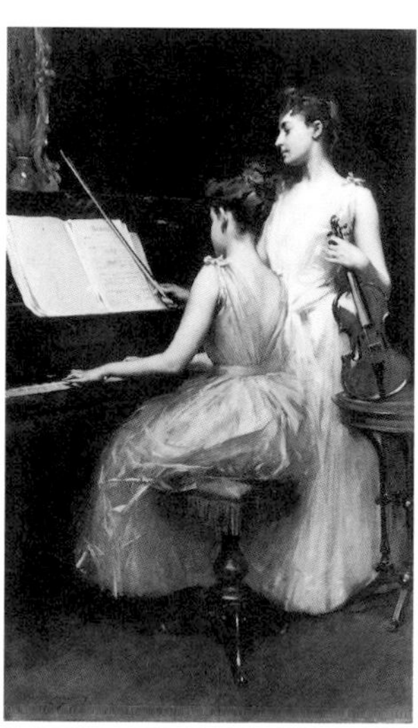

The Sonata. **#481. Lent by Mr. W. T. Evans, New York.** 1889. 44⅛ x 26¼. The Fine Arts Museums of San Francisco, Gift of Mrs. John D. Rockefeller III.

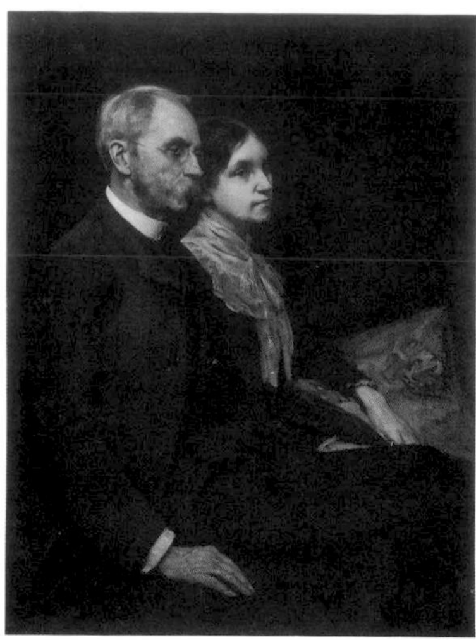

Portraits. **#530.** *The Artist's Mother and Father,* 1889. 48 x 36⅛. The Corcoran Gallery of Art, Museum Purchase, William A. Clark Fund.

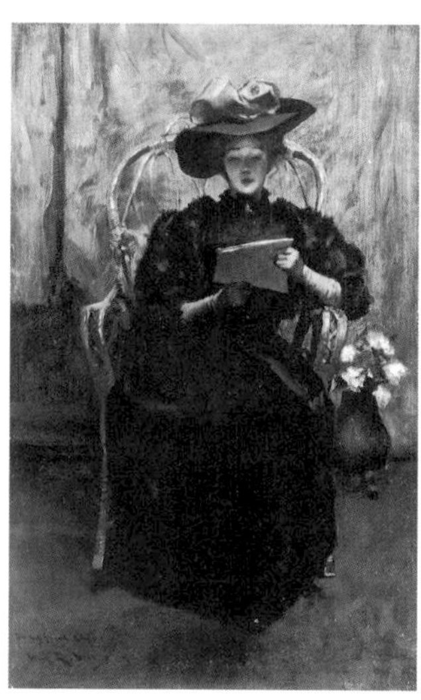

A Girl in Black. **#912. Lent by Mr. W. M. Chase, New York.** *The Red Room,* 1890 (oil on board). 16 x 10. Unlocated.[71] Photograph courtesy the Jordan Volpe Gallery, Inc., New York, NY.

A Lady in Green. **#940.** Unlocated.

WILES, L. M. (Lemuel Maynard). **New York.**
1826 Perry, NY–1905 New York, NY
Training — Albany, NY: Albany Academy (W. M. Hart); New York: J. F. Cropsey.

The Old Quarry. **#465.** [$200]. ca. 1891. 18 x 24. Unlocated. "A gray day. It is a delicate and subtle treatment in gray tones and is one of the best pictures this artist has painted"—Thomas B. Clarke Papers, Archives of American Art, roll N597, frame 514.

WITT, J. H. (John Henry/Harrison). **New York.**
1840 Dublin, IN–1901 New York, NY
Training — Cincinnati: J. O. Eaton.

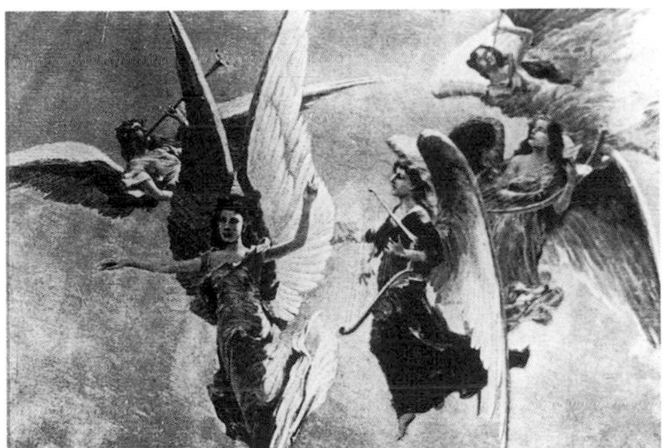

***The Celestial Choir.* #1023.** Unlocated. Illus: The New York Public Library, *The Artists File* (Alexandria, VA: Chadwyck-Healey, 1989).

WOODBURY, Charles Herbert. Boston.
1864 Lynn, MA–1940 Boston, MA
Training — Paris: Acad. Julian (William Bouguereau, Jules Joseph Lefebvre).

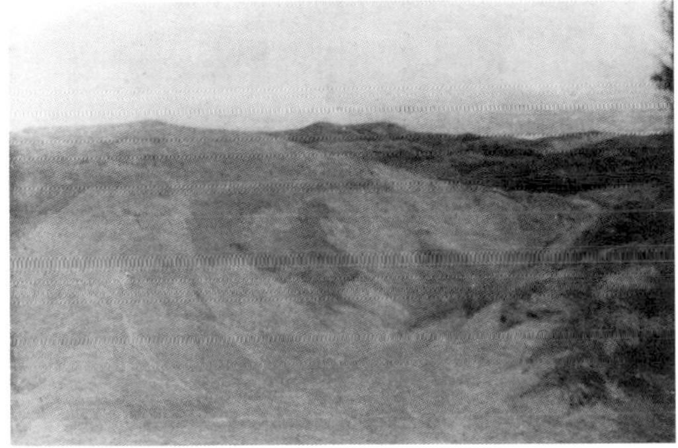

***North Sea Dunes.* #804.** [$1500]. Destroyed by the artist.[72] Illus: William H. Downes, "New England Art at the World's Fair," *New England Magazine* 8 (July 1893): 361. "Highly impressive composition, painted with great skill and force. It depicts an immense waste of sand hills and valleys seen from the landward side, with the figures of some peasant women introduced in a modest way to give some idea of the scale of size in the absence of buildings and vegetation. The bigness and desolation of the scene are memorable. . . . The ground in all its undulations and sweeping contours . . . the severity of the desert . . . the sea beyond . . ." —*Boston Daily Evening Transcript,* 21 Jan. 1893.

***The Tide River.* #1040.** [$2000]. ca. 1886. Unlocated. "A large canvas, which was most favorably received in New York, and now hangs in the Boston Museum of Fine Arts" — unidentified clipping from scrapbook in the possession of the artist's family; "With its breadth of treatment and richness of coloring" — Hubert H. Bancroft, *The Book of the Fair,* vol. 3 (Chicago: Blakely Printing Co., 1893), 686.

WOODWARD, William. New Orleans.
1859 Seekonk, MA–1939 New Orleans, LA
Training — Providence, RI: Rhode Island School of Design; Boston: Massachusetts Normal Art School; Paris: Acad. Julian (Gustave Boulanger, Jules Joseph Lefebvre).

***Persimmons.* #1285.** [$35]. ca. 1890. Unlocated.

WOODWELL, Johanna K. (Johanna Knowles/ Mrs. James D. Hailman). **Pittsburg.**
1871 Pittsburgh, PA–1958 Pittsburgh, PA
Training — Pittsburgh: Joseph R. Woodwell [her father].

***Study Head of a Young Lady.* #1035.** [$150]. Unlocated.

WOODWELL, Joseph R. (Joseph Ryan). **Pittsburg.**
1843 Pittsburgh, PA–1911 Pittsburgh, PA
Training — Paris; Munich; England.

***White Rocks, Magnolia, Mass.* #375.** [$500]. Unlocated.

***Rocks at Low Tide, Magnolia, Mass.* #844.** [$500]. Unlocated.

***A Rocky Coast, Magnolia, Mass.* #1160.** [$500]. Est. 26 wd. Unlocated.

***Cobblestone Beach, Magnolia, Mass.* #1165.** [$500]. Unlocated.

WOOLFOLK, E. Marshall (Eva Marshall). **Paris, France.**
United States–Residing 1905 Paris, France
Training — Paris: Raphaël Collin, Jules Adler.

***Washer-women, Nemours, France.* #1053.** [$150]. Unlocated.

WUERPEL, Edmund H. (Edmund Henry). **Paris, France.**
1866 Clayton, MO–1958 St. Louis, MO
Training— St. Louis: School of Fine Arts; Paris: Acad. Julian (William Bouguereau, Tony Robert-Fleury, G. J. M. A. Ferrier) Edmond-François Aman-Jean, Jean-Léon Gérôme, Henri-Lucien Doucet.

September Twilight. **#440. Lent by Dr. William Taussig, St. Louis.** Unlocated.

WYANT, A. H. (Alexander Helwig). **deceased.**
1836 Evans Creek, OH–1892 New York, NY
Training— New York; Karlsruhe, Germany: Hans Fredrik Gude.

Landscape. **#511. Lent by Mr. Thomas B. Clarke, New York.** 12 x 16. Sold (as *The Mountain Road*), American Art Association, New York, NY, 15 Feb. 1907, lot 40, to Fishel, Adler and Schwartz. Unlocated. "In the foreground at the left a rough road crosses a mountain ridge. Behind it, to the horizon, reaches a vast wilderness of many variations of surface. The smoke of brush fires here and there mingles with the moist vapors of a gray sky threatening showers. Signed at the left" —The Pennsylvania Academy of the Fine Arts, *Catalogue of the Thomas B. Clarke Collection of American Pictures* (Philadelphia, 1891), 123.

A North Woods Brook. **#517. Lent by Mr. Thomas B. Clarke, New York.** 12 x 16. Sold (as *North Woods*), American Art Association, New York, NY, 14–18 Feb. 1899, lot 46, to F. S. Smithers. Unlocated. "The vapors of early morning curl along the crests of the purple shadowed hills that form the horizon. In the middle plane, at the left, a ruined cabin shows its shattered walls on the further shore of a stream. In the foreground, from the right, cattle approach the water down a hilly track, on which grows a stunted tree. Signed at right" —The Pennsylvania Academy of the Fine Arts, *Catalogue of the Thomas B. Clarke Collection of American Pictures* (Philadelphia, 1891), 122–23.

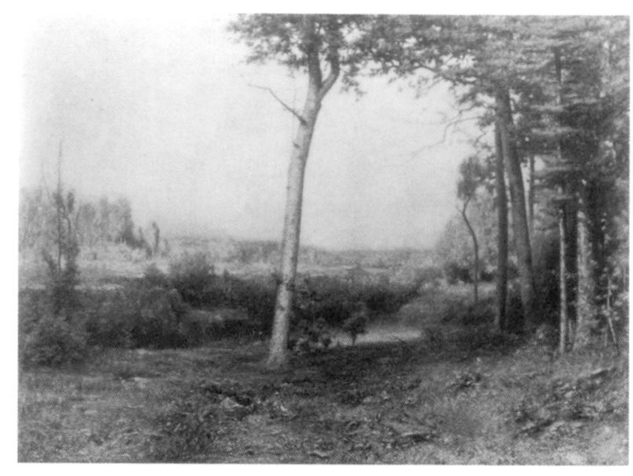

Forenoon in the Adirondacks. **#639.** [$1500]. **Lent by Mrs. A. L. Wyant, New York.** 1884. 33$^{1}/_{16}$ x 42¾. Collection Metropolitan Museum of Art by 1910. Sold, Parke-Bernet Galleries, New York, NY, 27–28 March 1956, lot 147. Unlocated. Illus: *Catalogue of the Collection of Foreign and American Paintings Owned by Mr. George A. Hearn* (New York, 1908; privately printed), 188.

In the Woods. **#735.** [$1200]. **Lent by Mrs. A. L. Wyant, New York.** Unlocated.

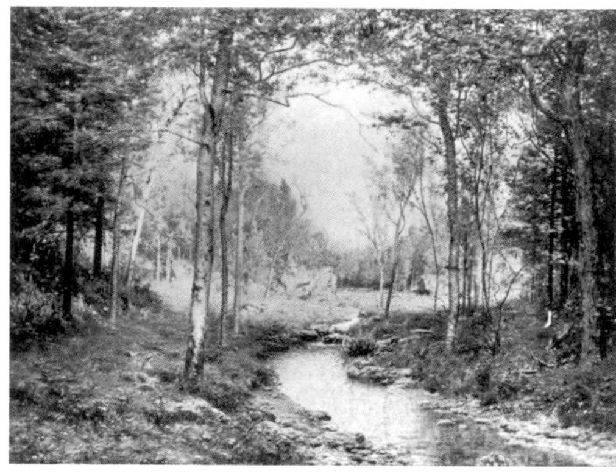

In the Adirondacks. **#918. Lent by Mr. W. T. Evans, New York.** n.d. (ca. 1877). 37 x 49. Collection Anthony E. Battelle, Massachusetts. Illus: *Catalogue of the Collection of Foreign and American Paintings Owned by Mr. George A. Hearn* (New York, 1908; privately printed), 190.

Evening. **#942.** [$2000]. **Lent by Mrs. A. L. Wyant, New York.** 14 x 20. Unlocated.

Sunset in the Woods. **#952. Lent by Mr. J. M. Lichtenauer, New York.** 10 x 14. Sold (as *Sunset in the Woods —Evening Glow*), American Art Association, New York, NY, 27 Feb. 1913, lot 98, to Henry Schultheis. Unlocated. "The spectator is well within the confines of a wood of great trees and second growth timber at the sunset hour. The foilage is thick and dark, with the green showing in patches.

Below the foliage line one looks amid the tangled trunks to a brilliant horizon of glowing red, whose radiance higher up percolates among the branches and is reflected in a pool of the central foreground" — American Art Association, *Collection of the Late J. M. Lichtenauer, Esq. of New York* (New York, 1913), lot 98.

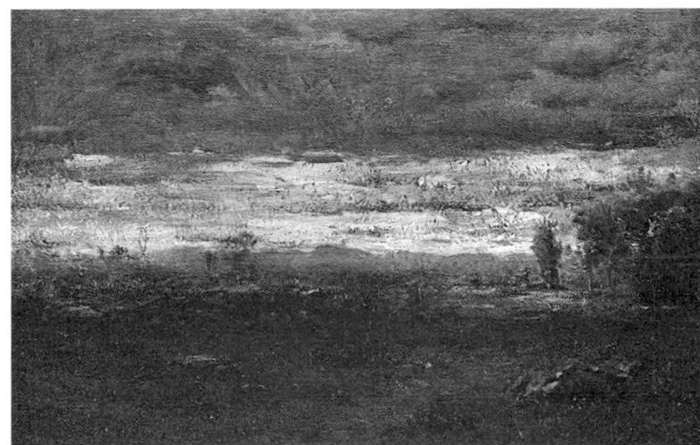

Clearing Off. **#982.** [$2000]. **Lent by Mrs. A. L. Wyant, New York.** n.d. (ca. 1891–92). 14 x 19. San Diego Museum of Art.

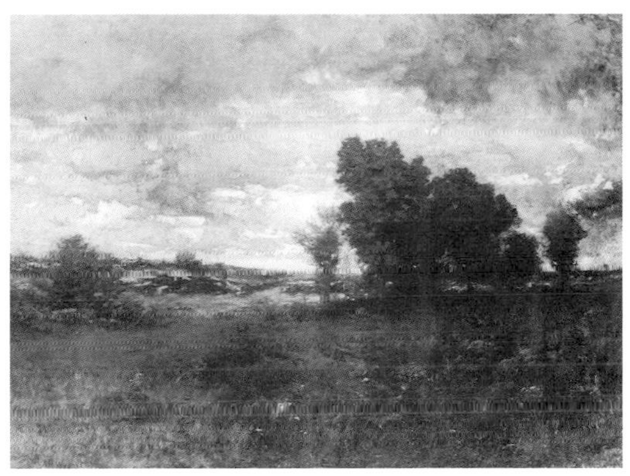

An October Day. **#989.** [$2000]. **Lent by Mrs. A. L. Wyant, New York.** n.d. (ca. 1888). 37 x 49¼. Museum of Art, Rhode Island School of Design, Gift of Jesse Metcalf.

Sunset. **#992. Lent by Mr. Frederick B. Pratt, Brooklyn, N.Y.** Unlocated.

YOUNG, Charles Morris. Gettysburg, Pa.
1869 Gettysburg, PA–1964 Radnor, PA
Training — Philadelphia: PAFA; Paris: Acad. Colarossi.

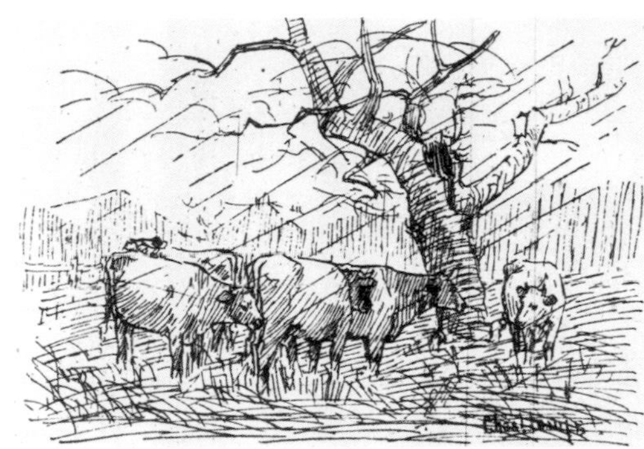

Wet Weather. **#397.** [$200]. ca. 1892. Unlocated. Illus: *Philadelphia Inquirer,* 1 March 1892. "A very nicely-wrought cattle piece, full of the signs of falling rain" — *New York Times,* 1 May 1892; "A group of cows assembled under a tree. The animals are well drawn and well grouped, and the effect is quiet, misty and artistic" — *The Item* [Philadelphia], 14 Feb. 1892.

The Harvest of Death (Wheat Field at Gettysburg after the battle). **#1114.** [$200]. Unlocated.

SCULPTURE

ADAMS, **Herbert** (Herbert Samuel). **Brooklyn.**

1858 West Concord, VT–1945 New York, NY
Training — Boston: Massachusetts Normal Art School; Paris: Acad. Julian (Jules Joseph Lefebvre, Gustave Boulanger, Antonin Mercié).

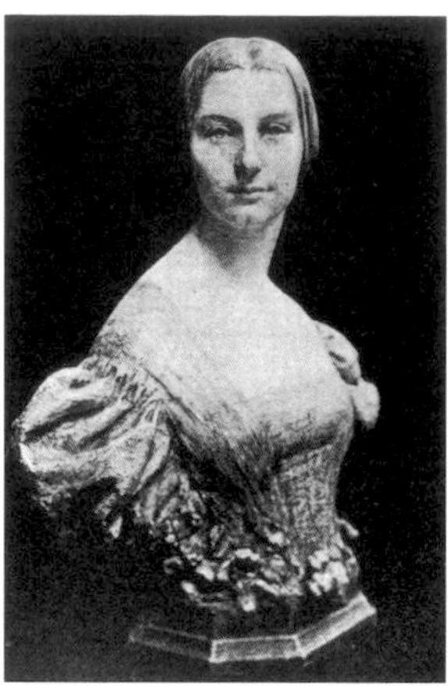

St. Agnes' Eve **(Plaster bust, colored). #76.** [$1000]. ca. 1892. Sold, World's Columbian Exposition, Chicago, IL, 1893. Unlocated. Illus: *Harper's Bazaar*, 14 May 1892, 396.

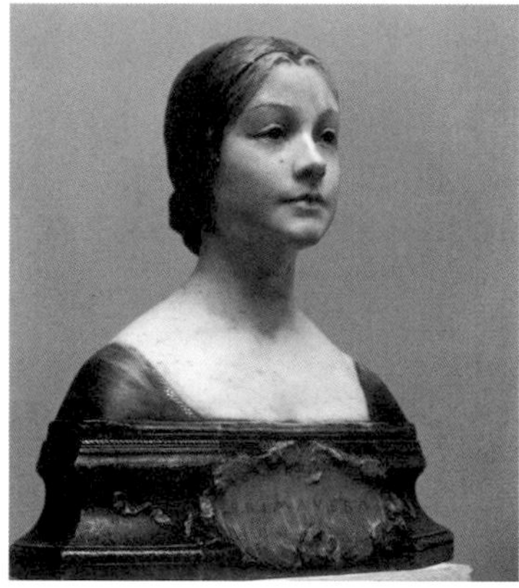

***Primavera* (Marble bust). #114.** [$1000]. n.d. (1890–92) (marble, polychromed). 21½ x 18⅞ x 9¾. The Corcoran Gallery of Art, Museum Purchase.

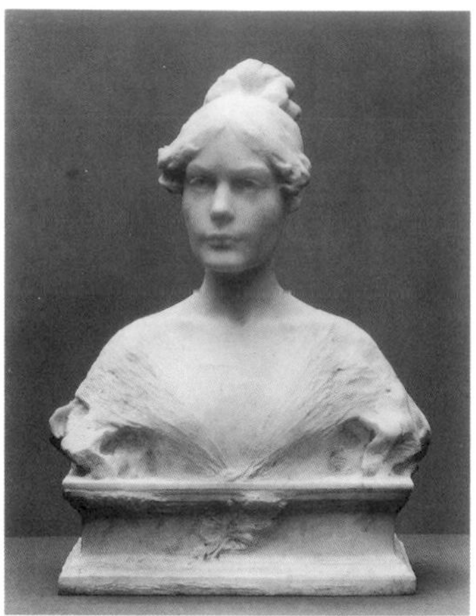

Portrait bust of a Lady **(Marble). #116.** *Adeline Valentine Pond Adams*, 1889. 27¼ x 22¾. The Hispanic Society of America, New York, NY.

BACHMANN, **Max** (Max T.). **Boston.**

1862 Brunswick, Germany–1921 New York, NY
Training — Berlin: Royal Academy (Albert Wolff).

The Son of Man **(Plaster). #96.** [$50 copies]. Unlocated.

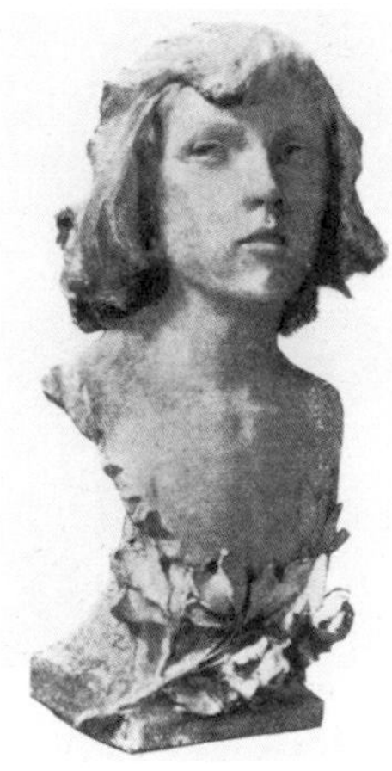

Bust of Miss O. (Adeline C. Okie) **(Plaster). #127. Owned by Dr. Okie, Boston.** Unlocated. Illus: William H. Downes, "New England Art at the World's Fair," *New England Magazine* 8 (July 1893): 367.

Mrs. F. Sheldon (Mrs. Frank Sheldon) **(Plaster bas-relief). #136.** Est. 24 x 16. Unlocated.

Portrait, bas-relief **(Plaster). #141.** Est. 24 x 16. Unlocated.

BALL, **Thomas. Florence, Italy.**
1819 Charlestown, MA–1911 Montclair, NJ
Training — Boston: Abel Bowen; largely self-taught.

Portrait of a Lady **(Plaster bust). #32.** Unlocated.

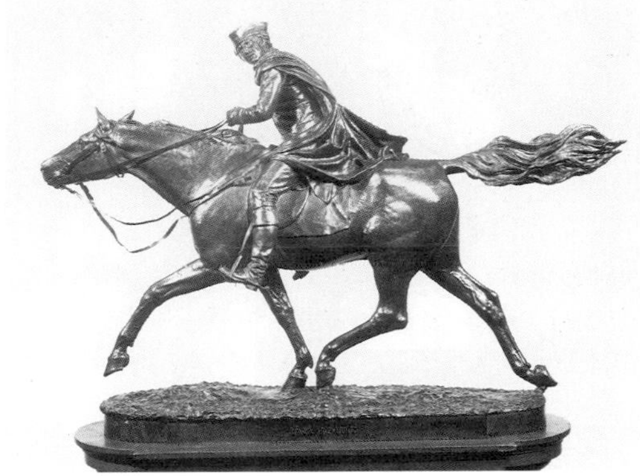

Paul Revere **(Equestrian statuette in bronze). #84.** 1883. 33⅛ x 12¼ x 31¾. Cincinnati Art Museum, Edwin and Virginia Irwin Memorial.

Portrait of a Gentleman **(Plaster bust). #109.** Unlocated.

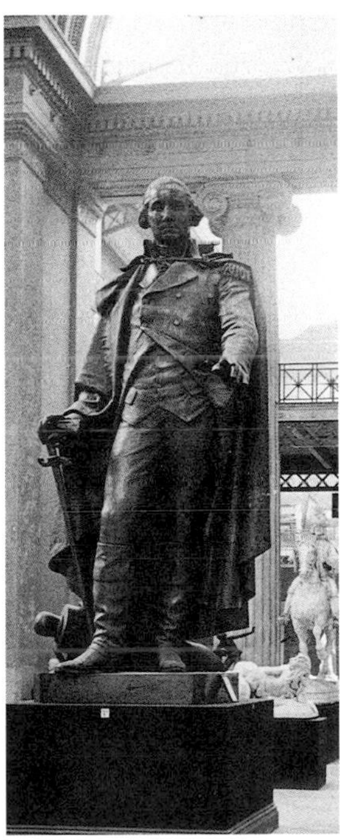

Colossal Statue of Washington **(Bronze). #110. Lent by Mr. E. F. Searles, Methuen, Mass.** *Monument to Washington*, 1889–1893. 180 h. (approx.). Forest Lawn Memorial-Park, Los Angeles, CA.

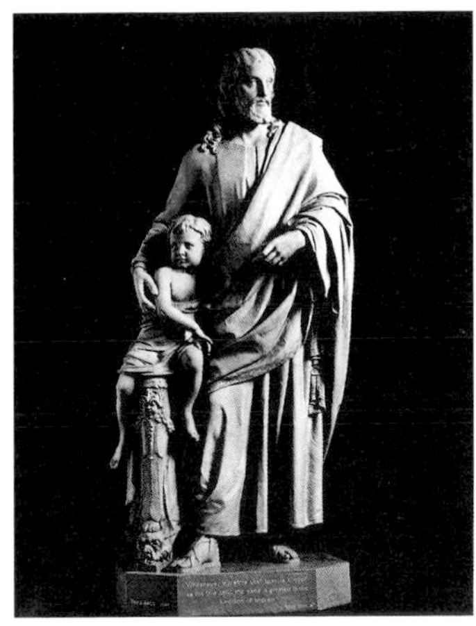

Christ and the Little Child **(Marble). #111. Lent by Mr. E. F. Searles, Methuen, Mass.** 1881. 96 x 34 x 42 (approx.). Presentation of Mary Provincial House, Methuen, MA. Photograph courtesy Index of American Sculpture, University of Delaware.

BARTLETT, **Paul W.** (Paul Wayland). **Paris, France.**
1865 New Haven, CT–1925 Paris, France
Training — Paris: EcBA (Pierre-Jules Cavelier), Jardin des Plantes (Emmanuel Frémiet), Acad. Julian.

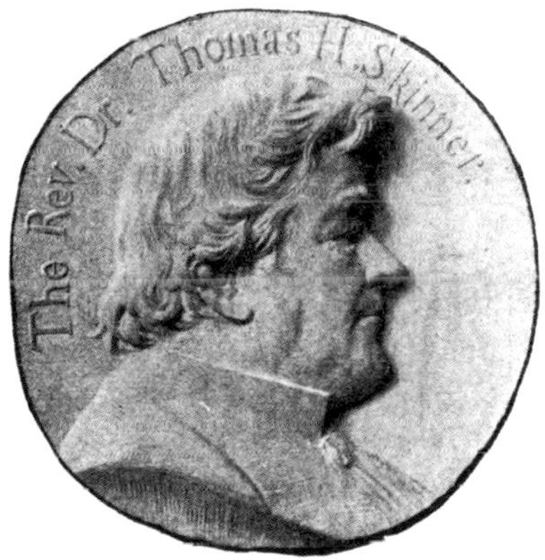

Medallion portrait of the Rev. Dr. Thomas H. Skinner **(Marble). #77.** ca. 1892. Unlocated. Illus: *Art Interchange* 28 (May 1892): 132.

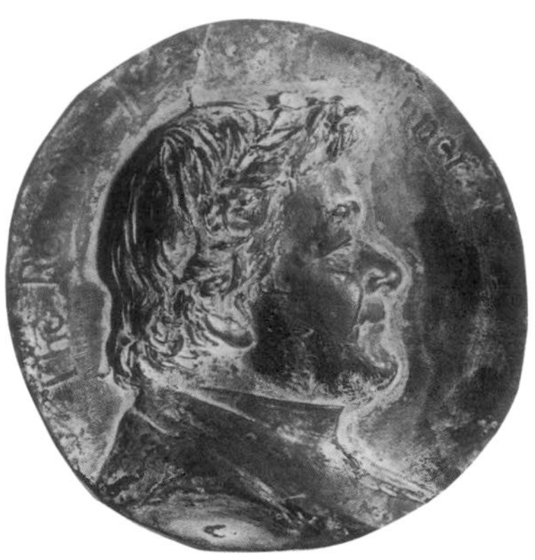

The Rev. Dr. Thomas H. Skinner. Bronze reduction, n.d. 4 15/16 diam. The Chrysler Museum, Norfolk, VA.

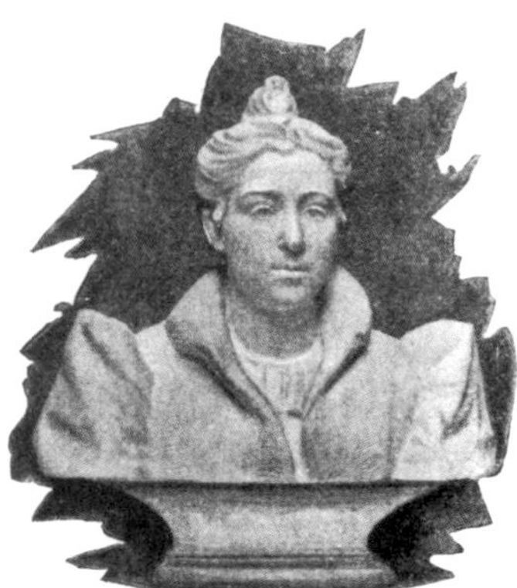

Bust of Mrs. B. (Emily Montgomery Skinner Bartlett) **(Marble). #119.** ca. 1892. Unlocated. Illus: *Art Interchange* 28 (May 1892): 132.

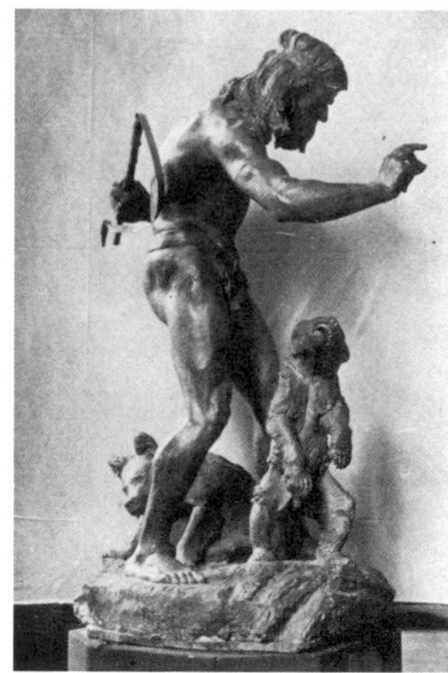

Bohemian and Bears **(Plaster). #124.** 1887. Over life-size. On loan to The Art Institute of Chicago from the artist by 1896. Presumably destroyed.[73] Illus (as *Primitive Man*): The Art Institute of Chicago, *Catalogue of Objects in the Museum* (Chicago, 1896).

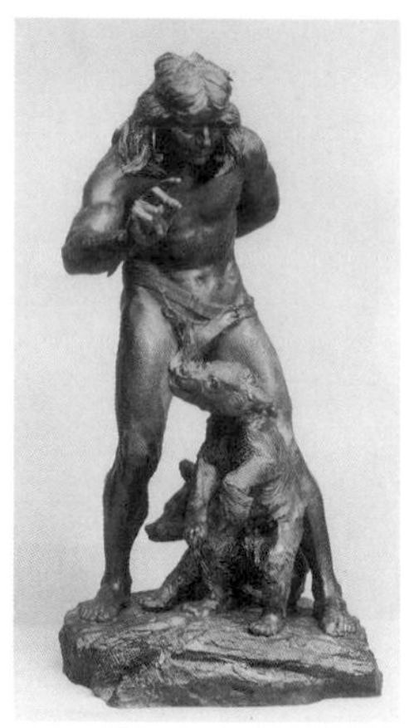

The Bohemian Bear Tamer. Bronze, cast 1889. 69⅜ x 33 x 45½. The Metropolitan Museum of Art, Gift of an Association of Gentlemen, 1891.

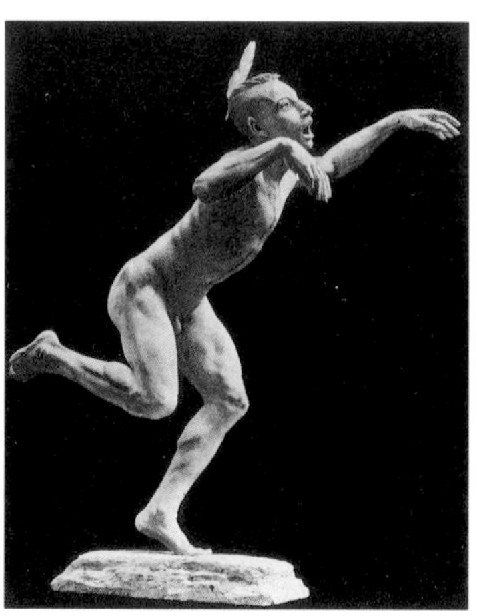

The Ghost Dance (study of the nude) **(Plaster). #132.** [$2000 in bronze]. 1889. Pennsylvania Academy of the Fine Arts until ca. 1950. Unlocated. Illus: Sadakichi Hartmann, *Modern American Sculpture* (New York: Paul Wenzel, [1918]), pl. 58.

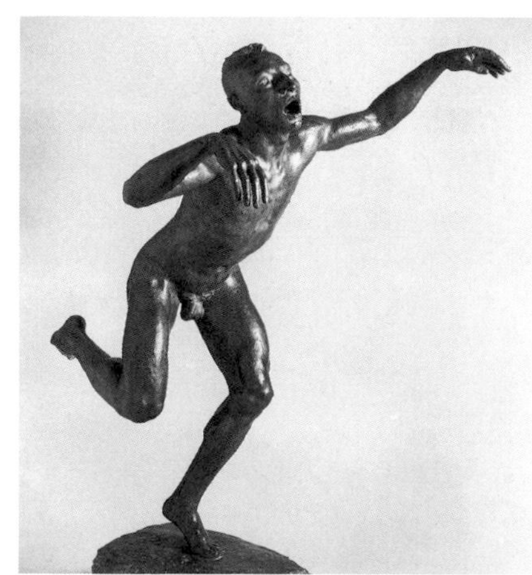

Sundance or *Ghost Dance*. Bronze, cast ca. 1889. 67⅛ x 38¼ x 60. National Museum of American Art, Smithsonian Institution, Gift of Mrs. Armistead Peter III.

BAUR, **Theodore. New York.**
1835 Wuertemberg, Germany–Residing 1896 New York, NY
Training — Munich: Royal Academy.

Panel of Joseph Jefferson as Rip Van Winkle, Bob Acres, and Dr. Pangloss **(Bronze). #103.** ca. 1892–93. Unlocated. ". . . A long relief, deeply undercut and full of figures and details, has been cast by the Henry Bonnard Company for Mr. Joseph Jefferson, and framed in heavy oak. . . . In the niche on the left stands Dr. Pangloss. . . ; in a corresponding niche on the right Bob Acres flourishes his pistol in the familiar hesitating way. A broad central space is given to a scene from 'Rip Van Winkle.' Rip is seated, and the village children are trooping about him. There is much detail — trees, ivy leaves, and houses in the background" — *New York Times*, 19 March 1893.

BISSELL, **George E.** (George Edwin). **New York.**
1839 New Preston, CT–1920 Mt. Vernon, NY
Training — Rome: English Academy; Florence; Paris: Aimé Millet, François Tabar, EcAD.

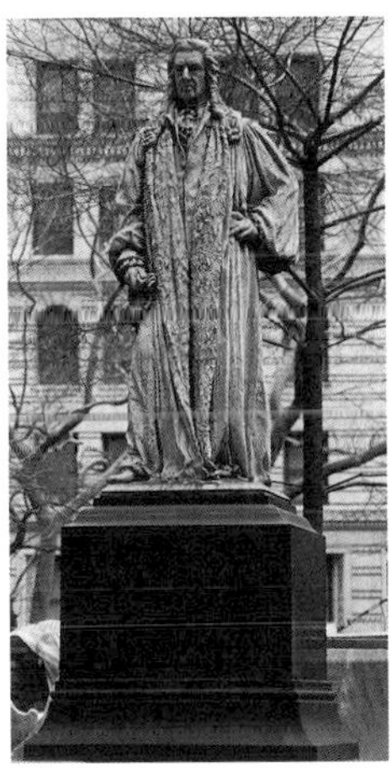

John Watts, last Royal Recorder of New York, and founder of the Leake and Watts Orphan House **(Bronze). #20.** ca. 1892. 84 h. (approx.). Trinity Church, New York, NY. Photograph by George Gurney.

BORGLUM, **J. Gurtzon** (John Gutzon de la Mothe). **Los Angeles, Cal.**
1867 Bear Lake, ID–1941 New York, NY
Training — Stephen Sinding; Los Angeles; San Francisco: Mark Hopkins Institute, Virgil Williams, William Keith, Elizabeth Collins; Paris: Acad. Julian (Jules Joseph Lefebvre), EcBA.

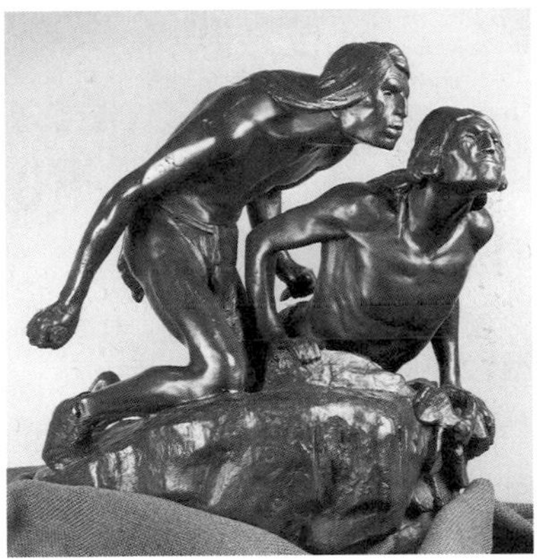

Indian Scouts **(Bronze). #147.** *Tribal Sentinels*, 1891. 13½ x 17½ x 11¾. Forest Lawn Memorial-Park, Glendale, CA.

BOYLE, J. J. (John J.). **Chicago.**
1851 New York, NY–1917 New York, NY
Training — Philadelphia: Franklin Institute, PAFA (Thomas Eakins, Joseph Bailly); Paris: Acad. Julian (Jean-Joseph Benjamin-Constant, J. P. Laurens), EcBA, Augustin Dumont, Aimé Millet.

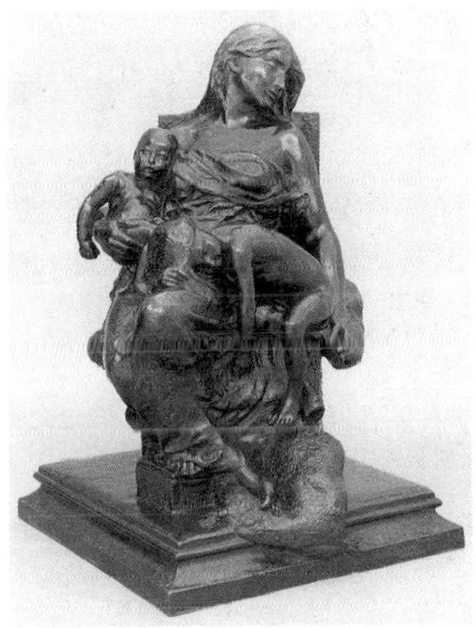

Tired Out* **(Bronze from *cire perdue*). #21. 1887. 22 x 14¼ x 14⅝. Courtesy of the Pennsylvania Academy of the Fine Arts, Philadelphia. Gift of Mrs. John J. Boyle.

BRADLEY, **Amy Aldis** (Amy Owen Aldis/Mrs. Richards Merry Bradley).[74] **Boston.**
1865 St. Albans, VT–1918 Boston, MA
Training — Paris: Augustus Saint-Gaudens, H. M. A. Chapu.

Daughter of the Pharaohs **(Plaster bust). #8.** [$150]. Unlocated.

Bust of a Boy **(Plaster). #100.** Unlocated.

BRINGHURST, Robert P. (Robert Porter). **St. Louis.**
1855 Jerseyville, IL–1925 University City, MO
Training — St. Louis: School of Fine Arts; Paris: EcBA, Augustin Dumont, Ernest-Eugéne Hiolle.

Faun — Fragment of a Fountain **(Plaster). #2.** [$3000 in bronze]. Unlocated.

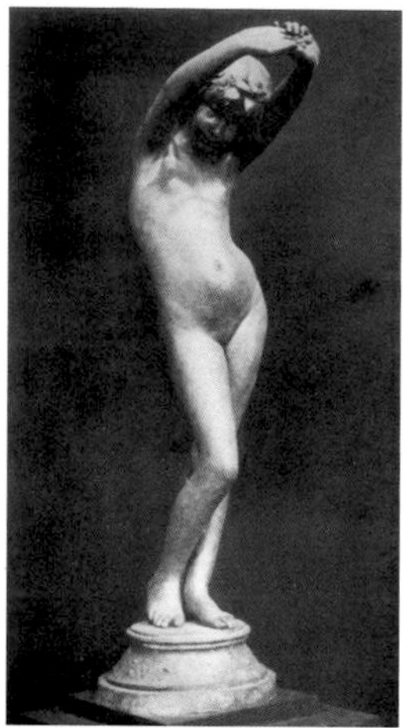

Awakening of Spring **(Terra cotta). #115.** ca. 1885. Unlocated. Illus: City Art Museum, St. Louis, *An Exhibition By Mr. Robert Porter Bringhurst and Mr. Frederick Oakes Sylvester* (St. Louis, 1911), 24.

Plaster, n.d. (ca. 1885). 56 h. The Art Institute of Chicago, 1898. Lost after transfer to The Art Institute's school, 1952. Unlocated.

BROOKS, Caroline S. (Caroline Shawk/Mrs. Samuel Brooks). **New York.**
1840 Cincinnati, OH–1913 St. Louis, MO
Training — St. Louis: Normal School.

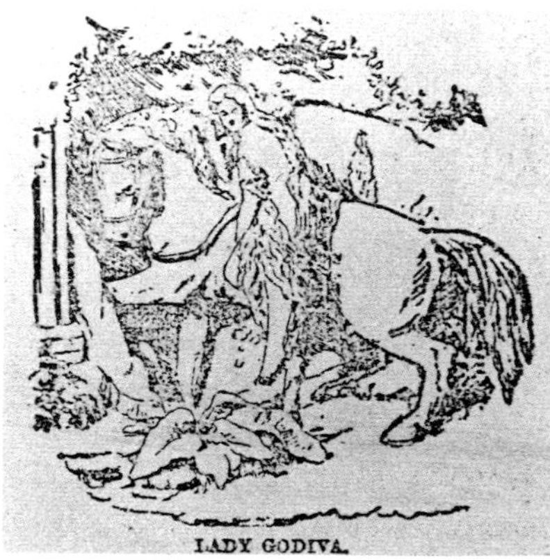

Lady Godiva Returning **(Relief in marble). #33.** 24 x 27 x 9½. Destroyed in San Francisco, CA, earthquake, 1906. Illus: Unidentified clipping, 2 Oct. 1891, The Art Institute of Chicago scrapbooks.

"La Rosa" (Vanderbilt Group) (Mrs. Marie Alicia Vanderbilt La Bau and her children, Lillian La Bau, Edith La Bau, Bertha La Bau, and Walter La Bau) **(Marble). #34.** 1886. Half life-size. Collection Mr. and Mrs. Albert G. Wheeler, Chicago, IL, 1910. Unlocated.

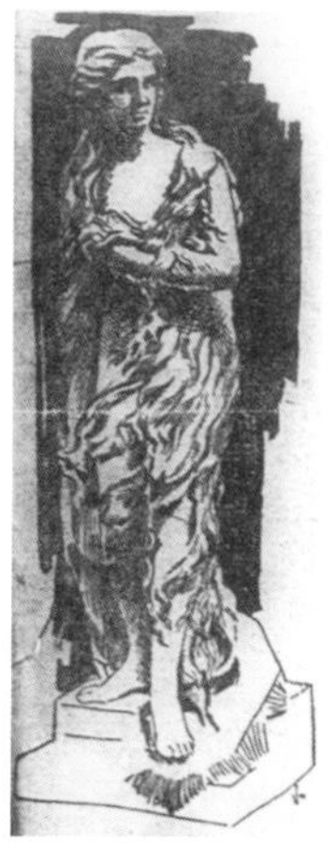

Lady Godiva **(Marble). #38.** *Godiva's Departure.* Destroyed in San Francisco, CA, earthquake, 1906. Illus: *Inter-Ocean,* Chicago, 14 June 1896.

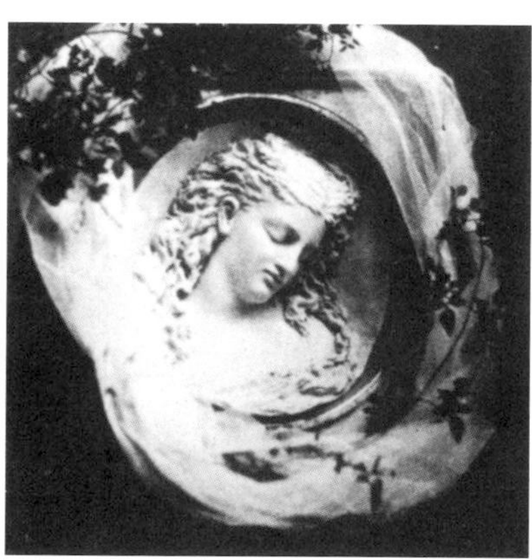

The Dreaming Iolanthe **(Relief in marble). #39.** Unlocated. Photograph courtesy Sellin Archives.

BROOKS, Carrie L. (Carol L./Mrs. Hermon Atkins MacNeil). **Chicago.**
1871 Chicago, IL–1944 New York, NY
Training — Chicago: Lorado Taft; Paris: Jean-Antoine Injalbert, Frederick W. MacMonnies.

Enid **(Head of a Child in plaster). #71. Lent by Mr. Watkins, Chicago.** Unlocated.

BUSH-BROWN, H. K. (Henry Kirke). **Newburgh, N.Y.**
1857 Ogdensburg, NY–1935 Washington, DC
Training — New York: NAD (Henry Kirke Brown); Paris: Acad. Julian (Antonin Mercié); Italy.

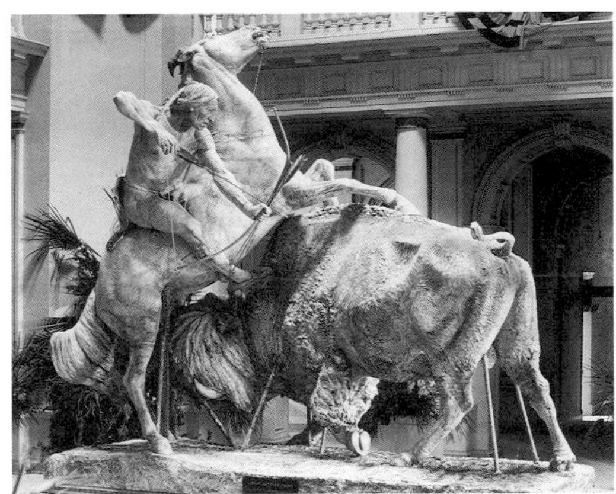

***The Buffalo Hunt* (Plaster). #56.** ca. 1893. In storage in New York, NY, warehouse, 1934. Unlocated. Photograph courtesy National Museum of American Art/National Portrait Gallery Library vertical files.

BYRNE, James A. (James Augustine). **Denver, Col.**
1835/36 Boston, MA–1908 Denver, CO

***Wounded Buffalo* (Plaster). #68.** Unlocated.

CALDER, A. Stirling (Alexander Stirling). **Philadelphia.**
1870 Philadelphia, PA–1945 New York, NY
Training — Philadelphia: PAFA (Thomas Eakins, Thomas Anshutz); Paris: Acad. Julian (H. M. A. Chapu), EcBA (J. A. J. Falguière).

***Cordelia* (Plaster bust). #4.** [$250]. ca. 1892. Unlocated.

***Boy with Ribbon* (Plaster). #79.** Unlocated.

CANNON, H. Legrand (Henry Legrand). **New York.**
1856 New York, NY–1895 New York, NY
Training — Augustus Saint-Gaudens, Jonathan S. Hartley.

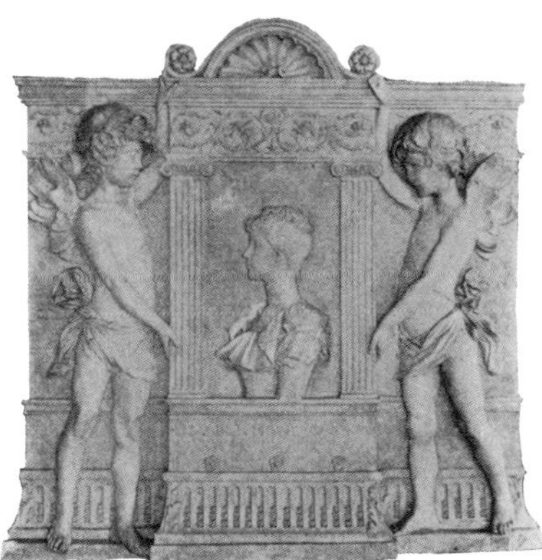

***Bas-relief of Elizabeth Mary Cannon* (Bronze). #137.** ca. 1893. Est. 48 x 43. Unlocated. Illus: *The Illustrated American* 17 (22 June 1895): 796.

CIANI, Vittorio A. (Vittorio Alfredo). **New York.**
1858 Florence, Italy–1908 Perth Amboy, NJ
Training — Rome: Academy of Fine Arts, G. Monteverde.

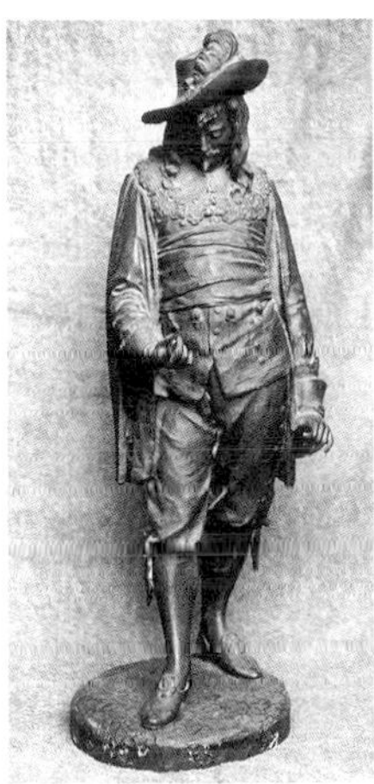

***A Cavalier* (Bronze statuette). #160.** n.d. 19½ x 8 x 6½.[75] Private collection, Metuchen, NJ.

CLARKE, Thomas Shields. Pittsburg.
1860 Pittsburgh, PA–1920 New York, NY
Training — Princeton; New York: ASL; Paris: P. A. J. Dagnan-Bouveret, Jean-Léon Gérôme, Tony Robert-Fleury, William Bouguereau, Henri-Lucien Doucet, Denys-Pierre Puech, Jean-Joseph Benjamin-Constant, H. M. A. Chapu, Acad. Julian (Jules Joseph Lefebvre).

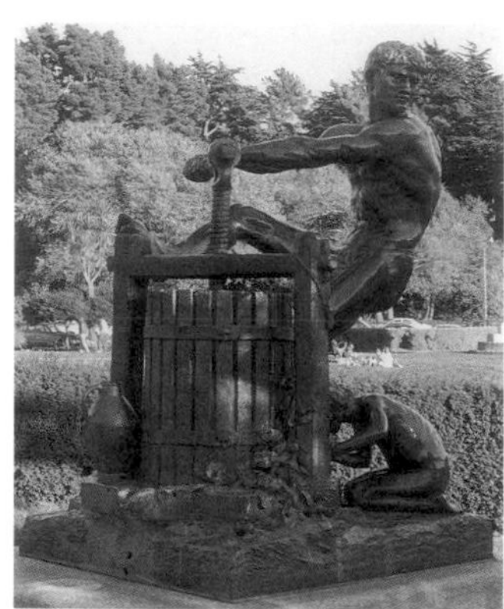

The Cider Press: a Fountain **(Bronze group). #43.** [$5000]. n.d. (1892). 90 x 51 x 56 (approx.). Golden Gate Park, San Francisco, CA. Photograph by Val Lewton.

COHEN, Katherine A. (Katherine M.). **Paris, France.**
1859 Philadelphia, PA–1914 Philadelphia, PA
Training — Philadelphia: The Philadelphia School of Design for Women, PAFA (Thomas Eakins); New York: ASL (Augustus Saint-Gaudens); Paris: Acad. Julian, Antonin Mercié, Denys-Pierre Puech, John J. Boyle, Frederick W. MacMonnies.

Bust of Henry Souther **(Plaster). #107.** [$100]. ca. 1890. Unlocated.

COPP, Ellen Rankin (Mrs. William H. Copp). **Chicago.**
1853 Atlanta, IL–Residing 1907 Chicago, IL
Training — Chicago: AIC (Lorado Taft); Munich: Fehr.

Relief portrait of Miss Harriet Monroe **(Bronze). #97.** 1893. Unlocated.

COX, Charles B. (Charles Brinton). **Philadelphia.**
1864 Philadelphia, PA–1905 Philadelphia, PA?
Training — Philadelphia: PAFA (Thomas Eakins); New York: NAD.

American Buffalo **(Bronze). #55.** [$100]. Unlocated.

CUSHING, Robert. New York.
1841 Ireland–1896 New York, NY
Training — New York: J. Q. A. Ward; Rome: Randolph Rogers.

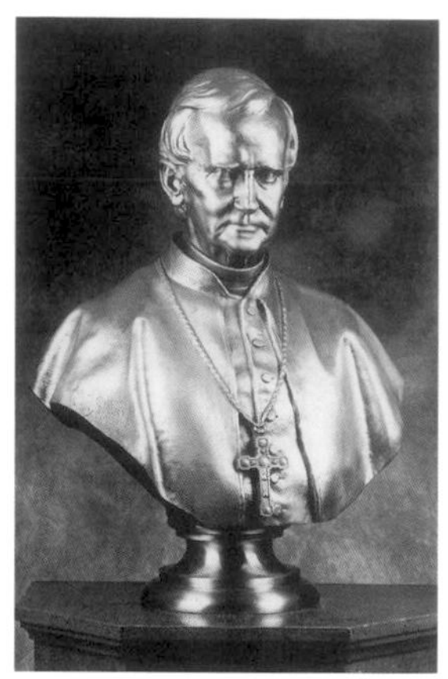

Bust of Cardinal McCloskey **(Bronze). #102.** [$750]. 1882. 29½ x 21½ x 13. Cardinal McCloskey Children's and Family Services, White Plains, NY.

DALLIN, C. E. (Cyrus Edwin). **Paris, France.**
1861 Springville, UT–1944 Arlington, MA
Training — Boston: Truman H. Bartlett; Paris: Acad. Julian (H. M. A. Chapu), Jean-Auguste Dampt.

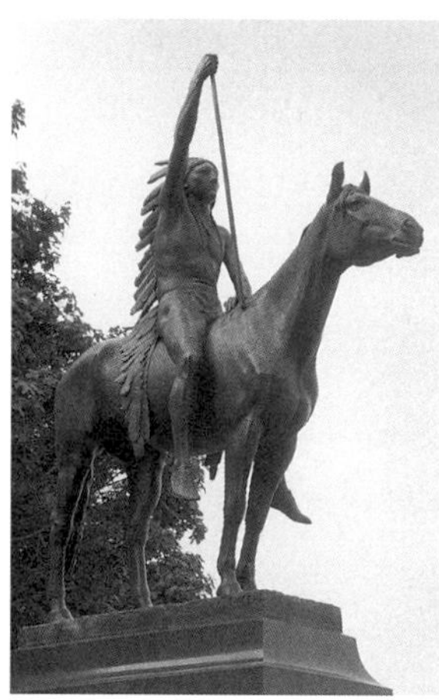

The Signal of Peace **(Bronze equestrian statue). #1.** [$6000]. 1890. Life-size. Lincoln Park, Chicago, IL. Photograph by George Gurney.

Portrait bust of Dr. I. [sic] F. Hamilton (Dr. John F. Hamilton) **(Marble). #64. Lent by Mrs. Fidelia B. Hamilton, Salt Lake City.** ca. 1892. Unlocated.

DONOGHUE, John (John Talbott). **London, England.**
1853 Chicago, IL–1903 New Haven, CT
Training — Chicago: Chicago Academy of Design; Paris: EcBA (François Jouffroy, J. A. J. Falguière).

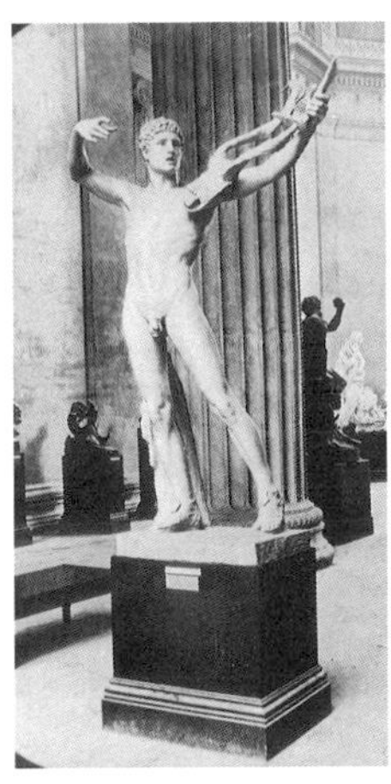

The Young Sophocles Leading the Chorus of Victory After the Battle of Salamis **(Plaster). #129.** 1885. 94 h. The Art Institute of Chicago, 1894. Presumably destroyed.[76] Photograph courtesy Ryerson and Burnham Libraries, The Art Institute of Chicago.

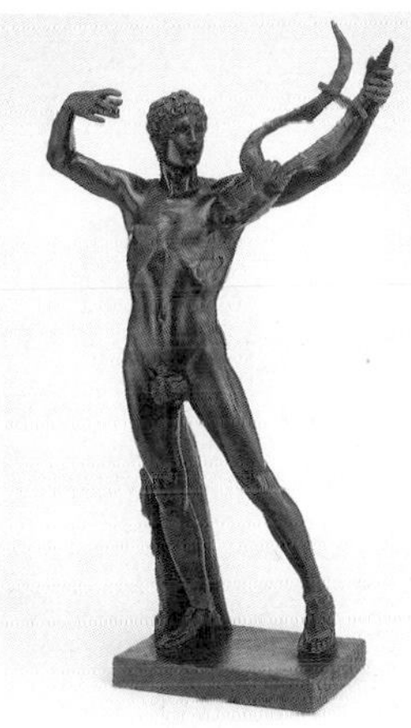

**Young Sophocles Leading Victory Chorus after Salamis.* Bronze, cast 1911. 94 x 53 x 32. The Art Institute of Chicago, Gift of Robert Allerton.

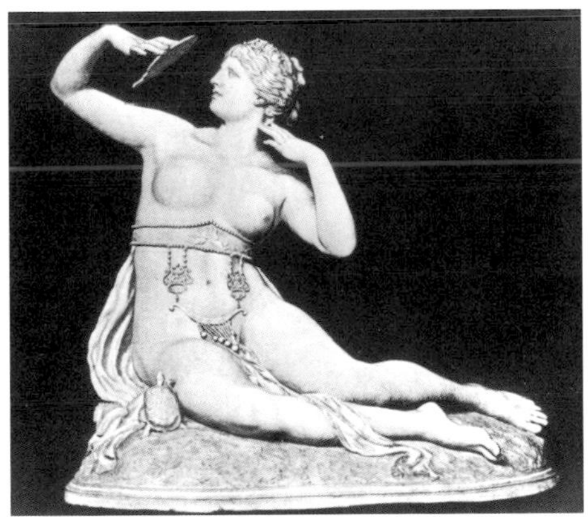

Kypros **(Plaster). #130.** ca. 1890. Unlocated. Illus (as *Venus*): Sadakichi Hartmann, *Modern American Sculpture* (New York: Paul Wenzel, [1918]), pl. 50.

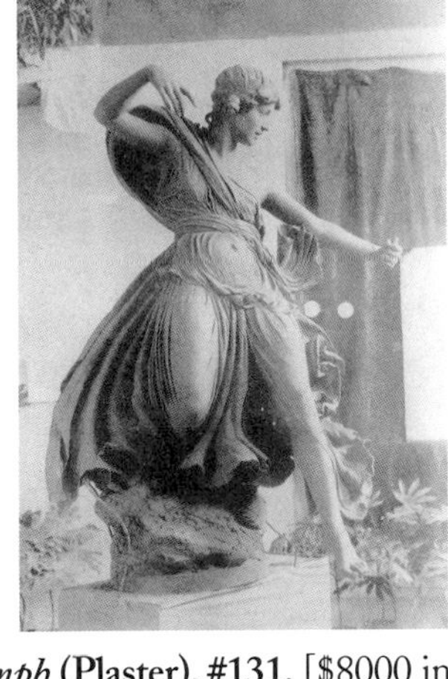

Hunting Nymph **(Plaster). #131.** [$8000 in marble]. 1886. Over life-size. Unlocated. Photograph courtesy Ryerson and Burnham Libraries, The Art Institute of Chicago.

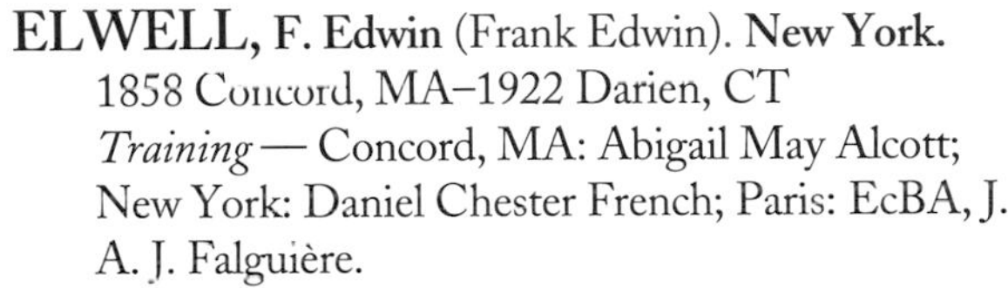

ELWELL, F. Edwin (Frank Edwin). **New York.**
1858 Concord, MA–1922 Darien, CT
Training — Concord, MA: Abigail May Alcott; New York: Daniel Chester French; Paris: EcBA, J. A. J. Falguière.

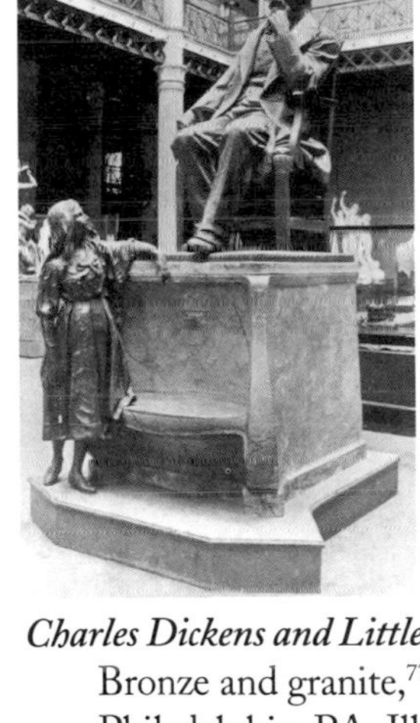

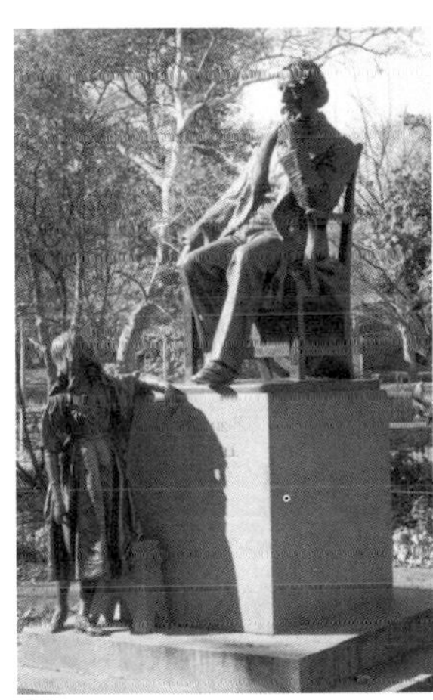

Charles Dickens and Little Nell **(Bronze). #26.** [$10,000]. Bronze and granite,[77] 1890. 80½ h. Clark Park, Philadelphia, PA. Illus *(left)*: *The White City, Beautifully Illustrated* (Chicago, 1894). Photograph *(right)* by George Gurney.

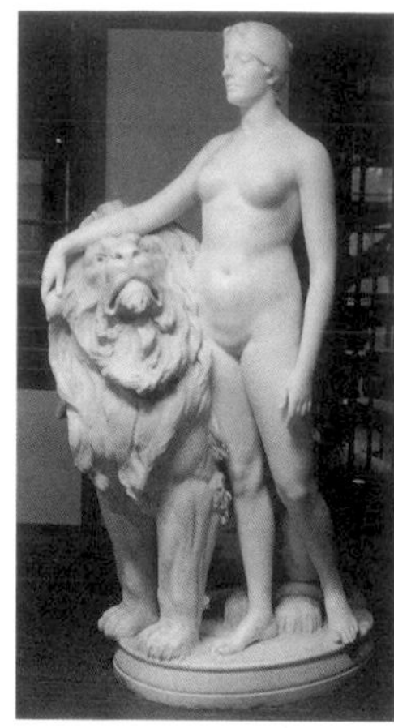

Intellect Dominating Brute Force; or Diana and the Lion **(Marble). #112.** [$6000]. 1893. 78 x 36 x 54 (approx.). Fabyan Villa, Kane County Forest Preserve, Geneva, IL. Photograph by George Gurney.

FJELDE, Jakob (Jakob H. G.). **Minneapolis, Minn.**
1859 Aalesund, Norway–1896 Minneapolis, MN
Training — Oslo: Bergslein; Copenhagen: Royal Academy; Rome: Bisson.

Bas-relief of Bert [*sic*] *Harwood* (Burt Harwood) **(Plaster). #139.** Est. 34 x 16. Unlocated.

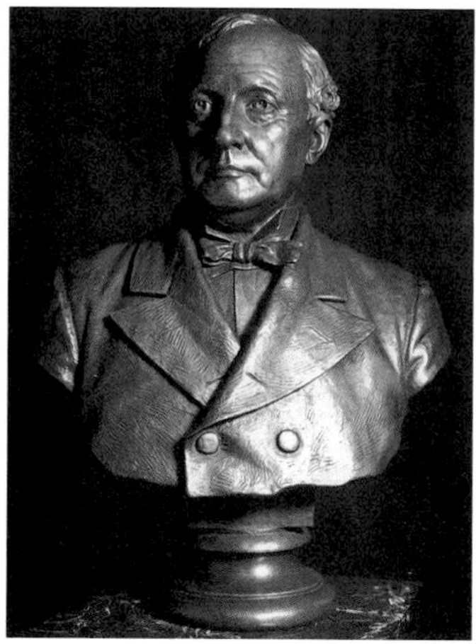

Bust of Judge Nelson **(Bronze). #156. Lent by U. S. District Court, St. Paul.** *Bust of Judge Rensselaer R. Nelson,* 1890. 28½ x 22 x 12. United States District Court, St. Paul, MN.

FRENCH, Daniel C. (Daniel Chester). **New York.**
1850 Exeter, NH–1931 Chesterwood, MA
Training — Boston: William Rimmer; New York: J. Q. A. Ward; Florence: Thomas Ball.

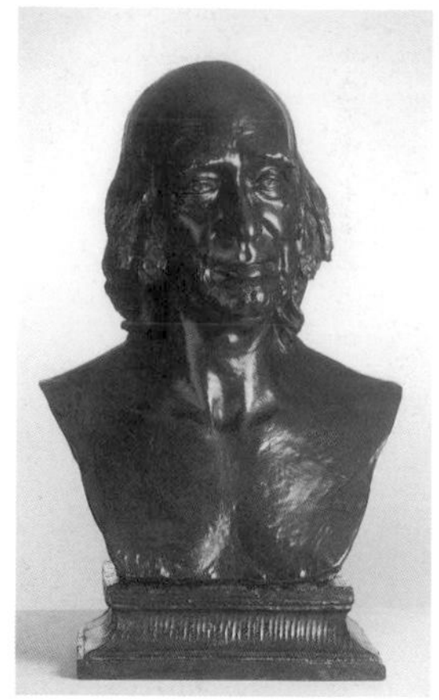

* *Bust of A. Bronson Alcott* **(Bronze). #74.** *Amos Bronson Alcott,* 1889. 22 x 11 x 7½. Chesterwood, a Museum Property of the National Trust for Historic Preservation, Stockbridge, MA.

The Angel of Death and the Sculptor **(Plaster). #145.** 1891. 82 x 100 x 25 (approx.). The Art Institute of Chicago, 1894. Destroyed, 1949.

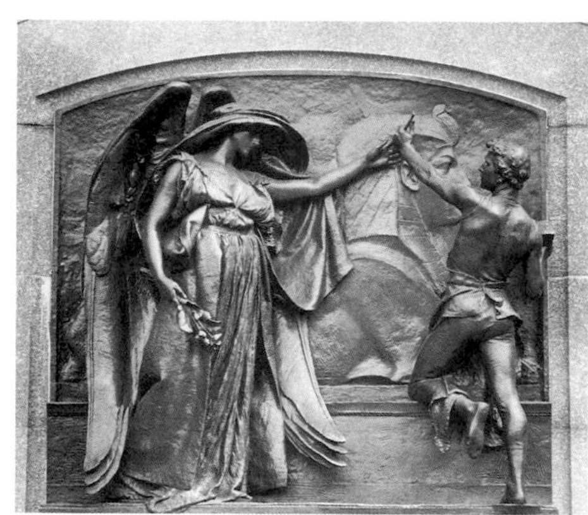

Milmore Memorial. Bronze, cast 1892. 82 x 100 x 25 (approx.). Forest Hill Cemetery, Jamaica Plain, MA. Photograph courtesy Bernie Cliff.

GELERT, J. (Johannes Sophus). **Chicago.**
1852 Nybel, Denmark–1923 New York, NY
Training — Copenhagen: Royal Academy; Paris; Berlin: Royal Academy (Albert Wolff, Rudolph Siemering); Rome.

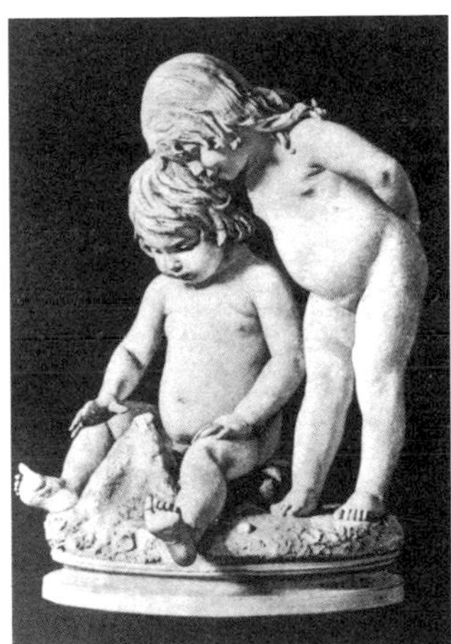

The Little Architect **(Plaster group). #28.** [$3000 in bronze]. ca. 1882. 37 h. Unlocated. Illus: Sadakichi Hartmann, *Modern American Sculpture* (New York: Paul Wenzel, [1918]), pl. 55.

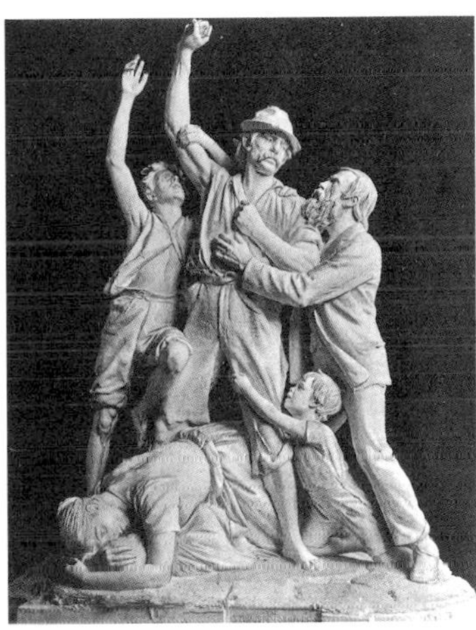

The Struggle for Work (A group of figures in plaster, represented as contending for a work ticket thrown from a factory window). **#93.** [$30,000 in bronze]. 1892. Presumably destroyed. Illus: Sadakichi Hartmann, *Modern American Sculpture* (New York: Paul Wenzel, [1918]), pl. 40.

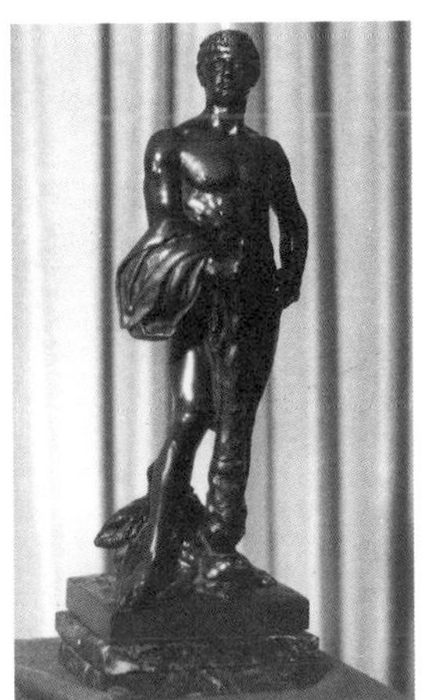

Theseus, Victor over the Minotaur **(Bronze statuette).** **#149.** [$500]. 1886. 17¼ x 6. Collection Robert A. Gelert, Sr., Palm Desert, CA.

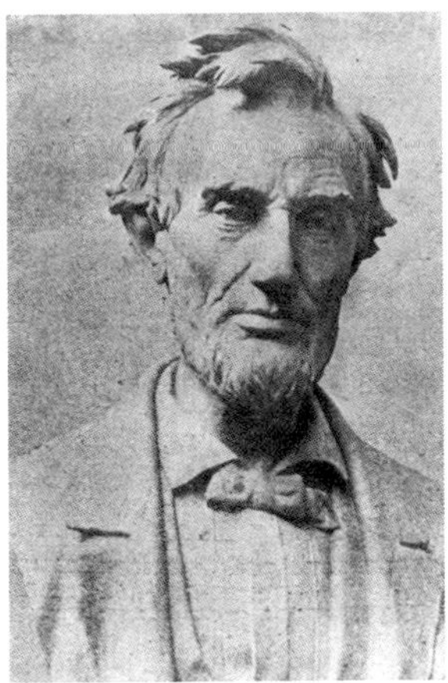

Bust of Abraham Lincoln, heroic size **(Plaster). #152.** [$1200 in bronze]. ca. 1892. Unlocated. Illus: *The Graphic* [Chicago], 13 Feb. 1892, 119.

Bronze later version, 1894. Life-size. Collection Robert A. Gelert, Sr., Palm Desert, CA.

GRAFLY, Charles. Philadelphia.

1862 Philadelphia, PA–1929 Philadelphia, PA
Training — Philadelphia: PAFA (Thomas Eakins, Thomas Anshutz); Paris: Acad. Julian (H. M. A. Chapu), Jean-Auguste Dampt.

A Bad Omen **(Plaster). #70.** [$1800]. 1891. Life-size. On permanent loan to the Detroit Institute of Art by 1899. Lost or destroyed during or after transfer to the University of Michigan, 1918. Unlocated.

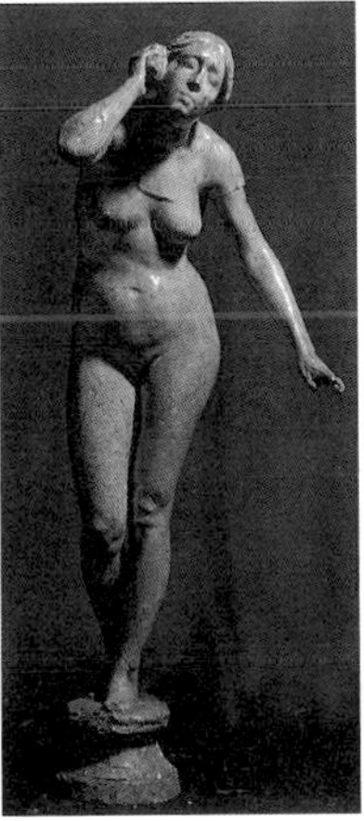

Mauvais Présage. Plaster study, 1891. 23 h. Courtesy of the Edwin A. Ulrich Museum of Art, The Wichita State University, Endowment Association Art Collection, Wichita, KS.

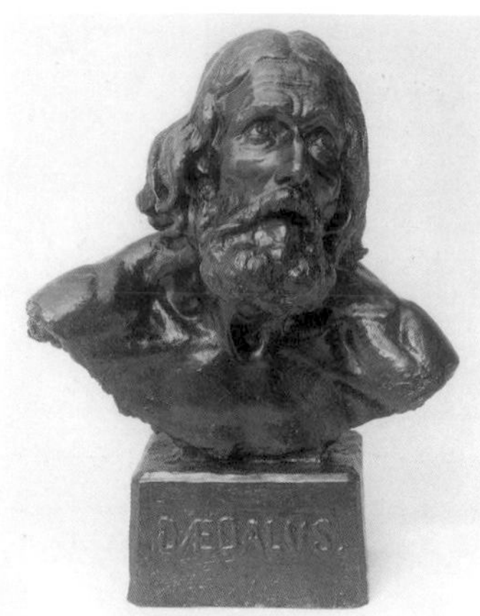

Daedalus (Bronze). **#123. Lent by the Pennsylvania Academy of the Fine Arts, Philadelphia.** Modeled 1889, cast 1892. 23¾ x 19 x 15. Courtesy of the Pennsylvania Academy of the Fine Arts, Philadelphia. Henry D. Gilpin Fund.

GRIFFITH, J. Milo (James Milo). **Chicago.**
1843 Werngoy, Wales–1897 London, England
Training — London: Lambeth School of Art, Royal Academy.

Nubian Captive **(Plaster). #6.** [$500 in bronze]. 1892. Unlocated.

Study of a Female Head **(Marble medallion). #9.** [$50]. 1891. Unlocated.

Sabrina, Goddess of the Severn **(Marble). #31.** 1883. Unlocated.

Dawn **(Marble medallion). #140.** [$200]. 1892. 16 diam. Unlocated. "... Figure of a winged child..." — Milo Griffith Scrapbook, National Museum of Wales.

Coursing during the time of Queen Elizabeth **(Bronze). #148.** [$200]. 1883. Est. 20 h. Unlocated. "Man and five dogs.... Carrying home dead deer." — Milo Griffith Scrapbook, National Museum of Wales.

HAMMOND, Jane Nye. Boston.
1857 New York, NY–1901 Providence, RI
Training — Boston: BMFA; Paris: Paul W. Bartlett, Raphaël Collin, Jean-Antoine Injalbert.

A Medallion **(Plaster). #66.** [$75]. Unlocated.

Lucie **(Bronze relief). #99.** [$150]. Unlocated.

HARTLEY, J. S. (Jonathan Scott). **New York.**
1845 Albany, NY–1912 New York, NY
Training — Albany, NY: Erastus D. Palmer; London: Royal Academy; Berlin; Rome; Paris.

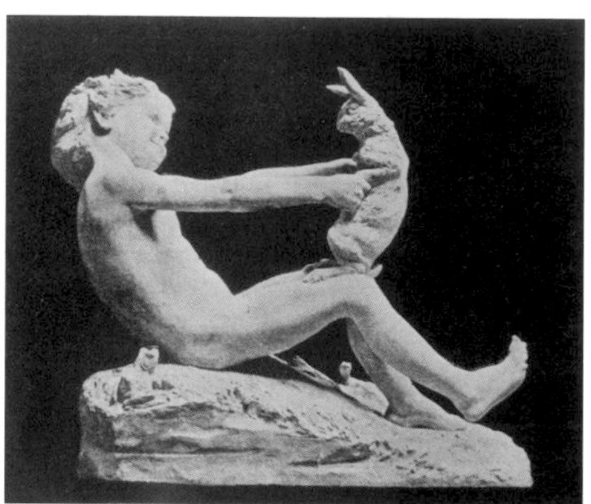

Pan **(Bronze group). #122.** [$500 copies]. **Lent by Dr. Fiske, Brooklyn, N.Y.** 1885. Unlocated. Illus (in plaster): The Art Club of Philadelphia, *Fifth Annual Exhibition, Oil Paintings and Sculpture* (Philadelphia, 1893), 20.

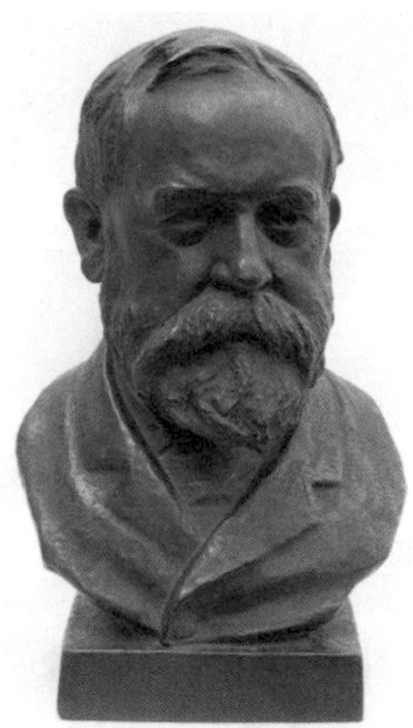

Bust of William Conant Church **(Bronze). #150. Lent by Col. W. C. Church, New York.** 1890. 18½ x 11½ x 10. Mary Church Kidd Collection, Mrs. Nancy Kidd, Westborough, MA. Photograph by George Gurney.

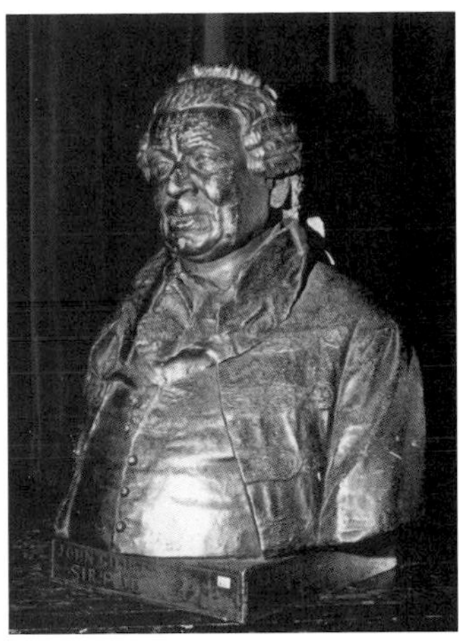

John Gilbert as Sir Peter Teazle **(Bronze). #158.** [$450]. 1889. 26 x 21 x 18. The Hampden-Booth Theatre Library, Players Club, New York, NY.

HYATT, **Harriet Randall** (Mrs. Alfred G. Mayor). **Boston.**
1868 Salem, MA–1960 Bethel, CT
Training — Boston: Cowles Art School (Dennis M. Bunker), Ross Turner, Henry H. Kitson, Ernest L. Major.

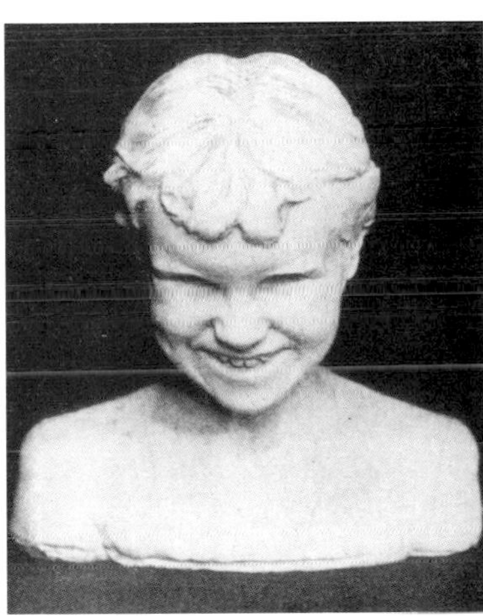

Head of Laughing Girl **(Plaster). #125.** [$35]. Unlocated. Illus (as *Head of a Laughing Child*): *The Arts* 3 (Oct. 1894): 103.

KEMEYS, **Edward. Chicago.**[78]
1843 Savannah, GA–1907 Washington, DC
Training — largely self-taught.

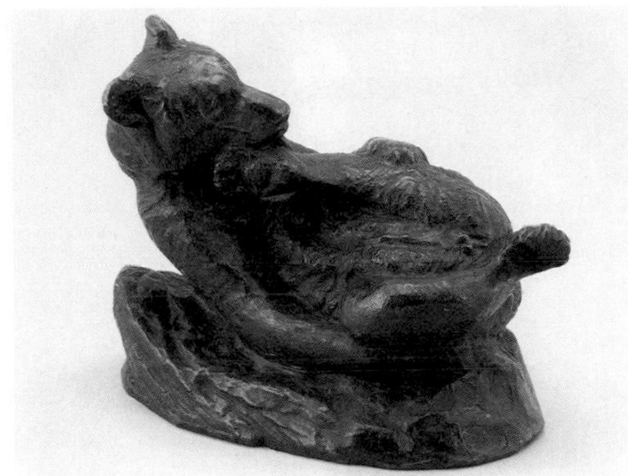

American Black Bear. **#25.** [$200 in bronze]. *Bear* or *The Soul of Contentment.* Bronze, 1886. 10½ x 12½. The Art Institute of Chicago, Gift of Margaret S. Watson.

Battle of the Bulls. **#27.** [$400 in bronze]. Before 1890. Est. 10 x 14 x 6. The Art Institute of Chicago, 1899. Deaccessioned and sold or given to Peoria, IL, ca. 1930. Unlocated. "Two buffalo standing end to end" — as seen in installation photograph.

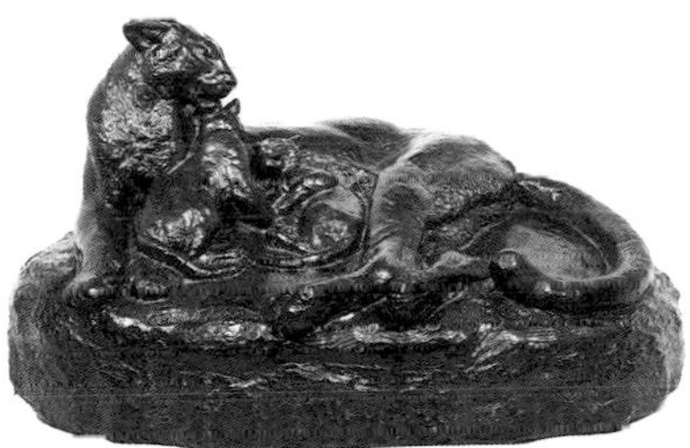

American Panther and her Cubs.* **#44. [$?000 (illegible) in bronze]. Plaster, 1878. 31⅝ x 60⅛ x 42⅝. National Museum of American Art, Smithsonian Institution, Gift of Edward Kemeys.

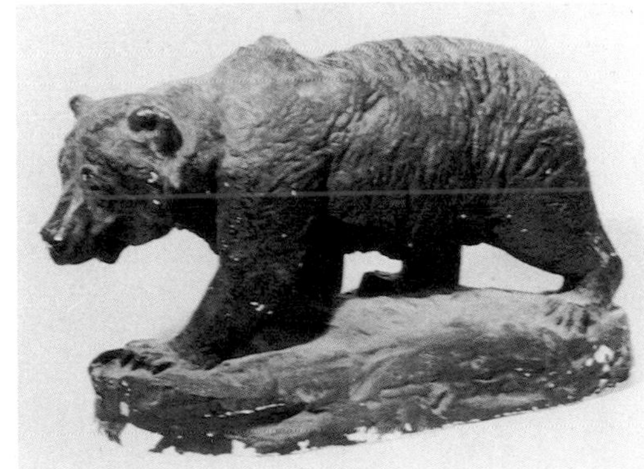

Old Ephriam. **#47.** [$400 in bronze]. Plaster, before 1885. 14½ x 24¼ x 7½. Formerly on loan to the National Museum of American Art, Smithsonian Institution, L.1907.1.32. Returned to Mr. J. Willis Johnson, San Angelo, TX, 1985.

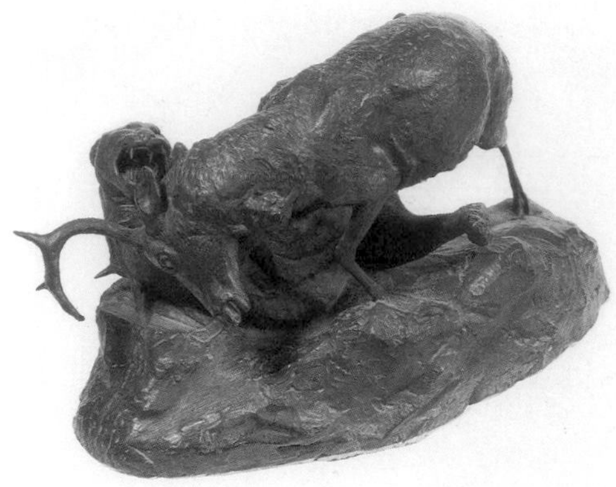

Fighting Panther and Deer. **#48.** [$2500 in bronze]. Bronze. 16¾ x 27½ x 12⅞. Formerly on loan to the National Museum of American Art, Smithsonian Institution, L.1907.1.2. Returned to Mr. Christopher Clark, Upperville, VA, 1971.

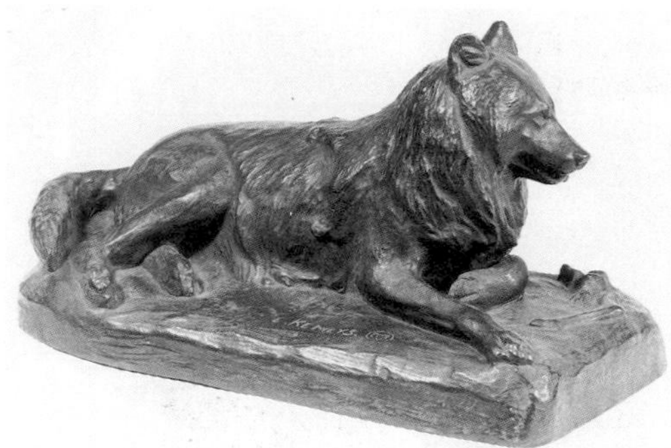

After the Feast. **#49.** [$150 in bronze]. *Grey Wolf and Carcass*. Bronze, 1878. 7½ x 14¼ x 7 3/16. Formerly on loan to the National Museum of American Art, Smithsonian Institution, L.1907.1.6. Returned to Mr. Christopher Clark, Upperville, VA, 1971.

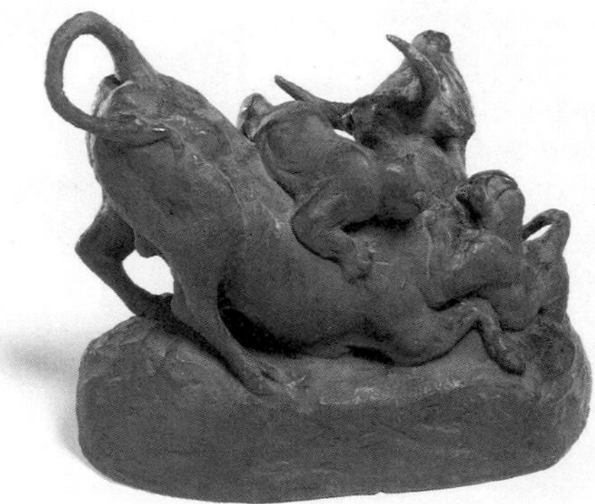

Texan Bull and Jaguars. **#50.** [$375 in bronze]. *Texan Bull Pulled Down by Jaguars*. Plaster, before 1891. 11 x 13⅛ x 6¼. National Museum of American Art, Smithsonian Institution, Gift of Edward Kemeys.

American Bison. **#51.** Unlocated.

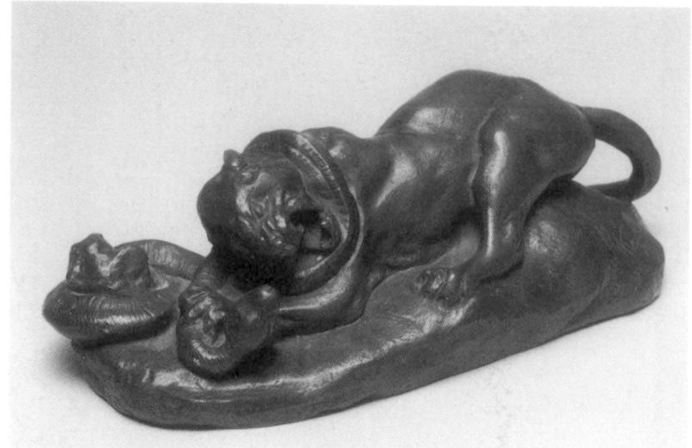

Jaguar and Boa-constrictor. **#52.** [$100 in bronze]. Bronze, 1877. 4⅛ x 11 7/16 x 5 3/16. Collection Dr. Marvin Reingold, Lawrence, NY.

American Bay Lynx. **#53.** [$125 in bronze]. Unlocated.

Grappling His Game. **#54.** [$1000 in bronze]. *Jaguar and Peccary*. Plaster, n.d. (before 1885). 13½ x 33 x 14½. Formerly on loan to the National Museum of American Art, Smithsonian Institution, L.1907.1.39. Returned to Mr. J. Willis Johnson, San Angelo, TX, 1985.

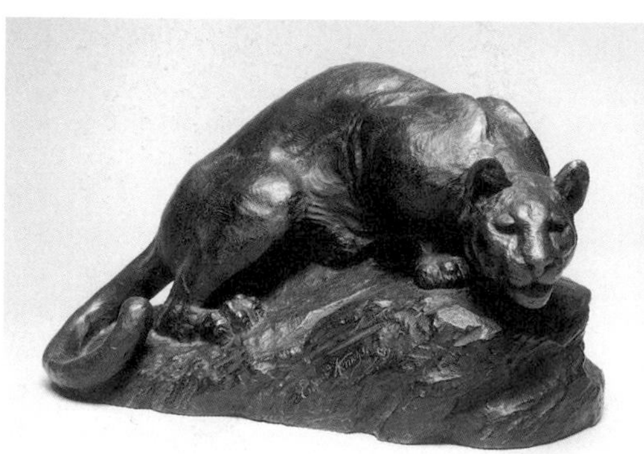

The Still Hunt. **#57.** [$350]. Bronze, n.d. 11¾ x 21 x 10¼ (approx.). Sold Christie's, New York, NY, 30 May 1986, lot 147. Unlocated. Photograph courtesy National Museum of American Art, Smithsonian Institution.

KITSON, Henry H. (Henry Hudson). **Boston.** 1863 Huddersfield, England–1947 Boston, MA *Training*— Huddersfield, England: Mechanics Institute; Paris: EcAD (Aimé Millet, Ganter), EcBA (Augustin Dumont, Jean-Marie Bienaime Bonnaissieux).

Christ Crucified **(Plaster). #104.** 1891. 95½ x 64⅞ x 21½ (approx.). Unlocated.

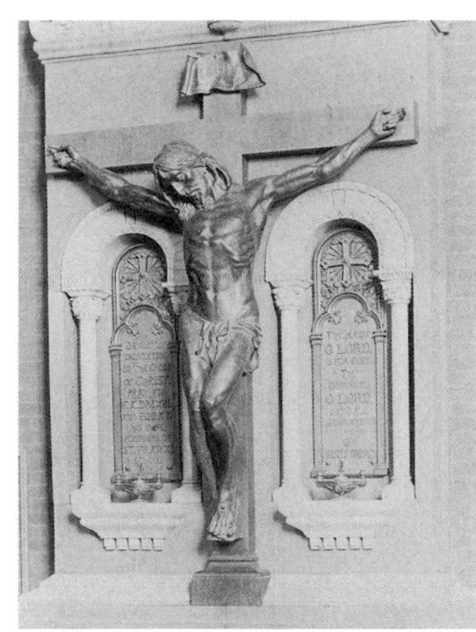

Bronze, 1891. 95½ x 64⅞ x 21½. Sacred Heart Church, Oxford, PA. Photograph (in former location at St. Francis Industrial School, Eddington, PA) courtesy Archives of the Sisters of the Blessed Sacrament, Bensalem, PA.

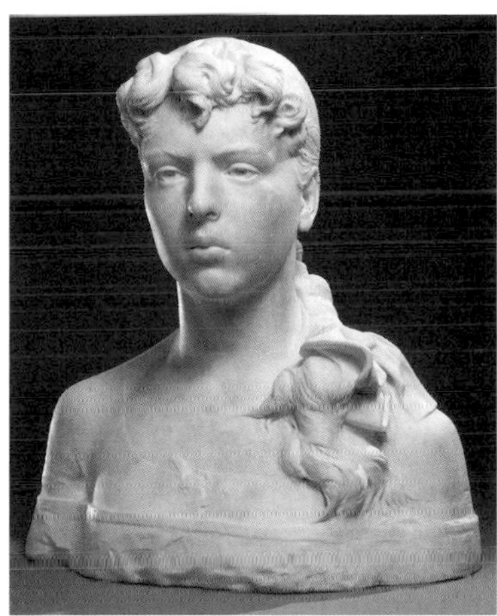

Portrait bust **(Marble). #117. Owned by Mrs. Ruggles, Boston.** *Miss Theo Alice Ruggles*, 1888.
20 x 18½ x 10¾. Museum of Fine Arts, Boston, Anonymous Gift in Memory of John and Helen Kitson.

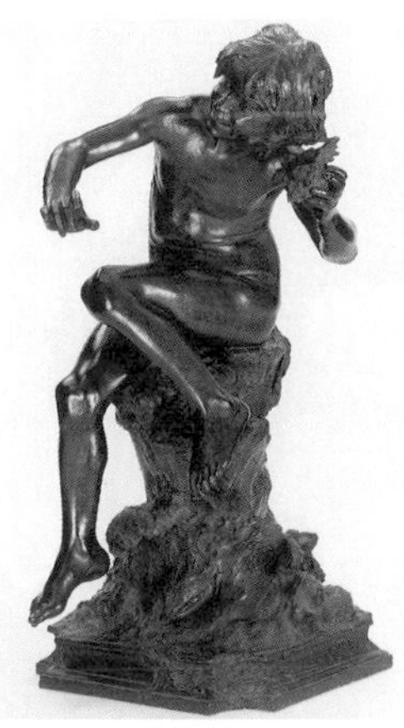

Music of the Sea **(Bronze). #118. Owned by Mrs. D. P. Kimball, Boston.** 1884. 44¾ x 24 x 29½. Museum of Fine Arts, Boston, Gift of David P. Kimball.

The Age of Stone **(Plaster). #146.** Not exhibited.

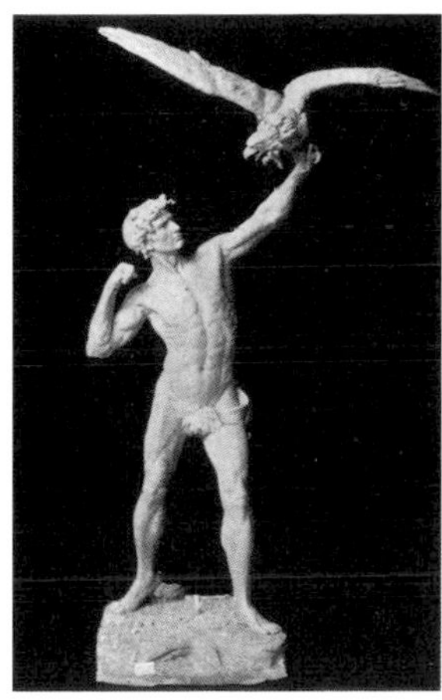

The Falconer (Plaster). Exhibited in place of #146. 1889. Over life-size. Presumably destroyed. Illus (as *Man and Eagle*): William H. Downes, "New England Art at the World's Fair," *New England Magazine* 8 (July 1893): 368.

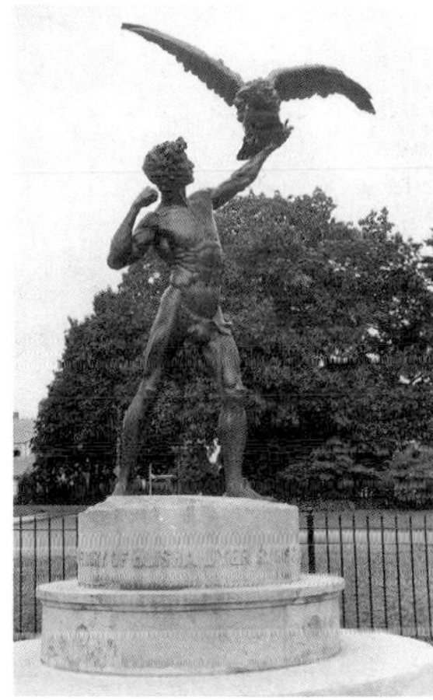

Elisha Dyer Memorial. Bronze, n.d. (1889). Over life-size. Roger Williams Park, Providence, RI. Photograph by Constance Worthington.

KRETSCHMAR, **Howard** (Howard Sigismund). **Chicago.**
1845 St. Louis, MO –1933 Dupage County, IL
Training — Munich: Royal Academy; Paris; Rome; Florence.

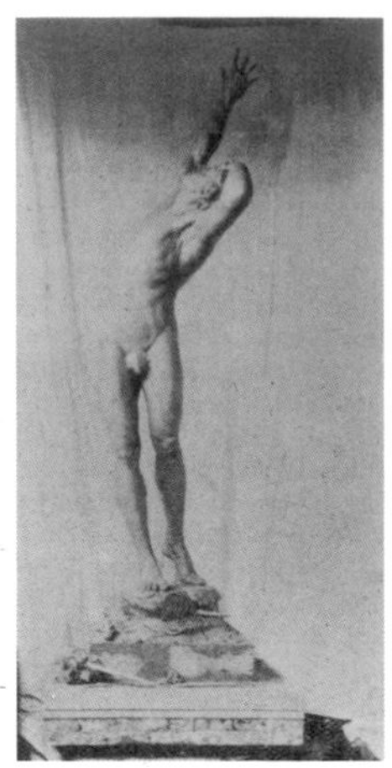

Tantalus (Plaster). #95. Unlocated. Illus: *The Arts* 3 (Oct. 1894): 115.

LINDSTROM, August (August Fredrik Lindström). Chicago.

1865 Vasteras, Sweden –1945 Vastmanland, Sweden
Training — Stockholm: Konstakademien.

Bust of John Ericsson (Plaster). #105. [$500]. Unlocated.

LOEHER, Aloys. Chicago.[79]

1850 Paderborn, Germany – 1906 Silver Spring, NY
Training — M. Widnmann; Vienna: K. Zumbusch.

Bust of Mrs. Jessie Bartlett Davis (Marble). #29. Lent by Mr. William Davis, Chicago. Unlocated.

MARTINY, Philip. New York.

1858 Strasbourg, France–1927 New York, NY
Training — Strasbourg, France: Eugene Dock; New York: Augustus Saint-Gaudens.

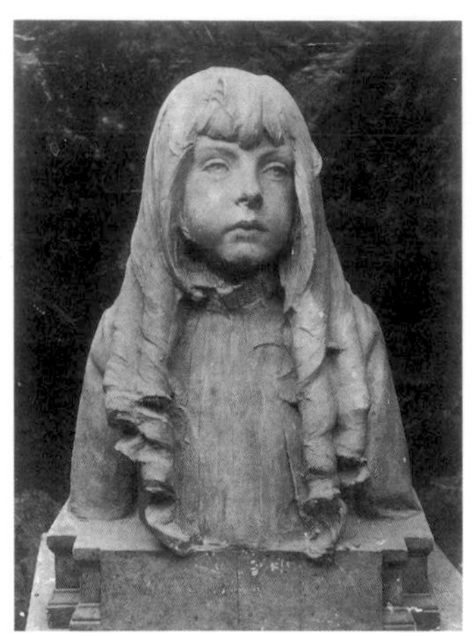

Portrait bust of a Child (Blanche Martiny) (Plaster). #73. ca. 1888. Unlocated.

MILLS, J. Harrison (John Harrison). New York.

1842 Bowmansville, NY–1916 Evans, NY
Training — Buffalo, NY: William Lautz.

Portrait medallion (Plaster). #10. Unlocated.

MURRAY, Samuel (Samuel Aloysius). Philadelphia.

1870 Philadelphia, PA–1941 Philadelphia, PA
Training — Philadelphia: PAFA (Thomas Eakins).

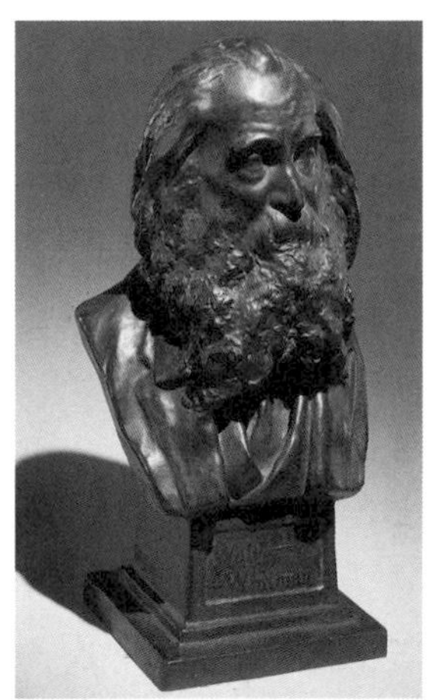

Portrait bust of Walt Whitman (Bronze). #59. Lent by Mr. Thomas B. Harned, Philadelphia. 1892. 13⅜ x 7⅛ x 5⅛. Hirshhorn Museum and Sculpture Garden, Smithsonian Institution.

Study of a Child's Head (William Brown) (Bronze). #61. Lent by Mrs. Brown, Philadelphia. 1892. Unlocated.

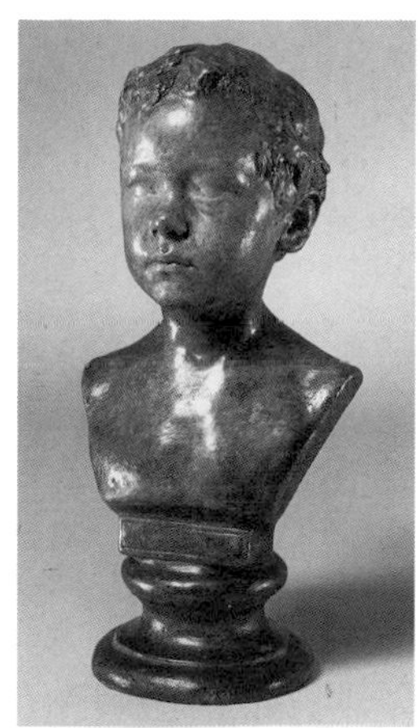

Boy's Head (William Brown). Plaster, 1892. 10⅛ x 4¾ x 4⅛. Hirshhorn Museum and Sculpture Garden, Smithsonian Institution.

---

† **NIEHAUS,** C. H. (Charles Henry). **New York.**
1855 Cincinnati, OH–1935 Cliffside Park, NJ
Training — Cincinnati: McMicken School of Design; Munich: Royal Academy.

Historical Door for Trinity Church, New York **(Plaster). #5. The panels represent: (1) Hendrick Hudson discovering Manhattan Island; (2) Barclay preaching to the Indians; (3) Washington entering St. Paul's after his Inauguration; (4) Consecration of the four Bishops, 1832; (5) Consecration of Trinity Church; (6) Dedication of the Reredos in Trinity Church, 1877.** [$2500 copies]. 1892. Two doors, each: 90⅛ x 41 (approx.); individual panels: 23¼ x 28. Presumably destroyed.

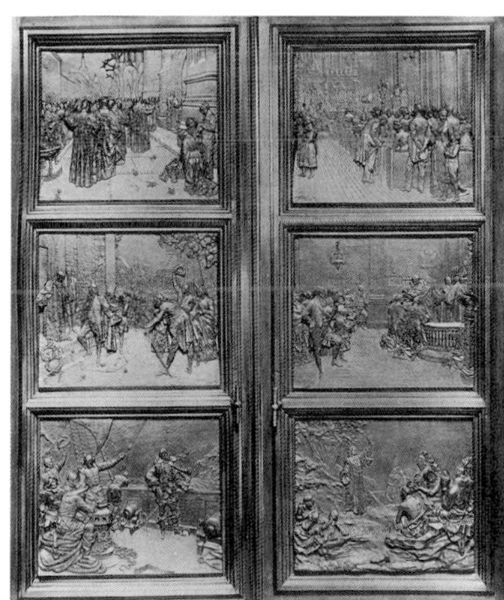

Bronze, 1892. 90¼ x 82. Trinity Church, New York, NY. Illus: Sadakichi Hartmann, *Modern American Sculpture* (New York: Paul Wenzel, [1918]), pl. 35.

Athlete **(Plaster). #11.** [$5000]. 1883. 85 h. (approx.). Destroyed by vandals in artist's studio, 1936.

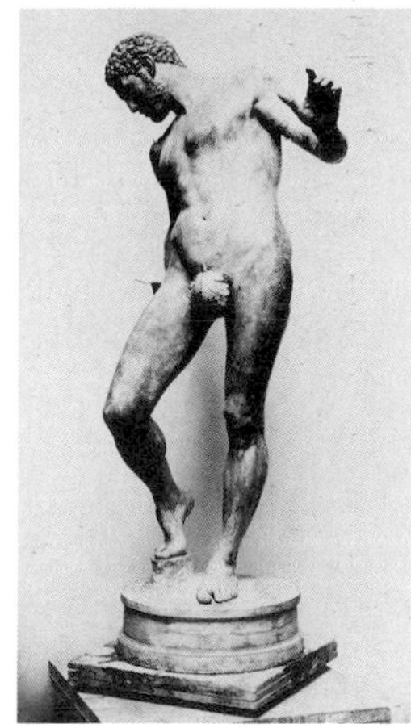

The Scraper. Bronze, cast 1912. 85 h. The Metropolitan Museum of Art, 1912. Sold, Parke-Bernet Galleries, New York, NY, 8 June 1956, lot 301. Unlocated. Illus: Archives of The Metropolitan Museum of Art.

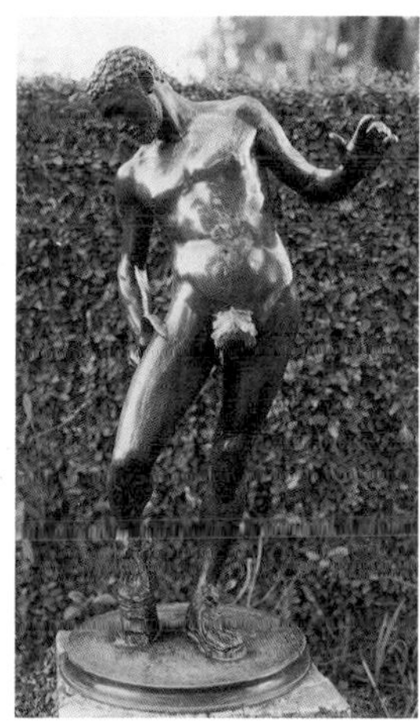

The Scraper. Bronze reduction, cast ca. 1935. 35½ h. Brookgreen Gardens, Murrells Inlet, SC.

O'DONOVAN, William Russell (William Rudolph). **New York.**
1844 Preston County, VA–1920 New York, NY
Training — self-taught.

Bust of Thomas Eakins **(Bronze). #154.** 1892. Unlocated.[80] "Mr. William Rudolph O'Donovan has had his portrait painted by Mr. Thomas Eakins as he worked in sculptor's apron at a portrait bust; but that bust was a portrait of the painter himself. Thus, as one hand washes another, the sculptor modeled the painter while the painter put on canvas the sculptor" *New York Times*, 5 April 1892.

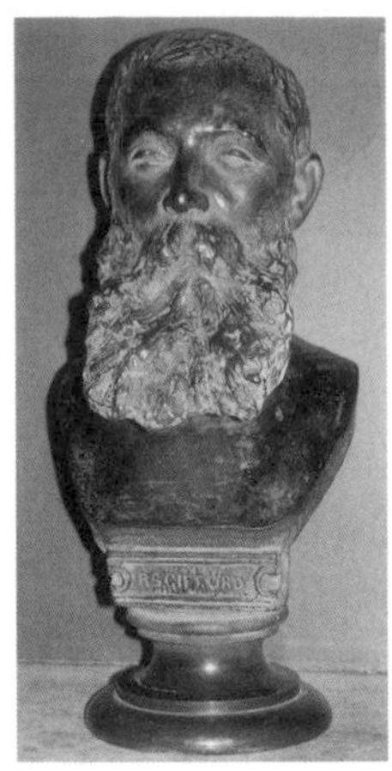

Bust of R. Swain Gifford **(Bronze). #155.** 1879. 23 x 10½ x 10. The Century Association, New York, NY. Photograph by George Gurney.

PARTRIDGE, William Ordway. Milton, Mass.
1861 Paris, France–1930 New York, NY
Training — Florence (Fortunato Galli); Paris: M. J. A. Mercié; Rome: Pio Welonski.

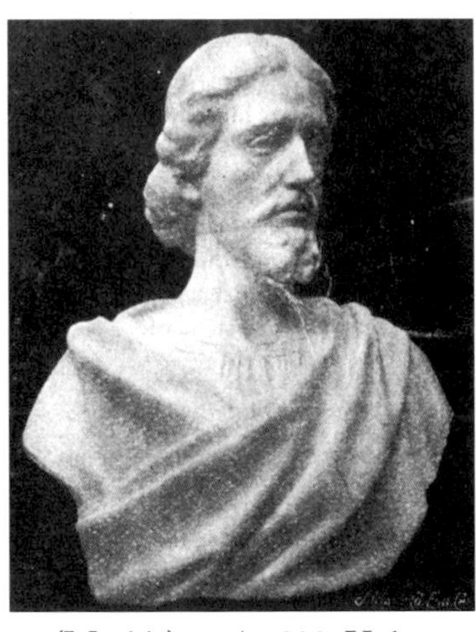

Head of Christ **(Marble). #15.** 1892. Unlocated. Illus: Scrapbook in the Collection of Mrs. William A. M. Burden, Courtesy of Dr. Marjorie P. Balge.

Plaster replica of statue of Shakespeare for Lincoln Park, Chicago. **#18.** 1893. 78 h. (approx.). Presumably destroyed.

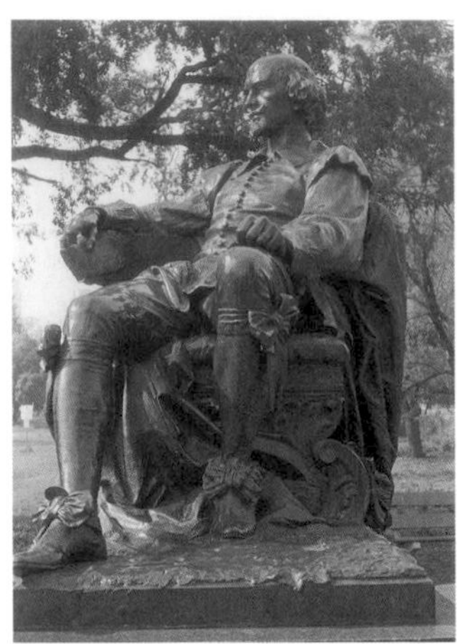

William Shakespeare. Bronze, cast 1893. 78 x 43¾ x 65. Lincoln Park, Chicago, IL. Photograph by George Gurney.

Madonna **(Plaster). #30.** ca. 1892. 24 h. (approx.). Unlocated.

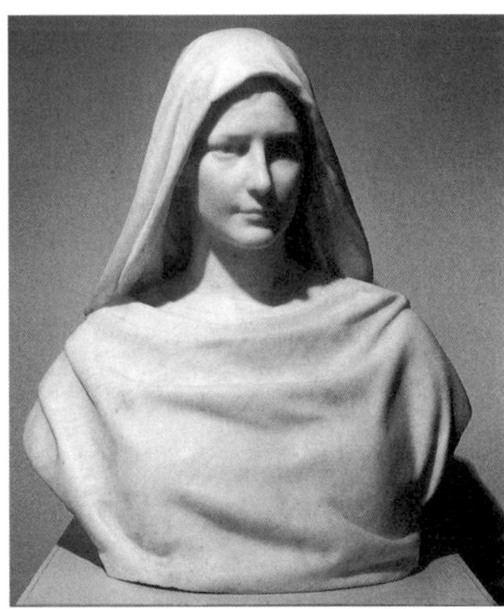

Maturity. Marble, n.d. (ca. 1892). 24 h. The Dayton Art Institute, Gift of Mrs. Charles Harries Simms.

Portrait bust of a Lady **(Marble). #41.** Unlocated.

Plaster replica of the statue of Alexander Hamilton for the Hamilton Club, Brooklyn. **#45.** 1892. 96 h. (approx.). Presumably destroyed.

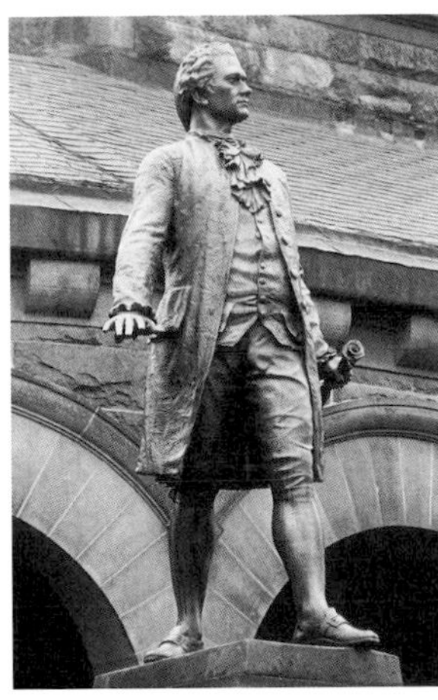

Alexander Hamilton. Bronze, cast 1893. 96 h. Hamilton Grange, New York, NY. Photograph by George Gurney.

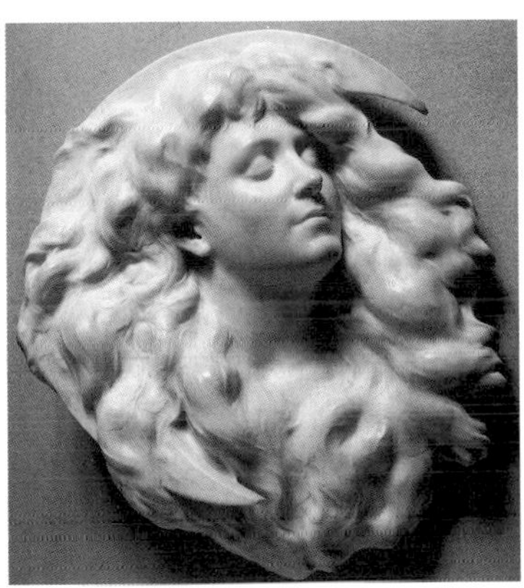

The Summer Night **(Relief in marble). #78.** [$1000]. *Midsummer Night's Dream,* 1892. 25 x 21½ x 7½. The Corcoran Gallery of Art, Gift of the Artist.

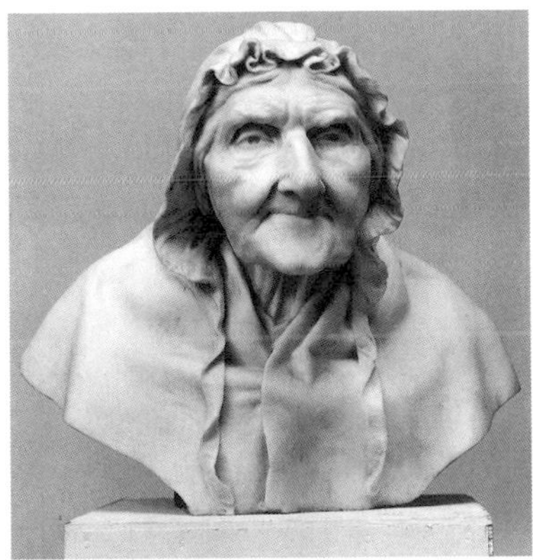

Nearing Home **(Marble bust). #82.** n.d. (modeled ca. 1887). 13½ x 21 x 13½. The Corcoran Gallery of Art, Gift of Mrs. William Ordway Partridge.

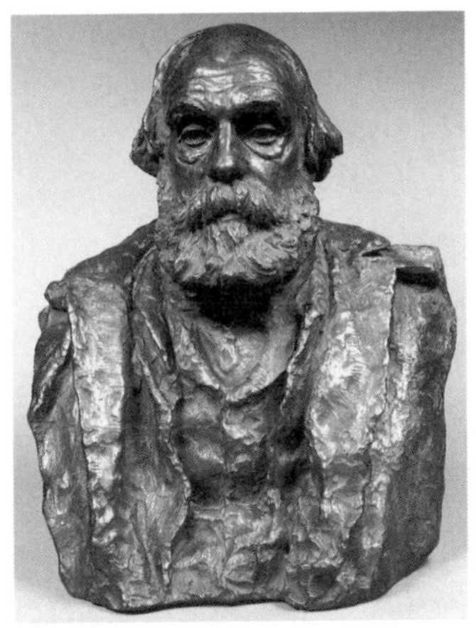

Portrait of Edward Everett Hale **(Bronze bust). #101.** 1891. 26 h. Union League Club of Chicago.

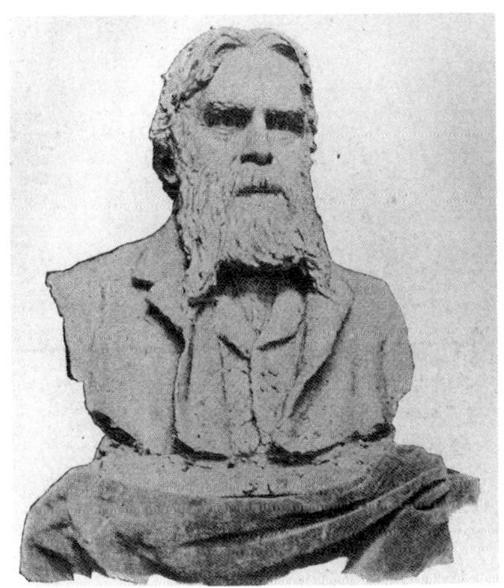

Bust of James Russell Lowell **(Plaster). #106.** 1891. 38 h. (approx.). Unlocated.[81] Illus: *The Outlook* 60 (1898): 857.

Plaster later version, 1903. 25 x 24 x 12. McKean County Historical Society, Smethport, PA.

A Dream **(Marble). #134.** 1892. 12½ diam. Yaddo, Saratoga Springs, NY, 1974. Unlocated.

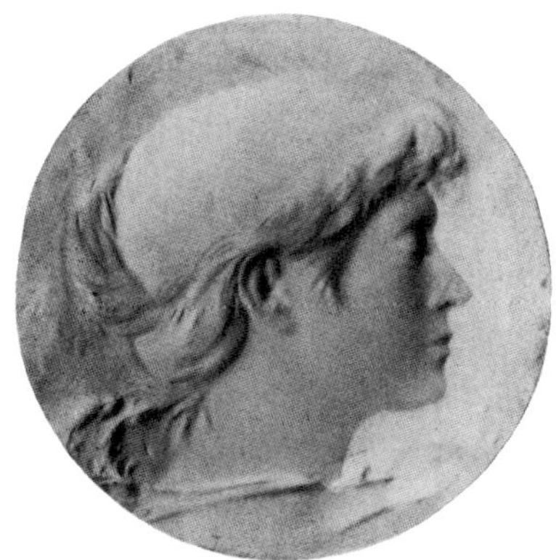

Plaster, n.d. 12½ diam. Collection Mrs. William A. M. Burden, New York, NY.

PETERSON, George D. Chicago.

1862 Wilmington, DE–Residing 1898 Chicago, IL
Training — Boston: Martin Millmore, BMFA; Paris: EcBA (H. M. A. Chapu, J. A. J. Falguière), Frederic Bartholdi.

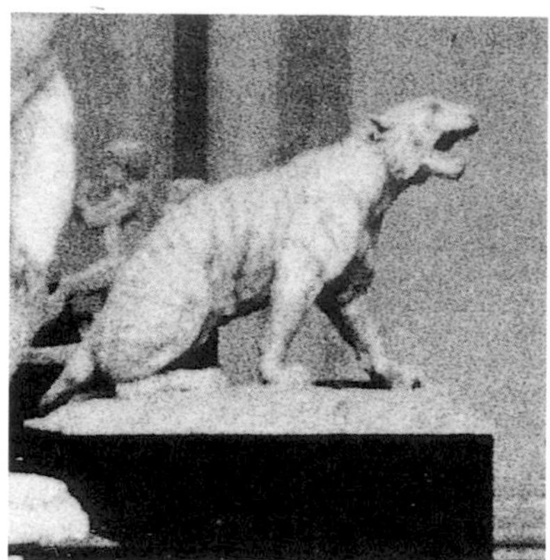

Tiger at Bay **(Plaster). #128.** [$5000 in bronze]. 1891 (painted plaster). On loan to The Art Institute of Chicago from R. Hamilton McCormick in 1896. Unlocated. Illus: Official Photographs of the World's Columbian Exposition by C. D. Arnold, vol. 8, pl. 63. Courtesy of The Chicago Public Library, Special Collections Department.

POTTER, Bessie O. (Bessie Onahotema/after 1899, Mrs. Robert W. Vonnoh; after 1948, Mrs. Edward Keyes). Chicago.

1872 St. Louis, MO–1955 New York, NY
Training — Chicago: AIC (Lorado Taft).

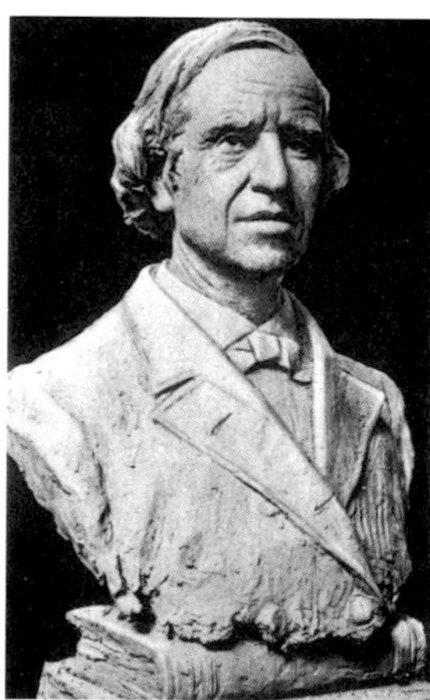

Portrait of Prof. David Swing **(Plaster bust). #108. Lent by Mr. J. I. Pearce, Chicago.** Unlocated. Illus: Sadakichi Hartmann, *Modern American Sculpture* (New York: Paul Wenzel, [1918]), pl. 56.

Portrait in Relief **(Plaster). #133. Lent by Mr. MacGillivray, Chicago.** Est. 24 x 13. Unlocated.

POWERS, Preston (William Preston). Denver, Col.

1843 Florence, Italy –1931 Florence, Italy
Training — Florence: Hiram Powers [his father].

Romola de 'Bardi **(Marble bust). #14.** 1893. Unlocated.

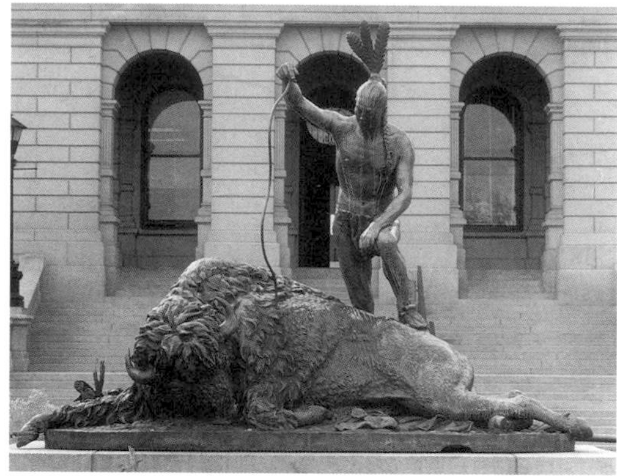

The Closing Era **(Bronze). #87.** Modeled 1891, cast 1893. Over life-size. East Lawn of Colorado State Capitol Building, Denver, CO. Photograph by Joe O'Connell.

PRESCOTT, Katherine (Katherine Tupper Hooper/ Mrs. Harry L. Prescott). Boston.

1851/52 Biddeford, ME–1926 Brookline, MA
Training — Boston: E. Boyd; New York: Frank Edwin Elwell.

Joy to the New Year, Peace to the Old **(Plaster medallion). #135.** [$12]. Est. 6 diam. Unlocated.

Ralph Waldo Emerson. **(Bronze medallion). #143.** [$25 in bronze]. Est. 8 x 5. Unlocated.

PROCTOR, A. Phimister (Alexander Phimister). New York.

1862 Bozanquit, Ontario, Canada–1950 Palo Alto, CA
Training — New York: NAD, ASL; Paris: Acad. Colarossi, Jardin des Plantes, Acad. Julian (Denys-Pierre Puech).

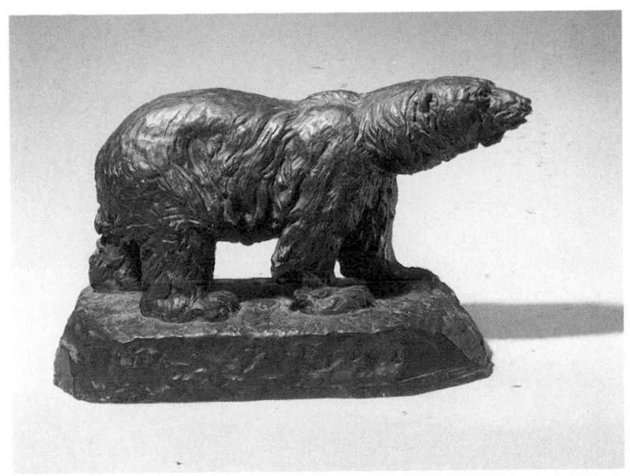

Polar Bear—cast of original study for life size figure on bridge, World's Columbian Exposition. **#80.** [$100 in bronze]. Bronze, modeled 1892, cast 1893. 8 x 11½ x 5½. Collection Christopher Hutchins.

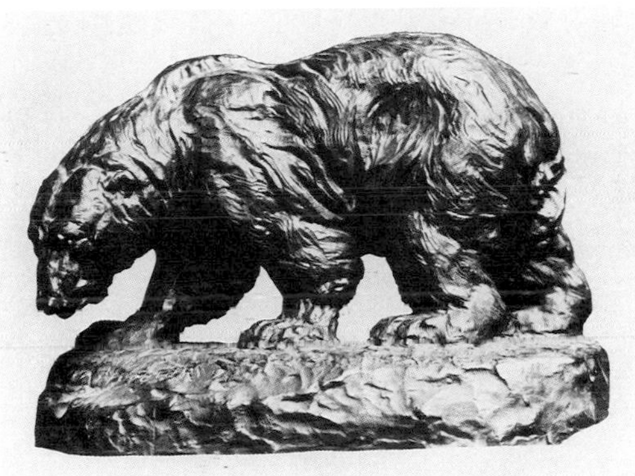

Polar Bear — cast of original study for life size figure on bridge, World's Columbian Exposition. **#81.** [$100 in bronze]. Bronze, modeled 1892, cast 1893. 7¾ x 10½ x 5⅛. Collection Phimister Proctor Church, Bainbridge Island, WA.

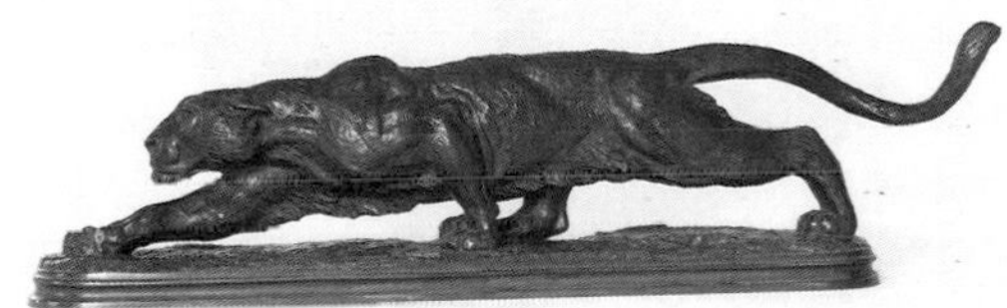

Panther **(Bronze). #85.** [$500]. *Stalking Panther,* 1891–92. 10¼ x 31 x 4½. The Corcoran Gallery of Art, Bequest of James Parmelee.

ROGERS, John. **New York.**
1829 Salem, MA–1904 New Canaan, CT
Training — Rome: Spence; largely self-taught.

Statue of Abraham Lincoln seated **(Plaster). #42.** 1892. Over life-size. Hallsville Grammar School, Manchester, NH, 1910. Unlocated.

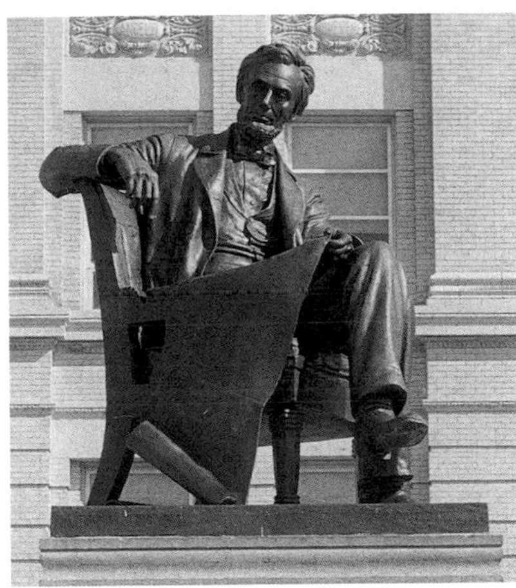

Bronze, cast 1910. Over life-size. Central High School, Manchester, NH. Photograph by George Gurney.

ROHL-SMITH, **Carl** (Carl Wilhelm Daniel). **Chicago.**
1848 Roskilde, Denmark–1900 Copenhagen, Denmark
Training — Copenhagen: Royal Academy (H. V. Bissen); Berlin: Royal Academy (Albert Wolff); Vienna.

Mato Wanartaka (Kicking Bear), Chief of the Sioux **(Plaster bust). #121.** [$300]. Unlocated.

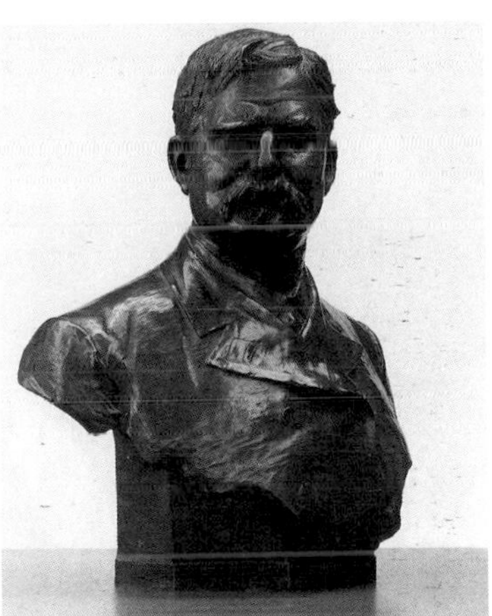

* *Bust of Henry Watterson* **(Bronze). #151. Lent by Mrs. Henry Watterson, Louisville.** 1890. 25 x 21½ x 14. Louisville Free Public Library, Louisville, KY.

† **RUCKSTUHL, F. Wellington** (also Ruckstull) (Frederick Wellington). **New York.**
1853 Breitenback, France–1942 New York, NY
Training — St. Louis: Washington University; Paris: Acad. Colarossi, Acad. Julian (Jules Joseph Lefebvre, Gustave Boulanger), Jean-Auguste Dampt, Antonin Mercié, Theodore Tholenaar.

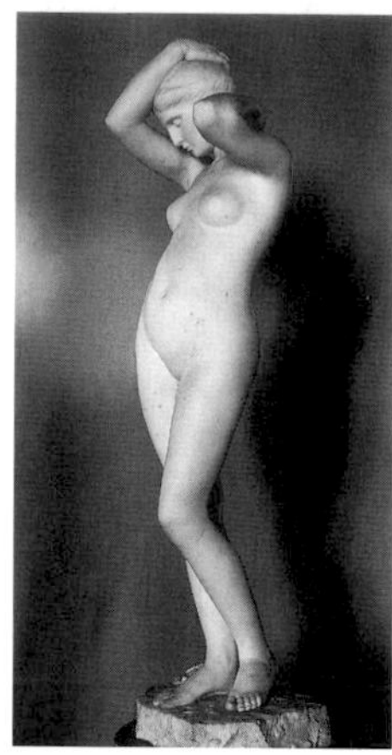

******Evening* **(Marble). #120.** [$10,000]. Modeled 1888, carved 1891. 72 x 20 x 20. The Metropolitan Museum of Art, Amelia B. Lazarus Fund, 1920.

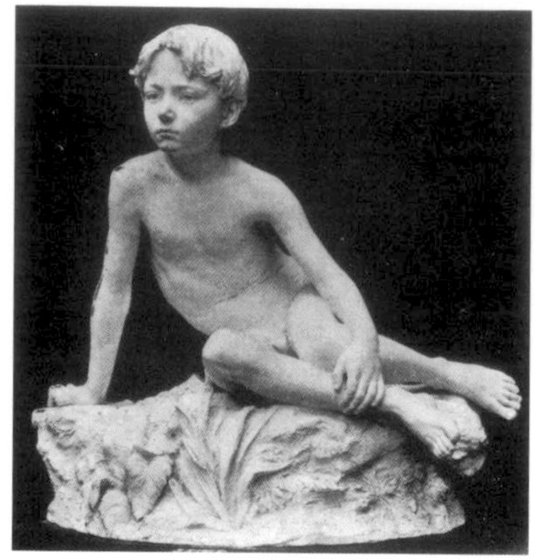

On the Banks of the Oise **(Bronze). #13.** [$1000 in bronze]. 1889. Estate of Dorothy P. Cavanaugh, 1986. Unlocated. Illus: William H. Downes, "New England Art at the World's Fair," *New England Magazine* 8 (July 1893): 369.

Portrait Bust of an Italian Child **(Bronze). #60.** ca. 1887. Unlocated.

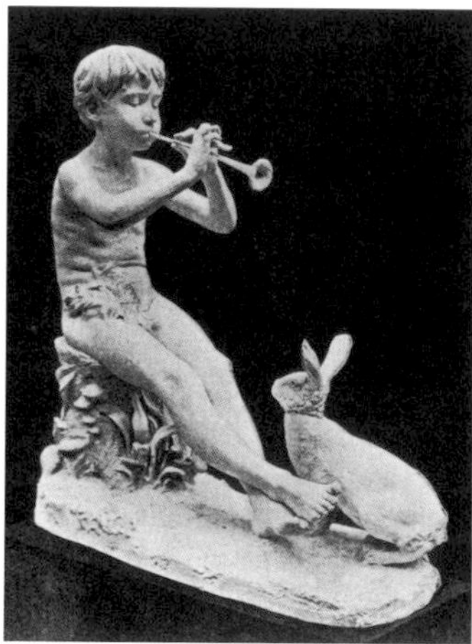

Young Orpheus **(Plaster). #126.** [$1000 in bronze]. ca. 1890. Unlocated. Illus: *Harper's Bazaar*, 14 May 1892, 396.

RUGGLES, Theo Alice (Mrs. Henry Hudson Kitson). **Boston.**
1871 Brookline, MA–1932 Boston, MA
Training — Henry H. Kitson; Paris: P. A. J. Dagnan-Bouveret, Gustave Courtois.

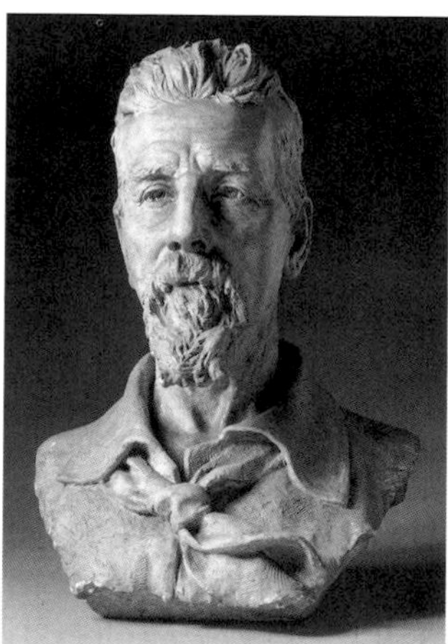

A New England Fisherman **(Plaster bust). #12.** 1892. 20½ x 14¾ x 11¾. Museum of Art, Rhode Island School of Design, Gift of Mrs. H. H. Kitson.

STAIR, Ida (Ida M. Obenchain/Mrs. Milton J. Stair). **Denver, Col.**
1857 Longansport, IN–1908 Denver, CO
Training — New York: William Merritt Chase, Kenyon Cox, Preston Powers; Chicago: AIC (Lorado Taft).

Left of Paradise **(Bas-relief in plaster). #65.** Unlocated. "A lovely intaglio of her children Gobin and Mildred . . . " — Artists Club Scrapbook, Chicago Historical Society.

TAFT, Lorado (Lorado Zadoc). **Chicago.**
1860 Elmwood, IL–1936 Chicago, IL
Training — Paris: EcAD, Petite École, Acad. Colarossi, EcBA (Augustin Dumont, Jules Thomas, Jean-Marie Bienaime Bonnaissieux), Antonin Mercié.

Portrait bust of Susan B. Anthony **(Marble). #92.** 1892. Presumably destroyed.

THOMPSON, J. S. (James S.). **Denver, Col.**
Unknown–1935/36 Italy
Training — Denver: University of Denver (William Preston Powers); Italy.

Head of a Cow-boy in bas-relief **(Marble). #88.** Unlocated.

TILDEN, Douglas. Paris, France.
1860 Chico, CA–1935 Berkeley, CA
Training — San Francisco: California School of Design (Virgil Williams, Marion F. Wells); New York: NAD (J. Q. A. Ward, H. Siddons Mowbray); Paris: Paul François Choppin.

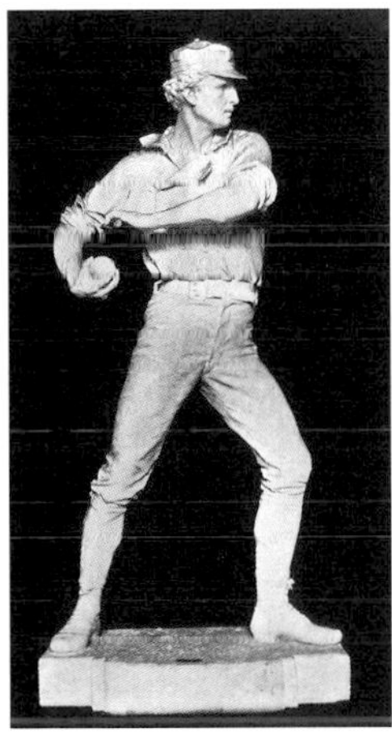

Base-ball Player **(Plaster). #3.** [$3500 in bronze]. 1889. Life-size. Presumably destroyed. Illus: Rand, McNally, *Fine Arts at the World's Columbian Exposition* (Chicago: Rand, McNally, 1894).

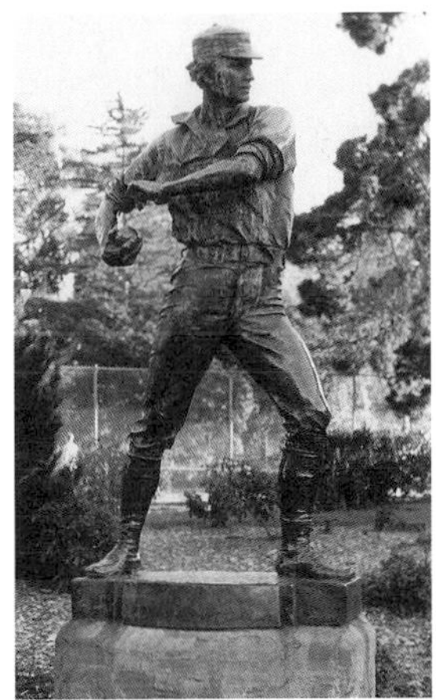

Bronze, 1889. 77 x 37 x 17. Golden Gate Park, San Francisco, CA. Photograph by Val Lewton.

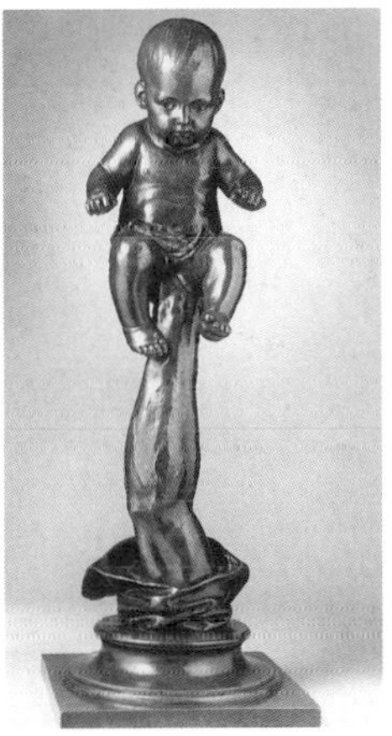

* *Young Acrobat* **(Bronze). #16.** [$250]. n.d. (ca. 1890–92). 33⅝ x 12 x 12. National Museum of American Art, Smithsonian Institution, Gift of Dr. Wayne H. Decker.

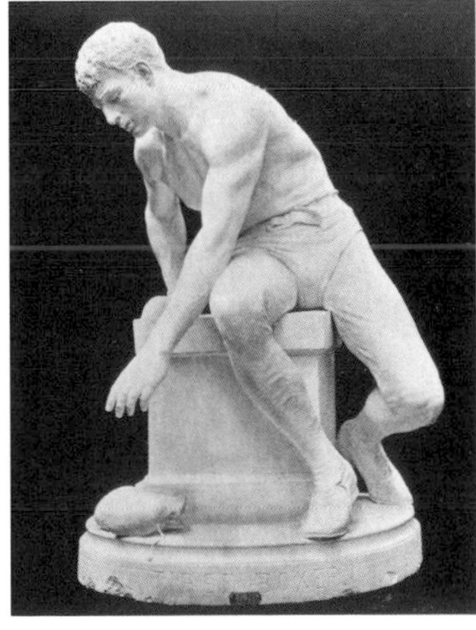

Tired Boxer **(Plaster). #19.** [$4000 in bronze]. 1890. Life-size. Collection The Art Institute of Chicago by 1896. Destroyed as "inferior work," 1922. Illus: *Buildings and Art at the World's Fair* (Chicago: Rand, McNally, 1894), 152.

Bronze, cast ca. 1891. Life-size. Collection Olympic Club, San Francisco, CA, 1893. Destroyed in San Francisco, CA, earthquake, 1906.

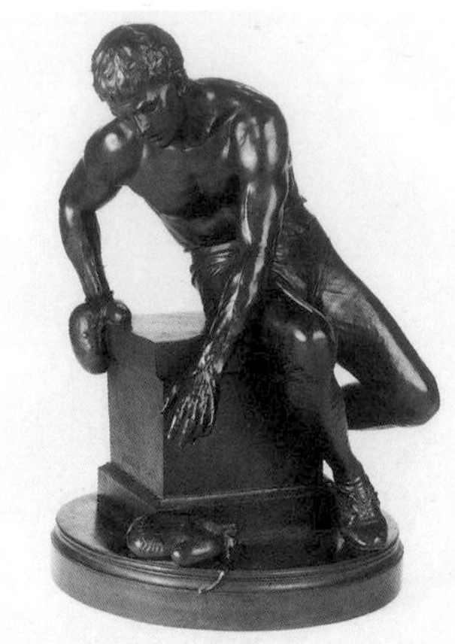

*Bronze reduction, cast 1892. 29¼ x 22 x 22. The Fine Arts Museums of San Francisco, Gift of Alice Vincilione and Mary L. Tiscornia.

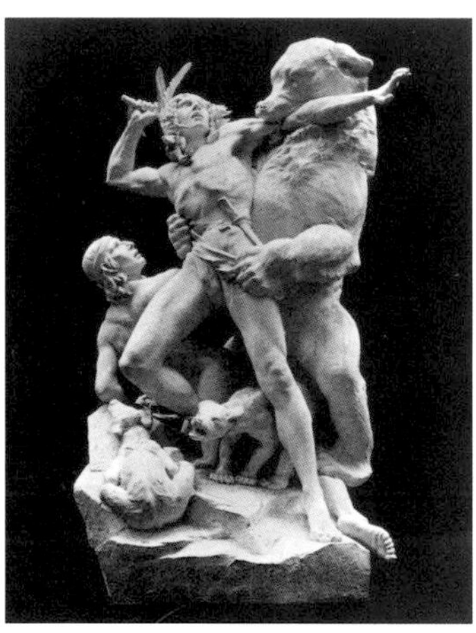

Indian Bear Hunt **(Bronze). #46.** [$15,000]. *Bear Hunt,* 1892. Over life-size. California School for the Deaf, Fremont, CA. Illus: *Fine Arts at the World's Columbian Exposition* (Chicago: Rand, McNally, 1894).

TRIEBEL, Frederick E. (Frederick Ernst). **Florence, Italy.**
1865 Peoria, IL–1944 New York, NY
Training — Florence: Academy of Fine Arts (Augusto Rivalta).

Bust of the Rev. Edwin B. Russell **(Marble). #83. Lent by the Rev. E. B. Russell, New York.** ca. 1887–1890. Unlocated.

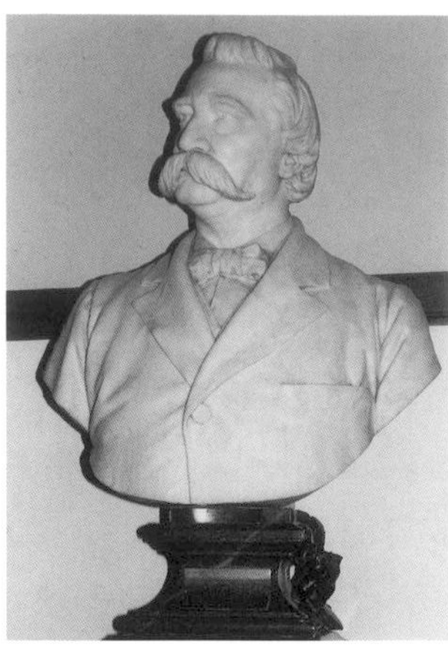

Bust of Gen. John A. Logan **(Marble). #86.** [$1300]. 1892. 32½ x 30 x 17½. Central Illinois Landmarks Foundation, Peoria, IL.

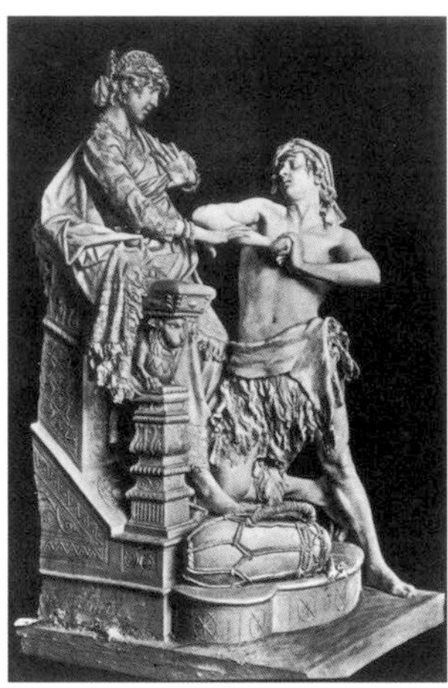

Love Knows no Caste **(Marble). #90.** [$6000 copies]. **Lent by Mrs. Joseph B. Greenhut, Peoria, Ill.** 1889. 60 x 40 x 30. Landmark City Hall, Peoria, IL. Illus: Sadakichi Hartmann, *Modern American Sculpture* (New York: Paul Wenzel, [1918]), pl. 52.

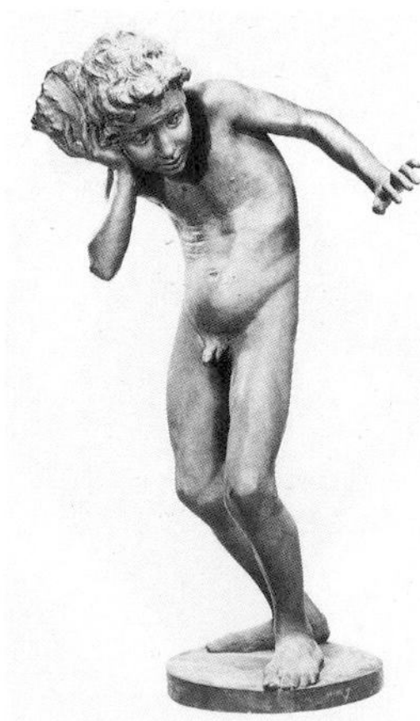

Mysterious Music **(Bronze). #91.** [$1200]. n.d. 43 h. Tokyo National Museum.

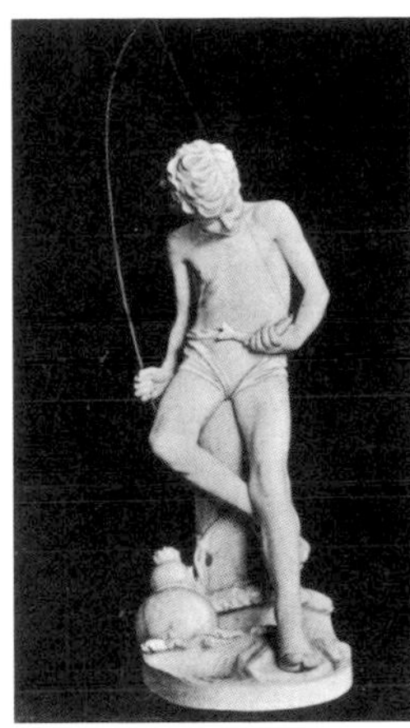

The First Fish **(Marble). #113.** [$2200]. Collection of the artist, 1943. Unlocated. Illus: Sadakichi Hartmann, *Modern American Sculpture* (New York: Paul Wenzel, [1918]), pl. 29.

Savonarola **(Plaster bas-relief). #142.** [$125 in marble]. Est. 16 x 12. Unlocated.

Donatello **(Plaster bas-relief). #144.** [$125 in marble]. Est. 16 x 12. Unlocated.

TURNER, **William G.** (William Green). **Florence, Italy.**
1833 Newport, RI–1917 Newport, RI
Training — Florence: Academy of Fine Arts.

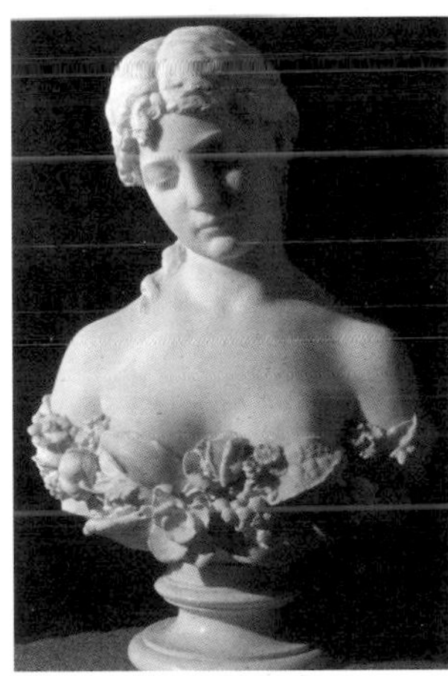

A Dream **(Marble bust). #62.** [$300]. *The Dreamer*, n.d. 27¼ x 17½ x 10¾. Newport Historical Society, Newport, RI.

Fisherman's Daughter **(Marble). #63.** [$700]. ca. 1876. Unlocated.

Rhoda **(Marble statuette). #69.** [$300]. Before 1876. Unlocated.

The Herald of Peace **(Bronze statue from *cire perdue*). #89.** [$600]. ca. 1876. Unlocated.

VARNEY, **Luella M.** (Mrs. Teodora Serrao). **Rome, Italy.**
1865 Angola, NY– after 1935
Training — Cleveland: Lewis Adams; Rome.

Portrait of Edith Van Buren **(Marble bust). #72.** Unlocated.

Portrait bust of a Lady **(Marble). #75.** Unlocated.

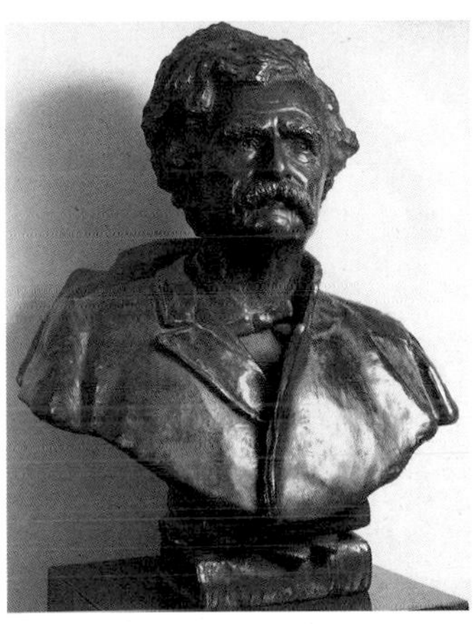

Mark Twain* **(Bronze bust). #153. [$1000]. 1892. 30 x 21 x 16. Cleveland Public Library. Photograph by Lynn Chambers Freska.

VOLK, **Leonard W.** (Leonard Wells). **Chicago.**
1828 Wellstown, NY–1895 Osceola, WI
Training — Rome; largely self-taught.

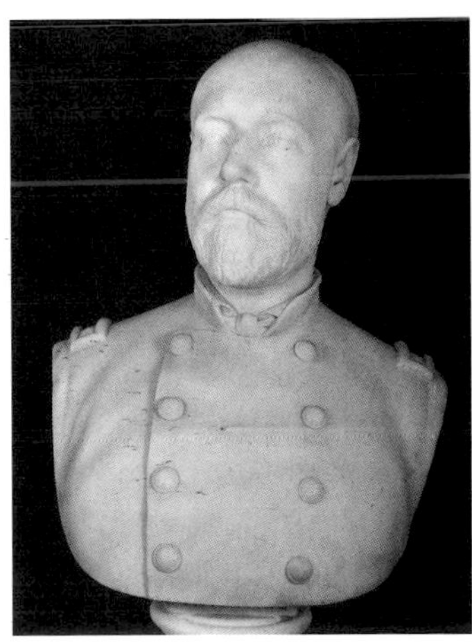

Bust of Colonel Herbert A. Hascall, U.S.A. **(Marble). #37. Presented to West Point Military Academy by Mrs.**

Mary C. Haskell. 1892. 23 x 19 x 12 (approx.). The West Point Museum, United States Military Academy, West Point, NY.

Bust of a Lady (Marble). #40. Unlocated.

Portrait of the late Col. Wm. Hale Thompson (Marble bust). #67. Lent by Mrs. W. H. Thompson, Chicago. Unlocated.

WARNER, Olin L. (Olin Levi). **New York.**
1844 West Suffield, CT–1896 New York, NY
Training — Paris: EcBA (François Jouffroy), Jean-Baptiste Carpeaux.

Diana Reclining (Plaster statuette). #7. 1887. 23½ h. (approx.). Presumably destroyed.

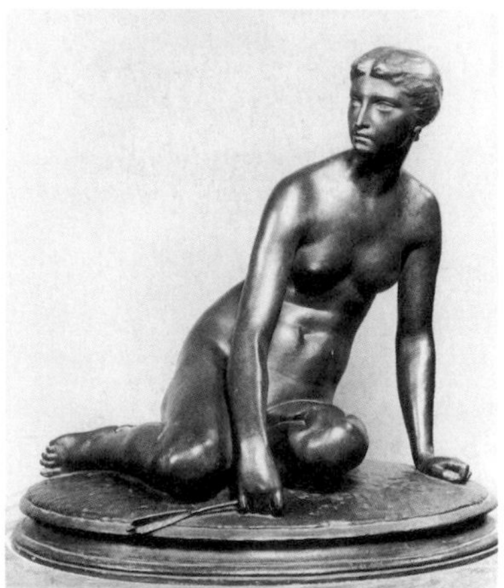

**Diana*. Bronze, cast 1897–98. 23½ h. The Metropolitan Museum of Art, Gift of the National Sculpture Society, 1898.

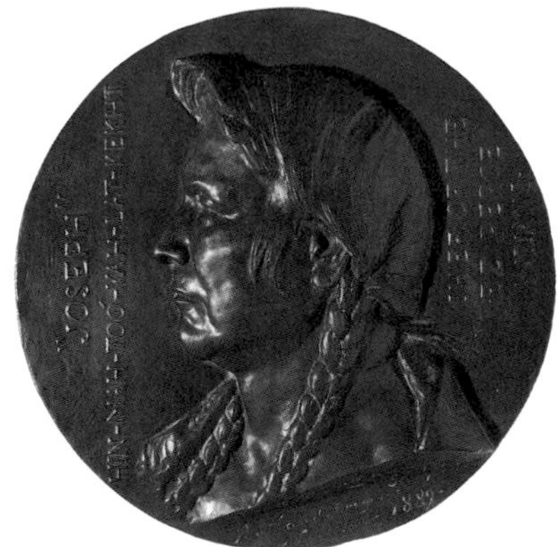

Medallion of Joseph, Chief of the Nez Perces Indians (Bronze). #36. *"Joseph," Hin-mah-too-yah-lat-kekht, Chief of the "Nez Percé" Indians*, 1889. 17⅝ diam. National Museum of American Art, Smithsonian Institution, Gift of Alison Warner Waterman in memory of her mother, Frances D. Warner.

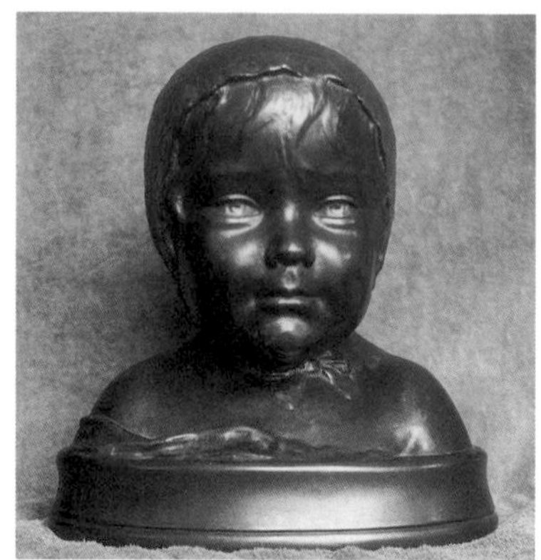

Rosalie Olin Warner (Bronze bust). #58. 1888. 10½x 9⅜ x 6¼. Private Collection, Haverford, PA. Photograph by George Gurney.

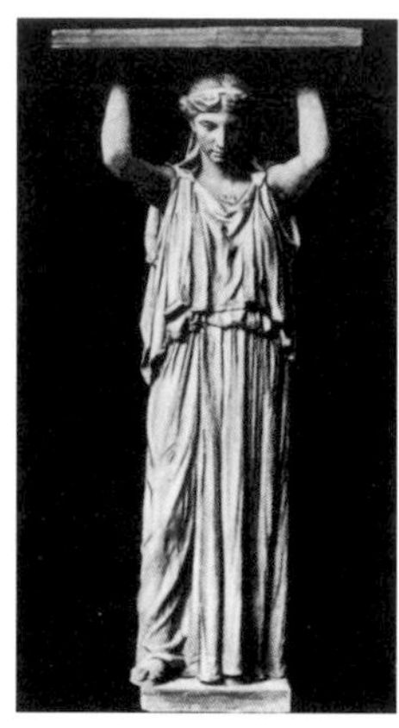

Model for a Caryatid (Plaster). #98. 1888. Life-size. Destroyed, ca. 1920. Illus: Sadakichi Hartmann, *Modern American Sculpture* (New York: Paul Wenzel, [1918]), pl. 52.

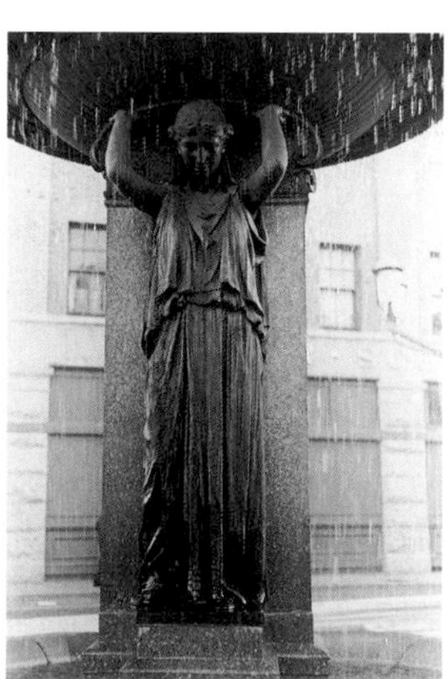

Caryatid. Bronze, cast 1888. Life-size. Skidmore Fountain Plaza, Portland, OR. Photograph by George Gurney.

* ***Bronze medallions of Columbia River Indians*** **(Bronze). #138.** 1891. National Museum of American Art, Smithsonian Institution, Gift of Alison Warner Waterman in memory of her mother, Frances D. Warner.

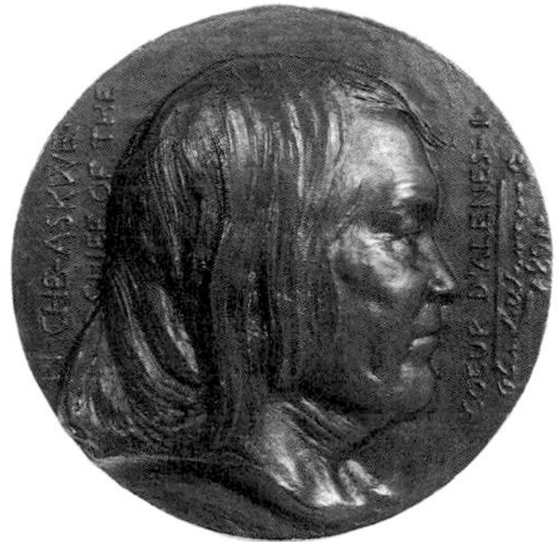

(a) ***N-che-askire, Chief of the Coeur d'Alenes.*** *N-che-askwe, Chief of the Coeur d'Alênes.* 7⅜ diam.

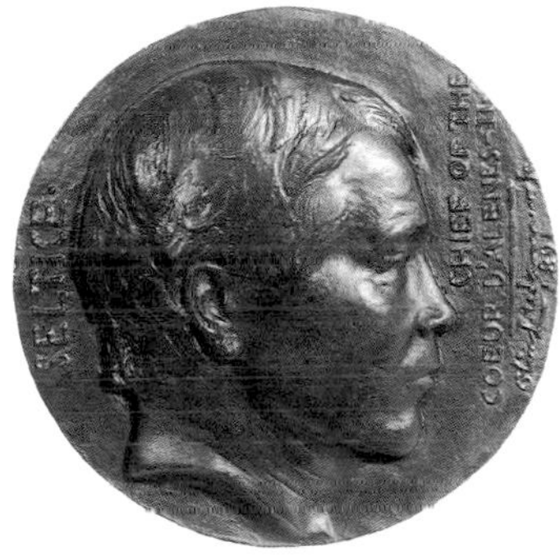

(b) ***Seltice, Chief of the Coeur d'Alenes.*** *Seltice, Chief of the Coeur d'Alênes.* 7⅝ diam.

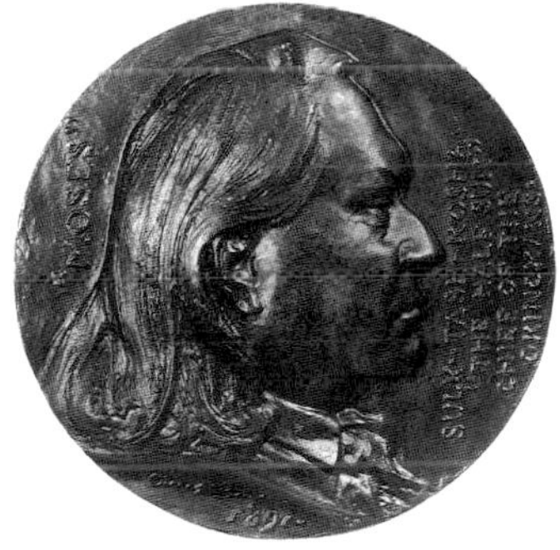

(c) ***Moses Sulk-tash-Kosha (The Half Sun), Chief of the Okinokans.*** *"Moses," Sulk-tash-kosha, "The Half Sun," Chief of the Okinokans.* 8½ diam.

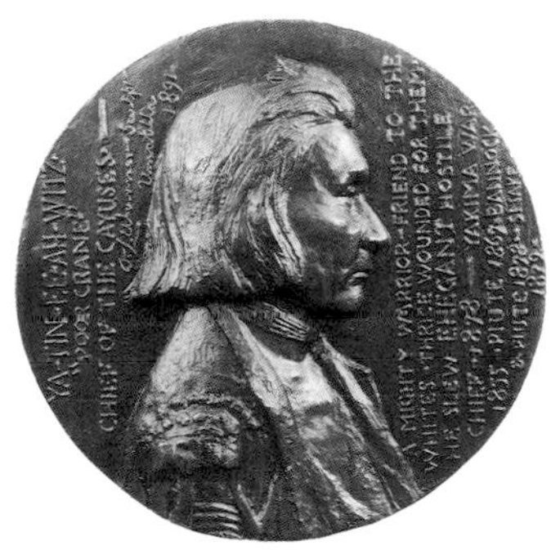

(d) ***Ya-tin-ee-ah-witz (Poor Crane), Chief of the Cayuses.*** *Ya-tin-ee-ah-witz, "Poor Crane," Chief of the Cayuse.* 11 diam.

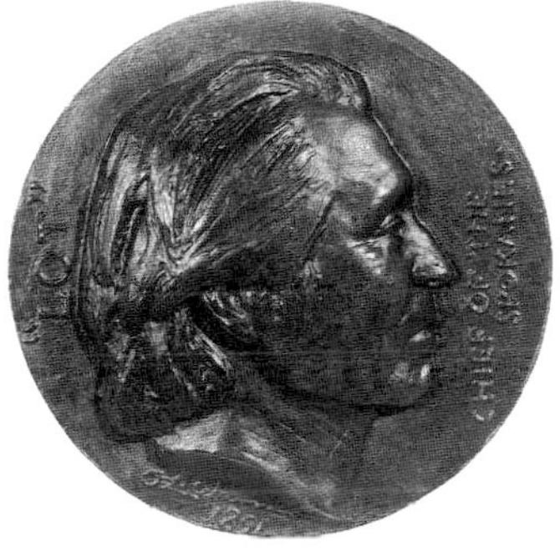

(e) ***"Lot," Chief of the Spokanes.*** 8¼ diam.

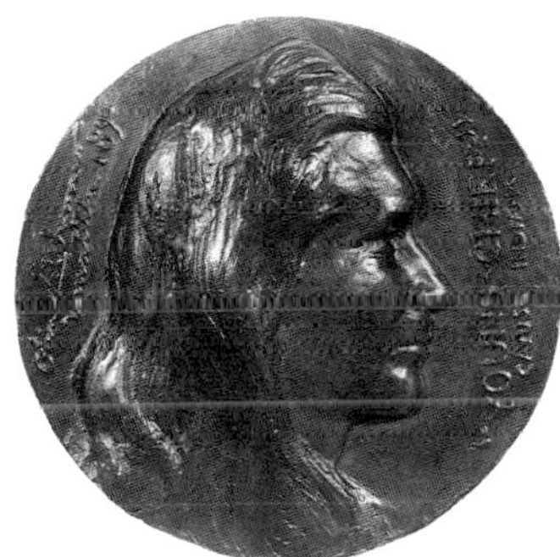

(f) ***Young Chief, Cayuse Indian.*** *Young-Chief, Cayuse Indian.* 7½ diam.

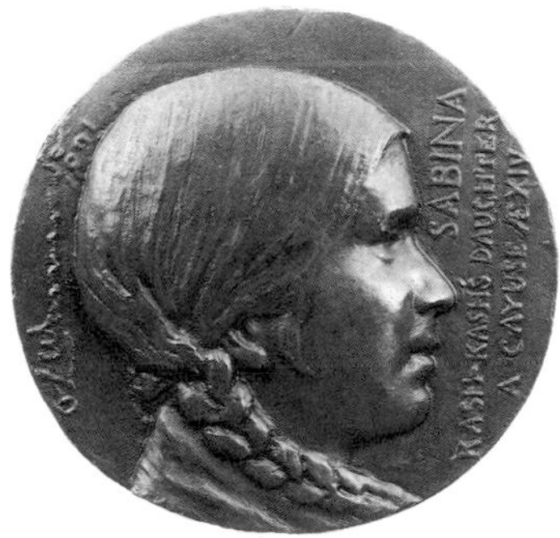

(g) ***Sabina —Kash-Kash's Daughter —A Cayuse, age fourteen.*** *Sabina, Kash-Kash's Daughter, a Cayuse AEXIV.* 5⅞ diam.

Bust of Mozart **(Plaster). #157.** 1892. 36 h. (approx.). Buffalo Liedertafel Society, Buffalo, NY, 1894. Presumably destroyed.

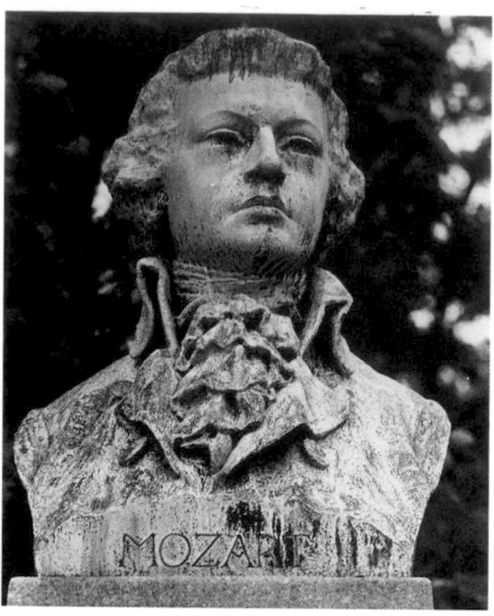

Bronze, cast 1892. 36 h. (approx.). Delaware Park, Buffalo, NY. Photograph by George Gurney.

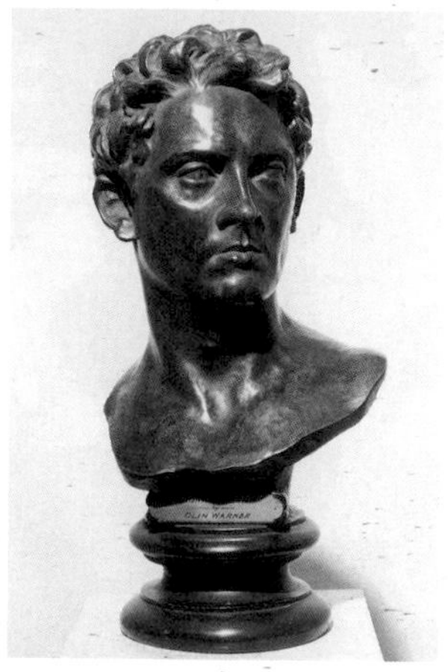

Portrait of J. Alden Weir **(Bronze bust). #159.** 1880. 22¾ h. American Academy and Institute of Arts and Letters. Photograph by Geoffrey Clements.

WESSELHOEFT, F. G. (Ferdinanda Emilie/Mrs. Willard J. Reed). **Cambridge, Mass.**[82]
ca. 1870–Residing 1951 Santa Barbara, CA

African Head **(Plaster). #17.** [$100]. Unlocated.

Titania and Bottom (Midsummer Night's Dream) **(Plaster). #22.** [$500]. Unlocated.

WHITE, Alfred (Alfred Richard). **Paris, France.**
1869/1870 Cincinnati, OH–1927 Cincinnati, OH
Training — Florence; Paris.

Portrait of Monsieur M. **(Plaster). #94.** [$250]. Unlocated.

WHITNEY, Anne. Boston.
1821 Watertown, MA–1915 Boston, MA
Training — Boston: William Rimmer; Rome; Munich; Paris.

Roma **(Plaster). #23.** 1893. Over life-size. Museum of Fine Arts, St. Louis, 1893. Lost in move to or from Washington University, St. Louis, MO.

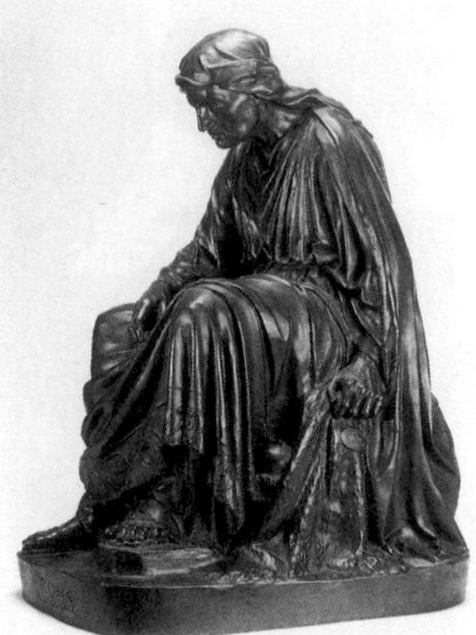

Bronze early version, cast 1890. 27 h. Davis Museum and Cultural Center, Wellesley College.

WUERTZ, Emil H. Chicago.
1856 St. Alban on the Rhine, Germany –1898 at sea on "La Bourgogne"
Training — Paris: Jean-Léon Gérôme, Auguste Rodin, Acad. Julian (H. M. A. Chapu, Antonin Mercié).

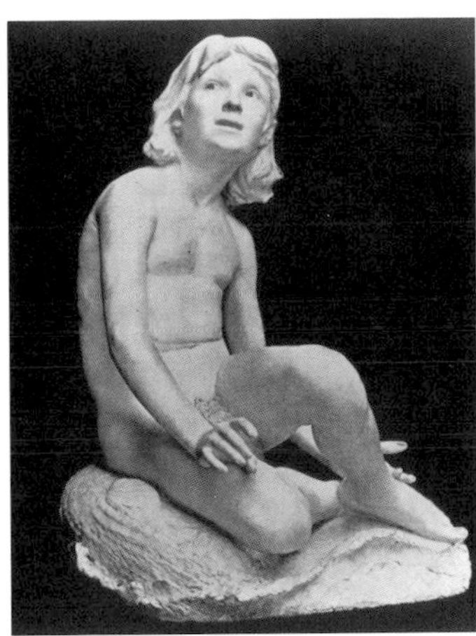

The Murmur of the Sea **(Plaster). #24.** [$2000 in marble]. 1890. The Art Institute of Chicago, 1898. Unlocated. Illus: *Buildings and Art at the World's Fair* (Chicago: Rand, McNally, 1894), 196.

ZEARING, H. H. (Henry/Harry H.). **Chicago.**
Unknown–Residing 1904 Chicago, IL

Bas-relief of Abraham Lincoln **(Bronze). #35.** [$50]. Unlocated.

NOTES

1. The artist is possibly David G. Anderson (born in New York) who exhibited in Paris Salons and was a pupil of Gustave Boulanger, Jules Joseph Lefebvre, and L. Doucet. Another possibility is that he is David I. Anderson who is listed in the American Art Annuals through 1915. All three, however, could be the same David Anderson.

2. Beckwith recorded his progress on this portrait in his diary for 1889 (Archives, National Academy of Design, New York City) in entries dated from 11 Mar. to 13 May. The artist used the same model for another painting, *The Diamond Broker*, sittings which are also recorded in his diary from 5 Oct. to 7 Dec. 1889.

3. Beckwith also recorded the sittings for this portrait of his sister-in-law in his diary for 1889 (Archives, National Academy of Design, New York City) in entries from 4 Mar. to 13 May.

4. An illustration of *Near Cloverdale*, provided by Mr. Closuit in 1973, can be found in the Inventory of American Paintings, National Museum of American Art, Smithsonian Institution.

5. This portrait, one other, and two miniatures of Evangeline Wilbour Blashfield were bequeathed to Theodora Wilbour, her sister, by Edwin H. Blashfield. See his will, dated 3 Feb. 1936, New York County Surrogate's Court.

6. Bregler mentions this portrait in his essay "Thomas Eakins as a Teacher," *The Arts* 17 (Mar. 1931): 377, where he recounts Eakins' interest in it: "'Charlie, have you seen Rembrandt's *The Woman Paring Her Nails*? It reminds me of your portrait of your Grandmother.' He was not one to flatter you, and I was staggered and did not reply. Even though coming from him, I did not feel it worthy of such a comparison. This portrait of my Grandmother always seemed to have pleased him, from the very first time that I had asked him to come to my room to see it." Susan Eakins also admired the painting. In a letter dated 18 July 1934, she notes that "Your 'grandmother' would be good to show anywhere." See Kathleen A. Foster and Cheryl Leibold, *Writing About Eakins: The Manuscripts in Charles Bregler's Thomas Eakins Collection* (Philadelphia: University of Pennsylvania Press, 1989), 304–5.

7. This painting was possibly sold as *Women at the Mosque* in the William Randolph Hearst sale, Gimbel Brothers and Saks Fifth Avenue, New York, NY (under the direction of Hammer Galleries, New York, NY), 1941, catalogue no. 39–7.

8. The painting was purchased from the World's Columbian Exposition by Mr. and Mrs. George Joslyn of Omaha, NE. Letters from J. G. Brown to Mr. Joslyn, located in the painting's registration file at the Joslyn Art Museum, indicate that the artist almost completely repainted the canvas in 1896 after Mrs. Joslyn attempted to wash it with lye soap. The painting today appears identical to pre-1896 photographs.

9. The artist was born Isaac Henry Stiefel but changed his name (to its Latin translation) as an adult.

10. In the *Art Amateur* of March 1893, a list of works accepted by the New York jury for the World's Columbian Exposition refers to this painting as a portrait of Miss Lawrence.

11. According to Churchill's biography in Richard Herndon, comp., and Edwin M. Bacon, ed., *Men of Progress* (Boston: New England Magazine, 1896), 552, he showed a "portrait of a lady" at the exposition.

12. This painting, or one of the same title, was with the Macbeth Gallery in 1901 and was exhibited at the Albright Art Gallery, Buffalo, in 1914 (Rose Clark to William MacBeth, 23 May 1901, Macbeth Gallery Papers, Archives of American Art, roll NMc5, frame 983; and *Catalogue of An Exhibition of Works by Buffalo Artists*, Albright Art Gallery, 1914, no. 72A).

13. *Early Morning* is most likely mistitled in the *Revised Catalogue*. Webb owned Coffin's *Early Moonrise* and lent it to the Paris Universal Exposition of 1889 and the National Academy of Design's Retrospective Exhibition of 1892, two exhibitions common to the histories of World's Columbian Exposition works. In a list of works accepted for the art gallery of the World's Columbian Exposition, published in the *New York Tribune* in January of 1893, *Early Moonrise* is again the title given to the painting.

14. The artist's place and date of birth have been variously recorded as Portland and Boston in 1855, 1865, and 1862, but it is most likely that Collins was born in Portland, ME, in 1855. See Forbes Watson, "Preliminary Fragment of Note on Alfred Quinton Collins," Forbes Watson Papers, Archives of American Art, roll D55, frames 361–62. Watson was Collins's brother-in-law. See also Doreen Bolger Burke, *American Paintings in the Metropolitan Museum of Art*, vol. 3 (New York: The Metropolitan Museum of Art, 1980), 176.

15. This painting was possibly sold as *The Grand Cañon of the Colorado, Arizona* (41½ x 35) at American Art Association, New York, NY, 25 Mar. 1903, lot 86, to a Mr. Dunham for $425.

16. A somewhat larger replica, painted in 1908, is in the collection of the Metropolitan Museum of Art, New York, NY.

17. John Wilton Cunningham was survived by his parents, the Rev. John W. and Mrs. S. I. Cunningham. They are listed in St. Louis city directories through 1911. See the *St. Louis Post-Dispatch*, 31 Aug. 1903 and 1 Sept. 1903, for obituaries.

18. See *Exhibition of Paintings by William T. Dannat* (New York: E. Gimpel & Wildenstein, 1915), Boston Museum of Fine Arts, Miscellaneous Exhibition Catalogues, Archives of American Art, roll MB509, frames 374–77.

19. The lender of the painting, as listed in early catalogues, was D. McNaughton. Donald McNaughton died in Chicago on 31 July 1893, while serving as the executive officer of the New York State World's Fair Commission. He resided in Wheatland, NY.

20. In 1883 Ida Joy resided in Paris and exhibited a painting in the Chicago Inter-State Industrial Exposition. In 1895 Ida Joy Didier resided with N. A. Didier and Paul Didier at 140 Ridge Ave. in Allegheny, PA (Paul Didier to John W. Beatty, 3 Oct. 1895, Carnegie Institute Papers, Archives of American Art, roll 1; and Pittsburgh/Allegheny, PA, city directories). N. A. Didier, Ida Joy's husband,

died in December of 1895 (see death record filed Allegheny County, PA), and his widow filed letters of administration there in 1897. Paul Didier died in 1928, survived by his wife, Victorene, and his two sons, Paul, Jr., of Harrisburg, PA, and Victor of Pittsburgh, as well as a sister, Mrs. Catherine Verstegen of Charleroi, Belgium. His will, filed 31 May 1928, in Allegheny County, PA, does not mention Ida Joy Didier. After 1897, we have located no further record of the artist.

21. *Reflections* (oil on wood, 1881), a loosely done painting or sketch, may be a study for this painting. See *Thomas Eakins, Susan Macdowell Eakins, Elizabeth Macdowell Kenton* (Roanoke, VA: North Cross School, 1977), no. 33. An error occurs in the *Revised Catalogue*. The lender's surname should read Macdowell.

22. The photograph included here represents the painting in its original state; its size was 60 x 40. The portrait has since been cut down to a head-and-shoulders format that measures 24 x 20.

23. M. E. Evans is listed in Florence N. Levy, ed., *American Art Annual* in 1903–04 (residing 154 W. 55th Street, New York, NY) and again in 1917 (residing 419 W. 119th Street, New York, NY). When she exhibited a painting at the National Academy of Design in 1902, her address given in the catalogue was 154 W. 55th Street. She moved to Los Angeles, CA, in 1906 and remained there until 1909 when she traveled to Mexico where she planned to stay for a year. It is unknown whether she returned to Los Angeles or went directly to New York.

24. The portrait has since been cut down to a bust format measuring 17 x 13.

25. The lender was Henry Wickes Goodrich, a lawyer in New York City and Nutley, NJ. Goodrich was a witness to Fowler's will, filed 1910, Westchester County, NY.

26. In an earlier edition of the catalogue, the title is given as *Portrait of Miss G. E.*

27. The painting is possibly *Sand Dunes at Naushon*, 1881 (18 x 30), which was sold at Skinner, Inc., Bolton, MA, 17 Nov. 1983, lot 71.

28. Gifford's largest and most important painting of this subject is *Padanaram Salt Vats* in the collection of the New Bedford Whaling Museum. This painting was exhibited at the St. Louis Louisiana Purchase Exposition in 1904 as *Salt Works Dartmouth*, and Gifford himself claimed that its only previous public exhibition was at the National Academy of Design (most likely in 1899 as *Dartmouth Salt Works*). Though this makes it improbable that it was exhibited at the World's Columbian Exposition as *Salt Works of Padanaram*, he may have repainted parts of the canvas after 1893 and shown it as a new work at the National Academy of Design in 1899.

29. Though the painting seems to be dated "93–94," an installation photograph verifies that it was exhibited at the World's Columbian Exposition. Later in 1893, Gifford exhibited it in the Philadelphia Art Club's Fifth Annual Exhibition, and in the spring of 1894, he showed it at the National Academy of Design. It is possible that he made minor changes to the painting prior to the spring Academy exhibition, thus dating the work "93–94."

30. This may be a portrait of Gustave Goldman, Martha's husband. See *Catalogue of The Exhibits of the State of Pennsylvania and of Pennsylvanians at The World's Columbian Exposition* ([Harrisburg], 1893), 117.

31. This is not the artist Lilian Bayliss Green (ca. 1878–1945) who also worked in Boston in the late nineteenth and early twentieth centuries.

32. At a time unknown to the present owner, this portrait was cut down to a ca. 30 x 25 inch bust, and the costume was repainted.

33. The *New York Times* of 1 August 1934 reports: "Mrs. Cecile Martin Harris requested yesterday the aid of the missing persons bureau in finding her 78-year-old artist husband, Charles X. Harris. According to Mrs. Harris, her husband left their home in West Hoboken, NJ, almost three years ago to go to Richmond, Va., to arrange an exhibition for the Virginia Historical Society, of which he is a member. He communicated with her at monthly intervals until last January, sometimes from Richmond but more often from other cities in the South. She last heard from him from Port Richie, Fla. This communication, she told detectives, was incoherent and she feared he had met with foul play. . . . Mrs. Harris said she and the artist were married in Washington, D.C. ten years ago."

34. Much confusion as to the identification of this painting has evolved from what seems to be an erroneous claim printed in the Parke-Bernet Galleries sales' catalogue when a painting by Hassam entitled *Midsummer Morning* was sold on 10 Feb. 1943, lot 116. The catalogue lists the World's Columbian Exposition, Chicago, 1893, as part of the painting's exhibition history. Now entitled *Figures in Sunlight*, this painting is in the collection of the Huntington Museum of Art in Huntington, WV. After undergoing conservation in 1975, the word and date "Chicago 1893" were revealed. It is likely that the setting for this painting, rather than part of its exhibition history, is the World's Columbian Exposition. Hassam exhibited "Midsummer" paintings in several exhibitions prior to the World's Columbian Exposition. The latter three are likely the same painting and also that one shown in the World's Columbian Exposition as *Midsummer Morning*:

27 Apr.–23 May 1891, Society of American Artists, Thirteenth Exhibition, New York, NY, no. 110, *Midsummer*. Owner, Eugene R. Knapp. "The brilliancy of color and beauty of effect in his 'Midsummer' (110), a tangle of wild flowers against an island-gemmed sea . . ."—*Art Amateur* 25 (June 1891): 6.

2–28 May 1892, Society of American Artists, Fourteenth Exhibition, New York, NY, no. 113, *Midsummer Morning, Celia Thaxter's Garden, Isle of Shoals*.

5–25 Dec. 1892, Society of American Artists, Retrospective Exhibition, New York, NY, no. 163, *Midsummer, An Island Garden*.

6–7 Feb. 1896, American Art Association, New York, NY, *Catalogue of the Oil Paintings, Water Colors, and Pastels by Childe Hassam*, no. 199, *Midsummer Morning, the Island Garden*.

35. It is clear from an installation photograph of Gallery 9, north wall, that this work is not the portrait of Mrs. Frederick W. Haynes now in the collection of the New-York Historical Society.

36. According to art historian Judith Herschman, Hitchcock repainted *Scarecrow* as *The Poppy Field*. She points out that the foregrounds are identical and the layers of paint in the center of *The Poppy Field* suggest the earlier version. The signature is similar as well.

37. Cut down and repainted by Homer in 1907, *Sailors Take Warning (Sunset)* was described in the Boston *Daily Evening Transcript* on 22 April 1893 as "the large canvas representing three girls standing on a rocky shore with the sun setting like a

scarlet globe in the mist behind them." In a 30 November 1907 letter from Homer to his brother, Charles, he describes reworking the painting: "I have just finished the picture by 'letting well enough alone'—which is the rule for grown artists *only.* This painting will not be new to you as it is the two girls & old pilot that has been hanging in my studio so long. Only I have made a new thing representing early evening—it is now *a very fine picture*" (Winslow Homer Papers, Archives of American Art, roll 2932). Autoradiographs taken by the Freer Gallery of Art in 1992 confirm that *Early Evening* was once composed of three girls standing on a rocky shore. Homer repainted most of the sky, from oranges and reds to a pale yellow, and added Prouts Neck junipers along the rocks.

38. According to American Art Association sales ledgers in the collection of the Archives of American Art, a painting of this title by Howe (72 x 96) was sold at American Art Association, New York, NY, 31 Jan.–2 Feb 1900, to Louis Stern. Only a watercolor of this title by Howe (15 x 30), however, is listed in the actual sale catalog, lot 93. Records indicate that the watercolor was also sold to Louis Stern.

39. *Norman Bull* was slightly repainted by the artist after its exhibition at the World's Columbian Exposition. This may have taken place ca. 1901 when the painting was exhibited at the 1901 Pan-American Exposition with the new title *Monarch of the Farm.*

40. A smaller version of this portrait was painted in 1894 for the Chamber of Commerce of the City of New York. The dimensions for the work shown at the exposition were taken from Huntington's *Account Book* (National Academy of Design Archives, New York, NY), p. 54.

41. A smaller painting of this subject (37 x 49) was offered for sale by Ipsen heirs at Vose Galleries, Boston, MA, in 1953. Records indicate that it did not sell and was apparently returned to the family.

42. This work was painted during the spring of 1883, during Herkomer's (a British painter and teacher) first visit to the United States. See an unidentified clipping from the "Herald," 24 June 1883, in the Thomas B. Clarke Papers, Archives of American Art, roll N598, frame 217.

43. This is possibly a portrait of Garth Wilkinson (Wilkie) James, brother of Henry James (Denver Art Museum curatorial files; letter from James L. Yarnell, 28 May 1991).

44. Macomber painted at least two works entitled *The Annunciation*, one measuring 50 x 40 inches, painted in 1915 and sold by Vose Galleries to the Fall River Public Library in 1951. The earlier version, shown at the World's Columbian Exposition, may have been in the collection of Mrs. S. D. Warren of Boston in 1914, as the 16 March 1914 issue of *The Mentor* claims that "'The Annunciation' is owned by Mrs. S. D. Warren."

45. Mrs. Reginald DeKoven was Anna Farwell, daughter of Sen. Charles B. Farwell of Illinois, whose portrait by Charles Boutwood was also shown at the exposition.

46. This painting is similar to the original version of *Love Locked Out* (46 x 26) which was exhibited at the Royal Academy in 1890 and is in the collection of the Tate Gallery in London. It differs from the original in that the image is reversed and wings have been added to the figure. Another version of the painting which more closely resembles the Tate version was offered for sale at Sotheby's Belgravia, London, 29 June 1976, lot 60, but did not sell.

47. Minor painted several works with this title during the 1880s and 1890s. Some examples which are candidates for the World's Columbian Exposition painting are: *Evening*, illustrated in *Sun and Shade* 1, no. 3 (1888), plate 2. *Evening* (lent by Mrs. Frederick Billings), shown in the Society of American Artists' 1892 retrospective exhibition. And, finally, the Corcoran Gallery of Art owned an *Eventide* (22 x 30½) which they purchased from the William T. Evans sale held through the American Art Association, New York, NY, in 1900. It was deaccessioned and sold through Parke-Bernet Galleries, New York, NY, in 1957.

48. In June of 1896, this painting was loaned by William Schaus (Messrs. Herman Schaus and A. W. Conover, Successors) to the "Second Annual Exhibition of Paintings in Aid of the 'Herald Free Ice Fund' and 'Tribune Fresh Air Fund,'" held at the American Art Galleries in New York, NY.

49. The lender is most likely Miss Martha E. French who appears in Chicago city directories through 1914.

50. Though the painting was executed ca. 1891 (it was exhibited in the spring exhibition at the National Academy of Design in 1891), it is inscribed "Copyright 1898," which is most likely close to the date that he finished the complete set of thirteen historical marine paintings.

51. Though biographical sources commonly list that Nehlig died in New York in 1909, no death certificate or obituary has yet been located. See Florence N. Levy, ed., *American Art Annual* 7 (1909–1910): 170, which states that he was "abroad" at this time.

52. This painting is possibly *Canal at Schleissheim, Near Munich, Bavaria*, 1883 (13 3/16 x 22¼) in the collection of the Cincinnati Art Museum.

53. In his scrapbook, now in the collection of the Dartmouth College Library, Parrish writes that the work, "was sent to Panama-Pacific Exhibition at San Francisco by its owner Mr. Mills (son of J. Harrison Mills) who says he bought it at Auction!"

54. There is a portrait of Phoebe Apperson Hearst, Peck's most prominent patron, at the University of California-Berkeley. The figure seems to be in fancy dress, and the costume would date from the early 1890s. This is a likely candidate for the exposition portrait, but no exposition label exists on the painting (letter from Mary Stoddard, Research Associate, Lowie Museum of Anthropology, 9 Oct. 1989).

55. Sophie Bendelari de Peralta is listed in the 1892 Boston city directory as "Paretta, S. Hotel Ludlow" and in the 1893 Boston city directory as "de Peralta, S. Mme, artist, Hotel Ludlow." She is not listed in Boston city directories after 1893, though, when exhibiting at the Boston Art Club in 1895, she cited her address as "Grundmann Studios, Boston." She exhibited two paintings in the 1882 spring exhibition of the National Academy of Design and is listed in the catalogue as "Sophie Bendelari, Rome, Italy."

56. For *Portrait of Alice*, *Reflection*, *Child in a Window*, and *Portrait of a Child* (Cornelia Wolcott), positive identification of the work shown in Chicago was made by Meredith Martindale and Pamela Moffat from cards in Lilla Cabot Perry's handwriting that remain with the artist's family.

57. This is most likely a portrait of Cornelia Wolcott, but, although Cornelia Wolcott's descendants have been traced, it remains unlocated.

58. This is most likely a portrait of Mrs. Ione Hinton Perry, the artist's mother.

59. The text printed along with the illustration of *The Night of the Nativity* in Smith's *Chefs-d'Oeuvre d'Art* states that the painting was purchased by the Buffalo Academy of Fine Arts after its exhibition at the American Art Association in New York in the summer of 1889. The Albright-Knox Art Gallery (formerly the Buffalo Academy) can find no record of it ever being in their collection, and since no lender appears in the WCE catalogue, it is doubtful if this work was ever purchased by the Buffalo Academy.

60. This is probably the *Portrait of Little Miss H.* shown at the Society of American Artists in 1891. See *Magazine of Art* 14 (1891): xxvi.

61. The painting was on long-term loan to the Metropolitan Museum of Art by the artist's wife, Mrs. Louise Richards, until her death around 1934. Mrs. Richards bequeathed the painting to her nieces Louise Parks Banes (Mrs. Lafayette Banes), Helen Parks Gallini (Mrs. Emil Gallini), and her nephew, Robert Parks. They expressed the wish to sell the painting, and the Metropolitan Museum suggested three New York dealers, John Levy Galleries, MacBeth Galleries, and Eric Newhouse Galleries. It is not known if the painting was ever sold by any of these dealers.

62. In most exhibition catalogues, including Salon records, the artist gives her name as Lucy Lee-Robbins.

63. The artist painted several portraits of her mother. One was shown at the Salon of 1887 (no. 1455) and described as a "full-length portrait of . . .a handsome lady, in a neat black evening dress with long train. . . . In the right hand she holds a red fan" (*The New York Herald* [Paris], 18 Jan. 1891). Another was shown at the new Salon in 1891 (no. 578) and was described in the *New York Times*, 13 July 1891, as "a full length portrait of her mother in white satin, pearls, gray hair, and a yellow toque."

64. Godfrey Mannheimer's daughter, Mamie Mannheimer Dessar (Mrs. Leonard A. Dessar), was asked to lend the painting to the Rosenthal Memorial Exhibition held in San Francisco in 1919. See William M. Kramer and Norton B. Stern, *San Francisco's Artist, Toby E. Rosenthal* (Northridge, CA: Santa Susan Press, 1978), 89–90.

65. The portrait was probably lent by Dora Wheeler (Mrs. Boudinot) Keith's mother, Mrs. Thomas Wheeler.

66. Frank Eugene Smith dropped his surname and was known as Frank Eugene by 1900. He made his reputation as a photographer in the Stieglitz circle.

67. Freer may not have lent this painting, as the catalogue indicates. The Freer Gallery of Art possesses the receipt of the works that Charles Freer lent to the World's Columbian Exposition, and this work does not appear on the receipt, nor is it in their collection.

68. This description is cited in a letter from May Brawley Hill, 28 Oct. 1987.

69. Weir's account book lists this painting as *Flowers*, 1883 (22 x 33) sold to J. R. Ball for $182. See an incomplete copy of the book in the National Museum of American Art's curatorial file for Weir's *Roses*, 1898.

70. A *Portrait de Mlle Von Hausen, du Théâtre-Royal-Braunschweig* was shown at the new Salon in 1892 by A. Vincent Renouf-Whelpley. The artist Annie Renouf, born Whelpley, is listed in Hans Wolfgang Singer, *Allgemeines Künstler-Lexicon* (Frankfurt, 1901) vol. 4, 43.

71. *The Red Room* is most likely the picture shown by Wiles in Chicago. It is inscribed from Wiles to William Merritt Chase and represents a girl in a black dress. Since the painting cannot be located, however, the existence of a confirming exhibition label is unknown.

72. Woodbury's scrapbook, in the possession of his family, recounts in two places that the painting was "cut up" and "destroyed" by the artist.

73. The sculpture remained at the Art Institute of Chicago at least through 1924. The *Chicago Evening Post*, 7 Oct. 1924, illustrates the work in the galleries. No records concerning the removal or destruction of the sculpture exist.

74. For additional information on Amy Aldis Bradley, see the Bradley family papers at the Schlesinger Library, Radcliffe College, Cambridge, MA.

75. The sculpture is now missing the sword.

76. Another plaster cast of the work (dated 1885, 92 ht.) was acquired by the University of Nebraska, Lincoln, from the Metropolitan Museum of Art in 1927. It has since been destroyed.

77. Shown at the World's Columbian Exposition in bronze and plaster, modifications were made to the base of the sculpture for its place in Clark Park. The base is now granite rather than plaster.

78. The *Revised Catalogue* does not indicate if Kemeys's works were exhibited in plaster or bronze. Though one early catalogue signifies that he exhibited all of his works in bronze, it is likely that some were shown in bronze and others in plaster.

79. Early catalogues give Loeher's address as Milwaukee, which is more indicative of his place of residence before and after the World's Columbian Exposition. Like many sculptors, Loeher may have temporarily moved to Chicago in 1892 to assist with the architectural sculpture at the fair. Loeher also exhibited *Columbian Shield (Deathless Shield of Homer)* (unlocated) in the Fine Arts Building. Though it does not appear in any version of the official catalogues, it can be seen in an installation photograph of the north court of the Fine Arts Building and is listed as a work accepted by the Chicago jury for exhibition in the Fine Arts Building in the Chicago *Inter-Ocean*, 7 March 1893.

80. A plaster relief portrait of Thomas Eakins by William O'Donovan is in the collection of the Pennsylvania Academy of the Fine Arts. It may give some indication of the appearance of the unlocated bronze bust.

81. A large marble bust of Lowell by Partridge was found in a New York City warehouse in April of 1957. See the *New York Times*, 28 April 1957, p. 58, and 5 May 1957, p. 127, for an illustration and articles that recount the discovery of this bust.

82. See Lilian Rixey, "Three Old Ladies. They Bought the 'Daily Worker,'" *Life*, 14 Oct. 1946, 2, 4, 6–8, for the most complete published account of the life of Ferdinanda Wesselhoeft Reed.

ACKNOWLEDGMENTS

When the World's Columbian Exposition opened on 1 May 1893, Halsey C. Ives, chief of the art department, must have experienced a monumental sense of accomplishment. In just two years he and his associates had pulled together an international exhibition of paintings, sculptures, watercolors, drawings, and architectural renderings that totaled more than 10,000 objects. A catalogue had been produced that was reasonably accurate under the circumstances, and although some of the objects were not in place on opening day, they were soon afterward. Such was the energy and vision of the men and women who were the motivating forces behind the fair that the sheer magnitude and complexity of the undertaking seem never to have daunted them. Considering the modes of communication and transportation and the reliance on manual typewriters and handwritten correspondence, what they accomplished can today be viewed with admiration and amazement.

Ives had considerably less time to bring his show together than we have had to produce this publication and the accompanying exhibition, but the task we set ourselves has proved to be equally challenging in its own way. In 1986 when the National Museum of American Art and the National Portrait Gallery first decided to celebrate the centennial of the American art shown in the Fine Arts Palace, two goals were envisioned. The first centered on locating and/or documenting as a permanent record the appearance of as many of the nearly 1,200 American paintings and sculptures in that show as possible. We were motivated by a desire to know the appearance of the original art exhibition in its entirety and to explore the widest range of possibilities from which our 1993 show might be chosen. Like all art historians, we hoped that this intensive research would lead us to hidden surprises. Our second objective focused on creating a meaningful exhibition that would go beyond a mere collection of works exhibited at the fair. We sought a selection of one hundred objects that would be both visually and aesthetically interesting yet also reflect the social and cultural context of the late nineteenth century. This effort has been an equally demanding quest. Over several years, as we repeatedly laid out the illustrations for discussion, certain groupings of objects based on subject matter emerged and became the basis for the four sections of the exhibition, as illustrated in the plate section of this publication.

When the World's Columbian Exposition closed in October 1893, Halsey Ives submitted a large request for funds to reimburse him for the official entertainment of visiting dignitaries. Presumably he wished to thank the scores of individuals who had been most generous in making the art exhibition possible. If we had Ives's resources, we would be pleased to do the same, but lacking them we must simply thank wholeheartedly the thousands of individuals who have responded to our inquiries and expressed interest and enthusiasm in this project.

Publication of this book was generously underwritten by the Elizabeth F. Cheney Foundation. We are particularly grateful to Lawrence Belles, president; Allan R. Drebin, treasurer; and Howard M. McCue III, secretary, for their support enabling us to provide future generations with a permanent record. We could not have initiated our research nor implemented the exhibition without the ongoing assistance of grants from the Smithsonian Institution Special Exhibition Fund. We appreciate the support of the panel that found the concept of the research and exhibition meritorious, and we wish to thank Tom L. Freudenheim, Assistant Secretary for the Arts and Humanities at the Smithsonian Institution, and his assistant Barbara Schneider, Program Manager, for their interest and advocacy.

We are most grateful to Robert Rydell, who took time from his numerous projects to share with us his intimate knowledge of the curious and compelling phenomenon of world's fairs. In supplying the perspective of a seasoned historian to this catalogue, he has considerably augmented our understanding of the cultural legacy of the 1893 fair.

In the early years of the project, three persons joined the team and made an inestimable impact. Brandon Brame Fortune, a curatorial assistant at the National Portrait Gallery, assumed the major responsibility for locating the portraits shown in 1893 and gathering the contemporary references and criticism associated with these works. Her ability to track and utilize genealogical data and to instruct numerous graduate students in primary documentary research has been fundamental to the successful discovery of many of the portraits still in private hands. As a summer intern at the National Museum of American Art, Michelle Mead rapidly absorbed the intricacies of locating missing works. She was persuaded to take a temporary position as an assistant and, fortunately for us, remained for over three years. While continuing her search for unlocated objects, she soon took on the monumental tasks of coordinating photographic requests and permissions. With others she became responsible for standardizing the catalogue information and ensuring its accuracy, ending her sojourn at the museum in an editorial capacity. Diane Dillon, a doctoral candidate at Yale University, scoured the country for paintings and sculptures and made extensive forays to investigate the condition and appropriateness of objects for the exhibition. Her research made her a key player in resolving the form and content of the show, providing crucial links to tie the material together. Brandon, Diane, and Michelle also deserve special credit for their extensive labor on the annotation and compilation of the catalogue and for their work on the labels for the exhibition and the text material in the plate section of this publication.

Many museums have generously ferreted out information on the history of objects in their collections, which has been crucial for the catalogue section of the publication. Those who have been particularly helpful include Nicki Thiras, Addison Gallery of American Art; Laura Catalano, Kari E. Horowicz, and Annette Masling, Albright-Knox Art Gallery; Doreen Bolger and Sarah Cash, Amon Carter Museum; Jack Perry Brown, Anndora Morginson, Milo Naeve, Lieschen A. Potuznik, Emily Romers, John Smith, and Mary Woolever, The Art Institute of Chicago; Lawrence Campbell, The Art Students League of New York; Joanna D. Catron, Belmont, The Gari Melchers Estate and Memorial Gallery; Debra Balken, Berkshire Museum; Joyce Butler, Brick Store Museum; Teresa A. Carbone and Barbara Dayer Gallati, The Brooklyn Museum; Lynnda Arrasmith, Canton Art Institute; Louise Lippincott, Carnegie Museum of Art; Linda Wesselman Jackson, Chesterwood; Genetta Gardner, Sarah S. Johnson, and Cathy G. Shaffer, Cincinnati Art Museum; Russ A. Pritchard, The Civil War Library and Museum, Philadelphia; Bruce Robertson, Cleveland Museum of Art; Karol Lawson, Columbus (Georgia) Museum; Rod Bouc and Lisa Weber Greenberg, Columbus Museum of Art; Marisa Keller, The Corcoran Gallery of Art; Robert J. Evans, Danforth Museum of Art; Susan Taylor, Davis Museum and Cultural Center; Dominique H. Vasseur, The Dayton Art Institute; Lauretta Dimmick and Lewis I. Sharp, Denver Museum of Art; Matthias Eberle and Christoph Stölzl, Deutsches Historisches Museum; Barbara Rothermel, Everhart Museum; Marie Frasz, Fabyan Villa; Margaret Burton, Forest Lawn Museum; Laveta Emory and Linda Merrill, Freer Gallery of Art; Steve Coomba and Kay Koeninger, Galleries of the Claremont Colleges; Tracey Bashkoff, Guild Hall Museum; Nancy Harm, Herbert F. Johnson Museum of Art; Jennifer Saville, Honolulu Academy of Arts; Holliday T. Day and Martin F. Krause, Indianapolis Museum of Art; Mary Ann Johnson, Jane Addams' Hull-House Museum; Jimmie Lee Buehler, John H. Vanderpoel Art Association; Penelope Smith, Joslyn Art Museum; Allen S. Weller, Krannert Art Museum; Ilene S. Fort, Los Angeles County Museum of Art; Sally Mills and Marc Simpson, M. H. de Young Memorial Museum; Deborah Davis Grazier, The Mattatuck Museum; Patricia P. Bladon, Memphis Brooks Museum of Art; Barbara File, Donna Hassler, Kathleen Luhrs, Carrie Rebora, and H. Barbara Weinberg, The Metropolitan Museum of Art; Alejandro Anreus, The Montclair Art Museum; Susan Else, Monterey Peninsula Museum of Art; Carmen T. Ruiz-Fischler, Museo de Arte de Ponce; Melody Ennis and Ann Slimmon, Museum of Art, Rhode Island School of Design; Trevor Fairbrother, Eleanor L. Jones, Charlotte Emans Moore, Theodore E. Stebbins, Jr., and Carol Troyen, Museum of Fine Arts, Boston; Phyllis M. Cohen, Museum of New Mexico, Museum of Fine Arts; Jan Seidler Ramirez, Museum of the City of New York; Babs Vaughan, Muskegon Museum of Art; David Derringer and Barbara Krulik, National Academy of Design; Cameran G. Castiel, Nicolai Cikovsky, Susan Davis, Elizabeth D. Pochter, and D. Dodge Thompson, National Gallery of Art; Charles C. Hill, National Gallery of Canada; Nancy Gwinn and Rhoda Ratner, National Museum of American History; Timothy Stevens, National Museum of Wales; Mel Ellis, New Britain Museum of American Art; Zolton Buki, New Jersey State Museum; Annette Blaugrund, New-York Historical Society; Harvey Jones and Arthur Monroe, Oakland Museum; Beverly Harrington, The Paine Art Center & Arboretum; Linda Bantel, Susan Danley, Elyssa Kane, Cheryl Leibold, and Jeanette Toohey, Pennsylvania Academy of the Fine Arts; Darrel L. Sewell and Claudia Ginanni, Philadelphia Museum of Art; Erika Passantino and Eliza Rathbone, The Phillips Collection; Mary C. Stoddard, The Phoebe A. Hearst Museum of Anthropology; Jerry Bloomer, R. W. Norton Art Gallery; Norma Sindelar, Saint Louis Museum of Art; Kay Williams, Sheldon Memorial Art Gallery; Edward R. Quick, Sheldon Swope Art Museum; Dean Porter, Snite Museum of Art; Martha Hoppin, Springfield Museum of Fine Arts; Michael Goodison, Smith College Museum of Art; Judith O'Toole, Sordoni Art Gallery; Carl Nold, State Museum of Pennsylvania; Margaret Molnar, Staten Island Museum of Arts & Sciences; David S. Brooke, John H. Brooks, and Beth Carver Wees, Sterling and Francine Clark Art Institute; Leslie Parris, Tate Gallery; Nancy Ames Petersen, Timken Museum of Art; Yoko Terasima, Tokyo National Museum; Anne O. Morris, The Toledo Museum of Art; James W. Cheevers, United States Naval Academy Museum; Lisa Calden, University Art Museum, Berkeley; David M. Carroll, Utah Museum of Fine Arts; Richard H. W. Brauer, Valparaiso University Museum of Art; Rebecca Lawton, Vassar College Art Gallery; Linda Ayres, Betsy Kornhauser, and Elizabeth McClintock, Wadsworth Atheneum; William R. Johnston, Walters Art Gallery; Thomas Lidtke, West Bend Gallery of Fine Arts; David Meschutt, West Point Museum; Richard C. Kugler and Judith N. Lund, Whaling Museum; Susan Strickler, Worcester Art Museum; and Wally Darnley, Worcester Historical Museum.

Without the close cooperation of many dealers and auction houses, the discovery of numerous unlocated works would have been extremely difficult. The shared knowledge has been much appreciated. To the dealers who have loaned works or assisted with private collectors, we owe sincere thanks: Edward Shein, American Art Search; Fred Hill, May Brawley Hill, Ida M. Smith, and Bruce Weber, Berry-Hill Galleries; Linda S. Cook, Butterfield & Butterfield; Odile Duff, Coe Kerr Gallery; Debra Force, Christie's; Rose O'Conner, Comenos Fine Arts; Janis Conner and Joel Rosenkranz, Conner-Rosenkranz; Michael Rose, David Ramus Fine Art; Robert D. Schwarz, Frank S. Schwarz & Son; Leslie Lynch Clinton, Freeman/Fine Arts of Philadelphia; Richard Green, London, England; M. P. Naud and Kathleen Burnside, Hirschl & Adler Galleries; Diane Jensen, Brookline, MA; David Dufour, Mary Lublin, and Vance Jordan, Jordan-Volpe Gallery; Melissa De Medieros, Knoedler & Co.; George J. Turak, Lagakos-Turak Gallery; Alexander R. Raydon, Raydon Gallery; Richard T. York, Richard York Gallery; Robin S. Reynolds, Skinner, Inc.; Lois Earl and Holly Goetz, Sotheby's; David Henry and Lisa N. Peters, Spanierman Gallery; Robert C. Vose, Jr. and Anne W. Schmoll, Vose Galleries; Elaine Banks, William Doyle Galleries; and William Vareika, William Vareika Fine Art.

The search for lost works was facilitated considerably by the invaluable assistance supplied by archives, historical societies, libraries, universities, and other institutions: Nancy A. Johnson, American Academy and Institute of Arts and Letters; Jane E. Lowenthal, Barnard College Archives; Hugh McLellan Russell, Belfast (ME) Free Library; Ruth Van Wagoner, Bergen County (NJ) Division of Cultural and Historic Affairs; Janice Chadbourne, Boston Public Library; Candace L. Ekdahl, Bradford Area (PA) Public Library; Brenda Marder, Brandeis University; Clyde H. Eller, Buffalo & Erie County (NY) Historical Society; Diane Morton, California School for the Deaf; Edmund Kenealy, Canton (MA) Public Library; Leslie H. Kenyon, Central Illinois Landmarks Foundation; Christiane Laude, Centre de Documentation Benjamin Franklin, Paris; Jay Cantor and Jonathan Harding, The Century Association, New York; Emily Clark, Eileen Flanagan, Riva Feshbach, Wendy Greenhouse, and Larry Viskochil, Chicago Historical Society; Laura Linard, Andrea Mark, and Galen R. Wilson, Chicago Public Library; Cynthia Fienga, Cleveland Public Library; Lou DeBruicker, Columbia Club, Indianapolis; Sarah Weiner, Columbia University; Sister Aline Plante, Congregation of the Presentation of Mary; Barbara A. Musselman, Cuyahoga County (OH) Public Library; Philip N. Cronenwett, Dartmouth College Library; Sister Michele Randall, Daughters of Charity of St. Vincent de Paul; Martha Utterback, Daughters of the Republic of Texas Library; Beverly Roelleke, Decatur (IL) Public Library; Kay Wisnia, Denver Public Library; Stacy Komitopoulos, Duquesne Club, Pittsburgh; Dorothy T. King, East Hampton (NY) Library; Rodrigo Aguirre De Carcer, Embassy of Spain, Washington, D.C.; Elizabeth Furdon, The Episcopal Diocese of Massachusetts; Mark Burnette, Evanston (IL) Historical Society; Brad Evans, Federal Reserve Bank; T. Gerard Connolly, Fordham University; John Chaney, The George Hail Library, Warren, RI; Penny Forrester, Greenville County (SC) Library; Fern DesChamps, Greenville County (Prescott, Ontario) Historical Society; Louise Ambler, Harvard University; Peter Blodgett, Henry E. Huntington Library; William T. La Moy, James Duncan Phillips Library, Essex Institute; Gillian Q. Blair, Jefferson County (NY) Historical Society; Edith E. Prout, Jenkintown (PA) Library; Caroline B. Matzen, Kingston (NY) Area Library; Carl Thomas Engel, Lake County Historical Society, Mentor, OH; Doris A. Most, Leake and Watts Children's Home; Marillyn D. Loomis, Archives, The Loomis-Chaffee School, Windsor, CT; Harriet Henderson, Louisville Free Public Library; Dina Malgeri, Malden (MA) Public Library; Steve Herald, Manistee (MI) County Historical Museum; Pamela Spoor, Manistee County Library; Sister Anna Mary Waickman, Marygrove Library, Detroit; Katherine H. Griffin, Massachusetts Historical Society; Jane M.

D'Alessandro, Melrose (MA) Public Library; Barclay Feather, Milton (MA) Academy; Page Talbot and Paula Feid, Moore College of Art, Philadelphia; Michael L. Olsen, New Mexico Highlands University; Gladys E. Bolhouse, Newport Historical Society; Joy C. Van Riper, Newark (NY) Public Library; R. Russell Maylone, Patrick Quinn, and Alice Snyder, Northwestern University; Kiran B. Patel, The Nutley (NJ) Free Public Library; Mary Sayre Haverstock, Ohio Artists' Project, Oberlin College Library; Michael Phipps, Omaha Public Library; Sonya Hung, Pasadena Public Library; Pat Gandy, Perth Amboy (NJ) Free Public Library; Claude Schoch, PhoneDisc USA; Curtis Harker and Glenna M. Laird, Salem County (NJ) Historical Society; Patrick Clougherty, Susan Cooney, Lorraine Jackson, and Alice V. N. Johnson, Salem (MA) Public Library; Susan Gleason and Libby Kane, Sarah Lawrence College; Donald G. Morton, Sedalia (MO) Public Library; Lorna Condon, Society for the Preservation of New England Antiquities; Sister Margaret M. O'Rourke, Sisters of the Blessed Sacrament; E. J. Wolleswinkel, Stichting Iconografisch Bureau, The Hague; Robin Carroll-Mann, Summit (NJ) Free Public Library; Carl L. Beck, James E. Cheek III, and Louise Trotter, Tennessee Wesleyan College; Julie S. Berkowitz and Dr. Russell W. Schaedler, Thomas Jefferson University, Philadelphia; Irene Martin, Toledo-Lucas County (OH) Public Library; Phyllis Barr, Trinity Church, New York; Amanda C. Jones, Ulster County (NY) Historical Society; Dennis Loy, Union League Club of Chicago; Roger Freedman, Union League Club, New York; Andrew Berner and Jane Reed, University Club, New York; Charles Lamb, University of Notre Dame Archives; Sandra Markham, University of Pennsylvania Archives; Nancy S. MacKechnie, Vassar College Library; Elizabeth D. Castner and Kristen Petersen, Waltham (MA) Historical Society; Pamela Simpson, Washington and Lee University; Dean M. Zimmerman, The Western Reserve Historical Society; Carol M. Russell, Wilton (MA) Library Association; and Richard Jones, Worcester Mechanics Hall Association.

To those scholars who opened their files and unselfishly shared their special expertise or knowledge of the period, we remain exceedingly grateful: Mildred Albronda, Julie A. Aronson, Margorie Balge, Faith Andrews Bedford, Jennifer A. Martin Bienenstock, Julie Brown, Laurene Buckley, Mary Alice Burke, Bruce W. Chambers, Greta E. Cooper, John Davis, Elizabeth de Veer, Betsy Fahlman, Ann Feldman, Madeleine Fidell-Beaufort, Diane P. Fischer, Abigail Booth Gerdts, William H. Gerdts, Mick Gidley, Jim Gilbert, Galina Gorokhoff, Kathryn Greenthal, Janet Headley, Susan Hobbs, Elaine Kilmurray, Virginia Couse Leavitt, Meredith Martindale, Pamela Moffat, Merl M. Moore, Jr., Keith N. Morgan, Alexander Nemerov, Robert Olpin, Michael Panhorst, Patricia Jobe Pierce, Ronald G. Pisano, Kathleen Pyne, the late Gary A. Reynolds, Michael Richman, Beverly Rood, Rona Schneider, David Sellin, Mary Smart, Thomas Somma, Regina Soria, Joy Sperling, Annette Stott, J. Gray Sweeney, Tara L. Tappert, Henri Tribout de Morembert, and James L. Yarnall.

For a project of this nature, often requiring considerable genealogical research, a variety of individuals, in many cases descendants of the artists or sitters, have provided previously unknown documentation as well as indispensable clues. Among those who kindly gave of their singular knowledge, we salute Edith F. Axelson, Joan Barnes, Lee Baxandall, Ifrene Benoist-Mechin, JoAnne W. Bowie, Phelps Brown, Richard and Jean Bryant, Mr. and Mrs. Anthony S. Bull, Joseph Warner Butler III, John H. Carnahan, Phimister P. Church, Donald Clifford, Adelaide N. Cooley, Virginia Anthony Cooper, James L. Coran, Jean D'Albis, John Davis, Wayne H. Decker, Genevieve Dobbin, Mary Rudd Dreyer, the Duke of Argyll, Mrs. Herbert A. Durfee, Jr., John Farquhar, Rolf Fjelde, Mr. and Mrs. Aymar H. Fowler, Alice Cooney Frelinghuysen, Arthur Garrity, Robert A. Gelert, Sr., Philip Gemmer, Kate Grinburg, Mrs. Eric Gugler, Dr. Anne Renouf Headley, Christian A. Herter, Jr., Harlow Higinbotham, Arthur Hoe, Hope Hogan, Reginald Hudson, David Huntoon, Ann Hutchison, William W. Jenney, Frances F. Jones, Richard A. Kellaway, Sidney and Norma Kosann, Mrs. Henry La Farge, Raymond Linder, Mary Haviland Mallet, Richard Manoogian, Betty Hoag McGlynn, Walter A. Nelson-Rees, Moritz E. Pape, Arthur J. Phelan, Jr., Blair Proctor, Eric Roussel, William D. Sawtell, M. Leonard Schoonman, Edith Scott, Harry Scott, Douglas Seaman, Barea Lamb Seeley, Dr. Stephen Sheppard, Elizabeth Sita, Mrs. C. Arthur Sloughfy, Theodore L. Steele, Carol Stussi, Michael Teague, Mary Trotter, John H. Turner, Alice B. Vincilione, Nelson H. White, David Williamson, and Alison Wilson.

Our greatest debt for their sustained support belongs to our colleagues at both the National Museum of American Art and the National Portrait Gallery. Elizabeth Broun generously gave us the benefit of her specialized knowledge about the fair and the period and has been indefatigable in her effort to secure funding for the exhibition. Alan Fern, with keen awareness of the historical importance of the fair, has given us his enthusiasm and support, which have been fundamental to the realization of this project. To William Truettner we owe a particular debt of gratitude for his help in defining the organization of the show and for his continuous sagacious advice.

Curators Jeremy Adamson, Lois M. Fink, Virginia

Mecklenburg, Ellen G. Miles, Richard Murray, Jacqueline Serwer, and Robert G. Stewart kindly lent their expertise to our research efforts. In the library, Cecilia Chin, Martin Kalfatovic, Patricia Lynagh, and Kathryn Trillas strove valiantly to fulfill our requests for rare books and catalogues. Our colleagues in the Archives of American Art— Betty Blum, Arthur Breton, Robert Brown, Paul J. Karlstrom, Judy Throm, and Joyce Tyler—played an important role in bringing archival material to our attention. Christine Hennessey and other members of the Inventories of American Painting and Sculpture aided our research most advantageously.

Registrar Suzanne Jenkins, with the assistance of Jack Birnkammer, kept a watchful eye on the endless details of insurance, packing, and shipping associated with an exhibition of this complexity. The rather overwhelming magnitude of our photographic requests was handled with aplomb by Kimberly Cody, Mildred Baldwin, Michael Fischer, Marianne Gurley, Rolland White, and Eugene Young. The improved appearance of some works may be credited to our conservators Ann Creager, Helen Ingalls, Lou Molnar-Ockershausen, Quentin Rankin, and Stefano Scafetta, all of whom were also most helpful in answering our endless conservation questions. The necessary repair of some frames and the construction of others were most skillfully handled by Martin Kotler. Nello Marconi and Al Elkins employed their skills in exhibition design to enhance further the commanding works in the show, while Beverly Cox made valuable suggestions that have added greatly to the visual coherence of the presentation. Bonnie Miller patiently explored our unusual suggestions about sponsors and coordinated our development efforts. Staff colleagues Karen Cassedy, Susan Cross, Jay Gaglione, Kevin Greene, Susan Haase, Angella Lyle, Christine Ossolinski, Lara Scott, and Deborah Thomas graciously supported our efforts in countless other ways.

At various stages in the project we were fortunate to have the assistance of an exceptionally talented group of research assistants, interns, and volunteers. Mary Fearon, Marie Louise Friendly, Jennifer Kabat, Anne Leonard, Bridget Manoogian, Glovenia Snead, and Claire Tieder were tremendously energetic and enthusiastic research assistants, spending hours at a time in the stacks at the Library of Congress and elsewhere, combing books and periodicals to locate lost works of art or resurrect information on little-known artists and lenders. Their devotion was matched by a gifted cadre of interns who made important contributions to our research efforts while also taking responsibility for so many of the tedious tasks required to make order out of chaos: Gretchen Bender, Susan Bollendorf, Ruth Sudweeks Clawson, Amy Comito, Alice DeWys, Sarah French, Kathy Gould, Adriane Herman, Nancy Holst, Joan James, Jessica Johnston, Marlene Kagen, Jackie Kodner, Carolyn McArthur, Kristin Norell, Leslie Olson, Amy Prochowski, Piper Rankine, Stephanie Rieke, Judy Shindel, Deborah Silverman, and Meg Steward. The uncommon crew of volunteers who rounded out our research team included Kim Donley, Julie Horan, Dawn Lewis, Katherine L. McCulloch, Cy Mill, Cynthia Mills, Pam Potter-Hennessey, and Marian Wardle.

On the editorial front, our thanks go to Terence Winch for his work on the catalogue of objects and the essay by Robert W. Rydell and to Janet Wilson for her work on the essays by Carolyn Carr, Brandon Fortune and Michelle Mead, and the other parts of the book. Our talented designer Polly Sexton handled a steady litany of special requests with unfailing grace and good humor. Steve Dietz remained amazingly calm while coordinating the entire production process, magically solving a myriad of editorial problems and tirelessly insisting on a topnotch product.

C.K.C.
G.G.

APPENDICES

APPENDIX A
United States Judges on the ***International Committee of Judges for the Department of Fine Arts***

Oil Painting
Thomas Allen
J. G. Brown
William Merritt Chase
C. da Cossa Conger
Henry F. Farny
R. Swain Gifford
Thomas Hovenden
John La Farge
Carl Marr
George W. Maynard
Gari Melchers
F. D. Millet
J. C. Nicoll
Walter Shirlaw
Worthington Whittredge
Mary M. Solari

Sculpture
Daniel Chester French
Olin L. Warner

Engraving, Etching, etc.
John P. Davis
Frederick Dielman
Mary Hallock Foote
Emily Sartain

APPENDIX B
Non-Competitors for Awards

Oil Painting
Henry Alexander
W. S. Allen
William T. Amsden
William J. Baer
E. A. Bell
Enella Benedict
R. A. Blakelock
Carle J. Blenner
Frank M. Boggs
Joseph H. Boston
Frederick A. Bridgman
J. B. Bristol
J. Appleton Brown
J. G. Brown
Matilda Browne
George B. Butler
Mary Buttles
Carlton T. Chapman
Rose Clark
Walter Clark
B. W. Clinedinst
Elizabeth R. Coffin
George W. Cohen
Mrs. Charlotte B. Coman
Lucy S. Conant
Eanger I. Couse
Lockwood de Forest
M. F. H. de Haas
Julia Dillon
Pauline A. Dohn
Mattie Dubé
Frant Dvorak
C. Harry Eaton
Charles Warren Eaton
Lydia Field Emmet
Joe Evans
Lucia Fairchild
William Bailey Faxon
Charles Noel Flagg
Mary B. O. Fowler
John A. Fraser
Elizabeth Gardner
Rosalie Lorraine Gill
C. A. Green
Frank Russell Green
Lillian Greene
Edward Grenet
John J. Hammer
Charles X. Harris
J. T. Harwood
Ida C. Haskell
C. Coventry Haynes
G. P. A. Healy
Edward L. Henry
Albert Herter
George Hetzel
Roswell S. Hill
Sarah Levis Hipple
Edith M. Howes
Benoni Irwin
Samuel Isham
Humphreys Johnston
Mrs. Dora Wheeler Keith
Susan M. Ketcham
James S. King
Robert Koehler
Ella Condie Lamb
Chester Loomis
Joseph Lyman
Mrs. Anna Lea Merritt
Charles H. Miller
Robert C. Minor
H. Humphrey Moore
Edward Moran
Walter Nettleton
Mrs. Marie Guise Newcomb
Charles Sprague Pearce
F. Winthrop Ramsdell
John Willard Raught
F. K. M. Rehn
William M. J. Rice
Edward F. Rook
Alexander Schilling
Jeannette Scott
Annie B. Shepley
Thomas W. Shields
Emily Slade
DeCost Smith
Henry P. Smith
F. W. Stokes
John R. Strickler
George Taggart
Stacy Tolman
A. Van Briggle
Kruseman Van Elten
L. E. Van Gorder
H. A. Vincent
Laurie Wallace
Albright Wigand
William Woodward
E. Marshall Woolfolk

Sculpture
Paul W. Bartlett
Douglas Tilden

APPENDIX C

Organizational Structure of the 1893 World's Fair

WORLD'S COLUMBIAN EXPOSITION
Private company of stockholders incorporated under Illinois law

BOARD OF DIRECTORS
Elected annually by stockholders; supervisory authority over other WCE bodies

WCE BOARD OF DIRECTORS' FINE ARTS COMMITTEE
Charles L. Hutchinson, Chicago, Chairman
James W. Ellsworth, Chicago
Potter Palmer, Chicago
Elbridge G. Keith, Chicago (replaces Palmer, April 1892)
Robert Waller, Chicago
Martin A. Ryerson, Chicago (replaces Waller, March 1891)
Eugene S. Pike, Chicago (replaces Ryerson, April 1892)
Charles T. Yerkes, Chicago

OFFICE OF THE
George Royal Davis

DEPARTMENT OF
Halsey C. Ives, Chief
Charles M. Kurtz, Assistant to Chief
Sara T. Hallowell, Assistant to Chief

ADVISORY COMMITTEES

NEW YORK
J. Q. A. Ward, Chairman
William B. Tuthill, Secretary

Sculpture
Augustus Saint-Gaudens
J. Q. A. Ward
Olin L. Warner

Oil Painting
William Merritt Chase
R. Swain Gifford
Eastman Johnson
H. Bolton Jones
F. D. Millet
Frederick Dielman (substitute for Millet)
George Willoughby Maynard (substitute for Millet)

PENNSYLVANIA
William Dalliba Dutton, Chairman
Clifford P. Grayson, Secretary

Sculpture
J. J. Boyle
Edmund A. Stewardson
Charles Grafly (substitute for Stewardson)

Oil Painting
John W. Beatty
Charles E. Dana
William Dalliba Dutton
Clifford P. Grayson
Joseph R. Woodwell

MASSACHUSETTS
J. Foxcroft Cole, Chairman
Thomas Allen (substitute for Cole)
Frederic P. Vinton, Secretary

Sculpture
Daniel Chester French

Oil Painting
Thomas Allen
John J. Enneking
I. M. Gaugengigl
Edmund C. Tarbell
Frederic P. Vinton

FLORENCE
Sculpture
William Couper
Larkin G. Mead
Waldo Story (rep. Rome)

JURIES OF SELECTION

NEW YORK
Sculpture
Augustus Saint-Gaudens
J. Q. A. Ward
Olin L. Warner
Daniel Chester French (rep. Massachusetts)
John J. Boyle (rep. Pennsylvania)

Oil Painting
William Merritt Chase
R. Swain Gifford
Eastman Johnson
H. Bolton Jones
F. D. Millet
George Willoughby Maynard (substitute for Millet)
I. M. Gaugengigl (rep. Massachusetts)
Edmund C. Tarbell (rep. Massachusetts)
John W. Beatty (rep. Pennsylvania)
Charles E. Dana (rep. Pennsylvania)

PENNSYLVANIA
Sculpture
J. J. Boyle
Charles Grafly
Daniel Chester French (rep. Massachusetts)
Olin L. Warner (rep. New York)

Oil Painting
John W. Beatty
Charles E. Dana
William Dalliba Dutton
Stephen Parrish (substitute for Dutton)
Clifford P. Grayson
Eastman Johnson (rep. New York)
H. Bolton Jones (rep. New York)
Joseph R. Woodwell (rep. Pennsylvania)

MASSACHUSETTS
Sculpture
Daniel Chester French
Olin L. Warner (rep. New York)
Charles Grafly (rep. Pennsylvania)

Oil Painting
Thomas Allen
John J. Enneking
I. M. Gaugengigl
Edmund C. Tarbell
Frederic P. Vinton
William Merritt Chase (rep. New York)
R. Swain Gifford (rep. New York)

FLORENCE
Sculpture
William Couper
Larkin G. Mead

WORLD'S COLUMBIAN COMMISSION

Created by act of Congress; Commissioners appointed by the governments of their respective states

WCC FINE ARTS COMMITTEE

Augustus G. Bullock, Worcester, MA, Chairman
William I. Buchanon, Sioux City, IA
Chauncey M. Depew, New York, NY
Michel H. de Young, San Francisco, CA
James M. Hodges, Baltimore, MD
Orson V. Tousley, Minneapolis, MN
Albert A. Wilson, Washington, DC
Thomas J. Woodward, New Orleans, LA

DIRECTOR-GENERAL

FINE ARTS—DEPARTMENT K

ADVISORY COMMITTEES

GREAT BRITAIN
Oil Painting
Edwin A. Abbey
Mark Fisher
John McLure Hamilton
John Singer Sargent

PARIS
Charles Sprague Pearce, Chairman
Walter McEwen, Secretary

Sculpture
Paul W. Bartlett
Frederick W. MacMonnies

Oil Painting
Frederick A. Bridgman
William T. Dannat
Walter Gay
Alexander Harrison
Gari Melchers
Charles Sprague Pearce
Julius L. Stewart
Edwin Lord Weeks

MUNICH
Carl Marr, Chairman
Orrin Peck, Secretary

Oil Painting
Walter Beck
J. Frank Currier
Carl Marr
Orrin Peck
Toby Rosenthal

ROME
Sculpture
Harriet Hosmer
Franklin Simmons
Waldo Story

Oil Painting
C. C. Coleman
William Stanley Haseltine
Elihu Vedder

JURIES OF SELECTION

NATIONAL JURY AT CHICAGO
Sculpture
Daniel Chester French, Boston
J. Gelert, Chicago
Carl Rohl-Smith, Chicago
Lorado Taft, Chicago
J. Q. A. Ward, New York
Olin L. Warner, New York
J. J. Boyle, Philadelphia
Robert P. Bringhurst, St. Louis

Oil Painting
Thomas Allen, Boston
Frederick W. Freer, Chicago
Walter McEwen, Chicago
J. H. Vanderpoel, Chicago
Henry Farny, Cincinnati
Gari Melchers, Detroit
C. C. Coleman, Italy
Douglas Volk, Minneapolis
J. G. Brown, New York
George Willoughby Maynard, New York
J. Francis Murphy, New York
Thomas Hovenden, Philadelphia
John H. Fry, St. Louis

PARIS
Oil Painting
Frederick A. Bridgman
William T. Dannat
Walter Gay
Alexander Harrison
Walter McEwen
Gari Melchers
Charles Sprague Pearce
Julius L. Stewart
Edwin Lord Weeks

MUNICH
Oil Painting
Walter Beck
J. Frank Currier
Carl Marr
Orrin Peck
Toby Rosenthal

ROME
Sculpture
Harriet Hosmer
Franklin Simmons
Waldo Story
Larkin G. Mead (rep. Florence)

Oil Painting
C. C. Coleman
W. S. Haseltine
Elihu Vedder

SELECTED BIBLIOGRAPHY

CONTEMPORARY SOURCES

Archival Materials

To date, the official records of the Department of Fine Arts at the fair have not been discovered. Some of this material was preserved in the papers of Charles M. Kurtz (see below), which were given to the Archives of American Art during the summer of 1991. Abbreviations for frequently cited sources are given in parentheses.

Archives of American Art, Smithsonian Institution, Washington, D.C. (AAA)
- Charles M. Kurtz Papers
- John Quincy Adams Ward Papers [filmed from originals held by the New-York Historical Society]

The Art Institute of Chicago, Archives (AIC)
- Bertha H. Palmer Papers

The Art Institute of Chicago, The Ryerson and Burnham Libraries
- C. D. Arnold Photograph Albums [Presentation Albums]
- Daniel H. Burnham Collection
- Art Institute Scrapbooks (1869–1956)

Chicago Historical Society, Library (CHS)
- John Barrett Kerfoot Scrapbooks on the World's Columbian Exposition of 1893

Chicago Historical Society, Manuscripts Division
- Bertha H. Palmer Papers
- World's Columbian Exposition, Board of Lady Managers Records
- World's Columbian Exposition, Executive Committee Minutes
- World's Columbian Exposition, Board of Directors' Minutes

Chicago Public Library, Special Collections Department (CPL)
- C. D. Arnold. Official Photographs of the World's Columbian Exposition
- James W. Ellsworth Papers

Library of Congress, Washington, D.C., Manuscripts Division (LC)
- Paul Wayland Bartlett Papers, Box 31

Metropolitan Museum of Art, New York City, Archives (MMAA)

National Archives, Washington, D.C. (NA)

Records of United States Participation in International Conferences, Commissions, and Expositions. Record Group 43:
- Final Report of the World's Columbian Commission, Thomas W. Palmer, President. Entry 576, Box 2343
- World's Columbian Exposition. Final Report of the World's Columbian Commission, John T. Dickinson, Secretary. 2 vols. Entry 577, Box 2348
- "Awards of the World's Columbian Exposition." 1893. [48 vols. containing copies of certificates of award.] Entry 578
- "List of Exhibitors at the World's Columbian Exposition held at Chicago, Illinois . . . for whom diplomas were prepared" Entry 579, Box 30

Records of the Department of the Treasury. Record Group 56:
- Minutes of the Meetings of the World's Columbian Commission, 1890–93. 5 vols. Entry 502
- World's Columbian Exposition. Scrapbook of Newspaper Clippings, 1891–92. 3 vols. Entry 507
- "Minutes of Meetings of The International Committee of Judges in the Department of Fine Arts (K)." Entry 512
- "Name Index to Registers of Awards." 1894–95. Entry 515
- "World's Columbian Commission Register of Awards." Entry 516
- "Name Indexes to Registers of Awards." 1894–95. Entry 517
- "Registers of Awards, Department K, Fine Arts." 1894–95. Entry 518

Records of the House of Representatives. Record Group 233:
- Kurtz, Charles M. Testimony in "Investigations of the Management of the World's Columbian Exposition Hearings." HR 52.A F3.4 (Committee on Appropriations), Box 26. (Spring 1892)

New York Public Library, Rare Books and Manuscripts Division
- Charles Henry Hart Papers

Newberry Library, Chicago

Charles L. Hutchinson Manuscripts
Private Collections
Harlow N. Higinbotham Papers
Saint Louis Art Museum, Archives
Halsey C. Ives Collection

Books

Adams, Henry. *The Education of Henry Adams. An Autobiography.* Boston and New York: Houghton Mifflin Company, 1918.

Arnold, C. D., and H. D. Higinbotham. *Official Views of the World's Columbian Exposition Issued by the Department of Photography.* Chicago: Press Chicago Photo-Gravure Co., 1893.

Art Club of Philadelphia. *Fifth Annual Exhibition of Oil Paintings and Sculpture.* Philadelphia, 1893.

Art Gems from the World's Columbian Exposition. Chicago: The Chicago Herald, 1893.

Art Treasures from the World's Fair. Chicago and New York: The Werner Co., 1895.

Artistic Guide to Chicago and the World's Columbian Exposition. Chicago: Columbian Art Company, 1892.

Bancroft, Hubert Howe. *The Book of the Fair: an historical and descriptive presentation of the world's science, art, and industry, as viewed through the Columbian Exposition at Chicago in 1893.* 4 vols. Chicago: Bancroft Company, 1893.

Banks, Charles Eugene. *The Artistic Guide to Chicago and the World's Columbian Exposition.* Chicago, 1893.

Beautiful Scenes of the White City. New York: George Cram, 1894.

Buel, James William. *The Magic City: A Massive Portfolio of Original Photographic Views of the Great World's Fair.* St. Louis: Historical Publishing Co., 1894.

Buildings and Art at the World's Fair; Containing Views of Grounds, . . . Supplemented with a Collection of Artotypes of the Most Famous Paintings and Statuary Exhibited. . . . Chicago: Rand, McNally & Co., 1894.

Burnham, D. H. *The Art of the World, illustrated in the paintings, statuary and architecture of the World's Columbian Exposition.* New York: Appleton, 1893–[1895].

California Midwinter International Exposition. *Official Catalogue. Department of Fine Arts.* San Francisco: Harvey, Whitcher & Allen, 1894.

Cameron, William E., Thomas W. Palmer, and Frances E. Willard. *The World's Fair: being a pictorial history of the Columbian Exposition.* Chicago: Chicago Publication & Lithograph Co., 1893.

Catalogue of the Sixty-third Annual Exhibition, Dec. 18, 1893 to Feb. 24, 1894. Philadelphia: Pennsylvania Academy of the Fine Arts, 1893.

Catalogue of Works of Art to be Exhibited at the World's Columbian Exposition, Chicago, 1893. Philadelphia: Pennsylvania Academy of the Fine Arts, 16 Jan. to 4 Feb. 1893.

The Chicago Record's History of the World's Fair. Chicago: The Chicago Daily News Co., 1893.

Classification of the World's Columbian Exposition, Chicago, U.S.A. Chicago, 1893.

Connecticut at the World's Fair: Report of the Commissioners from Connecticut of the Columbian Exposition. Hartford, 1893.

Dean, C. *The World's Fair City and Her Enterprising Sons.* Chicago, 1892.

Dean, Teresa. *White City Chips.* Chicago: Warren Publishing Co., 1895.

Department of Fine Arts, ed. [Charles M. Kurtz]. *World's Columbian Exposition, Official Publications, Revised Catalogue, Department of Fine Arts.* Chicago: W. B. Conkey Company, 1893.

Department of Publicity and Promotion, M. P. Handy, Chief. *World's Columbian Exposition, 1893. Official Catalogue. Part X. Department K. Fine Arts. Halsey C. Ives, Chief.* Chicago: W. B. Conkey Company, 1893.

The Economizer. How and Where to find the Gems of the Fair. Chicago: Rand, McNally & Co., 1893.

Farquhar, A. B., ed. *Catalogue of the Exhibits of the State of Pennsylvania . . . at the World's Columbian Exposition.* Pennsylvania, 1893.

Farquhar, A. B., ed. *Pennsylvania and the World's Columbian Exposition.* Harrisburg: E. K. Meyers, [1891].

Fine Arts at the World's Columbian Exposition; Being a Collection of Artotypes of the Most Famous Paintings and Statuary Exhibited at the World's Fair, Chicago, 1893. Chicago: Rand, McNally & Co., 1894.

Flinn, John Joseph, comp. *Official Guide to the World's Columbian Exposition in the City of Chicago.* Chicago: The Columbian Guide Co., 1893.

Forty Works of Art from the Sixty-third Annual Exhibition of the Academy of the Fine Arts. Philadelphia: The Levytype Company, 1894.

Gage, Lyman. *The World's Columbian Exposition: First Annual Report of the President.* Chicago: Knight & Leonard Company, 1891.

*The Government Collection of Original Views of the World's Columbian Exposition.*Chicago, 1895.

Halligan, Jewell N., and John McGovern. *Halligan's Illustrated World's Fair.* Chicago: The Illustrated World's Fair Publishing Co., 1890–93.

Handy, Moses P., ed. *The Official Directory of the World's Columbian Exposition May First to October Thirtieth, 1893.* Chicago: W. B. Conkey Co., 1893.

Higinbotham, H. N. *Report of the President to the Board of Directors of the World's Columbian Exposition 1892–1893.* Chicago: Rand, McNally & Co., 1898.

Hitchcock, Ripley. *The Art of the World, Illustrated in the Paintings, Statuary and Architecture of the World's Columbian Exposition.* 2 vols. New York: D. Appleton, 1895.

Holley, Marietta [Josiah Allen's wife]. *Samantha at the World's Fair.* New York: Funk & Wagnalls Company, 1893.

Howells, William Dean. *Letters of an Altrurian Traveller.* Ed. Clara M. Kirk and Rudolph King. Gainesville, FL: Scholars' Facsimiles and Reprints, 1961.

Information for Exhibitors and Others Interested in the Department of Fine Arts of the World's Columbian Exposition [Circular No. 2]. Chicago: World's Columbian Exposition, 1891.

Ives, Halsey C., intro. *The Dream City. Photographic Views of the World's Columbian Exposition*. St. Louis: N. D. Thompson Publishing Co., 1893.

Jackson, William Henry. *The White City as It Was*. Chicago: White City Art Company, 1894.

Johnson, Rossiter, ed. *A History of the World's Columbian Exposition*. 4 vols. New York: D. Appleton, 1897.

Kurtz, Charles M. ed. *Illustrations (Three Hundred and Thirty-Six Engravings) from the Art Gallery of the World's Columbian Exposition*. Philadelphia: George Barrie, 1893.

Larned, Walter Cranston. *Art Clippings from the Pen of Walter Cranston Larned and Other Critics At the Fair*. Ed. J. S. Merrill. Chicago: J. S. Merrill, 1893.

Millet, F. D., J. A. Mitchell, W. H. Low et al. *Some Artists at the Fair*. New York: Charles Scribner's Sons, 1893.

Northrup, Henry D., and N. H. Banks. *The World's Fair as Seen in One Hundred Days*. Philadelphia: Ariel Book Co., 1893.

Pierce, James Wilson. *Photographic History of the World's Fair*. Baltimore: R. H. Woodward & Co., 1893.

A Portfolio of Photographic Views of the World's Columbian Exposition. Chicago: Jewell N. Halligan Company, 1894.

Ralph, Julian. *Harper's Chicago and the World's Fair*. New York: Harper & Brothers, 1893.

Rand, McNally & Co.'s A Week at the Fair Illustrating Exhibits and Wonders of the World's Columbian Exposition. Chicago: Rand, McNally & Co., 1893.

Report of the Board of General Managers of the Exhibit of the State of New York at the World's Columbian Exposition. Albany: James B. Lyon, 1894.

Report of the Committee on Awards of the World's Columbian Exposition. 2 vols. Washington, D.C., 1901.

Report of the Massachusetts Board of World's Fair Managers. Boston: Wright & Potter Printing Co., 1894.

Report of the President to the Board of Directors of the World's Columbian Exposition. Chicago: Rand, McNally & Co., 1893.

Ridpath, John C., ed. *Art and Artists of All Nations. Over Four Hundred Photographic Reproductions of Great Paintings. . . . Including more than One Hundred and Forty of the Greatest Paintings Exhibited in the Department of Fine Arts at the World's Columbian Exposition*. New York: Arkell Weekly Company, 1894.

Ridpath, John C., ed. *Famous paintings of the world; a collection of photographic reproductions . . . including one hundred of the most notable paintings at the World's Columbian Exposition*. New York: Fine Art Publishing Company, 1894.

Shepp, James W., and D. B. Shepp. *Shepp's World's Fair Photographed*. Chicago and Philadelphia: Globe Bible Publishing Co., 1893.

Stevens, Mrs. Mark. *Six Months at the World's Fair*. Detroit: Detroit Free Press, 1895.

Sylvestre, Henri, Jr. *The Marvels in Art of the Fin de Siècle*. Philadelphia: Gebbie & Co., 1893.

Truman, Benjamin Cummings, ed. *History of the World's Fair*. Philadelphia: Mammoth Publishing Co., 1893.

Tuthill, William. "Report of the Fine Arts Exhibit." *Report of the Board of General Managers of the Exhibit of the State of New York, at the World's Columbian Exposition; transmitted to the Legislature April 18, 1894*. Albany: J. B. Lyon, 1894.

The Union League Club. *A Group of Paintings by American Artists Accepted for the Columbian Exposition*. New York, 1893.

Walton, William. *World's Columbian Exposition: Art and Architecture*. 3 vols. Philadelphia: George Barrie, 1893.

What to See and How to Find It. Gems of the Fair. Chicago: World's Fair & Chicago Guide Co., 1893.

White, Trumbull, and William Igleheart. *The World's Columbian Exposition, Chicago, 1893*. Philadelphia and St. Louis: P. W. Ziegler, [1893].

The Wonders of the World's Fair. Chicago: W. B. Conkey Co., 1894.

World's Columbian Exposition. *Catalogue of the Massachusetts Fine Art Exhibit at the Massachusetts Charitable Mechanics' Association Building . . . from January 16 to 28, Inclusive*. Boston, 1893.

World's Columbian Exposition, 1893. [Portfolio of views issued by the Department of Photography.] Chicago: National Chromograph Co., 1893.

World's Fairs from London 1851 to Chicago 1893. Chicago: Midway Publishing Co., 1892.

Yankee Doodle at the Fair, An Historical and Artistic Memorial. Philadelphia: George Barrie & Son, 1896.

Periodical Literature

"The American Art Exhibit at the Columbian Exposition." *The Studio* 7 (5 March 1892): 130–31.

"American Notes." *The Studio* 7 (12 Nov. 1892): 413.

"American Painting. III.—Melchers, McEwen, Shirlaw, Chase, Marr, Duveneck." *The Art Amateur* 29 (August 1893): 56–57.

"American Painting. IV.—Whistler, Dannat, Sargent." *The Art Amateur* 29 (Nov. 1893): 134.

"American Painting at the World's Fair. V.—Abbey, La Farge, Martin, Blakelock, Dewing, Twachtmann [*sic*]." *The Art Amateur* 30 (Feb. 1894): 74.

"American Paintings. Exhibits of Inness, Wyant and Tryon." *The Art Amateur* 28 (April 1893): 148.

"American Paintings." *The Art Amateur* 28 (March 1893): 116–17.

"American Pictures at the Union League Club." *The Critic* 22 (18 March 1893): 168.

"American Sculpture." *The Art Amateur* 29 (Oct. 1893): 108–9.

"American Sculpture." *The Art Amateur* 29 (Nov. 1893): 134.

Arnold, Elizabeth. "The Art Catalogue of the World's Fair." *Progress* 2 (Oct. 1893): 16–19.

"Art and Architecture at the World's Fair." *The Tribune Monthly* 5 (Sept. 1893): n.p.

"Art and Artists." *The Graphic* [Chicago], 27 May 1893, 350.

"Art and Artists." *The Graphic* [Chicago], 23 Oct. 1893, 293.

"Art and Artists." *The Graphic* [Chicago], 7 Jan. 1893, 6.

"The Art Display at the World's Fair." *The Studio* 7 (29 Oct. 1892): 389–90.

"The Art Gallery and Exhibit at Chicago." *The Art Interchange*

30 (May 1893): 119–21.
"Art Gossip." *The Art Interchange* 27 (Sept. 1891): 72.
"Art Gossip." *The Art Interchange* 27 (Oct. 1891): 108–9.
"Art Gossip." *The Art Interchange* 27 (Dec. 1891): 170–71.
"Art Gossip." *The Art Interchange* 30 (Jan. 1893): 8.
"Art Gossip." *The Art Interchange* 30 (June 1893): 152.
"Art Gossip." *The Art Interchange* 31 (July 1893): 6–7.
"Art in Boston—The Massachusetts Exhibit for the World's Fair." *The Studio* 8 (25 Feb. 1893): 109–10.
"Art in Chicago and Philadelphia." *The Magazine of Art* 14 (May 1891): xxiv.
Besant, Walter. "A First Impression." *Cosmopolitan Magazine* 15 (1893): 528–39.
Bowles, J. B. "Some Impressions of the Art Exhibit at the Fair—II. A Glance at the Loan Collection." *Modern Art* 1 (Autumn 1893): n.p.
Chasseloup-Laubat, Marquis de. "A Frenchman on the World's Fair and America." *The American Architect and Building News* 39 (28 Jan. 1893): 58–60.
Coffin, William A. "The Columbian Exposition.—I. Fine Arts: French and American Sculpture." *The Nation* 57 (3 Aug. 1893): 79–81.
Coffin, William A. "The Columbian Exposition.—II. Fine Arts: The United States Section." *The Nation* 57 (10 Aug. 1893): 96–99.
Coffin, William A. "The Columbian Exposition.—III. Fine Arts.: Pictures by American Artists—Sculptural and Pictorial Decoration." *The Nation* 57 (17 Aug. 1893): 114–16.
Coffin, William A. "The Columbian Exposition.—IV. The Ensemble." *The Nation* 57 (24 Aug. 1893): 132–33.
Coffin, William A. "The Columbian Exposition.—V. Fine Arts: The French Pictures and the Loan Collection." *The Nation* 57 (31 Aug. 1893): 150–52.
Coffin, William A. "The Columbian Exposition.—VI. Fine Arts. The British and the Non French Continental Sections. *The Nation* 57 (7 Sept. 1893): 168–69.
Cortissoz, Royal. "An American Critic on English Art at the Chicago World's Fair." *The Studio* 2 (16 Oct. 1893): 45–52.
Cortissoz, Royal. "An American Exhibition." Part III of "Art at the World's Fair." *Library of Tribune Extras* (1893): 11–13.
Downes, William H. "New England Art at the World's Fair." *New England Magazine, An Illustrated Monthly* n.s. 8 (July 1893): 352–77.
Forsyth, William. "Some Impressions of the Art Exhibit at the Fair, III. Portraiture—Holland and Japan—American Art—George Inness—Adolph Menzel—Impressionism—The French and their Skill." *Modern Art* 1 (Autumn 1893): n.p.
Hawthorne, Julian. "The Lady of the Lake. At the Fair." *Lippincott's Monthly Magazine* 52 (May 1893): 240–47.
Hawthorne, Julian. "A Description of the Inexpressible." *Lippincott's Monthly Magazine* 51 (April 1893): 496–503.
Hermant, Jacques. "Les Beaux Arts." *Gazette des Beaux-Arts* (1893): 451–61.
Howells, William Dean. "Letters of an Altrurian Traveller. II." *Cosmopolitan* 16 (Dec. 1893): 218–32.
Knaufft, Ernest. "Art at the Columbian Exposition." *Review of Reviews* 7 (June 1893): 551–63.
Kurtz, Charles M. "The American Art Exhibit at the Columbian Exposition." *The Studio* 7 (5 March 1892): 130–31.
Kurtz, Charles M. "Fine Arts. Department K." *World's Columbian Exposition Illustrated* 1 (Feb. 1892): 13.
K.[urtz], C.[harles] M. "News and Notes. World's Fair Art." *The Art Amateur* 26 (March 1892): 111.
"Literary Note." *The Studio* 8 (20 May 1893): 224.
"The Loan Exhibition at the Fine Arts Building. II.—Modern Painting." *The Art Amateur* 28 (April 1893): 126.
Low, Will H. "The Art of the White City." *Scribner's Magazine* 14 (Oct. 1893): 504–12.
Miller, Florence Fenwick. "Art in the Women's Section of the Chicago Exhibition." *Art Journal* n.s. 104 (Aug. 1893): xii–xvi.
Monroe, Lucy. "Chicago Letter." *The Critic* 22 (18 March 1893): 168.
Monroe, Lucy. "Chicago Letter." *The Critic* 22 (25 March 1893): 185–86.
Monroe, Lucy. "Chicago Letter." *The Critic* 22 (15 April 1893): 240–41.
Monroe, Lucy. "Chicago Letter." *The Critic* 22 (22 April 1893): 261.
Monroe, Lucy. "Chicago Letter." *The Critic* 22 (29 April 1893): 279.
Monroe, Lucy. "Chicago Letter." *The Critic* 22 (13 May 1893): 317.
Monroe, Lucy. "Chicago Letter." *The Critic* 22 (27 May 1893): 351–52.
Monroe, Lucy. "Chicago Letter." *The Critic* 23 (5 Aug. 1893): 91–92.
Monroe, Lucy. "Chicago Letter." *The Critic* 23 (12 Aug. 1893): 115.
Monroe, Lucy. "Chicago Letter." *The Critic* 23 (26 Aug. 1893): 141.
Monroe, Lucy. "Chicago Letter." *The Critic* 23 (9 Sept. 1893): 175.
Monroe, Lucy. "Chicago Letter." *The Critic* 23 (4 Nov. 1893): 191.
"Mr. Charles L. Hutchinson." *World's Columbian Exposition Illustrated* 1 (July 1891): 4.
"Painting and Sculpture at the World's Fair." *The Inland Architect and News Record* 22 (Nov. 1893): 35–36.
"Paintings for the World's Fair." *The Studio* 8 (11 Feb. 1893): 93–95.
"Pictures at the Chicago Exposition." *Art Journal* n.s. 103 (July 1893): ix–xii.
"Portraiture at the Fair." *The Art Interchange* 31 (Oct. 1893): 87–88.
Radford, J. A. "Art and the World's Fair." *The Canadian Magazine of Politics, Science, Art and Literature* 2 (1893–94): 128–30.
Schuyler, Montgomery. "Last Words about the World's Fair." *Architectural Record* 3 (Jan.–March 1894): 291–301.

"Sculpture at the Chicago Exhibition." *The Builder* [London] 65 (30 Sept. 1893): 240–42.
"Sculpture at the World's Fair. Part II." *The Studio* 8 (12 Aug. 1893): 285–86.
Stanton, Theodore. "Europe at the World's Fair. —II. The French Section." *The North American Review* 156 (Feb. 1893): 241–46.
"Topics of the Time. What the Columbian Exposition will do for America." *The Century Magazine* 44 (Oct. 1892): 953–55.
St. Cyr. "A Lesson From the Fair." *The Art Interchange* 31 (Sept. 1893): 56–57.
Van Brunt, Henry. "The Columbian Exposition and American Civilization." *Atlantic Monthly* 71 (May 1893): 577–88.
Van Dyke, John C. "Painting at the Fair." *The Century Magazine* 48 (July 1894): 439–46.
Van Rensselaer, M[arianna]. G[riswold]. "At the Fair." *The Century Magazine* 46 (May 1893): 3–13.
Villiers, F. "An Artist's View of Chicago and the World's Fair." *Journal of the Society of Arts* 42 (8 Dec. 1893): 49–54.
Wendell, Barrett. "Impressions at Chicago." *The Harvard Monthly* 27 (Oct. 1893): 1–14.
"Woman's Work." *World's Columbian Exposition Illustrated* 1 (July 1891): 14.
"World's Columbian Exposition." *Harper's Weekly* 34 (22 Nov. 1890): 912–16.
"World's Fair Notes." *The Studio* 7 (20 Feb. 1892): 113.
"World's Fair Notes." *The Studio* 8 (18 Feb. 1893): 107.
"World's Fair Notes." *The Studio* 8 (29 April 1893): 193.
"World's Fair Notes." *The Studio* 8 (13 May 1893): 215.
"World's Fair Notes." *The Studio* 8 (19 Aug. 1893): 297–98.
"The World's Fair. Women's Work in the Fine Arts." *The Art Amateur* 29 (Nov. 1893): 154.

Newspapers

Baltimore Sun

Taft, Lorado. "Art at the Fair. The First Letter of a Series by Prof. Lorado Taft." 9 Sept. 1893, p. 1, col. 7–8.
Taft, Lorado. "Art at the Fair. American Painters of Celebrity." 16 Sept. 1893, p. 1, col. 8–p. 2, col. 1.
Taft, Lorado. "Art at the Fair. Notable Pictures and Painters." 23 Sept. 1893, p. 1, col. 7–8.
Taft, Lorado. "Art at the Fair. Beautiful Creations of the Painter's Fancy." 30 Sept. 1893, p. 1, col. 8–p. 2, col. 1.
Taft, Lorado. "Art at the Fair. Some Excellent Work by American Figure Painters." 7 Oct. 1893, p. 1, col. 8–p. 2, col 1.
Taft, Lorado. "Art at the Fair. The Twelve Favorite Pictures in the Collection." 14 Oct. 1893, p. 2, col. 7–8.

Daily Evening Transcript, Boston

"The Fine Arts. The Art Department of the World's Fair in Chicago." 12 Nov. 1891, p. 7, col. 1–2.
"The Fine Arts." 29 Oct. 1892, p. 8, col. 5.
"The Fine Arts. Massachusetts Art and Artists and the World's Fair in Chicago." 14 Nov. 1892, p. 6, col. 3–4.
"The Fine Arts. Massachusetts Art at the World's Fair." 5 Dec. 1892, p. 6, col. 1–2.
"The Fine Arts. Art at the World's Fair." 30 Dec. 1892, p. 5, col. 3.
"The Fine Arts. The Retrospective Exhibit of American Pictures at the World's Fair." 10 Jan. 1893, p. 6, col. 3–5.
"The Pictures for Chicago." 10 Jan. 1893, p. 10, col. 5.
"The Fine Arts. The Boston Art Juries for the World's Fair Work." 11 Jan. 1893, p. 6, col. 3–4.
"Local Art Notes." 12 Jan. 1893, p. 4, col. 4.
"The Fine Arts. Massachusetts Art at Chicago." 13 Jan. 1893, p. 1, col. 4.
"Boston Art at Chicago." 14 Jan. 1893, p. 12, col. 1–2.
"The Fine Arts. The Philadelphia Exhibit of Works for the World's Fair." 17 Jan. 1893, p. 6, col. 4.
"The Fine Arts. Massachusetts Art for the World's Fair—Figures and Portraits." 19 Jan. 1893, p. 5, col. 1–2.
"The Fine Arts. The Landscapes and Marines in the Massachusetts Exhibit for the World's Fair." 21 Jan. 1893, p. 6, col. 4.
W. E. A. "Is It American Art?" 21 Jan. 1893, p. 6, col. 3–4.
"The Fine Arts. The Pictures for the World's Fair." 3 Feb. 1893, p. 10, col. 2.
"Technique and Our Artists." 4 Feb. 1893, p. 13, col. 4.
"American Art of the Future." 6 Feb. 1893, p. 6, col. 2.
"Art Notes." 16 Feb. 1893, p. 4, col. 6.
Gordon. "The War of the Artists." 23 Feb. 1893, p. 3, col. 4.
H. T. P. "The Artists and the Fair." 25 Feb. 1893, p. 9, col. 2.
"National Art Jury Begins Work." 7 March 1893, p. 10, col. 5.
"The Fine Arts. The National Jury and the Unhappy Number Threes." 7 March 1893, p. 6, col. 3.
"The Fine Arts. Studio and Gallery Notes." 20 Mar. 1893, p. 6, col. 4.
"Fine Arts. Studio and Gallery Notes." 27 March 1893, p. 6, col. 3.
"The Fine Arts. New England's Contribution to the Retrospective Exhibit of American Art at Chicago." 16 April 1893, p. 6, col. 1–2.
"The Fine Arts. Winslow Homer's Pictures at the World's Fair." 22 April 1893, p. 10, col. 3–5.
"The Fine Arts. Artists on Technique." 2 May 1893, p. 6, col. 1–2.
Church, Martin. "The Fine Arts. Art at the World's Fair." 11 May 1893, p. 5, col. 3–4.
"The Fine Arts. The Art Gallery of the World's Columbian Exposition Illustrated." 13 May 1893, p. 4, col. 1–2.
"The Fine Arts. American Subjects for American Artists." 24 May 1893, p. 6, col. 5–6.
"The Fine Arts. A Boston Artist's Comments on the Art Galleries of the World's Fair." 26 May 1893, p. 5, col. 1.
"The Fine Arts. Studio and Gallery Notes." 9 June 1893, p. 3, col. 7.
Robbins, M[ary]. C. "The Fine Arts. Flash Light Views of the Art at the World's Fair." 21 July 1893, p. 5, col. 1–2.
Bumpus, M. L. "The Fine Arts. American vs. French Art at Chicago." 16 Aug. 1893, p. 6, col. 1–2.
T. S. P. [Thomas Sergeant Perry]. "At the Greatest Show." 8

Sept. 1893, p. 4, col. 4.
"The Fine Arts. World's Fair Exhibits Still in Quod." 4 Jan. 1894, p. 5, col. 5.

Brooklyn Daily Eagle
C. M. S. [Charles M. Shean]. "Gallery and Studio. Further Reflections on Art at the World Fair." 16 Oct. 1892, p. 5, col. 6.
"Works of Art for the Fair. The Advisory Committee Begins Work in the Seventh Regiment Armory." 16 Jan. 1893, p. 1, col. 4.
C. M. S. [Charles M. Shean]. "Gallery and Studio. The Artists and the World Fair—Accusations of Mismanagement." 26 Feb. 1893, p. 5, col. 6–7.
C. M. S. [Charles M. Shean]. "Gallery and Studio. A Clerical Protest Against Immoral Art." 2 April 1893, p. 7, col. 1.
"Brooklyn's Tribute to Art." 27 June 1893, p. 2, col. 5.
C. M. S. [Charles M. Shean]. "Gallery and Studio. Awards of Prizes." 20 Aug. 1893, p. 13, col. 1–2.
C. M. S. [Charles M. Shean]. "Gallery and Studio. The Demeaning Effects of Realism in Art." 3 Sept. 1893, p. 8, col. 1.

Chicago Evening Journal
"Among Chicago Artists." 10 Feb. 1893, p. 4, col. 6.
"Art Jurors at Work." 6 March 1893, p. 2, col. 1.
"Studio and Gallery." 10 March 1893, p. 4, col. 5.
"Art at Jackson Park. Hanging of World's Fair Pictures Has Begun." 29 March 1893, p. 12, col. 1.
"In the World of Art." 4 April 1893, p. 4, col. 7.
"Why Art Goes Gadding." 4 Aug. 1893, p. 4, col. 3–4.
"Hopkinson Smith Criticised." 24 Aug. 1893, p. 4, col. 5.
"Mr. Whistler at the Fair." 26 Aug. 1893, p. 4, col. 7.

Chicago Evening Post
"Just the Right Man. C. M. Kurtz, Assistant Director." 13 Nov. 1891.

Chicago Herald
"Fine Arts Hampered. Little Progress in the Exhibit." 9 Oct. 1892, p. 10, col. 1–3.
"Looking at Pictures. Art as Viewed by Common Men." 14 May 1893, p. 33, col. 4–6.
"Genre and Portrait." 14 May 1893, p. 86, col. 1.
"What Not to Do in the Art Gallery." 28 May 1893, p. 28, col. 3–4.
"Canvas and Marble." 5 June 1893, p. 7, col. 1–2.
Mentor. "Imitations at Best. No American School at the Fair." 15 June 1893, p. 2, col. 1.
"Home Art is Inferior. Few Works of Merit at the Fair." 18 June 1893, p. 25, col. 1–3.
"Alienism in American Art." 18 June 1893, p. 28, col. 2–3.
"Morality and Art." 10 July 1893, p. 10, col. 1–2.
"Left Out the West." 12 July 1893, p. 3, col. 3.
"To Make the Awards. Many of the Judges Are Here Now." 13 July 1893, p. 9, col. 4.
"Thacher Down Again. Fine Arts Judges Scorn His Rules." 18 July 1893, p. 1, col. 5.
"Art Jurors at Work." 20 July 1893, p. 1, col. 7.
"Art Takes Its Turn. Painters and Sculptors to Meet." 30 July 1893, p. 11, col. 4–5.
"Artists Begin Their Congress." 1 Aug. 1893, p. 10, col. 2.
"Thacher Is Ignored. Art Jurors Make Their Own Rules." 4 Aug. 1893, p. 9, col. 1.
"Close of the Congress on Art." 6 Aug. 1893, p. 4, col. 2–3.
"Winners of Medals." 12 Aug. 1893, p. 1, col. 7–p. 2, col. 1–2.
"Medals to Painters." 13 Aug. 1893, p. 1, col. 6.
"Honors to Artists." 19 Aug. 1893, p. 9, col. 5.
"Lack Religious Note. Defect in World's Fair Fine Arts." 20 Aug. 1893, p. 12, col. 1.
"Art Lovers as Sunday Visitors." 4 Sept. 1893, p. 6, col. 2.
"Wrecking the Fair." 1 Nov. 1893, p. 3, col. 1.
"Failure of Art Sales." 5 Nov. 1893, p. 2, col. 4.
"Last Views of Art." 5 Nov. 1893, p. 13, col. 1.

Inter-Ocean, Chicago
"In Frenchmen's Eyes. What French Artists Think of American Art." 3 July 1892, p. 15, col. 4–5.
"Professor Ives Returns." 9 July 1892, p. 5, col. 2.
"World's Fair Doings. New York Attempts to Embarrass the Exposition." 16 Nov. 1892, p. 5, col. 1.
"World's Fair Doings. The Jury System of Awards Is Finally Adopted." 14 Jan. 1893, p. 5, col 2.
"Worlds Fair Doings. American Art Section. What Chief Ives Says of the American Art Exhibit." 24 Jan. 1893, p. 5, col. 1–2.
"About the Studios. New York Academicians and the Exposition. The Jury of Selection." 5 March 1893, p. 15, col. 3–5.
"Jury on Fine Arts." 7 March 1893, p. 5, col. 1.
"World's Fair Doings. Art Jury Considering American Canvases." 8 March 1893, p. 5, col. 1–3.
"Selections are Made." 9 March 1893, p. 5, col. 2.
"World's Fair Doings. The Art Jury Completes Its Work of Selection." 11 March 1893, p. 5, col. 1.
"About the Studios. Beautiful Masterpieces in Palace of Fine Arts." 7 May 1893, p. 27, col. 1–3.
"White City Chips. One Frenchman Thinks the Paintings Not Good." 1 July 1893, p. 6, col. 3–4.
"Brush and Palette. Lesson of the American Art Exhibit at the Fair." 2 July 1893, p. 24, col. 1–2.
"White City Chips. Picture of Levi Coffin's 'Underground Railroad.'" 8 July 1893, p. 5, col. 3–4.
"About the Studios. Works of the American Sculptors at the Exposition." 9 July 1893, p. 27, col. 1.
"In the Art Palace." 6 Aug. 1893, p. 23, col. 6.
"In the Art Palace. All Beautiful Works Are Not on the First Floor." 15 Oct. 1893, p. 27, col. 4–5.
"In the Art Palace. Old and New Schools of Thought in Religious Painting." 22 Oct. 1893, p. 23, col. 4–5.
"In the Art Palace. Some of the More Striking of the Paintings of Animals." 29 Oct. 1893, p. 29, col. 3–4.

Chicago Tribune
"Marquand for Art Director." 7 Jan. 1891, p. 6, col. 1–2.
"More Department Chiefs." 27 Jan. 1891, p. 8, col. 1.

"It's Still in a Tangle." 31 Jan. 1891, p. 8, col. 1.
"Mr. Marquand Still Hesitates." 2 Feb. 1891, p. 2, col. 4.
"Prof. Halsey Ives as Art Director." 30 March 1891, p. 6, col. 2.
"Exposition Notes." 3 May 1891, p. 2, col. 2.
"Halsey C. Ives, Art Director." 9 May 1891, p. 1, col 3–4.
"Want it on the Lake Front." 12 May 1891, p. 8, col. 2.
"Preparing for the Art Exhibit." 13 May 1891, p. 7, col. 2.
"Halsey C. Ives to Go to Europe." 6 June 1891, p. 9, col. 5.
"To Be in Jackson Park." 24 June 1891, p. 1, col. 1.
"The Fine Arts Department. . . ." 4 July 1891, p. 10, col. 1.
"Halsey C. Ives Going to Europe." 12 July 1891, p. 8, col. 3.
"Regarding the Fine Art Exhibits." 18 July 1891, p. 12, col. 2.
"Mr. Ives Looking for Paintings." 22 July 1891, p. 5, col. 4.
"Art Department of the World's Fair." 26 July 1891, p. 25, col. 5.
"Mr. Halsey C. Ives. . . ." 2 Aug. 1891, p. 29, col. 1.
"Art Exhibit Plans of France." 17 Sept. 1891, p. 8, col. 1.
"For Lighting the Art Galleries." 3 Oct. 1891, p. 12, col. 5.
"Will Benefit the World's Fair." 28 Nov. 1891, p. 10, col. 6.
"To Sail for Europe." 17 Dec. 1891, p. 13, col. 3.
"Interested in Art Exhibits. Director Ellsworth Says New York Will Make a Good Display." 4 Feb. 1892, p. 8, col. 1–2.
"Harm Done Abroad. Mr. Bryan and Mr. Ives Write Regarding the Matter." 31 Jan. 1892, p. 11, col. 3.
"Numerous Works of Art Received." 1 March 1893, p. 4, col. 6.
"Come to Be Judged. World's Fair Pictures Arriving in Great Numbers." 4 March 1893, p. 9, col. 1–2.
"Choosing Art Works." 7 March 1893, p. 8, col. 1.
"Few Western Paintings Taken. The Jury Quickly Disposes of a Great Number of Those Submitted." 8 March 1893, p. 3, col. 3.
"But Few Are Chosen. Ninety Out of 982 Pictures Selected for Exhibition." 9 March 1893, p. 9, col. 5.
"Art Works Chosen. The National Jury Finishes Its Exposition Duties." 11 March 1893, p. 9, col. 1–2.
"Selected by a Jury. Reproduction of the Pictures Chosen for the Exposition." 13 March 1893, p. 3, col. 1–5.
"The Fine Arts." 19 March 1893, p. 12, col. 3.
"Fine Arts Section Progress." 24 March 1893, p. 2, col. 7.
"Art at the Fair. Charles M. Kurtz Lectures on Paintings Received." 13 April 1893, p. 9, col. 7.
"Art Exhibit Grand. Display in the Palace Is Almost in Shape." 30 April 1893, p. 41, col. 7–p. 42, col. 1–7.
"Are Loaned to the Fair." 11 May 1893, p. 9, col. 4.
"They Ask for Juries." 12 May 1893, p. 1, col. 5–6.
"The Fine Arts." 14 May 1893, p. 37, col. 3–4.
"Hang Many Pictures. Work of Installation Being Pushed in the Art Building." 17 May 1893, p. 3, col. 1.
"Early Art in America." 18 May 1893, p. 2, col. 3–4.
"Secret Session of the Commission." 21 May 1893, p. 1, col. 7–p. 2, col. 1.
"America in the Arts." 21 May 1893, p. 26, col. 2.
"They Stand Firm." 22 May 1893, p. 1, col. 7.
"American Water Colors in Place." 22 May 1893, p. 2, col. 1.
"Want Jury Awards." 24 May 1893, p. 1, col. 7.
"Will Not Compete." 25 May 1893, p. 1, col. 5.
"Now It's Americans." 26 May 1893, p. 1, col. 1–p. 5, col. 4.
"Thacher Retreats." 27 May 1893, p. 1, col. 1–2.
"In the Exposition Art Gallery." 28 May 1893, p. 27, col. 3–4.
"Throngs at the Art Palace." 29 May 1893, p. 1, col. 2.
Townsend, George Alfred. "With Fair Artists." 4 June 1893, p. 25, col. 1–5.
"The Fine Arts." 11 June 1893, p. 27, col. 2–3.
"The Fine Arts." 18 June 1893, p. 27, col. 1.
"Pictures by California Artists." 25 June 1893, p. 12, col. 5.
"The Fine Arts." 25 June 1893, p. 27, col. 3.
"Fifteen Rare Old Miniatures." 26 June 1893, p. 2, col. 5–6.
"Fine Arts at the Fair." 2 July 1893, p. 25, col. 5–7–p. 32, col. 1.
"The Fine Arts at the Fair." 9 July 1893, p. 25, col. 4–7.
"Fine Arts at the Fair." 16 July 1893, p. 14, col. 1–3.
"Fine Arts at the World's Fair." 23 July 1893, p. 31, col. 3–4.
"Fine Arts at the Fair." 24 July 1893, p. 5, col. 1–4.
"Stories about World's Fair Artists." 31 July 1893, p. 12, col. 5–7.
"Trouble in Fine Arts Department." 5 Aug. 1893, p. 12, col. 4.
"Fine Arts at the Fair." 6 Aug. 1893, p. 14, col. 6.
"Awards in Painting." 19 Aug. 1893, p. 1, col. 3–4.
"Fine Arts at the Fair." 20 Aug. 1893, p. 24, col. 1–2.
"The Awards in the Art Department of the Fair." 27 Aug. 1893, p. 12, col 5.
"Art at the World's Fair." 27 Aug. 1893, p. 36, col. 1–3.
"The Fine Arts." 3 Sept. 1893, p. 27, col. 4–5.
"Brilliant Work of American Sculptors." 17 Sept. 1893, p. 34, col. 1–3.
"Art at the World's Fair." 17 Sept. 1893, p. 35, col. 3–5.
"Landscape and Its Painters." 24 Sept. 1893, p. 35, col. 1–3.
"Marine Paintings at the Fair." 1 Oct. 1893, p. 34, col. 1–2.
"Portraiture as Shown at the Fair." 8 Oct. 1893, p. 27, col. 1–4.
"Popular Successes of the Art Palace." 28 Oct. 1893, p. 35, col. 1–2.
"Art at the Fair." 1 Nov. 1893, p. 4, col. 4–5.
Ives, Halsey C. [On the Department of Fine Arts]. 1 Nov. 1893, p. 11, col. 1.
"Sales from the Art Gallery." 1 Nov. 1893, p. 13, col. 6–7.

Detroit Free Press
"American Artists." 4 June 1893, p. 1, col. 1.
"American Artists. Reasons Why They Should Paint Subjects Found in This Land." 11 June 1893, p. 25, col. 1–2.

New-York Daily Tribune
"Paintings for the Fair. A Large Number of Pictures Chosen." 22 Jan. 1893, p. 3, col. 4.
"Pictures for the Fair. New York's List of Oil Paintings." 29 Jan. 1893, p. 2, col. 4.
"Exhibits from American Artists Abroad." 11 Feb. 1893, p. 4, col. 2.
"Are the Artists Dissatisfied?" 24 Feb. 1893, p. 2, col. 3.
"Works of Art Selected by the Jury." 12 March 1893, p. 12,

col. 3.
"Notes of the Exposition. Disappointed Artists." 15 March 1893, p. 9, col. 2.
"A Dispute About High Art." 29 May 1893, p. 2, col. 1.
"Art at the World's Fair. I. The Contents of the Art Building at Chicago." 11 June 1893, p. 14, col. 5–6.
"Notes of the Fair. A Comparison with 1876." 18 June 1893, p. 16, col. 4–5.
"Art at the World's Fair. III. The American School and Its Brightest Ornaments." 19 June 1893, p. 5, col. 1–3.
"Art at the World's Fair. IX. The Loan Exhibition of 'Masterpieces' by Foreign Artists. Educational Possibilities in the Pictures at Chicago." 15 July 1893, p. 7, col. 4–5.
"The Art Jury." 20 July 1893, p. 7, col. 1.
"The Art Jury." 23 July 1893, p. 7, col. 3.
"Art at the World's Fair. XI. A Summary of the Sculpture in the Galleries." 26 July 1893, p. 9, col. 1–3.
"Medals and Diplomas for American Artists." 19 Aug. 1893, p. 2, col. 6.
"Sculptors Who Secure Awards." 23 Aug. 1893, p. 6, col. 6.
"The Art Jury in Chicago." 27 Aug. 1893, p. 6, col. 4–5.
"The Making of Art Awards." 21 Oct. 1893, p. 7, col. 1.

New York Evening Post
"Art News." 1 Oct. 1892, pt. 2, p. 2, col. 2.
"To Discuss Art Matters." 10 Nov. 1892, p. 5, col. 4.
"Art News." 19 Nov. 1892, pt. 2, p. 2, col. 6.
"Pictures for the Fair." 28 Jan. 1893, p. 2, col. 1–3.
J. C. V. D. [John C. Van Dyke] "Art at the Fair. The American Pictures. I." 31 July 1893.
"Art News." 14 Oct. 1893, p. 15, col. 2.

New York Herald
"Good Prospects for American Art at the World's Fair." 18 Sept. 1892, p. 30, col. 4–6.
"Art at Its Best Seen at the Fair." 30 April 1893, p. 14, col. 1–6.

New York Herald Tribune International, Paris
"All About Art. Leading American Painters and Sculptors in Rome Doubtful as to Their Reception at the World's Fair." 6 Jan. 1892, p. 2, col. 4.

New York Mercury
"Art Notes." 12 Feb. 1893, p. 12, col. 1–2.

New York Recorder
"General Art Notes. Prof. Ives and the Chicago Art Directorship." 19 April 1891.
"Art at the World's Fair. A Talk With Commissioner of Fine Art Ives." 31 May 1891.

New York Times
"Work on the Great Fair." 18 Oct. 1890, p. 1, col. 7.
"The Fine Arts Committee of the World's Columbian Exposition. . . ." 24 Oct. 1890, p. 8, col. 4.
"Halsey C. Ives. . . ." 28 March 1891, p. 1, col. 3.
"The Columbian Exposition." 29 March 1891, p. 2, col. 5.
"Chicago Will Be Strict. No Poor Works of Art to Be Shown at the Fair." 18 July 1891, p. 5, col. 4.
"Art at the Exposition." 6 Feb. 1892, p. 2, col. 1.
"Rules for Displays of Works of Art." 4 June 1892, p. 1, col. 5.
"Pictures for the Big Fair. Exhibits Proposed by American Artists Residing in Paris." 14 June 1892, p. 8, col. 2.
"Fine Arts at the Fair. H. C. Ives, Chief of the Department, Tells New-Yorkers About It." 11 Nov. 1892, p. 8, col. 5.
"Painting at the World's Fair." 14 Nov. 1892, p. 4, col. 4.
"Paintings for the Fair. Work Accomplished by the Jury of Selection." 29 Jan. 1893, p. 16, col. 5–6.
"Pictures for the Fair. The National Jury of Selection Is Now at Work." 8 Mar. 1893, p. 8, col. 5.
"American Art at Chicago. Painting and Sculpture Selected for Exhibition." 9 Mar. 1893, p. 5, col. 1.
"Art Notes." 4 June 1893, p. 4, col. 5.
"Art at Chicago." 22 June 1893, p. 5, col. 6.
"Art Department's Troubles." 19 July 1893, p. 8, col. 3.
"Art Jurors Have Their Way." 20 July 1893, p. 5, col. 2.
"Awards at the Fair." 23 July 1893, p. 5, col. 3.
"Some World's Fair Winners. Awards Announced by the Department of Arts." 19 Aug. 1893, p. 5, col. 4.
"Awards for Sculpture. Successful Exhibitors in the World's Fair Fine Arts Department." 22 Aug. 1893, p. 5, col. 4.
"Art Medals at the World's Fair." 27 Aug. 1893, p. 16, col. 6.
"More Light on Art Medals." 10 Sept. 1893, p. 4, col. 5.
"Art Notes." 7 Nov. 1893, p. 4, col. 6.

Philadelphia Press
"Pennsylvania Fine Arts. The Works in Oil, Water Color, and Architecture for Chicago." 15 Jan. 1893, p. 8, col. 4.
"New York Artists." 15 Jan. 1893, p. 8, col. 5.
"American Art at Chicago." 4 Feb. 1893, p. 2, col. 4.
"Art Knows No Shame." 18 June 1893, p. 23, col. 3.
"Art at the Fair." 6 Aug. 1893, p. 21, col. 1–7.
"Art Treasures at the Academy. Drift of Current Painting as Shown by the Selections from the Fair." 14 Jan. 1894, p. 23, col. 1–5.

Van Rensselaer, Mrs. M. G., and Reginald Coxe. "New Epoch in American Art. The Greatest Advance Has Been in the Number of Capable Artists and the Average of Public Intelligence in Art." Newspaper source unknown; ca. 1893; clipping from the Thomas B. Clarke Scrapbooks, Archives of American Art, roll N597, frames 527–28.

SELECTED SECONDARY SOURCES

The following books and articles represent a selection of recent studies of the World's Columbian Exposition, as well as a few recent works that have a direct bearing on the study of the art shown in Chicago. These references are included as an aid to the general study of the social and cultural context of the Chicago fair. Most of the more specific studies have appeared within the last five years. Other periodical literature may be found in the bibliographies of the earlier works cited here.

Adams, Judith A. *The American Amusement Park Industry, A*

History of Technology and Thrills. Boston: Twayne, 1991.

Appelbaum, Stanley. *The Chicago World's Fair of 1893*. New York: Dover Publications, 1980.

Badger, Reid. *The Great American Fair: The World's Columbian Exposition & American Culture*. Chicago: Nelson Hall, 1979.

Benedict, Burton et al. *The Anthropology of World's Fairs: San Francisco Panama-Pacific International Exposition, 1915*. Berkeley and London: Scolar Press, 1983.

Bennett, Tony. "The Exhibitionary Complex." *New Formations* 4 (Spring 1988): 73–102.

Blaugrund, Annette, ed. *Paris 1889: American Artists at the Universal Exposition*. Philadelphia: Pennsylvania Academy of the Fine Arts in association with Harry N. Abrams, New York, 1989.

The Books of the Fairs: Materials about World's Fairs, 1834–1916, in the Smithsonian Institution Libraries. Introduction by Robert W. Rydell. Chicago: American Library Association, 1992.

Bradbury, Malcolm. "Struggling Westward: America & the Coming of Modernism (I)." *Encounter* 60 (Jan. 1983): 55–60.

———. "Struggling Westward: America & the Coming of Modernism (II). *Encounter* 60 (Feb. 1983): 57–65.

Broun, Elizabeth. "American Painting and Sculpture in the Fine Arts Building of the World's Columbian Exposition, 1893." Ph.D. diss., University of Kansas, 1976.

Burg, David F. *Chicago's White City of 1893*. Lexington: University Press of Kentucky, 1976.

Burnham, Daniel H. *The Final Official Report of the Director of Works of the World's Columbian Exposition*. Introduction and bibliography by Joan E. Draper, preface by Thomas Hines. New York: Garland, 1989 [reprint of original report].

Burns, Sarah. "The Country Boy Goes to the City: Thomas Hovenden's *Breaking Home Ties* in American Popular Culture." *American Art Journal* 20 (1988): 59–73.

Cassell, Frank A., and Marguerite E. Cassell. "The White City in Peril: Leadership and the World's Columbian Exposition." *Chicago History* 12 (Fall 1983): 10–27.

Çelik, Zeynep. *Displaying the Orient: Architecture of Islam at Nineteenth-Century World's Fairs*. Berkeley: University of California Press, 1992.

Cordato, Mary Frances. "Representing the Expansion of Woman's Sphere: Women's Work and Culture at the World's Fairs of 1876, 1893, and 1904." Ph.D. diss., New York University, 1989.

Cronon, William B. *Nature's Metropolis: Chicago and the Great West*. New York: W. W. Norton, 1991.

Docherty, Linda Jones. "A Search for Identity: American Art Criticism and the Concept of the 'Native School,' 1876–1893." Ph.D. diss., University of North Carolina at Chapel Hill, 1985.

Doenecke, Justus D. "Myths, Machines, and Markets: The Columbian Exposition of 1893." *Journal of Popular Culture* 6 (Spring 1973): 535–49.

Downey, Dennis B. "Rite of Passage: The World's Columbian Exposition and American Life." Ph.D. diss., Marquette University, 1981.

Findling, John E., and Kimberly D. Pelle, eds. *Historical Dictionary of World's Fairs and Expositions, 1851–1988*. New York: Greenwood Press, 1990.

Gilbert, James. *Perfect Cities: Chicago's Utopias of 1893*. Chicago: University of Chicago Press, 1991.

Gillette, Howard. "White City, Capitol City." *Chicago History* 18 (1989–90): 26–45.

Goldstein, Leslie S. "Art in Chicago and the World's Columbian Exposition of 1893." M.A. thesis, University of Iowa, 1970.

Hales, Peter Bacon. "Photography and the World's Columbian Exposition: A Case Study." *Journal of Urban History* 15 (May 1989): 247–73.

Harris, Neil. *Cultural Excursions: Marketing Appetites and Tastes in Modern America*. Chicago: University of Chicago Press, 1990.

Hinsley, Curtis M. "The World as Marketplace: Commodification of the Exotic at the World's Columbian Exposition, Chicago, 1893." In *Exhibiting Cultures: The Poetics and Politics of Museum Display*, ed. Ivan Karp and Steven D. Lavine, 344–65. Washington, D.C.: Smithsonian Institution Press, 1991.

Holt, Elizabeth G. *The Expanding World of Art, 1874–1902: Vol. I, Universal Expositions and State-Sponsored Fine Arts Exhibitions*. New Haven: Yale University Press, 1988.

Kasson, John F. *Amusing the Million: Coney Island at the Turn of the Century*. New York: Hill & Wang, 1978.

Kerber, Stephen. "Florida and the World's Columbian Exposition of 1893." *Florida Historical Quarterly* 66 (July 1987): 25–49.

Knutson, Robert. "The White City—The World's Columbian Exposition of 1893." Ph.D. diss., Columbia University, 1956.

Lancaster, Clay. *The Incredible World's Parliament of Religions at the Chicago Columbian Exposition of 1893: A Comparative and Critical Study*. Fontwell, Sussex: Centaur Press, 1987.

Lewis, Russell. "Everything Under One Roof: World's Fairs and Department Stores in Paris and Chicago." *Chicago History* 12 (Fall 1983): 28–47.

Ling, Peter J. *America and the Automobile: Technology, Reform and Social Change*. [Chapter 5, "The Columbian Exposition—Manufacturing, Planning and the Consumer Culture."] Manchester: Manchester University Press, 1990.

Litwicki, Ellen M. " 'The Inauguration of the People's Age': The Columbian Quadricentennial and American Culture." *Maryland Historian* 20 (Spring/Summer 1989): 47–58.

Massa, Ann. "Black Women in the 'White City.'" *Journal of American Studies* 8 (Dec. 1974): 319–37.

Miller, Daniel T. "The Columbian Exposition of 1893 and the American National Character." *Journal of American Culture* 10 (Summer 1987): 17–22.

Miller, Ross. *American Apocalypse: The Great Fire and the Myth of Chicago*. Chicago: University of Chicago Press, 1990.

Mills, Cynthia. "Choosing the U.S. Fine Arts Display for the World's Columbian Exposition. Jury Selection at the World's Fairs." Unpublished graduate paper, University of Maryland, May 1991.

Moses, L. G. "Indians on the Midway: Wild West Shows and the Indian Bureau at World's Fairs, 1893-1904." *South Dakota History* 21 (Fall 1991): 205–29.

Parmet, Robert D., and Francis L. Lederer II. "Competition for the World's Columbian Exposition: The New York Campaign and the Chicago Campaign." *Journal of the Illinois State Historical Society* 65 (Winter 1972): 364–94.

Platt, Harold L. *The Electric City: Energy and the Growth of the Chicago Area, 1880–1930.* Chicago: University of Chicago Press, 1991.

Pohl, Frances K. "Historical Reality or Utopian Ideal? The Woman's Building at the World's Columbian Exposition, Chicago, 1893." *International Journal of Women's Studies* 5 (1982): 289–311.

Rudwick, Elliot M., and August Meier. "Black Man in the 'White City': Negroes and the Columbian Exposition, 1893." *Phylon* 26 (Winter 1965): 354–61.

Rydell, Robert W. *All the World's a Fair: Visions of Empire at American International Expositions, 1876–1916.* Chicago: University of Chicago Press, 1984.

Rydell, Robert W. "The Culture of Imperial Abundance: World's Fairs and the Making of American Culture." In *Consuming Visions: Accumulation and Display of Goods in America, 1880–1920*, ed. Simon J. Bronner. New York: W. W. Norton, 1989.

Sandweiss, Eric. "Around the World in a Day: International Participation in the World's Columbian Exposition." *Illinois Historical Journal* 84 (Spring 1991): 2–14.

Scott, Gertrude. "Village Performance: Villages at the Chicago World's Columbian Exposition, 1893." Ph.D. diss., New York University, 1991.

Seager, Richard Hughes. "The World's Parliament of Religions, Chicago, Illinois, 1893: America's Religious Coming of Age." Ph.D. diss., Harvard University, 1987.

Shindel, Judy. "Fair Reward: Art and Argument. The 'American' System of Awards at the 1893 World's Columbian Exposition and the Controversies It Sparked in the Fine Arts Department (K)." Smithsonian Internship Paper, American Studies Program, Smith College, Dec. 1991.

Susman, Warren I. "Ritual Fairs." *Chicago History* 12 (Fall 1983): 4–9.

Trachtenberg, Alan. *The Incorporation of America: Culture and Society in the Gilded Age.* New York: Hill & Wang, 1982.

Vignocchi, Bernice Elizabeth Gallagher. "Fair to Look Upon: An Analysis and Annotated Bibliography of Illinois Women's Fiction at the 1893 World's Columbian Exposition." Ph.D. diss., Northwestern University, 1990.

Weimann, Jeanne Madeline. *The Fair Women.* Chicago: Academy Chicago, 1981.

Weingarden, Lauren S. "A Transcendentalist Discourse in the Poetics of Technology: Louis Sullivan's Transportation Building and Walt Whitman's 'Passage to India.' " *Word & Image* 3 (Apr.–June 1987): 202–21.

Ziolkowski, Eric J. "Heavenly Visions and Worldly Intentions: Chicago's Columbian Exposition and the World's Parliament of Religions (1893)." *Journal of American Culture* 13 (Winter 1990): 9–15.

INDEX

Numbers in italics refer to captions.

References to endnotes are indicated by the page number followed by the endnote number, e.g. 114 n9 (page 114 note 9).